Less managing. More teaching. Greater learning.

 ## INSTRUCTORS...

Would you like your **students** to show up for class **more prepared**?
(Let's face it, class is much more fun if everyone is engaged and prepared...)

Want an **easy way to assign** homework online and track student **progress**?
(Less time grading means more time teaching...)

Want an **instant view** of student or class performance?
(No more wondering if students understand...)

Need to **collect data and generate reports** required for administration or accreditation?
(Say goodbye to manually tracking student learning outcomes...)

Want to **record and post your lectures** for students to view online?
(The more students can see, hear, and experience class resources, the better they learn...)

 ## With **McGraw-Hill's Connect,™**

INSTRUCTORS GET:

- Simple **assignment management**, allowing you to spend more time teaching.
- **Auto-graded** assignments, quizzes, and tests.
- **Detailed visual reporting** where student and section results can be viewed and analyzed.
- Sophisticated **online testing** capability.
- A **filtering and reporting** function that allows you to easily assign and report on materials that are correlated to learning objectives and Bloom's taxonomy.
- An easy-to-use **lecture capture** tool.
- The option to **upload course documents** for student access.

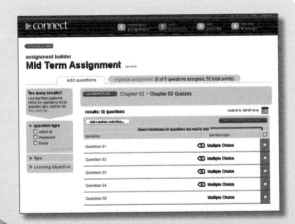

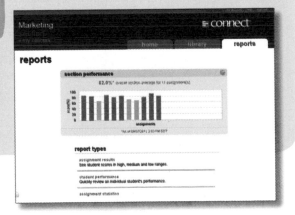

MARKETING

second canadian edition

McGraw-Hill Ryerson
Connect. Learn. Succeed.

MARKETING
SECOND CANADIAN EDITION

ISBN-13: 978-0-07-038548-1
ISBN-10: 0-07-038548-3

3 4 5 6 7 8 9 10 QVR 1 9 8 7 6 5 4 3 2

Printed and Bound in the United States

Executive Sponsoring Editor: *Leanna MacLean*
Executive Marketing Manager: *Joy Armitage Taylor*
Developmental Editors: *Andria Fogarty/Amy Rydzanicz*
Senior Editorial Associate: *Stephanie Hess*
Editorial Associate: *Erin Catto*
Photo/Permissions Editor: *Tracy Leonard*
Supervising Editor: *Graeme Powell*
Copy Editor: *Deborah Cooper-Bullock*
Production Coordinator: *Sharon Stefanowicz*
Cover and Interior Design: *Liz Harasymczuk*
Cover Image: *Paul Tearle/Getty Images (RF)*
Page Layout: *Laserwords Private Limited*
Printer: *QuadGraphics*

Library and Archives Canada Cataloguing in Publication

Marketing/Dhruv Grewal . . . [et al.].—2nd Canadian ed.

Includes bibliographical references and index.
ISBN 978-0-07-038548-1

1. Marketing—Textbooks. I. Grewal, Dhruv

HF5415.M29323 2012   658.8   C2011-906571-1

dedication

To those who had a strong positive influence on the early years of our careers:

James Littlefield, Professor of Marketing, Virginia Tech
Kent B. Monroe, John M. Jones Professor of Marketing, University of Illinois
A. Coskun Samli, Professor of Marketing, University of North Florida
Dianna L. Stone, Professor of Management, University of Central Florida
—*Dhruv Grewal*

James L. Ginter, Professor Emeritus, The Ohio State University
Roger A. Kerin, Harold C. Simmons Distinguished Professor of Marketing, Southern Methodist University
Mike Harvey, Hearin Professor of Global Business, The University of Mississippi
Bernard J. LaLonde, Professor Emeritus, The Ohio State University
Barton A. Weitz, J.C. Penney Eminent Scholar, The University of Florida
—*Michael Levy*

Ken Danns, Professor, University of Guyana
Leland Paul, Professor, University of Guyana
Vinod Kumar, Professor, Eric Sprott School of Business, Carleton University
Uma Kumar, Professor, Eric Sprott School of Business, Carleton University
—*Ajax Persaud*

Gordon McDougall, Professor Emeritus, School of Business and Economics, Wilfrid Laurier University
Auleen Carson, Retired Professor, School of Business and Economics, Wilfrid Laurier University
David Goodwin, Professor, Digital Arts Communication, University of Waterloo
Brad Davis, Professor of Marketing, School of Business and Economics, Wilfrid Laurier University
—*Shirley Lichti*

about the authors

Authors Michael Levy (left)
and Dhruv Grewal (right).

Dhruv Grewal, PhD (Virginia Tech), is the Toyota Chair in Commerce and Electronic Business and a Professor of Marketing at Babson College. He was awarded the 2010 AMS Cutco/Vector Distinguished Educator Award, the 2010 Lifetime Achievement Award in Retailing (AMA Retailing SIG), and in 2005 the Lifetime Achievement in Behavioral Pricing Award (Fordham University, November 2005). He is a Distinguished Fellow of the Academy of Marketing Science. He was ranked first in the marketing field in terms of publications in the top-six marketing journals during the 1991–1998 period and again for the 2000–2007 period. He has served as VP Research and Conferences, American Marketing Association Academic Council (1999–2001), and as VP Development for the Academy of Marketing Science (2000–2002). He was co-editor of *Journal of Retailing* from 2001 to 2007. He co-chaired the 1993 Academy of Marketing Science Conference, the 1998 Winter American Marketing Association Conference, the 2001 American Marketing Association Doctoral Consortium, and the American Marketing Association 2006 Summer Educators Conference.

He has published more than 95 articles in journals such as the *Journal of Retailing, Journal of Marketing, Journal of Consumer Research, Journal of Marketing Research,* and *Journal of the Academy of Marketing Science,* as well as other journals. He currently serves on numerous editorial review boards, such as the *Journal of Retailing, Journal of Marketing, Journal of the Academy of Marketing Science, Journal of Interactive Marketing, Journal of Business Research,* and *Journal of Public Policy & Marketing.*

He has won a number of awards for his teaching: 2005 Sherwin-Williams Distinguished Teaching Award, Society for Marketing Advances, 2003 American Marketing Association, Award for Innovative Excellence in Marketing Education, 1999 Academy of Marketing Science Great Teachers in Marketing Award, Executive MBA Teaching Excellence Award (1998), School of Business Teaching Excellence Awards (1993, 1999), and Virginia Tech Certificate of Recognition for Outstanding Teaching (1989).

He has taught executive seminars/courses and/or worked on research projects with numerous firms, such as IRI, TJX, RadioShack, Telcordia, Khimetriks, Profit-Logic, Monsanto, McKinsey, Ericsson, Council of Insurance Agents & Brokers (CIAB), Met-Life, AT&T, Motorola, Nextel, FP&L, Lucent, Sabre, Goodyear Tire & Rubber Company, Sherwin Williams, Esso International, Asahi, and numerous law firms. He has taught seminars in the United States, Europe, and Asia.

Michael Levy, Ph.D. (Ohio State University), is the Charles Clarke Reynolds Professor of Marketing and Director of the Retail Supply Chain Institute at Babson College. He received his Ph.D. in business administration from The Ohio State University and his undergraduate and M.S. degrees in business administration from the University of Colorado at Boulder. He taught at Southern Methodist University before joining the faculty as professor and chair of the marketing department at the University of Miami.

Professor Levy received the 2009 Lifetime Achievement Award from the American Marketing Association Retailing Special Interest Group. He was rated one of the Best Researchers in Marketing in a survey published in *Marketing Educator* in Summer 1997. He has developed a strong stream of research in retailing, business logistics, financial retailing strategy, pricing, and sales management. He has published more than 50 articles in leading marketing and logistics journals, including the *Journal of Retailing, Journal of Marketing, Journal of the Academy of Marketing Science,* and *Journal of Marketing Research.* He currently serves on the editorial review board of the *Journal of Retailing, International Journal of Logistics Management, International Journal of Logistics and Materials Management,* and *European Business Review.* He is co-author of *Retailing Management,* eighth edition (2012), the bestselling college-level retailing text in the world. Professor Levy was co-editor of the *Journal of Retailing* from 2001 to 2007. He co-chaired the 1993 Academy of Marketing Science conference and the 2006 Summer American Marketing Association conference.

Professor Levy has worked in retailing and related disciplines throughout his professional life. Prior to his academic career, he worked for several retailers and a housewares distributor in Colorado. He has performed research projects with many retailers and retail technology firms, including Accenture, Federated Department Stores, Khimetrics (SAP), Mervyn's, Neiman Marcus, ProfitLogic (Oracle), Zale Corporation, and numerous law firms.

Ajax Persaud, Ph.D., is an Associate Professor of Marketing and the founding Director of the Master of Science in Management program at the Telfer School of Management, University of Ottawa. Professor Persaud has more than 15 years of post-secondary teaching experience at colleges and universities in Canada and overseas. He has taught several undergraduate and graduate courses, including Marketing, Electronic Marketing, Digital Marketing Technologies, High-Tech Marketing, Marketing Strategy, New Product Development, Entrepreneurial Finance, R&D Management, Technology and Innovation Management, Economics, and Quantitative Methods. He has received several awards and nominations for teaching and research excellence. In 2005, he was awarded the University of Ottawa Excellence in Education Prize for excellence in teaching and research.

Professor Persaud has published material in journals, conference papers, and four books, including *E-Business Innovations: Cases and Readings* and *Managing Innovations Through Corporate Global R&D.* His research has been published in leading journals, such as *Journal of Product Innovation Management, IEEE Transactions on Engineering Management, Journal of Technology Transfer,* and the *Canadian Journal of Administrative Sciences.* He has also served as academic reviewer for many journals, including *Journal of Product Innovation Management, IEEE Transactions on Engineering Management,* and *Journal of Asia Pacific Marketing.*

As well, he has delivered many executive seminars and workshops and has consulted for many organizations in Guyana, Canada, and Europe. He is an active community volunteer, contributing both his time and his money, for many worthy causes and charities, focusing on education and disadvantaged children and youths.

Shirley Lichti, B.A., M.A., has taught in the School of Business and Economics (SBE) at Wilfrid Laurier University since 1993 as a part-time and full-time instructor. She has taught a range of undergraduate and graduate courses, including Introductory Marketing; Building and Managing Products, Services, and Brands; Integrated Marketing Communications; and Consumer Behaviour. Shirley has an extensive background in marketing, advertising, promotion, and training, which was developed during a 14-year career with IBM. She has worked in Canada, the Caribbean, and Japan.

A dedicated educator, Shirley was recognized with the 2002 SBE Outstanding Teacher Award. She was honoured to be included as one of Laurier's "Most Popular Professors" in the *Maclean's Guide to Canadian Universities* in 2003, 2004, 2005, and 2006. In 2007, Shirley was recognized by the Ontario Ministry of Training, Colleges and Universities with The LIFT Award for Teaching Excellence.

She also runs Marketing Magic, a Waterloo-based marketing communication consulting and training company. She has been a featured keynote speaker at conferences and has developed and delivered marketing seminars and workshops for many organizations. Her clients include small companies, ranging from the Stratford Festival to Fortune 500 companies such as Manulife Financial, Scotiabank, and Lexus Canada.

For more than 10 years, Shirley wrote a regular marketing column for *The Record.* She has been an active board member and volunteer in many organizations, including Communitech, the Business Success for Women Conference, K-W Business Women's Association, and the Sexual Assault Support Centre of Waterloo Region.

brief contents

table of contents

5 Consumer Behaviour 149

SECTION THREE Targeting the Marketplace 210

SECTION FOUR Value Creation 252

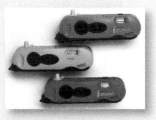

9 Product, Branding, and Packaging Decisions   287

SECTION FIVE Transacting Value   350

SECTION SIX   Value Delivery: Designing the Marketing Channel and Supply Chain   388

12 Marketing Channels: Distribution Strategy   389

13 Retailing   421

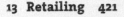

SECTION SEVEN   Value Communication   452

SECTION EIGHT   Marketing in the Global Environment   528

17 Ethics and Socially Responsible Marketing (On Connect)

what is marketing?

The function of marketing is multi-faceted, but its fundamental purpose is to create value. Consider these examples:

Not too long ago water was simply one of the most basic natural elements. It came out of a faucet in your home and was consumed for the purposes of drinking, washing, and so on. Firms such as Aberfoyle Springs, Clearly Canadian, Canadian Springs, and Montclair have created new products that customers find valuable by bottling water in attractive and easy-to-carry packages. Today, bottled water is a $35-billion worldwide industry with global consumption topping 154 billion litres, up 57 percent from five years earlier. And because of environmental concerns, companies that have introduced the convenience of bottled water, are facing unprecedented criticism related to the sea of plastic bottles hitting landfill and recycling sites. Many municipalities have banned bottled water outright.

Why do people buy lululemon yoga pants for well over $100 when they could buy another pair at Walmart for under $20? The answer lies in marketing brand value: lululemon has created a cache for its branded clothing with grassroots advertising and innovative fabrics and styles. When trendsetters start to wear these brands, others follow.

Regardless of your age, your gender, or the city in which you live, you already know something about marketing. You have been an involved consumer in the marketing process since childhood when, for example, you accompanied your mother or father to the grocery store and asked to buy a particular brand of cereal because you saw a friend eating it or heard about it on television. The prize inside the box of cereal was of value to you as a child; the nutritional information offered on the box panel was of value to your mother or father. Once you begin to explore the many ways in which companies and brands create value for their customers through marketing, you will also begin to appreciate the complex set of decisions and activities that are necessary to provide you with the products and services you use every day.

changes to the second canadian edition

The prevalence and power of the Internet has created a marketplace of more informed and savvy customers than ever before. Those who teach the marketers of the future need to account for the consumer's ability to assess the marketplace at their fingertips and discern good value from poor value. *Marketing*, Second Canadian Edition, is all about the core concepts and tools that help marketers create value for customers. Throughout this book you will find many examples that define how companies create value for customers through branding, packaging, pricing, retailing, service, and advertising. We introduce the concept of value in Chapter 1 and carry it through the entire text.

SECTION ONE   Assessing the Marketplace

The first section of the text contains three chapters and the central theme of the section is "Assessing the Marketplace." Following an introduction to marketing in Chapter 1, Chapter 2 focuses on how a firm deviielops a marketing plan. A central theme of the chapter is how firms can effectively create, capture, deliver, and communicate value to their customers. Finally, Chapter 3, Analyzing the Marketing Environment, focuses on how marketers can systematically uncover and evaluate opportunities.

Changes to Section One include:

- Revised Chapter Vignettes in Chapters 1 and 2, and a new Chapter Vignette for Chapter 3.
- The following new boxed features: Social Media Marketing, Entrepreneurial Marketing.
- New Sustainable Marketing boxes in Chapters 1 and 2.
- Revised coverage on marketing orientations in Chapter 1 to make it easier for students to appreciate the different ways marketing is practiced. Also, added a short discussion and an example showing how the four Ps need to be integrated and coordinated into a seamless whole rather than treated as individual components of the marketing mix.
- New content emphasizing the role of social media in marketing and the importance of sustainable marketing in Chapter 1.
- A new discussion about the pros and cons of the four growth strategies and the introduction of downsizing as a strategy to rationalize a business in Chapter 2.
- New content in Chapter 2 about sustainable competitive advantage.
- The expansion of the marketing strategies section in Chapter 2 to also cover locational excellence.
- A discussion of the recession in the economic factors section in Chapter 3.

SECTION TWO   Understanding the Marketplace

The second section of the book deals with "Understanding the Marketplace" and is composed of three chapters. Chapter 4, Marketing Research, identifies the various tools and techniques that marketers use to uncover these needs and ensure that they create goods and services that provide value to their target markets. Chapter 5, Consumer Behaviour, focuses on all aspects of understanding why consumers purchase products and services. The consumer decision process is highlighted. Chapter 6, Business-to-Business Marketing, focuses on all aspects pertaining to why and how business-to-business buying takes place.

Changes to Section Two include:

- New Chapter Vignettes.
- The following new boxed features: Social Media Marketing, Sustainable Marketing, Power of the Internet.
- New Entrepreneurial Marketing boxes in Chapters 5 and 6.
- New Chapter Case Studies in Chapters 5 and 6.
- New examples of strategies and tactics marketers use at each stage of the consumer process in Chapter 5.
- A new discussion about social risk and physiological risk in Chapter 5.
- A new section in Chapter 5 about how marketers can mitigate the various risks associated with the consumer buying decision.

- A new section in Chapter 5 focusing on the factors that influence the extent of alternative evaluation in the buying process.
- A new section in Chapter 6 about the challenges in reaching and serving B2B customers.
- A new section in Chapter 6 in the organizational culture section about building relationships.

SECTION THREE   Targeting the Marketplace

The third section of the book deals with "Targeting the Marketplace." Chapter 7 focuses on segmentation, targeting, and positioning. In this chapter, we focus on how firms segment the marketplace, pick a target market, and then position their good/service in line with their customers' needs and wants.

Changes to Section Three include:

- A new Chapter Vignette.
- The following new boxed features: Ethical Dilemma, Social Media Marketing, Sustainable Marketing, Power of the Internet, Entrepreneurial Marketing.
- A new Chapter Case Study.
- The addition of an appendix, Using Secondary Data to Assess Customer Lifetime Value (CLV), to demonstrate the expected financial contribution from a customer to a company's overall profitability over the course of the relationship.

SECTION FOUR   Value Creation

Marketing, Second Canadian Edition, devotes three chapters to **Value Creation**. The first two, Chapter 8, Developing New Products, and Chapter 9, Product, Branding, and Packaging Decisions, cover the development and management of products and brands. While many of the concepts involved in developing and managing services are similar to those of physical brands, Chapter 10, Services: The Intangible Product, addresses the unique challenges of the marketing of services.

Changes to Section Four include:

- A new Chapter Vignette in Chapter 8, and revised Chapter Vignettes for Chapters 9 and 10.
- The following new boxed features: Social Media Marketing, Sustainable Marketing.
- New Chapter Case Studies in Chapters 8 and 10, and a revised Chapter Case Study in Chapter 9.
- A simplified discussion of product mix and product line decisions in Chapter 9.
- A new discussion of metrics in Chapter 10 in a section titled "Evaluating Service Quality by Using Well-Established Marketing Metrics."

SECTION FIVE   Transacting Value

Pricing is the activity within a firm responsible for **Transacting Value** by bringing in money and affecting revenues. Chapter 11 examines the importance of setting the right price, the relationship between price and quantity sold, break-even analysis, the impact of price wars, and how the Internet has changed the way people shop.

Changes to Section Five include:

- A new Chapter Vignette.
- The following new boxed features: Social Media Marketing, Sustainable Marketing, Power of the Internet, Entrepreneurial Marketing.
- A new Chapter Case Study.
- An expanded discussion of competition that now includes four levels: oligopolistic competition, monopolistic competition, pure competition, and monopoly.
- A new discussion of daily deal companies, such as Groupon and WagJag, that reflects how companies are offering pricing deals to groups of consumers.

SECTION SIX   Value Delivery: Designing the Marketing Channel and Supply Chain

One important reason why Walmart has become the world's largest retailer is its **Value Delivery** system. It times the delivery of merchandise so the merchandise gets to stores just in time to meet customer demand. To achieve this, it has initiated many innovative programs with its vendors and developed sophisticated transportation and warehousing systems. *Marketing*, Second Canadian Edition, devotes two chapters to value delivery. Chapter 12 takes a look at marketing channels, distribution strategy, and supply chain, while Chapter 13 concentrates on retailing.

Changes to Section Six include:

- A new Chapter Vignette in Chapter 13, and a revised Chapter Vignette in Chapter 12.
- The following new boxed features: Social Media Marketing, Sustainable Marketing, Power of the Internet, and Entrepreneurial Marketing.
- A new section called "Data Warehouse" in Chapter 12 that discusses how companies can analyze consumer data as it relates to merchandise purchased.
- An updated and revised discussion of electronic data exchange in Chapter 12.
- The entire discussion on retailing in Chapter 13 has been refocused on "Factors for Establishing a Relationship with Retailers" to show students how retail partners are chosen, identifying the types of retailers a company may want to use, creating a retail strategy, and exploring a multichannel strategy. This last section in multichannel retailing contains significantly new content.

SECTION SEVEN   Value Communications

Today's methods of **Value Communication** are complex because of new technologies that add email, blogs, the Internet, and social media to the advertising mix that once utilized only radio and television to relay messages to consumers. *Marketing*, Second Canadian Edition, devotes two chapters to value communication. Chapter 14 introduces the breadth of integrated marketing communications. Chapter 15 is devoted to advertising, sales promotions, and personal selling.

Changes to Section Seven include:

- New Chapter Vignettes.
- The following new boxed features: Social Media Marketing, Sustainable Marketing, Power of the Internet, Entrepreneurial Marketing.
- Revised in-depth coverage of direct marketing in Chapter 14, which now includes more content from the last edition's retail chapter, where it previously fell under the "Non-Store Marketing" heading.
- Expanded information in Chapter 14, under "Electronic Media" heading, about fake blogs, online games, text messaging, social media, and mobile apps.
- New "Assess Impact by Using Marketing Metrics" section within "Steps in Planning an IMC Campaign" in Chapter 14.
- New content related to daily deal companies, such as Groupon and WagJag, in the "Sales Promotion" section in Chapter 15.

SECTION EIGHT   Marketing in the Global Environment

Most firms are involved in **Global Marketing** at some level. In less than 10 years, lululemon has been transformed into a global company and a great Canadian success story in the athletic and sportswear industry. But even small entrepreneurial firms are also involved because they get their materials, products, or services from firms located in other countries. Chapter 16 is devoted exclusively to this topic.

Changes to Section Eight include:

- A new Chapter Vignette.
- The following new boxed features: Ethical Dilemma, Social Media Marketing, Sustainable Marketing, Power of the Internet, Entrepreneurial Marketing.

features inside *Marketing,* second canadian edition

In addition to our emphasis on value in *Marketing,* Second Canadian Edition, you will also find integrated and highlighted coverage of ethics, entrepreneurship, Internet marketing, services, social media, sustainability, and globalization within the framework of the marketing discipline:

Marketing, Second Canadian Edition, contains an entire chapter on **Marketing Ethics** which is available on Connect. The chapter provides rich illustrations of corporate responsibility and introduces an ethical decision-making framework that is useful for assessing potential ethically troubling situations that are posed throughout the rest of the book. It can be used to set the tone for ethical material throughout the textbook as desired.

Ethical Dilemma 10.1 — Keeping Personal Information Private on Facebook

It's nearly impossible to discuss social media without talking about privacy. This topic is important for marketers to consider because it affects the usage and adoption of social media sites. Currently, 75 percent of social media users say their security is important or very important, and about one-quarter of social media users are concerned about identity theft online.[14] Sites such as ReclaimPrivacy.org even let you scan your profile to detect how much personal information you are sharing publicly.

People have shown concern about the collection and use of private information by Facebook, and how these details are shared. Facebook users were forced to grapple with more than 100 different settings to keep their personal information private, which was very confusing for users who were concerned about how this data was being used and who wanted to limit the use of the information.[17] In response to outcries from privacy watchdogs, Facebook simplified its system, paring it down to only 15 privacy settings.

Facebook co-founder, Mark Zuckerberg, faced intense

In addition, Chapters 2 to 17 each contain an **Ethical Dilemma box** with a compelling ethical discussion and end-of-chapter discussion questions that force students to consider and evaluate each situation. The Second Canadian Edition contains nine new Ethical Dilemmas.

Entrepreneurship. An entrepreneurial spirit pervades most marketing innovations and is necessary to keep firms growing and healthy. *Marketing,* Second Canadian Edition, nurtures that entrepreneurial spirit by providing examples of young entrepreneurial firms and successful entrepreneurs such as lululemon, Cora's Restaurants, Bullfrog Power, and more.

Entrepreneurial Marketing 7.1 — Chez Cora: The Business of Breakfast

When Cora Tsouflidou became a single mother to three teenage children, she bought a small eatery, worked hard, tripled its value, and sold it. From there she worked her way up from a hostess to the general manager in a well-known Montreal restaurant, mastering her foodservice industry knowledge along the way.[40]

These skills served her well when she bought a defunct 29-seat snack bar in Montreal's Ville St-Laurent in 1987 and launched the first Chez Cora restaurant. Plates garnished with a variety of artistically presented fresh fruits

most restaurant operations and thus appeal to franchisees, allowing them to spend more time with their families.

It's not surprising that Cora's image is used in advertising campaigns. She looks like a mom who really cares about family, which resonates with both customers and franchisees. Behind that colourful image is a self-made business woman who has won the Governor General's Award and the Ernst & Young Entrepreneur of the Year Award.[43] Cora's unique business plan has made Cora's one

And each chapter contains an **Entrepreneurial Marketing box** that depicts recognizable and interesting young entrepreneurial firms. There are 14 new Entrepreneurial Marketing boxes in the Second Canadian Edition.

Power of the Internet boxes, a new feature for the Second Canadian Edition, further explore the growing use of the Internet as a distribution channel as well as a marketing tool.

For example, Chapter 5 includes a discussion of how Canada's Expedia.ca allows its customers to approach their travel

Power of the Internet 5.1 — Evaluating Travel Alternatives with Expedia[20]

To illustrate how we evaluate alternatives in a buying decision, consider Expedia.ca, Canada's leading full-service online travel agency. Expedia.ca is a subsidiary of U.S.-based Expedia.com, the world's leading online travel service and the fourth-largest travel agency in the United States. Expedia.ca is well aware that Canadian travellers have high expectations in the competitive world of travel. Expedia's website (www.expedia.ca) makes alternative evaluation easy through a variety of innovations. It allows customers to plan their travel by date, price, interest, or

Consumers can use Expedia.ca to narrow their search from a universal set—all airlines—to their evoked set—say, only Air Canada, WestJet, and American Airlines. They can also search according to determinant attributes, such as the lowest price or the shortest flight. Some flyers use a noncompensatory decision rule; they will fly only Air Canada for international flights, no matter what the alternatives are, because they are members of the airline's frequent flyer program or prefer to support a Canadian airline. Others will use a compensatory decision rule, so

plans in many different ways; because consumers can search by price, interest, date, hotel, and packages, Expedia.ca is a major player on the competitive market today.

Social Media Marketing boxes, another new feature for the Second Canadian Edition, further explore the explosive growth of tools such as Facebook, YouTube, and Twitter, which help marketers communicate with their target markets and promote products or services to them.

For example, Chapter 13 discusses how Dell uses Twitter to tweet coupons or links to sales to sell products, generating millions of dollars in revenue.

Social Media Marketing 13.1 — **Dell Harnesses the Power of Social Media to Drive Sales**

Dell is well-known as the company that carved out a niche in the computer industry by selling direct to consumer, first by telephone and then by sales through its website. You'd think that selling online by using social media tools would be a natural progression. But it wasn't so straightforward.

Dell's chief blogger, Lionel Menchaca, wasn't convinced that Twitter had business potential at first. However, trying new social media tools was part of his job so he opened a Twitter account. He tweeted each time he

coupon or a link to a sale, and about half of the posts are Twitter-exclusive deals.[20] Incentives like these helped Dell build its number of followers to more than 1.4 million near the end of 2009.[21]

It took 18 months to generate the first million dollars in sales, but only six months more to double that figure. To date, Dell has earned just over $3 million on Twitter. This pales next to the company's overall revenue ($12.3 billion in the first quarter of 2009 alone).[22] Nevertheless, the model represents high growth potential for the company,

Sustainable Marketing boxes have been added to the Second Canadian Edition to encourage students to consider the environmental concerns that marketers face in bringing new products and services to the market. Bottled water companies, for example, have faced increased scrutiny and criticism over the use of plastic packaging and recycling issues. The boxes will help students see how smart marketers are embracing sustainability for the good of their companies as well as for consumers.

For example, in Chapter 12 we discuss Frito Lay Canada initiatives such as introducing a compostable bag for SunChips, optimizing delivery routes and switching to zero-emission electric vehicles.

Sustainable Marketing 13.1 — **IKEA's Never Ending List**

For most companies, sustainability means taking small steps in the hopes of making a positive long-term impact. However, initiatives by IKEA are taking a giant leap. As the world's largest furniture retailer, any sustainability efforts by IKEA will make a noticeable difference. With more than

light bulbs. IKEA not only integrates changes inside its stores, but also takes its initiative outside; it installed solar panels to 150 stores and distribution centres for electricity production.

Along with its in-store efforts, IKEA is making an effort to help customers consume in a more

Real Marketer Profile boxes are a new feature to the Second Canadian Edition and appear in eight chapters. They focus on the transition students make from attending post-secondary education to applying their marketing skills in the "real" world. While some of the profiles feature relatively new graduates who are still with their first employer, others show the career paths that grads have taken within a company or in a new role at a different organization.

Real Marketer Profile: **KELLI WOOD**

After graduating from Wilfrid Laurier University's Bachelor of Business Administration program with a specialization in Marketing, I decided to pursue my passion for sports by applying to work at Maple Leaf Sports and Entertainment (MLSE) in Toronto. MLSE proudly owns the Toronto Maple Leafs and the Toronto Raptors and is one of the most reputable sports and entertainment companies in the world

first over several hundred other candidates, but also got me the job of my dreams. I stayed at Toronto FC for almost five seasons, quarterbacking all marketing initiatives for the club, and being a part of the brand launch, the 2008 MLS All-Star Game, the International Friendly between Toronto FC and Real Madrid, and the 2010 MLS Cup. Our tiny team earned top honours across our industry breaking countless records for ticket

Reinforcing learning

Learning Objectives

Listed at the beginning of each chapter, Learning Objectives show students the main concepts discussed inside. These Learning Objectives are then presented in the margins throughout the chapter when they are introduced. At the end of each chapter, the Learning Objectives are revisited and reviewed, reinforcing for students the key sections in the chapter and allowing them to follow their own progress to know where they need help.

Chapter Vignette

Each chapter begins with a Chapter Vignette that helps to introduce and illustrate some of the main content that follows. These vignettes have been carefully selected to pique student interest and are designed to provide real-world examples of how the theory has been applied by a variety of companies. There are 12 new Chapter Vignettes in the Second Canadian Edition.

Overview
of Marketing

arketing is essentially about creating value for consumers and the company's shareholders. As you will learn throughout this book, creating value for consumers and the firm requires that marketers develop and nurture long-term, profitable relationships with consumers. This means that marketers must understand consumers' needs and wants and try to satisfy them through the goods and services they offer, the prices they charge, and the way they promote and deliver the goods and services. Let's take a look at how one of Canada's most successful and profitable high-tech companies, Research in Motion (RIM), is creating and delivering value to its consumers and shareholders with its BlackBerry.

The BlackBerry is one of Canada's most successful and innovative products. It changed not only the way business executives and professionals communicate, but also the speed and timeliness with which decisions are made. Users around the world attest that the BlackBerry enhances their ability to access key corporate information and connect with co-workers anywhere, anytime. The resulting efficiency means that business deals are made more quickly and key decisions are communicated to stakeholders even when they are on the golf course. The BlackBerry smartphone has become the one device that many business people can't live without.

The BlackBerry was designed for wireless email use. Within a few years of its release, it became the dominant device in the market. Not surprisingly, BlackBerry's market position is consistently challenged by new rivals, such as Apple's iPhone, HTC's Droid Incredible, and Palm's Pre. The iPhone launched in 2007 created huge buzz and took the smartphone market by storm, gaining more than 25 percent market share in less than three years and becoming the second most popular smartphone.

Learning Objectives

After studying this chapter, you should be able to

L01 Define marketing and explain its core concepts

L02 Illustrate how marketers create value for a product or service

L03 Summarize the four orientations of marketing

L04 Identify the role of customer relationship management in creating value

L06 Explain the importance of marketing both within and outside the firm

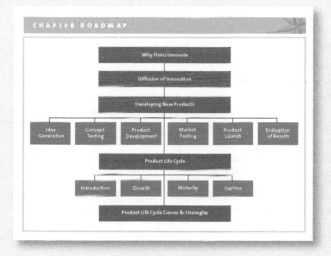

Chapter Roadmap

Each chapter consists of a Chapter Roadmap representing the main steps that describe a chapter. Then in the chapter, each step is explained in detail, allowing students to easily absorb and understand the information. The Chapter Roadmap serves as a useful study tool for students.

Unique End-of-Chapter Applications and Exercises

- **Marketing Applications.** Student-tested at Wilfrid Laurier University and the University of Ottawa, these Marketing Application questions encourage students to become more critical in their thinking of how marketing theory relates to practice. At least one of the Marketing Applications in each chapter poses an ethical dilemma based on material covered in the chapter.

- **Net Savvy.** Each chapter contains two exercises that drive students to the Internet to apply material covered in the text. For example, in Chapter 15, we direct students to the Concerned Children's Advertisers website (www.cca-kids.ca), one of the major self-regulatory bodies for children's advertising. We ask students to choose a PSA and discuss how these ads are used to deliver CCA's message.

- **End-of-Chapter Cases.** Each chapter ends with a two- or three-page case covering a current marketing idea, concept, or company.

Connect

McGraw-Hill Connect™ is a web-based assignment and assessment platform that gives students the means to better connect with their coursework, with their instructors, and with the important concepts that they will need to know for success now and in the future.

With Connect, instructors can deliver assignments, quizzes, and tests online. Questions are presented in an auto-gradable format and tied to the text's learning objectives. Instructors can edit existing questions and author entirely new problems. They can also track individual student performance–by question, by assignment, or in relation to the class overall—with detailed grade reports, and integrate grade reports easily with Learning Management Systems (LMS) such as WebCT and Blackboard. And much more.

The Connect Instructor Library provides all the critical resources instructors will need to build their courses, including a Test Bank, Instructor's Manual, and ready-made PowerPoint presentations:

- The **Test Bank** includes more than 2000 multiple-choice, true/false, and short essay questions. Each question is categorized according to learning objective, level of Bloom's taxonomy, correct answer, and text page reference.

- The computerized test bank is also available through EZ Test Online—a flexible and easy-to-use electronic testing program—that allows instructors to create tests from book-specific items. EZ Test accommodates a wide range of question types and allows instructors to add their own questions. Test items are also available in Word format (rich text format). For secure online testing, exams created in EZ Test can be exported to WebCT and Blackboard. EZ Test Online is supported at www.mhhe.com/eztest, where users can download a Quick Start Guide, access FAQs, or log a ticket for help with specific issues.

- The **Instructor's Manual** contains learning objectives, key terms with definitions, a detailed lecture outline, suggested Internet resources, and in-class activities.

- **PowerPoint slides** include key lecture points and images from the text. As an aid for instructors who wish to create their own presentations, an **Image Bank** containing all visual elements from the text is also available.

- **Videos** of more than 16 segments in a variety of lengths will provide flexibility for your class. Firms featured in the videos include Kraft, Dole, Ford, Frito Lay, as well as a long segment on the bottled water industry.

By choosing Connect, instructors are providing their students with a powerful tool for improving academic performance and truly mastering course material. Connect allows students to practise important skills at their own pace and on their own schedule. Importantly, students' assessment results and instructors' feedback are all saved online–so students can continually review their progress and plot their course to success.

Connect also provides 24/7 online access to an eBook—an online edition of the text—to aid them in successfully completing their work, wherever and whenever they choose.

Connect for Students

Connect provides students with a powerful tool for improving academic performance and truly mastering course material, plus 24/7 online access to an interactive and searchable eBook. Connect allows students to practise important skills at their own pace and on their own schedule. The Connect Student Resources Library includes Practice Quizzes, Active Exhibits, Videos, Interactives, and the Marketer's Showdown:

- The **Marketer's Showdown** consists of nine cases focusing on up-to-the-minute issues in the music, automotive, and soft-drink industries. These cases are designed to allow students to analyze the marketing problem, choose a proposed solution, and then watch their proposal debated by marketing professionals. After the debate, students have the opportunity to change their plan or stick to their guns, and then see the outcome of their decisions.

- The **Interactive Student Toolkits,** available for specific chapters, offer students interactive, gradable assignments that focus on challenging but pertinent concepts such as SWOT analysis, compensatory vs. noncompensatory consumer decision making, vendor evaluation analysis, marketing positioning map, service quality, breakeven analysis, customer lifetime value, and return on investment.

- **Self-Quizzes** that focus on key concepts and provide immediate feedback offer students the opportunity to determine their level of understanding.

Superior Service

Service takes on a whole new meaning with McGraw-Hill Ryerson and *Marketing*. More than just bringing you the textbook, we have consistently raised the bar in terms of innovation and educational research—both in operations management and in education in general. These investments in learning and the education community have helped us to understand the needs of students and educators across the country, and allowed us to foster the growth of truly innovative, integrated learning.

Integrated Learning. Your Integrated Learning Sales Specialist is a McGraw-Hill Ryerson representative who has the experience, product knowledge, training, and support to help you assess and integrate any of our products, technology, and services into your course for optimum teaching and learning performance. Whether it's helping your students improve their grades, or putting your entire course online, your *i*Learning Sales Specialist is there to help you do it. Contact your *i*Learning Sales Specialist today to learn how to maximize all of McGraw-Hill Ryerson's resources!

iLearning Services. McGraw-Hill Ryerson offers a unique *i*Services package designed for Canadian faculty. Our mission is to equip providers of higher education with superior tools and resources required for excellence in teaching.

Tegrity

Tegrity Campus is a service that makes class time available all the time by automatically capturing every lecture in a searchable format for students to review when they study and complete assignments. With a simple one-click start-and-stop process, you capture all computer screens and corresponding audio. Students replay any part of any class with easy-to-use browser-based viewing on a PC or Mac. Educators know that the more students can see, hear, and experience class resources, the better they learn. With Tegrity Campus, students quickly recall key moments by using Tegrity Campus's unique search feature. This search helps students efficiently find what they need, when they need it across an entire semester of class recordings. Help turn all your students' study time into learning moments immediately supported by your lecture. To learn more about Tegrity watch a two-minute Flash demo at http://tegritycampus.mhhe.com.

CourseSmart

CourseSmart brings together thousands of textbooks across hundreds of courses in an eTextbook format providing unique benefits to students and faculty. By purchasing an eTextbook, students can save up to 50-percent off the cost of a print textbook, reduce their impact on the environment, and gain access to powerful web tools for learning, including full text search, notes and highlighting, and email tools for sharing notes between classmates. For faculty, CourseSmart provides instant access to review and compare textbooks and course materials in their discipline area without the time, cost, and environmental impact of mailing print examination copies. For further details, contact your iLearning Sales Specialist or go to www.coursesmart.com.

Create Online

McGraw-Hill's Create Online gives you access to the most abundant resource at your fingertips—literally. With a few mouse clicks, you can create customized learning tools simply and affordably. McGraw-Hill Ryerson has included many of our market-leading textbooks within Create Online for eBook and print customization as well as many licensed readings and cases. For more information, go to www. mcgrawhillcreate.ca.

acknowledgements

We could not have completed this text without the help of others. In particular, we would like to thank Stacey Biggar, who diligently worked with us throughout the project as an invaluable research assistant, writer, and proofreader. We could not have met our many deadlines without her. Our thanks go as well to the many Wilfrid Laurier University students and professors who took the time to provide us with feedback on the chapter content, cases, and exercises.

Additionally, we would like to thank Priya Persaud, who worked as a research assistant on this book, and Gautam Lamba, who helped compile a comprehensive database of research articles. We would also like to thank Kashif Memon, University of Waterloo, for creating the content for the Grewal Connect site.

A special thanks to the many talented staff and freelance members at McGraw-Hill Ryerson—Leanna MacLean, Andria Fogarty, Amy Rydzanicz, Alison Derry, Tracy Leonard, Deborah Cooper-Bullock, and Joy Armitage Taylor. You made our jobs so much easier. It was a pleasure working with you.

We gratefully acknowledge feedback and constructive criticism from marketing colleagues across Canada.

Thomas Arhontoudis	George Brown College
Harp Arora	University of Waterloo
Arun Bhardwaj	NAIT
Mark Boivin	University of Calgary
Brian Broadway	Seneca College
Janice Brown	Seneca College
Alan Chapelle	Vancouver Island University
Jane-Michelle Clark	York University
Russell Currie	University of British Columbia
Glen Davis	Red River College
Ray Friedman	Lethbridge College
Markarand Gulawani	Grant MacEwan University
Dwight Heinrichs	University of Regina
Marion Hill	SAIT Polytechnic
Warveni Jap	Thompson Rivers University
Denyse Lafrance Horning	Nipissing University
Irene Lu	Carleton University
Elaine MacNeil	Cape Breton University
Michael Madore	University of Lethbridge
Diamond Meuse	Eastern College
Miguel Morales	St. Mary's University
David Moulton	Douglas College
Brent Pearce	Concordia University
Margery Taylor	George Brown College
William Thurber	York University

I would like to thank my wife, Vidya, and kids, Priya and Ryan, for their love, support, and humour that made writing this book enjoyable.   —Ajax Persaud

Thanks to John and Stephen, for your patience, support, and encouragement throughout the process of research and writing.   —Shirley Lichti

CHAPTER 1

Overview
of Marketing

Marketing is essentially about creating value for consumers and the company's shareholders. As you will learn throughout this book, creating value for consumers and the firm requires that marketers develop and nurture long-term, profitable relationships with consumers. This means that marketers must understand consumers' needs and wants and try to satisfy them through the goods and services they offer, the prices they charge, and the way they promote and deliver the goods and services. Let's take a look at how one of Canada's most successful and profitable high tech companies, Research In Motion (RIM), is creating and delivering value to its consumers and shareholders with its BlackBerry.

The BlackBerry is one of Canada's most successful and innovative products.[1] It changed not only the way business executives and professionals communicate, but also the speed and timeliness with which decisions are made. Users around the world attest that the BlackBerry enhances their ability to access key corporate information and connect with co-workers anywhere, anytime. The resulting efficiency means that business deals are made more quickly and key decisions are communicated to stakeholders even when they are on the golf course. The BlackBerry smartphone has become the one device that many business people can't live without.

The BlackBerry was designed for wireless email use. Within a few years of its release, it became the dominant device in the market. Not surprisingly, BlackBerry's market position is consistently challenged by new rivals, such as Apple's iPhone, HTC's Droid Incredible, and Palm's Pre. The iPhone, launched in 2007, created huge buzz and took the smartphone market by storm, gaining more than 25 percent market share in less than three years and becoming the second most popular smartphone.

Learning Objectives

After studying this chapter, you should be able to

LO1 Define marketing and explain its core concepts

LO2 Illustrate how marketers create value for a product or service

LO3 Summarize the four orientations of marketing

LO4 Identify the role of customer relationship management in creating value

LO5 Explain the importance of marketing both within and outside the firm

Google's Android, a recently launched operating system (OS) for smartphones, has more than doubled its market share in less than a year.[2]

To consolidate and grow its market position, RIM successfully entered into the consumer market segment with two hugely popular smartphones, the BlackBerry Curve and the BlackBerry Torch.[3] Consumers quickly adopted both of these smartphones, challenging the market segment where the iPhone is the current favourite. In response, Apple is now trying to gain a foothold in RIM's lucrative business market. The battle between the BlackBerry and the iPhone has many industry analysts pointing to the BlackBerry's weaknesses, such as a lack of applications and a challenging user interface. To silence its critics, RIM released the BlackBerry 6, with a new OS, user interface, and WebKit browser, while also revamping its BlackBerry App World. Although apps and web browsing are all the rage,[4] email access is what drives many voice-only customers to upgrade their plans to include data services, and this area has been the BlackBerry's strength.

The BlackBerry also uses wireless networks more efficiently than competing devices, which means that carriers such as Rogers and Bell can offer data services to BlackBerry customers for less money than customers pay to use competing products. In fact, telecom carriers are feeling the squeeze from data-hungry smartphones and have responded by introducing usage-based billing for data services.[5] This change could affect consumers' monthly bills, which could, in turn, influence their buying decision. RIM co-CEO Jim Balsillie has said that carriers are well aware of how profitable the BlackBerry is for their business and how strategically RIM is aligned with them. Clearly, the BlackBerry has some unique advantages over its competitors.

Despite fierce competition, RIM's sales grew from US$85 million in 2000 to US$19.9 billion in 2011. Within this same period, the company increased its workforce from about 1000 employees to more than 17 500 employees, of which 3200 are in sales, marketing, and customer support. RIM spent US$1.9 billion on sales and marketing in fiscal year 2010. Currently, RIM has more than 41 million subscribers globally. In addition to meeting its customer needs with an impressive portfolio of innovative products, RIM has made excellent customer service a top priority. It has increased the number of employees providing customer care, improved the number of service contracts to users, and developed training programs for corporate customers. This customer focus helps RIM ensure that BlackBerry is "Always On, Always Connected," satisfying users who demand information in real time. .::

What Is Marketing?

Unlike other subjects you may have studied, marketing is already very familiar to you. You start your day by agreeing to do the dishes in exchange for a freshly made cup of coffee. Then you fill up your car with gas. You attend a class that you have chosen and paid for. After class, you pick up lunch at the cafeteria, have your hair cut, download a few songs from iTunes, an online music store, and watch a movie. In each case, you have acted as the buyer and made a decision about whether you should part with your time and/or money to receive a particular service or type of merchandise. If, after you return home from the movie, you decide to auction a collectible item on eBay, you have become a seller. In each of these transactions, you were engaged in marketing because you were exchanging something of value that satisfies a need.

This chapter will look at the definition of marketing and at how marketing is used to create value in products or in services. We will see how the interrelated marketing mix—or four Ps—create, transact, communicate, and deliver value. As well, we will look at where marketing happens and how it has evolved over the years into today's concept of value-based marketing. Lastly, we will discuss why marketing is an important function for any successful firm. Refer to the chapter roadmap to guide you through the chapter contents.

The Canadian Marketing Association states that "**Marketing** is a set of business practices designed to plan for and present an organization's products or services in ways that build effective customer relationships."[6] What does this definition really mean? Good marketing is not a random activity; it requires thoughtful planning with an emphasis on the ethical implications of any of those decisions on consumers and society in general. Firms develop a **marketing plan** that specifies the marketing activities for a specific period of time. The marketing plan is broken down into various components—how the product or service will be conceived or designed, how much it should cost, where and how it will be

marketing
A set of business practices designed to plan for and present an organization's products or services in ways that build effective customer relationships.

marketing plan
A written document composed of an analysis of the current marketing situation, opportunities and threats for the firm, marketing objectives and strategy specified in terms of the four Ps, action programs, and projected or pro forma income (and other financial) statements.

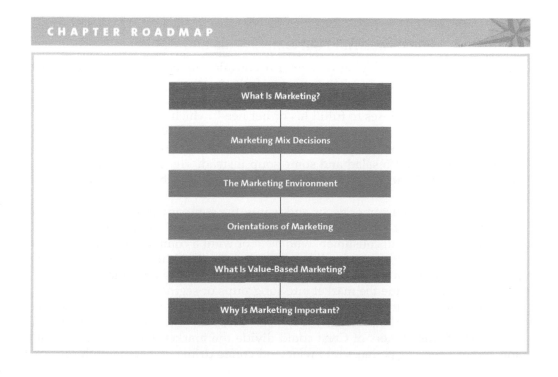

CHAPTER ROADMAP

- What Is Marketing?
- Marketing Mix Decisions
- The Marketing Environment
- Orientations of Marketing
- What Is Value-Based Marketing?
- Why Is Marketing Important?

L01   **EXHIBIT 1.1**   Core Aspects of Marketing

promoted, and how it will get to the consumer. In any exchange, the buyer and the seller should be satisfied with the value they obtained from a transaction. In our earlier example, you should be satisfied or even delighted with the song you downloaded, and Apple should be satisfied with the amount of money it received from you. The core aspects of marketing are shown in Exhibit 1.1. Let's see how they look in practice.

Marketing Is About Satisfying Customer Needs and Wants

Understanding and satisfying consumer needs and wants is fundamental to marketing success. A **need** is when a person feels deprived of the basic necessities of life, such as food, clothing, shelter, or safety. A **want** is the particular way in which the person chooses to fulfill his or her need, which is shaped by a person's knowledge, culture, and personality. For example, when we are hungry, we need something to eat. Some people want a submarine sandwich to satisfy that hunger, whereas others want a salad and some soup instead. The topic of understanding customer needs is described in detail in Chapter 5, which deals with consumer behaviour.

To understand customer needs and wants, the company must first identify the customers or **market** for its product or service. Generally, the market for a firm's offerings consists of all consumers who need or want a company's products or services and have the ability and willingness to buy them. Although marketers would prefer to sell their products and services to everyone, it is not practical to do so. Thus, marketers divide the market into subgroups or segments of people to whom they are interested in marketing their products, services, or ideas. For example, even though the marketplace for toothpaste users may include most of the people in the world, the makers of Crest could divide the market into adolescent, adult, and senior users, or perhaps into wine and coffee drinkers, people with sensitive

need
A person feeling physiologically deprived of basic necessities, such as food, clothing, shelter, and safety.

want
The particular way in which a person chooses to satisfy a need, which is shaped by a person's knowledge, culture, and personality.

market
Refers to the groups of people who need or want a company's products or services and have the ability and willingness to buy them.

| **EXHIBIT 1.2** | Exchange: The Underpinning of Seller–Buyer Relationships |

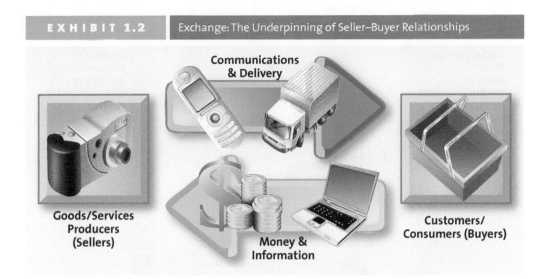

gums, and denture users. If you manufacture toothpaste that bleaches and removes stains, you want to know for which market segments your product is most relevant and then make sure that you build a marketing strategy that meets the needs and wants of the target groups or **target market**. The process of how companies segment the market for their products and services and then choose which segment to target and how best to reach that segment is described in Chapter 7. The process of identifying customer segments the company wants to target with its products and services requires market research. The types of market research that help marketers make good decisions about various aspects of the marketing mix are discussed in Chapter 4.

target market
The customer segment or group to whom the firm is interested in selling its products and services.

Marketing Entails Value Exchange

Marketing is about an **exchange**—the trade of things of value between the buyer and the seller so that each is better off as a result. As depicted in Exhibit 1.2, sellers provide goods or services, then communicate and facilitate the delivery of their offering to consumers. Buyers complete the exchange by giving money and information to the seller. Suppose you learn about a new Justin Bieber album when watching MTV, which gave a review of the album and mentioned that it was available online at iTunes. You go online and purchase the album. Along with gathering your necessary billing and shipping information, iTunes creates a record of your purchase: information that may be used in the coming months to inform you of the release of Bieber's next album or of his next concert in your area. Thus, in addition to making money on this particular transaction, iTunes can use the information you provided to facilitate a future exchange and solidify a relationship with you—additional value for both you and iTunes.

exchange
The trade of things of value between the buyer and the seller so that each is better off as a result.

When you purchase a new Justin Bieber album, you are engaging in a marketing exchange. You get the songs, and the exchange partners get money and information about you.

EXHIBIT 1.3 — Marketing Mix Decisions

L02

Product/Service
Brand
Size
Quality
Features
Packaging
Warranty

List Price
Discounts
Allowances
Costs
Payment Period
Credit Terms

Creating Value Product

Transacting Value Price

Target Market

Communicating Value Promotion

Delivering Value Place

Advertising
Sales Promotion
Personal Selling
Public Relations
Direct Marketing
Electronic Media

Marketing Channels
Distribution Intensity
Locations: retailers, online
Supply Chain
Logistics

Marketing Requires Product, Price, Place, and Promotion Decisions

marketing mix (four Ps)
Product, price, place, and promotion—the controllable set of activities that a firm uses to respond to the wants of its target markets.

Marketing traditionally has been divided into a set of four interrelated decisions known as the **marketing mix,** or **four Ps:** product, price, place, and promotion, as shown in Exhibit 1.3.[7] Together, the four Ps comprise the marketing mix, which is the controllable set of activities that the firm uses to respond to the wants of its target markets. But what does each of them mean and how do they work together to create value for consumers?

Product: Creating Value One main purpose of marketing is to create value by developing a variety of offerings, including goods, services, and ideas, to satisfy customer needs. Take, for example, water. Not too long ago, consumers perceived this basic commodity as simply water. It came out of a faucet and was consumed for drinking and washing. But taking a cue from European firms such as Perrier (France) and San Pellegrino (Italy), several Canadian-based firms, such as Clearly Canadian, Canadian Springs, and Montclair, have created a product with benefits that consumers find valuable. In addition to easy access to water, an essential part of this created value is the product's brand image, which lets users say to the world, "I'm healthy," "I'm smart," and "I'm chic."[8] Recently, however, there is growing opposition to bottled water, which not only makes it seem socially unacceptable, but also

Clearly Canadian has created a product with benefits that consumers find valuable.

has seen some organizations banning the sale of bottled water on their premises. For example, the University of Ottawa has banned the sale of bottled water on campus, declaring itself a bottled water–free zone; it has set aside $75,000 to install new water fountains across the campus.[9]

Goods are items that you can physically touch. Roots clothing, Molson Canadian beer, Kraft Dinner, and countless other products are examples of goods. Carmen Creek Gourmet Meats, a small Calgary-based company specializing in the marketing and distribution of grade A Canadian bison, demonstrates how a company offers value to customers. It provides exquisite gourmet bison meat that is raised, processed, and delivered using appropriate animal health practices. (See Entrepreneurial Marketing 1.1 later in this chapter.)

Unlike goods, **services** are intangible customer benefits that are produced by people or machines and cannot be separated from the producer. Air travel, banking, insurance, beauty treatments, and entertainment all are services. If you attend a hockey or football game, you are consuming a service. Getting money from your bank by using an ATM or teller is another example of using a service. In this case, cash machines usually add value to your banking experience by being conveniently located, fast, and easy to use.

Many offerings represent a combination of goods and services. When you go to Hakim Optical, for example, you can have your eyes examined (service) and purchase new contact lenses (good). If you enjoy Taylor Swift's music, you can attend one of her concerts, which can be provided only at a particular time and place. At the concert, you can purchase one of her CDs—a tangible good that provides you with a combination of a good and a service.

Ideas include thoughts, opinions, philosophies, and intellectual concepts that also can be marketed. Groups promoting bicycle safety go to schools, give talks, and sponsor bike helmet poster contests for the members of their primary target market: children. Then their secondary target market segment, parents and siblings, gets involved through their interactions with the young contest participants. The exchange of value occurs when the children listen to the sponsor's presentation and wear their helmets while bicycling, which means they have adopted, or become "purchasers," of the safety idea that the group marketed. In Chapters 8, 9, and 10 of this book, you will learn much more about the decisions, theories, applications, and strategies of product and services marketing.

Price: Transacting Value   Everything has a price, though it doesn't always have to be monetary. **Price,** therefore, is everything the buyer gives up—money, time, energy—in exchange for the product. Marketers must determine the price of a product carefully on the basis of the potential buyer's belief about its value. For example, Air Canada can take you from Toronto to Vancouver or New York. The price you pay depends on how far in advance you book the ticket, the time of year, whether you want to fly economy or business class, and more recently whether or not you have luggage to check in. Passengers are charged a fee if they have more than one piece of check-in luggage. If you value the convenience of buying your ticket at the last minute for a ski trip between Christmas and New Year's Day and you want to fly business class, you can expect to pay four or five times as much as you would for the cheapest available ticket. That is, you have traded off a lower price for convenience. For marketers, the key to determining prices is figuring out how much customers are willing to pay so that they are satisfied with the purchase and the seller achieves a reasonable profit. In Chapter 11, you will learn much more about pricing concepts, decisions, and strategies.

Many offerings are a combination of goods and services. At a Taylor Swift concert, you can enjoy the concert (a service) and buy her CD (a good).

goods
Items that can be physically touched.

services
Intangible customer benefits that are produced by people or machines and cannot be separated from the producer.

ideas
Include thoughts, opinions, philosophies, and intellectual concepts.

price
The overall sacrifice a consumer is willing to make—money, time, energy—to acquire a specific product or service.

Place: Delivering Value   The third P, place, describes all the activities necessary to get the product from the manufacturer or producer to the right customer when that customer wants it. Place decisions are concerned with developing an efficient system for merchandise to be distributed in the right quantities, to the right locations, and at the right time in the most efficient way in order to minimize systemwide costs while satisfying the service levels required by their customers.[10] Many marketing students initially overlook the importance of distribution management because a lot of distribution activities occur behind the scenes. But without a strong and efficient distribution system, merchandise isn't available when or where customers want it. They are disappointed, and sales and profits suffer. Place or distribution activities and decisions are discussed in detail in Chapter 12.

To illustrate how distribution delivers value, consider the experience of The Country Grocer, a small Ottawa-based independent grocery store. The Country Grocer was the first independently owned grocery store in Canada to offer online groceries. You might think that because the store is independent, customers would live within a couple of kilometres of it. On the contrary, The Country Grocer (www. thecountrygrocer.com) gets more than 30 percent of its online sales from the eastern Arctic (Iqaluit) and about 5 percent of its business from customers in the United States. Customers place their orders through the website, and The Country Grocer ensures that their purchases are delivered on time.[11]

Promotion: Communicating Value   Even the best products and services will go unsold if marketers cannot communicate their value to customers. Countless Internet companies failed in the late 1990s, at least partly because they did not communicate successfully with their customers. Some such firms had great products at very fair prices, but when customers could not find them on the Internet, the companies failed. Promotion is communication by a marketer that informs, persuades, and reminds potential buyers about a product or service to influence their opinions or elicit a response. Promotion generally can enhance a product or service's value, as happened for Parasuco jeans. The company's provocative advertising has helped create an image that says more than "Use this product and you will look good." Rather, the promotion sells youth, style, and sex appeal.

The four Ps work together. Although marketers deliver value through each of the four Ps individually, they can deliver greater value to consumers by configuring the four Ps as a whole rather than by treating them as separate components. That is, the product or service offered must satisfy the target customers' specific needs and wants, be priced appropriately, be available at locations where customers want it, and be promoted in a manner and through media that are consistent with the target consumers. For instance, luxury or high-fashion items from retailers such as Coach, Louis Vuitton, and Swarovski are well-made, priced at a premium, available at exclusive locations, and promoted only in certain media where the advertisements emphasize style, fashion, sex appeal, and so on.

Parasuco is known for its provocative advertising, which appears on billboards and uses celebrities to market its denim lines.

Marketing Is Shaped by Forces and Players Within the Firm

A company's marketing activities are shaped by factors that are both internal to the firm and external to the firm, as shown in Exhibit 1.4. The consumer is the centre of all marketing activities, and offering the best value possible will attract customers to products and keep them loyal. For marketers to deliver the best value to their customers, they must leverage the full potential of their internal capabilities; work effectively with their partners (i.e., suppliers, distributors, and other intermediaries, such as financial institutions, advertising agencies, and research firms); and constantly evaluate and respond to the competitive environment.

EXHIBIT 1.4 Understanding the Marketing Environment

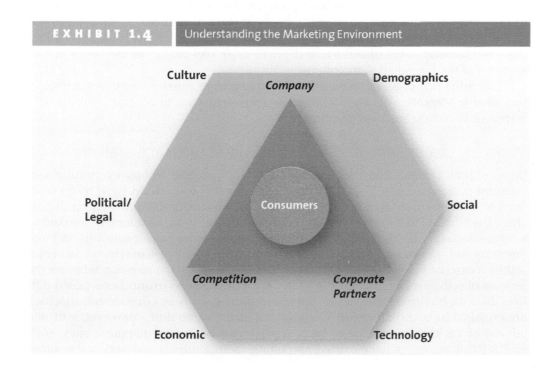

As described in the chapter vignette, RIM's success rests in the unique email capability of the BlackBerry, coupled with excellent customer service. RIM harnesses its internal capabilities by creating a customer-driven organization, where all internal departments and functions share information and work collaboratively toward a common goal, balance costs with benefits, and build strong relationships with customers. In addition, RIM relies on corporate partners, such as Rogers, TELUS, and Bell, to sell its BlackBerry devices, so it is hardly surprising to hear RIM co-CEO Jim Balsillie making the point that carriers are aware of how profitable the BlackBerry is for their businesses. RIM's competitors have improved the value they offer to customers; thus, it is imperative for RIM to enhance its value to customers, or else it could be overtaken by the competition. Suppliers or even natural disasters can exert substantial influence on a company's marketing activities, sometimes with devastating consequences. In March 2011, a tsunami and earthquake in Japan destroyed several nuclear reactors, disrupting power and industrial production in Japan. This natural disaster also affected North American companies that relied on Japanese suppliers or inputs. For example, both Honda and Toyota severely cut back on the production of their 2011-model vehicles because of a shortage of electronic components and other parts that were usually imported from Japan. This reduction created a huge shortage of vehicles among Japanese dealerships in Canada and the United States during the spring season, one of the best seasons for new-car sales.[12]

Marketing Is Shaped by Forces and Players External to the Firm

External forces such as cultural, demographic, social, technological, economic, and political and legal changes shape a company's marketing activities, as shown in Exhibit 1.4. For instance, two current social trends that are reshaping the marketing activities of most firms are concerns about the environment and obesity. In response to these concerns, marketers are beginning to use more environmentally friendly packaging for their products; some companies are even using alternative materials in the products themselves. In response to the obesity trend, marketers try to distinguish their products by using labels such as non-fat, low-fat, fat-free, sugar-free, and cholesterol-free. Similarly, food retailers are responding to demographic changes in Canada's population composition. Because the proportion of Chinese and South Asian people in Canada is on the rise and is forecasted to increase in the next decade, many food retailers have developed products and services that cater specifically to the needs of these groups. Sobeys's FreshCo store format demonstrates a prime example of a retailer trying to reach out and serve these Canadians. The store's layout, merchandise, level of service, and prices cater specifically to the needs of this segment of the Canadian demographic.

The influence of all of these forces is discussed in greater detail in Chapter 3. Sustainable Marketing 1.1 shows how marketers are trying to become more socially responsible in their business practices.

Marketing Can Be Performed by Both Individuals and Organizations

Imagine how complicated the world would be if you had to buy everything you consumed directly from producers or manufacturers. You would have to go from farm to farm buying your food and then from manufacturer to manufacturer to purchase the table, plates, and utensils you need to eat that food. Fortunately, marketing intermediaries, such as retailers, accumulate merchandise from producers in large amounts and then sell it to you in smaller amounts. The process in which businesses sell to consumers is known as **B2C (business-to-consumer)** marketing, whereas the process of selling merchandise or services from one business to another is called **B2B (business-to-business)** marketing. Some companies, such as GE (General Electric), are engaged in both B2B and B2C marketing at the same time. However, with the advent of various auction sites, such as eBay and Kijiji, and payment sites, such as PayPal, consumers have started marketing their products and services to other

**B2C
(business-to-consumer)**
The process in which businesses sell to consumers.

**B2B
(business-to-business)**
The process of selling merchandise or services from one business to another.

Sustainable Marketing 1.1

Green Your Marketing Practices

The idea of sustainable development, or sustainability, is popular these days among groups representing various segments of society such as the media, environmentalists, nonprofit organizations, politicians, business executives, and even consumers. But what exactly does sustainability mean, how widespread is the adoption of sustainable development practices and policies among businesses, and what are the benefits of sustainability?

You might be surprised to learn that sustainability seems to mean different things to different people. For instance, a recent global survey of 1749 business executives by McKinsey & Company reported that 55 percent say that sustainability is about managing environmental issues such as greenhouse gas emissions, energy efficiency, waste management, green-product development, and water conservation. Further, 48 percent say it is about governance issues such as complying with regulations, maintaining ethical practices, and meeting accepted industry standards, and 41 percent say it includes the management of social issues such as working conditions and labour standards.[13] In a nutshell, it seems that organizations that practise sustainability must strive to conduct their business in such a way as to minimize harm to the environment, follow good governance practices, and comply with social standards.

Indeed, a truly comprehensive and proactive approach to sustainability requires that businesses develop practices and policies around all three perspectives: environmental, governance, and social. This means that sustainability practices and policies must be embedded in all facets of the organization, from human resource management to manufacturing, marketing, production, planning, investments, and corporate strategy. Also, sustainability must involve all employees, from the CEO to the employee on the shop floor. Implementing a comprehensive sustainability program is quite expensive and so many businesses tend to do the bare minimum or implement low-cost programs. In fact, according to the McKinsey Global Survey, 36 percent of executives believe that the main benefit of sustainability is that it improves corporate and brand reputation, while less than 20 percent believe that it improves operational efficiency, lowers costs, presents growth opportunities (new markets and products), or strengthens competitive position.

Clearly, we are in the early stages in the adoption of sustainability policies and practices, and it is not unusual for there to be experimentation and feelings of euphoria, uncertainty, and confusion. Organizations and executives tend to get better as their learning improves over time. We expect to see a greater number of organizations being more proactive in implementing sustainability policies and practices. Throughout this book, we will present various examples of sustainable marketing efforts undertaken by Canadian companies.

---

consumers, which requires a third category in which consumers sell to other consumers, or **C2C (consumer-to-consumer)** marketing. These marketing transactions are illustrated in Exhibit 1.5. Individuals can also undertake activities to market themselves. When you apply for a job, for instance, the research you do about the firm, the resumé and cover letter you submit with your application, and the way you dress for an interview and conduct yourself during it are all forms of marketing activities. Accountants, lawyers, financial planners, physicians, and other professional service providers also market their services.

C2C (consumer-to-consumer) The process in which consumers sell to other consumers.

| **EXHIBIT 1.5** | Marketing Can Be Performed by Both Individuals and Organizations |

Firm (Makes Monitors) — B2B → Firm (Dell Sells PCs & Monitors) — B2C → Consumer A — C2C → Consumer B

Social Media Marketing 1.1

What Is Social Media?

When you hear the term *social media*, chances are you immediately think of Facebook, YouTube, MySpace, Twitter. Initially, many of these sites were viewed as places where people connected just for fun. Things have changed dramatically over the last couple of years. Today, marketers are euphoric about the marketing potential of these sites. Not surprisingly, a major preoccupation of marketers these days concerns developing an integrated social media marketing strategy. So, what exactly is social media?

It's not an understatement to say that there are as many definitions of *social media* as there are flavours at a Baskin-Robbins ice cream store. In fact, a quick Google search revealed more than 25 definitions, an indication of the diversity of these media. Considering the various definitions of and the use of social media leads us to the following simple definition:

Social media is the use of Internet tools and software by individuals to easily and quickly create and share content, such as information, knowledge, and insights, with people who have similar interests to foster dialogue, social relationships, and personal identities. Participants act as both publishers and consumers by creating, sharing, or remixing content, such as videos, images, and texts. Social media conversations and relationships may move freely between the online and physical context. That is, they may originate online and continue offline, or vice versa. Openness, authenticity, and transparency are key elements of effective social media.[14]

Social media is important to marketers for several reasons. First, more than 90 percent of Canadian Internet users are actively engaged with social media, with each visitor interacting with it for an average of 6.5 hours per month and downloading an average of 120 videos per month.[15] Social media is an excellent way to reach these consumers. Second, consumers are already carrying on conversations about companies, their brands and services; therefore, to be part of the conversation or to initiate conversations, companies must participate in social media. Third, social media enables marketers to accomplish many marketing goals, such as promoting corporate social responsibility, building customer relationships, enhancing customer service, building or defending their brands, engaging customers in research and new product development, and recruiting talent.

Although social media is currently very popular among retail businesses and the consumer packaged goods industry, interest from firms of all sizes, all industries, and all types (B2B, B2C, and C2C) are increasing daily. To illustrate how marketers are embracing this ever-changing world of social media, we have developed Social Media Marketing boxes for each chapter of this book.

For a visual look at the impact of social media on the world around us, you may want to view a video called *Social Media Revolution*, which is available on YouTube.

Sources: "What is Social Media? A not so critical review of concepts and definitions," http://blog.metaroll.com/2008/11/14/what-is-social-media-a-not-so-critical-review-of-concepts-and-definitions/ (accessed December 2, 2009); Joseph Thornley, "Social networking isn't just about Facebook," http://www.itworldcanada.com/blogs/ahead/2009/04/08/social-networking-isnt-just-about-facebook/48460/ (accessed December 2, 2009); Joseph Thornley, "What is 'social media'?" http://propr.ca/2008/what-is-social-media/ (accessed December 2, 2009); ComScore, www.comscore.com, 2009.

social media
The use of Internet tools to easily and quickly create and share content to foster dialogue, social relationships, and personal identities.

Regardless of whether organizations or individuals are engaged in B2B, B2C, or C2C marketing, one thing seems to be clear: social media is quickly becoming an integral part of their marketing and communications strategies. Social media was widely used in the 2011 federal election in Canada, as politicians tried to win the hearts and minds of Canadians. Even more dramatically, social media played a major role in the crises observed in several Mideast countries. Social media was used to organize protesters and to report news of events in these countries to the rest of the world as they unfolded in real time. Social Media Marketing 1.1 shows how marketers are using social media to reach out to their customers.

Marketing Occurs in Many Settings

Most people think of marketing as a way for firms to make profits, but marketing works equally well in the nonprofit sector. Think about what influenced your selection of your college or university, other than family, friends, and convenience. It's likely that your college has a sophisticated marketing program to attract and retain students. Hospitals, theatres, charities, museums, religious institutions, politicians, and even governments rely on marketing to communicate their message to their constituents.

A Piece of Africa buys art from African artists and, through its website (www.bizinsa.com/ apieceofafrica), makes that art available to customers all over the world, thereby creating a market that otherwise would not exist.

In addition, marketing isn't useful only in countries with well-developed economies. It can also jump-start the economies of less developed countries by actually putting buyers and sellers together to create new markets. A Piece of Africa, for example, buys art from African artists and, through its website, makes that art available to customers all over the world, thereby creating a market that otherwise would not exist. Customers become exposed to an array of products from various countries that previously would have been available only through expensive galleries, and the tribal artists can spend their earnings locally, which stimulates the local economy. Furthermore, A Piece of Africa donates 3 percent of the online sales to goodwill projects in Africa, which solidifies its socially responsible appeal.

Marketing is often designed to benefit an entire industry, which can help many firms simultaneously. The dairy industry has used a very successful, award-winning campaign with its slogan "Got Milk?" aimed at different target segments. This campaign has not only created high levels of awareness about the benefits of drinking milk, but also increased milk consumption in various target segments,[16] possibly through the use of celebrities such as Hilary Duff and athletes such as soccer superstar David Beckham. Overall, this campaign benefits the entire dairy industry, not just one dairy farmer.

Now that we've examined what marketing is and how it creates value, let's consider how it fits into the world of commerce, as well as into society in general.

The dairy industry's "Got Milk?" ad campaign has created high levels of awareness about the benefits of drinking milk and has increased milk consumption by using celebrities such as David Beckham in its ads.

Marketing Helps Create Value

Marketing didn't get to its current prominence among individuals, corporations, and society at large overnight. Over the last 100 years, marketing has evolved from an activity designed simply to produce and sell products to an integral business function aimed at creating value for consumers and the company's shareholders. As we have examined marketing practices over the years, we have observed four different marketing orientations or philosophies: product orientation, sales orientation, market orientation, and value-based orientation.

LO3

Product Orientation   Product-oriented companies focus on developing and distributing innovative products with little concern about whether the products best satisfy customers' needs. This philosophy is best illustrated by a famous quote made around the turn of the twentieth century by Henry Ford, the founder of Ford Motor Company, who remarked, "Customers can have any colour they want so long as it's black." Manufacturers believed that a good product would sell itself, and retail stores typically were considered places to hold the merchandise until a consumer wanted it. Companies with a product orientation generally start out by thinking about the product they want to build; they try selling the product after it is developed rather than starting with an understanding of the customers' needs and then developing a product to satisfy those needs.

Sales Orientation   Companies that have a sales orientation basically view marketing as a selling function where companies try to sell as many of their products as possible rather than focus on making products consumers really want. These firms typically depend on heavy doses of personal selling and advertising to attract new customers. Companies with a selling orientation tend to focus on making a sale or on each transaction rather than building long-term customer relationships. They generally believe that if consumers try their products, they will like them.

Market Orientation   Market-oriented companies start out by focusing on what consumers want and need before they design, make, or attempt to sell their products and services. They believe that customers have choice and make purchase decisions based on several factors, including quality, convenience, and price. Basically, the "customer is king," and the market is a buyer's market since consumers wield tremendous power. In this orientation, marketers' role is to understand and respond to the needs of consumers and to do everything possible to satisfy them.

Value-Based Orientation   Most successful firms today are market oriented.[17] That means they have gone beyond a production or sales orientation and attempt to discover and satisfy their customers' needs and wants. Better marketing firms recognized that there was more to good marketing than simply discovering and providing what consumers wanted and needed; to compete successfully, they would have to give their customers greater value than their competitors.

value
Reflects the relationship of benefits to costs, or what the consumer *gets* for what he or she *gives.*

Value reflects the relationship of benefits to costs, or what you *get* for what you *give.*[18] In a marketing context, customers seek a fair return in goods and/or services for their hard-earned money and scarce time. They want products or services that meet their specific needs or wants and that are offered at competitive prices. The challenge for firms is to find out what consumers are looking for and to attempt to provide those goods and services but still make a profit.

Every value-based marketing firm must implement its strategy according to what its customers value. Depending on the specific product or service for sale, these valuable benefits could include speed, convenience, size, accuracy, price, cost-savings, or user-friendliness. Sometimes providing greater value means providing a lot of merchandise for relatively little money, such as Subway's foot-long subs for $5 or a diamond for 40 percent off the suggested retail price at Costco. But value is in the eye of the beholder and doesn't always come inexpensively.

Entrepreneurial Marketing 1.1 — Carmen Creek: Meeting Customer Needs[19]

In 2002, Kelly Long, Pieter Spinder, and Dean Andres joined forces to create Carmen Creek Gourmet Meats. The award-winning, Calgary-based company specializes in the marketing and distribution of grade A Canadian bison, which the Heart and Stroke Foundation's Health Check approves as a healthy substitute for red meat. Carmen Creek saw its revenues increase 15 times during its first year of operation and 18 times during its second year. The company was a finalist for the 2008 Ernst and Young Entrepreneur of the Year Award and won the 2008 Calgary Chamber of Commerce RBC Small Business of the Year Award. Carmen Creek attributes its success to its distinctive marketing strategy: it positions itself as a bison-specific producer with a commitment to quality and consistency to reach targeted markets.

Carmen Creek brings value to its three target markets, consumers, retailers (e.g., Safeway Canada), and foodservice businesses (e.g., Moxie's Classic Grill restaurant), in a variety of ways. Consumers can choose from an assortment of fresh and frozen bison meat, including bison burgers, bison steak, and prime rib. Retailers are provided with support in the form of recipe cards, a 1-800 help line, shelf danglers, shelf talkers, and in-store sampling booths. Foodservices customers are offered support through menu inserts, table toppers, and server incentives. In addition, Carmen Creek promises all of its customers exquisite gourmet bison meat that is grown, processed, and delivered using appropriate animal health practices, exceptional attention to detail, and superior safety. It provides all of this while guaranteeing the best prices that it can offer.

Carmen Creek's quality products and competitive pricing is allowing it to successfully satisfy the demands of North American and European customers. Its commitment to building a value chain that embraces producers, processors, and customers is allowing Carmen Creek to

Carmen Creek Gourmet Meats brings value to its customers beyond monetary cost and price.

break into new markets. On February 27, 2007, Carmen Creek acquired all the shares of Grande Prairie Bison Company, along with its strong European customer base and distribution network. This acquisition opened the door for Carmen Creek to expand its European presence. The company is actively pursuing new European markets in Belgium, Luxembourg, and the Netherlands to add to its list of international customers, which currently includes Australia and Germany.

Carmen Creek carefully focuses the distribution of its investments in Canada, the United States, and Europe. Couple this with its diversified product offerings under a consistent and supported brand, and you get a recipe for success. The company's approach to market development and its unique strategy has launched Carmen Creek Gourmet Meats to the top of both *Profit* 50's list of Canada's emerging growth companies and *Profit* 100's list of Canada's fastest growing companies.

Satisfied Louis Vuitton customers probably believe the Vuitton clothing, bags, or shoes they buy are good value because they have received many benefits for a reasonable price. Similarly, teenagers may be willing to pay a premium for Apple's iPhone because of its extraordinary design and packaging, even though cheaper substitutes are available. This is the power of marketing in general and branding in particular. Value-based marketing is examined in greater detail in the following section; however, the story of Carmen Creek described in Entrepreneurial Marketing 1.1 illustrates aspects of value beyond monetary cost and price.

What Is Value-Based Marketing?

Consumers make explicit and/or implicit trade-offs between the perceived benefits of a product or service and their costs. Customers naturally seek options that provide the greatest benefits at the lowest costs. Marketing firms attempt to find the most desirable balance between providing benefits to customers and keeping their costs down, as illustrated in Exhibit 1.6.

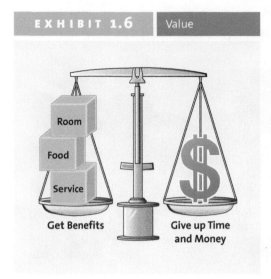

To better understand value and to develop a **value-based marketing** orientation, a business must also understand what customers view as the key benefits of a given product or service and how to improve on them. For example, some benefits of staying at a Four Points by Sheraton hotel might include the high level of service quality provided by the personnel, the convenience of booking the room via Sheraton's website, and the overall quality of the room and meals offered. In broader terms, some critical benefits may be service quality, convenience, and merchandise quality.

The other side of the value equation entails the firm's ability to provide either a better product/service mix at the same cost or the same level of quality and convenience for a lower cost. The customer's potential cost elements, in terms of value-based marketing strategies, for the Sheraton hotel in our example would include the price of the room and meals, the time it takes to book a room or check in at the hotel, and the risk of arriving at the hotel and finding it overbooked.

value-based marketing
Focuses on providing customers with benefits that far exceed the cost (money, time, effort) of acquiring and using a product or service while providing a reasonable return to the firm.

How Firms Compete on the Basis of Value

With such a simple formula, marketers should be able to deliver value consistently, right? Well, not exactly. In today's quickly changing world, consistently creating and delivering value is quite difficult. Consumer perceptions change quickly, competitors constantly enter markets, and global pressures continually reshape opportunities. Thus, marketers must keep a vigilant eye on the marketplace so they can adjust their offerings to meet customer needs and keep ahead of their competition.

Value-based marketing, however, isn't just about creating strong products and services; it should be at the core of every firm's functions. For example, Walmart does not serve those customers who are looking to impress their friends with conspicuous consumption. Rather, this store is for people who want convenient one-stop shopping and low prices—and on those values, it consistently delivers. But good value is not limited to just low prices. Although Walmart carries low-priced pots, pans, and coffee pots, cooking enthusiasts may prefer the product selection, quality, and expert sales assistance at a Paderno outlet. The prices there aren't as low as at Walmart, but Paderno customers believe they are receiving good value when they shop there because of the selection, quality, and service they receive. Even nonprofit organizations need to focus on creating value to ensure the services they provide to stakeholders are of high quality while also minimizing the total fundraising required.

How Firms Become Value-Driven

Firms become value-driven by focusing on three activities (see Exhibit 1.7). First, they share information about their customers and competitors across their own organization and with other firms that might be involved in getting the product or service to the marketplace, such as manufacturers and transportation companies. Second, they strive to balance their customers' benefits and costs. Third, they concentrate on building relationships with customers.

Sharing Information In a value-based, market-oriented firm, marketers share information about customers and competitors that has been collected through customer relationship management, and integrate it across the firm's various departments. The fashion designers for Zara, the Spain-based fashion retailer, for instance, collect purchase information and research customer trends to determine what their customers will want to wear in the next few weeks; simultaneously, the logisticians—those persons in charge of getting the merchandise to the stores—use the same purchase history to forecast sales and allocate appropriate merchandise to individual stores. Sharing and coordinating such information represents a critical success factor for any firm. Imagine what might happen if Zara's advertising department were to plan a special promotion but not share its sales projections with those people in charge of creating the merchandise or getting it to stores.

Fashion designers for Zara, the Spain-based fashion retailer, collect purchase information and research customer trends to determine what their customers will want to wear in the next few weeks. They share this information with other departments to forecast sales and coordinate deliveries.

Balancing Benefits with Costs Value-oriented marketers constantly measure the benefits that customers perceive against the cost of their offering. In this task, they use available customer data to find opportunities in which they can better satisfy their customers' needs and in turn develop long-term loyalties. Such a value-based orientation has helped Canadian Tire and Walmart outperform other department stores, and WestJet Airlines and Southwest Airlines outperform mainstream carriers. Also, as noted in the chapter vignette, RIM offers its customers not only the innovative, feature-packed portfolio of BlackBerry products, but also high-quality customer service at a competitive price. By establishing contracts with wireless carriers such as AT&T and BellSouth, it gained a solid footing before competitors such as Nokia entered the market. RIM's marketing savvy in making customer value the centrepiece of its strategy is one of the reasons why it has been able to beat the competition.

Until recently, it sometimes cost more to fly within Europe than to fly from the United States to Europe. But low-frills, low-cost carriers such as Ryanair and easy-Jet,[20] modelled on Southwest Airlines and JetBlue Airways, now offer customers what they want: cheap intra-Europe airfares. Like their American counterparts, Ryanair and easyJet offer no food service and generally fly to and from out-of-the-way airports, such as Stansted, which is about 55 kilometres northeast of London. But many customers find value despite such minor inconveniences. Consider, for example, the London to Salzburg, Austria, route for $65 or the London to Sweden flight for $70. Values such as these are also what have given low-cost carriers in the United States approximately 25 percent of the market share. They are so popular that conventional airlines have started their own low-frills/low-cost airlines: Singapore Airlines provides Tiger Airways and Australia's Qantas offers Jetstar.

To provide a great value, U.K.-based easyJet offers no food service and generally flies to and from out-of-the-way airports.

LO4

transactional orientation
Regards the buyer–seller relationship as a series of individual transactions, so anything that happened before or after the transaction is of little importance.

relational orientation
A method of building a relationship with customers based on the philosophy that buyers and sellers should develop a long-term relationship.

customer relationship management (CRM)
A business philosophy and set of strategies, programs, and systems that focus on identifying and building loyalty among the firm's most valued customers.

Building Relationships with Customers   During the past decade or so, marketers have begun to realize that they need to think about their customer orientation in terms of relationships rather than transactions.[21] A **transactional orientation** regards the buyer–seller relationship as a series of individual transactions, so anything that happened before or after the transaction is of little importance. For example, used-car sales typically are based on a transactional approach; the seller wants to get the highest price for the car, the buyer wants to get the lowest price, and neither expects to do business with the other again.

A **relational orientation,** in contrast, is based on the philosophy that buyers and sellers should develop a long-term relationship. According to this idea, the lifetime profitability of the relationship matters, not how much money is made during each transaction. For example, UPS works with its shippers to develop efficient transportation solutions. Over time, UPS becomes part of the fabric of the shippers' organizations, and their operations become intertwined. In this scenario, UPS and its shippers have developed a long-term relationship.

Firms that practise value-based marketing also use a process known as **customer relationship management (CRM),** a business philosophy and set of strategies, programs, and systems that focus on identifying and building loyalty among the firm's most valued customers.[22] Firms that employ CRM systematically collect information about their customers' needs and then use that information to target their best customers with the products, services, and special promotions that appear most important to those customers.

LO5

Why Is Marketing Important?

Marketing was once only an afterthought to production. Early marketing philosophy went something like this: "We've made it; now how do we get rid of it?" Today, marketing has evolved into a major business function that crosses all areas of a firm or organization, as illustrated in Exhibit 1.8. Marketing works with other departments, such as research and development (R&D), engineering, and production, to ensure that high-quality, innovative products that meet customers' needs are available in the right quantity, at the right price, and at the right place, that is, wherever they want to purchase it. It creates mutually valuable relationships between the company and its suppliers, distributors, and other external firms that are involved in the firm's marketing process. It identifies those elements that local customers value and makes it possible for the firm to expand globally. Marketing has had a significant impact on consumers as well. Without marketing, it would be difficult for any of us to learn about new products and services. You may even decide to pursue a career in marketing after you graduate. Even if you pursue a career in another field, marketing knowledge will help you market yourself in ways that could land you your dream job.

These brands can be found in many countries.

Marketing Expands Firms' Global Presence

A generation ago, Coca-Cola was available in many nations, but Levi's and most other American and Canadian brands were not. But today most jeans, including those by Levi Strauss & Co. and Parasuco, are made in places other than Canada and the United States and are available nearly everywhere. Thanks to MTV and other global entertainment venues, cheap foreign travel, and the Internet, you share many of your consumption behaviours with college and university students in countries all over the globe. The best fashions, music, and even food trends disseminate rapidly around the world.

EXHIBIT 1.8	Importance of Marketing

Can Be
Entrepreneurial

Expands Global
Presence

Pervasive Across
Organization

Enriches Society

Importance of Marketing

Makes Life Easier

Pervasive Across
Supply Chain

Starbucks has adjusted its menu to meet customer wants in the Japanese market more effectively.

Take a look at your next shopping bag. Whether it contains groceries or apparel, you will find goods from many countries: produce from Mexico, jeans from Italy, T-shirts from China. Global manufacturers and retailers continue to make inroads into the Canadian market. Companies such as Honda, Sony, and Heineken sell as well in Canada as they do in their home countries. Sweden's fashion retailer H&M operates in 38 countries, including Canada.[23] Its upscale competitor Spain's Zara operates in more than 80 countries, including Canada.[24] Starbucks even adjusted its menu to meet customer wants in the

Japanese market more effectively. How does marketing contribute to a company's successful global expansion? Understanding customers is critical. Without the knowledge that can be gained by analyzing new customers' needs and wants on a segment-by-segment, region-by-region basis—one of marketing's main tasks—it would be difficult for a firm to expand globally. Power of the Internet 1.1 shows how the Internet has expanded the reach of marketers and changed marketing practices.

Marketing Is Pervasive Across the Organization

In value-based marketing firms, the marketing department works seamlessly with other functional areas of the company to design, promote, price, and distribute products. Consider the Scion, a car and brand designed by Toyota for the less affluent youth market, which sometimes has been referred to as Generation Y.[26] Scion's marketing department worked closely with engineers to ensure that the new car exceeded customers' expectations in terms of design but remained affordable. The company also coordinated the product offering with an innovative communications strategy. Because Generation Y is famous for its resistance to conventional advertising, Scion introduced a virtual road race in which participants received mileage points for sending Scion e-cards. The more "places" they visited, the more mileage points they received. At the end of the competition, each driver's points were totalled and compared with other racers' scores. The driver with the most points won an onboard navigation system worth more than $2000. In addition, when Scion was a new car, the marketing department worked closely with the distribution department to ensure that advertising and promotions reached all distributors' territories and that distribution existed where those promotions occurred. Thus, marketing was responsible for coordinating all these aspects of supply and demand.

Toyota introduced a virtual road race in which participants received mileage points for sending Scion e-cards. At the end of the competition, the driver with the most points won an onboard navigation system worth more than $2000.

Power of the Internet 1.1

Internet Marketing: Past, Present, and Future[25]

The Internet was released for commercial use in 1993. Immediately, the media, entrepreneurs, and others began to hype it as the "new marketing channel" that would revolutionize business practices. For entrepreneurs and investors, it was a time of euphoria, experimentation, and instantaneous wealth; for established companies, it was a time of uncertainty and fear. Many traditional businesses with established brands thought that the Internet was just another fad; while others did not quite understand how to integrate it with their existing businesses. Fear of making mistakes that could harm their brands led many companies to create "online" businesses that were separate from their core "bricks-and-mortar" or "offline" businesses. For instance, Procter & Gamble's online business was called reflect.com and Kmart's company in the United States was called bluelight.com.

The apprehension that established marketers had for jumping on the dot-com bandwagon seemed justified when in 2000 the explosive growth of Internet businesses collapsed within a couple of months. The dot-com bust provided established marketers with breathing room to reflect on how they could incorporate the Internet into their business and marketing strategies. Around 2004, almost a decade later, marketers came to realize that an effective marketing strategy requires an integration of online and offline businesses to provide customers with a seamless "multi-channel marketing" experience.

When marketers initially pursued Internet marketing, they were mostly excited about designing the best website by using the latest publishing software and technology available. Although most websites were originally text-based, marketers quickly adopted multimedia technologies since their goal was to create an appealing website that would attract visitors and keep them on the site. Little thought was given as to whether or not customers needed or valued these features. The early focus on the technology and the product is reminiscent of the product-oriented market era of early twentieth century. Two decades later, in 2012, we observe that although websites are much more complex technologically, their focus has shifted to the consumer: that is, how marketers can use the technology to identify and fulfill customer needs and deliver the best customer value while generating profits. This focus seems more in line with the value-based orientation described in the book. But, how did we get from a technology focus to a value-based focus? What were some of the steps along the way?

From Static Websites to Social Media to Mobile Marketing

Rewind to 1993 when the commercial Internet came into being; websites were *static, text-based* sites, which marketers used to "push" information to customers about their products and companies. Customers wishing to make a purchase had to call a telephone number listed on the website. Shortly thereafter, email marketing became widespread, and the main focus was on how to create the perfect email and ensure it reached the target customers. Second-generation websites became more *dynamic and interactive;* that is, they provided information to customers' requests in real time, made greater use of multimedia technology, and offered modest interactivity. The next development was *e-commerce* capability, that is, the ability to order and pay for goods and services online. This capability laid the foundations for the explosive growth of online marketing since marketers could now reach customers worldwide through their online stores and customers could order products and services anytime, anywhere. The era of instant gratification and ultimate shopping convenience seemed closer than ever. E-commerce transactions grew exponentially year after year, and they continue to grow unabated. B2C, B2B, and C2C via auction sites became possible and grew exponentially. The next phase in the evolution of Internet marketing was *personalization and customization*, where customers were given the ability to customize the look and feel of a website, and the products shown, to suit their preferences. Today, thanks to social networking sites such as Myspace, YouTube, Facebook, Flickr, and Twitter, and portable devices such as smartphones, *social media and mobile* marketing is all the rage. What will be next?

The Internet is much more sophisticated and complex now than it was in the 1990s. It has changed and will continue to change. No one can predict the transformations with certainty; however, it seems reasonable to think that in the short term at least three aspects of Internet marketing will keep marketers awake at night. One aspect is figuring out how to create a winning multichannel marketing strategy that can evolve as new technologies are developed and deployed (see Chapter 13 for more information on multichannel marketing). A related challenge is how to develop and implement an effective and efficient mobile marketing strategy, given the marketing potential of smartphones and the increasing trend among Canadians to upgrade their cellphones to smartphones. The other dilemma is to figure out a profitable social media marketing strategy, given that social media marketing is in its infancy and is yet to generate profits for companies.

If the closing decade of the twentieth century was a period of euphoria, experimentation, and confusion with the Internet, then the first decade of the twenty-first century is a period of Internet maturation. Marketers have expanded their use of the Internet for marketing communications to such an extent that it has replaced TV, radio, and print advertising as the key advertising medium. In addition, consumers have made the Internet their first source for information. Mobile, multichannel, and social media marketing are the next likely frontiers for Internet marketing.

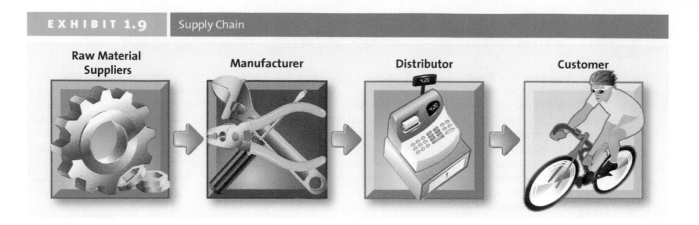

EXHIBIT 1.9   Supply Chain

Raw Material Suppliers → **Manufacturer** → **Distributor** → **Customer**

Marketing Is Pervasive Across the Supply Chain

Firms typically do not work in isolation. Manufacturers buy raw materials and components from suppliers, which they sell to retailers or other businesses after they have turned the materials into their products (see Exhibit 1.9). Every time materials or products are bought or sold, they are transported to a different location, which sometimes requires that they be stored in a warehouse operated by yet another organization. The group of firms and set of techniques and approaches firms use to make and deliver a given set of goods and services is commonly referred to as a **supply chain.** Excellent supply chains effectively and efficiently integrate their supply chain partners—suppliers, manufacturers, warehouses, stores, and transportation intermediaries—to produce and distribute goods in the right quantities, to the right locations, and at the right time. Supply chain management is discussed in detail in Chapter 12; but, for now, let's consider the value of the supply chain in marketing.

Often, some supply chain participants take a transactional orientation in which each link in the chain is out for its own best interest. Manufacturers, for example, want the highest price, whereas retailers want to buy the product at the lowest cost. Supply chain members do not enjoy any cooperation or coordination. But for the supply chain to provide significant value to the ultimate customer, the parties must establish long-term relationships with one another and cooperate to share data, make joint forecasts, and coordinate shipments. Effectively managing supply chain relationships often has a huge impact on a firm's ability to satisfy the consumer, which results in increased profitability for all parties.

Consider Loblaw, Canada's largest food distributor, and its relationships with its manufacturers and trading partners. A couple of years ago, Loblaw's supply chain system suffered from several inefficiencies that drove up its costs substantially.[27] For example, inaccurate demand forecasts led trading partners to stock huge inventory to meet unpredictable demand. Inefficient use of customer data meant that stock replenishment was made by estimation rather than true customer data. Disconnected supply chain systems, limited collaboration, reduced information sharing, and supply variability led to poor quality information on which to base sales forecasts, production plans, and replenishment schemes. The company has since made many changes to improve the efficiency of its supply chain. Loblaw's participation in a radio frequency identification (RFID) pilot project for the grocery industry conducted by the Canadian RFID Centre has helped it improve its operations. Preliminary results seem to indicate that Loblaw has improved its inventory management and use of promotions.

supply chain
The group of firms and set of techniques and approaches firms use to make and deliver a given set of goods and services.

Marketing Makes Life Easier

Marketers provide you, as a consumer, with product and service choices, as well as information about those choices, to ensure that your needs are being met. They balance the product or service offering with a price that makes you comfortable with your purchase. After the sale, they provide reasonable guarantees and return policies. Marketing's responsibility also includes offering pleasant and convenient places for you to shop, appropriate opening hours for you to shop, products and services in the form you want, and purchase options. These are often referred to as time, place, form, and ownership utility. When your Shoppers Drug Mart store is open 24-hours a day, 7 days a week, it is providing more time utility than another store that is open only from 9 a.m. to 5 p.m. Similarly, when Loblaw carries several brands of potato chips in various sizes, it is catering to different customer needs, or offering form utility. When car dealerships offer customers the option to buy or lease a car, they are providing ownership utility. In essence, marketers make your life easier, and in these ways, they add value.

Marketing Provides Career Opportunities

Marketing also offers a host of career opportunities that require a variety of skills. On the creative side, positions such as artists, graphic designers, voice talent, animators, music composers, and writers represent just a few of the opportunities available to talented individuals. On the analytical side, marketing requires database analysts, market researchers, and inventory managers who can quickly digest information, cross-reference data, and spot trends that might make or break a company. On the business side, marketing requires strategists, project/product/brand managers, sales associates, and analysts who are capable of designing and implementing complex marketing strategies that increase the bottom line.

Marketing Enriches Society

Should marketing focus on factors other than financial profitability, such as good corporate citizenry? Many of Canada's best-known corporations seem to think so, because they encourage their employees to participate in activities that benefit their communities and invest heavily in socially responsible actions and charities. For example, HP Canada donated equipment packages to two First Nations communities as part of a pilot project to increase the literacy and technology skills of local youths. More than 700 at-risk youths in these communities will now have access to leading-edge technology. According to the president of the RCMP Foundation, HP's gift will aid its efforts to divert youths toward positive activities and away from the negative choices of drinking alcohol, doing drugs, participating in violence, and dropping out of school.[28] Canadian companies recognize that a strong social orientation is in both their and their customers' best interest. It shows the consumer that the firm can be trusted with their business. Also, investors view firms that operate with high levels of corporate responsibility and ethics as safe investments. Similarly, firms have come to realize that good corporate citizenship through socially responsible actions should be a priority because it will help their bottom line in the long run.[29]

Marketing Can Be Entrepreneurial

Whereas marketing plays a major role in the success of large corporations, it also is at the centre of the successes of numerous new ventures initiated by entrepreneurs, or people who organize, operate, and assume the risk of a business venture.[30] Key to the success of many such entrepreneurs is that they launch ventures that aim to satisfy unfilled needs. Some examples of successful ventures (and their founders) that understood their customers and added value include:

- Research In Motion (Mike Lazaridis)
- *The Oprah Winfrey Show* and other ventures (Oprah Winfrey)

Mike Lazaridis is best known for inventing the BlackBerry and for founding the highly successful company RIM, which was described in the chapter vignette. Mike Lazaridis and two of his friends, Doug Fregin and Mike Barnstijn, launched their

entrepreneurial venture, Research In Motion Limited (RIM) in 1984, while they were still university students. Headquartered in Waterloo, Ontario, RIM has offices in North America, Europe, and Asia-Pacific. The company continues to grow and is recognized as the global leader for wireless, mobile communication, particularly among business executives, managers, and professionals. In 2007, Lazaridis was listed in *Forbes* magazine as one of the world's richest people. He also appeared on the *Time* list of the 100 most influential people in 2005.[31]

Another extraordinary entrepreneur and marketer is Oprah Winfrey. A self-made billionaire before she turned 50, Oprah went from being the youngest person and first African-American woman to anchor news sta-

Mike Lazaridis, co-CEO of Research In Motion, is best known for inventing the BlackBerry.

tion WTVF-TV in Nashville, Tennessee, to being only the third woman in history to head her own production studio. Under the Oprah Winfrey banner, you can find Harpo Productions; *O, The Oprah Magazine*; *O at Home* magazine; Harpo Films; and the Oxygen TV network. In addition, Oprah's philanthropic contributions are vast and varied. Through the Oprah Winfrey Foundation and Oprah's Angel Network, women around the world have raised more than US$50 million for scholarships, schools, women's shelters, and youth centres.[32]

Both of these distinguished entrepreneurs had a vision about how certain combinations of products and services could satisfy unfilled needs. Each understood the marketing opportunity (i.e., the unfilled need), conducted a thorough examination of the marketplace, and developed and communicated the value of their products and services to potential consumers.

When you think of Oprah Winfrey, think big: Harpo Productions; O, The Oprah Magazine; O at Home magazine; Harpo Films; the Oxygen TV network, not to mention her philanthropic work with the Oprah Winfrey Foundation and Oprah's Angel Network.

LO1 Define marketing and explain its core concepts

In definition form, "marketing is a set of business practices designed to plan for and present an organization's products or services in ways that build effective customer relationships." Marketing strives to *create value* in many ways. If marketers are to succeed, their customers must believe that the firm's products and services are valuable; that is, the products and services are worth more to the customers than they cost.

Marketers also enhance the value of products and services through various forms of *communication*, such as advertising and personal selling. Through communications, marketers educate and inform customers about the benefits of their products and services and thereby increase their perceived value.

Marketers facilitate the *delivery of value* by making sure the right products and services are available when, where, and in the quantities their customers want. Better marketers are not concerned about just one transaction with their customers; they recognize the value of loyal customers and strive to develop *long-term relationships* with them.

LO2 Illustrate how marketers create value for a product or service

Value represents the relationship of benefits to costs. Firms can improve their value by increasing benefits, reducing costs, or both. The best firms integrate a value orientation into everything they do. If a move doesn't increase benefits or reduce costs, it probably shouldn't occur. Marketers also have found that providing good value is one of the best ways to maintain a sustainable advantage over their competitors.

Firms become value driven by finding out as much as they can about their customers and those customers' needs and wants. They share this information with their partners, both up and down the supply chain, so the entire chain collectively can focus on the customer. The key to true value-based marketing is the ability to design products and services that achieve the right balance between benefits and costs—not too little, not too much.

Finally, value-based marketers aren't necessarily worried about how much money they will make on the next sale. Instead, they are concerned with developing a lasting relationship with their customers so those customers return again and again.

LO3 Summarize the four orientations of marketing

Firms that are *production-oriented* tend to believe that a good product will sell itself. Manufacturers are concerned with product innovation, not with satisfying the needs of individual consumers, and keep producing with the assumption that people will buy it. Marketing with this orientation is simply about informing the customer that a product exists, if used at all.

In the case of a *sales orientation*, firms rely on a sales team to sell. Production is maximized and then heavy doses of personal selling and advertising help distribute and sell the product. The role of marketing is focused only on the sale of products.

If a firm is *market-oriented*, it celebrates the customer. Here the customer can decide what is best for them, based on the attributes of a product or service. Rather than simply produce and sell, manufacturers with this orientation seek to learn customer needs and wants and design products to fit the customers. Marketing plays an important role to communicate the different attributes, or value, created by each product.

Most successful firms today have transcended other views and instead support a *value-based orientation*. In addition to discovering needs and wants, it is critical to deliver more value to customers than competitors. Value reflects the relationship of benefits to costs, or what you get for what you give. Marketing plays an integral role not only in creating and delivering that valuable product, but also in communicating the value, especially in relation to other products available, and transacting the value through to customers.

LO4 Identify the role of customer relationship management in creating value

Building strong relationships with customers is important to creating value and is the central concept of the relational orientation. Unlike the transactional orientation, here firms adopt a business strategy that identifies customers and focuses on building strong relationships with them. This is known as *customer relationship management (CRM)*, and it maximizes the long-term value of the buyer–seller relationship rather than trying to maximize the profit from each transaction. CRM often includes collecting customer information to target specific promotions or offers to customers who would benefit most.

LO5 Explain the importance of marketing both within and outside the firm

The marketing function is important both within and outside the firm. Many brands and stores now appear in multiple countries, which complicates the challenge for marketers. Successful firms integrate marketing throughout their organizations so that marketing activities coordinate with other functional areas, such as product design, production, logistics, and human resources.

Marketing also helps facilitate the smooth flow of goods through the supply chain, all the way from raw materials to the consumer. From a personal perspective, the marketing function facilitates your buying process, and knowledge of marketing will help you in virtually any career you may decide to pursue.

Marketing also can be important for society through its embrace of solid, ethical business practices. For instance, a firm clearly has "done the right thing" when it sponsors charitable events, but that effort also helps endear customers to the firm. Finally, marketing is a cornerstone of entrepreneurialism.

Not only have many great companies been founded by outstanding marketers, but an entrepreneurial spirit pervades the marketing decisions of firms of all sizes.

Key Terms

- B2B (business-to-business), 12
- B2C (business-to-consumer), 12
- C2C (consumer-to-consumer), 13
- customer relationship management (CRM), 20
- exchange, 7
- goods, 9
- ideas, 9

- market, 6
- marketing, 5
- marketing mix (four Ps), 8
- marketing plan, 5
- need, 6
- price, 9
- relational orientation, 20
- services, 9

- social media, 14
- supply chain, 24
- target market, 7
- transactional orientation, 20
- value, 16
- value-based marketing, 18
- want, 6

Concept Review

1. What is marketing and why is it important?

2. Is the marketing mix (the four Ps) enough to guarantee successful marketing? Explain.

3. Explain how a strike at one of a company's supplier firms or a new technology would influence the company's marketing efforts?

4. Discuss the main elements of value-based marketing. List four ways in which marketing helps to create value.

5. Explain the relationship between customer value and customer satisfaction.

6. Generally, all companies are in business to generate profits and increase shareholder value. Yet, the Canadian Marketing Association's definition of marketing given on page 5 does not explicitly mention profits or shareholder value. Why do you think these are not included in the definition? Should they be included?

7. Today, many marketers are not interested in selling their products and services to everyone who wants them; instead, they want to sell them only to selected target markets. What do you think the main reasons are for targeting specific market segments?

8. Give reasons why you think understanding customer needs and wants is fundamental to marketing success. How can marketers go about understanding customer needs and wants?

9. Which marketing orientation would most likely help a company build strong customer relationships that are profitable? Why?

10. Explain how customer value is created or increased when the company's marketing department works closely with other departments within the firm as well as with the firm's suppliers and customers.

Marketing Applications

1. When apparel manufacturers develop their marketing strategies, do they concentrate on satisfying their customers' needs or wants? What about a utility company? A cellphone company?

2. Choose a product that you use every day. Describe its four Ps.

3. Provide examples of three firms that are involved in both B2C and B2B marketing.

4. Pick a firm that you believe provides its customers with good value. Justify your answer by explaining how the firm competes on value.

5. Assume you have been hired by the marketing department of a major consumer products manufacturer such as Colgate-Palmolive. You are having lunch with some new colleagues in the finance, manufacturing, and logistics departments. They are arguing that the company could save millions of dollars if it just got rid of the marketing department. Develop an argument that would persuade them otherwise.

6. Why do marketers find it important to embrace societal needs and ethical business practices? Provide an example of a societal need or ethical business practice being addressed by a specific marketer.

7. Visit the website of Rogers Communications (www.rogers .com) and compare the four Ps marketing mix for the BlackBerry Bold and the BlackBerry Torch. What factors might explain the differences you observe?

8. For many consumers, the difference between Dasani water made by Coca-Cola (www.dasani.com) and Aquafina water made by Pepsi (www.aquafina.com) is hardly noticeable. However, both companies and their loyal customers would argue that there are many differences between these two brands of water. What is your view? Explain how customer perceptions and emotions may influence the way they value a company's product.

9. As described in this chapter, customer relationship management is a very important aspect of value-based marketing. Pick any one of Canada's major retailers (e.g., The Bay (www.hbc.com), Loblaw (www.loblaws.ca), or Shoppers Drug Mart (www.shoppersdrugmart.ca), and explain how it goes about building strong customer relationships with its customers.

10. RIM's PlayBook is seen as a competitor to Apple's iPad 2. Visit Apple's website (www.apple.com) and the Rogers Communications website (www.rogers.com) to learn more about these two products. What do you think the main value proposition is for each product? Eventually, which product do you think will come out as the winner and why?

Net Savvy

1. Happy Planet (www.happyplanet.com), a Vancouver-based organic juice producer, is an emerging player in the organic beverage market. It supplies all of Canada and some of the United States with organic juice. Visit its website and describe how the company delivers value above and beyond that provided by traditional grocery retailers. Describe the ways in which the company communicates this value through its website.

2. Montréal Biodôme (http://www2.ville.montreal.qc.ca/ biodome/) has developed an excellent reputation in international scientific and cultural circles for the diversity of its collection. Visit its website and describe the ways in which it creates value for patrons. What else could Montréal Biodôme do to offer even more value to its patrons?

Chapter Case Study

TABLET WAR: RIM'S PLAYBOOK VERSUS APPLE'S IPAD[33]

Background

Research In Motion (RIM), Canada's premier high-tech company, invented the smartphone when it created its innovative BlackBerry in 1999. Being first to market, the BlackBerry enjoyed tremendous, unrivalled success with a near-monopoly of the business enterprise market; almost overnight BlackBerry became the standard for mobile communications and the ways companies do business and communicate with clients changed forever. BlackBerry was the de facto market leader for about a decade until its first serious rival—the now legendary Apple iPhone—came along in 2007. It is often said that while RIM's BlackBerry created the smartphone market, Apple's iPhone revolutionized the smartphone market, taking it by storm and creating huge buzz.

The iPhone offered touchscreen features with a sleek design that made it look light years ahead of the BlackBerry. Even though it was priced higher than the BlackBerry, supply could not keep up with demand for several months after it was introduced. No wonder the iPhone gained 25 percent market share within its first year. While the BlackBerry was seen as a device for business people and professionals, the iPhone was seen as a smartphone for the average consumer. This strategy worked handsomely for Apple. Recognizing the huge competitive threat, RIM spent the next several months developing a BlackBerry for the consumer market. The race to catch up with Apple had begun in earnest.

While RIM was playing catch-up, Apple had another trick up its sleeve, the much talked about iPad. For Apple, the iPad was seen as a huge gamble since it was neither

The PlayBook is small but powerful, offering multitasking, Flash, and professional quality features and experiences.

laptop nor phone, although it looked like a supersized iPhone and worked seamlessly with the iPhone and with iTunes. Many analysts and commentators questioned its positioning in the market; but, at that time, consumer sentiment seemed to suggest that anything by Apple was good, a notion echoed by sales numbers. The iPad was a huge success, and the critics were proved wrong. The iPad was to the tablet market what the iPhone was to the smartphone market: it created huge buzz and excitement, and took the tablet market by storm, this time in less than a year. Apple sold more than 20 million iPads and became the de facto market leader for tablets. RIM was left playing catch-up again as it prepared to launch its PlayBook. And, with the iPad near-monopoly of the tablet market, analysts seemed to agree that "The PlayBook would need to have a lot more muscle in the hardware, so the user could do more things, faster. It would need new software, too, because RIM's aging operating system was past its prime."[34]

PlayBook Launch

By the time RIM was ready to launch its PlayBook on April 19, 2011, Apple had already launched iPad 2, which had many more features that its first iPad version. In addition, it had worked out all the iPad's major bugs and offered consumers access to more than 65 000 apps specifically designed for the iPad and more than 350 000 apps from its iPhone that are compatible with the iPad.[35] In contrast, the PlayBook was launched with about 3000 apps designed for tablets. None of the BlackBerry's 27 000 apps were optimized to run on the PlayBook.[36] Additionally, both the iPad and the iPad2 were launched with much fanfare, long lineups, and media frenzy. The iPad was not available for preorder before its official launch. In contrast, RIM's PlayBook was launched with lukewarm response from the media, not much fanfare, and virtually no lineups either in Canada or the United States. Consumers were able to preorder the PlayBook.

One analyst suggested that RIM's low-key approach was probably a deliberate strategy "so you couldn't compare the two launches."[37] Other analysts and commentators were much harsher in their evaluation of the PlayBook and RIM. For instance, Walt Mossberg, an influential technology blogger for the *Wall Street Journal*, wrote, "So far the tablet 'revolution' has remained obstinately an iPad revolution with no other device coming even close to challenging Apple's dominance in the market. It would appear that the PlayBook is not going to cause Apple CEO Steve Jobs to lose much sleep."[38] Similarly, Tony Bradley of *PCWorld* wrote, "The BlackBerry PlayBook seems to have some significant drawbacks. Many reviews call the RIM tablet a rushed, or unfinished work in progress."[39] Not to be outdone, the influential market research firm, Gartner Group released a report days before the PlayBook was launched, declaring that 85 percent of tablets will run on systems designed by Apple or Google by 2015 and RIM will be running a distant third.[40]

Is it all doom and gloom for RIM and its PlayBook? Are these criticisms justified? What should RIM do to combat these negative perceptions? To help you make up your mind, let's look at the PlayBook and RIM's marketing more closely and compare them with Apple's iPad.

Product

Exhibit 1.10 presents the main features of both the PlayBook and the iPad. What does the Play-Book really offer customers? According to Mike Lazaridis, RIM's co-CEO, "The BlackBerry Play-Book is an amazing tablet that is already being widely praised as a multi-tasking powerhouse with an uncompromised web experience and an ultra-portable design."[41] The PlayBook offers professional-quality, consumer-friendly experiences that raise the bar of mobile computing:

> This ultra-portable tablet looks and feels great, measuring less than half an inch thick and weighing less than a pound. It features a vivid 7-inch high-resolution display that is highly-responsive with a fluid touch screen experience. It also offers industry leading performance, uncompromised web browsing with support for Adobe® Flash® Player 10.1, true multitasking, HD multimedia, advanced security features, out-of-the-box enterprise support and a robust development environment.[42]

The BlackBerry PlayBook with WiFi is available in three models: 16 GHz, 32 GHz, and 64 GHz.[43]

Despite the unique product features and benefits of the PlayBook, some critics claimed that it was a disappointment because it did not capitalize on RIM's core strengths. Specifically, the first iteration of the PlayBook did not offer email, calendar, and messenger on a standalone basis. Instead, PlayBook users had to tether or sync the PlayBook with their BlackBerry and the Black-Berry Bridge software to access these features. Analysts argued that these features were clear competitive advantages of RIM, and they were puzzled as to why they were not available. In its defence, RIM noted that the approach of tethering the BlackBerry with the PlayBook offered two key advantages: enhanced security and freedom from establishing yet another wireless data plan.

EXHIBIT 1.10	Comparison of PlayBook and iPad Product Features[44]	
Features	**PlayBook**	**iPad**
Size	194 mm × 130 mm × 10 mm	241 mm × 186 mm × 8.8 mm
Screen	LCD touchscreen	LED backlit
Weight	425 g	601 g
Processor	1 GHz dual-core	1 GHz dual-core
Memory	1 GB RAM	N.A. estimates – 512 MB
Storage	16, 32, and 64 GB	16, 32, and 64 GB
Multitasking	Yes	No
Camera	Dual 1080p HD	720p HD
WiFi	Yes	Yes
3G/Cellular	No	Yes
Bluetooth	Yes	Yes
Videoconferencing	Yes	No (but has video mirroring and a front-facing camera)
HDMI Output	Yes	No

Both of these criteria are key concerns for corporate clients. With tethering, users could access all the information on their BlackBerry through the PlayBook, a larger format suited for increased productivity, and once the Bridge connection is terminated, all the information is cleaned off the PlayBook. This deletion means that security concerns are virtually nonexistent. Also, users do not need additional data plans because they can use their existing BlackBerry plan, so their costs are limited to the cost of purchasing the PlayBook. The BlackBerry PlayBook combo offered consumers a one-stop solution to wireless communication.

The security features of the PlayBook are widely recognized as the best in the industry and are far superior to Apple's iPad. Thus, it's no wonder that the new Ritz-Carlton hotel in Toronto bought iPads for its restaurant menus but PlayBooks for its check-in system, which handles financial data, such as customer credit card numbers. The PlayBook's security, multitasking, presentation, and tethering features and capabilities has led many to regard the PlayBook, at its launch, as a device designed primarily for existing BlackBerry customers, especially its corporate clients.

Now let's take a brief look at Apple's iPad. When Apple launched the new mobile tablet in April 2010, customers lined the sidewalks, waiting for their chance to purchase Apple's newest product. Combining many of the advantages of smartphones and laptop computers, Apple's version allows users to browse the Internet, read and send email, listen to music, watch HD movies and TV shows, read e-books, play games, and view photos. To make the iPad more appealing, the iPad came with dozens of preloaded apps and gave customers access to more than 140 000 apps through its apps store.[45]

Consumers

What factors do consumers consider when buying tablets? Multiple factors, each with varying degrees of importance, affect their decision. Some buyers want apps and are influenced by the number and quality available. Other factors include price, features, benefits, prior experience with a product, loyalty, and so on. However, it seems that consumers' initial interest in a product such as the tablet is driven by what we would call "wow factors": the one or two features of a product that captivate them. These factors will vary for different consumers. We informally asked a few owners of both the PlayBook and the iPad (a convenience sample) what factors wowed them. The wow factors of the PlayBook included its ability to multitask and videoconference, its presentation, its speed, its light weight and small size, and its price, which is lower than the cost of its chief rival. The wow factors of the iPad included its front-facing camera, apps, and sleek design. What is it about these devices that wow you?

Price

RIM has priced its feature-packed PlayBook at a discount compared with both of Apple's iPad models. Exhibit 1.11 compares the price of both devices.

EXHIBIT 1.11	Comparison of PlayBook and iPad Prices[46]		
Model	**PlayBook**	**iPad + WiFi**	**iPad + WiFi + 3G**
16 GB	$499	$519	$649
32 GB	$599	$619	$749
64 GB	$699	$719	$849

Distribution

Prior to the launch of the PlayBook, RIM announced that the tablet would be widely available in more than 20 000 retail outlets in the United States and Canada. Exhibit 1.12 lists the distributors. In contrast, the iPad is sold through Apple's stores, its website, and selected distributors, such as specialty electronics stores (e.g., Future Shop).

From Leader to Follower

Now that RIM has launched the PlayBook, two questions come into play. First, how was RIM, an innovative company that created the smartphone category, overtaken by Apple, a new player in the smartphone market that is now setting the pace? Comments by Lazaridis exemplify RIM's new status as a follower: "[The iPad] validated what we were doing; it gave us extra insight. That's why we went out and we beefed up the horsepower of the thing [PlayBook] to run QNX rather than what we were building ourselves." Second, what is in store for RIM and the PlayBook in the future? Can RIM regain its leader status? We examine these questions below.

A recent *Globe and Mail* report observed that RIM had been struggling for years with the challenge of moving beyond the smartphone. RIM's corporate customers were clamouring for a BlackBerry laptop that combined RIM's exceptional security features with a larger screen and keyboard; but, RIM never delivered on this need.[47] Instead, RIM focused on developing new products such as the BlackBerry Bold to defend its market share against a growing number of competitors, including Apple, HTC, and Samsung Electronics. RIM was trying to capture a larger share of the consumer market with phones such as the BlackBerry Storm, which had a touchscreen but ultimately failed. RIM was also investigating new avenues for growth, such as embedding RIM products into cars for hands-free calling.[48] Did RIM miss the tablet trend, starting work on its tablet too late? Was the executive team too risk averse, not wanting to bet on new technologies? Did RIM become too big, too fast, a victim of its own success? Did it lack focus?

EXHIBIT 1.12	PlayBook Distributors in Canada and the United States	
Distributors in Canada		**Distributors in the United States**
Bell	Staples	AT&T
Best Buy	Tbooth Wireless	Best Buy
Chapters Indigo	TELUS	BlackBerry from Wireless Giant
Costco	The Source	Cbeyond
Future Shop	Videotron	Cellular South
Mobilicity	Walmart	Cincinnati Bell
MTS Allstream	WIND Mobile	Office Depot
Rogers	WIRELESS etc.	RadioShack
SaskTel	WIRELESSWAVE	ShopBlackBerry.com
Sears		Sprint
ShopBlackBerry.com		Staples
		Verizon Wireless

The Future

Some analysts expect PlayBook sales to take off after a slow start. National Bank Financial analyst Kris Thompson projects that RIM will sell just under 500 000 PlayBooks in the first quarter, which ends in May 2011, about 3.6 million in fiscal 2012, and more than 6 million in 2013.[49] Compared to sales of the iPad, these forecasts are very modest.

Clearly, the launch of the PlayBook marks only the beginning of the road ahead for RIM. In the short-term, RIM needs to fix several "bugs." For starters, the company has to significantly boost the number of apps dedicated to the PlayBook to compete with Apple and Google. Fortunately for RIM, the PlayBook's new OS will enable users to run apps designed for Google's Android system. This compatibility could result in tens of thousands of apps being available to PlayBook users. RIM also has the opportunity to leverage the products of thousands of people all over the world who are developing apps; however, RIM's challenge will be overcoming its highly secured system, which poses a serious obstacle for app developers.

RIM's executive team made two major strategic decisions that could generate tremendous benefits for the company: its relationship with Adobe and its purchase of QNX. Early on in the PlayBook design process, RIM decided to work with Adobe. The move made sense for both firms because Adobe wanted to get back at Apple for refusing to allow Adobe's Flash-based multimedia on any of its handheld devices. Flash is a common piece of software that runs interactive features, such as video, on websites. Its absence on the iPad and iPhone is why many videos on the Internet won't play on those devices. For RIM, the Adobe partnership not only helps further differentiate PlayBook—it can run a lot of Internet video and TV that the iPad can't—but also gives RIM access to Adobe's millions of app developers, which could potentially help RIM close the "app gap" with Apple.

Technology analysts see the PlayBook's OS, known as QNX Neutrino, as one of the keys to RIM's success, and perhaps its resurgence. QNX makes some of the best OSs on the planet. The OSs are so reliable that they are used in critical infrastructure such as nuclear power plants, where a software crash could be potentially catastrophic. A version of QNX's OS even powers the Canadarm at the International Space Station. According to RIM, QNX will become the standard for every piece of hardware the company makes from now on, including its phones. QNX will enhance RIM's already secure system and provide it with a distinct competitive advantage over BlackBerry OS 6.

Another positive for RIM is its large base of diehard BlackBerry corporate users. The cost and security infrastructure of the BlackBerry and PlayBook, combined with the large numbers of BlackBerry users who are accustomed to the BlackBerry, provide RIM with a strong basis to compete in the marketplace. Also, the company's global presence could yield strong growth opportunities.[50]

Questions

1. Who do you think the PlayBook's primary customers were at the time of its launch? Who were the customers for the iPad?

2. Do you think that both devices provided adequate value to their customers? Which of these two tablets do your prefer and why?

3. What main factors do you think RIM considered before it priced the PlayBook lower than the iPad? Do you think the lower price will entice customers to buy the iPad instead of the PlayBook?

4. Media reports suggest that the launch of the PlayBook was low-key. Why do you think RIM opted for a low-key launch? Do you think this strategy was appropriate, or should RIM have tried to create greater buzz?

5. What marketing strategies could RIM use to expand its customer base?

6. Which features of the PlayBook offer the most value to customers and its partners (e.g., advertisers)?

7. RIM's critics suggest that RIM has missed the emerging tablet trend because the PlayBook launched a year after the iPad, after almost 20 million iPads had already been sold. Why do you think RIM seems to have initially missed the emerging tablet trend?

8. Do you think that the PlayBook will ever dethrone the iPad in the tablet market? If you were hired to engineer a strategy to dethrone the iPad, what would you do and why?

CHAPTER 2

Developing
a Marketing Plan and Marketing Strategies

As we learned in Chapter 1, the business environment in which a firm operates can present marketers with new opportunities to grow and expand their business, and pose threats to their existing businesses. Additionally, problems or challenges may arise because of poor implementation of a marketing program or the firms may experience declining performance. Under these circumstances, the firm must take corrective action to adjust its marketing strategy to address weaknesses, threats, and/or opportunities. Let's look at how The Walt Disney Company (Disney), the world's leader in theme-park entertainment, handles such a situation.

Managers at Disney noticed that attendance at their theme parks was declining.[1] Visitors cited long lines and high ticket prices as the major deterrents to visiting the theme park. Disney was challenged to adjust its strategy to create a better in-park experience and deliver more value for the $63-a-day ticket price.

Their answer was to create a strategy heavy on technology that makes the park experience more personal and relevant to each visitor. To reinvent the customer experience, influence visitor behaviour, and ease crowding throughout the parks, it combined global positioning satellites, smart sensors, wireless technology, and mobile devices.

Consider "Pal Mickey." The 26-centimetre doll, available for rent or purchase, is equipped with a central processing unit, an internal clock, small speakers, and an infrared sensor. As patrons move through the park, the sensor acquires wireless data uploads from beacons concealed in lampposts, rooftops, and bushes. When the doll receives information, it giggles and vibrates, which means "It's time to tell a secret" about shorter lines for rides in the area, the time of the upcoming parade, or trivia about the area in which the patron is walking. Pal Mickey also contains 700 prerecorded messages to keep kids entertained with jokes and games while they wait in line. Pal Mickey speaks Spanish too!

The concept of working with data to create a more individual experience has migrated to other applications as well. For example, Disney plans to send text messages about dinner reservations, fireworks displays, and tee times via a visitor's cellphone or PDA. If a visitor spends a long time in the Dinosaur Exhibit at Animal Kingdom and purchases dinosaur merchandise, Disney figures that he or she might like to receive a special email notification about an upcoming DVD release about dinosaurs. With Disney's digital-imaging services, park visitors can even view pictures taken throughout the day on their hotel TV sets and purchase them with the touch of a button.

Realizing that Mickey Mouse's popularity is declining due to intense competition from Nickelodeon, Pixar, and DreamWorks characters, Disney is rebranding Mickey's personality to appeal to the new generation of children and consumers. The new Mickey will be slowly unveiled, first in the video game *Epic Mickey* for the Nintendo Wii. According to *The New York Times*, the game will "show the character's darker side." The new Mickey is multifaceted and can be at times "cantankerous and cunning, as well as heroic, as he traverses a forbidding wasteland."[2]

Disney's executives know that Mickey is not just any mouse; he's a $5 billion mouse, and by tinkering with Mickey's personality they run the risk of alienating their core customers.[3] Should Disney embark on a strategy to rebrand Mickey to appeal to a new generation of consumers, or should it focus on its core consumers? .::

In the first part of this chapter, we examine the various levels of strategic planning and discuss each of the steps involved in developing a marketing plan. We then consider ways of analyzing a marketing situation, as well as identifying and evaluating marketing opportunities. We also consider how the implementation of the marketing mix increases customer value. Finally, we examine some specific strategies marketers use to grow a business. Refer to the chapter roadmap to guide you through the chapter contents.

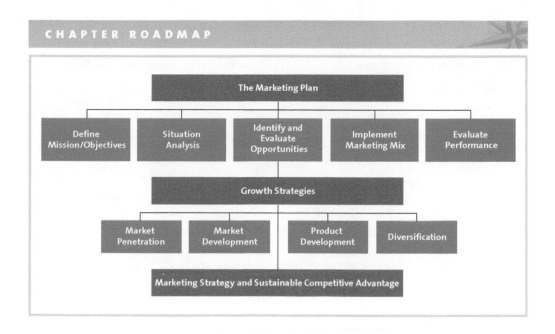

Levels of Strategic Planning in Corporations

Effective marketing doesn't just happen. Firms such as Rona, Future Shop, The Bay, and Disney carefully plan their marketing strategies to react to changes in the environment, the competition, and their customers by creating a marketing plan. Strategic planning in most organizations occurs on at least two levels, the corporate level and the functional level (see Exhibit 2.1). Corporate level planning is done by the company's top management and focuses on the overall direction of the entire company. Senior managers decide on the business of the company, define the company's mission or vision, and set objectives or goals for the company. Corporate level planning focuses on the long-term direction of the company, which is updated regularly to respond to changes in the business environment. Generally, large corporations have various business functions such as human resources, R&D, finance, manufacturing, and marketing. Each of these functions usually undertakes some form of planning. The marketing function develops marketing plans for the company's various products, brands, and markets. These plans could take the form of annual plans or three- to five-year plans.

In addition to corporate and functional level strategic planning, large companies that operate several business lines may see each of their strategic business units (SBUs) develop strategic plans for their products and the markets they serve. An SBU is a division of the company that can be managed somewhat independently from other divisions since it markets a specific set of products to a clearly defined group of customers. For example, Disney has four business units—media networks, parks and resorts, studio entertainment, and consumer products—that focus on different customer segments with different products. Each of these units develops plans for the products and markets under their control. It is important to recognize that the marketing function may also be involved in both corporate-level and SBU-level planning because of its focus on creating value for customers and the company. Marketing can advise top management where business opportunities exist as well as possible threats to their businesses. Similarly, marketing can advise SBUs of changing consumer trends or recommend that SBUs develop customer service and loyalty programs for all business units. In the remainder of this chapter, we focus on the **marketing planning process** for a particular product, brand, or market.

marketing planning process
A set of steps a marketer goes through to develop a marketing plan.

EXHIBIT 2.1	Levels of Strategic Planning		
Levels of Planning	**Scope**	**Duration**	**Strategic Focus**
Corporate planning	Entire firm	Long-term (5 years)	Define the company's mission, set company's goals, and establish the business portfolio
Strategic business unit (SBU)/Division planning (applies only to large firms with more than one distinct line of business)	Single SBU within the firm	Medium to long-term (3 to 5 years)	Set goals and establish portfolio of products and markets for the business unit
Functional planning (e.g., marketing planning)	Product portfolio, single product, brand or market	Short-term to medium term (1 to 3 years)	Develop marketing plans for specific products, brands, or markets

L01 The Marketing Plan

A marketing plan is a written document composed of an analysis of the current marketing situation, opportunities and threats for the firm, marketing objectives and strategy specified in terms of the four Ps, action programs, and projected or pro forma income (and other financial) statements.[4] The three major phases of the marketing plan are planning, implementation, and control.[5]

Although most people do not have a written plan that outlines what they are planning to accomplish in the next year, and how they expect to do it, firms do need such a document. It is important that everyone involved in implementing the plan knows what the overall objectives for the firm are and how they are going to be met. Other stakeholders, such as investors and potential investors, also want to know what the firm plans to do. A written marketing plan also provides a reference point for evaluating whether or not the firm met its objectives.

A marketing plan entails five steps, depicted in Exhibit 2.2. In Step 1 of the **planning phase**, marketing executives, in conjunction with other top managers, define the mission and objectives of the business. For the second step, they evaluate the situation by assessing how various players, both inside and outside the organization, affect the firm's potential for success (Step 2). In the **implementation phase**, marketing managers identify and evaluate different opportunities by engaging in a process known as segmentation, targeting, and positioning (STP) (Step 3). They then are responsible for implementing the marketing mix by using the four Ps (Step 4). Finally, the **control phase** entails evaluating the performance of the marketing strategy by using marketing metrics and taking any necessary corrective actions (Step 5).

As indicated in Exhibit 2.2, it is not always necessary to go through the entire process for every evaluation (Step 5). For instance, a firm could evaluate its performance in Step 5, and then go directly to Step 2 to conduct a situation analysis without redefining its overall mission.

We will first discuss each step involved in developing a marketing plan. Then we consider ways of analyzing a marketing situation, as well as identifying and evaluating marketing opportunities. We also examine some specific strategies marketers use to grow a business. Finally, we consider how the implementation of the marketing mix increases customer value. A sample marketing plan outline and a marketing plan are provided in Appendix 2A, following this chapter.

planning phase
Where marketing executives and other top managers define the mission and objectives of the business, and evaluate the situation by assessing how various players, both inside and outside the organization, affect the firm's potential for success.

implementation phase
Where marketing managers identify and evaluate different opportunities by engaging in a process known as segmentation, targeting, and positioning. They then develop and implement the marketing mix by using the four Ps.

control phase
The part of the strategic marketing planning process when managers evaluate the performance of the marketing strategy and take any necessary corrective actions.

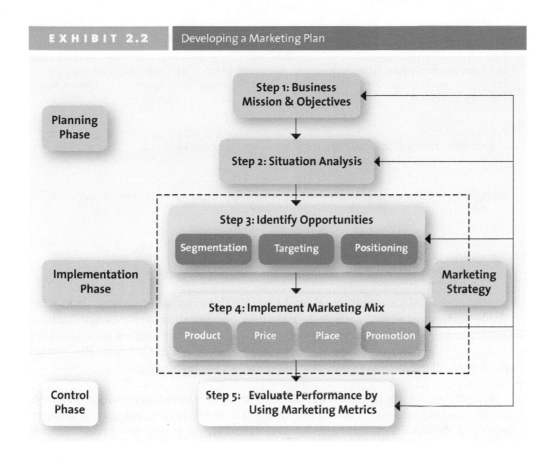

EXHIBIT 2.2 Developing a Marketing Plan

Step 1: Define the Business Mission and Objectives

The **mission statement**, a broad description of a firm's objectives and the scope of activities it plans to undertake,[6] attempts to answer two main questions: What type of business are we? and What do we need to do to accomplish our goals and objectives? These fundamental business issues must be answered at the highest corporate levels before marketing executives can get involved. Most firms want to maximize shareholders' wealth by increasing the value of the firm's stock and paying dividends.[7] However, owners of small, privately held firms frequently have other objectives, such as achieving a specific level of income and avoiding risks. (See Exhibit 2.3 for several mission statement examples.)

Nonprofit organizations, such as the Heart and Stroke Foundation, specify nonmonetary objectives such as improving the health of Canadians through research, health promotion, and advocacy. Tim Horton's mission is very focused: delivering superior quality products and services to customers and being the quality leader in what it does.[8] Disney's mission statement is sufficiently broad to encompass the many different types of businesses it operates. For all three organizations, marketing holds the primary responsibility of enhancing the value of the company's products for its customers and other constituents, whether or not the company pursues profit. Another key goal or objective often embedded in a mission statement is how the firm is building a sustainable competitive advantage.

Step 2: Conduct a Situation Analysis

After developing its mission, a firm next must perform a **situation analysis**, using a SWOT analysis that assesses both the internal environment with regard to its

mission statement
A broad description of a firm's objectives and the scope of activities it plans to undertake; attempts to answer two main questions: What type of business is it? and What does it need to do to accomplish its goals and objectives?

situation analysis
Is the second step in a marketing plan; uses a SWOT analysis that assesses both the internal environment with regard to its **s**trengths and **w**eaknesses and the external environment in terms of its **o**pportunities and **t**hreats.

EXHIBIT 2.3	Mission Statements

The Heart and Stroke Foundation mission is to improve the health of Canadians by preventing and reducing disability and death from heart disease and stroke through research, health promotion, and advocacy.

Tim Hortons states its mission this way: "Our guiding mission is to deliver superior quality products and services for our customers and communities through leadership, innovation and partnerships. Our vision is to be the quality leader in everything we do."

Disney, with its many business units, broadly describes its mission as its commitment to producing creative entertainment experiences based on storytelling.

Sources: "About Us," www.heartandstrokefoundation.ca; "Company Facts," www.timhortons.com/ca/en/about/2908.html; and "Company Overview," www.corporate.disney.go.com.

strengths and weaknesses (internal analysis) and the external environment in terms of its opportunities and threats (external analysis). Situation analysis also includes an examination of market trends, customer analysis, and competitive analysis. Additionally, the firms should assess the opportunities and uncertainties of the marketplace due to changes in cultural, demographic, social, technological, economic, and political forces (CDSTEP).

A SWOT analysis is designed to help the firm determine areas in which it is strong and can compete effectively and areas where it is weak and vulnerable to competitive attacks. It also enables the firm to understand where it has sustainable competitive advantage or unique advantages that cannot be easily copied by competitors and how it can leverage those advantages in response to new opportunities arising from changes in its external environment. By understanding its competitive strengths and weaknesses, the firm will be better positioned to address weaknesses and deal with threats arising from its external business environment. A SWOT analysis requires the firm to undertake a critical assessment of its resources, capabilities, organization, strategies, and performance in relation to competitors. Similarly, the firm must conduct a careful analysis of changes in the environment and understand how they affect its business, whether they represent threats or opportunities. Strengths and weaknesses are within the control of the firm, and it can take actions to alleviate weaknesses and consolidate its strengths. Opportunities and threats are outside of the control of the firm; therefore, the firm can decide only how it wants to respond.

Exhibit 2.4 lists several general elements that are usually examined when conducting a SWOT analysis. The relevance of specific elements will depend on the nature of the firm. This list is for illustration purposes and is by no means exhaustive.

To illustrate the application of Exhibit 2.4, let's look at a SWOT analysis for Disney, pictured in Exhibit 2.5. The strengths (Exhibit 2.5, upper left) are positive and internal attributes of the firm. Disney is one of the world's best-known brands, ranking ninth among the top 100 global brands. The Disney name is so well recognized globally that when people see the name on any of Disney's products they know they will be entertained. Disney is a diverse company that operates in four distinct businesses: media networks, studio entertainment, parks and resorts, and consumer products, where it has global marketing reach and distribution. These diverse businesses provide opportunities for growth and reduce the firm's overall risk. The company's cable stations appeal to a broad range of interests and age groups, with channels such as ABC, Lifetime, A&E, Toon Disney, SOAPnet, and ESPN.[9] Disney also produces and distributes movies worldwide under the names of Walt Disney Pictures, Touchstone, Miramax, and Dimension. Its consumer products segment licenses the Walt Disney name and uses Disney Stores and catalogues in direct retail distribution.

EXHIBIT 2.4	Examples of Elements Considered in a SWOT Analysis	

Environment	Evaluation	
	Positive	**Negative**
Internal	**Strengths** • Superior resources and capabilities • Superior management, marketing, technical talent • Strong brand • Superior product offerings • Extensive marketing reach • Wide distribution networks (national/global) • Strong financial resources • Excellent geographic location • Proprietary technologies/Intellectual property • Strong base of loyal customers	**Weaknesses** • Little or no brand recognition • Lack of financial resources • Lack of other resources and capabilities • Lack of marketing, management, and technical talent • Limited market reach or distribution network • No propriety technology • Poor location • Limited customer base or loyalty • Lack of credibility
External	**Opportunities** • CDSTEP changes that offer opportunities for the firm to serve new markets with existing products and/or pursue completely new market opportunities • When existing firms exit the market because of financial or other difficulties (i.e., reduced competition) • When a firm acquires another firm, the acquiring firm gets market access, new customers, new technology and expertise, and financial resources	**Threats** • Political or regulatory changes (e.g., new laws affecting business or products) • New entrants into the industry or market • New technology that could render existing technology or business practices obsolete • Natural or man-made disasters • Recession or economic downturn that affects consumers' purchasing power and confidence • Changes in socio-cultural or demographic trends

Every firm has weaknesses, and Disney is no different. The weaknesses (Exhibit 2.5, upper right) are negative attributes of the firm. For instance, Disney relies heavily on its relationships with cable operators to expand its distribution. Without them, the company's continued growth would be in jeopardy. The linked nature of Disney's businesses can have a domino effect. If a movie is not successful, then its merchandise will not sell either. Finally, foreign operations are fraught with risk. Euro Disney, for instance, was not successful when it first opened. Similarly, the Hong Kong Disneyland Resort has not yet lived up to expectations; its Magic Kingdom theme park has steadily lost money since opening in 2005.[10] This negative situation could tarnish Disney's image and future growth in Asia.[11]

The opportunities (Exhibit 2.5, lower left) are positive aspects of the external environment. Like Disney's strengths, it has many opportunities, not the least of which is its ability to build its current brand and businesses both in the United States and globally. For instance, increasing affluence in international markets presents opportunities for Disney to expand into those markets, which is precisely what Disney has done. Disney launched its Disney Channel and Toon Disney channel in India, and Disney's Asian TV service is available in seven Asia-Pacific regions: Australia, Korea, Malaysia, South Korea, Singapore, Brunei, and the Philippines.[12] The growth opportunities in these and other markets are enormous.

Threats (Exhibit 2.5, lower right) are negative aspects of the external environment. For Disney, stiff competition in all markets can negatively impact its businesses. For example, Disney's studio and broadcasting services face stiff competition from other TV networks (such as CBS and Fox), satellite television, and cable television. These competitors could affect Disney's ability to raise advertising revenues from its

Home release of some Disney videos, such as Pirates of the Caribbean *and* Finding Nemo, *demonstrate consistently strong sales.*

EXHIBIT 2.5	SWOT Analysis for Disney

Environment	Evaluation	
	Positive	**Negative**
Internal	**Strengths** • Superior capabilities and resources: it is the largest media and entertainment company in the world, with assets valued at more than US$60 billion • Global marketing reach and distribution in its four diverse business lines: media networks, studio entertainment, parks and resorts, and consumer products • Well-known brand image: Disney ranked ninth in the top 100 global brands for 2010 • Innovative: Known for developing new, innovative attractions • Its characters (e.g., Mickey, Winnie the Pooh) are well-known and liked by consumers globally • Disney Store sells exclusively Disney merchandise and maintains control of the merchandises' marketing	**Weaknesses** • Overreliance on relationships in certain business lines and markets • Revenue concentration: about 80% of Disney's revenues are from the United States, resulting in an over-dependence on the U.S. market • Standardization strategy: exporting U.S. offering to international markets rather than developing offering that suits the local markets • Lacklustre performance of Hong Kong Disneyland Resort and some business lines have hurt the Disney brand
External	**Opportunities** • Increasing affluence in emerging economies makes it more attractive for Disney to expand into international markets • Expansion possibilities in existing business in the United States • Expansion possibilities for cruise line business • New attractions could be built in theme parks	**Threats** • Increasing competitive pressures • Its properties could be a target for a terrorist attack • Regulatory changes in media and entertainment • Recession or serious economic downturn in any of its markets

media properties. Similarly, Disney's parks and resorts business faces stiff competition for visitors from the likes of Paramount Parks and smaller local U.S.-based amusement parks around the country. Finally, the media business is heavily regulated in both the United States and internationally, which could limit Disney's ability to offer certain programs; for example, there are restrictions on commercial time during children's programming. In addition, any economic trend that affects businesses in general will also affect Disney.

L03

Step 3: Identify and Evaluate Opportunities by Using STP (Segmentation, Targeting, and Positioning)

After completing the situation analysis, the next step is to identify and evaluate opportunities for increasing sales and profits by using **STP** (segmentation, targeting, and positioning). With STP, the firm must first understand customer needs and wants through market research, then divide the market or customers into distinct subgroups or segments, determine which of those segments it should pursue or target, and finally decide how it should position its products and services to best meet the needs of those chosen targets. The criteria to evaluate target segments are discussed in detail in Chapter 7.

STP
The processes of segmentation, targeting, and positioning that firms use to identify and evaluate opportunities for increasing sales and profits.

Segmentation Many types of customers appear in any market, and most firms cannot satisfy everyone's needs. For instance, among Internet users, some users do research online, some shop, some look for entertainment, and many do all three. Each of these groups might be a **market segment** consisting of consumers who respond similarly to a firm's marketing efforts. The process of dividing the market into distinct groups of customers where each individual group has similar needs, wants, or characteristics— who therefore might appreciate products or services geared especially for them in

market segment
A group of consumers who respond similarly to a firm's marketing efforts.

EXHIBIT 2.6	Hertz Market Segmentation				
	Segment 1	**Segment 2**	**Segment 3**	**Segment 4**	**Segment 5**
Segments	Single people and couples who want to have a bit of fun	Business customers and families who prefer a luxurious ride	Environmentally conscious customers	Families	Commercial customers
Cars Offered	Fun Collection	Prestige Collection	Green Collection	SUV/minivan & crossover	Commercial Van/Truck
	Corvette ZHZ	Infiniti QX56	Toyota Prius	Toyota Rav 4	Ford Cargo Van
	Chevrolet Camaro	Cadillac Escalade	Ford Fusion	Ford Explorer	

similar ways—is called **market segmentation**. For example, Disney targets Pleasure Island to singles and couples, Epcot to families with older children and adults, and the Magic Kingdom to families with younger children. Firms identify segments in various ways. For instance, Disney may use demographics, such as gender, age, and income, to identify the young families it is pursuing for the Magic Kingdom but psychological or behavioural factors, such as people who like to party or go dancing, to identify the singles and couples it is pursuing for Pleasure Island. As shown in Exhibit 2.6, some of the segments that car rental company Hertz targets include single people and couples who want to have a bit of fun, business customers and families who prefer a luxurious ride, and consumers who are environmentally conscious. Firms may also segment consumers based on benefits sought or socio-cultural factors, which will be discussed in Chapter 7.

Targeting   After a firm has identified the various market segments it might pursue, it evaluates each segment's attractiveness and decides which to pursue by using a process known as **target marketing** or **targeting**. For example, Disney realizes that the Magic Kingdom's primary appeal is to young families, so the bulk of its marketing efforts for this business are directed toward that group. Similarly, potato chip manufacturers have divided the market into many submarkets or segments. Frito Lay Canada, for instance, makes its cheesy Doritos (R) tortilla chips for the teen segment and makes its Lay's (R) wasabi and curry potato chips for Asian-Canadians.[13] The criteria used to evaluate the attractiveness of a target segment are also described in Chapter 7. After identifying its target segments, a firm must evaluate each of its strategic opportunities. A method of examining which segments to pursue is described in the Growth Strategies section later in the chapter. Firms typically are most successful when they focus on those opportunities that build on their strengths relative to those of their competition.

Positioning   Finally, when the firm decides which segments to pursue, it must determine how it wants to be positioned within those segments. Because positioning is what consumers think and feel about a brand or product, marketers try very hard through their various marketing efforts to shape consumers' perceptions regarding their brand or product. All marketers would like consumers to think of their brand or product in the way the company wants to present it to them. Disney, for instance, defines itself as an entertainer, and most consumers perceive

market segmentation
The process of dividing the market into distinct groups of customers where each individual group has similar needs, wants, or characteristics—who therefore might appreciate products or services geared especially for them in similar ways.

target marketing/targeting
The process of evaluating the attractiveness of various segments and then deciding which to pursue as a market.

PepsiCo Canada targets several markets with many different types of chips and carbonated beverages.

Disney as an entertainment provider. Similarly, Abercrombie & Fitch defines its brand as casual luxury, and most consumers see its products as offering casual luxury. **Market positioning** involves the process of defining the marketing mix variables so that target customers have a clear, distinct, desirable understanding of what the product does or represents in comparison with competing products.

market positioning
Involves the process of defining the marketing mix variables so that target customers have a clear, distinct, desirable understanding of what the product does or represents in comparison with competing products.

Set Marketing Objectives   Normally the marketing manager is responsible for setting the specific marketing objectives for the product or brand over the life of the plan. These objectives may include market share, revenues and profitability targets, unit sales volume, and brand awareness. Depending on the duration of the plan, these objectives usually cover one year to five years. In Step 4 of the strategic marketing planning process, the firm implements its marketing mix and allocates resources to different products and services.

L04 Step 4: Implement Marketing Mix and Allocate Resources

When the firm has identified and evaluated different growth opportunities by performing an STP analysis, the real action begins. The company has decided what to do, how to do it, and how many resources the firm should allocate to it. In the fourth step of the planning process, marketers implement the marketing mix—product, price, promotion, and place—for each product and service on the basis of what it believes its target markets will value (Exhibit 2.7). At the same time, it makes important decisions about how it will allocate its scarce resources to its various products and services. Each element of the four Ps must be fully integrated to achieve a coherent strategy.

Product and Value Creation   Products, which include services, constitute the first of the four Ps. Because the key to the success of any marketing program is the creation of value, firms attempt to develop products and services that customers perceive as valuable enough to buy. For many consumers, the products offered by Starbucks contain enough value that they will pay upwards of $4 for a single cup of coffee. Still, there are millions of consumers who see no value in coffee products or suffer heartburn from drinking coffee. Knowing this, P&G, the consumer products giant, introduced Folgers Simply Smooth, a coffee designed to be gentle on people's stomachs. Simply Smooth will not appeal to traditional coffee buyers, who value other elements of a coffee product, but it may create a new category of coffee drinkers, which would enable P&G to reach customers who typically would not have consumed any coffee products.[14] You'll learn more about product and branding decisions in Chapters 8 and 9.

Folgers created value for a product and market that didn't previously exist.

A Stomach-Friendly Coffee from Folgers

Price and Value for Money   Recall that the second element of the marketing mix is price. As part of the exchange process, a firm provides a product or a service, or some combination thereof, and in return it receives money. Value-based marketing requires that firms charge a price that customers perceive as giving them good value for the products and services they receive. Clearly, it is important for a firm to have a clear focus in terms of what products to sell, where to buy them, and what methods to use in selling them. But pricing is the only activity that actually brings in money by influencing revenues. If a price is set too high, it will not generate much volume. If a price is set too low, it may result in lower-than-necessary margins and profits. Therefore, marketers should base price on the value that the customer perceives. Pricing decisions and strategies are discussed in detail in Chapter 11.

Place and Value Delivery   For the third P, place, the firm must be able to, after it has created value through a product and/or service, make the product or service readily accessible when and where the customer wants it. Consider Lee Valley Tools, a small Ottawa-based company that has grown to become one of the world's leading mail-order and retail suppliers of innovative woodworking and gardening tools. The company was founded more than 30 years ago as a catalogue mail-order supplier of woodworking and gardening tools by entrepreneur Leonard Lee. Over the years, Lee has opened 11 stores across Canada and launched a fully-functional e-commerce website, leevalley.com. To make its products

| EXHIBIT 2.7 | Developing the Marketing Mix |

Promotion Strategy

Place Strategy

Target Mkt. & Positioning

Product & Service Strategy

Price Strategy

and services accessible to all of its customers, Lee Valley has integrated its stores and catalogue operations with its Internet operations and used place to create value in its delivery process. Through its website, Lee Valley is able to reach a wider market segment more efficiently and cost-effectively. Thus, Lee Valley turned the integration of its different channels into a seamless customer experience, a key value driver for the company.[15] Chapters 12 and 13 deal with in-depth place, or distribution, decisions. Although many companies have developed sophisticated website and online marketing strategies to deliver place value for their customers, the same cannot be said for nonprofit organizations. As described in Power of the Internet 2.1, the overwhelming majority of Canadian nonprofit organizations have been unable to leverage the power of the Internet to raise funds, recruit volunteers, and communicate with their clientele.

Promotion and Value Communication   The fourth P of the marketing mix is promotion. Marketers communicate the value of their offering, or the value proposition, to their customers through a variety of media, including TV, radio, magazines, buses, trains, blimps, sales promotion, publicity, the sales force, and the Internet. It is now possible for firms in out-of-the-way locations to expand their market area to the whole world. For example, Canadians living in places such as Africa, Australia, and New Zealand can order their favourite authentic Canadian products that they cannot find in these countries through the Ottawa-based Country Grocer website, www.thecountrygrocer.com.[16] Similarly, Cupcakes by Heather and Lori (see Entrepreneurial Marketing 2.1 on page 55), located in the Lower Mainland of Vancouver, British Columbia—sells millions of cupcakes each week to customers across Canada and the United States.[17] These retailers and thousands like them have added value to their offerings through their efficient and effective communications strategies, which will be discussed in more detail in Chapters 14 and 15.

The Salvation Army is one of few not-for-profit organizations that leverages the Internet effectively.

Marketers therefore must consider which are the most efficient and effective methods to communicate with their customers, which goes back to understanding customers, the value created, and the message being communicated. Recently, an increasing number of companies are using the Internet and their own websites to advertise and communicate with their customers and build closer relationships. For example, apart from enabling customers to order tools through its website, Lee Valley uses it to tell customers of upcoming training seminars that are held in its physical stores. These seminars teach customers about the use and care of the tools and demonstrate new, innovative tools being developed. The website also contains a variety of technical articles on woodworking and gardening

More than 161 000 nonprofit organizations operate in Canada, providing invaluable services within their communities. Usually, these organizations convey their visions, core values, and missions through traditional channels of communication, such as print media, public service announcements, word of mouth, and promotional events. These methods of communication are both cost- and resource-intensive. Since nonprofit organizations operate mainly on donations, they must use funds allocated to marketing and promotion in the most effective way, which means maximizing their reach by using the least costly resources.

Most nonprofit organizations have recognized that the Internet provides a cost-effective way to reach a wide audience and deliver great value. As a result, they are now moving toward the Internet as a source of sharing their visions, providing information about their services, and achieving their purposes. However, even with an online presence, many nonprofits are not leveraging the full capabilities of the Internet to maximize their reach and achieve their goals. A study conducted by professors Ajax Persaud and Judith Madill of the Telfer School of Management at the University of Ottawa found that the majority

of charities have a very basic website. Nonprofits are using the Internet to communicate their mission and provide information about services; but, they are not doing much to fundraise, recruit volunteers, or build relationships with donors, volunteers, and other constituents, all of which are key to achieving their purposes. Very few nonprofit websites provide information about volunteering opportunities or online donations. The Salvation Army is one of the few nonprofit organizations that allow visitors to donate directly on its website, view their donation history, and review their donation before submitting. Although, nonprofit organizations have made websites part of their marketing strategy, they could do more to enhance the effectiveness of their online efforts.

Having an online presence creates the opportunity to deliver greater value. Private corporations are taking advantage of this opportunity with sophisticated websites that serve customers and build relationships. In stark contrast, nonprofit organizations are not harnessing the full potential of the Internet. They need to make improvements so that they can use their websites to deliver effective content and value for visitors.[18]

that help customers learn more and enjoy their favourite activities. The regular e-newsletter, which customers sign up for, provides technical information, trade-show dates, company news, special event dates, and other topics of interest to woodworkers and gardeners. Customers can even send letters about their experiences with specific tools, which are posted publicly on the company's website. Lee Valley is building loyal customer relationships one customer at a time.

Research has shown that this type of campaign is much more effective than either mail or TV advertising. Nevertheless, marketers must balance the effectiveness of their value communication activities with their costs. In addition to the Internet, many Canadian companies spend a large portion of their marketing budgets on sales promotions because Canadian consumers are increasingly becoming more value-conscious. In fact, spending on sales promotion has exceeded spending on advertising in Canada.[19] Sponsorship of charitable and community-based events is gaining in popularity in Canada as companies try to demonstrate social responsibility. Corporate sponsorships of charitable events have always been viewed with suspicion from some segments of society, while others have embraced it as a beneficial activity. Ethical Dilemma 2.1 examines the financial relationships between corporations and charities that raise questions concerning the credibility of charities and the motivations of corporate donors.

In addition to developing the four Ps and allocating resources, marketing managers must develop schedules: timelines for each activity and the personnel responsible for the respective activity to avoid bottlenecks and ensure smooth and timely implementation of the marketing mix activities. Also, marketers must design the organization that will be responsible for putting the plan into action. This organization is usually represented in the form of an organizational chart. In most established companies, the marketing organization already exists and marketing managers must simply assign responsibilities to various employees within the marketing department. The marketing organization is usually responsible for the day-to-day operational decisions involved in executing the plan.

| **Ethical Dilemma 2.1** | **Corporate "Do"nations or "Don't"nations for Charities[20]** |

Many Canadians rely on the services offered by charities and many charities rely on corporate donations to fund these services. Charities are admired for the services they offer, the programs they deliver, the resources they provide, and the goodwill that they build within the community. Most charities advocate a specific cause, such as cancer research or women's rights. They seek to promote awareness and generate solutions for the betterment of their constituents. Charities are heavily reliant on the work of volunteers and the donations of individuals to achieve their missions. While Canadians are generous donors, with an average of 85 percent of Canadians contributing to charities,[21] corporations are still the primary source of funding for charities. This issue raises questions about the partnerships formed between charities and corporations. Complications arise when charities partner with corporations that sell products or represent ideas that conflict with the charity's message or purpose. Nearly every charitable organization is facing this challenge.

Consider the Heart and Stroke Foundation, whose mandate is to eliminate cardiovascular disease and promote healthy living. One of its leading donors is the Boston Pizza Foundation. Critics say that two slices of the restaurant's pepperoni pizza contain 400 calories and 900 milligrams of sodium—hardly a step in the right direction to fight against cardiovascular disease! Also consider the Canadian Cancer Society, which is adamant about the need for protection against harmful environmental carcinogens. Nevertheless, its top donors include companies that have been highly criticized by environmentalists for releasing carcinogens and polluting the environment. These companies include Suncor Energy, Syncrude Canada, and Husky Energy.

With such a dependence on corporate donations, is it possible for charitable organizations to stay true to their missions and motivate positive change without being compromised in the process? Should charities continue to accept donations from corporations they are struggling against?

Step 5: Evaluate Performance by Using Marketing Metrics

The final step in the planning process includes evaluating the results of the strategy and implementation program by using marketing metrics. A metric is a measuring system that quantifies a trend, dynamic, or characteristic. Metrics are used to explain why things happened and to project the future. They make it possible to compare results across regions, business units, product lines, and time periods. The firm can determine why it achieved or did not achieve its performance goals with the help of these metrics. Understanding the causes of the performance, regardless of whether that performance exceeded, met, or fell below the firm's goals, enables firms to make appropriate adjustments.

Typically, managers begin by reviewing the implementation programs, and their analysis may indicate that the strategy (or even the mission statement) needs to be reconsidered. Problems can arise both when firms successfully implement poor strategies and when they poorly implement good strategies.

Customers purchase Lee Valley woodworking and gardening tools by catalogue, by phone, by website, or in store.

Who Is Accountable for Performance?   At each level of an organization, the business unit and its manager should be held accountable only for the revenues, expenses, and profits that they can control. Expenses that affect several levels of the organization, such as the labour and capital expenses associated with operating a corporate headquarters, shouldn't be arbitrarily assigned to lower levels. In the case of a store, for example, it may be appropriate to evaluate performance objectives based on sales, sales associate productivity, and energy costs. If the corporate office lowers prices to get rid of merchandise and therefore profits suffer, then it's not fair to assess a store manager's performance based on the resulting decline in store profit.

Performance evaluations are used to pinpoint problem areas. Reasons why performance may be above or below planned levels must be examined. Perhaps the managers involved in setting the objectives aren't very good at making estimates. If so, they may need to be trained in forecasting.

Actual performance may be different than the plan predicts because of circumstances beyond the manager's control. For example, there may have been a recession. Assuming the recession wasn't predicted, or was more severe or lasted longer than anticipated, there are several relevant questions: How quickly were plans adjusted? How rapidly and appropriately were pricing and promotional policies modified? In short, did the manager react to salvage an adverse situation, or did those reactions worsen the situation?

Performance Objectives and Metrics   Many factors contribute to a firm's overall performance, which make it hard to find a single metric to evaluate performance. One approach is to compare a firm's performance over time or to competing firms, using common financial metrics such as sales and profits. Another method of assessing performance is to view the firm's products or services as a portfolio. Depending on the firm's relative performance, the profits from some products or services are used to fuel growth for others.

Financial Performance Metrics   Some commonly used metrics to assess performance include revenues, or sales, and profits. For instance, sales are a global measure of a firm's activity level. However, a manager could easily increase sales by lowering prices, but the profit realized on that merchandise (gross margin) would suffer as a result. Clearly, an attempt to maximize one metric may lower another. Managers must therefore understand how their actions affect multiple performance metrics. It's usually unwise to use only one metric because it rarely tells the whole story.

In addition to assessing the absolute level of sales and profits, a firm may wish to measure the relative level of sales and profits. For example, a relative metric of sales or profits is its increase or decrease over the prior year. Additionally, a firm may compare its growth in sales or profits relative to other benchmark companies (e.g., Pizza Pizza may compare itself to Pizza Hut).

The metrics used to evaluate a firm vary depending on (1) the level of the organization at which the decision is made and (2) the resources the manager controls. For example, while the top executives of a firm have control over all of the firm's resources and resulting expenses, a regional sales manager has control over only the sales and expenses generated by his or her salespeople.

Social Responsibility Performance Metrics   As Canadian companies become more convinced of the importance of social responsibility, we will likely see an increasing number of companies report corporate social responsibility metrics, such as their impact on the environment, their ability to diversify their workforce, their energy conservation initiatives, and their policies on protecting the human rights of their employees and the employees of their suppliers. Sustainable Marketing 2.1 presents an example that illustrates the importance of having such performance metrics.

To illustrate how a firm evaluates its performance and makes appropriate adjustments, let's consider the case of Canada's Fairmont Hotels and Resorts, the largest luxury hotel company in North America. Recently, the company developed a guest data warehouse to maintain guest profile information across all its properties; to target guest segments with personalized communications, incentives, and discounts; to better manage its loyalty program; and to acquire new guests and build loyalty. This data warehouse is seamlessly integrated with Fairmont's website and the hotel's central reservation and property management systems. It can gather guest information from all touchpoints (media through which customers come into contact with Fairmont). As a result of this guest warehouse, Fairmont is able to maximize its revenues by focusing its marketing and brand-building efforts on higher-value guest segments. It can also, for the first time, measure the effectiveness of segmented marketing initiatives.[22]

Sustainable Marketing **2.1**	**Birks: A Diamond in the Rough?**[23]

When striving to achieve sustainability, small changes can make a huge difference. Birks & Mayors, founder of Birks, realizes the impact that small changes can have on its economic, environmental, and social performance. In an industry where sustainability is very challenging because of the nature of the supply chain, Birks is attempting to distinguish itself through corporate social responsibility and by turning sustainability into its new gold standard. Birks is trying to purchase ethically sourced diamonds, gold, and silver whenever possible. It relies on strategic partnerships to guarantee that products meet its strict social and environmental standards. Birks is reinforcing its commitment to the environment by introducing recyclable shopping bags. It also encourages employees to suggest ways that the company can improve its sustainable performance. These are some of the steps that Birks is taking to fulfill its mandate of being as sustainable as possible by addressing the controllable aspects of its operations.

Birks' sustainability efforts can drive success and create a competitive advantage. However, its efforts will have little impact unless it takes steps to make stakeholders aware of the positive changes it is implementing. Before it can inform stakeholders about positive improvements, Birks needs to have a method of measuring the results of the changes. This need highlights the importance of performance metrics. Adequate analytical metrics enable organizations to capture crucial qualitative and quantitative information that allows for tracking the success of sustainability strategies. Such tracking will allow Birks to consistently meet its established environmental and social standards and provide greater transparency and credibility for stakeholders. Once analytical metrics are used to enlighten stakeholders, Birks can leverage its sustainability initiatives as a point of differentiation. Clear and compelling communication to stakeholders about how the changes are making a huge difference in the jewellery industry will likely allow Birks continued financial stability within a sustainable enterprise.

Birks is turning sustainability into a new gold standard.

Strategic Planning Is Not Sequential

The planning process in Exhibit 2.2 on page 39 suggests that managers follow a set sequence when they make strategic decisions. Namely, after they've defined the business mission, they perform the situation analysis, identify opportunities, evaluate alternatives, set objectives, allocate resources, develop the implementation plan, and, finally, evaluate their performance and make adjustments. But actual planning processes can move back and forth among these steps. For example, a situation analysis may uncover a logical alternative, even though this alternative might not be included in the mission statement, which would mean that the mission statement would need to be revised. Or, the development of the implementation plan might reveal that insufficient resources have been allocated to a particular product for it to achieve its objective. In that case, the firm would need to either change the objective or increase the resources; alternatively, the marketer might consider not investing in the product at all.

Now that we have gone through the steps of the strategic marketing planning process, let's look at some strategies that have been responsible for making many marketing firms successful. We begin by looking at portfolio analysis, then product-market growth strategies, and finally four macro strategies that companies use to create and maintain sustainable competitive advantage.

Portfolio Analysis   In portfolio analysis, for example, management evaluates the firm's various products and businesses—its "portfolio"—and allocates resources according to which products are expected to be the most profitable for the firm in the future. Portfolio analysis is typically performed at the **strategic business unit (SBU)** or

strategic business unit (SBU)

A division of the company that can be managed somewhat independently from other divisions since it markets a specific set of products to a clearly defined group of customers.

The tabs on this screenshot show some of the business lines of President's Choice, which is a brand within the Loblaw group of companies.

product line level of the firm, though managers can also use it to analyze brands or even individual items. An SBU is a division of the company that can be managed somewhat independently from other divisions since it markets a specific set of products to a clearly defined group of customers. For example, Loblaw Companies Limited consists of its general merchandise, drugstores, President's Choice brand, and financial products and services operations.[24] Each of these is an SBU. A product line, in contrast, is a group of products that consumers may use together or perceive as similar in some way. There are several product lines within Loblaw's PC Financial services SBU: PC banking, PC MasterCard, mortgages, and insurance.

product line
A group of products that consumers may use together or perceive as similar in some way.

relative market share
A measure of the product's strength in a particular market, defined as the sales of the focal product divided by the sales achieved by the largest firm in the industry.

market growth rate
The annual rate of growth of the specific market in which the product competes.

BOSTON CONSULTING GROUP'S PORTFOLIO ANALYSIS

One of the most popular portfolio analysis methods, developed by the Boston Consulting Group (BCG), requires that firms classify all their products into a two-by-two matrix, as depicted in Exhibit 2.8.[25] The circles represent brands, and their sizes are in direct proportion to the brands' annual sales—that is, larger circles correspond to higher levels sales and smaller circles indicate lower levels of sales. The horizontal axis represents the **relative market share**. In general, market share is the percentage of a market accounted for by a specific entity,[26] and it is used to establish the product's strength in a particular market. It is usually discussed in units, revenue, or sales. A special type of market share metric, relative market share, is used in this application because it provides managers with a product's relative strength, compared to that of the largest firm in the industry.[27] The vertical axis is the **market growth rate**, or the annual rate of growth of the specific market in which the product competes. Market growth rate thus measures how attractive a particular market is. Each quadrant has been named on the basis of the amount of resources it generates for and requires from the firm.

Stars. Stars (upper left quadrant) occur in high-growth markets and are high–market share products. That is, stars often require a heavy resource investment in such things as promotions and new production facilities to fuel their rapid growth. As their market growth slows, stars will migrate from heavy users of resources to heavy generators of resources and become cash cows.

Cash cows. Cash cows (lower left quadrant) are in low-growth markets but are high–market share products. Because these products have already received heavy investments to develop their high market share, they have excess resources that can be spun off to those products that need it. For example, in Exhibit 2.8, Brand C uses its excess resources to fund products in the question mark quadrant.

Question marks. Question marks (upper right quadrant) appear in high-growth markets but have relatively low market shares; thus, they are often the most managerially intensive products in that they require significant resources to maintain and potentially increase their market share. Managers must decide whether to infuse question marks with resources generated by the cash cows, so that they can become stars, or withdraw resources and eventually phase out the products. Brand A, for instance, is currently a question mark, but by infusing it with resources, the firm hopes to turn it into a star.

Dogs. Dogs (lower right quadrant) are in low-growth markets and have relatively low market shares. Although they may generate enough resources to sustain themselves, dogs are not

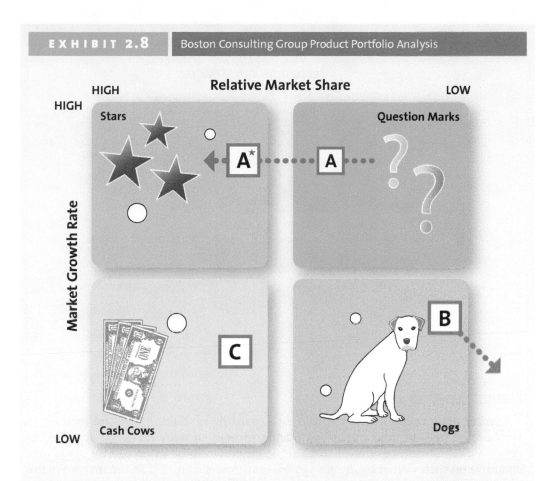

EXHIBIT 2.8   Boston Consulting Group Product Portfolio Analysis

destined for stardom and should be phased out unless they are needed to complement or boost the sales of another product or for competitive purposes. In this case, the company has decided to stop making Brand B.

Although quite useful for conceptualizing the resource allocation task, the BCG approach, and others like it, are often difficult to implement in practice. In particular, it is difficult to accurately measure both relative market share and industry growth. Furthermore, other measures could easily serve as substitutes to represent a product's competitive position and the market's relative attractiveness. Another issue for marketers is the potential self-fulfilling prophecy of placing a product into a quadrant. That is, suppose a product is classified as a dog although it has the potential of being a question mark. The firm might reduce support for the product and lose sales to the point that it abandons the product, which might have become profitable if provided with sufficient resources.

Because of these limitations, many firms have tempered their use of matrix approaches to achieve a more balanced approach to allocating their resources. Instead of assigning allocation decisions to the top levels of the organization, many firms start at lower management levels and employ checks and balances to force managers at each level of the organizational hierarchy to negotiate with those above and below them to reach their final decisions.

Growth Strategies   L05

Firms consider pursuing various market segments as part of their overall growth strategies, which may include the four major strategies shown in Exhibit 2.9.[28] The rows distinguish those opportunities a firm possesses in its current markets from those it has in new markets, whereas the columns distinguish between the firm's current marketing offering and that of a new opportunity. Let's consider each of them in detail.

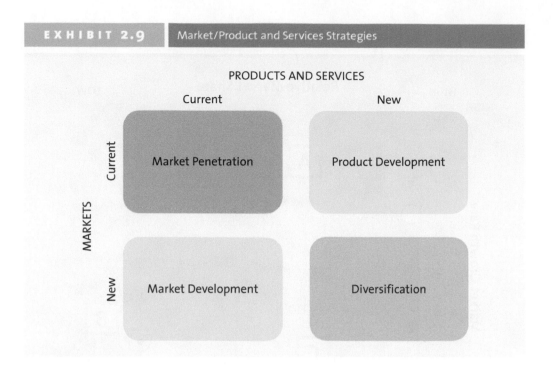

EXHIBIT 2.9   Market/Product and Services Strategies

Market Penetration

A **market penetration strategy** employs the existing marketing mix and focuses the firm's efforts on existing customers. Such a growth strategy might be achieved by encouraging current customers to patronize the firm more often or buy more merchandise on each visit or by attracting new consumers from within the firm's existing target market. A market penetration strategy generally requires greater marketing efforts, such as increased advertising, additional sales and promotions, or intensified distribution efforts in geographic areas in which the product or service is already sold.

For example, Canada's Fairmont Hotels and Resorts offer customers numerous promotions and discount packages all year round for staying at its hotels and resorts. Its "Only One Way Summer Rates" discount package offers customers a discount on one-night accommodation at the Fairmont during the summer months. With this promotion, customers who book for a minimum of two nights before a certain date and pay with any American Express® Card receive up to a $50 food and beverage credit per night for stays between May and September or can earn double airline miles from its participating airline partners.[29] Its President Club membership program offers its 800 000 members—half of them Canadians—many benefits, such as allowing them to reserve Adidas apparel and footwear in their personal sizes, plus selected equipment, and having it waiting in their rooms as part of its Fairmont Fit Program.[30] These promotions and discounts entice existing Fairmont customers to patronize the firm more often and spend more money on each visit. Other market penetration tactics that firms use include advertising, loyalty or rewards programs, and improved store atmospherics (e.g., layout, lighting, music) to enhance the shopping experience.

Market Development

A **market development strategy** employs the existing marketing offering to reach new market segments, whether domestic or international or segments not currently served by the firm. International expansion is generally riskier than domestic expansion because firms must deal with differences in government regulations, cultural traditions, supply chain considerations, and language. Fairmont formed a joint venture in 2007 with Jin Jiang International Group, the largest hotel group in China, to renovate, reopen, and manage The Peace Hotel, a Shanghai landmark for more than a century. In 2010, the hotel was opened under the name the Fairmont Peace Hotel. In the future, the company plans to open Fairmont properties in Vancouver, Cairo, Abu Dhabi, South Africa, and other parts of Asia and the Middle East where it has very few hotels and resorts.[31] Similarly, Forever 21, a Los Angeles–based pioneer of "cheap chic" clothing that sells "ripped-from-the-runway" fashion aimed at teens and college and university students, has opened more than a dozen stores in Canada over the last few years. It plans to follow the footsteps of H&M of Sweden and Zara of Spain and open more stores across Canada.[32]

Market development may also include segments the firms are not currently serving but that represent great opportunities. For example, for many years RIM's BlackBerry was marketed to business professionals in the B2B segment or enterprise market; but, increased competition from Apple's iPhone in 2007 led RIM to develop the BlackBerry Pearl for the consumer market.

Product Development

The third growth strategy option, a **product development strategy**, offers a new product or service to a firm's current target market. Fairmont wanted to migrate its existing customers to its website from existing channels, so it developed a website that simplifies the booking steps, shortens the time frame required to complete the booking process, and provide relevant, value-added packages and promotions during the booking process. To further enhance its e-business initiative, Fairmont now offers visitors secured wired and wireless connectivity throughout its properties. According to Fairmont's vice-president of technology, "We have guests that actually host their own servers, and who actually work out of our hotels, out of meeting rooms, and out of guestrooms. Some even run mail servers." The idea is to make professional visitors as productive in their hotel rooms as they are in the corporate office.[33] Similarly, RIM's introduction of its PlayBook in response to Apple's hugely successful iPad is an attempt by RIM not only to offer its customers a full suite of products to satisfy their evolving technology needs, but also to ward off competition from Apple and other entrants into the tablet market.

> **product development strategy**
> A growth strategy that offers a new product or service to a firm's current target market.

Diversification

A **diversification strategy**, the last of the growth strategies from Exhibit 2.9, introduces a new product or service to a market segment that is currently not served. Diversification opportunities may be either related or unrelated. In a related diversification opportunity, the current target market and/or marketing mix shares something in common with the new opportunity. In other words, the firm might be able to purchase from existing vendors, use the same distribution and/or management information system, or advertise in the same newspapers to target markets that are similar to their current consumers. In contrast, in an unrelated diversification, the new business lacks any common elements with the present business. As part of its related diversification strategy, Fairmont entered a lower market segment by acquiring Delta Hotels and Resorts.[34] Similarly, in an unrelated diversification, Fairmont took a 35-percent investment stake in the Legacy Hotels Real Estate Investment Trust (REIT).[35]

> **diversification strategy**
> A growth strategy whereby a firm introduces a new product or service to a market segment that it does not currently serve.

While all four growth strategies present unique challenges for marketers, a market penetration strategy is the easiest to implement since it focuses on promoting existing products to existing customers. In this case, marketers know both their products and markets. With market development or product development, marketers have experience with one element and must learn the other element. Diversification requires marketers to go outside of both their current products and markets, and the risks of making mistakes are substantially greater with this strategy. The particular growth strategy a company chooses depends on its goals and capabilities, among other things. Also, marketers tend to pursue multiple growth strategies simultaneously.

Marketers may also develop strategies for **downsizing** their business operations by either exiting markets or reducing their product portfolios. They may exit markets or abandon products for many reasons, for example, because they have entered new markets where they have little or no experience; diversified into markets or products that do not quite fit with current products, markets, or capabilities; developed products that offer very little value for customers; or encountered declining demand for some products.

Marketing Strategy and Sustainable Competitive Advantage

A **marketing strategy** identifies (1) a firm's target market(s), (2) a related marketing mix—the four Ps, and (3) the bases upon which the firm plans to build a sustainable competitive advantage. A **sustainable competitive advantage** is an advantage over the competition that is not easily copied and thus can be maintained over a long period of time.

Starbucks and Tim Hortons appeal to different target markets, and they implement their marketing mixes—the four Ps—in different ways. In essence, they have very different marketing strategies. Although both stores' customers seek a good cup of coffee and a tasty pastry, Starbucks attempts to reach customers who want a coffee-drinking experience that includes a warm, social atmosphere and personable baristas to make their esoteric drinks. And people are willing to pay relatively high prices for this. Tim Hortons customers, on the other hand, aren't particularly interested in having an experience. They just want a good tasting cup of coffee at a fair price, and they want to get in and out of the store quickly.

Building a Sustainable Competitive Advantage

What about these companies' respective marketing mixes would provide a sustainable competitive advantage? After all, there are stores and restaurants that sell coffee and pastries in every neighbourhood in which there is a Starbucks or a Tim Hortons, and many of these establishments have great coffee and pastries. If Starbucks or Tim Hortons lowered their prices, their competition in the area would match the reduction. If they introduced a peppermint swirl cappuccino for the holiday season, other stores in the area could do the same. Thus, just because a firm implements an element of the marketing mix more effectively than its competition, it does not necessarily mean that it is sustainable. Establishing a competitive advantage means that the firm, in effect, builds a wall around its position in the market. When the wall is high, it will be difficult for competitors outside the wall to enter the market and compete for the firm's target customers.

Over time, all advantages will be eroded by competitive forces; but, by building high, thick walls, firms can sustain their advantage, minimize competitive pressure, and boost profits for a longer time. Thus, establishing a sustainable competitive advantage is key to long-term financial performance.[36]

There are four overarching strategies that focus on aspects of the marketing mix to create and deliver value and to develop sustainable competitive advantages, as we depict in Exhibit 2.10:[37]

- **Customer excellence:** Focuses on retaining loyal customers and excellent customer service.
- **Operational excellence:** Achieved through efficient operations and excellent supply chain and human resource management.
- **Product excellence:** Having products with high perceived value and effective branding and positioning.
- **Locational excellence:** Having a good physical location and Internet presence.

Entrepreneurial Marketing 2.1

Starting a Business Is No Cake-Walk![38]

Best friends Heather White and Lori Joyce always shared a childhood dream of owning a company together. Their dream faded into the background as the pair grew up and grew apart, as their jobs and academic pursuits took them in different directions. However, both Heather and Lori found themselves working in New York when the tragic events of 9/11 took place. The tragedy was an eye-opener for both women, and through the shock and devastation they found inspiration. They decided to follow their childhood aspirations and start a business together. Both women shared a passion for eating delicious cupcakes and were inspired to start a cupcake business after visiting a New York bakery shortly after 9/11. In April 2002, they opened their first store, Cupcakes by Heather and Lori, in Vancouver.

Since neither of the women had any experience in business, or in baking for that matter, they knew their cupcake venture would be a challenge. Although they had no experience, they did have a vision. Heather and Lori wanted their product to be timeless. They imagined that their store would be like a magic cupcake factory, which they represented by decorating with colours such as candy pink, dark chocolate brown, and soft vanilla: colours that matched their whimsical cupcakes, cakes, and other confectionaries. Their vision helped them define their strong brand values, position their brand and their product, choose effective advertising and promotional strategies, and seek out new business opportunities.

Both Heather and Lori were firmly committed to the quality of their cupcakes and felt that quality would differentiate their brand. Their values were based on old-fashioned personalized service with clients and vendors, and employees who were always cheerful, sweet, and friendly. They wanted their cupcakes to be "a sweet treat escape for customers in all age groups, both male and female." With a clear vision and strong brand values, the girls were ready to introduce their cupcakes to the world. They decided to use unconventional guerilla marketing tactics to accomplish this. They used experiential

Heather White and Lori Joyce built their cupcake business on a clear vision and strong brand values.

marketing and ensured that everyone in the media knew about and were given a sample of their cupcakes.

The media tasted their delicious cupcakes and loved them so much that the women now have their own reality TV show, "The Cupcake Girls." The 13-episode docu-soap airs on the W Network and follows their journey of expanding their cupcake empire. They currently have three corporate bakeries and six franchise locations across Vancouver's Lower Mainland and are seeking additional expansion opportunities. Customers can place custom orders online at the company's website (www.cupcakesonline.com), but the company's aggressive growth strategy goes beyond an online presence. Heather and Lori's objective is to establish Cupcakes bakeries in strategically chosen communities in North America and beyond through their Franchise and Area Development initiative. Their decision to franchise the Cupcakes brand that they worked so hard to create is their latest step down the path of their cupcake journey, which started out with a dream and a vision. Heather and Lori's fulfillment of their childhood dream was their biggest accomplishment. The rest of their success is just frosting on the cupcake!

Customer Excellence   Customer excellence is achieved when a firm develops value-based strategies for retaining loyal customers and provides outstanding customer service.

Retaining loyal customers.   Sometimes, the methods a firm uses to maintain a sustainable competitive advantage help attract and maintain loyal customers. For instance, having a strong brand, unique merchandise, and superior customer service all help solidify a loyal customer base. But in addition, having loyal customers is, in and of itself, an important method of sustaining an advantage over competitors.

EXHIBIT 2.10 | Macro Strategies for Developing Customer Value

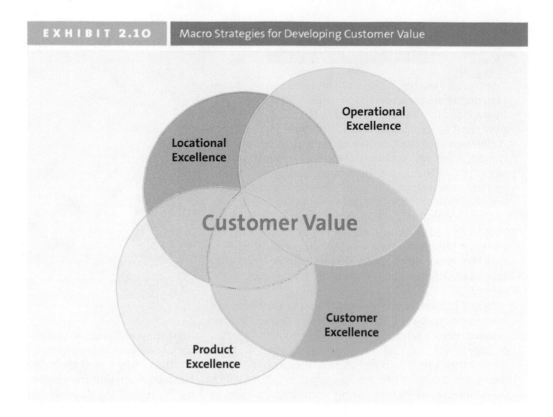

Loyalty is more than simply preferring to purchase from one firm instead of another;[39] it means that customers are reluctant to patronize competitive firms. For example, loyal Apple customers will continue to buy Apple's iPod, iPhone, iPad, and other Apple products rather than RIM's BlackBerry or PlayBook, even though RIM's products offer superior capability and performance, a lower price, and matching customer service.

More and more firms realize the value of achieving customer excellence through focusing their strategy on retaining their loyal customers. For instance, a good dry cleaner doesn't think in terms of washing and pressing a single shirt for $2. Instead, the store is concerned with satisfying the customer who spends $25 per week, 50 weeks a year, for 10 years or more. This customer isn't a $2 customer; he or she is a $12,500 customer. Viewing customers with a lifetime value perspective, rather than on a transaction-by-transaction basis, is key to modern customer retention programs.[40] We will examine how the lifetime value of a customer is calculated in Appendix 7A.

Marketers use several methods to build customer loyalty. One such way involves developing a clear and precise positioning strategy. For instance, loyal Bell Sympatico High Speed Internet consumers value its fast, efficient, and helpful customer service so much that they would not move to other service providers even though they might save a few dollars by switching. Another method of achieving customer loyalty creates an emotional attachment through loyalty programs.[41] Loyalty programs, which constitute part of an overall customer relationship management (CRM) program, prevail in many industries, from airlines to hotels to movie theatres to retail stores. Three-quarters of Canadians and Americans belong to at least one loyalty program.[42] Although the benefits to consumers of loyalty programs are limited since only a small percentage of customers save enough points to claim their rewards, loyalty programs are a boon to marketers. With such programs, companies can combine membership data with customer purchase data to develop a deeper understanding of the customer. Companies often use this data to tailor their offering to better meet the needs of their loyal customers. For instance, by analyzing their databases, financial institutions, such as Bank of Montreal, develop profiles of customers who have defected in the past and use that information to identify customers who may defect in the future. Once it identifies these customers, the firm can implement special retention programs to keep them.

Customer service. Marketers may also build sustainable competitive advantage by offering excellent customer service,[43] though consistently offering excellent service can prove difficult. Customer service is provided by employees, and invariably, humans are less consistent than machines. Firms that offer good customer service must instill its importance in their employees over a long period of time so that it becomes part of the organizational culture. Although it may take considerable time and effort to build a reputation for customer service, once a marketer has earned a good service reputation, it can sustain this advantage for a long time because a competitor is hard pressed to develop a comparable reputation.

Operational Excellence A second way to achieve a sustainable competitive advantage is via operational excellence, which is accomplished through a firm's efficient operations, excellent supply chain management, strong relationships with suppliers, and excellent human resource management (which yields productive employees).

Efficient operations. All marketers strive for efficient operations to get their customers the merchandise they want, when they want it, in the required quantities, and at a lower delivered cost than that of their competitors. By so doing, they ensure good value to their customers, earn a profit, and satisfy their customers' needs. In addition, efficient operations enable firms to either provide their customers with lower priced merchandise or, even if their prices are not lower than those of the competition, to

Some firms develop a sustainable competitive advantage through operational excellence with efficient operations and excellent supply chain management.

use the additional margin they earn to attract customers away from competitors by offering even better service, merchandise assortments, or visual presentations. For example, TELUS, Canada's second largest telecommunications company, has more than 6.9 million wireless subscribers, 4.7 million wireline network access lines and 1.2 million Internet subscribers. Customer service is a key differentiator in this industry because price competition is fierce. Assessing its customer service performance, TELUS found that its customer service management application was cumbersome and inefficient for its customer service representatives (CSRs) to use. For example, CSRs had to undergo extensive training and took a long time to learn the application before they became comfortable. Also, several screens asked CSRs to enter the same information repeatedly and multiple applications were required to serve the same customer. Thus, the possibility for errors was substantial and CSRs spent considerable amounts of time trying to resolve customer inquiries—valuable time that could be spent upselling and cross-selling to customers. To rectify the situation, TELUS implemented its Smart Desktop, a much easier and more efficient application, at more than 1000 customer service sites at a cost of $6.5 million. The results on operational efficiency are impressive: training time for existing staff and new hires was considerably reduced as well as the volume of call transfers—estimated savings were more than $1.3 million. Additionally, CSR upselling and cross-selling activities increased by more than 25 percent across all products and more than 125 percent in one of its products. TELUS won a CIPA Silver Award of Excellence in Efficiency for its efficiency and operational improvements.[44]

Excellent supply chain management and strong supplier relations.   Firms achieve efficiencies by developing sophisticated distribution and information systems as well as strong relationships with vendors. Similar to customer relationships, vendor relations must be developed over the long term and generally cannot be easily offset by a competitor.[45] Firms with strong relationships may gain exclusive rights to (1) sell merchandise in a particular region, (2) obtain special terms of purchase that are not available to competitors, or (3) receive popular merchandise that may be in short supply.

The supply chain of Netflix represented a remarkable innovation when the company first started; with its 50 high-tech distribution centres, it can deliver movies to 97 percent of its subscribers overnight.[46] When the DVDs arrive back at its facilities, Netflix immediately sorts them for distribution to the next customer, and it sorts its mailed bundles by postal code so that its postal service provider doesn't have to, which earns Netflix a better shipping rate. Netflix Canada has also pursued a more recent innovation designed to streamline movie distribution and provide superior customer service. It has signed a deal with Paramount Pictures to bring new movies and TV titles to Canadian subscribers for viewing on computers and TV sets through online streaming. According to Ted Sarandos, Netflix's chief content officer, the agreement will allow subscribers to watch some of Paramount's latest hit films as well as a range of the studio's recent and classic favourites anytime they want.[47]

Like Netflix, many companies are looking to new technologies to improve their operations and strengthen their customer relationships. Social Media Marketing 2.1 illustrates how companies are embedding social media in their marketing strategies.

Human resource management.   Employees play a major role in the success of all firms. Those who interact with customers when providing services are particularly important for building customer loyalty. Knowledgeable and skilled employees committed to the firm's objectives are critical assets that support the success of companies such as WestJet, Delta Hotels and Resorts, and The Bay.[49]

J.C. Penney chairman and CEO Mike Ullman believes in the power of the employee for building a sustainable competitive advantage.[50] He said, "The associates are the first customers we sell. If it doesn't ring true to them, it's impossible to communicate and inspire the customer." To build involvement and commitment among its employees, J.C. Penney's has dropped many of the traditional pretenses that defined an old-style hierarchical organization. For instance, at the Plano, Texas, corporate headquarters, all employees are on a first-name basis, have a flexible workweek, and may attend leadership workshops intended to build an executive team for the future.

Product Excellence   Product excellence, the third way to achieve a sustainable competitive advantage, occurs by having products with high perceived value and effective branding and positioning. Some firms have difficulty developing a competitive advantage through their merchandise and service offerings, especially if competitors can deliver similar products or services easily. However, others have been able to maintain their sustainable competitive advantage by investing in their brand itself; positioning their product or service by using a clear, distinctive brand image; and constantly reinforcing that image through their merchandise, service, and promotion. For instance, *The Globe and Mail* and Interbrand's top Canadian brands—RBC Financial Group, Shoppers Drug Mart, Bell, Tim Hortons, Molson, Rona, and Loblaw—are all leaders in their respective industries, at least in part because they have strong brands and a clear position in the marketplace.[51]

One of the world's leading consumer electronics brands, Apple overtook the mobile music market and displaced established market leaders, such as Sony, with its iPod and iTunes combination. Although critics claimed that there was nothing

Social Media Marketing 2.1

Social Media: A Game Changer![48]

Business analysts and executives are quickly realizing that social media is a game changer for marketers because it has the potential to fundamentally improve the way they manage their operations (operational excellence), communicate and interact with customers (customer excellence), and even shape the products they make (product excellence).

Observing how today's consumers make extensive use of the social media in their purchase decisions, Susan Doniz, P&G's chief information officer (CIO) of Global Business Services in Canada, remarked that "Today's consumers are no longer happy to be talked to; they want to be talked *with*." Similarly, Cam Murray, Fidelity Investments Canada's CIO observed that in the new era, "The new employee, the new investor, the new investment advisor of the future is going to conduct business totally different than the way I thought." The implications are clear: if marketers are to serve customers how they want to be served, businesses have to rethink the way they organize and manage their operations. Essentially, if customers are already having conversations in social media about companies' brands, marketers must do more than just listen and monitor; they have to become part of the conversation, and even open up new conversations.

P&G Canada did just that recently. Realizing that new moms, expectant moms, and moms in general are among the most active communities online, P&G created a blogging area on its website and opened it up for postings from mothers about its Pampers diapers. The company

went a step further by bringing some of the more popular mommy bloggers in and asking them what they liked or didn't like about Pampers, knowing full well that the moms would go back and blog about it. The company has learned a lot from this experience and is now very active in social media. P&G even developed a tool, PeopleConnect, with a Facebook-like platform to enable its employees to put up their own blogs, join wikis, and form their own groups. The groups are open for everyone to read or collaborate with.

Similarly, Fidelity, although much more cautious in its approach, has begun to use blogs, wikis, podcasts, and chat to encourage collaboration. The growing enthusiasm within the company for the use of social media has resulted in the creation of a social networking tool dubbed Innovation Station. With Innovation Station, employees can post their ideas on a variety of subjects, such as products and marketing, cost-efficiency, and even green workspaces. According to Cam Murray, the real benefit comes from the refinement of ideas as other employees comment on initial posts.

Murray concludes that social media will have a profound effect on the way companies do business, pointing to a recent decision by General Motors to cancel its Buick crossover, based largely on the many negative comments on the model that appear on Twitter. The bottom line is that consumers want to shape the products that companies make, and they will do it whether the company wants it or not—thanks to the power of social media!

revolutionary about the iPod technology, the fact still remains that Apple not only redesigned the mobile music device to make it an accessory that consumers felt proud to carry and display, but also revolutionized how music is purchased and consumed with its iTunes store. The iPhone and iPad are two other hugely successful products that have further consolidated Apple's brand image as a world-class innovative technology company with an enviable reputation for building high-quality, well-designed, and fashionable products. How did Apple come from behind to dislodge established market leaders and create such buzz around its technology? According to various reports, Apple's CEO, Steve Jobs, sees Apple as a marketing company first: understanding customer needs and satisfying those needs is what it does best. Technology comes second.

Locational Excellence Location is particularly important for retailers and service providers. Many say the three most important things in retailing are location, location, location. Most people will not walk or drive very far when looking to buy a cup of coffee. A competitive advantage based on location is sustainable because it is not easily duplicated.

Tim Hortons and Starbucks have developed a strong competitive advantage with their location selection. They have such a high density of stores in some markets that it makes it very difficult for a competitor to enter a market and find good locations.

Real Marketer Profile: KELLI WOOD

After graduating from Wilfrid Laurier University's Bachelor of Business Administration program with a specialization in Marketing, I decided to pursue my passion for sports by applying to work at Maple Leaf Sports and Entertainment (MLSE) in Toronto. MLSE proudly owns the Toronto Maple Leafs and the Toronto Raptors and is one of the most reputable sports and entertainment companies in the world. In 2006, in partnership with the City of Toronto, MLSE purchased the rights to launch a Major League Soccer (MLS) team in the Toronto market. Luckily for me a marketing position for Toronto FC was posted just weeks after I graduated.

I had to find a creative way to apply for the job, as I knew that competition would be fierce because so many people want to follow their passion to work in sports, and very few marketers get the chance to build a brand from scratch. I figured that the best way to get a marketing job was to demonstrate how I could uniquely market and position the most important brand that I could ever manage: myself.

My creative resumé not only helped me get interviewed first over several hundred other candidates, but also got me the job of my dreams. I stayed at Toronto FC for almost five seasons, quarterbacking all marketing initiatives for the club, and being a part of the brand launch, the 2008 MLS All-Star Game, the International Friendly between Toronto FC and Real Madrid, and the 2010 MLS Cup. Our tiny team earned top honours across our industry, breaking countless records for ticket sales, sponsorship and creative work, and were awarded one of the most prestigious industry awards in 2009 by being named *Strategy Magazine*'s Brand of the Year.

In March 2011, I left MLSE to join Sid Lee, a Montreal-based advertising agency. Working on the account team for an international creative powerhouse is a big leap from being on the client side of a niche, local brand. I've always had a passion for creativity, and the new position gives me the opportunity to be closer to the work, learn about new strategies, and gain experience in marketing to different segments and product categories by working with new brands.

WestJet Airlines provides good service at a good price—a good value—and they have fun doing it!

Multiple Sources of Advantage

In most cases, however, a single strategy, such as low prices or excellent service, is not sufficient to build a sustainable competitive advantage. Firms require multiple approaches to build a wall around their position that stands as high as possible. For

example, WestJet has achieved success by providing customers with good value that meets their expectations, offering good customer service, maintaining good customer relations, and offering great prices. The company has consistently positioned itself as a carrier that provides good service at a good value—customers get to their destination on time for a reasonable price. At the same time, its customers don't have extraordinary expectations and don't expect food service, seat assignments, or flights out of certain airports.[52] By fulfilling all of these strategies, WestJet has developed a huge cadre of loyal customers and has built a very high wall around its position as the value player in the Canadian airline industry.

Learning Objectives Review

LO1   Describe how a firm develops and implements a marketing plan

A marketing plan is composed of an analysis of the current marketing situation, its objectives, the strategy for the four Ps, and appropriate financial statements. A marketing plan represents the output of a three-phase process: planning, implementation, and control. The planning phase requires that managers first define the firm's mission and vision, which helps to answer the questions "What business are we in now?" and "What do we intend to be in the future?" In the planning phase, managers conduct a situation analysis to evaluate how various players, both inside and outside the organization, affect the firm's potential for success. In the second phase, implementation, the firm identifies and evaluates different opportunities through a process known as segmentation, targeting, and positioning, and develop the marketing mix, the four Ps. Specifically, managers focus on implementing the marketing mix, allocate resources, design the marketing organization, and develop schedules and action plans. Finally, in the control phase, the firm must evaluate its performance to determine what worked, what didn't, and how performance can be improved in the future.

LO2   Conduct a SWOT analysis and explain its use in marketing planning

Recall that SWOT stands for strengths, weaknesses, opportunities, and threats. A SWOT analysis occurs during the second step in the strategic planning process, the situation analysis. By analyzing what the firm is good at (its strengths), where it could improve (its weaknesses), where in the marketplace it might excel (its opportunities), and what is happening in the marketplace that could harm the firm (its threats), managers can assess their firm's situation accurately and plan its strategy accordingly.

LO3   Explain how a firm chooses what group(s) of people to pursue with its marketing efforts

Once a firm identifies different marketing opportunities, it must determine which are the best to pursue. To accomplish this task, marketers go through a segmentation, targeting, and positioning (STP) process. Firms segment various markets by dividing the total market into those groups of customers with different needs, wants, or characteristics who therefore might appreciate products or services geared especially toward them. After identifying the different segments, the firm goes after, or targets, certain groups on the basis of the firm's perceived ability to satisfy the needs of those groups better and more profitably than competitors. To complete the STP process, firms position their products or services according to the marketing mix variables so that target customers have a clear, distinctive, and desirable understanding of what the product or service does or represents relative to competing products or services.

LO4   Describe how the marketing mix increases customer value

The marketing mix consists of the four Ps—product, price, promotion, and place—and each P contributes to customer value. To provide value, the firm must offer a mix of products and services at prices their target markets will view as indicating good value. Thus, firms make trade-offs between the first two Ps, product and price, to give customers the best value. The third P, promotion, informs customers and helps them form a positive image about the firm and its products and services. The last P, place, adds value by getting the appropriate products and services to customers when they want them and in the quantities they need.

LO5   Describe how firms grow their businesses

Firms use four basic growth strategies: market penetration, market development, product development, and diversification. A market penetration strategy directs the firm's efforts toward existing customers and uses the present marketing mix. In other words, it attempts to get current customers to buy more. In a market development strategy, the firm uses its current marketing mix to appeal to new market segments, as might occur in international expansion. A product development growth strategy involves offering a new product or service to the firm's current target market. Finally, a diversification strategy takes place when a firm introduces a new product or service to a new customer segment. Sometimes a diversification strategy relates to the firm's current business, such as when a women's clothing manufacturer starts making and selling men's clothes, but a more risky strategy is when a firm diversifies into a completely unrelated business. Great marketing firms also employ strategies to achieve their sustainable competitive advantage: customer excellence through retaining loyal customers and providing excellent customer service, operational excellence through efficient supply chain management and operations, locational excellence by having a good physical location and Internet presence, and product excellence through branding and positioning.

Key Terms

- control phase, 38
- customer excellence, 54
- diversification strategy, 53
- downsizing, 54
- implementation phase, 38
- locational excellence, 54
- market development strategy, 52
- market growth rate, 50
- market penetration strategy, 52
- market positioning, 44
- market segment, 42
- market segmentation, 43
- marketing planning process, 37
- marketing strategy, 54
- mission statement, 39
- operational excellence, 54
- planning phase, 38
- product development strategy, 53
- product excellence, 54
- product line, 50
- relative market share, 50
- situation analysis, 39
- STP, 42
- strategic business unit (SBU), 49
- sustainable competitive advantage, 54
- target marketing/targeting, 43

Concept Review

1. Briefly describe the activities involved at each of the three phases of the marketing planning process: (1) planning, (2) implementation, and (3) control.

2. What is meant by a mission or vision statement? What purpose does a mission statement serve and how does it influence marketing planning?

3. What does SWOT mean? List two benefits of SWOT analyses. What do you think the differences are between a SWOT analysis for the entire firm and a SWOT analysis for a product?

4. What type of information is required to conduct a SWOT analysis and where do marketers typically look for this information?

5. Why are segmentation, targeting, and positioning (STP) crucial for identifying and evaluating market opportunities? How does STP influence the development of the marketing mix—four Ps?

6. Describe the four growth strategies that firms typically pursue. Use a fast-food restaurant or a grocery chain in Canada (e.g., Loblaw, Safeway, or Food Basics) to illustrate each of the four growth strategies.

7. Of the four growth strategies described in the chapter, which is the most risky? Which is the easiest to implement? Why?

8. Identify and describe the four strategies that firms could use to grow their business. What other strategies could companies use to compete in the market?

9. What are the four components of the BCG Matrix? When would "stars" be preferred over "cash cows"?

10. Explain why in the BCG Matrix all products start out as questions marks and either end up as stars, cash cows, or dogs.

Marketing Applications

1. How has WestJet created a sustainable competitive advantage?

2. Perform a SWOT analysis for your college or university.

3. Describe the primary target markets for the Toronto Blue Jays, Victoria's Secret, and Gatorade. How do these three firms position their products and services so that they appeal to their respective target markets?

4. Pick your favourite product, service provider, or retailer. How do marketers add value to it through the implementation of the four Ps?

5. Choose three retailers. You believe the first builds customer value through product excellence, the second through operational excellence, and the third through customer excellence. Justify your answer.

6. Visit the website of your bank and try to identify how it uses STP to develop various types of bank accounts (products) and charge different fees (price) for different types of accounts.

7. Select a company with which you are familiar or surf the Internet to find a company that has pursued a diversification strategy as one of its growth strategies. How successful was the company's diversification strategy? What factors do you think account for its success or failure?

8. Imagine that you have just developed and launched a new sports bike for cycling enthusiasts and your business has become an instant success. You would like to capitalize on this success and fame to grow your

business. Explain how you would go about expanding your business over the next three years.

9. Using the sports bike scenario from the previous question, describe what kinds of analysis you might conduct before deciding which growth strategies to implement.

10. You and a few of your classmates are planning to open a new spa facility near the campus of your university. Explain how you would segment the market for your services, which segment you would target, and how you would position your spa to the chosen target market.

Toolkit

SWOT ANALYSIS

Assume you are a marketing analyst for a major company and are trying to conduct a situation analysis by using SWOT analysis. Use the toolkit provided on Connect and complete the SWOT grids for each company by using the appropriate items.

Net Savvy

1. Petro-Canada is considered a progressive company in terms of its values and the mission statement that drives its business. Visit its website (www.petro-canada.ca) and review the portion that discusses the company, its mission, and its values. Discuss aspects of its mission and values that might be considered progressive. Do you believe its progressive attitude creates a special position in the market that contributes to a sustainable competitive advantage?

2. More and more firms seem to be entering the dating service industry. Visit eHarmony (www.eharmony.com) and tour its website to find the types of activities and methods such companies use to help match compatible couples. Analyze the environment that might affect Internet dating services by using a SWOT analysis.

Chapter Case Study

TORONTO FOOTBALL CLUB: REBIRTH TO EXCITEMENT[53]

The sold-out crowd of 20 148 roared at the first home game of the Toronto FC (Football Club).[54] On April 28, 2007, fans of all ages and backgrounds united to cheer on their team as it battled the Kansas City Wizards.[55] Many were dressed from head to toe in Toronto FC gear, waving scarves of red and white. The crowd went into hysterics when Toronto player Andy Welsh had a chance to score but was denied. Despite the high-energy of the crowd, Kansas was too tough a challenge for Toronto FC, and the final score was 1–0.[56]

This game was the first re-appearance of professional soccer in Canada since 1984, when the Toronto Blizzards folded after their governing league was dismantled. Despite past challenges for the sport, the future looked promising. Excitement from the recent FIFA World Cup still lingered, and soccer had become the most televised sport in Canada. At any given time, fans have the opportunity to watch one of more than 500 soccer games on cable television—more than anywhere else in the world.[57] Even veteran English soccer fans were impressed with the excitement from Toronto fans.[58]

Bringing the Toronto FC to life required a venue where games could be played. The approval of the expansion team couldn't happen until a stadium was planned. Negotiations between municipal, provincial, and federal governments as well as private enterprises and the Major League Soccer (MLS) organization required immense coordination and concrete business plans. In October 2006 a tentative deal was struck, delivering the funds for a new $62.8 million stadium with five key financiers. The open-air BMO Field, with a total capacity of 20 000, was completed just in time for Toronto FC's first game.[59]

The portfolio of teams managed by Maple Leaf Sports and Entertainment (MLSE) lent great expertise to the new team. Some of Canada's leading sports franchises handled by the company include the Toronto Maple Leafs and the Toronto Raptors. While success on the field can often create new fans, the company knew it wasn't all about winning. For example, the Leafs haven't won a Stanley Cup since 1967, yet year after year the strong brand provides value and consistently sells out the Air Canada Centre.

For the Toronto FC, success would ultimately be measured by continued fan enrolment, making sure that new fans joined the franchise more quickly than any that left. Even before the team set foot on the new field, the company had to form a strategy for long-term business success, which included the following objectives:

1. Build a strong brand to establish the new team.
2. Over-deliver value in all interactions with fans.

The first step in building the brand was to ensure that they had an excellent understanding of the soccer fan base in order to develop appropriate marketing strategies that would ensure the team was embraced not only by Torontonians, but also by Canadians. MLSE quickly learned that Toronto has tens of thousands of fanatical soccer fans that follow the game closely on TV and play the game at one of the many local clubs in Toronto. In addition, thousands of other Torontonians really love the sport but play only recreationally, without belonging to a club. Not surprisingly, this fan base is diverse and fragmented—that is, they come from many different countries around the world and so their loyalties are toward different countries or teams. MLSE also learned that diehard soccer fans want a truly authentic, international experience whether they watch the game at a stadium or on TV. Thus, MLSE's challenge was bringing this diverse, fragmented fan base together to rally around a local soccer team, while at the same time providing a truly authentic experience. According to Paul Beirne, senior director of business operations for Toronto FC, "We wanted to be their local soccer club. You might be a Liverpool supporter sitting beside an Everton supporter, but you could share your love for Toronto FC and enjoy your mutual distaste for each other's teams."[60] Also, listening to and engaging soccer fans by meeting them on their turf will be key to making them feel that Toronto FC is their local soccer club.

Armed with this understanding of the fan base, MLSE created the slogan "All for One" to attract diehard soccer fans from all backgrounds to Toronto FC. To engage the fans, Toronto FC held pub crawls across the city, where patrons could discuss the potential for a successful pro soccer team in Toronto with the team's head coach, players, and staff. MLSE even provided patrons with the chance to vote on the final team name.[61] Advertising and promotion focused on creating a grassroots, local experience by drawing from ethnic street art, using handmade signs, and featuring the Toronto FC's logo and tagline in English, French, Spanish, Italian, Portuguese, and Mandarin. Toronto's multicultural neighbourhoods were flooded with these advertising messages through print, out-of-home executions (outdoor advertising tactics), streetcar wraps, and bumper stickers. Team emblems and merchandise were created with red and white colours and a generic name with the hope that fans would begin to develop nicknames organically.[62] Later, when games began, the matches were broadcast publicly on CBC so fans could watch at home. In the community, MLSE worked hard to give back to the less fortunate by fundraising for Right to Play, a charitable organization that engages children and youth in regular, organized sports activities.[63]

To further enhance the authentic experience that soccer fans crave, MLSE chose to name the team Toronto *Football Club* rather than using *soccer club* to hearken back to the roots of the sport. They also chose not to have mascots or cheerleaders, which is in keeping with the origins of the sport that grew out of local athletic associations. The team's primary colour, red, often represents champions in the sport. The stadium atmosphere also reinforced a sense of authenticity. The food served during games goes beyond hot dogs and pretzels; it includes international fare. To reinforce the authenticity and localness of Toronto FC, the MLSE leveraged its partnerships with BMO, Carlsberg, and Adidas. BMO's name is on all Toronto FC gear; Carlsberg, the authentic football beer brand, has a patio on one side of the pitch; and Adidas sells Toronto FC apparel and merchandise in its stores. The BMO stadium was positioned as the place where soccer fans can come not only to enjoy the game live, but also to celebrate their love of the sport. One popular initiative involved attaching Toronto FC scarves to tickets to the team's first home game of the inaugural season so fans could sport them in the stands, which is a regular spectacle at matches overseas. Membership cards were also given out with season ticket purchases to encourage fans to become members of the club.[64]

One critical decision in providing value was ticket pricing. A major pricing objective for MLSE was that prices were set to ensure full brand accessibility. With a certain supply of 20 000 seats and uncertain demand, MLSE needed to be strategic. Introductory prices were set low by league standards in hopes that corporations and hard-core fans would consume many of the season tickets. Ticket prices were initially set lower at launch in an aim to over-deliver value to fans. Season tickets were $285–$1820 per season; single tickets were $525–$1840 per season; youth tickets were $304–$874 per season; and single game group pricing was as low as $19 per ticket. Toronto FC were interested in attracting fans with a deep-rooted love for the game: those fans who used to sit at home and watch soccer on Italian and other European stations, who had a favourite team or player in another country, and who really got fired up about soccer. This pricing coupled with news of player acquisitions and potential game schedules created a surprisingly large demand for ticket sales, and the available 14 000 season's ticket packages quickly sold out. Most surprising though was the diversity of fan demographics, including much unexpected interest from young career professionals.[65] The remaining 6000 seats were reserved for half-season packages and single game sales, to allow accessibility for fans from all income brackets.

Other key decisions for providing value included bringing popular teams to Toronto. High-calibre international teams such as SL Benfica and Aston Villa were expensive to host but guaranteed that many fans would be interested in watching the matches. Even if the cost of these teams exceeded the revenues they brought in for Toronto, the games ensured the enrolment growth in the franchise. Toronto FC also reinforced its connection to the international football world by arranging friendly games with reputable international teams. For example, a match against star-studded La Liga juggernaut Real Madrid set the fans at BMO Field, and all of Toronto, ablaze with football frenzy.[66] Toronto's season began slowly. The season opener on April 7, 2007, against Chivas USA in California ended in a loss of 1–0. One loss rolled into another and another. The Toronto FC players couldn't seem to score a goal or rack up a win for four games straight. The loss couldn't silence the Toronto fans, though. Their passion shone and continued to support the team, selling out every single home game. The players' hard work and their devoted followers were finally rewarded on May 11, 2007, when the club conquered Chicago Fire with a 3–1 win.[67] The stadium erupted with cheers and praise.

Frenzied fans fuel Toronto FC.

With sold-out season tickets, the focus for MLSE has become future success. Since starting with 18 corporate partners in the 2007 season, Toronto FC now boasts around 40. The team experienced revenue growth of 25 percent from 2007 to 2008 and 10 percent from 2008 to 2009. There is a long waiting list for seasons' tickets; the club is sold out of merchandise and is trying to find more. With consistently sold-out crowds and a growing number of independent supporter groups such as the Red Patch Boys and Tribal Rhythm Nation, propping up the atmosphere, in year three it is safe to say that Toronto FC's momentum is showing no signs of slowing down.[68]

Questions

1. What do you think the company's mission is? Comment on the appropriateness of its mission.

2. Conduct a situation analysis for Toronto FC by using a SWOT analysis. To what extent are the company's objectives appropriate for long-term success?

3. What do you perceive as Toronto FC's competitive advantage? To what extent is this competitive advantage sustainable over time?

4. Who do you think is Toronto FC's target market?

5. Describe how the Toronto FC uses its four Ps strategy to keep existing fans loyal to the franchise.

6. What can the Toronto FC do to keep the momentum going? What will keep the fans coming back?

Writing
a Marketing Plan

Have a plan. Follow the plan, and you'll be surprised how successful you can be. Most people don't have a plan. That's why it's easy to beat most folks.

—Paul "Bear" Bryant, football coach, University of Alabama

Why Write a Marketing Plan?[1]

As a student, you likely plan out much in your life—where to meet for dinner, how much time to spend studying for exams, which courses to take next semester, how to get home for winter break, and so on. Plans enable us to figure out where we want to go and how we might get there.

For a firm, the goal is not much different. Any company that wants to succeed (which means any firm whatsoever) needs to plan for a variety of contingencies, and marketing represents one of the most significant. A marketing plan—which we defined in Chapter 2 as a written document composed of an analysis of the current marketing situation, opportunities and threats for the firm, marketing objectives and strategy specified in terms of the four Ps, action programs, and projected or pro forma income (and other financial) statements—enables marketing personnel and the firm as a whole to understand their own actions, the market in which they operate, their future direction, and the means to obtain support for new initiatives.[2]

Because these elements—internal activities, external environments, goals, and forms of support—differ for every firm, the marketing plan is different for each firm as well. However, several guidelines apply to marketing plans in general; this appendix summarizes those points and offers an annotated example.

Marketing Plan Versus Business Plan

Of course, firms consider more than marketing when they make plans and therefore commonly develop business plans as well. Yet as this book highlights, marketing constitutes such an important element of business that business plans and marketing plans coincide in many ways.[3] Both marketing and business plans generally encompass the following:

1. Executive summary
2. Company overview
3. Objectives/goals, usually according to strategic plan and focus
4. Situation analysis
5. STP analysis (market/product/customer analysis)
6. Marketing strategy
7. Financial projections
8. Implementation plan
9. Evaluation and control metrics

However, a business plan also includes details about R&D and operations, and both documents may feature details about other key topics, depending on the focus of the company and the plan.

Structure of a Marketing Plan

This section briefly describes each of the elements of a marketing plan.[4]

Executive Summary

The executive summary essentially tells the reader why he or she is reading this marketing plan—what changes require consideration, what new products need discussion, and so forth—and suggests possible actions to take in response to the information the plan contains.

Company Overview

In this section, the plan provides a brief description of the company, including perhaps its mission statement, background, and competitive advantages.

Objectives/Goals

This section offers more specifics about why readers are reading the marketing plan. What does the company want to achieve, both overall and with this particular marketing plan?

Situation Analysis

Recall from Chapter 2 that a situation analysis generally relies on SWOT considerations; therefore, this section describes the strengths, weaknesses, opportunities, and threats facing the company.

STP Analysis

The analysis proceeds by assessing the market in which the company functions, the products it currently offers or plans to offer in the future, and the characteristics of current or potential customers.

Marketing Strategy

The marketing strategy may be very specific, especially if the plan pertains to, for example, a stable product in a familiar market, or it may be somewhat open to varied possibilities, such as when the firm plans to enter a new market with an innovative product.

Financial Projections

On the basis of the knowledge already obtained, the marketing plan should provide possible developments and returns on the marketing investments outlined in the marketing strategy.

Implementation Plan

This portion of the marketing plan includes the timing of promotional activities, when monitoring will take place, and how expansions likely will proceed.

Evaluation and Control Metrics

The firm must have a means of assessing the marketing plan's recommendations; the marketing plan therefore must indicate the methods for undertaking this assessment, whether quantitatively or qualitatively.

Appendix

The final section(s) offers additional information that might be of benefit, such as a list of key personnel, data limitations that may influence the findings, and suggestions of the plan, relevant legislation, and so forth.

Information Sources[5]

When writing a marketing plan, you likely can turn to a variety of your firm's in-house information sources, including annual reports, previous marketing plans, published mission statements, and so on. In addition, various sources offer suggestions and examples that may provide you with direction and ideas. Exhibits 4.2 and 4.3 on pages 123 and 124 also list many sources that you may find very helpful.

- Knowthis.com—"a knowledge source for marketing" (www.knowthis.com/principles-of-marketing-tutorials/how-to-write-a-marketing-plan/)
- Encyclopedia of American Industries—introduces industry structure; arranged by SIC and NAICS codes
- Standard & Poor's NetAdvantage—surveys of more than 50 different industries, with financial data about companies in each industry
- Investext Plus—brokerage house reports
- IBISWorld—market research on thousands of industries; classified by NAICS code
- Statistics Canada surveys on virtually all aspects of business, the economy, social statistics, and population data—a vast variety of statistics on a range of topics
- Statistics Canada Census—detailed statistical data gathered every 10 years on all aspects of the Canadian population
- LifeStyle Market Analyst—lifestyle information about geographic areas, lifestyle interest groups, and age and income groups
- Mediamark Reporter—information about demographics, lifestyles, product and brand usage, and advertising media preferences

- Arbitron/Scarborough—local market consumer information for various media in 75 local markets for consumer retail shopping behaviour, product consumption, media usage, lifestyle behaviour, and demographics
- Simmons Study of Media and Markets—products and consumer characteristics; various media audiences and their characteristics
- Rand McNally Commercial Atlas and Marketing Guide—maps and tables showing demographic, industrial, transportation, railroad, airline, and hospital data
- Annual & 10-K reports from Thomson ONE Banker, Edgar, and LexisNexis—business descriptions, product listings, distribution channels, possible impact of regulations and lawsuits, and discussions of strategic issues
- MarketResearch.com Academic—market research reports on a variety of consumer products
- Mintel Reports Database—market research reports focusing on consumer products, lifestyles, retailing, and international travel industry

Linguistic and Visual Suggestions

Again, recall that all marketing plans differ, because all firms differ. However, just as rules exist that dictate what makes for good writing, some rules or guidelines apply to all well-written marketing plans

- Maintain a professional attitude in the writing and presentation.
- Keep descriptions and summaries concise. Get to the point.
- Use standard, edited English.
- Proofread the entire plan multiple times to catch grammatical, spelling, or other such errors that could dampen the professionalism of the writing.
- Adopt a businesslike tone; avoid flowery or jargon-filled writing.
- Employ direct, rather than passive, and present, rather than past, tense whenever possible (e.g., "We plan to achieve 30 percent growth in two years" rather than "The plan was that 30 percent growth would be achieved by the firm within two years").
- Be positive.
- Yet avoid meaningless superlatives (e.g., "Our goal is tremendous growth").
- Be specific; use quantitative information whenever possible.
- Insert graphics to convey important concepts succinctly, including photos, graphs, illustrations, and charts.
- However, avoid using so many visual elements that they clutter the plan.
- Lay out the plan clearly and logically.
- Organize sections logically, using multiple levels of headings, distinguished clearly by font differences (e.g., bold for first-level heads, italics for second-level heads).
- Consider the use of bullet points or numbered lists to emphasize important points.
- Exploit modern technology (e.g., graphics software, page-layout software, laser printers) to ensure the plan looks professional.
- Adopt an appropriate font to make the text easy to read and visually appealing—avoid using anything smaller than 10-point font at a minimum.
- Avoid unusual or decorative fonts; stick with a common serif type to make the text easy to read.
- Consider binding the report with a clear cover and an attractive title page.
- Generally aim for a plan that consists of 15–30 pages.

PeopleAhead Marketing Plan Illustration[6]

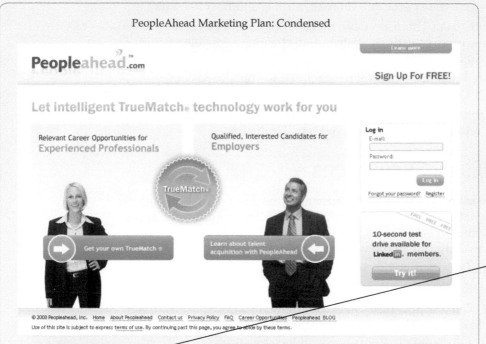

PeopleAhead Marketing Plan: Condensed

Instead of using separate "Executive Summary" and "Company Overview" sections, this marketing plan begins with a general overview that includes both aspects and answers the key questions: "What type of business are we?" and "What do we need to do to accomplish our objectives?" (see Chapter 2).

1. Executive Summary

PeopleAhead focuses on career advancement done right. Instead of making job search a one-time event, PeopleAhead provides a platform for people to find, advance, and develop their careers by sharing career goals, discussing professional development plans, and socializing with other professionals.

As this plan does, a marketing plan should start with a positive, upbeat assessment of what the company does and what it hopes to continue doing.

PeopleAhead culminates the career advancement experience with its proprietary TrueMatch® technology, which identifies synergies between the companies hiring talent (employers) and PeopleAhead members (job candidates) who wish to be hired. By anonymously presenting only prequalified career opportunities to members, who confirm their interest and recommend others, PeopleAhead transforms the ineffective online hiring process into a highly efficient career-matching system. PeopleAhead was founded by Carlos Larracilla and Tom Chevalier to improve people's lives by helping them achieve their career aspirations. The vision for PeopleAhead was conceived of in January 2006, with a notion that personality alignment is critical to matching the right people with the right career opportunities. Since then, the idea has grown and morphed into a company that matches the right person with the right career opportunity by aligning personality, competencies, experience, and interests.

Note the personalization of the company founders, which may help readers feel connected to the company.

Tom and Carlos combine human resources, system development, and sales experience to deliver a groundbreaking, TrueMatch®-branded talent matching network that makes it easier for people to achieve their career aspirations and improves the way companies identify individuals who will be able to contribute to their long-term success. The organizational chart of PeopleAhead is available in Appendix A.

2. Strategic Objectives

2.1. Mission

PeopleAhead's mission is to help individuals with career advancement and improve the human capital in companies. The site will act as a networking platform for professionals and career matching as opposed to job and resumé-posting searches.

2.2. Goals

- Use brand-matching technology: TrueMatch®
- Build critical mass of users.
- Drive traffic to the website through marketing blitzes.
- Utilize word-of-mouth advertising from satisfied users.

2.3. Business Summary

- *Business Customers:* This group provides PeopleAhead's revenues. Customers purchase contact information about the Top Ten PROfiles gleaned from the individual member base that have been sorted and ranked by the TrueMatch® technology. PeopleAhead will focus on small and medium businesses (see Market Segmentation section), because these entities are underserved by large competitors in the online recruitment market, and because research shows that this demographic has a less efficient recruitment process that would benefit most readily from PeopleAhead's services. Within this segment, customers include HR managers who are responsible for the sourcing of candidates, functional area managers who require new talent for their team, and executives whose business objectives rely on human capital and efficiency of operations.
- *Individual Members:* This group does not pay for services but is the main source of data points for PeopleAhead's TrueMatch® system. PeopleAhead will focus on building a base of individual members who range from recent graduates to individuals with 5–7 years of continuous employment. Ideal members are those who are currently employed or will be graduating within nine months and are "poised" to make a career change. These individuals can utilize the services to the fullest extent and are valuable candidates for business customers.

2.4. Competitive Advantage

- *TrueMatch® offers a branded technology,* marketed to both business customers and individual candidates for its "black box" value proposition, which establishes PeopleAhead as the category leader for recruitment-matching software. This technology provides a point of differentiation from competitors, which may have technically similar matching software but constantly need to reinforce their marketing messages with explanations of their value proposition.
- *For individual candidates,* PeopleAhead will be the favoured career advancement platform online, where individuals enthusiastically create a history and have connections (invited friends, co-workers, and mentors) in place that will make PeopleAhead a staple among their favourite websites. PeopleAhead delivers TrueMatch® career opportunities, professional development plans that let people establish a professional record, and valuable career advancement tools, including automatic position feedback, "recommend-a-friend," and team-based career networking.
- *For business customers,* PeopleAhead makes online sourcing and qualification of candidates quick and efficient by prequalifying potential candidates, seeking recommendations for hard-to-find individuals, and delivering only the Top 10 most highly qualified candidates who have preconfirmed interest in the available position.

The paragraph provides a general outline of the firm's objectives; the bulleted list offers more specific goals, and the subsequent sections go into more detail about the various factors that may influence these objectives.

By referring to another section, the plan makes clear where it is heading and enables readers to cross-reference the information.

The plan acknowledges both a general, potential target market and the ideal targets.

As Chapter 2 suggests, the plan notes PeopleAhead's sustainable competitive advantage as part of its overall mission statement.

PeopleAhead will be the most effective candidate-company matching platform available in the market, delivering prequalified, preconfirmed candidates.

In discussing both the external market and the internal advantages of PeopleAhead, the plan carefully distinguishes between individual job candidates and businesses, thus differentiating the focus and objectives according to this segmentation.

3. Situation Analysis—Online Recruitment

Online recruitment is the system whereby companies use the Web to locate and qualify prospective candidates for available positions. The methods employed by online recruitment service providers to serve this market range from resumé aggregation to assessment test application to linking strategies. However, the common underlying objective is to locate candidates who would not be found by traditional recruitment methods and use computing power to qualify candidates quickly and with more accuracy than would be possible manually.

3.1. Industry Analysis

Large online recruitment websites make this a tedious process by requiring companies to search through many resumés manually to find the "right" candidate. Other sites solicit recommendations for positions. However, resumés are often "enhanced," such that almost all candidates appear qualified, and information found in the resumé or provided through a recommendation is simply not sufficient to make an educated hiring decision. Companies need more information and intelligent tools that make this screening process more accurate.

3.1.1. Market Size

The market size for both member segments in 2005 was as follows:

Figures provide a visually attractive break in the text and summarize a lot of information in an easy-to-read format.

Individual Members Segments

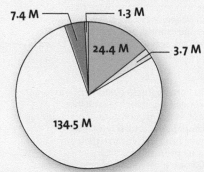

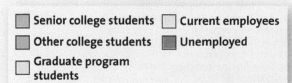

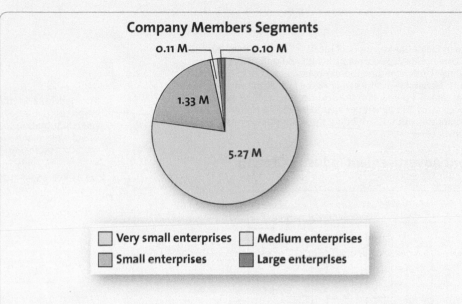

Company Members Segments

0.11 M   0.10 M

1.33 M

5.27 M

- ▢ Very small enterprises
- ▢ Medium enterprises
- ▢ Small enterprises
- ▇ Large enterprises

The most critical issue in examining market size is the relationship between the number of companies and the number of workers employed, because sales are based on the number of positions (profiles purchased), not the number of companies that use the service.

The following figure shows the number of people employed by each enterprise market segment as of January 2006, according to the U.S. Department of Labor. This segment information will be useful in defining PeopleAhead's target market.

Employment by Enterprise Type

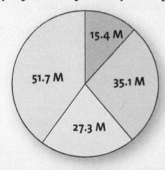

15.4 M

51.7 M

35.1 M

27.3 M

- ▨ Very small enterprises
- ▢ Medium enterprises
- ▢ Small enterprises
- ▢ Large enterprises

3.1.2. Market Growth

PeopleAhead will operate in the online recruitment market. The growth of this industry is subject to two primary constraints: U.S. economic health and online recruitment advertisement adoption rates. Understanding these constraints will help to identify PeopleAhead's opportunity. General indicators suggest the U.S. economy (GDP) will grow at an average annual rate of 4 percent for the next decade.[7] Online recruitment advertising is expected to grow by 35 percent per year to reach $7.6 billion by 2010.[8] Not only is the market expanding, but it is exhibiting rapid adoption by new entities, as the following graph shows.[9]

> Another visually attractive graph summarizes complicated information easily. The use of high-quality colour can add a professional feel to a marketing plan.

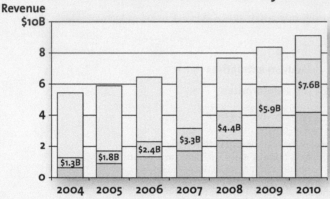

Recruitment Advertisement Industry Growth

Revenue

- $1.3B (2004)
- $1.8B (2005)
- $2.4B (2006)
- $3.3B (2007)
- $4.4B (2008)
- $5.9B (2009)
- $7.6B (2010)

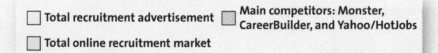

☐ Total recruitment advertisement

☐ **Main competitors: Monster, CareerBuilder, and Yahoo/HotJobs**

☐ Total online recruitment market

3.1.3. Market Needs

- **The right person for the right position:** The right employee for one company or position is not the same for all others. Not only must companies locate intelligent individuals with relevant experience, but they also prefer people who are aligned with the position requirements in terms of personality, competencies, and fit with the company culture.

- **Prescreening qualification tools:** Increasing the number of candidates through online recruitment can be advantageous, but it can also be a hindrance. When sourcing candidates, recruiters need tools that help them qualify applicants.

- **Time savings:** Companies need to complete the online sourcing and qualification of candidates quickly. Leaving positions unfilled can cause critical performance gaps to emerge within the company.

3.1.4. Market Trends

The methods by which online recruitment service providers deliver candidates has been undergoing a migration from resumé aggregation and search services such as Monster and CareerBuilder to new Web 2.0 methodologies that include passive recruitment, "meta tagging," and social networking.

The underlying objective of these Web 2.0 services is to allow individuals to remain on a few trusted websites while enabling companies to access those individuals for financial purposes. In parallel, the focus is moving from aggregation of unique visitors toward engaging existing users more intensively. Internet users are growing familiar with sites that encourage socializing, collaborating, and distributing private information online to help to improve network benefits and need to be engaged to maintain contact.

3.2. SWOT Analysis

	Positive	Negative
Internal	**Strengths**	**Weaknesses**
	• Industry best practices: The networking model used by PeopleAhead draws on the industry accepted "best practices" contact protocols drawn from multiple industries, including online feedback, recruitment, and social networking and offline professional networking. TrueMatch® software aligns business objectives with appropriate candidates. • Team expertise: The combined talents of the founders include human resources, system development, sales, and marketing. • Web development expertise: PeopleAhead has partnered with an award-winning European software development provider. This company provides quality usually reserved for high-budget projects, at terms that are favourable for a start-up company.	• Absence of industry "influentials": As a start-up, PeopleAhead does not currently have resources to attract influential industry managers. • Inability to guarantee critical mass: As is true of many Internet companies, the business must solve the "chicken and egg" puzzle to build critical mass. • Verifying efficiency of matching capabilities: In theory, the system has an absolute guarantee of effectiveness; computations make decisions rather than humans. However, the matching capabilities must be verified as accurate to gain widespread acceptance. • Broad target market: Because PeopleAhead is targeting a wide range of businesses, the product being developed has not been "customized" ideally for each segment.
External	**Opportunities**	**Threats**
	• Service gap: Recruiters are not pleased with current online recruitment vendors. • Industry gap: Job turnover is every 3.5 years per person. • Demand for productive candidates. • Online recruitment advertising: Growing by 35% per year, to reach $7.6 billion by 2010.[10]	• Convergence: existing competitors may form strategic alliances and establish powerful positions before PeopleAhead can establish itself. • Inability to protect model: Very little intellectual property created by online websites is protected by law. Although PeopleAhead will

(continued)

Before engaging in a firm-specific SWOT analysis (see Chapter 2), this marketing plan assesses the external market environment further and thus establishes a basis for the subsequent SWOT analysis.

Using a table and bullet points, the plan summarizes a lot of information succinctly and clearly.

Note that the analysis uses outside sources to support its claims.

External	**Opportunities**	**Threats**
	• Fragmented business models: Online recruitment is fragmented by recruitment methodology: active (people who need jobs), passive (people who are not looking but would move if enticed), poised (people unsatisfied with jobs they have), and network (finding people of interest based on who or what they know).	pursue aggressive IP protection strategies, the model could be copied or mimicked by competitors. • Inadequate differentiation: Inability to explain our differentiation would relegate PeopleAhead to (unfair) comparisons with competitors. Without differentiation, PeopleAhead will not be able to create scale through network effects.

3.3. Competition

Most online recruitment websites compete in the active recruitment market, including Monster, CareerBuilder, and Yahoo/HotJobs. The pervasive segment includes job seekers who actively look for jobs, post their resumés, and search for jobs on company websites. Most active recruiters offer free services to users and charge companies on a fee basis. Companies can post jobs and search for candidate resumés in the database (average fee for local searches is $500 and nationwide is $1000). In this first-generation online recruitment business model, competitors face the challenge to make the process more user-friendly and reduce the effort required to make these sites deliver results.

- **Monster:** Monster.com is the sixteenth most visited website in the United States, with more than 43 million professionals in its viewer base. Monster earns revenue from job postings, access to its resumé database, and advertisements on websites of partner companies.
- **Careerbuilder:** Careerbuilder.com has experienced 75 percent growth for the past five years. This job post/resumé search company uses its media ownership to attract "passive" candidates from partner websites. It achieves growth through affiliate partnerships that host job searches on affiliated web pages, such as Google, MSN, AOL, USA Today, Earthlink, BellSouth, and CNN. Job posting is the primary activity, sold together with or separately from resumé searches.
- **Passive Recruitment:** The second generation of online recruitment locates candidates who are not necessarily looking for jobs but who could be convinced to move to a new position if the right opportunity was presented. The most recognized competitors in this category include Jobster, LinkedIn, and H3 (Appendix B).

3.4. Company Analysis

PeopleAhead's mission is simple: improve people's lives through career advancement. PeopleAhead recognizes that career advancement means many things to many people and provides a fresh perspective on career networking that is flexible yet powerful:

- **Users are not alone:** Finding a job is not easy. Why search solo? PeopleAhead unites groups of friends, co-workers, and mentors to create natural, team-based career discovery.
- **Job posting is not natural:** People spend countless hours searching job listings and posting resumés, only to be overlooked because their writing style or resumé format does not match an overburdened recruiter's preference. Good people make

---

If PeopleAhead chooses to adopt a competitor-based pricing strategy (see Chapter 11), detailed information about how other recruitment firms work will be mandatory.

Information about competitors' revenues, customers, growth, and so forth often is available publicly through a variety of sources.

For information that may not belong in the main text, an appendix offers an effective means to provide detail without distracting readers.

This section offers the "product" component of the market/product/customer analysis. Because PeopleAhead's product is mostly a service (see Chapter 10), it focuses on some intangible features of its offering.

great companies, not resumés. PeopleAhead's TrueMatch® technology matches the right people with the right position. No posting, no applying—just good, quality matches.

- **Professionals being professionals:** There is a place online for social networking, pet networking, and music networking. So why is there no outlet for career networking online—the activity that consumes the majority of our professional lives? PeopleAhead is a place where professionals share their experiences, achievements, and objectives with other professionals that care and can be found by employers who value their professionalism.

3.5. Customer Analysis

PeopleAhead's R&D efforts show that the impetus to improve recruitment effectivity is pervasive and that unmet needs revolve around a few core issues: the ability to find qualified talent, establishing a fit between the candidate and the company culture, verifying the candidate's career progression, and working quickly and cost-effectively. The following customer characteristics represent ideal attributes that align with PeopleAhead's service offering. This information might be used in conjunction with the Marketing Strategy.

3.5.1. Business Customer

- **Industry:** Because companies that value human capital are more likely to take a chance on a start-up that promotes professional development, the broadly defined professional services industry, including insurance, banking, and consulting, is the primary focus.
- **Functional area:** PeopleAhead's system identifies "people" people, so positions that require human interaction are more aligned with system capabilities than those with stringent skill requirements, sets such as programming or accounting.
- **Size:** Large businesses (>1000 employees) have high-volume requirements and demand vendors with proven track records; small businesses (<25 employees) hire fewer people and may not justify acquisition costs. PeopleAhead aligns best with medium-sized customers.
- **Hiring need:** PeopleAhead serves two types of searches very well: those with too many applicants and those with too few applicants. By drawing applicants that most systems overlook and delivering only the most qualified applicants, the system assures the right candidate is identified quickly.

3.5.2. Individual Member

- **Background:** People who value professional development and are familiar with computer networking technologies; most are likely college-educated, motivated by career success, and aware of their professional competencies/deficiencies.
- **Situation:** Members should have a professional development plan to share with others who can help them achieve their objectives—likely people who are inquisitive about their professional future and not content with their current situation. The common industry terminology for this group of people is "poised candidates."
- **Outlook:** Proactive people who research, plan, self-educate, and talk about their career. Probably the clearest example of proactivity is a student who devotes time, effort, and financial resources toward career advancement.

The last—and some would say most important—piece of the analysis puzzle: customers.

Although the introduction to this appendix and the plan's organization suggest that analyses of competitors, products, and customers are separate, as this plan shows a firm usually cannot address one without considering the other. Here, in the Business Customer section, the plan notes what PeopleAhead's competitors fail to do and therefore why it offers a more valuable service.

Understanding a target customer is not just about numbers. PeopleAhead tries to consider what customers think and feel when searching for jobs too.

4. Marketing Strategy

4.1. Market Segmentation

4.1.1. Business Customers

- **Small enterprises.** Businesses with 10–99 employees. Companies with less than 10 employees are categorized as "Very Small Enterprises" and will not be a primary target market.
- **Medium enterprises.** Businesses with 100–1000 employees.

4.1.2. Individual Members

- **Senior college students.** Students in the process of searching for a first career.
- **Graduate program students.** Mid-career candidates searching for new career opportunities, such as internships, part-time during enrollment, or full-time after graduation.
- **Current employees.** Persons who are currently employed but are poised to locate better career opportunities.
- **Unemployed.** Persons searching for a job not included in previous segments.

4.2. Target Market

PeopleAhead plans to focus resources on small to medium enterprises (SMEs) in the New England Metro market, including Boston, Providence, Hartford, Stamford, Norwalk, Worcester, and Springfield. Online recruitment companies compete for national recruitment spending, but most job seekers are locally based, so market penetration is possible by covering a single geographical location. By maintaining this focus, PeopleAhead will be better equipped to build a critical mass of users that represent the job-seeking population and thus improve both users' and customers' experience, customer service, and the use of financial resources.

4.3. User Positioning

To the proactive professional, PeopleAhead is career advancement done right—providing a platform to discover, plan, and advance careers by uniting friends, co-workers, and mentors with companies searching for the right talent.

5. Marketing Mix

5.1. Products/Services Offered

The first planned offering is **group profiling**; users self-associate with groups to share development plans. Access to groupings is permission based and similar to social networking. Members will be able to share professional experiences with people they know. Group profiling may prompt "voyeur" networking, such that members join to view the profiles of the people they know.

PeopleAhead will then open **group profiling to business customers**, who will be granted access to groups of members to target people they want to hire.

The next added feature will be **user feedback** on professional development plans. PeopleAhead will track data from successful member profile matches to provide feedback for members who have not been matched successfully.

The plan continues with the same segmentation throughout. Here the plan discusses targeting and what makes each segment attractive.

By already identifying key markets in the previous section, the plan provides a foundation for a more specific targeting statement in this section.

The final step in the STP process: positioning for the segmented, targeted market.

PeopleAhead's mission

Given its own section in this plan, a discussion of the marketing mix constitutes a key element of the strategic planning process (see Chapter 2).

According to well-known marketing concepts, the marketing mix consists of the four Ps: product (service here), price, place (distribution here), and promotion.

The product (service) offering must establish the value for consumers: Why should they expend effort or resources to obtain the offering?

5.2. Price

In addition to a basic pricing schedule, PeopleAhead will offer bulk pricing and contract pricing to business customers to satisfy unique customer needs. The pricing model is expected to remain constant, but customer feedback will be analyzed to ensure alignment with their requirements.

Continuing the new customer acquisition plan, PeopleAhead will encourage new trials by offering promotional pricing to new customers.

5.3. Distribution

- **PeopleAhead Challenge:** The PeopleAhead Challenge will act as a primary user acquisition strategy. Selection will be focused on successful target segments demanded by customers.
- **Direct Sales:** Direct customer contact is the preferred method of communication during the first six months. Telesales is the anticipated eventual sales model, due to reduced costs and quicker customer sales cycle, but it limits intimacy between the customer and PeopleAhead. During the initial stages, intimacy and excellent customer service are more highly desired than reduced cost, and direct sales achieves that objective.
- **Industry Events:** Attendance at HR industry and recruitment events will supplement direct sales efforts.
- **Challenge Groups:** Word-of-mouth distribution by PeopleAhead members.

5.4. Promotion

- **Public Profiling:** When the product is ready, with proper precautions for protecting competitive advantages, PeopleAhead can increase its Web presence. Strategies include contributing articles to recruitment publishers, writing op/ed pieces, public profiling of the founders on websites such as LinkedIn, Ziggs, and ZoomInfo, and blogging.
- **Blogger Community Testimonials:** Influential users of blogs will be invited to try the system and be granted "exclusive" access to the inner workings of the site. A subsequent linking blitz will put opinion pieces in front of recruiters, job seekers, and the investment community.
- **Strategic Alliances:** PeopleAhead offers a product that complements the services offered by many large organizations. Partner opportunities exist with
  a. Universities, colleges, academic institutions
  b. Professional associations, clubs, industry affiliation groups
  c. Online associations, groups, blogs
  d. Professional services firms, outplacement firms, and executive search firms

Strategic alliances serve multiple purposes: They can help PeopleAhead increase public exposure, increase the user base, expand product offerings, and increase revenue opportunities. These benefits will be considered and partnerships proposed prior to the official launch. For strategic purposes, PeopleAhead prefers to focus on product development in the near term (three months) and then reassess potential alliances after system efficacy has been proven.

> Making the product (service) available where and when consumers want it may seem somewhat easier for PeopleAhead because of the vast development of the Internet; however, the firm still needs to consider how it can ensure people know where and how to access its offering.

> The plan offers a specific time frame, which recognizes the potential need to make changes in the future, as the market dictates.

Is your company looking
for the right talent?

Peopleahead.com

delivers:

▸Target marketing for hard-to-fill
positions

▸Qualified & pre-confirmed candidates

▸Intelligent candidate ranking tools

▸Results

6. Financials

Start-up costs consist primarily of website design and development, legal representation (business formation, contract negotiation, and intellectual property protection), and general overhead. PeopleAhead projects start-up expenditures of $70,000 during inception, of which $30,000 has been funded by the founding team.

After the website launches, the cost structure will consist of sales agent salaries, general and administrative operating costs, and marketing. In the first year, marketing expenses are projected to be $6250 per month. Monthly overhead likely will reach $24,750 and remain constant.

A. Projected Income Statement

Pro Forma Income Statement

	Year 1	Year 2	Year 3	Year 4	Year 5
Sales	$56,453	$2,683,665	$8,170,655	$16,312,843	$30,921,013
Gross Margin	$54,194	$2,316,318	$7,383,829	$14,780,329	$28,244,172
Gross Margin %	96.00%	86.31%	90.37%	90.61%	91.34%
Net Profit	($156,906)	$717,403	$3,356,768	$7,035,155	$14,180,041

The marketing plan needs to identify not only costs, but also potential revenues to cover those costs.

Certain assumptions or marketing research form the basis for its estimation of start-up costs.

This section contains a lot of numbers in a small space; the graphs and tables help to depict those numbers clearly and visually.

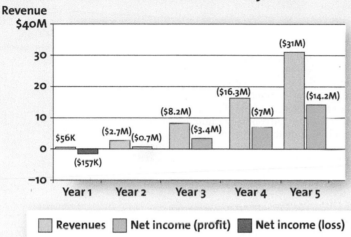

Revenue and Net Income Projections

7. **Implementation Plan**

The launch of PeopleAhead will use a phased approach, beginning with building brand awareness. Brand awareness should be developed through the founders' visible presence at professional events, online searches, membership in professional associations, networking, and strategic alliances. This visibility will help to gain investment capital.

> This plan divides the objectives into three categories: overall objective, marketing, and financial. Although this is a marketing plan, it must also include other aspects that influence marketing, such as financial status.

7.1. Objective—Growth

- During the first six months of commercial availability, the primary objective is to expand both the user and customer base to maintain a 100:1 user to customer ratio.
  - **Business Customers:** Sign 24 regular customers and 72 occasional customers. Execute 117 position matches.
  - **Individual Members:** Convert 10 000 people to PeopleAhead members.

7.2. Marketing Objectives—Growth

- **PeopleAhead Challenge:** Pursue groups that were effective during Beta trial and represent a cohesive set of profiles. Expand and refine the Challenge to reflect lessons learned.
- **Increase member networking activity:** Increase user numbers through networking initiated by existing members. Improve user experience to promote networking.
- **Increase profile completeness:** Increase user engagement with platform.
- **Generate traffic.**
- **Public relations campaign (PR):** Increase awareness of PeopleAhead brand through concentrated PR efforts directed at the target market of customers and users.

7.3. *Financial Objectives*

- **Efficient marketing expenditures:** 9000 target users (10 000 year-end total − 1000 during beta) × $5.00 target acquisition cost = $45,000 budget.
- **Revenue:** $482.50 per position × 117 positions = $56,452.50 revenue.

> By offering quantitative, direct goals, PeopleAhead ensures that it can measure its progress toward those goals.

7.4. *Key Success Factors*

- **Economical marketing to relevant constituents:** PeopleAhead needs to establish communication (distribution) channels that pinpoint relevant constituents in a manner consistent with mission values. Limited by resources, chosen channels must aggregate many relevant eyes with free, minimal, or deferred costs involved.
- **Crafting of brand identity:** The contrast between PeopleAhead and competitors lies not only in product differentiation, but also in the company's mission statement and delivery. One-time job search is available from thousands of online recruitment sources. Social networking has been covered from diverse angles, attracting many different audiences. The challenge is to associate www.PeopleAhead.com and True-Match® technology with "career advancement done right." The goal is to become the only company that a person thinks of for long-term career discovery, advancement, and development.
- **Efficient value delivery:** The base of customers (both individual and business) needs to receive the proposed value in a timely manner, with consideration given to quality versus quantity of results, alignment with existing objectives, and overall experience with the PeopleAhead brand.
- **Critical mass of business customers and individual users:** The matching process requires that both customers and users exist in the system from the outset of commercialization. This need brings to the forefront the "chicken and egg" scenario; establishing either customers or users requires the other constituent to exist already. The exact number that constitutes "critical mass" ranges from 100 users per position to 10 users per position, depending on compatibility between each constituency.
- **System effectivity:** The ability of PeopleAhead's TrueMatch® software to provide relevant candidate recommendations is critical. The effectiveness of the software depends on the algorithms that match users with positions and the networking protocol that initiates recommendations between users and the people they know. Proposing an inappropriate match could jeopardize the credibility of the system.
- **Intellectual property (IP) strategy:** PeopleAhead is engaged in two primary segments of online enterprise: online recruitment and social networking. Existing competitors have made many efforts to protect their methodologies through U.S. patents. However, precedent has not been established for the legal assertions made by these companies. As a result, PeopleAhead will assume an offensive IP strategy, consisting of diligent IP infringement review, patent application where appropriate, and aggressive trade secret protection of best practices.
- **Financial support:** The founders' investment is sufficient to form the business core and take delivery of PeopleAhead's website and software. Financial support will be required to fund operations, execute the IP strategy, and secure customers and users to meet financial targets. Without funding, PeopleAhead will not be able to proceed beyond the product development stage.
- **Sales process:** PeopleAhead's business model requires the acquisition of both business customers who have available positions and users who will be matched with those positions. These two constituents may be reached through different sales processes without overlap.

8. Evaluation and Control

PeopleAhead will evaluate user profiles to identify sets of profiles that are valuable to new business customers, which will aid in the selection of subsequent target market customers.

8.1. Business Customer

> The evaluation section retains the segmentation scheme established previously between business customers and individual members.

Face-to-face meetings, phone conversations, and email survey contacts with people from a range of industries, company sizes, and functional areas provide a means to (1) build relationships with prospective customers, (2) understand customer needs, and (3) ensure alignment between PeopleAhead's product and customers' recruitment preferences. A summary of the key findings is listed here:

- **Employee fit:** Will the applicant fit our corporate culture? Will the applicant fit with the team we're considering? Will the applicants' competencies fit with the position requirements?
- **Pay for performance:** Objections to recruitment services focus not on price (though it is a consideration) but rather on lack of performance.
- **Unqualified applicants:** Many people who want a job apply, whether they are qualified or not. Recruiters then must scan resumés and weed out unqualified applicants instead of getting to know the qualified applicants.
- **Hard costs vs. soft costs:** Most companies track the recruitment costs of hiring providers, but few measure the time costs of hiring, opportunity costs of hiring the wrong employee, or productivity costs of leaving a position unfilled. Recruitment performance must be easy to measure. Value selling is difficult in human resources departments.
- **Valuable recommendations:** Most recruiters use online recruitment as a necessary but ineffective means of candidate sourcing, secondary to recommendations. Recommendations include the recommender's judgment of the candidate's fit with the available position.

8.2. Individual Members

Periodic surveys of various prospective users of online recruitment services indicate (1) current services, (2) methods that work well, and (3) biggest problems with online recruitment providers. The following is a qualitative summary of the key findings:

- **Willingness to try:** Careers are important to people; they are averse to spending time uploading resumé information to online recruitment websites only because of the lack of perceived value. They will spend time when the career opportunities are perceived as valuable.
- **Frustration:** Job seekers are frustrated with available online recruitment providers. Networking is the favoured method for career advancement.
- **Lack of differentiation:** Regardless of the qualifications a job seeker possesses, it is difficult to make them evident in a traditional resumé.
- **Motivation shift over time:** Early professionals are motivated by financial rewards. Mid-career professionals recommend people because it helps the people they know. Late career professionals hope to improve their own job search opportunities.

Appendix A. Organizational Chart of PeopleAhead

Appendix B. Competition: Passive Recruiters

> Additional useful information that might clutter the plan should appear in an appendix. The appendices are not included in this illustration.

CHAPTER 3

Analyzing the Marketing Environment

As we learned in Chapter 2, it is important for firms to continuously monitor their internal and external environments to identify new opportunities or threats to its business. Such analyses help firms identify areas where they are vulnerable to competition and areas where they are dominant. Firms then develop strategies or action plans to attack the competition or defend their market position. Let's see how Canadian Tire, an icon of Canadian retailing, has used knowledge of its environment to maintain its position for almost 100 years.

Canadian Tire's legacy started with a single Hamilton Tire and Garage Limited store just west of Toronto, which was purchased by brothers John and Alfred Billes in 1922. They renamed the company Canadian Tire Corporation in 1927 and grew it into a powerhouse. Today, Canadian Tire has five business units: Canadian Tire Retail (CTR), Canadian Tire Financial Services, Canadian Tire Petroleum, PartSource, and Mark's (formerly Mark's Work Wearhouse). CTR has a network of more than 485 retail stores that offer everything from automotive parts and services to sports, leisure, and home equipment and products. CT Petroleum is one of the largest independent retailers of gasoline, with a network of 287 agent-operated gas bars, 266 convenience stores, 74 car washes, 13 pit stops, and 86 propane stations. CT Financial Services, through its Options MasterCard, has more than 5 million credit card customers. PartSource, an automotive parts specialty chain that sells to professional automotive installers and "do-it-yourselfers," consists of 86 stores. Mark's consists of 372 stores of which 43 are franchises. Mark's has 39 percent market share in the industrial clothes market.[1] Canadian Tire, through its various businesses, employs more than 57 000 people and earned revenues of C$10.32 billion, with profits of C$453 million, in 2010.

Learning Objectives

After studying this chapter, you should be able to

LO1 Identify the factors in a firm's microenvironment

LO2 Explain how the factors in a firm's microenvironment influence its marketing strategy

LO3 Identify the factors in a firm's macroenvironment

LO4 Explain how the factors in a firm's macroenvironment influence its marketing strategy

LO5 Identify today's important social trends and describe why they affect marketing decisions

Canadian Tire is one of the most trusted brands in Canada. It has a unique assortment of products and services, a modern store network, and global sourcing capabilities. It is also the market leader in 17 of the top 20 selling categories, such as backyard, exercise, and household consumables.[2] The company does an excellent job of leveraging its trusted Canadian Tire brand across its multiple businesses.[3] Because of Canadian Tire's level of success over the years, one wonders about its secret for success and whether it has always been smooth sailing for the company.

Canadian Tire has received lumps, bumps, and bruises on several occasions. For example, in 1982, Canadian Tire debuted in the United States, but the venture failed miserably, and by 1985 Canadian Tire was forced to withdraw.[4] In 1992, the company decided to take another stab at the U.S. market under the name Auto Source. It again failed and bailed out in 1995, after three years and huge losses.[5] Despite these and other challenges, Canadian Tire has emerged as a successful and well-managed business. Its success has been attributed to many things, including its vision, good strategic planning, and excellent execution of its marketing strategies. However, one important element that cannot be discounted is its ability to understand and manage its microenvironment and macroenvironment.

For example, when global giants Walmart, Home Depot, and Lowes entered the already crowded Canadian market, many industry analysts feared that their deep pockets and aggressive business strategies would spell the end of Canadian Tire. However, as we have seen over the last decade, Canadian Tire has not only held its own against these global behemoths, but also steadily grew. The company implemented a wide range of strategies aimed at improving cost-efficiencies and productivity, enhancing customer service, bolstering its brands, growing its businesses, strengthening its loyalty program, and renewing its store concepts. For example, it continuously changed its store formats in response to changing demographic and social trends. In 2003, it launched its 20/20 store format,[6] which featured an updated layout, new and expanded product assortments, a customer care centre, new store signage, and a redesigned exterior store facade. Recently, the company rolled out its latest store formats, dubbed Smart stores and Small Market stores.[7] Smart stores have a racetrack floor plan that offers more space for high-growth categories and helps customers find products more easily through better signage and logical product adjacencies. Small Market stores include a Mark's store and a gas bar. The company has responded to advancing technology by integrating its website into its physical store operations and upgraded its information technology and communication infrastructure. It has adopted a wide range of environmental technologies aimed at reducing its carbon footprint. And it grew through the acquisition of Mark's Work Wearhouse, pursuing a broader target market that includes children and young women.

Like other retailing businesses, Canadian Tire cannot escape the challenges of the economy and other external factors that affect its businesses, but it must find a way to minimize the impact. In a conference call with investors to explain its 2010 first-quarter results, Canadian Tire's executives noted that the unseasonably warm winter resulted in poor sales of winter products but that sales of outdoor, home, and backyard products picked up earlier than usual. Similarly, sales at PartSource were down because of the warm winter weather. Further, improvements in employment in resource-based Alberta and British Columbia led to increased sales of industrial wear at Mark's. The Financial Services division had to set aside a greater amount for loan losses because of higher bankruptcies among its customers. However, lower interest costs helped to improve the financial situation. Moreover, the executives remarked that complying with new government regulations, specifically the harmonized sales tax, will increase their costs. These costs are estimated at $8 million for government regulation, up to $5 million for tax changes, and $8 million related to the issuance of chip and pin cards.[8] Government-mandated increases in the hourly minimum wage, such as from $8.75 to $10.25 in March 2010, could increase labour costs.[9]

What do you think Canadian Tire's sustainable competitive advantages are? What factors in the macroenvironment seemed to impact Canadian Tire's business strategy? .::

A Marketing Environment Analysis Framework

As the chapter vignette suggests, marketers who understand and manage the changes in their marketing environments are able to adapt their product and service offerings to meet new challenges and opportunities. Canadian Tire, for example, introduced three new store formats between 2003 and 2008, based on its understanding of the marketplace. Many marketers get their ideas for new products or services from monitoring and studying the marketing environment, as demonstrated in the case of Kobo and eBooks at the end of this chapter. Analyzing the marketing environment also helps marketers assess their continued strengths and the value of their products and services, and any weaknesses resulting from changes in the marketing environment.

Our chapter roadmap shows how companies analyze their marketing environment starting with a framework. At the heart of the analysis is, as always, the consumer. Consumers may be influenced directly by the firm's microenvironment, including the immediate actions of the focal company, the company's competition, and the corporate partners that work with the firm to make and supply products and services to consumers. The firm, and therefore consumers indirectly, is influenced by the macroenvironment, which includes influences such as culture and demographics,

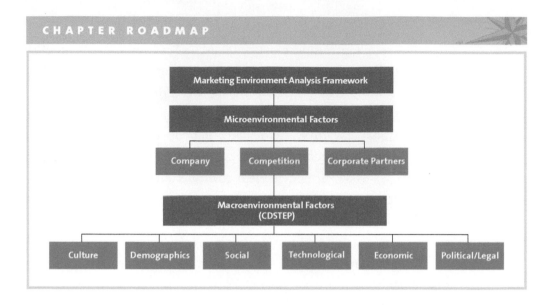

as well as social, technological, economic, and political/legal factors. We'll discuss each of these components in detail in this chapter and suggest how they interrelate. Exhibit 3.1 also illustrates these ideas.

One of the goals of value-based marketing is to provide greater value to consumers than competitors offer. This provision requires that the marketing firm looks at the entire business process from a consumer's point of view.[10] Consumers' needs and wants, as well as their ability to purchase, are affected by a host of factors that change and evolve over time. Firms use a variety of tools to keep track of their competitors' activities and communicate with their corporate partners. Furthermore, they monitor their macroenvironment to determine how such factors influence consumers and how they should respond to them. Sometimes, firms can even anticipate trends. For example, pharmaceutical companies have done an excellent job of monitoring

EXHIBIT 3.1   Understanding the Marketing Environment

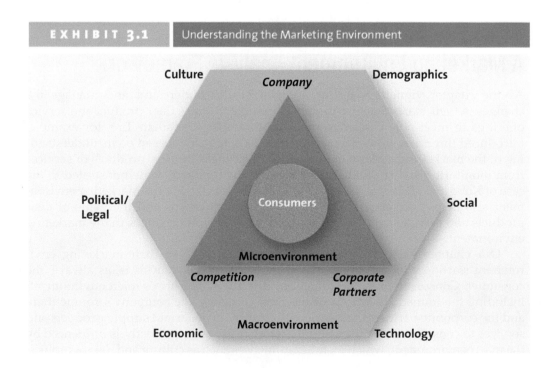

market trends and consumers and responding to consumers' needs. On the basis of observing and monitoring the aging baby boomer generation of consumers, they have made and marketed drugs to lower cholesterol, improve sexual performance, slow aging, and stem hair loss.

Microenvironmental Factors

LO1

Exhibit 3.2 illustrates the factors affecting consumers' microenvironment: the company (i.e., its capabilities), its competition, and its corporate partners.

Company Capabilities

LO2

In the firm's microenvironment, the first factor that affects the consumer is the firm itself. Successful marketing firms focus their efforts on satisfying customer needs that match their core competencies. The primary strength of Apple, for instance, rests in the design, manufacture, distribution, and promotion of Macintosh computers. But, it has successfully leveraged its core competency in the digital audio player arena with its iPod, iPhone, and iPad. It recognized a trend among consumers for sleek but functional portable devices, which can become one of their personal accessories. Marketers can use an analysis of the external environment, like the SWOT analysis described in Chapter 2, to categorize an opportunity as either attractive or unattractive and, if it appears attractive, to assess it relative to the firm's existing competencies.

Competition

Competition also significantly affects consumers in the microenvironment. Greater competition may mean more choices for consumers, which influences their buying decisions. It is critical that marketers understand their firm's competitors, including their strengths, weaknesses, and likely reactions to the marketing activities their own firm undertakes. When Colgate introduced Colgate Total toothpaste, promising total

| **EXHIBIT 3.2** | Understanding the Microenvironment |

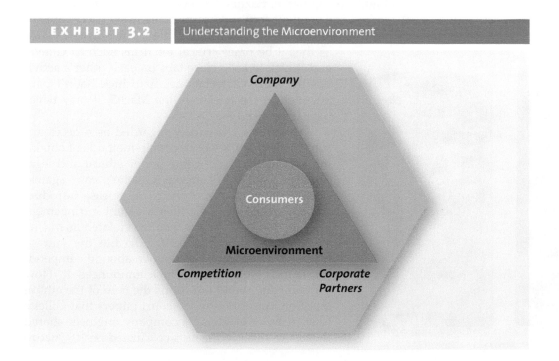

protection of your teeth, P&G responded with Crest Pro-Health, which promises to protect all areas where dentists check most.[11]

competitive intelligence (CI)
Used by firms to collect and synthesize information about their position with respect to their rivals; enables companies to anticipate changes in the marketplace rather than merely react to them.

Firms use **competitive intelligence (CI)** to collect and synthesize information about their position with respect to their rivals. In this way, CI enables companies to anticipate changes in the marketplace rather than merely react to them.[12] In Canada, an Ipsos Reid study conducted on behalf of the Marketing Research and Intelligence Association reports that while overall awareness of various business intelligence components ranges from medium to high among CI decision makers and business executives, existing CI activities are fairly limited in practice, and require more resources and attention in the future. The study found that less than half of decision makers say that their company is involved in various CI initiatives.[13]

The strategies to gather CI can range from simply sending a retail employee to a competitive store to check merchandise, prices, and foot traffic to more involved methods, such as

- Reviewing public materials, including websites, press releases, industry journals, annual reports, subscription databases, permit applications, patent applications, and tradeshows.

- Interviewing customers, suppliers, partners, or former employees.

- Analyzing a rival's marketing tactics, distribution practices, pricing, and hiring needs.

These more sophisticated CI strategies are implicitly obvious in the modern razor market. Although men and women have been shaving for thousands of years, it wasn't until 1901 that anyone tried to sell a disposable, thin piece of metal sharp enough to shave hair. In its first year of production, the Gillette Safety Razor Company, as it was known then, sold 50 razor sets. The following year it sold 12 million— obviously, the company anticipated a need well. Today, American men spend almost $2 billion annually on razors and blades. Gillette, the Canadian market leader with a 76-percent market share, changed the landscape again when it launched the enormously successful Mach3, a three-blade razor.[14] Not to be outdone, Energizer Holdings, the owner of Schick, introduced the Quattro razor, the world's first four-blade razor. The resulting battle for the title of "best razor" and for market share has resulted in a costly promotional and pricing battle. Razors that normally retail for up to $10 are being given away for free, and coupons for the corresponding razor blades appear everywhere.[15] Gillette has since introduced a razor with five blades. In situations such

*Who copied whom?
Gillette and Schick
introduced similar
razors almost
simultaneously.*

as this, it becomes critical for firms such as Gillette and Schick to keep close tabs on each other's activities by using CI techniques. If Schick hadn't paid attention to the release of the Mach3, it may never have introduced the Quattro.

Although CI is widely regarded as a necessary function in today's world, certain methods of obtaining information have come under ethical and legal scrutiny. Take, for example, Gillette's case against Schick. Within hours of the press release introducing the Quattro, Gillette filed a patent infringement lawsuit, claiming that the Quattro violated its Mach3 system's technology patent.[16] To file the suit so quickly, Gillette must have known about the impending launch well before Schick announced it. How the company found out forms the core of the ethical question. According to the court papers that Gillette filed two weeks later, "A company engineer shared the results of scientific tests conducted on 10 Quattro cartridges obtained by the company." Schick questioned how Gillette obtained the cartridges in an ethically appropriate manner prior to their commercial release. But Schick's ethical argument apparently held little sway, as the U.S. Appeals Court ruled that Gillette's patent could extend to four or even five blades and was not limited to the number of blades currently installed in the Mach3.[17] Armed with this ruling, Gillette and Schick continue to compete head-to-head. Gillette released the manual- and battery-operated Fusion, one-upping the Quattro's four blades with five. Schick, in anticipation of the Fusion, created three stylized versions of the Quattro (the Schick Quattro Chrome, Midnight, and Power) to appeal to shavers on a more aesthetic level.[18]

Another misuse of CI can be seen in Air Canada's case against WestJet. A lawsuit occurred based on allegations that WestJet management used the password of a former Air Canada employee to access a website maintained by Air Canada to download confidential information. WestJet countersued by alleging Air Canada used private investigators to search through recycling material at the home of a WestJet executive. WestJet later accepted full responsibility for its misconduct, which was unethical and unacceptable. Even worse, this practice was undertaken with the knowledge and discretion of the highest management levels of WestJet and was not halted until discovered by Air Canada. WestJet apologized to its competitor and Air Canada top executive Robert Milton. WestJet has also paid $5 million to Air Canada for its investigation and litigation costs, and made a $10-million donation to children's charities in the names of both airlines.[19]

Corporate Partners

Few firms operate in isolation. For example, automobile manufacturers collaborate with suppliers of sheet metal, tire manufacturers, component part makers, unions, transport companies, and dealerships to produce and market their automobiles successfully. Even firms such as Dell, which makes its own computers and sells them to customers, must purchase components, consulting services, advertising, and transportation from others. Parties that work with the focal firm are its corporate partners. Consider an example that demonstrates the role these partners play and how they work with the firm to create a single, efficient manufacturing system. Unlike most outdoor clothing manufacturers that use synthetic nonrenewable materials, Nau makes outdoor and ski clothing from renewable sources such as corn and recycled

Nau works with its corporate partners to develop outdoor and ski clothing from renewable resources such as corn and recycled plastic bottles.

plastic bottles. The company was founded by a team of entrepreneurs who left companies such as Nike and Patagonia. To develop clothing from sustainable materials that were rugged and beautiful, these founders turned to manufacturing partners around the world to develop new fabrics, such as PLA (polylactic acid), a fast-wicking biopolymer made from corn. To complement the new fabrics, the company uses only organic cotton and wool from "happy sheep," provided by partners in the ranching industry that embrace animal-friendly practices. Thus, not only does Nau represent the cutting edge of sustainability and green business, but it also clearly demonstrates how "going green" can prompt companies to work more closely with their partners to innovate.[20]

Macroenvironmental Factors

In addition to understanding the company itself, their competition, and their corporate partners, marketers must also understand the **macroenvironmental factors** that operate in the external environment, namely, the **c**ulture, **d**emographics, **s**ocial trends, **t**echnological advances, **e**conomic situation, and **p**olitical/legal environment, or CDSTEP, as shown in Exhibit 3.3.

Culture

Culture   We broadly define **culture** as the shared meanings, beliefs, morals, values, and customs of a group of people.[21] Transmitted by words, literature, and institutions, culture gets passed down from generation to generation and learned over time. You participate in many cultures. For example, your family has a cultural heritage so perhaps your mealtime traditions include eating rugelach, a traditional Jewish pastry, or sharing corned beef and cabbage to celebrate your Irish ancestry on St. Patrick's Day. Your school or workplace also shares its own common culture. In a broader sense, you also participate in the cultural aspects of the town and country in which you live. The challenge for marketers is to have products or services identifiable by and

macroenvironmental factors
Aspects of the external environment—**c**ulture, **d**emographics, **s**ocial trends, **t**echnological advances, **e**conomic situation, and **p**olitical/legal environment (CDSTEP)—that affect companies.

culture
The shared meanings, beliefs, morals, values, and customs of a group of people.

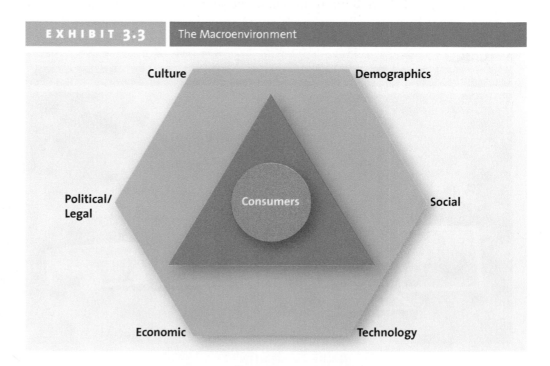

EXHIBIT 3.3   The Macroenvironment

relevant to a particular group of people. Our various cultures influence what, why, how, where, and when we buy. Two dimensions of culture that marketers must take into account as they develop their marketing strategies are the culture of the country and that of a region within a country.

Country Culture   The visible nuances of a **country's culture**, such as artifacts, behaviour, dress, symbols, physical settings, ceremonies, language differences, colours and tastes, and food preferences, are easy to spot. But the subtle aspects of culture generally are trickier to identify and navigate. BMW's Mini and other global automobile manufacturers have successfully bridged the cultural gap by producing advertising that appeals to the same target market across countries. The pictures and copy are the same. The only thing that changes is the language.

Regional Subcultures   The region in which people live in a particular country affects the way they react to different cultural rituals, or even how they refer to a particular product category. A resident of Quebec is 25 percent less likely to buy a hot prepared meal or reheatable meal than a resident of Ontario. This difference is attributed to Quebec women's desire to cook and be involved in their family's lives. As well, Quebec consumers are less price sensitive when grocery shopping than residents of Ontario. In Quebec, the most popular stores are IGA and Metro, as compared with No Frills and Food Basics in Ontario.[22] These kinds of differences can be the insight that helps a marketer make a strong connection with a consumer, rather than communicating the same way to all Canadians.

Another example of a regional subcultural difference is how we refer to our beverages. For instance, 37 percent of Canadians refer to carbonated beverages as *soda*, whereas another 40 percent call it *pop*, and an additional 17 percent call any such beverage a "Coke," even when the drink is a Pepsi. Eat lunch in British Columbia,

country culture
Entails easy-to-spot visible nuances that are particular to a country, such as dress, symbols, ceremonies, language, colours, and food preferences, and more subtle aspects, which are trickier to identify.

Some firms, such as BMW's Mini, have successfully bridged the cultural gap by producing advertising that appeals to the same target market across countries.

and you'll have the best luck ordering a *pop*, but if you head to Quebec for dinner, you'd better order a *soft drink*. Imagine the difficulty these firms have in developing promotional materials that transcend regional boundaries.[23]

Demographics

demographics
Characteristics of human populations and segments, especially those used to identify consumer markets, such as age, gender, income, race, ethnicity, and education.

Demographics indicate the characteristics of human populations and segments, especially those used to identify consumer markets. Typical demographics such as age—which includes generational cohorts—gender, income, race, and ethnicity are readily available from market research firms such as Nielsen, Ipsos Reid, Leger Marketing, and Statistics Canada. For instance, Nielsen collects information about TV viewership and sells it to networks and potential advertisers. The networks then use this information to set their advertising fees, whereas advertisers use it to choose the best shows on which to advertise. For a show popular among the desirable 18- to 35-year-old viewing segment, a network can charge the highest fees. But advertisers also might want to know whether a show is more popular with women than men or with urban or rural viewers. Demographics thus provide an easily understood "snapshot" of the typical consumer in a specific target market.

In the next few sections, we examine how firms use such demographics to assess their customers' needs and position themselves to deliver better value for those customers.

generational cohort
A group of people of the same generation—typically have similar purchase behaviours because they have shared experiences and are in the same stage of life.

Generational Cohorts   A group of people of the same generation, **generational cohorts**, have similar purchase behaviours because they have shared experiences and are in the same stage of life. For instance, baby boomers made up of people between the ages of 48 and 66, and generation Xers or people between the ages of 36 and 47, both gravitate toward products and services that foster a casual lifestyle; however, they tend to do so for different reasons.[24] The aging baby boomers, who grew up with jeans and khakis and brought casual dressing into the business arena, are often trying to maintain their youth. Gen Xers, in contrast, typically wear jeans and khakis because they are less impressed with the symbols of conspicuous consumption that their parents seem to have embraced. Although there are many ways to cut the generational pie, we discuss five major groups: tweens, gen Y, gen X, baby boomers, and seniors.

Tweens.   Tweens—not quite teenagers but not young children either—sit in beTWEEN. The importance of **tweens** to marketers stems from their immense buying power, estimated at $2.9 billion annually in Canada and $260 billion annually in the United States.[25] Canadian tweens also influence another $20 billion annually in family purchases. Marketers feel the tween effect in many areas, but particularly in the cellphone market. Tween users make great use of advanced features such as web surfing, photo capabilities, and texting. Although smartphones, such as the BlackBerry and Treo, historically targeted business users, companies today recognize the massive market for the features of these products among the tween segment.

tweens
Generational cohort of people who are not quite teenagers but are not young children either (ages 9 to 12); they're in beTWEEN.

Marketers position their products and services differently depending on which generational cohort they are targeting.

In Canada, tweens spend their money mainly on food and drinks, electronics (gaming consoles and games, digital music players, cellphones, and computers) and clothing. They learn about new products mainly from TV shows and friends. Although they enjoy the attention they get from marketers, they are not an easy group to market to. Three in four Canadian tweens make shopping decisions jointly with their parents.[26] Tweens are also known as speeders, because they do everything at lightning speed.[27] Since tweens are the first generation born after the emergence of the Internet, technology has no novelty for them. They communicate with friends via instant messenger while talking on a cellphone and flipping through TV channels, all simultaneously. As a result, marketers are inventing increasingly innovative ways to reach tweens through the Internet. Marketers must be careful with this cohort though; once they get bored, tweens are gone, off doing something else. So firms need to engage them quickly and with sincerity. Many companies, such as McCain Foods with its frozen pizza and Sony with its PlayStation, have developed innovative media campaigns to market to this group.

Watch out for tweens. They are fast, multitasking, technology-savvy, and easily bored.

And what do tweens like? In the food industry, they lean toward products such as Heinz's green ketchup and Yoplait's Yop. For toys and clothing, they have made Build-A-Bear Workshop, Claire's, and Limited Too immensely popular. However, because they have little of their own money, tweens tend to be value conscious, which makes them key targets for retailers such as The Gap, Hollister, American Eagle Outfitters, and Old Navy.

Generation Y. **Generation Y**, also called millennials or the "echo boom" generation, represent just over 7 million Canadians, or about 21 percent of the population.[28] This group also varies the most in age, ranging from teenagers to young adults who have their own families.[29] Generation Y grew up in a more media-intensive and brand-conscious era than their parents. Thus, they are more skeptical about what they hear in the media, which makes marketing to this group even more challenging. If a gen Y member believes the sell is "too hard," they won't buy. Regardless of where they live, they watch an hour less TV than an average household, use the Internet at work for personal reasons, and expect a healthy option at fast-food restaurants.[30] Gen Yers are Internet- and technology-savvy and love digital electronics such as cellphones, digital music players, digital cameras, and video games. In the next 10 years or so, many gen Yers will be starting new families and will be prime targets for homes and durable household products such as appliances, furniture, and gardening equipment and tools. In addition, now that gen Y is entering the workplace, it is becoming apparent that its members have different expectations and requirements than those of other cohorts. Gen Y puts a strong emphasis on balancing work and life; these young adults want a good job, but they also want to live in a location that supports their lifestyle.

generation Y
Generational cohort of people between the ages of 13 and 32; the biggest cohort since the original postwar baby boom.

Exhibit 3.4 provides comparisons between baby boomers and their children: members of generation X and generation Y.

generation X
Generational cohort of people between the ages of 36 and 47.

Multitasking is no big deal for gen Y.

Generation X. The next group, **generation X**, are people between the ages of 36 and 47. This group represents more than 5 million Canadians, or about 15 percent of the Canadian population.[31] Unlike their baby boomer parents, gen X is the first generation of latch-key kids: those who grew up in homes in which both parents worked. These young adults, having grown up in times of economic recession, are more likely than previous generations to be unemployed, carry higher debt loads, travel the world, and move far away from their parents; they are also more likely to live longer with their parents, compared with baby boomers, who, at their age, couldn't wait to move away from home.[32]

EXHIBIT 3.4	Generational Cohort Comparisons	
Baby Boomers	**Generation X**	**Generation Y**
Diversity as a cause	Accept diversity	Celebrate diversity
Idealistic	Pragmatic/cynical	Optimistic/realistic
Mass movement	Self-reliant/individualistic	Self-inventive/individualistic
Conform to the rules	Reject rules	Rewrite the rules
Killer job	Killer life	Killer lifestyle
Became institutions	Mistrust institutions	Irrelevance of institutions
TV	PC	Internet
Have technology	Use technology	Assume technology
Task-technology	Multitask	Multitask fast
Other boomers	Friend-not family	Friends-family

Source: "Gen Y and the future of mall retailing," *American Demographics*, December 2002 24. (11) p. J1. Used by permission of Crane Communications.

Gen Xers possesses considerable spending power because they tend to wait to get married and buy houses later in life. They're much less interested in shopping than their parents but are far more cynical, which tends to make them astute consumers. They demand convenience and tend to be less likely to believe advertising claims or what salespeople tell them. Marketing to gen X is difficult, but word-of-mouth advertising from people they know and trust can give marketers the credibility needed to market to this cohort. Because of their experience as children of working parents who had little time to shop, gen X developed shopping savvy at an early age and knew how to make shopping decisions by the time they were teenagers. As a result, they grew more knowledgeable about products and more risk averse than

No matter how old they get, baby boomers will always love rock 'n' roll.

other generational cohorts. Finally, gen X is much less interested in status products than older generations, not because they can't afford luxury brands but because they just don't see the point. Many companies such as Harley-Davidson and the Starwood Hotels and Resorts chain have developed products targeted specifically to gen X.

Baby Boomers. After World War II, the birth rate in Canada rose sharply, resulting in a group known as the **baby boomers**, who are between the ages of 48 and 66. They are the largest cohort of Canadians, representing 30 percent of the population. Although the baby boomer generation spans 18 years, experts agree that its members share several traits that set them apart from those born before World War II. First, they are individualistic. Second, leisure time represents a high priority for them. Third, they believe that they will always be able to take care of themselves, partly driven by their feeling of economic security, even though they are a little careless about the way they spend their money. Fourth, they have an obsession with maintaining their youth. Fifth and finally, they will always love rock 'n' roll.

baby boomers
Generational cohort of people born after World War II; are between the ages of 48 and 66.

The baby boomers' quest for youth, in both attitude and appearance, provides a massive market for anti-aging products, cosmetics, pharmaceuticals, and biotechnology. Boomers spend $30 billion per year on these products.[33] Salon services used to be a purely feminine domain, but with boomers turning 50 at the rate of seven per minute, providers are recognizing the potential of positioning themselves as being in the rejuvenation business. In ways that previous generations would have considered unthinkable, men have begun pampering themselves with salon services such as manicures, facials, and pedicures. Indeed, many boomers, including older baby boomers, are driving sports cars and going on adventure-based vacations.

Seniors. **Seniors** are over the age of 65 and make up Canada's fastest-growing group.[34] Between 1981 and 2006, the number of seniors in Canada grew from 2.4 million to 4.3 million. Their share of the population increased from 9.6 percent to 13.7 percent. Fifty-six percent of seniors are women. According to Statistics Canada, between 2006 and 2026 the number of seniors is projected to increase from 4.3 million to 8 million and will make up 21.2 percent of the Canadian population. But just because they are a large and growing segment, are they necessarily an important market segment for marketers to pursue? They're more likely to complain, need special attention, and take time browsing before making a purchase compared with younger groups. However, they generally have time to shop and money to spend.

seniors
North America's fastest-growing generational cohort; people aged 65 and older.

In the past, seniors were very conservative with their savings because they wanted something to pass on to their children. But that attitude appears to be changing. Perhaps you have seen the bumper sticker: "I am spending my children's inheritance!"[35] Older people seem to be buying goods and services at the same pace as younger generations. What do they spend their money on? Travel, second homes, luxury cars, electronic equipment, investments, home furnishings, and clothing are frequent purchases. Internet use among seniors more than quadrupled between 2000 and 2010—from 16 percent in 2000 to 66 percent in 2010.[36] Seniors use the Internet for emailing (90 percent), searching for travel information and making travel arrangements (59 percent), obtaining weather reports (56 percent), and banking electronically (40 percent). Only 26 percent have embraced e-commerce in the sense of placing an order online; although 54 percent use the Internet for searching for information.

Specifically, seniors tend to like "made in Canada" items and recognizable brand names (but generally not designer labels), value, quality, and classic styles. They're typically loyal and willing to spend but are extremely quality conscious and demand hassle-free shopping, particularly in terms of convenient locations. Because most mature customers don't need the basics, they prefer to buy a few high-quality items rather than a larger number of low-quality items.[37]

Income The median income of Canadian families in 2008 was approximately $63,900.[38] Canadians may be classified into distinct groups based on their income

The Fuel Cell Car and Experiment Kit appeals to an affluent consumer at specialty retailer Hammacher Schlemmer.

and other factors such as background, education, and occupation: upper class, middle class, working class (or low-income earners), and under class (at or below poverty). *Upper class* consumers are very affluent, and their spending patterns are not influenced by economic conditions. They have high discretionary incomes and tend to purchase luxury items. Their family income is usually in excess of $70,000. They are more likely to be highly educated and work in managerial and executive roles. About 48 percent of Canadian households are in the upper class.[39] *Middle class* families earn between $30,000 to $70,000, with the majority tending toward the higher end of this scale. They can afford a good life most of the time. They tend to be careful about their spending and are often value-conscious.

Approximately 38 percent of Canadian households fall in the middle class. *Working class*, or low-income families, earn between $20,000 and $30,000, barely sufficient income to cover their basic needs. *Under class* families earn less than $20,000 and often rely on assistance to cover their basic needs. Just under 15 percent of Canadian households belong to the working class and the under class. According to a report published by the Canadian Centre for Policy Alternatives, the richest 20 percent of Canadians spend 6 or 7 times more in every shopping category than the poorest 20 percent of Canadians.[40] Family income distribution in Canada varies by province, education level, gender, and profession. This broad range in incomes creates marketing opportunities at both the high and low ends of the market.

Although some marketers choose to target only affluent population segments, others have had great success delivering value to middle- and low-income earners. Consider, for example, the toys presented by the specialty retailer Hammacher Schlemmer versus the mass appeal of Walmart's toy sections. Toy buyers at Walmart are looking for inexpensive products; those at Hammacher Schlemmer go to great lengths to find unusual toys such as the Fuel Cell Car and Experiment Kit pictured.[41] Or note the variety of cellphone plans, from unlimited access to prepaid cards, designed to enable everyone to use a phone.[42]

Another aspect of the income demographic relates to the concept of value. Why are customers searching for this value more today than in recent decades? During the first three decades after World War II, most families experienced real income growth; but, between 1980 and 2005, that growth began to idle. Between 1980 and 2005, median earnings among the top 20 percent of earners increased by 16.4 percent. In contrast, median earnings among those in the bottom 20 percent fell 20.6 percent. Median earnings among those in the middle 20 percent stagnated, increasing by only 0.1 percent.[43] In 2010, the richest families, on average, earned about 10 times more than the poorest families!

Education Studies show that higher levels of education lead to better jobs and higher incomes.[44] Moreover, average annual earnings are higher for those with degrees than for those without. For example, 60 percent of Canadians with just a high school education level earn less than $20,000 per year and 60 percent with university degrees earn more than $80,000. In 2007, the median earnings for Canadians with a bachelor's degree were $45,000, a master's degree $60,000, and a doctorate $65,000. Those with a college diploma earned on average $35,000, and those with less than a high school education earned considerably less.[45]

For some products, marketers can combine education level with other data such as occupation and income to obtain pretty accurate predictions of purchase behaviour. For instance, a full-time college or university student with a part-time job may have relatively little personal income but will spend his or her disposable dollars differently than would a high school graduate who works in a factory and earns a similar income. College and university students tend to be engaged in playing sports and going to nightclubs, whereas the high school graduate more likely watches sports and goes to bars. Marketers are therefore quite cognizant of the interaction among education, income, and occupation.

Since women are such an important segment of their customers, Rona, the giant home improvement chain, has designed their stores with women in mind.

Gender Years ago, gender roles appeared clear, but those male/female roles have been blurred. This shift in attitude and behaviour affects the way many firms design and promote their products and services. For example, more firms are careful about gender neutrality in positioning their products and, furthermore, attempt to transcend gender boundaries whenever they can.

From cars to copiers, sweaters to sweeteners, women make the majority of purchasing decisions and then influence most of the remainder. For instance, despite the traditional view that hardware stores appeal mostly to men, women shoppers are so important to Rona, the home improvement chain, that the stores have been designed with women in mind.[46] Furthermore, women now head more than 20 percent of Canadian households.[47] Clearly, the working women's segment is a large, complex, and lucrative market.

But that doesn't mean marketers have forgotten about men. The days of commercials that show Mom alone with the kids are over. To reflect changing family roles, commercials for most children's gear now include Dad interacting with the kids and being involved in purchase decisions. Although the gap is narrowing, men still earn more money than women. In 2008, women earned an average of 71.3 percent of what men earned—that is, women earned $44,700, while men earned $62,600. The difference is much lower for women aged 25 to 29 entering the workforce; these women earned 15 percent less than men, or 85 cents for each dollar earned by men.[48]

Women are no longer the only family member doing the grocery shopping.

Ethnicity Statistics Canada data shows that the ethnic composition of Canada has changed over the last two decades and will continue to change in the next decade. Current research shows that 1 out of every 5 Canadians was not born here, accounting for nearly 70 percent of Canada's population growth. If this trend continues, Canada's population growth will be attributed almost exclusively to immigration by 2030.[49] The two fastest-growing groups are the Chinese (from Hong Kong, mainland China, and Taiwan) and South Asians (from India, Pakistan, Sri Lanka, and Bangladesh). It is estimated that ethnic groups or visible minorities will make up about 8.5 million or 23 percent of Canada's population by 2017 because of immigration and increasing

Sobeys' FreshCo stores were designed with the needs of ethnic consumers in mind.

birth rates among various ethnic groups.[50] Many new immigrants choose to settle in Montreal, Toronto, or Vancouver; however, areas such as Calgary, Edmonton, Winnipeg, and London are growing in popularity. These groups of South Asians and Chinese are typically young, educated, and wealthy. Currently, more than a quarter of all visible minorities in Canada are under 14 years; thus, they are likely to have considerable influence over the economy in the future. South Asians are the largest ethnic group in Ontario.[51]

What does this ethnic demographic shift mean for marketers? Simply put, the growing number of ethnic groups or visible minorities represents both a challenge and a marketing opportunity. The challenge is for marketers to understand the culture, value, and spending patterns of the various groups and figure out the best way to communicate and serve them. The creative director of Fat Free Communications, a Toronto ad agency, argues that most bank advertising employs "very superficial ways of acknowledging the (ethnic) community, which a lot of people in the community actually find irritating." Chris Bhang, a vice-president at Allard Johnson Communications, admonishes marketers to "be colloquial, be creative but be relevant."[52]

In terms of marketing opportunity, it is estimated that ethnic groups spend more than $42 billion on retail goods and services, and the average Chinese household spends $63,500 per year, compared with the Canadian average of $58,500. In general, ethnic Canadians spend more than their white counterparts on big-ticket items such as cars, clothing, and home furnishings. Many also have an affinity for brand-name products because they equate them with quality.[53]

Recognizing this huge opportunity and believing that much of its future growth will come from ethnic markets, Canadian grocery heavyweight Sobeys has recently developed a new store concept, FreshCo, specifically targeted to the unique needs of the ethnic consumer. The company started in Ontario by converting some existing Price Chopper stores in particularly diverse Brampton and Mississauga markets to the new FreshCo model. It has since opened stores in Hamilton, Oakville, and Brantford, and plans to open more locations in the coming years. The concept is a value-driven store with low prices like No Frills or Food Basics but with a focus on fresh produce, halal meats, and freshly baked breads (unlike most discount banners) to meet the demands of ethnic clientele. As well, the layout of the store is different. After the store's layout guides consumers through the fresh produce, bakery, and meat departments, as in a typical retail grocery store, the natural flow of the store takes shoppers through the extended international foods aisle, which highlights Asian, West Indian, Middle Eastern, and Eastern European food products, before the customers reach the centre grocery aisles.[54] Sobeys has also committed to adapting the FreshCo store assortments to match the demographics of the surrounding neighbourhood, including teaming up with local suppliers.[55] The success of FreshCo will depend, in part, on the success that Sobeys marketers have in getting grocery shoppers to move away from smaller ethnic grocery stores and other ethnic-targeted stores—such as T&T Supermarket, which was acquired by Loblaw in 2009—that are the typical grocery choice for ethnic consumers.

It's no doubt that other grocery stores will respond to remain competitive. Some of the tactics retailers are taking to accommodate the ethnic consumer include adapting signs and flyers to feature different languages, choosing ethnic-targeted media to advertise, celebrating important ethnic holidays such as Chinese New Year, Ramadan, Eid, and Hanukkah with events, promotions, and seasonal products, and offering ethnic merchandise for sale and making sure it is merchandised correctly.[56]

Social Trends

Social trends shape consumer values in Canada, the United States, and around the world. Social trends tend to change over time in their popularity and importance, and savvy marketers work hard to identify emerging trends to understand whether they present an opportunity or pose a threat to their business. Here, we discuss a few current social trends that have gained prominence recently. This list is by no means exhaustive but includes greener consumers, marketing to children, privacy concerns, and the time-poor society.

Greener Consumers[57]   **Green marketing** involves a strategic effort by firms to supply customers with environmentally friendly merchandise. Although this "green" trend is not new, it is growing. Many consumers, concerned about everything from the purity of air and water to the safety of beef and salmon, believe that each person can make a difference in the environment. A study found that more than 90 percent of Canadians feel that individuals can take action to reduce air pollution. For example, more than half of Canadian households now recycle their soft-drink bottles, cardboard boxes, and newspapers. In many cities across Canada, the use of pesticides on lawns is banned and many consumers are trying alternative, environmentally friendly lawn care treatment. Also, a growing number of cities across Canada are introducing the "green bin" program that encourages consumers to recycle their food and yard waste to make compost for gardening. Initial results suggest that this program is hugely successful everywhere it has been introduced.

For companies selling environmentally friendly products, this trend represents a great opportunity. However, firms that sell products considered harmful to the environment may find this trend a threat to their business and must innovate to stay in business. The Sustainable Marketing boxes throughout this book provide many examples of how individual Canadians and businesses are taking actions to reduce the harmful effects of their consumption and production decisions.

Social Media Marketing 3.1 shows how the Toronto Zoo used Twitter to spread important information about protecting the environment.

The demand for green-oriented products has been a boon to the firms that supply them. For instance, marketers encourage consumers to replace their older versions of washing machines and dishwashers with water- and energy-saving models and to invest in phosphate-free laundry powder and mercury-free, rechargeable batteries. Canada's love affair with recycling also has created markets for recycled building products, packaging, paper goods, and even sweaters and sneakers. Similarly, this raised energy consciousness has spurred the growth of more-efficient appliances, lighting, and heating and cooling systems in homes and offices.

green marketing
Involves a strategic effort by firms to supply customers with environmentally friendly merchandise.

Spawned by environmental concerns and rising gas prices, consumers are demanding more fuel-efficient hybrid cars.

"I guess it is easy being green."

Presenting the 36 mpg Ford Escape Hybrid, the most fuel-efficient SUV on Earth.* How green is that?
www.fordvehicles.com

ESCAPE HYBRID

*Based on Automobile Revue, Transport Canada and US EPA. EPA estimated 36 city/31 hwy mpg, FWD. Actual mileage will vary. ©The Muppets Holding Company, LLC. All Rights Reserved.

Social Media Marketing 3.1   Saving the Planet One Tweet at a Time

Twitter is a very powerful tool. In addition to being an ideal forum for sharing updates, news, and opinions, its ability to measure, count, and categorize tweets helps to monitor popular news stories and track growing trends. Adding a hash mark (#) ahead of words in a tweet enables searching and tracking. This feature helped the Toronto Zoo spread important messages about the environment.

Known as the symbol for wildlife and preservation, the polar bear was the centre of an online campaign asking Twitter users to promote environmental messages and help to educate others about global warming. The microsite PolarTweets.com was created to scan Twitter for tweets related to the polar bears, global warming, and other green themes. When these green topics were mentioned often, the site showed a polar bear safely atop an "iceberg" of twitter keywords, far away from the ocean. Fewer green conversations resulted in the iceberg shrinking, bringing the bear closer to the ocean and illustrating its real-life plight. In only two weeks, the site saw more than 2000 visitors and moved the bear farther from the ocean.[58]

When visitors came to the site to see the updates, facts about the environment were displayed. For example, one fact read "25% of the Arctic Sea has already disappeared. Without action, the polar bears could disappear too." The site then went on to encourage tweets about the fact. The site was touted as the first ever to monitor eco-activity in real time.[59] The reactive iceberg of eco-words also provided an incentive to tweet for the cause.

Health-conscious consumers continue to fuel the markets for organic foods, natural cleaning and personal care products, air- and water-filtration devices, bottled water, and organic fertilizers. By offering environmental responsibility, these green products add an extra ounce of value that other products don't have, as illustrated in Entrepreneurial Marketing 3.1.

Marketing to Children[60]   In the past 20 years, child obesity has doubled in Canada, leading to skyrocketing rates of high blood pressure, high cholesterol, early signs of heart disease, and Type 2 diabetes among children. In response, the Center for Science and the Public Interest (CSPI) has proposed *Guidelines for Responsible Food Marketing to Children*, which outlines a variety of changes to advertising directed at children. The CSPI notes that children are highly impressionable, and most food advertising to these young consumers touts high-calorie, low-nutrition products, associated in advertising with various toys, cartoons, and celebrities. The new guidelines require advertisers to market food in reasonably proportioned sizes. The advertised food items also must provide basic nutrients, have less than 30 percent of their total calories from fat, and include no added sweeteners. The advertising also cannot be aired during children's programming, and companies cannot link unhealthy foods with cartoon and celebrity figures. For example, Burger King no longer uses SpongeBob SquarePants to promote burgers and fries. Other organizations such as the Chronic Disease Prevention Alliance of Canada (CDPAC) and health and citizens' groups are also working to ensure proper advertising to children.

Privacy Concerns   More and more consumers worldwide sense a loss of privacy. At the same time that the Internet has created an exploding volcano of accessibility to consumer information, improvements in computer storage facilities and the manipulation of information have led to more and better credit check services. In addition, consumers are constantly reminded that their identity may not be their own, as in the humorous series of Citibank commercials that depict unsuspecting credit card users who have had their identities stolen. In one, a sweet-looking older woman describes her new pickup truck in a deep, masculine voice-over.

Canadians are becoming increasingly conscious about how their purchase and consumption decisions impact the environment. In an effort to offset the harmful environmental effects of the products they consume, many Canadians are reducing their carbon footprint by subscribing to a wide variety of environmentally friendly initiatives. They believe that each person can make a difference, and they are taking whatever action they can to reduce negative environmental effects.

Tom Heintzman, president of Bullfrog Power, recognizes this growing social trend. He is capitalizing on the green trend by providing Canadian consumers with an energy alternative, helping them reduce their carbon footprint. Heintzman believes that it is important for Canadians to consider clean energy, especially since the Kyoto Protocol expires in 2012 and its goals have not been achieved. As a result of this lack of progress, Heintzman believes it's important for individuals to lead. By making clean energy choices available, he believes that individuals can exert their unique power to change the world.

Heintzman's company, Bullfrog Power, is based in Toronto and provides 100 percent green electricity. The company opened in Ontario in September 2005 and has since successfully expanded its operations and services to British Columbia, Alberta, Nova Scotia, New Brunswick, and Prince Edward Island. Bullfrog Power addresses climate change and environmental issues that are growing social trends. The company uses electricity that comes from wind and hydro facilities instead of more-polluting sources such as coal, oil, nuclear, and natural gas. Bullfrog Power ensures that the amount of electricity used by its consumers is matched by the amount of renewable electricity that the company's wind turbines and low-impact water generators channel into the local grid. This option means that residents do not need to purchase any additional equipment or wiring to switch to a greener energy alternative, which appeals to consumers because it is simple for them to take action to create a greener environment.

The change toward a greener environment is being embraced, despite the fact that green energy can be more costly. Bullfrog Power is a relatively expensive product. It is targeted toward a specific demographic that has a high level of income and a high level of education and is therefore more aware of environmental issues. These individuals are willing to pay more for products that align with their values. By understanding important social trends and targeting specific demographics, Bullfrog Power is reshaping the electricity landscape and leading the switch to greener energy.

Although these commercials promote a new credit card with identity theft protection, most consumers have no such protection. In April 2011, Epsilon, a Dallas, Texas–based marketing firm that controls the email databases of more than 2500 business clients and sends more than 40 billion marketing messages to consumers per year on behalf of its clients, reported that hackers had breached its system. Epsilon's list of clients includes some of the biggest U.S. corporations with global reach: AIR MILES, Best Buy, Marriott, Hilton Hotels, JPMorgan Chase, Citigroup, Capital One Financial, Walgreens, Kroeger, U.S. Bancorp, and several others. American investigators regard this data breach as one of the biggest in U.S. history.[62] Thus, it is hardly surprising that more than three-quarters of Canadians are concerned about the security and privacy of the information they provide over the Internet.[63]

The Time-Poor Society   Reaching a target market has always been a major challenge, but it is made even more complicated by several trends that increase the difficulty of grabbing those markets' attention. First, in the majority of families, both parents work, and the kids are busier than ever. For example, on average, Canadians worked 8.9 hours during a typical workday, but 25 percent said they devote more than 10 hours a day to their work. Thus, Canadians have less time for leisure and to spend with family. In 2011, Canadian workers spent about 200 hours less with family per year than they did two decades earlier.[64]

Second, consumers today have hundreds of shows and programs available to them through TV, radio, PDAs, DVDs, smartphones, personal computers, and the Internet. With many shows and programs available on the Internet, consumers can choose when,

Time-poor consumers multitask to cope with their lack of leisure time.

Self-checkout lanes speed the shopping process, but do they improve customer service?

where, and what shows they want to watch or listen to at their convenience. By fast-forwarding thorough the commercials, they can catch an entire one-hour show in approximately 47 minutes, which means they miss all the messages marketers are attempting to send them.

Third, many consumers attempt to cope with their lack of leisure time by multitasking: watching TV or listening to music while talking on the telephone or doing homework. Their divided attention means they simply cannot focus as well on the advertisements that appear in those media.

Marketers are thus faced with the challenge of finding more creative ways to get their marketing messages out to consumers under these ever-changing media consumption trends. Some marketers have responded to the challenge of getting consumers' attention by, for example, moving some of their advertising expenditures from traditional venues such as TV and print media to instant messaging, Internet-based reviews and ads, social media ads, movie screens, fortune cookies, baggage claim conveyor belts, billboards, and ads in airports and on taxis, buses, and mass transport vehicles.[65] Retailers are doing their part by making their products available to customers whenever and wherever they want. For instance, retailers such as Sears Canada and The Bay are becoming full-fledged multichannel retailers that offer stores, catalogues, and Internet shopping options. Others, such as Metro, Shoppers Drug Mart, and Walmart, have extended their hours of operation so that their customers can shop during hours that they aren't working. In addition, automated processes such as self-checkout lanes and electronic kiosks speed the shopping process and provide customers with product and ordering information.

To find and develop methods to make life easier for many diverse consumers in a time-poor society, marketers often rely on technology, another macroenvironmental factor and the topic of the next section.

Technological Advances

technological advances
Technological changes that have contributed to the improvement of the value of both products and services in the past few decades.

Technological advances have accelerated greatly during the past few decades, improving the value of both products and services. The world has realized the commercial successes of smartphones, including the iPhone, BlackBerry, and Android; MP3 players; access to the Internet virtually everywhere through WiFi and 4G on tablet computers (iPad, PlayBook); and digital and video cameras. Flat-screen and high-definition televisions, as well as video on demand, have begun to change the way we view TV, and their impact is expected only to increase in the next few years. Exhibit 3.5 showcases some of the recent major achievements in technology.

On the retail side, firms are able to track an item from the moment it is manufactured, through the distribution system, to the retail store, and into the hands of the final consumer by using radio frequency identification device (RFID) chips that are affixed to the merchandise. Because they are able to determine exactly how much of

EXHIBIT 3.5	Advances in Technology						
	Cellphone	LCD Televisions	MP3 Player	Internet Access	Digital Camera	iPhone	iPad
Year Introduced	1984	1988	1991	1993	1998	2007	2010
Sales	$115.5 Million	$924 Million	$719 Million	$582 Million	$828 Million	$360 Million	$9.8 Billion*

*Fiscal year sales ending September 2010: $4.9 billion. First-quarter sales of 2011, ending December 25, 2010: 7.33 million units, at an estimated price of $664/unit, which includes accessories and other related services.

Sources: www.apple.com/pr/library/2011/01/18results.html; SEC 10K filing.

each product is at a point in the supply chain, retailers also can communicate with their suppliers—instantaneously over the Internet—and collaboratively plan to meet their inventory needs.

Other areas of technical advance include how we bring media into our homes. Popular movies are now on Blu-ray disc or high-definition digital video disc (HD DVD), and the latest sportscasts are available via high-definition television (HDTV). Gaming consoles have come a long way as well. With faster central processing units and stronger graphics, both Sony's PlayStation 3 and Microsoft's Xbox 360 are capable of online networking and data and photo storage. The Nintendo Wii has also revolutionized home gaming with its hand-held remote that detects movement in three directions. Kinect for Xbox 360 has gone one step further by eliminating hand-held remotes during game play altogether. Rather than sitting on the couch to play a game with friends, you can now literally get into the action and swing to hit a homerun or jump up to volley a ball. All three consoles feature 3-D perspectives that greatly increase the challenge of the games. Not only do these technological advances result in higher quality products, they also create buzz and a sense of novelty for their industries, as well as new opportunities to communicate with consumers. Power of the Internet 3.1 describes some of the latest offerings along these lines.

Different technology adoption levels also matter to marketers when communicating a new product or using a new media type. As noted so far and as described throughout this book in the Social Media Marketing boxes, not only are marketers trying to make social media an integral part of their marketing strategy, but also consumers are using social media to share information and their experiences and frustrations with products, services, and marketers. The relative ease with which consumers can use social media has really increased the power of consumers to affect a firm's marketing strategy. Some firms have embraced social media as a way to get excellent feedback from consumers, which is then used to design new or redesign existing products, services, and marketing campaigns and strategies. Moreover, even traditional media such as TV networks are encouraging consumers to share their experiences, gripes, and frustrations through their websites; these consumer accounts are then aired. For example, the CBC show *The National* has a Go Public link on its website, which encourages consumers to share their stories; one story is reported on every night that the show airs.[67] One recent story concerned Sears's Kenmore stoves, which consumers said would turn on by themselves, posing a very dangerous and

Power of the Internet 3.1

Brands, Calling at Your Service, Sir[66]

On your next ski vacation, you can take most of the guess-work out of your trip just by turning to your cellphone.

Unsure of the conditions on the mountain? Check out the North Face Snow Report, an application that provides official weather reports and snow conditions. It also enables users to tweet about the conditions they see in real time, so your fellow ski bums can clue you in to deteriorating conditions.

It might be a long drive to get to the mountain with the best snow, so you also might download the SitOrSquat app from Charmin, which gives you a list of bathrooms, categorized by amenities, in your chosen area. For example, if you need a washroom with handicap access, you can narrow your search to find one. You can also get a rating from other users or add a new facility you find.

If your travelling companions include species other than humans, download Purina's petcentric app to find a restaurant that will let you bring Fido in for a meal, a park that encourages dog visitors, and a hotel that permits animals who want to stay the night. If you can't find an accommodating hotel, petcentric offers a list of nearby kennels.

Finally, imagine that you've arrived late at the hotel, gotten the dog settled in, and need some food before you turn in early so you can hit the slopes first-thing in the morning. If you order from Domino's Pizza, the company's website allows you to track exactly where your pizza is, from the moment you place your order to the minute it leaves the store on its way to you.

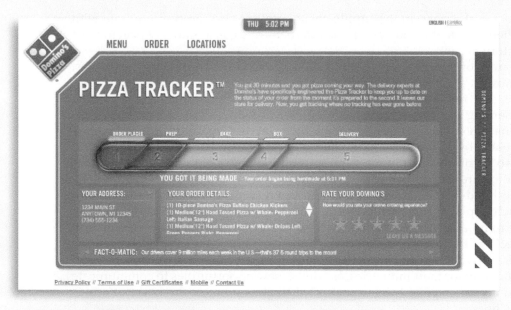

Domino's Pizza Tracker allows customers to track where their pizza is, from the moment they place their order to the minute it leaves the store on its way to them.

unsafe situation. And, because they were dissatisfied with the response from Sears, the consumers went public with their story. Needless to say, this story generated a lot of negative publicity for Sears.

As well as posing a serious threat to marketers, this mixture of social media and traditional media is also an opportunity for marketers to demonstrate their customer care efforts and gain free publicity. The key challenge for marketers is to spot emerging technology trends very early and to assess their likely impact, positive or negative, on business. They must then develop appropriate strategies for responding to the trends. Although most of the examples used here are based on information and communication (ICT) technologies, marketers will be affected by virtually all major technological advances, regardless of fields or applications, from clean technology to biotechnology, nanotechnology, medical technology, and so on.

Economic Situation   Marketers monitor the general **economic situation**, both in their home country and abroad, because it affects the way consumers buy merchandise and spend money. Some major factors that influence the state of an economy include the rate of inflation, foreign currency exchange rates, interest rates, and recession.

Inflation refers to the persistent increase in the prices of goods and services.[68] Increasing prices cause the purchasing power of the dollar to decline; in other words, a dollar buys less than it used to.

In a similar fashion, **foreign currency fluctuations** can influence consumer spending. For instance, on January 21, 2007, C$1.00 was worth US$0.6179, the lowest exchange rate ever between these two currencies. In less than four months (at the beginning of May 2007), the value of the Canadian dollar relative to the U.S. dollar increased to $0.9071[69]—a 32-percent increase—and in less than nine months the Canadian dollar increased to $1.10. Such rapid increases in the exchange rate between the currencies of Canada and the United States, our largest trading partner, has both negative and positive consequences for Canadian marketers, depending on whether they are exporters or importers and whether they report their earnings in Canadian or U.S. dollars. The exchange rate changes also have serious implications for consumers as well. As the value of the Canadian dollar increases compared with the U.S. dollar, merchandise made in Canada and exported to the United States becomes more costly to Americans, and Canadian exporting companies suddenly find that they have lost a good chunk of their cost advantage. However, imports of products made in the United States cost less for both Canadian importers and consumers.

Another, perhaps unexpected result of the strengthening of the Canadian dollar compared with the U.S. dollar, is that it might allow Canadian manufacturers to win and American manufacturers to lose—that is, imports of raw material from the United States are cheaper. During such inflationary times, "made in America" claims become more important, which means that Canadian manufacturers and U.S. retailers that specialize in Canadian merchandise must decide whether they should attempt to maintain their profit margins or accept a lower price to keep their customer base. It is not always easy for marketers to respond quickly to such rapid increases; but, marketers who monitor the economic environment have the advantage, as they will be able to adjust their strategies if they foresee the increase.

Interest rates represent the cost of borrowing money. For example, when customers borrow money from a bank, they agree to pay back the loan, plus the interest that accrues. The interest, in effect, is the cost to the customers or the fee the bank charges those customers for borrowing the money. Likewise, if a customer opens a savings account at a bank, he or she will earn interest on the amount saved, which means the interest becomes the fee the consumer gets for "loaning" the money to the bank. If the interest rate goes up, consumers have an incentive to save more, because they earn more for loaning the bank their money; when interest rates go down, however, consumers generally borrow more.

For instance, when the Bank of Canada cut its overnight lending rate, the rate at which it lends to banks, by 4.25 percent to 0.25 percent in April 2009, record numbers of Canadians took advantage of the historic low interest rates and took out mortgages. The 0.25 percent interest rate broke the previous record low of 1.12 percent, which was set in 1958, 50 years earlier. The cut was considered absolutely necessary to deal with the worsening global economic and financial crisis. According to the Bank of Canada governor and the finance minister, cheap credit has led to a situation in Canada where the average Canadian income-to-debt ratio

economic situation
Economic changes that affect the way consumers buy merchandise and spend money; see *inflation, foreign currency fluctuations, interest rates,* and *recession.*

inflation
Refers to the persistent increase in the prices of goods and services.

foreign currency fluctuations
Changes in the value of a country's currency relative to the currency of another country; can influence consumer spending.

interest rates
Represent the cost of borrowing money.

is 150—that is, for every $1 earned, Canadians owe $1.50. If this situation continues, it could exert negative consequences on the economy and ultimately on consumers and marketers.[70]

recession
A period of economic downturn when the economic growth of the country is negative for at least a couple of consecutive quarters.

Finally, **recession** is a period of economic downturn when the economic growth of the country is negative for at least a couple of consecutive quarters. We experienced this in 2008–2009. In a recession, the stock market declines sharply, unemployment increases, business and consumer confidence falls, and spending by both businesses and consumers is severely reduced. Indeed, thousands of consumers lose their jobs during a recession; thus, their purchasing power is greatly reduced. Even people who have jobs tend to spend cautiously because of uncertainty as to whether they will lose or keep their jobs.

In recessionary times, consumers alter their spending patterns by postponing big-ticket or discretionary items and look for the best deals for items they need—that is, they become even more value conscious, wanting the most value for their money. Marketers must adjust their marketing strategies accordingly. Most marketers try to cut costs, lower prices to keep their existing customers and to attract new customers, and may even introduce slightly lower quality goods or reduce the level of services offered in order to manage costs. In a recession, some industries do well and others struggle. Marketers must be vigilant in monitoring the environment and understanding the impact economic downturn has on their business.

How do these four important economic factors—inflation, foreign currency fluctuations, interest rates, and recession—affect a firm's ability to market goods and services? Shifts in the four economic factors make marketing easier for some and harder for others. For instance, when inflation increases, consumers probably don't buy less food, but they may shift their expenditures from expensive steaks to less-expensive hamburgers. Grocery stores and inexpensive restaurants win, but expensive restaurants lose. Consumers also buy less discretionary merchandise. For instance, the sale of expensive jewellery, fancy cars, and extravagant vacations will decrease; but, curiously, the sale of low-cost luxuries, such as personal care products and home entertainment, tends to increase. It appears that, instead of rewarding themselves with a new Lexus or a health spa vacation, consumers buy a few cosmetics and rent a movie. As noted above, lower interest rates encourage more consumers to borrow to finance purchases, especially of big-ticket or discretionary items such as cars, houses, furniture, and home entertainment systems. Not surprisingly, the building industry and housing market did extremely well in the period leading up to the recent recession. As consumers switch from more- to less-expensive goods and services and demand greater value, marketers who were able to adjust their offering did much better than those who did not change their value offering.

Tourists from other countries flock to the United States to shop because the value of the dollar is low compared with their own currency.

Political/Legal Environment

political/legal environment
Comprises political parties, government organizations, and legislation and laws that promote or inhibit trade and marketing activities.

The **political/legal environment** comprises political parties, government organizations, and legislation and laws that promote or inhibit trade and marketing activities. Organizations must fully understand and comply with any legislation regarding fair competition, consumer protection, or industry-specific regulation. Since the turn of the century, the government has enacted laws that promote both fair trade and competition by prohibiting the formation of monopolies or alliances that would damage a competitive marketplace, fostering fair pricing practices for all suppliers and consumers, and promoting free trade agreements among foreign nations.

Ethical Dilemma 3.1 — BP's Dividend Announcement: Slick or Shoddy?[71]

Not so long ago British Petroleum (BP) was Wall Street's sweetheart. Its share prices soared to a value of $60.50, and it was named *Fortune* 500's fourth largest corporation, with operations in more than 100 countries. It was one of three companies shortlisted to win the U.S. government's Safety Award for Excellence. On April 20, 2010, the day of the Deepwater Horizon oil spill, it was scheduled to accept an award for "outstanding safety and pollution prevention performance" in offshore drilling. However, instead of accepting a green award, BP was waist-deep in slick, black goop.

The Deepwater Horizon oil spill is the world's most destructive oil spill to date, devastating the economy and ecology of the Gulf Coast and the surrounding region. There were different estimates of how much oil was actually spilling on a daily basis; but, millions of barrels of oil leaked into the Gulf Coast over the more than 80-day debacle. Kilometres of oil threatened the livelihood of wildlife and inhabitants in the surrounding area. In spite of the catastrophic effects on the environment and the livelihood of the people in the affected area, 58 days into the leak and with no solution in sight, BP announced that it would pay the dividends due to its shareholders. Not surprisingly, this announcement made instant headlines across the world, generating negative reactions from various sections of society. Under intense pressure from the U.S. government, BP backed down and agreed to suspend dividend payments for the rest of the year.

Given the state of affairs and considering that BP saw no clear solution at the time it declared the dividends, do you think that it was appropriate for BP to consider offering its shareholders their promised dividends while local fishers, small businesses, and cities and towns along the Gulf Coast and other affected areas were suffering severe financial hardships?

Legislation also has been enacted to protect consumers in a variety of ways. First, regulations require manufacturers to abstain from false or misleading advertising practices that might mislead consumers, such as claims that a medication can cure a disease when in fact it causes other health risks. Second, manufacturers are required to identify and remove any harmful or hazardous materials (e.g., asbestos) that might place a consumer at risk. Third, organizations must adhere to fair and reasonable business practices when they communicate with consumers. For example, BP seems to have ignored its own safety procedures and warning signal, which resulted in the largest oil spill in U.S. history, with devastating consequences to the environment and the people of the Gulf Coast, as described in Ethical Dilemma 3.1.

Last but not least, the government enacts laws focused on specific industries and on consumers. These laws may be geared toward increasing competition, such as the deregulation of the telephone and energy industries. Or, they may be in response to current events or to achieve specific objectives, such as when the governments of Ontario and British Columbia introduced the harmonized sales tax (HST) to improve the competitiveness of Canadian businesses, or when the federal government introduced the one-year home renovation tax credit to encourage consumers to spend during the recession. As described in the chapter vignette, implementing the government-mandated HST will cost Canadian Tire millions of dollars. Similarly, the government has developed laws to regulate consumer behaviour, such as banning smoking, mandating child car seats, and requiring drivers to use only hands-free cellphones.

Generally, government regulations may have a negative or positive impact on marketers. On the positive side, certain laws create an opportunity for marketers to sell more of their products, as was the case with Bluetooth devices or car seats. Also, regulation may help to create a level playing field for competition and set standards for marketers to follow. In other cases, regulation tends to increase the cost of compliance; compliance usually requires more paperwork, time, effort, and money and may cause delays when government approval is needed. A short list of some of the most significant legislation affecting marketing interests appears in Exhibits 3.6 and 3.7.

EXHIBIT 3.6	Major Federal Legislation to Protect Competition and Consumers

Access to Information Act	Income Tax Act
Bankruptcy Act	Interest Act
Bills of Exchange Act	Investment Canada Act
Broadcasting Act	Lobbyist Registration Act
Canada Agricultural Product Standards Act	Official Languages Act
Canada Corporations Act	Patent Act
Canada Dairy Products Act	Personal Information Protection and Electronic
Canada Human Rights Act	Documents Act (PIPEDA)
	Privacy Act
Canada Small Business Financing Act	Small Loans Act
Competition Act	Standards Council of Canada Act
Consumer Packaging and Labelling Act	Textile Labelling Act
Copyright Act	Trade-Marks Act
Criminal Code	True Labelling Act
Electricity and Gas Inspection Act	Weight and Measures Act
Food and Drugs Act	Winding-up Act

EXHIBIT 3.7	Marketing Practices Covered by the Competition Act

Law	Description
Price	
Price fixing	Sellers conspire to set the price of a product, usually higher than it would be in a free market
Price discrimination	Charging different prices to different (competing) buyers for goods of the same quality and of the same quantity
Predatory pricing	Pricing that is intended to drive competitors out of the market or keep competitors from entering the market—usually low prices
Resale price maintenance	Manufacturers or channel members try to influence the price at which the product is sold to subsequent purchasers
Bid rigging	Sellers collude to set prices in response to bids or quotations for products
Promotion	
Misleading advertising	All types of advertising about a product or service that are false or misleading
Bait-and-switch	Sellers try to attract customers to their stores by offering a low price on a product (bait); but, once the customers are in the store, sellers try to persuade them to buy a higher-priced item (switch)
Referral selling	Incentives offered to consumers to provide the names of other potential consumers
Distribution (Place)	
Refusal to deal	A seller refuses to sell products or services to legitimate buyers
Exclusive dealing	A seller refuses to sell to other channel members unless that member agrees to buy exclusively from that particular seller
Pyramid selling	Schemes where salespersons are paid to recruit other salespeople, and each new salesperson pays for the right to recruit other salespeople, with some of that money going to earlier recruiters. Participants are often asked to buy a specific quantity of goods or are knowingly sold unreasonable quantities of goods and are not allowed to return the goods on commercially reasonable terms.

Learning Objectives Review

LO1 Identify the factors in a firm's microenvironment

The three factors in a firm's microenvironment are its capabilities, corporate partners, and competition. Understanding these three factors is key to serving its customers, who should be at the heart of all its marketing decisions and activities. The factors help decide the business activities the firm should engage in and how it should design and deliver its marketing offers.

LO2 Explain how the factors in a firm's microenvironment influence its marketing strategy

Successful marketing firms focus their efforts on satisfying customer needs that match their core competencies. Everything a firm does should utilize its strengths and revolve around the customer; without the customer, nothing gets sold. Firms must discover their customers' wants and needs and then be able to provide a valuable product or service that will satisfy those needs. If there were only one firm and many customers, a marketer's life would be a piece of cake. But because this setup rarely occurs, firms must monitor their competitors to discover how they might be appealing to their customers. Marketing life certainly would be difficult, if not impossible, without corporate partners. Good marketing firms work closely with their suppliers, marketing research firms, consultants, and transportation firms to coordinate the extensive process of discovering what customers want and getting it to them when and where they want it. Each of these activities—identifying corporate strengths, discovering customer needs, and working with corporate partners—is central to the firm's marketing strategy and helps add value to firms' products and services.

LO3 Identify the factors in a firm's macroenvironment

The factors in the firm's external environment are culture, demographics, social trends, technological advances, economic situation, and political/legal environment (CDSTEP). A clear understanding of these factors enables marketers to understand whether they pose threats or present new opportunities.

LO4 Explain how the factors in a firm's macroenvironment influence its marketing strategy

To be successful, marketers must understand fully what is going on outside their firm. For instance, what are the chances that a fast-food hamburger restaurant would be successful in a predominantly Hindu neighbourhood? Right—not very good. Marketers must be sensitive to such cultural issues to be successful, and then they must also consider competitors as well as customer demographics—age, gender, income, race, ethnicity, and education—to identify specific customer groups. In any society, major social trends influence the way people live. Understanding these trends—such as green marketing, marketing to children, privacy issues, and the time-poor society—can help marketers serve their customers better. Furthermore, in no other time in history has technology moved so rapidly and had such a pervasive influence on the way we live. Not only do marketers help to develop technologies for practical, everyday uses, but technological advances also help marketers provide consumers with more products and services more quickly and efficiently. In addition, the general state of the economy influences how people spend their disposable income. When the economy is healthy, marketing grows relatively easy. But when the economy gets bumpy, only well-honed marketing skill can yield long-term successes. Naturally, all firms must abide by the law, but many legal issues also affect marketing directly. These laws can be broken into those that pertain to competitive practices, such as antitrust legislation, and those designed to protect consumers from unfair or dangerous practices, such as warning labels on cigarette packages. Basically, a clear understanding of these macroenvironmental factors will enable marketers to design marketing strategies that are better suited to the needs of their target customers.

LO5 Identify today's important social trends and describe why they affect marketing decisions

Social trends have a tremendous impact on what consumers purchase and consume. Understanding these trends—such as price sensitivity, health and wellness, green marketing, privacy issues, and the time-poor society—can help marketers serve their customers better by offering them products and services that closely match their needs and wants.

Key Terms

- baby boomers, 97
- competitive intelligence (CI), 90
- country culture, 93
- culture, 92
- demographics, 94
- economic situation, 107
- foreign currency fluctuations, 107
- generation X, 95
- generation Y, 95
- generational cohort, 94
- green marketing, 101
- inflation, 107
- interest rates, 107
- macroenvironmental factors, 92
- political/legal environment, 108
- recession, 108
- seniors, 97
- technological advances, 104
- tweens, 94

Concept Review

1. List the three elements a firm must assess before looking externally (i.e., the microenvironment).

2. List and describe the elements of a firm's macroenvironment. Select a Canadian company that you think has done a great job at managing the macroenvironmental factors and discuss what it has done.

3. List five ways in which baby boomers, generation X, and generation Y are different.

4. If a store permanently offers extended shopping hours, what macroenvironmental factor(s) is it appealing to?

5. List some of the important social and cultural trends affecting the Canadian market.

6. Besides language, explain why using the same advertisement for Ontario and for Quebec wouldn't be equally successful.

7. Why should marketers care about engaging tweens quickly and sincerely?

8. How do changes in the value of the Canadian dollar vis-à-vis the U.S. dollar affect Canadian companies that sell to American consumers?

9. Why is understanding cultures and subcultures so important in marketing?

10. The Chinese and South Asian consumer segment is a rapidly growing segment in Canada. What opportunities and challenges does this trend pose for food and grocery retailers? What strategies could they use to market effectively to this segment of consumers?

Marketing Applications

1. Assume you are going to open a new store. Describe it. Who are your competitors? What would you do to monitor your competitors' actions?

2. In which generational cohort do you belong? What about your parents? How would you approach buying a car differently than your parents? What about buying an outfit to wear to a party? How can firms use their knowledge of generational cohorts to market their products and services better?

3. How can firms use customer demographics such as income, education, and ethnicity to market to their customers better?

4. Identify some of the changes in the gender landscape. Describe how they might affect the marketing practices of (a) men's apparel retailers, (b) do-it-yourself home improvement retailers, and (c) upscale salon services.

5. Identify some recent technological innovations in the marketplace and describe how they have affected consumers' everyday activities.

6. Do you feel that firms are invading or could invade your privacy? Why or why not?

7. Why should Canadian companies selling goods in the United States care about the value of the U.S. dollar?

8. Time-poor consumers have adopted various approaches to "buy" themselves more time, such as (a) voluntarily simplifying their complex lives, (b) using new technologies for greater empowerment and control, (c) using their time productively when travelling or commuting, and (d) multitasking. Identify and describe some products and services that consumers use to implement each of these strategies.

9. Identify a company that you believe does a particularly good job of marketing to different cultural groups. Justify your answer.

10. You have recently been hired by a major department store in its marketing department. Your boss informs you that you are going to supervise a field research study. You arrive at your assigned store and find that the study consists of shadowing customers. The store has set up a "private" shopping event for store credit card holders. All who attend must swipe their cards to receive the special discount coupon book. The shadow shoppers (who the store manager hired) are given hand-held devices loaded with a specific customer's information and past purchase behaviour. Thus, each shadow shopper knows the name, address, income, family size, and spending patterns for the customer she or he is observing. You begin to feel uncomfortable about this study since the consumers have no idea they are being tracked, nor do they know the level of confidential information about them that a stranger can access. You are also concerned that the shadow customers are not regular employees or employees of an established marketing research provider. What, if anything, would or should you do about your concerns?

Net Savvy

1. Seventh Generation is the leading brand of nontoxic, environmentally safe household products in Canada (they are sold at Home Depot). Visit Seventh Generation's website (www.seventhgeneration.com) and review the philosophy behind the business. Next, review the site to identify the products that the company offers. Briefly summarize some of the consumer trends you note, and describe the ways in which the company's products address the wants and needs of its customers.

2. The Internet has been a double-edged sword for consumers. On the one hand, it provides easy access to many businesses and sources for information. On the other hand, consumers must give up some of their privacy to access this information. The Privacy Rights Clearinghouse provides information to consumers about privacy and opt-out strategies. Visit its website (www.privacyrights.org) and review the privacy survival guide. From that document, select and describe three actions you might take to protect your own privacy.

Chapter Case Study

CAN E-BOOKS REPLACE PRINT BOOKS AND KILL THE CHAIN BOOKSTORE?[72]

E-books have been with us for more than a decade now, but they have largely remained a niche market.[73] In fact, early e-book readers (or e-readers), such as the Rocket eBook in 1998 and the Sony LIBRIé in 2004, failed to gain widespread consumer acceptance. However, recent evidence indicates an increase in the demand for e-books and e-readers. Many industry analysts view this resurgence in demand as the tipping point for e-books to move from a niche market to a mainstream market. Despite the numerous opportunities facing the industry, it still must overcome many challenges to achieve its full potential. Nevertheless, the e-book landscape is getting increasingly crowded as new competitors enter the market. The latest entrant is Kobo, a small Canadian e-book service provider. Kobo is not just another player; it has entered the market with a vastly different approach that it hopes will forever change the way people buy and read books. Its goal is to enable e-book consumers to be able to read any book, anytime, anywhere, and on any device of their choice. Kobo's open software application allows consumers to read e-books on any e-reader, which is in stark contradiction to the industry norm of using a closed system. For example, only the Kindle e-reader can plug into Amazon's e-book store and download titles. Can Kobo, the small Canadian upstart, really change industry practices and emerge as the global market leader for e-books? Can e-books replace print books and spell the death of the chain bookstore? What will it take for this to happen?

E-books: The Concept and Benefits

Generally, *e-books* refers to digital content such as books, newspapers, and magazines that are offered in a format that can be read by various technology devices, including laptops, smartphones, tablets, and dedicated e-book readers such as Amazon's Kindle, Barnes & Noble's Nook, and the Kobo eReader. Some common e-book formats are PDF, ePub, and Publt. Most e-books are text-based, with virtually no interactivity or multimedia elements. Since e-books can be read from a variety of devices, consumers do not necessarily have to purchase an e-reader. However, e-readers seem to provide a better reading experience and offer more features than other devices. Except for Kobo's open, cross-platform e-reader application system, most applications currently in the market are closed or proprietary systems. This restriction means that consumers who buy Amazon's Kindle can purchase and download e-books from Amazon's store, but those with other e-readers, such as Barnes & Noble's Nook or a Sony e-reader, cannot plug in and load titles from Amazon since they are meant only for the Kindle. These types of closed systems limit consumer choices, stifle competition and innovation, and hamper the development of the industry. The Kobo software application, ePub, is an open system designed to give consumers access to content regardless of the readers they choose.

How and why do consumers purchase e-books? E-books can be bought as downloads from the websites of e-book service providers or their retailers. Consumers with dedicated e-readers could purchase books directly from their e-book provider via WiFi, 3G, or a computer or device that is connected to the Internet, depending on the capability of their e-readers. Consumers with e-readers that do not have WiFi or 3G capability must first download the e-book on another Internet-connected device and then transfer the e-book to their e-reader via USB or Bluetooth.

E-books are appealing for many reasons and each consumer will have his or her own motivation for choosing e-books. Environmentally conscious consumers may choose e-books because they save on paper, ink, printing, and all the harmful effects the printing industry has on the environment. Consumers who prefer to read on a screen will find e-books appealing since they can adjust the typeface, type size, and backlight on their devices to make reading easier. Consumers who like to read and do not want to carry around several books will find the e-reader a convenient alternative since they can carry multiple books in one small device. Consumers who want to purchase any title, anytime, anyplace will also find e-readers, especially those with WiFi or 3G capability, very appealing. For price conscious consumers, e-books are often cheaper than books, but they may have to incur additional cost to buy an e-reader. For publishers, e-books are faster and cheaper to produce and distribute than print books. They are also much easier to update or correct. Thus, e-book providers could offer customers a better price and still earn a good margin. For authors and content providers who own copyrights to their works, e-books offer a cheaper and faster way for their works to be published.

The Opportunities and Challenges

The resurgence in demand for e-books can be traced back to three broader social trends. First, a growing number of publishers and content providers are increasing the amount of content they make available via e-books. Second, it is a growing trend for people to carry PDAs and spend a considerable amount of time reading on a small, mobile screen. People who grew up with the Internet and cellphones are particularly likely to do this. Consequently, making the transition to an e-reader should be relatively easy for them. Third, the trend among people of all ages to communicate, interact, collaborate, and socialize through mobile devices and mobile media could make the acceptance of e-books and e-readers more plausible. In fact, in April 2010, less than four years after Amazon launched the Kindle, its e-book sales surpassed sales of hard-copy books, with 105 e-books sold for every 100 print books.[74]

Despite the benefits of e-books, the industry must overcome challenges before e-books become a widespread phenomenon. A major stumbling block is the cost and quality of e-book readers. Industry analysts argue that current e-reader prices, which range from $139 to $300, are far too expensive to make using them an economical choice for the mass market. Also, the e-readers in the market today lack many basic features needed to create a functional and enjoyable reading experience. In addition, the practice where every e-book service provider has its own proprietary e-book application fragments the market and undermines its long-term vibrancy. Finally, today's e-books are primarily text-based and offer very little multimedia, interactive, and "smart" features that could enrich the reading experience. For instance, an e-book on weight loss could enable readers to interact with it by entering, for example, their weight, age, sex, and other relevant information, and immediately suggest a diet and exercise plan based on the information provided. Essentially, the technology must keep pace with the needs of consumers for convenience, affordability, and functionality.

Kobo, the Canadian Player

What role can Kobo play to change the game? Kobo was launched in December 2009, with backing from Indigo Books and Music, Borders, REDgroup Retail, and Cheung Kong Holdings. Indigo Books and Music controls about 60 percent of the company. In March and June 2010, Kobo entered the United Kingdom and the United States, respectively. It also established distribution channels in the European Union, Australia, New Zealand, Hong Kong, and other territories. Additionally, Kobo established partnerships with publishers, manufacturers, and retailers around the world in order to source content, distribute its e-reader device and application, and get its application preloaded on various technologies, such as smartphones, tablets, and laptops. Kobo has more than 2 million e-books, covering a wide range of genres and bestsellers from around the world. It has readers in more than 200 countries and has access to 100 million consumers through its distribution partners.

The Kobo application is available for free download at the App Store, BlackBerry App World, Palm App Catalog, Android Marketplace, or at www.kobobooks.com. Kobo features thousands of free e-books, so users can try eReading for free. Kobo's eReader application allows users to read e-books in both standard ePUB and PDF formats. The eReader application supports a range of hardware options with various screen types, including eInk and LCD screens. It does not have 3G or WiFi connectivity, a colour screen, or audio playback features like the Kindle or the Nook, as these elements would drive up the price. Therefore, e-books must first be purchased through Kobo's website, using a computer or a smartphone, and then transferred to the Kobo eReader via Bluetooth or USB.

Basically, the Kobo eReader device and software application aims to make electronic reading more enjoyable, affordable, and accessible. Experts say that its most crucial feature is that it operates on an open platform. When you buy a Kobo e-book, it can be downloaded on your Kobo device or, if you prefer, your desktop, laptop, smartphone, or a Sony e-reader. According to Kobo, consumers who buy a Kobo eReader can switch to another device at any time and transfer the books they have already bought to the new device. This means that the library a consumer creates with Kobo is easily portable to another device.

Kobo eReader, priced at US$139 (the lowest e-reader price in the market), is currently the smallest of the e-readers. It is capable of holding up to 1000 e-books. Amazon's Kindle 3, the most popular e-reader, also sells for US$139; it can carry up to 1500 e-books. Both have the capability of storing more e-books by using external memory. A comparison of the Kobo eReader with other leading devices is presented in the table below, which is adapted from Forrester Research.

Brand	Amazon Kindle 3 & Kindle DX	Sony Reader Digital Book	Barnes & Noble Nook	Alex eReader	Pandigital Novel	Kobo*
Price (US$)	$139–$329	$229–$299	$149–$249	$399	$199	$139
Screen Size (inches)	Kindle 3:6 Kindle DX 9.7	6	6	6	7	6
Wireless	Yes	No	Yes	Yes	No	No
Touchscreen	No	Yes	Yes	Yes	No	No
Colour	No	Some models	Some models	No	No	No

For a more detailed comparison of these and other models on more dimensions, visit http://ebook-reader-review.toptenreviews.com.

Source: Forrester Research, Inc.

In addition, the following quotations give a flavour of the media perceptions of Kobo's device and system.

The $149 price point is one of the lowest around for an e-book reader and compared to a couple of others I have tried lately. I think the hardware on the Kobo eReader is better than most of these other devices.—**ZDNet**

By adopting the cross-platform ePub standard, Kobo is lining up with those trying to prove to the world's new digital book consumers that there's a better way ahead than Amazon's Kindle, which has proprietary software locking its titles into its own device.—**BBC News**

Kobo is so far the best and most comprehensive service we have used to buy and read books, especially for non-US residents. . . . The Kobo app puts Amazon's rushed-out Kindle for iPhone to shame.—**Wired**

The Future

Not every publisher in the book industry seems willing to concede the future of reading to technology companies. Penguin Books, for example, seems unwilling at this moment to accept the ePub format embraced by Kobo and others. Penguin Books wants to embed audio, video, and streaming into its digital content. The ePub format, which is the standard for e-books at present, is designed to support traditional narrative text but not this cool stuff. Thus, it seems that establishing an e-book standard is premature until a better understanding of the full potential of e-books and e-reader technology is obtained.

Questions

1. Briefly explain what the competitive advantages of Kobo's e-book system are. Are these advantages sustainable over time?

2. What factors in Kobo's microenvironment do you think are responsible for Kobo's success?

3. Identify and describe the macroenvironmental factors that could influence the success of Kobo's business.

 Practise and learn online with Connect. Connect allows you to practise important concepts at your own pace and on your own schedule, with 24/7 online access to an eBook, practice quizzes, interactivities, videos, study tools, additional resources, and more.

CHAPTER 4

E.D. SMITH

Triple Fruits™*

1/3 MORE FRUIT
1/3 LESS SUGAR
THAN OUR JAM WITH PECTIN

WBERRY
ERRY & RED PLUM

500 mL

Marketing
Research

So far, we have learned that effective marketing requires that marketers develop a deep and clear understanding of their company's strengths and weaknesses, their customers' needs, wants, and purchase characteristics, competitors' strengths and weaknesses, and their external environment by examining the CDSTEP factors. But how do marketers acquire such an understanding? Simply put, marketers conduct marketing research, which helps them make better decisions in order to ensure their company's survival, continued growth, and expansion. Let's consider the experience of E.D. Smith, a company that has been serving Canadians for more than a century in a highly competitive market. Few companies can boast this longevity.

For more than 125 years, E.D. Smith has provided Canadians with delicious, high-quality jams and spreads. To stay ahead in the highly competitive jam market, it needed to solicit feedback from consumers to make its products even better. Many companies turn to consumer focus groups and survey feedback from customers for this data. But E.D. Smith did even better than that: it went face-to-face with customers in the jam aisle. In cooperation with its research company, E.D. Smith polled more than 3000 consumers across the country to better understand how to improve existing products and how to market them effectively.

E.D. Smith's marketing team feels strongly about talking directly with consumers. Interacting right in the aisle generates more genuine comments. Also, by talking to shoppers who are about to buy jam, researchers can uncover real insights and get at what's really on grocery shoppers' minds at the point of purchase. The results are more real and researchers observe more emotional responses than what's revealed in a survey or questionnaire. And customers

Learning Objectives

After studying this chapter, you should be able to

LO1 Describe the five steps in the marketing research process

LO2 Explain the differences between secondary data and primary data, and specify when each should be used

LO3 Identify various internal and external secondary data sources

LO4 Describe various primary data collection techniques

LO5 Outline ethical issues firms encounter when conducting marketing research

get to test the products! On-the-spot taste tests helped the research team at E.D. Smith learn that most consumers found jams to be far too sweet. Promotional tools were also investigated. Consumers said they were most likely to take advantage of a coupon as a way to try a new product.

Acting on its new research findings, E.D. Smith made big changes to stay competitive. Three new product lines were introduced into the market: reduced-sugar jams, triple fruit spreads with reduced sugar, and even a no-sugar-added line of spa-inspired jams.[1] As well, packaging was redesigned to clearly communicate the no-sugar feature. Coupons attached to store shelves encouraged customers to try these innovative products. Using the information from the grocery store studies to develop new products has helped E.D. Smith retain its leadership in the jam aisle.

How would you describe the method used by E.D. Smith to get customer feedback? What other methods could E.D. Smith researchers have used to get the feedback they needed? What are the limitations of the approach E.D. Smith used? What criteria do you think is most important in deciding what research method to use? ..::

marketing research
A set of techniques and principles for systematically collecting, recording, analyzing, and interpreting data that can aid decision makers involved in marketing goods, services, or ideas.

As the E.D. Smith example shows, **marketing research** is a key prerequisite to successful decision making; it consists of a set of techniques and principles for systematically collecting, recording, analyzing, and interpreting data that can aid decision makers involved in marketing goods, services, or ideas.[2] When marketing managers attempt to develop their strategies, marketing research can provide valuable information that will help them make segmentation, positioning, product, place, price, and promotion decisions. Marketing research is also key to understanding topics such as consumer and B2B buying behaviour (Chapters 5 and 6), global marketing and cultural differences (Chapter 16), new product development, branding, and customer service (Chapters 8 to 10), and for assessing the effectiveness of pricing, promotions, and product and service delivery strategies (Chapters 11 to 15).

As shown in our chapter roadmap, we will discuss the five steps in the marketing research process, as well as the various types of data used in marketing research and data collection methods. We will also examine the circumstances under which it is ethical to collect and use customer information in marketing research.

Firms invest millions of dollars in marketing research every year. Canada's market research industry is valued at just under a half-billion dollars. Some of the major players in Canada's multimillion dollar market research and polling industry include Angus Reid, COMPAS, Harris/Decima, EKOS Research Associates, Ipsos Reid, Leger Marketing, Pollara, and The Strategic Counsel. In addition, there are foreign-owned firms with offices in Canada, such as Nielsen Canada and Forrester Research. Why do marketers find this research valuable? First, it helps reduce some of the uncertainty under which they currently operate. Successful managers know when research might help their decision making and then take appropriate steps to acquire the information they need. Second, marketing research provides a crucial

CHAPTER ROADMAP

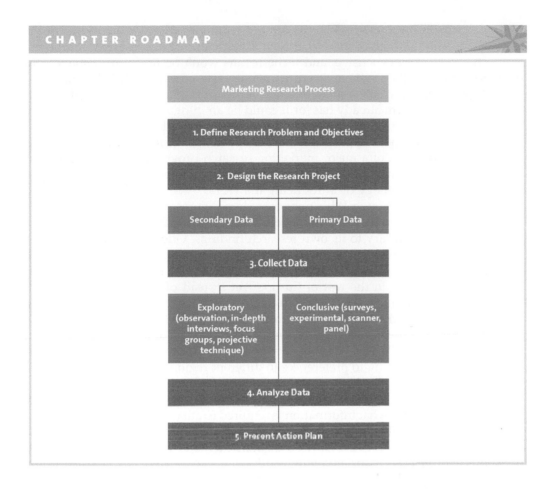

link between firms and their environments, which enables firms to be customer-oriented because they build their strategies by using customer input and continual feedback. Third, by constantly monitoring their competitors, firms can anticipate and respond quickly to competitive moves. Fourth, ongoing marketing research can identify emerging opportunities and new and improved ways of satisfying consumer needs and wants from changes in the external environment.

If you think market research is applicable only to corporate or retailing ventures, think again. Nonprofit organizations and governments also use research to serve their constituencies better. Political parties have been slicing and dicing the voting public for decades to determine relevant messages for different demographics. Politicians desperately want to understand who makes up the voting public to determine how to reach them. They want to know not only your political views, but also your media habits, such as what magazines you subscribe to, so they can target you more effectively.[3] To do so, they rely on the five-step marketing research process we describe in this chapter.

Politicians and nonprofit organizations do research to understand their constituencies.

The Marketing Research Process

L01

Managers consider several factors before embarking on a marketing research project. First, will the research be useful? Will it provide insights beyond what the managers already know and reduce uncertainty associated with the project? Second, is top management committed to the project and willing to abide by the results of the research? Related to both of these questions is the value of the research. Marketing research can be very expensive, and if the results won't be useful or management does not abide by the findings, it represents a waste of money. Third, should the marketing research project be small or large? A project might involve a simple analysis of data that the firm already has, or it could be an in-depth assessment that costs hundreds of thousands of dollars and takes months to complete.

Consider Whirlpool's approach to the European market for washing machines.[4] Although the findings of a major marketing research program indicated that there were significant regional differences in consumer preferences, managers stayed committed to their strategy of introducing the World Washer, which could be sold in all EU markets. Although Whirlpool considered its research to be a worthwhile project, it was not particularly valuable to the firm because it continued to pursue a strategy that was contrary to its own research findings. Offering the same machine to different regions failed to address different preferences in the marketplace, such as Britons' preference to wash laundry more frequently by using quieter machines than their neighbours in the rest of Europe. Yet instead of a localization strategy, Whirlpool relies on innovation to design its new products. One of its new washing machines in Europe, the Aqua Steam, can inject steam into the washing machine to remove stains at high temperatures or even sterilize baby clothing.[5] While the company maintained its "World Washer" strategy, its European competitors continued to innovate by responding to preferences in different regions by offering products to meet their special needs.

Because research is both expensive and time-consuming, it is important to establish in advance exactly what information is required to answer specific research questions, and how that information should be obtained. Researchers assess the value of a project through a careful comparison of the benefits of answering some of their questions and the costs associated with conducting the research. For instance, going back to Whirlpool's European washing machine study, suppose the company had a choice of conducting in-depth interviews with several hundred washing machine owners at a cost of $200 per interview or doing an online survey with the same number of respondents but at a cost of only $2 per questionnaire. Which data collection method should Whirlpool use? Clearly the questionnaires are much less expensive, but the in-depth interviews provide richer information that would be virtually impossible to access through questionnaires. As this simple example shows, there are always value trade-offs in marketing research. Researchers can always design a more expensive study and eke out more and better information; but, in the end, they should choose the method that will provide them with the information they need at the lowest cost.

The marketing research process itself consists of five steps, as shown in Exhibit 4.1. Although the stages of the marketing research process are shown as a step-by-step progression, of course, research doesn't always happen this way. Sometimes, researchers go back and forth from one step to another as the need arises. For example, marketers may establish a specific research objective, which they follow with data collection and preliminary analysis. If they uncover new information during the data collection step or if the findings of the analysis spotlight new research needs, they might redefine their objectives and begin again from a new starting point. A major automobile manufacturer once set out to identify consumer responses to its new company logo, only to discover in preliminary focus groups that some

While Whirlpool chose to pursue a "World Washer" strategy in Europe that was contrary to its own research findings, its European competitors continued to innovate by responding to preferences in different regions.

Whirlpool Corporation
Building unmatched loyalty one customer at a time.

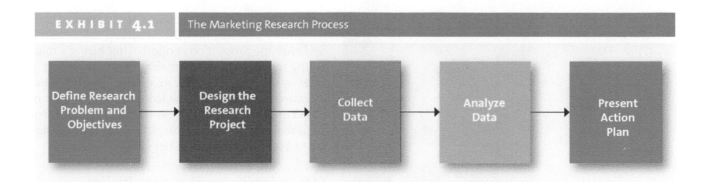

EXHIBIT 4.1 | The Marketing Research Process

Define Research Problem and Objectives → Design the Research Project → Collect Data → Analyze Data → Present Action Plan

of the respondents thought the company had gone out of business! Clearly, those researchers had to regroup and set out in a different direction with an entirely different objective.

Another important step when embarking on a research project is to plan the entire project in advance. For example, when setting up a questionnaire, marketers should consider the data collection process and anticipate the types of analyses that might produce meaningful results for decision makers. For example, open-ended questions on a questionnaire can slow down the coding process and make it difficult to run some sophisticated statistical analyses. If the decision makers want a sophisticated analysis fast, a questionnaire filled with open-ended questions may not be the best choice. By planning the entire research process well in advance of starting the project, researchers can avoid unnecessary alterations to the research plan as they move through the process. Now let's examine each step of the research process in more detail.

The major advantage of using primary data collection such as focus groups for market research is that marketers can tailor the research to fit the pertinent research questions. But primary data is usually more expensive and takes longer to collect than secondary data.

Step 1: Define the Research Problem and Objectives

Correctly defining the marketing problem is one of the most important elements of the marketing research process. To underscore the importance of this first step, some marketing researchers claim that this aspect is the most difficult of the marketing research process. Why? If you define the problem incorrectly, you will more than likely end up with the wrong solution even though the rest of the process is done perfectly. On the contrary, if you define the problem correctly but fail to carry out the rest of the process correctly, you may end up with results that may be useless or even misleading. Once the research problem is defined, marketers must specify the research objectives or questions to be answered. Marketing research efforts and resources can be wasted if the research objectives are poorly defined.[6] Poor design arises from three major sources: basing research on irrelevant research questions, focusing on research questions that marketing research cannot answer, or addressing research questions to which the answers are already known. However, timely and focused marketing research could help companies refine their marketing efforts and campaigns. Thus, market researchers devote considerable effort to defining the problem and trying to separate the symptoms of a problem from the actual problem.

For example, Wendy, the owner of a small clothing store in downtown Ottawa that caters to girls between the ages of 10 and 16, thought that the declining sales she was observing in her store were due to inadequate or poor advertising. Thus, she increased her advertising and promotions to boost sales and regain her lost

The objective of a company's research project is to evaluate its position in the marketplace relative to its competitors. For example, a company could research the position of its men's cologne brand.

customers. Unfortunately, this effort provided only temporary benefits, and the declining sales continued after the promotions ended. After hiring a marketing researcher, Wendy realized that the declining sales were just a symptom of the real problem: outdated merchandise. She learned that the current target market of 10 to 16 year olds is quite different from their predecessors, the girls who were this age when Wendy first opened her store.

Step 2: Design the Research Project

The second step in the marketing research project involves design. In this step, researchers identify the type of data needed and determine the type of research necessary to collect it. Recall that the objectives of the project drive the type of data needed, as outlined in Step 1. Let's look at how this second step works by using a hypothetical example about marketing cologne.

A marketer of a national brand of men's cologne sets out to evaluate its position in the marketplace relative to its competitors (i.e., a benchmarking project). The specific purpose of the marketing research is twofold: to determine the brand's current relative market share (Chapter 2) and to assess how that position will change in the next few years.

Identifying the type of data needed for the first purpose—determining relative market share—is fairly straightforward. It requires finding the company's sales during a particular time frame relative to the largest firm in the industry.

Identifying the type of data needed for the second purpose—assessing the extent to which the firm's market position will improve, stay the same, or deteriorate—is not as easy to obtain. For instance, the company's marketers might want to assess customers' brand loyalty, because if the company enjoys high levels of loyalty, the future looks rosier than if loyalty is low. The company's relative market share in relation to that of its competitors over time can also shed light on the future of its market position. The firm will want to know which firms have been gaining market share and which are losing.

The marketer must now decide whether the data required to make a decision should be obtained from secondary sources or primary sources.

LO2

secondary data
Pieces of information that have been collected prior to the start of the focal project.

LO3

Secondary Data   are pieces of information that have been collected prior to the start of the focal research project. Secondary data include both external and internal data sources. A marketing research project often begins with a review of the relevant secondary data. Secondary data might come from free or very inexpensive external sources such as census data, information from trade associations, the Internet, books, journal articles, and reports published in magazines and newspapers. Although readily accessible, these inexpensive sources may not be specific or timely enough to solve the marketer's research needs and objectives. Primary data, in contrast, are those data collected to address the specific research needs/questions currently under investigation. Some primary data collection methods include focus groups, in-depth interviews, and surveys.

A marketing research project often begins with a review of the relevant internal and external secondary data, such as the company's own records and other published sources, including those listed in Exhibits 4.2 and 4.3. Generally, secondary data can be quickly accessed at a relatively low cost. For example, Statistics Canada data on retail trade provides data about sales of different types of retail establishments either free or inexpensively. These patterns may be the only accurate sources available to a new small business that wants to determine the size of its potential market. For such a firm, gathering accurate and comprehensive data on its own would be quite difficult. Researchers must ensure that the secondary data they use, especially from external sources, are current, are relevant, and can shed light on the research problem or objectives.

EXHIBIT 4.2	Sample List of Sources for Secondary Data

Guides, Indexes, and Directories
Business Periodicals Index
Canadian Almanac and Directory
Canadian News Index
Canadian Periodical Index
Canadian Small Business Index and Directory
Canadian Trade Index
Directory of Canadian Associations
Fraser's Canadian Trade Directory
Predicasts F&S Index
Scott's Directories
Standard Periodical Directory

Statistics Canada and Other Government Publications
Annual Retail Trade
Canadian Economic Observer
Canada Yearbook
Family Expenditure Guide
Market Research Handbook
Statistics Canada Catalogue
Western Economic Diversification Canada
Ontario Ministry for Economic Development and Trade
Department of Foreign Affairs and Trade
U.S. Census
Stat-USA

Periodicals and Newspapers
Advertising Age
Adweek
American Demographics
Business Horizons
Canadian Business
Canadian Consumer
Canadian Grocer
Forbes
Fortune
Harvard Business Review
Journal of Advertising
Journal of Marketing Management
Journal of Personal Selling and Sales Management
Journal of Small Business Management
LexisNexis
Marketing Magazine
Marketing & Media Decisions
Marketing News
Canadian Grocer
Sales and Marketing Management
The Globe and Mail
Financial Post
Financial Post Magazine
The Wall Street Journal

Trade Sources
Aberdeen Research
Nielsen
Conference Board of Canada
Dun & Bradstreet Canada
Financial Post Publishing
Find/SVP
Gale Research
Interactive Advertising Bureau
Jupiter Research
Forrester Research
MacLean Hunter Research Bureau
MapInfo Canada
Predicasts International

Online Sources
Websites of competitors
White papers from industry associations
Search engines
Industry publication websites
Competitive annual reports
Business and strategy sites (e.g., www.canadianbusiness.com)
News alerts and online news searches (e.g., Google Alerts)
Finance sites for publicly traded companies (e.g., Yahoo! Finance)
Wikipedia (Always validate data from here!)
The Free Library (www.thefreelibrary.com)

Databases
CANSIM (Statistics Canada)
CompuServe
Dialog
Dow Jones
Factiva
FPinfomart
Infoglobe
SEDAR
SymphonyIRI Group

Source: Adapted from Crane, Kerin, Hartley, Berkowitz, and Rudelius, *Marketing*, 6th Canadian ed. (Whitby ON: McGraw-Hill Ryerson, 2007).

EXHIBIT 4.3	Syndicated Data Providers in Canada and the United States and Their Services
Bureau of Broadcasting Measurement (http://bbm.ca)	Provides broadcast measurement and consumer behaviour data, as well as intelligence to broadcasters, advertisers, and agencies on audience behaviours during and after broadcasts.
GfK Mediamark Research Inc. (www.gfkmri.com)	Supplies multimedia audience research pertaining to media and marketing planning for advertised brands.
GfK NOP (www.gfknop.com)	The mKids US research study tracks mobile telephone ownership and usage, brand affinities, and entertainment habits of American youth between 12 and 19 years of age.
Ipsos Canada, Harris/Decima, Leger Marketing, Angus Reid, SES Research, EKOS Research Associates, The Strategic Counsel, Pollara, and COMPAS	Provides polling services and marketing research on all aspects of marketing, including loyalty, branding, media analysis, pricing, position, image enhancement, customer satisfaction, focus groups, online panels, and surveys across many industries.
J.D. Power and Associates (www.jdpower.com)	Widely known for its automotive ratings, the company produces quality and customer satisfaction research for a variety of industries.
National Purchase Diary Group (www.npd.com)	Tracking services provide information about product movement and consumer behaviour in a variety of industries.
Nielsen (www.nielsen.com)	With its market measurement services, the company tracks the sales of consumer packaged goods, gathered at the point of sale in retail stores of all types and sizes.
Print Measurement Bureau (www.pmb.ca)	Provides single-source data on print readership, non-print media exposure, product usage, and lifestyles of Canadians. It uses an annual sample of 24 000 to measure the readership of more than 115 publications and consumer usage of more than 2500 products and brands.
Research and Markets (www.researchandmarkets.com)	Promotes itself as a "one-stop shop" for market research and data from most leading publishers, consultants, and analysts.
Roper Centre for Public Opinion Research (www.ropercenter.uconn.edu)	The General Social Survey is one of the United States's longest running surveys of social, cultural, and political indicators.
Simmons Market Research Bureau (www.smrb.com)	Reports on the products American consumers buy, the brands they prefer, and their lifestyles, attitudes, and media preferences.
Yankelovich (www.yankelovich.com)	The MONITOR tracks the consumer attitudes, values, and lifestyles shaping the American marketplace.

Sometimes, however, secondary data are not adequate to meet researchers' needs. Because the data initially were acquired for some purpose other than the research question at hand, they may not be completely relevant. For instance, Statistics Canada's Census is a great source for demographic data about a particular market area, and it can be easily accessed at a low cost. However, the data are collected only every 10 years, so they quickly become outdated. For example, if a firm were interested in opening a retail flooring store in 2014, it would have to rely on Statistics Canada Census data collected in 2006, which would be eight years old. If it hoped to locate in an area where housing starts are projected to grow rapidly in the next three to four years, these data would not include any of these new housing developments and thus would not provide much in the way of insights.

Although the secondary data described above is either free or inexpensive and can be quickly accessed, they may not always be adequate to answer the research objective. Under these circumstances, marketers may find it useful to purchase external secondary data called **syndicated data**, which are data available for a fee from commercial research firms such as SymphonyIRI Group, National Purchase Diary Panel, Nielsen, and Leger Marketing. Exhibit 4.3 contains information about various firms that provide syndicated data. For our hypothetical cologne example, the pertinent data available from these sources might include the prices of various colognes, sales figures, growth or decline in the category, and advertising and promotional spending. Consumer packaged goods firms that sell to wholesalers often lack the means to gather pertinent data directly from the retailers that sell their products to consumers, which makes syndicated data a valuable resource for them. Some syndicated data providers also offer information about shifting brand preferences and product usage in households, which they gather from consumer panels.

For example, Leger Marketing, one of the largest Canadian-owned independent marketing research and polling firms, has an online panel of 350 000 people that represents various consumer segments of the Canadian population. This impressive panel makes it possible for Leger Marketing to complete surveys among the general public and more-specific consumer segments. It is therefore hardly surprising that Leger Marketing can offer marketers a 48-hour service—a solution for businesses and decision makers who wish to receive reliable information quickly from a large representative sample of consumers regarding their marketing campaigns, products, and brands. Leger Marketing offers its clients strategic advice in a wide array of areas, including media and advertising analysis, marketing planning, market research, product launch, segmentation analysis, positioning, customer satisfaction and loyalty strategies, pricing and packaging strategies, mystery shoppers, and image assessment. It also offers website analytics, which marketers can use to evaluate and improve the performance of their websites.[7]

Finally, when it comes to secondary data, marketers must pay careful attention to how the secondary data were collected. Despite the great deal of data available on the Internet and elsewhere, easy access does not ensure that the data are trustworthy. Without knowing the research design, for instance, information pertaining to the purpose of the research, sample size, respondents, response rate, questions asked, and so on, researchers could make wrong or misleading inferences or conclusions. As described in Power of the Internet 4.1, the Internet is a huge repository of all sorts of information about consumers, including shopping behaviours, attitudes, perceptions, and even emotions. Marketers are increasingly relying on technologies to mine this data to help them learn more about customers so they can serve them better. In Appendix 7A, we will detail how secondary data can be used to assess customer lifetime value (CLV), a popular marketing metric to determine a customer's value to a firm.

Primary Data In many cases, the information researchers need is available only through **primary data**, or data collected to address the specific research needs/ questions currently under investigation. Marketers collect primary data by using a variety of means, such as observing consumer behaviour, conducting focus groups, or surveying customers by using the mail, telephone, in-person interviews, or the Internet. Primary data collection can help eliminate some of the problems inherent to secondary data.

A major advantage of primary research is that it can be tailored to fit the research questions; however, it also has its own set of disadvantages. For one thing, it is usually more costly to collect primary than secondary data, and the collection typically takes longer. Furthermore, marketers often require extensive training and experience to design and collect primary data that are unbiased, valid, and reliable. For a summary of the advantages and disadvantages of each type of research, see Exhibit 4.4. Biased data results when, for example, the sample does not represent the entire population, researchers inject their own biases by the way they ask questions or try to get respondents to answer in specific ways, or the respondents may be the wrong people or provide answers they think researchers want to hear.

syndicated data
Data available for a fee from commercial research firms such as SymphonyIRI Group, National Purchase Diary Panel, Nielsen, and Leger Marketing.

primary data
Data collected to address the specific research needs/questions currently under investigation. Some primary data collection methods include focus groups, in-depth interviews, and surveys.

Power of the Internet 4.1

Market Research: Out with the Old and In with the New?[8]

Today, most consumers turn to the Internet *first* when they are searching for information about a product or company. The increasing adoption of smartphones with web-browsing capability enables consumers to access the Internet anywhere, anytime. This availability means that consumers are always accessible to marketers. Apart from using their websites to share information with consumers, conduct commerce, and build relationships with customers, marketers use the Internet to varying degrees for research purposes. Marketers use online methods to obtain feedback from consumers about their level of satisfaction with their products and services, to analyze visitors web-surfing patterns, and to gauge consumers' attitudes, perceptions, behaviours, and emotions toward their products and marketing efforts. Consumers are invited to participate in short online surveys, quick polls, and contests, usually with the promise of the possibility of winning a prize or receiving an incentive. This type of customer feedback is inexpensive, easy to execute, and quick, helping marketers gather data and analyze it very quickly.[9]

In addition, marketers use a wide variety of web tools and applications, such as web analytics software to analyze website traffic patterns, Twitter's Trending Topics to find out what topics people think are worth sharing, and Google Hot Trends to learn what people are searching for at any particular moment. Real-time experiments can also be conducted to test a researcher's hypothesis about the popularity of a product or website and to provide immediate results. Social media, digital tools, and online conversations also create a variety of detailed metrics that market researchers can use to gain information about consumers' attitudes and opinions. Marketers can even connect a customer's online survey results with his or her transaction details, including what was purchased, how much was spent, whether items were on sale, whether coupons were used, the time of day, and the name of the cashier who served the customer.[10]

Indeed, the speed and ease with which data can be gathered and analyzed through the Internet has major appeal to marketers. But is this information of high quality? Marketing professor and consultant Jim Barnes warns that although the Internet generates tremendous volumes of useful information, the information is typically very tactical and not particularly insightful: it does not allow marketers to gain a deep understanding of their customers. While marketers are getting customer satisfaction information, they may be missing out on deeper thinking on what motivates, disappoints, satisfies, frustrates, impresses, or delights customers.[11] Further, the information is not representative of the customer base since it captures the views of *only* consumers who opt to participate. The importance of eliminating bias and ensuring that quality research is being conducted is being overshadowed by the constant availability and convenience of Internet data.[12] The use of online data calls into question the reliability and validity of the research results. In addition, marketers face huge challenges to make sense of the phenomenal amount of data gathered through the Internet.

Do these drawbacks mean marketers should not use Internet research? Far from it, as online research does provide useful insights. However, marketers must recognize the limitations associated with Internet research and work diligently to obtain reliable and valid data on which to make strategic decisions. How can market researchers balance the Internet's powerful capabilities with its limitations to harness its full potential as a market research tool?

EXHIBIT 4.4	Advantages and Disadvantages of Secondary and Primary Data		
Type	**Examples**	**Advantages**	**Disadvantages**
Secondary Research	• Census data • Sales invoices • Internet information • Books • Journal articles • Syndicated data	• Saves time in collecting data because they are readily available • Reduces data collection costs	• Information may not be precisely relevant to information needs • Information may not be as timely as needed • Sources may not be original; therefore, usefulness is an issue • Methodologies for collecting data may not be relevant or may contain bias in the subject matter
Primary Research	• Observed consumer behaviour • Focus groups • In-depth interviews • Surveys • Experiments	• Is specific to the immediate data needs and topic at hand • Offers behavioural insights generally not available from secondary research	• Information is usually more costly to collect • Data typically takes longer to collect • It often requires more sophisticated training and experience to design and collect unbiased, valid, and reliable data

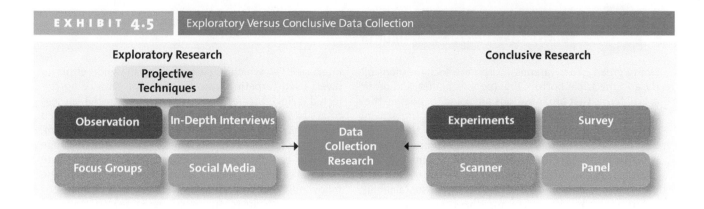

EXHIBIT 4.5 | Exploratory Versus Conclusive Data Collection

Data collection through primary research requires that the researcher makes several important decisions. These decisions include which methods to use (see Exhibit 4.5 for a list of various methods), what types of sampling plan is best in light of the research objective, what types of research instruments (e.g., questionnaire, observation) to use, how the research instrument should be designed (described below), and how best to contact potential respondents (telephone, online, in-person, or mail). Improper execution of any of these important aspects of primary data collection could seriously reduce the reliability and validity of the research study.

Simply put, **reliability** is the extent to which you will get the same result if the study is repeated under identical situations.[13] For example, on a Saturday in August you randomly stop shoppers in a mall and ask them to fill out a short questionnaire about why they shop at that particular mall. Let's say your data analysis shows that the reason they shop at that mall is because they get very good deals. Now, if you were to repeat the study in the same mall, using the same questionnaire, on another Saturday, and randomly ask shoppers to fill out the questionnaire, you should find the same result: people shop at the mall because they get good deals. If you found otherwise, then the reliability of your study is called into question. **Validity** is the extent to which the study actually measures what it is supposed to measure.[14] For example, suppose you want to measure consumers' trust in online retailers by using a questionnaire. Validity seeks to determine whether the questions you asked on the questionnaire actually measure online trust or if it measures some other construct. It is important to note that a market research study must be both reliable and valid for it to be useful.

One very important aspect of market research that can affect the reliability and validity of a study is the sampling plan. Often it is too difficult, impractical, or costly to study the entire group of consumers, so marketers usually select a **sample**, a segment or subset of the population that adequately represents the entire population of interest. For example, if you are interested in studying the loyalty of Canadian teenage boys to brand name clothing, then your population is all Canadian teenage boys and your sample is the small subset of boys selected for your study. How you select the sample is also very important. Three important questions that must be answered are (1) who should be surveyed, (2) how big should the sample be, and (3) what types of **sampling** procedure to use, for example, simple random sampling, convenience sampling, stratified sampling, or cluster sampling. More details on the sampling procedure are provided on Connect. Each of these sampling procedures has their advantages and disadvantages, and the decision as to which one to use will depend on the research objectives of the study. Although there is a formula in statistics to calculate required sample size, as a rule of thumb, sample sizes should be large enough to ensure the reliability of the study. Generally, larger samples tend to yield more reliable results up to a certain point.

reliability
The extent to which the same result is achieved when a study is repeated under identical situations.

validity
The extent to which a study measures what it is supposed to measure.

sample
A segment or subset of the population that adequately represents the entire population of interest.

sampling
The process of picking a sample.

| Sustainable Marketing 4.1 | Embedding Sustainability in the Organizational Culture[15] |

Going green, eco-awareness, corporate social responsibility, and the triple bottom line (people, planet, and profit) are all terms that organizations are using to redefine their organizational strategies. Many companies are striving to incorporate sustainability practices into their corporate cultures. They realize that to stay competitive they need to embrace sustainability strategies that will create long-term value for stakeholders. However, with little information available on how to implement sustainability practices, organizations are apprehensive about how to make sustainability a part of their corporate culture.

Research is being jointly conducted by the Network for Business Sustainability, which operates out of Ivey School of Business, and Canadian Business for Social Responsibility, which is a nonprofit business organization. The objective of the research is to provide organizations with a framework for incorporating sustainability into their corporate culture. The project is designed so that information and data can be collected from a few organizations that are successfully implementing sustainability initiatives. These organizations include LoyaltyOne, which is using eco-friendly Smart cars as company transportation when employees need to travel for business, and

InterfaceFLOR, which is part of a Canada-wide effort to divert used carpeting from landfills. The data being collected is linked to factors that contribute to the success of a sustainability strategy. Success is largely attributed to commitment from both employees and management. Interviews and panel discussions are conducted to gauge levels of commitment. Questions used to demonstrate the level of organizational commitment may include the following: What types of initiatives are being undertaken? How much of our resources are being devoted to these initiatives?

After the data is collected, it will be compiled, analyzed, and interpreted into useful and meaningful information. This information will be presented in a report about best sustainable practices. The report will provide a reference point for many organizations that are striving to make corporate sustainability a part of their cultures.

Because a systematic research process was used to define the objectives, design the study, collect relevant data, and interpret results, many organizations are being provided with reliable information that could enable them to successfully develop and implement their own sustainability strategies and cultures.

LO4

Step 3: Collect Data

Depending on the nature of the research problem, the data collection method can employ either an exploratory method or a conclusive research method.

exploratory research
Attempts to begin to understand the phenomenon of interest; also provides initial information when the problem lacks any clear definition.

As its name implies, **exploratory research** attempts to begin to understand the phenomenon of interest; it also provides initial information that helps the researcher more clearly formulate the research problem or objectives. Exploratory research is more informal and qualitative than conclusive research methods and includes observation, following social media sites, in-depth interviews, focus groups, and projective techniques (see Exhibit 4.5). Sustainable Marketing 4.1 shows how researchers are using exploratory research methods to develop a better understanding of how organizations can build sustainability into their organizational culture.

conclusive research
Provides the information needed to confirm preliminary insights, which managers can use to pursue appropriate courses of action.

If the firm is ready to move beyond preliminary insights gained from exploratory research, it is likely ready to engage in **conclusive research**, which provides the information needed to confirm those insights and which managers can use to pursue appropriate courses of action. For marketing researchers, because it is often quantitative in nature, conclusive research offers a means to confirm implicit hunches through surveys, formal studies such as specific experiments, scanner and panel data, or some combination of these (see Exhibit 4.5, right side). Conclusive research also enables researchers to test their prediction or **hypothesis**, which is a statement or proposition predicting a particular relationship among multiple variables. The following is an example of a hypothesis: customer satisfaction leads to or is positively related to customer loyalty.

hypothesis
A statement or proposition predicting a particular relationship among multiple variables that can be tested through research.

We now examine each of these primary data collection techniques, starting with the exploratory and ending with the conclusive. Many research projects use exploratory research as the first phase of the research process and then follow it up with conclusive research.

Exploratory (Qualitative) Research Methods

Observation   An exploratory research method, **observation** entails examining purchase and consumption behaviours through personal means or the use of technology, such as video camera or other tracking devices. For example, researchers might observe customers while they shop or when they go about their daily lives, during which processes they use a variety of products. Observation can last for a very brief period of time (e.g., two hours watching teenagers shop for clothing in the mall), or it may take days or weeks (e.g., researchers live with families to observe their use of products). When consumers are unable to articulate their experiences, observation research becomes particularly useful. How else could researchers determine which educational toys babies choose to play with or confirm purchase details that consumers might not be able to recall accurately? As Ethical Dilemma 4.1 describes, observational research can even be used to understand the differences among consumers when they shop in retail stores.

This family is being observed while cooking.

observation
An exploratory research method that entails examining purchase and consumption behaviours through personal or video camera scrutiny.

ethnography
An observational method that studies people in their daily lives and activities in their homes, work, and communities.

in-depth interview
A research technique in which trained researchers ask questions, listen to and record the answers, and then pose additional questions to clarify or expand on a particular issue.

Ethnography is an observational method that studies people in their daily lives and activities in their homes, work, and communities. It is often used when market researchers believe that potential respondents may be unable to express in a useful way their experiences with a product or service. This type of research yields insights and intimate details that respondents may not want to reveal. It is increasingly being used by companies (e.g., Unilever, P&G, Miller Brewing Co.). Ethnographic studies require highly trained researchers. They often use video cameras, audio recording devices, and diaries to keep detailed records of their observations. Analysis of ethnographic data requires very experienced and knowledgeable market researchers to make sense of hours of video tapes, audio tapes, or a volume of notes from the researcher's diary.

P&G sends video crews to households around the world to gain insights into life's daily routines.[16] This exercise yields priceless insights into consumer behaviour that could not be captured by using traditional methods such as interviews or focus groups. For example, people have selective memories and might tell a market researcher that they brush their teeth three times a day for two minutes each time. Camera crews capture a different picture though, sometimes leading to new products. Watching people sort laundry showed researchers piles of clothes that never went into the washing machine, which resulted in the creation of Dryel, a home dry-cleaning kit.[17]

In-Depth Interviews   An **in-depth interview** is an exploratory research technique in which trained researchers ask questions, listen to and record the answers, and then pose additional questions to clarify or expand on a particular issue. For instance, in addition to simply watching teenagers shop for apparel, interviewers might stop them one at a time in the mall to ask them a few questions, such as "We noticed that you went into and came out of Abercrombie & Fitch very quickly, and without buying anything. Why was that?" If the subject responds that no one had bothered to wait on her, the interviewer might ask a follow-up question, such as "Oh? Has that happened to you before?" or "Do you expect sales assistance in that store?" The results often provide insights that help managers better understand the nature of their industry, as well as important trends and consumer preferences, which can be invaluable for developing marketing strategies.

In-depth interviews have quite a few benefits. They can provide a historical context for the phenomenon of interest, particularly when they include industry

A consumer is being interviewed.

Ethical Dilemma 4.1

Getting Up-Close-and-Personal with Shoppers[18]

Successful marketing starts with knowing your customers: the more intimately you know them, the more likely you will be able to serve them. The key to learning about consumers is to get into their heads. This feat is terribly difficult, if not impossible, but is the challenge marketers face, especially in a fiercely competitive world where competition is global.

In addition, marketing professionals and researchers know that there is often a huge disconnect between what consumers tell them in surveys and focus groups and what the customers actually do when shopping in stores. Thus, many companies conduct in-store research, such as mall intercepts, distributing in-store trials, free samples, store displays, and simply observing consumers shop, to get a better understanding of consumers' attitudes and behaviours. Recently, Frito Lay Canada placed GPS devices on grocery carts to determine consumers' shopping patterns as they moved through a store. The device tracked the aisles consumers visited, the time they spent at particular spots, and so on. Frito Lay then translated that information into actionable game plans, going to its retailers and implementing merchandising tactics that responded to the findings.

Indeed, the use of observational research methods where consumers may be unaware that they are being studied is on the rise. In some cases, researchers obtain consent from the consumers they are watching and videotaping; but, in other cases, they do not. The ethical dilemma for marketing researchers centres on whether using observational techniques in which the subjects are not informed that they are being studied, such as viewing customers in a mall or a retail store, violates the rule of fair treatment. Observing uninformed consumers might lead to important insights that would not otherwise be discovered; but do the results justify the methodology?

Do you believe it is ethical for a firm to record the movements and activities of customers as they shop in a store? Would your opinion be different if the customers were informed that they were being watched?

experts or experienced consumers. They also can communicate how people really feel about a product or service at the individual level, a level that rarely emerges from other methods that use group discussions. Finally, marketers can use the results of in-depth interviews to develop surveys.

In-depth interviews, however, are relatively expensive and time-consuming. One interview may cost $200 or more, depending on its length and the characteristics of the people used in the sample. For instance, if the sample requires medical doctors, the costs of getting interviews will be higher than intercepting teenagers at a mall.

Focus Group   In **focus groups**, a small group of persons (usually 8 to 12) comes together for an in-depth discussion about a particular topic. Using an unstructured method of inquiry, a trained moderator guides the conversation on the basis of a predetermined general outline of the topics of interest. Researchers usually record the interactions on videotape or audiotape so they can carefully comb through the interviews later to catch any patterns of verbal or nonverbal responses.

In particular, focus groups gather qualitative data about initial reactions to a new or existing product or service, opinions about different competitive offerings, or reactions to marketing stimuli, like a new ad campaign or point-of-purchase display materials.

The Jones Apparel Group, for example, used focus groups to develop new products and an advertising campaign for its L.e.i. brand. A Fortune 500 company that produces apparel and accessories under the brand names Nine West, Jones New York, and Anne Klein New York,[19] Jones Apparel Group believed the L.e.i. brand was not connecting with its target market—juniors 13 to 17 years of age—and wanted to give the brand a facelift. To identify why consumers were not buying the brand, it conducted extensive focus groups, which revealed that juniors wanted the brand to be more inspirational and patriotic. Jones Apparel Group also discovered, because the focus groups told it so, that juniors were spending a lot of time online. Therefore, it has increased its use of the Internet, including sponsoring a contest on Myspace that involved consumers uploading photos of themselves waving the American flag. So far, the response to the brand update has been "outstanding."[20]

Virtual focus groups have started to make inroads into the market researchers' toolkit. Lego, for instance, invited more than 10 000 kids to participate in a virtual focus group to get ideas for new products.[21] The participants saw short lists of proposed toys and clicked on the ones they liked. They ranked their choices and even suggested new ideas. These ideas were fed, in turn, to other potential customers and were rated against the ideas from Lego's own toy creators. The new suggestions, in turn, got creative juices flowing among still other potential customers. The resulting product, the Star Wars Imperial Destroyer, was different from anything else in Lego's 73-year history—it was Lego's largest and most expensive set ever, at 3100 parts and with a $300 price tag. Its first production run sold out in less than five weeks.

Projective Technique   A **projective technique** is a type of qualitative research in which subjects are provided a scenario and asked to express their thoughts and feelings about it. For example, consumers may be shown a cartoon that has a consumer looking at a shelf display in a supermarket with a text box above the consumer. The respondent would write in their thoughts on the issue in the text box. Thus, the cartoon allows respondents to visualize the situation and project their thoughts or feelings by filling out the text box.

Social Media   Social media sites are a booming source of data for marketers. Marketers believe that social media can provide valuable information that could aid them in their marketing research and strategy endeavours. These social media sites can provide insights into what consumers are saying about the firm's own products or its competitor's products. Companies are learning a lot about their customers' likes, dislikes, and preferences not only by monitoring their past purchases, but also by monitoring their interactions with social network sites such as Facebook. Customers appear keen to submit their opinions about their own and friends' purchases and interests to polls and

focus group
A research technique in which a small group of persons (usually 8 to 12) comes together for an in-depth discussion about a particular topic, with the conversation guided by a trained moderator using an unstructured method of inquiry.

projective technique
A type of qualitative research in which subjects are provided a scenario and asked to express their thoughts and feelings about it.

Lego's Star Wars Imperial Destroyer, at 3100 parts and with a $300 price tag, was designed with the help of virtual focus groups.

blogs. Marketers are paying attention to online reviews about everything from restaurants to running shoes to jeans.[22]

Some firms are learning to use social media in very creative ways. The market research firm Communispace actually builds branded online communities for companies, such as Kraft. When it considered the launch of its South Beach product line, Kraft hired Communispace to create a virtual community of target consumers: 150 women who wanted to lose weight and 150 "health and wellness" opinion leaders. The participants openly shared their frustrations and difficulties with managing their weight because the community environment prompted them to sense that everyone on the site struggled with similar issues and concerns. By monitoring the community, Kraft learned that it would need to educate consumers about the South Beach Diet and would need to offer products that could address cravings throughout the day, not just at mealtimes. Six months after the line's introduction, Kraft had earned profits of $100 million.[23]

Many companies, including Ford Motor Company, PepsiCo, Coca-Cola, and Southwest Airlines, have added "heads of social media" to their management teams. These heads of social media take responsibility for scanning the Internet for blogs, postings, tweets, or Facebook posts in which customers mention their experience with a brand. By staying abreast of this continuous stream of information, a firm can gather the most up-to-date news about itself, its products, and its services, as well as its competitors. These social media searches allow companies to learn about customers' perceptions and resolve customer complaints they may never have heard about through other channels.[24]

One question that must be going through your mind at this stage is which of these primary qualitative data collection techniques are used most frequently. Generally, focus groups and in-depth interviews are used more frequently than personal observations, especially ethnography. Deciding which technique to use depends on several important considerations, such as the objective of the research, the cost to undertake the research, the time required to undertake the research, how soon the results are needed, and whether the marketer has the research expertise in-house or has to hire a market research firm to do the research, especially with methods such as ethnography and projective techniques. Normally, marketers have to make a trade-off between these considerations to get the results in a timely and cost-effective manner. Often a company may use several methods together to get actionable results.

Conclusive (Quantitative) Research Methods

Conclusive research is intended to verify insights and to aid decision makers in selecting a specific course of action.[25] Conclusive research can be descriptive in nature, such as when it profiles a typical user or non-user of a particular brand according to a survey. It can also be experimental, such as when a soft-drink producer conducts a taste test to determine which formulation of a green, high-caffeine drink is preferred by customers. Conclusive research can also be collected from the merchandise that is scanned at a store, or from a group of customers, known as a panel, who record all of their purchases. In this section, we will discuss four conclusive research techniques: survey, experiment, scanner, and panel.

Survey Research   Survey research is probably the most popular type of conclusive research method used in marketing research. It is widely used to study consumers' attitudes, preferences, behaviours, and knowledge about products and brands. It is generally more cost-effective than other methods for reaching a large sample of consumers. Survey questionnaires usually yield quantitative data that can be easily analyzed by using sophisticated statistical methods to examine the relationships among variables. However, it suffers from a few shortcomings. Consumers may be unable to answer some of the questions on the questionnaire, may not be able recall the information, or may even interpret the questions differently from what the researchers

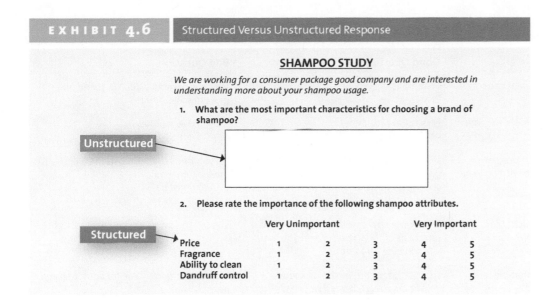

| EXHIBIT 4.6 | Structured Versus Unstructured Response |

SHAMPOO STUDY

We are working for a consumer package good company and are interested in understanding more about your shampoo usage.

1. **What are the most important characteristics for choosing a brand of shampoo?**

Unstructured

2. **Please rate the importance of the following shampoo attributes.**

Structured

	Very Unimportant			Very Important	
Price	1	2	3	4	5
Fragrance	1	2	3	4	5
Ability to clean	1	2	3	4	5
Dandruff control	1	2	3	4	5

intended. Some may even try to answer the questions according to what they think the researchers want. Another big problem, especially in the data analysis phase, is when respondents answer some but not all the questions on the questionnaire. Incomplete data makes the analysis and interpretation of the data more complicated and tricky.

A **survey** is a systematic means of collecting information from people that generally uses a questionnaire. A **questionnaire** is a form that features a set of questions designed to gather information from respondents and thereby accomplish the researchers' objectives. Survey questionnaires can take different forms: phone, mail, or fax, delivered via the Internet, or even conducted in person, for example, mall intercepts. Individual questions on a questionnaire can be either unstructured or structured. **Unstructured questions** are open-ended and allow respondents to answer in their own words. An unstructured question like "What are the most important characteristics for choosing a brand of shampoo?" yields an unstructured response. However, the same question could be posed to respondents in a structured format by providing a fixed set of response categories, such as price, fragrance, ability to clean, and dandruff control, and then asking respondents to rate the importance of each. **Structured questions** thus are closed-ended questions for which a discrete set of response alternatives, or specific answers, is provided for respondents to evaluate (see Exhibit 4.6).

Developing a questionnaire is part art and part science. The questions must be carefully designed to address the specific set of research questions. Moreover, for a questionnaire to produce meaningful results, its questions cannot be misleading in any fashion (e.g., open to multiple interpretations), and they must address only one issue at a time. Furthermore, they must be worded in vocabulary that will be familiar and comfortable to those being surveyed. More specifically, the questions should be sequenced appropriately: general questions first, more specific questions next, and demographic questions at the end. Finally, the layout and appearance of the questionnaire must be professional and easy to follow, with appropriate instructions in suitable places. For some tips on what *not* to do when designing a questionnaire, see Exhibit 4.7.

Marketing surveys can be conducted either online or offline, but online marketing surveys offer researchers the chance to develop a database quickly with many responses, whereas offline marketing surveys provide a more direct approach that includes interactions with the target market.

survey
A systematic means of collecting information from people that generally uses a questionnaire.

questionnaire
A form that features a set of questions designed to gather information from respondents and thereby accomplish the researchers' objectives; questions can be either unstructured or structured.

unstructured questions
Open-ended questions that allow respondents to answer in their own words.

structured questions
Closed-ended questions for which a discrete set of response alternatives, or specific answers, is provided for respondents to evaluate.

EXHIBIT 4.7	What Not to Do When Designing a Questionnaire	
Issue	**Good Question**	**Bad Question**
Avoid questions the respondent cannot easily or accurately answer.	When was the last time you went to the grocery store?	How much money did you spend on groceries last month?
Avoid sensitive questions unless they are absolutely necessary.	Do you take vitamins?	Do you dye your hair?
Avoid double-barrelled questions, which refer to more than one issue with only one set of responses.	1. Do you think Jack Layton would make a good prime minister? 2. Do you think Elizabeth May would make a good prime minister?	Do you think that Elizabeth May or Jack Layton would make a good prime minister?
Avoid leading questions, which steer respondents to a particular response, irrespective of their true beliefs.	Please rate how safe you believe a Volvo is on a scale of 1 to 10, with 1 being not safe and 10 being very safe.	Volvo is the safest car on the road, right?
Avoid one-sided questions that present only one side of the issue.	To what extent do you feel fast food contributes to adult obesity? 1: Does not contribute, 5: Main cause	Fast food is responsible for adult obesity: Agree/Disagree
Avoid questions with implicit assumptions, which presume the same point of reference for all respondents.	Should children be allowed to drink Coca-Cola in school?	Since caffeine is a stimulant, should children be allowed to drink Coca-Cola in school?
Avoid complex questions and those that may seem unfamiliar to respondents.	What brand of wristwatch do you typically wear?	Do you believe that mechanical watches are better than quartz watches?

Source: Adapted from A. Parasuraman, Dhruv Grewal, and R. Krishnan, *Marketing Research*, 2nd ed. (Boston, MA: Houghton Mifflin, 2007), Ch. 10.

Web surveys have steadily grown as a percentage of all quantitative surveys. Many online survey tools let researchers quickly design a survey, launch it, download the data, and analyze the data even as the survey is progressing, as well as at the end of the data collection. SurveyMonkey and Qualtrics are two popular online survey tools with vastly different capabilities, services, and pricing models. Online surveys have a lot to offer marketers with tight deadlines and small budgets.[26] Response rates are relatively high. Typical response rates run from 1 to 2 percent for mail and 10 to 15 percent for phone surveys. For online surveys, in contrast, the response rate can reach 30 to 35 percent, or even higher in B2B research. It is inexpensive. An average 20-minute phone interview can cost $30 to $40, compared with $7 to $10 for an online interview. Costs likely will continue to fall more as users become more familiar with the online survey process. Results are processed and received quickly. Reports and summaries can be developed in real time and delivered directly to managers in simple, easy-to-digest reports, complete with colour, graphics, and charts. Traditional phone or mail surveys require laborious data collection, tabulation, summary, and distribution before anyone can grasp their results. The Internet can also be used to collect data other than that available from quantitative surveys. If consumers give a firm permission to market to them, the firm can collect data about

Online marketing surveys enable researchers to develop a database quickly with many responses at a relatively low cost.

EXHIBIT 4.8	A Hypothetical Fast-Food Survey

Please take a few minutes to tell us about your experience at McDonald's and Wendy's. For each question, please respond by checking the box that applies or writing your response in the space provided.

Please Evaluate Your Experience at McDonald's

A. McDonald's	Strongly Disagree	Disagree	Neither Agree or Disagree	Agree	Strongly Agree
	1	2	3	4	5
McDonald's food tastes good	☐	☐	☐	☑	☐
McDonald's is clean	☐	☐	☐	☑	☐
McDonald's has low prices	☐	☐	☐	☑	☐

B. Wendy's	Strongly Disagree	Disagree	Neither Agree or Disagree	Agree	Strongly Agree
	1	2	3	4	5
Wendy's food tastes good	☐	☐	☐	☑	☐
Wendy's is clean	☐	☐	☐	☑	☐
Wendy's has low prices	☐	☐	☐	☑	☐

C. McDonald's

	Never	1-2 times	3-4 times	More than 5 times
In the last month, how many times have you been to McDonald's?	☐	☐	☐	☑
On average, how much do you spend each visit at McDonald's?	$ _____			
What is your favourite item at McDonald's?	_____			

D. Please Tell Us About Yourself

	under 16	17-24	25-35	36+
What is your age?	☐	☐	☐	☐
What is your gender?	Male ☐	Female ☐		

their usage of its website and other Internet applications. In addition, open-ended questionnaires can be used to collect more in-depth qualitative data.

Marketing researchers typically use different types of scales to measure certain concepts such as attitudes, perceived quality, perceived value, loyalty, and convenience. Assume you were part of a research team at McDonald's tasked to find out how its customers evaluated its food and facilities. The team prepared a survey like the one in Exhibit 4.8, which would be administered to customers. Let's examine this questionnaire. Section A measures the customer's experience in McDonald's, Section B measures the customer's experience in Wendy's, Section C measures the customer's habits at McDonald's, and Section D measures customer demographics.

Furthermore, suppose the research team administered the survey to 1000 customers. The results of the first question, "McDonald's food tastes good," were as follows:

1	2	3	4	5
Strongly Disagree	**Disagree**	**Neither Agree nor Disagree**	**Agree**	**Strongly Agree**
N = 50	N = 50	N = 100	N = 300	N = 500

Their responses are indicated by "N = ." Marketers could report several metrics. But two common metrics would be that 80 percent $[(300 + 500)/1000]$ of respondents had high satisfaction since they responded to "Agree" or "Strongly Agree." It could also be reported that satisfaction was high because the mean was 4.15 $[(50 \times 1 + 50 \times 2 + 100 \times 3 + 300 \times 4 + 500 \times 5)/1000]$ on the 5-point scale.

experimental research
A type of quantitative research that systematically manipulates one or more variables to determine which variable has a causal effect on another variable.

Experimental Research   **Experimental research** is a type of quantitative research that systematically manipulates one or more variables to determine which variable(s) have a causal effect on another variable. In the hypothetical McDonald's example, the research team was trying to determine the most profitable price for a new combo item (a hamburger, fries, and a drink). Assume that the fixed cost of developing the item is $300,000, and the variable cost, which is primarily composed of the cost of the food itself, is $2.00. McDonald's puts the item on the menu at four different prices in four different markets (see Exhibit 4.9). In general, the more expensive the item, the less it will sell. But, by running this experiment, the restaurant chain determines the most profitable item is the second least expensive item ($5.00). These findings suggest some people may have believed the most expensive item ($7.00) was too expensive, so they refused to buy it. The least expensive item ($4.00) sold fairly well, but McDonald's did not make as much money on each item sold. In this experiment, the changes in price likely caused the changes in quantities sold and therefore affected the restaurant's profitability.

scanner research
A type of quantitative research that uses data obtained from scanner readings of UPC codes at checkout counters.

Scanner Research   **Scanner research** is a type of quantitative research that uses data obtained from scanner readings of UPC codes at checkout counters. Whenever you go into your local grocery store, your purchases are rung up by using scanner systems. The data from these purchases are likely to be acquired by leading marketing

EXHIBIT 4.9	Hypothetical Pricing Experiment for McDonald's				
	1	**2**	**3**	**4**	**5**
Market	**Unit Price**	**Market Demand at Price (in Units)**	**Total Revenue (Col. 1 × Col. 2)**	**Total Cost of Units Sold ($300,000 Fixed Cost; $2.00/unit Variable Cost)**	**Total Profits (Col. 3 − Col. 4)**
1	$4	200 000	$800,000	$700,000	$100,000
2	5	150 000	750,000	600,000	150,000
3	6	100 000	600,000	500,000	100,000
4	7	50 000	350,000	400,000	(50,000)

research firms, such as SymphonyIRI Group or Nielsen. They use this information to help leading consumer packaged goods firms (e.g., Kellogg's, PepsiCo, and Sara Lee) assess what is happening in the marketplace. For example, a firm can determine what would happen to sales if it reduced its price by 10 percent in a given month. Did sales increase, decrease, or stay the same?

Panel Research **Panel research** is a type of quantitative research that involves collecting information from a group of consumers (the panel) over time. The data collected from the panellists may be from a survey or a record of purchases. This data provides consumer packaged goods firms with a comprehensive picture of what individual consumers are buying or not buying. Walmart's Asda subsidiary in the United Kingdom uses an 18 000-customer panel it calls "Pulse of the Nation" to help it determine which products to carry. Asda sends emails to each participant with product images and descriptions of potential new products. The customers' responses indicate whether they think the product should be carried in the stores. As a thank you for participating, those customers who respond are automatically entered in a draw for free prizes.[27]

panel research
A type of quantitative research that involves collecting information from a group of consumers (the panel) over time; data collected may be from a survey or a record of purchases.

Now that we have discussed the various secondary and primary data collection methods, we can see that both primary data and secondary data have certain inherent advantages and disadvantages. Exhibit 4.10 highlights some of the differences between exploratory and conclusive research methods.

Regardless of how marketers collect data, research can be an expensive process for entrepreneurs working on a shoestring budget. Entrepreneurial Marketing 4.1 suggests a host of avenues entrepreneurs might pursue.

Step 4: Analyze Data

The next step in the marketing research process—analyzing and interpreting the data—should be both thorough and methodical. To generate meaningful information,

EXHIBIT 4.10	Differences Between Exploratory and Conclusive Research	
Research Project Components	**Exploratory Research**	**Conclusive Research**
Research purpose	General: to generate preliminary insights about people, relationships, feelings, perceptions, a situation, or even the discovery of new ideas	Specific: to verify insights and aid in selecting a course of action
Data needs	Fuzzy	Clear
Data sources	Ill defined	Well defined
Data collection form	Open-ended, rough	Usually structured
Sample	Relatively small, often not randomly drawn; subjectively selected to maximize generalization of insights	Relatively large and randomly drawn; objectively selected to permit generalization of findings
Data collection	Often flexible; no set procedure	Generally rigid; well-laid-out procedure
Data analysis	Typically nonquantitative—mainly interpretive and subjective based on content analysis	Formal; typically quantitative—descriptive or predictive based on statistical analysis
Inferences/Recommendations	More tentative than final	More final than tentative
Researcher skills	Need strong interpersonal communication, observational, interpretation of text or visual data skills	Need strong statistical analysis and interpretation of numbers skills

Sources: A. Parasuraman, D. Grewal, and R. Krishnan, *Marketing Research*, 2nd ed. Copyright © 2007 by Houghton Mifflin Company; J. Hair Jr., R. Bush, and D. Ortinau, *Marketing Research in the Digital Information Environment*, 4th ed. McGraw-Hill Irwin, 2009. Adapted with permission.

Marketing Research on a Shoestring Budget

Imagine your company needs some research conducted but has a relatively small budget. Fortunately, marketing research does not have to have a high price tag, though it always takes drive and knowledge. Here are some ways to uncover the information you and your company might need without breaking the bank.

Objective: What is it that you need to know?

● *Network.* Use the directory on your cellphone to call friends and professional colleagues. In most cases, researchers probably already know people in the industry who will be able to share their knowledge. They can help marketers determine what their objectives should be in upcoming research projects.

Customer Analysis: Who are your customers, and what do they want?

● *Customers.* Talk with current and prospective customers. Ask them the right questions, and they will provide the necessary answers. This approach is remarkably cheap because it entails only the researcher's labour, though it will require a large time commitment. Marketers need to take care how they ask the questions; people tend to provide answers that they think the questioner wants to hear or that seem socially acceptable.

● *Online.* Use a search engine such as Google by typing in some appropriate keywords.

● *Statistics Canada.* Statistics Canada is an important source of information. At www.statcan.gc.ca, industry, demographic, and economic reports are accessible for free. Although not known for its ease of use, the website offers a wealth of information.

Competitive Analysis: What are your competitors doing?

Secondary Sources: Many are listed in Exhibit 4.2 on page 123 in this chapter.

● *Websites.* Visit competitors' websites, if they have them. Learn about their products and services, pricing, management teams, and philosophies. Read their press releases. You can even infer what parts of the businesses are thriving by reading their career pages.

● *SEC Filings.* If competitors are public, they are required to file 10K forms annually with the Securities Exchange Commission (SEC). Search for SEC filings by using http://finance.yahoo.com or http://money.msn.com, both of which provide sales and expense numbers, in addition to other important information in the footnotes.

● *University Libraries Electronic Databases.* Most Canadian universities subscribe to several electronic business databases that provide information on Canadian companies. These databases are usually accessible remotely by students, staff, and alumnus at no cost to users. A sample of these databases include Canadian Business Resource, Canadian Business & Current Affairs, Factiva, *Financial Post* databases, MarketResearch.com, Mergent Online, Mergent WebReports, ProQuest Asian Business and Reference, and ProQuest European Business. Many of these databases provide company profiles, financial data, contact information, and short stories or case studies on company successes, failures, and innovations.

● *Go There.* If competitors are smaller mom-and-pop stores, visit them. Hang out in front of the store armed with a pad and paper and count the number of people who walk in. Then calculate the percentage of people that walk out having purchased something. Use logic and judgment. Have the customers purchased items that appear to have high profit margins? Find out where and what competitors are advertising.

● *NAICS Codes.* For a wider view of the competitive industry, review the North American Industry Classification System (NAICS) codes. The NAICS identifies companies operating in an industry sector with a six-digit code. The government websites at www.ic.gc.ca/ic_wp-pa.htm and www.statcan.gc.ca help pinpoint the correct NAICS code and can generate an industry-specific report. For example, if you want to identify women's clothing stores, you would go to number 44812. The first two digits, 44, identify merchandise retailers (as would 45). The third digit breaks down the merchandise retailers further. For example, retailers selling clothing and clothing accessories are in classification 448, while general merchandise retailers are in classification 452. The fourth digit subdivides clothing and accessory retailers (448) into clothing stores (4481), shoe stores (4482), and jewellery and luggage stores (4483). The fifth digit provides a further breakdown into men's clothing stores (44811) and women's clothing stores (44812). The sixth digit (not shown here) is used to capture differences in the three North American countries using the classification scheme: the United States, Mexico, and Canada.

Classification by Type of Merchandise

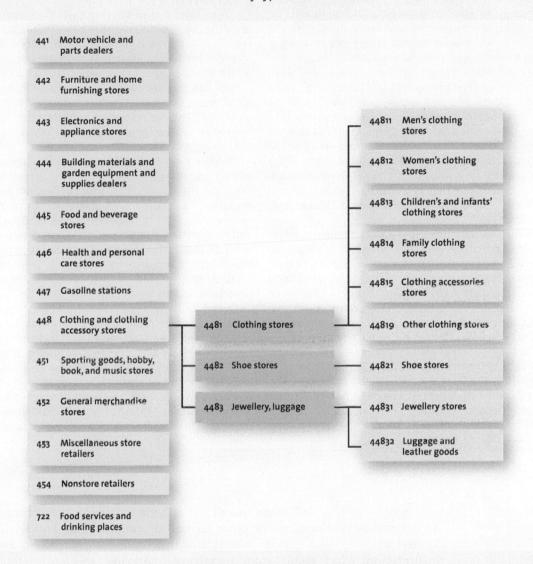

Focus Groups, Surveys, and Analyst Reports: What detailed information can you gather?

- *Be Specific.* Determine precisely what information is required; it is very costly to pay for research that does not assist in a decision or provide strategic direction.

- *Surveys.* Determine what form will provide the most value. Phone surveys cost about $40 per interview, mailings average from $5000 to $15,000 for 200 responses, and email and Internet-based surveys are usually much cheaper.

- *Focus Groups.* Although focus groups can be more expensive, there are ways to cut corners. Develop the questions in-house, and don't outsource the moderator or facility. It is important, however, to find the right participants.

- *Analyst Reports.* Prewritten reports, covering a broad price range and a wide variety of questions, are available for purchase from the hundreds of companies that write and sell reports. Two of the best known are www.forrester.com and www.hoovers.com.

Social Media Marketing 4.1   Mining Social Media[28]

Traditionally, in the offline world, marketers rely on a range of marketing techniques such as observations, focus groups, interviews, surveys, and experiments to assess their marketing efforts and campaigns. With the advent of online marketing, marketers began using a range of analytic web tools to track and evaluate their websites and online marketing campaigns, as well as to get a deeper understanding of their customers' online shopping habits and behaviour. Companies such as Google Analytics, Webtrends, Omniture, and several others have developed a wide range of real-time metrics of online activities to gauge the effectiveness of online marketing activities. These metrics range from visitor behaviour while on a website (e.g., what pages consumers visit and how long they spend on each page) to transaction data to advertising effectiveness measures (e.g., click-through rates).

Unlike individual company websites where marketers have control over their sites and can easily monitor visitors' browsing and shopping behaviour, marketers have little control over social media sites; therefore, monitoring these sites could prove challenging. Also, unlike individual company websites where products are promoted, bought, and sold, social media sites are about conversations and information sharing: people voluntarily and spontaneously talk to one another about products, services, brands, companies, and themselves. The views expressed are usually not influenced by the pressure or bias introduced by a researcher's set of questions. Hence, social media sites are alluring because they allow marketers to obtain the real sentiments of people in an unobtrusive way. Tracking and mining this kind of information across multiple sites is regarded as a virtual gold mine.

Given the value of tracking customers' sentiments in social media, it is not surprising that numerous vendors (e.g., Sysomos, Infegy, JamiQ, Radian6) offer a wide array of social media monitoring technologies. In addition, a recent Forrester Research survey of 145 global marketers in both B2B and B2C companies indicated that the use of social media as a marketing tool is on the rise, and what's more, more than 50 percent of marketers said they would be increasing their spending on social media marketing in the coming months.

Since social media is about chatter, conversations, and communities, it is considered a huge reservoir of rich behavioural data and is an enticing medium for marketers to use to conduct market research. Some marketers see social media as a place where they can quickly, easily, and inexpensively recruit people to participate in market research studies and obtain results faster than by traditional market research methods. This method may be particularly appealing to small companies or marketing departments with limited research budgets.

A substantially reduced role for traditional market research could be counterproductive. Thus, a major challenge for marketers is to figure out how to integrate traditional market research methods with web analytics and social media to yield valid marketing insights. One important consideration in this regard is to determine what research questions can be best answered through the different approaches and the extent to which the combined methods triangulate findings from the individual approaches.

---

data
Raw numbers or other factual information of limited value.

information
Data that has been organized, analyzed, interpreted, and converted into a useful form for decision makers.

researchers analyze and make use of the collected data. In this context, **data** can be defined as raw numbers or other factual information that, on their own, have limited value to marketers. However, when the data are interpreted, they become **information**, which results from organizing, analyzing, and interpreting the data, and putting it into a form that is useful to marketing decision makers. For example, a checkout scanner in the grocery store collects sales data about individual consumer purchases. Not until those data are categorized and examined do they provide information about which products and services were purchased together or how an in-store promotional activity translated into sales.

For example, in our hypothetical cologne benchmarking example at the beginning of the chapter, the firm learns from secondary data sources that its product is priced lower than its competition, it spends more money on traditional advertising in fashion magazines, and it is slowly losing market share to a new upstart competitor. Putting these disparate data points together provides information that indicates the need to find out what is so good about the competitor's new cologne. The firm commissions a series of focus groups, which is useful in developing a survey of users of its cologne and of its competitor. The survey provides conclusive information that the firm uses to change its strategy. In particular, it found that its product's scent was a little too strong and wasn't as appealing to its younger target market. It also discovered that peers have a tremendous influence on scent preferences. So the company decided to tone down the scent and reapportion its promotional budget to include more innovative social media initiatives through Twitter, Facebook, and YouTube. Data analysis might be as simple as calculating the average purchases of different customer segments or as complex as forecasting sales by market segment by using elaborate statistical techniques. Social Media Marketing 4.1 shows how marketers are tapping into the rich qualitative data from social media to learn more about consumers and their shopping behaviour.

Continuing with our McDonald's example, the results of the survey found in Exhibit 4.8 on page 135 are summarized in Exhibit 4.11. They indicate that McDonald's and Wendy's scored the same on the cleanliness of the restaurant, but McDonald's had lower prices, while Wendy's food tasted better. McDonald's may want to improve the taste of its food to better compete with Wendy's.

Coinstar, a worldwide leader of self-service coin-counting machines, uses sophisticated regression models to identify and rank potential locations for its machines.

The purpose of converting data to information is to describe, explain, predict, and/or evaluate a particular situation. For example, Wendy, the downtown Ottawa-based retailer of tweens clothing, learned that her core customers live in various suburbs around downtown. This piece of data takes on new meaning when she learns that none of these customers were drawn to her store by a clever and expensive direct mail campaign. By analyzing data she collected through a survey, she discovered that her core customers are working professionals who are drawn to the store when they walk by it on their way to and from work, not people from the upscale apartments in the downtown region that she targeted with her direct mail advertisements.

Data analysis might be as simple as calculating the average purchases of different customer segments or as complex as forecasting sales by market segment by using elaborate statistical techniques. Coinstar, a worldwide leader in self-service coin counting, has begun analyzing marketing research in increasingly sophisticated ways. The company operates machines in more than 10 000 supermarkets in Canada, the United States, and the United Kingdom. Consumers use the machines, which can count up to 600 coins per minute, to process large volumes of change that they exchange for a voucher good for cash or groceries. Since it was founded in 1991, the company has tried to identify new and profitable locations on an ongoing

EXHIBIT 4.11	Survey Results for McDonald's and Wendy's

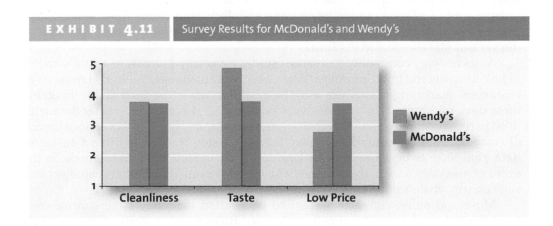

basis as demand for its services continues to grow. When the company was small, coming up with "best guesses" of prime locations based on intuition worked out well, but Coinstar researchers recently developed regression models to identify and rank potential locations for its "green machines." This approach greatly improved Coinstar's ability to find prospective locations and forecast those areas that had the best potential for growth and profitability. The company can now capitalize on the estimated $7.7 billion in coins sitting in people's homes, waiting to be converted to paper money or grocery purchases.[29]

It is important for market researchers to analyze and interpret the data in an objective manner. They should not try to hide or colour-coat findings that are different from what they had hoped for. Misinterpreting the findings or manipulating the statistics in a way to suit the researcher's hunch or prediction could lead to the wrong decision, which could have serious consequences for marketers. The temptation to lie with statistics is something market researchers must always be aware of and try to avoid.

Step 5: Present Action Plan

In the final phase of the marketing research process, the analyst prepares the results and presents them to the appropriate decision makers, who undertake appropriate marketing actions and strategies. A typical marketing research presentation includes an executive summary, the body of the report (which discusses the research objectives, methodology used, and detailed findings), the conclusions, the limitations, and appropriate supplemental tables, figures, and appendices. To be effective, a written report must be short, interesting, methodical, precise, lucid, and free of errors.[30] Furthermore, the reports should use a style appropriate to the audience, devoid of technical jargon, and include recommendations that managers can actually implement.

Let's go back to the hypothetical McDonald's scenario. According to the research findings, the company is doing fine in terms of cleanliness (as are its competitors), it is perceived to have lower prices, and the taste of its food could be improved. Based on the analysis and insights gained, McDonald's could hire gourmet chefs to improve its menu and food offerings. It would also want to highlight these additional offerings in its advertisements and promotions by pointing out how they were created by gourmet chefs. McDonald's should also consider performing additional pricing research to determine whether its lower prices are positively impacting sales and profits, or whether it should price more competitively with Wendy's.

L05 The Ethics of Using Customer Information

As we will note in Chapter 17, upholding strong business ethics requires more than a token nod to ethics in the mission statement. A strong ethical orientation must be an integral part of a firm's marketing strategy and decision making. In Chapter 17, we will discuss how marketers have a duty to understand and address the concerns of the various stakeholders in the firm.

As technology continues to advance rapidly, especially in terms of a firm's ability to link data sets and build enormous databases that contain information on millions of customers, marketing researchers must be careful to not abuse their ability to access these data, which can be very sensitive. Unauthorized sharing of customer data with third parties or for purposes other than legitimate company business is a serious breach of customer trust. Also, marketers must take every step possible to protect customer data from security breaches from hackers and other unauthorized individuals. In the event of a security breach, the company must quickly notify its affected customers and state clearly what steps it is taking to protect their data and privacy.

More and more, consumers want to be assured that they have control over the information that has been collected about them through various means, such as a website or product registration or rebate form. Consumers' anxiety has become so intense that the Canadian government has implemented various regulations, such as the Privacy Act, that govern the collection, use, disclosure, and retention of personal information by federal government institutions, and the Personal Information Protection and Electronic Documents Act (PIPEDA), which governs the collection, use, disclosure, and retention of personal information by certain parts of the private sector.[31] When conducting marketing research, researchers must assure respondents that the information they provide will be treated as confidential and used solely for the purpose of research. Without such assurances, consumers will be reluctant to either provide honest responses to marketing research inquiries or even agree to participate in the first place.

It is extremely important to adhere to ethical practices when conducting marketing research. The Canadian Marketing Association, for example, provides three guidelines for conducting marketing research: (1) it prohibits selling or fundraising under the guise of conducting research, (2) it supports maintaining research integrity by avoiding misrepresentation or the omission of pertinent research data, and (3) it encourages the fair treatment of clients and suppliers. Numerous codes of conduct written by various marketing research societies all reinforce the duty of researchers to respect the rights of the subjects in the course of their research. The bottom line: Marketing research should be used only to produce unbiased, factual information.

Learning Objectives Review

L01 Describe the five steps in the marketing research process

There are five steps in the marketing research process. The first step is to define the research problem and objectives, which sounds so simple that managers often gloss over it. But this step is crucial to the success of any research project because, quite basically, the research must answer those questions that are important for making decisions. In the second step, designing the research project, researchers identify the type of data that are needed, whether primary or secondary, on the basis of the objectives of the project from Step 1, and then determine the type of research that enables them to collect those data. The third step involves deciding on the data collection process and collecting the data. Depending on the research objectives and the findings from the secondary data search, researchers will choose either exploratory or conclusive research. Exploratory research usually involves observation, in-depth interviews, or projective techniques, whereas if the project calls for conclusive research, the researchers may perform a survey, an experiment, or use scanner and panel data. The fourth step is to analyze and interpret the data, and the fifth and final step is to present an action plan. Although these steps appear to progress in a linear fashion, researchers often work backward through the process as they learn at each step.

L02 Explain the differences between secondary data and primary data, and specify when each should be used

Secondary data are pieces of information that have been collected from other sources, such as the Census, internal company sources, the Internet, books, articles, trade associations, or syndicated data services. Primary data are data collected to address specific research needs/questions under investigation, usually through observation, focus groups, interviews, surveys, or experiments. Research projects typically start with secondary research, which provides a background for what information is already known and what research has been done previously. Also, compared with primary research, secondary research is quicker, easier, and less expensive, and it requires less methodological expertise. However, secondary research likely was collected for reasons other than those pertaining to the specific problem at hand, which means the information may be dated, biased, or simply not specific enough to answer the research questions. Primary research, in contrast, can be designed to answer very specific questions, but it also can be expensive and time-consuming.

L03 Identify various internal and external secondary data sources

External secondary data are pieces of information that have been collected from other sources, such as Statistics Canada, the Internet, books, articles, magazines, newspapers, trade associations, scanner data, panel data, or syndicated data services. Internal secondary data are derived from internal company records such as sales, customer lists, and other company reports.

L04 Describe various primary data collection techniques

Exploratory research methods include observation, in-depth interviewing, focus groups, and projective techniques. Conclusive research is used to verify the insights gained from exploratory research and to aid in choosing a course of action. Conclusive research methods involve experiments, surveys, scanner, and panel research. With both exploratory and conclusive research methods, the specific methods managers choose depends foremost on the marketing research objectives, which must be balanced by other considerations such as costs, timeliness, and usefulness of the results. Many managers use exploratory research methods as the first phase of the research process in order to get a deeper insight into the situation.

L05 Outline ethical issues firms encounter when conducting marketing research

Marketing researchers have obligations to their subjects and to society to behave in an ethical manner. This responsibility means that marketing researchers must take every precaution to ensure the confidentiality of the data they collect from consumers and the privacy of study participants. Researchers should never misrepresent the purpose of a study; for example, a sales pitch should never be cast as a marketing research study. Similarly, marketing researchers should collect information on consumers only for the sole purpose of conducting marketing research endeavours. Information should not be collected under the guise of marketing research when the intent is to sell products or fund-raise. Finally, the results of research studies should be reported fully. If data or parts of the study are ignored, the results might be misinterpreted.

Key Terms

- conclusive research, 128
- data, 140
- ethnography, 129
- experimental research, 136
- exploratory research, 128
- focus group, 131
- hypothesis, 128
- in-depth interview, 129
- information, 140

- marketing research, 118
- observation, 129
- panel research, 137
- primary data, 125
- projective technique, 131
- questionnaire, 133
- reliability, 127
- sample, 127
- sampling, 127

- scanner research, 136
- secondary data, 122
- structured questions, 133
- survey, 133
- syndicated data, 125
- unstructured questions, 133
- validity, 127

Concept Review

1. Is marketing research really necessary? Defend your answer.

2. Briefly describe the steps in the marketing research process. Explain why it is important to clearly define the research problem and objectives from the very outset of the process.

3. What is the difference between secondary and primary data? What are some of the advantages of each type of data? When should each type of data be used?

4. In data collection methods, researchers may choose between exploratory research methods or conclusive research methods, or use both methods. What considerations guide their choice of data collection methods?

5. Today, information and communications technologies (ICT), including the Internet, are changing not only the way marketing is practiced, but also how market research is conducted. In response, many companies are using a wide variety of observational methods (e.g., GPS, RFID, video cameras, audio devices, ethnography) to gather customer data. Discuss the ethical issues underlying the increasing use of observational research methods that use technology.

6. Marketing research is designed to help marketers make better decisions on various aspects of their businesses.

The quality of research findings is as good as the quality of the data on which they are based. What are some things marketers could do to ensure that they obtain the best quality data?

7. Explain the main advantages and disadvantages of using the Internet for marketing research versus conventional offline methods.

8. Identify and explain the ways in which the design of a market research study could reduce the reliability and validity of the study. Can a market research study that has high reliability lack validity? Can a study that has high validity lack reliability? Explain your answers.

9. What do you think are some of the differences between exploratory data collection methods, which are mainly qualitative, and conclusive research methods, which are more quantitative in nature? Which type of method should a researcher prefer and why?

10. Explain some of the problems and challenges market researchers face in the data analysis and interpretation stage of the marketing research process. Should they report these problems when presenting their action plan? Why or why not?

Marketing Applications

1. A large department store collects data about what its customers buy and stores these data in a data warehouse. If you were the store's buyer for children's clothing, what would you want to know from the data warehouse that would help you be a more successful buyer?

2. Identify a nonprofit organization that might use marketing research, and describe one example of a meaningful research project that it might conduct. Discuss how this project would be useful to the organization.

3. Marketing researchers do not always go through the steps in the marketing research process in sequential order. Provide an example of a research project that might not follow this sequence.

4. A new men's clothing store is trying to determine whether there is a significant market for its type of merchandise in a specific location where it is considering putting a store. Would it be most likely to use primary or secondary data, or a combination of the two, to answer this question?

5. A high-tech firm has just developed a new technology to correct bad vision without surgery or contact lenses. The company needs to estimate the demand for such a service. Would it use primary or secondary data, or a combination of the two?

6. A bank manager notices that by the time customers get to the teller, they seem irritated and impatient. She wants to investigate the problem further, so she hires you to design a research project to figure out what is bothering the customers. What type of research method would you recommend? Is it an exploratory or conclusive method?

7. Snapple has developed a new beverage, and it wants to determine whether it should begin to market it throughout Canada. The company used two separate studies for the advertising campaign:

   - A focus group to identify the appropriate advertising message for the new beverage
   - A survey to assess the effectiveness of the advertising campaign for the new Snapple beverage

   Which study was exploratory and which was conclusive?

8. What other studies would you recommend that Snapple undertake?

9. Suppose your university wants to modify its course scheduling procedures to better serve students. What are some secondary sources of information that might be used to conduct research into this topic? Describe how these sources might be used. Describe a method you could use to gather primary research data about the topic. Would you recommend a specific order in obtaining each of these types of data? Explain your answer.

10. Tony is planning to launch a new shampoo and is trying to decide what features and price would interest consumers. He sends a request for proposal to four marketing research vendors, and three respond, as described in the table below. Which vendor should Tony use? Explain your rationale for picking this vendor over the others.

Vendor A	**Vendor B**	**Vendor C**
The vendor that Tony has used in the past, it estimates it can get the job done for $200,000 and in two months. The vendor plans to do a telephone-based survey analysis and use secondary data.	Tony's key competitor has used this vendor, which claims that it can get the job done for $150,000 and in one month. This vendor plans to do a telephone-based survey analysis and use secondary data. During a discussion pertaining to its price and time estimates, the vendor indicates it will draw on insights it has learned from a recent report prepared for one of Tony's competitors.	This well-known vendor has recently started to focus on consumer packaged goods clients. It quotes a price of $180,000 and a time of one month. The vendor plans to conduct an Internet-based survey analysis and use secondary data.

Net Savvy

1. Go to the website of either Harris/Decima (www.decima.com) or Ipsos Canada (www.ipsos.ca), which administer public opinion polls. Search the site for results from any recent survey that is available for free. Print out the results. Identify the objective(s) of the survey. Discuss one of the major findings, and provide an interpretation of the data.

2. Select two online survey tools (e.g., SurveyMonkey, Qualtrics, Zoomerang, Survey Solutions) and compare and contrast them in terms of their features, capabilities, ease of use, support service, pricing models, clientele, and any other characteristics you think would be useful for a market researcher to know.

Chapter Case Study

MOBILE SURVEYS PROVIDE REAL-TIME CUSTOMER INSIGHTS[32]

Shoeless Joe's Sports Grill is an award-winning restaurant and bar located primarily in Ontario cities, such as Ajax, Whitby, Oshawa, Pickering, Peterborough, and Cornwall, and in the Greater Toronto Area. It offers customers a casual dining and bar experience, where they can relax and enjoy a meal and drinks while watching on huge TV screens their favourite sports or games, be it the Stanley Cup finals, the Super Bowl, World Cup Soccer, or a great UFC matchup. Shoeless Joe's offers patrons exceptional food, service, and entertainment in an atmosphere that appeals to today's discriminating diners.[33] Shoeless Joe's goal is to set the industry standard among sports-themed restaurants and bars for service, environment, quality, and profits.

The thriving restaurant, established in 1985, was named after the legendary baseball star Joe "Shoeless" Jackson. Initially, Shoeless Joe's was not as successful as its namesake. When Fred Lopreiato and his nephew Nick purchased Shoeless Joe's in 1987, it was a struggling Toronto-based restaurant, with no theme; it was certainly not a well-known brand. However, Fred and Nick had a game plan; they had always imagined the enormous potential of a sports-themed restaurant. The pair converted the restaurant into a more casual venue with an inviting, informal atmosphere, catering to customers—sports fans, families, and individuals—between the ages of 25 and 49.

The reinvented Shoeless Joe's turned out to be a winner, with a 50-percent increase in profits after the first year and another 35-percent increase the following year.[34] The restaurant continued to be extremely successful, so much so that Fred and Nick opened a second location in 1991. As the adage goes, success breeds success, and this was precisely the case with Shoeless Joe's. Fred and Nick had to decide whether to open more company-owned restaurants or franchise their business. They opted for franchising since they felt that it was the most effective way to grow their business. Thus, in 1997 the first Shoeless Joe's franchise was launched in Toronto. Since then Shoeless Joe's has opened more than 40 franchises across Ontario. Fred and Nick plan to open 10 to 15 new franchises in 2011: an ambitious expansion strategy for such a small company, particularly in these tough economic times.

Although Fred and Nick remain excited about the growth potential for their business and intend to pursue an aggressive expansion strategy, they are not willing to compromise on two fundamental principles, even if it means delaying their expansion. The two principles that have always guided their successful expansion are finding the right franchisees and finding the most suitable locations. Finding the right franchisee is an intense, personal process involving in-depth interviews and analysis with potential franchisees to determine the right fit. Finding the right

Shoeless Joe's used in-depth interviews to find franchisees and mobile surveys to collect consumer perceptions and opinions.

location is a more complex task requiring the consideration of many important variables, most of which are usually outside the control of the company. These variables include neighbourhood demographic factors, physical surroundings, accessibility, real estate, and market trends, among many others. To assist it in making the right location choice, Shoeless Joe's leverages technology to help it gather and analyze key information that will provide useful insights easily and quickly. To help it execute its aggressive expansion strategy, Shoeless Joe's used Pitney Bowes Business Insight's (PBBI) location intelligence solutions and consulting service.

Pitney Bowes is a leading global provider of expertise and technology tools that help companies find the best business solution in the most cost-effective way. Shoeless Joe's was the first company in Canada to implement PBBI's FACES (Faster, Accurate, Current, Economical Surveys) tool to gain access to real-time customer data.[35] FACES is a new mobile consumer survey system that gauges consumer perceptions and opinions on customer service or any other business dimension. It is a unique and professional survey system that uses current technology to collect consumer data at the point of experience. FACES catalogues data in a secure database, conducts sophisticated analysis, and delivers actionable insight, all in real time.

With this unique system, consumers may feel more inclined to participate in a survey because it is fast, easy, interactive, and less intrusive than the traditional paper-and-pen method of collecting information. The FACES survey enables Shoeless Joe's to create customized surveys to assist it in collecting consumer data. This system is extremely useful and efficient because, unlike conventional survey tools, Shoeless Joe's can make adjustments to the survey questions to keep target customers' profiles up to date and accessible. This creates a more streamlined process and helps Shoeless Joe's gain a better understanding of target customers by creating in-depth customer profiles.

In its initial project, Shoeless Joe's created a survey with 10 questions and deployed it in 4 of its 38 locations.[36] Survey questions included asking customers about where they were from, where they were headed next, their spending patterns, the frequency of their visits to the restaurant, their level of satisfaction, the competition, and so on.

Shoeless Joe's still uses the system. On busy nights, two staff members are responsible for conducting the survey, going from table to table by using an electronic mobile device, such as a PDA or a smartphone, to collect survey information from patrons. The FACES system allows Shoeless Joe's to quickly download the survey data and perform analysis that gives a snapshot of the results. Having real-time customer information collected by staff members is extremely valuable for Shoeless Joe's decision-making process, helping the company to better understand its competition and to evaluate potential areas for expansion. The information provided also equips Shoeless Joe's with the insights it needs to make decisions regarding real estate, marketing, merchandising, and branding.

Questions

1. What do you consider to be the strengths and limitations of the FACES tool that Shoeless Joe's is using to capture information to make location decisions based on customers' insights?

2. What are the methodological drawbacks of the way in which Shoeless Joe's employees go about collecting survey responses from customers?

3. How do the drawbacks identified in the previous question affect the validity and reliability of the data collected? Discuss.

4. Would you recommend that Shoeless Joe's also uses other methods to collect the data it needs? What are the advantages of the methods you would recommend over the method it currently uses?

 Practise and learn online with Connect. Connect allows you to practise important concepts at your own pace and on your own schedule, with 24/7 online access to an eBook, practice quizzes, interactivities, videos, study tools, additional resources, and more.

CHAPTER 5

Consumer
Behaviour

I n every chapter so far, we have emphasized the fact that the consumer should be at the heart of all marketing decisions and strategies. We have also emphasized the need for marketers to develop a deep understanding of consumer needs and wants in order to satisfy those needs with value-based offerings. Marketers who can recognize customers' needs even before customers articulate those needs could acquire strategic competitive advantage over competitors. In trying to satisfy consumer needs, one particularly difficult challenge for marketers is to understand why consumers prefer one brand, store, or service provider over another and if the factors that influence their purchase behaviour change over time or with the types of purchases. Let's look at how Toyota, one of the world's leading car manufacturers, identified and satisfied consumers' need for a different type of car with its Prius hybrid.

Toyota was arguably the first car manufacturer to recognize that consumer concerns about the harmful effects of their carbon footprints would one day lead to a market for more fuel-efficient cars. Recognizing this nascent consumer need a decade before its competition, Toyota started researching for a solution that would meet consumer needs. The answer after more than a decade of research was the now hugely successful Toyota Prius, a hybrid gas–electric car. Prior to the car's launch, skeptics and critics questioned its appeal and consumer's acceptance. However, Toyota's gamble paid off: it sold more than two million Prius worldwide between the car's launch in 1997 and March 2011.[1] Approximately 50 percent of the global sales of the Prius are in the United States and Canada. For several years the demand for the Prius exceeded supply, and customer waiting lists in some areas averaged six-month waits.

Learning Obectives

After studying this chapter, you should be able to

LO1 Describe the steps a customer goes through when buying a product or service

LO2 Identify what determines how much time consumers will spend searching for information before buying a product or service

LO3 Summarize how psychological, social, and situational factors influence consumers' buying behaviour

LO4 Explain how involvement influences the consumer buying decision process

The Prius provides an excellent example in which a company identified a consumer need even before it was articulated and brought a product to market to satisfy that need. Not surprisingly, Toyota is reaping the benefits of superior profits and has been the market leader from the Prius's inception, despite stiff competition recently from competitors such as Honda, Nissan, General Motors, and Ford. In spite of this success, automotive data shows that the top-selling cars in Canada are gas-guzzling sports utility vehicles and other mid- and full-sized vehicles. This information begs the question, who is the target market for the much smaller, quieter, and fuel-efficient Prius, and what motivates these consumers to purchase it?

The hybrid-car market is still a niche market consisting of consumers who are excited about new technologies (technology enthusiasts), who are environmentally conscious, and who are value conscious (i.e., looking for high fuel economy and low maintenance at affordable prices). The Prius seems equally popular with middle-aged, upper-class men and women who seek to show off their personality and be trendsetters. Government incentives and increasing value for money through new features and greater room in the newer models are two key drivers behind the strong purchase of the Prius.

Unfortunately, to date the Prius has not yet made inroads into the mass market. One of the main reasons for this is price, since these consumers are reluctant to pay a price premium for green products and "green" does not yet appear to be a determinant attribute in mass-market consumers' buying decisions.[2] The decision regarding which car to buy is a complex one that involves such variables as emotional response, personal style, and specific criteria including vehicle appearance, mileage, price, reliability, and safety. This plethora of considerations makes the car buyer's decision anything but simple. What must Toyota do to take the Prius into the mass-market segment? .::

All of us purchase goods and services; therefore, we are all consumers at one time or another. But we are also complex and irrational creatures who cannot always explain our own actions, making the job of marketing managers even more difficult because without a deep understanding of consumers' behaviour, they will not be able to properly satisfy the needs and wants of their customers.

To understand consumer behaviour, we must ask *why* people buy products or services, or even specific brands. Using principles and theories from sociology and psychology, marketers have been able to decipher many consumer actions and develop basic strategies for dealing with their behaviour. Generally, people buy one product or service instead of another because they perceive it to be the better value for them; that is, the ratio of benefits to costs is higher for that product or service than

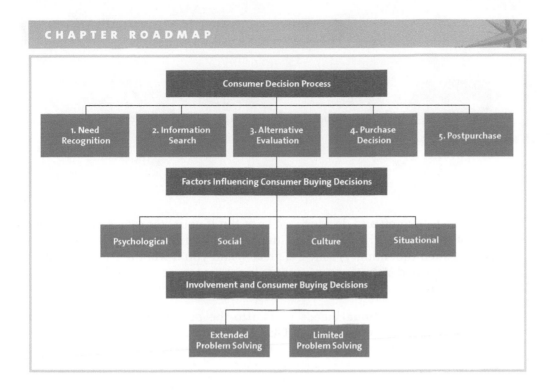

for any other.[3] However, "benefits" can be subtle and far from rationally conceived, as we shall see. Consider the tens of thousands of Canadians who purchased Apple's iPhone 4G on the very first day it was released in Canada. In making the decision to abandon or replace their feature phone with the iPhone, they must have asked themselves

- What is the additional overall value I am getting for the price I am paying for the iPhone 4G?
- What will friends, family, and co-workers think about my latest gadget?

As outlined in the chapter roadmap, we begin this chapter by exploring the process that consumers go through when buying products and services. Then we discuss the psychological, social, and situational factors that influence this consumer decision process. We end the chapter with a discussion of how the level of consumer involvement influences the buying decision process. Throughout the chapter, we illustrate what firms can do to influence consumers to purchase their products and services. The chapter roadmap outlines the major topics covered in this chapter.

The Consumer Decision Process

L01

The consumer decision process model represents the steps that consumers go through before, during, and after making purchases. Because marketers often find it difficult to determine how consumers make purchasing decisions, it is useful for us to break down the process into a series of steps and to examine each step individually,[4] as in Exhibit 5.1.

Step 1: Need Recognition

The consumer decision process begins when consumers recognize they have an unsatisfied need and want to go from their actual, needy state to a different, desired state. The greater the discrepancy between these two states, the greater the **need recognition** will be. For example, your stomach tells you that you are hungry, and you would rather not have that particular feeling. If you are only a little hungry, you

need recognition
The beginning of the consumer decision process; occurs when consumers recognize they have an unsatisfied need and want to go from their actual, needy state to a different, desired state.

EXHIBIT 5.1	The Consumer Decision Process

Need Recognition → Information Search → Alternative Evaluation → Purchase Decision → Post-purchase

may pass the feeling off and decide to eat later. But if your stomach is growling and you cannot concentrate, the need—the difference between your actual (hungry) state and your desired (not hungry) state—is greater, and you'll want to eat immediately to get to your desired state. Consumer needs like these can be classified as functional, psychological, or both.[5]

functional needs
Pertain to the performance of a product or service.

Functional Needs   **Functional needs** pertain to the performance of a product or service. For years, materials such as GORE-TEX, Polartec, and Thinsulate have been viewed as functionally superior to others that might be used in rugged, high-performance outerwear. Knowing that consumers seek out these materials, high-end outdoor manufacturers, such as North Face, prominently display the material content on each piece of clothing and equipment they offer.

psychological needs
Pertain to the personal gratification consumers associate with a product or service.

Psychological Needs   **Psychological needs** pertain to the personal gratification consumers associate with a product and/or service. Shoes, for instance, provide a functional need: to keep feet clean and protect them from the elements. So why would anyone pay $500 to $1500 for shoes that may do neither? Because that consumer is seeking a way to satisfy psychological needs. Christian Louboutin's shoes, with their signature red soles, may be the hottest shoes on the market.[6] Sarah Jessica Parker was

Do Christian Louboutin's shoes satisfy functional or psychological needs?

spotted in a pair on the set of the *Sex and the City* movie, a pair showed up in an episode of *Dirty Sexy Money*, and BMW featured the shoes in a commercial. Nicole Kidman, Catherine Deneuve, Cameron Diaz, Ashley Olsen, Gwyneth Paltrow, and Angelina Jolie have also been photographed wearing Louboutin shoes. As a result of all this media attention, there is a strong demand for Louboutin shoes by women who just love exciting (and expensive) shoes. Not surprisingly, when designers at Yves Saint Laurent made a red suede shoe with a red sole, Louboutin immediately responded by filing a lawsuit against Yves Saint Laurent.[7]

Both these examples highlight that the vast majority of products and services are likely to satisfy both functional and psychological needs, albeit in different degrees. Whereas the functional characteristics of GORE-TEX are its main selling point, it also maintains a fashionable appeal for mountain climber wannabes. In contrast, Christian Louboutin shoes satisfy psychological needs that overshadow the functional needs they serve. You can get a $15 haircut at First Choice Haircutters or spend $80 or more to get basically the same thing at an upscale salon. Are the two haircuts objectively different? The answer might vary depending on which you believe represents a good haircut and good value. One person might value getting a really good deal; another might enjoy the extra attention and amenities associated with a fancy salon.

A key to successful marketing is determining the correct balance of functional and psychological needs that best appeals to the firm's target markets. Harley-Davidson, for instance, produces motorcycles that do much more than get their riders to the mall and back. Harleys are a way of life for motorcycle enthusiasts who want to ride and have fun. Even though other manufacturers, such as Yamaha, Honda, Suzuki, and Kawasaki, offer functional, dependable, and fast motorcycles, they cannot compete with the Harley mystique.

So, what can marketers do at the need recognition stage to influence consumer purchase decisions? Marketers use numerous tactics to either remind customers of a need or create new needs. Researching and understanding what products and services customers need or want and why, are the first steps in developing appropriate tactics. Common tactics marketers employ include using reminder advertising for their products, creating awareness about a new product and its capabilities, showing how a product could enhance consumers' image, and even altering the physical layout of a store or where products are placed in stores. For example, placing products near checkout lanes or placing products that customers buy together (e.g., eggs and bread) near each other means when customers come to buy one item (eggs), they are reminded of the other item (bread).

Step 2: Information Search

LO2

The second step, after a consumer recognizes a need, is to search for information about the various options that exist to satisfy that need. The length and intensity of the search are based on several factors, including the degree of perceived risk associated with purchasing the product or service and the importance of the product to the consumer. If the way your hair is cut is important to your appearance and self-image, you may engage in an involved search for the right salon and stylist. Alternatively, an athlete looking for a buzz cut might go to the closest, most convenient, and cheapest barber shop. Regardless of the required search level, there are two key types of information: internal and external.

On the one hand, in an **internal search for information**, the buyer examines his or her own memory and knowledge about the product or service, gathered through past experiences. For example, every time Brad, who likes to shop online and loves action movies, wants to watch a movie, he orders it through Zip.ca. He relies on his memory of past experiences when making this purchase decision. On the other hand, in an **external search for information**, the buyer seeks information outside his or her personal knowledge base to help make the buying decision. Consumers might fill in their personal knowledge gaps by talking with friends, family, or a salesperson. They can also scour commercial media for unsponsored and (it is hoped) unbiased information, such as that available through *Consumer Reports*, or peruse sponsored media such as magazines, TV, or radio. One source of information consumers turn to more and more frequently is the Internet.[8] With the explosive growth of smartphones with web-browsing capability and of social media, consumers turn to the Internet for information in real time simply because they have their phones with them all the time. Sometimes consumers get commercial exposure to products or services without really knowing it.

Social Media Marketing 5.1 shows how today's consumers increasingly make use of and rely on social media for information on all sorts of decisions, including their purchase decisions.

Factors Affecting Consumers' Search Processes It is important for marketers to understand the many factors that affect consumers' search processes. Among them are the following:

- *The perceived benefits versus perceived costs of search.* Is it worth the time and effort to search for information about a product or service? For instance, most families spend a lot of time researching the automobile market before they make a purchase because cars are a relatively expensive and important purchase with

Internal search for information
Occurs when the buyer examines his or her own memory and knowledge about the product or service, gathered through past experiences.

external search for information
Occurs when the buyer seeks information outside his or her personal knowledge base to help make the buying decision.

Social Media Marketing 5.1   The Twitterati Effect

During the information search step in the consumer decision process, it's quite likely for the potential purchaser to turn to social media for input. The information available—be it complimentary or not, or unsolicited or not—can alter the buying process.

A good example of this in action appears on the Canadian Product Reviews forum at smartcanucks.ca. The open nature of this message board allows consumers to log in, share their thoughts on products they've tried, explain their points of view, and offer advice. A quick glance at the board clearly shows diversity of opinion, with subject lines such as "Expensive yes, but worth every penny" to "I've really had it with them this time!"[9] Similar to corporate websites, such as Best Buy's, which encourage feedback and reviews on each product, the smartcanucks.ca forum allows a fast exchange of information to aid in the decision-making process.

But where social media has had the biggest impact is the "Twitterati" effect,[10] when famous stars and Twitter celebrities share feedback about a product. A great example of this is when popular blogger Heather Armstrong tweeted to her 1.4 million followers "STILL BROKEN. DO NOT BUY MAYTAG" and went on to explain how her washing machine had been repaired three times but was still broken. In another example, Kelly Osbourne posted photos showing the chemical burns she received after using Impulse body spray and urged her fans not to buy the product.[11] These messages reach such a large audience so quickly that they can be a real public relations crisis for companies. In some cases, these negative tweets have turned out to be a golden opportunity for competitive products. Representatives of Axe body spray actually appeared in media releases regarding the Impulse body spray incident, expressing their concern for Osbourne's injuries. It is difficult to measure Axe's loss or gain in this situation, since it was under scrutiny as a producer of body sprays; but, the company's product was still favoured as an alternative to Impulse.

Social media allows people to share and spread their messages so rapidly that things can quickly snowball out of control. Tim Hortons had committed a donation of refreshments to a meeting for the National Organization for Marriage, a group that opposes gay marriage. Interest groups got ahold of this information and began sending out tweet after tweet about it, some with facts and some with inaccurate information, which spread ferociously. Tim Hortons had to back out of the event because hundreds of consumers boycotted Tim Hortons and its products because of the conflict of interest.[12]

Social media has changed the game because people blog, tweet, and post to discuss what they are passionate about. This results in strong engagement and a desire to share the message widely, as occurred in the Tim Hortons case. Also, others no longer have to seek out this information; they simply log on to various media and have opinions presented to them. Unfortunately, there is no way to avoid social media. Even companies with a low level of commitment to social media can find themselves caught in the middle of a flurry, since it is consumers, not companies, who start these discussions. In the days of social media, it is still essential to address consumer inquiries and concerns quickly and effectively, and tools such as Twitter have changed dealing with customer complaints from a 9-to-5 world to a 24-7 situation.

---

significant safety implications, whereas they likely spend little time researching which inexpensive plastic toy car to buy for the youngest member of the family.

internal locus of control
Refers to when consumers believe they have some control over the outcomes of their actions, in which case they generally engage in more search activities.

external locus of control
Refers to when consumers believe that fate or other external factors control all outcomes.

- *The locus of control.* People who have an **internal locus of control** believe they have some control over the outcomes of their actions, in which case they generally engage in more search activities. With an **external locus of control**, consumers believe that fate or other external factors control all outcomes. In that case, they believe it doesn't matter how much information they gather; if they make a wise decision, it isn't to their credit, and if they make a poor one, it isn't their fault. For example, if Brad believes he can get a better deal when buying his first car, he will conduct an extensive search for information and try to use the information when negotiating his purchase. However, if Brad feels that regardless of what information he has, he can do little to influence the outcome of the deal, he will not engage in an extensive search.

- *Actual or perceived risk.* Five types of risk associated with purchase decisions can delay or discourage a purchase: performance, financial, social, physiological, and psychological. The higher the risk, the more likely the consumer is to engage in an extended search.

Performance risk involves the perceived danger inherent in a poorly performing product or service. An example of performance risk might be the possibility that Brad's sports car does not start or breaks down on the day he is supposed to take his girlfriend out for a drive to show off his new car.

Financial risk is risk associated with a monetary outlay and includes the initial cost of the purchase, as well as the costs of using the item or service. Car manufacturers, for instance, recognize that extended warranties help alleviate financial risk because consumers fear extensive postpurchase repair costs. For example, Brad bought two additional years of warranty over the manufacturer's standard "3-year, 60 000 kilometre" coverage for his sports car to reduce his financial risk within the first five years of buying the car.

Social risk involves the fears that consumers suffer when they worry others might not regard their purchases positively. When buying a dress, consumers like Katie, Brad's girlfriend, consider what her friends would think. Alternatively, since a job interview is so important, Katie might make a conscious effort to assert a distinctive identity or make a statement by buying a unique, more stylish, and possibly more expensive dress than her friends would typically buy.

Physiological risk could also be called **safety risk**. Whereas performance risk involves what might happen if a product does not perform as expected, physiological (or safety) risk refers to the fear of an actual harm should the product not perform properly. Although physiological risk is typically not an issue with apparel, it can be an important issue when buying other products, such as a car. External agencies and government bodies publish safety ratings for cars to help assuage this risk. Consumers compare the safety records of their various choices because they recognize the real danger to their well-being if the automobile they purchase fails to perform a basic task, such as stopping when the driver steps on the brakes. A recent example of this is the safety recalls associated with Toyota cars that failed to stop when the brakes were applied and instead accelerated. Sales of affected brand of Toyota cars fell off sharply and consumers purchased competitive brands, such as General Motors and Ford.[13]

Finally, **psychological risks** are those risks associated with the way people will feel if the product or service does not convey the right image. For example, Brad looked up reviews of the various sports cars and asked his friends their opinions because he wanted people to perceive his choice as a really good one.

- *Type of product or service.* Another factor that affects the depth and type of search a consumer undertakes is the type of product or service—specifically, whether it is a specialty, shopping, or convenience product.

Specialty goods/services are products or services toward which the customer shows a strong preference and for which he or she will expend considerable effort to search for the best suppliers. Because Brad wants the best sports car for his money, he searches carefully on the Internet for reviews and talks to friends who own sports cars before he starts shopping. Similarly, environmentally minded consumers, who would consider purchasing only a Prius or another hybrid car, would devote lots of time and effort to selecting just the right one.

Shopping goods/services are products or services, such as apparel, fragrances, and

performance risk
Involves the perceived danger inherent in a poorly performing product or service.

financial risk
Risk associated with a monetary outlay; includes the initial cost of the purchase, as well as the costs of using the item or service.

social risk
Involves the fears that consumers suffer when they worry others might not regard their purchases positively.

physiological (safety) risk
Risk associated with the fear of an actual harm should the product not perform properly.

psychological risk
Associated with the way people will feel if the product or service does not convey the right image.

Soda and bread are generally considered convenience goods (left). Shoes and T-shirts are shopping goods (middle). Products made by designers such as Polo Ralph Lauren are specialty goods (right).

specialty goods/services
Products or services toward which the customer shows a strong preference and for which he or she will expend considerable effort to search for the best suppliers.

shopping goods/services
Products or services, such as apparel, fragrances, and appliances, for which consumers will spend time comparing alternatives.

convenience goods/services
Products or services for which the consumer is not willing to spend any effort to evaluate prior to purchase.

appliances, for which consumers will spend a fair amount of time comparing alternatives. When Brad decides to buy a new pair of sneakers for himself, he will go from store to store shopping—trying shoes on, comparing alternatives, and chatting with salespeople.

Convenience goods/services are those products or services for which the consumer is not willing to spend any effort to evaluate prior to purchase. They are commodity items that are frequently purchased, usually with very little thought. Items such as pop, bread, and soap typically fall into this category.

Consumers can spend considerable time searching for both specialty and shopping goods or services; the difference lies in the kind of search. In some cases, the consumer's specific perceptions and needs help define the kind of search—and the type of product. For Brad, getting a haircut is a convenience purchase, so he visits the fastest, most convenient location. Brad's girlfriend, however, has tried various salons, each time comparing the haircut she received with her previous experiences. For her, a haircut is a shopping service. Finally, Brad's dad patronizes their neighbourhood barber shop because he perceives it to be the best in town. He often waits a few days for an appointment and pays a bit more than he would pay in similar barber shops. For him, getting a haircut is a specialty service.

Knowing that consumers go through various levels of information search, marketers must try to understand the sources of information customers use to search for information and the importance of each source. With this knowledge, marketers could implement various tactics, including providing information about their products or even educating customers about their product in general or a product category as a way to build trust and credibility (e.g., teaching consumers about digital cameras or photography while promoting their own brand of camera). In addition, tactics aimed at reducing the various risks should be communicated to customers. For example, marketers can provide guarantees through which defective products can be returned for a full refund or replaced at the company's expense, or that allow consumers to return products if they are not completely satisfied with them. Marketers also sometimes reduce the perception of risk by showing consumers that others have purchased the product and are proud owners or users.

Step 3: Alternative Evaluation

evaluative criteria
Consist of a set of salient, or important, attributes about a particular product that are used to compare alternative products.

Once consumers have recognized a problem and explored the possible options, they must sift through the choices available and evaluate the alternatives. Alternative evaluation often occurs while consumers are engaged in the process of information search. For example, a vegetarian consumer might learn about a new brand of yogourt that he or she can immediately rule out as a viable alternative because it contains some animal by-products. Consumers forgo alternative evaluations altogether when buying habitual (convenience) products; you'll rarely catch a loyal skim milk drinker buying a carton of 4-percent milk.

When you get your hair cut, do you consider it to be a convenience, shopping, or specialty purchase?

When consumers begin to evaluate different alternatives, they often base their evaluations on a set of important attributes or evaluative criteria. **Evaluative criteria** consist of a set of salient, or important, attributes about a particular product that are used to compare alternative products. For example, a consumer looking to buy a new HDTV might take into consideration such things as features, selling price, looks, and popularity of the different brands. At times, however, it becomes difficult to evaluate different brands or stores because there are so many choices, especially when those choices involve technical criteria, as in the HDTV market.

To simplify the potentially complicated decision process, consumers use shortcuts such as determinant attributes and consumer decision rules. **Determinant attributes** are product or service features that are *important* to the buyer and on which competing brands or stores are perceived to *differ*.[14] Because many important and desirable attributes are equal among the various choices, consumers look for something special—a determinant attribute—to differentiate one brand or store from another and on which to base their choice. Determinant attributes may appear perfectly rational, such as low gas consumption per mileage for a sports car, or they may be more subtle and psychologically based, such as the shapes, colour, and look of the car.

Consumer decision rules are the set of criteria that consumers use consciously or subconsciously to quickly and efficiently select from among several alternatives. These rules take several different forms: compensatory, noncompensatory, or decision heuristics.

What evaluative criteria would you consider when choosing one of these shampoos?

determinant attributes Product or service features that are important to the buyer and on which competing brands or stores are perceived to differ.

consumer decision rules The set of criteria consumers use consciously or subconsciously to quickly and efficiently select from among several alternatives.

Compensatory   A **compensatory decision rule** assumes that the consumer, when evaluating alternatives, trades off one characteristic against another, such that good characteristics compensate for bad characteristics.[15] For instance, when Brad was looking to buy a new car he considered several factors, such as mileage, style, price, and accessories. Even if the car is priced a little higher than Brad was planning to spend, the superb mileage offsets, or *compensates* for, the higher price.

Although Brad probably would not go through the formal process of making the purchasing decision based on the model described in Exhibit 5.2, it illustrates how a compensatory model would work. Brad assigns weights to each factor depending on their importance to him. These weights must add up to 1.0. So, for instance, mileage is the most important with a weight of 0.4, and style is least important with a weight of 0.1. Then Brad assigns weights to how well each of the cars might perform, with 1 being very poor, and 10 being very good. For instance, he thinks Toyota has the best mileage, so he assigns it a 10. Brad multiplies each performance rating by its importance rating to get an overall score for each car. The rating for Toyota in this example is the highest of the three cars ($[0.4 \times 10] + [0.1 \times 8] + [0.3 \times 6] + [0.2 \times 8] = 8.2$).

Noncompensatory   Sometimes, however, consumers use a **noncompensatory decision rule**, in which they choose a product or service on the basis of a subset of its characteristics, regardless of the values of its other attributes.[16] Thus, Brad might find a car with a lot of accessories and great mileage that costs considerably more than he is willing to spend but rejects the car simply on the basis of price. Because the Nissan offers a better price (he rated the price of a Toyota as 6 and a Nissan as 10 on the 10-point scale), he decides that the strength of the good points of the Toyota does not compensate for its biggest weakness—a high ticket price. Thus, based on compensatory decision rules, Brad should choose the Toyota car; but, using a noncompensatory decision rule, the price of the cars, Brad chose the Nissan.

The distinctive style of these lululemon yoga pants is a determinant attribute that distinguishes the product from other brands.

Decision Heuristics   Not everyone uses compensatory or noncompensatory decision rules. Some people use **decision heuristics**, which are mental shortcuts that help them narrow down their choices. Some examples of these heuristics follow:

- *Price.* Consumers can choose the more expensive option, thinking they are getting better quality along with the higher price ("You get what you pay for"), or they might buy the product priced

compensatory decision rule
Is at work when the consumer is evaluating alternatives and trades off one characteristic against another, such that good characteristics compensate for bad ones.

noncompensatory decision rule
Is at work when consumers choose a product or service on the basis of a subset of its characteristics, regardless of the values of its other attributes.

decision heuristics
Mental shortcuts that help consumers narrow down choices; examples include price, brand, and product presentation.

EXHIBIT 5.2	Compensatory Versus Noncompensatory Choices for Buying a Car				
	Mileage	**Style**	**Price**	**Accessories**	**Overall Score**
Importance Weight	0.4	0.1	0.3	0.2	
Toyota	10	8	6	8	8.2
Honda	8	9	8	3	7.1
Nissan	6	8	10	5	7.2

Evaluations are based on a 1 (very poor) to 10 (very good) scale.
Based on the noncompensatory decision rule (based on price), Nissan is the best candidate for purchase.

in the middle of the alternatives, neither the most expensive nor the cheapest, thinking that it is a good compromise between the two extremes.[17]

- *Brand.* Always buying brand name goods allows some consumers to feel safe with their choices. Purchasing a national brand, even if it is more expensive, gives many consumers the sense that they are buying a higher quality item.[18] For example, many consumers buy the more expensive Tylenol or Advil pain relief tablets over Shoppers Drug Mart's Life-brand pain tablets because they believe it is a higher quality product, despite identical ingredients.

- *Product presentation.* Many times, the manner in which a product is presented can influence the decision process. For example, two similar homes that are comparably priced will be perceived quite differently if one is presented in a perfectly clean and uncluttered condition, with fresh flowers and the smell of chocolate chip cookies wafting through it, whereas the other appears messy, has too much furniture for the rooms, and emits an unappealing smell. Consumers want to see that some effort has been put into the selling process, and just the way the product is presented can make or break a sale.[19]

Generally, the extent of alternative evaluation depends on several factors, such as the types of products or services (specialty, shopping, or convenience), the importance of the purchase, the perceived risks, and the expressive value of the purchase (i.e., to what extent the customers feel the product reflects an aspect of their personality). Shopping products tend to involve greater evaluation than convenience products. The purchase of highly expressive products that carry greater risks and that are more important to consumers involve more evaluation than the purchase of products that are less expressive or that have lower perceived risks.

Marketers can assist consumers in their evaluation process not only by educating them about the company's products, but also by providing detailed comparison information on price, technical specifications, unique features and benefits, and so on. Marketers may even provide free samples or trials of their products, which may enable consumers to compare the actual products. Power of the Internet 5.1 illustrates how Expedia.ca has created value for Canadian consumers by making travel alternatives readily available.

Step 4: Purchase Decision

Once consumers have considered the possible alternatives and evaluated the pros and cons of each, they can move toward a purchase decision. Value is a strong driver of consumers' purchase decisions. Customers seek out and purchase the products and services that they believe provide them with the best value. They don't always patronize the store or purchase the brand or item on which they had originally decided. Their choice may not be available at the retail store or there may be some other stumbling block.

| Power of the Internet 5.1 | Evaluating Travel Alternatives with Expedia[20] |

To illustrate how we evaluate alternatives in a buying decision, consider Expedia.ca, Canada's leading full-service online travel agency. Expedia.ca is a subsidiary of U.S.-based Expedia.com, the world's leading online travel service and the fourth-largest travel agency in the United States. Expedia.ca is well aware that Canadian travellers have high expectations in the competitive world of travel. Expedia's website (www.expedia.ca) makes alternative evaluation easy through a variety of innovations. It allows customers to plan their travel by date, price, interest, or activity. Travellers can book flights, hotel accommodations, car rentals, cruises, and vacation packages with the click of a mouse. The site also offers travel tools, such as travel alerts, flight status checks, seat selectors, airport information, currency converters, driving directions, weather reports, and passport information.

Consumers can use Expedia.ca to narrow their search from a universal set—all airlines—to their evoked set—say, only Air Canada, WestJet, and American Airlines. They can also search according to determinant attributes, such as the lowest price or the shortest flight. Some flyers use a noncompensatory decision rule; they will fly only Air Canada for international flights, no matter what the alternatives are, because they are members of the airline's frequent flyer program or prefer to support a Canadian airline. Others will use a compensatory decision rule, so they will fly WestJet from Ottawa to Calgary, depending on which airline has the best combination of the lowest price, shortest flight, and minimum number of stops. Finally, some travellers choose an airline on the basis of key product signals, such as legroom, number of in-flight movie options, or quality of the food.

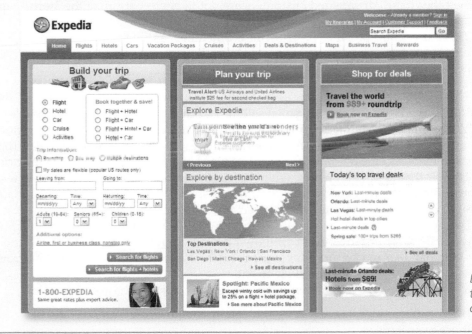

Expedia.ca makes every travel customer his or her own travel agent.

After consumers purchase the product or service, they usually consume it, or "put it to the test." A special type of consumption is called **ritual consumption**, which refers to a pattern of behaviours tied to life events that affect what and how we consume. These behaviours tend to have symbolic meanings and vary greatly by culture. They might take the form of everyday rituals, such as Brad going to Tim Hortons for his daily morning coffee or you brushing your teeth, or they can be reserved for special occasions, such as rites of passage or holiday rituals. Many firms try to tie their products and services to ritual consumption; just imagine, where would Hallmark be without holidays? Several situational factors, such as the following, help facilitate purchases: having the merchandise in stock that customers want, offering multiple payment options (e.g., cash, cheque, credit card, debit card, interest-free loans, no down payment), having many checkout lanes open and placing the checkouts conveniently in the store, installing digital displays to entertain customers waiting in

ritual consumption Refers to a pattern of behaviours tied to life events that affect what and how people consume.

line,[21] and offering such tactics as delivery, price-match guarantee, a warranty, or a simple return policy. Additional factors that affect whether the purchase decision is made immediately or later, such as store atmospherics, shopping situation, and temporal states, are discussed below.

In the case of online shopping, consumers may abandon their shopping carts just before checkout or at the payment stage. Retailers use various tactics to increase the chances that customers will convert their positive evaluations into purchases by making it easier to purchase merchandise. For example, Zappos.com and Overstock.com create urgency by alerting customers when an item in their shopping cart is almost sold out. Other online retailers, such as Gilt, offer items for a specified 36-hour period or until they run out, and Neiman Marcus runs two-hour, online-only sales. Many retailers send reminder emails to visitors about items in carts they have abandoned.[22]

Step 5: Postpurchase

The final step of the consumer decision process is postpurchase behaviour. Marketers are particularly interested in postpurchase behaviour because it entails actual, rather than potential, customers. On the one hand, marketers hope to create satisfied customers who become loyal, purchase again, and spread positive word of mouth. On the other hand, dissatisfied customers are not likely to patronize the store again and will spread negative word of mouth.

There are three possible postpurchase outcomes, as illustrated in Exhibit 5.3: customer satisfaction, postpurchase cognitive dissonance (buyer's remorse), and customer loyalty (or disloyalty).

Customer Satisfaction Setting unrealistically high consumer expectations of the product through advertising, personal selling, or other types of promotion may lead to higher initial sales, but it eventually will result in dissatisfaction when the product fails to achieve these high performance expectations. This failure can lead to dissatisfied customers and the potential for negative word of mouth. For example, Starbucks recognized that it should worry when its market research suggested that it was not meeting customer expectations in terms of speed of service. With higher-than-average coffee cup prices, customers expect fast and precise service.[23]

But setting customer expectations too low is an equally dangerous strategy. Many retailers, for instance, don't "put their best foot forward"; no matter how good their merchandise and service may be, if their store is not clean and appealing from the entrance, customers are not likely to enter.

Marketers can take the following steps to ensure postpurchase satisfaction:

- Build realistic expectations—not too high and not too low—and deliver on those expectations.
- Demonstrate correct product use; improper usage can cause dissatisfaction.
- Stand behind the product or service by providing money-back guarantees and warranties.
- Encourage customer feedback, which cuts down on negative word of mouth and helps marketers adjust their offerings.
- Periodically make contact with customers and thank them for their support. This contact reminds customers the marketer cares about their business and wants them to be satisfied. It also provides an opportunity to correct any problems. Customers appreciate human contact, though it is more expensive for marketers than email or postal mail contacts.

postpurchase dissonance
An internal conflict that arises from an inconsistency between two beliefs, or between beliefs and behaviour; buyer's remorse.

Postpurchase Cognitive Dissonance **Postpurchase dissonance** (or buyer's remorse) is an internal conflict that arises from an inconsistency between two beliefs, or between beliefs and behaviour. For example, you might have buyer's remorse after

EXHIBIT 5.3   Postpurchase Outcomes

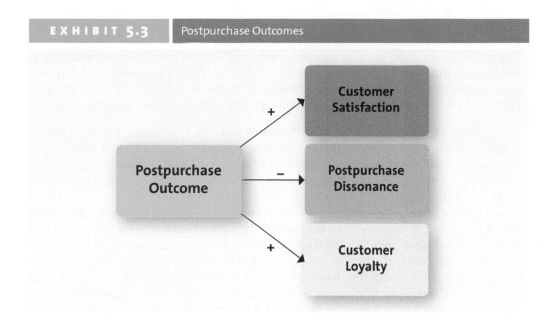

purchasing an expensive TV because you question whether a high-priced TV has appreciably better quality than a similar-size TV at a lower price. Thus, postpurchase cognitive dissonance is a feeling of regret, guilt, or grave uneasiness, which generally occurs when a consumer questions the appropriateness of a purchase after his or her decision has been made. This usually occurs when consumers feel, for example, that they made the purchase without all the information they needed, they were persuaded by a salesperson, they liked the good features of the product or service but do not like the negative aspects of the product or service, or if immediately following the purchase they see the product or service advertised elsewhere at a better value. Postpurchase dissonance is especially likely for products that are expensive, infrequently purchased, highly expressive, and associated with high levels of risk.

Aware of the negativity involved with postpurchase dissonance, marketers direct efforts at consumers after they have made the purchase to address the issue. For example, after Brad bought a Honda Civic, Honda Canada sent him a letter thanking him for his purchase and positively reinforcing the message that he made a wise decision by mentioning the high quality of the product's design and production. Included with the letter was a customer satisfaction survey (CSI) that asks about Brad's satisfaction with the dealership, salesperson, and other aspects of his purchase experience. Brad also received additional information about Honda services available to Honda Civic owners. To reduce the dissonance, Brad can take several actions:

Consumers often feel dissonance when purchasing products or services.

- Pay attention to positive information about the Honda Civic, such as looking up reviews by owners and car buffs on the Internet.
- Get positive feedback from friends about his new sports car.
- Seek negative information about sports cars he did not buy. Reading these reviews makes him feel more comfortable with his purchase decision.

Customer Loyalty   Customer loyalty develops over time with multiple repeat purchases of the product or brand from the same marketer. In the postpurchase stage of the decision-making process, marketers attempt to build and nurture a loyal relationship with their customers from

the very first purchase and with each subsequent purchase. They want customers to be satisfied with their purchase every time and buy from the same company again. Loyal customers will only buy certain brands and shop at certain stores, and they do not consider other brands or firms in their decision. As we explained in Chapter 2, such customers are therefore very valuable to firms, and marketers have designed customer relationship management (CRM) programs specifically to retain them.

Undesirable Consumer Behaviour Although firms want satisfied, loyal customers, sometimes they fail to attain them. Passive consumers are those that don't repeat purchase or fail to recommend the product to others. More serious and potentially damaging, however, is negative consumer behaviour, such as negative word of mouth and rumours.

negative word of mouth
Occurs when consumers spread negative information about a product, service, or store to others.

Negative word of mouth occurs when consumers spread negative information about a product, service, or store to others. When customers' expectations are met or even exceeded, they often don't tell anyone about it. But when consumers believe that they have been treated unfairly in some way, they usually want to complain, often to many people. The Internet has provided an effective method of spreading negative word of mouth to millions of people instantaneously through personal blogs, Twitter, and corporate websites. To lessen the impact of negative word of mouth, firms provide customer service representatives—whether online, on the phone, or in stores—to handle and respond to complaints. If the customer believes that positive action will be taken as a result of the complaint, he or she is less likely to complain to family and friends or through the Internet.

L03 Factors Influencing Consumer Buying Decisions

The consumer decision process can be influenced by several factors, as illustrated in Exhibit 5.4. First, are psychological factors, which are influences internal to the customer, such as motives, attitudes, perceptions, learning, and lifestyles. Second, social factors, such as family, reference groups, and culture, also influence the decision process. Third, situational factors, such as the specific purchase situation, a particular shopping situation, and temporal states (the time of day), affect the decision process.

Every decision people make as consumers will take them through some form of the consumer decision process. But, like life itself, this process does not exist in a vacuum.

Psychological Factors

Although marketers themselves can influence purchase decisions, a host of psychological factors affects the way people receive marketers' messages. Among them are motives, attitudes, perceptions, learning, and lifestyles. In this section, we examine how such psychological factors can influence the consumer decision process.

motive
A need or want that is strong enough to cause the person to seek satisfaction.

Motives In Chapter 1, we argued that marketing is all about satisfying customer needs and wants. When a need, such as thirst, or a want, such as a Diet Coke, is not satisfied, it motivates us, or drives us, to get satisfaction. So, a **motive** is a need or want that is strong enough to cause the person to seek satisfaction.

People have several types of motives. One of the best-known paradigms for explaining these motive types was developed by Abraham Maslow more than 30 years ago.[24] Maslow categorized five groups of needs, namely, physiological (e.g., food, water, shelter), safety (e.g., secure employment, health), love (e.g., friendship, family), esteem (e.g., confidence, respect), and self-actualization (people engage in personal growth activities and attempt to meet their intellectual, aesthetic, creative, and other such needs). The pyramid in Exhibit 5.5 demonstrates the theoretical progression of those needs.

physiological needs
Relate to the basic biological necessities of life: food, drink, rest, and shelter.

Physiological needs deal with the basic biological necessities of life: food, drink, rest, and shelter. Although for most people in developed countries these basic needs

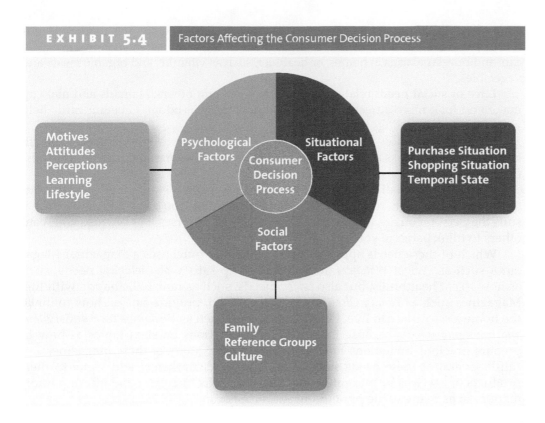

EXHIBIT 5.4 Factors Affecting the Consumer Decision Process

are generally met, there are those in both developed and less-developed countries who are less fortunate. However, everyone remains concerned with meeting these basic needs. Marketers seize every opportunity to convert these needs into wants by reminding us to eat at Taco Bell, drink milk, sleep on a Simmons Beautyrest mattress, and stay at a Marriott.

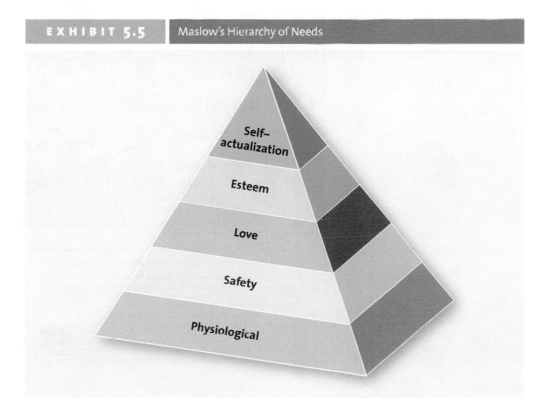

EXHIBIT 5.5 Maslow's Hierarchy of Needs

safety needs
Pertain to protection and physical well-being.

love (social) needs
Relate to our interactions with others.

esteem needs
Allow people to satisfy their inner desires.

self-actualization
Occurs when you feel completely satisfied with your life and how you live.

Safety needs pertain to protection and physical well-being. The marketplace is full of products and services that are designed to make you safer, such as airbags in cars and burglar alarms in homes, or healthier, such as vitamins and organic meats and vegetables.

Love or social needs relate to our interactions with others. Haircuts and makeup make you look more attractive, and deodorants prevent odour. Greeting cards help you express your feelings toward others.

Esteem needs allow people to satisfy their inner desires. Yoga, meditation, health clubs, and many books appeal to people's desires to grow or maintain a happy, satisfied outlook on life.

Finally, **self-actualization** occurs when you feel completely satisfied with your life and how you live. You don't care what others think. You drive a Prius because it suits the person you are, not because some celebrity endorses it or because you want others to think better of you.

Which of these needs applies when a consumer purchases a magazine? Magazines such as *Weight Watchers*, for instance, help satisfy *physiological* needs, such as how to eat healthfully, but also *esteem* needs, such as how to be happy with life. Magazines such as *Family Circle*, on the other hand, provide tips on how to make the home a *safer* place to live. Finally, magazines such as *Weddings* help satisfy *love and belonging* needs, because they provide instructions on such topics as how to prepare gracious invitations for friends and family. Many of these magazines can fulfill several of these needs simultaneously. Good marketers add value to their products or services by nudging people up the needs hierarchy and offering information on as many of the pyramid needs as they can.

Taco Bell satisfies physiological needs.

Ads for crime prevention satisfy safety needs.

Attitude We have attitudes about almost everything. For instance, we don't like this class, but we do like the instructor. We like where we live, but we don't like the weather. An **attitude** is a person's enduring evaluation of his or her feelings about and behavioural tendencies toward an object or idea. Attitudes are learned and long-lasting, and they might develop over a long period of time, though they can also abruptly change. For instance, you might like your instructor for much of the semester—until she returns your first exam. One thing we all have in common is that our attitudes have the ability to influence our decisions and actions.

An attitude consists of three components. The **cognitive component** reflects what we *believe* to be true, the **affective component** involves what we *feel* about the issue at hand—our like or dislike of something—and the **behavioural component** comprises the *action(s)* we take based on what we know and feel. For example, Ed and Tracy Lee see an ad for a Volvo that shows a family of five driving down the road, the kids strapped into their car seats and mom and dad talking in the front. An announcer lists the features included with each model, as well as government safety ratings that indicate Volvo is the safest brand on the road in its class. On the basis of this advertisement, Ed and Tracy believe that the government statistics must be true and that the car is therefore safe (cognitive component). Watching the happy family looking comfortable while driving this safe car allows Ed and Tracy to feel that they would like to have this car for their family (affective). Thus encouraged, they go to the Volvo dealership closest to them to make a purchase (behavioural).

Ideally, agreement exists among these components. When there is incongruence among the three however, cognitive dissonance might occur. Suppose, for instance, that though Ed and Tracy believe the Volvo is safe and like the car, they buy another brand because it is cheaper. It is likely that they will experience the discomfort of buyers' remorse, or cognitive dissonance.

Although attitudes are pervasive and usually slow to change, the important fact from a marketer's point of view is that they can be influenced and perhaps changed through persuasive communications and personal experience. Marketing communication—through salespeople, advertisements, free samples, or other such methods—can attempt to change what people believe to be true about a product or service (cognitive) or how they feel toward it (affective). If the marketer is successful, the cognitive and affective components work in concert to affect behaviour. Continuing with our example, suppose that prior to viewing the ad, Ed and Tracy thought that a Toyota Camry was the safest car on the road, but they liked the looks of the Volvo. The ad positively influenced the cognitive component of their attitude toward Volvo, making it consistent with the affective component.

Which hierarchy of needs do these magazines fulfill?

attitude
A person's enduring evaluation of his or her feelings about and behavioural tendencies toward an object or idea; consists of three components: *cognitive*, *affective*, and *behavioural*.

cognitive component
A component of *attitude* that reflects what a person believes to be true.

People buy Volvos because they believe they are safe (cognitive component of an attitude), because they like them (affective), and because they have many convenient dealerships to visit (behavioural).

affective component
A component of *attitude* that reflects what a person feels about the issue at hand—his or her like or dislike of something.

behavioural component
A component of *attitude* that comprises the actions a person takes with regard to the issue at hand.

perception
The process by which people select, organize, and interpret information to form a meaningful picture of the world.

Perception   Another psychological factor, **perception**, is the process by which we select, organize, and interpret information to form a meaningful picture of the world. Perception influences our acquisition and consumption of goods and services through our tendency to assign meaning to such things as colour, symbols, taste, and packaging. Culture, tradition, and our overall upbringing determine our perceptual view of the world. For instance, Tracy has always wanted a Volvo because her best friend in college had one, and they had a great time driving across the country together one summer. However, based on his past experiences, Ed has a different perception. Ed thinks Volvos are slow, stodgy, unfashionable, and meant to be driven by little old ladies with grey hair—though they are safe! Volvo has worked hard in recent years to overcome this long-standing, negative perceptual bias that Ed and many others hold by creating faster cars with more stylish designs and by using promotion to reposition the brand to portray a more positive image.

In trying to influence perceptions, marketers must understand and focus on the four components of perception: *selective exposure, selective attention, selective comprehension,* and *selective retention*. People who look at the news and sports channels only, but not the comedy or women's TV network channels, are engaged in selective exposure because they are excluding other programs or channels. Similarly, consumers who only listen to messages that are consistent with their beliefs, and not others, are practicing selective attention. For instance, although someone may look at the sports channel, he or she may watch hockey, soccer, or baseball but not boxing or wrestling because these may be too violent for his or her taste. Selective comprehension occurs when consumers interpret a marketing message in a way that is different from what the marketer intends. For example, a Dolce & Gabbana ad was intended to be edgy and sexual but consumers felt that it reinforced stereotypes about rape and degraded women. Knowing this, marketers can target their communications in those media that maximize exposure to their target market and create messages that are consistent with their beliefs and attitudes so that they will pay attention to the messages and interpret them in the intended way. Finally, selective retention describes the situation where consumers do not remember all the information they see, read or hear. Marketers can provide the information in various other forms such as print, online, and other displays to reinforce their message.

learning
Refers to a change in a person's thought process or behaviour that arises from experience and takes place throughout the consumer decision process.

Learning   **Learning** refers to a change in a person's thought process or behaviour that arises from experience and takes place throughout the consumer decision process. For instance, after Brad recognized that he wanted a sports car, he started looking for ads and searching for reviews and articles on the Internet. He learned from each new piece of information, so that his thoughts about sports cars were different from what they were before he had read anything. In addition, Brad liked the salesperson at the dealership who served him. Brad learned from this experience, and it became part of his memory to be used in the future, possibly so he would recommend the dealership or salesperson to his friends.

Learning affects both attitudes and perceptions. Throughout the buying process, Brad's attitudes shifted. The cognitive component changed for him when he learned that the dealership offers various additional services at low costs to Honda Civic owners. Once he started getting the additional services (e.g., free car washes, special rates for car detailing), he realized how much he liked the service, which indicates the affective component, and he then subscribed to it—the behavioural component. Each time Brad was exposed to information about the service, he learned something different that affected his perception of the dealership. Before he tried it, Brad hadn't realized how friendly and helpful the people at the dealership were; thus, his perception of the dealership service changed through learning.

lifestyle
Refers to the way consumers spend their time and money to live.

Lifestyle   **Lifestyle** refers to the way consumers spend their time and money to live. For many consumers, the question of whether the product or service fits with their actual lifestyle, which may be fairly sedentary, or their perceived lifestyle, which might be outdoorsy, is an important one. Some of the many consumers sporting

North Face jackets certainly need the high-tech, cold weather gear because they are planning their next hike up Mount Robson and want to be sure they have sufficient protection against the elements. Others, however, simply like the image that the jacket conveys—the image that they might be leaving for their own mountain-climbing expedition any day now—even if the closest they have come to this trip has been shovelling their driveway. Similarly, people buy the Hummer luxury four-wheel drive SUV so that they can get over almost any off-road obstacle, but they also like the leather seats with lumbar support, six-speaker audio system preloaded with XM satellite radio, remote keyless entry system, and the fact that they can whiz over speed bumps at the local grocery store.

A person's perceptions and ability to learn are affected by their social experiences, which we discuss next. Furthermore, Sustainable Marketing 5.1 shows how consumers' changing attitudes and lifestyles are influencing the types of foods they buy and consume.

Social Factors

Exhibit 5.4 on page 163 illustrates that the consumer decision process is also influenced by the external, social environment, which consists of the customer's family, reference groups, and culture.[25]

Family Many purchase decisions are made about products or services that the entire family will consume or use. Thus, firms must consider how families make purchase decisions and understand how various family members might influence these decisions.

When families make purchase decisions, they often consider the needs of all the family members. In choosing a restaurant, for example, all the family members may participate in the decision making. In other situations, however, different members of the family may take on different roles. For example, Brad recalled that when he was a kid, his dad and two older brothers were the ones who looked through car magazines and *Consumer Reports* to search for information about a new car. But once the family arrived at the dealership, his dad, not his brothers, decided which model and colour to buy, and his mom negotiated the final deal.

Despite that example, children and adolescents play an increasingly important role in family buying decisions. For instance, the tween segment alone in Canada is estimated to spend more than $3 billion per year on personal items such as snacks, soft drinks, electronics, and apparel. Tweens in Canada also indirectly influence family purchases in excess of $20 billion on big ticket items such as recreation, vacations, technology, and the family car.[26]

Influencing a group that holds this much spending power is vitally important. Traditional food retailers are already caught in a squeeze between Walmart, which lures low-end customers, and specialty retailers, such as Whole Foods, which target the high end. Knowing how children influence food-buying decisions is a strategic opportunity for traditional supermarkets and their suppliers to exploit. Getting this group to prefer one store, chain, or product over another can make a difference in the bottom line, as well as in the chances for survival in a difficult marketplace.[27]

Reference Groups A **reference group** is one or more persons an individual uses as a basis for comparison regarding beliefs, feelings, and behaviours. A consumer might have various reference groups, including family, friends, co-workers, or famous people the consumer would like to emulate. These reference groups affect buying decisions by (1) offering information, (2) providing rewards for specific purchasing behaviours, and (3) enhancing a consumer's self-image.

reference group
One or more persons an individual uses as a basis for comparison regarding beliefs, feelings, and behaviours.

Family members often influence buying decisions.

Sustainable Marketing 5.1   Consumers Warm Up to Organic Foods

Organic agriculture, previously seen as a niche market that originated approximately 15 years ago, is registering rapid growth, with global sales estimated to be growing at 10 to 20 percent annually.[28] This flourishing global market for organic food was valued at about US$30 billion in 2005, and the growth of demand for organic food is expected to continue. This increased demand has been attributed to various food scares, including concerns about the use of pesticides and food additives, and the increased use of genetically modified organisms in food production.[29] The organic industry integrates all aspects of a pesticide-free, fertilizer-free production process by using specific standards and is subject to a rigorous certification system.

What Is Organic Food?

There is often confusion about the true definition of *organic* among consumers. When comparing organic food to conventional food products, consumers of organic food generally describe it as "pesticide free" and "hormone free," with "no chemicals," "no pollutants," "no antibiotics," and "no genetically modified organisms"; thus, it is considered "natural." They also describe organic products as more nutritious, tasty, better looking, fresher, and without a uniform shape.

The Organic Food Consumer Profile

Although consumers of organic food differ in terms of their socio-demographic profile, we can say that they are mainly women, who buy in larger quantities and more frequently than men. Although age is not an important factor, younger consumers show a higher willingness to buy organic because of their greater environmental concerns but cannot always afford to. Families often introduce organic foods with the arrival of a baby, which leads to substantial changes in food consumption habits. In 2001, a total of 71 percent of Canadians had at least tried organic foods. Among those people who have tried organics, 18 percent are frequent buyers, 22 percent are infrequent buyers, and 31 percent are occasional buyers.[30]

Consumer's Motivations to Buy Organic Food

In Canada, consumers identify health, the environment, and supporting local farmers as being the principal values that explain their organic food consumption.[31] Interestingly, consumers express that a socially responsible behaviour motivates them: to support local farmers or the local economy. More generally, in several different European countries, studies highlighted the following consumers' life values: values centred on the human being, on the environment, and on animals' well-being. Overall, organics are perceived as less associated with health risks than their conventional counterparts. For Canadians, health motivation is more an avoidance motivation (e.g., to avoid ingesting chemicals) than an approach motivation (e.g., to acquire nutritional benefits). Consumers' desire to maximize their personal health and well-being is another important motivation. The main reasons preventing consumers from buying organic foods are their high price, their lack of wide availability, their unsatisfactory quality, consumer satisfaction with current purchases, consumers' lack of familiarity with organic foods, consumer mistrust of organic labels, limited choice, and lack of perceived value.

Trust in Organic Food

Consumers rely on several indicators in order to trust the products. Therefore, marketers can use different tactics to encourage consumers not only to trust the brand and the label, but also to trust partners, such as producers. For now, when it comes to consumption of organic products, brand does not yet appear to be the main source of trust. Labelling and certification issues prevail, as consumers are either unfamiliar with or confused by labels or do not know to what degree they can trust certification labels. Generally, consumers want to learn more about the source of organic products and the production practices they are produced under. Regular consumers of organic food are developing a greater level of trust and confidence for specific organic certifications. New consumers at an early stage of their learning curve just rely on what is labelled as "organic."

Consumers' trust of points of sale seems to be an important factor in deciding where they buy organic foods. Supermarkets are increasingly successful but must deal with a lack of trust, especially for regular consumers of organic food, whereas specialty shops are associated with personal relationships, knowledge, and trust.

Consumer knowledge and awareness are important in the organic foods market: a segment of the potential market is not yet informed about them, and those consumers who have general knowledge do not have enough detailed information to differentiate the food's unique attributes. Therefore, knowledge and awareness about organics can affect perceptions and attitudes, and ultimately, buying decisions.

Reference groups provide information to consumers directly through conversation or indirectly through observation. For example, when Emily, a second-year business student at the University of British Columbia saw that almost all her colleagues had a smartphone (iPhone, BlackBerry, or Android), she quickly decided it was time for her to purchase a smartphone in order to fit in with her peers.

Some reference groups also influence behaviours by rewarding behaviour that meets with their approval or chastising those who engage in behaviour that doesn't. For example, smokers are often criticized by their friends and made to smoke outside or in restricted areas.

Consumers can identify and affiliate with reference groups to create, enhance, or maintain their self-image. Customers who want to be seen as "earthy" might buy Birkenstock sandals, whereas those wanting to be seen as "high fashion" might buy Christian Louboutin shoes, as we discussed earlier in this chapter.

A survey of Canadian and American teenagers showed that Hollister, American Eagle, West Coast Brands, and Abercrombie & Fitch are the most popular brands among this group.[32] Some stores, such as Abercrombie & Fitch, play on these forms of influence and hire sales associates they hope will serve as a reference group for customers who shop there. These hip, attractive, and somewhat aloof employees are encouraged to wear the latest store apparel—thereby serving as living mannequins for customers to emulate.

Culture   We defined culture in Chapter 3 as the shared meanings, beliefs, morals, values, and customs of a group of people. Your cultural group might be as small as your reference group at school or as large as the country in which you live or the religion in which you participate. For instance, the culture at Brad's college evokes a "high-achiever" attitude. This reputation influences, to some extent, the way he spends his leisure time, the types of people he hangs out with, and the kinds of products he buys. Culture is one of the most pervasive factors influencing consumer behaviour. Therefore, marketers must work hard to understand how it is different not only in Canada but in those countries to which they plan to market their products. Marketing strategies that may work in Canada or North America may not work well in Japan or India because consumers in those countries are culturally different, as discussed in Chapter 16. Additionally, even within Canada, there are cultural differences between various subgroups or subcultures. A subculture is a group of people whose beliefs and values are different from the rest of the larger society in which they live. Examples of subcultures in Canada include French-Canadian subculture, Chinese Canadian subculture, South-Asian subculture, and Acadian subculture. Research has shown that Chinese- and Asian-Canadians prefer to do business with marketers who truly understand their culture and needs rather than those who have very superficial ways of acknowledging their community, which a lot of people in the community actually find irritating.[33]

Situational Factors

Psychological and social factors typically influence the consumer decision process the same way each time. For example, your motivation to quench your thirst usually drives you to drink a Pepsi, and your reference group at the workplace coerces you to wear appropriate attire. But sometimes, **situational factors**, or factors specific to the situation, override, or at least influence, psychological and social issues. These situational factors are related to the purchase and shopping situation, as well as to the temporal state, as illustrated in Exhibit 5.4. Entrepreneurial Marketing 5.1 describes how Montreal's BIXI has been embraced by consumers as a desirable mode of transportation in busy, crowded cities.

situational factors
Factors affecting the consumer decision process; those that are specific to the purchase and shopping situation and temporal state that may override, or at least influence, psychological and social issues.

Purchase Situation   Customers may be predisposed to purchase certain products or services because of some underlying psychological trait or social factor, but these factors may change in certain purchase situations. For instance, Priya Persaud, a Vancouverite, considers herself a thrifty, cautious shopper—someone who likes to get a good deal. But her best friend is getting married, and she wants to buy the couple a silver tray. If the tray were for herself, she would probably go to Stokes, Bowring, or possibly even Walmart. But since it is for her best friend, she went to Birks. Why? To purchase something fitting for the special occasion of a wedding.

Entrepreneurial Marketing 5.1   **Collaborative Consumption and Montreal's BIXI**[34]

Many of us have heard the saying "sharing is caring." Today's entrepreneurs are taking this concept not only to heart, but also to a completely new level and scale unimaginable just a few years ago. In business, the concept of sharing and caring is developing into an emerging trend, which researchers are calling "collaborative consumption." The practice of collaborative consumption is becoming such a dominant cultural force in today's society that it is the subject of a new book, *What's Mine Is Yours: The Rise of Collaborative Consumption*, co-authored by Rachel Botsman and Roo Rogers. Collaborative consumption is a socio-economic trend based on the idea of making the maximum use of a product through sharing, swapping, bartering, trading, or renting in order to minimize adverse environmental effects. It is centred on the mindset of reducing our carbon footprints, and consumers pay for the benefit of having *access* to a product rather than having to pay more to *own* it.

The huge shift to collaborative consumption is being facilitated by advances in technologies, social media, and peer-to-peer online platforms, where people can share and exchange information. The trend is changing not only what we consume, but also how we consume. Areas where collaborative consumption is beginning to take root include transportation (e.g., car sharing, carpooling, ride sharing, bike sharing), apparel (e.g., clothes and accessories swapping), food, living spaces, household appliances, money (e.g., social lending, virtual currencies, time banks), workspaces, travel, accommodation, space (e.g., storage, parking, spare rooms), and book swapping.[35]

The City of Montreal has gotten into the act of collaborative consumption in a big way with its entrepreneurial venture BIXI system. The $15 million BIXI system was officially launched in May 2009. The term *BIXI* results from combining the words *bike* and *taxi*. The BIXI system is modelled on bike-sharing programs in Europe, such as the famous Vélib network in Paris. Consumers are showing growing interest in Montreal's patented bike-sharing model. Consumers can subscribe to the service on a yearly, monthly, or daily basis.

The BIXI system began with a fleet of 3000 bikes that are available for short-term rental around Montreal's downtown core. The city has set up 300 stations where bikes can be stored and picked up. After consumers pick up the bikes, they can ride it for the first 30 minutes for free, and they can return the bikes to any station around Montreal. The bikes are made of aluminum and are theft-proof, as they are equipped with GPS chips that automatically lock the brakes if the bike is not returned. Cyclists, residents, and tourists alike, have enthusiastically embraced the BIXI system, leading to its tremendous success within a short time. Montreal's BIXI system has been so successful that other cities, such as London, England, and Boston, United States, have licensed the system. The system was also introduced in Ottawa and Toronto in 2011.[36]

The success of the BIXI system is not the only benefit of the venture; it is also benefiting Montreal residents. Consumers who are interested in the green movement now have a transport system that fits into their green lifestyle.

Montreal's BIXI program offers 3000 bikes for rent at 300 stations.

Shopping Situation Consumers might be ready to purchase a product or service but for a variety of reasons be completely derailed once they arrive in the store. Marketers use several techniques to influence consumers at this choice stage of the decision process. Consider the following techniques:

- *Store atmosphere*. Some retailers and service providers have developed unique images that are based at least in part on their internal environment, also known as their atmospherics.[37] Research has shown that, if used in concert with other aspects of a retailer's strategy, music, scent, lighting, and even colour can positively influence the decision process.[38] For example, Abercrombie & Fitch aggressively positions itself as a lifestyle brand called "Casual Luxury." Its stores are plastered with photos of physically attractive young models, blasted with loud dance music through powerful speakers, and pumped full of the company's signature cologne, Fierce. The stores are also staffed with attractive models, young salespeople who embody the Abercrombie & Fitch lifestyle: attractive, athletic, popular, enthusiastic, and outgoing.[39] Restaurants, such as Rainforest Cafe, have developed internal environments that are not only pleasant, but also consistent with their food and service.

- *Salespeople*. Well-trained sales personnel can influence the sale at the point of purchase by pointing out the advantages of one item over another and by encouraging multiple purchases. The salesperson at Birks, for instance, explained to Priya why one platter was better than the next and suggested some serving pieces to go with it.

- *Crowding*. Customers can feel crowded because there are too many people, too much merchandise, or lines that are too long. If there are too many people in a store, some people become distracted and may even leave.[40] Others have difficulty purchasing if the merchandise is packed too closely together. This issue is a particular problem for shoppers with mobility disabilities.

- *In-store demonstrations*. The taste and smell of new food items may attract people to try something they normally wouldn't. Similarly, some fashion retailers offer "trunk shows," during which their vendors show their whole line on a certain day. During these well-advertised events, customers are often enticed to purchase that day because they get special assistance from the salespeople and can order merchandise that the retailer otherwise does not carry.

- *Promotions*. Retailers employ various promotional vehicles to influence customers once they have arrived in the store. For instance, an unadvertised price promotion can alter a person's preconceived buying plan. Multi-item

Abercrombie & Fitch stores blast loud dance music through powerful speakers and pump the company's signature cologne, Fierce, into the air.

In-store demonstrations entice people to buy.

discounts, such as "buy one, get one free" sales, are popular means to get people to buy more than they normally would. Because many people regard clipping coupons from the newspaper as too much trouble, some stores make coupons available in the store. Another form of promotion is offering a "free" gift with the purchase of a good or service. This type of promotion is particularly popular with cosmetics.

● *Packaging.* It is difficult to make a product stand out in the crowd when it competes for shelf space with several other brands. This problem is particularly difficult for consumer packaged goods, such as groceries and health and beauty products. Marketers therefore spend millions of dollars designing and updating their packages to be more appealing and eye-catching than their competitors'.

Temporal State   Our state of mind at any particular time can alter our preconceived notions of what we are going to purchase. For instance, some people are "morning people," whereas others function better at night. In turn, a purchase situation may have different appeal levels depending on the time of day and the type of person the consumer is. Mood swings can also alter consumer behaviour. Suppose Priya received a parking ticket just prior to shopping at Birks. It is likely that she would be less receptive to the salesperson's influence than if she came into the store in a good mood. Her bad mood may even cause her to have a less positive postpurchase feeling about the store. Unfortunately, such temporal factors are usually beyond the control of even the most creative marketer.

As we've seen, people's lives are lived in different contexts and consumer decisions are made in unique contexts. Marketers who understand this fact are better positioned to serve their target consumers. All the factors that affect the consumer decision process that we have discussed—psychological factors, social factors, and situational factors—are all impacted by the level of consumer involvement, the subject of the next section.

L04   Involvement and Consumer Buying Decisions

involvement
The consumer's degree of interest or concern in the product or service.

Consumers engage in two types of buying process/decisions depending on their level of involvement: extended problem solving for high-priced, risky, infrequent, or highly expressive purchases; and limited problem solving, which includes impulse buying and habitual purchases/decision making. **Involvement** is the consumer's degree of interest or concern in the product or service.[41] Consumers may have different levels of involvement for the same type of product. One consumer behaviour theory, the elaboration likelihood model, illustrated in Exhibit 5.6, proposes that high- and low-involvement consumers process different aspects of a marketing message or advertisement.

If both types of consumers viewed ads for hybrids produced by Toyota and Ford, the high-involvement consumer (e.g., Katie who is researching hybrids) will scrutinize all the information provided (e.g., gas savings, eco-friendly) and process the key elements of the message deeply. As a consequence, Katie, an involved consumer, is likely to either end up judging the ad to be truthful and form a favourable impression of the product or alternatively view the message as superficial and develop negative product impressions (i.e., her research suggests the product is not as good as it is being portrayed).

In contrast, a low-involvement consumer will likely process the same advertisement in a less thorough manner. Such a consumer might pay less attention to the key elements of the message (e.g., gas savings, eco-friendly) and focus on

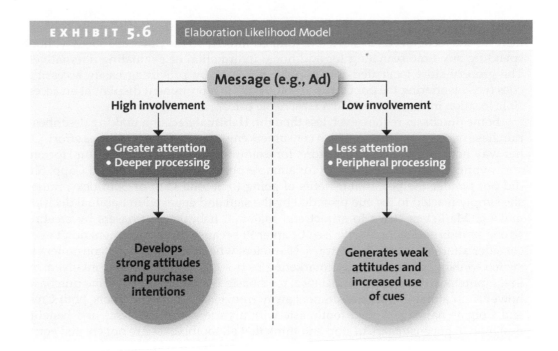

EXHIBIT 5.6   Elaboration Likelihood Model

heuristic elements such as brand name (Toyota), price, and the presence of a celebrity endorser. The impressions of the low-involvement consumer are likely to be more superficial.

Extended Problem Solving

As we noted in the beginning of this chapter, the buying process begins when consumers recognize that they have an unsatisfied need. Katie recognized her need to have access to transportation when she went away to college. She sought information by asking for advice from her friends, by reading consumer reports, and by researching online. Once she decided that a car and not a bike or the bus was her best option, she visited several car dealerships to test drive the models she was interested in and to find out which dealer offered the best price. Finally, after considerable time and effort spent analyzing her alternatives, Katie purchased a Toyota Prius. This process is an example of **extended problem solving**, which is common when the customer perceives that the purchase decision entails a great deal of risk. The potential risks associated with Katie's decision to buy her car include financial (Did I pay too much?), physiological (Will it keep me safe in an accident?), social (Will my friends think I look cool?), performance (Will the car perform as expected?), and psychological (Will the car convey the right image of me?) risks. To reduce her perceived risk, Katie spent a lot of effort searching for information about cars before she actually made her purchase.

Limited Problem Solving

Limited problem solving occurs during a purchase decision that calls for, at most, a moderate amount of effort and time. Customers engage in this type of buying process when they have had some prior experience with the product or service and the perceived risk is moderate. Limited problem solving usually relies on past experience more than on external information. For some people even a car purchase could require limited effort.

A common type of limited problem solving is **impulse buying**, a buying decision made by customers on the spot when they see the merchandise.[42] When Katie went to the grocery store to do her weekly shopping, she saw a display case of popcorn and Dr Pepper near the checkout counter. Knowing that some of her friends were going to her place to watch a movie later, she stocked up. The popcorn and pop

extended problem solving
A purchase decision process during which the consumer devotes considerable time and effort to analyzing alternatives; often occurs when the consumer perceives that the purchase decision entails a great deal of risk.

limited problem solving
Occurs during a purchase decision that calls for, at most, a moderate amount of effort and time.

impulse buying
A buying decision made by customers on the spot when they see the merchandise.

were an impulse purchase. Katie didn't go through the entire decision process; instead, she recognized her need and jumped directly to the purchase stage without spending any time searching for additional information or evaluating alternatives. The grocery store facilitated this impulse purchase by providing easily accessible cues (i.e., by offering the popcorn and soft drinks in a prominent display, at an accessible location in the store, and at a reasonable price).

habitual decision making
A purchase decision process in which consumers engage with little conscious effort.

Some purchases require even less thought. **Habitual decision making** describes a purchase decision process in which consumers engage with little conscious effort. On her way home from the grocery store, for example, Katie drove past a Tim Hortons and swung into the drive-through for a maple pecan Danish and an Iced Capp. She did not ponder the potential benefits of going to Second Cup or Starbucks; rather, she simply reacted to the cue provided by the sign and engaged in habitual decision making. Marketers strive to attract and maintain habitual purchasers by creating strong brands and store loyalty (see Chapter 9) because these customers don't even consider alternative brands or stores. Marketers who are trying to get consumers to switch to their brands often use marketing tactics that require greater involvement in the purchase decisions. For instance, toothpaste is a habitual or routine purchase; however, in attempt to lure customers away from each other's products, both Crest and Colgate have developed toothpaste with a variety of ingredients and benefits designed to get customers to stop and think that all toothpastes are not created equal and that toothpaste is just not toothpaste—it offers various health benefits. The same thing can be said of bread and a host of other consumer packaged goods.

Learning Objectives Review

 Describe the steps a customer goes through when buying a product or service

Consumers generally start their decision process by recognizing that they must buy something to satisfy a need or want. Sometimes the needs are simple: I need food because I am hungry. Often, however, they become more complex: I want to buy my girlfriend an engagement ring.

Once they recognize the need, consumers start searching for information. Generally, the more important the purchase, the more time and effort the consumer will spend on the search process. Firms facilitate this search by providing promotional materials and personal selling. Once they have enough information, consumers can evaluate their alternatives and make a choice.

In the next step of the decision process, consumers purchase and use the product or service. But the process doesn't simply stop there. After the sale, the consumer is either satisfied with the purchase or experiences postpurchase dissonance. Every marketer wants satisfied customers, but when instead they are confronted with dissatisfied customers who are in some way unsure about their purchase, marketers must proactively turn the situation around. If they don't, the customer may be gone for good.

LO2 **Identify what determines how much time consumers will spend searching for information before buying a product or service**

A variety of factors affect consumers' searches for information about a potential purchase. First, they consider the time and effort associated with searching versus the benefits derived from the search. Second, people who have an internal locus of control—those who believe they have control over the outcomes of their actions—are more likely to spend time searching for information than those with an external locus of control. Third, consumers who perceive a high performance, financial, social, physiological, or psychological risk associated with the purchase will spend relatively more time searching for information than those who do not. Finally, consumers will spend more time searching for information for specialty goods than for shopping or convenience goods, respectively.

LO3 **Summarize how psychological, social, and situational factors influence consumers' buying behaviour**

First and foremost, firms must design their products and services to meet their customers' wants and needs, but understanding certain aspects of consumer behaviour can help as well. For instance, it is important to understand people's motives (i.e., what drives them to buy), their attitudes (i.e., how they feel about a product or service), and their perceptions (i.e., how information about that product or service fits into their worldview). Knowledge about these psychological characteristics helps firms design and provide products and services that their customers want and need.

In addition, people don't live in a vacuum. Consumers are influenced by their family, their reference groups, and their culture. Understanding these social groups and people's roles within them provides important insights into consumers' buying behaviour. Finally, though consumers already carry a host of psychological and social factors along with them on a shopping expedition, certain other factors can influence a purchase at the point of sale. For instance, customers might change their buying behaviour because the purchase situation is different than the one they are used to. Also, things can happen to customers, both positive and negative, once they are in a store that might alter their preconceived notion of what they plan to purchase. Finally, people can be just plain finicky, and being in an unusually good or extremely bad mood can also alter a purchase decision. The more firms understand these psychological, social, and situational factors, the more likely they will be to influence purchase decisions.

LO4   Explain how involvement influences the consumer buying decision process

How much time a consumer spends making a purchasing decision depends on the product or service being purchased. Some purchasing decisions require limited problem solving because the perceived risk of the purchase is low or the consumer has previous experience purchasing the product or service. Impulse and habitual purchases fall in this category. Sometimes, however, consumers enter into complex buying behaviour because the perceived risk of the purchase is great.

Key Terms

- affective component, 166
- attitude, 165
- behavioural component, 166
- cognitive component, 165
- compensatory decision rule, 158
- consumer decision rules, 157
- convenience goods/services, 156
- decision heuristics, 158
- determinant attributes, 157
- esteem needs, 164
- evaluative criteria, 156
- extended problem solving, 173
- external locus of control, 154
- external search for information, 153
- financial risk, 155

- functional needs, 152
- habitual decision making, 174
- impulse buying, 173
- internal locus of control, 154
- internal search for information, 153
- involvement, 172
- learning, 166
- lifestyle, 166
- limited problem solving, 173
- love (social) needs, 164
- motive, 162
- need recognition, 151
- negative word of mouth, 162
- noncompensatory decision rule, 158
- perception, 166

- performance risk, 155
- physiological needs, 162
- physiological (safety) risk, 155
- postpurchase dissonance, 160
- psychological needs, 152
- psychological risk, 155
- reference group, 167
- ritual consumption, 159
- safety needs, 164
- self-actualization, 164
- shopping goods/services, 156
- situational factors, 169
- social risk, 155
- specialty goods/services, 156

Concept Review

1. Give three reasons why it is important for marketers to understand the factors that influence consumers' purchasing decisions.

2. List the five steps of the consumer buying decision process. What should be the primary focus of marketing strategy at the alternative evaluation stage? The purchase stage?

3. What are the primary factors that affect consumers' search processes? What marketing strategies can marketers employ to ensure that customers get the information they need in order to make their shopping decisions?

4. Briefly explain how the extent of problem solving influences consumers' buying behaviour and describe four strategies marketers could use to facilitate consumer purchasing in each case. Give examples of products you would classify as high-involvement purchases.

5. Identify and briefly explain the five psychological factors that influence consumer buying decisions.

6. What marketing tactics could be used to break through customers' selective perception (i.e., selective exposure, selective attention, selective comprehension, and selective retention)?

7. How can marketers use Maslow's hierarchy-of-needs model to develop successful marketing programs for their target market?

8. Briefly explain how social and situational considerations influence customer buying decisions.

9. Perceived risks are a key determinant of consumer buying decisions. Explain what is meant by perceived risks and identify tactics marketers could use to mitigate these risks.

10. Culture is one of the most important but least understood influences on consumer buying decisions. Explain how marketers can ensure that their marketing efforts are suited to their culturally diverse target market. What are the challenges involved in developing such efforts?

Marketing Applications

1. Describe two products: one you just purchased without much thought and one that took some deliberation on your part. Why did you spend a different amount of time and effort deciding on your purchases of the two products?

2. Assume you are in the market to buy a new car. What kind of car would you consider? What type of need(s) would you be satisfying if you purchased that particular type of car?

3. Explain the factors that affect the amount of time and effort that a consumer might expend when choosing an optometrist for contact lenses. How would your answer change if the consumer were looking for contact lens cleaning solution?

4. When evaluating different alternatives for a Saturday night outing at a fine restaurant, explain how a consumer would use decision heuristics to narrow down the choice of restaurants. Give examples of heuristics such as price, brand, and presentation in your answer.

5. What can retailers do to make sure that they have satisfied customers after the sale is complete?

6. Tazo blends exotic green teas, spearmint, and rare herbs to create a tea called Zen. Using Maslow's hierarchy of needs, explain which need(s) are being fulfilled by this tea.

7. Identify and describe the three social factors that influence the consumer decision process. Provide an example of how each of these might influence the purchase of the necessary products and services for a family vacation.

8. Nike has developed a new shoe for long-distance runners that is designed to minimize wear and tear on the joints and tendons. Develop a theme for an advertising strategy that ensures all three components of attitude are positively covered.

9. What can a marketer do to positively influence a situation in which a consumer is ready to buy but has not yet done so?

10. You were recently hired by a retail and catalogue company that promotes itself as a Canadian firm selling only Canadian-made goods. The products featured in advertising and in the catalogues tell the stories of the firms that produced the goods in Canada. The sales response to the firm's Made in Canada position has been incredible and growth has been impressive. One day while speaking to a vendor, you learn a shipment of merchandise will be delayed since the product is coming from overseas and is late. A few days later you hear a similar story. As it turns out, the firm just barely earns the Made in Canada label. Although technically the products meet the standard to be classified as Canadian-made, you worry that the firm is not being truthful to its customers. You decide to write a letter to the vice-president of marketing detailing your concerns. What would you put in the letter?

Toolkit

CONSUMER BEHAVIOUR

Jill is trying to decide, once and for all, which soft-drink company is her favourite. She has created a chart to help her decide. She has rated Coca-Cola, Pepsi-Cola, and Jones Soda in terms of price, taste, variety, and packaging. She has also assessed how important each of these four attributes is in terms of her evaluations. Use the toolkit provided on Connect to determine which cola Jill will choose by using a compensatory model. Which cola would she choose if she used a noncompensatory model? If you were Jill, which model would you use, the compensatory or the noncompensatory? Why?

Net Savvy

1. Visit the Harley-Davidson website (www.harley-davidson.com) and review the information provided about its Harley Owners Group (H.O.G.). Describe the efforts the company makes to maintain customer loyalty through its programs. What are the benefits to H.O.G. members? Discuss how these measures might be effective in creating value for members.

2. Customers use a variety of methods to provide feedback to companies about their experiences. Planetfeedback. com was developed as one such venue. Visit its website (www.planetfeedback.com) and identify the types of feedback that customers can provide. Look over the feedback about Ford, and summarize some of the most recent comments. What is the ratio of positive to negative comments about Ford during the last year or so? Describe the effect these comments might have on customer perceptions of Ford.

Chapter Case Study

WEIGHT WATCHERS VERSUS JENNY CRAIG[43]

Ever wanted to lose weight? For about 30 million Canadians, the answer is yes, according to the National Health and Nutrition Examination Survey (NHANES) conducted between 2007 and 2009.[44] For weight-loss companies, that's the right answer.

The weight-loss industry in Canada and the United States, worth more than $50 billion in 2004, is growing steadily because lifestyles and food choices are working against the desire to lose weight. Most Canadians spend their days sitting in front of a computer and their evenings sitting in front of a TV; about 68 percent of Canadians live sedentary lives. No wonder that 56 percent, or more than 1.2 million, Canadian youths aged 15 to 19 years old are either overweight or obese. The corresponding number for adults is 51 percent, or more than 14.2 million Canadians.[45] Restaurant meals, prepared foods, and high-fat/high-sugar snacks have replaced home-cooked meals, whole grains, and fresh produce. These habits are fattening profits for the weight-loss industry as well as expanding belt sizes. By the time you factor in diet pills, specially packaged weight-loss meals and snacks, diet programs, and a whole range of products and services promising bodies fit for bathing suits, you've got a market projected to be worth more than $586.3 billion annually in the United States and Canada.[46] Two recognized diet behemoths, Weight Watchers and Jenny Craig, share a substantial piece of the pie. Both stress flexibility to fit a wide range of lifestyles, and both showcase their success stories. But each approaches dieting differently in their quest for new members.

The Big Two

Founded in 1963, Weight Watchers International now boasts groups in more than 30 countries worldwide. The program encourages members to track their daily food intake, exercise, hunger levels, and emotions related to eating. Dieters record meals and snacks in a paper or electronic journal. All foods are assigned point values, calculated based on calories, fat, and fibre, and members have a daily point allotment based on individual weight and lifestyle. Although members can follow the Weight Watchers regimen without support, the company notes that the most successful members are those who weigh in at weekly group sessions and attend meetings. During these half-hour meetings, a group leader discusses a particular topic, such as holiday eating, measuring and weighing foods for portion control, or eating out. Members are given an opportunity to swap ideas and recipes that have worked for them, admit their mistakes and request support, and be acknowledged for successes. Weight Watcher members can prepare their own food, dine out, or purchase Weight Watcher–prepared or endorsed dinners, snacks, and desserts at most grocery stores. Other Weight Watcher products that help with portion control and healthy habits, such as food scales, cookbooks, and water bottles, are sold online and at meetings.

Jenny Craig promises a unique and comprehensive plan for food, body, and mind.[47] Members eat meals and snacks prepared and packaged by Jenny Craig, supplemented by fresh fruits and vegetables. Jenny Craig's foods control portions and accommodate busy schedules by reducing meal prep time. Members meet weekly on a one-on-one basis with a personal counsellor and are encouraged to develop an exercise program. Like its major competitor, Jenny Craig offers customized programs for men and teenagers and for those who prefer to lose weight on their own rather than travel to a centre.

Other diet programs abound but, while many people lose weight on these regimens, the loss tends to be temporary because the diets are based on unsustainable eating patterns, such as eliminating major food groups. Additionally, the big diet companies offer social reinforcement and flexibility, which appears to help people remain committed to their weight-loss programs.

Defining the Difference

Jenny Craig recently launched an advertising campaign that shows its spokeswoman in a lab coat claiming, "Jenny Craig clients lost twice as much weight, on average, as those on the largest weight-loss program." Inarguably, Weight Watchers is the program referred to, and Weight Watchers sued in response.[48] The claim, it says, is bogus and based on two separate studies that

Jenny Craig uses Jason Alexander, who played George Costanza on the TV series Seinfeld, *as its spokesperson to appeal to men.*

were spaced a decade apart. However, the lawsuit indicates the serious nature of the struggle for members. The competition is particularly intense in the early months of the year, when Canadians return to the scales after indulging during the holidays.

The two diet giants are locked in another battle as well, this one targeted at men.[49] While a completely different program isn't needed—both sexes need to cut calories and increase exercise—marketing specifically to men has the power to bring in new members. While the Weight Watchers' men's program is the same as the women's program, the men's website is tailored to male interests and concerns, focusing more on working out and less on the eating plan. The men's site also mentions the link between obesity and erectile dysfunction, implying that a man's sex life might improve if he loses weight.

Jenny Craig's men's program is also very similar to its women's program but is tweaked to accommodate differences in food cravings and issues with portion control. Men on this program, Jenny Craig promises, can still have a beer and fries once in a while. To further entice men to their program, Jenny Craig uses Jason Alexander, who played George Costanza on the TV series *Seinfeld*, as its spokesperson.

Technology Support for Dieters

Dieters have a variety of electronic devices to help track food consumption and exercise. Using any Internet-ready device, Weight Watcher members can check point values for foods, including meals at popular restaurants, and add snacks or meals to their daily journal. Similar services and applications for fitness training are available via cellphone applications. Using a camera-equipped cellphone, for example, dieters can photograph a meal and send the picture to a registered dietitian, who replies with recommendations for modifying portions or food choices. Theoretically, this approach is more honest than keeping a food diary since dieters may be tempted not to record full amounts. These services require fees.

Questions

1. Trace how you might go through the steps in the consumer decision process if you were thinking of going on a diet and using either of these diet programs.

2. How have Weight Watchers and Jenny Craig created value?

3. Identify the determinant attributes that set the Weight Watchers' and Jenny Craig's programs apart from each other. Use those attributes to develop a compensatory purchasing model like the one found in Exhibit 5.2 on page 158.

4. How can Weight Watchers and Jenny Craig increase the probability of customer satisfaction?

5. Which factors examined in the chapter do you think would have the most impact on consumers' propensity to go on a diet and choose either of these diet programs?

 Practise and learn online with Connect. Connect allows you to practise important concepts at your own pace and on your own schedule, with 24/7 online access to an eBook, practice quizzes, interactivities, videos, study tools, additional resources, and more.

CHAPTER 6

Business-to-Business Marketing

Most of us know that RBC Royal Bank is Canada's largest commercial bank; however, not many people know that RBC buys more than $3 billion worth of goods and services each year from its approved vendors in a variety of B2B transactions.[1] So, what kinds of goods and services are purchased, and how does a company become an approved vendor? These purchases include a wide range of items from toilet paper to office supplies to advertising and a host of other products and services that are used for the bank's operations. In addition, RBC buys goods and services in support of its sponsorship events and community causes, which totalled more than $105 million in 2009. In 2010, as a partner of the Olympic and Paralympic Winter Games and the Olympic and Paralympic Torch Relays, RBC purchased millions of dollars worth of goods. In fact, just prior to the 2010 Winter Olympic Games, RBC updated its Vendor Information Form (described below) to include a new category listing for Vancouver 2010. The Vendor Information Form allowed potential vendors the opportunity to highlight their interest in providing a product or service during the Games.

To be considered a potential vendor, a business must first register with RBC by completing and submitting a Vendor Information Form, which requires that potential vendors provide information about their company and products and services. This information is entered into RBC's Potential Vendor Database, where it is kept for two years. RBC's procurement group, which is responsible for all purchases of goods and services for all RBC's business units, use this database as the primary source of vendor information to assess the market for new sourcing opportunities. RBC contacts vendors whose products and services it is interested in.

In addition to registering on RBC's website by using the Vendor Information Form, potential vendors must meet other requirements if they want to be one of the many small, medium, and large businesses supplying RBC. First, vendors must offer high-quality goods and services with top-notch customer service and have e-procurement capability because RBC wants to efficiently and cost-effectively buy goods and services. Second, vendors must meet RBC's Green Sourcing Initiative, which employs environmental screening mechanisms by using its Green Procurement Questionnaire to help identify and select the most appropriate vendor for RBC. These mechanisms weigh and score the social and environmental policies and practices of potential and existing products and providers. This latter condition is aimed at helping RBC's suppliers to increase their environmental stewardship, an important element of RBC's goal to reduce its carbon footprint. RBC's centralized, structured, and technology-driven buying process is designed to improve the efficiency of the buying process and help ensure that RBC gets good value for the billions of dollars it spends annually. What do you think are some of the strengths and drawbacks of RBC's centralized buying process? ..::

business-to-business (B2B) marketing
The process of buying and selling goods or services to be used in the production of other goods and services, for consumption by the buying organization, or for resale by wholesalers and retailers.

Business-to-business (B2B) marketing refers to the process of buying and selling goods or services to be used in the production of other goods and services, for consumption by the buying organization, or for resale by wholesalers and retailers. Therefore, B2B marketing involves manufacturers, wholesalers, retailers, and service firms that market goods and services to other businesses but not to the ultimate consumer. The distinction between a B2B and a B2C transaction is not the product or service itself; rather, it is the ultimate purchaser and *user of* that product or service. Had your jeans been sold to an industrial supply firm, which then sold them to a custodial firm whose employees would wear them on the job, the transaction would still be a B2B transaction because the jeans are being purchased and used by a business rather than by an individual household consumer.

In this chapter, we will look at the different types of B2B markets and examine the B2B buying process with an eye toward how it differs from the B2C buying process, which we discussed in Chapter 5. Several factors influence the B2B buying process, and we discuss these as well. Finally, the chapter concludes with a discussion about the role of the Internet and its influence on the way B2B marketing is conducted. The chapter roadmap guides you through the major topics covered in this chapter.

L01 B2B Markets

Just like organizations that sell directly to final consumers in B2C transactions, B2B firms focus their efforts on serving specific types of customer markets to create value for those customers.[2] For instance, RBC maintains a dedicated group of account executives to service its small business and commercial banking clients. As the largest

CHAPTER ROADMAP

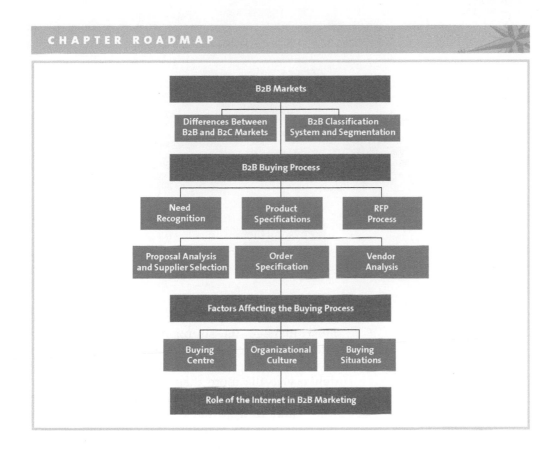

Canadian commercial bank, RBC manages assets of more than $620 billion, and its online capabilities generate a tremendous amount of traffic and span many different service requirements, including cash management, foreign exchange, international trade, borrowing and credit, online banking, and investment advice.

As in RBC's case, many firms find it more productive to focus their efforts on key industries or market segments rather than on ultimate consumers. Cossette Communication Group and BBDO Canada, two of Canada's largest advertising agencies, provide advertising, public relations, and other marketing communications services to large and small business clients across Canada. Similarly, Canada's Magna International designs, develops, and manufactures automotive systems, assemblies, modules, and components primarily for sale to original equipment manufacturers (OEMs) of cars and light trucks in North America, Europe, Asia, South America, and Africa.[3]

In the chapter vignette, we saw how various manufacturers and resellers market their products to RBC by registering as a vendor on RBC's e-procurement system. Basically, manufacturers, resellers, institutions, and governments are all involved in B2B transactions (see Exhibit 6.1). Therefore, in the next sections, we describe each of these B2B organizations.

Manufacturers or Producers

Some of the biggest B2B buyers are manufacturers and producers. Manufacturers, for example, buy raw materials, components, and parts that allow them to manufacture their own goods. For example, The Clorox Company requires a vast variety of inputs to manufacture more than 150 earth-friendly, natural personal care products under the brand Burt's Bees, including plastic for the product containers, perfumes, and beeswax.[4] To match the rapidly growing demand for its skin

| EXHIBIT 6.1 | B2B Markets |

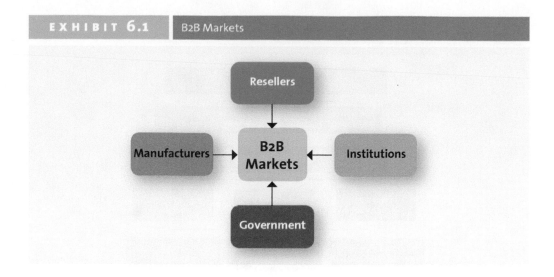

Burt's Bees purchases raw materials from around the world in B2B transactions.

moisturizers, hair products, and lip balms, Clorox must manage its suppliers and transportation intermediaries closely to minimize any inventory shortages or overages, as well as to ensure on-time delivery to the more than 30 000 retail outlets in the United States, United Kingdom, Canada, Hong Kong, and Taiwan that carry its products.[5] Thus, not only does the manufacturer purchase products from other firms to make its products, but it also works with its corporate partners, such as transportation companies and retailers, to facilitate the movement of the raw supplies to the factory and finished products to the stores.

Today, many B2B companies are demanding, as a condition for doing business, that suppliers demonstrate social responsibility by putting in place policies and practices to reduce their carbon footprint. Sustainable Marketing 6.1 explains how a small company saves money while improving its corporate image as a socially responsible organization by implementing eco-friendly printing technology.

Resellers

resellers
Marketing intermediaries that resell manufactured products without significantly altering their form.

Resellers are marketing intermediaries that resell manufactured products without significantly altering their form. For instance, wholesalers and distributors buy jeans from 7 For All Mankind and sell them to retailers (a B2B transaction), and retailers in turn resell those same jeans to the ultimate consumer (a B2C transaction). Wholesalers, distributors, and retailers are all resellers. The Retail Council of Canada estimates that in 2009 there were about 220 000 retail establishments in Canada, which employed two million Canadians and generated sales of $415 billion. Retail trade accounted for 13 percent of total employment in 2009.[6] Similarly, the wholesale sector consisted of 120 000 firms, employed 758 352 Canadians, and generated sales of $532.5 billion in 2008.[7] The role of wholesalers, retailers, and other intermediaries involved in the distribution of goods is discussed in greater detail in Chapters 12 and 13.

Institutions

Institutions, such as hospitals, educational organizations, prisons, religious organizations, and other nonprofit organizations, also purchase all kinds of goods and

| Sustainable Marketing 6.1 | Eco-friendly Printing Produces Cost-Savings[8] |

Thistle Printing Limited is a small business based in Toronto, Ontario. The 79-year-old company prints posters, newsletters, business cards, catalogues, and books for other businesses. Although it is a small firm, Thistle Printing is aiming to stand out from competitors by implementing a series of sustainable eco-changes. The printing industry is not known for being particularly environmentally friendly because of its paper consumption and hazardous waste creation. However, Thistle Printing is trying to differentiate itself as an eco-friendly organization by capturing, cleaning, and reusing chemicals from its printing process.

Thistle Printing views sustainability as a process, not an endpoint, and, as a result, it is introducing a series of changes that will alleviate its impact on the environment. It hired a green consulting firm, EcoSafe, to conduct a three-month pollution prevention assessment. As a result of the findings from this assessment, Thistle Printing has installed a solvent recycler and a closed-loop fountain recirculation system, which will reduce the amount of harmful chemicals emitted in its printing process. These changes were costly, but Thistle Printing realizes that implementing sustainable changes will cut costs in the long run and positively impact its bottom line. Implementing the new eco-friendly changes initially cost Thistle Printing approximately $39,000, but the changes will save more than $30,400 per year.

In addition to the monetary benefits, making sustainable environmental changes will appeal to customers who are increasingly embracing the green culture. The sustainable changes that Thistle Printing has made are not going unnoticed. The company has won eco-awards from the Toronto Region Sustainability Program and the industry magazine *PrintAction*.

Thistle Printing plans to continue its commitment to sustainability.

services for the people they serve. For instance, there are 161 000 nonprofit organizations in Canada, employing about 2 million people and generating revenues in excess of $110 billion annually.[9]

Government

In most countries, the central government tends to be one of the largest purchasers of goods and services. For example, the Canadian federal government spends about $240 billion annually on procuring goods and services. If you add in the amounts spent by provincial and municipal governments, as well as the academic, social, and health sectors, this amount increases to more than $550 billion annually. In 2010, the federal government alone spent more than $10 billion on science and technology and about $3.75 billion on culture. The bulk of the federal government's buying of goods and services is done centrally by Public Works and Government Services Canada on behalf of more than 85 departments, agencies, Crown corporations, and Special Operating Agencies.[10] Information about government buying can be obtained from Business Access Canada or from MERX.[11] MERX is the most complete source of Canadian public tenders, private tenders, U.S. tenders, and private-sector construction news available in Canada. MERX makes it possible for businesses of any size to have easy and affordable access to billions of dollars in contracting opportunities with the

MERX is the most complete source of public tenders, private tenders, U.S. tenders, and private-sector construction news available in Canada.

Government of Canada, participating provincial and municipal governments, the U.S. Government, state and local governments, and the private sector.[12]

Key Challenges of Reaching B2B Clients

For marketers to be effective and successful at B2B marketing, they must master three key challenges for each business customer they want to serve. The first challenge is to identify the right persons or decision makers within the organizations who can authorize or influence purchases. Second, marketers must understand the buying process of each of its potential clients. The third challenge is to identify the factors that influence the buying process of potential clients. B2B markets differ in varying degrees on these three dimensions; hence, marketers must invest the time and resources to understand these challenges. For example, institutional buyers, such as nursing homes and universities, tend to have relatively small budgets and therefore seek the best value when buying products and services for their organizations. That is, if two suppliers are offering roughly similar products, they may opt for the supplier with the lower price. Governments, on the other hand, make much larger purchases, but their buying processes must not only satisfy strict policy guidelines and directives set by the government, but also meet international trade rules set by the World Trade Organization (WTO) or the North American Free Trade Agreement (NAFTA). Additionally, government purchases are subject to public scrutiny and can be subjected to legal challenges or be cancelled or modified. Governments consider a wide range of factors in their purchases and may not always purchase from the vendor with the lowest price. Institutional organizations are not under such public scrutiny and rarely disclose their purchase decisions and practices, although they may try to make their buying processes transparent. Finally, private sector companies, such as manufacturers, producers, and resellers rarely, if ever, disclose their buying criteria or buying process. They are likely to engage in reciprocal buying, a situation where two companies agree to buy each other's products as appropriate.

To address the complexity of B2B markets, many companies have salespeople or a sales team dedicated to specific clients. For instance, many companies wishing to sell to the government (e.g., IBM, Microsoft) have business–government relations experts or departments.

Let us now explore in a little more detail, some of the unique characteristics of B2B markets that distinguish them from B2C markets. Exhibit 6.2 lists the key characteristics of B2B and B2C buying behaviour.

L02 Differences Between B2B and B2C Markets

Market Characteristics In B2C markets, consumers buy goods to satisfy their own individual or household needs and are heavily influenced by price, personal tastes, brand reputation, or personal recommendations of friends and family. In B2B markets, demand for goods and services is derived from B2C sales in the same supply chain. More specifically, **derived demand** is the linkage between consumers' demand for a company's output and its purchase of necessary inputs to manufacture or assemble that particular output. For instance, the demand for raw denim used to make 7 For All Mankind jeans is derived from the sale of the jeans to consumers. Thus, demand for raw material and semifinished goods purchased by business firms tend to fluctuate more, and more frequently. In addition, demand in many business markets is inelastic—that is, the total demand for goods is not affected much by price changes in the short run. For instance, a small increase in the price for raw denim will not cause a huge drop in the demand for denim in the apparel industry in the short run. Another characteristic of B2B markets is that the number of business buyers is substantially fewer than in B2C markets, and the

derived demand
The linkage between consumers' demand for a company's output and its purchase of necessary inputs to manufacture or assemble that particular output.

EXHIBIT 6.2	Characteristics of B2B Buying as Compared with B2C Buying

Market Characteristics
- Demand for business products is derived
- Fewer customers, more geographically concentrated, and orders are larger
- Demand is more inelastic, fluctuates more, and more frequently

Product Characteristics
- Products are technical in nature and purchased based on specifications
- Mainly raw and semifinished goods are purchased
- Heavy emphasis is placed on delivery time, technical assistance, after-sale service, and financing assistance

Buying Process Characteristics
- Buying decision is more complex
- Buying may involve competitive bidding, negotiated pricing, and complex financial arrangements
- Buying involves qualified, professional buyers who follow a more formalized buying process
- Buying criteria and objective are specified, as are procedures for evaluating and selecting vendors and products
- Multiple people with varied interests participate in purchase decisions
- Reciprocal arrangements exist, and negotiations between buyers and sellers are common
- Buyers and sellers usually work closely to build close long-term relationships
- Online buying over the Internet is common

Marketing Mix Characteristics
- Direct selling is the primary form of selling and physical distribution is often essential
- Advertising is technical in nature, and promotions emphasize personal selling
- Price is often negotiated, inelastic, frequently affected by trade and quantity discounts. Price usually includes a service or maintenance component

business buyers are more concentrated in big cities, towns, and industrial areas. Also, the sizes of the orders are substantially larger than consumer purchases. For example, Bombardier announced that corporations placed orders worth almost US$4.7 billion for its *CSeries*, *Global 7000*, and *Global 8000* aircraft at the 2011 Paris Air Show.[13]

Product Characteristics   In B2B markets, the products ordered are primarily raw materials and semifinished goods that are processed or assembled into finished goods for the ultimate consumers. For example, Dell orders all the computer components from different suppliers and then assembles the computers before shipping to the final consumer. In certain B2B markets (e.g., aerospace, medical, pharmaceutical, shipping, defence), the products are very technical and sophisticated in nature and must conform to technical standards specified by the buyer. Thus, the raw materials, components, and semifinished goods undergo rigorous testing before shipping. Also, orders must be delivered on the dates agreed to by both buyers and sellers. Technical services and financing assistance are important aspects of B2B buying behaviour. Companies such as Bombardier often provide vendor financing—a practice where a company provides its customer with a loan that is used to buy goods from the company.[14] In B2C markets, consumers buy finished goods for their own personal consumption.

Buying Process Characteristics Generally, for routine purchases or small-dollar-value purchases, only one or a few individuals within a department or the company may be responsible for the buying decision. However, for purchases of highly technical or complex products involving thousands or millions of dollars, the buying effort is much more structured, formalized, and professional.

More people are usually involved in complex buying decisions. They are usually technically trained and qualified professionals, and they represent different interests (e.g., managerial, technical, and departmental) within the organization. The group of people involved in the buying decision is often referred to as the buying centre, which is described in detail below. Most companies have formal policies and procedures to guide buying decisions that must be closely followed by the people involved in the buying decisions. Examples of such procedures include rules governing competitive bidding, negotiated pricing, complex financial arrangements, buying criteria, and objectives, as well as procedures for evaluating competitive bids.

Another major difference between B2B and B2C buying lies in the nature of the relationship between the firm and its suppliers. Generally, the buying decision is based on negotiations, which for complex purchases could be quite extended. The negotiated contract normally covers a range of concerns, including price, delivery, warranty, technical specifications, and claim policies. In B2B markets, buyers and sellers strive to develop close relationships with each other and so will often provide help or advice to ensure a win-win situation for both parties. For example, Shepherd Thermoforming and Packaging, a leading Canadian manufacturer of plastic products ranging from your hot tub to your chocolate tray, Tylenol package, smoke detector cover, and other plastic accoutrement in your homes and cars, noted that its B2B customers often chose to come in and work with its engineering staff to create the desired look and product functionality that they needed.[15]

In addition, some firms may engage in reciprocal buying arrangements—a practice where two firms agree to buy each other's products and services. Clearly, reciprocal buying has both negative and positive consequences for both the buying and selling firms involved, as well as for other suppliers. Two such consequences are that it excludes other vendors from participating in the buying process and may limit the firms to each other's products, which may not be the best thing.

Marketing Mix Characteristics Another major difference between the typical B2B and B2C transaction is the role of the salesperson. On the one hand, while salespeople are an important component of the communications mix for B2C transactions such as sales of real estate, insurance, jewellery, consumer electronics, and high-end apparel, most fast-moving consumer goods (FMCG) found in grocery and discount stores are not sold with the aid of salespeople. On the other hand, in most B2B sales, the salesperson is an integral component of the transaction. Pharmaceutical manufacturers rely primarily on sales representatives to promote their drugs to doctors. Also, many manufacturers provide trade and quantity discounts to resellers for carrying their products.

LO3 B2B Classification System and Segmentation

North American Industry Classification System (NAICS) codes
A classification scheme that categorizes all firms into a hierarchical set of six-digit codes.

Statistics Canada collects data about business activity in Canada through its classification scheme, which categorizes all firms into a hierarchical set of six-digit **North American Industry Classification System (NAICS) codes.**[16] The NAICS was developed jointly by Canada, the United States, and Mexico to provide comparable statistics about business activity in all of North America. The NAICS codes replaced the Standard Industrial Classification (SIC) system that had been in use since the 1930s. The NAICS groups economic activity into 20 sectors and 928 Canadian industries. The NAICS six-digit numerical system works as shown in Exhibit 6.3. The first two digits represents the sector in the economy (e.g., 51 is the information sector); the third digit represents the subsector (e.g., 515 is "Broadcasting except Internet"); the fourth digit represents the industry group; the fifth digit represents a specific

EXHIBIT 6.3	Telecommunications NAICS Codes
NAICS Code	**Level**
51	Information
515	Broadcasting except Internet
5151	Radio and Television Broadcasting
51511	Radio Broadcasting
515111	Radio Networks

Source: www.ic.gc.ca/cis-sic/cis-sic.nsf/IDE/cis-sic51defe.html (accessed July 6, 2010).

subgroup within the industry; and the full six-digits refer to the country-level or national industry. The NAICS system is revised periodically to add new industries or to consolidate or delete others.

The NAICS classification system can be quite useful to B2B marketers for segmenting and targeting markets. Suppose, for instance, that a high-tech telecommunications components manufacturer has developed a new product that will significantly speed data transmission. Which of the types of firms listed under NAICS classification 515111 (radio networks) would be the most worthwhile to pursue as customers? To answer this question, the components manufacturer would first do research, probably by having company sales representatives conduct interviews, to determine which types of firms would find the new component most useful for their products. Then, using the NAICS data collected by Statistics Canada or the U.S. Census Bureau, the manufacturer could assess the number, size, and geographical dispersion of firms within each type, which might indicate both the product's potential and the types of firms that constitute the target market.

In addition, to NAICS, marketers may segment B2B markets in several other ways, including geographic location (e.g., by country, provinces, region, cities), firm size (e.g., by the number of employees in the firm or by sales volume), account size (by small, medium, and large accounts or purchase size), and types of products purchased.

The NAICS classification system could help a high-tech telecommunications components manufacturer identify groups of customers to pursue.

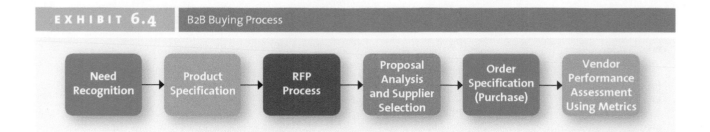

EXHIBIT 6.4   B2B Buying Process

Need Recognition → Product Specification → RFP Process → Proposal Analysis and Supplier Selection → Order Specification (Purchase) → Vendor Performance Assessment Using Metrics

L04 The B2B Buying Process

The B2B buying process (Exhibit 6.4) parallels the B2C process, though it differs in many ways. Both start with need recognition, but the information search and alternative evaluation stages are more formal and structured in the B2B process. Typically, B2B buyers specify their needs in writing and ask potential suppliers to submit formal proposals, whereas B2C buying decisions are usually made by individuals or families and sometimes are unplanned or impulsive. In contrast, B2B buying decisions often are made by committees after a great deal of consideration. Finally, in B2C buying situations, customers evaluate their purchase decision and sometimes experience postpurchase dissonance. Formal performance evaluations of the vendor and the products sold generally do not occur, as they do in the B2B setting. As discussed in greater detail below in "Buying Situations," it is worth noting that not all B2B purchases go through each stage or go through each stage with the same intensity. For example, a routine purchase of office stationery will likely not go through all the stages of the buying decision process. However, the purchase of a computerized call centre system for the company will likely go through all the stages more rigorously than buying a few replacement computers for office use. Let's examine all six stages within the context of Toyota purchasing tires for its vehicles from Goodyear, Dunlop, and Firestone.[17]

Toyota recognized the need to change tire suppliers when customers complained that their current supplier's tires did not perform adequately on snow-packed and off-the-road surfaces.

In B2B transactions, it is important to seek information to recognize a need.

Stage 1: Need Recognition

In the first stage of the B2B buying process, the buying organization recognizes, through either internal or external sources, that it has an unfilled need. For instance, Toyota's design teams might realize that their suppliers have increased the prices of the types of tires they use. At the same time, customers have complained that the tires they are currently using do not work very well on their all-wheel-drive vehicles. Toyota's own driving tests on snow-packed and off-the-road surfaces also indicate the need for a change. Through suppliers' salespeople, tradeshow demonstrations, ads in trade journals, Internet searches, and white papers, the company also has become aware of the benefits of different tire manufacturers.

Stage 2: Product Specification

After recognizing the need, the organization considers alternative solutions and comes up with potential specifications that suppliers might use to develop their proposals to supply the product. Because a significant share of Toyota vehicles are made and sold in North America, the company has made a strong commitment to engaging in long-term, mutually beneficial relationships with North American suppliers. In 2007, for instance, it spent nearly $29 billion for parts and materials from hundreds of North American suppliers and business partners.[18] Rather than working in a vacuum to determine its specifications for the new tires, Toyota's design teams and engineers actually go on site to vendors' plants to develop the specifications for prototypes with their experts.

request for proposals (RFP) A process through which buying organizations invite alternative suppliers to bid on supplying their required components.

ToyotaSupplier.com is used to post RFPs so current and potential suppliers can get information on Toyota's purchasing policies and on relevant news articles.

Stage 3: RFP Process

The **request for proposals (RFP)** is a common process through which buying organizations invite alternative suppliers to bid on supplying their required components. The purchasing company may simply post its RFP needs on its website, work through various B2B linkages (which we discuss later in this chapter), or contact potential suppliers directly. Toyota, for example, has set up ToyotaSupplier.com so current and potential suppliers can get information on its purchasing policies and on relevant news articles.[19] As discussed in Entrepreneurial Marketing 6.1, responding to RFPs can be time-consuming and costly.

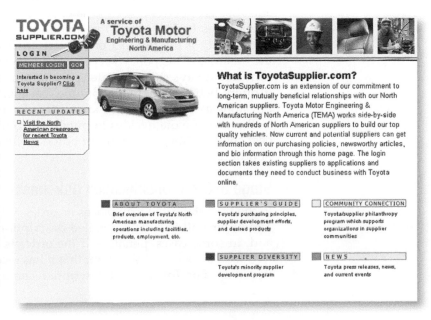

What is ToyotaSupplier.com?
ToyotaSupplier.com is an extension of our commitment to long-term, mutually beneficial relationships with our North American suppliers. Toyota Motor Engineering & Manufacturing North America (TEMA) works side-by-side with hundreds of North American suppliers to build our top quality vehicles. Now current and potential suppliers can get information on our purchasing policies, newsworthy articles, and bio information through this home page. The login section takes existing suppliers to applications and documents they need to conduct business with Toyota online.

Entrepreneurial Marketing 6.1 — Tilting Pixels on the Web[20]

Matt Inglot had to get his father to register his first company, Lizard Soft, because, at the time, Inglot was still in high school. The company offered web hosting and custom software applications, and was Inglot's first taste of entrepreneurship. The experience made him realize that his future held possibilities other than getting a degree and going to work for a company like Microsoft. Inglot's next venture, Tilted Pixel, was formed out of necessity in 2005 when the start-up company he worked for went bankrupt. As a second-year university student pursuing a double degree in business and computer science, Inglot had bills to pay and so he started developing websites. He bought a friend dinner and a beer in exchange for designing his logo, which is still in use today at the Waterloo-based company. Soon he was working on his first client's website, at a price of only $300 because Inglot had no idea how much to charge.

Inglot knew from the start that he wanted to build a scalable web development company, so after two years, he rented office space and hired employees. Business growth necessitated two important changes: adjusting his approach to further education and developing a business plan. Inglot switched to part-time studies, making Tilted Pixel his full-time endeavour. He developed a business strategy to generate higher revenues in order to cover his increased overhead. New procedures and a proposal template for quotations were created. His sales process became more formalized. He also raised prices to reflect the added-value services of the company's consultative approach, which helped clients achieve success online.

Tilted Pixel's customer mix changed too. Although Inglot was still targeting mostly small to medium-sized businesses, now he focused on those with at least $1 million in revenues: an amount that ensured the companies had a marketing budget. The company found a niche in the local food segment. A website it designed for FoodLink (www.foodlink.ca) featured an online map to help consumers learn about and find local food. This work helped land more business. Tilted Pixel beat out 97 other competitors in a request for proposal (RFP) to develop a website for a Toronto-based food company. Since most new business comes by referral and through networking, Tilted Pixel rarely responds to RFPs unless there is a high chance of success. One RFP the company received had 23 pages of bidding requirements before it got to a description of the website specifications. Inglot said the cost to respond could never be recouped if he won the business.

Today the company has five employees and a proprietary web development platform. It plans to expand into major cities in Canada after Inglot graduates. He aims to shake up the industry and a few pixels, saying, "What Second Cup did for coffee, and what McDonald's did for fast food, Tilted Pixel will do for web development."

Stage 4: Proposal Analysis and Supplier Selection

The buying organization, in conjunction with its critical decision makers, evaluates all the proposals it receives in response to its RFP. Firms are likely to narrow the process to a few suppliers, often those with which they have existing relationships, and discuss key terms of the sale, such as price, quality, delivery, and financing. Some firms have a policy that requires them to negotiate with several suppliers, particularly if the product or service represents a critical component or aspect of the business. This policy keeps suppliers on their toes; they know that the buying firm can always shift a greater portion of its business to an alternative supplier if it offers better terms. For example, because Toyota negotiates with Dunlop and Firestone as well, Goodyear knows that it cannot grow lax in the benefits it offers. In the end, Toyota decides to purchase from Goodyear because Goodyear has the best combination of strength of brand, ability to deliver, product quality, and ease of ordering.

Stage 5: Order Specification (Purchase)

In the fifth stage, the firm places its order with its preferred supplier (or suppliers). The order will include a detailed description of the goods, prices, delivery dates, and, in some cases, penalties if the order is not filled on time. The supplier then will send an acknowledgement that it has received the order and fill it by the specified date. For Toyota, this description includes the specific sizes and number of tires it wants, the price it will agree to pay for those tires, the date it expects to receive them, and the result if the wrong tires are delivered or the correct tires are delivered after the due date.

Stage 6: Vendor Performance Assessment Using Metrics

Just as in the consumer buying process, firms analyze their vendors' performance so they can make decisions about their future purchases. The difference is that, in a B2B setting, this analysis is typically more formal and objective. Let's consider how Toyota might evaluate Goodyear's performance, as in Exhibit 6.5, using the following steps:

1. The buying team develops a list of issues that it believes are important to consider in the evaluation of the vendor.

2. To determine how important each of these issues (in column 1) is, the buying team assigns an importance score to each (column 2). The more important the issue, the higher a score it will receive, but the importance scores must add up to 1. In this case, the buying team believes that product quality and strength of brand are most important, whereas meeting the delivery dates and the ease of ordering are less important.

3. In the third column, the buying team assigns numbers that reflect its judgments about how well the vendor performs. Using a 5-point scale, where 1 equals "Poor Performance" and 5 equals "Excellent Performance," the buying team decides that Goodyear has fairly high performance on all issues except ease of ordering.

4. To get the overall performance of the vendor, in the fourth column, the team combines the importance of each issue and the vendor's performance scores by multiplying them together. Note that Goodyear performed particularly well on the most important issues. As a result, when we add the importance/performance scores in column 4, we find that Goodyear's overall evaluation is quite high: 4.6 on a 5-point scale!

In Stage 4, proposal analysis and supplier selection, Toyota decides to purchase from Goodyear because Goodyear has the best combination of strength of brand, ability to deliver, product quality, and ease of ordering.

Although most B2B organizations utilize the buying process described above as a way to ensure they get the best value for their money, some organizations simply

EXHIBIT 6.5	Evaluating a Vendor's Performance		
1 Key Issues	2 Importance Score	3 Vendor's Performance	4 Importance/ Performance
Strength of brand	0.30	5	0.15
Meets delivery dates	0.20	4	0.8
Product quality	0.40	5	2.0
Ease of ordering	0.10	3	0.3
Total	**1.0**		**4.6**

Ethical Dilemma 6.1

Value Village Cozies Up to Charities

We have all received phone calls from charitable organizations, such as the Cerebral Palsy Association of Canada or the Canadian Diabetes Association, asking for donations of cash or household items and clothing. Most of us are more than willing to donate to these causes, believing that our donations are going to the needy. But have you ever stopped to wonder where your gently used clothing and household items are actually going?

Many of us assume that these charities distribute them to families in need. But did you know that nonprofit organizations such as the Cerebral Palsy Association of Canada and the Canadian Diabetes Association actually sell the items they receive to Value Village, a privately owned, U.S., for-profit corporation? Charities claim that the money received from Value Village is used to fund their programs and help them fulfill their mission since they receive little financial support from government sources.

Unlike the Salvation Army or the Women In Need Society (WINS), Value Village is not a nonprofit thrift store; it is a multimillion dollar corporation. Value Village has a distinct business model. It has formed alliances with local nonprofit organizations and purchases donated items from them by weight at a pre-set bulk rate, which is never made public. Critics, however, have indicated that the rates are extremely low and the charities have very little negotiating power.

Not surprisingly, claims are mounting that Value Village is taking advantage of people's goodwill to make a profit. They point out that Value Village is benefiting from the good name of nonprofit organizations because people believe that they are donating to a charity and not to a profit-seeking entity. Additionally, other nonprofit thrift organizations, such as the Salvation Army, are also seeking donations to help generate funds to run their programs. So is it fair that Value Village may be benefiting from the guise of falling into the same category as other thrift stores?

Value Village points out that it has never attempted to position itself as anything but a for-profit organization. It defends its unique business model, which involves partnering with local charities in a B2B setting. It is proud of its contribution to the community: providing support to local charities while offering quality affordable goods to its customers. Value Village is also proud of its efforts to embrace the green culture by recycling unwanted goods and keeping them out of landfills.

Is Value Village being a good corporate citizen with its unique business model? Or is it a profit-seeking corporation that is unfairly taking away much needed donations from nonprofit organizations? Are charities that sell donated items to Value Village engaging in unethical business practices by not publicly informing donors of their business model?

operate based on a sole source or on longer-term business relationships, as in the case of Value Village, which is described in Ethical Dilemma 6.1.

L05 Factors Affecting the B2B Buying Process

The six-stage B2B buying process may be influenced by three factors within the purchasing organization: the buying centre, the buying organization's philosophy or corporate culture, and the buying situation.

The Buying Centre

buying centre
The group of people typically responsible for the buying decisions in large organizations.

In most large organizations, several people typically are responsible for the buying decisions. These **buying centre** participants can range from employees who have a formal role in purchasing decisions (e.g., the purchasing or procurement department), to members of the design team that is specifying the particular equipment or raw material needed, to employees who will be using a new machine that is being ordered. All these employees are likely to play different roles in the buying process, which vendors must understand and adapt to in their marketing and sales efforts.

initiator
The buying centre participant who first suggests buying the particular product or service.

We can categorize six different buying roles within a typical buying centre. One or more people may take on a certain role, or one person may take on more than one of the following roles: "(1) **initiator**, the person who first suggests buying the

Many people are involved in making B2B purchasing decisions.

particular product or service; (2) **influencer**, the person whose views influence other members of the buying centre in making the final decision; (3) **decider**, the person who ultimately determines any part of or the entire buying decision—whether to buy, what to buy, how to buy, or where to buy; (4) **buyer**, the person who handles the paperwork of the actual purchase; (5) **user**, the person(s) who consumes or uses the product or service; and (6) **gatekeeper**, the person(s) who controls information or access, or both, to decision makers and influencers."[21]

To illustrate how a buying centre operates, consider purchases made by a hospital. Where do hospitals obtain their X-ray machines, syringes, and bedpans? Why are some medical procedures covered in whole or in part by insurance, whereas others are not? Why might your doctor recommend one type of allergy medication instead of another?

The Initiator—Your Doctor   When you seek treatment from your physician, he or she *initiates* the buying process by determining the products and services that will best address and treat your illness or injury. For example, say that you fell backwards off your snowboard and, in trying to catch yourself, shattered your elbow. You require surgery to mend the affected area, which includes the insertion of several screws to hold the bones in place. Your doctor promptly notifies the hospital to schedule a time for the procedure and specifies the brand of screws she wants on hand for your surgery.

The Influencer—The Medical Device Supplier, the Pharmacy   For years, your doctor has been using ElbowMed screws, a slightly higher-priced screw. Her first introduction to ElbowMed screws came from the company's sales representative, who visited her office to demonstrate how ElbowMed's screws were far superior to those of its competition. Your doctor recognized ElbowMed as good value. Armed with empirical data and case studies, ElbowMed's sales rep effectively *influenced* your doctor's decision to use that screw.

The Decider—The Hospital   Even though your doctor requested ElbowMed screws, the hospital ultimately is responsible for *deciding* whether to buy ElbowMed screws. The hospital supplies the operating room, instrumentation, and surgical supplies, and therefore, the hospital administrators must weigh a variety of factors to determine not only whether the ElbowMed screw is best for patients, but also whether using ElbowMed screws involves a cost that various insurance providers will reimburse.

The Buyer—Hospital's Materials Manager   The actual *buyer* of the screw will likely be the hospital's materials manager, who is charged with buying and maintaining inventory for the hospital in the most cost-effective manner. Whereas ElbowMed screws are specific to your type of procedure, other items, such as gauze and sutures, may be purchased through a group purchasing organization (GPO), which obtains better prices through volume buying.

The User—The Patient   Ultimately though, the buying process for this procedure will be greatly affected by the *user,* namely, you and your broken elbow. If you are

influencer
The buying centre participant whose views influence other members of the buying centre in making the final decision.

decider
The buying centre participant who ultimately determines any part of or the entire buying decision—whether to buy, what to buy, how to buy, or where to buy.

buyer
The buying centre participant who handles the paperwork of the actual purchase.

user
The person who consumes or uses the product or service purchased by the buying centre.

gatekeeper
The buying centre participant who controls information or access to decision makers and influencers.

uncomfortable with the procedure or have read about alternative procedures that you prefer, you may decide that ElbowMed screws are not the best treatment.

The Gatekeeper—The Insurance Company   Your insurer may believe that ElbowMed screws are too expensive and that other screws deliver equally effective results. Therefore, it might refuse to reimburse the hospital in full or in part for the use of the screws.

In the end, the final purchase decision must take into consideration every single buying centre participant.

Organizational Culture

organizational culture
Reflects the set of values, traditions, and customs that guides a firm's employees' behaviour.

autocratic buying centre
A buying centre in which one person makes the decision alone, though there may be multiple participants.

democratic buying centre
A buying centre in which the majority rules in making decisions.

consultative buying centre
A buying centre in which one person makes the decision, but he or she solicits input from others before doing so.

consensus buying centre
A buying centre in which all members of the team must reach a collective agreement that they can support a particular purchase.

A firm's **organizational culture** reflects the set of values, traditions, and customs that guides its managers' and employees' behaviour. The firm's culture often comprises a set of unspoken guidelines that employees share with one another through various work situations. For example, a new employee might be told that the workday begins at 9:00 a.m.; however, in observing co-workers, he or she learns that most workers arrive at 8:30 a.m. and thus decides to start arriving earlier.

Organizational culture can have a profound influence on purchasing decisions, and corporate buying centre cultures might be divided into four general types: autocratic, democratic, consultative, and consensus, as illustrated in Exhibit 6.6. Knowing which buying centre culture is prevalent in a given organization helps the seller decide how to approach that particular client, how and to whom to deliver pertinent information, and to whom to make the sales presentations.

In an **autocratic buying centre**, though there may be multiple participants, one person makes the decision alone, whereas the majority rules in a **democratic buying centre**. **Consultative buying centres** use one person to make a decision, but he or she solicits input from others before doing so. Finally, in a **consensus buying centre**, all members of the team must reach a collective agreement that they can support a particular purchase.[22]

Cultures act like living, breathing entities that change and grow, just as organizations do. Even within some companies, culture may vary by geography, division, or functional department. Whether you are a member of the buying centre or a supplier trying to sell to it, it is extremely important to understand its culture and the roles of the key players in the buying process. Not knowing the roles of the key players in that case could waste a lot of time—both yours and the buying centre's—and could even alienate the real decision maker.

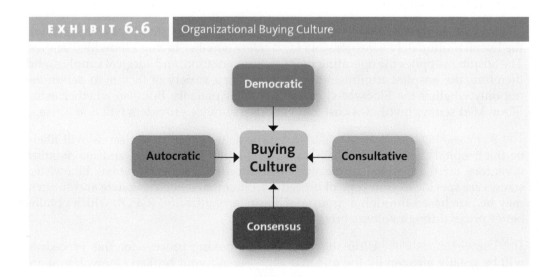

EXHIBIT 6.6   Organizational Buying Culture

Building B2B Relationships   In B2B contexts, there are a vast variety of ways to enhance relationships, and these methods seem to be advancing and evolving by the minute. For example, blogs and social media can build awareness, provide search engine results, educate potential and existing clients about products or services, and warm up a seemingly cold corporate culture.[23] An expert who offers advice and knowledge about products increases brand awareness, and a blog is a great medium for this information. Web analytics, such as traffic on the website and the number of comments, can offer tangible evaluations, but a better measure is how often the blog gets mentioned elsewhere, the media attention it receives, and the interaction, involvement, intimacy, and influence that it promotes.

The LinkedIn social network is mainly used for professional networking in the B2B marketplace. Twitter, the microblogging site, is also valuable for B2B marketers, because they can communicate with other businesses as often as they want. Companies such as TweetDeck make it easier for companies using Twitter to manage their followers, update their posts, track analytics, and even schedule Tweets, just as they would to manage a traditional marketing campaign.[24] Staples has come up with another means to exploit online technology to improve its B2B relationships, as Power of the Internet 6.1 describes.

The majority of B2B marketers use white papers for their marketing efforts, and 71 percent of B2B buyers regularly read them prior to making a purchase.[25] When executives confront an unfulfilled business need, they normally turn to white papers. Their B2B partner may have a technologically advanced solution, but buyers have to understand the solution before they can consider a purchase. A good white paper provides information about the industry and its challenges in an educational context, rather than a promotional sense, to avoid seeming like simply propaganda. That is, the goal of white papers is to provide valuable information that a businessperson can easily understand and that will help the company address its problems with new solutions.

Buying Situations

The type of buying situation also affects the B2B decision process. Most B2B buying situations can be categorized into three types: new buys, modified rebuys, and straight rebuys (see Exhibit 6.7). To illustrate the nuances between these three buying situations, we portray how Dell develops relationships with some of its business customers after first targeting them.

Dell has been very successful in the B2B market, primarily because it is flexible, maintains a customer focus, and provides complete product solutions at value prices.

EXHIBIT 6.7	Buying Situations

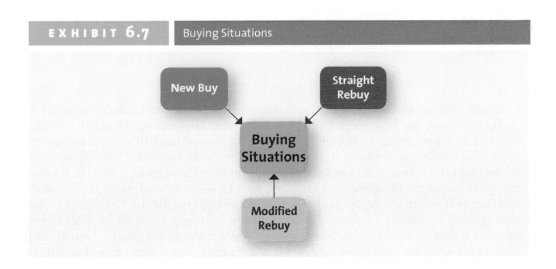

Power of the Internet 6.1

Staples Businesses stickK to It!

New Year's resolutions are hard to keep, whether for individuals or for companies. To offer some support for small businesses, Staples has launched a new website in partnership with stickK.com. The "stickK to It! Business Challenge" encourages users to set goals and then put up their own money to increase their accountability. If they succeed, they can earn Staples EasyPoints and redeem them for merchandise and services.

Approximately 65 000 users on the site have entered into 42 000 contracts and pledged $4.5 million.[26] Although anyone can enter into a contract, the focus is on small businesses, most of which never measure their performance to determine whether they are successful or whether they have met their goals. The tough modern economy makes it even more difficult for small businesses to focus on specific goals, especially when they have that next phone call to make, another email to respond to, and one more client to soothe.

For Staples, the initiative may lead to the acquisition of more small-business customers. The retailer gains brand recognition because of its nontraditional marketing campaign, and customers will start using Staples products when they reach their goals. If these original small businesses grow into medium-sized or large businesses, Staples likely will continue to enjoy their loyalty, in the form of a much larger business account.

To improve its relationships with its customers, Staples developed the "stickK to it! Business Challenge," which encourages customers to set goals and put up their own money to increase their accountability.

Dell uses strong sales relationships and database marketing to understand what its customers want and how to fulfill those wants. First, Dell advertises heavily to educational and government institutions during the second and third quarters of the year, which coincide with the start of their buying cycle. Second, Dell's salespeople understand the financial and resource constraints that these groups face, so it offers complete packages of software, hardware, and IT services and provides installers who not only set up the equipment, but also remove old hardware. Third, Dell works closely with its buyers to obtain feedback and solicit help from its product development teams so that production is geared toward customer needs. Fourth, Dell divides its accounts into three categories: acquisition, development, and retention.

Working with key decision makers, the company maintains consistent contact with each account and maximizes every dollar it allocates toward technology spending.[27]

In a **new buy** situation, a customer purchases a good or service for the first time,[28] which means the buying decision is likely to be quite involved because the buyer or the buying organization does not have any experience with the item. In the B2B context, the buying centre is likely to proceed through all six steps in the buying process and involve many people in the buying decision. Typical new buys might range from capital equipment to components that the firm previously made itself but now has decided to purchase instead. For example, the University of Ottawa bought its first video-conferencing equipment and facility to enhance its distance-education capability. Prior to this, the school relied mainly on its audiographics network, which carried the voices of professors, students, and teaching aides over two telephone lines, one for voice and one for the graphics portion of the course over the Internet.

In a **modified rebuy**, the buyer has purchased a similar product in the past but has decided to change some specifications, such as the desired price, quality level, customer service level, and options. Current vendors are likely to have an advantage in acquiring the sale in a modified rebuy situation, as long as the reason for the modification is not dissatisfaction with the vendor or its products. For example, a few years ago, many universities across Canada replaced their huge CRT monitors in their students' labs with flat-screen LCD monitors.

A **straight rebuy** occurs when the buyer or buying organization simply buys additional units of products that had previously been purchased. A tremendous amount of B2B purchases are likely to fall in the straight rebuy category. For example, a couple of years after the purchase of its first video-conferencing equipment, the University of Ottawa was satisfied with its initial purchase and bought some more. Currently, the university has five video-conferencing rooms that can seat between 18 and 88 students.

These varied types of buying situations call for very different marketing and selling strategies. The most complex and difficult is the new buy because it requires the buying organization to make changes in its current practices and purchases. As a result, several members of the buying centre will likely become involved, and the level of their involvement will be more intense than in the case of modified and straight rebuys. In new buying situations, buying centre members also typically spend more time at each stage of the B2B buying process, similar to the extended decision making process that consumers use in the B2C process. In comparison, in modified rebuys, the buyers spend less time at each stage of the B2B buying process, similar to limited decision making in the B2C process (see Chapter 5).

In straight rebuys, however, the buyer is often the only member of the buying centre involved in the process. Similar to a consumer's habitual purchase, straight rebuys often enable the buyer to recognize the firm's need and go directly to the fifth step in the B2B buying process, skipping the product specification, RFP process, and proposal analysis and supplier selection steps.

Regardless of the situation, more and more firms have begun to use the Internet to help facilitate buying for both buyers and sellers. Let's look at the various ways in which the Internet has transformed B2B marketing.

Role of the Internet in Business-to-Business Marketing

L06

As consumers, we often use the Internet to research products and buy them for ourselves, our family, and our friends. In a similar fashion, the B2B market has been radically altered in recent years through Internet technologies. For instance, the Internet has become the communication mode of choice, and sometimes of necessity, for connecting divisions and employees located in disperse locations. Consider a salesperson on

---

new buy
In a B2B setting, a purchase of a good or service for the first time; the buying decision is likely to be quite involved because the buyer or the buying organization does not have any experience with the item.

modified rebuy
Refers to when the buyer has purchased a similar product in the past but has decided to change some specifications, such as the desired price, quality level, customer service level, and options.

straight rebuy
Refers to when the buyer or buying organization simply buys additional units of products that had previously been purchased.

Social Media Marketing 6.1   Monitoring and Defending Your Brand

Today, with the explosion of social media, many companies, big and small, are beginning to test the waters with one-off campaigns. A major challenge most companies face is integrating social media into their marketing strategy. While businesses are trying to figure this out, consumers are busy using social media to express and spread both their positive and negative thoughts about brands and service encounters. For example, Dominos Pizza experienced a huge decrease in sales based on negative word of mouth that spread as a result of an unflattering employee video posted to YouTube. This example shows that businesses must urgently integrate social media into their marketing to not only defend their brands and reputation, but also to use it to their advantage.

Enter Microsoft's Looking Glass technology, touted as one of the most powerful and perhaps controversial social media tracking solutions because it allows businesses to keep a log of what has been said, by whom, when, and where. Microsoft's Looking Glass allows marketers to aggregate and monitor social media sites for their brands and companies by combining feeds from social networking sites such as Facebook, YouTube, Myspace, Twitter, and blogs, and by connecting these with customer relationship management systems, company databases, service centres, and more. The product will track the sentiments given in content on these sites and will automatically rate each posting as either positive or negative. Based on the ranking of the comments, the marketing team will see how customers are responding to their product and marketing campaigns. Microsoft boasts that Looking Glass will not only let marketers see whether their messages are on target, but also allow them to discover customer segments of which they are not currently aware. By allowing companies to listen to, participate in, and analyze social media, Looking Glass enables businesses to make the social media actionable, quickly and efficiently putting it to use as they create marketing campaigns.[30]

---

a sales call far from his or her company headquarters. By logging on to the company's database, the salesperson can quickly find information about product availability and order status and even consult with his or her supervisors about important negotiating points, such as price and discounts. Current trends suggest that B2B marketing will continue to rely increasingly on the Internet. Some companies, such as Intel, have even set ambitious goals, such as moving half of all advertising online.[29] Social Media Marketing 6.1 shows how companies are developing online tools to enable other businesses to enhance their social media strategy.

Another increasingly common use of the Internet involves virtual trade shows. Not unlike a traditional tradeshow—in which companies fly representatives to a convention site, set up complicated display booths, and attempt to convince potential buyers walking by the convention space to come to the booth to review their wares—today companies can set up "booths" inside a virtual space and engage in product demonstrations and conversations with potential clients. The virtual space can also host educational seminars and networking areas, just as a real-world trade show would do. Such virtual trade shows provide considerable savings, because the company has no need to fly a representative anywhere or purchase an expensive booth display. They also provide impressive ease of use for both the seller and the business customer. Members of the buying centre can log on to the site whenever it is convenient, and the sellers can update their products, inventory levels, and pricing with the click of a button. Their widespread appeal has pushed virtual trade shows into consumer products, job fairs, and corporate training arenas—so far, at least.[31]

The Internet is equally useful for communications between businesses through private exchanges and auctions (see Exhibit 6.8). A **private exchange** occurs when a specific firm (either buyer or seller) invites others to participate in online information exchanges and transactions. These exchanges help streamline procurement or distribution processes. Like Toyota with its ToyotaSupplier.com, as detailed in our discussion of the B2B buying process, IBM, General Motors, Ford, General Electric, Walmart, and

private exchange
Occurs when a specific firm (either buyer or seller) invites others to participate in online information exchanges and transactions; can help streamline procurement or distribution processes.

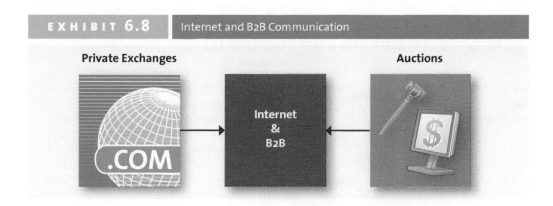

EXHIBIT 6.8 | Internet and B2B Communication

other large firms have formed private exchanges and included their key suppliers. Some, such as IBM and GE, have even mandated that their suppliers must deal with them primarily through such online exchanges, which provides tremendous cost savings through the elimination of periodic negotiations and routine paperwork, as well as the ability to form a supply chain that can respond quickly to the buyer's needs.

At another level, manufacturers and suppliers can work together to design better products.[32] Manufacturers and retailers collect detailed information about their customers' preferences and other market trends, which they can share with those key suppliers involved in product design. This collaborative design process results in products that more closely match customer needs, thus creating and delivering higher customer value.

Private exchanges have also formed on the manufacturer-to-retailer side of the supply chain and, in service industries, between skilled workers and small- to medium-sized companies. The website Guru.com, for example, was founded to help freelance professionals connect with companies that need their services, whether those services entail graphic design and cartooning or finance and accounting advice. Currently, 724 000 professionals list their offerings on this service-oriented professional exchange, and more than 30 000 companies regularly visit the site to post work orders.[33] Guru.com thus provides value to both companies and freelancers by offering not only a site for finding each other, but also by providing dispute resolution, escrow for payments, and a means to rate freelancer quality.[34]

Furthermore, B2B transactions have increasingly turned to online auctions, whether English or reverse. In an **English auction**, goods and services are simply sold to the highest bidder. Thus, if a PC manufacturer has a number of unsold PCs, it can auction them through an exchange (perhaps even through eBay) and sell them to the buyer that bids the highest price for them. In a **reverse auction**, however, the buyer provides specifications to a group of sellers, who then bid down the price until the buyer accepts a specific bid. Firms such as Dell, HP, Motorola, Palm, and Sun have lowered their procurement and component costs by using reverse auctions.[35]

Thus, in various ways, B2B marketing both differs from and mirrors the B2C process we detailed in Chapter 5. The differences in the six stages of the buying process make sense in light of the many unique factors that come into play. The constitution of the buying centre (initiator, influencer, decider, buyer, user, and gatekeeper), the culture of the purchasing firm (autocratic, democratic, consultative, or consensus), and the context of the buying situation (new buy, modified rebuy, straight rebuy) all influence the B2B buying process in various ways, which means that sellers must be constantly aware of these factors if they want to be successful in their sales attempts. Finally, just as it has influenced everywhere else we look, the Internet has radically changed some elements of the B2B world, increasing the frequency of both private electronic exchanges and auctions.

English auction
Goods and services are simply sold to the highest bidder.

reverse auction
The buyer provides specifications to a group of sellers, who then bid down the price until the buyer accepts a specific bid.

Real Marketer Profile: RYAN BURGIO AND SOUROV DE

Sourov De: My first job out of school was with Unilever Canada as an assistant brand manager (ABM). I graduated from Wilfrid Laurier University with an Honours Bachelor of Business Administration and learned about the job through the Laurier Career Centre's email notifications about companies looking to hire marketing and business grads. I saw the job posting and applied with a resumé by email. I knew the job posting would be competitive, and I really wanted Unilever's HR manager to notice my application. The email address of the HR manager was written in the job posting, and the email address included the HR

manager's name. So I thought, what the heck, I'll call Unilever's main line, ask for the HR manager by name, and politely ask her if she received my email and resumé. I had nothing to lose, and I thought that a personal call would be a great way to get noticed. Talking to the HR manager was a lot easier than I thought; I got through to her right away, and I ended up joking around with her about how my last name is abnormally short. I think she liked my personality and initiative.

While at Unilever, I was the ABM of a $9-million marketing campaign to nationally relaunch Suave Hair Care. After working at Unilever, I left the corporate marketing world to pursue an entrepreneurial career. I helped manage the launch of the *Eat, Shrink and Be Merry* cookbook brand into the U.S. market. After the launch, my business partner, Ryan Burgio, and I launched The Stryve Group, a sales and marketing consultancy that helps companies get more sales leads. I made the career move from corporate brand management to entrepreneurship because I find the work I do now more personally meaningful. I enjoy the challenge of thinking innovatively and building a venture from the ground up.

Starting a marketing and sales consultancy at the age of 26 has been the most interesting and exciting project I've worked on. Building our company, The Stryve Group, has been an incredible exercise in marketing. Every day we work on refining what our company's value proposition is, who our ideal clients are, and how to get our marketing message out to those clients in the most effective way.

I love marketing because it's a mixture of psychology, science, art, business strategy, and competition. Ultimately, I think we are all trying to sell or market our ideas or ourselves, whether or not we're in the "business of marketing." Marketing is a passion of mine because I see its application in the world around me in almost everything people do on a daily basis.

Ryan Burgio: I was incredibly lucky to gain employment through my experience with the co-op program at Wilfrid Laurier University (Honours Economics and Business Administration). During my second work term, I was employed by Daggerwing Group, a management and marketing consulting firm that works with senior executives to improve business results from marketing, sales, and customer management activities. I was offered a full-time position after completion of my work term.

Daggerwing Group provided a dynamic work environment that allowed me to work on a variety of interesting and challenging client projects. As a senior associate, I consulted with clients on areas such as marketing analytics, campaign execution, organizational structure, business development, and customer relationship management.

My time at Daggerwing Group was very satisfying; however, my passion for entrepreneurship soon overcame me. I became involved in the launch of Janet and Greta Podleski's bestselling cookbook *Eat, Shrink and Be Merry!* into the U.S. market. That experience and my time at Daggerwing Group gave me an incredible understanding of marketing, so I decided to parlay that knowledge into the launch of The Stryve Group, a sales and marketing consultancy. My business partner Sourov De and I have built The Stryve Group since it launched in 2008 and have loved every minute of it.

I have never encountered anything more exciting or interesting than building my own business step-by-step, day-by-day, challenge-by-challenge. It's been an amazing experience throughout. At The Stryve Group, we've had the opportunity to work on a variety of projects, but my favourite has been working with a retail chain in the United States on the launch of a new concept of retail outlets. The opportunity to see our marketing work drive business results has been incredible.

Why did I pursue entrepreneurship? I think the following quote characterizes my feelings: "An entrepreneur equals a quixotic mix of smarts plus stubbornness that eventually makes you unemployable by anybody but yourself."[37]

I love marketing because it is the ultimate blend of business and creativity, of right-brain and left-brain capabilities. One moment I can be using statistical analysis to measure the effectiveness of a campaign, and the next I'm analyzing colour palettes for a website design. No other aspect of business allows you the opportunity to do both.

Learning Objectives Review

L01 Describe the nature and composition of B2B markets

The B2B market comprises four groups of organizations: manufacturers/producers, resellers, governments, and institutions. Manufacturers such as HP and Dell spend huge amounts to buy raw materials and parts for the computers, printers, and other products they produce. Similarly, producers such as farmers spend a great deal of money to buy fertilizers, seeds, and other agricultural products for their crops. Resellers are mainly wholesalers, distributors, and retailers who distribute the goods of manufacturers. In Canada, wholesale and retail trades are among the largest sectors of the economy. The government sector—federal, provincial, and municipal—in Canada and in most other countries is the largest buyer in a country. Institutions such as nonprofit organizations, universities, and prisons also spend millions of dollars buying finished products for their organizations and clients. The B2B market is substantially larger than the B2C market in terms of both volume and value of their purchases.

L02 Explain the key differences between B2B buying and B2C buying

B2B markets are different from B2C markets in terms of (1) the characteristics of market demand; (2) the types, value, and volume of products bought; (3) the nature of the buying process, which is more formalized and professional, and involves more people; and (4) the nature of the marketing mix—personal and online selling is more prevalent and prices are negotiated and inelastic in the short run. At first glance, the B2B buying process looks similar to the consumer process described in Chapter 5. It starts with need recognition and ends with an evaluation of the product's or service's performance. But it is really quite different, primarily because of its formality. For instance, in the second stage, product specification, the buying group spells out very specific requirements for the products or services it wants to purchase. Then, in the RFP process of the third stage, the buying firm announces its need for a product or service and solicits formal proposals. In the fourth stage, buyers analyze the various proposals and select a supplier. Unlike the consumer process, the fifth stage, in which the B2B firm places the order, is very formal and spells out every detail of the sales contract.

L03 Explain the ways B2B firms classify and segment their markets

The basic principles behind market segmentation remain the same for both B2B and consumer markets. Specifically, B2B firms want to divide the market into groups of customers with different needs, wants, or characteristics and that therefore might appreciate products or services geared especially toward them. On a broad level, B2B firms divide the market into four types: manufacturers or producers, resellers, institutions, and government. Each of these types is described in more detail in the summary for Learning Objective 1. To assist in their market segmentation, B2B businesses can use the NAICS, developed by Canada, the United States, and Mexico, to identify potential customers by type and then develop marketing strategies to reach them. Businesses may also segment B2B markets by account size and types of products purchased.

L04 Describe the B2B buying process

Similar to the B2C buying process, the B2B process consists of several stages: need recognition, product specification, the RFP process, proposal analysis and supplier selection, order specification (purchase), and vendor performance assessment using metrics. The B2B process tends to be more formalized and structured than the B2C buying process. Also, suppliers and customers tend to be more involved in the B2B buying process, which is dependent to a large extent on the close relationships between the company and its suppliers and customers.

L05 Describe the factors that influence the B2B buying process

In B2B situations, it is likely that several people, organized into a buying centre, will be involved in making the purchase decision. The vendor must understand the relationships among the participants of the buying centre to be effective. A firm's organizational culture can also influence the decision process. For instance, if a firm is trying to sell to a young, high-tech computer component manufacturer, it might be advised to send salespeople who are fluent in technology-speak and can easily relate to the customer. Finally, the buying process depends to a great extent on the situation. If a firm is purchasing a product or service for the first time, the process is much more involved than if it is engaging in a straight rebuy.

L06 Summarize how the Internet has enhanced B2B marketing

The Internet has done more to change the way B2B marketing is conducted than any previous innovation. The Internet has not only made it easier for people to communicate within firms, but also facilitated the transfer of information among companies. Buyers can purchase products and services over the Internet through private exchanges, which are set up by one firm that invites other participants, and through B2B Internet auctions. These exchanges and auctions have created opportunities to streamline the procurement process, opened up markets to new buyers and sellers, and provided for more competitive market pricing.

Key Terms

- autocratic buying centre, 196
- business-to-business (B2B) marketing, 182
- buyer, 195
- buying centre, 194
- consensus buying centre, 196
- consultative buying centre, 196
- decider, 195
- democratic buying centre, 196

- derived demand, 186
- English auction, 201
- gatekeeper, 195
- influencer, 195
- initiator, 194
- modified rebuy, 199
- new buy, 199
- North American Industry Classification System (NAICS) codes, 188

- organizational culture, 196
- private exchange, 200
- request for proposals (RFP), 191
- resellers, 184
- reverse auction, 201
- straight rebuy, 199
- user, 195

Concept Review

1. Explain how marketers may use NAICS codes to segment B2B markets. List two other ways marketers may segment B2B markets. Support your answer with appropriate examples.

2. List and discuss the unique characteristics of B2B markets relative to B2C markets.

3. What are the major differences between the consumer buying process discussed in Chapter 5 and the B2B buying process discussed in this chapter?

4. Explain why all B2B purchases may not go through all the stages of the B2B buying decision process and why some may go through the process in a more systematic and rigorous manner. Give examples of buying situations to support your answer.

5. What are the key bases for distinguishing between new buys, modified buys, and straight rebuys? Support your answer with three clear examples.

6. List five specific ways in which the Internet has enhanced B2B buying and decision making.

7. Explain the concept of the buying centre. What factors may influence the behaviour of the buying centre? What is the role of gatekeepers in buying centres, and how do they influence the buying decision?

8. Explain how understanding the role, structure, and behaviour of a buying centre may help a marketer sell to B2B buyers.

9. This book claims that the six-step B2B buying process is similar to the five-step B2C buying process. How would you go about mapping the B2B process to fit the B2C process?

10. How does understanding the organizational culture and buying centre's culture of a potential B2B customer help a salesperson who is targeting that organization?

Marketing Applications

1. Provide an example of each of the four key types of B2B organizations.

2. Mazda is trying to assess the performance of two manufacturers that could supply music systems for its vehicles. Using the information below, determine which manufacturer Mazda should use.

Performance Evaluation of Brands			
Issues	**Importance Weights**	**Manufacturer A's Performance**	**Manufacturer B's Performance**
Sound	0.4	5	3
Cost	0.3	2	4
Delivery time	0.1	2	2
Brand cache	0.2	5	1
Total	**1**		

Notes: Performance is rated on a 5-point scale, where 1 is "Poor" and 5 is "Excellent."

3. Imagine you have written this book and are going to attempt to sell it to your school. Identify the six members of the buying centre. What role would each play in the decision process? Rank them in terms of how much influence they would have on the decision, with 1 being most influential and 6 being least influential. Will this ranking be different in other situations?

4. Provide an example of the three types of buying situations that the bookstore at your school might face when buying textbooks.

5. Describe the organizational culture at your school or job. How is it different from the one at the last school you attended or the last job you had?

6. Nike manufactures shoes and sportswear. How has the Internet changed the way this company communicates with its suppliers and retail customers?

7. You have just started to work in the purchasing office of a major oil processing firm. The purchasing manager has asked you to assist in writing an RFP for a major purchase. The manager gives you a sheet detailing the specifications for the RFP. While reading the specifications you realize that they have been written to be extremely favourable to one bidder. How should you handle this situation?

8. You have recently been hired by Cognos, Canada's premier business intelligence solution provider, as a salesperson for its suite of business intelligence applications. Pick one prospective company you plan to sell to and explain how you would go about identifying the persons in the different roles in the buying centre for the chosen company. How would you try to target the needs of the different members in the buying centre?

9. Cognos has developed a new business intelligence application that it would like to sell to some of its existing customers. You are part of the sales team. How would your approach to selling to an existing customer be different from selling to a new customer?

10. You are the owner of a mid-sized company (about 450 employees) that has a call centre that specializes in providing 24-hour technical support for individual computer owners. One day a sales rep from Dell, HP, or Lenovo approaches you with a business proposal that goes something like this: If you buy all of your computer supplies from us, we will make you our exclusive call centre operator for all of Ontario and Quebec. Assume that all the conditions of the offer made to you are favourable. Will you accept the offer? Do you think that accepting such an offer is ethical?

Toolkit

B2B VENDOR ANALYSIS

Help David evaluate two software vendors. He has created a chart to help him decide which one to pick. He has rated the two vendors on brand strength, timeliness of deliveries, product quality, and ease of ordering. His firm is generally most interested in quality and then in timeliness. Reputation is somewhat important. The ease of ordering is least important. Use the toolkit provided on Connect to specify the importance weights and help David pick the best software vendor.

Net Savvy

1. Browse the Public Works and Government Services Canada website (www.tpsgc-pwgsc.gc.ca) to learn more about how you may sell goods and services to the federal government. Using the information on the website, describe the buying process used by the federal government and explain how the electronic tendering system supports buying and selling between Canadian companies and the Government of Canada.

2. Mark's Work Wearhouse, a Canadian company that currently operates mainly in the B2C market, has hired you as its government–business relations officer with the primary task of helping the company move into the B2B marketplace, selling its merchandise primarily to government departments. Explain how you would go about getting Mark's ready to do business with the Canadian government. Hint: You will find loads of helpful information on the following websites: Public Works and Government Services Canada (www.tpsgc-pwgsc.gc.ca), Business Access Canada (https://buyandsell.gc.ca), and Industry Canada (www.ic.gc.ca).

Chapter Case Study

THE GLOBE AND MAIL CRUISES TO NEW ADVERTISING CLIENTS

When you think of *The Globe and Mail*, Canada's leading national newspaper, its excellent coverage of business and politics, both nationally and internationally, likely comes to mind. Its readership is primarily business professionals, politicians, academics, and others in executive or leadership positions. Few people would associate *The Globe and Mail* with luxury cruises but that is precisely what the newspaper recently offered its readers and business partners. As we will learn, although the patrons for the cruises were mainly consumers, specifically *Globe and Mail* readers, a tremendous amount of B2B marketing was involved with this promotion.

The cruise idea developed as *The Globe and Mail* was redesigning its newspaper and introducing a new section to the paper, Globe Life. Launched in 2007, Globe Life focused on issues related to food, wine, work–life balance, parenting, relationships, and lifestyle, topics which *The Globe and Mail* was not known for covering. Thus, its immediate challenge was to attract advertisers to this new section of the newspaper and to get current readers interested in Globe Life. To do this, The Globe marketing executives wanted a creative promotion that included all the topics covered in Globe Life. Enter Sanjay Goel, president of Cruise Connections, one of *The Globe and Mail*'s existing advertising clients, who suggested that a luxury cruise could be a great way for the newspaper to recruit new advertisers and readers and to attract existing advertisers and readers to Globe Life.

To accomplish its goals, The Globe needed to create something that provided value to passengers (*The Globe and Mail* readers), advertisers, and the paper itself. The cruises attracted readers as passengers and advertisers as event sponsors, creating unique on-board benefits for both. *The Globe and Mail*'s celebrity chef Massimo Capra, food columnist Lucy Waverman, wine critic Beppi Crosariol, and journalists were brought on board to engage passengers on topics about food and wine, areas that reinforce Globe Life's contents. The paper's journalists conducted on-board seminars, forums, Q & As, and demonstrations, and led shore excursions. An existing advertiser, Lifford Wine Agency, ran wine tastings and seminars. The cruise was designed to reach out to advertising clients with unique offerings that were new touchpoints beyond what the *Globe and Mail* newspaper or website offered.

To determine how a cruise could deliver great value for all parties involved, the company developed a business model, collected information, and conducted a thorough analysis of the cost and revenues of offering a luxury cruise. Based on its analysis, The Globe decided to launch the Caribbean Odyssey cruise in 2007 and the Mediterranean Odyssey in 2009. Unlike the Caribbean cruise concept, which was the plan of an advertising client, the idea for the Mediterranean Odyssey came from the passengers of the Caribbean cruise. For both cruises, The Globe had to partner with several other organizations for a variety of products and services to bring the cruise to fruition. For example, the company had to recruit sponsors and advertisers whose products and services were related to the topics covered in Globe Life, such as food, wine, and lifestyles. Similarly, it had to get the necessary approvals from cruise providers and government bureaucrats in the countries and cities it planned to visit. All these B2B transactions, according to Sean Humphrey, *The Globe and Mail*'s marketing director, required intense and personalized discussions and negotiations over time.

As Humphrey noted, selling the idea of a cruise to advertisers and sponsors is a much more complex task than simply selling advertising space. Thus, *The Globe and Mail*'s ad managers identified potential advertisers and developed personalized slide presentations for each based on how receptive each advertiser would likely be to the idea. Once potential advertisers were identified, a high-level marketing team was assembled to meet with potential clients and make a formal sales pitch. The team consisted of the director of marketing, the vice-president of marketing, and Sanjay Goel. Goel was involved in the presentations because he had the expertise to speak about how on-board experience would benefit advertisers. According to Humphrey, the presentation and recruitment process differed from one client to the next; however, they all had basically the same question: What kind of experience and exposure could *The Globe and Mail* cruise offer their brand?

Attracting passengers to the cruise was done primarily through mass media: TV, travel magazines, and *The Globe and Mail* newspaper and its website. To entice readers, the company ran a contest that offered a few free cabins as prizes. The Caribbean Odyssey sold out and generated a lot of consumer and media buzz for Globe Life—exactly what *The Globe and Mail* had hoped.

As noted previously, the idea for the Mediterranean Odyssey came from *Globe and Mail* readers who went on the Caribbean cruise. The itinerary for the Mediterranean Odyssey began in Turkey and went on to Crete, Malta, Corsica, and three cities in Italy, including Pompeii, Florence, and Rome. The two-week cruise finished in Monte Carlo, Monaco. Many special extras were planned for the benefit of both passengers and advertisers. In Istanbul, an excursion was arranged to the well-known Blue Mosque to observe morning prayers on the first day of Ramadan. While visiting the ruins at Ephesus, passengers were treated to a private concert by Montreal jazz singer Nikki Yanofsky in an open-air amphitheatre. In Tuscany, a respected cooking school offered lessons and patrons could visit world-famous wineries. Although museums are usually closed on Mondays in Florence, The Globe negotiated an exclusive tour of the famed Uffizi and Accademia Galleries. And, in Rome, passengers enjoyed a private cardinal-led tour of the Vatican Museums, followed by a concert by the pope's choir in the Sistine Chapel.

To host these activities, *The Globe and Mail* required the cooperation of foreign governments. Cruise Connections was instrumental in setting up links to the Turkish government, the Italian government, and Turkish Airlines, which were anxious to be part of the Mediterranean Odyssey. In exchange for the Turkish and Italian governments' approval of and cooperation with the planned activities, *The Globe and Mail* offered them special advertising packages promoting the regions visited during the cruise.

In addition, these countries were given substantial exposure and promotion both editorially and promotionally in the newspaper. In return, the governments agreed to promote and subsidize the unique events taking place in their countries. Turkey was eager for the publicity and promotion since Turkish Airlines was about to resume flights to Toronto, and it wanted Canadians to consider Turkey as a tourist destination. Prior to the cruise, Turkish Airlines had stopped flying into Toronto because of political differences between the Harper and Turkish governments, concerning comments made by the Canadian government about the Armenian conflict that took place years ago.

Through its cruise vendor, Cruise Connections, The Globe engaged the services of Vanguard Travel in Turkey to create and promote all the events that took place there. For instance, Vanguard Travel worked closely with senior bureaucrats within the Turkish government to make the Blue Mosque visit and the concert at Ephesus possible, as both venues are government properties and the governments' permission and cooperation were critical.

Advertisers coming on board were asked to create unique activities that would engage passengers and help them to learn more about their brands. For example, one client created the concept of a BMW driver-training event in Monte Carlo as a way of engaging cruise passengers with its brand. Essentially, advertisers on-board were in a sort of 11-day focus group with *Globe and Mail* readers, its journalists, chefs, wine critics, and marketers. The result was that advertisers learned more about The Globe brand and what it could deliver for them. Also, the advertisers had a captive audience of affluent and influential *Globe and Mail* readers, whom they learned more about, helping them to reach out and better serve these consumers. According to The Globe's marketing director, the cruise helped break the stereotype among advertisers that the typical *Globe and Mail* audience is 60 to 70 years old, white, male, and working on Bay Street. Many advertisers came to realize that *The Globe and Mail* audience consists of the affluent and influential in Canada from all different ethnic backgrounds and from sectors including retail, technology, banking, and finance. Suddenly, advertisers were faced with a captive audience of wealthy individuals for 11 days.

The Mediterranean Odyssey cruise launched in 2009 in the midst of the worst economic recession since the Great Depression of the 1920s. Likewise, there was a strong downward trend in advertising spending by all companies. Therefore, as an incentive to attract advertisers, *The Globe and Mail* offered a free cabin to advertisers who exceeded their contracted advertising expenditure with the company by a certain amount. The required expenditure was determined on a case-by-case basis. This incentive generated more than 30 new advertisers for *The Globe and Mail* and $1.5 million in advertising revenues.

As mentioned earlier, offering a cruise is outside the core business of *The Globe and Mail*, which is in the business of providing news to Canadians. Therefore, offering a cruise was not without risk. In addition, the timing of the cruise in 2009 heightened the risk because Canada was in the midst of a major economic crisis: people were losing their jobs, consumer confidence was low, and companies were cutting back drastically on spending. Thus, the decision to go ahead with the cruise was carefully scrutinized. The decision to proceed involved several executives from within *The Globe and Mail* and its parent company, CTV Globe Media. Five groups of executives representing different interests were involved in the decision making. These executives included the director of marketing, the vice-president of marketing and business development, the vice-president of advertising sales, *The Globe and Mail* publisher, and the chief financial officer of CTV Globe Media. Each executive scrutinized the business case from a different perspective. For example, the director of marketing looked at the business case to determine whether the company could sell all the cabins, that is, consumer uptake. The advertising sales executive evaluated how much revenue could be brought in through sponsorship and ad incentives. The CFO looked at the business case from the perspective of all the different forecasted numbers coming together as a whole and determining the risk factors (the big picture). After much discussion, all the executives agreed and decided to go ahead with the cruise.

Questions

1. Based on the information presented in the case, what are some of the differences between the B2B and B2C buying decision process?

2. To what extent does the buying process followed in this case reflect the buying process described in this book? What factors account for any differences observed?

3. Who are the members of the buying centre, and what role did each play in the buying decision?

4. Of the four organizational buying cultures described in the text—autocratic, democratic, consultative, and consensus—which one best describes the way the decision was made to go ahead with the Mediterranean Odyssey cruise? Explain your rationale.

 Practise and learn online with Connect. Connect allows you to practise important concepts at your own pace and on your own schedule, with 24/7 online access to an eBook, practice quizzes, interactivities, videos, study tools, additional resources, and more.

CHAPTER 7

Segmentation, Targeting, and Positioning

I n previous chapters we have learned that effective marketing requires that marketers need a clear understanding of their customers' needs, wants, and purchase characteristics. Now we will take a look at how marketers identify which customers are the best fit by following a process of segmenting the market, choosing the desired target markets, and positioning their products and services in the minds of these consumers.

Coca-Cola creates many different products to help it meet the needs of its consumers. Today, the Coca-Cola Company is one of the largest consumer packaged goods companies in the world; but, when it first introduced Coca-Cola in 1886, sales averaged a modest nine drinks per day.[1] Its growth, driven largely by a remarkably disciplined approach to marketing, has led to Coke products being sold in more than 200 countries at an astounding rate of 1 billion servings per day.[2] Yet Coca-Cola continually faces the unique challenge of a mature cola market, which means growth rates overall are low and to increase sales it must either take customers away from other beverage companies or encourage existing customers to drink more cola—neither of which is an easy task.

Part of the company's solution pertains to its approach to new product development.[3] For example, Coke creates unique products for various specific market segments. Because those unique products appeal to specific groups, Coke can increase its sales without cannibalizing the sales of its other products. Have you ever stopped drinking soft drinks in an attempt to limit the amount of caffeine you drink? Coke wants you to know that it feels your pain and therefore offers Caffeine-Free Coca-Cola and Diet Coke. Still like your caffeine but want to minimize the amount you drink right before bedtime? Why not purchase a case

Learning Objectives

After studying this chapter, you should be able to

LO1 Describe the STP process

LO2 Describe the bases marketers use to segment a market

LO3 Identify the criteria for determining the attractiveness of a segment and whether it is worth pursuing (targeting)

LO4 Explain how a firm decides what type of segmentation strategy to use: undifferentiated, differentiated, concentrated, or micromarketing

LO5 Explain what positioning is and describe how firms do it

of each, saving your regular Coke for when you need a midday pick-me-up and your Caffeine-Free Coke for your after-dinner thirst? By introducing decaffeinated versions of its traditional drinks, Coca-Cola could increase the number it sells each day without cannibalizing sales because the consumers targeted by these products had already been avoiding Coca-Cola to reduce their caffeine intake.

Through its efforts to identify and target such specific market segments, Coca-Cola has grown its stable of consumer brands to more than 400 products.[4] Consider the plight of Diet Coke. "Real men" didn't want to drink a diet product which they stigmatized as a "girly" drink that only women consumed. But Coca-Cola had a plan: the high-profile launch of Coke Zero avoided the dreaded word *diet*[5] and specifically targeted men through its packaging, promotions, and image. By targeting men between the ages of 18 to 34 years who wanted to drink a low-calorie cola but would not purchase Diet Coke, the company increased its sales of Coke-branded products by one-third.[6]

A successful new product introduction needs to combine an innovative product with a marketing campaign that communicates the value of that new product to the targeted segment. Thus, for the Coke Zero launch, Coca-Cola designed a campaign supported by advertisements on TV and radio, in print, on outdoor billboards, and online, as well as through widespread sampling programs and opportunities. Little mention was made of the lack of calories or dietetic element of the new offering; instead, the advertising was focused on the similarity of the taste between Coke and Coke Zero and used dark, bold colours. The marketing campaign even included a fantasy football game, "Fantasy Football Fever," available on the Coke Zero website, that was regularly featured in ESPN fantasy sports podcasts.

By using gender to segment the diet cola market, Coca-Cola was able to customize the advertising for Coke Zero to appeal to men, whereas Diet Coke ads concentrated on women. Coke Zero became one of the most successful launches in the company's long history.[7]

Some people like fruit-based drinks, while others like highly caffeinated energy drinks. Some people want a diet product; others care primarily about how well the product hydrates after a workout. Still other people demand affordable beverages, whereas some prefer the drinks to be organic. More likely though, a group of people desires a drink that is dark in colour, cola-flavoured, and caffeinated. Another group demands a drink that is light in colour, citrus-flavoured, and low calorie. Each of these product attributes potentially appeals to a different group of people, or market segment. .:

In Chapter 1, we learned that marketing is about satisfying consumers' wants and needs. A company could make one type of beverage and hope that every customer would buy it, but that's the kind of mistake that causes companies to go out of business. Beverage manufacturers could analyze the market to determine the different types of drinks people want and then make several varieties that cater to the wants of specific groups. It is not enough just to make the product, however. Drink manufacturers, such as Coca-Cola, must position their products in the minds of their target market so those consumers understand why a particular drink meets their needs better than competitive brands do.

In Chapter 2, we described the steps involved in a marketing plan: The manager first defines the firm's mission and objectives and then performs a situation analysis. The third step of the marketing plan is to identify and evaluate opportunities by performing an STP (segmentation, targeting, and positioning) analysis, which makes up the topic of this chapter. In Chapters 3 and 16 we discuss how understanding the marketing environment and conducting systematic, rigorous research is crucial in giving marketers a better knowledge and understanding of their consumers, which is subsequently used to develop effective STP strategies to better serve their customers.

In the chapter vignette, Coca-Cola identified the various groups of cola drinkers that would respond similarly to the firm's marketing efforts. These are also known as market segments. Those who like caffeine-free regular cola are one market segment; people who prefer diet cola constitute a different segment. After evaluating the attractiveness of different market segments, Coca-Cola decided to concentrate its new product line on one group of consumers—its target market—because it believes it could satisfy this group's needs better than its competitors could. As we noted in Chapter 2, the process of dividing the market into groups of customers who have different needs, wants, or characteristics and who therefore might appreciate products or services geared especially for them is called market segmentation.

Once the target market was identified, Coca-Cola had to convince members of the targeted group that when it comes to soft drinks, their choice should be Coke Zero. It achieved this task by defining the marketing mix variables so that the target customers had a clear, distinctive, desirable understanding of what the product or services do or represent, relative to competing products—a process we described in Chapter 2 as market positioning. To achieve its market positioning, Coca-Cola designed a lifestyle advertising campaign that has positioned Coke Zero as the only diet drink with the taste of regular Coca-Cola. The idea is to get customers to recall Coke Zero at the need recognition stage of the consumer buying process described in Chapter 5. The company has also made sure that the drink is available almost anywhere its customers would want to buy it.

In this chapter, we discuss how a firm conducts a market segmentation or STP analysis. As shown in our chapter roadmap, we first discuss market segmentation, or how a segmentation strategy fits into a firm's overall strategy and objectives and which segments are worth pursuing. Then we discuss how to choose a target market or markets by evaluating each segment's attractiveness and, on the basis of this evaluation, choosing which segment or segments to pursue. Finally, we describe how a firm develops its positioning strategy.

The Segmentation-Targeting-Positioning Process `L01`

The segmentation, targeting, and positioning process is shown in Exhibit 7.1.

Step 1: Establish Overall Strategy or Objectives

As discussed in Chapter 2, the first step in the planning process is to articulate the mission and the objectives of the company's marketing strategy clearly. The

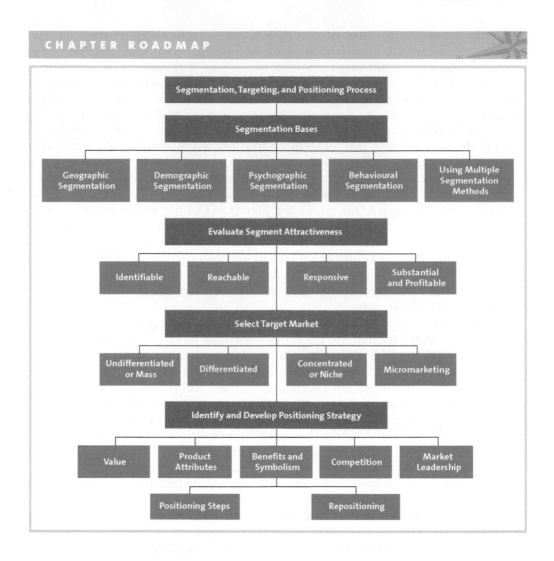

CHAPTER ROADMAP

segmentation strategy must then be consistent with and derived from the firm's mission and objectives, as well as its current situation—its strengths, weaknesses, opportunities, and threats (SWOT). Coca-Cola 's objective, for instance, is to increase sales in a mature industry. The company recognized its strengths were its globally recognized brand name and its ability to place new products on retailers' shelves. Its primary weakness was that it didn't have a product line for the emerging market

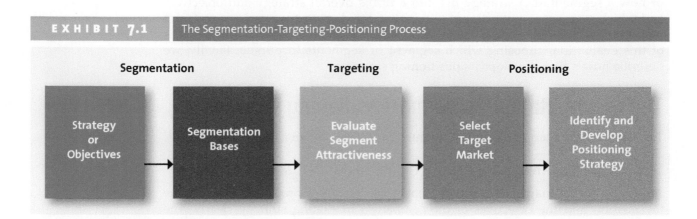

EXHIBIT 7.1   The Segmentation-Targeting-Positioning Process

segments. Identifying this potentially large and profitable market segment before many of its mainstream competitors offered a great opportunity, though following through on that opportunity could lead to a significant threat: competitive retaliation. Coca-Cola's decision to pursue a target market of health-conscious men is clearly consistent with its overall strategy and objectives.

Now let's take a look at the methods, or bases, that can be used to segment the market.

Step 2: Segmentation Bases

LO2

The second step in the segmentation process is to use a formal approach to segment the market. This step develops descriptions of the different segments, their needs, wants, and characteristics, which helps firms better understand the profile of the customers in each segment. With this information, they can distinguish the customer similarities within a segment and dissimilarities across segments. Soft-drink marketers, for instance, have broken up the carbonated-beverage landscape into caffeinated or decaffeinated, regular (with sugar) or diet, and cola versus something else. This segmentation method is based on the benefits that consumers derive from the products.

Marketers use various segmentation bases, including geographic, demographic, psychographic, and behavioural, or a combination of these segmentation approaches (see Exhibit 7.2).

Geographic Segmentation **Geographic segmentation** organizes customers into groups on the basis of where they live. Thus, a market could be grouped by country (Canada, Germany, China), by region (Atlantic Canada, Western Canada), by areas within a region (province, city, neighbourhoods, area codes), or by climate and topography (warm, cold and snowy, mountainous). Not surprisingly, geographic segmentation is most useful for companies whose products satisfy needs that vary by region.

geographic segmentation The grouping of consumers on the basis of where they live.

Firms can provide the same basic goods or services to all segments even if they market globally or nationally; but, better marketers make adjustments to meet the needs of smaller geographic groups. For instance, a national grocery store chain, such as Sobeys or Loblaws, runs similar stores with similar assortments in various locations across Canada. Within those similar stores though,

EXHIBIT 7.2	Bases for Segmenting Markets
Segmentation Base	**Sample Segments**
Geographic	Continent, (North America, Asia, Europe, Africa), country, region (West Coast, Prairies, Central, Maritimes), province, city, urban, suburban, rural, climate
Demographic	Age, gender, income, education, occupation, race, marital status, family size, family life cycle, religion, ethnic background (white, black, Asian, Indian, German, Irish, Arab), generational cohort (baby boomer, generation X, generation Y), home ownership
Psychographic	Lifestyle (innovators, thinkers, achievers, experiencers, believers, strivers, makers, survivors), personality/self-concept (conservative, liberal, adventuresome, outgoing, health- and fitness-conscious), social class (upper class, middle class, working class)
Behavioural	Benefits sought (convenience, economy, prestige, quality, speed, service, environmental impact), usage (heavy, moderate, light, non-user, ex-user, potential user, first-time user), loyalty (not loyal, somewhat loyal, completely loyal)

a significant percentage of the assortment of goods will vary by region, city, or even neighbourhood, depending on the different needs of the customers who surround each location.

Consider a new superstore in Surrey, British Columbia, designed to cater specifically to the surrounding South East Asian (Punjabi) neighbourhood. In the produce section, piles of shiny, green *pasilla* chiles sit beside paddle-shaped cactus leaves and bumpy, brown yucca roots. At the meat counter, a customer greets a clerk in Punjabi and asks him to marinate some meat.

And, as you will read in the chapter case study, M&M Meat Shops used geographic segmentation to launch stores in the urban core of large cities, moving away from its traditional suburban–outlet-only strategy.

demographic segmentation
The grouping of consumers according to easily measured, objective characteristics such as age, gender, income, and education.

Demographic Segmentation   **Demographic segmentation** groups consumers according to easily measured, objective characteristics such as age, gender, income, education, race, occupation, religion, marital status, family size, family life cycle, and home ownership. These variables represent the most common means to define segments because they are easy to identify. For example, car makers often consider market segments defined by their income levels. Kellogg's uses age to define segments for its line of breakfast cereals. Froot Loops and Rice Krispies are for kids, while Special K and All-Bran are for adults. In addition, demographically segmented markets are easy to reach. For instance, if McCain's or Pizza Hut wants to advertise their newest pizza to kids, they can easily determine that the best time for TV ads would be during cartoons shown on Saturday morning or after school on weekdays. By considering the viewer profiles of various TV shows, McCain's and Pizza Hut can find those that fit its target market's demographic profile.

One demographic variable, gender, plays a very important role in how firms market products and services. Social Media Marketing 7.1 illustrates how one marketer used webisodes to target young women. Other marketers know that TV viewing habits vary significantly between men and women. Men tend to channel surf—switching quickly from channel to channel—and watch primetime shows more often if they are action-oriented and have physically attractive cast members. Women, in contrast, tend to view shows to which they can personally relate through the situational plot or characters and shows recommended by friends.[8]

Firms such as Gillette use an important demographic factor, gender, to sell different types of razors to men (Fusion ad on the left) and women (Venus ad on the right).

Social Media Marketing 7.1   Canadians: Social Media Leaders

When it comes to social media, Canadians lead the world. According to a recent report by comScore, a leading market research firm, 85 percent of Canadians online (more than 20 million Canadians) stream video, viewing an average of 120 videos per month. Furthermore, 90 percent of Canadians who are online visit a social networking site, spending an average of 6.5 hours on these sites per month, viewing an average of 804 pages per month, with an average of 35 visits per month. Our nearest competitor is the United Kingdom, and its numbers are much lower than Canada's. In the United Kingdom, 81 percent of the online population visits a social networking site, spending an average of 4.5 hours on these sites per month, viewing 539 pages and visiting 22 times per month.

In Canada, with respect to demographic profiles, social networking sites are equally popular with both males and females, as well as across all age groups. However, women on average spend 1.8 hours more time on these sites than men and view 245 more pages than their male counterparts. Geographically, Ontario leads the way in terms of the proportion of the online population that visits social networking sites. Overall, the top three sites among Canadians, from most to least favourite, are Facebook, Blogger, and WordPress.com. In contrast, the top three sites in the United States are Myspace, Facebook, and Blogger. Among younger Canadians (18 to 35 years), Myspace, Facebook,

Flickr, and Blogger are the most popular sites, whereas older Canadians (35 years and older) prefer LinkedIn, Twitter, and Classmates.com.

So, what does this all mean for Canadian marketers? For starters, if they want to connect with their customers, they must actively participate in the social media space with carefully crafted, integrated social media marketing strategies. Some marketers are designing their campaigns to maximize participation from their target markets.

As a case in point, consider the webisode series InYourFace.com. Launched by Marcelle Cosmetics, the series promoted a new line of skin-care products targeted at 15 to 27 year olds. The webisodes featured the skin care trials and tribulation of two fictional Montreal college students. To ensure that the product spoke to teens and young adults in a new way, viewers were invited to share suggested scripts for the characters as well as plot angles. Cash prizes were offered for the best angles and themes, the best lines for the characters, and the best submission of an original episode.

Sources: State of the Nation: Canada, Online Presentation, comScore. com, 2009 (accessed December 3, 2009); "Interactive website declares war on acne." www.clickweekly.com/articles/September 29_2009/ pimples.htm (accessed December 5, 2009); and Katie Bailey, "Marcelle gets in teen's faces with webisodes," www.mediaincanada.com/articles/mic/20090929/marcelle.html (accessed December 5, 2009).

Thus, a company such as Gillette, which sells razors for both men and women, will consider the appeal of various shows when it buys advertising time on TV. Also, as discussed in Chapter 3, the growth of ethnic Canadians from mainland China, Hong Kong, Taiwan, Philippines, and South East Asia (India, Pakistan, Sri Lanka) has led companies to develop marketing mixes and strategies targeted to these groups.

However, demographics may not be useful for defining the target segments for other companies. For example, demographics are poor predictors of the users of activewear, such as jogging suits and athletic shoes. At one time, firms such as Nike assumed that activewear would be purchased exclusively by young, active people, but the health and fitness trend has led people of all ages to buy such merchandise. Furthermore, relatively inactive consumers of all ages, incomes, and education find activewear more comfortable than traditional street clothes. Because it is relatively easy to gather demographic information, demographic variables are often used for segmenting markets. Depending on the nature of the product and market, however, marketers may find it more advantageous to combine demographic segmentation with other segmentation bases, described below, to derive a richer understanding of their potential customers. The Nike example shows that stereotyping could lead to poor STP strategies rather than a deep understanding of market segments.

psychographics
This segmentation base delves into how consumers describe themselves; allows people to describe themselves by using those characteristics that help them choose how they occupy their time (behaviour) and what underlying psychological reasons determine those choices.

Psychographic Segmentation   Of the various methods for segmenting, or breaking down the market, **psychographics** is the one that delves into how consumers

Marketers such as Benetton want their ads to appeal to one's self-concept. "I'm like them, so I should buy their products."

describe themselves. Usually marketers determine (through demographics, buying patterns, or usage) into which segment an individual consumer falls. But psychographics allows people to describe themselves by using those characteristics that help them choose how they occupy their time (behaviour) and what underlying psychological reasons determine those choices.[9] For example, a person might have a strong need for inclusion or belonging, which motivates him or her to seek out activities that involve others, which then influences the products he or she buys to fit in with the group. If a consumer becomes attached to a group that enjoys literary discussions, he or she is motivated to buy the latest books and spend time in stores such as Chapters. Such self-segmentation by the consumer could be very valuable knowledge for bookstore managers trying to find new ways of attracting customers. Determining psychographics involves knowing and understanding three components: self-values, self-concept, and lifestyles.

self-values
Goals for life, not just the goals one wants to accomplish in a day; a component of *psychographics* that refers to overriding desires that drive how a person lives his or her life.

Self-values are life goals, not just the goals one wants to accomplish in a day. In this context, they refer to overriding desires that drive how a person lives his or her life. Examples of self-value goals might include self-respect, self-fulfillment, or a sense of belonging. This motivation causes people to develop self-images of how they want to be and then determine a way of life that will help them arrive at these ultimate goals. From a marketing point of view, self-values help determine the benefits the target market may be looking for from a product. Lexus uses the tagline "Relentless Pursuit of Perfection" and BMW uses "'Someday' Just Arrived" to target these values. In this sense, the underlying, fundamental, personal need that pushes a person to seek out certain products or brands stems from his or her desire to fulfill a self-value, or goal.

self-concept
The image a person has of himself or herself; a component of *psychographics*.

How does that underlying goal affect the individual? It does so through **self-concept**, or the image people have of themselves.[10] A person who has a goal to belong may see, or want to see, himself or herself as a fun-loving, gregarious type whom people wish to be around. Marketers can make use of this image through communications that show their products being used by groups of laughing people who are having a good time. The connection emerges between the group fun and the product being shown and connotes a certain lifestyle. TV commercials for dating services such as eHarmony use this technique to sell their services. L'Oréal uses the tagline, "Because I'm Worth It," for its hair colour products.

Lifestyles, the third component of people's psychographic makeup, are the ways we live.[11] If values provide an end goal and self-concept is the way one sees oneself in the context of that goal, lifestyles are how we live our lives to achieve goals. Someone with a strong sense of belonging who sees himself as a "people person" will probably live in a well-populated area that allows for many activities. He likely will join clubs or partake in activities that attract like-minded people. Marketers thus have a built-in target group with similar interests and buying desires. lululemon quickly built a global empire of sportswear clothing and accessories based not on demographics but on the philosophy of a healthy, balanced, fun-filled lifestyle. Similarly, Rollerblade makes different skates for people with different lifestyles—the Astro ABT for regular skaters who want comfort, Crossfire II 4D Air Carbon for those looking for a perfect blend of speed, versatility, and comfort, and the Problade 07 for racers.

The most widely used psychographic system is the **VALS**™, owned and operated by Strategic Business Insights (SBI).[12] On the basis of their answers to the VALS™ questionnaire (www.strategicbusinessinsights. com/vals/presurvey.shtml), consumers are classified into the eight segments in the two dimensions shown in Exhibit 7.3. On the vertical dimension, segments are described by their resources, including their income, education, health, energy level, and degree of innovativeness. The upper segments have more resources and are more innovative; those on the bottom have fewer resources and are less innovative.

The horizontal dimension shows the segment's primary motivation. Consumers buy many products and services because of their primary motivations—that is, how they see themselves in the world and how that self-image governs their activities. The three universal primary motives are ideals, achievement, and self-expression. People who are primarily motivated by ideals are guided by knowledge and principles, whereas those who are motivated by achievement look for products and services that demonstrate success to their peers. Exhibit 7.4 provides a description of the VALS™ types.

VALS™ enables firms to identify target segments and their underlying motivations. It shows correlations between psychology and lifestyle choices. For instance, a Japanese auto manufacturer repositioned its product line to better understand consumer perceptions of its product mix. The insights which resulted from the VALS™ analysis led to an advertising campaign that increased sales by 60 percent in six months.[13] In another case, VALS was used to help a medical centre identify those customers most interested in and able to afford cosmetic surgery. By identifying the underlying motivations of its target customers, the centre's ad agency developed a campaign that was so successful it had to be pulled early to avoid overbooking its scheduling capabilities.

Rollerblade makes different skates for people with different lifestyles, ranging from weekend warriors to racers.

lifestyles
Refers to the way a person lives his or her life to achieve goals; a component of *psychographics*.

VALS™
A psychographical tool developed by Strategic Business Insights, classifies consumers into eight segments: Innovators, Thinkers, Believers, Achievers, Strivers, Experiencers, Makers, or Survivors.

Using the VALS Questionnaire in a survey "thinkers" (left) can be identified and contrasted with "makers" (right). "Thinkers" are motivated by ideals, whereas "makers" are prompted to buy based on their need for self-expression in a physical, hands-on way.

EXHIBIT 7.3   VALS™ Framework

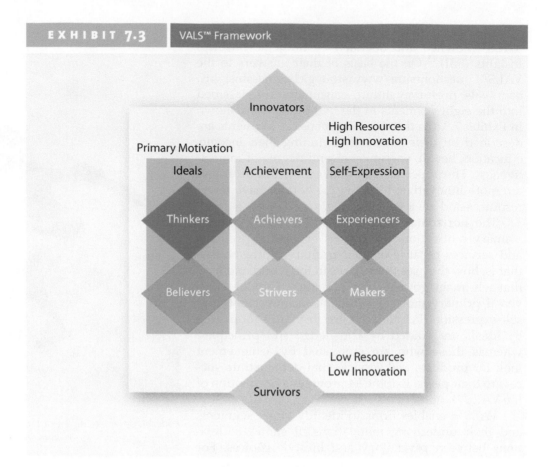

Source: www.strategicbusinessinsights.com/vals/ustypes.shtml (accessed June 7, 2011).

Firms are finding that psychographics are a very good complement to demographics to produce an in-depth profile and predict consumer behaviour. For instance, first-year college students and some day labourers may share similar demographics such as their age, education, and income, but they spend their income quite differently because of their very different mindsets. Likewise, Harpreet and Javinder are both 30 years old, married and college graduates. From a demographic standpoint they are the same, yet Harpreet is risk averse while Javinder is a risk taker. Harpreet is socially conscious. Javinder is focused on himself. Lumping these two men in the same target market does not make sense because they think and act very differently.

There are limitations to using psychographic segmentation however. Psychographics are not as objective as demographics, and it is harder to identify potential customers. With demographics, for example, a firm such as Nike can easily identify its customers as men or women and then direct its marketing strategies to each group differently. The problem is that not all men are alike, as we saw with Harpreet and Javinder. Women are not all alike either! Since it can be difficult to identify and target "thinkers" versus "makers," psychographic segmentation is often used in conjunction with other segmentation methods.[14]

behavioural segmentation
Groups consumers based on the benefits they derive from products or services, their usage rate, their user status, and their loyalty.

Behavioural Segmentation   **Behavioural segmentation** groups consumers on the basis of the benefits they derive from products or services, their usage rates of products or services, their user status, and their loyalty. As discussed in Sustainable Marketing 7.1, some universities are considering interest in sustainability initiatives as a way to segment and target both students and their parents. Because marketing

EXHIBIT 7.4	Description of VALS™ Categories

Innovators	Thinkers	Believers	Achievers
• Successful, sophisticated, take-charge people • High self-esteem • Change leaders • Established and emerging business leaders • Very active consumers • Purchases reflect cultivated taste for finer things	• Mature, satisfied, comfortable • Value responsibility • Well-educated, knowledge seekers • Respect for authority • Conservative, practical consumers • Like durability and clear value	• Conservative conventionalists • Concrete beliefs around family, religion, community • Deep-rooted moral codes • Established routines • Predictable, loyal consumers • Choose familiar products and established brands	• Goal-oriented lifestyles • Deep commitment to career and family • Respect for authority • Value stability, self-discovery • Active consumers • Favour prestige products that demonstrate their success, time-saving products
Strivers	**Experiencers**	**Makers**	**Survivors**
• Trendy and fun-loving • Money defines success • Favour stylish products • Active yet impulsive consumers • Shopping is a social activity and a display of status • Spend as much as they can	• Seek variety and excitement • Active in sports and social activities • Enthusiastic, impulsive consumers • Spend high proportion of income on fashion and entertainment • Want to look good and have cool stuff	• Practical people with constructive skills • Value self-sufficiency • Traditional views of family and work • Suspicious of new ideas • Unimpressed by material possessions • Prefer value over luxury	• Believe the world is changing too quickly • Comfortable with familiarity • Concerned with safety and security • Always focused on meeting needs not fulfilling wants • Cautious consumers • Loyal to favourite brands • Love a good deal

Source: The VALS™ Types. www.strategicbusinessinsights.com/vals/ustypes.shtml (accessed June 6, 2010).

is about satisfying consumers' needs and wants, dividing the market into segments whose needs and wants are best satisfied by the product benefits can be very powerful. It is also relatively easy to portray a product's or service's benefits in the firm's communication strategies: their usage rates of products or services, their user status, and their loyalty. Some companies track consumer behaviour and use it for better customer experiences or interactions with the firm. For example, as discussed in Power of the Internet 7.1, Amazon makes recommendations to customers while they are browsing its site by matching their profiles to those of other customers.

As mentioned previously, **benefit segmentation** looks at the benefits customers derive from products or services. Because marketing is all about satisfying needs and wants, dividing the market into segments according to which consumers' needs and wants your offerings can best satisfy makes a lot of sense.

An excellent illustration of benefit segmentation can be found in the RBC Royal Bank's approach. Although it considers that its customers may fall into as many as 80 market segments, its primary categorization centres on the benefits that customers seek from a bank. RBC divides personal (i.e., nonbusiness) customers into five primary benefit groups: Youth, Nexus, Borrowers/Builders, Wealth Accumulators, and Wealth Preservers.[15] As the names of these segments suggest, RBC approaches them according to the benefits they want their banks to provide, such as the accumulation or the preservation of their wealth.

The flyPhone, a multimedia cellphone manufactured by Firefly Mobile, offers another good illustration of benefit segmentation. The flyPhone combines an MP3 player, video player, camera, and game player; but, because the flyPhone is particularly targeted at tweens, it also includes sophisticated parental controls. Parents can limit incoming or outgoing calls and prevent new addresses or numbers from

benefit segmentation
Groups consumers based on the benefits they derive from products or services.

Sustainable Marketing 7.1   Corporate Knights: Sustainability-Focused Education

When you were evaluating universities, you probably considered their location, the program you wanted to pursue, and even how well they fared in *Maclean's* Annual University Rankings. But did on-campus sustainability initiatives ever cross your mind? Toby Heaps, editor-in-chief at Corporate Knights, thinks it will be an important factor in the future. Founded in 2002, the media company publishes the world's largest circulation magazine with an explicit emphasis on corporate responsibility.[16] It also publishes an annual Global 100 Most Sustainable Corporations in the World list and the Knight Schools Guide to sustainable education in Canada.

Heaps thinks that adopting more sustainable practices can help universities target students who want a "greener" post-secondary education. During a recent sustainability seminar offered to university professors, he suggested that the education system needs to become more interdisciplinary. For example, double degrees could be introduced to incorporate sustainability, or students could be encouraged to major or minor in an area related to sustainability.

Dalhousie University in Halifax set the goal of creating a program in which any student from any faculty could pursue a double major in sustainability, a first in Canada. Only a couple of years later, the program welcomed its first students. It has already gained international recognition by being short-listed for a 2009 World Innovation Summit for Education Award.[17] Dr. Deborah Buszard, a Dalhousie plant biologist who researches the use of plants in built environments, believes that sustainability should be added to the list of subjects every student should study.

According to Heaps, most sustainability initiatives on campus are

Students at Wilfrid Laurier University implemented eco-takeout containers on the campus.

student-driven and so it makes sense that universities could segment markets based on student interests and motivations and then use this information to attract these target students as well as their parents.

For example, at the University of British Columbia (UBC), a student-driven grassroots movement has been launched to increase awareness and inspire actions toward more sustainable living. Students can take the Sustainability Pledge to show their commitment and empower others to become active leaders in the transition toward sustainability at UBC and beyond.[18] In addition to taking the pledge, students are connected to sustainability initiatives, courses, workshops, and events. UBC addresses sustainability through a number of on-campus themes, including energy, materials, water, and community. But not just students are being targeted; there's information about sustainability efforts on web pages intended for parents of prospective students too.

At Wilfrid Laurier University in Waterloo, Ontario, a student-driven initiative resulted in hiring a sustainability coordinator. Sarah English says that students raised the money to pay her salary because it was an issue they passionately cared about. English cites numerous projects already in place, including a partnership with Sustainable Waterloo, a not-for-profit company dedicated to helping organizations decrease carbon emissions, to introducing composters in residences, to switching to green seal–certified cleaning products, to implementing eco-takeout container programs designed to reduce dependence on disposable containers, and to increasing the availability of reusable containers.

---

being added to the phone.[19] Using a benefit segmentation approach, Firefly Mobile designed a phone that appeals to both parents and their children: tweens get the benefit of a cool phone, and their parents enjoy the benefits of providing a cool product while still limiting cost and protecting their children.[20]

Hollywood is a constant and effective practitioner of benefit segmentation. Although all movies may seem to provide the same service—entertainment for a few hours—film producers know that people visit the theatre or rent films to get a variety of benefits and so they market them accordingly. Need a laugh? Try the latest comedy. Want to cry and then feel warm and fuzzy? Take in a romance movie. By the time you leave the theatre you will feel heartwarmingly happy because the lead characters are sure to have overcome their differences to find love.

Firms have long known that it pays to retain loyal customers. Loyal customers are those who feel so strongly that the firm can meet their relevant needs best that any competitors are virtually excluded from their consideration—that is, these customers buy almost exclusively from the firm.[21] These loyal customers are the most profitable in the long term.[22] In light of the high cost of finding new customers and the profitability of loyal customers, today's companies are using **loyalty segmentation** and investing in retention and loyalty initiatives to retain their most profitable customers. Canadians are crazy about loyalty cards, with nearly 9 in 10 adults (87 percent) actively participating in at least one loyalty program, whether it's retail or air travel. Loyalty card participation cuts across all demographics, for instance, 96 percent of affluent consumers actively participate in a loyalty program, 78 percent of young adults (18 to 25 years old), 90 percent of seniors (60 years or older), and 95 percent of women (25 to 49) do as well. In the United States, only 39.5 percent of the general population actively participates in a loyalty program.[23]

Airlines, for instance, definitely believe that all customers aren't created equal. At Air Canada, the customers who have flown the most miles with the company, the "Super Elite," receive a distinctive card, personalized Air Canada Super Elite luggage tags, special access to Aeroplan Reward seats, priority reservation waitlist, preferred seat selection, Air Canada concierge service, priority airport check-in, extra checked-baggage allowance, priority boarding, guaranteed reservations for full-fare tickets, and priority baggage handling, among other benefits.[24] None of these special services are available to the occasional flyer.

Usage rate (heavy users, regular users, light users, occasional users) as well as user status (current users, ex-users, potential users) can also be used as segmentation variables. For example, fast-food restaurants often use promotional coupons to target occasional visitors to their restaurant or to entice people who have never visited their restaurants to come in and try their food and services.

Using Multiple Segmentation Methods Although all segmentation methods are useful, each has its unique advantages and disadvantages. For example, segmenting by demographics and geography is easy because information about who the customers are and where they are located is readily available, but these characteristics don't help marketers determine their customer needs. Because "birds of a feather flock together," companies use a combination of geographic, demographic, and lifestyle characteristics, called **geodemographic segmentation**, to classify consumers.[25] Consumers in the same neighbourhoods tend to buy the same types of cars, appliances, and apparel, shop at the same types of retailers, and behave similarly to media and promotions. One of the most widely used tools for geodemographic segmentation in Canada are **PSYTE cluster** profiles, developed by Compusearch. The PSYTE system groups all neighbourhoods in Canada into 60 different lifestyles clusters with specific locations. The information in Exhibit 7.5 describes three PSYTE clusters.[26] PRIZM CE, a tool developed by Environics Research, groups Canadians into one of 66 lifestyle types—with names such as Cosmopolitan Elite, Electric Avenues, Les Chics, and Lunch at Tim's—and is also widely used in Canada. The system provides a Canadian segmentation model that has linked geodemographics to psychographics, incorporating "Social Values" data from Environics Research with demographics and product preferences to explain consumer behaviour.[27]

Geodemographic segmentation can be particularly useful for retailers because customers typically patronize stores close to their neighbourhood. Thus, retailers can use geodemographic segmentation to tailor each store's assortment to the preferences of the local community. If a toy chain discovers that one of its stores is surrounded by "Big Sky Families," it can adjust its offerings to include less expensive merchandise. This kind of segmentation is also useful for finding new locations; retailers identify their "best" locations and determine what type of people live in the

loyalty segmentation
Strategy of investing in retention and loyalty initiatives to retain the firm's most profitable customers.

geodemographic segmentation
The grouping of consumers on the basis of a combination of geographic, demographic, and lifestyle characteristics.

PSYTE clusters
The grouping of all neighbourhoods in Canada into 60 different lifestyles clusters.

EXHIBIT 7.5	PSYTE Cluster		
Cluster Name	**Urban Lower Middle (U4): Urban Bohemia**	**Suburban Affluent (S1): Suburban Affluence**	**Suburban Affluent (S1): Asian Heights**
Description	From body piercing to tattoos, Urban Bohemia includes a diverse population by design. A neighbourhood with a youthful skew, this cluster occupies itself in a variety of artistic, retail, and generally creative employment. Men and women employed in cultural, artistic, and entertainment-related jobs abound. Household maintainers under age 25, many with college degrees, are also found in this cluster.	This cluster with a flair for fine living represents both old and new wealth. Because wealth accumulates throughout life stages, this cluster exhibits an older skew with many empty nests. Suburban Affluence indexes high on managerial and technical employment and are married with children.	Asian ancestries combined with hard work and growing wealth create and mould these upscale neighbourhoods. Asian Heights represents the affirmation of dreams cultivated through generations of immigrants and often through hardship. These families boost local economies as well as family prospects. Asian Heights indexes high on Chinese, Korean, and Japanese immigration as well as households of six or more persons.
Average Household Income	$46,000	$166,000	$96,000

Source: http://tetrad.com/pcensus/can/psyteadv_clusters.pdf (accessed June 1, 2007).

area surrounding those stores, according to the geodemographic clusters. They can then find other potential locations where similar segments reside. Geodemographic systems, such as PSYTE and PRIZM CE, can also help marketers track and compare sales performance among various clusters in different locations.

Knowing what benefits customers are seeking or how the product or service fits a particular lifestyle is important for designing an overall marketing strategy, but such segmentation schemes present a problem for marketers attempting to identify specifically which customers are seeking these benefits. Thus, firms often employ a combination of segmentation methods, using demographics and geography, as discussed above, to identify and target marketing communications to their customers, and then using benefits or lifestyles to design the product or service and the substance of the marketing message. See Real World Segmentation Example for an example of how multiple segmentation methods can combine to develop a richer segmentation strategy for financial markets.

Developing a market segmentation strategy over the Internet usually is somewhat easier than developing it for traditional channels. Power of the Internet 7.1 explains why.

REAL WORLD SEGMENTATION EXAMPLE

Segmenting the Financial Services Market by Using Demographics and Lifestyles[28]

LIMRA, a financial services research and consulting organization, which operates in Canada and the United States, surveyed its consumers to determine their personal financial objectives and the type of lifestyle they wanted when they retired. The survey yielded four identifiable segments for middle-income households, as described in the chart below.

Steve Hall is a financial consultant who is prospecting for new customers. What can he do with combined demographic and lifestyle LIMRA data? The demographic data can identify the type of people in a segment, how firms might reach these people through the media or other selling vehicles, and how profitable the segments may be. For instance, Steve has found a group of "Worker Bees" who are self-employed, over 40, and have relatively high incomes. The lifestyle data then can be used to help design products and promotional messages that are relevant to this group. For instance, Steve historically would study a customer's portfolio and his or her attitude toward taking financial risks before preparing a retirement package for that customer. But knowing the type of lifestyles to which these "Worker Bees" aspire when they retire enables the sales agent to better match customers' lifestyles and the financial planning process. Since the "Worker Bees" are very entrepreneurial and love to work, Steve designs a sales presentation that stresses how much money they need to save over the coming years to maintain their relatively modest lifestyle and enable them to continue to work as long as they wish or are physically able.

The financial services consulting firm LIMRA targets four identifiable segments based on demographics and lifestyle data to best meet the needs of middle-income households getting ready to retire.

Demographic and Retirement Lifestyle Segmentation for the Financial Services Market

	Pragmatic Planners	Worker Bees	Grand Thinkers	Status Quo
DEMOGRAPHIC CHARACTERISTICS	✓ Single ✓ No dependent children ✓ Educated ✓ Moderate income ✓ Have discretionary income ✓ Under 45 years old	✓ Couples ✓ Less formal education ✓ High income ✓ High investable assets ✓ Over 40 ✓ Self-employed	✓ Couples ✓ Broad education levels ✓ Moderate incomes ✓ Broad age ranges	✓ Couples ✓ With dependent children ✓ Less formal education ✓ Broad income range ✓ Over 40
PERCENTAGE OF MIDDLE-MARKET HOUSEHOLDS	30 percent	15 percent	34 percent	21 percent
RETIREMENT LIFESTYLE GOALS	✓ Save to buy home ✓ Eliminate or reduce debt ✓ Save for retirement ✓ Maintain modest but comfortable standard of living ✓ Spend time with family ✓ Enjoy leisure activities	✓ Start or expand business ✓ Save for retirement ✓ Maintain modest but comfortable living standard ✓ Start or run business ✓ Keep working in a capacity similar to today's	✓ Save to buy home ✓ Protect family in case of death ✓ Eliminate or reduce debt ✓ Save for retirement ✓ Maintain modest but comfortable standard of living ✓ Spend time with family ✓ Enjoy leisure activities	✓ Protect family in case of death ✓ Protect family in case of disability ✓ Eliminate or reduce debt ✓ Save for retirement ✓ Maintain modest but comfortable standard of living ✓ Spend time with family

Source: Pete Jacques, "Aspirational Segmentation," *LIMRA's MarketFacts Quarterly* 22 (Spring 2003), p. 2.

L03 ## Step 3: Evaluate Segment Attractiveness

The third step in the segmentation process involves evaluating the attractiveness of the various segments. To undertake this evaluation, marketers first must determine whether the segment is worth pursuing by using several descriptive criteria: Is the segment identifiable, reachable, responsive, and substantial and profitable? (See Exhibit 7.6.)

Identifiable   Firms must determine who is within their market to be able to design products or services to meet their needs. It is equally important to ensure that the segments are distinct from one another because too much overlap between segments means that distinct marketing strategies aren't necessary to meet segment members' needs.

The Gap has identified several distinct segments to pursue. Recognizing that many of its core customers had families, The Gap opened GapKids and babyGap. Its research also indicated an opportunity to compete with Victoria's Secret in the women's intimate apparel market, so it opened GapBody. Finally, though The Gap is largely successful with middle-of-the-road customers, it was too expensive for some customers and not fashion-forward enough for others. Its Old Navy and Banana Republic stores appeal better to these markets.

Reachable The best product or service cannot have any impact if that market cannot be reached (or accessed) through persuasive communications and product distribution. Consumers must know the product or service exists, understand what it can do for them, and recognize how to buy it.

La Senza is one of Canada's leading specialty retailers of women's lingerie and apparel. It is composed of La Senza Lingerie, La Senza Girl, La Senza Express, La Senza International, La Senza Spirit, and lasenza.com, and it sells through stores and the Internet. La Senza Girl does not sell through the Internet but has a straightforward plan for reaching its target customers: girls between 7 and 14 years of age.[32] The company simply uses its website to attract its targeted customers to explore its merchandise and fashions so that they can be comfortable and knowledgeable when they visit the physical stores to shop. Advertisements appear in media that are consistent with the lifestyle La Senza Girl is trying to portray: lively, attractive, stylish, fun, and cool.

Firms trying to reach university students have a much more difficult time because students' media habits are quite diverse, and generally they are cynical about firms

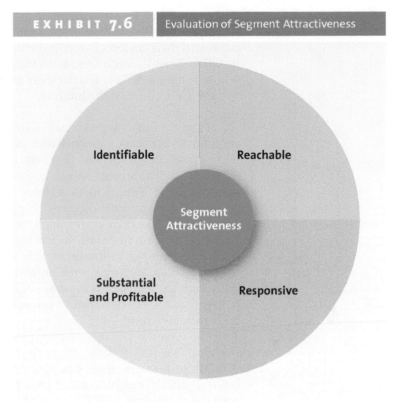

EXHIBIT 7.6 | Evaluation of Segment Attractiveness

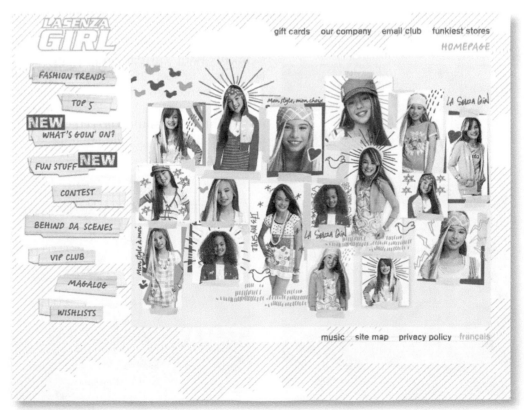

La Senza must ensure any new segment it considers is identifiable, reachable, responsive, substantial, and profitable.

that try too hard to sell to them. High-end fashion jeans companies, for instance, often underpromote their lines or promote them very subtly through traditional media because if their customers start to believe the brand is too mainstream, they won't buy it. Other hard-to-reach segments are composed of people with disabilities or those whose religious beliefs restrict their media choices. For example, Amish Mennonites eschew TV, radio, and the Internet.

Responsive For a segmentation strategy to be successful, the customers in the segment must react similarly and positively to the firm's offering. If, through its distinctive competencies, the firm cannot provide products or services to that segment, it should not target it. For instance, suppose La Senza is considering introducing a line of formal dress wear for its large and very lucrative 18- to 35-year-old customer segment. People in this market are currently purchasing formal dress wear at stores such as The Bay, Holt Renfrew, and Les Ailes de la Mode (Wings of Fashion). In contrast, La Senza has built a reputation for carrying a full range of intimate, stylish, and sexy daywear and sleepwear bras, panties, camisoles, pyjamas, and nightshirts and competes best in this apparel line. Although the formal dress wear segment meets all the other criteria for a successful segment, La Senza should not pursue it because the market probably will not be responsive to it.

Substantial and Profitable Once the firm has identified its potential target markets, it needs to measure their size and growth potential. If a market is too small or its buying power insignificant, it won't generate sufficient profits or be able to support the marketing mix activities. Although The Gap had identified potential new target markets to pursue, it was imperative for the company to determine whether the market for women's intimate apparel was small or large. If it was relatively small, the company would fit the products into its regular stores. If it was large, the products would require their own space. The Gap experimented cautiously with the new concept by first placing a section of intimate apparel in some of its stores. Over time, Gap managers realized the potential of the concept and began to roll out GapBody stores.

Marketers must also focus their assessments on the potential profitability of each segment, both current and future. Some key factors to keep in mind in this analysis include market growth (current size and expected growth rate), market competitiveness (number of competitors, entry barriers, product substitutes), and market access

The Gap has identified several distinct segments to pursue. Two of its brands: Gap (right) and Gap Kids (left) appeal to different target markets.

(ease of developing or accessing distribution channels and brand familiarity). Some straightforward calculations can help illustrate the profitability of a segment:[33]

Segment profitability = (Segment size × Segment adoption percentage × Purchase behaviour × Profit margin percentage) − Fixed costs

where

Segment size = Number of people in the segment

Segment adoption percentage = Percentage of customers in the segment who are likely to adopt the product/service

Purchase behaviour = Purchase price × Number of times the customer would buy the product or service during a given time period

Profit margin percentage = (Selling price − Variable costs) ÷ Selling price

Fixed costs = Advertising expenditure, rent, utilities, insurance, administration, salaries

Several segments may appear to be equally profitable according to this formula. In some cases, however, it is more accurate to evaluate the profitability of a segment over the lifetime of one of its typical customers—that is, through customer lifetime value (CLV), the total value of purchases of the customer over a lifetime of patronage. For example, Ken Danns has been a loyal Costco customer for the last five years, spending about $300 per week at Costco. He plans to continue patronizing Costco for at least another five years. To Costco, Ken Danns is not a $300 customer but a $156,000 customer if he patronizes Costco for 10 years ($300 × 52 week × 10 years). To address the issue of CLV, marketers consider factors such as how long the customer will remain loyal to the firm, the defection rate (percentage of customers who switch on a yearly basis), the costs of replacing lost customers (advertising, promotion), whether customers will buy more or more-expensive merchandise in the future, and other such factors.[34] See Appendix 7A for more details on determining the lifetime value of customers.

Now that we've evaluated each segment's attractiveness (Step 3), we can select the target markets to pursue (Step 4).

Step 4: Select Target Market

`L04`

The fourth step in the STP process is selecting a target market. The key factor likely to affect this decision is the marketer's ability to pursue such an opportunity or target segment. Thus, as we mentioned in Chapter 2, a firm is likely to assess both the attractiveness of the opportunity (opportunities and threats based on the SWOT

Which segment will be more profitable to Mark's, its traditional market for rugged work clothes (right), or the fashion-forward segment (left)?

IT'S LIKE SIGNING A CARD WITH YOUR VOICE.

NEW *RECORDABLE* CARDS WITH MUSIC

Rock Mom's day with a personalized voice message, introducing a song from an artist she knows. Record as many times as you like to say the perfect thing. Then whether she's far away or sitting right next to you, Mom will know exactly how you feel.

See the Mother's Day collection at your Hallmark Gold Crown store. And check out the card demonstration at Hallmark.com/AddYourVoice.

Hallmark GOLD CROWN

How has Hallmark selected its target markets?

undifferentiated segmentation strategy (mass marketing)
A marketing strategy a firm can use if the product or service is perceived to provide the same benefits to everyone, with no need to develop separate strategies for different groups.

analysis—i.e., profitability of the segment) and its own competencies (strengths and weaknesses based on SWOT analysis) very carefully.

What could be a more undifferentiated market segment strategy than greeting cards? After all, they are available in grocery stores, discount stores, drug stores, and specialty card stores. Each year, 90 percent of households purchase at least one greeting card. Everyone needs greeting cards from time to time, right? Then how does Hallmark, a greeting card company with more than $4.4 billion in annual sales and a brand recognized around the globe, segment its market?[35]

First, using a geographic segmentation strategy, Hallmark is continuing its global expansion, particularly to India and China. Also, it is using a benefit segmentation strategy by targeting those seeking the convenience of sending a card over the Internet. The industry was worried that e-cards, which are generally free, would negatively affect traditional card sales, but in fact the availability of e-cards has helped to boost sales. Hallmark has a link on its home page for a free iPhone app to promote its brand name via the Internet. Internet users are exposed to traditional advertising, and Hallmark can sell and promote its movies made for the Hallmark Channel and sell gifts, ornaments, and other popular personal expression items. Exhibit 7.7 provides an illustration of how a firm such as Hallmark might match its competencies with the attractiveness of various alternative segments and use this process to pick the best fit.

Establishing a basic segmentation strategy is not always as easy and clear as it was for La Senza. Exhibit 7.8 illustrates several segmentation strategies. Sometimes it makes sense to not segment at all. In other situations, a firm should concentrate on one segment or go after multiple segments at once. Finally, some firms choose to specialize in their product or service line to meet the needs of very small groups—perhaps even one person at a time. We discuss each of these basic segmentation types next.

Undifferentiated Segmentation Strategy, or Mass Marketing   When everyone might be considered a potential user of its product, a firm uses an **undifferentiated segmentation strategy** (see Exhibit 7.8). If the product or service is perceived to provide the same benefits to everyone, there simply is no need to develop separate strategies for different groups. Although not a common strategy in today's complex marketplace, an undifferentiated strategy can be effective for very basic items, such as salt, sugar, or greetings cards. However, even those firms that offer salt, sugar, or greeting cards now are trying to differentiate their products, as is the case with Hallmark.

An undifferentiated strategy also is common among smaller firms that offer products or services that consumers

Kettleman's Bagel Co. differentiates itself with its "no-wall" experience. When customers walk into its bagel shop, the first thing they see is the Kettleman's Bagel Roller working and rolling fresh bagels.

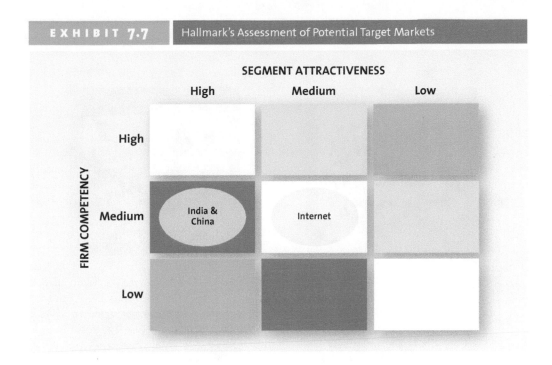

EXHIBIT 7.7　　Hallmark's Assessment of Potential Target Markets

perceive to be indistinguishable, such as a neighbourhood bakery. But again, more marketing-savvy entrepreneurs typically try to differentiate themselves in the marketplace. The corner bakery thus becomes "Kettleman's Bagel" or "The Great Canadian Bagel." By making their commodity-like products appear special, these companies add value for the customer and differentiate themselves from their competition.

What about gasoline? Everyone with a car needs it. Yet gasoline companies have vigorously moved from an undifferentiated strategy to a differentiated one by segmenting their market into low-, medium-, and high-octane gasoline users. Esso even uses its Speedpass to differentiate its quick service to consumers: with just a swipe at the pump with Speedpass, you are ready to pump gas—no need to swipe cards, enter personal information, or sign receipts. Plus customers earn Esso Extra points or Aeroplan Miles on every eligible purchase made at Esso. Points can be redeemed for gas, car washes, snacks, and travel rewards.

Differentiated Segmentation Strategy　　Firms using a **differentiated segmentation strategy** target several market segments with a different offering for each (see Exhibit 7.8). La Senza, for instance, employs three store formats—La Senza, La Senza Girl, and La Senza Express—to appeal to three different segments respectively: (1) confident, fashion-forward 18- to 35-year-old women; (2) younger girls; and (3) women looking for the ultimate destination for bras and panties for everyday and trend-forward styles.[36] In a similar fashion, Adidas Group appeals to various segments through its various companies, including Adidas Reebok (athletic shoes), Rockport (comfortable walking shoes), and TaylorMade-Adidas Golf lines of clothing and footwear.

Firms embrace differentiated segmentation because it helps them obtain a bigger share of the market and increase the market for their products overall. The more retail formats La Senza develops to reach different market segments, the more apparel and accessories it can and will sell. Offering several different lingerie lines enable La Senza to appeal to more customer segments than if it had just one line. Furthermore, providing products or services that appeal to multiple segments helps diversify the business thereby lowering the company's overall risk. For example, if a line directed

differentiated segmentation strategy A strategy through which a firm targets several market segments with a different offering for each.

| EXHIBIT 7.8 | Segmentation Strategies |

Mass or Undifferentiated

Differentiated

Concentrated

Micromarketing One-to-One

toward one segment is performing poorly, the impact on the firm's profitability can be offset by revenue from another line that is doing well.

But a differentiated strategy can be expensive. Consider La Senza's investment in accessories alone. The firm must develop, manufacture, transport, store, and promote the accessories separately for each of its store concepts.

Concentrated (Niche) Segmentation Strategy   When an organization selects a single, primary target market and focuses all its energies on providing a product to fit that market's needs, it is using a **concentrated or niche segmentation strategy** (see Exhibit 7.8). Entrepreneurial start-up ventures often benefit from using a concentrated strategy, which allows them to employ their limited resources more efficiently. The story of Cora's restaurants in Entrepreneurial Marketing 7.1 is an example of a niche strategy since it focuses on serving breakfast and brunch only; restaurants are open only until 3 p.m. Gennum Corporation of Burlington, Ontario, is another example of a niche strategy; it is the world's leading innovator in microcircuitry for hearing aids—a niche market.

For example, if you've ever shopped at Abercrombie & Fitch (A&F), chances are you're younger than 30 years of age. Since its inception, A&F has pursued a calculated concentrated segmentation strategy by deliberately targeting the young and good-looking crowd with a hip, edgy strategy. Thus, when older or "unhip"

concentrated (or niche) segmentation strategy A marketing strategy of selecting a single, primary target market and focusing all energies on providing a product to fit that market's needs.

consumers don't find it appealing, that doesn't bother the company one bit. Its whole brand experience is designed to create an impression of exclusivity for its 18- to 22-year-old customers.[37] For instance, rather than display items in brightly lit windows, as most clothing retailers do, it carefully shutters off the outside of its stores so that customers have to enter to see the merchandise. Once inside, they confront not a brightly lit interior that helps customers find what they're looking for but rather a dark, loud environment with an almost overwhelming scent of heavy cologne. The stores are carefully designed to make shopping an emotional experience

for core customers; but, for the parents of these customers, that experience is usually unpleasant. But then, they're not part of the target market A&F is trying to attract.[38]

Abercrombie & Fitch targets the 18- to 22-year-old market with a hip, edgy image.

Micromarketing[39]   Take a look at your collection of belts. Have you ever had a belt made to match your exact specifications? When a firm tailors a product or service to suit an individual customer's wants or needs, it is undertaking an extreme form of segmentation called **micromarketing** or **one-to-one marketing** (see Exhibit 7.8). Small producers and service providers generally can tailor their offering to individual customers more easily, whereas it is far more difficult for larger companies to achieve this degree of segmentation. Nonetheless, companies such as Dell and Lands' End have capitalized on Internet technologies to offer "custom-made" computers, dress shirts, chinos, and jeans. Firms, such as Build-a-Bear Workshop, that interact on a one-to-one basis with many people to create custom-made products or services are engaged in **mass customization**, providing one-to-one marketing to the masses. Prior to the Internet era, micromarketing was almost impossible to achieve except for within small, entrepreneurial firms. However, the Internet has made it possible for firms of all sizes and markets to engage in micromarketing.

micromarketing (one-to-one) marketing An extreme form of segmentation that tailors a product or service to suit an individual customer's wants or needs.

mass customization The practice of interacting on a one-to-one basis with many people to create custom-made products or services; providing one-to-one marketing to the masses.

Nike and its many customers seem to have taken this concept to heart. The success of its online make-your-own-shoe feature, and a tiny SoHo studio that has seen a steady stream of celebrities customizing their kicks, led Nike to take its ID program mainstream. A new NikeID "lab" is now open at Niketown on 57th Street in Manhattan, where consumers make an appointment to sit down at a computer and put their own stamp on a pair of sneakers. Three to four weeks later, custom sneakers arrive at their doorstep. This studio has more features than its online version (http://nikeid.nike.com), which attracts 3 million unique visitors each month. There also are consultants assigned to each "designer" to help them realize their shoe fantasies. Customers pick everything from colour and materials to the fit. They can also add a "signature" on the back of the shoe. Nike looks to the ID program as a way to ramp up its personal connection with customers, and the offerings, including apparel, will continue to expand.

The degree to which firms should segment their markets—from no segmentation to one segment to multiple segments to one-to-one segments—depends on the balance the firm wants to achieve between the added perceived customer value that segmentation can offer and its cost.

Sometimes firms' target market selection also can raise serious ethical concerns. Ethical Dilemma 7.1 examines the issue of marketing high-end designer clothing to teens.

Entrepreneurial Marketing 7.1   Chez Cora: The Business of Breakfast

When Cora Tsouflidou became a single mother to three teenage children, she bought a small eatery, worked hard, tripled its value, and sold it. From there she worked her way up from a hostess to the general manager in a well-known Montreal restaurant, mastering her foodservice industry knowledge along the way.[40]

These skills served her well when she bought a defunct 29-seat snack bar in Montreal's Ville St-Laurent in 1987 and launched the first Chez Cora restaurant. Plates garnished with a variety of artistically presented fresh fruits made Cora's dishes both unique and popular. Her homey, healthy food was a hit, which led to franchising the first Chez Cora in Quebec, followed by franchising Cora's Breakfast and Lunch across the rest of the country. Today, there are more than 100 Cora's restaurants, all of which have traditional family-style breakfast and lunch menus featuring new dishes created and tested by Cora herself.

When deciding to open a new franchise, the company starts with a demographic analysis to determine whether there are enough people in an area to feed a Cora's restaurant.[41] Psychographics and behavioural segmentation are also important to identify and attract customers who are interested in healthy lifestyles and want the benefit of nutritious meals.

A unique strategy attracts franchisees based on their desired lifestyle. Restaurants serve only breakfast and lunch and thus are open between 6 a.m. and 3 p.m., an approach born out of necessity from Cora's early days as a single mom. These hours are considerably shorter than most restaurant operations and thus appeal to franchisees, allowing them to spend more time with their families.

It's not surprising that Cora's image is used in advertising campaigns. She looks like a mom who really cares about family, which resonates with both customers and franchisees. Behind that colourful image is a self-made business woman who has won the Governor General's Award and the Ernst & Young Entrepreneur of the Year Award.[42] Cora's unique business plan has made Cora's one of the fastest-growing restaurant chains in Canada.

Cora's serves up healthy fare featuring a variety of colourful fruits with each meal.

Step 5: Identify and Develop Positioning Strategy

positioning
The mental picture that people have about a company and its products or services relative to competitors.

The last step in developing a market segmentation strategy is **positioning**. Positioning is the mental picture or perception—the thoughts, feelings, and impressions—that people have about a company, its products and brands relative to competing products, brands, or companies. This mental picture is formed from multiple sources such as friends, family, relatives, reference groups, published articles in magazines and newspapers, reports and stories from radio, TV, and the Internet, as well as the customer's own experience. Regardless of whether companies want them to or not, consumers form their own ideas and feelings about a product or brand, and it is those very ideas and emotions that drive them toward or away from a brand or company. Basically, positioning is what determines consumers' *preference* for a company's products or brands. Preference is when consumers *want* a company's brand and will not accept competitors' substitutes. For example, Internet surfers prefer Google over Yahoo! for online searching and Apple's iPod over Sony's Walkman MP3 players for mobile music. Preference drives market share and revenues; both Apple and Google are the dominant players in their space. Recognizing the strategic importance of positioning, many companies work very hard to shape consumers' perceptions of their brands. Positioning is one of the most important but difficult and least understood aspects of marketing strategy development. Why?

What happens when marketing to a segment works too well? Take, for example, designer labels targeting teens 13 to 17 years of age. In 2007, designer labels accounted for 15.4 percent of teen clothing purchases; just three years earlier, these labels earned only 9.6 percent. Yet among adults older than 18 years of age, the 7-percent market share designer labels maintain has remained constant.[43] So what can explain these trends?

High-end designers are taking advantage of teens' desire for fashion and bragging rights to sell apparel to younger consumers by targeting them intensively with advertising and product placements. Luxury brands targeting kids include Dolce & Gabbana and Armani, which have created their own separate teen lines, as well as Michael Kors, Coach, Dooney & Bourke, and Dior, which target young consumers with accessories. Even retailers are cashing in on the trend; department stores such as Nordstrom have added Burberry and Prada products to their children's departments. As a result, tweens are showing up to school with their $225 Dooney & Bourke gym bags in tow.[44]

The effects of intense advertising to kids also appear in the form of more sophisticated brand opinions among younger and younger consumers. Four years ago, 15 percent of teens claimed to love Armani; today that level has reached 27 percent. In schools across the country, the effects of increased advertising to kids has also resulted in massive increases in "fashion bullying"—that is, when students are targeted because they do not wear the "right" clothing or designers. More than one-third of all middle school students say that they have been bullied because of what they wear. Although this form of bullying certainly is not new, guidance counsellors say that fashion bullying has reached a new level of intensity as more designers launch collections targeted at kids.

Fashion companies face an ethical dilemma: How much should they target teens? Clearly, these companies hope to gain lifetime aficionados by reaching out to consumers at a young age, with the goal of turning them into loyal repeat customers. However, some advertising appears to be encouraging fashion bullying. Furthermore, luxury purchases such as designer handbags and totes are specifically created to be exclusive. When teens buy luxury goods at more than twice the rate of the general population, it suggests that parents are funding a fashion habit that they may not engage in themselves and that may not be sustainable for those children when they grow up and have to pay their own way. Should the designers care? What do you think?

Should fashion companies target teens?

It is difficult because it is not easy to shape consumers' perceptions in the way marketers may want. It is also difficult because while marketers must keep their positioning fresh to keep abreast with the ever-changing marketplace, consumers' perceptions are enduring and do not change easily. Positioning is very risky for marketers because if it is not done correctly, the brand may not succeed in the marketplace. Effective positioning, therefore, requires that marketers not only shape their customers' thinking and feelings, but also evolve these feelings as they reposition their products and brands to keep up with the dynamic marketplace. For example, HP successfully repositioned itself from a boring, stodgy printer company to a consumer electronics powerhouse. It is now a leading computer company.

Market positioning involves a process of defining the marketing mix variables so that target customers have a clear, distinctive, desirable understanding of what the product does or represents in comparison with competing products. Effective positioning is about letting consumers know what the company's unique value proposition is and for whom it is intended. Clarity of this message is crucial for successful positioning. For example, Abercrombie & Fitch offers casual luxury to young, sexy, athletic- and cheerleading-type university students. Its advertising messages, models, store design, and merchandise all reinforce this message. It does not make clothing for overweight, fat, or obese people because it does not want to be perceived as being all things to all people. Rather, it determines its target market's needs and wants and tries to deliver the best value to its customers.

From the preceding discussion, it is obvious that a firm's positioning strategies must focus on the value a product or service offers the target consumer, or how it is better than competitors' products and services. When positioning against competitors, the objective is to play up how the brand being marketed provides the desired benefits better than those of competitors. Positioning strategies are realized by communicating particular messages (i.e., the **positioning statement**) in persuasive communications through different media. Usually, firms position their products and services according to value, product attributes, benefits and symbolism, and against competition (see Exhibit 7.9). Let's explore each of these in a bit more detail.

positioning statement
Expresses how a company wants to be perceived by consumers.

Value   Value is a popular positioning method because the relationship of price to quality is among the most important considerations for consumers when they make a purchase decision. Value positioning may open up avenues to attract new customer segments that the company previously had neglected. For example, while Proctor & Gamble's (P&G's) competitors, such as Unilever and Colgate, found success with lower-priced "value" products such as Suave shampoo and Alberto VO5, P&G seemed to ignore that 80 percent of the world could not afford its products. In an attempt to correct this oversight, P&G company managers are now working globally to understand "price-sensitive customers" in various regions and sharing strategies

EXHIBIT 7.9	Positioning Strategies	
Positioning Strategy	**Company**	**Examples of Ad Jingles**
Value Price/Quality	Buy.com Dell Gillette Walmart WestJet	"Canada's low-price Internet superstore" "To deliver the most energy-efficient products in the industry" "The best a man can get" "Save money. Live better." "No frill, low-fare, air travel in Canada"
Product Attributes	American Express Energizer KFC Intel (leadership)	"Don't leave home without it" "It keeps going and going" "Finger Lick'n Good" "Leap ahead"
Benefits/Symbolism	3M Abercrombie & Fitch Canon (self-expression) Kodak (personal meaning) Lexus L'Oréal (self-concept)	"3M Innovation" "Casual luxury" "Express yourself" "Share moments. Share life" "Relentless Pursuit of Excellence" "Because I'm worth it"
Competition	Avis Capital One (differentiation) ING Direct (head to head)	"We try harder" "Hands in your pocket" "The unmortgage, save your money"

to promote P&G products. For example, they've taken flagship products such as Ivory soap and dropped the price 10 to 15 percent below that of rivals such as Dial. In the kids' toy market, Mega Bloks uses a low-price, value-based strategy, whereas its competitor, Lego, relies on a high-price positioning strategy.

Other value-based positioning strategies emphasize that consumers are offered the best product or service but must pay a premium price to cover the additional cost. Air Canada's Super Elite flyer program, described earlier in this chapter, is an example of this type of positioning. Balmshell lip gloss is another example; it was introduced at Holt Renfrew, a high-end retailer, at a premium price relative to existing lip gloss. Or, a company may go after a competitor by offering a comparable product at a lower price. This strategy is often observed for high-end products or luxury brands such as hotels and sports cars. Some companies claim that they are offering the same value for much less money. This type of positioning is common among wireless service providers (e.g., Roger's, Bell, TELUS), cable/satellite TV and radio providers (Sirius, Roger's), electronics retailers (Future Shop), and department stores (Zellers). Companies such as Internet Superstore, Buy.com, and TigerDirect emphasize that consumers are getting the best computer deals anywhere but at much lower prices. Finally, companies may use value positioning that lets consumers know they are getting much less but they are also paying much less. WestJet, dollar stores (e.g., Buck or Two, Dollar Store), and countless retailers targeting cost-conscious consumers commonly use this strategy.

Product Attributes   Another common positioning strategy focuses on those attributes that are most important to the target market. Car company Volvo traditionally positioned itself for the safety-conscious driver but now wants to stretch its safety image to one focused on driving performance and excitement. The company expects the positioning adjustment to be difficult but achievable, because so many of Volvo's boxier vehicles remain on the road today, which reinforces its more conservative image. Volvo's goal is not to abandon the safety perception associated with the brand but rather to expand its image to compete with other top luxury brands.[45] Positioning strategies that are based on product attributes tend to focus on product leadership, emphasizing dimensions such as innovation, quality,

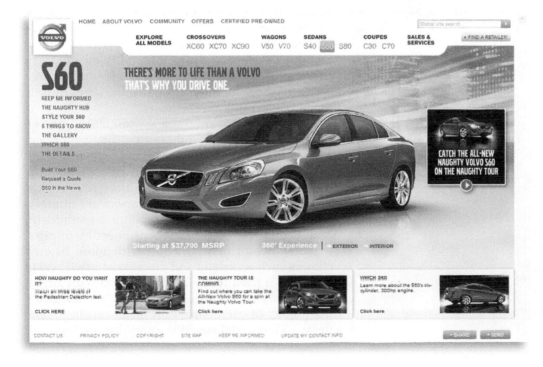

Can Volvo reposition its cars to be more exciting with higher performance without losing its traditional position that appeals to safety-conscious drivers?

performance, design, and reliability. 3M and HP focus on their innovations while Rockport focuses on comfort and a wide selection of shoes for all occasions. Cora's, a product-attributes success story, is able to compete in the highly competitive restaurant market by attracting a target market that wants a healthy and homey breakfast (see Entrepreneurial Marketing 7.1.)

Benefits and Symbolism   This type of positioning emphasizes the benefits of the brand as well as the psychological meaning of the brand to consumers. For example, JACOB is about comfort in a casual, modern style, and JACOB lingerie is about femininity, European elegance, and unparalleled comfort. La Senza Express is the ultimate destination dedicated to bras and panties, and Abercrombie & Fitch is about casual luxury.[46] The meanings created by these brands are often the reasons why consumers buy them rather than lesser known brands that sometimes offer similar benefits or quality. For established companies, a well-known symbol can also be used as a positioning tool, especially to appeal to loyal customers. What comes to mind when you think of Colonel Sanders, the Jolly Green Giant, the Gerber Baby, or Tony the Tiger? Or consider the Nike swoosh or the Ralph Lauren polo player. These symbols are so strong and well known that they create a position for the brand that distinguishes it from its competition.

Competition   Firms can choose to position their products or services *head-to-head* against a specific competitor or an entire product/service classification on similar attributes within the target market. Using head-to-head positioning, Avis positioned itself alongside Hertz with its message "Avis is only no. 2 in rental cars. So why go with us? We try harder (When you're not the biggest, you have to.)."[47] Head-to-head positioning often leads to price wars such as the "cola wars" and "airline wars," which are good for consumers but bad for businesses. Marketers must be careful that they don't position their product too closely to their competi-

The Jolly Green Giant is such a well-known symbol that it can be used as a positioning tool.

What if you ate vegetables just because you liked them?

Healthy for dinner, but with its delicious 3 cheese blend, you'll want it all the time. For the love of vegetables.

tion because they risk confusing customers or facing legal challenges. If, for instance, their package or logo looks too much like a competitor's, they might be opening themselves up to a trademark infringement lawsuit. Numerous store brands have been challenged for having packaging confusingly similar to that of national brands. McDonald's, for example, sues anyone who uses the *Mc* prefix. It sued Quality Inns International when it named its no-frills chain McSleep Inns.[48] On the contrary, courts have allowed parody jeans for full-figured women to be sold under the Lardashe label, despite the objections of Jordache jeans.

Firms can also choose a *differentiation* strategy by going after a less competitive, smaller market niche.[49] For instance, Goodrich tires were promoted as "The Other Guys," or the ones without the blimp, to set them apart from Goodyear tires. McDonalds, which is historically known as the world's number-one beef burger joint has responded to industry critics and health-conscious consumers by improving the "health of its menu" with more healthy choices such as salads and chicken sandwiches. In doing so, it tried to avoid competition with archrivals Wendy's and Burger King while minimizing the impact of cannibalization of its existing menu items. Thus, McDonald's carefully picked and named its new salads and chicken sandwiches. This move paid off brilliantly for McDonald's because, for the first time in its more than 50-year history, it overtook the number-one chicken joint—KFC—when it racked up chicken sales of $5.2 billion in just one year.[50]

Market Leadership Instead of positioning head-to-head, companies, especially market leaders, may emphasize their leadership position within their industry. Canadian companies such as the RBC Royal Bank, Loblaw, and Canadian Tire, and global companies such as Amazon, Intel, HP, Google, and eBay play up their status as market leaders in their respective industry. Each of these companies is the leader in their industry and so consumers often perceive them as setting the standards of their industry.

Now that we have identified the various methods by which firms position their products and services, we discuss the actual stages they go through in establishing that position.

Positioning by Using Perceptual Mapping

Now that we've identified the various methods by which firms position their products and services, let's look at what they do next. When developing a positioning strategy, firms go through five important steps. Before you read about these steps though, take a look at Exhibit 7.10, a hypothetical perceptual map of the soft-drink industry. A **perceptual map** displays, in two or more dimensions, the position of products or brands in the consumer's mind. We have chosen two dimensions for illustrative purposes: strong versus light taste (vertical) and fun versus healthy

perceptual map
Displays, in two or more dimensions, the position of products or brands in the consumer's mind.

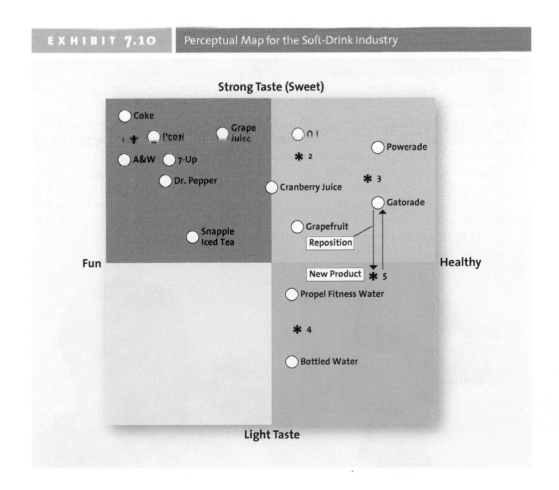

EXHIBIT 7.10 | Perceptual Map for the Soft-Drink Industry

ideal point
The position at which a particular market segment's ideal product would lie on a *perceptual map*.

(horizontal). Also, though this industry is quite complex, we have simplified the diagram to include only a few players in the market. The position of each brand is denoted by a small circle, and the numbered asterisks denote consumers' **ideal points**—where a particular market segment's ideal product would lie on the map.

To derive a perceptual map such as this, marketers follow five steps.

1. **Determine consumers' perceptions and evaluations of the product or service in relation to competitors'.** Marketers determine their brand's position by asking consumers a series of questions about their and competitors' products. For instance, they might ask how the consumer uses the existing product or services, what items the consumer regards as alternative sources to satisfy his or her needs, what the person likes or dislikes about the brand in relation to competitors, and what might make that person choose one brand over another.

2. **Identify competitors' positions.** When the firm understands how its customers view its brand relative to competitors', it must study how those same competitors position themselves. For instance, Powerade ("Liquid Hydration") positions itself closely to Gatorade ("Is It in You?"), which means they appear next to each other on the perceptual map and appeal to target market 3. They are also often found next to each other on store shelves, are similarly priced, and are viewed by customers as sports drinks. Gatorade also knows that its sports drink is perceived to be more like Powerade than like its own Propel Fitness Water (located near target market 4), Coca-Cola (target market 1), or Sunkist orange juice (target market 2).

3. **Determine consumer preferences.** The firm knows what the consumer thinks of the products or services in the marketplace and their positions relative to one another. Now it must find out what the consumer really wants—that is, determine the "ideal" product or service that appeals to each market. For example, a huge market exists for traditional Gatorade, and that market is shared by Powerade. Gatorade also recognizes a market, depicted as the ideal product for segment 5 on the perceptual map, of consumers who would prefer a less sweet, less calorie-laden drink that offers the same rejuvenating properties as Gatorade. Currently, no product is adequately serving market 5.

4. **Select the position.** Continuing with the Gatorade example, the company has three choices to appeal to the "less sweet sports drink" target market 5. It could develop a new product to meet the needs of market 5. Alternatively, it could adjust or reposition its marketing approach—its product and promotion—to sell original Gatorade to market 5 (arrow pointing down from Gatorade to the ideal point for segment 5). Finally, it could ignore what target market 5 really wants and hope that consumers will be attracted to the original Gatorade because it is closer to their ideal product than anything else on the market (arrow pointing up from the ideal point for segment 5 to Gatorade).

Gatorade with football player Jason Taylor (left) and Powerade with soccer player David Beckham (right) are positioned to compete for target market 3 in Exhibit 7.10.

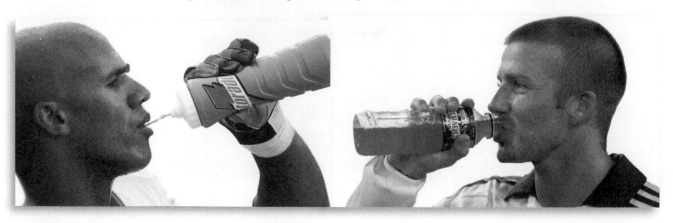

5. **Monitor the positioning strategy.** Markets are not stagnant. Consumers' tastes shift, and competitors react to those shifts. Attempting to maintain the same position year after year can spell disaster for any company. Thus, firms must always view the first three steps of the positioning process as ongoing, with adjustments made in step 4 as necessary.

Repositioning

Sometimes firms try to change their positioning. For example, many so-called junk-food companies are trying to reposition themselves as offering healthier choices. A group of Wilfrid Laurier University students examined consumer behaviour with respect to repositioning junk food as a healthy alternative. They observed the trend among junk-food companies to use terms such as *multigrain* to insinuate that their food was healthy.[51] The students observed that Pizza Pizza introduced a multigrain dough that contains omega-3 fat, a healthy ingredient. Also, the company website advertising has a natural and healthy appearance to communicate its nutritional repositioning and create a perception of health. While multigrain dough is better than typical white dough, pizza is still a high-fat food with elevated levels of sodium, and toppings such as pepperoni, cheese, and sausage far outweigh the health benefits of a multigrain crust. Do you think Pizza Pizza will ever be seen as a provider of healthy food or will its pizza always be seen as junk food?

Tiffany & Co. has long been known for luxury jewellery that is most often purchased by wealthy individuals. In the 1990s, the company, following a trend of "affordable luxury," tried to reposition by expanding its product assortment to appeal more to the middle class. Tiffany introduced a silver charm bracelet priced at $110 that became very popular with teenagers and resulted in explosive sales growth for the company. Although it was a financial success, at least in the short term, the image of inexpensive silver jewellery alienated older, more affluent customers who now viewed Tiffany as a common brand. In response, the company increased prices on its silver product by 30 percent in an attempt to reclaim its position as a luxury jeweller.

Good marketers constantly re-evaluate their brand's position to determine when to reposition it. Companies should reposition their brands to keep up with changes in the marketplace or to put a fresh spin on their stale and stodgy brand. Many companies that operate on the idea "if it ain't broke, then don't fix it" often find out too late that their brand needs a serious makeover. The result is that their positioning is so badly damaged that it takes years and huge budgets to rebuild. Proactive companies change or tinker with their positioning to keep up with market dynamics. For example, for most of General Electric Company's history, its positioning was based on product—"We Bring Good Things to Life"—which served GE very well. More recently, GE replaced that positioning with one that focuses on its rich history of innovation: "Imagination at Work."

As the Tiffany's example described earlier shows, repositioning is not an easy task because consumers' perceptions do not change readily, even though the marketplace is changing rapidly. One disadvantage of repositioning is that if it's not done well, the company risks alienating its core customers while simultaneously failing to attract new customers. A major advantage of successful repositioning is that it strengthens the brand in the marketplace, thereby allowing the company to keep its core customers

GE repositioned itself from a manufacturer of excellent products to an innovator, in keeping with marketing trends where innovation is seen as the basis of competitive advantage.

satisfied while drawing new customers to the brand. For example, Cadbury successfully repositioned itself from a leading brand for older customers to a brand for a younger target market (25 to 35 year olds) because customer loyalty among its older customers had been dropping. To do this, Cadbury refreshed its brand by updating the look of its packaging, displays, and marketing communications to portray a more cheerful and lively appearance, and by launching an advertising campaign that depicted the product being enjoyed in a work environment. By doing so, Cadbury increased its customer loyalty rating by 5 percent between 2004 and 2005. In a contrary example, McDonald's Arch Deluxe failed when it was positioned as the "adult hamburger" in much the same way that Happy Meals are positioned for children. This move actually alienated kids and their Happy Meals, and failed to secure an adult audience. The $100-million campaign was abandoned, and some store sales declined. Not surprisingly, the campaign is called the McFlop.

brand repositioning (rebranding)
A strategy in which marketers change a brand's focus to target new markets or realign the brand's core emphasis with changing market preferences.

Brand repositioning refers to a strategy in which marketers change a brand's focus to target new markets or realign the brand's core emphasis with changing market preferences.[52] As manufacturers were driving prices of appliances down and steel was pushing material costs up, Whirlpool began to see its appliances become a commodity. The company needed an innovation that would justify higher prices and increase its market share. The design chief of Whirlpool fought against traditional mindsets and brought in usability researchers, graphic artists, and engineers to design new appliances. The Duet® laundry pair, a matching set of stylish washers and dryers, is a result of one of these teams. The appliance demands the highest price in the front-loading washer/dryer market and owns 20 percent of this market. Whirlpool has brought appliances into a realm that previously didn't exist. Appliances can be "cool": Paris's Louvre Museum has exhibited the Whirlpool next-generation concept products and the Smithsonian awarded Whirlpool its annual National Design Award in Corporate Achievement.[53]

Whirlpool has successfully repositioned its washer/dryer market with the newly designed Duet® line. It is so stylish that it has been displayed in Paris's Louvre Museum and has won a design award from the Smithsonian.

New marketing opportunities also may spur firms to reposition their brands. The growing youth segment, its purchasing power, and its increasing influence on household purchasing decisions has made firms in various industries sit up and take notice. Since buying the Elizabeth Arden unit from Unilever in 2000, FFI Fragrances has repositioned several of the firm's cosmetics lines to attract younger consumers, using celebrities such as Kate Beckinsale, Kirsten Dunst, Sarah Jessica Parker, and Catherine Zeta-Jones in its advertisements.[54] Some magazines have also been repositioned, moving from the overcrowded young teen segment to slightly older teens, such as *YM*'s repositioning of its publication to cater to 19 year olds.[55]

Repositioning can change the quality image of the brand, as noted in the Tiffany example. However, WestJet successfully repositioned itself from a no-frills low-cost leader to a considerably higher quality airline by adding luxuries such as leather seats and seat-back LCD TV screens. Repositioning also breathes life into old brands. Such revitalization sometimes can result from changing the packaging and/or altering the characteristics of the brand.[56] Aqua Velva aftershave lotion changed its packaging to a more convenient bottle, and Arm & Hammer started advertising a variety of uses for its baking soda, including deodorizing refrigerators.[57]

Although repositioning can improve the brand's fit with its target segment or boost the vitality of old brands, it is not without costs and risks. Firms often need to spend tremendous amounts of money to make tangible changes to the product and packages, as well as intangible changes to the brand's image through advertising. These costs may not be recovered if the repositioned brand and messages are not credible to the consumer or if the firm has mistaken a fad for a long-term market trend.

Learning Objectives Review

L01 Describe the STP process

The STP process is a systematic process consisting of five stages. First, marketing managers establish the overall objectives of their marketing strategy. Next, they identify the various market segments and develop a profile for each segment. Then the segments are evaluated to determine their attractiveness and fit with the company's competencies. This information is then used to select the segment(s) they would like to serve (i.e., targeting). Finally, marketing managers develop a positioning strategy that is consistent with the target market in order to communicate their unique value proposition.

L02 Describe the bases marketers use to segment a market

There is really no one "best" method to segment a market. Firms choose from various segmentation bases depending on the type of product/service they offer and their goals for the segmentation strategy. For instance, if the firm wants to identify its customers easily, geographic or demographic segmentation likely will work best. But if the firm is trying to dig deeper into why customers might buy its offering, then lifestyle, benefits, or loyalty segmentation work best. Geodemographic segmentation provides a nice blend of geographic, demographic, and psychographic approaches. Typically, a combination of several segmentation methods is most effective.

L03 Identify the criteria for determining the attractiveness of a segment and whether it is worth pursuing (targeting)

Marketers use several criteria to assess a segment's attractiveness. First, the customer should be *identifiable*—companies must know what types of people are in the market so they can direct their efforts appropriately. Second, the market must be *reachable*—the firm must be able to reach the segment through effective communications and distribution. Third, the firm must be *responsive* to the needs of customers in a segment. It must be able to deliver a product or service that the segment will embrace. Finally, the market must be *substantial* enough to be worth pursuing. If relatively few people appear in a segment, it is probably not cost-effective to direct special marketing mix efforts toward them. Additionally, the segment must be *profitable*, both in the near term and over the lifetime of the customer.

LO4 **Explain how a firm decides what type of segmentation strategy to use: undifferentiated, differentiated, concentrated, or micromarketing**

Most firms use some form of segmentation strategy. An *undifferentiated strategy* is really no segmentation at all and only works for products or services that most consumers consider to be commodities. The difference between a *differentiated* and a *concentrated strategy* is that the differentiated approach targets multiple segments, whereas the concentrated targets only one. Larger firms with multiple product/service offerings generally use a differentiated strategy; smaller firms or those with a limited product/service offering often use a concentrated strategy. Firms that employ a *micro-marketing* or *one-to-one marketing strategy* tailor their product/service offering to each customer—that is, it is custom-made. In the past, micromarketing was reserved primarily for artisans, tailors, or other craftspeople who would make items exactly as the customer wanted. Recently, however, larger manufacturers and retailers have begun experimenting with custom-made merchandise as well. Service providers, in contrast, are largely familiar with customizing their offering. Hair salons could not flourish if every customer got the same cut.

LO5 **Explain what positioning is and describe how firms do it**

Positioning is the P in the STP (segmentation, targeting, and positioning) process. It refers to how customers think about a product, service, or brand in the market relative to competitors' offerings. Firms position their products and services according to several criteria. Some focus on their offering's *value*—customers get a lot for what the product or service costs. Others determine the most *important product attributes* for customers and position their offering on the basis of those attributes. *Benefits and symbols* can also be used for positioning, though few products or services are associated with symbols that are compelling enough to drive people to buy. Companies may also use their dominant position in their market—*market leadership*—to position their products or services. Finally, *competition* is one of the most common positioning methods and relies on the favourable comparison of the firm's offering with the products or services marketed by competitors (head-to-head). Companies may also choose to compete by differentiating their value proposition.

Key Terms

- behavioural segmentation, 220
- benefit segmentation, 221
- brand repositioning (rebranding), 242
- concentrated (or niche) segmentation strategy, 232
- demographic segmentation, 216
- differentiated segmentation strategy, 231
- geodemographic segmentation, 223
- geographic segmentation, 215
- ideal point, 240
- lifestyles, 219
- loyalty segmentation, 223
- mass customization, 233
- micromarketing (one-to-one marketing), 233
- perceptual map, 239
- positioning statement, 236
- positioning, 234
- psychographics, 217
- PSYTE clusters, 223
- self-concept, 218
- self-values, 218
- undifferentiated segmentation strategy (mass marketing), 230
- VALS™, 219

Concept Review

1. How do segmentation, targeting, and positioning add value to a company's value proposition?

2. Outline the steps in the STP process. What are some of the key decisions marketers have to make at each step?

3. List the bases that can be used to segment a market for a product or service. Which of these bases is considered to be the most difficult to use and which is the easiest? Why?

4. Describe the segmentation bases you think Coca-Cola used to develop its target segment. What kinds of products do you think this segment was buying before Coca-Cola introduced its Coke Zero brand? Thinking back to the consumer buying decision process, what kind of strategies do you think were necessary to get this segment to switch to Coke Zero?

5. List the four types of targeting strategies companies can use to serve selected market segments. What are the main points to consider before selecting one or some combination of these strategies? What are the advantages and disadvantages of each strategy, and how can competitors influence the strategy a company chooses?

6. Explain the difference between positioning and a positioning statement. Why do you think marketers find market positioning one of the most difficult aspects of the STP process? How can marketers try to influence the positioning of their products or services in the marketplace?

7. List four types of strategies companies could use to position their products or services in the marketplace. When Home Depot says, "You Can Do It, We Can Help," for what type of positioning is it striving?

8. What is a perceptual map? How is it used in developing positioning strategies or identifying market opportunities?

9. Why should marketers consider repositioning their brand? Explain what is meant by repositioning and the major challenges and risks inherent in repositioning.

10. An online news article suggests that Sony is thinking of repositioning its PlayStation 3 game console as a computer. Do you think that Sony can do this successfully? Give reasons. Do you think consumers will ever see the PlayStation as a computer? Why or why not?

Marketing Applications

1. You have been asked to identify various strategies for segmenting a market, which then will be used to choose one strategy for your sporting goods shop. List and discuss each of the overall strategies that can be used to develop a segmentation approach. Provide an example of each of the four strategies the sporting goods shop might use.

2. What overall segmentation strategy would you suggest for a small entrepreneur starting a business? Justify why you would recommend that particular approach.

3. The concept of mass customization seems like a contradiction in terms. How and why would a retailer use mass customization?

4. Various methods are used to segment markets. Identify the typical customer for each of the four methods discussed in the text.

5. You have been asked to evaluate the attractiveness of several potential market segments. What criteria should you use to evaluate those segments? Why are these appropriate criteria?

6. A small-business owner is trying to evaluate the profitability of different segments. What are the key factors he or she must consider? For how long should the business owner conduct the evaluation?

7. Think about the various hotel brands that you know (e.g., Marriott, Holiday Inn, Super 8). How do those brands position themselves in the market?

8. Put yourself in the position of an entrepreneur who is developing a new product to introduce into the market. Briefly describe the product. Then, develop the segmentation, targeting, and positioning strategy for marketing the new product. Be sure to discuss (a) the overall strategy, (b) characteristics of the target market, (c) why that target market is attractive, and (d) the positioning strategy. Provide justifications for your decisions.

9. Think of a specific company or organization that uses various types of promotional material to market its offerings. (The Internet, magazine ads, newspaper ads, catalogues, newspaper inserts, direct mail pieces, and flyers might all be sources of promotional materials.) Locate two or three promotional pieces for the company and use them as a basis to analyze the segment(s) being targeted. Describe the basic segmentation strategy reflected in these materials, and describe characteristics of the target market according to the materials. Be sure to include a copy of all the materials used in the analysis.

10. You have been hired recently by a large bank in its credit card marketing division. The bank has relationships with a large number of colleges and universities and prints a wide variety of credit cards featuring college and university logos, images, and the like. You have been asked to oversee the implementation of a new program targeting first-year students at the schools with which the bank has a relationship. The bank has already purchased the names and home addresses of the incoming students. You have been told that no credit checks will be required for these cards as long as the student is older than 18 years of age. The bank plans a first-day-of-school marketing blitz that includes free hats, T-shirts, and book promotions, as well as free pizza, if the students simply fill out an application. Do you think it is a good idea to offer this program to these new students?

Toolkit

MARKET POSITION MAP ANALYSIS

Assume you are a brand manager for a major manufacturer. You have identified a number of market segments and are trying to understand how its products are positioned relative to other manufacturers'. Use the toolkit provided on Connect to conduct a market position analysis.

Net Savvy

1. Go to the L'Oréal Canada website (www.lorealparis.ca) and try to describe the segmentation approach it uses to group customers. Apply the vocabulary presented in this chapter to describe its segmentation strategy. Then click on "Haircare," and look for "Re-Nutrition." Who do you think is the target market for this product? How would you describe L'Oréal's product positioning in Canada?

2. Suppose you want to open a specialty coffee and treats shop near your university campus. You think collecting

some demographic data will be a helpful starting point. Your first hunch is to use StatsCan but, from prior experience, you realize this will be difficult and time-consuming. Help is on the way. Go to SRC's FreeDemographics website (www.freedemographics.com) and register to use this free service. Use this site to generate a report on the demographics of the area where you want to locate your coffee shop. How helpful is this site?

Chapter Case Study

M&M MEAT SHOPS: USING DEMOGRAPHICS TO DRIVE DECISIONS[58]

Known as the store with hundreds of meal ideas but only one aisle, M&M Meat Shops is Canada's largest retail chain of specialty frozen foods, with more than 470 locations coast to coast. The demand for ready-to-heat food is increasing as home-cooked meals become more difficult in time-strapped households, an important demographic for the company.

The first store opened in October 1980, based on a consumer insight by founders Mark Nowak and Mac Voisin that it was not possible to buy restaurant-quality steaks in retail outlets. Neither Nowak, a lawyer, nor Voisin, an engineer, had much marketing experience. However, when the company started offering franchises, they recognized the need to have a segmentation methodology to help them assess potential new locations.

M&M Meat Shops uses demographics as well as a segmentation system, MOSAIC, to gain insights into their trade areas and their customers, and to help refine M&M Meat Shops' understanding of who has the best lifestyle fit for the company.

Demographic data helps the company understand whether a trade area has potential. It is demographics that highlight whether an area is, for example, experiencing growth or decline in population, whether the area is home to more apartment dwellers than home owners, as well as what the dominant language is. Segmentation systems pick up where univariate demographics leave off and help define neighbourhoods more thoroughly. Two neighbours with similar incomes, religious backgrounds, and housing can have very different lifestyles and buying habits, and it's vitally important for a marketer to be able to identify these differences.

The M&M Max Card allows the company to track 94 percent of all sales transactions, gathering valuable information about consumer shopping habits.

Although its head office personnel have worked with PSYTE Canada Advantage (described earlier in this chapter), today M&M Meat Shops uses a sophisticated segmentation, MOSAIC, that classifies its customer data into one of 150 different lifestyle clusters. The MOSAIC system incorporates thousands of variables from as many areas as possible (e.g., occupation dwellings, ethnicity, mobility, house value, household income, language), which provides M&M Meat Shops with a more precise look at its trade areas and helps define its customer base.

In Ontario, one of the top clusters for M&M Meat Shops is known as "Wine with Dinner." This group is university-educated, athletic, and lives in single-detached homes with larger-than-average families. They have an average household income of $70,000 and spend a lot of money on home decor and gardening.

Using information produced through segmentation analysis efforts, M&M Meat Shops selects which target markets to pursue. Its target customer is typically a woman (age 35 and older) with a family, with a very active family life that includes two or more children. These consumers are time-starved and need convenient food options. Having identified the best target markets, the company turns its efforts to finding more consumers who fit the profile and reaching them with relevant campaigns.

As the country becomes much more multicultural, ongoing analysis is conducted to understand the changing Canadian population. According to the 2006 Census, the face of Canada continues to change at a fairly rapid pace. In the five years between the 2001 and 2006 Censuses, 1.6 million new residents called Canada home, of which 1.2 million, or 75 percent of those residents, were new immigrants. These new Canadians are a potentially huge market for retailers, one that is anticipated to grow. By 2017, one in five Canadians are expected to be a member of a visible minority. Armed with such insights, M&M Meat Shops has begun to research the complexities of ethnic marketing.

Although M&M Meat Shops is predominantly a suburban chain, it has launched a new urban concept called M&M Meat Shops Uptown. The first locations were in downtown Toronto and feature edgier decor than the suburban outlets. This new concept is designed to fit the urban lifestyle, with extended hours of operation as well as the inclusion of specialty products, such as indoor grills and computer kiosks, to help customers create their own menus and download recipes.[59]

Other expansion plans for M&M Meat Shops included a foray into the United States. Determining where to open the first U.S. stores was a massive undertaking. One step in this research was to compare the company's top Canadian MOSAIC clusters to U.S. MOSAIC clusters to check for similarities in lifestyle. (The Canadian and U.S. clusters are totally different.) Because these lifestyle systems are a combination of demographic and psychographic information, they help identify areas in the United States that have very similar lifestyles to M&M Meat Shops' strongest Canadian markets.

Ohio was identified as a good fit; however, the entry into the U.S. market was ill-timed, coinciding with the recession of late 2008 and throughout 2009. The company quickly changed direction. Instead of sticking with its original strategy of opening suburban stores in strip malls, it has gone to a store-within-a-store format. Three outlets have been opened in Toledo, Maumee, and Columbus in The Andersons Store. In business since 1952, this U.S. retailer offers general merchandise, home improvement, and outdoor lawn-care products, specialty foods, and wine. The format has been a success, and additional stores are planned.

Knowing it pays to retain loyal customers, the company's MAX program rewards its most loyal customers. The program also provides the company with valuable consumer insights. M&M Meat Shops says that 94 percent of all sales transactions are tracked through the program and that 93 percent of customers, or 5.7 million Canadians, have a MAX card. Data collected from the card, such as postal codes, are used to understand how far customers travel to outlets—useful information when determining locations of new stores. It also helps more narrowly focus advertising efforts to reach the core customer profile.

Segmentation data and loyalty program data are provided to franchisees to help them to increase market penetration in their trade areas and even to determine what mix of products to stock. M&M's approach adds value to franchisees, helping them to first attract and then keep their best customers.

M&M Meat Shops uses census data combined with its MAX card loyalty program to better serve growing ethnic markets. For example, butter chicken was featured in sales flyers during Diwali celebrations.

Questions

1. Describe the type of segmentation strategy M&M Meat Shops uses to serve its suburban markets. Provide support for your answer.

2. Why would a different strategy be needed for its Uptown urban store locations?

3. Why do companies such as M&M Meat Shops need to use a combination of segmentation approaches when identifying potential target markets?

4. What are some key demographic differences M&M Meat Shops should consider for future expansion in the U.S. market?

5. Besides adapting its advertising to reflect different cultural holidays, what are some other ways M&M Meat Shops could reach out to Canada's growing ethnic population?

Practise and learn online with Connect. Connect allows you to practise important concepts at your own pace and on your own schedule, with 24/7 online access to an eBook, practice quizzes, interactivities, videos, study tools, additional resources, and more.

Using Secondary Data to Assess Customer Lifetime Value (CLV)

This appendix examines how secondary data from customer transactions can help determine the value of a customer over time. Specifically, **customer lifetime value (CLV)** refers to the expected financial contribution from a particular customer to the firm's profits over the course of their entire relationship.[1]

To estimate CLV, firms use past behaviours to forecast future purchases, the gross margin from these purchases, and the costs associated with servicing the customers. Some costs associated with maintaining customer relationships include communicating with customers through advertising, personal selling, or other promotional vehicles to acquire their business initially and then retain them over time.

Measures of CLV typically apply to a group or segment of customers and use available secondary data. A basic formula for CLV,[2] with the assumption that revenues and profits arrive at the start of the year, is as follows:

$$CLV = \frac{\sum_{t=1}^{T}[\text{profit at t} \times \text{retention rate}^{t-1}]}{(1 + i)^{t-1}} - \text{acquisition costs}$$

To implement this CLV formula, we must answer the following questions:

1. How many years (t) can we expect to do business with a customer? The total number of years is denoted by T.

2. What can we expect the annual profits to be from an individual customer or an average customer? These profits are based on sales minus the costs of merchandise and the costs of serving and retaining the customer.

3. What is the retention rate, that is, the average percentage of customers who continue to purchase from the firm from one time

customer lifetime value (CLV)
The expected financial contribution from a particular customer to the firm's profits over the course of their entire relationship.

period to another? A 90 percent retention rate means that if we have 100 customers in the first year, we will have 90 at the beginning of the second year.

4. What is the discount rate (i)? The discount rate is based on the idea that a dollar is worth less in the future than it is today, so the company can use it to adjust future profits and determine a customer's value today for the customer's purchases in the future. For example, if the discount rate is 10 percent, $100 in profits at the beginning of year 2 are worth only $90.91 (100/(1 + 0.1)) at the beginning of year 1.

Consider Gregory Missoni, a fairly new client of Very Clean Cleaners who switched from his other dry cleaner because Very Clean sent him $100 worth of coupons in a direct mailing. .::

Very Clean Cleaners should consider a customer's lifetime value to determine its service levels.

Greg just picked up his $200 shirt from Very Clean and found that the dry cleaner had broken a brown button and replaced it with a white button. When he complained, the clerk acted as if it were no big deal. Greg explained to the clerk that it was a very expensive shirt that deserved more careful handling and then asked to speak with the manager. At this point, how important is it that the manager makes sure Greg is satisfied, so that he will continue to bring his dry cleaning to Very Clean Cleaners? To answer this question, the manager uses the following information:

- It cost Very Clean $100 to acquire Greg as a customer. Thus, the acquisition cost is $100.
- Very Clean expects Greg to remain a client for 5 years (time horizon T = 5 years).
- Very Clean expects to make a $1000 profit each year from Greg's dry cleaning.
- On average, 10 percent of customers defect to another cleaner each year. Therefore, the expected retention rate is 90 percent.
- The discount rate is 10 percent per year (i in this illustration). For simplicity, Very Clean assumes all profits are accrued at the beginning of the year.

Applying the formula, such that CLV equals the profits from years 1 to 5, less the acquisition costs, we obtain the following:

$$\text{CLV} = \underbrace{\frac{\$1000 \times (0.90)^0}{(1 + 0.1)^0}}_{\textbf{Year 1}} + \underbrace{\frac{\$1000 \times (0.90)^1}{(1 + 0.1)^1}}_{\textbf{Year 2}} + \underbrace{\frac{\$1000 \times (0.90)^2}{(1 + 0.1)^2}}_{\textbf{Year 3}}$$

$$\underbrace{\frac{\$1000 \times (0.90)^3}{(1 + 0.1)^3}}_{\textbf{Year 4}} + \underbrace{\frac{\$1000 \times (0.90)^4}{(1 + 0.1)^4}}_{\textbf{Year 5}} - \$100$$

Or

$$CLV = \$1000 + \$818.2 + \$669.4 + \$547.7 + \$448.1 - \$100 = \$3383.40$$

Let's see how the formula works. The expected profit from Greg is $1000 per year. Very Clean assumes profits accrue at the beginning of the year, so the profits for the first year equal $1000; they are not affected by the retention rate or the discount rate.

However, the retention and discount rates have effects on the profits for the subsequent time periods. In the second year, the retention rate, which Very Clean determined was 90 percent (i.e., 90 percent of customers continue to do business with it) modifies profits, such that expected profits in the second year equal $1000 × 90% = $900. Moreover, the discount rate is applied such that the profits received in the second year are worth less than if they had been received in the first year. Therefore, the $900 received at the beginning of the second year must be divided by 1.1, which is equivalent to $818.20.

Using similar calculations for the third year, the expected profits adjusted for retention are $1000 × 0.9 × 0.9 = $810. The discount rate then reduces the profit to $810 ÷ 1.1^2 = $669.40 in today's dollars. (Note that the discount rate is squared because it refers to two years in the future.) After calculating the adjusted and discounted profits for the fourth and fifth years in similar fashion, we realize the sum of estimated discounted profits for five years is $3483.40. However, we still must subtract the $100 spent to acquire Greg, which provides a CLV of $3383.40.

According to this analysis, it would be a good idea for the manager to take a long-term perspective when evaluating how to respond to Greg's complaint about his button. Greg cannot be viewed as a $2.50 customer, as he would be if Very Clean determined his value based on the cost of laundering his shirt, nor should he be viewed as a $200 customer, based on the cost of the shirt. He actually is worth a lot more than that.

For illustrative purposes, we have simplified the CLV calculations in this example. We assumed that the average profits remain constant at $1000. But firms usually expect profits to grow over time, or else grow, level off, and then perhaps decline. Retention costs, such as special promotions used to keep Greg coming back, also do not appear in our illustration, though such additional costs would reduce annual profits and CLV. Finally, we assume a five-year time horizon; the CLV obviously would differ for longer or shorter periods. For an infinite time horizon, with first period payments upfront, the formula becomes fairly simple:[3]

$$CLV = \text{profits} \times \left[1 + \frac{\text{retention rate}}{(\$1 + \text{discount rate} + \text{retention rate})} \right]$$

$$- \text{acquisition costs}$$

$$= \$1000 \times \left[1 + \frac{0.9}{(1 + 0.1 - 0.9)} \right] - \$100$$

$$= \$1000 \times (1 + 4.5) - \$100$$

$$= \$5500 - \$100 = \$5400$$

This illustration thus explains how firms can use secondary data to calculate CLV; it further demonstrates the importance of knowing a customer's lifetime value when executing marketing tactics and strategies. Several CLV problems can be accessed on Connect.

CHAPTER 8

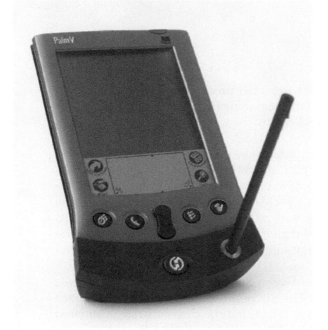

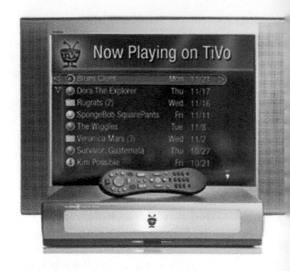

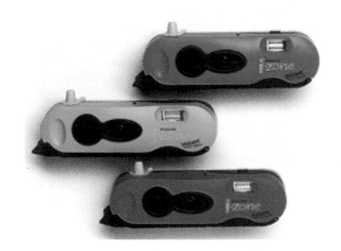

SECTION FOUR

Value Creation

Developing
New Products

Having examined the processes marketers use to segment markets and identify which customers to target, let's look at how new products are developed to meet the needs and wants of those customers. Few three-letter words are more exciting than *new*. It brings forth an image of freshness, adventure, and excitement. Yet *new* is also a complex term because it might mean adding something new to an existing product, introducing a new flavour, or creating new packaging that provides added value.

When stellar new products enter the market, many people's first response goes something like this: "What a great idea! Why didn't somebody think of this before?" To the team at Inventables, the answer would be, "Because no one used our program to spark his or her creativity before." The company's motto "Explore What's Possible," illustrates its dedication to building a living showcase of what's possible in order to deliver inspiration and innovation to the dreamers of the world.[1]

Inventables hires "technology hunters," people with some experience in materials science, to search the world for what is new and interesting. By interviewing designers, scouring trade shows, reviewing trade journals and magazines, conducting research in foreign markets, and talking with the network of informants the company has developed, it ensures it has access to the most recent breakthroughs in science, technology, and material innovation. For example, Inventables noted recent developments in nanoscience and now lists luminescent nanocrystals within its research portfolio.

Not sure what luminescent nanocrystals can do for you? That's okay—you aren't Inventables' main customer. Instead, Inventables offers its research and innovation expertise to

Learning Objectives

After studying this chapter, you should be able to

LO1 Identify the reasons firms innovate

LO2 Describe the diffusion of innovation theory and how managers can use it to make product line decisions

LO3 Explain the stages involved in developing new products and services

LO4 Describe the product life cycle and summarize how it is used to make product line decisions

product companies looking for new applications. It's those applications that one day will be in your hand. For example, imagine a paint that contains luminescent nanocrystals; the walls of your dorm room could glow like the light sticks that children carry on Halloween and concert fans love to wave to demand an encore from their favourite band.

Inventing is hard work, and Inventables tries to take some of the legwork out of it for consumer goods (e.g., Avon, Kraft, Tupperware), consumer electronics (e.g., Bissell, Samsung, Whirlpool), toys (e.g., Disney, Fisher-Price, Mattel), and other organizations that it counts as its clients (e.g., BMW, Hallmark, the U.S. Army). After identifying, researching, and summarizing what is new and exciting, Inventables gathers various concepts, ideas, and materials into its Innovation Centre, a display that contains actual samples that product developers may explore. Each sample is tagged with a brief description and suggestions about how the related technology might be applied. The Centre gets delivered to each company that orders it and can be updated regularly with new findings. Each company deals with the Centre in its own way, either by encouraging product developers to interact with it daily or by hosting innovation sessions during which everyone comes together to play and experiment with the sample materials.

The items that Inventables provides to its customers come from five categories: materials, mechanisms, electronics, processes, and "wow" products. Included items must demonstrate something new, solve a problem in an unconventional way, or be found only in a niche market but remain largely unknown elsewhere.

Thus, when the watchmaker Fossil signed up to receive Inventables' services, it received exposure to a combination push-button/LCD switch. Previously, the switch had been used primarily as a cheaper alternative to a digital touchscreen or as an interface element in automation equipment. These applications certainly did not fit the watch industry but, by playing with the item in their own hands, developers at Fossil realized that the technology could change the way people use stopwatches. Instead of having to find and press a tiny button on a watch's side—which, as almost any runner will tell you, becomes an especially challenging task after a strenuous run—people instead could just slap at the face of the watch to turn off the timer.

In addition to its sample suggestions, Inventables maintains a portfolio of ideas that are not quite ready for production yet, with the understanding that it sure would be great if someone figured out how to make them work. Imagine, for example, a clear toaster that enables you to watch your bread cook, eliminating burnt toast forever. Why didn't someone think of that before? .:

As a key element of a firm's marketing mix (four Ps) strategies, product strategies are central to the creation of value for the consumer. A **product** is anything that is of value to a consumer and can be offered through a marketing exchange. In addition to *goods*, such as toothpaste, or *services*, such as a haircut, products might also be *places* (e.g., Whistler, British Columbia), *ideas* (e.g., "stop smoking"), *organizations* (e.g., Canadian Blood Services), *people* (e.g., Avril Lavigne), or *communities* (e.g., Facebook.com) that create value for consumers in their respective competitive marketing arenas.

Imagine living 200 years ago. You cook your meals on a stove fuelled by coal or wood. As a student, you do your homework by hand, illuminated only by candlelight. You get to school on foot, by horseback, or in a horse-drawn carriage, if you're really fortunate. Your classroom is small and basic, and you have very few classmates. The professor simply lectures and writes on a chalkboard.

Fast-forward to today. You finish your homework on a laptop with word-processing software that appears to have a mind of its own and can correct your spelling automatically. Your climate-controlled room has ample electric light. While you work on your laptop, you can also talk with a friend by using the hands-free headset of your wireless phone. On your way to school, in your car, you pick up fast food from a convenient drive-through window while browsing or listening to your personal selection of songs playing through your car speakers, connected wirelessly to your iPod. Your friend calls to discuss a slight change to an assignment, so you pull over to grab your BlackBerry, make the necessary changes, and email the assignment from your smartphone to your professor. When you arrive at university, you sit in a 200-person classroom where you plug in your laptop, taking notes on it and using it to digitally record the lecture. The professor adds notes on the day's PowerPoint presentations by using her new tablet computer. You have already downloaded the PowerPoint presentations and add similar notes through your own laptop. After class, to complete your planning for a last-minute party, you send out a Facebook invitation to your friends and ask for responses to get a head count. Then you instant message your roommate, telling her to get food and drinks for the right number of people, which she orders through an online grocer that will deliver later in the day.

Our lives are defined by the many new products and services developed through scientific and technological advances and refined either with the help of outside idea generation companies or by firms' internal product development teams. Whereas scientific research opens up the world of ideas, technological research transforms these ideas into interesting and useful services, tangible products, and processes.

This chapter deals with the first P in the marketing mix: product, specifically new products. (Refer to the chapter roadmap to guide you through the chapter contents.) Product branding and packaging will be examined in the next chapter. Now we explore how companies add value to firms' product and service offerings through innovation. We also look at the process firms go through to develop new products and services. We conclude the chapter with an examination of how new products and services are adopted by the market and how firms change their marketing mix as the product or service moves through its life cycle.

product
Anything that is of value to a consumer and can be offered through a marketing exchange.

Why Do Firms Create New Products?

L01

New market offerings provide value to both firms and customers. But the degree to which they do so depends on how new they really are. When we say a "new product," we don't necessarily mean that the product has never existed before; completely new-to-the-market products represent fewer than 10 percent of all new product introductions each year. (Refer to Sustainable Marketing 8.1 for an example

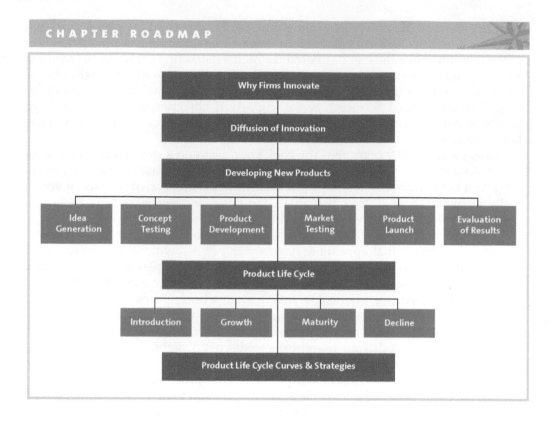

of a "new product" that improves on an existing concept.) It is more useful to think of the degree of newness of a product on a continuum from "new-to-the-world"—as HDTV was a few years ago—to "slightly repositioned," such as the repositioning of Kraft's Capri Sun brand of ready-to-drink beverages, which was repackaged in a bigger pouch to appeal more to teens. Regardless of where on the continuum a new product fits, firms have to innovate.

Innovation
The process by which ideas are transformed into new products and services that will help firms grow.

Innovation is the process by which ideas are transformed into new products and services that will help firms grow. Without innovation and its resulting new products and services, firms would have only two choices: continue to market current products to current customers or take the same product to another market with similar customers.

Although innovation strategies may not work in the short run—some estimates indicate that only about 3 percent of new products actually succeed—overriding long-term reasons compel firms to introduce new products and services. Firms innovate for a number of reasons, as we discuss next.

Changing Customer Needs

When they add new products to their offerings, firms can create and deliver value more effectively by satisfying the changing needs of their current and new customers or simply by keeping customers from getting bored with the current product or service offering. For example, Unilever's Dove Beauty Bar product line successfully extended the brand into hair, face, and skin-care lines, all under the Dove umbrella. Today, Dove loyalists can enjoy not only bar soap, but also antiperspirants and deodorants, moisturizing lotions, cleansers, toners, shampoo, conditioner, and much more.[2] Sometimes, companies can identify problems and develop products that customers never knew they needed. For example, a car wash offers a basic wash; a wash and polish; or a wash, polish, and undercarriage wash. Customers may never

| Sustainable Marketing **8.1** | **Making Your Next Move Green** |

Moving is stressful! Before you can even start packing you have to go to local stores to snag free boxes. If they don't have enough, you have to buy some. Having to buy, build, and dispose of all those boxes is a needless hassle and expense. And, worst of all, those cardboard boxes may contain dirt, bacteria, and other things you really don't want all over your stuff.

Now there's a better, more sustainable solution. Founded in 2008 in Vancouver by Doug Burgoyne, Frogbox will rent you reusable plastic boxes, an eco-friendly alternative to traditional cardboard moving boxes. Burgyone estimates that Greater Vancouver uses about 450 000 cardboard moving boxes every month and Seattle uses about 1 million.[3]

Unlike cardboard boxes, the Frogbox solution has a low impact on the environment, as its boxes can be reused hundreds of times. The boxes are 2.4 cubic feet (70 litres). To put this in perspective, approximately 25 boxes would be needed to move the contents of a one-bedroom apartment.

Frogbox will rent you as many boxes as you need for a week or longer, and it can deliver them and pick them up when you've finished with your move. The boxes stack neatly inside each other and don't require any assembly, eliminating the need to spend hours building and taping cardboard boxes.

The Frogbox name is fitting because both the company and frogs have a connection to the sustainable environment. And Frogbox donates 1 percent of gross revenues to frog habitation restoration.[4] But its sustainability efforts are hopping in other areas too. For example, the company uses solar energy to power its website and waste-generated biodiesel to fuel its fleet vehicles.

The company has big goals. Currently, it has locations in Vancouver, Seattle, and Toronto but wants to expand into the top 30 cities in North America in the next five years. Frogbox aims to redefine how people move, making it easier on you, easier on your wallet, and, best of all, easier on the planet.

Frogbox offers an eco-friendly alternative to traditional cardboard moving boxes.

have thought about washing the undercarriage of their car prior to their exposure to the new service offering. In other cases, the firms take a well-known offering and innovate to make it more interesting, as Dyson has done for the vacuum cleaner. According to the company's mythology, James Dyson caught sight of a local sawmill that used a cyclone to collect sawdust from the air, and then decided to apply the concept to a vacuum cleaner so he could create a vacuum that won't lose suction. The experience he had developing and protecting his innovative technology also formed the company's present innovation process, which relies heavily on secrecy, protection of ideas, and risk taking.

Market Saturation

The longer a product exists in the marketplace, the more likely it is that the market will become saturated. Without new products or services, the value of the firm

By adding new products, Unilever's Dove brand creates and delivers value more effectively by satisfying the changing needs of its current and new customers or simply by keeping customers from getting bored with its current product offerings.

will ultimately decline. Suppose, for instance, that Reebok adopted a strategy of producing the same sneakers year after year. Because many people don't actually wear out their shoes within a year, they would have no incentive to buy new ones. But people tend to get tired of the same old shoes and seek variety.[5] By introducing new lines several times a year, Reebok is able to sustain its growth.

Likewise, car companies can't expect that people will keep their cars until they stop running.[6] If that were the case, there would be no need to come up with new and innovative models; companies could just stick with the models that sell well. But few consumers actually keep the same car until it stops running. Even those who want to stay with the same make and model often want something new, just to add some variety to their lives. Therefore, car companies revamp their models every year, whether by including new features, such as GPS or a more powerful engine, or by redesigning the entire look of the vehicle. This change lets firms sustain their growth by getting consumers excited by the new looks and new features, prompting many car buyers to exchange their old vehicle years before its functional life is over.

Managing Risk Through Diversity

Through innovation, firms often create a broader portfolio of products, which helps them diversify their risk and enhance firm value better than a single product can.[7] If some products in a portfolio are doing poorly, others may be doing well. As we saw in the chapter vignette, tapping innovative ideas allows companies to create new products to add to their existing portfolio. Firms with multiple products are better able to withstand external shocks, including changes in consumer preferences or intensive competitive activity. For this reason, firms such as 3M demand that a specific percentage of their sales each year must come from new products introduced within the previous few years. And, in the cereal aisle, Kellogg's offers many variations of its longstanding basic Special K product, including cereal bars and protein shakes. This diversification enables the company to achieve better results than it would with just one kind of Special K cereal.

Fashion Cycles

In industries that rely on fashion trends and experience short product life cycles—including apparel, arts, books, and software—most sales come from new products. For example, a motion picture generates

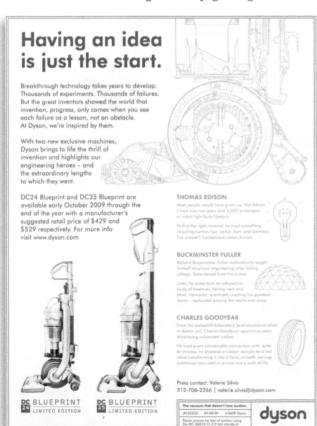

Dyson added value by taking a well-known product, the vacuum cleaner, and redesigning it so that it won't lose suction.

most of its theatre, DVD, and cable TV revenues within a year of its release. If the same selection of books were always available for sale, with no new titles, there would be no reason to buy more. Consumers of computer software and video games demand new products in much the same way that fashion mavens demand new apparel styles.

To generate sales, apparel fashion designers produce entirely new product selections a few times a year.

Innovation and Value

New product introductions, especially new-to-the-world products that create new markets, can add tremendous value to firms. These new products, services, or processes are called **pioneers**, breakthroughs or "disruptive" because they establish a completely new market or radically change both the rules of competition and consumer preferences in a market.[8] Generally, disruptive products require a higher level of learning from consumers and offer much more benefits than predecessor products (see Exhibit 8.1). For example, consumers had to spend a lot of time learning about the Internet to adopt it; but, now that they have mastered this, its benefits have changed the way they work, play, and interact with people. On the other hand, WiFi does not require a lot of learning yet offers consumers tremendous flexibility and freedom in the way they work, communicate, and interact—anytime and anywhere once there is a WiFi hot spot or if they subscribe to mobile wireless. Some examples of pioneers include minicomputers, the Intel microprocessor, Canon's desktop photocopiers, Microsoft's Windows operating system, eBay's online auction model, and the BlackBerry.[9]

pioneers
New product introductions that establish a completely new market or radically change both the rules of competition and consumer preferences in a market; also called *breakthroughs*.

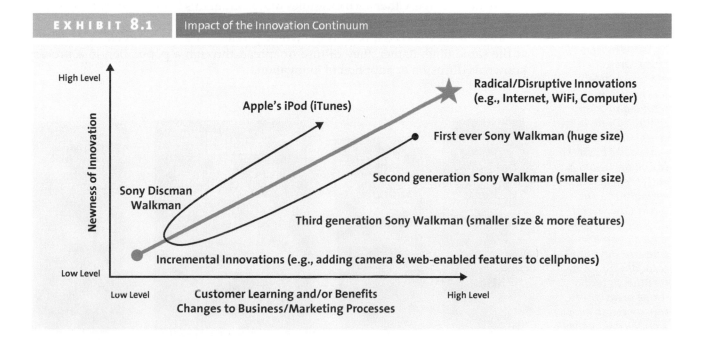

EXHIBIT 8.1 Impact of the Innovation Continuum

Newness of Innovation (vertical axis, Low Level to High Level)

Customer Learning and/or Benefits / Changes to Business/Marketing Processes (horizontal axis, Low Level to High Level)

- Apple's iPod (iTunes)
- **Radical/Disruptive Innovations** (e.g., Internet, WiFi, Computer)
- Sony Discman Walkman
- **First ever Sony Walkman (huge size)**
- **Second generation Sony Walkman (smaller size)**
- **Third generation Sony Walkman (smaller size & more features)**
- **Incremental Innovations (e.g., adding camera & web-enabled features to cellphones)**

first movers

Product pioneers that are the first to create a market or product category, making them readily recognizable to consumers and thus establishing a commanding and early market share lead.

Pioneers have the advantage of being **first movers**; as the first to create the market or product category, they become readily recognizable to consumers and thus establish a commanding and early market share lead. As an example, for decades consumers bought and used the Sony Walkman for mobile music, which required them to buy and carry tapes or CDs. Apple's iPod eliminated the need for CDs with its iTunes service—a radically new service associated with a digital mobile device. Freedom and convenience—the ability to carry more than 10 000 songs plus photos and videos and to share these with friends—have dramatically changed the concept of mobile music players as first introduced by Sony. Studies also have found that market pioneers can command a greater market share over a longer time period than later entrants can.[10]

This finding does not imply, however, that all pioneers succeed.[11] In many cases, imitators capitalize on the weaknesses of pioneers and subsequently gain advantage in the market. Because pioneering products and brands face the uphill task of establishing the market alone, they pave the way for followers, which can spend less marketing effort creating demand for the product category and instead focus directly on creating demand for their specific brand. Also, because the pioneer is the first product in the market, it often has a less sophisticated design and may be priced relatively higher, leaving room for better and lower priced competitive products. As the Sony example in Exhibit 8.1 shows, every subsequent generation of the Sony Walkman had increasingly more features but the Apple iPod not only imitated the idea of mobile music, it radically changed the way mobile music is bought, sold, and consumed. Even the device—the iPod—offers a revolutionary look and feel compared to the Walkman. Will Apple's iPad do the same for the e-book category?

Not all new products succeed in the marketplace. In fact, the majority of new products are failures. As many as 95 percent of all consumer goods fail, and products across all markets and industries suffer failure rates of 50 to 80 percent.[12] Why? There are many reasons, but the following are most common: (1) they offer consumers too few benefits compared with existing products; (2) they are too complex or require substantial learning and effort before consumers can use them, and (3) bad timing—that is, they are introduced at a time when consumers are not ready for such new products or services. As the iPod example shows, new products succeed because they offer substantial benefits that customers like and want even though they may not be inexpensive. Other such examples discussed in this book so far include lululemon clothing and BlackBerry.

Even if they succeed, new-to-the-world products are not adopted by everyone at the same time. Rather, they diffuse or spread through a population in a process known as diffusion or adoption of innovation.

Have you ever heard of any of these products? No wonder. They all failed. Orajel (left), a "fluoride-free" toothpaste, was targeted to young children. Dunk-A-Balls cereal (centre) was shaped like basketballs so children could play with them before eating them. The Garlic Cake (right) was supposed to be served as an hors d'oeuvre. But the company forgot to mention potential usage occasions to consumers, so people wondered why they would want to eat one.

Adoption of Innovation

L02

The process by which the use of an innovation—whether a product or a service—spreads throughout a market group, over time and over various categories of adopters, is referred to as **diffusion of innovation**[13] or adoption of innovation. The theory surrounding diffusion or adoption of innovation helps marketers understand the rate at which consumers are likely to adopt a new product or service. It also gives them a means to identify potential markets for their new products or services and predict their potential sales, even before they introduce the innovations.

As the consumer adoption cycle in Exhibit 8.2 shows, the number of users of an innovative product or service spreads through the population over time and generally follows a bell-shaped curve. A few people buy the product or service at first, then increasingly more buy, and finally fewer people buy as the degree of the diffusion slows. For example, it took close to 20 years to get about 90 percent of Canadians to use ATMs (automated teller machines) but within five years more than 60 percent of Canadians adopted the Internet. Comparing the iPod and Sony Walkman, Merrill Lynch analyst, Steve Milunovich observes that after only 2.5 years, iPod shipments were approximately 1 million units ahead of the Walkman's pace after being on the market for the same period of time in the 1980s when the Walkman was first released.[14] Apple's iPad reached 1 million units in its first 28 days—less than half the 74 days it took for the iPhone to reach the same milestone.[15]

Purchasers can be divided into five groups according to how soon they buy the product after it has been introduced.

Innovators

Innovators are those buyers who want to be the first on the block to have the new product or service. These buyers enjoy taking risks, are regarded as highly knowledgeable, and are not price sensitive. You probably know someone who is an innovator—or perhaps you are one for a particular product or service category. For example, the person who stood in line for days to be sure to get a ticket for the very first showing of the latest superhero movie is an innovator in that context. Firms that invest in the latest technology, either to use in their products or services or to make the firm more efficient, also are considered innovators. Typically, innovators

diffusion of innovation
The process by which the use of an innovation, whether a product or a service, spreads throughout a market group over time and over various categories of adopters.

innovators
Those buyers who want to be the first to have the new product or service.

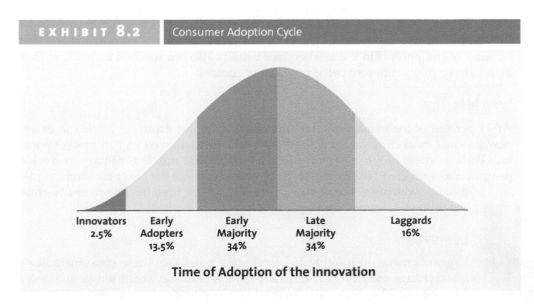

| EXHIBIT 8.2 | Consumer Adoption Cycle |

| Innovators 2.5% | Early Adopters 13.5% | Early Majority 34% | Late Majority 34% | Laggards 16% |

Time of Adoption of the Innovation

Source: Adapted from Everett M. Rodgers, *Diffusion of Innovation* (New York: The Free Press, 1983).

keep themselves very well informed about the product category by subscribing to trade and specialty magazines, talking to other "experts," searching the Internet, and attending product-related forums, seminars, and special events. Typically, innovators represent only about 2.5 percent of the total market for any new product or service.

However, these innovators are crucial to the success of any new product or service because they help the product gain market acceptance. Through talking and spreading positive word of mouth about the new product, they prove instrumental in bringing in the next adopter category, known as early adopters.

Early Adopters

early adopters
The second group of consumers in the diffusion of innovation model, after *innovators*, to use a product or service innovation; generally don't like to take as much risk as innovators.

The second subgroup that begins to use a product or service innovation is the **early adopters**. They generally don't like to take as much risk as innovators but instead wait and purchase the product after careful review. Early adopters tend to enjoy novelty and often are regarded as the opinion leaders for particular product categories. Thus, this market waits for the first reviews of the latest Harry Potter movie, before purchasing a ticket, though they likely still go a week or two after it opens. They don't stand in line to grab the first Nintendo 3DS; only after reading the innovators' complaints and praises do they decide whether it is worth the cost.

Members of this group, which represents about 13.5 percent of all buyers in the market, act as opinion leaders who spread the word to the next big groups: early majority and late majority. As a result, early adopters are crucial for bringing the other three buyer categories to the market. If the early adopter group is relatively small, the number of people who ultimately adopt the innovation likely will also be small.

Early Majority

early majority
A group of consumers in the diffusion of innovation model that represents approximately 34 percent of the population; members don't like to take much risk and therefore tend to wait until bugs are worked out.

The **early majority**, which represents approximately 34 percent of the population, is crucial because few new products and services can be profitable until this large group buys them. If the group never becomes large enough, the product or service typically fails.

The early majority group differs in many ways from buyers in the first two stages. Its members don't like to take as much risk and therefore tend to wait until "the bugs" are worked out of a particular product or service. If we continue our application to movies, this group probably rents the latest Harry Potter movie from a video store when it first comes out on video. Thus, they experience little risk, because all the reviews are in, and their costs are lower because they're renting the movie instead of going to the theatre. When early majority customers enter the market, the number of competitors in the marketplace usually also has reached its peak, so these buyers have many different price and quality choices.

Late Majority

late majority
The last group of buyers to enter a new product market.

At 34 percent of the market, the **late majority** is the last group of buyers to enter a new product market; when they do, the product has achieved its full market potential. Perhaps these movie watchers wait until the latest movie is always in stock or just put it low on their Netflix queue, to be delivered after the other consumers interested in watching it have already seen it. By the time the late majority enters the market, sales tend to level off or may be in decline.

laggards
Consumers who like to avoid change and rely on traditional products until they are no longer available.

Laggards may never adopt a new product or service.

Laggards

Laggards make up roughly 16 percent of the market. These consumers like to avoid change and rely on traditional products until they are no longer available.[16] In some cases, laggards may never adopt a certain product or service. When the final Harry Potter movie eventually shows up on regular TV networks, they are likely to go ahead and watch it. Other examples of laggards are households that still use rotary phones versus touchtone models or listen to music on audiocassettes because they do not own an MP3 player. Very few companies actively pursue these customers.

Using the Adoption Cycle

Using the diffusion of innovation theory or adoption cycle, firms can predict which types of customers will buy their new product or service immediately after its introduction, as well as later as the product gets more and more accepted by the market. With this knowledge, the firm can develop effective promotion, pricing, and other marketing strategies to push acceptance among each customer group. However, because different products are adopted at different rates, marketers must understand what the diffusion curve for the new product looks like, as well as the characteristics of the target customers in each stage of the diffusion. The speed with which products are adopted depends on several product characteristics, illustrated in Exhibit 8.3.

EXHIBIT 8.3 Factors Affecting Product Diffusion Speed

Compatibility

Relative Advantage → Factors Affecting Product Diffusion ← Observability

Complexity and Trialability

Relative Advantage If a product is perceived to be better than substitutes, then the diffusion will be relatively quick. Many believe, for example, that Starbucks' meteoric rise to success is because it is a superior substitute to doughnut or traditional coffee shops. Similarly, the BlackBerry was adopted by business consumers over other devices because it offered substantially more benefits that these consumers needed (as described in Chapter 1's opening vignette).

Compatibility Most business professionals and executives have to make decisions in a timely fashion and be able to communicate their decisions in a timely manner also; they need real-time information to do this. The BlackBerry is compatible with this mode of operation, and so its popularity is hardly surprising. Similarly, the ritual of "having a coffee" is well ingrained in many cultures, including Canadian culture. "Having a coffee" is consistent with people's past behaviour, their needs, and their values. Since people are accustomed to drinking coffee, it has been relatively easy for Starbucks to acquire customers in Canada. The diffusion has been much slower in countries such as China and Japan, where tea has been the traditional drink.

What has made BlackBerry so successful? It has a strong relative advantage to other smartphones. It is compatible with people's current behaviour. Products are easily observable by others. It is not complex and is easy to try.

Observability The ubiquitous Starbucks logo can be easily seen on cups in and around Starbucks stores. On the one hand, when products are easily observed, their benefits or uses are easily communicated to others, thus enhancing the diffusion process. A Botox treatment to reduce wrinkles, on the other hand, is not easily observed by others and therefore has diffused more slowly. Many examples of how the BlackBerry was used to close business deals or to make life-saving decisions are reported in many newspapers and magazines on the Internet. Indeed, you can see the BlackBerry being used everywhere from the workplace to the road to sports venues and even in bars. This presence allows others to easily observe the benefits of the technology

Boots designed by Elizabeth LeGear can hold credit cards, a cellphone, and keys.

when people are working even when they are on the golf course or in a taxi.

Complexity and Trialability   Products that are relatively less complex are also relatively easy to try. These products will generally diffuse more quickly than those that are not. Purchasing a tall non-fat latte, for instance, is a lot easier than purchasing a new car with a GPS system. Purse 'n Boots are women's boots with interior pockets that hold a cellphone, credit cards, change, and keys. Designed in Calgary by Elizabeth LeGear, the patent-pending boots offer an innovative solution. Until distribution moves beyond online only (www.elizabethanneshoes.com), trialability may prove to be a challenge. The BlackBerry is very simple to use and business consumers can try it at a minimal cost before adopting it through the entire organization.

The diffusion of innovation theory thus comes into play in the immediate and long-term aftermath of a new product or service introduction. But before the introduction, firms must actually develop those new offerings. Therefore, in the next section, we detail the process by which most firms develop new products and services and how they initially introduce them into the market.

How Firms Develop New Products

L03   The new product development process begins with the generation of new product ideas and culminates in the launch of the new product and the evaluation of its success. The stages of the new product development process, along with the important objectives of each stage, are summarized in Exhibit 8.4. Although this exhibit depicts linear and sequential stages, in reality, the process is iterative, consisting of a number of feedback loops at various stages. Generally the process is a team effort with the new product team composed of members from various functions: marketing, design, engineering, manufacturing, procurement, and finance, all of whom play different roles at different stages of the process. Marketing plays a crucial role in the new product development process by communicating customer needs and wants and marketplace preferences and attitudes to the research and development (R&D) and engineering group.

Bear in mind that it's not always necessary to take a new product through each stage in the process. Substantially new products will likely follow the process fairly closely, while products imitating a successful product from a competitor, having a low development cost, or involving incremental changes (such as line extensions) may skip one or more steps. For example, P&G launched its Folgers brand of

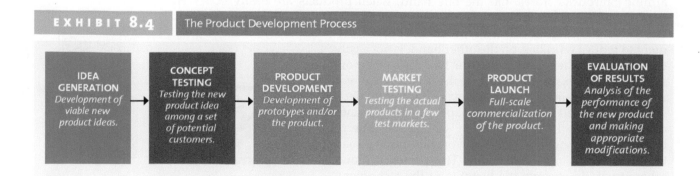

EXHIBIT 8.4   The Product Development Process

| **IDEA GENERATION** *Development of viable new product ideas.* | **CONCEPT TESTING** *Testing the new product idea among a set of potential customers.* | **PRODUCT DEVELOPMENT** *Development of prototypes and/or the product.* | **MARKET TESTING** *Testing the actual products in a few test markets.* | **PRODUCT LAUNCH** *Full-scale commercialization of the product.* | **EVALUATION OF RESULTS** *Analysis of the performance of the new product and making appropriate modifications.* |

decaffeinated crystal coffee without market testing. Although skipping stages in the new product development process is very risky, companies often do it to reduce costs or launch new products quickly.

Idea Generation

To generate ideas for new products, a firm can use its own internal R&D efforts, collaborate with other firms and institutions, license technology from research-intensive firms, brainstorm, research competitors' products and services, and/or conduct consumer research. Sometimes new product ideas come from employees, customers, suppliers, and partners or are generated by attending trade shows and conferences. Companies also generate ideas by using reverse engineering or, in more extreme cases, even by digging through a competitor's garbage. See Exhibit 8.5 for an example of how employee ideas resulted in a new product. Firms that want to be pioneers rely more extensively on R&D efforts, whereas those that tend to adopt a follower strategy are more likely to scan the market for ideas. Let's look at each of these idea sources.

Internal Research and Development McDonald's director of culinary innovation, Dan Coudreaut, faces the challenge of dreaming up new products that can be prepared by entry-level help across all of the chain's locations, made from ingredients available in industrial quantities all year round.[17] He launched the Angus Burger after seeing rivals such as Burger King introduce new cheeseburgers that lifted sales. The Angus Burger was subjected to six months of team cooking and market research before eventually being tested with restaurant owners in key markets to ensure staff could reliably reproduce the recipe. More than a year may be spent in extensive internal R&D playing around with a recipe before unveiling a new product.

Many firms have their own R&D departments, in which scientists work to solve complex problems and develop new ideas.[18] Historically, firms such as IBM in the computer industry, Rubbermaid in the consumer goods industry, 3M in the industrial goods industry, and Merck and Pfizer in the pharmaceuticals industry have relied on R&D efforts for their new products. In other industries, such as software, music, and motion pictures, product development efforts also tend to come from internal ideas

EXHIBIT 8.5	Sources of Ideas

Post-it® Notes were not a planned product. Spencer Silver was working at the 3M research laboratories in 1970 trying to find a strong adhesive. He developed a new adhesive, but it was even weaker than what 3M already manufactured. It stuck to objects but could easily be lifted off.

No one knew what to do with the adhesive but Silver didn't discard it. Then one Sunday, four years later, another 3M scientist named Arthur Fry was singing in the church's choir. He used markers to keep his place in the hymnal, but they kept falling out of the book. Remembering Silver's adhesive, Fry used some to coat his markers. Success! With the weak adhesive, the markers stayed in place, yet lifted off the pages without damaging them. 3M began distributing Post-it® Notes nationwide in 1980—10 years after Silver developed the super weak adhesive. Today, they are one of the most popular office products available.

Source: Adapted from Post-it® Note History, www.ideafinder.com/history/inventions/postit.htm (accessed June 5, 2011).

and investments. Power of the Internet 8.1 discusses how the Internet can be used as a new and powerful way to invite customers into the research lab.

The product development costs for firms are quite high, and the resulting new product or service has a good chance of being a technological or market breakthrough. Firms expect such products to generate enough revenue and profits to make the costs of R&D worthwhile; however, R&D investments generally are considered continuous investments, so firms may lose money on a few new products. In the long run though, these firms are betting that a few extremely successful new products, often known as blockbusters, can generate enough revenues and profits to cover the losses from other introductions that might not fare so well.

Licensing   For many new scientific and technological products, firms buy the rights to use the technology or ideas from other research-intensive firms through a licensing agreement. This approach saves the high costs of in-house R&D, but it means that the firm is banking on a solution that already exists but has not been marketed. For example, many pharmaceutical firms license products developed by biotechnology firms such as Amgen, Biogen, and Genentech. Because most biotechnology firms are smaller, tend to be very research focused, and lack the resources and expertise to market their own innovations, they are content to obtain some development financing and royalties on sales of their product from the pharmaceutical firms.[19]

Brainstorming   Firms often engage in brainstorming sessions during which a group works together to generate ideas. One of the key characteristics of a brainstorming session is that no idea can be immediately accepted or rejected. The moderator of the session may channel participants' attention to specific product features and attributes, performance expectations, or packaging, but only at the end of the session do the members vote on the best ideas or combinations of ideas. Those four to eight ideas that receive the most votes are carried forward to the next stage of the product development process.

Competitors' Products   A new product entry by a competitor may trigger a market opportunity for a firm, which can use reverse engineering to understand the competitor's product and then bring an improved version to market. **Reverse engineering** involves taking apart a competitor's product, analyzing it, and creating an improved product that does not infringe on the competitor's patents, if any exist. This copycat approach to new product development is widespread and practised by even the most research-intensive firms. Copycat consumer goods show up in grocery and drugstore products, as well as in technologically more complex products such as automobiles and computers. For example, China Unicom Ltd., the state-controlled telecommunications giant ranked as China's second-biggest mobile operator, launched Red-Berry, a new product aimed squarely at BlackBerry.[20]

reverse engineering
Involves taking apart a competitor's product, analyzing it, and creating an improved product that does not infringe on the competitor's patents, if any exist.

Customer Input   Listening to the customer is essential for successful idea generation.[21] Prior studies have found that as much as 85 percent of all new business-to-business (B2B) product ideas come from customers.[22] Because customers for B2B products are relatively few in number, firms can follow their use of products closely and survey them often for suggestions and ideas to improve those products. The firm's design and development team then works on these suggestions, sometimes in

Staples observed how customers opened their mail in the kitchen and so developed the Mailmate shredder to look like a kitchen appliance.

Power of the Internet 8.1

Your Ideas in Action at Starbucks

Consumers use the Internet as a part of their daily lives to share information, discuss interests, and air grievances. Starbucks recognized that its loyal consumers wanted to share ideas for new products and a website (MyStarbucksIdea.com) was launched to make it easy for them to do so. Since its customers know better than anyone how and what they want the company to serve them, Starbucks is encouraging customers to submit their ideas, revolutionary or otherwise.

This example of corporate democracy in action allows anyone who signs up for an account to make suggestions. Others can discuss and vote on the ideas in an online forum while Starbucks watches to see which ideas are the most popular. All "Ideas in Action" have icons beside them to note whether they are under review, reviewed, in the works, or launched.

Involving consumers in this way is a gold mine for Starbucks because it provides a way to invite customers into the research lab, so to speak. Integrating customer views into a company's new product development process can provide an untapped source of new ideas, refinements to existing products, and access to

Customer feedback led to a "splash stick" to prevent drinks from spilling.

a knowledgeable test market—all at little or no cost.

One example of a new product introduction that resulted from consumer feedback was the addition of soy-based beverages to cater to lactose-intolerant customers. Although the website is a great place for Starbucks to get feedback on new products customers want, ideas are not restricted to that category. Feedback is also welcome in other categories, including "experience ideas" (ordering, payment, pickup, atmosphere, locations) and "involvement ideas" (building communities, social responsibility.)

Some of the posted ideas include[24]

- Create a splash stick to prevent spills from drink lid.

- Don't throw out used Starbucks cards. Instead give people a 25-cent credit for reloading them.

- Add ice cubes made from coffee to iced coffee drinks so the beverage doesn't become diluted.

- Offer gluten-free food.

- Showcase local art in stores to provide a new experience for customers and shine a light on local artists.

consultation with the customer. This joint effort between the selling firm and the customer significantly increases the probability that the customer eventually will buy the new product. Power of the Internet 8.1 illustrates how companies use the Internet to solicit and incorporate customer feedback in the new product development process.

Customer input comes from a variety of sources. Staples observed how people use products in their homes and noticed that people opened their mail in the kitchen but waited to shred it until they got to their office. Using this information, Staples designed the Mailmate, a stainless steel shredder that looks like a kitchen appliance so it blends in with the kitchen decor and customers can shred their mail instantly after opening it.[23]

In the food and beverage industry, in which new product failure rates are as high as 78 percent, Kraft minimizes its risk through a careful new product development process that includes consumer research. Frito Lay is the third-fastest-growing food company in Canada. Its Lightly Salted Lay's potato chips were developed after research showed that saturated fats and trans fats are at the top of consumers' concerns but that sodium also ranks high. Sales were beyond their expectations.[25] Innovation is the lifeblood of Frito Lay's business. Some years, innovation has accounted for more than 100 percent of its growth in Canada—without it, sales would be flat.[26]

A particularly successful customer input approach is to analyze **lead users**, those innovative product users who modify existing products according to their own ideas

lead users
Innovative product users who modify existing products according to their own ideas to suit their specific needs.

These innovative consumers are called lead users because they modify existing products according to their own ideas to suit their specific needs.

concepts
Brief written descriptions of a product or service; its technology, working principles, and forms; and what customer needs it would satisfy.

concept testing
The process in which a concept statement that describes a product or a service is presented to potential buyers or users to obtain their reactions.

to suit their specific needs.[27] These lead users have customized the firm's products; other customers might wish to do so as well. Thus, studying lead users helps the firm understand general market trends that might be just on the horizon. Manufacturers and retailers of fashion products often spot new trends by noticing how trendsetters have altered their clothing and shoes. For instance, designers of high-fashion jeans distress their products in different ways depending on signals they pick up "on the street." One season, jeans appear with whiskers, the next holes, the next paint spots. Products developed by paying attention to lead users include Gatorade, protein-based shampoo, Liquid Paper correction fluid, mountain bikes, chocolate milk, desktop publishing, and the World Wide Web.

At the end of the idea-generation stage, the firm should have several ideas that it can take forward to the next stage: concept testing.

Concept Testing

Ideas with potential are developed further into **concepts**, which in this context refer to brief written descriptions of the product; its technology, working principles, and forms; and what customer needs it would satisfy.[28] A concept might also include visual images of what the product would look like.

Concept testing refers to the process in which a concept statement is presented to potential buyers representative of the target market or users to obtain their reactions. These reactions enable the developer to estimate the sales value of the product or service concept, possibly make changes to enhance its sales value, and determine whether the idea is worth further development.[29] If the concept fails to meet customers' expectations, it is doubtful it would succeed if it were to be produced and marketed. Because concept testing occurs very early in the new product introduction process, even before a real product has been made, it helps the firm avoid the costs of unnecessary product development.

The concept for an electric scooter might be written as follows:

The product is a lightweight electric scooter that can be easily folded and taken with you inside a building or on public transportation. The scooter weights 25 pounds [11 kg]. It travels at speeds of up to 15 miles [24 km] per hour and can go about 12 miles [19 km] on a single charge. The scooter can be recharged in about two hours from a standard electric outlet. The scooter is easy to ride and has simple controls—just an accelerator button and a brake. It sells for $299.[30]

Concept testing progresses along the research techniques described in Chapter 4. The firm likely starts with exploratory research, such as in-depth interviews or focus groups, to test the concept, after which it can undertake conclusive research through Internet or mall-intercept surveys. Video clips on the Internet might show a virtual prototype and the way the product or service works so that potential customers can evaluate it.[31] In a mall-intercept survey, an interviewer would provide a description of the concept to the respondent and then ask several questions to obtain his or her feedback.

The most important question pertains to the respondent's purchase intentions were the product or service be made available. Marketers also should ask whether the product would satisfy a need that other products currently are not meeting. Depending on the type of product or service, researchers might also ask about the expected frequency of purchase, how much customers would buy, whether they would buy it for themselves or as a gift, when they would buy, and whether the price information (if provided) indicates a good value. In addition, marketers usually collect some demographic information so they can analyze which consumer segments are likely to be most interested in the product.

Some concepts never make it past this stage, particularly if respondents seem uninterested. Those that do receive high evaluations from potential consumers, however, move on to the next step, product development.

Product Development

Product development or **product design** entails a process of balancing various engineering, manufacturing, marketing, and economic considerations to develop a product's form and features or a service's features. An engineering team develops a product prototype that is based on research findings from the previous concept testing step, as well as their own knowledge about materials and technology. A **prototype** is the first physical form or service description of a new product, still in rough or tentative form that has the same properties as a new product but is produced through different manufacturing processes, sometimes even crafted individually.[32]

Product prototypes are usually tested through alpha and beta testing. In **alpha testing**, the firm attempts to determine whether the product will perform according to its design and whether it satisfies the need for which it was intended.[33] Rather than using potential consumers, alpha tests occur in the firm's R&D department. For instance, Ben & Jerry's alpha tests all its proposed new ice cream flavours on its own employees at its corporate headquarters in Vermont. It may be a great job, but it also sounds rather fattening!

As discussed in Ethical Dilemma 8.1, many people, consumer groups, and governmental agencies are concerned when alpha testing involves tests on animals, particularly when it comes to pharmaceuticals and cosmetics.

In contrast, **beta testing** uses potential consumers, who examine the product prototype in a "real use" setting to determine its functionality, performance, potential problems, and other issues specific to its use. The firm might develop several prototype products that it gives to users, and then survey those users to determine whether the product worked as intended and to identify any issues that need resolution.

Household products manufacturer Kimberly-Clark uses virtual testing in the beta-testing phase of its product development process. The consumer goods company uses a virtual store aisle that mimics a real-life shopping experience by creating a realistic picture of the interior of the store. A retina-tracking device records the movement of a test customer who "shops" the virtual aisle of a store and chooses certain products to investigate further in the virtual simulation. Thus, consumer companies can demonstrate the likely success, or failure, of a product without actually having to produce it for a market and, potentially, expose its secrets to competitors.[34]

Market Testing

The firm has developed its new product or service and tested the prototypes. Now it must test the market for the new product with a trial batch of products; although, as mentioned earlier, companies sometimes skip this step because of competitive, timing, or cost pressures. These tests can take two forms: premarket testing or test marketing.

Premarket Tests Firms conduct **premarket tests** before they actually bring a product or service to market to determine how many customers will try and then continue to use

Ben & Jerry's uses alpha testing with its own employees to make sure its products have the right taste and feel.

product development (product design)
Entails a process of balancing various engineering, manufacturing, marketing, and economic considerations to develop a product.

prototype
The first physical form or service description of a new product, still in rough or tentative form, that has the same properties as a new product but is produced through different manufacturing processes, sometimes even crafted individually.

alpha testing
An attempt by the firm to determine whether a product will perform according to its design and whether it satisfies the need for which it was intended; occurs in the firm's R&D department.

beta testing
Having potential consumers examine a product prototype in a real-use setting to determine its functionality, performance, potential problems, and other issues specific to its use.

Ethical Dilemma 8.1

Should Firms Test on Animals?

Product testing on animals has been a primary issue for animal right activists for years.[35] As public opposition to animal testing increases, so do many companies' declarations that they "do not test products on animals." However, such statements can be misleading because even though the whole product may not have tested on animals, the individual ingredients may have been. To help clarify any confusion, companies can apply to the Coalition for Consumer Information on Cosmetics (CCIC), a national group formed by eight animal welfare group members, and be certified as "cruelty free." They can then purchase the trademarked Leaping Bunny Logo from CCIC for use on their labels.

One of the founding principles of The Body Shop, and one that has resonated well with its customers, is that its products are free of animal testing. While the website for The Body Shop states that it has never tested or commissioned testing of its ingredients or products on animals, many of the ingredients in its products were in fact tested on animals by other companies. This discrepancy caused confusion and resulted in the company changing the labels on its products from "not tested on animals" to "against animal testing" because it is impossible to avoid ingredients ever tested on animals.[36] Another major cosmetics manufacturer, P&G, has eliminated animal testing on more than 80 percent of its products. It uses a combination of vitro testing, computer modelling, and historical data to determine the safety of new products and ingredients. These methods are more expensive than more traditional methods, but P&G claims that the results are better. If performed correctly, new chemicals can either be dropped from consideration or pushed forward in as little as three days compared with the six months previously required for animal testing.

In other fields, animal welfare groups continue to push to stop the use of animal testing altogether. The People for the Ethical Treatment of Animals (PETA) publicly cites companies it accuses of engaging in animal testing and praises those that do not. Other groups promote propaganda, encourage pressure from consumers, and lobby legislatures, yet the industry continues to push back, citing consumer choice, expense, and free trade.

The European Union has passed a ban on animal testing altogether. As of 2009, any cosmetic tested on animals, even in other parts of the world, cannot be sold in the European Union. However, the cosmetic industry is worried that this ban will not only affect their companies' sales, but also their customers' ability to find the products they want. The E.U. cosmetics industry successfully lobbied for an extension on certain areas of toxicity testing to provide more time to find alternatives. The cosmetic industry believes it will be difficult to find alternative testing methods in time. If it cannot, then it will have fewer ingredients to make the products consumers want.

The issues involved in animal testing for cosmetics are complex. At the broadest level, should firms be allowed to develop products that customers want, even if there is some potential harm to the environment or to those animals that share the environment with humans? More specifically, should firms be allowed to test products on animals, even when those products are not specifically designed to improve the health and well-being of their human users? After all, these products may make their users more attractive, but they will not save their lives. Does the testing that is performed endanger the lives or health of the animals?

---

the product or service according to a small group of potential consumers. One popular proprietary premarket test version is called Nielsen BASES. During the test, potential customers are exposed to the marketing mix variables, such as the advertising, and then surveyed and given a sample of the product to try.[37] After some period of time, during which the potential customers try the product, they are surveyed about whether they would buy/use the product again. This second survey indicates an estimation of the probability of a consumer's repeat purchase. From these data, the firm generates a sales estimate for the new product that enables it to decide whether to introduce the product, abandon it, redesign it before introduction, or revise the marketing plan. An early evaluation of this sort—that is, before the product is introduced to the whole market—saves marketers the costs of a nationwide launch if the product fails.

Sometimes firms simulate a product or service introduction,[38] in which case potential customers view the advertising of various currently available products or services along with advertising for the new product or service. They receive money to buy the product or service from a simulated environment, such as a mock web page or store, and respond to a survey after they make their purchases. This test thus can determine the effectiveness of a firm's advertising as well as the expected trial rates for the new product.

premarket test
Conducted before a product or service is brought to market to determine how many customers will try and then continue to use it.

Test Marketing   A method of determining the success potential of a new product, **test marketing** introduces the offering to a limited geographical area (usually a few cities) prior to a national launch. A test marketing effort uses all the elements of the marketing mix. It includes promotions such as advertising and coupons, just as if the product were being introduced nationally, and the product appears in targeted retail outlets, with appropriate pricing. On the basis of the results of the test marketing, the firm can estimate demand for the entire market. McDonald's tested its McCafé concept—cappuccinos, lattes, European-style pastries—in 70 Atlantic Canada locations to determine whether it should roll them out across the country.[39]

Test marketing costs more and takes longer than premarket tests, which may provide an advantage to competitors that could get a similar or better product to market first. For this reason, some firms, such as Newman's Own Organics, launch new products (e.g., its Fig Newmans™) without extensive consumer testing and rely instead on intuition, instincts, and guts.[40]

However, test marketing offers a key advantage: The firm can study actual consumer behaviour, which is more reliable than a simulated test. Canada Post piloted Fetch, a service that allows people to access advertisers' information via email and cellphones without compromising their privacy, in Calgary. The city has a relatively young demographic profile, precisely the target demographic Canada Post wanted to reach; plus, residents tend to be technically inclined. It turned out to be a good choice, and the pilot exceeded expectations.[41] Labatt chose Calgary and Edmonton as the test markets for its Brazilian Brahma beer. As a test market, Calgary offers an attractive demographic in terms of income levels, lifestyle, and a relatively youthful population.

Other cities are used for test markets for a variety of reasons. London, Ontario, is often chosen because its population is reflective of a "typical" Canadian city. Winnipeg is a good location to test shampoos and skin lotions for dry skin because of its cold winters. Petro-Canada tested a new, upscale convenience store and restaurant concept called Neighbours in Oakville, Brampton, and Vaughan, all Ontario cities with residents who earn slightly higher incomes, before rolling out more locations across the province.

Many firms use BehaviorScan to improve the probability of success during the test marketing phase of a new product introduction. BehaviorScan utilizes consumer panel data collected passively at the point of sale in stores and through home scanning to measure individual household first-time trial and repeat purchases. New products are placed in stores within one week of introduction, rather than the typical 8- to 12-week period. Since more sales data are collected in a shorter period of time than conventional test-marketing methods, first-year sales can be estimated after just 16 to 24 weeks in the test market.[42] Once the market demand is estimated, the product is released nationally.

However, sometimes test marketing can result in tipping your hand to competitors, who carefully monitor sales and pre-emptively launch their own products. For instance, Kellogg's tracked sales of Toast'ems during test marketing by General Foods. Noting they were becoming popular, they quickly went national with Pop-Tarts before the test was finished. General Foods invented freeze-dried coffee and was in the midst of test marketing its Maxim brand when Nestlé launched Taster's Choice, which went on to become the leading brand.[43]

Product Launch

If the market testing returns with positive results, the firm is ready to introduce the product to the entire market. Frito Lay originally launched its Wasabi and Spicy

test marketing
Introduces a new product or service to a limited geographical area (usually a few cities) prior to a national launch.

Petro-Canada test-marketed a new, upscale restaurant and convenience store concept in Southwestern Ontario to gauge consumer response.

Curry Lay's chips in Toronto and Vancouver, where the largest number of Asian-born Canadians reside. Sales of the curry flavour were three to four times higher than expected; however, Wasabi didn't enjoy much success.[44]

A product launch is the most critical step in the new product introduction and requires tremendous financial resources and extensive coordination of all aspects of the marketing mix. If the new product launch is a failure, it may be difficult for the product—and perhaps the firm—to recover. Some products show great promise through their launches, though, as Exhibit 8.6 describes.

So what does a product launch involve? First, on the basis of the research it has gathered on consumer perceptions and the tests it has conducted, as well as any competitive considerations, the firm confirms its target market(s) and decides how the product will be positioned. Then the firm finalizes the remaining marketing mix variables for the new product, including the marketing budget for the first year.[45]

Promotion   The test results help the firm determine an appropriate integrated marketing communications strategy.[46] For products that are somewhat complex or conceptually new, marketers may need to provide for more consumer education about the product's benefits than they would for simpler and more familiar products. For technical products, technical support staff must be trained to answer any customer questions that may arise immediately after the launch. RIM promotes the BlackBerry Bold as small, smart, and stylish to attract consumer markets and offers troubleshooting tips for top issues via its technical solution centre.

Place   The firm must have an adequate quantity of products available for shipment and to keep in stock at relevant stores. The product offering should also be as complete as possible. For example, a firm launching a new printer should ensure it has an adequate supply of the related cartridges or toners. Interested consumers can purchase a BlackBerry Bold from any Bell, Rogers, or TELUS wireless products location. This accessibility not only provides the new product in a convenient location, but also allows the opportunity for tailored customer service and subscription to appropriate service plans.

Price   The firm needs to ensure that it gets the price right. It is sometimes easier to start with a higher price and offer promotions (e.g., coupons, rebates) and then over time to lower the price than it is to introduce the new product at a low price and then

---

EXHIBIT 8.6	Best New Products[47]

Below is sampling of winners as voted by Canadians in the Best New Product Awards.

Award Category	Product	Category
Best in Food & Beverage Category and Best in Show	Europe's Best Antioxidant Fruit Blend	Frozen Fruit
Best in Health and Beauty Category	Trojan Fire & Ice Condoms	Condoms
Best in Household Products Category	Arm & Hammer Double Duty Cat Litter	Pet Care

Source: http://bestnewproductawards.biz/canada/index.html (accessed June 8, 2011).

try to raise it. The BlackBerry Bold is a premium telecommunications product commanding a fitting price of $549.95 without a service contract. However, carriers entice new buyers by bundling a reduced price for the Bold if a service plan is included. The price can drop by hundreds of dollars, or even to zero with a long-term contract.[48]

Timing The timing of the launch may be important, depending on the product.[49] Hollywood studios typically release movies targeted toward general audiences (i.e., those rated G or PG) during the summer when children are out of school. New automobile models traditionally are released for sale during September, and fashion products are launched just before the season of the year for which they are intended.

Evaluation of Results

After the product has been launched, marketers must undertake a critical postlaunch review to determine whether the product and its launch were a success or a failure and what additional resources or changes to the marketing mix are needed, if any. Firms measure the success of a new product by three interrelated factors: (1) its satisfaction of technical requirements, such as performance; (2) customer acceptance; and (3) its satisfaction of the firm's financial requirements, such as sales and profits.[50] If the product is not performing sufficiently well, poor customer acceptance will result, which in turn leads to poor financial performance. The new product development process, when followed rationally and sequentially, helps avoid such domino-type failures. The product life cycle, discussed in the next section, helps marketers manage their products' marketing mix during and after its introduction.

The Product Life Cycle

The **product life cycle** (PLC) defines the stages that new products move through as they enter, get established in, and ultimately leave the marketplace and thereby offers marketers a starting point for their strategy planning. Exhibit 8.7A illustrates a typical product life cycle, including the industry sales and profits over time. In their life cycles, products pass through four stages: introduction, growth, maturity, and decline. When

L04

product life cycle
Defines the stages that new products move through as they enter, get established in, and ultimately leave the marketplace and thereby offers marketers a starting point for their strategy planning.

EXHIBIT 8.7A | Product Life Cycle

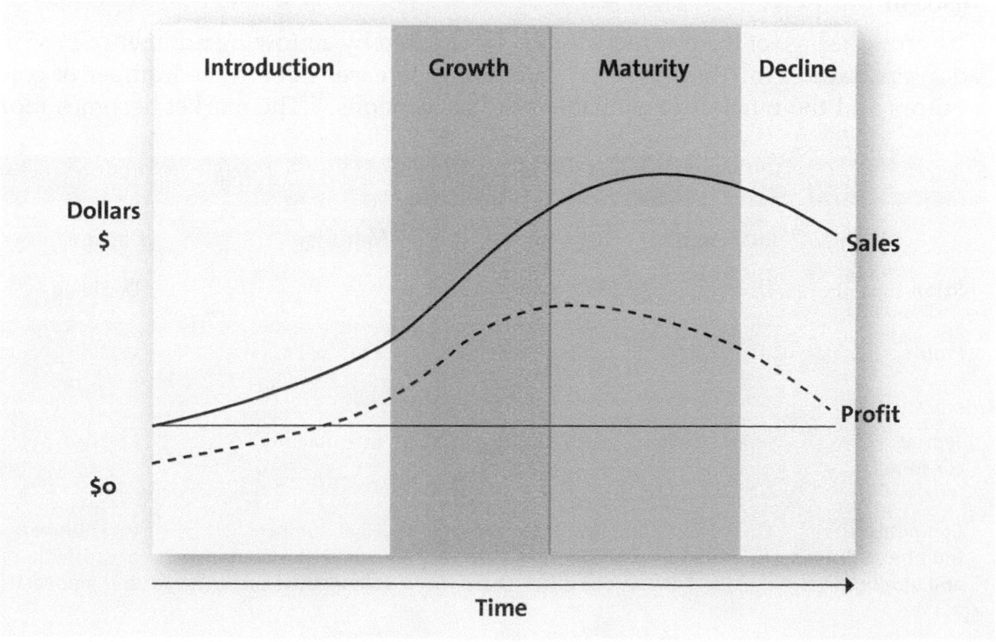

introduction stage
Stage of the product life cycle when innovators start buying the product.

growth stage
Stage of the product life cycle when the product gains acceptance, demand and sales increase, and competitors emerge in the product category.

innovators start buying the product, the product enters the **introduction stage** of its life cycle. In the **growth stage**, the product gains acceptance, demand and sales increase, and competitors emerge in the product category. In the **maturity stage**, industry sales reach their peak, so firms try to rejuvenate their products by adding new features or repositioning them. If these efforts succeed, the product achieves new life.[51] If not, it goes into the **decline stage** and eventually exits the market.

Not every product follows the same life cycle shape; many products stay in the maturity period for a very long time. For example, "white good" categories, such as clothes washers, clothes dryers, and refrigerators, have been in the maturity stage for a very long time and will remain there indefinitely until a superior product comes along to replace them.

The product life cycle also offers a useful tool for managers to analyze the types of strategies that may be required over the life of their products. Even the strategic emphasis of a firm and its marketing mix (four Ps) strategies can be adapted from insights about the characteristics of each stage of the cycle, as we summarize in Exhibit 8.7B.

Let's look at each of these stages in depth.

Introduction Stage

The introduction stage for a new, innovative product or service usually starts with a single firm, and innovators are the ones to try the new offering. Some new-to-the-world products and services that defined their own product category and industry include the telephone (invented by Alexander Graham Bell in 1876), the transistor semiconductor (Bell Laboratories in 1947), the Walkman portable cassette player (Sony in 1979), the Internet browser (Netscape in 1994), iTunes (Apple in 2001), and BlackBerry (RIM in 2003) and Blu-ray (Sony in 2006). See Exhibit 8.8 for an example of how BlackBerry has moved from introduction to subsequent stages of the product life cycle. Sensing the viability and commercialization possibilities of this market-creating new product, other firms soon enter the market with similar or improved products at lower prices. The same pattern holds for less innovative products such as apparel, some CDs, or even a new soft-drink flavour. The introduction stage is characterized by initial losses to the firm because of its high start-up costs and low levels of sales revenue as the product begins to take off. If the product is successful, firms may start seeing profits toward the end of this stage.

These new-to-the-world products defined their own product category and industry. The telephone (top) was invented in 1876, and the Sony Walkman (bottom) came out in 1979.

Growth Stage

The growth stage of the product life cycle is marked by a growing number of product adopters, rapid growth in industry sales, and increases in both the number of competitors and the number of available product versions.[52] The market becomes more

EXHIBIT 8.7B	Characteristics of Different Stages of the Product Life Cycle			
	Introduction	**Growth**	**Maturity**	**Decline**
Sales	Low	Rising	Peak	Declining
Profits	Negative or low	Rapidly rising	Peak to declining	Declining
Typical consumers	Innovators	Early adopters and early majority	Late majority	Laggards
Competitors (number of firms and products)	One or few	Few but increasing	High number of competitors and competitive products	Low number of competitors and products

EXHIBIT 8.8	Product Life Cycle Strategies, BlackBerry Example		
	Introduction	**Growth**	**Maturity**
Product	Basic product offered	New product variations introduced	Diversify brands and models into a full product line
Price	High price	Prices drop slightly	Full complement of price points in product line
Place	Selective distribution	Build distribution outlets; add dealers to reach new business markets	Build more intensive distribution to reach consumer markets
Promotion	Build word of mouth and product awareness among early adopters	Build awareness in broader markets and media channels	Stress brand differences and benefits

segmented and consumer preferences more varied, which increases the potential for new markets or new uses of the product or service.[53] Innovators start rebuying the product, and early majority consumers enter.

Also during the growth stage, firms attempt to reach new consumers by studying their preferences and producing different product variations—varied colours, styles, or features—which enables them to segment the market more precisely. The goal of this segmentation is to ride the rising sales trend and firmly establish the firm's brand, so as not to be outdone by competitors. In recognizing the growing demand for and appeal of organic products, many food manufacturers are working hard to become the first brand that consumers think of when they consider organic products. Del Monte was the first of the major canned vegetable sellers to go organic, releasing organic versions of its tomatoes, green beans, corn, and sweet peas, along with an organic chicken broth product under its College Inn line. The cans feature bold "organic" banners across the front and promise that no pesticides were used to produce the food items. Even though Del Monte products have been around for more than 100 years, in this growth category, the company must work to establish its distinctive appeal in the organic market in particular.[54]

As firms ride the crest of increasing industry sales, profits in the growth stage also rise because of the economies of scale associated with manufacturing and marketing costs, especially promotion and advertising. At the same time, firms that have not yet established a stronghold in the market, even in narrow segments, may decide to exit in what is referred to as an "industry shakeout."

Maturity Stage

The maturity stage of the product life cycle is characterized by the adoption of the product by the late majority and intense competition for market share among firms. Marketing costs (e.g., promotion, distribution) increase as these firms vigorously defend their market share against competitors. At the same time, they face intense competition on price as the average price of the product falls substantially compared with the shifts during the previous two stages of the life cycle. Lower prices and increased marketing costs begin to erode the profit margins for many firms. In the later phases of the maturity stage, the market has become quite saturated, and practically all potential customers for the product have already adopted the product. Such saturated markets are prevalent in developed countries; in Canada, most consumer packaged goods found in grocery and discount stores are already in the maturity stage.

Firms may pursue several strategies during this stage to increase their customer base and/or defend their market share, such as entering into new markets and market segments and developing new products or promotions. Social Media Marketing 8.1 shows

maturity stage
Stage of the product life cycle when industry sales reach their peak, so firms try to rejuvenate their products by adding new features or repositioning them.

decline stage
Stage of the product life cycle when sales decline and the product eventually exits the market.

how PepsiCo works to keep its products from falling into the decline stage. See Exhibit 8.9 for additional strategies for extending the maturity stage of the product life cycle.

Entry into New Markets or Market Segments   Because the market is saturated at this point, firms may attempt to enter new geographical markets, including international markets (as we will discuss in Chapter 16), that may be less saturated. For example, Whirlpool has started manufacturing washing machines for Brazil, China, and India that it prices lower than those it sells in North America to attract the large consumer base of lower-income consumers in these countries.[55] In many developing economies, the large and growing proportion of middle-class households is just beginning to buy the home, kitchen, and entertainment appliances that have been fairly standard in Canadian households for several decades. In India alone, the roughly 487 million middle-class consumers will spend $420 billion on a variety of consumer products in the next four years.[56]

However, even in mature markets, firms may be able to find new market segments. Emerging new trends or changes in consumer tastes may fragment mature markets, which would open new market opportunities. As the popularity of the Internet increased, for example, firms such as Expedia, Orbitz, Priceline, and Travelocity found that they could provide the easy access and convenience of online bookings for air travel, hotel stays, and car rentals. Consumers who prefer such access and convenience, as well as the ability to compare prices across different service providers, increasingly are using the Internet to make their travel plans.

New market opportunities also may emerge through simple product design changes, such as in the market for "wipes." Just a few years ago, baby wipes accounted for most of the sales of personal wipes, but P&G's Oil of Olay Facial Cleansing Cloths and Unilever's Ponds Age-Defying wipes have recently gained significant market share.[57] In the household sector, products such as P&G's Swiffer, the electrostatic wipe for mopping floors, have expanded the market greatly. Clorox has added premoistened Armor All wipes to its do-it-yourself car cleaning line[58] and the Clorox® ToiletWand™ for consumers who don't enjoy unsightly and unsanitary

EXHIBIT 8.9	Strategies for Extending the Product Life Cycle
Strategy	**Example**
Develop new uses for products	• Baking soda is now promoted for deodorizing refrigerators, as an environmentally friendly cleaning product, and much more.
Modify the product: • Change quality • Boost performance • Alter appearance	• Add graphite to tennis racquets and golf clubs • Enhance computer chip speed • Introduce new scent; modify packaging; change colours
Increase frequency of use	• Dentyne gum is promoted as a way to help clean your teeth when you can't brush after a meal.
Increase the number of users	• Tums have always contained calcium, but when this fact was promoted, people concerned about bone density began to purchase the product.
Find new users	• Club Med introduced vacations geared to baby boomers, seniors, golfers, and those looking for cruises after some of their original target market of swinging singles got married and had children.
Reposition product	• Suntan lotion has evolved to become sunscreen protection. • Vitamin D is sold as a cancer deterrent.
Tweak marketing strategy	• Greeting cards are sold in supermarkets. • Upscale cosmetics are sold in drug stores.

Social Media Marketing 8.1   PepsiCo Amps Its Game to Stave Off Decline

Launched in 2001 to compete against Red Bull and Monster, AMP Energy has become a mega brand for PepsiCo. The energy drink category has witnessed explosive growth, with dozens of new entrants bursting onto the scene, including RockStar, Full Throttle and NRG. In such a fiercely competitive market, the battle for market share and consumer attention is intense.

As products mature, marketers must respond with creative, new strategies to extend the product life cycle. AMP Energy has done this by rejuvenating the line by developing new products such as the Energy Shot and adding trendy new flavours such as green tea and lemonade. Promotional efforts to keep the product top of mind with consumers are another tactic to keep the product from slipping into decline.

By tying video games to the Amp Your Game (AYG) tour, marketers designed the promotion to connect with the important, energy drink–consuming target market of 18 to 24 year olds on campuses across Canada. The AYG tour visited 40 schools with a plan to give out 100 000 samples of AMP Energy. It also offered a tempting $100,000 Rock Off! grand prize for the best rock band. Each campus stop featured a two-hour live Rock Band 2 competition on the PlayStation 3 platform.[60] Free access to the latest video game titles was provided on all gaming platforms as part of the tour as well.

Because this target market included very heavy users of social media, AMP Energy launched a Facebook fan page to give competitors in the tour a way to rally their friends and solicit their votes. Canadians use Facebook more than almost any other country. In this case,

the AYG Facebook page became an anchor point for students to connect on campus events and voting. The finale, held at Toronto's Yonge and Dundas Square, was streamed to thousands of fans via the world's first live Facebook feed, helping to create an emotional connection to the brand.

The tour was a success. AYG attracted 15 200 new Facebook fans, who cast 61 000 votes. The sampling goal was exceeded, with a total of 151 398 cans distributed,[61] increasing brand preference, encouraging future purchase, and extending the product life cycle for AMP Energy.

The Amp Your Game tour featured live rock band competitions on campuses across Canada.

toilet brushes hanging around in their bathrooms.[59] Although the household cleaning and cosmetic markets are both well established and mature, marketers working in these product categories saw trends early and moved to create new products that offer value for consumers.

Development of New Products Despite market saturation, firms continually introduce new products with improved features or find new uses for existing products because they need constant innovation and product proliferation to defend market share during intense competition. Firms such as 3M, P&G, and HP, for instance, continuously introduce new products. Innovations by such firms ensure that they are able to retain or grow their respective market shares.

Just a few years ago, baby wipes accounted for most of the sales of personal wipes. Firms have seen the opportunity to enter new markets, so products have proliferated.

Sometimes new products are introduced by less-than-famous companies. Even in a product category as old as food, entrepreneurs such as Rachna and Mona Prasad keep coming up with new innovations, as we discuss in Entrepreneurial Marketing 8.1. And KFC was able to build on its expertise with an existing product line when it developed Kentucky Grilled Chicken, an innovative product for a mature market.

Decline Stage

Firms with products in the decline stage either position themselves for a niche segment of diehard consumers or those with special needs, or they completely exit the market. The few laggards who have not yet tried the product or service enter the market at this stage. Take vinyl long-playing records (LPs) for example. In an age of CDs and Internet-downloaded music in MP3 and other formats, it may seem surprising that vinyl records are still made and sold. Although the sales of vinyl LPs have been declining in the past 15 years, about 2 million are sold in the United States each year. In Canada, vinyl sales declined from $913,000 in 2000 to $608,000 three years later compared with CD sales that same year of $686,976,000.[62] Still, diehard music lovers prefer the unique sound of a vinyl record to the digital sound of CDs and music in other formats. Because the grooves in vinyl records create sound waves that are similar to those of a live performance, and therefore provide a more authentic sound, nightclub DJs, discerning music listeners, and collectors prefer them. Even some younger listeners have been buying vinyl records, influenced perhaps by their parents' collections, the sound, or simply the uniqueness of an LP. In Edmonton, independent and high-profile bands alike are competing for limited record-pressing resources, a sign that vinyl is in vogue again.[63] The nostalgia factor associated with the old albums has given new life to the older medium.

Aiding this continued demand is the fact that there are simply too many albums of music from the predigital era that are available only on vinyl. It may take many years, maybe even decades, for all the music from earlier generations to be digitized. Many collectors are attracted to old albums for their history, as evidenced by the recent sale of a one-of-a-kind Velvet Underground recording for US$25,200.[64]

KFC used its expertise in chicken preparation to introduce Kentucky Grilled Chicken to stimulate sales in a mature market.

The Shape of the Product Life Cycle Curve

In theory, the product life cycle curve is assumed to be bell-shaped with regard to sales and profits. In reality, however, each product or service has its own individual shape; some move more rapidly through their product life cycles than others, depending on how different the product or service is from products currently in the market and how valuable it is to the consumer. New products and services that consumers accept very quickly have higher consumer adoption rates very early in their product life cycles and move faster across the various stages.

For example, DVD players and DVDs moved much faster than VCRs across the life cycle curve and have already reached the maturity stage, likely because consumers, who already owned VCRs, were accustomed to recording TV shows and playing prerecorded movies and programs. It also was easy to switch VCR customers to DVD technology because DVDs were more durable and had better resolution than videotapes. Finally, prices for DVDs and DVD players dropped more quickly and drastically than did VCR prices, which made the new technology a better value.

Lastly, as shown in Exhibit 8.10, the type of product affects variations in the shape of the product life cycle curve. When first introduced, microwaves were considered high-learning products and spent much longer in the introduction stage than subsequent low-learning products such as microwave popcorn. Fads move

Entrepreneurial Marketing 8.1

Gourmantra: Spice Business Heats Up

Rachna Prasad invited all her friends to a housewarming party, promising them a great home-cooked Indian meal. But she wasn't sure she could actually pull it off, so she asked her mother for help. Her mother didn't have time to cook but did come up with a novel solution. She packaged up all the necessary spices for the meal in just the right proportions and gave her daughter detailed preparation instructions. Rachna's friends raved about the meal. When asked for her secret, she gave them the leftover spice blends and cooking instructions from her mother.

Friends regularly requested these spice blends after that, leaving Rachna wondering if a business opportunity could be built around authentic home-cooked Indian meals that required minimal preparation time. To test the market, Rachna, her mother Rekha, and her sister Mona, a part-time student in Wilfrid Laurier University's MBA program, booked a booth at the Markham Fair in Ontario. When their product sold out within hours, they started their company, Rasika.

While still at Laurier, Mona entered the Launch-Pad $50K Venture Creation Competition, hoping to win enough money to buy a commercial grade spice grinder that would allow them to grow the business. She won third place against 400 other competitors. Buoyed by this success, they rebranded the company, changing its name from Rasika to Gourmantra, and hired a graphic designer to create professional packaging. The prepackaged spice blends, designed to make the cooking process simple, are made with the highest grade of spices and are free of oils, preservatives, artificial colours, and MSG. All consumers need to do is add chicken, lamb, beef, shrimp, chickpeas, or vegetables. Four meal flavour kits are currently available: Chana Masala, Korma, Tandoori, and Butter Chicken.

Rachna and Mona introduced Gourmantra to consumers through sampling programs and fairs in southern Ontario, positioning the company to enter the Canadian market via retailers such as Safeway, Sobeys, Loebs, Longos, Metro, Walmart, and other grocery chains. They have since expanded distribution across 18 U.S. states. This new line of at-home meal kits is now spicing up the Indian food category by taking the guesswork out of preparing authentic dishes.

Gourmantra's prepackaged spice blends offer convenience to consumers, taking the guesswork out of Indian cooking.

through the stages very quickly while fashion products tend to be cyclical in nature. For example, wide ties for men and suit lapels may be out of style today but may well become fashionable again in the future.

Strategies Based on Product Life Cycle: Some Caveats

Although the product life cycle concept provides a starting point for managers to think about the strategy they want to implement during each stage of the life cycle of a product, this tool must be used with care. The most challenging part of applying the product life cycle concept is that managers do not know exactly what shape each product's life cycle will take, so there is no way to know precisely what stage a product is in. If, for example, a product experiences several seasons of declining sales, a manager may decide that it has moved from the growth stage to the decline stage and stop promoting the product. As a result, of course, sales decline further.

EXHIBIT 8.10 | Variations on the Product Life Cycle Curve

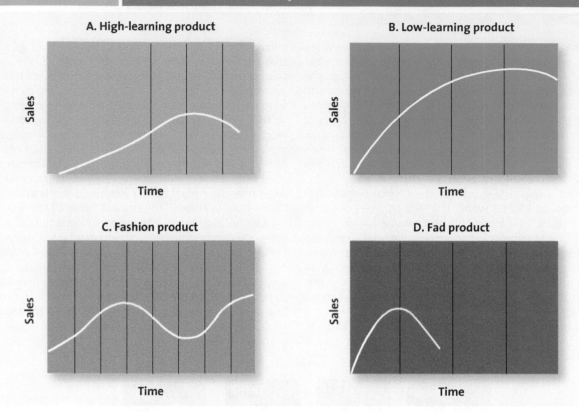

The manager then believes he or she made the right decision because the product continues to follow a predetermined life cycle. But what if the original sales decline was due to a poor strategy or increased competition—issues that could have been addressed with positive marketing support? In this case, the product life cycle decision became a self-fulfilling prophecy, and a growth product was doomed to an unnecessary decline.[65]

Fortunately, new research, based on the history of dozens of consumer products, suggests that the product life cycle concept is indeed a valid idea, and new analytical tools now provide "rules" for detecting the key turning points in the cycle.[66] In the pharmaceutical industry, where breakthrough innovations are few and far between, firms use the product life cycle to identify the consumer promotions needed at each stage to get the most out of their existing brands.[67]

Learning Objectives Review

 Identify the reasons firms innovate

Firms need to innovate to respond to changing customer needs, prevent decline in sales, avoid market saturation, diversify their risk, and respond to short product life cycles. New products and services keep current customers coming back for more and induce new customers into the market. Risky, new-to-the-world products have tremendous potential because they are the first in the market to offer something that has never before been available.

 Describe the diffusion of innovation theory and how managers can use it to make product line decisions

The diffusion of innovation theory can help firms predict which types of customers will buy their products or services immediately upon introduction, as well as later as the products/services gain more acceptance in the market. The firms can then develop marketing strategies to encourage acceptance among each customer group. Diffusion of innovation also can help predict sales.

LO3 **Explain the stages involved in developing new products and services**

When firms develop new products, they go through several steps. First, they generate ideas for the product or service by using several alternative techniques, such as internal research and development, licensing, brainstorming, tracking competitors' products or services, or working with customers. Second, firms test their concepts by either describing the idea of the new product or service to potential customers or showing them images of what the product would look like. Third, the design process entails determining what the product or service will actually include and provide; fourth, firms test-market their designs. Fifth, if everything goes well in the test market, the product is launched. Sixth, firms must evaluate the new product or service to determine its success.

LO4 **Describe the product life cycle and summarize how it is used to make product line decisions**

The product life cycle helps firms make marketing mix decisions on the basis of the product's stage in its life cycle. In the introduction stage, companies attempt to gain a strong foothold in the market quickly by appealing to innovators. During the growth stage, the objective is to establish the brand firmly. When the product reaches the maturity stage, firms compete intensely for market share, and many potential customers already own the product or use the service. Eventually, most products enter the decline phase, during which firms withdraw marketing support and eventually phase out the product. Knowing where a product or service is in its life cycle helps managers determine its specific strategy at any given point in time.

Key Terms

- alpha testing, 269
- beta testing, 269
- concept testing, 268
- concepts, 268
- decline stage, 275
- diffusion of innovation, 261
- early adopters, 262
- early majority, 262
- first movers, 260

- growth stage, 274
- innovation, 256
- innovators, 261
- introduction stage, 274
- laggards, 262
- late majority, 262
- lead users, 267
- maturity stage, 275
- pioneers, 259

- premarket test, 270
- product, 255
- product development (product design), 269
- product life cycle, 273
- prototype, 269
- reverse engineering, 266
- test marketing, 271

Concept Review

1. Explain how new product or service innovations add value to the firm.

2. Sketch and describe the diffusion of innovation curve. How can marketers use the information provided by this curve to make marketing strategies and decisions?

3. Identify and discuss the factors that influence the adoption of new products.

4. List the steps in the new product development process. Describe some of the sources companies use to generate ideas for new products at the beginning of this process.

5. Why might a company need to exercise caution during the test marketing stage of the new development process?

6. What other factors besides the product itself does a company need to finalize during the product launch stage?

7. Do all products go through each and every stage of this process? Explain your answer.

8. What is the product life cycle (PLC)? Describe the characteristics of each stage of the PLC in terms of sales, profits, typical consumers, competition, and four Ps strategies.

9. Describe some of the strategies companies can use to extend the life of a mature product.

10. Explain why the product life cycle is not a fail-proof tool in managing products.

Marketing Applications

1. Some people think that a product should be considered "new" only if it is completely new to the market and has never existed before. Describe or give examples of other types of new products.

2. RIM has introduced the PlayBook featuring a touchscreen. How quickly do you think this product will diffuse among the Canadian population? Describe the types of people that you expect will be in each of the diffusion of innovation categories.

3. Are there any advantages for companies that are the first to introduce products that create new markets? Justify your answer. If you see advantages, explain why some new products fail.

4. Identify and describe the ways that companies generate new product ideas. Which of these ways involve the customer? How can firms assess the value of the ideas that customers generate?

5. Describe an example of a new product or service that is targeted at the student market. Using the concept testing discussion in this chapter, describe how you would conduct a concept test for this product or service.

6. A number of portable MP3 players are currently available in the market. How might the design and value provided by MP3 players make this product more appealing to consumers than, say, portable CD players?

7. Mazda is about to introduce a new model and is currently in the market testing phase of the new product development process. Describe two ways that Mazda might conduct initial market testing prior to launching this new model.

8. What shampoo do you use? What stage of the product life cycle is it in? Is the shampoo manufacturer's marketing strategy—its four Ps—consistent with the product's stage in its life cycle? Explain.

9. In what stage of the product life cycle is a new model of a Palm Pre? Is Palm's marketing strategy—its four Ps—consistent with the product's stage in its life cycle? How is it different from that of the shampoo in the previous question? Explain.

10. You have recently been hired by a cosmetics company for its product development group. The firm's brand is a top-selling, high-end line of cosmetics. The head of the development team has just presented research that shows that tween girls, aged 11 to 15, are very interested in cosmetics and have money to spend on them. The decision is made to create a line of tween cosmetics based on the existing adult line. As the product moves through development you begin to notice that the team seems to lean toward a very edgy and sexual theme for the line, including naming the various lines "Envy," "Desire," "Prowess," and "Fatal Attraction." You begin to wonder if this concept is too much for girls in the targeted age group. Explain your thoughts.

Net Savvy

1. Go to the *Canadian Living* Best New Products Awards website (www.canadianliving.com/life/best_new_product_awards/) and search for an interesting new product. Is this an innovative, new-to-the-world product? Discuss the extent to which the new product has the properties that would be important for new product design and development.

2. The automotive industry is constantly adding new and different products to cars and trucks. Conduct an Internet or library database search for innovative new automotive technologies. Choose products that fit each stage of the product life cycle, and justify your choices.

Chapter Case Study

APPLE'S "iPRODUCTS": THE GREAT CONSUMER HOPE[68]

Apple manufactures and sells computer, music, and phone hardware, along with related software. Since its incorporation in 1977[69] under the name Apple Computer Incorporated, Apple has introduced products that challenge conventional approaches in the electronics industry. It pioneered modular design with the Apple II, engineered the initial graphical interfaces with the Macintosh, and offered the PowerBook as the first laptop to include a built-in track pad.[70] But the road to marketing success is long and requires research, planning, product alterations, and creative contemplations. These requirements make it all the more rare to witness the success of Apple's newest generation of products: the iPod, iPhone, and iPad.

The iPod

In 2001, Apple changed how consumers listen to music when it entered the portable music player market. Apple founder Steve Jobs saw the iPod designed, built, and placed on shelves in less than a year. It quickly became the cool product of choice for listening to and trading the latest sounds and has expanded to various models that music enthusiasts have snapped up. Furthermore, its introduction and subsequent acceptance has spawned an entire industry composed of companies that market compatible accessories.

The iPod was the first portable music player with the capability to download and store thousands of songs digitally. Its sales have reached more than 4 million per year. The concept began in response to consumer wants and in an environment that was ready for a product that would change the tide in the practice of pirating digital forms of music. Jobs saw the need for a good quality player that would allow its users to legally download and customize their music and to trade songs. In less than three years, his invention had already been termed "a cultural phenomenon" by *Brandweek* magazine.

Apple's road to success was not without hurdles. Jobs had to persuade the major music labels to allow their artists' songs to be downloaded for 99 cents each, or about $9.99 per album. After being burned by sites such as Roxio's Napster, which allowed peer-to-peer downloading for free, the music industry was hesitant to open its doors to such a proposal. Jobs sold the idea to the recording industry by making sure it would get its cut and relying on his credibility as a well-known name in computers and the head of Pixar Animation Studios. iPod owners would purchase songs via Apple's iTunes Music Store software, accessed through the iMac. The concept represented a cultural change for how people would access, purchase, and listen to music. The support of the industry soon became overwhelming; iTunes now offers more than 1 million tracks, representing five major music labels and 600 independents.

Being first in the market with a very desirable product meant Apple was able to command upward of $400 for the 40 GB (10 000 songs stored) iPod model. More than 1000 accessories have been rolled out, including car adapters, custom carrying cases, and home speakers.

When other companies realized the power of the iPod, they began cobranding with Apple so that they could get a piece of the action. HP, Bose, Volkswagen of America, and BMW—which built adapters into some of its cars' stereo systems—are just a few examples. Other smaller companies marketed iPod accessories, allowing Apple to extend the iPod's reach even further in the retail market.

The iPod's most distinguishing feature was the white cord that connects the player to its earbuds; this cord identifies iPod users as they go about their daily business, whether that means walking across campus, dancing down the sidewalk, or driving in their BMWs. Anyone can spot a

Anyone can spot a member of the iPod "club."

member of the iPod "club." The introductory multimedia advertising campaign therefore focused on a simple, silhouetted dancing figure with a highlighted iPod and earphones.

Since its introduction, Apple has sold more than 100 million iPods, making it the market leader with a 74 percent market share in the MP3 arena.[71] According to most consumers and technology experts, the success of the iPod resulted from its incredible ease of use. By combining a music store, software, and portable player into one simple system, Apple eliminated the problems consumers faced with other music players and thus created value by simplifying the digital music experience.

The iPhone

If the iPod changed how people listened to music, then the iPhone changed how they bought and used cellphones. When Apple decided to develop the iPhone, it made two important decisions. First, it would redesign the buying process for cellphones. Second, Apple would introduce new iPod features unique to the iPhone. But first it had to overcome significant barriers.

Although Apple dominated the dedicated MP3 player market, more and more phone manufacturers were adding music playback to their handsets. Primary phone manufacturers, such as Nokia and Motorola, already had existing relationships with cellular carriers, so they achieved a distinct advantage in the market, where cellular carriers dominated the distribution market for handsets. (Only 0.05 percent of all cellphones were sold by noncarriers.)[72] To address this problem, Apple partnered with Cingular, now AT&T. But it could not negotiate price support, which meant that consumers would have to pay the entire $699 list price.

To improve the cellphone purchasing process, Apple relied on simplification to make the ordeal as painless as possible. Customers who disliked shopping for phones could buy online and register through iTunes. Those who wanted to be among the first to get their hands on an iPhone could turn to AT&T sales locations and Apple stores, which provided no-risk trials. Apple even took control of the customer service and troubleshooting functions for the iPhone to ensure it determined all aspects of the user experience.

Then, to differentiate the iPhone from anything else available on the market, Apple developed unique features that were unavailable to iPod owners. In creating special value for technologically savvy, forward-thinking consumers, Apple designed the iPhone with a touchscreen, wireless capabilities, and a much larger viewing screen. By late 2007, Apple added these features to its iPod Touch.

Despite the high purchase price of the iPhone and the widespread tendency for consumers to get locked into long-term contracts with their existing cellular carriers, on the first day the iPhone was available, consumers lined up in the streets in hopes of having an opportunity to purchase it. In 2007, *Time* named the iPhone the "Invention of the Year."[73]

The iPad

With the introduction of the iPad in 2010, Jobs appeared set to define a new category of wireless device, bringing to the market a product to bridge the gap between smartphones and netbooks. Billed by some as the Kindle-killer, the iPad offers consumers utility in a number of areas: reading (books, magazines, newspapers), gaming, networking, browsing, and watching videos. Although it wasn't primarily designed as an e-reader, the iPad was greeted as a potential lifesaver of the publishing industry. Five of North America's largest trade book publishers—Penguin, HarperCollins, Simon & Schuster, Macmillan, and Hachette—were enlisted as early suppliers of Apple's iBook store.[74] Enthusiasm for the iPad by publishers stems at least partly from the hope that it will give them more influence. Unlike the deal struck with Amazon, which has them selling book titles for the Kindle wholesale, publishers are trying to negotiate a deal to retain ownership of titles and license Apple to distribute them on a commission basis.

Newspaper publishers quickly got on board. *The New York Times* unveiled a new iPad app and created a new Reader Applications division, which will focus on the development of a digital reader experience similar to a print platform.[75] Shortly after, *The Globe and Mail* introduced its Globe2Go platform to allow subscribers to receive the print edition of the newspaper on the mobile reader of their choice.

Although the iPad was initially met with skepticism on the part of some analysts who wrote that the tablet market had never really taken off, Apple sold 300 000 units on the first day of sales,[76] 1 million units in its first 28 days (less than half the 74 days it took for the iPhone to reach the same milestone[77]), and 2 million units in less than 60 days.[78] Moreover, with each new Apple "iProduct," the price point has successfully been raised, with the iPad priced at $879.

The iFuture

As CEO, Jobs has a reputation in the marketplace for his creative genius and for personally seeing new products successfully from the initial idea to the product launch. He has been credited with an uncanny ability to spot the next revolutionary innovation that will change the landscape of the marketplace. That's a tough reputation to maintain. And yet, only four months after the introduction of the iPad, Apple surpassed Microsoft as the largest technology company in the world based on market capitalization.[79] Having reinvented Apple as a provider of must-have tech gadgets, can Jobs maintain the company's explosive growth as a digital media giant? Will Apple morph into a small electronics marketer? Will it take a different direction in the not-so-distant future? The answer depends on so many factors that it defies speculation. For the time being, Apple will enjoy its recent successes and prepare for the next big thing.

The Globe and Mail *introduced Globe2Go to allow subscribers to receive the print edition of the newspaper on e-readers such as the iPad.*

Questions

1. One critical factor that affects the success of a product innovation is the ability to offer a differentiated product that delivers unique and superior value to customers. Discuss the extent to which Apple successfully accomplished this with the iPhone and the iPad.

2. How would you classify the iPod, iPhone, and iPad today in terms of each product's stage in the product life cycle? Why?

3. Provide a description of what you think each type of adopter would be for an iPad. Do you think we are seeing late majority adopters or laggards yet?

4. Do you think the iPad will continue to be a success? What factors support your position?

5. Apple has introduced several winning products over the last few years—iPod, iPhone, and iPad—in markets where the company was a newcomer that successfully challenged market leaders. How would you describe Apple's product innovation strategy in the mobile devices market? Based on your analysis, what do you think Apple's next winning innovation might be? What are some of the barriers it may need to consider?

Practise and learn online with Connect. Connect allows you to practise important concepts at your own pace and on your own schedule, with 24/7 online access to an eBook, practice quizzes, interactivities, videos, study tools, additional resources, and more.

CHAPTER 9

Product, Branding,
and Packaging Decisions

Since its debut in 1957, Dove has grown to become a global brand sold in more than 80 countries. Launched as a beauty bar that wouldn't dry skin the way soap did, Dove is now the world's top cleansing brand.[1] Dove products can be found in one of every four homes in Canada.[2]

At the heart of the brand is the original Dove beauty bar. Containing one-quarter moisturizing cream, Dove's brand promise is to gently cleanse skin while moisturizing. This simple benefit positioning has been successfully leveraged in multiple personal-care categories. After more than four decades of building a strong brand, Unilever extended the brand into new product lines, including moisturizing body wash, antiperspirant and deodorant, face care, shampoos and conditioners, and styling aids.

Some brand extensions fail because there isn't a strong fit with the core brand, for example, Ben-Gay Aspirin, Vaseline Aftershave, or 7-Up lip balm. New Dove products fit well with the core brand. And, Unilever had organizational competencies in the new product categories. For instance, it already had expertise in face care (Ponds), hair care (Thermasilk, Salon Selectives, Finesse), and antiperspirants (Degree).

Consumer insights were used to drive brand extension ideas. The deodorant extension was based on consumer research that identified a need for a mild moisturizing product that would not irritate razor burn from shaving underarms. Brand consistency was achieved across new products because all extensions supported the moisturization functional attribute.

This brand consistency has helped develop solid brand associations. The Dove brand image has always been associated with moisture and mildness. Feminine imagery is often used to convey the properties of the brand. The logo, an abstract image of a dove, connotes universal feminine attributes such as peace,

Learning Objectives

After studying this chapter, you should be able to

LO1 List the components of a product

LO2 Identify the types of consumer products

LO3 Explain the difference between a product mix's breadth and a product line's depth

LO4 Identify the advantages that brands provide firms and consumers

LO5 Summarize the components of brand equity

LO6 Describe the types of branding strategies used by firms

LO7 State how a product's packaging and label contribute to a firm's overall strategy

mildness, and softness. The image is further exemplified in packaging where curved bottle shapes and lines are used. Even the core product, the Dove beauty soap bar, is curved so that it contours to the shape of a woman's body.

The simple Dove value proposition has remained unchanged for more than 50 years: its brand promise of mildness and moisturization is still relevant and compelling to consumers. Dove built a strong brand by continually delivering on its brand promise, making it a trusted brand not only with consumers, but also with professionals—Dove is the number one dermatologist-recommended cleansing bar.

In 2010, Dove extended the brand to include a line of men's products, Men+Care. Although the packaging is decidedly masculine, using dark colours and angular lines, the value proposition remains unchanged, focusing on moisturizing qualities.

By staying true to the brand promise, Dove not only created a valued product, but also built strong brand equity, high customer awareness, and intense loyalty. .::

This chapter is the second that deals with the first P in the marketing mix: product. In the last chapter, you learned that developing new products is key to a firm's marketing mix and central to the creation of value for consumers. Continuing our discussion, we now explore how companies add value to their offerings by developing an assortment of products and product lines and by creating strong brands.

As shown in our chapter roadmap, this chapter begins with a discussion of the complexity and types of products. Next we examine how firms adjust their product

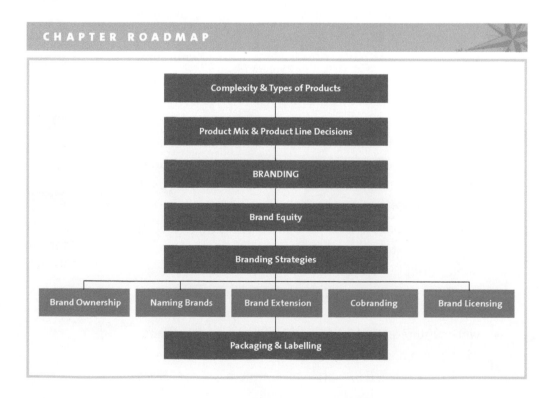

CHAPTER ROADMAP

Complexity & Types of Products

Product Mix & Product Line Decisions

BRANDING

Brand Equity

Branding Strategies

Brand Ownership | Naming Brands | Brand Extension | Cobranding | Brand Licensing

Packaging & Labelling

lines to meet and respond to changing market conditions. Then we turn our attention to branding: Why are brands valuable to the firm, and what are the different branding strategies firms use? We also never want to underestimate the value of a product's packaging and labelling in product strategies and promotion. Packaging and labelling must send out a strong message from the shelf: Buy me! The final section of this chapter examines packaging and labelling issues.

Complexity of Products and Types of Products

L01

Complexity of Products

There is more to a product than its physical characteristics or its basic service function. Marketers involved with the development, design, and sale of products think of them in an interrelated fashion as depicted in Exhibit 9.1. At the centre is the **core customer value**, which defines the basic problem-solving benefits that consumers are seeking. When Mars manufactures M&M's, Snickers, and other confectionary products and when Trek designs its bicycles, this is their core question: What are customers looking for? With Mars, is it a sweet, great-tasting snack, or is it an energy boost? With Trek, is the bike being used for basic green transportation (a cruiser), or is it for speed and excitement (a road, hybrid, or mountain bike)?

Marketers convert core customer value into an *actual product*. Attributes such as the brand name, features/design, quality level, and packaging are considered, though the importance of these attributes varies depending on the product. The Trek Madone 6 Series features a carbon frame that is light, stiff, and comfortable; an advanced shifting system; and other high-tech features. Not only is it beautiful to look at, but customers can also choose from three different fits: pro, performance, and touring.

The **associated services** in Exhibit 9.1, also referred to as the **augmented product**, include the nonphysical aspects of the product, such as product warranties, financing, product support, and after-sale service. The amount of associated services varies depending on the product. The associated services for a package of M&M's may include only a customer complaint line, which means they are relatively less important than the associated services for a Trek bicycle. The frame of the Madone 6 Series bicycle is guaranteed for the lifetime of the original owner. Trek sells its bikes only

core customer value
The basic problem-solving benefits that consumers are seeking.

associated services (or augmented product)
The nonphysical attributes of the product, including product warranties, financing, product support, and after-sale service.

EXHIBIT 9.1	Product Complexity

Actual Product
Brand Name   Packaging
Quality Level   Features/Design

Core
Customer
Value

Associated Services

Financing
Product Warranty
Product Support

to shops that have the expertise to properly service them. Every possible consumer question is answered on Trek's comprehensive website. Trek even has a financing program that allows customers to purchase a new bike on credit.

When developing or changing a product, marketers start with the core customer value to determine what their potential customers are seeking. Then they make the actual physical product and add associated services to round out the offering.

Types of Products

Marketers consider the types of products they are designing and selling because it impacts how they promote, price, and distribute their products. There are two primary categories of products and services based on who is buying them: consumers or businesses (Chapter 6 discusses products for businesses).

consumer products
Products and services used by people for their personal use.

Consumer products are products and services used by people for their personal use. Marketers further classify these products by the way they are used and purchased.

L02

Specialty Products/Services   Specialty products/services are products or services toward which customers show such a strong preference that they will expend considerable effort to search for the best suppliers. Road bike enthusiasts, like those interested in the Trek Madone 6 Series, will devote lots of time and effort to selecting just the right bike. Other examples might include luxury cars, legal or medical professionals, or designer apparel.

Shopping Products/Services   Shopping products/services are products or services, such as furniture, apparel, fragrances, appliances, and travel alternatives, for which consumers will spend a fair amount of time comparing alternatives. When people need new sneakers, for instance, they will go from store to store shopping—trying shoes on, comparing alternatives, and chatting with salespeople.

Convenience Products/Services   Convenience products/services are those products or services for which the consumer is not willing to spend any effort to evaluate prior to purchase. They are frequently purchased commodity items, usually purchased with very little thought, such as common beverages, bread, or soap.

Unsought Products/Services   Unsought products/services are products consumers either do not normally think of buying or do not know about. Because of their very nature, these products require lots of marketing effort and various forms of promotion. When new-to-the-world products, such as GPS systems, are first introduced, they often represent unsought products. Do you have cold hands and don't know what to do about it? You must not have heard yet of HeatMax HotHands Hand Warmers, air-activated packets that provide warmth for up to 10 hours.

product mix
The complete set of all products offered by a firm.

product lines
Groups of associated items, such as those that consumers use together or think of as part of a group of similar products.

product category
An assortment of items that the customer sees as reasonable substitutes for one another.

Product Mix and Product Line Decisions

The complete set of all products offered by a firm is called its **product mix**. Colgate-Palmolive's product mix is shown in Exhibit 9.2. The product mix typically consists of various **product lines**, which are groups of associated items, such as items that consumers use together or think of as part of a group of similar products. Colgate-Palmolive's product lines include oral care, personal care, household care, fabric care, and pet nutrition.

Within each product line, there are often multiple product categories. A **product category** is an assortment of items that the customer sees as reasonable substitutes for one another. For example, in the oral care product line, Colgate-Palmolive offers several categories with a variety of offerings to choose from in each: toothpaste,

EXHIBIT 9.2	Colgate-Palmolive Product Mix

	Product Lines **product line breadth** ⟶				
	Oral Care	**Personal Care**	**Household Care**	**Fabric Care**	**Pet Nutrition**
Product Categories ↑ product line depth ↓	*Toothpaste* (Colgate Total) *Toothbrush* (Colgate Plus) *Kids' products* (Colgate Barbie Bubble Fruit toothpaste) *Whitening products* (Colgate Simply White) *Floss* (Colgate Total Dental Floss) *Oral first aid* (Colgate Orabase)	*Deodorants* (Speed Stick) *Bar soap* (Irish Spring) *Body wash* (Soft Soap) *Hand wash* (Soft Soap) *Men's toiletries* (Skin Bracer Aftershave)	*Dishwashing liquid* (Palmolive) *Automatic dishwashing liquid* (Palmolive) *Household cleaners* (Ajax) *Dish wipes* (Palmolive)	*Laundry detergents* (Fab) *Fabric softener* (Fleecy)	Hill's Pet Nutrition, Inc.–subsidiary *Dog food* (Science Diet) *Cat food* (Science Diet)

Source: www.colgate.com.

whitening products, toothbrushes, kid's oral-care products, floss, and oral first aid. Each category within a product line may use the same or different **brands**, which are the names, terms, designs, symbols, or any other features that identify one seller's good or service as distinct from those of other sellers.[3] For instance, Colgate-Palmolive offers several brands of toothbrushes (e.g., 360°, Motion Whitening, Massager, Navigator).

The product mix reflects the breadth and depth of a company's product lines. A firm's **product mix breadth** (sometimes also referred to as variety) represents the number of product lines offered by the firm; Colgate-Palmolive has five, as indicated by the five columns in Exhibit 9.2. **Product line depth**, in contrast, is the number of products within a product line. Within Colgate-Palmolive's oral-care line, for example, it offers toothpaste, toothbrushes, kids' products, and so forth. Its pet nutrition product line, however, comprises fewer offerings and therefore has less depth.

Within each product category are a number of individual items called **stock keeping units (SKUs)**, which are the smallest unit available for inventory control. For instance, within the toothpaste category, Colgate-Palmolive offers 49 Colgate SKUs that represent various sizes, flavours, and configurations of Colgate Herbal White, Colgate Total, and Colgate Fresh Confidence.[4] Each individual product is a unique SKU. The 100-millilitre size of Colgate Total Clean Mint is one SKU, while the 100-millilitre package of Colgate Total Whitening Paste is a second SKU. The same size package of Colgate Total Advanced Fresh Gel represents a third SKU. The category depth is the number of SKUs within a category. Each SKU has its own unique product code (UPC) code as well.

The decision to expand or contract product lines and categories depends on several industry-, consumer-, and firm-level factors. Among the industry factors, firms expand their product lines (breadth) when it is relatively easy to enter a specific market (entry barriers are low) and/or when there is a substantial market opportunity.[5] When firms add new lines to their product mix, they often earn significant sales and profits, as was the case with Doritos' Cool Ranch product line, Ford's Explorer line, and Chrysler's minivans.[6]

brand
The name, term, design, symbol, or any other features that identify one seller's good or service as distinct from those of other sellers.

 L03

product mix breadth
The number of product lines, or variety, offered by the firm.

product line depth
The number of products within a product line.

stock keeping units (SKUs)
Individual items within each product category; the smallest unit available for inventory control.

Starbucks increased its product mix breadth by adding Natural Fusions flavoured coffee. It was a natural extension when it learned that more than 60 percent of its consumers enjoyed flavoured coffees.

However, adding unlimited numbers of new products can have adverse consequences. Too much variety in the product mix is often too costly to maintain, and too many brands may weaken the firm's brand reputation.[7] In the past several years, for example, Heinz has gone through a major restructuring, consolidating its global operations and increasing concentration on those products and markets that were doing well. In Europe, it reduced the number of different Heinz ketchup options (as indicated by the bottle designs available) from 24 to 12.[8]

Now let's look at why firms change their product mix's breadth, depth, or number of SKUs, as well as product line decisions for services.

Change Product Mix Breadth

Exhibit 9.3 offers a hypothetical example of a company with four product lines in its product mix. Firms may change their product mix breadth by either adding to or deleting entire product lines.

Increase Breadth   Firms often add new product lines to capture new or evolving markets, increase sales, and compete in new venues (e.g., addition of Product Line D in Exhibit 9.3) With the introduction of VIA Ready Brew, Starbucks changed the way people thought about instant coffee. The new line is expected to produce more than a billion dollars in sales.[9] And when the company learned that more than 60 percent of its consumers enjoyed flavoured coffee, it introduced Natural Fusions, a line of

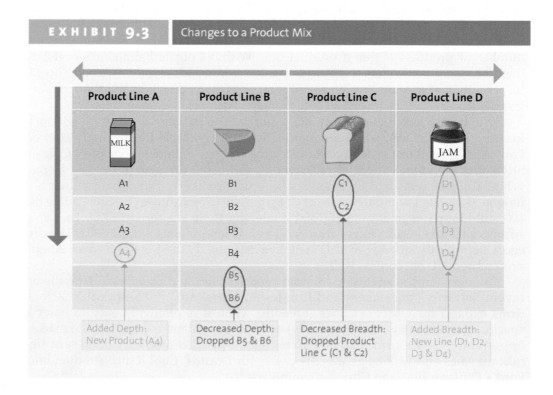

EXHIBIT 9.3	Changes to a Product Mix		
Product Line A	**Product Line B**	**Product Line C**	**Product Line D**
MILK			JAM
A1	B1	C1	D1
A2	B2	C2	D2
A3	B3		D3
A4	B4		D4
	B5		
	B6		
Added Depth: New Product (A4)	Decreased Depth: Dropped B5 & B6	Decreased Breadth: Dropped Product Line C (C1 & C2)	Added Breadth: New Line (D1, D2, D3 & D4)

premium coffee available for sale in grocery stores in vanilla, cinnamon, and caramel flavours. As part of Starbucks' business strategy, it was a natural way to grow its consumer products business.[10]

Decrease Breadth   Sometimes it is necessary to delete entire product lines to address changing market conditions or meet internal strategic priorities (e.g., deletion of Product Line C in Exhibit 9.3). A few years ago, SC Johnson sold off many products in its skin-care line, including its successful Aveeno brand, to Johnson & Johnson.[11] The firm no longer competes in the skin-care business; but, it remains a strong competitor in its original product lines, such as home cleaning (Pledge, Windex), air care (Glade), and home storage (Saran, Ziploc).[12]

Change Product Line Depth

As with product line breadth, firms occasionally either add to or delete from their product line depth (see Exhibit 9.3).

Increase Depth   Firms may add new products within a line to address changing consumer preferences or pre-empt competitors while boosting sales (e.g., addition of A4 in Exhibit 9.3). Levi Strauss & Co. introduced its Signature line of low-cost jeans to be sold through Walmart. Jeans in the Signature line are priced at only $21 to $23 a pair, almost half the price of the popular Levi's 505 and 501 brands (the "red tab" line) sold through department stores.[13] The firm's decision was an attempt to get a much-needed sales boost in the face of tough competition from the likes of Diesel and Parasuco and to reach new target markets by selling through other retailers. A firm may also add new products to its product line to serve new target segments. For instance, Seiko developed the Seiko LaSalle watch for a lower market segment that wants to wear a Seiko watch but cannot afford its luxury brand.

Decrease Depth   From time to time, it is necessary to delete product categories to realign resources (e.g., deletion of B5 and B6 in Exhibit 9.3). The decision to delete products is never taken lightly. Generally, substantial investments have been made to develop the brand and manufacture the products. Consumer goods firms, such as P&G and Unilever, make pruning decisions regularly to eliminate unprofitable items and refocus their marketing efforts on more profitable items. For example, when executives at consumer goods giant Unilever noted flat sales and declining profits, they recognized they were carrying a lot of excess baggage. The company took decisive action to divest itself of 400 core brands, such as Ragu pasta sauces and Sunlight laundry detergent, reducing its portfolio from 1600 brands. This move made Unilever more competitive with rivals such as P&G and freed up resources for future acquisitions, such as Ben & Jerry's.[14]

Change Number of SKUs

A very common and ongoing activity for many firms is the addition or deletion of SKUs in existing categories to stimulate sales or react to consumer demand. Fashion manufacturers and their retailers, for instance, change their SKUs every season. Generally, these changes are minor, such as a different colour or fabric. Sometimes though, the change is more drastic, such as when jeans manufacturers lowered the waistline and flared the legs of their products.

Product Line Decisions for Services

Many of the strategies used to make product line decisions for physical products can also be applied to services. For instance, a service provider such as a bank typically offers different product lines for its business and retail (consumer) accounts; those product lines are further divided into categories based on the needs of different target markets.

On the retail side, banks offer savings and chequing accounts to individual consumers. The different types of accounts thus are equivalent to SKUs. The RBC Royal Bank is Canada's largest bank, as measured by assets, and serves more than 14 million personal, business, public sector, and institutional clients through offices in North America and 34 countries around the world.[15] It offers a variety of chequing account products to meet the needs of its different target markets. For example, the RBC VIP account has high monthly fees and offers an all-inclusive package covering multiple accounts, unlimited transactions, and a free premium Visa card. Students can take advantage of an RBC No Limit Banking for Students account with unlimited debits, a no-fee credit card, and moderate monthly fees. For customers who use fewer than 15 transactions per month, the RBC Day to Day Banking account offers very low monthly fees.[16]

Branding

A company lives or dies based on brand awareness. Consumers can't buy products that they don't know exist. Branding provides a way for a firm to differentiate its product offerings from those of its competitors and can be used to represent the name of a firm and its entire product mix (General Motors), one product line (Chevrolet), or a single item (Corvette). Both Snapple and Tropicana make and sell fruit drinks; yet, a consumer may choose one over the other because of the associations that the brands evoke. Brand names, logos, symbols, characters, slogans, jingles, and even distinctive packages constitute the various brand elements firms use,[17] which they usually choose to be easy for consumers to recognize and remember. For example, most consumers are aware of the Nike Swoosh logo and would recognize it even if the word *Nike* did not appear on the product or in an advertisement. Exhibit 9.4 summarizes these brand elements.

EXHIBIT 9.4	What Makes a Brand?
Brand Element	**Description**
Brand name	The spoken component of branding, it can either describe the product or service/product characteristics and/or be composed of words invented or derived from colloquial or contemporary language. Examples include Comfort Inn (suggests product characteristics), Apple (no association with the product), or Accenture (invented term).
URLs (uniform resource locators) or domain names	The location of pages on the Internet, which often substitutes for the firm's name, such as Yahoo! and Amazon.
Logos and symbols	Logos are visual branding elements that stand for corporate names or trademarks. Symbols are logos without words. Examples include the Nike Swoosh and the Mercedes star.
Characters	Brand symbols that could be human, animal, or animated. Examples include the Pillsbury Doughboy and the Jolly Green Giant.
Slogans	Short phrases used to describe the brand or persuade consumers about some characteristics of the brand. Examples include State Farm's "Like A Good Neighbour" and Tim Hortons "Always Fresh."
Jingles	Audio messages about the brand that are composed of words or distinctive music. Examples are Intel's four-note sound signature that accompanies the "Intel Inside" slogan.

Source: Adapted from Kevin Lane Keller, *Strategic Brand Management*, 2nd ed. (Upper Saddle River, NJ: Prentice Hall, 2003).

Value of Branding for the Customer and the Marketer

Brands add value to merchandise and services beyond physical and functional characteristics or the pure act of performing the service.[18] Let's examine some ways in which brands add value for both customers and the firm (see Exhibit 9.5).

LO4

When customers see an ad for Coca-Cola, they immediately make associations with familiar attributes, such as taste, to help them make quick decisions.

Brands Facilitate Purchasing Brands are often easily recognized by consumers and, because they signify a certain quality level and contain familiar attributes, brands help consumers make quick decisions.[19] Imagine how much time it would take to buy groceries if the brands on the shelves were unfamiliar! This would also be the case for purchases such as cars. When consumers see a brand such as Honda, they immediately know what it is, its level of quality and engineering, its relative status, how much it generally costs, and, most important, whether they like it and want to buy it. Brands enable customers to differentiate one firm or product from another. Without branding, how could we easily tell the difference between a Honda and a Toyota without looking very closely?

Brands Establish Loyalty Over time and with continued use, consumers learn to trust certain brands. They know, for instance, that Band-Aid® bandages always perform in the exact same way. Many customers become loyal to certain brands in much the same way that you or your friends likely have become loyal to your college or university. They wouldn't consider switching brands and, in some cases, feel a strong affinity to certain brands. For instance, Coca-Cola drinkers don't drink Pepsi, and wouldn't touch a Dr Pepper. As a result of this loyalty, these companies can maintain great depth in their product lines since their customers will buy other brands within their product mix.

Brands Protect from Competition and Price Competition Strong brands are somewhat protected from competition and price competition. Because such brands are more established in the market and have a more loyal customer base, neither competitive pressures on price nor retail-level competition is as threatening to the firm. For instance, Lacoste is known for its golf shirts. Although many similar brands are available and some retailers offer their own brands, Lacoste is perceived to be of superior quality and garners a certain status among its users; therefore, it can command a premium price.

Brands Reduce Marketing Costs Firms with well-known brands can spend relatively less on marketing costs than firms with little-known brands because the brand sells itself. People have become familiar with lululemon's white, stylized "A"

EXHIBIT 9.5 Value of Branding

- Brands Facilitate Purchasing
- Brands Establish Loyalty
- Brands Protect from Competition
- Brands Reduce Marketing Costs
- Brands Are Assets
- Brands Impact Market Value

Value of Branding

The fact that consumers are familiar with lululemon as a brand helps the company reduce marketing costs.

logo, so its advertisements don't need to explain who the company is or what it does. People just know.

Brands Are Assets   Brands are also assets that can be legally protected through trademarks and copyrights and thus constitute a unique ownership for the firm. Firms sometimes have to fight to keep their brands "pure." Rolex and other Swiss watch companies are ever watchful to ensure that the value of their brands is not diluted with counterfeit merchandise or sales through unauthorized dealers. Likewise, Tiffany & Co.'s iconic blue box is instantly recognizable and associated with high-quality items.

Brands Impact Market Value   Having well-known brands can have a direct impact on the company's bottom line. The value of a brand can be calculated by assessing the earning potential of the brand over the next 12 months;[20] see examples of Canada's most valuable brands in Exhibit 9.6.

L05 ## Brand Equity

To understand branding, we look at three areas: brand equity, brand ownership, and brand names, as illustrated in Exhibit 9.7. The value of a brand translates into **brand equity**, or the set of assets and liabilities linked to a brand that add to or subtract from the value provided by the product or service.[21] Coca-Cola ranks number one on the best global brands list with a value of $67 billion; McDonald's is sixth, with a value of just over $32 billion.[22] Like the physical possessions of a firm, brands are assets the firm can build, manage, and harness over time to increase its revenue, profitability, and overall value. Firms spend millions of dollars on promotion, advertising, and other marketing efforts throughout a brand's life cycle. These marketing expenditures, if done carefully, result in greater brand recognition, awareness, and consumer loyalty for the brand.

Tiffany & Co. works hard to protect its brand, including its famous blue box.

Ralph Lauren has mastered the art of building brand equity by defining its own version of value. The name Ralph Lauren, the ubiquitous polo player, and associated brands such as Purple Label, Black Label, Blue Label, Lauren, Polo Ralph Lauren, and others have engendered a loyal following throughout North America and the rest of the world. Ralph Lauren merchandise can command prices 50 to 100 percent higher than similar-quality merchandise from lesser known and appreciated designers and manufacturers. The brand, under the tight control of its parent company, has been licensed for tabletop, bed and bath, furniture, paints, broadloom, and gift items.[23] These licensed products are manufactured and distributed by firms other than Ralph Lauren, but the brand association earns them greater value and brand equity.

How do we know how "good" a brand is, or how much equity it has? Experts look at four

EXHIBIT 9.6	Canada's 10 Most Valuable Brands		
Rank	**Brand**	**Sector**	**2010 Brand Value (C$M)**
1	Thomson Reuters	Business Services	9,413
2	TD Canada Trust	Financial Services	6,668
3	RBC Financial Group	Financial Services	6,171
4	BlackBerry	Consumer Electronics	6,000
5	Shoppers Drug Mart	Retail	3,425
6	Tim Hortons	Restaurant	2,654
7	Bell	Telecom	2,452
8	Rogers	Telecom	2,276
9	Scotiabank	Financial Services	2,159
10	BMO Financial Group	Financial Services	1,972

Source: The Business Week/Interbrand Annual Ranking of the Best Canadian Brands 2010, www.interbrand.com/en/Interbrand-offices/Interbrand-Toronto/Best-Canadian-Brands-2010.aspx (accessed April 27, 2011).

aspects of a brand to determine its equity: brand awareness, perceived value, brand associations, and brand loyalty.

Brand Awareness   **Brand awareness** measures how many consumers in a market are familiar with the brand and what it stands for, and have an opinion about that brand. The more aware or familiar customers are with a brand, the easier their decision-making process will be. Familiarity matters most for products that are bought without much thought, such as soap or chewing gum. However, brand awareness is also important for infrequently purchased items or items the consumer has never purchased before. If the consumer recognizes the brand, it probably has attributes that make it valuable.[24] For those who have never purchased a Toyota, for instance, just being aware of the brand can help facilitate a purchase. Certain brands gain such predominance in a particular product market over time that they become synonymous with the product itself; that is, the brand name starts being used as the generic product category. Examples include Kleenex tissue, Clorox bleach, Xerox copiers, Band-Aid bandages, and Rollerblade inline skates. Companies must be vigilant in protecting their brand names, because if they are used so generically, over time, the brand itself can lose its trademark status. Thermos, trampoline, linoleum, and yo-yo are all examples of brands that lost their trademark status. Aspirin has become a generic brand in the United States; however, it remains a registered trademark in Canada.[25]

Marketers create brand awareness through repeated exposures of the various brand elements (brand name, logo, symbol, character, packaging, or slogan) in the firm's communications to consumers. Such communication media include

brand equity
The set of assets and liabilities linked to a brand that add to or subtract from the value provided by the product or service.

brand awareness
Measures how many consumers in a market are familiar with the brand and what it stands for; created through repeated exposures of the various brand elements (brand name, logo, symbol, character, packaging, or slogan) in the firm's communications to consumers.

EXHIBIT 9.7   Brand Overview

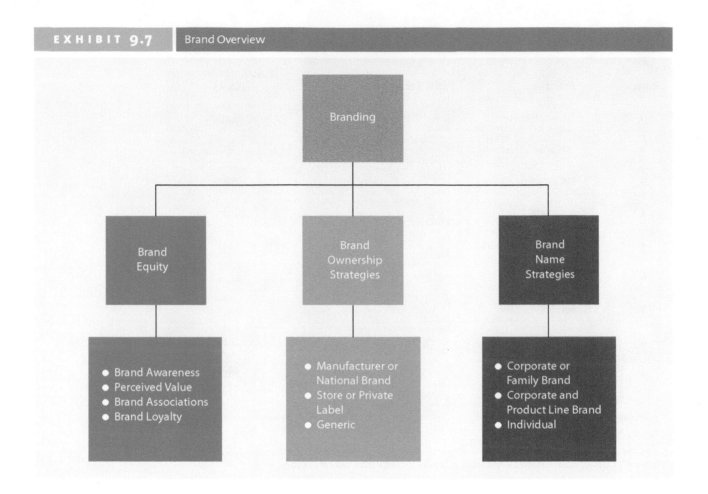

advertising and promotions, personal selling, sponsorship and event marketing, publicity, and public relations (see Chapters 14 and 15).[26] Because consumer awareness is one of the most important steps in creating a strong brand, firms are willing to spend tremendous amounts of money advertising the brand, including more than $3 million for just one 30-second spot on TV during the Super Bowl.

These brands have such predominance in their product market that the brand name is used as the generic product category.

Perceived Value   Brand awareness alone does not ensure a strong brand. Consumers could be aware of a brand but have a negative opinion of its value or the firm's reputation. **Perceived value**, therefore, is the relationship between a product or service's benefits and its cost. Customers usually determine the offering's value in relationship to that of its close competitors. If they feel an inexpensive brand is about the same quality as a premium brand, the perceived value of the cheaper choice is high. Many private-label brands are less expensive than brands developed by manufacturers. These brands, commonly found in supermarkets or drugstores, have seen a rise in popularity in recent years because of their high perceived value.

Good marketing raises customers' quality perceptions relative to price; thus, it increases perceived value. Many customers tend to associate higher prices with higher quality, but they also have become more informed and perceptive in recent years. Retailers such as Zellers and Giant Tiger specialize in providing great value. Certainly, merchandise at these stores is not always of the highest possible quality, and the apparel is not the most fashion-forward. But customers don't necessarily want to buy a wastebasket or paring knife that will last for 50 years and be suitable for display in a living room, nor do they need to show up at school looking like they came from a fashion-show runway. Instead, they want products to do what they were designed to do and be available at a reasonable price. First Choice Haircutters, a national haircutting chain, provides "Affordable, Professional Haircare"—usually at one-half to one-third salon prices. Its customers perceive the chain to be a great value because the haircut is better than good and the price is more than reasonable.

First Choice Haircutters, a national haircutting chain, provides its customers with great value because the haircut is better than good and the price is more than reasonable.

Brand Associations   **Brand associations** reflect the mental links that consumers make between a brand and its key product attributes, such as a logo, slogan, or famous personality. These brand associations often result from a firm's advertising and promotion efforts. For example, Walmart conveys its low prices with advertising that stresses price cuts and the slogan "Save Money, Live Better." Associations with specific attributes help create differentiation between the brand and its competitors, as when Volvo stresses that its cars are made with consumer safety in mind. Firms also attempt to create specific associations for their brands with positive consumer emotions, such as fun, friendship, good feelings, family gatherings, and parties. As mentioned in the chapter vignette, the Dove brand image has always been associated with moisture and mildness. Power of the Internet 9.1 illustrates some ways that Nutella has used the Internet to change brand associations and build strong relationships with customers.

Firms sometimes even develop a personality for their brands, as if the brand were human. **Brand personality** refers to a set of human characteristics associated with a brand,[27] which has symbolic or self-expressive meanings for consumers.[28] Brand personality elements include male, female, young, old, fun-loving, and conservative, as well as qualities such as fresh, smooth, round, clean, or floral.[29] McDonald's has created a fun-loving, youth-oriented brand personality with its golden arches, brightly lit and coloured restaurants, exciting and youthful packaging and advertising, and spokesperson and mascot Ronald McDonald, the clown.

Brand Loyalty   **Brand loyalty** occurs when a consumer buys the same brand's product or service repeatedly over time rather than buying from multiple suppliers within the same category.[30] Therefore, brand-loyal customers are an important source of value for firms. First, such consumers are often less sensitive to price. In return, firms

perceived value
The relationship between a product or service's benefits and its cost.

brand association
The mental links that consumers make between a brand and its key product attributes; can involve a logo, slogan, or famous personality.

brand personality
Refers to a set of human characteristics associated with a brand, which has symbolic or self-expressive meanings for consumers.

brand loyalty
Occurs when a consumer buys the same brand's product or service repeatedly over time rather than buying from multiple suppliers within the same category.

Power of the Internet 9.1

Branding on the Net

For marketers, the Internet is more than just the information highway. It can be the ultimate channel for branding a product. Marketers use the Internet to

- Create awareness and hype for new brands and marketing campaigns

- Teach consumers more about the company and its products

- Educate them as to which products best suit their needs

- Help customers decide which products to buy by giving them tools to help compare price, features, and quality

- Encourage trial

- Project a positive image of the brand to consumers

In short, the Internet can help build a strong, lasting brand impression in the minds of consumers. Ferrero Canada created a national campaign to reposition its Nutella hazelnut spread as a healthy breakfast choice and launched a website (www.nutella.ca) and the Better Breakfast Challenge. For each mom who signed up for the challenge, Nutella donated $1 to Breakfast for Learning, a nonprofit organization that supports child nutrition programs in Canada.[31]

Savvy marketers offer interactive websites that allow customers to play games, enter contests or take quizzes, chat, and share their experiences. These activities are provided not just for fun, but also to build consumer trust and develop positive associations with the brand. The Nutella site offers nutrition facts, a "Breakfast Builder" based on a child's age and gender, healthy living tips, an "Activity Challenge," recipes, a newsletter, and contests. Marketing research has shown that customers who have a very positive attitude toward a site and brand are more likely to shop at the site or purchase the brand.

The site was promoted by online banner ads directing users to Nutella.ca for free product samples. The company also sent out samples with major daily newspapers in hopes that readers would try the spread at breakfast while reading the paper.[32]

Try our
Breakfast Builder

The Better Breakfast Challenge and Nutella website helped reposition the hazelnut spread as a healthy breakfast option.

sometimes reward loyal consumers with loyalty or customer relationship management (CRM) programs, such as points that customers can redeem for extra discounts or free services, advance notice of sale items, and invitations to special events sponsored by the company. Second, the marketing costs of reaching loyal consumers are much lower because the firm does not have to spend money on advertising and promotion campaigns to attract these customers. Loyal consumers simply do not need persuasion or an extra push to buy the firm's brands. Third, a high level of brand loyalty insulates the firm from competition because, as we noted in Chapter 2, brand-loyal customers do not switch to competitors' brands, even when provided with a variety of incentives.

Firms can manage brand loyalty through a variety of CRM programs. They create associations and clubs to provide a community feeling among loyal customers,[33] such as Harley-Davidson's Harley Owners Group (H.O.G.), which the company formed in 1983 so Harley owners could meet with other owners in their communities. More than 1000 H.O.G. chapters worldwide host a total of almost 1 million members. Other firms, such as airlines, hotels, long-distance telephone providers, credit card companies, and retailers, have developed frequent buyer/user programs to reward their loyal customers. The better CRM programs attempt to maintain some continuous contact with loyal customers by sending them birthday cards or having a personal sales associate contact them to inform them of special events and sales.

Branding Strategies

Firms institute a variety of brand-related strategies to create and manage key brand assets, such as the decision to own the brands, establishing a branding policy, extending the brand name to other products and markets, cooperatively using the brand name with that of another firm, and licensing the brand to other firms.

Brand Ownership

Brands can be owned by any firm in the supply chain, whether manufacturers, wholesalers, or retailers. There are three basic brand ownership strategies: manufacturer or national brands, private-label or store brands, and generic brands (see Exhibit 9.8). **Manufacturer brands** are owned and managed by the manufacturer, are also known as **national brands**, and include Nike, Mountain Dew, KitchenAid, and Marriott. The majority of the brands marketed in Canada are manufacturer brands. Manufacturing firms spend millions of dollars each year to promote their brands. For example, P&G spends about $100 million in media expenditures annually to promote its Tide brand

Dove has rewarded consumers for their loyalty with double points at Shoppers Drug Mart.

L06

manufacturer brands (national brands) Brands owned and managed by the manufacturer.

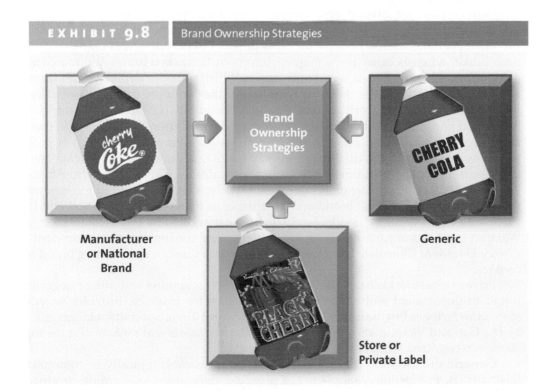

| EXHIBIT 9.8 | Brand Ownership Strategies |

Manufacturer or National Brand

Brand Ownership Strategies

Generic

Store or Private Label

President's Choice, a private-label developed and marketed by Canada's largest food distributor, Loblaw, is successfully positioned as a premium, high-quality private label with moderate prices.

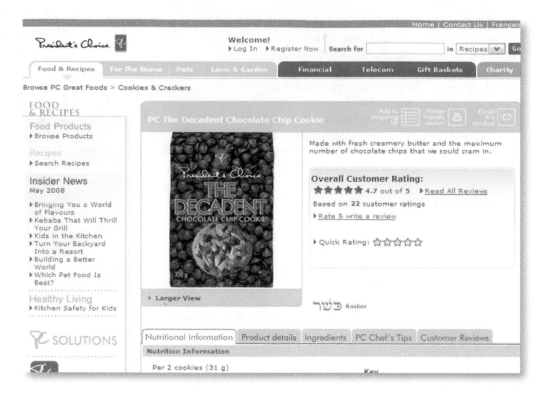

of liquid and powdered detergents.[34] By owning their brands, manufacturers retain more control over their marketing strategy, are able to choose the appropriate market segments and positioning for the brand, and can build the brand and thereby create their own brand equity.

Brands that are owned and managed by retailers, in contrast, are called **private-label brands** or **store brands**. Some manufacturers prefer to make only private-label merchandise because the costs of national branding and marketing are prohibitive, whereas other firms manufacture both their own brand and merchandise for other brands or retailers. For instance, Whirlpool sells appliances under its own name and also makes them for Sears under the Kenmore brand. Wholesalers also sometimes develop private-label brands. President's Choice, a private label developed and marketed by Canada's largest food distributor, Loblaw, is extremely successful in Canada and parts of the United States.[35] President's Choice is positioned as a premium, high-quality private label with moderate prices.[36] Private-label brands are particularly common in supermarkets, discount stores, and drugstores. Their popularity among consumers depends on several factors, including consumer preferences for a lower-cost brand and the trust consumers have in the store and its brand. Such private-label brands, especially those marketed by large chains such as Walmart and Costco, are fast gaining in popularity and consumer loyalty. President's Choice Decadent Chocolate Chip Cookies has become Canada's bestselling brand of cookies.[37]

Private-label brands have also gained popularity in apparel and other categories found in department and specialty stores. The Bay, for instance, provides several store brands, including Beaumark, Mantles, Truly, and Togo. Specialty retailers, such as The Gap and Victoria's Secret, stock only their own labels and rank among the top 20 most recognized apparel and accessory brands.[38]

Generic products are those sold without brand names, typically in commodities markets. For instance, shoppers can purchase unbranded salt, grains, produce,

---

private-label brands (store brands)
Brands developed and marketed by a retailer and available only from that retailer.

generic
A product sold without a brand name, typically in commodities markets.

meat, or nuts in grocery stores. Hardware stores often sell unbranded screws, nuts, and lumber. However, even in these markets, the popularity and acceptance of generic products has declined. Consumers question the quality and origin of the products, and retailers have found better profit potential and the ability to build brand equity with manufacturer and store brands. For example, many fruits and vegetables sold through supermarket chains now carry either the manufacturer's brand name (e.g., Dole bananas) or the store's.

All of General Electric's brands carry the GE brand name, so they all benefit from the brand awareness associated with the corporate name.

Naming Brands and Product Lines

Firms use several very different strategies to name their brands and product lines (see Exhibit 9.9).

Corporate or Family Brand   A firm can use its own corporate name to brand all its product lines and products, such as the General Electric Company, which brands its appliances prominently with the GE brand name. Similarly, all products sold through The Gap stores (Gap, GapKids, babyGap, GapMaternity, GapBody) bear only The Gap brand name. When all products are sold under one **corporate brand** or **family brand**, the individual brands benefit from the overall brand awareness associated with the family name.

Corporate and Product Line Brands   A firm also could use combinations of the **corporate and product line brands** to distinguish its products. For example, Kellogg's uses its family brand name prominently on its cereal brands (e.g., Corn Flakes, Froot Loops, Rice Krispies) helping to maintain its powerhouse status on grocery store shelves. In other cases, the individual brand's name is more prominently displayed on the package than the Kellogg's name, as in the case of Pop-Tarts,

corporate brand (family brand)
The use of a firm's own corporate name to brand all of its product lines and products.

corporate and product line brands
The use of a combination of family brand name and individual brand name to distinguish a firm's products.

EXHIBIT 9.9	Brand Name Strategies

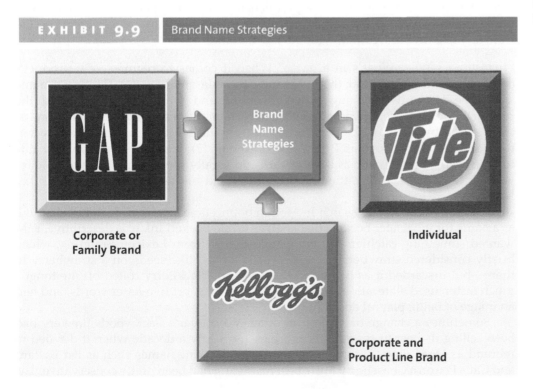

Corporate or Family Brand

Brand Name Strategies

Individual

Corporate and Product Line Brand

Depending on the brand, sometimes Kellogg's uses its family brand name prominently on its cereal brands, while other times the individual brand's name is more prominently displayed on the package.

individual brands
The use of individual brand names for each of a firm's products.

Eggo, and Nutri-Grain. In addition, Kellogg's owns non-cereal and breakfast food brands, such as Cheez-It and Famous Amos, which are not overtly associated with the family brand.

Individual Brands   A firm can use **individual brand** names for each of its products. For example, in its house and home products line, P&G markets various detergent products (Tide, Gain, Cheer, Downy, Febreze), paper products (Bounty, Charmin), household cleaners (Mr. Clean, Swiffer), and dishwashing products (Cascade, Dawn, Joy). Furthermore, it markets brands in various other product lines, such as personal and beauty products (Olay, Old Spice, Secret, CoverGirl), health and wellness products (Pepto-Bismol, Oral-B, Puffs), baby products (Pampers, Luvs), and pet nutrition and care products (Iams).[39] Similarly, Loblaw operates across Canada under the following brands: Atlantic Superstore, Dominion, Extra Foods, Fortinos, Loblaws, Maxi, No Frills, Provigo, Your Independent Grocer, and Zehrs. Sobeys operates under the following retail banners: Sobeys, IGA Extra, IGA, Foodland, and Price Chopper. Individual brands allow a company to compete within one category, for example, laundry detergent, offering a variety of products to different target markets. And if one brand experiences problems, other products with unique brand names are protected from any negative association with the failed brand.

Choosing a Name   What's in a name? When it comes to naming new products, companies should consider the following desirable qualities: (1) The brand name should be descriptive and suggestive of benefits and qualities associated with the product. For example, the name *Sunkist* evokes images of oranges ripening on the trees kissed by the sun. (2) The brand name should be easy to pronounce, recognize, and remember, such as Tide, Crest, or Kodak. (3) The company should be able to register the brand name as a trademark and legally protect it. (4) For companies looking to global markets, the brand name should be easy to translate into other languages.

Did you know that Research In Motion bounced around the idea of PocketLink as a name for what later became BlackBerry? While PocketLink was descriptive, RIM wanted something catchier. The company got help from Lexicon Branding, which briefly considered strawberry—the keyboard looked like seeds on a strawberry to them—but discarded it as being too slow a word. BlackBerry rolled off the tongue much faster, used alliteration, was composed of two short five-letter words, and had an image of being playful and friendly.[40]

Sometimes a change of name is in order. Vancouver's Backwoods Brewery had been selling its beer to restaurants and bars for nearly a decade when it decided to rebrand as Dead Frog. Competing against whacky wine names such as Fat Bastard and Cat's Pee on a Gooseberry Bush, beer marketing had been pretty conservative. The

company wanted a memorable
but irreverent name that would
appeal to a younger audience.[41]
And chances are that a band
called Rainbow Butt Monkeys
never would have become a hit
sensation. While it may have
been memorable, band mem-
bers received a better reception
after they changed their name
to Finger Eleven.

Crest uses a brand extension strategy since it uses the same brand name for many related products.

Brand Extension

A **brand extension** refers to the use of the same brand name for new products
being introduced to the same or new markets.[42] The dental hygiene market, for
instance, is full of brand extensions; Colgate, Crest, and Butler all sell toothpaste,
toothbrushes, and other dental hygiene products. Roots has extended its brand
from athletic clothing to leather bags, yoga wear and accessories, and even a line of
baby clothes. Brand extensions are also common in global expansions. For example,
Coca-Cola, Nike, and Levi's are sold the world over under the same name. In some
cases, firms use the same wording and lettering in their logos when extending their
brands globally.

brand extension
The use of the same brand name for new products being introduced to the same or new markets.

There are several advantages to using the same brand name for new products.
First, because the brand name is already well established, such as the Dove example
discussed in the chapter vignette, the firm can spend less in developing consumer
brand awareness and brand associations for the new product.[43] Gillette's Braun
brand started selling kitchen appliances (coffeemakers, toasters, food processors,
blenders, juicers), and then extended into various other product categories, including
shaving (dry razors, beard care), beauty care (cordless hair stylers), oral care (power
toothbrushes), and steam irons.[44]

Second, if the brand is known for its high quality, that perception will carry over
to the new product. Following its success in the PC market, Dell extended its brand
name to monitors, printers, hand-held computers, digital jukeboxes, LCD TVs, servers, and network switches, among other products.[45]

Third, the marketing costs for a new product by an established brand are lower
because consumers already know and understand the brand. Moreover, consumers
who have adopted the core brand are more likely to try the extension. Anyone who
has treated a blister from wearing uncomfortable shoes with a Johnson & Johnson
Band-Aid may choose to buy the company's new Anti-Blister Stick to reduce rubbing
and prevent the blister in the first place.

Life Savers unsuccessfully attempted a brand extension strategy with its line of soft drinks.

Fourth, when brand extensions are used for
complementary products, a synergy exists between
the two products that can increase overall sales. For
example, Frito Lay markets both chips and dips
under its Frito-Lay and Doritos brand names.[46]
When people buy the chips, they tend to buy the
dips as well.

Fifth, successful brand extensions can result
in cross category trial and boost sales because
adopters of the new extended brand may try other
products in the brand family they are not already
using. For example, consumers who had not used
the Neutrogena brand before trying the Neutrogena
On-the-Spot Acne Patch might be encouraged to try

Entrepreneurial Marketing 9.1   Exploring Virgin Territories

Sir Richard Branson's first business venture was a magazine called *Student*, launched in 1968 when he was only 17.[49] Two years later, he started a mail-order record company called Virgin, but the business was adversely affected by a postal strike the very next year. He then opened his first Virgin record store, followed by a recording studio and a record label. In 1984, Branson started Virgin Atlantic Airways. The Virgin label can now be found on a broad array of product categories and markets, including health clubs (Virgin Active), book publishing (Virgin Books), travel and tourism (Virgin Holidays, Virgin Express, Virgin Limobike, Virgin Trains), cellphones (Virgin Mobile), and cosmetics (Virgin Cosmetics). These product categories currently enjoy group sales of more than $8 billion and maintain approximately 35 000 employees.[50]

The Virgin name has been placed on products and product categories far removed from its core businesses: air travel and music stores (the firm sold its record business to Thorn EMI in 1992). These developments have challenged the conventional wisdom that successful brand extensions must occur in similar product categories. However, Virgin's

Sir Richard Branson has successfully extended the Virgin brand beyond its core businesses of air travel and music stores. One of his latest ventures is Virgin Home Loans.

core emphasis on value has made most of its extensions successful. Some believe that the success of the Virgin brand extensions is due not to the quality of any particular Virgin product but to the characteristics associated with the family brand: being irreverent, entertaining, and unconventional.

Although it may appear that there are no limits to extending the Virgin brand name, the firm has experienced some failures, especially in the alcoholic and cola beverages markets. Its brand of vodka was a failure, and Virgin Cola was never introduced in Canada, failed in the United States, and achieved only a 3-percent market share in the United Kingdom. The primary risk that Virgin runs from extending its brand too far is not being able to satisfy all the customers of all its brands. As long as the customer has a nice flight on Virgin Atlantic, he or she may try Virgin Mobile. But if that same person has a bad experience with his or her cellphone contract, Virgin Atlantic—and the other Virgin brands—may lose a customer forever.

---

brand dilution

Occurs when a brand extension adversely affects consumer perceptions about the attributes the core brand is believed to hold.

Neutrogena moisturizing lotion, especially if their experience with the acne patch has been positive.[47]

Not all brand extensions are successful, however. Some can dilute brand equity.[48] **Brand dilution** occurs when the brand extension adversely affects consumer perceptions about the attributes the core brand is believed to hold.[51] For example, Cadbury's association with fine chocolates and candy was weakened when the company extended its brand name to mainstream food products such as mashed potatoes and soups.[52] And while Life Savers soft drinks did well in prelaunch taste tests, they didn't do well in subsequent sales. If the brand extension is very similar to the core brand, it even could cause cannibalization of sales from the core brand. Entrepreneurial Marketing 9.1 examines the rise and extension of Sir Richard Branson's brand, Virgin.

To prevent the potentially negative consequences of brand extensions, firms must consider the following caveats:

- Marketers should carefully evaluate the fit between the product class of the core brand and that of the extension.[53] If the fit between the product categories is high, consumers will consider the extension credible, and the brand association will be stronger for the extension. When Starbucks introduced VIA, its line of instant coffee, it made sense to consumers.

- Firms should carefully evaluate consumer perceptions of the attributes of the core brand and seek out similar attributes for the extension because brand-specific associations are very important for extensions.[54] For example, if HP printers were associated with reliability, performance, and value, consumers would expect the same brand-specific attributes in other products that carried the HP brand name.

- Firms should refrain from extending the brand name to too many products and product categories to avoid diluting the brand and damaging brand equity. While Donald Trump has been quite successful lending his name to real estate properties and TV shows, he was unsuccessful in extending his name to branding steaks.

- Firms should consider whether the brand extension will be distanced from the core brand, especially if the firm wants to use some but not all of the existing brand associations. When Marriott introduced its budget line of hotels, it downplayed the Marriott name, calling the new chain Fairfield Inn. And did you even know that Marriott International owns 99 percent of the Ritz-Carlton chain of luxury hotels? Not many people do, and that ignorance is by the company's design. The information is buried on the Ritz-Carlton web page.[55]

Cobranding

Cobranding is the practice of marketing two or more brands together, on the same package or promotion. Primarily because of credit card companies, such as Visa and MasterCard, the practice has greatly increased in the past decade. Airlines were among the first to cobrand with credit card companies (such as the CIBC Aeroplan Visa Card), but, recently, firms in other industries, such as banking, retail, and restaurants, have begun forming similar alliances, resulting in cards such as BMO Mosaic MasterCard, TD Gold Visa, and President's Choice MasterCard, to name a few. Starbucks was the first in the quick-service restaurant industry to offer its own credit card, the RBC Starbucks Duetto in alliance with Visa.[56] Not all cobranding efforts are a success: RBC discontinued the Duetto card after seven years when it failed to attract enough customers to make it financially viable.

Cobranding enhances consumers' perceptions of product quality[57] by signalling otherwise unobservable product quality through links between the firm's brand and a well-known quality brand. For example, NutraSweet's claim to be a sugar substitute that was safe and left no aftertaste got a boost after both Coca-Cola and Pepsi started offering products that contained it. The cobranding of Intel, with its "Intel Inside" logo, helped boost the brand reputations of PC manufacturers that chose to use Intel chips. Loblaw partnered with Mattel in a cobranding agreement for its affordable fashion line, Joe Fresh, to create a limited edition collection of Barbie-branded sleepwear and underwear.[58]

Cobranding can also be a prelude to an acquisition strategy. FedEx entered into a cobranding arrangement with Kinko's, whereby it provided FedEx delivery services at Kinko's retail outlets.[59] Then, in early 2004, FedEx acquired Kinko's for an estimated $2.4 billion and has rebranded Kinko's as FedEx Kinko's.[60]

However, there are, of course, some risks to cobranding, especially when customers for each of the brands are vastly different. For example, the Burger King and Häagen-Dazs cobranding strategy failed because the customer profiles for each brand were too different.[61] Tim Hortons found that its customers responded enthusiastically to its efforts to cobrand with Cold Stone Creamery ice cream in the United States and is now testing the concept in Canada.[62] Cobranding may also fail if the brands' owners cannot resolve financial disputes about revenue or royalty sharing.[63] Finally, the firms that own the brands may change their

cobranding
The practice of marketing two or more brands together, on the same package or promotion.

priorities, as a result of which the cobranded product may no longer be available. In this scenario, the customer relationships and loyalty created with the cobranded product would be lost.[64]

Brand Licensing

brand licensing
A contractual arrangement between firms, whereby one firm allows another to use its brand name, logo, symbols, or characters in exchange for a negotiated fee.

Brand licensing is a contractual arrangement between firms, whereby one firm allows another to use its brand name, logo, symbols, and/or characters in exchange for a negotiated fee.[65] Brand licensing is common for toys, apparel, accessories, and entertainment products, such as video games; in the United States, it generates more than $100 billion in retail sales per year.[66] The firm that provides the right to use its brand (licensor) obtains revenues through royalty payments from the firm that has obtained the right to use the brand (licensee). These royalty payments sometimes take the form of an upfront, lump-sum licensing fee or may be based on the dollar value of sales of the licensed merchandise.

Several aspects of a brand can be licensed. Popular apparel designers, such as Ralph Lauren, Calvin Klein, and Eddie Bauer, and luxury goods manufacturers often license the right to use their brand name on a variety of products. The Porsche name is used by Grundig radios and also appears on watches, luggage sets, and tennis racquets. The computer world has even capitalized on the Porsche brand name with the game *Need for Speed: Porsche Unleashed*. Canadian Tire has built on the growing popularity of NASCAR racing to become the official automotive retailer of NASCAR in Canada.[67] One very popular form of licensing is the use of characters created in books and other media. Such entertainment licensing has generated tremendous revenues for movie studios such as Disney, Lucas Films (think of the *Star Wars* memorabilia), and New Line (licensor of *Lord of the Rings* toys and collectibles), as well as for comic book publishers such as Marvel Entertainment (*Spider-Man*). A long-standing staple of licensing has been major league sports teams that play in the NBA, NFL, or NHL, as well as various collegiate sports teams.

Licensing is an effective form of attracting visibility for the brand and thereby building brand equity while also generating additional revenue. There are, however, some risks associated with it. For the licensor, the major risk is the dilution of its

*The famous tennis player Rene "the alligator" Lacoste (left in 1927 photo) co-founded a firm that made a white, knit shirt, with an alligator emblazoned on the left breast.
The brand is still sold today (right) at Lacoste boutiques and stores across Canada.*

brand equity through overexposure of the brand, especially if the brand name and characters are used inappropriately.[68]

Consider, for instance, the famous—or possibly infamous—alligator shirt. In 1933, the company founded by Frenchman David Lacoste (the licensor), famous as a tennis player and for his nickname "the alligator," entered into a licensing agreement with Andre Gillier (the first licensee) to produce a high-quality, white, knit shirt with a ribbed collar, short sleeves, and a crocodile emblazoned on the left breast. The line expanded to include other casual apparel items, and in 1966, the Lacoste name was licensed to American manufacturer Izod (the second licensee). Alligator-emblazoned apparel could be found in better department stores and country club golf and tennis shops into the late 1980s. But Izod also began to sell the alligator apparel in discount stores, and quality and sales suffered. The alliance continued until 1992, when Lacoste severed its ties with Izod. Lacoste has since regained its prestigious image and can be found in boutiques and exclusive specialty department stores around the world.[69]

Licensors also run the risk of improperly valuing their brand for licensing purposes or entering into the wrong type of licensing arrangement. For example, Marvel Entertainment's previous deals with movie studios for the use of its comic book characters were "undervalued," because the firm took lump-sum licensing fees upfront rather than pegging its royalty fees to sales. As a result, the firm probably left money on the table for deals on the first *X-Men* and *Blade* films.[70] In entertainment licensing, both licensors and licensees run the risk that characters based on books and movies will be only a fad. Moreover, the success or failure of merchandise based on movies is directly affected by the success or failure of the movie itself.[71]

Packaging

L07

Packaging is an important brand element with more tangible or physical benefits than the other brand elements because packages come in different types and offer a variety of benefits to consumers, manufacturers, and retailers. Consumers typically seek convenience in terms of storage, use, and consumption.

But packaging also serves to protect products. Wrappers and exterior cartons protect eggs from being broken and help prevent tampering with products such as toothpaste. Packaging provides the UPC label used by retail scanners as well as contents, directions, and other additional product information. The package can also be an important marketing tool for the manufacturer if it is used to convey the brand's positioning. Cosmetics giant Estée Lauder considers packaging to be primarily about brand image, so its packages portray a modern, sophisticated look that is immediately recognizable.[72] Packaging is considered by many marketers to be the last frontier in advertising because of its role in promoting products to consumers on the floor of the store at the point of purchase. As discussed in Social Media Marketing 9.1, Polar Ice drove users to its website through packaging changes. Packaging may also affect consumers' emotions and drive impulse buying. The shapes of fragrance, perfume, and deodorant bottles and containers are good examples of marketers extending the use of packaging beyond a distribution function to encourage purchase and differentiation. Many children also pressure their parents to buy products, like breakfast cereal, more because of the packaging than for the product. In these instances, packaging acts as a point of differentiation and makes consumers feel proud to own the brand.

Some packaging changes are designed to make the product more ecological, such as PepsiCo's response to concerns about the waste associated with bottled water. To reduce the amount of plastic it uses, PepsiCo

Coca-Cola's Fridge Packs boosted sales. Consumers were able to store 12 cans in their refrigerators conveniently, making it easy to grab a cold drink whenever they wanted one.

Social Media Marketing 9.1   Mia Tweets Polar Ice to Success

Corby's Polar Ice vodka has become a Canadian success story. In the last 10 years, sales have grown 377 percent, from 85 000 cases to 320 000 cases, making Polar Ice the third largest vodka brand in Canada.[73]

Social media has played a prominent role in Corby's recent marketing effort to launch a new website (www. polarice.ca). The company incorporated Twitter and Facebook into the site, offering a unique brand experience for a target market of 19- to 25-year-old fun-seekers who are early adopters of technology and engaged in social media.

The website landing page features a "socialscape" scene, which changes depending on which province users come from. For example, users from British Columbia see the Vancouver skyline and mountains, while those from Ontario see a Toronto cityscape that features the CN Tower. Lighthouses are prominent for Maritime provinces, and an Inukshuk displays for visitors from Nunavut. These customized backgrounds help build a stronger relationship with consumers since the user can better relate.

User-generated tweets mashed up from the Polar Ice Twitter account@mia_at_polarice are featured on the site. "Mia" is a persona created to reflect the target market. The brand personality is very young and modern, is full of confidence, has a sense of style, has nothing to hide, and is a very social fun-seeker. Drawing on actual tweet posts allows Corby to incorporate user-generated content while still maintaining control of the brand.

Kelly Kretz, senior brand manager at Corby, said she was floored by how natural communication is between the target market and "Mia." She thinks it's because Mia represents a person and not a company. The Facebook page has generated more than 26 million impressions and has more than 3600 fans.[74] Ads on Facebook direct fans to the website. The Twitter profile has 1700 followers and is ranked seventh for those using the "vodka" tag.

The brand's social media efforts are also supported in packaging. For example, neck tags on bottles direct buyers to the website. A contest featured on the site invited all HIV-positive artists to share designs for a special edition bottle of Polar Ice launched in 2010 to help raise money and awareness for the Canadian AIDS Society.[75]

---

has decreased the weight of its water bottles by 20 percent, which means less plastic in landfills.

Sometimes packaging changes can backfire though, such as when Tropicana changed its packaging to feature a picture of a glass of juice, rather than the familiar straw in an orange. Customers balked, and said the new image was reminiscent of a generic bargain brand. The company poorly misjudged its customers' loyalty to its existing brand position, as exemplified by its packaging. Frito Lay's efforts to launch compostable SunChips packaging resulted in many consumers complaining that the bags were too noisy.

Many consumers experience "wrap rage"—a great frustration with packaging that makes it seemingly impossible to get at the actual products. So companies are moving away from traditional clamshells, which are the curved plastic package around many electronics goods, because they are so difficult to open. Costco has replaced the clamshells with packaging made of coated paperboard; it still requires scissors to be opened but is flat and therefore can be opened easily.

Retailers' priorities for packaging, however, differ. They want convenience in terms of displaying and selling the product. For customers, Coca-Cola's Fridge Pack of 12 cans offers a compact shape and convenience when carrying it home and storing it in their refrigerators; for retailers, the packaging offers the means to easily stack the packages on their shelves.

In addition, items may often be packed into larger cartons, pallets, or containers to facilitate shipment and storage from the manufacturer to the retailer. These shipping packages benefit the manufacturer and the retailer in that they protect the shipment during transit; aid in loading, unloading, and storage; and allow cost efficiencies because of the larger order and shipment sizes.

Because packaging is critical to the firm's brand positioning and shelf appeal, many innovations in design and materials have occurred in the past few decades. Some examples include[76]

- **Stand-up, reclosable zipper pouches**. Capri Sun's stand-up pouch juice drink took the lead; now a variety of products and pouch types are available, including pouches with reclosable zippers. You can even buy tuna in a stand-up pouch and cheese in reclosable zipper pouches.

- **Aluminum beverage cans**. First introduced in 1965, cans dominated the beverage market by 1985. Even some water and energy drink brands now are available in aluminum cans.

- **Aseptic packaging**. Tetra Pak and IP provided designs and machinery that increased the shelf life of beverages without refrigeration. They are used primarily by juice marketers but also by some soup companies.

- **Child-resistant/senior-friendly packages**. Products that are harmful to children under the age of five years, such as drugs and medicines, solvents, chemicals, and pesticides, now are packaged with child-resistant tops. Seniors appreciate packages that are light, easy to handle, easy to read, and easy to open. Responding to consumer feedback, McNeil Consumer Healthcare in Canada developed the E-Z Open cap, a non-child-resistant closure specifically targeted to customers with arthritis.[77]

- **Green and biodegradable packaging**. Today's environmentally conscious consumers are demanding less packaging and want to be able to easily recycle it. See Sustainable Marketing 9.1 to read about Coca-Cola's new, fully recyclable PlantBottle. Vancouver-based Earthcycle Packaging launched compostable palm fibre–based packaging for items such as takeout food and produce. Palm fibre takes about 90 days to decompose and is being used by Loblaw and Walmart.[78] And P&G converted all of its liquid laundry brands (e.g., Tide, Gain, Cheer) to a concentrated formula in containers half the previous size. Retailers appreciated the storage and shelf-space savings of the smaller packages.[79]

Labelling

Labels on products and packages provide information the consumer needs for his or her purchase decision and consumption of the product. In that they identify the product and brand, labels are also an important element of branding and can be used for promotion. The information required on them must comply with general and industry-specific laws and regulations, including the constituents or ingredients contained in the product, where the product was made, directions for use, and/or safety precautions.

Many labelling requirements stem from various laws, including the Competition Act, the Consumer Packaging and Labelling Act and Regulations, the Food and Drugs Act, and the Hazardous Materials Act. Several federal agencies, industry groups, and consumer watchdogs carefully monitor product labels. The Food and Drugs Act regulates the information on food, drugs, and cosmetics package labels. Quaker Canada had to wait for Health Canada approval before it could state on its labels that oat fibre helps reduce cholesterol. The Consumer

Innovative packages can enhance a product's positioning and shelf appeal. Consider reclosable packages, child-resistant/senior-friendly packages, ring-pull aluminum cans, aseptic drink bottles, and twist-off tops.

Sustainable Marketing 9.1 · Message in a Bottle

Most consumers are accustomed to seeing ads from Coca-Cola telling them about the great product inside the bottle. Recently, the company has been sending a message about the bottle itself. A sustainable packaging goal to reduce its environmental footprint led the company to the introduction of the PlantBottle. Coca-Cola's commitment to responsible citizenship includes conservation of natural resources and protection of the soil, water, and climate required to sustain life on Earth.[80] Like bottles used in the past, PlantBottle is fully recyclable. Unlike previous petroleum-based PET plastic bottles, this new bottle has a lower reliance on non-renewable resources and reduces carbon emissions, with 30 percent of materials coming from sugar cane and molasses.

The bottle was introduced in Canada for the Vancouver Olympics and contains a little green symbol to help consumers recognize the change to more environmentally friendly packaging. The plan has been to carefully and specifically launch in green-conscious

Coca-Cola's fully recyclable Plant Bottle has won awards for packaging innovation.

cities; for example, the bottle was introduced in Copenhagen, Denmark, just in time for the conference on climate change.[81]

Coca-Cola's sustainability efforts go well beyond the PlantBottle. It works with a number of organizations, including the Bill and Melinda Gates Foundation, to help implement sustainable farming practices in various parts of the world. It also works with WWF (World Wildlife Fund/World Wide Fund for Nature) on the Better Sugar Initiative to promote improvements in the key environmental and social impacts of sugarcane production and primary processing.[82]

PlantBottle has already been recognized a unique new technology. It won a gold award at the DuPont Awards for Packaging Innovation for its demonstrated breakthrough packaging innovation.[83] In the first full year of using the PlantBottle product, Coca-Cola hopes to produce up to two billion bottles.[84] Now that's a message in a bottle.

The packaging and label for BioBest Maximmunité highlight the fact that the product contains probiotic cultures.

Packaging and Labelling Act covers food products and ensures that the claims made by the manufacturer are true and that labels accurately reflect ingredients and quantities. All this has to be done in both of Canada's official languages, French and English.

Manufacturers' claims on labels also can be subject to criticisms by various consumer groups. In the United Kingdom, the consumer watchdog group ITC ruled that Danone's Shape yogourt was not "virtually fat free," as its label claimed. The Dairy Industry Federation guidelines state that only products containing less than 0.3 grams of fat per every 100 grams could be called "virtually fat free," but Danone's Shape yogourt contained three times that amount.[85]

Ethical Dilemma 9.1 illustrates some of the problems companies face in promoting the types of ingredients they use in their products, as well as the associated labelling concerns. These concerns are further compounded when the products are sold across international borders.

A product label is much more than just a sticker on the package; it is a communication tool. Many of the elements

on the label are required by laws and regulations (i.e., ingredients, fat content, sodium content, serving size, calories), but other elements of the label remain within the control of the manufacturer. How manufacturers use labels to communicate the benefits of their products to consumers varies by the product. For example, the label for BioBest Maximmunité highlights the fact that the drink contains probiotic cultures. Many other products highlight other specific ingredients, vitamin content, or nutrient content. This focus signals to consumers that the product offers these benefits. Although often overlooked, the importance of the label as a communication tool should not be underestimated.

Ethical Dilemma 9.1

What's Behind a Seal of Approval?

Today's shoppers want to buy more nutritious foods and avoid those that are unsound. With consumers becoming increasingly focused on healthful eating, many companies have jumped on the bandwagon, putting "seals of approval" on their products. For example, Kraft Foods introduced Sensible Solution, a green flag currently used on more than 500 products, promoted as a way for consumers to more easily choose great-tasting foods that are better for them. Smart Spot is PepsiCo's better-for-you signal to consumers. Even restaurants are getting into game, seizing the opportunity to market select menu items as healthful fare. Swiss Chalet promotes the Heart and Stroke Foundation's Health Check symbol on entrees and side dishes that meet the program's nutrient criteria.

But what's in a seal? To bear the Smart Spot symbol, products must meet one of the following criteria:

- Contain at least 10 percent of the daily value of a targeted nutrient (i.e., protein, fibre, calcium, iron, vitamin A, vitamin C) and meet limits for fat, saturated fat, trans fat, cholesterol, sodium, and added sugar

- Be formulated to have specific health or wellness benefits

- Have a reduction in calories or nutrients such as fat, sodium, or sugar[86]

Sound good? It might until you dig a little deeper. Diet Pepsi sports a Smart Spot label because it has no sugar, no calories, and no carbs. However, nutritionists argue that people should drink juice, water, or milk if they really want to make a healthy choice. Plus there's the matter of the aspartame sweetener to consider. Baked Cheetos get the nod because they are baked and have no cholesterol or trans fats. But they are still high in calories (34 Cheetos contain 130 calories, 45 of which are from fat) and contain no fibre, vitamins, or minerals.

As for what's cooking in Kraft's kitchens, its Oreo Thinsations are packaged in convenient 100-calorie packages.

Have you seen these better-for-you labels on products in grocery stores? Would you buy organic candy floss?

While these cookies are lower in fat than conventional Oreo cookies, in the end, those 100 calories are still empty and sugary.

Does Swiss Chalet fare any better? Menu items marked with the Health Check symbol appear to be very nutritious and a good choice for consumers who are concerned about their health. However, very few menu items earn the symbol, and some items, such as salads, must be eaten without dressing to qualify.

A recent twist to the health labelling trend is seen in companies promoting organic junk food. To some consumers the organic label has become a seal of approval. Yet, are organic Pop-Tarts any better for you than regular ones? What about Pure Fun Organic Cotton Candy? Critics claim it's just a way to give health-conscious consumers an excuse to eat junk food.[87]

While most of these companies are working hard to provide consumers with healthier choices, you have to question whether these better-for-you labels are just a marketing ploy. What do you think? Are health symbols self-serving or sincere?

Real Marketer Profile: STACEY BIGGAR

I studied Business Administration at Wilfrid Laurier University, specializing in Brand Communications and taking part in the co-op program.

I found my first job through Workopolis.ca. I searched for jobs, like I'd experienced on co-op, and tailored my cover letter and resumé to each posting that sounded interesting. My first job was in the Marketing department at Parmalat Canada with brands such as Black Diamond cheese and Astro yogurt.

Some days consisted of managing agency partners to design coupons and websites; other days were dedicated to writing business proposals for new product launches, or attending commercial shoots for new TV ads. Outside of the office, I've attended focus group research sessions, promotional activations, and in-store demonstrations of new products to consumers.

My most exciting project so far has been bringing BioBest yogourt with Plant Sterols to market, right from business case to live product. It was one of the first food products in Canada ever to contain plant sterols, proven to lower cholesterol. The focus on launching quickly meant efficiency was essential, demanding smart decisions, fast.

The need for speed to market also challenged me to work closely with our cross-functional team and agency partners to reduce timelines to less than one-third of what they typically would be. We were able to launch in less than four months after receiving approval for using plant sterols in Canada!

Since then, I have changed jobs and now focus on longer-term planning, communication strategy, and innovations for the Becel margarine brand at Unilever Canada. This new position is a contrast to typical brand management roles as it is completely separate from the day-to-day business management but plays a key role in the health of the brand.

The most exciting part about marketing is that every day is different. One day is brainstorming innovations and the next is balancing budgets with invoice payments. The variety keeps things very engaging. It's also fulfilling to see your products and projects in market. It's great to watch TV and see your communication strategy in action or to browse the grocery aisle and see your flavour decisions and packaging choices come to life.

Learning Objectives Review

LO1 List the components of a product

The product itself is important but so are its associated services, such as support or financing. Other elements combine to produce the core customer value of a product: the brand name, quality level, packaging, and additional features.

LO2 Identify the types of consumer products

These products tend to be classified into four groups: specialty, shopping, convenience, and unsought products. Each classification involves a different purchase situation and consumer goal.

LO3 Explain the difference between a product mix's breadth and a product line's depth

Breadth, or variety, entails the number of product lines that a company offers. Depth involves the number of categories in one specific product line. Firms grow their product lines

by adding either new product categories or new SKUs within a product category. The decision to add products should be made carefully. Excessive product line expansions can confuse consumers and dilute the appeal of the brand's core products. Sometimes, products or product lines become unprofitable, the firm's priorities change, or consumer preferences shift. When this happens, firms must prune their product lines by deleting items or possibly even entire product categories.

LO4 Identify the advantages that brands provide firms and consumers

Brands facilitate the consumer search process. Some customers are loyal to certain brands, which essentially protects those brands from competition. In addition, brands are valuable in a legal sense, in that trademarks and copyrights protect firms from counterfeiters and knock-off artists. Firms with well-known brands can spend relatively less on marketing because the brand and its associations help sell the product. Finally, brands have real market value as a company asset.

LO5 **Summarize the components of brand equity**

Brand equity summarizes the value that a brand adds, or subtracts, from the offering's value. It comprises brand awareness, or how many consumers in the market are familiar with the brand; brand associations, which are the links consumers make between the brand and its image; and brand loyalty, which occurs when a consumer will buy only that brand's offer. Brand equity also encompasses the concept of perceived value, which is a subjective measure that consumers develop to assess the costs of obtaining the brand.

LO6 **Describe the types of branding strategies used by firms**

Firms use a variety of strategies to manage their brands. First, they must decide whether to offer national, private-label, or generic brands. Second, they have a choice of using

an overall corporate brand or a collection of product line or individual brands. Third, to reach new markets or extend their current market, they can extend their current brands to new products. Fourth, firms can cobrand with another brand to create sales and profit synergies for both. Fifth, firms with strong brands have the opportunity to license their brands to other firms.

LO7 **State how a product's packaging and label contribute to a firm's overall strategy**

Like brands, packaging and labels help sell the product and facilitate its use. The package holds the product, and its label provides product information. The package also provides additional consumer information on its label and facilitates transportation and storage for both retailers and their customers. Labels have become increasingly important to consumers because they supply important safety, nutritional, and product usage Information.

Key Terms

- associated services (augmented product), 289
- brand, 291
- brand association, 299
- brand awareness, 297
- brand dilution, 300
- brand equity, 297
- brand extension, 305
- brand licensing, 308
- brand loyalty, 299
- brand personality, 299

- cobranding, 307
- consumer products, 290
- core customer value, 289
- corporate and product line brands, 303
- corporate brand (family brand), 303
- generic, 302
- individual brands, 304
- manufacturer brands (national brands), 301

- perceived value, 299
- private-label brands (store brands), 302
- product category, 290
- product mix, 290
- product mix breadth, 291
- product line depth, 291
- product lines, 290
- stock keeping units (SKUs), 291

Concept Review

1. Explain the differences between product mix breadth and product line depth. Why is understanding this difference important?

2. Explain why branding is important to marketers. What value do customers derive from purchasing and using brand name products?

3. What is brand equity? Describe the strategies marketers could employ to increase the value of their brand equity.

4. Differentiate between a national brand, generic brand, and store brand. Should retailers carry all three types of brands? Why?

5. Describe the desirable qualities companies should consider when choosing product names.

6. What are the advantages of using the same brand name and extending it to new products?

7. Explain how brand licensing differs from cobranding.

8. What is cobranding? When does it make sense for a company to use a cobranding strategy?

9. Explain how marketers increase the value of their product offering through packaging. Discuss the ethical issues surrounding product packaging and labelling. How might some of these issues be resolved?

10. Explain how labelling could be used as a marketing weapon rather than just providing legally required information.

Marketing Applications

1. Prepared foods at Whole Foods Market, the world's largest retailer of organic foods, are very profitable. To make them even more profitable, suggest two strategies that would alter the product mix breadth and depth.

2. Visit a grocery store and look for Colgate Total toothpaste on the shelves. How many different SKUs (including all sizes and flavour variations) are sold at the store? What are the advantages and disadvantages of having so many different variations?

3. Suppose you have just been hired by a jewellery manufacturer as a marketing consultant. The manufacturer has been making private-label jewellery for 75 years but is thinking about developing its own brand of jewellery. Discuss the advantages and disadvantages of such a strategy.

4. Identify a specific brand that has developed a high level of brand equity. What specific aspects of that brand establish its brand equity?

5. Are you loyal to any brands? If so, pick one and explain why you believe you are loyal, beyond that you simply like the brand. If not, pick a brand that you like and explain how you would feel and act differently toward the brand if you were loyal to it.

6. Ford Motor Company owns several brands: Ford, Lincoln, Mercury, Mazda, and Aston Martin. Within each brand are many models, each of which has a unique identifying name. Wouldn't it be easier to just identify them all as Fords? Justify your answer.

7. Unlike Ford Motor Company, BMW has only one brand and gives each car it makes a number instead of a name, for example, the BMW Series 3, Series 5, or Series 7. What are the advantages to BMW of this approach?

8. Identify a specific company that has recently introduced a new brand extension to the marketplace. Discuss whether you believe the brand extension example you provided will benefit or harm the firm.

9. Do you think all food sold in a grocery store should have an ingredient and nutrition label? Consider the perspectives of consumers, the manufacturer, and the store.

10. You are hired by a small bakery interested in distributing its product through supermarkets. The market for the bakery's products has been steadily growing and it is time to expand distribution now that the bakery has expanded its production capacity. You have an appointment with the manager of a local grocery chain. The manager is familiar with the bakery's products and is excited about the possibility of having them in the store. He has asked you to come up with a plan to package your products in a way that makes them attractive to shoppers, keeps baked goods fresh, and uses the least amount of packaging possible to satisfy even the most stringent environmentalist. You've never had to deal with this issue before. At the bakery, goods are packed in paper bags after being selected from protective glass displays. Come up with a package that works for the retailer and is affordable for the bakery.

Net Savvy

1. Visit the P&G website (www.pg.ca). Identify and briefly describe its different *product lines*. Now identify one of its *product categories*, and discuss the *product line breadth* of that particular category. Be sure to justify your answers.

2. Interbrand Corporation is a leading brand consultancy firm headquartered in New York that conducts research on the monetary value of different brands. Visit the company's website (www.interbrand.com) and access the most recent "Best Global Brands" survey. Identify the top five brands, their brand values, and their countries of origin. Describe changes in the rankings of these firms from the previous year. Why do you think the rankings changed? Identify the brands with the greatest increase and the greatest decrease in terms of percentage change in brand value from the previous year.

Chapter Case Study

BAND-AID® BRAND PRODUCTS: BUILDING ON THE VALUE OF THE BRAND[88, 89]

Part of global giant Johnson & Johnson's Consumer Products Company, Band-Aid is widely known as a leader in the wound-care market. With its dominant share of the market, the brand is widely recognized and respected by consumers and health-care professionals alike. Known as an innovator of wound-care products, the company continues to introduce new products that exploit creative technologies, one of which led *Good Housekeeping* magazine to name Band-Aid Brand Liquid Bandage a "Good Buy" award winner. From its early beginnings to today, the company has excelled at providing value to its customers and demonstrated that people across the world can trust the brand.

The Brand Begins

Necessity is the mother of invention, and in the case of Band-Aid the saying applies. Back in 1920,

Band-Aids come in a variety of sizes and styles. These packages are made for children.

when Earl Dickson came home from his cotton-buying job at Johnson & Johnson, he would always find a hot meal that his wife Josephine had prepared for him. He also found visible burns and cuts on Josephine from her kitchen labours, which prompted Earl to piece together gauze squares and adhesive tape to cover her wounds. Soon, Earl decided to prepare ready-made bandages in this fashion, with pieces of gauze at intervals along the tape so that Josephine could cut the premade strip and tend to her wounds throughout the day. When the product was first launched in the market, the bandages were made by hand, were not sterile, and had annual sales of just $3000.

The Company Today

Today, Band-Aid products are machine-made and completely sterile. A visit to the company's website (www.bandaid.com) reveals the distance Band-Aid has come from the early tape and gauze product, as well as the modern demand for over-the-counter first-aid products in a variety of categories.

In keeping with its long history of product innovations, the company continues to invest in new product development and marketing (Exhibit 9.10). Band-Aids come in a host of styles, including those with popular characters for kids; uniquely shaped bandages for various parts of the body; antibiotic Band-Aids to help fight germs; waterproof products with aloe to treat burns; scar-healing strips; bandages in clear plastic, stretchy cloth, and round and square shapes; and treated and untreated pads. Moreover, the Band-Aid franchise has expanded to include various ointments, gauze, tapes, and kits for a plethora of first-aid needs. For example, One-Step Cleansing + Infection Protection Foam antiseptic cleans and heals wounds without the need for antibiotic ointment; Calamine Spray dries rashes from poison ivy; Bug-Bite Relief Patches relieve itching and prevent scratching; and FIRST AID TO GO!® Mini First-Aid Kits include essential travel-sized products.

But new product introductions by Band-Aid don't come cheap; of the $28-million marketing budget for 2003, $17 million was earmarked for three new product extensions. Advanced Healing Blister Block, a round, waterproof cushioning strip to heal and prevent foot blisters, received $7 million in marketing support to tout its ability to promote fast, natural healing. Finger Care Tough Strips obtained a marketing budget of $5 million and was rolled out as an extension of regular finger-care products. Finally, Extra Large Tough Strips were also supported with $5 million for marketing.[90] Previous years' launches were similarly supported, including Liquid Bandages ($7 million), Water Block Bandages ($8 million), and Hurt-Free Antiseptic Wash ($5 million).

The company is in an enviable position. People around the world see the value of Band-Aid products to heal, prevent, and repair minor nicks, cuts, scrapes, wounds, and bruises. Continued product innovations and line expansions likely will help the company continue to be the most recognized name in tape, bandages, and gauze.

EXHIBIT 9.10	Examples of Band-Aid Product Innovations

Year	Product Innovation
1920	Band-Aid brand adhesive bandages—7.5-cm wide and 46-cm long—introduced to the market
1924	First machine-made, sterile bandages
1940	Packaging adds red strings to open bandage packages
1951	Plastic strips
1956	Decorated bandages
1958	Sheer vinyl bandages
1994	Sport-strip bandages
1997	Antibiotic adhesive bandages with ointment on the pad
2000	Advanced healing strips for wound care
2001	Liquid bandage that promotes fast healing
2003	Scar-healing technology that fades red and raised scars
2007	Plus Antibiotic bandages to reduce infection and scars
2009	Anti-Blister Stick to reduce rubbing on skin and prevent blisters

Source: www.bandaid.com.

Questions

1. Visit the company's website (www.bandaid.com) and identify and describe the different product lines that it markets. How would you describe its product line breadth?

2. Review the different product categories in each of the company's product lines. Which has the greatest breadth? Which has the least?

3. Look at the new products that the company offers. Identify which are extensions of the Band-Aid brand name and which are not. Discuss the extent to which the brand extensions might dilute brand equity.

4. Review the company's products designed for children. To what extent do these use manufacturer (national) branding? Private-label (store) branding? Licensed branding? Justify your answers. What added values do these products offer compared with regular Band-Aid protection products?

 Practise and learn online with Connect. Connect allows you to practise important concepts at your own pace and on your own schedule, with 24/7 online access to an eBook, practice quizzes, interactivities, videos, study tools, additional resources, and more.

CHAPTER 10

Services:
The Intangible Product

When you want to get rid of old furniture, ancient appliances, or yard waste, who would you call? According to an Ipsos Reid study, 1-800-GOT-JUNK? is the leading branded junk removal option. It was founded in Vancouver in 1989 by Brian Scudmore as a way to put himself through university. Today, the $150-million business operates in more than 330 cities in Canada, the United States, and Australia. Its goal is to become the world's largest junk removal company, the Starbucks of the trash business.[1]

The company has paid careful attention to branding, right down to the blue and green colours used on trucks. Brands help add tangibility, a crucial component for services companies that otherwise sell the invisible; for example, Got-Junk consumers have no tangible reminder of the service that has been provided except perhaps for more space in the garage or basement. The gleaming trucks send a signal of quality and professionalism to customers. Rather than buying top of mind awareness via traditional advertising, Got-Junk builds buzz at the local level with its brightly coloured trucks, lawn signs, and enthusiastic employees. The company's public relations staff has successfully generated more than 1000 articles, further raising awareness and communicating their message to millions of consumers through appearances on *Dr. Phil* and *Oprah*. In Ontario, a cost-effective customer acquisition campaign gave consumers who ordered the company's services a $20 gift certificate for The Beer Store. Teaming up with The Beer Store made sense because its large and reliable base of male customers was the main target audience for Got-Junk's service.[2]

Finding and keeping employees who deliver outstanding customer service is another key to success for services companies. Hiring great people and treating them well

Learning Objectives

After studying this chapter you should be able to

LO1 Identify how marketing a service differs from marketing a product by applying the principles of intangibility, inseparability, inconsistency, and inventory

LO 2 Explain why it is important that service marketers understand and manage customer expectations

LO 3 Describe strategies that firms can use to help employees provide better service

LO4 Summarize three service recovery strategies

is a core belief at Got-Junk and results in the ability to deliver an exceptional customer experience. Recruitment became a lot easier after the company was ranked as the number one company to work for in British Columbia two years in a row. Scudmore was also named Entrepreneur of the Year by the International Franchise Association.[3] The public recognition not only garnered media attention, but also helped attract new employees in a tough labour market. Since services businesses rely on employees to act as company ambassadors, Got-Junk provides staff with bright blue fleece shirts emblazoned with the company logo, helping to present a uniform—no pun intended—image to customers. Strategies to keep staff pumped and motivated to stay with the company are critical, so employees are encouraged to submit their suggestions to a "Can you imagine?" wall at head office. Ideas so far include having a toy junk truck in McDonald's Happy Meals and wrapping the logo on a 737 jet.[4]

The company is dedicated to responsible junk removal and continually monitors its environmental performance, measuring the amount of junk collected and where it goes. It recycles as much of the junk it collects as possible and donates reusable household or commercial items to local charities. A published audit report shows that 40.6 percent is recycled, 16.2 percent is converted to energy, and 4.5 percent is reused.[5]

Got-Junk has big plans to build success along the lines of Starbucks, FedEx, or Southwest Airlines. Their slogan proves they've learned from Nike, too. It's "Just Get It Done." .::

customer service
Specifically refers to human or mechanical activities firms undertake to help satisfy their customers' needs and wants.

Got-Junk turns trash into cash, an example of a firm that provides services as opposed to products. Whereas a service is any intangible offering that involves a deed, performance, or effort that cannot be physically possessed,[6] **customer service** specifically refers to human or mechanical activities that firms undertake to help satisfy their customers' needs and wants. By providing good customer service, firms add value to their products or services.

In this chapter, we examine the unique characteristics of services that differentiate them from products. Then, as shown in the chapter roadmap, we discuss how companies can provide great service and use elements in the Gaps Model to help them meet customer expectations. Lastly, we look at how companies can recover from inevitable service failures.

Exhibit 10.1 illustrates the continuum from a pure service to a pure product. Some firms lie somewhere in the middle and include some service and some product or sell products with an "embedded" service element (e.g., restaurants). As we noted in Chapter 2, even firms engaged primarily in selling a product, such as apparel stores, typically view service as a method to maintain a sustainable competitive advantage. This chapter moves on to take an inclusive view of services as anything from pure service businesses to a business that uses service as a differentiating tool to help it sell physical products.

CHAPTER ROADMAP

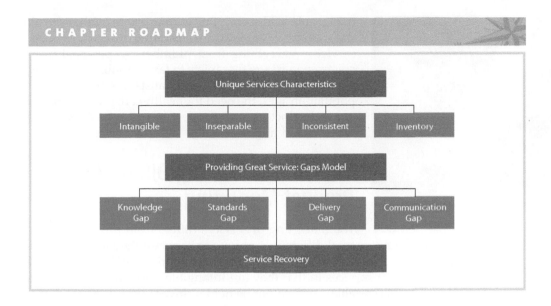

Economies of developed countries such as Canada have become increasingly dependent on services. For example, the service sector makes up more than 70 percent of Canada's economy, the lion's share of jobs, and is growing far faster than goods-producing industries. This dependence and the growth of service-oriented economies in developed countries have emerged for several reasons.

First, it is generally less expensive for firms to manufacture their products in less-developed countries. Even if the goods are finished in Canada, some of their components likely were produced elsewhere. In turn, the proportion of service production to goods production in Canada, and other similar economies, has steadily increased over time.

Second, household maintenance activities, which many people performed by themselves in the past, have become quite specialized. Food preparation, lawn maintenance, house cleaning, laundry and dry cleaning, hair care, and automobile maintenance all are often performed by specialists in the modern economy.

Third, people place a high value on convenience and leisure. Most households have little time for the household maintenance tasks mentioned in the previous

EXHIBIT 10.1 | The Service–Product Continuum

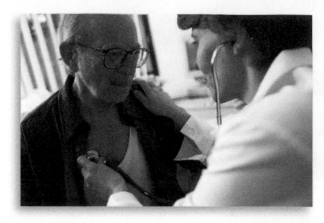

As the population ages, the need for health-care professionals increases.

L01

intangible
A characteristic of a service; it cannot be touched, tasted, or seen like a pure product can.

paragraph, and many are willing to pay others to do their chores. People are demanding more specialized services—everything from plumbers to personal trainers, from massage therapists to tax specialists, from lawyers to travel and leisure specialists. As the Canadian population ages, the need for health-care professionals—not only doctors and nurses, but also assisted-living facilities and nursing homes—also increases.

Services Marketing Differs from Product Marketing

The marketing of services differs from product marketing because of four fundamental differences unique to services: they are intangible, inseparable, variable, and perishable.[7] To help remember these differences, think of them as the four Is of services in that they are intangible, inseparable from their providers, inconsistent (variable), and cannot be held in inventory (perishable). (See Exhibit 10.2.) These differences make marketing services considerably more challenging than marketing products. This section examines these four differences and discusses how they affect marketing strategies.

Intangible

As the title of this chapter implies, the most fundamental difference between a product and a service is that services are **intangible**; they cannot be touched,

EXHIBIT 10.2	Core Differences between Services and Goods

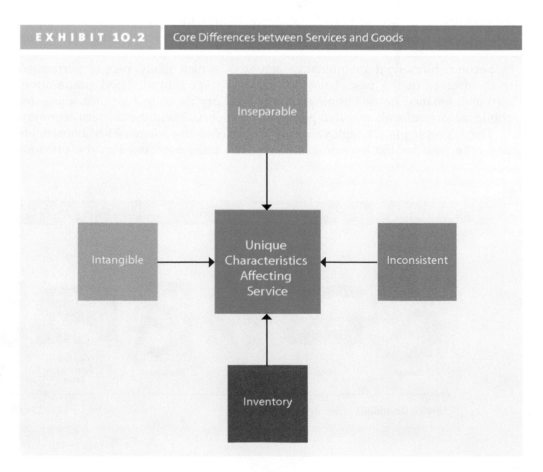

tasted, or seen like a pure product can. When you get a physical examination, you see and hear the doctor, but the service itself is intangible. This intangibility can prove highly challenging to marketers. For instance, it makes it difficult to convey the benefits of services. Try describing whether the experience of visiting your dentist was good or bad and why. Health-care service providers (e.g., physicians, dentists) offer cues to help their customers experience and perceive their service more positively, such as a waiting room stocked with TV sets, computer games, and toys for children; upscale beverages; and comfortable chairs to create an atmosphere that appeals to the target market.

Similarly, Starbucks has always enhanced its service offering by providing a comfortable and cozy atmosphere for drinking coffee, working, reading, or chatting with friends. It adds tangibility to its service by creating a warm and inviting environment and offering free WiFi to customers nationwide. RBC Royal Bank offers clients *my*FinanceTracker, an online financial management tool that tracks expenses, categorizes transactions, and provides advanced budgeting capabilities for personal banking and credit card accounts.[8] The tool improves RBC's service offering and adds tangibility to the banking experience by helping clients save time and money. Refer to Social Media Marketing 10.1 to see how Cineplex Entertainment adds tangibility to its services.

Furthermore, a service is also difficult to promote because it can't be shown directly to potential customers. Marketers must therefore creatively employ symbols and images to promote and sell services, as Walt Disney World does in using its advertising to evoke images of happy families and nostalgic memories of Mickey Mouse and previous visits to the theme park. Likewise, Cirque du Soleil, considered Canada's top cultural export, adds tangibility to its performances with mesmerizingly staged acrobatics, which are backed by a live orchestra playing an original score. The entire circus experience is carefully coordinated to create memorable impressions—the Porta Potties on its big-top sites even have running water.[9] Fans can also buy a wide variety of Cirque du Soleil–branded merchandise (e.g., music, videos, books, clothing, and accessories) to extend their positive memories of the performances. In another example, professional medical services provide appropriate images of personnel doing their jobs in white coats surrounded by high-tech equipment. Dentists provide patients with tangible evidence of their visits in the form of free toothbrushes. Educational institutions promote the quality of their services by touting their famous faculty and alumni, as well as their accreditations. They also often use images of happy students sitting spellbound in front of a fascinating professor or going on to lucrative careers of their own.

Because of the intangibility of services, the images marketers use reinforce the benefit or value that a service provides. Professional service providers, such as doctors, lawyers, accountants, and consultants, depend heavily on consumers' perceptions of their integrity and trustworthiness. Yet the promotional campaigns some of these professionals use have been criticized by their peers and consumer welfare groups. Tension is created when service providers such as personal injury lawyers use aggressive marketing tactics to attract clients to their service but still attempt to maintain a perception of integrity and trustworthiness or when invasion of privacy becomes an issue, as discussed in Ethical Dilemma 10.1.

At Starbucks, customers can have a drink, buy iTunes gift cards, and surf the Internet by using the stores' free WiFi access.

Inseparable Production and Consumption

Another difference between services and products is that services are produced and consumed at the same time—that is, service and

Social Media Marketing 10.1   Cineplex Creates a Community Around Entertainment

The launch of an online social networking community (mycineplex.com) gave Cineplex Entertainment an opportunity to experiment with social media. Following the website's initial success, the company quickly added a Facebook page, contests, polls, and Q & A sessions to encourage fan interaction. It posted videos on YouTube and initiated social bookmarking efforts to increase brand awareness and communicate the message that mycineplex was more than just a place to check out showtimes.

Membership at mycineplex is free, adding tangibility to an otherwise intangible service. The online community enhances the entertainment experience for movie lovers who can review and discuss their movie thoughts with other fans. Members benefit from access to unique services such as exclusive contests, access to advance screenings, personalized e-newsletters, and online and mobile ticketing.[10] For example, Cineplex ran a members-only contest to promote the release of the blockbuster movie of Dan Brown's novel *Angels & Demons*. The contest gave fans a chance to win prizes, demonstrating some of the more concrete perks of membership.

The site also helps Cineplex deal with the issue of service perishability. Empty seats in theatres can't be held in inventory for future use. By using social media tools such as Facebook and Twitter, Cineplex can more fully engage members to provide them with timely updates. The interactivity of the website gives members more reasons to visit theatres more often, reducing reliance on mainstream media and increasing the time they spend building a relationship with Cineplex. And it seems as though these efforts are working; in spite of the financial market meltdown in 2008, theatre attendance grew 16 percent in the final quarter of 2008.[11]

---

inseparable
A characteristic of a service: it is produced and consumed at the same time—that is, service and consumption are inseparable.

consumption are **inseparable**. Because service production can't be separated from consumption, astute service marketers provide opportunities for their customers to get directly involved in the service. Health-care providers have found, for instance, that the more control they allow their patients in determining their course of treatment, the more satisfied those patients are.[12]

Because the service is inseparable from its consumption, customers rarely have the opportunity to try the service before they purchase it. And after the service has been performed, it can't be returned. Imagine telling your dentist that you want a "test" cavity filled before he or she starts drilling a real one or asking to try out a new look before your stylist lops several inches off your hair. Because the purchase risk in these scenarios can be relatively high, services sometimes provide extended warranties and 100-percent satisfaction guarantees, such as First Choice Haircutters, which promotes "Affordable, Professional Haircare. Guaranteed." Many hotels (e.g., Comfort Inn, Comfort Suites, Quality Inn, Sleep Inn, Clarion) post claims advising guests, "If you are not satisfied with your accommodations or our service, please advise the front desk of a problem right away and give them an opportunity to correct the situation. If the hotel staff is unable to satisfy you, they will give you up to one night's free stay."[13]

Inconsistent

inconsistent
A characteristic of a service: its quality may vary because it is provided by humans.

The more humans that are needed to provide a service, the more likely that the service's quality will be **inconsistent** or variable. A hair stylist may give bad haircuts in the morning because he or she went out the night before; yet, that stylist still may offer a better service than the undertrained stylist working at the next station. A restaurant, which offers a mixture of services and products, generally can control its food quality but not the variability in food preparation or delivery. If a consumer has a problem with a product, it can be replaced, remade, destroyed, or, if it is already in the supply chain, recalled. In many cases, the problem can even be fixed before the product gets into consumers' hands. But an inferior service can't be recalled; by the time the firm recognizes a problem, the damage has been done.

Keeping Personal Information Private on Facebook

It's nearly impossible to discuss social media without talking about privacy. This topic is important for marketers to consider because it affects the usage and adoption of social media sites. Currently, 75 percent of social media users say their security is important or very important, and about one-quarter of social media users are concerned about identity theft online.[14] Sites such as ReclaimPrivacy.org even let you scan your profile to detect how much personal information you are sharing publicly.

Facebook privacy has been an especially hot topic. Concerns over lack of privacy in 2010 led to the introduction of Quit Facebook Day, pioneered by Torontonians Joseph Dee and Matthew Milan.[15] Rather than demand that 400-million users abandon the site forever, the initiative was intended to bring privacy and respect concerns to the forefront. Young people are privacy savvy and understand that online profiles are important for managing their online reputation. About half of people aged 18 to 29 have deleted comments that others have made on their profile, and a similar number have untagged photos that had included their name.[16] Such attentiveness is critical when career aspirations and personal lives can cross, such as when potential employers search social media profiles before making hiring decisions.

People have shown concern about the collection and use of private information by Facebook, and how these details are shared. Facebook users were forced to grapple with more than 100 different settings to keep their personal information private, which was very confusing for users who were concerned about how this data was being used and who wanted to limit the use of the information.[17] In response to outcries from privacy watchdogs, Facebook simplified its system, paring it down to only 15 privacy settings.

Facebook co-founder, Mark Zuckerberg, faced intense scrutiny over these issues. He agreed that having fewer privacy settings is better, and said that users need control of their own information. "People are finding . . . value in sharing; as long as they have control of that, they are comfortable with that."[18]

Public outcry about a lack of privacy doesn't seem to have slowed the use of social media sites. Despite consumer claims of being concerned with privacy, only 35 percent of users choose high security settings to protect their personal information, and more than 80 percent have no concerns about sharing their name, gender, and email address. The most common complaint is that unsecure social media sites result in increased, unwanted advertisements.[19] Marketers must understand and respond to concerns such as these or risk backlash from consumers.

Some marketers of services strive to reduce service inconsistency through training and standardization. Enterprise Rent-A-Car, for instance, has worked to standardize its service delivery across North America and, to that end, provides extensive training to its associates. Go to any Enterprise outlet at any airport and chances are you will be greeted in the same personalized way. The airport shuttle drivers will load and unload your bags. When you get off the shuttle, you will be greeted by name, and your car will be ready to go in minutes. This smooth and pleasant service transaction is the result of the company's very specific service standards and excellent training program.

Enterprise Rent-A-Car reduces its service inconsistency through training and standardization. You get the same great service everywhere you go.

Marketers also can use the inconsistent nature of services to their advantage. A micromarketing segmentation strategy can customize a service to meet customers' needs exactly (see Chapter 7). Technology services company Nerds On Site will come to your home or office and take care of any repair or service your PC might need: setting up a network, cleaning your hard drive, or designing or hosting your website. Each customer's needs are different, so Nerds On Site employs a cadre of consultants who possess a variety of skills. Clients are matched with their

Nerds on Site match clients with a "Primary Nerd" to ensure personalized service.

very own "Primary Nerd" on the basis of their needs, which allows for a fully personalized service offering.

Such micromarketing can be expensive to deliver though, particularly for a firm that offers multiple services. Consumers also may get confused or even irritated if they must pay for each little service. Imagine a hotel that charged separately for each bed, towel, bar of soap, minute of TV use, and lap in the swimming pool. Instead, service providers usually bundle their services into one package and charge a single price. For example, Club Med resorts offer all-inclusive amenity packages for one price, which includes, for example, a flight from Montreal to Club Med Punta Cana, Dominican Republic, and then accommodations, meals, snacks, bar service, and sports and entertainment activities once you arrive for about $1800 for seven nights—include a friend for $1300 more![20]

In an alternative approach, some service providers tackle the inconsistency issue by replacing people with machines. For simple transactions such as getting cash, using an ATM is usually quicker and more convenient—and less variable—than waiting in line for a bank teller. Self-checkout machines are multiplying in grocery and discount stores at blistering speed. Even libraries are installing self-checkout machines for books. Canadians are accustomed to serving themselves and quickly adopt new technology. An Ipsos Reid/NCR study showed that 56 percent of Canadians are more likely to shop at stores with self-service than those without.[21]

Self-checkouts are successful and increase customer loyalty because they appeal to shoppers who want to move quickly and believe they can zip through checkouts faster by using the machines. Although expensive, the machines reduce labour expenses; one cashier can oversee the operation of four to eight self-checkouts. And the machines don't have to be trained; nor do they ever come to work late or with a bad attitude, thereby reducing service inconsistency.

The technological delivery of services sometimes causes additional problems. Customers may not embrace the idea of replacing a human with a machine for business interactions or have problems using the technology. In addition, the technology may not perform adequately, such as self-checkout scanners that fail to scan all merchandise or ATMs that run out of money or are out of order.

Do self-checkout machines increase or reduce consumers' perception of service?

The Internet has reduced service inconsistency in several areas. Customers can purchase travel items (e.g., airline tickets, hotel rooms, rental cars), concert and movie tickets, insurance, mortgages, and merchandise directly via the Internet or by cellphone. Cineplex launched mobile applications for BlackBerry, iPhone, and Android smartphones to allow customers to buy movie tickets faster. The apps not only reduce inconsistency for movie goers, but also reduce costs for theatres. And if the customer wants more information than is available online, websites provide ways to contact customer service personnel by email or telephone.

Beyond online benefits, the Internet has also reduced service inconsistency. At the William Lutsky YMCA in Edmonton, members can use FitLinxx, a computerized system, to track their workout performance. New users establish goals, workouts, and schedules, and receive detailed workout programs (e.g., at least 14 abdominal muscle workouts pop up when users select "abs"). FitLinxx learns users' programs, coaches them individually throughout workouts, and tracks progress over time. Not only does the system have health benefits for users, who always get a consistent workout; it has also boosted customer retention, and users typically exercise more often than average.[22]

Inventory

Services are perishable because they cannot be held in **inventory** or stored for use in the future. You can't stockpile a yoga class like you could a six-pack of beer, for instance. The perishability of services provides both challenges and opportunities to marketers in terms of the critical task of matching demand and supply. As long as the demand for and the supply of the service match closely, there is no problem; but, unfortunately, this perfect matching rarely occurs. A ski area, for instance, can be open as long as there is snow, even at night, but demand peaks on weekends and holidays, so ski areas often offer less expensive tickets during off-peak periods to stimulate demand. Airlines, cruise ships, movie theatres, and restaurants confront similar challenges and attack them in similar ways. Airlines offer promotional pricing to encourage people to book flights during the off-season, and movie theatres routinely discount matinee showings when demand is typically lower. Looking to increase facility usage and reach new audiences, Cineplex Galaxy started broadcasting NHL games live in five Canadian cities in 2006. For some hockey fans, it's the next best thing to being there, and at a ticket price of $10.95, fans pay only a fraction of the cost of watching, for example, the Toronto Maple Leafs at the Air Canada Centre, which costs between $23 and $381 a ticket.[23]

Balancing the ups and downs of demand and capacity is challenging. As noted earlier, unlike products, services can't be stockpiled in inventory. For services companies, excess demand results in having to turn customers away in peak periods, while excess capacity may mean less desirable expense to revenue ratios. For example, dental hygienists, rent, and other expenses still need to be paid even if customers forget their appointments, so dental offices maximize capacity by making advance reminder calls to patients or by charging cancellation fees to clients who do not show up for their appointments without adequate notice. Hotel reservation systems offer guaranteed late arrivals, ensuring that revenue is not forfeited by holding rooms until very late in the day. Dealing with the ups and downs of weather can also pose a challenge to some businesses, as discussed in Entrepreneurial Marketing 10.1.

Inventory
A characteristic of a service: it is perishable and cannot be stored for future use.

Since services are perishable, service providers such as ski areas offer less expensive tickets at night to stimulate demand.

| Entrepreneurial Marketing 10.1 | The Calypso Adventure |

Guy Drouin is banking on the fact that regardless of how the economy is doing, people still want to have fun. And he hopes they'll do it at Calypso Park, Canada's largest themed water park. Drouin has been preoccupied with theme parks ever since 1963, when his father started charging a fee to tobogganers who wanted to sled down his Quebec City hill. When Drouin took over the business in 1971, he modernized things, added cross-country ski trails and skating tracks, and hosted the park's first off-season event, a motorcycle competition.[24] Over the next 10 years, he continued to expand Valcartier Vacation Village's winter activities, and in 1980 he introduced water features.

At the time, there were very few water parks. Since then, they've taken off; there are more than 1000 in North America, according to the World Waterpark Association. Approximately 80 million people visited water parks in Canada, the United States, and Mexico during the summer of 2008, with attendance growing by 3 to 5 percent annually over the last five years.[25]

And so it was a logical next step for Drouin to expand his business by building Calypso Park, a new park that opened in 2010. Located in Limoges, Ontario, the park features 35 waterslides and a wide variety of other activities, including two international-calibre beach volleyball courts. Although Limoges is a small town, the 100-acre water park is only 20 minutes from Ottawa and 75 minutes from Montreal. The location in the Ottawa-Gatineau region was carefully chosen based on consumer demographics. According to Statistics Canada, the average family income was $75,200, compared to the national average of $68,800.[26] Best of all, there was no real competition within a 100-kilometre radius.

Being at the mercy of the weather makes managing the ups and downs of capacity and demand at a Calypso Park challenging. People still go to amusement parks when it rains; but, they only go to a water park when it's sunny. Only open in the summer, bad weather can spell disaster for Calypso, a challenge its Quebec cousin, Valcartier Vacation Village has avoided by being open year-round. It's a water park in the summer and an outdoor enthusiast's playground in the winter.

To help counter weather concerns, Drouin maintains Calypso's water temperature at 27-degrees Celsius, toasty enough to keep park attendance high even if the air temperature is cool.[27] Another perk for park visitors is "Money at my fingertip," a point of sale payment system that uses biometric technology to give guests access to their money for food, beverages, or other merchandise.[28] The convenience of being able to make purchases without having to carry money, especially when you're wearing a swimsuit, helps deal with service inconsistency and adds to the overall park experience. Attention to details such as these should ensure that the warm Caribbean atmosphere of Calypso Park makes a big splash with customers.

Water features such as Pirate's Aquaplay make Calypso Park an exciting adventure.

L02 Providing Great Service: The Gaps Model

Certainly, providing great service is not easy, and it requires a diligent effort to analyze service processes step by step in order to improve them. We now examine what is known as the Gaps Model, which is designed to highlight those areas where customers believe they are getting less or poorer services than they expect (the gaps) and how these gaps can be closed.

service gap
Results when a service fails to meet the expectations that customers have about how it should be delivered.

Customers have certain expectations about how a service should be delivered. When the delivery of that service fails to meet those expectations, a **service gap** results. The Gaps Model (Exhibit 10.3) is designed to encourage the systematic examination of all aspects of the service delivery process and prescribe the steps needed to develop an optimal service strategy.[29]

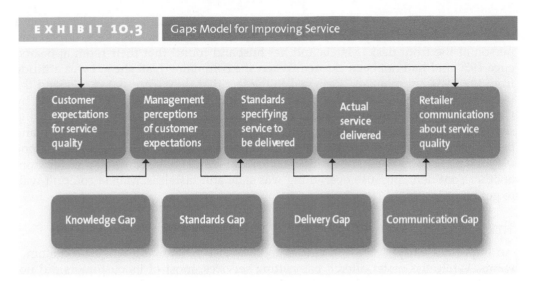

EXHIBIT 10.3	Gaps Model for Improving Service

Source: Michael Levy and Barton Weitz, *Retailing Management*, 6th ed. (Burr Ridge, IL: McGraw-Hill, 2007). Adapted from Valerie Zeithaml, A. Parasuraman, and Leonard Berry, *Delivering Quality Customer Service* (New York: The Free Press, 1990) and Valerie Zeithaml, Leonard Berry, and A. Parasuraman, "Communication and Control Processes in the Delivery of Service Quality," *Journal of Marketing* 52, no. 2 (April 1988), pp. 35–48.

As Exhibit 10.3 shows, there are four service gaps:

1. The **knowledge gap** reflects the difference between customers' expectations and the firm's perception of those customer expectations. Firms can close this gap by matching customer expectations with actual service through research.

2. The **standards gap** pertains to the difference between the firm's perceptions of customers' expectations and the service standards it sets. Firms can narrow this gap by setting appropriate service standards and measuring service performance.

3. The **delivery gap** is the difference between the firm's service standards and the actual service it provides to customers. This gap can be closed by getting employees to meet or exceed service standards.

4. The **communication gap** refers to the difference between the actual service provided to customers and the service that the firm's promotion program promises. Generally firms can close this gap if they are more realistic about the services they can provide and manage customer expectations effectively.

As we discuss the four gaps, we will apply them to the experience that Marcia Kessler had with a motel in Muskoka, Ontario. She saw an ad for a weekend package that quoted a very reasonable daily rate and listed the free amenities available at Paradise Motel: free babysitting services, a piano bar with a nightly singer, a free continental breakfast, a heated swimming pool, and newly decorated rooms. When she booked the room, Marcia

knowledge gap
Reflects the difference between customers' expectations and the firm's perception of those expectations.

standards gap
Pertains to the difference between the firm's perceptions of customers' expectations and the service standards it sets.

delivery gap
The difference between the firm's service standards and the actual service it provides to customers.

communication gap
Refers to the difference between the actual service provided to customers and the service that the firm's promotion program promises.

What service gaps did Marcia experience while on vacation at the Paradise Motel in Muskoka?

discovered that the price advertised was not available during the weekend, and a three-day minimum stay was required. After checking in with a very unpleasant person at the front desk, Marcia and her husband found that their room appeared circa 1950 and had not been cleaned. When she complained, all she got was attitude from the assistant manager. Resigned to the fact that they were slated to spend the weekend, she decided to go for a swim. Unfortunately, the water was "heated" by Georgian Bay and hovered around 10 degrees. No one was using the babysitting services because there were few young children at the resort. It turns out the piano bar singer was the second cousin of the owner, and he couldn't carry a tune, let alone play the piano very well. The continental breakfast must have come all the way from another continent, because everything was stale and tasteless. Marcia couldn't wait to get home.

The Knowledge Gap: Knowing What Customers Want

An important early step in providing good service is knowing what the customer wants. While the motel offered babysitting services, most of its customers did not have kids, had not brought them on their trip, or simply did not want to use the service. However, all guests want their rooms cleaned prior to check-in.

To reduce the knowledge gap, firms must understand the customers' expectations, which can be accomplished through customer research and by increasing the interaction and communication between managers and employees.

Understanding Customer Expectations Customers' expectations are based on their knowledge and experiences.[30] Marcia's expectations were that her room would be ready and clean when she got there, the swimming pool would be heated, the singer would be able to sing, and the breakfast would be fresh.

Expectations vary according to the type of service. Marcia's expectations might have been higher, for instance, if she were staying at a Fairmont rather than the Paradise Motel. At Fairmont, she might expect employees to know her by name, be aware of her dietary preferences, and have placed fresh fruit of her choice and fresh-cut flowers in her room before she arrived.

People's expectations also vary depending on the situation. Marcia may be satisfied with both the preceding hotel properties, depending on the circumstances. If she were travelling on business, the Paradise Motel might be fine, but if she were celebrating her tenth wedding anniversary, she probably would prefer the Fairmont. Regardless of these choices, however, the service provider needs to know and understand the expectations of the customers in its target market.

Evaluating Service Quality by Using Well-Established Marketing Metrics To meet or exceed customers' expectations, marketers must determine what those expectations are. Yet because of their intangibility, the **service quality**, or customers' perceptions of how well a service meets or exceeds their expectations, often is difficult for customers to evaluate.[31]

Customers generally use five distinct service dimensions to determine overall service quality: reliability, responsiveness, assurance, empathy, and tangibles (Exhibit 10.4).

If you were to apply the five service dimensions to your own decision-making process when you selected a university—which provides the service of education—you might find results like those in Exhibit 10.5.

If your expectations include an individualized experience at a state-of-the-art institution, perhaps University B is a better alternative for you. But if you are relying heavily on academic performance and career placement from your university experience, then University A might be a better choice. If a strong culture and tradition are important to you, University A offers this type of environment. What were your expectations, and how did your university choices fall within these service dimensions?

service quality
Customers' perceptions of how well a service meets or exceeds their expectations.

EXHIBIT 10.4	Building Blocks of Service Quality

RELIABILITY:
The ability to perform the service dependably and accurately.

RESPONSIVENESS:
The willingness to help customers and provide prompt service.

ASSURANCE:
The knowledge of and courtesy by employees and their ability to convey trust and confidence.

EMPATHY:
The caring, individualized attention provided to customers.

TANGIBLES:
The appearance of physical facilities, equipment, personnel, and communication materials.

Marketing research (see Chapter 4) provides a means to better understand consumers' service expectations and their perceptions of service quality. This research can be extensive and expensive, or it can be integrated into a firm's everyday interactions with customers. Today, most service firms have developed voice-of-customer programs and employ ongoing marketing research to assess how well they are meeting their customers' expectations.

EXHIBIT 10.5	Collegiate Service Dimensions

	University A	University B
Reliability	Offers sound curriculum with extensive placement services and internships.	Curriculum covers all the basics but important courses are not always available. Career placement is haphazard at best.
Responsiveness	Slow to respond to application. Very structured visitation policy. Rather inflexible with regard to personal inquiries or additional meetings.	Quick response during application process. Open visitation policy. Offers variety of campus resources to help with decision making.
Assurance	Staff seems very confident in reputation and services.	Informal staff who convey enthusiasm for institution.
Empathy	Seems to process student body as a whole rather than according to individual needs or concerns.	Very interested in providing a unique experience for each student.
Tangibles	Very traditional campus with old-world look and feel. Facilities are manicured. Dorm rooms are large, but bathrooms are a little old.	New campus with modern architecture. Campus is less manicured. Dorm rooms are spacious with newer bathrooms.

A systematic **voice-of-customer (VOC) program** collects customer insights and intelligence to influence and drive business decisions. For instance, Dell launched IdeaStorm.com, an online forum that allows people to submit ideas for improving its products and services. The community votes on the best ideas and if they make sense, the company will act on them. When IdeaStorm.com contributors wanted Linux pre-installed on their PCs and notebooks Dell surveyed 100 000 customers to get more insights and ended up implementing the idea. Three months after launching IdeaStorm.com more than 3500 ideas had been posted.[32] Aeroplan uses online surveys and conducts in-person "kitchen table" meetings with selected members, asking them everything from what their redemption experience is like to what new services and improvements they'd like to see.[33] Feedback from FedEx's VOC program, involving in-person meetings with business customers, resulted in the development of its intra-Canada deferred (two-day) service.[34]

Sustainable Marketing 10.1 provides a glimpse into how the voice-of-customer insights can be applied to employees in the green building industry.

An important marketing metric to evaluate how well firms perform on the five service quality dimensions (Exhibit 10.4), the concept of the **zone of tolerance** refers to the area between customers' expectations regarding their desired service and the minimum level of acceptable service—that is, the difference between what the customer really wants and what he or she will accept before going elsewhere.[35] To define the zone of tolerance, firms ask a series of questions about each service quality dimension that relate to

- The desired and expected level of service for each dimension, from low to high.
- Customers' perceptions of how well the focal service performs and how well a competitive service performs, from low to high.
- The importance of each service quality dimension.

Exhibit 10.6 illustrates the results of such an analysis for Lou's Local Diner, a family-owned restaurant. The rankings on the left are based on a 9-point scale, on which 1 is low and 9 is high. The length of each box illustrates the zone of tolerance for each service quality dimension. For instance, according to the length of the reliability box, customers expect a fairly high level of reliability (top of the box) and will also accept only a fairly high level of reliability (bottom of the box). On the other end of the scale, customers expect a high level of assurance (top of the box) but will accept a fairly low level (bottom of the box). This difference is to be expected, because the customers also were asked to assign an importance score to the five service quality dimensions so that the total equals 100 percent (see bottom of Exhibit 10.6). Looking at the average importance score, we conclude that reliability is relatively important to these customers, but assurance is not. So customers have a fairly narrow zone of tolerance for service dimensions that are fairly important to them and a wider range of tolerance for those service dimensions that are less important. Also note that Lou's Local Diner always rates higher than its primary competitor, Well-Known National Chain, on each dimension.

Further note that Well-Known National Chain scores below the zone of tolerance on the tangibles dimension, meaning that customers are not willing to accept the way the restaurant looks and smells. Lou's Local Diner, in contrast, performs above the zone of tolerance on the responsiveness dimension—maybe even too well. Lou's may wish to conduct

voice-of-customer (VOC) program
An ongoing marketing research system that collects customer insights and intelligence to influence and drive business decisions.

zone of tolerance
The area between customers' expectations regarding their desired service and the minimum level of acceptable service—that is, the difference between what the customer really wants and what he or she will accept before going elsewhere.

Lou's Local Diner always rates higher than its primary competitor, a well-known national chain, on each service quality dimension.

| EXHIBIT 10.6 | Customers' Evaluation of Service Quality |

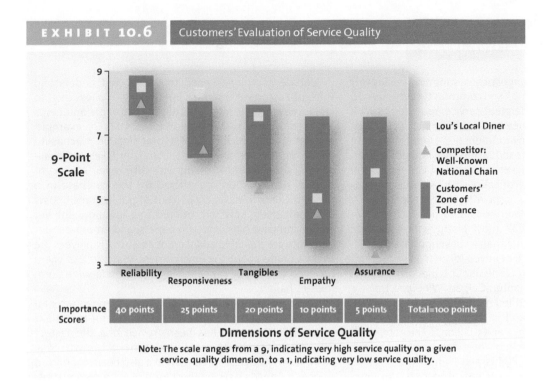

Note: The scale ranges from a 9, indicating very high service quality on a given
service quality dimension, to a 1, indicating very low service quality.

further research to verify which responsiveness aspects it is performing so well, and then consider toning those aspects down. For example, being responsive to customers' desires to have a diner that serves breakfast 24 hours a day can be expensive and may not add any further value to Lou's Local Diner, because customers would accept more limited times.

A very straightforward and inexpensive method of collecting consumers' perceptions of service quality is to gather them at the time of the sale. Service providers can ask customers how they liked the service—though customers often are hesitant to provide negative feedback directly to the person who provided the service—or distribute a simple questionnaire. Starbucks customers can rate their experience by visiting the web survey at the bottom of their receipts. Using this method, a customer does not have to make the complaint directly to the barista who may have caused the problem, but Starbucks still gets almost instantaneous feedback. The company must take care not to lose much of this information, which can happen if there is no effective mechanism for filtering it up to the key decision makers. Furthermore, in some cases, customers cannot effectively evaluate the service until several days or weeks later. Automobile dealers, for instance, often call their customers a week after they perform a service like an oil change to assess their service quality.

Another excellent method for assessing customers' expectations is making effective use of customer complaint behaviour. Even if complaints are handled effectively to solve customers' problems, the essence of the complaint is too often lost on managers. For instance, a large PC retailer responded to complaints about the lack of service from salespeople and issues with products by providing an email address for people to contact the service department. Contacting the company proved to be difficult when the problem was that the computer wasn't working.[36]

Even firms with the best formal research mechanisms in place must put managers on the front lines occasionally to interact directly with the customers. Unless the

Sustainable Marketing 10.1   Walking the Green Building Talk

When you are Canada's largest consulting firm exclusively dedicated to green buildings and communities, you need to do more than just provide great service. You need to walk the talk. Enermodal Engineering, the foremost LEED (Leadership in Energy and Environmental Design) consulting firm, designed its new headquarters, A Grander View, on the banks of the Grand River in Kitchener, Ontario, to the highest LEED Platinum certifications. Unlike other companies that may have difficulty showing their services directly to potential customers, Enermodal can point to its own building, which is Canada's most energy-efficient office, using 82 percent less energy than a conventional office.

Established in 1980 by University of Waterloo engineering graduate Stephen Carpenter, Enermodal has offices in Kitchener, Toronto, Edmonton, Calgary, Winnipeg, Halifax, and Vancouver. It has certified more than 45 percent of all LEED Canada buildings and is currently working on sustainability projects worth over $5 billion.[37] The company's projects vary from public schools, hospitals, and a sportsplex, to a Museum of Human Rights and 23 new buildings on Toronto's scenic waterfront. It also worked with Fifth Town Artisan Cheese, a socially and environmentally responsible producer of handmade cheese in Picton, Ontario, to build an award-winning state-of-the-art green factory and retail outlet. One of its notable features is a subterranean cheese-aging cave that reduces the energy required to maintain a steady cool temperature year-round.[38]

In 2009, Enermodal became one of the first companies in the Region of Waterloo to become a Gold pledging partner with Sustainable Waterloo's Regional Carbon Initiative. Sustainable Waterloo is a nonprofit organization helping corporations reduce their environmental impact. Carpenter has committed Enermodal to a reduction target of 100 percent in 10 years.[39] Carbon neutrality encompasses everything from building energy use and business travel to employee commuting. Policies to reduce energy use by computers include programming them to go into "idle" mode after five minutes without use and into "sleep" mode after 30 minutes, saving 7 to 15 percent of the computer's operating energy with no loss in performance. Vacancy sensors turn off lights when rooms are not in use and the use of ultra-low plumbing fixtures and a rainwater cistern reduce indoor water use by 80 percent.[40] Business travel is minimized through the use of a video conferencing system. And when business trips are unavoidable, Enermodal employees can use a high-efficiency carshare vehicle at the office instead of their own potentially more gas-intensive vehicle.

Service companies need to collect and understand voice-of-customer insights. Enermodal applies this to employees in their roles as internal customers and helps them lead more sustainable lives as well. For example, catered lunches have a local and/or organic purchasing policy for all company events; company bikes are available for employee use, along with bike repair kit; incentives of up to $3000 are offered for the purchase of a high-efficiency vehicle; 60 percent of public transit costs are reimbursed; staff are offered free low-flow shower heads, compost bins, and rain barrels; and employee garden plots are available at A Grander View.[41] Employees are so passionate about the environment that some of them travelled to work by canoe during the Canada-wide Commuter Challenge.

Senior management recognizes that environmental sustainability is key to attracting and keeping top talent as well.[42] Enermodal has been named one the fastest growing firms in North America, with annual growth of 35 percent over the past three years. It's also been recognized as one of Canada's 50 greenest employers,[43] demonstrating to customers and employees that the company walks the green building talk.

Some Enermodal employees travelled to work by canoe during the annual Canada-wide Commuter Challenge.

managers who make the service quality decisions know what their service providers are facing every day, and unless they can talk directly to the customers with whom those service providers interact, any customer service program they create will not be as good as it could be.

The Standards Gap: Setting Service Standards

Say the Paradise Motel in Muskoka set out to determine its customers' service expectations and gained a pretty good idea of them. Its work is still far from over; the next step is to set its service standards and develop systems to ensure high-quality service. How can it make sure that every room is cleaned by 2:00 p.m.? That the food is checked for freshness and quality every day? The firm needs to set high service standards, enforce these standards, and train employees on how to perform their tasks to these standards. Managers must lead by example and demonstrate high service standards, which will permeate throughout the organization.

Service providers, like this housekeeper at a hotel, generally want to do a good job, but they need to be trained to know exactly what a good job entails.

L03

Achieving Service Goals Through Training To deliver consistently high-quality service, firms must set specific, measurable goals based on customers' expectations; to help ensure that quality, the employees should be involved in the goal setting. For instance, although the most efficient process at Paradise Motel would be to start cleaning rooms at 8:00 a.m. and finish by 5:00 p.m., many guests want to sleep late and new arrivals want to get into their room as soon as they arrive. A customer-oriented standard would mandate that the rooms get cleaned between 10:00 a.m. and 2:00 p.m.

Service providers generally want to do a good job, as long as they know what is expected of them. Motel employees should be shown, for instance, exactly how managers expect them to clean a room and what specific tasks they are responsible for performing.

While front-line service employees can be taught specific tasks related to their jobs, it is simply not enough to tell employees to "be nice" or "do what customers want." A quality goal should be specific: "Greet every customer you encounter with 'Good morning/afternoon/evening, Sir or Miss.'" Try to greet customers by name.

In extreme cases, such training becomes even more crucial. From long ticket lines to cancelled flights to lost baggage, customer service incidents are on the rise in the airline industry. Faced with mounting complaints, airlines are responding with better employee training geared toward identifying and defusing potentially explosive situations. For example, Delta Airlines has implemented a "Customer First" training program for its ground operations, customer service agents, flight attendants, and pilots that mandates specific performance measures and standardized practices throughout Delta's service areas. Policies for service during delays, such as providing snacks on board or trucking food out to waiting planes and offering status updates every 15 minutes, have given employees the tools and guidelines they need to better service their customers.[44]

Commitment to Service Quality Service providers take their cues from management. If managers strive for excellent service, treat their customers well, and demand the same attitudes from everyone in the organization, it is likely employees will do the same. Take, for example, WestJet CEO, Gregg Saretsky. Named one of Canada's most respected CEOs in the tenth annual Canada's Most Respected Corporations Survey, executives such as Saretsky are perfectly happy to clean cabins and lend a hand on flights when they are passengers. WestJet's legendary reputation for customer service has resulted in revenues of $2.3 billion and years of record-breaking net earnings.[45] This commitment to service quality has been modelled by company executives from the start. When WestJet launched in 1996, executive vice-president Don Bell spent a lot of time in the airline's call centre fielding questions and booking flights for customers.[46]

Employees who understand that operating on time is a critical component to service quality and guest experience work hard to improve on-time performance. In 2010, 81.9 percent of flights arrived within 15 minutes of their scheduled time.[47] Sales agents also strive to provide the highest standard of customer service. Their efforts were recognized when the Sales Super Centre was named the Best Call Centre in the country in an airline survey conducted by *Canadian Business Magazine's* consumer reports department. An employee profit-sharing plan provides rewards beyond public recognition. The vast majority of employees belong to the WestJet Employee Share Purchase Plan, making them owners of the company and giving them all the more reason to ensure high levels of service quality. This has resulted in WestJet being named as one of Canada's Best Employers and in its induction into Canada's Most Admired Corporate Cultures Hall of Fame.

The Delivery Gap: Delivering Service Quality

The delivery gap is where "the rubber meets the road," where the customer directly interacts with the service provider. Even if there are no other gaps, a delivery gap always results in a service failure. Marcia experienced several delivery gaps at the Paradise Motel: the unclean room, the assistant manager's attitude, the unheated swimming pool, the poor piano bar singer, and the stale food.

Delivery gaps can be reduced when employees are empowered to act in the customers' and the firm's best interests and are supported in their efforts so they can do their jobs effectively.[48] Technology can also be employed to reduce delivery gaps (see Exhibit 10.7).

empowerment
In the context of service delivery, means allowing employees to make decisions about how service is provided to customers.

Empowering Service Providers In this context, **empowerment** means allowing employees to make decisions about how service is provided to customers. When front-line employees are authorized to make decisions to help their customers, service quality generally improves.[49] Best Buy, for instance, has re-engineered its organizational structure to empower employees to be more involved in the day-to-day running of the business and to make adjustments as necessary. The new employee-centric culture has helped Best Buy significantly lower its employee turnover rate. Happy employees make for happy customers.[50]

However, empowering service providers can be difficult and costly. In cases in which the service is very repetitive and routine, such as at a fast-food restaurant, it might be more efficient and easier for service providers to follow a few simple rules. For instance, if a customer doesn't like his hamburger, ask him what he would like instead or offer him a refund. If an exceptional circumstance that does not fit the rules arises, then a manager should handle the issue.

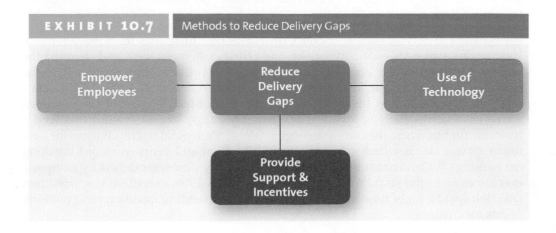

| **EXHIBIT 10.7** | Methods to Reduce Delivery Gaps |

The Keg is successful, in part, because it empowers its employees to satisfy customers.

Empowerment becomes more important when price points edge higher and services are more individualized. The Keg Steakhouse & Bar hires the best staff and empowers them through superlative training programs. Staff members are professional—their friendliness, warmth, personality, and enthusiasm are all part of The Keg dining experience. It is because of this that The Keg was recognized for the eighth year in a row as one of the 50 Best Employers in Canada.[51]

Providing Support and Incentives   A service provider's job can often be difficult, especially when customers are unpleasant or less than reasonable. The old cliché "Service with a smile" remains the best approach. To ensure that service is delivered properly, management needs to support the service provider.

First, managers and co-workers should provide emotional support to service providers by demonstrating a concern for their well-being and by standing behind their decisions. Because it can be very disconcerting when a waiter is abused by a customer who believes her food was improperly prepared, for instance, restaurant managers must be supportive and understanding and work to help employees get through their often emotional reaction to the berating they might experience.[52] When the waiter is empowered to rectify the situation by giving the customer new food and a free dessert, the manager also must stand behind the waiter's decision, not punish her for giving away too much, and thereby provide the needed support.

Second, the support that managers provide must be consistent and coherent throughout the organization. Patients expect physicians to provide great patient care by using state-of-the-art procedures and medications; yet, many doctors must squeeze more people into their office hours. These conflicting goals can be so frustrating and emotionally draining on physicians and other health-care providers that some have found work outside of medicine.

Third, a key part of any customer service program is providing rewards to employees for excellent service. Numerous firms have developed a service reputation by ensuring that their employees recognize the value the firm places on customer service, offering VIP clubs and "employee of the month" service awards. Some companies encourage associates or their managers to stand up and recount their great customer service episodes from the past week.[53]

Using Technology Technology has become an increasingly important method for facilitating the delivery of services. Since the mid-1990s, with the widespread usage of the Internet, firms have invested heavily in technologies that have enabled customers to buy more quickly, more easily, and with more information than in the past. Electronic kiosks, for instance, have found their way into many service venues. Ticketing kiosks at airports allow customers to get boarding passes and seat assignments, often in less than a minute. You can renew your licence plate stickers, order vanity plates, change your address, or pay fines at ServiceOntario kiosks located in major shopping centres in the province. Not only are kiosks convenient, they are also open much longer hours than Ministry of Transportation offices and the service experience is much more consistent for users. As previously noted, electronic kiosks and other technologies can reduce the inconsistency of providing a service. Kiosks and self-checkout machines can also help close the delivery gap.

Web-enabled services have also changed the way firms do business with other companies. Already, Cisco Systems, the leading supplier of networking equipment and networking management for the Internet, receives in excess of 80 percent of new orders electronically and resolves more than 80 percent of its customer issues through self-service mechanisms.[54]

Using technology to facilitate service delivery can provide many benefits, such as access to a wider variety of services, a greater degree of control by the customer over the services, and the ability to obtain information. Management also benefits from the increased efficiency in service processes through reduced servicing costs and, in some cases, can develop a competitive advantage over less service-oriented competitors.[55] See Power of the Internet 10.1 for examples of how technology can strengthen customer relationships, enhance loyalty, and increase revenue.

The Communication Gap: Communicating the Service Promise

The communication gap pertains to the difference between the service promised and the service actually delivered. A customer of an Internet provider was convinced to cancel her service to sign up with a new one after hearing advertisements for "great service" at a lower cost. During the first three weeks of the service, she was able to access the Internet only half a dozen times because of technology failures. She was further disappointed because when she called technology support she had to pay long-distance rates since an 800 number was not available to her. When she did get through, she was told to call back because no one was in that department at the moment. She expected reliable service and helpful customer representatives but instead received spotty service, as well as difficult and expensive technology support.[56]

Although firms have difficulty controlling service quality because it can vary from day to day and provider to provider, they do have control over how they communicate their service package to their customers. If a firm promises more than it can deliver, customers' expectations won't be met. An advertisement may lure a customer into a service situation once; but, if the service doesn't deliver on the promise, the customer may never return. Dissatisfied customers also are likely to tell others

Fairmont Hotels & Resorts is the largest luxury hotel company in North America, with 38 properties in Canada, the United States, Mexico, and the Caribbean. To meet its worldwide expansion objectives, Fairmont recognized the need to build its brand as a provider of unrivalled customer service in all markets.

Inspired by its mission statement, "Turning moments into memories for our guests," Fairmont created an e-business strategy to support its most loyal customers: business visitors. More than 50 percent of Fairmont's customers are mobile professionals attending conventions or business meetings.

Working with Accenture and Cisco, Fairmont developed a new website and online booking engine. The goals were to enhance its ability to market its properties to individual travellers, persuade potential guests to choose Fairmont as their hotel of choice, and provide guests with unmatched online service.

To start, it created a more personalized, transaction-based experience for website visitors. For example, its new online booking system recognizes clients when they log on and preloads information stored in their guest's profile, such as President's Club status (the guest loyalty program) and preferences. Guests can view rooms, rates, availability, and promotional packages offered at each of Fairmont's properties. And they can confirm, update, or cancel their reservations in real time, regardless of their original booking source.

Another part of the e-business solution strengthened guest data warehouse capabilities, allowing Fairmont to maintain guest profile information across properties, to target guest segments with personalized communications, incentives, and discounts, to better manage its loyalty program, and to acquire new guests and build loyalty. Individual tracking provided the ability to follow visitors globally across the hotel chain, which meant Fairmont could improve its customer service capabilities by better understanding their guests' preferences, booking channels, and spending patterns.

Fairmont's e-business strategy was designed to boost customer loyalty by crafting personalized guest services and picking up nuances in travel habits through self-selected options on the Fairmont website as well as information input by employees at the property level. By leveraging this information, Fairmont was able to gather data that allowed them to personalize and enhance the guest experience and establish targeted marketing campaigns tailored to the preferences of unique market segments.

Fairmont's new website was a finalist for a Webby Business Award and won major hospitality awards. Marketing costs were reduced for its call centre, President's Club fulfillment, promotion, and brochures. New guests were attracted via the Internet and sales increased because of last-minute Internet-based promotions. Overall, its e-business strategy resulted in dramatic increases in customer satisfaction rates and customer loyalty by strengthening relationships with travellers via personalized offers.

Source: Adapted from www6.lexisnexis.com/publisher/EndUser?Action=UserDisplayFullDocument&orgId=616&topicId=12552&docId=I:59938758o&start=20 (accessed April 20, 2007).

about the underperforming service, using word of mouth or, increasingly, the Internet, which has become an important channel for dissatisfied customers to vent their frustrations.

The communication gap can be reduced by managing customer expectations. Suppose you need an operation, and the surgeon explains, "You'll be out of the hospital in five days and back to your normal routine in a month." You have the surgery and feel well enough to leave the hospital three days later. Two weeks after that, you're playing tennis again. Clearly, you will tend to think your surgeon is a genius. However, regardless of the operation's success, if you had to stay in the hospital for 10 days and it took you two months to recover, you would undoubtedly be upset.

Promising only what you can deliver, or possibly even a little less, is an important way to control the communication gap.[57] For instance, when FedEx first issued its next-day delivery guarantee—"Absolutely, Positively There by 10:30 a.m."—it achieved a competitive advantage until others matched its promise. Now FedEx often gives next-day service when the customer has paid only for second-day service. If the package arrives on the second day, it meets expectations. If it arrives a day early, it exceeds them.

When a service failure occurs, such as receiving a poor meal at a restaurant, a firm's goodwill can be recovered by giving the customer a free dessert.

A relatively easy way to manage customer expectations considers both the time the expectation is created and the time the service is provided. Expectations typically are created through promotions, whether in advertising or personal selling. For instance, if a salesperson promises a client that work can be performed in one day, and it actually takes a week, the client will be disappointed. However, if the salesperson coordinates the work with those responsible for the service delivery, the client's expectations likely will be met.

Customer expectations can also be managed when the service is delivered. For example, recorded messages can tell customers who have telephoned a company how many minutes they will have to wait before the next operator is available.

L04 Service Recovery

Despite a firm's best efforts, sometimes service providers fail to meet customer expectations. When this happens, the best course of action is to attempt to make amends with the customer and learn from the experience. Of course, it is best to avoid a service failure altogether, but when it does occur, the firm has a unique opportunity to demonstrate its customer commitment.[58] Effective service recovery efforts can significantly increase customer satisfaction, purchase intentions, and positive word of mouth, though customers' post-recovery satisfaction levels usually fall lower than their satisfaction level prior to the service failure.[59]

The Paradise Motel in Muskoka could have made amends with Marcia Kessler after its service failures if it had taken some relatively simple, immediate steps: the assistant manager could have apologized for his bad behaviour and quickly upgraded her to a suite and/or given her a free night's lodging for a future stay. The motel could also have given her a free lunch or dinner to make up for the bad breakfast. None of these actions would have cost the motel much money. Yet by not taking action, the motel lost Marcia, who over time could have been responsible for several thousand dollars in sales. Furthermore, Marcia is likely to spread negative word of mouth about the motel to her friends and family because of its failure to recover. Quite simply, effective service recovery entails (1) listening to the customer, (2) providing a fair solution, and (3) resolving the problem quickly.[60]

Listening to the Customer

Firms often don't find out about service failures until a customer complains. Whether the firm has a formal complaint department or the complaint is offered directly to the service provider, the customer must have the opportunity to air the complaint completely, and the firm must listen carefully to what he or she is saying.

Customers can become very emotional about a service failure, whether the failure is serious (a botched surgical operation) or minor (the wrong change at a restaurant). In many cases, the customer may just want to be heard, and the service provider should give the customer all the time he or she needs to "get it out." The very process of describing a perceived wrong to a sympathetic listener is therapeutic in and of itself. Service providers therefore should welcome the opportunity to be that sympathetic ear, listen carefully, and appear anxious to rectify the situation to ensure it doesn't happen again.[61]

Finding a Fair Solution

Most people realize that mistakes happen. But when they happen, customers want to be treated fairly, whether that means distributive or procedural fairness.[62] Their perception of what *fair* means is based on their previous experience with other firms, how they have seen other customers treated, material they have read, and stories recounted by their friends.

When handling returns or other services issues, it is important to use procedures that are perceived to be fair by the customers.

Distributive Fairness **Distributive fairness** pertains to a customer's perception of the benefits he or she received compared with the costs (inconvenience or loss). Customers want to be compensated a fair amount for a perceived loss that resulted from a service failure. If, for instance, a person arrives at the airport gate and finds her flight is overbooked, she may believe that taking the next flight that day and receiving a travel voucher is adequate compensation for the inconvenience. But if no flights are available until the next day, the traveller may require additional compensation, such as overnight accommodations, meals, and a round-trip ticket to be used at a later date.[63]

The key to distributive fairness, of course, is listening carefully to the customer. One customer, travelling on vacation, may be satisfied with a travel voucher, whereas another may need to get to the destination on time because of a business appointment. Regardless of how the problem is solved, customers typically want tangible restitution—in this case, to get to their destination—not just an apology. If providing a tangible restitution isn't possible, the next best thing is to assure the customer that steps are being taken to prevent the failure from recurring.

Procedural Fairness With regard to complaints, **procedural fairness** refers to the perceived fairness of the process used to resolve them. Customers want efficient complaint procedures over whose outcomes they have some influence. Furthermore, customers tend to believe they have been treated fairly if the service providers follow specific company guidelines, though rigid adherence to rules can have damaging effects. For example, requiring a manager's approval for every return, no matter how small, can take several minutes and therefore can irritate everyone in the checkout line.

Consider the local convenience store that sells cigarettes. The store owner has implemented a policy that everyone under 19 years of age who attempts to purchase them must show valid identification. If the store clerks comply, the customers see and accept it as part of the purchasing protocol and perceive it as fair for everyone.

distributive fairness Pertains to a customer's perception of the benefits he or she received compared with the costs (inconvenience or loss) that resulted from a service failure.

procedural fairness Refers to the customer's perception of the fairness of the process used to resolve complaints about service.

Resolving Problems Quickly

The longer it takes to resolve a service failure, the more irritated the customer will become and the more people he or she is likely to tell about the problem. To resolve service failures quickly, firms need clear policies, adequate training for their employees, and empowered employees. Health insurance companies, for instance, have made a concerted effort in recent years to avoid service failures that occur because customers' insurance claims have not been handled quickly or to the customers' satisfaction.

Companies should welcome complaints and make it easy for customers to provide feedback, listening carefully to what customers have to say. Although customers may be complaining, they are nevertheless exhibiting a degree of loyalty and a genuine desire to get their problem fixed. Of customers who do complain, 56 to 70 percent will do business with the company again if the complaint is resolved. That goes up to 96 percent if the complaint is resolved quickly!

It may seem overly simple, but to recover effectively from service failures, firms must not only listen to the customers' complaints but act on them. It is the implementation of this simple rule that offers firms such challenges.

Real Marketer Profile: BYRON PASCOE

I got involved in providing the service of comedy entertainment in high school, working with friend Paul Telner, who was a stand-up comedian. During my undergraduate business degree at Wilfrid Laurier University, I formed a company with Paul and other friends called Let It Out Entertainment, focusing on comedy TV. After I graduated, we sold programming to American cable TV (G4), CBC (late-night pilot), and MuchMusic (segments, half-hour prime-time specials).

My official title has been Business Manager, which means anything it needs to mean on a daily basis. Because our company has just a few full-time members, I wear many hats. My partners were all on the creative side, and I was on the business side. During filming days, I was the production manager, production assistant, driver, and so on. On other days, I took care of financing, insurance, legalities, staffing, and preparation for shoots. I also tried to create business opportunities and strengthen third-party relationships by ensuring that the group attended all the major Canadian entertainment events. Sometimes you need to show up at the annual festivals and conferences so everyone knows you're still in the game.

We made a conscious effort to develop our online presence by bringing our content not just to our main dot-com, but also to the third-party sites where people go to find content, namely YouTube. Key elements of a successful YouTube presence are transferable to other third-party sites and perhaps other digital marketing experiences. My advice? Post engaging content on a recurring schedule. Cross-promote the content with the best partners available, for example, collaboration videos with well-known YouTube stars. At the end of the day, it is vital to put yourself in your customer's shoes at all parts of the business cycle.

Our comedic style has always been reality comedy. Presently, I am focused on a reality comedy aggregator brand called Bag of Misfits (www.youtube.com/bagofmisfits), which has been promoted on Mashable, USA Today, ABC's *The View*, and in Canada in *24 Hours*. My roles for this site include being the liaison with all our content partners, managing the graphics, increasing awareness, and seeking advertising opportunities and partnerships. We launched with The Cheezburger Network, which owns and operates Fail Blog, the most watched comedy channel on YouTube. It has had more than 1 billion video views. Currently, we are working with AuditionBooth.com: Paula Abdul's digital casting website. This site allows us to cast new talent for our brand and concurrently creates awareness for our brand.

Selling an intangible, whether it's a TV format to get pilot order or a comedy digital destination to get an advertiser on board, starts way before the pitch. It includes having your bases covered on the digital communications, so that when someone looks for you online, they will actually find you instead of finding someone else. When selling a personality, the person needs to have big numbers of people who follow wherever you take them. It's a lot easier to sell a TV format if the star has a million YouTube subscribers, as opposed to someone who can't be found on the site.

It's also about having the best partnerships available. It's much easier to sell an advertising package to a company if you represent both your digital brand, as well as the brand of 20 of your partners, each with their own online presence. Strength in numbers. You are only as strong as your network, so build up the network and then go after the people who are spending the money.

There is an element of marketing in every position. What I love most about this is bringing what I've learned in one role, and the relationships I've made, to my next role. It's a ripple effect that leads to each new project becoming stronger than the last.

Learning Objectives Review

L01 **Identify how marketing a service differs from marketing a product by applying the principles of intangibility, inseparability, inconsistency, and inventory**

First and foremost, services are intangible—they can't be seen or touched—which makes it difficult to describe a service's benefits or promote it to others. Service providers attempt to reduce the impact of the service's intangibility by enhancing its delivery with more tangible attributes, such as a nice atmosphere or price benefits. Second, services are produced and consumed at the same time. Third, services are more inconsistent than products, though service providers attempt to reduce this variability through standardization, training, service bundling, and technology. Fourth, because consumers can't stockpile services, marketers provide incentives to stagger demand over time.

LO2 Explain why it is important that service marketers understand and manage customer expectations

A knowledge gap occurs when marketers don't understand what their customers want. They may not be providing customers enough or the right service, in which case customers will be disappointed. To understand customer expectations, marketers analyze service quality through comprehensive studies and by interacting with customers.

LO3 Describe strategies that firms can use to help employees provide better service

First, firms should provide training to employees regarding how to do their job and interact with customers. Second, they need to demonstrate a strong commitment to service

by setting high standards and enforcing these standards, and lead through example. Third, they can empower service providers to solve service issues and problems. Fourth, they should provide employees with both emotional support and the tools they need to do a good job. Fifth, the service program should be consistent throughout the organization. Sixth, service providers need incentives that encourage them to do a good job.

LO4 Summarize three service recovery strategies

In the best-case scenario, the service does not fail in the first place. But failures are inevitable, and when they do happen, the firm must make amends to the customer. Listen carefully to the customer. Let the customer air his or her complaint. Find a fair solution to the problem that not only compensates the customer for the failure but also follows procedures that the customer believes are fair. Resolve the problem quickly.

Key Terms

- communication gap, 331
- customer service, 322
- delivery gap, 331
- distributive fairness, 343
- empowerment, 338
- inconsistent, 326
- inseparable, 326
- intangible, 324
- inventory, 329
- knowledge gap, 331
- procedural fairness, 343
- service gap, 330
- service quality, 332
- standards gap, 331
- voice-of-customer (VOC) program, 334
- zone of tolerance, 334

Concept Review

1. Describe the four dimensions in which services marketing is different from product marketing.

2. Why is intangibility described as the most fundamental difference between products and services?

3. Discuss the actions companies can implement to minimize the potential negative impact of service inconsistency on the delivery of customer service.

4. How can companies deal with the perishability of their services?

5. Identify the components of the Gaps Model. Describe each component and explain the strategies companies can implement to reduce the gaps in service delivery.

6. Describe the five dimensions of service quality that consumers often use to judge the quality of a service experience.

7. Explain how the use of technology can help companies deliver higher quality service.

8. Discuss why underpromising and overdelivering is an important way to control the communication gap.

9. What is meant by service recovery? How can companies use service recovery to ensure that a service failure does not lead to a lost customer?

10. Explain the differences between distributive and procedural fairness in the context of service recovery.

Marketing Applications

1. Those companies from which you purchase products and services are not pure sellers of services, nor are they pure sellers of products. What services does a department store provide? What goods does a dentist provide?

2. You have been sitting in the waiting room of your doctor's office for an hour. With the knowledge that products are different than services, develop a list of the things the office manager could do to improve the

overall service delivery. Consider how the office might overcome problems of intangibility, inseparability, inconsistency, and inventory issues associated with services.

3. You have conducted a zone of tolerance analysis for a local dry cleaner. You find that the length of the reliability and responsiveness boxes are much greater than those of the other three service quality dimensions. You also find that the dry cleaner is positioned above the zone box on reliability but below the box on responsiveness. What should you tell the manager of the dry cleaner to do?

4. Design a simple system for collecting customer information about the services of your local dry cleaner.

5. Think back to your last job. What training did your employer provide regarding how to interact with customers and provide good customer service? What could your employer have done to prepare you better to interact with customers?

6. Provide a specific situation in which a service provider could have avoided a service failure if he or she had been empowered by an employer to do so. What should that person have done?

7. What types of support and incentives could your university provide advisers to help make them more attentive to students' needs?

8. What technologies do you use that help facilitate your transactions with a specific retailer or service provider? Would you rather use the technology or engage in a face-to-face relationship with a person? How, if at all, would your parents' answer be different to these two questions?

9. A local health club is running a promotional campaign that promises you can lose an inch a month off your waist if you join the club and follow its program. How might this claim cause a communication gap? What should the club do to avoid a service failure?

10. You are hired by a career consulting firm that promises to market new graduates to high-paying employers. The firm provides potential clients with an impressive client list. It charges the clients a fee, and then a separate finder's fee if the client gets a position. The firm aggressively markets its services and has a large client base. You learn that the firm simply takes any submitted resumés and posts them to a variety of online job search engines. The firm never actually contacts any firms on its clients' behalf. The CEO, himself a recent university grad, tells you that the firm never promises that the firm will contact potential employees themselves, only that they have access to and will distribute clients' resumés. What do you think of the career consulting firm's practices?

Toolkit

SERVICES ZONE OF TOLERANCE

Use the toolkit provided on Connect to assess the zone of tolerance for several service providers.

Net Savvy

1. What services does WestJet offer (www.westjet.com)? Compare its services to those offered by Air Canada (www.aircanada.ca) by using the five service quality dimensions (tangibility, responsiveness, reliability, assurance, and empathy).

2. Evaluate the ease with which you can make hotel reservations when using Fairmont's (www.fairmont.com) Internet reservation system. Check out the hotel's privacy policy. Are you comfortable with their use of cookies to identify visitors when they return to the site?

Chapter Case Study

PUTTIN' ON THE RITZ[64]

Luxury hotels are booming, and hotels are adding more and more expensive rooms to compete for the highest-end customers.[65] Despite the vast number of hotels in the luxury hotel market, though, the undisputed leaders remain Ritz-Carlton hotels. Ritz-Carlton competes by simply offering the best service. So what exactly does this hotel chain do differently than its competitors, and how does it maintain its advantage based on superior service?

Ritz-Carlton, owned by the hotel group Marriott International, consists of 70 hotels in 24 countries around the world. Ritz-Carlton hotels employ 38 000 people and train their employees to create the perfect service experience.[66] The history of Ritz-Carlton began in 1927 with the opening of the Ritz-Carlton Boston, a hotel renowned for the lengths it would go to for its guests, such as re-upholstering the chairs in Winston Churchill's room in red fabric to match his favourite colour or redecorating the decor of Joan Crawford's room with a theme of peppermint Lifesavers, her favourite candies.[67]

Ritz-Carlton's superior customer service also is based on highly trained employees who care for their guests, as well as a sophisticated customer relationship management (CRM) system that ensures that Ritz-Carlton guests receive consistent and superlative service.

Attention to Employees

Ritz-Carlton combines extensive employee training and careful hiring practices to create an environment that embraces the customer. For example, employees are instructed to never say the word *no* to a guest, and each concierge receives a $2000 daily fund for each guest that the concierge can use to solve problems for hotel customers. Ritz guests are often surprised by the little things that hotel employees do, but this high-quality service gets reinforced by constant training. For instance, on every shift, on every Ritz-Carlton property, a 15-minute meeting acts as a refresher to remind employees to act on one of the 12 "Service Values" that constitute the company's "Gold Standard."

Training is only one part of the excellent customer service; before it even gets to that point, Ritz-Carlton starts by hiring the right kind of employees. It looks for people who are warm and caring and works to instill in them the Ritz-Carlton motto, "We Are Ladies and Gentlemen Serving Ladies and Gentlemen."[68] Before the opening of the Ritz-Carlton Dallas, each employee had undergone more than 80 hours of training. Of the 400 employees who would run the hotel, half transferred in from other Ritz hotels to ensure that the new opening would maintain the customer service and attention to every detail for which the company continues to be so well known.

The Ritz-Carlton's motto is "We Are Ladies and Gentlemen Serving Ladies and Gentlemen."

Sophisticated IT Systems

To support its performance, the Ritz-Carlton uses a CRM system called Mystique that collects information about guests, from their special requests to informal observations by employees. This system is relatively difficult to implement because observations need to be actionable and confirmed by various aspects of the customer's stay. For example, if a customer orders a martini with pearl onions three times, the bartender should enter it into the system as the customer's favourite drink; but, if that same customer orders a similar martini only once, it likely is not something worth noting. Yet employees are constantly trying to wow their customers, so any knowledge that helps them do so in the future provides value to both employees and customers.

Ritz-Carlton's goal is to encourage guests to engage actively with the Ritz-Carlton brand. Its research shows that customers who connect with the brand spend 23 percent more than other customers. That makes customer service an important driver of company value. After all, a mere 4 percent increase in customer engagement would be worth approximately $40 million in sales to the company! Employees are trained how to engage their customers, realizing, for example, that a rock star and a retired corporate executive probably should be treated differently. Employees are taught to alter their style depending on the situation, because their interactions should differ when greeted by a guest who says, "Good evening, young man; how are you?" versus another who utters, "Hey dude, how's it going?"

Recognition of the Best

Finally, beyond the impressive loyalty that Ritz-Carlton enjoys from its customers, it has earned some of the most prestigious awards in quality, including the Malcolm Baldrige National Quality Award. To share what it has learned with other companies, Ritz-Carlton recently created a customer service training program that costs $1700 per person. Now banks, hospitals, law firms, and car dealerships—industries often criticized for providing poor service—send their employees to training programs to improve their own level of service. Even employees of Lexus dealerships and Starbucks have been attendees at Ritz-Carlton training programs.

Students in Ritz-Carlton's training program learn about how the hotel chain provides the best service to its customers and how they might borrow some of its techniques in their own industry. The people who do the laundry, maintain the landscaping, park guests' cars, and open the doors at the hotels are all involved in training employees from other companies that turn to the Ritz-Carlton for help. They offer advice on how to help guests or customers in their own areas of expertise and also on how to perform outside of their job description, when called on, even during busy periods, to ensure superb customer service all the time.

Questions

1. Using the building blocks (five dimensions) of service quality (see Exhibit 10.4 on page 333), evaluate the Ritz-Carlton hotel chain. Do you think the Ritz-Carlton places equal emphasis on all five dimensions or do one or two stand out as being critical? Explain your answer.

2. Compare the Ritz-Carlton's service quality performance with that of the most recent hotel in which you stayed.

3. Using the Gaps Model, identify the service gaps you might have noticed during your most recent hotel stay. How might those gaps be closed?

 Practise and learn online with Connect. Connect allows you to practise important concepts at your own pace and on your own schedule, with 24/7 online access to an eBook, practice quizzes, interactivities, videos, study tools, additional resources, and more.

CHAPTER 11

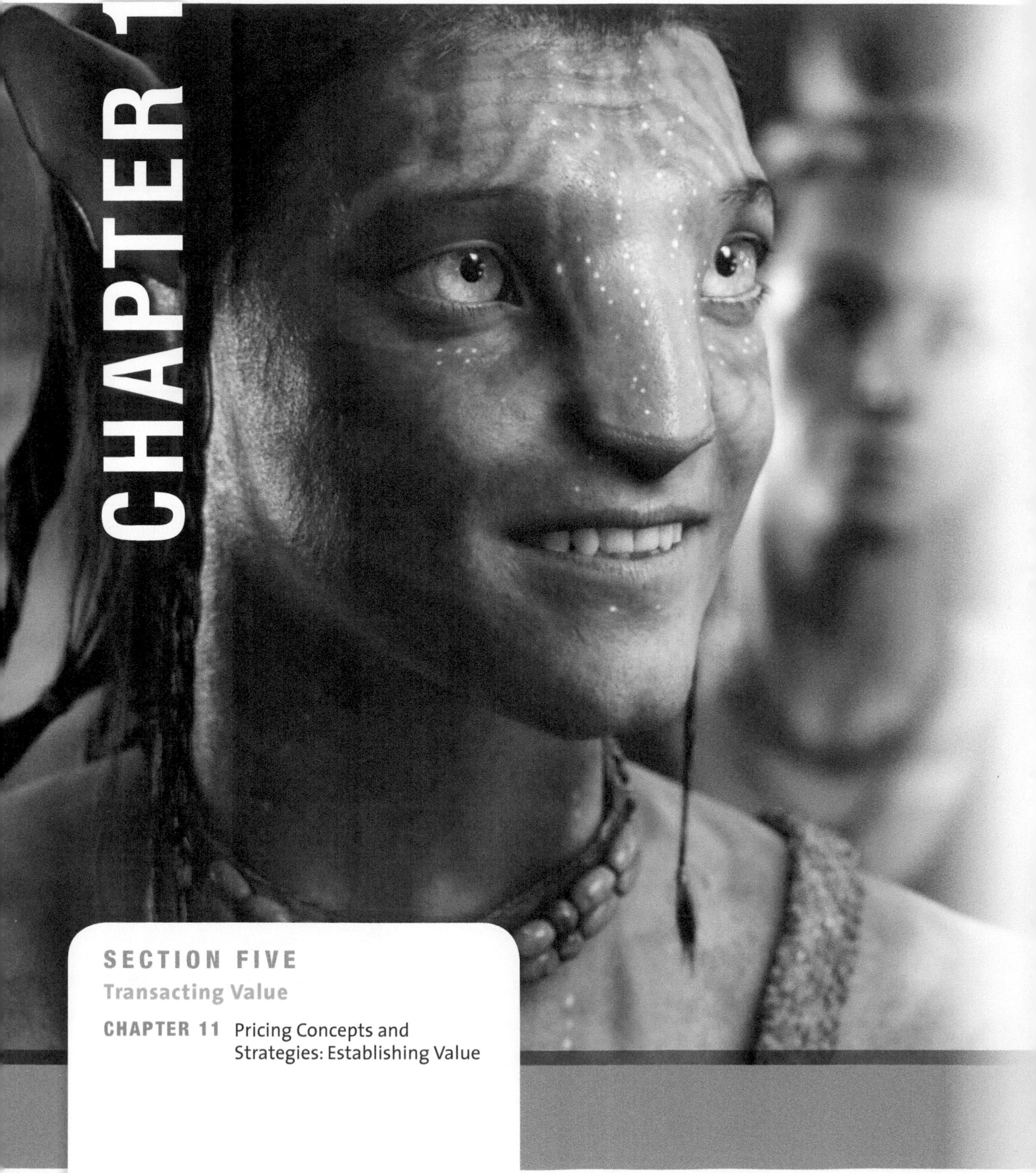

SECTION FIVE

Transacting Value

CHAPTER 11 Pricing Concepts and Strategies: Establishing Value

Pricing Concepts and Strategies: Establishing Value

When you go to the movies, do you care if it's a traditional, 3-D, or IMAX film? Each appeals to a different set of consumer preferences and beliefs about pricing. Is it better to spend the extra money to get a more immersive movie experience? Or should you save your money and wait until the film is released on DVD and then watch it at home? Is *Avatar* in 3-D on the big screen really that much better?

These different philosophies about price reflect the concept of value. As more and more 3-D and IMAX films have been released, Cineplex Entertainment has changed its technology strategy to keep pace. With 131 theatres and 1353 screens, Cineplex is the largest exhibitor of digital, 3-D, and IMAX projection technologies in Canada.[1] In the last year, it has nearly doubled the number of digital projectors installed to 238, of which 199 are capable of using RealD 3-D technology.

Although 3-D technology has been around since 1890, the hardware and processes required to produce and display films was expensive. Even today the cost of converting to digital projection is not cheap: up to $150,000 per screen or more. These costs are reflected in premium-priced tickets, ranging from $3 to $5 more than tickets to see traditional movies.[2] So you may be surprised to learn that even during the recent recession, although consumers cut back on expensive vacations and big-ticket items, they continued to go to the cinema.

Thanks to movies such as *Avatar* and *Alice in Wonderland*, Cineplex recorded its highest ever first-quarter box office revenues in 2010, with 3-D and IMAX films making up 33.9 percent of box office revenue, compared to 7 percent in the same period a year prior.[3] By identifying and meeting customer needs and wants associated with the evolving entertainment experience, Cineplex delivered value to consumers and stakeholders.

Learning Objectives

After studying this chapter you should be able to

LO1 Explain what price is and its importance in establishing value in marketing

LO2 Illustrate how the five Cs—company objectives, customers, costs, competition, and channel members—influence pricing decisions

LO3 Describe various pricing strategies and tactics and their use in marketing (e.g., cost-based pricing, competitor-based pricing, value-based pricing, new product pricing, psychological pricing, and pricing tactics targeted to channel members and consumers)

LO4 Summarize the legal and ethical issues involved in pricing

As long as consumers value the benefits the higher price signifies, they likely will spend the extra money to see 3-D movies. Yet there will always be others who will opt for lower priced alternatives. Thus, knowing how consumers arrive at their perceptions of value is critical to developing successful pricing strategies. A good pricing strategy must consider other factors too, so developing this strategy is a formidable challenge to all firms. Do it right, and the rewards to the firm will be substantial. Do it wrong, and failure will be swift. Even if a pricing strategy is implemented well, consumers, economic conditions, markets, competitors, government regulations, and even a firm's own products and services change constantly—and that means that a good pricing strategy today may not remain an effective pricing strategy tomorrow. .::

L01 A lot rides on marketers setting the right price, so it's important to understand the role price plays in the marketing mix. As shown in the chapter roadmap, we explain what "price" is as a marketing concept, why it is important, how marketers set pricing objectives, and how various factors influence price setting. Then, we extend this foundation by focusing on specific pricing strategies as well as the psychological aspects of pricing. Lastly, we describe various B2B and consumer pricing tactics and some important legal and ethical issues associated with pricing.

Imagine that a consumer realizes that to save money on a particular item, she will have to drive an additional 20 kilometres. She may judge that her time and travel costs are not worth the savings, so even though the price tag is higher at a nearby store, she judges the overall cost of buying the product there to be lower. To include aspects of price such as this, we define price as the overall sacrifice a consumer is willing to make to acquire a specific product or service. This sacrifice usually includes the money that must be paid to the seller to acquire the item; but, it also may involve other sacrifices, whether nonmonetary, such as the value of the time necessary to acquire the product or service, or monetary, such as travel costs, taxes, and shipping costs, all of which the buyer must give up to take possession of the product.[4]

Consumers judge the benefits a product delivers against the sacrifice necessary to obtain it, and then make a purchase decision based on this overall judgment of value. Thus, a great but overpriced product can be judged as low in value and may not sell as well as an inferior but well-priced item. In turn, we cannot define price without referring to the product or service associated with it. The key to successful pricing is to match the product or service with the consumer's value perceptions.

That key raises a related question: If firms can price their products or services too high, can they price them too low as well? Quite simply, yes. A price set too low may signal low quality, poor performance, or other negative attributes about the product or service. Consumers don't necessarily want a low price all the time or for all products. Rather, they want high value, which may come with a relatively high or low price, depending on the bundle of benefits the product or service delivers.

Price is the only element of the marketing mix that generates revenue. Every other element in the marketing mix may be perfect, but with the wrong price, sales simply will not occur. Research has consistently shown that consumers usually rank

CHAPTER ROADMAP

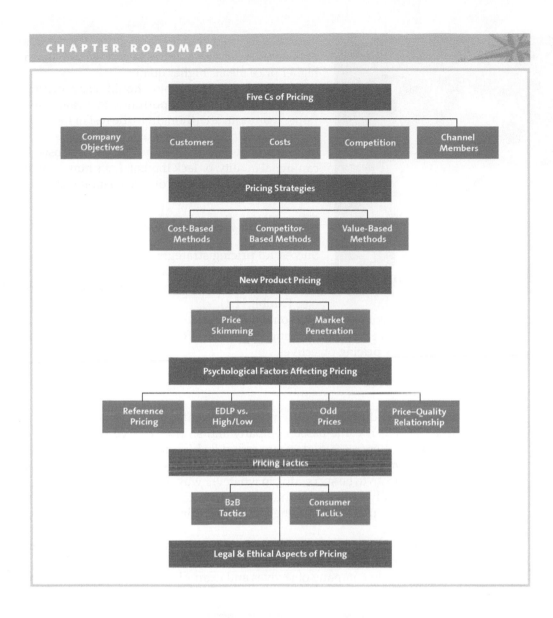

price as one of the most important factors in their purchase decisions.[5] So if the firm wants to deliver value and value is judged by the benefits relative to the cost, then pricing decisions are absolutely critical to the effort to deliver value.

Price is the most challenging of the four Ps to manage, partly because it is often the least understood. Historically, managers have treated price as an afterthought to their marketing strategy, setting prices according to what competitors were charging or, worse yet, by adding up their costs and tacking on a desired profit to set the sales price. Prices rarely changed except in response to radical shifts in market conditions. Even today, pricing decisions often fail to reflect our current understanding of the role of price in the marketing mix.

Moreover, managers have held an overly simplistic view of the role of price, considering it simply the amount of money a consumer must part with to acquire a product or service. We now know that price is not just a sacrifice but an information cue as well. That is, consumers use the price of a product or service to judge its quality,[6] particularly when they are less knowledgeable about the product category. For example, most college and university students know little about fine wine, so if a student found herself in the Vintages section of the liquor store and had to make a decision about which bottle to

When shopping for wine, most of us infer that a higher price means higher quality.

purchase, she might judge the quality of the various options according to their prices and assume that a higher price means higher quality.

In summary, marketers should view pricing decisions as a strategic opportunity to create value rather than as an afterthought to the rest of the marketing mix. Price communicates to the consumer more than how much a product or service costs; it can signal quality, or lack thereof. Let's now turn to the five basic components of pricing strategies.

The Five Cs of Pricing

Successful pricing strategies are built through the five critical components: company objectives, customers, costs, competition, and channel members (see Exhibit 11.1).

We examine these components in some detail because each makes a significant contribution to formulating good pricing decisions.[7] To start, the first step is to develop the company's pricing objectives.

L02 ## Company Objectives

By now, you know that different firms embrace different goals. Walmart, for example, wants to be seen as a value-based company and so uses everyday low pricing (EDLP), whereas Holt Renfrew's high prices reflect its high-fashion image.

Each firm then embraces an objective that seems to fit with where management thinks the firm needs to go to be successful, in whatever way they define success. These specific objectives usually reflect how the firm intends to grow. Do managers want it to grow by increasing profits, increasing sales, decreasing competition, or building customer satisfaction?

Company objectives are not as simple as they might first appear; they often can be expressed in slightly different forms that mean very different things. Exhibit 11.2 introduces some common company objectives and examples of their implications for

EXHIBIT 11.1	Five Cs of Pricing

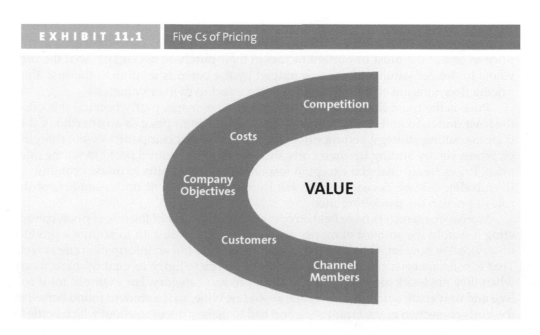

EXHIBIT 11.2	Company Objectives and Pricing Strategy Implications
Company Objective	**Examples of Pricing Strategy Implications**
Profit-oriented	Institute a companywide policy that all products must provide for at least an 18 percent profit margin to reach a particular profit goal for the firm.
Sales-oriented	Set prices very low to generate new sales and take sales away from competitors, even if profits suffer.
Competitor-oriented	Set prices very low to discourage more competitors from entering the market. Set prices higher than competitor to signal higher quality or market leadership. Match competitor prices to show similar value.
Customer-oriented	Target a market segment of consumers who highly value a particular product benefit and set prices relatively high (referred to as premium pricing).

pricing strategies. These objectives are not always mutually exclusive, because a firm may embrace two or more noncompeting objectives.

Profit Orientation Even though all company objectives may ultimately be oriented toward making a profit, firms implement a **profit orientation** by focusing on target profit pricing, maximizing profits, or target return pricing.

- Firms usually implement **target profit pricing** when they have a particular profit goal as their overriding concern. To meet this targeted profit objective, firms use price to stimulate a certain level of sales at a certain profit per unit.

- The **maximizing profits strategy** relies primarily on economic theory. If a firm can accurately specify a mathematical model that captures all the factors required to explain and predict sales and profits, it should be able to identify the price at which its profits are maximized. Gathering the data on all these relevant factors and coming up with an accurate mathematical model is an extremely difficult undertaking.

- Other firms, less concerned with the absolute level of profits and more interested in the rate at which their profits are generated relative to their investments, typically use **target return pricing** and other pricing strategies designed to produce a specific return on their investment.

Sales Orientation Firms using a **sales orientation** to set prices believe that increasing sales will help the firm more than increasing profits. For example, a new health club might focus on unit sales or market share and therefore be willing to set a lower membership fee and accept less profit at first. In contrast, a high-end jewellery store, such as Tiffany & Co. might focus on dollar sales and maintain higher prices. This store relies on its prestige image, as well as the image of its suppliers, to generate sales. Even though it sells fewer units, it can still generate high dollar sales levels.

Finally, some firms may be more concerned about their overall market share than about dollar sales per se because they believe that market share better reflects their success relative to the market conditions than do sales alone. A firm may set low prices to discourage new firms from entering

profit orientation
A company objective that can be implemented by focusing on target *profit pricing, maximizing profits,* or *target return pricing.*

target profit pricing
A pricing strategy implemented by firms when they have a particular profit goal as their overriding concern; uses price to stimulate a certain level of sales at a certain profit per unit.

maximizing profits strategy
A mathematical model that captures all the factors required to explain and predict sales and profits, which should be able to identify the price at which its profits are maximized.

target return pricing
A pricing strategy implemented by firms less concerned with the absolute level of profits and more interested in the rate at which their profits are generated relative to their investments; designed to produce a specific return on investment, usually expressed as a percentage of sales.

Tiffany & Co. keeps its prices high even during a recession to protect its prestigious image symbolized by its famous blue box.

Want to fly from London to Milan? You can do it on Ryanair for 19€, or about $24.

sales orientation
A company objective based on the belief that increasing sales will help the firm more than will increasing profits.

competitor orientation
A company objective based on the premise that the firm should measure itself primarily against its competition.

competitive parity
A firm's strategy of setting prices that are similar to those of major competitors.

customer orientation
Pricing orientation that explicitly invokes the concept of customer value and setting prices to match consumer expectations.

the market, encourage current firms to leave the market, take market share away from competitors—all to gain overall market share. For instance, Ireland's discount airline Ryanair regularly lowers their fares to rates below their competition's prices to gain market share. In all the above cases, profits are of lesser concern; the focus is on increasing sales.

Adopting a market share objective does not always imply setting low prices. Rarely is the lowest-price offering the dominant brand in a given market. Heinz ketchup, Philadelphia cream cheese, Crest toothpaste, and Nike athletic shoes have all dominated their markets, yet all are premium-priced brands. Thus, companies can gain market share simply by offering a high-quality product at a fair price, as long as they generate high-value perceptions among consumers. Although the concept of value is not overtly expressed in sales-oriented strategies, it is at least implicit because for sales to increase, consumers must see greater value.

Competitor Orientation

When firms undertake a **competitor orientation**, they strategize according to the premise that they should measure themselves primarily against their competition. Some firms focus on **competitive parity**, which means they set prices that are similar to those of their major competitors. Value is only implicitly considered in competitor-oriented strategies, in the sense that competitors may be using value as part of their pricing strategies, so copying their strategy might provide value.

Customer Orientation

A **customer orientation** explicitly invokes the concept of value. Sometimes a firm may attempt to increase value by focusing on customer satisfaction and setting prices to match consumer expectations. Or a firm can use a "no-haggle" price structure to make the purchase process simpler and easier for consumers, thereby lowering the overall price and ultimately increasing value. Some car companies have embraced the "no-haggle" price policy to do just that.

Firms also may offer very high-priced, "state-of-the-art" products or services in full anticipation of limited sales. These offerings are designed to enhance the company's reputation and image and thereby increase the company's value in the minds of consumers. For example, Paradigm, a Canadian speaker manufacturer in Mississauga, Ontario, produces what many audiophiles consider a high-value product, offering speakers priced as low as $320 per pair. However, Paradigm also offers a high-end pair of speakers for $8500. Although few people will spend $8500 on a pair of speakers, this "statement" speaker communicates what the company is capable of and can increase the image of the firm and the rest of its products—even that $320 pair of speakers. For an unprecedented 19 years in a row, Paradigm has been rated number one best price/value by *Inside Track*.[8] Setting prices with a close eye to how consumers develop their perceptions of value can often be the most effective pricing strategy, especially if it is supported by consistent advertising and distribution strategies.

After a company has a good grasp on its overall objectives, it must implement pricing strategies that enable it to achieve those objectives. As the second step in this process, the firm should look toward consumer demand to lay the foundation for its pricing strategy.

Customers

The second C of the five Cs of pricing is the most important because it is about understanding consumers' reactions to different prices. Consumers want value, and as you may recall, price is half of the value equation.

To determine how firms account for consumers' preferences when they develop pricing strategies, we must first lay a foundation of traditional economic theory that helps explain how prices are related to demand (consumers' desire for products) and how managers can incorporate this knowledge into their pricing strategies.

Demand Curves and Pricing   A **demand curve** shows how many units of a product or service consumers will demand during a specific period of time at different prices. Although we call them "curves," demand curves can be either straight or curved, as Exhibit 11.3 shows. Of course, any static demand curve assumes that everything else remains unchanged. For example, marketers creating a demand curve must assume that the firm will not increase its expenditures on advertising and that the economy will not change in any significant way.

Exhibit 11.3 illustrates the common downward-sloping demand curve in which, as price increases, demand for the product or service decreases. In this case, consumers will buy more CDs as the price decreases. We can expect to uncover a demand curve similar to this one for many, if not most, products and services.

The horizontal axis measures the quantity demanded for the CDs in units and plots it against the various price possibilities indicated on the vertical axis. Each point on the demand curve then represents the quantity demanded at a specific price. So, in this instance, if the price of a CD is $10 per unit ($P_1$), the demand is 1 000 000 units (Q_1), but if the price were set at $15 ($P_2$), the demand would be only 500 000 units (Q_2). The firm will sell far more CDs at $10 each than at $15 each. Why? Because of the greater value this price point offers.

Knowing the demand curve for a product or service enables a firm to examine different prices in terms of the resulting demand and relative to its overall objective. In our preceding example, the music retailer will generate a total of $10,000,000 in sales at the $10 price ($10 × 1 000 000 units) and $7,500,000 in sales at the $15 price ($15 × 500 000 units). In this case, given only the two choices of $10 or $15, the $10 price is preferable as long as the firm wants to maximize its sales in terms of dollars and units. But what about a firm that is more interested in profit? To calculate profit, it must consider its costs, which we cover in the next section.

Can you tell the difference between the $8500 and the $320 Paradigm speaker?

demand curve
Shows how many units of a product or service consumers will demand during a specific period at different prices.

EXHIBIT 11.3	Demand Curves for Compact Discs

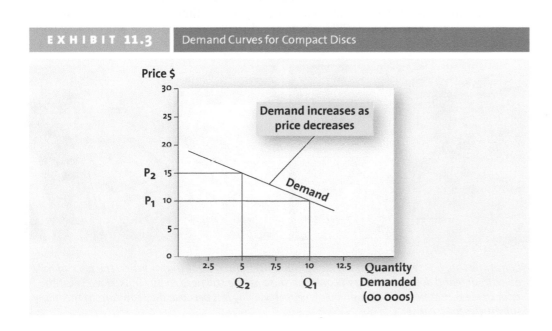

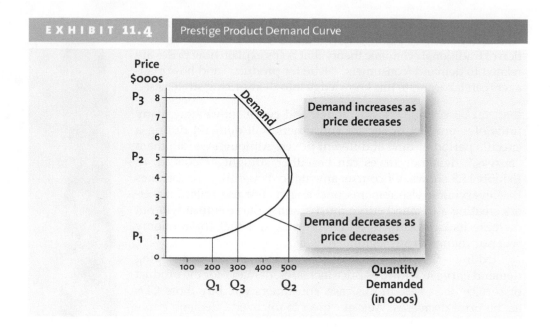

EXHIBIT 11.4   Prestige Product Demand Curve

Interestingly enough, not all products or services follow the downward-sloping demand curve for all levels of price depicted in Exhibit 11.3. Consider **prestige products or services**, which consumers purchase for their status rather than their functionality. The higher the price, the greater the status associated with it and the greater the exclusivity, because fewer people can afford to purchase it. Most important, in this case, a higher price also leads to a greater quantity sold—up to a certain point. When customers value the increase in prestige more than the price differential between the prestige product and other products, the prestige product attains the greater value overall.

Exhibit 11.4 illustrates a demand curve for a hypothetical prestige service, such as a Caribbean cruise. As the graph indicates, when the price increases from \$1000 (P_1) to \$5000 (P_2), the quantity demanded actually increases from 200 000 (Q_1) to 500 000 (Q_2) units. However, when the price increases to \$8000 (P_3), the demand then decreases to 300 000 (Q_3) units, after peaking at about 500 000.

Although the firm likely will earn more profit selling 300 000 cruises at \$8000 each than 500 000 cruises at \$5000 each, we do not know for sure until we consider

Consumers are less sensitive to the price of milk (left) than to steak (right). When the price of milk goes up, demand does not fall significantly because people still need to buy milk. However, if the price of steak rises beyond a certain point, people will buy less because they can turn to the many substitutes for steak.

costs. However, we do know that more consumers are willing to book the cruise as the price increases initially from $1000 to $5000 and that most consumers will choose an alternative vacation as the price increases further from $5000 to $8000.

Price Elasticity of Demand Although we now know something about how consumers react to different price levels, we still need to determine how consumers respond to actual changes in price. Consumers are generally less sensitive to price increases for necessary items, such as milk, because they have to purchase these items even if the price climbs. When the price of milk goes up, demand does not fall significantly. However, if the price of steak rises beyond a certain point, people will buy less because there are many substitutes. Marketers need to know how consumers will respond to a price increase (or decrease) for a specific product or brand so they can determine whether it makes sense for them to raise or lower prices.

Price elasticity of demand measures how changes in a price affect the quantity of the product demanded. We can calculate it with the following formula:

$$\text{Price elasticity of demand} = \frac{\% \text{ change in quantity demanded}}{\% \text{ change in price}}.$$

In general, the market for a product or service is price sensitive (or **elastic**) when the price elasticity is less than -1: that is, when a 1-percent decrease in price produces more than a 1-percent increase in the quantity sold. In an elastic scenario, relatively small changes in price will generate fairly large changes in the quantity demanded, so if a firm is trying to increase its sales, it can do so by lowering prices.

The market for a product is generally viewed as price insensitive (or **inelastic**) when its price elasticity is greater than -1: that is, when a 1-percent decrease in price results in less than a 1-percent increase in quantity sold. Generally, if a firm must raise prices, it is helpful to do so with inelastic products or services because in such a market, fewer customers will stop buying or reduce their purchases—customers just don't notice or care about the lower price.

Consumers are generally more sensitive to price increases than to price decreases.[9] Also, the price elasticity of demand usually changes at different points in the demand curve unless the curve is actually a straight line, as in Exhibit 11.3. For instance, a prestige product or service, such as our Caribbean cruise example in Exhibit 11.4, enjoys a highly inelastic demand curve up to a certain point, so price increases do not affect sales significantly. But when the price reaches that certain point, consumers start turning to other alternatives because the value of the cruise has finally been reduced by the extremely high price.

The Canadian economy has experienced the full force of this elasticity phenomenon during the past few years, as the U.S. dollar has lost ground to other major world currencies. In January 2002, the exchange rate was $0.62 for a U.S. dollar. By 2011, the Canadian currency had appreciated significantly and the exchange rate was above parity. An American family planning a two-week vacation in 2002 would have found that a US$5000 budget stretched nicely to more than C$8000. However, the same family would have been left with $5000 or less to spend because of currency fluctuations a decade later. Not surprisingly, a Consumer Confidence Survey by the U.S. Conference Board indicates that U.S. tourism intentions have softened,[10] as Canada is no longer perceived as such a good bargain.

Factors Influencing Price Elasticity of Demand We have illustrated how price elasticity of demand varies across different products and at different

price elasticity of demand Measures how changes in a price affect the quantity of the product demanded; specifically, the ratio of the percentage change in quantity demanded to the percentage change in price.

elastic Refers to a market for a product or service that is price sensitive; that is, relatively small changes in price will generate fairly large changes in the quantity demanded.

inelastic Refers to a market for a product or service that is price insensitive; that is, relatively small changes in price will not generate large changes in the quantity demanded.

Travelling to Canada on vacation is much more expensive for Americans today than it was a few years ago because of the strong Canadian dollar.

If there are many close substitutes for a product, customers will be sensitive to small price changes, and the product will be highly price elastic. If, for instance, Skippy raises its price, many customers will switch to another brand.

income effect
Refers to the change in the quantity of a product demanded by consumers because of a change in their income.

substitution effect
Refers to consumers' ability to substitute other products for the focal brand, thus increasing the price elasticity of demand for the focal brand.

cross-price elasticity
The percentage change in demand for Product A that occurs in response to a percentage change in price of Product B.

complementary products
Products whose demand curves are positively related, such that they rise or fall together; a percentage increase in demand for one results in a percentage increase in demand for the other.

points along a demand curve, as well as how it can change over time. What causes these differences in the price elasticity of demand? We discuss a few of the more important factors next.

Income effect.   Generally, as people's income increases, their spending behaviour changes: They tend to shift their demand from lower-priced products to higher-priced alternatives. That is, consumers may buy steak instead of ground beef and splurge on a movie a week instead of one per month. In turn, when the economy is good and consumers' incomes are rising overall, the price elasticity of steak or movies may actually drop, even though the price remains constant. Conversely, when incomes drop, consumers turn to less expensive alternatives or purchase less. This **income effect** refers to the change in the quantity of a product demanded by consumers because of a change in their income.

Substitution effect.   The **substitution effect** refers to consumers' ability to substitute other products for the focal brand. The greater the availability of substitute products, the higher the price elasticity of demand for any given product will be. For example, there are many close substitutes for the various brands of peanut butter. If Skippy raises its prices, many consumers will turn to Jif, President's Choice, or another brand because they can easily find lower-priced substitutes. Extremely brand-loyal consumers, however, are willing to pay a higher price because in their minds, Skippy still offers a better value than the competing brands.

Keep in mind that marketing plays a critical role in making consumers brand loyal, making the price elasticity of demand for some brands very low. For example, Polo Ralph Lauren sells millions of its classic polo shirt at $65, while shirts of equal quality but without the polo player logo sell for much less. Getting consumers to believe that a particular brand is unique or extraordinary in some way makes other brands seem less substitutable.

Cross-price elasticity.   **Cross-price elasticity** is the percentage change in the quantity of Product A demanded compared with the percentage change in price in Product B. For example, when the price of Blu-ray players dropped rapidly, the demand for Blu-ray discs also increased rapidly. Products such as Blu-ray discs and Blu-ray players are **complementary products**, which are products whose demands are positively related, such that they rise or fall together. In other words, a percentage increase in the quantity demanded for Product A results in a percentage increase in the quantity demanded for Product B.[11] However, when the price for Blu-ray players dropped, the demand for DVD players went down, so Blu-ray players and DVD players are **substitute products** because changes in their demand are negatively related.

Prior to this point, we have focused on how changes in prices affect how much customers buy. Clearly, knowing how prices affect sales is important, but it cannot give us the whole picture. To know how profitable a pricing strategy will be, we must also consider the third C, costs.

Costs

To make effective pricing decisions, firms must understand their cost structures so they can determine the degree to which their products or services will be profitable at different prices. In general, prices should *not* be based on costs because consumers make purchase decisions based on their perceived value; they care little about the firm's costs to produce and sell a product or deliver a service. Consumers use just the price they must pay and the benefits they may receive to judge value; they will not pay a higher price for an inferior product simply because the firm cannot be as cost-efficient as its competitors.

If, for instance, a CD were available at both Chapters and Walmart, most consumers would buy it at Walmart, where it likely will be priced lower. But many consumers see additional benefits to shopping at Chapters because it also offers a good selection of books, they can find their choice more easily, or they enjoy buying a CD while sipping a latte they have purchased from the same place. If these consumers did not value these benefits, Chapters would not survive.

Although companies incur many different types of costs as a natural part of doing business, there are two primary cost categories: variable and fixed.

Variable Costs **Variable costs** are those costs, primarily labour and materials, which vary with production volume. As a firm produces more or less of a good or service, the total variable costs increase or decrease at the same time. Because each unit of the product produced incurs the same cost, marketers generally express variable costs on a per-unit basis. Continuing with our CD example, the variable costs include the labour needed to burn each CD; the costs of the blank CDs, jewel cases, and labels; and royalties paid to the artist. Each of these costs is incurred each time the producer makes a new CD.

In the service industry, variable costs are far more complex. A hotel, for instance, incurs certain variable costs each time it rents a room, including the costs associated with the labour and supplies necessary to clean and restock the room. Note that the hotel does not incur these costs if the room is not booked. Suppose that a particular hotel calculates its total variable costs to be $20 per room; each time it rents a room, it incurs $20 in variable costs. If the hotel rents out 100 rooms on a given night, the total variable cost is $2000 ($20/room × 100 rooms).

Variable costs tend to change depending on the quantity produced. If a record producer creates five CDs, it must pay a set amount for each one. If it makes 500, though, it can probably get the discs at a lower price by buying in bulk. Though not always the case, variable costs per unit may go up or down (for all units) with significant changes in volume.

Fixed Costs **Fixed costs** are those costs that remain essentially at the same level, regardless of any changes in the volume of production. Typically, these costs include items such as rent, utilities, insurance, administrative salaries (for executives and higher-level managers), and the depreciation of the physical plant and equipment. Across reasonable fluctuations in production volume, these costs remain stable; whether the producer makes 5 or 500 CDs, the rent it pays for the building in which it burns the CDs remains unchanged.

Total Cost Finally, the **total cost** is simply the sum of the variable and fixed costs. For example, in one year, our hypothetical hotel incurred $100,000 in fixed costs. We also know that because the hotel booked 10 000 room nights, its total variable cost is $200,000 (10 000 room nights × $20/room). Thus, its total cost is $300,000.

Next, we illustrate how to use these costs in simple analyses that can inform managerial decision making about setting prices.

Break-Even Analysis and Decision Making

A useful technique that enables managers to examine the relationships among cost, price, revenue, and profit over different levels of production and sales is called the break-even analysis. Central to this analysis is the determination of the **break-even point**, or the point at which the number of units sold generates just enough revenue to equal the total costs. At this point, profits are zero.

How do we determine the break-even point? Although profit, which represents the difference between the total cost and the total revenue (total revenue or sales = selling price of each unit sold × number of units sold) can indicate how much money the firm is making or losing at a single period of time, it cannot tell managers

substitute products
Products for which changes in demand are negatively related—that is, a percentage increase in the quantity demanded for Product A results in a percentage decrease in the quantity demanded for Product B.

variable costs
Those costs, primarily labour and materials, which vary with production volume.

fixed costs
Those costs that remain essentially at the same level, regardless of any changes in the volume of production.

total cost
The sum of the *variable* and *fixed costs*.

break-even point
The point at which the number of units sold generates just enough revenue to equal the total costs; at this point, profits are zero.

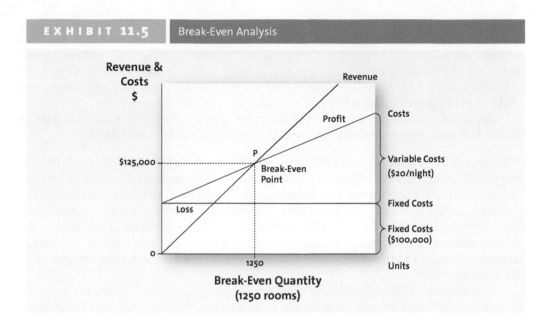

EXHIBIT 11.5 | Break-Even Analysis

how many units a firm must produce and sell before it stops losing money and at least breaks even. (Please visit Connect for online tutorials and exercises on break-even analysis and other financial concepts.)

Exhibit 11.5 presents the various cost and revenue information we have discussed in a graphic format.

Let's use the hotel example to illustrate the break-even analysis. Recall that the fixed costs are $100,000 and the variable costs are $20/room rented. If the rooms rent for $100 per night, how many rooms must the hotel rent over the course of a year to break even? If we study the graph carefully, we find the break-even point at 1250, which means that the hotel must rent 1250 rooms before its revenues equal its costs. If it rents fewer rooms, it loses money; if it rents more, it makes a profit. To determine the break-even point in units mathematically, we must consider fixed costs and the **contribution per unit**, which is the price less the variable cost per unit. We use the following formula to calculate the break-even point in units:

> **contribution per unit**
> Equals the price less the variable cost per unit; variable used to determine the break-even point in units.

$$\text{Break-even points (units)} = \frac{\text{Fixed costs}}{\text{Contribution per unit}}.$$

In this case,

$$\text{Break-even points (units)} = \frac{\$100,000}{100-20=\$80} = 1250 \text{ room nights.}$$

When the hotel has crossed that break-even point of 1250 rooms, it will then start earning profit at the same rate of the contribution per unit. So if the hotel rents 2500 rooms—1250 rooms more than the break-even point—its profit will be $100,000 (1250 rooms × $80 contribution per unit).

Although a break-even analysis cannot actually help managers set prices, it does help them assess their pricing strategies because it clarifies the conditions in which different prices may make a product or service profitable. It becomes an even more powerful tool when performed on a range of possible prices for comparative purposes. For example, the hotel management could analyze various prices, not just $100, to determine how many hotel rooms it would have to rent at what price to make a $200,000 profit.

Naturally, however, a break-even analysis has limitations. First, it is unlikely that a hotel has one specific price that it charges for each and every room, so the price it would use in its break-even analysis probably represents an average price that

In a hotel, the cost of the physical structure (left) is fixed—it is incurred even if no rooms are rented. The costs to clean towels and sheets (right) are variable—the more rooms that are rented, the more the costs.

attempts to account for these variances. Second, prices often get reduced as quantity increases because the costs decrease, so firms must perform several break-even analyses at different quantities.

Third, a break-even analysis cannot indicate for sure how many rooms will be rented or, in the case of products, how many units will sell at a given price. It tells the firm only what its costs, revenues, and profitability will be given a set price and an assumed quantity. To determine how many units the firm actually will sell, it must bring in the demand estimates we discussed previously.

Competition

Because the fourth C, competition, has a profound impact on pricing strategies,[12] we use this section to focus on its effect, as well as on how competitors react to certain pricing strategies. There are four levels of competition—monopoly, oligopolistic, monopolistic, and pure—and each has its own set of pricing challenges and opportunities (see Exhibit 11.6).

In a **monopoly**, one firm provides the product or service in a particular industry, and as such results in less price competition. For example, in the utilities industry, there is only one provider of power in each region of the country—Hydro One in most of Ontario and SaskPower in Saskatchewan. Power companies operate more efficiently when there is one service provider, so the government regulates the pricing of utility monopolies to prevent them from raising prices uncontrollably. Monopolies have had a long history in the United States, starting with Standard Oil, which the government broke up in 1911. Both professional baseball and football leagues have been involved in monopolistic controversies over the years, as has software giant Microsoft and the diamond supplier De Beers. A monopoly that restricts competition by controlling an industry can be deemed illegal and broken apart by the government.

monopoly
Occurs when only one firm provides the product or service in a particular industry.

When a market is characterized by **oligopolistic competition**, only a few firms dominate. Firms typically change their prices in reaction to competition to avoid upsetting an otherwise stable competitive environment. Often cited examples of oligopolistic markets include the banking industry, the retail gasoline industry, and commercial airline travel.

oligopolistic competition
Occurs when only a few firms dominate a market.

Sometimes reactions to prices in oligopolistic markets can result in a **price war**, which occurs when two or more firms compete primarily by lowering their prices.

price war
Occurs when two or more firms compete primarily by lowering their prices.

EXHIBIT 11.6 Four Levels of Competition: Can you match each photo to its respective type of competition?

Less Price Competition | More Price Competition

Monopoly
One firm controls the market

Oligopoly
A handful of firms control the market

Fewer Firms

Monopolistic Comp.
Many firms selling differentiated products at different prices

Pure Competition
Many firms selling commodities for the same prices

Many Firms

monopolistic competition
Occurs when many firms sell closely related but not homogeneous products; these products may be viewed as substitutes but are not perfect substitutes.

pure competition
Occurs when different companies sell commodity products that consumers perceive as substitutable; price usually is set according to the laws of supply and demand.

Price wars often appear in the airline industry when a low-cost provider enters a market in which established carriers already exist. But what motivates firms to enter price wars?[13] In the airline example, the new entrants might want to gain market share, whereas the established airlines drop their prices to preserve their market share. Other reasons include avoiding the appearance of being insensitive to consumers and simply overreacting to a price decrease offered by competitors. In many cases, companies do not need to respond to price cuts with price cuts of their own[14] because consumers do not buy solely on the basis of price. Better service, higher quality, and brand loyalty might be used as competitive strategies instead.

Monopolistic competition occurs when there are many firms competing for customers in a given market but their products are differentiated. When so many firms compete, product differentiation rather than a strict pricing competition tends to appeal to consumers. This form of competition is the most common. Hundreds of firms make wristwatches, and the market is highly differentiated. For example, Timex is known for durability, Swatch for style, Armani for fashion, and Rolex for prestige.

With **pure competition**, consumers perceive a large number of sellers of standardized products or commodities as substitutable, such as grains, spices, gold, or minerals. In such markets, price usually is set according to the laws of supply and demand. For example, wheat is wheat, so it does not matter to a commercial bakery whose wheat it buys. However, the secret to pricing success in a pure competition market is not necessarily to offer the lowest price because doing so might create a price war and erode profits. Instead, some firms have brilliantly decommoditized their products. For example, coffee beans used to be regarded as all the same, and then Juan Valdez and the Colombian Coffee Growers Federation made their "100%

| Ethical Dilemma 11.1 | **White-Label ABM Fees Red-Flagged** |

It's Friday night and you're at a bar with friends. As usual, you didn't bring along enough cash. No problem. There's an ABM in the lobby. Just pop in your bank card and withdraw $20. It's easy. It's convenient. And, it's expensive. Depending on the type of ABM machine you used, that $20 transaction could cost you a whole lot more. While you could withdraw money from your own bank's ABM for little or nothing, machines run by independents use a pricing approach that adds surcharges between $1.50 and $6.15.

Today in Canada, about two-thirds of cash machines are white-label—that is, privately owned—as opposed to being owned by banks.[15] The machines have multiplied dramatically in the past decade, springing up in bars, convenience stores, movie theatres, and truck stops across the country. Critics charge that the white-label industry has grown outside the strict federal laws that govern the banks. The lack of restrictions has attracted entrepreneurs only too happy to seize the opportunity for profits inherent in white-label fees. There are currently between 200 to 250 companies involved in Canada's white-label industry, representing 35 000 privately owned machines that handle about 135 million transactions a year.[16]

With few barriers to entry—a used ABM can be purchased on eBay for as low as $1500—the appeal of white-label machines is attractive. What's more, Canadians don't seem to mind the high fees, relishing the convenience of having ready cash close at hand. However, with a largely unregulated market, the RCMP has recently raised questions about a possible link between privately owned ABMs and money laundering. Even though Canada is in the midst of tightening laws against money laundering, it won't affect new ABM rules.[17] And machines stocked with dirty money aren't the only concern. ABMs could be an ideal way to disperse counterfeit funds, a problem that has captured the attention of Bank of Canada officials. In light of this scrutiny, it's interesting to note that the birth of the white-label business is a direct result of the Competition Bureau's 1996 decision to force Interac to open up the market to nonfinancial institutions.[18]

In the meantime, Canadians were charged more than $420 million last year to access their own money.[19] Even if customers are willing to pay these fees, should the white-label industry be allowed to charge what the market will bear or should it be regulated via a fee cap?

Colombian Coffee" special, ensuring that coffee drinkers now know the difference between their beans and everything else. In some cases, pure competition opens the market to new players who are able to charge higher prices based on the convenience they offer, as demonstrated in Ethical Dilemma 11.1.

When a commodity can be differentiated somehow, even if simply by a sticker or logo, there is an opportunity for consumers to identify it as distinct from the rest, and in this case, firms can at least partially extricate their product from a pure competitive market.

Channel Members

Channel members—manufacturers, wholesalers, and retailers—can have different perspectives when it comes to pricing strategies. Consider a manufacturer that is focused on increasing the image and reputation of its brand but working with a retailer that is primarily concerned with increasing its sales. The manufacturer may desire to keep prices higher to convey a better image, whereas the retailer wants lower prices and will accept lower profits to move the product, regardless of consumers' impressions of the brand. Unless channel members carefully communicate their pricing goals and select channel partners that agree with them, conflict will surely arise.

Channels can be very difficult to manage, and distribution outside normal channels does occur. A **grey market**, for example, employs irregular but not necessarily illegal methods; generally, it legally circumvents authorized channels of distribution to sell goods at prices lower than those intended by the manufacturer.[20] Many manufacturers of consumer electronics therefore require retailers to sign an agreement that demands certain activities (and prohibits others) before they may become authorized dealers. But if a retailer has too many high-definition TVs in stock, it may sell them at just above its own cost to an unauthorized discount dealer. This move places the

grey market
Employs irregular but not necessarily illegal methods; generally, it legally circumvents authorized channels of distribution to sell goods at prices lower than those intended by the manufacturer.

TV sets and other consumer electronics are commonly sold in the grey market.

merchandise on the street at prices far below what authorized dealers can charge, and in the long term, it may tarnish the image of the manufacturer if the discount dealer fails to provide sufficient return policies, support, service, and so forth.

To discourage this type of grey market distribution, some manufacturers, such as Fujitsu, have resorted to large disclaimers on their websites, packaging, and other communications to warn consumers that the manufacturer's product warranty becomes null and void unless the item has been purchased from an authorized dealer.[21]

Other Influences on Pricing

Thus far, we have focused mainly on product- and firm-specific factors—the five Cs—that influence pricing. Now we turn to broader factors that have a more sweeping effect on pricing in general: the Internet and economic factors.

The Internet

The shift among consumers to acquiring more and more products, services, and information online has made them more price sensitive and opened new categories of products to those who could not access them previously. Gourmet foods, books, music, movies, electronics, and even contact lenses (see Power of the Internet 11.1) are just a few of the product categories that present a significant online presence. Because they have gained access to rare cheeses, breads, meats, spices, and confections, consumers are demanding more from their local grocery stores in terms of selection and variety and have become more sensitive about prices. Furthermore, consumers' ability to buy electronics at highly discounted prices online has pushed bricks-and-mortar stores to attempt to focus consumers' attention on prepurchase advice and expertise, consulting services, and after-sales service—and away from price.

The Internet also provides search engines and online auction sites, such as eBay and Kijiji, that enable consumers to find the best prices for any product, new or used, quickly, which again increases their price sensitivity and reduces the costs associated with finding lower-price alternatives.[22] Not only do consumers know more about prices, they know more about the firms, their products, their competitors, and the markets in which they compete.

A more recent trend affecting pricing has been the rapid growth of online daily coupon promotions from companies such as Groupon or WagJag. In Toronto, The Butchers promoted $175 of organic meat for $55 through Dealfind. It sold 11 500 coupons in three days, worth $632,500, and set a North American record for the largest promotion by an independent store in a single city.[23] Although The Butchers had been in business for more than 10 years, the online coupon promotion resulted in huge growth in its customer base.

Economic Factors

Two interrelated trends that have merged to impact pricing decisions are the increase in consumers' disposable income and status consciousness. Some consumers appear willing to spend money for products that can convey status in some way. For example, when Holt Renfrew introduced the limited-edition I'm Not a Plastic Bag cotton tote by British accessories designer Anya Hindmarch, people camped out in front of the Bloor flagship store to buy one. A total of 3000 bags were received at

Power of the
Internet 11.1

Clearly a Winning Strategy

Would you buy glasses or contact lenses over the Internet? You might for the right price. Roger Hardy and his sister Michaela Tokarksi founded Clearly Contacts in 2000 in a Vancouver basement office that had a computer, a phone, and a Ping-Pong table. In a few short years, it has become the world's fastest growing online retailer of eyeglasses and contact lenses. While working for a contact lens manufacturer, Hardy realized that the margins were extremely high. He knew there had to be a better, cheaper way for consumers to buy eye-care products and so he set out to change that, defining his mission as "Saving the World from Overpriced Eyeglasses."[24]

In the past, the prescription glasses market has been dominated by opticians. The Clearly Contacts business model eliminates the middleman, automates the order process, and ships direct to consumers for 50 to 70 percent less than traditional eye-care retailers. Prices range from $38 to $198, great value for designer brands such as Prada, Dior, Armani, and Fendi.[25] Still, Hardy discovered that although consumers were willing to purchase books or clothes over the Internet, they had reservations about buying eyeglasses online. Curtis Petersen, director of acquisition and retention for Clearly Contacts notes that it's a more complex purchase. You have to convince consumers to change their behaviour and do something a little different to complete the purchase.[26] A Virtual Mirror application lets customers see how some of the 500 designs would look on their faces. Free shipping and liberal payment terms help minimize the risk of the purchase.

To persuade Vancouverites to try the products, the company decided to give 3000 pairs of designer glasses away for free in June 2010. Consumers signed up online to get a coupon code for the glasses. Clearly Contacts' strategy was to get the high-quality glasses in the hands of consumers to dispel concerns about buying them on the Internet. The company ran a similar promotion in Toronto the year before with a one-day offer of free prescription eyeglasses. It was so successful that it brought the company's website down for more than two hours. In spite of the crash, it managed to give away 1000 pairs of designer glasses by 1:00 p.m.[27] and generated positive word of mouth advertising.

Most of Clearly Contact's advertising budget is spent online on banner ads and search engine optimization, very appropriate for an online retailer. It appears the company has found a winning formula, having captured about 10 percent of the eyeglasses market and earned a spot on Profit 100's Top Fastest Growing Companies in Canada. With operations in North America, Europe, and Asia, more than 2 million customers, and revenues of $119 million,[28] it is clearly on its way to becoming the world's largest online optical store.

Would the right price entice you to buy contacts or glasses online?"

Holt Renfrew stores across Canada, and they sold out in less than an hour at $18 each.[29] Products once considered only for the very rich, such as Rolex watches and Mercedes-Benz cars, are now owned by more working professionals. Although such prestige products are still aimed at the elite, more and more consumers are making the financial leap to attain them.

At the same time, however, a countervailing trend finds customers attempting to shop cheap. The popularity of everyday low price retailers, such as Walmart and Giant Tiger, among customers who can afford to shop at department and specialty stores illustrates that it is cool to save a buck. Retailers such as H&M and Loblaws, with its Joe Fresh line of clothing, have introduced disposable chic and cross-shopping into Canadians' shopping habits. In this context, **cross-shopping** is the pattern of buying both premium and low-priced merchandise or patronizing both expensive, status-oriented retailers and price-oriented retailers. These stores offer fashionable merchandise at great values—values so good that if items last for only a few wearings, it doesn't matter to the customers. The net impact of these contradictory trends on prices has been

cross-shopping
The pattern of buying both premium and low-priced merchandise or patronizing both expensive, status-oriented retailers and price-oriented retailers.

Limited-edition cotton totes by British designer Anya Hindmarch sold out in less than an hour at $18 each at Holt Renfrew stores.

that some prestige items have become more expensive, whereas many other items have become cheaper.

Finally, the economic environment at local, regional, national, and global levels influences pricing. Starting at the top, the growth of the global economy has changed the nature of competition around the world. Many firms maintain a presence in multiple countries: products get designed in one country, the parts are manufactured in another, the final product assembled in a third, and after-sales service is handled by a call centre in a fourth. By thinking globally, firms can seek out the most cost-efficient methods of providing goods and services to their customers.

On a more local level, the economy still can influence pricing. Competition, disposable income, and unemployment all may signal the need for different pricing strategies. For instance, rural areas are often subjected to higher prices because it costs more to get products there and because competition is lower. Similarly, retailers often charge higher prices in areas populated by people who have more disposable income and enjoy low unemployment rates.

L03   Pricing Strategies

Coming up with the "right" price is never easy. If RIM had decided to price BlackBerry Bold at a low point initially, how would it have affected future sales—both its own and of potential competitors? Firms embrace different objectives, face different market conditions, and operate in different manners; thus, they employ unique pricing strategies that seem best for the particular set of circumstances in which they find themselves. Even a single firm needs different strategies across its products and services and over time as market conditions change. Thus, the choice of a pricing strategy is specific to the product/service and target market. Although firms tend to rely on similar strategies when they can, each product or service requires its own specific strategy because no two are ever exactly the same in terms of the marketing mix. Cost-based, competitor-based, and value-based strategies are discussed in this section.

Cost-Based Methods

cost-based pricing method Determines the final price to charge by starting with the cost, without recognizing the role that consumers or competitors' prices play in the marketplace.

As their name implies, **cost-based pricing methods** determine the final price to charge by starting with the cost. Cost-based methods do not recognize the role that consumers or competitors' prices play in the marketplace. Although relatively simple compared with other methods used to set prices, cost-based pricing requires that all costs can be identified and calculated on a per-unit basis. Moreover, the process assumes that these costs will not vary much for different levels of production. If they do, the price might need to be raised or lowered according to the production level. Thus, with cost-based pricing, prices are usually set on the basis of estimates of average costs.

Competitor-Based Methods

competitor-based pricing method An approach that attempts to reflect how the firm wants consumers to interpret its products relative to the competitors' offerings.

Most firms know that consumers compare the prices of their products with the different product/price combinations competitors offer. Thus, using a **competitor-based**

pricing method, they may set their prices to reflect the way they want consumers to interpret their own prices relative to the competitors' offerings. For example, setting a price very close to a competitor's price signals to consumers that the product is similar, whereas setting the price much higher signals greater features, better quality, or some other valued benefit.

Another competitor-based method is **premium pricing**, which means the firm deliberately prices a product above the prices set for competing products to capture those consumers who always shop for the best or for whom price does not matter. For example, whether or not a $250,000 Ferrari is that much better than a $230,000 Ferrari, some consumers will pay the additional $20,000 to get what they perceive as the very best.

This Ferrari Scaglietti uses premium pricing.

Value-Based Methods

Value-based pricing methods include approaches to setting prices that focus on the overall value of the product offering as perceived by the consumer. Consumers determine value by comparing the benefits they expect the product to deliver with the sacrifice they will need to make to acquire the product. Of course, different consumers perceive value differently. Sometimes a value-based pricing strategy can be a bit unconventional, as discussed in Social Media Marketing 11.1. So how does a manager use value-based pricing methods? We consider two key approaches.

Improvement Value Method With this method, the manager must estimate the improvement value of a new product or service. This **improvement value** represents an estimate of how much more (or less) consumers are willing to pay for a product relative to other comparable products. For example, suppose a major telecommunications company has developed a new cellphone. Using any of a host of research methods, such as consumer surveys, the manager could get customers to assess the new product relative to an existing product and provide an estimate of how much better it is, or its improvement value.

Cost of Ownership Method Another value-based method for setting prices determines the total cost of owning the product over its useful life. Using the **cost of ownership method**, consumers may be willing to pay more for a particular product because, over its entire lifetime, it will eventually cost less to own than a cheaper alternative.[30]

Consider, for example, that an energy-efficient fluorescent light bulb costs $3 and is expected to last 6000 hours. Alternatively, a conventional light bulb costs $1 but its average life is only 1500 hours. Even though the fluorescent bulb is expected to last four times longer than a conventional bulb, it costs only three times as much. Using the cost of ownership method, and considering the cost per hour, the fluorescent bulb manufacturer could charge $4 for each bulb to give it an equivalent cost to a conventional bulb. However, given its research indicated that many consumers would be reluctant to spend $4 for a bulb, the manufacturer chose to charge only $3, thereby offering customers greater value.

Although value-based pricing strategies can be quite effective, they also necessitate a great deal of consumer research to be implemented successfully. Sellers must know

premium pricing
A competitor-based pricing method by which the firm deliberately prices a product above the prices set for competing products to capture those consumers who always shop for the best or for whom price does not matter.

value-based pricing method
Focuses on the overall value of the product offering as perceived by consumers, who determine value by comparing the benefits they expect the product to deliver with the sacrifice they will need to make to acquire the product.

improvement value
Represents an estimate of how much more (or less) consumers are willing to pay for a product relative to other comparable products.

cost of ownership method
A value-based method for setting prices that determines the total cost of owning the product over its useful life.

Is the improvement value on the new BlackBerry Torch sufficiently greater than competitive products that RIM can charge a higher price for it?

Imagine making money 365 days of the year, just for putting on a shirt! Jason Sadler struck gold with this innovative way to make money. Instead of selling you the shirt off his back, he wears a company's T-shirt for a day to promote it. Days were sold at face value, so the first day of the year costs $1, while the last day of the year sells for $365. To ensure that companies received value for the benefits received, Sadler took many photographs of himself wearing the shirt throughout the day, which he then posted to his website (IWearYourShirt.com), a daily blog, Flickr, YouTube, Ustream.tv, and Twitter.

Sadler attracted media attention across North America and internationally, fuelling interest and sales. His Twitter profile has attracted more than 21 000 avid followers.[31] Daily videos posted to YouTube range from hundreds of views to just under 10 000. Crazy you say? Sadler's first year's inventory was quickly sold out, earning him about $83,000, including sponsorships,[32] just for wearing a different T-shirt every day.

Unconventional perhaps, however, companies bought into Sadler's value-based pricing strategy, resulting in a sold out 2009 calendar. Sales were booked well into the fall of 2010, in spite of an increase in price to $2 for the January 1 slot. While the price doubled, so did the promotion, with two guys wearing the T-shirts, maximizing exposure for companies. Pretty impressive for a business model built solely around social media.

Using value-based pricing, Jason Sadler got companies to pay him to wear their T-shirts.

how consumers in different market segments will attach value to the benefits delivered by their products. They also must account for changes in consumer attitudes because the way customers perceive value today may not be the way they perceive it tomorrow.

New Product Pricing

Developing pricing strategies for new products is one of the most challenging tasks a manager can undertake. When the new product is just another "me-too" product, similar to what already appears on the market, this job is somewhat easier because the product's approximate value has already been established. But when the product is truly innovative, or what we call "new to the world," determining consumers' perceptions of its value and pricing it accordingly becomes far more difficult.

Consider, for example, the value to consumers of innovations such as airbags. They can prevent serious lifelong disabilities and even save lives. So how do car manufacturers attach value to benefits like those? To make it even more complex, automobile companies have to consider the value of an airbag that never deploys. Good marketing research can uncover the value of an innovation in the eyes of the consumer. Let's turn our attention to two distinct pricing strategies for new products: skimming and penetration.

Price Skimming

In many markets, and particularly for new and innovative products or services, innovators and early adopters (see Chapter 8) are willing to pay a higher price to obtain the new product or service. This strategy, known as **price skimming**, appeals to these segments of consumers who are willing to pay the premium price to have the innovation first. Did any of your friends wait in line for hours desperate to be the first to own the iPhone 4? If so, they are likely part of the innovator segment of the market, which made them willing to pay top dollar to get the new product and its exciting enhancements. After this high-price market segment becomes saturated and sales begin to slow down, companies generally lower the price to capture (or skim) the next most price-sensitive market segment, which is willing to pay a somewhat lower price. This process can continue until the demand for the product has been satisfied, even at the lowest price points. Luxury products are often an exception. For example, Louis Vuitton does not lower the price of its bags, but rather, keeps prices high to support its prestige image.

For price skimming to work, the product or service must be perceived as breaking new ground in some way, offering consumers new benefits currently unavailable in alternative products. Firms use skimming strategies for a variety of reasons. Some may start by pricing relatively high to signal high quality to the market. Others may decide to price high at first to limit demand, which gives them time to build their production capacities. Similarly, some firms employ a skimming strategy to try to quickly earn back some of the high R&D investments they made for the new product. Finally, firms employ skimming strategies to test consumers' price sensitivity. A firm that prices too high can always lower the price; but, if the price is initially set too low, it is almost impossible to raise it without significant consumer resistance.

For a skimming pricing strategy to be successful, competitors cannot be able to enter the market easily; otherwise, price competition will likely force lower prices and undermine the whole strategy. Competitors might be prevented from entering the market through patent protections, their inability to copy the innovation (because it is complex to manufacture, its raw materials are hard to get, or the product relies on proprietary technology) or the high costs of entry.

Skimming strategies also face a significant potential drawback in the relatively high unit costs often associated with producing small volumes of products. Therefore, firms must consider the trade-off between earning a higher price and suffering higher production costs.

Price skimming also can cause some discontent for consumers. Those who purchase early and pay a higher price may feel somewhat cheated when the prices drop. For instance, when first introduced in 2007, iPhones sold for $599. While early adopters did line up to buy them, the price dropped to $399 within months. To avoid negative responses, some firms differentiate their products in some way. For example, publishers generally release a new book first in hardcover and later in softcover at a lower price.

Market Penetration Pricing

Instead of setting the price high, firms using **market penetration pricing** set the initial price low for the introduction of the new product or service. Their objective is to build sales, market share, and profits quickly. In direct opposition to a skimming strategy, the low market penetration price encourages consumers to purchase the product immediately rather than waiting for the price to drop. With price skimming, profits are generated through margin, whereas with penetration pricing, profits flow through volume. Although it is not always the case, many firms expect the unit cost to drop significantly as the accumulated volume sold increases, an effect known as the **experience curve effect**. With this effect, as sales continue to grow, the costs continue to drop, allowing even further reductions in the price.

price skimming
A strategy of selling a new product or service at a high price that *innovators* and *early adopters* are willing to pay to obtain it; after the high-price market segment becomes saturated and sales begin to slow down, the firm generally lowers the price to capture (or skim) the next most price-sensitive segment.

market penetration pricing
A pricing strategy of setting the initial price low for the introduction of the new product or service, with the objective of building sales, market share, and profits quickly.

experience curve effect
Refers to the drop in unit cost as the accumulated volume sold increases; as sales continue to grow, the costs continue to drop, allowing even further reductions in the price.

Apple used a price skimming strategy when it introduced the iPhone but quickly lowered the price to attract more customers.

In addition to offering the potential to build sales, market share, and profits, penetration pricing discourages competitors from entering the market because the profit margin is relatively low. Furthermore, if the costs to produce the product drop because of the accumulated volume, competitors that enter the market later will face higher unit costs, at least until their volume catches up with the early entrant.

A penetration strategy also has its drawbacks. First, the firm must have the capacity to satisfy a rapid rise in demand—or at least be able to add that capacity quickly. Second, low price does not signal high quality. Of course, a price below their expectations decreases the risk for consumers to purchase the product and test its quality for themselves. Third, firms should avoid a penetration pricing strategy if some segments of the market are willing to pay more for the product; otherwise, the firm is just "leaving money on the table."

Psychological Factors Affecting Value-Based Pricing Strategies

Understanding the psychology underlying the way consumers arrive at their perceptions, make judgments, and finally invoke a choice is critical to effective pricing strategies, so marketers must examine some of the more important psychological processes that influence consumers' reactions to and use of price. When consumers are exposed to a price, they assign meaning to it by placing it into a category, such as "expensive," "a deal," "cheap," "overpriced," or even "fair."

In this section, we examine some of the factors that influence this psychological process of adding meaning to, or evaluating, price.[33] But first, let's look at how one woman with an incredible vision launched a new product based on a unique concept in Entrepreneurial Marketing 11.1.

Consumers' Use of Reference Prices

reference price
The price against which buyers compare the actual selling price of the product and that facilitates their evaluation process.

external reference price
A higher price to which the consumer can compare the selling price to evaluate the purchase.

A **reference price** is the price against which buyers compare the actual selling price of the product and that facilitates their evaluation process. In some cases, the seller itself provides an **external reference price**, a higher price to which the consumer can compare the selling price to evaluate the deal.[34] Typically, the seller labels the external reference price as the "regular price" or an "original price." When consumers view the "sale price" and compare it with the provided external reference price, their perceptions of the value of the deal will likely increase.[35] In the advertisement shown to the right, Sears has provided an external reference price, in smaller print and labelled "Reg.," to indicate that $24.99 is the regular price of Lee jeans. In addition, the advertisement highlights the current "sale" price of $21.99. Thus, the external reference price suggests to consumers that they are getting a good deal and will save money.

Consumers may also rely on an **internal reference price** to judge a price offering by accessing price information stored in their memory—perhaps the last price they paid or what they expect to pay.[36] For instance, when a consumer has been seated in a restaurant and first views the price of a large pepperoni pizza, she has only her internal reference price for comparison. If the price of the pizza on the menu is $12 and the consumer's internal reference price is $10 because she recalls that as the price she usually pays for a large pepperoni pizza at another restaurant, she may judge the menu price as high.

In this ad, Sears provides an external reference price of $24.99, in small print, to reflect the regular price of Lee jeans.

A more complex element of reference prices is the relationship among them. That is, external reference prices influence internal reference prices.[37] When consumers are repeatedly exposed to higher reference prices, their internal reference prices shift toward the higher external reference prices, assuming their initial internal reference price was not too far away from it. The net effect is that consumers will perceive the product or service in question to have a relatively lower selling price, and it therefore becomes a better deal in their perceptions.

Everyday Low Pricing (EDLP) Versus High/Low Pricing

With an **everyday low pricing (EDLP)** strategy, companies stress the continuity of their retail prices at a level somewhere between the regular, nonsale price and the deep-discount sale prices their competitors may offer.[38] By reducing consumers' search costs, EDLP adds value; consumers can spend less of their valuable time comparing prices, including sale prices, at different stores. For example, Walmart relies on EDLP to communicate to consumers that, for any given group of often purchased items, its prices are lower than those of any other company in that market. This claim does not necessarily mean that every item that consumers may purchase will be priced lower at Walmart than anywhere else—in fact, some competitive retailers will offer lower prices on some items. However, on average, Walmart's prices tend to be lower.

Alternatively, some retailers prefer a **high/low pricing** strategy, which relies on the promotion of sales, during which prices are temporarily reduced to encourage purchases. In the end, which consumers prefer which strategy depends on how those consumers evaluate prices and quality. Some prefer not to expend the time to find the lowest price and favour EDLP as an efficient way to get low prices. Alternatively, other consumers may relish the challenge of getting the lowest price or be so price sensitive that they are willing to expend the time and effort to seek out the lowest price every time.

internal reference price
Price information stored in the consumer's memory that the person uses to assess a current price offering—perhaps the last price he or she paid or what he or she expects to pay.

everyday low pricing (EDLP)
A strategy companies use to emphasize the continuity of their retail prices at a level somewhere between the regular, nonsale price and the deep-discount sale prices their competitors may offer.

high/low pricing
A *pricing* strategy that relies on the promotion of sales, during which prices are temporarily reduced to encourage purchases.

Entrepreneurial Marketing 11.1

Sweet Smell of Success

Most entrepreneurs start their businesses in hopes of making a profit. While this goal is part of Barbara Stegemann's plan, she has another driving motivation: changing the face of the Afghan heroin industry. Her Halifax company, The 7 Virtues Communications Group, has helped large companies and government organizations adapt to their changing environments. Now she's promoting sustainable business development in war-torn Afghanistan by encouraging a group of male and female farmers to abandon their poppy fields to grow orange blossoms for use as fragrance oil.

A feasibility study conducted in 2004 showed that Afghans were well-positioned to tap into the US$18.4 billion international flavour and fragrance market.[39] The study determined that essential oils were high in value and low in volume; in other words, like the opium produced from poppies, small quantities are worth a lot of money. Stegemann was inspired by her friendship with Captain Trevor Greene, who served in Afghanistan. In spite of sustaining serious injuries during his stay, he was ready to return to the country. "Perfume not Poppies" became her philosophy as she set out to capture

Psychological pricing and a "Perfume not Poppies" philosophy is helping to sell 7 Virtues perfume.

some of the $600 million Canadians spend annually on perfume.[40]

Stegemann met with officials from the Canadian International Development Agency, the Afghan embassy in Ottawa, and the Canada Afghanistan Business Council. These connections led to an extraordinary partnership with an Afghan company, Gulestan, owned by Abdullah Arsala, that produces essential oils.[41] The first cup of orange blossom oil cost Stegemann $2000, enough to produce 1000 bottles of perfume. The new product was introduced on March 8, 2010,[42] International Women's Day, a fitting day since most of the orange blossoms farmers are women. Next year Stegemann promised to buy their entire crop, which would allow her to produce 8000 to 12 000 bottles.

Psychological pricing is often used in the fragrance industry, as consumers seek must-have products. Priced at $70 for 50 millilitres, 7 Virtues is not inexpensive; but, price hasn't been a deterrent. In fact, the story behind 7 Virtues is helping the perfume to fly off shelves. In spite of the relatively high price point, on launch day, nearly one-third of Stegemann's stock sold.[43]

But even this categorization gets more complicated, in that it needs to include quality perceptions as well. Some consumers perceive that stores that use EDLP carry lower quality goods, whereas high/low pricing stores tend to carry better quality items. In part, this perception forms because consumers view the initial price at a high/low store as the reference price. In the end, however, the consumer's decision, once again and as always, comes down to value.

Odd Prices

odd prices
Prices that end in odd numbers, usually 9, such as $3.99.

Have you ever wondered why prices rarely end in round amounts, like $3.00 or $23.00? In various product categories, **odd prices**, or those that end in odd numbers, usually 9, are very common, such as $3.99, $11.99, and $7.77. Although not documented, most marketers believe that odd pricing got its start as a way to prevent sales clerks from just pocketing money. Because the price was odd, the clerk would have to open the cash register for change, which required that the sale be rung up on the register.

Today, it seems that odd pricing may be so traditional that sellers are afraid to round off their prices for fear that consumers will respond negatively. Also, some sellers may believe that consumers mentally truncate the actual price, making the perceived price appear lower than it really is. For example, if the price is $21.99, consumers may focus more on the $21 than on the 99 cents, which may cause them to perceive the price as significantly lower than $22.00, even though that difference is only a penny. The main finding from research on the odd pricing approach is that odd prices signal to consumers that the price is low.[44] So if sellers want to suggest that a deal is to be had, odd prices may be appropriate.

The Price–Quality Relationship

Imagine that you have an important date tonight, and you are cooking a special, romantic, Italian dinner. You go to the grocery store to buy the food and realize that your recipe for the antipasto appetizer calls for lupini beans (a large bean usually imported from Italy). You've never even heard of lupini beans, much less purchased or used them in a recipe. Luckily, the store has three different brands of lupini beans. But how do you choose which brand to buy? The three choices are priced at $3.99, $3.79, and $3.49. Are you going to risk the success of this dinner to save a mere

Odd prices signal to consumers that the price is low.

50 cents on a can of beans? Probably not. Without other information to help you make a choice, you will likely go for the $3.99 can of beans because, like most consumers, you believe that they must be of higher quality because they cost more.

But not all consumers rely on price to judge quality. When consumers know the brands, have had experience with the products, or have considerable knowledge about how to judge the quality of products objectively, price becomes less important.[45] The store, brand name, product warranties/guarantees, and where the product was produced also represent information consumers use to judge quality. Even free tap water can be promoted as high quality, as discussed in Sustainable Marketing 11.1. Nonetheless, price generally plays a critical role in consumers' judgments of quality.[46] Given the various psychological pricing factors that come into play for consumers, marketers must consider how they function when they set prices. In the next section, we discuss how to apply psychological factors in the pricing decisions for new products.

Pricing Tactics

It is important to distinguish clearly between pricing strategies and pricing tactics. A *pricing strategy* is a long-term approach to setting prices broadly in an integrative effort (across all the firm's products) based on the five Cs (company objectives, customers, costs, competition, and channel members) of pricing. **Pricing tactics**, in contrast, offer short-term methods to focus on select components of the five Cs. Generally, a pricing tactic represents either a short-term response to a competitive threat (e.g., lowering price temporarily to meet a competitor's price reduction) or a broadly accepted method of calculating a final price for the customer that is short term in nature. We separate our discussion of pricing tactics into those aimed at intermediaries in a business-to-business (B2B) setting and those directed at end consumers.

Business-to-Business Pricing Tactics and Discounts

The pricing tactics employed in B2B settings differ significantly from those used in consumer markets. Among the most prominent are seasonal and cash discounts, allowances, quantity discounts, and uniform delivered versus geographic pricing (see Exhibit 11.7).

Seasonal Discounts A **seasonal discount** is an additional reduction offered as an incentive to retailers to order merchandise in advance of the normal buying season. For instance, Lennox may offer its air conditioning dealers an additional seasonal

pricing tactics
Short-term methods, in contrast to long-term pricing strategies, used to focus on company objectives, customers, costs, competition, or channel members; can be responses to competitive threats (e.g., lowering price temporarily to meet a competitor's price reduction) or broadly accepted methods of calculating a final price for the customer that is short term in nature.

seasonal discount
Pricing tactic of offering an additional reduction as an incentive to retailers to order merchandise in advance of the normal buying season.

Sustainable Marketing 11.1   H₂O to Go

Ah, summer time. Outdoor festivals, concerts, great weather, and fun with friends. And when the sun beats down, you may reach for a cold bottle of water. If you live in the Region of Waterloo in Ontario, officials are hoping it will be filled with tap water. The Region is on a mission to increase awareness and appreciation for the high-quality tap water available to its residents. Though it's a convenience most of us take for granted, the United Nations estimates that more than 1 billion people live without access to clean, safe drinking water.[47]

To make it easy for locals to access tap water when attending public events, the Region has purchased a mobile water wagon that will travel to outdoor festivals and other community events. All residents have to do is bring along a reusable, refillable bottle. When it's empty, they can top it up for free from the water wagon. The initiative is sponsored by the Municipal Tap Water Providers. Members represent different levels of government responsible for water supply and distribution, including the Region of Waterloo, the City of Kitchener, Kitchener Utilities division, the City of Cambridge, and the City of Guelph.

As consumers become increasingly aware of protecting their environment, efforts such as the water wagon enable them to make their community more sustainable. Currently, more than 15 000 plastic water bottles are recycled at Waterloo Region's recycling plant every day.[48] The Region is hoping its mobile drinking station with its slogan "Bring It! Fill It! Drink It!" will help the environment and reduce waste. Some consumers may balk at drinking tap water, and yet that's exactly what they pay for when they buy bottled water products such as Dasani and Aquafina. Check the labels and you'll see the letters

Consumers attending public events in Waterloo Region can get free water for refillable containers from a mobile wagon.

PWS, which stand for *public water source*; in other words, tap water.

The question is whether the Region can change old habits and consumer behaviour to convince residents to bring their refillable bottles. There's real value to consumers on a number of levels, and with free access to water from the mobile drinking station, the price is right. Still, it may take time for consumers to switch from buying bottled water to getting it at no charge. The water wagon initiative is a starting point and a visible reminder to residents that water is a valuable resource, one that needs to be conserved.

---

discount if they place their orders and receive delivery before April 1, prior to the warm months when air conditioner sales are highest. If it can ship earlier in the season, Lennox can plan its production schedules more easily and lessen its finished goods inventory. Its dealers, however, must weigh the benefits of a larger profit because of the discount versus the extra cost of carrying the inventory for a longer period of time.

cash discount
Tactic of offering a reduction in the invoice cost if the buyer pays the invoice prior to the end of the discount period.

Cash Discounts   A **cash discount** reduces the invoice cost if the buyer pays the invoice prior to the end of the discount period. Typically, it is expressed in the form of a percentage, such as "3/10, n/30," or "3 percent, 10 days, net 30," all of which means the buyer can take a 3-percent discount on the total amount of the invoice if the bill is paid within 10 days of the invoice date; otherwise, the full, or net, amount is due within 30 days. Why do B2B sellers offer cash discounts to customers? By encouraging early payment, they benefit from the time value of money. Getting money earlier rather than later enables the firm to either invest the money to earn a return on it or to avoid borrowing money and paying interest on it. In both instances, the firm is better off financially.

EXHIBIT 11.7	B2B Pricing Tactics
Tactic	
Seasonal discounts	An additional reduction offered as an incentive to retailers to order merchandise in advance of the normal buying season.
Cash discounts	An additional reduction that reduces the invoice cost if the buyer pays the invoice prior to the end of the discount period.
Allowances	Advertising or listing allowances (additional price reductions) offered in return for specific behaviours. *Advertising allowances* are offered to retailers if they agree to feature the manufacturer's product in their advertising and promotional efforts. *Listing allowances* are offered to get new products into stores or to gain more or better shelf space.
Quantity discounts	Providing a reduced price according to the amount purchased.
Uniform delivered versus geographic pricing	With *uniform delivered pricing*, the shipper charges one rate, no matter where the buyer is located. With *geographic pricing*, different prices are charged depending on the geographical delivery area.

Allowances   Another pricing tactic that lowers the final cost to channel members is allowances, such as advertising or listing allowances, offered in return for specific behaviours. An **advertising allowance** offers a price reduction to channel members if they agree to feature the manufacturer's product in their advertising and promotional efforts. **Listing allowances** are fees paid to retailers simply to get new products into stores or to gain more or better shelf space for their products. Some argue that slotting allowances are unethical because they put small manufacturers that cannot readily afford allowances at a competitive disadvantage. Demanding large listing allowances could be considered a form of bribery—that is, paying off the retailer to get preferential treatment.

Quantity Discounts   A **quantity discount** provides a reduced price according to the amount purchased. The more the buyer purchases, the higher the discount and, of course, the greater the value.

A **cumulative quantity discount** uses the amount purchased over a specified time period and usually involves several transactions. This type of discount encourages resellers to maintain their current supplier because the cost to switch must include the loss of the discount. For example, automobile dealers often attempt to meet a quota or a sales goal for a specific period, such as a quarter or a year. If they meet their quotas, they earn discounts on all the cars they purchased from the manufacturer during that period in the form of a rebate cheque. For this very reason, you will often find good deals on cars at the end of a quarter or fiscal year. If the dealership can just sell a few more cars to meet its quota, the rebate earned can be substantial, so taking a few hundred dollars less on those last few cars is well worth the opportunity to receive a rebate worth many times the amount of the losses.

A **noncumulative quantity discount**, though still a quantity discount, is based only on the amount purchased in a single order. Therefore, it provides the buyer with an incentive to purchase more merchandise immediately. Such larger, less frequent orders can save manufacturers order processing, sales, and transportation expenses. For example, a jeans store might get a 40-percent discount off the manufacturer's suggested retail price for placing a $500 order; a 50-percent discount for an order of $501 to $4999, and a 60-percent discount for an order of greater than $5000.

advertising allowance
Tactic of offering a price reduction to channel members if they agree to feature the manufacturer's product in their advertising and promotional efforts.

listing allowances
Fees paid to retailers simply to get new products into stores or to gain more or better shelf space for their products.

quantity discount
Pricing tactic of offering a reduced price according to the amount purchased; the more the buyer purchases, the higher the discount and, of course, the greater the value.

cumulative quantity discount
Pricing tactic that offers a discount based on the amount purchased over a specified period and usually involves several transactions.

noncumulative quantity discount
Pricing tactic that offers a discount based on only the amount purchased in a single order.

Uniform Delivered Versus Geographic Pricing These pricing tactics are specific to shipping, which represents a major cost for many manufacturers. With a **uniform delivered pricing** tactic, the shipper charges one rate, no matter where the buyer is located, which makes things very simple for both the seller and the buyer. **Geographic pricing**, however, sets different prices depending on a geographical division of the delivery areas. For example, a manufacturer based in Montreal might divide Canada into five different zones and use different shipping rates for each zone to reflect the average shipping cost for customers located therein. This way, each customer in a zone is charged the same cost for shipping. Geographic pricing can be advantageous to the shipper because it reflects the actual shipping charges more closely than uniform delivered pricing can.

Pricing Tactics Aimed at Consumers

When firms sell their products and services directly to consumers, rather than to other businesses, the pricing tactics they use naturally differ. In this section, we analyze some tactics for products and services aimed directly at consumers: price lining, price bundling, and leader pricing (see Exhibit 11.8).

Price Lining When marketers establish a price floor and a price ceiling for an entire line of similar products and then set a few other price points in between to represent distinct differences in quality, the tactic is called **price lining**.

Consider the specific price lines used by Moores Clothing for Men. The firm prices its sports jackets at different price points. For example, its house brand, Joseph & Feiss, sells for around $119. Move up to a middle-range price point and you can buy an Alfred Sung jacket for between $159 and $199. At the top end of the line, you can find a pure wool Pronto Uomo sports jacket for $229.

While it may be difficult to determine which is the better jacket, having options at different price points means Moores can satisfy a range of tastes and budgets.

Price Bundling When firms are stuck with a slow-moving item, to encourage sales, they sometimes will "bundle" it with a faster-moving item and price the bundle below what the two items would cost separately. Sometimes, however, firms bundle products together just to encourage customers to stock up so they won't purchase competing brands, to encourage trial of a new product, or to provide an incentive to purchase a less desirable product or service to obtain a more desirable one in the same bundle. This practice of selling more than one product for a single, lower price is called **price bundling**.

We present a price bundling example in Exhibit 11.9. Imagine we have four different offerings for sale: home phone line, long-distance, Internet, and satellite TV services. Customers use combinations of these products and services differently, and each customer has unique needs. Subscribing to each service separately is the most expensive option, as shown in the first line. However, if customers bundle together three or more services, they can take advantage of lower prices.

uniform delivered pricing
The shipper charges one rate, no matter where the buyer is located.

geographic pricing
The setting of different prices depending on a geographical division of the delivery areas.

price lining
Consumer market pricing tactic of establishing a price floor and a price ceiling for an entire line of similar products and then setting a few other price points in between to represent distinct differences in quality.

price bundling
Consumer pricing tactic of selling more than one product for a single, lower price than what the items would cost sold separately; can be used to sell slow-moving items, to encourage customers to stock up so they won't purchase competing brands, to encourage trial of a new product, or to provide an incentive to purchase a less desirable product or service to obtain a more desirable one in the same bundle.

EXHIBIT 11.8	Pricing Tactics Aimed at Consumers
Tactic	
Price lining	Establishing a price floor and a price ceiling for an entire line of similar products and then setting price points in between to represent distinct differences in quality.
Price bundling	Pricing of more than one product for a single, lower price.
Leader pricing	Building store traffic by aggressively pricing and advertising a regularly purchased item, often priced at or just above the store's cost.

EXHIBIT 11.9	An Illustration of Price Bundling					
	Home Phone Basic	**Internet Performance**	**Bell TV Digital Cable**	**Bell Mobility Uber 30 Plan**	**Total**	**Annual Savings**
Regular price	$34.95	$41.95	$35.00	$30.00		
Bundled price	$29.95	$31.95	$30.00	$25.00		
Student example: Internet and cellphone						
Full price services		$41.95		$30.00	$ 71.95	
Full price with added service		$41.95	$35.00	$30.00	$106.95	
Bundled services		$31.95	$30.00	$25.00	$ 86.95	$240.00
Family example: Home phone, Internet, Cable TV, and cellphone						
Full price services	$34.95	$41.95		$30.00	$106.90	
Full price with added service	$34.95	$41.95	$35.00	$30.00	$ 141.90	
Bundled services	$29.95	$31.95	$30.00	$25.00	$ 116.90	$300.00

Source: Prices from "Bell Bundle." http://bundle.bell.ca/en/on/home/calculate-your-bundle (accessed July 2, 2010).

Let's look at how Bell uses price bundling to add value for its customers. For example, a student away at university on a tight budget may elect to subscribe to only the essentials: Internet and a cellphone. Regular price for these items would be $71.95/month. Through their bundled service offering, Bell can entice the student to also sign up for cable TV by reducing the price of the Internet service when the cable TV service is added. The company benefits from enhancing the relationship with the customer and by collecting additional revenue. While the student's monthly bill will rise slightly to $86.95, he will save $240.00/year from the unbundled service prices and should now be able to enjoy playoff hockey matches while at home!

Similarly, a family could be currently subscribing to home phone, cellphone, and Internet service through Bell for $106.90/month, while obtaining its cable TV service from another provider. Again, by bundling the services, Bell can entice the family to switch its cable TV service to Bell by reducing the price of the other services. Adding the new service increases the monthly fee to $116.90, but the family saves $300.00/year compared to the regular-priced services and will also enjoy the convenience of receiving a single bill each month.

Leader Pricing **Leader pricing** is a tactic that attempts to build store traffic by aggressively pricing and advertising a regularly purchased item, often priced at or just above the store's cost. The rationale behind this tactic is that, while in the store to get the great deal on, say, milk, the consumer will also probably pick up other items he or she needs. The store has priced these items at higher profit margins, so their purchase will more than cover the lower markup on the milk. Imagine the marketing potential of various combinations of products; the store uses leader pricing on cocktail sauce, which gives employees the perfect opportunity to ask, "How about a pound of fresh shrimp to go with the cocktail sauce you're purchasing?"

leader pricing
Consumer pricing tactic that attempts to build store traffic by aggressively pricing and advertising a regularly purchased item, often priced at or just above the store's cost.

Consumer Price Reductions

The final price a customer pays for a product or service often has been adjusted from the original price because marketers have used various techniques designed to enhance value. Some of these techniques include markdowns, quantity or seasonal discounts, coupons, and rebates.

markdowns
Reductions retailers take on the initial selling price of the product or service.

Markdowns   **Markdowns** are the reductions retailers take on the initial selling price of the product or service.[49] An integral component of the high/low pricing strategy we described previously, markdowns enable retailers to get rid of slow-moving or obsolete merchandise, sell seasonal items after the appropriate season, and match competitors' prices on specific merchandise. Retailers must get rid of merchandise that isn't selling because holding on to such items hurts the retailer's image and ties up money in inventory that could be used more productively elsewhere.

Retailers also use markdowns to promote merchandise and increase sales. Particularly when used in conjunction with promotions, markdowns can increase traffic into the store, which many retailers view as half the battle. Once customers are in the store, retailers always hope they will purchase other products at regular prices.

size discount
The most common implementation of a quantity discount at the consumer level; the larger the quantity bought, the less the cost per unit (e.g., per gram).

Quantity Discounts for Consumers   We have already discussed how firms use quantity discounts in the B2B marketplace, but the most common implementation of a quantity discount at the consumer level is the **size discount**. For example, there are three sizes of General Mills' popular cereal Cheerios: 425-gram, 575-gram, and 1.5-kilogram boxes, priced at approximately $4.19, $4.49, and $6.89, respectively. The larger the quantity, the less the cost per gram, which means the manufacturer is providing a quantity discount. Most grocery stores now post the price per 100 grams on the shelves so consumers can easily compare value for money. The goal of this tactic is to encourage consumers to purchase larger quantities each time they buy. In turn, these consumers are less likely to switch brands and often tend to consume more of the product, depending on the product usage characteristics. Typically, buying a larger package of toilet tissue does not mean consumers will use it faster, but buying a larger box of cereal may encourage them to eat more of it or to eat it more often.[50]

coupon
Provides a stated discount to consumers on the final selling price of a specific item; the retailer handles the discount.

rebate
A consumer discount in which a portion of the purchase price is returned to the buyer in cash; the manufacturer, not the retailer, issues the refund.

Seasonal Discounts   Seasonal discounts are price reductions offered on products and services to stimulate demand during off-peak seasons. You can find hotel rooms, ski-lift tickets, snowmobiles, lawn mowers, barbecues, vacation packages, flights to certain destinations, and Christmas cards at discounts during their "off" seasons. Some consumers even plan their buying around these discounts, determined to spend the day after Christmas stocking up on discounted wrapping paper and bows for the following year.

Customers get a size discount for buying larger sizes. With Cheerios, the larger the box, the less it costs per gram.

Coupons and Rebates   Coupons and rebates both provide discounts to consumers on the final selling price. However, for the **coupon**, the retailer handles the discount, whereas the manufacturer issues the refund in the case of the **rebate**, which is defined as a portion of the purchase price returned to the buyer in the form of cash.

The goal of coupons is to prompt consumers to try a product, reward loyal customers, or encourage repurchases. By saving the consumer money, firms add value to their products. Whereas a coupon provides instant savings when presented, a rebate promises savings, usually mailed to the consumer at some later date. The "hassle factor" for rebates is higher than for coupons; the consumer must first buy the item during a specified time period, then mail in the required documentation—which usually includes the original sales receipt—and finally wait four to six weeks (or more!) for a cheque to arrive. Although consumers may believe this process adds value when the potential rebate is $50, they might question whether a rebate for a couple of dollars is worth their time and effort. From the marketer's viewpoint, however, rebates offer greater control than coupons and provide valuable customer information. Coupons and rebates are considered to be sales promotion tools as well as pricing tactics so you'll read more about them in Chapter 15.

With so many different pricing strategies and tactics, it is no wonder that unscrupulous firms find ample opportunity to engage in pricing practices that can hurt consumers. We now take a look at some of the legal and ethical implications of pricing.

Legal and Ethical Aspects of Pricing

L04

Prices tend to fluctuate naturally and respond to varying market conditions. Thus, though we rarely see firms attempting to control the market in terms of product quality or advertising, they often engage in pricing practices that can unfairly reduce competition or harm consumers directly through fraud and deception. A host of laws and regulations at both the federal, provincial, and municipal levels attempt to prevent unfair pricing practices, but some are poorly enforced, and others are difficult to prove.

Deceptive or Illegal Price Advertising

Although it is always illegal and unethical to lie in advertising, a certain amount of "puffery" is typically allowed (see Chapter 15). But price advertisements should never deceive consumers to the point of causing harm. For example, a local car dealer's advertising that it had the "best deals in town" would likely be considered puffery. In contrast, advertising "the lowest prices, guaranteed" makes a very specific claim and, if not true, can be considered deceptive.

Deceptive Reference Prices   Previously, we introduced external reference prices, which create reference points for the buyer against which to compare the selling price. If the reference price is bona fide, the advertisement is informative. If the reference price has been inflated or is just plain fictitious, however, the advertisement is deceptive and may cause harm to consumers. The Competition Bureau fined Suzy Shier $1 million after an investigation revealed that the company placed price tags on garments showing a "regular" price and a "sale" price when in fact the clothes had not been sold in any significant quantity for any reasonable time at the "regular" price.[51] But it is not easy to determine whether a reference price is bona fide. What standard should be used? If an advertisement specifies a "regular price," just what qualifies as regular? How many units must the store sell at this price for it to be a bona fide regular price: Half the stock? A few products? Just one? Finally, what if the store offers the item for sale at the regular price but customers do not buy any? Can it still be considered a regular price? In general, if a seller is going to label a price as a regular price, the Better Business Bureau suggests that at least 50 percent of the sales have occurred at that price.[52]

Loss Leader Pricing   As we discussed previously, leader pricing is a legitimate attempt to build store traffic by pricing a regularly purchased item aggressively but still above the store's cost. **Loss leader pricing** takes this tactic one step further by lowering the price below the store's cost. No doubt you have seen "buy one, get one free" offers at grocery and discount stores. Unless the markup for the item is 100 percent of the cost, these sales

loss leader pricing
Loss leader pricing takes the tactic of *leader pricing* one step further by lowering the price below the store's cost.

Is this a legitimate sale or is the retailer using deceptive reference prices?

obviously do not generate enough revenue from the sale of one unit to cover the store's cost, which means it has essentially priced the total for both items below cost.

Bait and Switch   Another form of deceptive price advertising occurs when sellers advertise items for a very low price without the intent to really sell any. This **bait-and-switch** tactic is a deceptive practice because the store lures customers in with a very low price on an item (the bait), only to aggressively pressure these customers into purchasing a higher-priced item (the switch) by disparaging the low-priced item, comparing it unfavourably with the higher-priced model, or professing an inadequate supply of the lower-priced item. Again, the laws against bait-and-switch practices are difficult to enforce because salespeople, simply as a function of their jobs, are always trying to get customers to trade up to a higher-priced model without necessarily deliberately baiting them. The key to proving deception centres on the intent of the seller, which is also difficult to prove.

Predatory Pricing

When a firm sets a very low price for one or more of its products with the intent to drive its competition out of business, it is using **predatory pricing**. Predatory pricing is illegal under the Competition Act because it constrains free trade and represents a form of unfair competition. It also tends to promote a concentrated market with a few dominant firms (an oligopoly).

But again, predation is difficult to prove. First, one must demonstrate intent—that is, that the firm intended to drive out its competition or prevent competitors from entering the market. Second, the complainant must prove that the firm charged prices lower than its average cost, an equally difficult task.

Price Discrimination

There are many forms of price discrimination, but only some of them are considered illegal under the Competition Act. When firms sell the same product to different resellers (wholesalers, distributors, or retailers) at different prices, it can be considered **price discrimination**; usually, larger firms receive lower prices.

We have already discussed the use of quantity discounts, which is a legitimate method of charging different prices to different customers on the basis of the quantity they purchase. The legality of this tactic stems from the assumption that it costs less to sell and service 1000 units to one customer than 100 units to 10 customers. But quantity discounts must be available to all customers and not be structured in such a way that they consistently and obviously favour one or a few buyers over others. Still, some marketers have found ways to get around these rules, for example, offering "preferred member" pricing. The Competition Act requires companies to demonstrate only that their price discounts do not restrict competition. While quantity discounts may be a grey area, it is perfectly legitimate to charge a different price to a reseller if the firm is attempting to meet a specific competitor's price. In addition, a barter agreement, in which buyers and sellers negotiate a mutually agreed upon price, is commonplace and absolutely legal in retail settings such as car sales and collectibles markets.

Price Fixing

Price fixing is the practice of colluding with other firms to control prices. Recently, the five largest music companies—Universal Music, Sony Music, Warner Music, BMG Music, and EMI—and three of the largest music retailers—Musicland Stores,

---

bait and switch
A deceptive practice of luring customers into the store with a very low advertised price on an item (the bait), only to aggressively pressure them into purchasing a higher-priced item (the switch) by disparaging the low-priced item, comparing it unfavourably with the higher-priced model, or professing an inadequate supply of the lower-priced item.

predatory pricing
A firm's practice of setting a very low price for one or more of its products with the intent of driving its competition out of business; illegal under the Competition Act.

price discrimination
The practice of selling the same product to different resellers (wholesalers, distributors, or retailers) or to the ultimate consumer at different prices; some, but not all, forms of price discrimination are illegal.

price fixing
The practice of colluding with other firms to control prices.

Is this price discrimination illegal?

ADMISSION PRICES
General Admission $9.25
Bargain Matinee $7.00
Friday-Sunday and Holiday periods before 4:00 PM
Monday-Thursday during Non-Holiday periods before 6:00 PM
Children (2 -12) $6.50
Seniors (60 & Over)

Trans World Entertainment, and Tower Records—agreed to pay $67.4 million and distribute $75.7 million in CDs to public and nonprofit groups to settle a lawsuit for alleged price fixing during the late 1990s.[53] And Tate & Lyle, which makes Splenda, a low-calorie sweetener, agreed to pay $650,000 to settle a lawsuit in British Columbia that accused sugar substitute companies of conspiring to fix prices in the 1980s and 1990s.[54]

This particular case of price fixing is especially interesting because it includes both horizontal and vertical price fixing. **Horizontal price fixing** occurs when competitors that produce and sell competing products collude, or work together, to control prices, effectively taking price out of the decision process for consumers. In this particular case, prosecutors alleged that horizontal price fixing had occurred among the record companies, which specified pricing terms associated with the sale and distribution of CDs. **Vertical price fixing** occurs when parties at different levels of the same marketing channel (e.g., manufacturers and retailers) collude to control the prices passed on to consumers. In the music industry case, prosecutors alleged that the music companies colluded with music retailers to maintain retail prices for CDs.

As these legal issues clearly demonstrate, pricing decisions involve many ethical considerations. In determining both their pricing strategies and their pricing tactics, marketers must always balance their goal of inducing customers, through price, to find value and the need to deal honestly and fairly with those same customers. Whether another business or an individual consumer, buyers can be influenced by a variety of pricing methods; it is up to marketers to determine which of these methods works best for the seller, the buyer, and the community.

horizontal price fixing
Occurs when competitors that produce and sell competing products collude, or work together, to control prices, effectively taking price out of the decision process for consumers.

vertical price fixing
Occurs when parties at different levels of the same marketing channel (e.g., manufacturers and retailers) collude to control the prices passed on to consumers.

Learning Objectives Review

LO1 Explain what price is and its importance in establishing value in marketing

Price is the only element of the marketing mix that generates revenues. It is also half the value equation. Although costs and other factors should be taken into consideration when setting prices, the most important factor is how the customer views the price in relationship to what he or she receives.

LO2 Illustrate how the five Cs—company objectives, customers, costs, competition, and channel members—influence pricing decisions

Successful pricing strategies are built on the five Cs—company objectives, customers, costs, competition, and channel members. Company goals and objectives set the framework for pricing strategies. Companies focusing on image set high prices, while those that focus on value tend to use everyday low prices. Understanding customers' reactions to different prices help marketers set prices that are consistent with their customers' attitudes and preferences. The demand curve and price elasticity of demand are two related tools that marketers use to gauge customers' sensitivity to prices changes. Customers' income and the availability of substitute products also influence customers' reaction to price changes. The third C, costs, is a major determinant of pricing. Cost of producing a good helps marketers determine the possible prices they can charge and the levels of profitability they can expect. Break-even analysis is a helpful tool that is used to help marketers determine the

price level at which the number of units sold exactly covers the cost of producing the good. The fourth C, competition, influences pricing because a firm usually pays close attention and reacts to a competitor's moves. Intense competition may produce price wars. The level of competition is usually determined by the market structure of the industry. That is, whether the industry structure is oligopolistic, monopolistic, pure competition, or a monopoly. The final, C, channel members—manufacturers, wholesalers, retailers—influence prices because they play a key role in getting the product to the final consumer, and they are independent and usually have their own objectives and competitive situation to deal with. The company may want to set a certain price level for its products in order to reflect quality and value, but retailers may decide they want to move more volume and so reduce the price, hence the possibility for conflict. Also, manufacturers may give discounts to channel members, which may influence the price the ultimate consumer pays.

LO3 Describe various pricing strategies and tactics and their use in marketing (e.g., cost-based pricing, competitor-based pricing, value-based pricing, new product pricing, psychological pricing, and pricing tactics targeted to channel members and consumers)

The various methods of setting prices each have their own set of advantages and disadvantages. The fixed percentage and markup approaches are quick and easy but fail to reflect the competitive environment or consumer demand.

Although it is always advisable to be aware of what competitors are doing, using competitor-based pricing should not occur in isolation without considering consumers' reactions. Taking a value-based approach to pricing, whether the improvement value or the total cost of ownership, in conjunction with these other methods provides a nicely balanced method of setting prices.

Companies tend to use different pricing strategies and tactics for different products or different markets. Pricing strategies are a long-term approach to pricing products, whereas price tactics focus more on the short-term aspects of the five Cs of pricing. The various pricing strategies can be grouped into three broad categories: cost-based strategies, value-based strategies, and competitor-based strategies. Cost-based strategies are based on the firm ascertaining the cost of producing and marketing the product, and then adding some markup for profit. Competitor-based pricing is based on a firm understanding what competitors are doing and reacting accordingly. Firms may choose to set prices below, at, or above competitors' prices. Value-based pricing is based on a firm understanding consumers' perceptions of value as reflected in the price of the product (e.g., cheap, expensive, bargain). Consumers' assessments of value may be influenced by their reference prices of similar products or may use marketers' prices to infer a price–quality relationship. Marketers often use price skimming or penetration pricing when they introduce new products in the marketplace based on the nature of the product and their marketing goals, for example, whether they want to gain market share, show price leadership, or signal innovation.

Companies may use a wide variety of pricing tactics from two categories: (1) business-to-business pricing tactics and discounts, and (2) pricing tactics aimed at consumers. B2B pricing tactics and discounts usually include seasonal discounts, cash discounts, quantity discounts, allowances, and geographic pricing. Pricing tactics aimed at consumers include markdowns, quantity and seasonal discounts, and coupons and rebates.

LO4 **Summarize the legal and ethical issues involved in pricing**

There are almost as many ways to get into trouble by setting or changing a price as there are pricing strategies and tactics. Three of the most common legal issues pertain to advertising deceptive prices. Specifically, if a firm compares a reduced price with a "regular" or reference price, it must actually have sold that product or service at the regular price. Advertising the sale of products priced below the retailer's cost constitutes an unfair competitive practice, as does bait-and-switch advertising. Charging different prices to different customers is sometimes, but not always, illegal, whereas any collusion among firms to fix prices is always illegal.

Key Terms

- advertising allowance, 377
- bait and switch, 382
- break-even point, 361
- cash discount, 376
- competitive parity, 356
- competitor orientation, 356
- competitor-based pricing method, 368
- complementary products, 360
- contribution per unit, 362
- cost of ownership method, 369
- cost-based pricing method, 368
- coupon, 380
- cross-price elasticity, 360
- cross-shopping, 367
- cumulative quantity discount, 377
- customer orientation, 356
- demand curve, 357
- elastic, 359
- everyday low pricing (EDLP), 373
- experience curve effect, 371
- external reference price, 372
- fixed costs, 361

- geographic pricing, 378
- grey market, 365
- high/low pricing, 373
- horizontal price fixing, 383
- improvement value, 369
- income effect, 360
- inelastic, 359
- internal reference price, 373
- leader pricing, 379
- listing allowances, 377
- loss leader pricing, 381
- markdowns, 380
- market penetration pricing, 371
- maximizing profits strategy, 355
- monopolistic competition, 364
- monopoly, 363
- noncumulative quantity discount, 377
- odd prices, 374
- oligopolistic competition, 363
- predatory pricing, 382
- premium pricing, 369
- prestige products or services, 358
- price bundling, 378

- price discrimination, 382
- price elasticity of demand, 359
- price fixing, 382
- price lining, 378
- price skimming, 371
- price war, 363
- pricing tactics, 375
- profit orientation, 355
- pure competition, 364
- quantity discount, 377
- rebate, 380
- reference price, 372
- sales orientation, 356
- seasonal discount, 375
- size discount, 380
- substitute products, 361
- substitution effect, 360
- target profit pricing, 355
- target return pricing, 355
- total cost, 361
- uniform delivered pricing, 378
- value-based pricing method, 369
- variable costs, 361
- vertical price fixing, 383

Concept Review

1. Explain the importance of pricing in the marketing mix from the perspective of the firm and the consumer.

2. List the five Cs of pricing. Which one do you consider to be the most important and why?

3. Explain how companies try to determine consumers' sensitivity to price changes. What factors influence their price sensitivity?

4. Why is it important for firms to determine costs when setting prices?

5. Why does a company need to understand a product's break-even point?

6. How has the Internet changed the way some people use price to make purchasing decisions?

7. What is the major difference between pricing strategies and pricing tactics? Give three examples of each.

8. Explain how psychological factors may influence a firm's pricing strategy.

9. In what conditions should a price skimming strategy be used? When is it appropriate to use a market penetration strategy?

10. Explain the four types of illegal or unethical pricing practices.

Marketing Applications

1. You and your two roommates are starting a pet grooming service to help put yourself through university. There are two other well-established pet services in your area. Should you set your price higher or lower than that of the competition? Justify your answer.

2. One roommate believes the most important objective in setting prices for the new pet grooming business is to generate a large profit, while keeping an eye on your competitors' prices; the other roommate believes it is important to maximize sales and set prices according to what your customers expect to pay. Who is right and why?

3. Assume you have decided to buy an advertisement in the local newspaper to publicize your new pet grooming service. The cost of the ad is $1000. You have decided to charge $40 for a dog grooming, and you want to make $20 on each dog. How many dogs do you have to groom to break even on the cost of the ad? What is your break-even point if you charge $50 per dog?

4. On your weekly grocery shopping trip, you notice that the price of ground beef has gone up 50 cents a kilogram. How will this price increase affect the demand for ground beef, ground turkey, and hamburger buns? Explain your answer in terms of the price elasticity of demand.

5. Zinc Energy Resources Co., a new division of a major battery manufacturing company, recently patented a new battery that uses zinc-air technology. The unit costs for the zinc-air battery are as follows: battery housing, $8; materials $6; and direct labour, $6 per unit. Retooling the existing factory facilities to manufacture the zinc-air batteries amounts to an additional $1 million in equipment costs. Annual fixed costs include sales, marketing, and advertising expenses of $1 million; general and administrative expenses of $1 million; and other fixed costs totalling $2 million. Please answer the following questions.

a. What is the total per-unit variable cost associated with the new battery?

b. What are the total fixed costs for the new battery?

c. If the price for the new battery was set at $35, what would the break-even point be?

6. How do pricing strategies vary across markets that are characterized by monopoly, monopolistic, oligopolistic, and pure competition?

7. Though not illegal, many firms operating over the Internet have been experimenting with charging different consumers different prices for the same product or service. Since stores in different parts of the country might have different prices, some websites require postal code information before providing prices. Why would retailers charge different prices in different markets or postal codes? Is it ethical for retailers to do so? Is it a good business practice?

8. Suppose you have been hired as the pricing manager for a grocery store chain that typically adds a fixed percentage onto the cost of each product to arrive at the retail price. Evaluate this technique. What would you do differently?

9. Coupons and rebates benefit different channel members. Which would you prefer if you were a manufacturer, a retailer, and a consumer? Why?

10. Imagine that you are the newly hired brand manager for a T-shirt company whose new line is about to come out. Because of a major fashion magazine's very positive review of the line, the company wants to reposition the brand as a premium youth brand. Your boss asks what price you should charge for the new T-shirt line. The current line, considered mid-range retail, is priced at $20. What steps might you undertake to determine what the new price should be?

Toolkit

BREAK-EVEN ANALYSIS

A shoe manufacturer has recently opened a new manufacturing plant in Asia. The total fixed costs are $50 million. It plans to sell the shoes to retailers for $50, and its variable costs (material and labour) are $25 per pair. Calculate the break-even volume. Now see what would happen to the break-even volume if the fixed costs were increased to $60 million because of the purchase of new equipment, or the variable costs were decreased to $20 because of a new quantity discount provided by the supplier. Use the toolkit provided on Connect to experiment with changes in fixed cost, variable cost, and selling price to see what happens to break-even volume.

Net Savvy

1. Several different pricing models can be found on the Internet. Each model appeals to different customer groups. Go to www.ebay.com and try to buy this book. What pricing options and prices are available? Do you believe that everyone will choose the least expensive option? Why or why not? Now go to www.amazon.ca. Is there more than one price available for this book? If so, what are those prices? If you had to buy another copy of this book, where would you buy it, and why would you buy it there?

2. Prices can vary depending on the market being served. Because Dell sells its computers directly to consumers all around the world, the Dell website makes it easy to compare prices for various markets. Go to www.dell.com. Begin on the Dell Canada site and determine the price of a Dimension 3000 desktop computer. Next go to the Dell U.K. website and another country of your choice to find the price of the same computer. (If you need to convert currency, go to www.xe.com.) How does the price of the desktop computer vary? What would account for these differences in price?

Chapter Case Study

BATTLE ROYALE: APPLE VERSUS AMAZON[55]

As commentators far and wide have acknowledged, Apple radically changed the music industry when it introduced the iPod and its affiliated iTunes site. The very way musicians and media companies marketed music had to change in response, and one of the most significant changes occurred with regard to pricing.

Apple set the pricing model. Most songs on iTunes sell for around 99 cents, and album costs usually equal the single-song price multiplied by the number of songs on that album. In creating this pricing model, Apple also instituted a technology unique to digital music, namely, digital rights management (DRM). This technology ensures that songs will expire or prevents them from being shared multiple times or between multiple devices. Thus, one consumer cannot download a song, copy it innumerable times, and share it with all of her friends. Although DRM technology therefore protects copyright holders, it also seems to frustrate consumers.

Apple also dictated that its iPods, iPhones, and related devices would play only songs equipped with its own proprietary FairPlay DRM solution or those without any DRM protection at all. Producers were faced with an either–or choice: Use iTunes or go DRM free. And many music companies, including Warner Music Group, swore they would never allow their songs to be sold without DRM protection.

Apple has thus far refused to license FairPlay to any other music players. Therefore, the company has almost a stranglehold on the digital music market and limits the markets for media companies to iPod or iPhone owners who use the FairPlay DRM.

Everything changed when Amazon.com started selling music downloads of Universal and EMI songs without any DRM protection at all. The days in which music companies could tell listeners when and how they might listen to their songs essentially were over. The online retailer's offering contains about 2 million songs that sell, on average, for 40 percent less than they would cost through iTunes.

The likely result seems to be an all-out price war. In just a few years, Apple and iTunes could be forced to engage in the kind of deep discounting that Tower Records and CD Warehouse undertook in the years before digital downloads swept both aside. Such a price war could help rejuvenate the sales of songs and albums, and perhaps lower prices for consumers.

The price war also could quickly decrease the margins of music stores such as Amazon and Apple. In announcing its new music store, Amazon didn't say how the discounts would affect its margins, but the implications cannot be minor.

Yet according to one music industry insider, the industry "needs to have a lot of successful retailers or they won't have a growing market. You can't satisfy consumers if there is only one place to buy music. In every industry, you see market growth when there are lots of different places to buy the product."

The music companies that have signed up with Amazon currently are making less on each copy sold, and the copies include no protections against copying or expiration dates. The situation appears likely headed into a price war, which will mean smaller margins for all the players.

Questions

1. Who are the key players in this industry?

2. Why do you think different music companies, such as Warner and Universal, have taken such different stances on DRM protection?

3. What would represent an effective response by Apple to Amazon's lower prices? Should it lower download prices to match the offer? Why or why not?

4. If a price war will reduce margins, as the case suggests, why would any company embrace this strategy?

 Practise and learn online with Connect. Connect allows you to practise important concepts at your own pace and on your own schedule, with 24/7 online access to an eBook, practice quizzes, interactivities, videos, study tools, additional resources, and more.

CHAPTER 12

Marketing Channels:
Distribution Strategy

Zara International (www.zara.com), a fast-growing Spanish apparel retailer and an inexpensive but chic subsidiary of Inditex (Industria de Diseño Textil), operates about 1422 fashionable clothing stores in 76 countries, including 19 in Canada.[1] The chain takes in annual sales of more than $3 billion—an impressive number for a company founded only 35 years ago. The first Zara shop opened its doors in 1975 in La Coruña in the northwestern region of Spain's Galicia. Nearby is Zara's ultramodern headquarters and its 500 000 square metre distribution centre that supplies all its stores.

In a tribute to Zara's "with it" image, according to *Vogue*, even French customers of Zara stores identify Zara as being of French origin. Various fashion pages continue to feature celebrities such as Cindy Crawford shopping at a Zara store in Canada; Chelsea Clinton visiting the Zara store in Ankara, Turkey; the children of the Spanish royal family regularly frequenting the Zara store on Madrid's upscale Velazquez Street; and tourist buses making sightseeing stopovers at the Zara store on Paseo de Gracia in Barcelona. Today, Zara shops can be found in upscale neighbourhoods such as New York's 5th Avenue, Paris's Champs Elysées, London's Regent Street, and Tokyo's Shibuya Shopping Centre.

Inditex (www.inditex.com), which owns and operates Zara, is made up of almost 100 companies that all deal with activities related to textile design, production, and distribution. Inditex also operates seven other chains: Kiddy's Class, Pull and Bear, Massimo Dutti, Bershka, Stradivarius, Oysho, and Zara Home. But Zara International is the largest and the oldest of its chains, providing close to 80 percent of its revenues.

Although Zara competes with local retailers in most of its markets, analysts consider its three closest competitors

Learning Objectives

After studying this chapter you should be able to

LO1 Explain the importance of distribution and the interrelationships among distribution channels, supply chain management, and logistics management

LO2 Identify how distribution channels add value to businesses and consumers

LO3 Describe distribution channel design and management decisions and strategies

LO4 Explain how logistics and supply chain management affect distribution strategy

to be The Gap, Sweden's Hennes & Mauritz (H&M), and Italy's Benetton. There are, however, important differences in the ways the four firms operate. The Gap and H&M own most of their stores but outsource all their manufacturing. In contrast, Benetton has invested relatively heavily in manufacturing, but licensees run its stores. Zara not only owns a majority of its stores, it also produces the majority of its own clothes, mostly at its ultramodern manufacturing complex in northwestern Spain. In another departure from the pack, Zara makes more than 40 percent of its own fabric—far more than most of its rivals.

From its base in Spain, Zara also operates its own flexible worldwide distribution network. Controlling the supply chain gives Zara flexibility that its competitors can only dream about. It also allows Zara to operate with minimal inventory buildups because its stores get deliveries twice a week, and newly supplied items rarely remain on the retail shelves for more than a week. In this sense, Zara has one of the most sophisticated supply chains of any apparel retailer. Zara takes only four to five weeks to design a new collection and then about a week to manufacture it. Its competitors, by comparison, need an average of six months to design a new collection and another three weeks to manufacture it. How does Zara do it?

The company derives its competitive advantage from an astute use of information and technology. All its stores are electronically linked to the headquarters in Spain. Store managers, together with a fleet of sharp-eyed, design-savvy trendspotters on Zara's staff, routinely prowl fashion hot spots such as university campuses and happening nightclubs. Their job is to function as the company's eyes and ears, to spot the next wave. Using wireless handheld devices, they send images back to corporate headquarters so that designers can produce blueprints for close-at-hand manufacturers to start stitching, resulting in garments that will be hanging in Zara stores within weeks.

In effect, Zara's designers have real-time information when they make decisions, with the commercial team, about the fabric, cut, and price of a new line of garments. This combination of real-time information sharing and internalized production means that Zara can work with almost no stock and still have new designs in its stores twice a week. Its lightning-quick logistics system keeps fashion fresh and inventory lean, enabling the company to sell much of its stock at full price; unsold items represent less than 10 percent of its inventory, in contrast with the 17 to 20 percent industry average.[2] Customers love the results of this high-velocity operation. They queue up in long lines at Zara's stores on designated delivery days, a phenomenon dubbed "Zaramania" by the press. .::

In this chapter, we discuss the third P, place, which includes all activities required to get the right product to the right customer when that customer wants it. Students of marketing often overlook or underestimate the importance of place in the marketing mix simply because it happens behind the scenes. Yet distribution channels, or place, add value for customers because they get products to customers efficiently: quickly and at low cost.

As shown in our chapter roadmap, we begin by understanding the importance of distribution, how distribution channels are designed, how they are structured, and how they are managed. Then we move to a discussion of the supply chain and the critical role it plays in distribution strategy. Lastly we end the chapter by examining how logistics management integrates activities from the efficient flow of raw materials through to the delivery of finished goods.

The Importance of Distribution

So far in this book, we've examined how companies conduct in-depth market research, gain insights into consumer and business behaviour, carefully segment markets and select the best target markets, develop new products and services, and set prices that signal good value. However, even if they execute these activities flawlessly, if they are unable to secure appropriate distribution channels that reach prospective customers, their products and services are unlikely to ever meet their revenue targets.

Convincing intermediaries, such as wholesalers and retailers, to carry new products can prove to be more difficult than you might think. For example, a typical grocery store may carry between 30 000 and 40 000 different items. But a good number of these would have to be cleared off the shelves to make room for all the new foods, beverages, household goods, pet products, and other miscellaneous items launched each year. With dozens of new products being introduced each day, the fight for shelf space is fierce. For many companies, distribution is not only difficult, it's also expensive and involves paying listing fees to get shelf space, as we discuss later in the chapter.

All goods and services organizations need a well–thought out distribution strategy—even organizations that physically make money. On October 21, 2004, the Royal Canadian Mint released the world's first coloured circulation coin, a quarter that featured a red poppy to pay homage to the 117 000 Canadians who died in battle.[3] Normally coins are distributed through banks. However, very few consumers receive coins at banks. The Mint needed a distribution partner that could get its coins into circulation quickly, as Remembrance Day was fast approaching. It chose Tim Hortons because of its many outlets across the country and its ability to reach so many Canadians. And since consumers could pay for their Tim Hortons' purchases only in cash at that time, they were almost certain to get some poppy quarters along with their double-doubles. This successful distribution strategy was reused when the Mint released its second coloured circulation coin, a 25-cent piece featuring the iconic pink ribbon, to help raise awareness of the Canadian Breast Cancer Foundation. The coins were distributed exclusively at Shoppers Drug Mart stores.[4]

A good distribution strategy is key to the successful launch of a new product. As seen in Entrepreneurial Marketing 12.1, getting distribution is not always easy. A well–thought out distribution strategy that is well integrated with other elements of the marketing mix can result in increased revenues. For example, Brick Brewing Co. in Waterloo, Ontario, prides itself on being an industry innovator. It introduced 473-millilitre brown plastic bottles that chill faster, stay cold longer, and are lightweight and unbreakable, making Brick the first Canadian company to put beer in

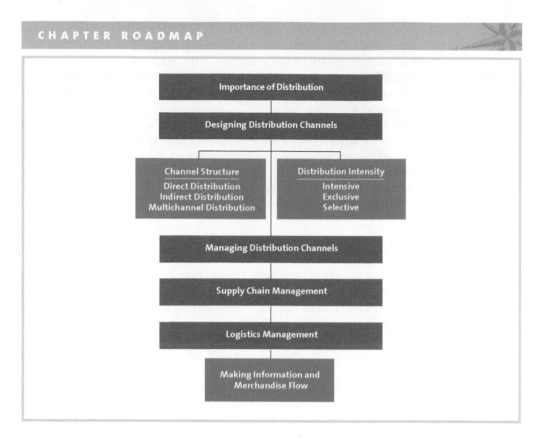

CHAPTER ROADMAP

Importance of Distribution

Designing Distribution Channels

Channel Structure
Direct Distribution
Indirect Distribution
Multichannel Distribution

Distribution Intensity
Intensive
Exclusive
Selective

Managing Distribution Channels

Supply Chain Management

Logistics Management

Making Information and Merchandise Flow

The Royal Canadian Mint released the world's first coloured circulation coin, featuring the poppy, via Tim Hortons outlets, followed by a 25-cent breast cancer coin through Shoppers Drug Mart stores.

plastic bottles.[5] While this might sound like a product or packaging decision, the plastic bottle was closely tied to distribution strategy because it allowed Brick to expand its sales to outlets where glass bottles were prohibited, such as university residences, sports events, and concert venues. It also let the company compete against canned beer distribution without having to invest in expensive canning equipment.

Although increased sales and access to more consumers is often desirable, that's not always the case. Over the years, companies such as Walmart, Zellers, and Esso have asked to carry M&M Meat Shops products. These retailers would have dramatically expanded the company's distribution reach; however, the company decided against such deals, sensing the move would ultimately hurt the brand. M&M Meat Shops prides itself on offering high quality, whereas retailers such as Walmart focus on low price.

Distribution Channels, Supply Chain, and Logistics Are Related

People often talk about distribution channel management, supply chain management, and logistics management as if they were the same thing. It's because these business practices are closely interrelated. A **distribution channel** is the set of institutions that

Entrepreneurial Marketing 12.1 | **Bottling Nostalgia**

As a kid, Brian Alger couldn't get enough of the Pop Shoppe. The discount soft-drink company was started in 1969 in London by two business grads who realized they could sell the pop they made from their own stores. By eliminating the middleman and traditional retail channels, they were able to offer 20 different flavours of pop at a great price. Consumers flocked to the stand-alone stores to buy mix-and-match flavours in cases of 24. In only six years, the business grads expanded beyond Canada's borders, into the United States, with stores in 11 states.[6] Selling pop at only 10 cents a bottle, the Pop Shoppe offered a cheap alternative to conventional soft drinks. At its peak in 1977, the company was selling 1 million bottles a day. Yet by 1983 the company was out of business, partly because of the price wars launched by Coca-Cola and PepsiCo.

In 2002, when Alger learned that the Pop Shoppe's trademarks had lapsed, he re-registered them. Two years later, he re-introduced several soft-drink flavours, including Lime Ricky and Cream Soda. But he made some important changes. First, he launched as a premium brand instead of bringing the products back to the market as a discount brand. There were simply too many cheap private-label brands already on store shelves, and he knew he couldn't compete on price.[7] Secondly, he decided against opening Pop Shoppe retail outlets. While consumers were willing to make a special trip to its stores to purchase and refill returnable glass bottles in the 1970s, the concept had run its course and was no longer convenient or economically feasible.[8]

As a one-man operation, Alger has no employees, no corporate office, and no warehouse. He communicates with suppliers, partners, and distributors from his home office in Grimsby, Ontario. Distribution proved to be a challenge. He couldn't get access to convenience store pop fridges, which were already full of better known brands. While the grocery store channel was attractive,

The Pop Shoppe's unconventional distribution strategy has led to sales success.

he couldn't justify the listing fees, which ran as high as $100,000 to secure shelf space. Every distributor turned him down cold. Then he met Beverage World, a distributor/wholesaler of niche drinks in Hamilton, Ontario. The company was looking for an exclusive deal with a new premium brand. The contract with Beverage World let Alger partner with an established retailer that could handle sales, warehousing, shipping, and more.

By 2006, stores such as Costco, Kitchen Table, and Hasty Market picked up the Pop Shoppe line. Then Zellers came on board, and Alger had national distribution. He has since gained distribution through a New Brunswick restaurateur with regional stores.[9] He's now on his way to becoming the number one premium soft drink in the country. But the Canadian market is small, worth only $25 million, and so Alger is eyeing expansion to U.S. markets. To do that, he'll need a distribution strategy with some real fizz.

---

transfer the ownership of and move goods from the point of production to the point of consumption; as such, it consists of all the institutions and marketing activities in the marketing process.[10] The terms *distribution channel* and *supply chain* are virtually the same and are often used interchangeably. As indicated in Exhibit 12.1, distribution channels make products available to consumers, whether they are individuals or businesses. In some cases, companies use direct market channels to deliver their goods to consumers; in other instances, distribution is accomplished indirectly through the use of intermediaries.

As we noted in Chapter 1, **supply chain management** refers to a set of approaches and techniques firms employ to efficiently and effectively integrate their suppliers, manufacturers, warehouses, stores, and transportation intermediaries into a seamless value chain in which merchandise is produced and distributed in the right quantities, to the right locations, and at the right time, as well as to minimize systemwide costs while satisfying the service levels their customers require.[11] As we learned in

distribution channel
The institutions that transfer the ownership of and move goods from the point of production to the point of consumption.

EXHIBIT 12.1 Distribution Components

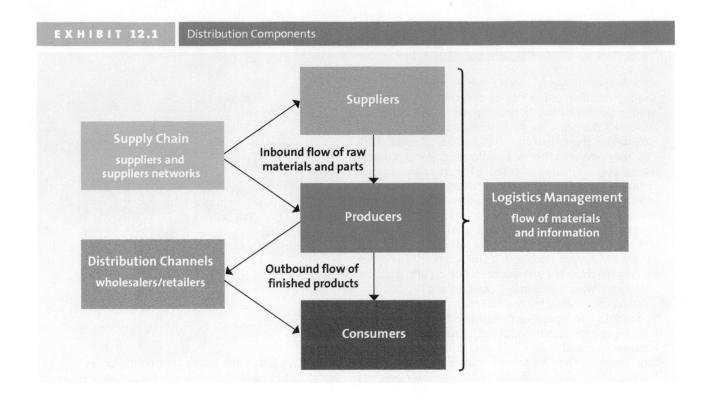

the chapter vignette, Zara employs a completely integrated supply chain because the company owns or at least has considerable control over each phase. As a result, it is able to conceive of, design, manufacture, transport, and ultimately sell high-fashion apparel much more quickly and efficiently than any of its major competitors.

A simplified supply chain would be one in which manufacturers make products and sell them to intermediaries such as retailers or wholesalers. This chain becomes much more complicated if we include suppliers of materials to manufacturers and all of the manufacturers, wholesalers, and stores in a typical supply chain. **Wholesalers** are firms that buy products from manufacturers and resell them to retailers, and **retailers** sell products directly to consumers. Manufacturers ship to a wholesaler, or, in the case of many multistore retailers, to the retailer's distribution centre or directly to stores. The more intermediaries that are involved in the supply chain, the greater the complexity and number of transactions involved for a company to reach consumers.

Although the above discussion reflects the typical flow of manufactured goods, many variations to this supply chain exist. Some retail chains, such as Home Depot and Costco, function as both retailers and wholesalers; they act as retailers when they sell to consumers directly and as wholesalers when they sell to other businesses, such as building contractors or restaurant owners. When manufacturers such as Dell or Avon sell directly to consumers, they are performing both production and retailing activities. When Dell sells directly to a university or business, it becomes a business-to-business (B2B) transaction, but when it sells to the students or employees individually, it is a business-to-consumer (B2C) operation.

Supply chain management focuses on the relationships among members of the supply chain and distribution channel and the need to coordinate efforts to provide customers with the best value.

Logistics management describes the integration of two or more activities to plan, implement, and control the efficient flow of raw materials, in-process inventory, and finished goods from the point of origin to the point of consumption. These activities may include, but are not limited to, customer service, demand forecasting,

supply chain management
Refers to a set of approaches and techniques firms employ to efficiently and effectively integrate their suppliers, manufacturers, warehouses, stores, and transportation intermediaries into a seamless value chain in which merchandise is produced and distributed in the right quantities, to the right locations, and at the right time.

wholesalers
Those firms engaged in buying, taking title to, often storing, and physically handling goods in large quantities, and then reselling the goods (usually in smaller quantities) to retailers or industrial or business users.

retailers
Sell products directly to consumers.

distribution communications, inventory control, materials handling, order process-ing, parts and service support, plant and warehouse site selection, procurement, packaging, return goods handling, salvage and scrap disposal, traffic and transporta-tion, and warehousing and storage.[12] Supply chain management takes a systemwide approach to coordinating the flow of merchandise and includes both distribution management and logistics management.

Distribution channel management, supply chain management, and logistics management are related but have been handled differently in the past. Distribution channel management traditionally has been the responsibility of marketing depart-ments, under the direction of a marketing vice-president. Logistics was traditionally the responsibility of operations, under a vice-president of operations. Although their goals were similar, they often saw solutions differently, and sometimes they worked at cross-purposes. For instance, the marketing department's goal might have been to make sales, whereas logistics wanted to keep costs low. Firms have come to realize there is tremendous opportunity in coordinating marketing and logistics activities not only within a firm, but also throughout the supply chain.

logistics management
The integration of two or more activities for the purpose of planning, implementing, and controlling the efficient flow of raw materials, in-process inventory, and finished goods from the point of origin to the point of consumption.

Distribution Channels Add Value

L02

Distribution channels are composed of various entities that are buying, such as retailers or wholesalers; selling, such as manufacturers or wholesalers; or helping facilitate the exchange, such as transportation companies. Like interactions between people, these relationships can range from close working partnerships to one-time arrangements. In almost all cases though, they occur because the parties want some-thing from one another. For instance, Home Depot wants hammers from Stanley Tool Company; Stanley wants an opportunity to sell its tools to the public; and both com-panies want UPS to deliver the merchandise.

Each channel member performs a specialized role. If one member believes that another isn't doing its job correctly or efficiently, it usually can replace that member. So, if Stanley isn't getting good service from UPS, it can switch to FedEx. Likewise, if Home Depot believes its customers don't perceive Stanley tools to be a good value, it may buy from another tool company. Home Depot could even decide to make its own tools or use its own trucks to pick up tools from Stanley. However, even if a channel member is replaced, the function it performed remains, so someone needs to complete it.

Distribution channels perform a variety of transactional, logistical, and facilitat-ing functions, as noted in Exhibit 12.2. One important role played by intermediaries is to reduce the number of marketplace contacts, resulting in more efficient systems. Intermediaries also match the requirements of individual consumers to the goods that manufacturers produce; handle physical distribution and storage of goods, mak-ing them available for customers to purchase; facilitate searches by both buyers and sellers; and standardize exchange transactions. While channel functions may shift

The Home Depot and Stanley Tool Company have a mutually beneficial partnership. The Home Depot buys tools from Stanley because its customers find value in Stanley products. Stanley sells tools to Home Depot because it has established an excellent market for its products.

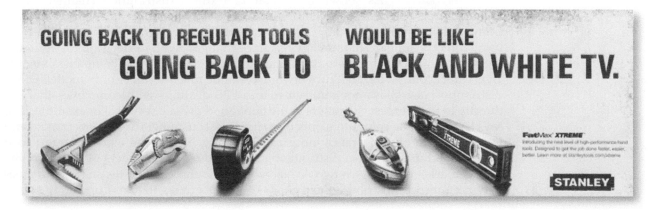

EXHIBIT 12.2	Functions Performed by Intermediaries

Transactional Function

Buying—purchase goods for resale to other intermediaries or consumers
Risk Taking—ownership of inventory that can become outdated
Promotion—promote products to attract consumers
Selling—transact with potential customers

Logistical Function

Physical Distribution—transport goods to point of purchase
Storing—maintain inventory and protect goods

Facilitating Function

Gather Information—share competitive intelligence about customers or other channel members
Financing—extend credit and other financial services to consumers

from one intermediary or channel member to another, it's important to recognize that they cannot be eliminated. As noted in the Home Deport example above, these functions must be completed by some organization to get the right products to the right customers when they want them.

In this section, we examine how distribution channels are structured, as well as the appropriate level of distribution intensity.

LO3 Designing Distribution Channels

Channel Structure

When a firm is just starting out or entering a new market, it doesn't typically have the option of designing the "best" distribution channel structure—that is, choosing from whom it buys or to whom it sells. A new retailer selling children's clothing, for instance, will be primarily concerned about getting the right assortment and needs to scout the market to get just the right mix. Some manufacturers won't want to sell to this new retailer initially because its credit isn't established or the manufacturers already have enough of their products represented by other retailers in the area. The problem can be equally daunting for manufacturers entering a new market, whose primary concern will be to find retailers that want to take a chance on their line. Every company must develop a distribution strategy for how it will sell goods to consumers. The distribution system may take the form of direct distribution, indirect distribution, and multichannel distribution, or some combination of these forms.

Direct Distribution   As shown in Exhibit 12.3, direct distribution channels allow manufacturers to deal directly with consumers. Many products and services are distributed this way. For decades, Dell's distribution strategy was based exclusively on using direct channels. This strategy has since changed, with its decision to begin selling select personal computers at Walmart and other stores. Other companies, such as TigerDirect.com, Avon, and Tupperware, continue to use a direct-only model. Direct distribution also plays a significant role in B2B dealings with companies that sell directly to their largest customers in the public and private sectors. For example, IBM sells its mainframe computers directly to its largest customers in the government and in the banking and insurance industries. Recently, Nestlé, the world's largest food company, adopted a direct distribution strategy to reach customers in Brazil, sailing a supermarket barge down two Amazon River tributaries.[13] Lastly, some companies may be forced to distribute their goods directly because they are unable to secure

Ethical Dilemma 12.1

Listing Fees: Needless or Necessary?

Most consumers never think about how products make it to grocery store shelves. Often they don't realize that suppliers can pay thousands of dollars in listing fees to have their products stocked. In the world of grocery marketing, shelf space and position are critical. Listing fees can determine whether an item gets placed at eye level or down on a bottom shelf where it's harder to find.

In Canada, listing fees can range from a few hundred dollars, to $25,000 per item per store, to $1 million per item per grocery chain. When it comes to getting listed, Val Laidlaw, director of customer marketing at Dare Foods of Kitchener, Ontario, says the first task is to get retailers onside and convince them your product will do well. Retailers don't care if your product helps you gain market share. They care only if it will help them by growing a category, bringing new consumers to the category, or adding to their profit.

Many large grocery store chains charge listing fees to cover their costs in rearranging the store shelves and the warehouse to accommodate the new product. Plus, adding a new product has administration costs. The fee depends on many variables, including potential sales volume, trade allowances, product promotion offered (e.g., samples, in-store demos, promotional pricing, co-op advertising), product category, and company size. Grocery retailers know that large companies such as Kraft or Colgate-Palmolive can afford listing fees. However, some category leaders don't have to pay them because retailers know they simply must stock popular products such as Coke and Tide. Also, if there is high consumer demand for the product, there may be no listing fee.

The size of the category within a store plays an important role in obtaining space, too. With products such as cookies and crackers, offering enough money in listing fees will likely get you on the shelves since consumers are likely to try new products in these categories. However, the frozen-food section of a grocery store is very expensive to expand, making it very tough to get new products listed. SKUs that don't perform well are de-listed within six months of hitting the shelves. Based on the Nielsen definition of a successful new product, failure rates are around 70 percent.

Grocery stores have a right to be selective when choosing from 100 000 plus items if they have room for only 40 000 items. However, critics say listing fees curb fair access to the market and erode consumer choice since small companies can't afford the fees. And the fees ultimately get passed on to consumers in the form of higher prices. What do you think? Are listing fees needless or necessary?

Source: Adapted from Shirley Lichti, "Listing Fees Can Decide a Food Product's Fate." www.marketingmagic.ca/articles/ListingFees.htm (accessed June 27, 2010).

shelf space in retail outlets or are unable to pay the high listing fees demanded by retailers for the shelf space. For example, many large grocery store chains charge listing fees that cover their costs in rearranging the store shelves and the warehouse, plus the administration costs associated with adding a new product. Ethical Dilemma 12.1 examines the issue of listing fees in more depth.

EXHIBIT 12.3 | Direct and Indirect Distribution

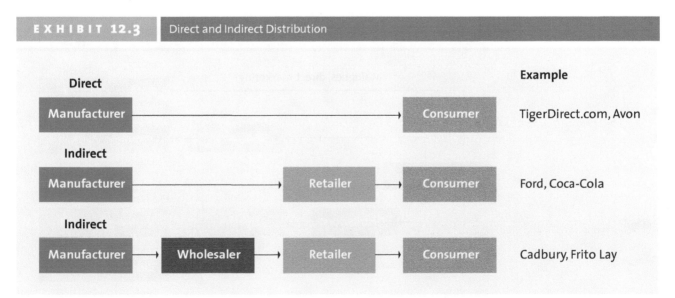

				Example
Direct				
Manufacturer	→		Consumer	TigerDirect.com, Avon
Indirect				
Manufacturer	→	Retailer	→ Consumer	Ford, Coca-Cola
Indirect				
Manufacturer	→ Wholesaler	→ Retailer	→ Consumer	Cadbury, Frito Lay

Indirect Distribution   With indirect distribution channels, one or more intermediaries work with manufacturers to provide goods and services to consumers. In some cases, there may only be one intermediary involved. Many automotive manufacturers, such as Ford, General Motors, and Daimler Chrysler use indirect distribution with dealers acting as the retailer, as shown in Exhibit 12.3. Typically only one intermediary is used in the case of large retailers such as The Bay. Wholesalers are often used when a company does not buy in sufficient quantity to make it cost-effective for a manufacturer to deal directly with a retailer. The use of wholesalers is quite common for low-cost or low-unit value items such as candy and chips, as shown in the last example in Exhibit 12.3.

When developing its distribution strategy, a company may choose to use a push strategy or a pull strategy. With a push strategy, a manufacturer focuses its promotional efforts—for example, personal selling or sales promotion—on channel members to convince them to carry its product. This strategy literally pushes the product through distribution channels to end consumers. Sometimes, if channel members are reluctant to stock new products, manufacturers may use a pull strategy. In this case, promotional efforts are directed at consumers to build demand for products that, in turn, may convince retailers to carry them. Consumers who see TV commercials or print advertisements or who receive direct mail information or coupons regarding new products may approach local retailers and request that they stock these products, thus pulling them through the distribution channels. When Greb Industries first started selling Hush Puppies in Canada, retailers were skeptical about stocking the shoes. So Charles Greb launched a TV ad campaign that featured a lovable basset hound and promoted the "barefoot comfort" of the shoes. Consumers responded enthusiastically and pressured retailers to carry the brand.[14]

Multichannel Distribution   Today, many companies are embracing a multichannel, or hybrid, approach to distribution. As shown in Exhibit 12.4, companies such as Sony are better able to reach both consumers and business customers by using a combination of both direct and indirect distribution channels. In very large cities, Sony may sell directly via its own branded stores, while in other areas it may sell indirectly through retailers such as Best Buy and Future Shop. Some companies engage a sales force to deliver products to customers while others pursue a direct marketing approach through the use of catalogues. Sears Canada sells directly at its retail stores as well as online and through the use of catalogues.

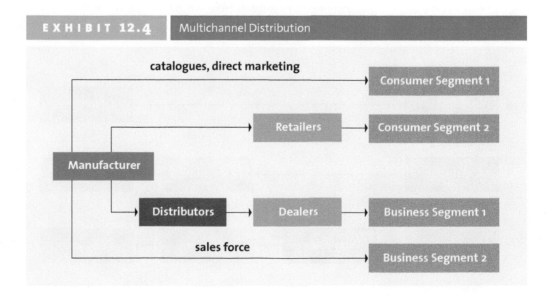

EXHIBIT 12.4   Multichannel Distribution

When choosing which channels and retailers through which to sell, the manufacturer should consider where the end customer expects to find the product, as well as some important retailer characteristics.

Customer Expectations Distribution channel management is an integral part of any marketing strategy. A key part of any strategy is to determine customer expectations. From a retailer's perspective, it is important to know from which manufacturers its customers want to buy. Manufacturers, in contrast, need to know where their target market customers expect to find their products and those of their competitors. Customers generally expect to find certain products at some stores but not at others. For instance, children's apparel manufacturer OshKosh B'Gosh would not choose to sell to Holt Renfrew or Giant Tiger because its customers would not expect to shop at those stores for children's clothing. Instead, Holt Renfrew might carry imported clothing from France, and Giant Tiger will probably offer bargain closeouts. But OshKosh's customers would definitely expect to find its clothing offerings at major department stores, such as The Bay or Sears.

Companies need to stay abreast of changes in where customers buy products and what products they request, and then change their distribution strategies accordingly. As an example, when country singer Garth Brooks realized that the majority of his CDs were purchased at Walmart, he signed an exclusive distribution deal with the retailer that eliminated his record label. Similarly, 70s Rock and Roll Hall of Fame band The Eagles released *Long Road out of Eden*, its first new studio album in 28 years, exclusively at Walmart. Other bands, such as Journey and Foreigner, have since taken the same path. Although decisions such as these may limit distribution to just one retailer, artists benefit from increased promotion and an increased share of the profits. Social Media Marketing 12.1 describes how General Mills was able to get access to shelf space for gluten-free products, a niche market with a lot of demand from consumers.

Channel Member Characteristics Several factors pertaining to the channel members themselves will help determine the distribution structure. Generally, the larger and more sophisticated the channel member, the less likely that it will use intermediaries. A small specialty toy manufacturer will probably use a group of independent salespeople to help sell its line; whereas a large manufacturer such as Mattel will use its own sales force. In the same way, an independent grocery store might buy merchandise from a wholesaler; but, Walmart, the world's largest grocer, only buys directly from the manufacturer. Larger firms often find that by performing the distribution functions themselves, they can gain more control, be more efficient, and save money. Large national convenience store chains often prefer to deal with one regional supplier when it comes to buying products such as ice. This preference has helped Arctic Glacier dominate the packaged ice industry with about 50 to 60 percent of the market share.[15]

Distribution Intensity

When setting up distribution for the first time or introducing new products, firms decide the appropriate level of **distribution intensity**—the number of channel members to use at each level of the supply chain. Distribution intensity commonly is divided into three levels: intensive, exclusive, and selective (see Exhibit 12.5).

Intensive Distribution An **intensive distribution** strategy is designed to get products into as many outlets as possible. Most consumer packaged goods companies,

distribution intensity
The number of channel members to use at each level of the supply chain.

intensive distribution
A strategy designed to get products into as many outlets as possible.

The Arctic Glacier bag is familiar across North America. The Winnipeg-based company has become a market leader, adding value to water by turning it into ice.

Social Media Marketing 12.1

Social Media Allows Big Brands to Target Niche Markets

Last year, General Mills noticed a clear trend: gluten-free products were the most consumer requested item. However, a full-scale new product launch was unlikely: only 2 percent of the population has Celiac disease, and another 10 percent try to avoid gluten.[16] A market this small simply couldn't sustain the investment necessary for a full-scale launch. Getting distribution would be extremely difficult.

General Mills knew that this niche market was not only important, but also completely ignored. It developed a gluten-free Chex breakfast cereal and followed it up with a line of gluten-free Betty Crocker baking mixes. The first challenge it faced was getting shelf space for these niche products. With most stores reducing their product assortments by 15 percent or more, it seemed impossible. However, the competition for shelf space actually helped. Instead of listing many different brands in a category, retailers are now taking only the top few brands plus some private labels. General Mills was able to leverage

General Mills used social media to promote its gluten-free products and pave the way for mainstream distribution.

its status as a number one brand and heavily promoted its key point of difference.[17] This meant that while the new products might have lower volumes, they could still be distributed through well-established channels.

Rather than promote the new products with mass media, General Mills used direct marketing and social media to speak to the right consumer. It partnered with major Celiac disease foundations and invested in search-engine optimization—an important step since most people who are newly diagnosed with Celiac disease jump online to find out which foods they can eat. Dena Larson, marketing manager–baking products at General Mills, explained that despite being small in numbers, consumers with Celiac disease are well connected. Rumours that General Mills was developing gluten-free baking products generated a lot of buzz on Twitter, and social media tools continue to help people with Celiac disease share information and tips about gluten-free products as they come to market.[18]

such as PepsiCo, P&G, Kraft, and most other nationally branded products found in grocery and discount stores, strive for and often achieve intensive distribution. PepsiCo, for instance, wants its product available everywhere: grocery stores, convenience stores, restaurants, and vending machines. Timex watches, starting at around $60, can also be found in many locations. The more exposure these products get, the

---

EXHIBIT 12.5   Distribution Intensity

Intensive

Selective

Exclusive

| Power of the Internet **12.1** | **Google Brings e-Books to Your Browser** |

Search-engine giant Google changed the face of the Web, distributing volumes of digitized information to consumers. Now it plans to transform the online book market with the launch of Google Editions. Although the company has been digitizing books for years, available under the Google Books tab, this new venture promises to diversify its revenue sources, which today come almost exclusively from search advertising. A bookstore project was considered as early as 2006 but stalled because web browsers weren't able to support the service.[19] More recent technology is now paving the way for Google to achieve intensive distribution and provide publishers with the infrastructure needed to support direct-to-consumer sales.[20]

Google Editions will offer millions of consumers online access to millions of books. Consumers can buy digital copies of the books from Google or from book retailers who offer the service on their own sites. To ensure buy-in from distributors, in this case booksellers, Google has proposed a different model than Amazon or Apple, one which places no restrictions on how the books are accessed or for what type of device, which means consumers would be able to read books on any device that can connect to the Internet, not just on e-readers. No separate apps or interfaces will be required,[21] and books, which are fully searchable, stay on an electronic bookshelf, allowing readers to come back to them at any point in the future. The Google model also means that book retailers would retain the lion's share of the revenues; by selling e-books directly to consumers rather than via competitive platforms, book retailers would retain 63 percent of revenues.[22]

Although Amazon.com is the dominant book retailer today, a Forrester Research study noted it was facing attacks by competitors, who were launching new features and improving their relationships with publishers. Enter Google Editions with its direct-to-consumer sales model. Google is facing significant legal challenges from a Google Book Search Copyright class action lawsuit from authors and publishers who claim that Google Books violates their copyrights. Although the technology is available to offer this service and that consumers may benefit from the service, Google must overcome legal hurdles before it can proceed. In addition, Google must provide consumers with a compelling experience to entice them to use this new service. The company can already display up to 20 percent of the contents of in-print books from browser-based Google Books. Will users find enough value in Google's model to make them prefer and pay for a dedicated e-book over a cached version of the book accessed from their browser?

more they sell. Refer to Power of the Internet 12.1 to see how Google plans to achieve intensive distribution of e-books by distributing them directly to anyone with a web browser.

Exclusive Distribution   Manufacturers also might use an **exclusive distribution** policy by granting **exclusive geographic territories** to one or very few retail customers so no other customers in the territory can sell a particular brand. Exclusive distribution can benefit manufacturers by assuring them that the most appropriate customers represent their products. Cosmetics firms such as Estée Lauder, for instance, limit their distribution to a few select, higher-end retailers in each region. They believe that if they sell their products to drugstores, discount stores, and grocery stores, this distribution would weaken their image. Likewise, Rolex watches are sold only by high-end jewelers and a few retail outlets in keeping with their prestigious brand image.

In cases of limited supply or when a firm is just starting out, providing an exclusive territory to one customer helps ensure enough inventory to offer the customer an adequate selection. For instance, Cervélo is a Canadian bicycle manufacturer that makes lightweight racing bikes. It selects its authorized dealers carefully. By controlling sales territories, it guarantees dealers adequate supply, which gives them a strong incentive to push Cervélo's products. Dealers know there will be no competing retailers to cut prices, so their profit margins are protected, which also gives them an incentive to carry more inventory and use extra advertising, personal selling, and sales promotions.

Selective Distribution   Between the intensive and exclusive distribution strategies lies **selective distribution**, which uses a few selected customers in a territory. Similar

exclusive distribution
Strategy of granting exclusive rights to sell to one or very few retail customers so no other customers can sell a particular brand.

exclusive geographic territories
Territories granted to one or very few retail customers by a manufacturer using an exclusive distribution strategy; no other customers can sell a particular brand in these territories.

selective distribution
Lies between the intensive and exclusive distribution strategies; uses a few selected customers in a territory.

Most consumer packaged goods companies, such as PepsiCo (top), strive for intensive distribution—it wants to be everywhere. But cosmetics firms such as Estée Lauder (bottom) use an exclusive distribution strategy by limiting its distribution to a few select, higher-end retailers in each region.

channel conflict
Results when supply chain members are not in agreement about their goals, roles, or rewards.

to exclusive distribution, selective distribution helps a seller maintain a particular image and control the flow of merchandise into an area, so many shopping goods manufacturers use it. Recall that shopping goods are those products for which consumers are willing to spend time comparing alternatives, such as most apparel items, home items such as branded pots and pans, sheets, and towels, branded hardware and tools, and consumer electronics. Seiko uses a selective distribution strategy for its watches to match its more upscale image and pricing. Retailers still have a strong incentive to sell the products but not to the same extent as if they had an exclusive territory.

Managing Distribution Channels

If a distribution channel is to run efficiently, the participating members must cooperate. Oftentimes, however, channel members have conflicting goals. For instance, Stanley wants Home Depot to carry all its tools but not those of its competitors so that Stanley can maximize its sales. But Home Depot carries a mix of tool brands so it can maximize the sales in its tool category. When channel members are not in agreement about their goals, roles, or rewards, **channel conflict** results. For example, in England, singer and songwriter Prince infuriated retailers with his decision to have a newspaper, *The Mail*, include free copies of his new *Planet Earth* CD. After the giveaway was announced, Columbia Records' corporate parent, Sony Music, said it would not release the CD for retail sale in the United Kingdom.[23]

Channel conflict can be resolved through good negotiations. But when the issues can't be worked out, relationships can fall apart, and the firms may go their separate ways. In other cases, conflict may lead to a stronger supply chain. In the mid-1980s, P&G was having trouble selling to Walmart; in their relationship, there was no sharing of information, no joint planning or sales forecasting, and no systems coordination. So Sam Walton, founder of Walmart, ventured out on a canoe trip with Lou Pritchett, P&G's vice-president of sales. On this trip, they started a process of examining how the two firms could mutually profit by working together. The conflict thus ultimately resulted in a much stronger partnership between the two firms in which they currently work together to establish sales forecasts and determine how to best restock P&G merchandise on Walmart's shelves. All parties benefit. Customers get lower prices and high product availability, and because P&G produces according to demand, there is less need for inventory, so its salespeople spend less time in the stores. Finally, Walmart achieves higher sales and lower inventory costs.[24]

Companies can manage distribution channels by developing strong relationships with supply chain partners. Or they can coordinate the channel by using a vertical marketing system.

Managing Channels Through Vertical Marketing Systems

Although conflict is likely to occur in any distribution channel, it is generally more pronounced when the channel members are independent entities. Distribution channels that are more closely aligned, whether by contract or ownership, share common goals and therefore are less prone to conflict.

In an independent distribution channel (the left panel of Exhibit 12.6), the several independent members—a manufacturer, a wholesaler, and a retailer—each attempt

| EXHIBIT 12.6 | Independent Versus Vertical Distribution Channel |

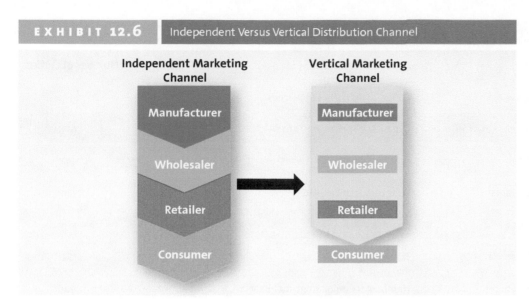

vertical marketing system
A supply chain in which the members act as a unified system; there are three types: *administrated*, *contractual*, and *corporate*.

administered vertical marketing system
A supply chain system in which there is no common ownership and no contractual relationships, but the dominant channel member controls the channel relationship.

contractual vertical marketing system
A system in which independent firms at different levels of the supply chain join together through contracts to obtain economies of scale and coordination and to reduce conflict.

to satisfy their own objectives and maximize their own profits, often at the expense of the other members. None of the participants has any control over the others.

For instance, the first time Zara purchases cotton fabric from Tessuto e Colore in Northern Italy, both parties try to extract as much profit from the deal as possible, and after the deal has been consummated, neither party feels any responsibility to the other. Over time, Zara and Tessuto might develop a relationship in which their transactions become more routine and automatic, such that Zara depends on Tessuto for fabric, and Tessuto depends on Zara to buy a good portion of its output. This scenario represents the first phase of a **vertical marketing system** (the right panel of Exhibit 12.6) in which the members act as a unified system because they realize that each party can maximize their individual benefits by working together to make the distribution system more efficient rather than individually or at cross-purposes. There are three types, or phases, of vertical marketing systems, each with increasing levels of formalization and control. The more formal the vertical marketing system, the less likely conflict will ensue.

Zara and Tessuto e Colore might develop a vertical marketing system in which transactions have become routine and automatic, such that Zara depends on Tessuto for fabric, and Tessuto depends on Zara to buy a good portion of its output.

Administered Vertical Marketing System   The Zara/Tessuto channel relationship offers an example of an **administered vertical marketing system**. In an administered vertical marketing system, there is no common ownership and no contractual relationships, but the dominant channel member controls the channel relationship. In our example, because of its size and relative power, Zara imposes some control over Tessuto; it dictates, for instance, what Tessuto should make and when it should be delivered. Zara also has a strong influence over the price. If either party doesn't like the way the relationship is going, however, it can simply walk away.

Contractual Vertical Marketing System   Over time, Zara and Tessuto may formalize their relationship by entering into contracts that dictate various terms, such as how much Zara will buy each month, at what price, and the penalties for late deliveries. In **contractual vertical marketing systems** like this, independent firms at different levels of the supply chain join together through contracts to obtain economies of scale and coordination and to reduce conflict.[25]

EXHIBIT 12.7	The 10 Largest Franchises in Canada		
Rank	**Franchise**	**Type**	**Number of Outlets**
1	Tim Hortons	Coffee, doughnuts, sandwiches	2902
2	Subway	Submarine sandwiches, salads	2457
3	McDonald's	Hamburgers, chicken, salads	1421
4	YUMI Restaurants	Pizza Hut, Taco Bell, KFC	1261
5	Shoppers Drug Mart	Pharmacy	1090
6	H&R Block Canada	Tax preparation	1047
7	A&W Food Services	Hamburgers, onion rings, root beer	700
8	Cara Operations	Harvey's, Kelseys, Montana's, Milestones, Swiss Chalet	686
9	Jan-Pro Cleaning Systems	Commercial Janitorial Services	600
10	Jani-King Canada	Commercial Janitorial Services	593

Source: Canadian Franchise Association "Franchise Facts."

franchising

A contractual agreement between a *franchisor* and a *franchisee* that allows the franchisee to operate a retail outlet, using a name and format developed and supported by the franchisor.

Franchising is the most common type of contractual vertical marketing system; franchising companies and their franchisees account for $90 billion in Canadian retail sales—an astonishing 26 percent of all retail sales in this country—and employ more than 1 million people.[26] **Franchising** is a contractual agreement between a franchisor and a franchisee that allows the franchisee to operate a retail outlet, using a name and format developed and supported by the franchisor. Exhibit 12.7 lists some of Canada's favourite franchises.

In a franchise contract, the franchisee pays a lump sum plus a royalty on all sales in return for the right to operate a business in a specific location. The franchisee also agrees to operate the outlet in accordance with the procedures prescribed by the franchisor. The franchisor typically provides assistance in locating and building the business, developing the products or services sold, management training, and advertising. To maintain the franchisee's reputation, the franchisor also makes sure that all outlets provide the same quality of services and products.

A franchise system combines the entrepreneurial advantages of owning a business with the efficiencies of vertical marketing systems that function under single ownership (a corporate system, as we discuss next). Franchisees are motivated to make their stores successful because they receive the profits, after they pay the royalty to the franchisor. The franchisor is motivated to develop new products, services, and systems and to promote the franchise because it receives royalties on all sales. Advertising, product development, and system development are all done efficiently by the franchisor, with costs shared by all franchisees. Canada has the second largest franchise industry in the world, outdone only by the United States, that generates more than $100 billion in annual sales.[27]

Corporate Vertical Marketing System Because Zara deals with "fast fashion," it is imperative that it have complete control over the most fashion-sensitive items. So Zara manufactures these items itself and contracts out its less fashionable items to other manufacturers.[28] The portion of its supply chain that Zara owns and controls is called a **corporate vertical marketing system**. Because Zara's parent company Inditex owns the manufacturing plants, warehouse facilities, retail outlets, and design studios, it can dictate the priorities and objectives of that supply chain, and thus conflict is lessened.

Supply Chains Add Value

Why would a manufacturer want to use a wholesaler or a retailer? Don't these supply chain members just cut into their profits? Wouldn't it be cheaper for consumers to buy directly from manufacturers? In a simple agrarian economy, the best supply chain may in fact follow a direct route from manufacturer to consumer: the consumer goes to the farm and buys food directly from the farmer. But how will the food get cooked? The consumer doesn't know how to make a stove, nor does she have the materials to do so. The stove maker who has the necessary knowledge must buy raw materials and components from various suppliers, make the stove, and then make it available to the consumer. If the stove maker isn't located near the consumer, the stove must be transported to where the consumer has access to it. To make matters even more complicated, the consumer may want to view a choice of stoves, hear about all their features, and have the stove delivered and installed.

Each participant in the supply chain thus adds value. The components manufacturer helps the stove manufacturer by supplying parts and materials. The stove maker then turns the components into the stove. The transportation company gets the stove to the retailer. The retailer stores the stove until the customer wants it, educates the customer about product features, and delivers and installs the stove. At each step, the stove becomes more costly but also more valuable to the consumer.

Exhibits 12.8A and 12.8B show how using supply chain partners can provide value overall. Exhibit 12.8A shows three manufacturers, each of which sells directly to three consumers in a system that requires nine transactions. Each transaction costs money—for example, the manufacturer must fill the order, package it, write up the paperwork, and ship it—and each cost is passed on to the customer. Exhibit 12.8B shows the same three manufacturers and consumers; but, this time they go through a single retailer. The number of transactions falls to six, and as transactions are eliminated, the supply chain becomes more efficient, which adds value for customers by making it more convenient and less expensive to purchase merchandise.

Supply Chain Management Streamlines Distribution

Supply chain management offers the twenty-first century's answer to a host of distribution problems faced by firms. As recently as the early 1990s, even the most innovative firms needed 15 to 30 days—or even more—to fulfill an order from the warehouse to the customer. The typical order-to-delivery process had several steps: order creation, usually using a telephone, facsimile, or mail; order processing, using a manual system for credit authorization and assignment to a warehouse; and physical delivery. Things could, and often did, go wrong. Ordered goods were not available. Orders were lost or misplaced. Shipments were misdirected. These mistakes lengthened the time it took to get merchandise to customers and potentially made the entire process more expensive and frustrating, a familiar scenario for many of us.

Faced with these predicaments, firms began stockpiling inventory at each level of the supply chain (retailers, wholesalers, and manufacturers), but keeping inventory where it is not needed becomes a huge and wasteful

corporate vertical marketing system
A system in which the parent company has complete control and can dictate the priorities and objectives of the supply chain; it may own facilities such as manufacturing plants, warehouse facilities, retail outlets, and design studios.

L04

How many companies are involved in making and getting a stove to your kitchen?

EXHIBIT 12.8A | Direct Supply Chain with No Retailer

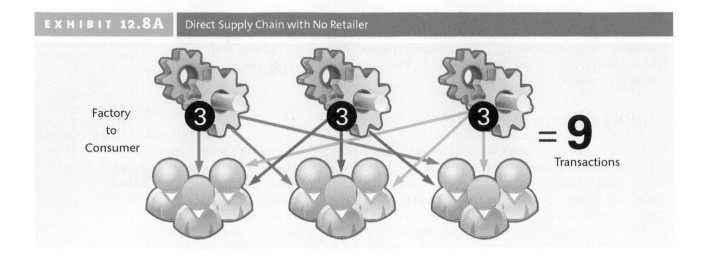

Factory to Consumer

3 3 3 = **9** Transactions

expense. If a manufacturer has a large stock of items stuck in a warehouse, it not only forgoes profits by not selling those items, but also must pay to maintain the warehouse.

Therefore, more recently, firms have swung in the other direction. As noted in the chapter vignette, Zara gains its competitive advantage by bringing fashions to the store and its customers much faster than other clothing retailers. It holds minimal inventory, produces new fashion quickly, and rarely gets stuck with old inventory. Deliveries are made to stores once a week, and the clothes rarely remain on shelves for more than a week. But this speedy system is not limited to the retail side; Zara also takes only four to five weeks to design a new collection and then about a week to manufacture it; so it continually cycles through its inventory of fabric and materials needed to make its clothing. Its competitors, in comparison, need an average of six months to design a new collection and another three weeks to manufacture it.

EXHIBIT 12.8B | Indirect Supply Chain with Retailer

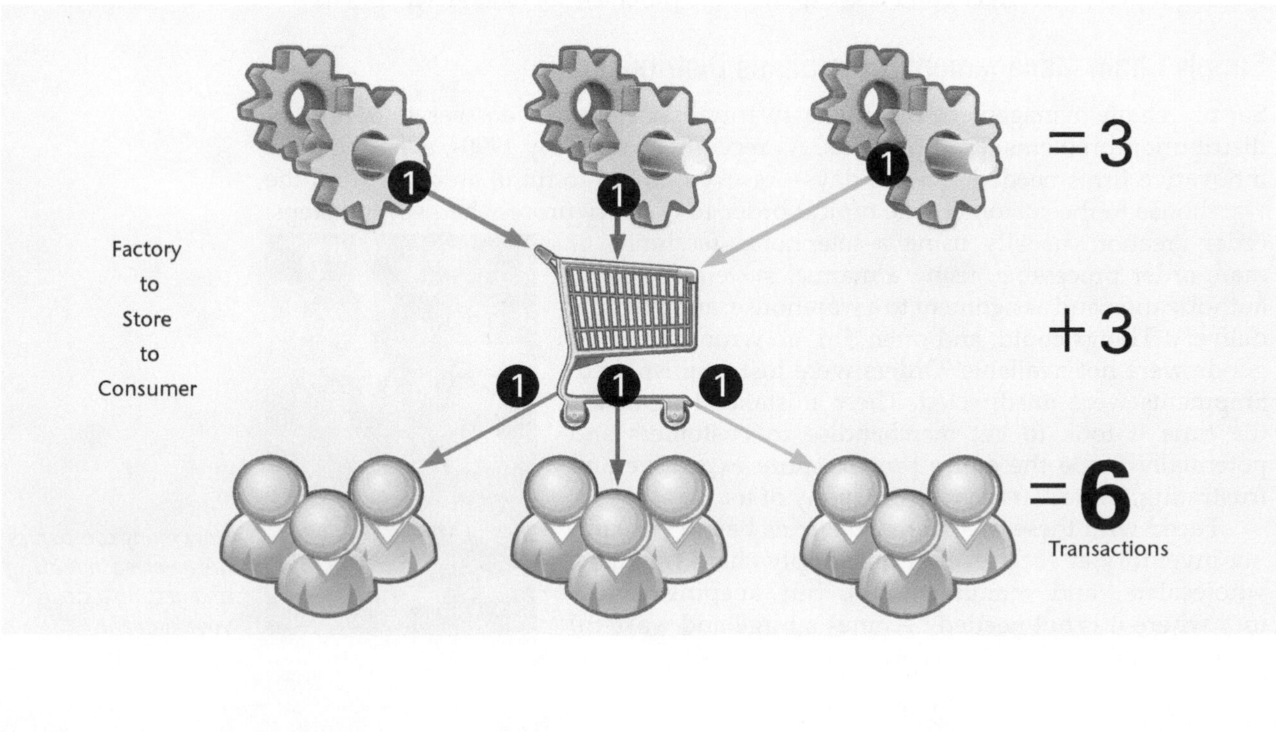

Factory to Store to Consumer

1 1 1 = 3

1 1 1 + 3

= **6** Transactions

Supply Chain Management Affects Marketing

Every marketing decision is affected by and has an effect on the supply chain. When products are designed and manufactured, how and when the critical components reach the factory must be coordinated with production. The sales department must coordinate its delivery promises with the factory or distribution centres. A **distribution centre**, a facility for the receipt, storage, and redistribution of goods to company stores or customers, may be operated by retailers, manufacturers, or distribution specialists.[29] Furthermore, advertising and promotion must be coordinated with those departments that control inventory and transportation. There is no faster way to lose credibility with customers than to promise deliveries or run a promotion and then not have the merchandise when the customer expects it. Entrepreneur Michael Dell got into the computer business and developed his firm into one that provides better value to customers with great supply chain management. The company builds roughly 50 000 made-to-order computers a day and carries just four days' worth of parts inventory. Online sales account for nearly half of its orders. Using state-of-the-art technology, Dell monitors every aspect of the supply chain, including supplier report cards that compare individual performance to preset criteria.

Five interrelated activities emerge in supply chain management: designing distribution channels (discussed earlier in this chapter), making information flow, managing the relationships among supply chain partners, making merchandise flow, and managing inventory. In the next few sections, we examine these remaining activities.

distribution centre
A facility for the receipt, storage, and redistribution of goods to company stores or customers; may be operated by retailers, manufacturers, or distribution specialists.

Logistics Management: Making Information Flow

Information flows from the customer to stores, to and from distribution centres, possibly to and from wholesalers, to and from product manufacturers, and then on to the producers of any components and the suppliers of raw materials. To simplify our discussion and because information flows are similar in other supply chain links and B2B channels, we shorten the supply chain in this section to exclude wholesalers, as well as the link from suppliers to manufacturers. Exhibit 12.9 illustrates the flow of information that starts when a customer buys a Sony HDTV at Future Shop. The flow follows these steps:

universal product code (UPC)
The black and white bar code found on most merchandise.

Michael Dell makes made-to-order computers on this assembly line.

- **Flow 1 (Customer to Store).** The sales associate at Future Shop scans the **universal product code (UPC)** tag, the black and white bar code found on most merchandise, on the HDTV packaging, and the customer receives a receipt. The UPC tag contains a 13-digit code that includes the manufacturer of an item and information about special packaging and special promotions. In the future, RFID tags, discussed later in this chapter, may replace UPC codes.

- **Flow 2 (Store to Buyer).** The point-of-sale (POS) terminal records the purchase information and electronically sends it to the buyer at Future Shop's corporate office. The sales information is incorporated into an inventory management system and used to monitor and analyze sales and to decide to reorder more HDTVs, change a price, or plan a promotion. Buyers also send information to stores on overall sales for the chain, how to display merchandise, upcoming promotions, and so on.

- **Flow 3 (Buyer to Manufacturer).** The purchase information from each Future Shop store is

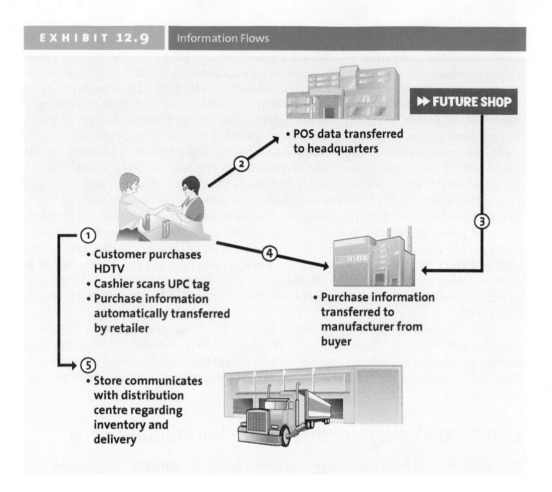

EXHIBIT 12.9 | Information Flows

typically aggregated by the retailer as a whole, which creates an order for new merchandise and sends it to Sony. The buyer at Future Shop may also communicate directly with Sony to get information and negotiate prices, shipping dates, promotional events, or other merchandise-related issues.

- **Flow 4 (Store to Manufacturer).** In some situations, the sales transaction data are sent directly from the store to the manufacturer, and the manufacturer decides when to ship more merchandise to the distribution centres and the stores. However, if the merchandise is reordered frequently, the ordering process can become automatic and virtually bypass the buyer.

- **Flow 5 (Store to Distribution Centre).** Stores also communicate with the Future Shop distribution centre to coordinate deliveries and check inventory status. When the store inventory drops to a specified level, more HDTVs are shipped to the store and the shipment is sent to the Future Shop computer system.

In Flow 3, the retailer and manufacturer exchange business documents through a system called electronic data interchange.

Data Warehouse

Consumers' purchase data collected at the point of sale (information flow 2 in Exhibit 12.9) goes into a huge database known as a data warehouse. The information stored in the data warehouse is accessible on various dimensions and levels, as depicted in the data cube in Exhibit 12.10.

As shown on the horizontal axis, data can be accessed according to the level of merchandise aggregation: SKU (item), vendor, category (e.g., dresses), or all merchandise.

EXHIBIT 12.10 | Retail Data Warehouse

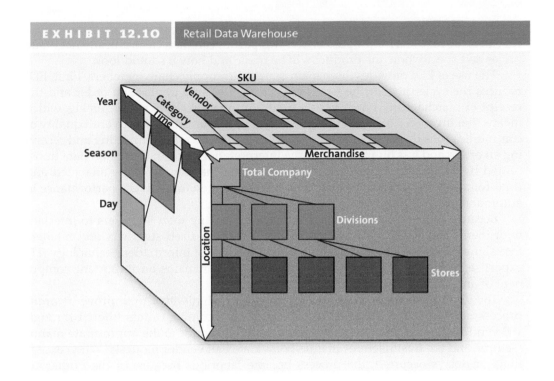

Along the vertical axis, data can be accessed by level of the company: store, divisions, or the total company. Finally, along the third dimension, data can be accessed by point in time: day, season, or year.

The CEO might be interested in how the corporation is generally doing and could look at the data aggregated by quarter for a merchandise division, a region of the country, or the total corporation. A buyer may be more interested in a particular manufacturer in a certain store on a particular day. Analysts from various levels of the retail operation extract information from the data warehouse to make a plethora of marketing decisions about developing and replenishing merchandise assortments.

In some cases, manufacturers also have access to this data warehouse. They communicate with retailers by using electronic data interchange and use supply chain systems known as vendor-managed inventory and collaborative planning, forecasting, and replenishment.

Electronic Data Interchange

Electronic data interchange (EDI) is the computer-to-computer exchange of business documents from a retailer to a vendor and back. In addition to sales data, purchase orders, invoices, and data about returned merchandise can be transmitted back and forth.

Many retailers now require vendors to provide them with notification of deliveries before they take place by using an **advanced shipping notice**, an electronic document that the supplier sends the retailer in advance of a shipment to tell the retailer exactly what to expect in the shipment. If the advanced shipping notice is accurate, the retailer can dispense with opening all the received cartons and checking in merchandise. In addition, EDI enables vendors to transmit information about on-hand inventory status, vendor promotions, and cost changes to the retailer, as well as information about purchase order changes, order status, retail prices, and transportation routings.

electronic data interchange (EDI)
The computer-to-computer exchange of business documents from a retailer to a vendor and back.

advanced shipping notice
An electronic document that the supplier sends the retailer in advance of a shipment to tell the retailer exactly what to expect in the shipment.

Using EDIs, suppliers can describe and show pictures of their products, and buyers can issue requests for proposals. The two parties can then electronically negotiate prices and specify how the product will be made and how it should look.

The use of EDI provides three main benefits to supply chain members. First, EDI reduces the cycle time, or the time between the decision to place an order and the receipt of merchandise. When EDI is used, information flows more quickly, which means that inventory turnover is higher. Second, EDI improves the overall quality of communications through better record keeping; fewer errors in inputting and receiving an order; and less human error in the interpretation of data. Third, the data transmitted by EDI are in a computer-readable format that can be easily analyzed and used for a variety of tasks, ranging from evaluating vendor delivery performance to automating reorder processes.

Because of these benefits, many retailers are asking their suppliers to interface with them by using EDI. However, small to medium-sized suppliers and retailers face significant barriers, specifically, cost and the lack of information technology (IT) expertise, to becoming EDI-enabled. However, EDI remains an important component of any vendor-managed inventory system.

Toy giant Hasbro, for example, launched an EDI initiative to improve its order processing. Before this, roughly 70 percent of all incoming orders filtered through 100 vendors in Asia. Each order was sent from the vendor to the appropriate manufacturer, and the manufacturer manually reviewed all vendor requests. When exceptions or delays occurred, the process became laborious because of the numerous faxes and phone calls needed to resolve any issue. After Hasbro implemented EDI for its manufacturers, 80 percent of the orders needed no human interaction at all. As a result, the Asian operations were able to handle a 100-percent increase in their order volume without any additional resources.[30]

Managing Supply Chains Through Strategic Relationships

There is more to managing supply chains than simply exercising power over other members in an administered system or establishing a contractual or corporate vertical marketing system. There is also a human side.

In a conventional distribution channel, relationships between members often are based on the argument over the split of the profit pie: if one party gets ahead, the other party falls behind. Sometimes this type of transactional approach is acceptable if the parties have no interest in a long-term relationship. If Harry Rosen sees a trend for very narrow white belts, it would be interested in purchasing from a vendor in which an ongoing relationship would be built. Harry Rosen would not purchase from a vendor on a one-time basis just to get a one-time good price because long-term relationship building is important to the company's business practices.

More often than not, firms seek a **strategic relationship**, also called a **partnering relationship**, in which the supply chain members are committed to maintaining the relationship over the long term and investing in opportunities that are mutually beneficial. In a conventional or administered supply chain, there are significant incentives to establishing a strategic relationship, even without contracts or ownership relationships. Both parties benefit because the size of the profit pie has increased, so both the buyer and the seller increase their sales and profits. These strategic relationships are created explicitly to uncover

**strategic relationship
(partnering relationship)**
A supply chain relationship that the members are committed to maintaining long term, investing in opportunities that are mutually beneficial; requires mutual trust, open communication, common goals, and credible commitments.

Hasbro makes toys and games such as this Trivial Pursuit Star Wars Edition. It communicates efficiently with its vendors with EDI.

and exploit joint opportunities, so members depend on and trust each other heavily; share goals and agree on how to accomplish those goals; and are willing to take risks, share confidential information, and make significant investments for the sake of the relationship. Successful strategic relationships require mutual trust, open communication, common goals, and credible commitments.[31]

Mutual Trust   Mutual trust holds a strategic relationship together. When vendors and buyers trust each other, they're more willing to share relevant ideas, clarify goals and problems, and communicate efficiently. Information shared between the parties thus becomes increasingly comprehensive, accurate, and timely. With trust, there's also less need for the supply chain members to constantly monitor and check up on each other's actions, because each believes the other won't take advantage, even given the opportunity. RFID systems that enable sealed cartons to be checked into a distribution centre without being opened would be impossible without mutual trust.

Open Communication   To share information, develop sales forecasts together, and coordinate deliveries, Harry Rosen and its suppliers maintain open and honest communication. This maintenance may sound easy in principle, but most businesses don't tend to share information with their business partners. But open, honest communication is a key to developing successful relationships because supply chain members need to understand what is driving each other's business, their roles in the relationship, each firm's strategies, and any problems that arise over the course of the relationship.

Common Goals   Supply chain members must have common goals for a successful relationship to develop. Shared goals give both members of the relationship an incentive to pool their strengths and abilities and exploit potential opportunities together. For example, Harry Rosen and its local suppliers recognize that it is in their common interest to be strategic partners. Harry Rosen needs the quick response local manufacturers afford, and those manufacturers recognize that if they can keep Harry Rosen happy, they will have more than enough business for years to come. So if Harry Rosen needs a special production run to make an emergency shipment, suppliers will work to meet the challenge. If one of Harry Rosen's suppliers has difficulty getting a particular fabric or financing its inventory, it is in Harry Rosen's best interest to help it because they are committed to the same goals in the long run.

Harry Rosen grew from a single 500-square foot Toronto tailor shop to a national upscale menswear chain. It works hard to develop strategic partnerships with its suppliers based on mutual trust, open communications, common goals, and credible commitments.

Credible Commitments   Successful relationships develop because both parties make credible commitments to, or tangible investments in, the relationship. These commitments involve spending money to improve the products or services provided to the customer.[32] For example, if Harry Rosen makes a financial commitment to its suppliers to help them develop state-of-the-art manufacturing facilities and computer systems for improved communication, it is making a credible commitment—putting its money where its mouth is.

Just like many other elements of marketing, managing the supply chain can seem like an easy task at first glance: Put the merchandise in the right place at the right time. But the various elements and actors involved in a supply chain create unique and compelling complexities and require that firms work carefully to ensure they are achieving the most efficient and effective chain possible.

RFID tags make receiving and checking merchandise accurate, quick, and easy.

Logistics Management: Making Merchandise Flow

To explore the different types of merchandise flows, consider the following scenario.[33] Merchandise is shipped from Sony to Future Shop's distribution centres or from Sony directly to stores. If the merchandise goes through distribution centres, it is then shipped to stores and then to the customer.

Inbound Transportation

Because its distribution centres typically are quite busy, a **dispatcher**—the person who coordinates deliveries to Future Shop's distribution centres—assigns a time slot for each shipment of HDTVs to arrive. If the truck misses the time slot, it is fined. Although many manufacturers pay transportation expenses, some retailers negotiate with their vendors to absorb this expense. These retailers believe they can lower net merchandise cost and control their merchandise flow better if they negotiate directly with truck companies and consolidate shipments from many vendors.

dispatcher
The person who coordinates deliveries to distribution centres.

Receiving and Checking

Receiving refers to the process of recording the receipt of merchandise as it arrives at a distribution centre or store. Checking is the process of going through the goods upon receipt to ensure they arrived undamaged and that the merchandise ordered was the merchandise received.

Today, many distribution systems use EDI designed to minimize, if not eliminate, these processes. The advance shipping notice tells the distribution centre what should be in each box. The recipient scans the UPC label on the shipping carton or the radio frequency identification tag, which identifies the carton's contents, and those contents then are automatically counted as being received and checked. **Radio frequency identification (RFID) tags** are tiny computer chips that automatically transmit to a special scanner all the information about a container's contents or individual products.

radio frequency identification (RFID) tags
Tiny computer chips that automatically transmit to a special scanner all the information about a container's contents or individual products.

Storing and Cross-Docking

There are three types of distribution centres: traditional, cross-docking, and combinations. A traditional distribution centre is a warehouse in which merchandise is unloaded from trucks and placed on racks or shelves for storage. When the merchandise is needed in the stores, a worker goes to the rack, picks up the item, and places it in a bin. A conveyor system or other material-handling equipment transports the merchandise to a staging area, where it is consolidated and made ready for shipment to stores.

The second type, called a cross-docking distribution centre, is one to which vendors ship merchandise prepackaged in the quantity required for each store. The merchandise already contains price and theft detection tags. Because the merchandise is ready for sale, it goes straight to a staging area rather than into storage. When all the merchandise going to a particular store has arrived in the staging area, it is loaded onto a truck, and away it goes.

Most modern distribution centres combine the two previous approaches. It is difficult for a firm to operate without some storage facilities, even if merchandise is stored for only a few days. For instance, some merchandise, such as tent stakes at Mountain Equipment Co-op, has relatively slow sales but must be carried because it rounds out an assortment. These items are good candidates for storage in a distribution centre, even if the rest of the merchandise is cross-docked. Also, no matter how good a sales forecasting system may be, sometimes the merchandise arrives before it is needed in the stores. In these cases, the retailer must have a system to store the merchandise temporarily.

Getting Merchandise Floor-Ready

Floor-ready merchandise is merchandise that's ready to be placed on the selling floor immediately. Getting merchandise floor-ready entails ticketing, marking, and, in the case of apparel, placing garments on hangers. Ticketing and marking refers to creating price and identification labels and placing them on the merchandise. It is more efficient for a retailer to perform these activities at a distribution centre than in its stores because the work is time-consuming and messy. Some retailers force their suppliers to ship merchandise floor-ready, thus totally eliminating this expensive, time-consuming process for themselves.

In a cross-docking distribution centre, merchandise moves from vendors' trucks to the retailer's delivery trucks in a matter of hours.

Shipping Merchandise to Stores

Shipping merchandise to stores is quite complex for multistore chains. A Future Shop distribution centre will run approximately 100 trucks to its stores per day. To handle such complex transportation problems, distribution centres use a sophisticated routing and scheduling computer system that considers the rate of sales in the store, road conditions, and transportation operating constraints to develop the most efficient routes possible. (Refer to Sustainable Marketing 12.1 for an example of how Frito Lay Canada deals with optimizing routes and its fleet of vehicles.) As a result, stores receive an accurate estimated time of arrival, and the supply chain maximizes vehicle use. In Canada, different shipping methods are chosen depending on the nature of the goods, costs, location of customers relative to manufacturers, and needs of the customers. These methods include air (e.g., Air Canada), rail (e.g., Canadian Pacific Railway), land (e.g., Challenger Motor Freight), and sea (e.g., SEA-CAN.)

Inventory Management Through Just-In-Time Systems

Customers demand specific SKUs, and they want to be able to buy them when needed. At the same time, firms can't afford to carry more than they really need of an SKU, because to do so is very expensive. Suppose, for instance, a shoe store carries $1 million worth of inventory at its own expense. Experts estimate that it would cost between 20 and 40 percent of the value of the inventory, or $20,000 to $40,000 per year, to hold that inventory! So firms must balance having enough inventory to satisfy customer demands with not having more than they need.

To help reconcile these seemingly conflicting goals, many firms have adopted just-in-time inventory systems. **Just-in-time (JIT) inventory systems**, also known as **quick-response (QR)** systems in retailing, are inventory management systems designed to deliver less merchandise on a more frequent basis than traditional inventory systems. The firm gets the merchandise "just-in-time" for it to be used in the manufacture of another product, in the case of parts or components, or for sale when the customer wants it, in the case of consumer goods. The benefits of a JIT

just-in-time (JIT) inventory systems
Inventory management systems designed to deliver less merchandise on a more frequent basis than traditional inventory systems; the firm gets the merchandise "just in time" for it to be used in the manufacture of another product; also known as *quick response (QR)* systems in retailing.

quick response (QR)
An inventory management system used in retailing; merchandise is received just in time for sale when the customer wants it.

Sustainable Marketing 12.1 — Driving the Bottom Line

If you like Frito-Lay SunChips, you may have noticed the new packaging: a 100-percent compostable bag. Made primarily of the plant-based material polylactic acid, the bag will completely break down in 14 weeks. It's all part of Frito Lay Canada's "Leave No Trace" sustainability vision. The company has set clear goals to use less water, electricity, and fuel and to reduce waste for everything it makes, moves, and sells.[34] At Frito Lay, financial achievement is gauged by social and environmental performance. And so, in spite of consumer complaints about the "noisy" SunChips bag, Frito Lay stuck with the bag in Canada, even though it was withdrawn in the United States.

With one of the largest private delivery fleets in Canada, Frito Lay is keenly aware of the profound effect efficient vehicles can have on its carbon footprint. It has taken measures to enhance fleet performance, including the use of custom-designed vehicles that weigh less than comparable models, new low-emission engine technology, and even low-drag mud flaps and belly fairings. Optimization of delivery routes has allowed Frito Lay to reduce the number of trucks it uses for distribution, an amazing feat given it is one of the fastest-growing consumer packaged goods companies in Canada. Strategic sequencing of vendors on routes also resulted in reducing the number of kilometres travelled by 3 percent and diesel consumption by 7 percent.[35]

More recently Frito Lay Canada became the first food manufacturer to make zero-emission electric vehicles part of its delivery fleet.[36] The initial six trucks introduced have a range of 60 kilometres per day, meeting the daily needs of the majority of routes from its distribution centres in Brampton, Ottawa, Surrey, and Laval. The electricity the vehicles use is offset by renewable energy credits, and even the batteries will be recycled at the end of their lives.

The company's sustainability initiatives go far beyond fleet management. Its efforts in other areas have resulted in reducing electricity consumption by more than 20 percent and water consumption by 30 percent since 1999. Steam stack heat recovery systems are in place at all its plants to capture waste heat from the exhaust manufacturing line and divert it to warm its buildings, to dry starch, and to heat water and oil.[37] Since 1999, it has also reused 40 million cardboard shipping cartons, the equivalent of saving more than 300 000 trees annually.

Commitment to sustainable growth is a core Frito Lay Canada value, one which helps the company keep pace with an ever-changing market. It views sustainability as a journey and thus has many more initiatives planned for the future.

Frito Lay's electric trucks are an important part of its sustainability initiatives.

---

lead time
The amount of time between the recognition that an order needs to be placed and the arrival of the needed merchandise at the seller's store, ready for sale.

system include reduced **lead time** (by eliminating the need for paper transactions by mail and overnight deliveries), increased product availability, and lower inventory investment. JIT systems lower inventory investments, but product availability actually increases.

To illustrate a JIT system, consider P&G's five-step process. Managers start with demand data, which they obtain directly from their retailers. They work closely with these retailers to develop sales forecasts and shipping schedules that better align P&G's production with demand at the retail store. This effort reduces both excess inventory and out-of-stock situations. Most importantly, P&G produces just enough to meet demand. To achieve this balance, the company has moved from producing every product once a month to a system in which it produces every item every day, which it then delivers to the customer the following day.[38]

Real Marketer Profile: MARK MONTPETIT

I'm sitting in the lounge at Billy Bishop Airport, sipping a latte; my flight has been delayed. I am about to fly to Calgary to present to the grocery director of one of Canada's largest retailers. I work in the world of category management; the way I explain it to friends is that I'm an expert in the science of grocery. I serve as an advisor to a major retailer on every facet of its category (grocery retailers divide their business into subcategories, such as popcorn), consulting on everything from pricing to assortment to feature activity.

I represent ConAgra Foods, a large North American consumer packaged goods company, with top-selling brands in the majority of categories in which it competes. Today, our North American yearly sales exceed $12 billion, with Canada contributing to this achievement.

You may be asking, "What's in it for the manufacturer?" Well, first of all, we are only advisors on categories where we are the market leader. Therefore, we are vested in the category and driven to see it succeed. We use our internal knowledge (e.g., upcoming product launches, investments in media) and align our corporate strategy with the retailer's strategy. This delivers better execution at retail: selling the right products at the right time.

You may also be asking, "How is this marketing?" While we affect many aspects of the marketing mix, we have the most impact on place. We bring retailers insights on how their shoppers shop specific categories. There is nothing more frustrating than not being able to find your favourite product in a retail environment. Retailers often have too many products on the shelf (causing out-of-stocks or creating a confusing section for the shopper). Sometimes retailers are simply not listing the products that the shopper is looking for. As a category analyst, I make sure that shoppers can find the products they are looking for and enhance their overall shopping experience.

The most challenging part of my job is also the most rewarding. The challenge in category management is selling your ideas to the retailers; while you must leverage data and research, you must often rely on your relationship with the change agent to ultimately influence change. While both sides may agree that your recommendation will benefit the category, you must often overcome competing priorities (e.g., time, corporate strategies). There is nothing more satisfying than instituting a change at a retailer and watching as both the retailer and manufacturer reap the rewards.

I've just received notice that my plane will soon be boarding. I have three presentations in my hand, which I will study throughout the three-hour trip. If the category director is to act on my recommendations, I will need to know each category better than the category managers themselves.

Learning Objectives Review

 LO1 Explain the importance of distribution and the interrelationships among distribution channels, supply chain management, and logistics management

Companies cannot take the distribution of products for granted. Appropriate distribution channels must be identified and channel members need to be convinced to carry these new products, both of which are integral to a successful distribution strategy. A distribution channel is the set of institutions and marketing activities that transfer the ownership of and move goods from the manufacturer or producer to the consumer. Supply chain management refers to the effort to coordinate suppliers, manufacturers, warehouses, stores, and transportation intermediaries so that the merchandise the customer wants is produced in the right quantities and sent to the right locations at the time the customer wants it. In this sense, the supply chain is considered to be longer and covers more aspects of the distribution strategy since it extends backwards to include suppliers. Logistics concentrates on the physical movement and control of the products, whereas supply chain management includes the managerial aspects of the process as well.

LO2 Identify how distribution channels add value to businesses and consumers

Without distribution channels, consumers would be forced to find raw materials, manufacture products, and somehow get them to where they could be used, all on their own. Each channel member adds value to the product by performing one of these functions. Supply chain management creates value for each firm in the chain and helps bind together many company functions, including manufacturing, inventory management, transportation, advertising, and marketing.

LO3 **Describe distribution channel design and management decisions and strategies**

Sometimes, particularly when firms are starting out, companies cannot choose their ideal partners but instead take any partners they can get to obtain the materials or customers they need. In general, the larger and more sophisticated the company, the more likely it will perform some supply chain activities itself rather than use third-party intermediaries. When deciding on the distribution channel structure, firms can choose from direct, indirect, and multichannel distribution. Firms that want as much market exposure as possible use intensive distribution, whereas firms that either want to maintain an exclusive image or are not large enough to sell to everyone tend to use an exclusive distribution strategy. Somewhere in the middle lies a selective distribution strategy.

LO4 **Explain how logistics and supply chain management affect distribution strategy**

For a supply chain to operate properly, the flow of information and merchandise must be coordinated, and supply chain members must work together to their mutual benefit. In more sophisticated supply chains, information flows seamlessly between supply chain members through EDI. Many of the best supply chains use a JIT or QR inventory management system, which provides the right amount of inventory just when it is needed. The JIT systems thus improve product availability and reduce inventory investments. The increasing use of RFID technology is expected to have a revolutionary impact on distribution channels, supply chain management, and logistics management in the future. The expectation is that the overall system of producing and delivering will become much more sophisticated and efficient.

The more closely aligned the supply chain members are with each other, the less likely there will be significant conflict. An administered supply chain occurs when a dominant and powerful supply chain member has control over the other members. In a contractual supply chain (e.g., franchising), coordination and control are dictated by contractual relationships between members. Corporate supply chains can operate relatively smoothly because one firm owns the various levels of the chains. Supply chains also can be effectively managed through strong relationships developed with supply chain partners. To create such relationships, the partners must trust each other, communicate openly, have compatible goals, and be willing to invest in each other's success.

Key Terms

- administered vertical marketing system, 403
- advanced shipping notice, 409
- channel conflict, 402
- contractual vertical marketing system, 403
- corporate vertical marketing system, 405
- dispatcher, 412
- distribution centre, 407
- distribution channel, 393
- distribution intensity, 399
- electronic data interchange (EDI), 409
- exclusive distribution, 401
- exclusive geographic territories, 401
- franchising, 404
- intensive distribution, 399
- just-in-time (JIT) inventory systems, 413
- lead time, 414
- logistics management, 395
- quick response (QR), 413
- radio frequency identification (RFID) tags, 412
- retailers, 394
- selective distribution, 401
- strategic relationship (partnering relationship), 410
- supply chain management, 394
- universal product code (UPC), 407
- vertical marketing system, 403
- wholesalers, 394

Concept Review

1. Explain why having a well thought out distribution strategy is important to a company's success.

2. Explain the factors that must be considered when designing a distribution strategy.

3. Explain the differences between direct, indirect, and multichannel distribution systems. What role do technologies and consumer behaviour play in the rise of multichannel distribution?

4. Describe the functions performed by intermediaries. Why would companies choose to have intermediaries fulfill these functions rather than perform them themselves?

5. Explain how customer expectations and channel member characteristics impact a company's distribution strategy.

6. Explain intensive, selective, and exclusive distribution intensity. Under what circumstances would it be best to use each of these strategies?

7. Describe how companies manage distribution channels by using vertical marketing systems.

8. Explain how supply chain management and logistics management add value to a company's consumer offerings.

9. Explain how supply chain management improves marketing activities.

10. What are the major elements of a logistics management system? Explain the benefits of a well-run just-in-time inventory management system.

Marketing Applications

1. Explain distribution strategy and identify the major activities that distribution channels, supply chain, and logistics management involve. Identify several ways that supply chain management adds value to a company's offerings, with regard to both consumers and business partners.

2. You are hired by a small bakery that is interested in distributing its product through supermarkets. The market for the bakery's products has been steadily growing and it is time to expand distribution now that the bakery has expanded its production capacity. You have an appointment with the manager of a local grocery chain. The manager is familiar with the bakery's products and is excited about the possibility of having them in the store. He presents the contract and you notice a $10,000 fee for stocking the product. When you ask about the fee, you are told it is simply the cost of doing business and that the bigger bakeries are not in favour of adding your product line to the chain. You know that the bakery cannot afford to pay the fee. What should you do now?

3. Discuss the advantages and disadvantages of Dell's decision to change from using a direct distribution strategy to a multichannel approach to distribution.

4. Research the "160 kilometre diet" trend and discuss how growing consumer awareness of shipping costs and environmental concerns has led to a push for more locally produced foods.

5. Give an example of a retailer that participates in an independent (conventional) supply chain and one involved in a vertical marketing system. Discuss the advantages and disadvantages of each.

6. In what ways can the flow of information be managed in the supply chain? How can the ready flow of information increase a firm's operating efficiencies?

7. Describe how B2B transactions might employ EDI to process purchase information. Considering the information discussed in Chapter 6 about B2B buying situations, determine which buying situation (new task, modified rebuy, or straight rebuy) would most likely align with the use of EDI technology. Justify your answer.

8. Discuss the advantages to a retailer such as SportChek of expending the time and effort to get merchandise floor-ready at either the point of manufacture or in the distribution centre rather than having retail store staff members do it in the stores. Provide the logic behind your answer.

9. Why would a large company such as Nike want to develop strategic partnerships with locally owned running stores? Describe what Nike would have to do to maintain such relationships.

10. You are hired as an assistant brand manager for a popular consumer product. One day in an emergency meeting, the brand manager informs the group that there is a problem with one of the suppliers and that he has decided to send you over to the manufacturing facilities to investigate the problem. When you arrive at the plant, you learn that a key supplier has become increasingly unreliable in terms of quality and delivery. You ask the plant manager why he doesn't switch suppliers since this is becoming a major problem for your brand. He informs you that the troubled supplier is his cousin, whose wife has been very ill, and he just can't switch right now. What course of action should you take?

Net Savvy

1. Dell is considered exemplary in its ability to manage its supply chain efficiently. Go to the company's website (www.dell.com) and go through the process of configuring a computer to purchase. Print a copy of the computer system you have designed, making note of the delivery date and price. Describe how Dell has revolutionized computer sales and delivery. Is there any indication that Dell has partnered with other companies to sell peripheral equipment such as printers or scanners? How would this partnership add value to customers?

2. The chapter vignette highlighted ways that Zara, a division of Inditex, successfully manages its supply chain. Visit Inditex's website (www.inditex.com) and review the company's commitment to social responsibility, particularly the section that pertains to its code of conduct. Considering the discussion in this chapter about strategic relationships, how does Inditex address the factors necessary for mutually beneficial partnerships according to its code of conduct?

Chapter Case Study

WALMART: PIONEER IN SUPPLY CHAIN MANAGEMENT[39]

Walmart dominates the retailing industry in terms of its sales revenue, its customer base, and its ability to drive down costs and deliver good value to customers. After all, the world's largest corporation takes pride in having received numerous accolades for its ability to continuously improve efficiency in the supply chain, while meeting its corporate mandate of "Save Money. Live Better."

Tight inventory management is legendary at Walmart; its just-in-time techniques, some of which are homegrown, allow the firm to boast one of the best supply chains in the world. Walmart has not only transformed its own supply chain, but also influenced how vendors throughout the world operate because it has the economic clout to request changes from suppliers and get them. For example, retailers everywhere are now placing much more emphasis on vendors' on-time and accurate deliveries. To meet these requirements, vendors have had to upgrade their inventory management and delivery systems to ensure they are doing business the way their large retailer customers prefer.[40] Recognized for its ability to obtain merchandise from global sources, Walmart also pioneered the strategy of achieving high levels of growth and profitability through its precision control of manufacturing, inventory, and distribution. Although the company is not unique in this regard, it is by far the most successful and most influential corporation of its kind and has put into practice various innovative techniques.

And when Walmart does something, it does it on a massive scale. Walmart's computer system, for example, is second only to that of the Pentagon in storage capacity. Its information systems analyze more than 10 million daily transactions from point-of-sale data and distribute their analysis in real time, both internally to its managers and externally via a satellite network to Walmart's many suppliers, who use the information for their production planning and order shipment.

Much of the popularity of supply chain management has been attributed to the success of Walmart's partnership with P&G. During the 1980s, the two collaborated in building a software system that linked P&G to Walmart's distribution centres, taking advantage of advances in the world's telecommunications infrastructure. When a Walmart store sold a particular P&G item, the information flowed directly to P&G's planning and control systems. When the inventory level of P&G's products at Walmart's distribution centre got to the reorder point, the system automatically alerted P&G to ship more products; this information in turn helped P&G plan its production. Walmart was also able to track when a P&G shipment arrived at one of its distribution warehouses, which enabled it to coordinate its own outbound shipments to stores. Both Walmart and P&G realized savings from the better inventory management and order processing, savings that in turn were passed on to Walmart's consumers through its low prices.

A history of success doesn't mean that Walmart executives can coast. Changes in social values, economic fluctuations, technological advances, and other market factors demand that Walmart continue its search for innovative ways to keep consumer prices down.

Walmart's Innovations

Walmart has pioneered many innovations in the purchase and distribution processes of the products it sells. More than 20 years ago, Walmart drove the adoption of UPC bar codes throughout the retail industry; it also pioneered the use of EDI for computerized ordering from vendors. Its hub-and-spoke distribution network ensures goods are brought to distribution centres around the country and then directed outward to thousands of stores, each of which are within a day's travel. Through the use of cross-docking, one of its best-known innovations, goods get trucked to a distribution centre from suppliers and then are immediately transferred to trucks bound for stores, without ever being placed into storage.[41] In addition, Walmart uses a dedicated fleet of trucks to ship goods from warehouses to stores in less than 48 hours and to replenish store inventories about twice a week. Thus, with flow-through logistics, the company speeds the movement of goods from its distribution centres to its retail stores around the world.

Today, the retail giant continues to push the supply chain toward greater and greater efficiency, prioritizing customer needs while employing new technologies and greener practices. One of the early adopters of using RFID technology to increase efficiency in its supply chain, Walmart discovered the value of balancing vision with technology maturity levels after mandating that its suppliers apply RFID tags to crates and pallets bound for its stores.[42] Some companies thrived by using the new technology. Others, including Walmart itself, ran into trouble. At the time of the mandate, RFID technology was in its infancy, and costs for planning, hardware, software, and training were prohibitive for many suppliers. Additionally, the technology was new enough that the industry lacked best practices for implementation. Indeed, it lacked any examples that might help newcomers avoid pitfalls. Walmart repealed its edict but continues to probe the usefulness of the technology.

In response to criticism from consumer groups, Walmart tackled environmental sustainability in its supply chain and, as is frequently the case because of the company's size, became a trendsetter for other retailers. After vowing to reduce its greenhouse gas emissions by the equivalent of taking nearly 4 million cars off the roads for a year, Walmart directed its suppliers to think green throughout the full product life cycle.[43] Suppliers are required to pay for sustainability efforts, a price most accept willingly to retain their relationship with Walmart. Many also recognize that reducing energy use will benefit them as energy costs rise. Harnessing energy, increasing recycling, reducing waste, and minimizing packaging and transportation all reduce cost in the supply chain and also appeal to today's consumers and preserve global resources.

In a third innovation, Walmart is consolidating its global sourcing.[44] The new model focuses on increasing the percentage of products purchased directly from suppliers and buying from global merchandising centres rather than through individual countries. Third-party procurement providers, who previously enjoyed a substantial business from the retail giant, will find themselves increasingly bypassed in the supply chain. In addition to eliminating the cost of a middleman, this effort may give Walmart increased control over inbound freight. Better control, in turn, can lower inventory costs. Thus, Walmart's continuous use of innovations leads to lower inventory and operating costs, which enables Walmart to keep its lean costs.

Walmart continues to hone its management of the flow of products and information among its suppliers, distribution centres, and individual stores through technology to increase its control of logistics and inventory. Thoughtful use of innovation has put Walmart at the top of the retailing game. Not all organizations can pull off this approach so well; Walmart is a unique case in which a single, very powerful firm took primary responsibility for improving performance across its own supply chain. By developing a superior supply chain management system, it has reaped the rewards of higher levels of customer service and satisfaction, lower production and transportation costs, and more productive use of its retail store space. Fundamentally, this accomplishment boils down to Walmart's ability to link together suppliers, manufacturers, distributors, retail outlets, and, ultimately, customers, regardless of their location. Although operational innovation isn't the only ingredient in Walmart's success, it has been a crucial building block for its strong competitive position.

Questions

1. How does an individual firm such as Walmart "manage" a supply chain, particularly considering that supply chains include multiple firms with potentially conflicting objectives? Describe some of the conflicts that could arise in such a circumstance.

2. What are some of the ways that Walmart's supply chain management system has provided it the benefits of higher levels of product availability and lower merchandise acquisition and transportation costs? Provide specific examples of each benefit.

 Practise and learn online with Connect. Connect allows you to practise important concepts at your own pace and on your own schedule, with 24/7 online access to an eBook, practice quizzes, interactivities, videos, study tools, additional resources, and more.

CHAPTER 13

Retailing

As fast as the dry cleaners, as friendly as the concierge at a hotel—can Apple stores leap tall buildings too?[1] Apple retail stores, crucial for the company's success and accounting for 20 percent of the company's revenue, have led to its recognition as one of *Fortune*'s Most Admired Companies. Before it opened its own retail stores, Apple allowed product sales through large retailers, which meant the company depended on these electronics retailers. The retailers had no special incentive to market Apple products, nor did they have the training necessary to sell the technologically advanced items. Apple therefore realized that the only way it could ensure its unique products really stood out was by taking the responsibility for selling into its own hands.

In the course of this decision, Apple spent significant time and effort designing its stores. The company leased warehouse space to create a prototype store that it could then replicate all over the country. After a few iterations, the ultimate Apple Store emerged, based on a design that considered how customers shop for products, not just the product categories themselves. Apple's largest flagship store in Boston looks like a glass cube with a glowing Apple logo. Even some of the smaller stores carry this theme, with ceilings that make the stores appear as if they are lit by the sun. In Canada, most Apple retail locations are housed in malls; yet, all are designed to be bright, open, and inviting. Computers are connected to the Internet, and customers are free to surf the Internet and chat online. If you are in need of an Internet café, Apple Stores even provide the service for free!

The Apple Store has become more than just a retailer to sell its iPods, iPhones, iPads, and so forth. The store offers an array of free services and is designed to allow customers to try out the different products before buying them. This

Learning Objectives

After studying this chapter, you should be able to

LO1 Explain the issues manufacturers consider when choosing retail partners

LO2 Identify what types of retailers are available to distribute products

LO3 Describe how retailers use the four Ps to create value for customers

LO4 Describe the multichannel options available to retailers

LO5 Explain why traditional retailers are evolving into multichannel retailers

benefit is especially important for early adopters who want to try new technologies as soon as they are available. For customers who need more assistance with products or who are pressed for time, the store offers personal shopping. A customer can make an appointment with a "Specialist" at a store to learn about the products of interest, without being obligated to make a purchase. For free technical services, the store offers a Genius Bar, with "Geniuses" who have been trained at the corporate headquarters on Apple products.

The stores also offer free workshops, focusing on everything from the basics of using Apple products to using Adobe Photoshop to create business presentations. For professional photographers, musicians, and filmmakers, workshops teach the detailed applications that they can use to optimize their finished products. The Apple stores also offer camps for children, workshops for families, and more.

When customers enter the store, a person wearing an orange shirt, the "Concierge," directs them where they need to go. The store avoids checkout counters; instead, salespeople use EasyPay: mobile wireless credit-card readers to check out customers right on the sales floor.

Apple also can brag about achieving the best-per-square-foot sales in the country—$4500 per square foot, far more than Best Buy at $930, and even Tiffany & Co. at $2746.[2] If companies had middle names, "innovative" would be Apple's. The company continues to demonstrate its willingness to do what it takes to be unique, while still producing the best technology and the best customer service in the retail industry. ..::

---

retailing
The set of business activities that add value to products and services sold to consumers for their personal or family use; includes products bought at stores, through catalogues, and over the Internet, as well as services such as fast-food restaurants, airlines, and hotels.

Retailing sits at the end of the supply chain, where marketing meets the consumer. As Apple realized before it started to open its retail stores, regardless of how strong a firm's strategy is or how great the product or service is, if it isn't available when the customer wants it, where he or she wants it, at the right price, and in the right size, colour, and style, it simply won't sell. It is primarily the retailer's responsibility to make sure that these customers' expectations are fulfilled.

In this chapter and as shown in the chapter roadmap, we explain how manufacturers choose retailers to carry their products and we discuss the types of retailers currently operating in Canada. Then we examine how retailers create value by implementing marketing mix strategies. We follow this with a discussion of how multichannel options are changing the face of retailing and the ongoing evolution toward multichannel marketing.

Retailing is defined as the set of business activities that add value to products and services sold to consumers for their personal or family use. Our definition of retailing includes products bought at stores, through catalogues, and over the Internet, as well as services such as fast-food restaurants, airlines, and hotels. Some retailers claim they sell at "wholesale" prices, but if they sell to customers for their personal use,

CHAPTER ROADMAP

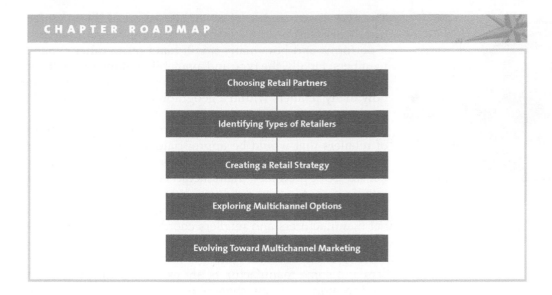

they are still retailers, regardless of how low their prices may be. Wholesalers, in contrast, are those firms engaged in buying, taking title to, often storing, and physically handling goods in large quantities, and then reselling the goods (usually in smaller quantities) to retailers or industrial or business users (as defined in Chapter 12).

Retailing today is changing, both in Canada and around the world. No longer do manufacturers rule many marketing channels, as they once did. Retailers such as Walmart, Carrefour (a French hypermarket), Home Depot, Loblaws, and Metro (a German retail conglomerate)[3]—the largest retailers in the world—dictate to their suppliers what should be made, how it should be configured, when it should be delivered, and, to some extent, what it should cost. These retailers are clearly in the driver's seat.

Retailing in the aggregate is a big business. Virtually every penny you personally spend, except for taxes, goes to retailers. Food, rent, clothing, tuition, insurance, and haircuts are all either retail services or goods provided by retailers. Even nonprofit organizations such as the Salvation Army, Goodwill Industries, and the Ontario Science Centre have retail operations. Canadian retail sales in 2009 were $448.6 billion,[4] representing more than 227 000 retail establishments. Retailing is Canada's third largest industry by size, employing approximately 2 million people.[5]

This chapter examines how and why manufacturers use retailers. The manufacturer's strategy depends on its overall market power and on how consistent a new product or product line is with its current offerings.

Exhibit 13.1 illustrates four factors manufacturers consider when developing strategies for working with retailers.[6] In choosing retail partners, the first factor, manufacturers assess how likely it is for certain retailers to carry their products. Manufacturers also consider where their target customers expect to find the products, because those are exactly the stores in which they want to place their products.

EXHIBIT 13.1   Factors for Establishing a Relationship with Retailers

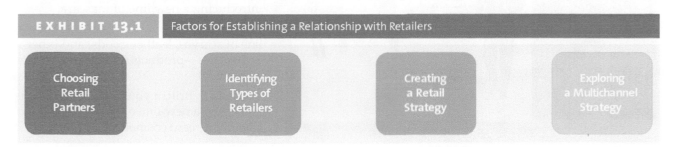

Even nonprofit organizations such as Goodwill Industries have retail operations.

multichannel strategy
Selling in more than one channel (e.g., store, catalogue, kiosk, and Internet).

The overall size and level of sophistication of the manufacturer will determine how many of the supply chain functions it performs and how many it will hand off to other channel members. Finally, the type and availability of the product and the image the manufacturer wishes to portray will determine how many retailers within a geographic region will carry the products.

In the second factor, manufacturers identify the types of retailers that would be appropriate to carry its products. Although the choice is often obvious—such as a supermarket for fresh produce—manufacturers may have a choice of retailer types for some products.

As we discussed in Chapter 12, a hallmark of a strong marketing channel is that manufacturers and retailers coordinate their efforts in it. In the third factor, manufacturers and retailers therefore develop their strategy by implementing the four Ps.

Finally, many retailers and some manufacturers are exploring a **multichannel strategy** in which they sell in more than one channel (e.g., store, catalogue, kiosk, and Internet). The fourth factor therefore consists of examining the circumstances in which sellers may prefer to adopt a particular strategy. Although these factors are listed consecutively, manufacturers may consider them all simultaneously or in a different order.

L01 Choosing Retail Partners

Imagine trying to buy a suit for a job interview without being able to visit a retailer. You would have to figure out exactly what size, colour, and style of suit you wanted. Then you'd have to contact various manufacturers, whether in person, by phone, or over the Internet, and order the suit. Assuming it fit you reasonably well, you might still need to take it to a tailor to have the sleeves shortened. Then you'd have to go through the same process for a shirt or blouse, accessories, and shoes. It would not be very convenient.

Moores Clothing for Men creates value by helping men put it all together. Their wardrobe consultants provide fashion advice, and their tailors make sure everything fits properly.

Retailers such as Moores Clothing for Men create value by pulling it all together for you. The store offers a broad selection of suits, shirts, ties, and other accessories that it has carefully chosen in advance. You can see, touch, feel, and try on each item while in the store. You can buy one suit or shirt at a time or buy several shirts to go with your new suit. Finally, the store provides a salesperson to help you coordinate your outfit and a tailor to make the whole thing fit perfectly.

When choosing retail partners, manufacturers must look at the basic channel structure, where their target customers expect to find the products, and channel member characteristics. As discussed in Chapter 12, distribution intensity is also a factor to be considered. Consider the following scenarios:

- **Scenario 1**: Cosmetics conglomerate Estée Lauder's subsidiary brand MAC is introducing a new line of mascara.
- **Scenario 2**: Estée Lauder is introducing a line of scarves, leather goods, and other accessories—products not currently in its assortment.
- **Scenario 3**: Britt, a young entrepreneur, is launching a new line of environmentally friendly (green) cosmetics.

Each of these scenarios is different and requires the manufacturer to consider different alternatives for reaching its target markets through retailers.

Channel Structure

The level of difficulty a manufacturer has in getting retailers to purchase its products is determined by the degree to which the channel is vertically integrated, as described in Chapter 12; the degree to which the manufacturer has a strong brand or is otherwise desirable in the market; and the relative power of the manufacturer and retailer.

Scenario 1 represents a corporate vertical marketing system. Because MAC is made by Estée Lauder and operates its own stores, when the new mascara line gets introduced, the stores will simply receive the new line automatically. They have no choice.

However, when an established firm such as Estée Lauder enters a new market with scarves, leather, and accessories, as is the case in Scenario 2, it cannot just place the products with any retailer. It must determine where its customers would expect to find higher-end scarves, leather goods, and accessories, and then use its established relationships with cosmetics buyers, the power of its brand, and its overall reputation to leverage its position in this new product area.

In Scenario 3, our young entrepreneur Britt would have an even more difficult time getting a retailer to buy and sell her green cosmetics line, because she lacks power in the marketplace—she is small, and her brand is unknown. It would be difficult to get buyers to see her, let alone consider her line. She might face relatively high listing fees (see Chapter 12) just to get space on retailers' shelves. But like Estée Lauder in Scenario 2, when choosing retailers to which to sell, Britt should consider where the end customer expects to find her products, as well as some important retailer characteristics.

Customer Expectations

From a retailer's perspective, it is important to know from which manufacturers its customers want to buy. Manufacturers, in contrast, need to know where their target market customers expect to find their products and those of their competitors. Customers generally expect to find certain products at some stores but not at others. For example, Estée Lauder would not choose to sell to Zellers or Giant Tiger because its customers would not expect to shop at those stores for high-end cosmetics or clothing. Instead, Zellers might carry less expensive cosmetic brands, such as Revlon and Maybelline, and bargain closeouts probably appear at Giant Tiger. But Estée Lauder's customers would definitely expect to find its clothing offerings at major department stores such as The Bay and Sears.

Channel Member Characteristics

Several factors pertaining to the channel members themselves will help determine the channel structure. Generally, the larger and more sophisticated the channel member, the less likely that it will use supply chain intermediaries. Britt will probably use a group of independent salespeople to help sell her line of green cosmetics, whereas a large manufacturer such as Estée Lauder will use its own sales force that already has existing relationships in the industry. In the same way, an independent grocery store might buy merchandise from a wholesaler; but, Walmart, the world's largest grocer, only buys directly from the manufacturer. Larger firms often find that by performing the channel functions themselves, they can gain more control, be more efficient, and save money.

Identifying Types of Retailers   `L02`

Although it may seem clear which type of retailer Estée Lauder and Britt may wish to pursue when attempting to place their new lines, the choice is not always easy.

Manufacturers need to understand the general characteristics of different types of retailers so they can determine the best channels for their product. For instance, the characteristics of a retailer that are important to a food manufacturer may be quite different than those of a cosmetics manufacturer. In the next few sections, we examine the various types of retailers, identify some major players, and discuss some of the issues facing each type.

Food Retailers

The food retailing landscape is changing dramatically. Not too long ago, people shopped for food primarily at traditional grocery stores. Today, however, you can buy food at drugstores, discount stores, warehouse clubs, and convenience stores. Pharmacy chains such as Shoppers Drug Mart offer milk, bread, and even fresh fruit in some locations. Walmart and the Real Canadian Superstore both provide supercentres whose product mix contains 30 to 40 percent food items. Food sales represent about 50 percent of the total sales in warehouse clubs such as Costco. Convenience stores now offer more than a slushie and gasoline; for example, Petro-Canada Neighbours stores provide upscale sandwiches and salads. And retailers such as Zellers and IKEA have in-store restaurants, making it easy for customers to shop longer. And, of course, restaurants also compete for consumers' food dollars. The characteristics of the three major categories of food retailers—**conventional supermarkets**, **big-box food retailers**, and convenience stores—are summarized in Exhibit 13.2.

All this competition can mean trouble for traditional grocery stores. Yet some continue to thrive because they offer their target customers great value—they are conveniently located, make shopping easy, have fair prices, and find special products and services that are important to their customers. Pete's Frootique, a Halifax-based grocery store, effectively competes on selection and service. Knowledgeable staff members offer information about the selection of produce, storage, and cooking tips, and an in-house registered dietitian helps shoppers understand which foods can re-energize their health.[7]

conventional supermarket Offers groceries, meat, and produce with limited sales of nonfood items, such as health and beauty aids and general merchandise, in a self-service format.

big-box food retailer Comes in three types: supercentre, hypermarket, and warehouse club; larger than a *conventional supermarket*; carries both food and nonfood items.

EXHIBIT 13.2	Food Retailer Characteristics	
Category	**Description**	**Examples**
Conventional Supermarket	Offers groceries, meat, and produce with limited sales of nonfood items, such as health and beauty aids and general merchandise, in a self-service format.	Safeway is a popular supermarket in western Canada; Sobeys is common on the East Coast.
Big-Box Food Retailer	Comes in three types: supercentres, hypermarkets, and warehouse clubs. Larger than conventional supermarkets, they carry both food and nonfood items.	Supercentres and warehouse clubs are popular in Canada, whereas hypermarkets tend to flourish in Europe and South America. Hypermarkets (Carrefour) and warehouse clubs (Costco) generally carry a greater percentage of food.
Convenience Store	Provides a limited number of items at convenient locations in small stores with speedy checkout.	Stores such as 7-Eleven generally charge higher prices than most other types of food stores. Most convenience stores also sell gasoline, which accounts for more than 55 percent of their annual sales.

General Merchandise Retailers

The main types of **general merchandise retailers** are discount stores, specialty stores, category specialists, department stores, drugstores, off-price retailers, and extreme value retailers. Many of these general merchandise retailers sell through multiple channels, such as the Internet and catalogues, as discussed later in this chapter.

Discount Stores A **discount store** offers a broad variety of merchandise, limited service, and low prices. Walmart and Zellers dominate the discount store industry in Canada and vie for similar target markets. But because their competencies are slightly distinct, they both can survive. Walmart pioneered the everyday low-price concept, and its efficient operations have allowed it to offer the lowest-priced basket of merchandise in every market in which it competes—which doesn't necessarily mean that Walmart has the lowest price on every item in every market. But it does try to be the lowest across a wide variety. Zellers, in contrast, has concentrated on merchandising. Opting for quality and style, Zellers offers exclusive lines by Martha Stewart and Hilary Duff, providing good value without being cheap. Recently Zellers stores have been sold to U.S. retailing giant, Target Corp., which plans to convert about 150 of the stores to Target by 2014.

Specialty Stores **Specialty stores** concentrate on a limited number of complementary merchandise categories in relatively small stores. These stores tailor their retail strategy toward very specific market segments by offering deep but narrow assortments and sales associate expertise. For example, Payless ShoeSource is the largest specialty family footwear retailer in the western hemisphere. Payless stores feature fashionable, quality footwear and accessories for women, men, and children at affordable prices in a self-selection format.

Estée Lauder's MAC line of cosmetics sells in the company's own retail specialty stores, as well as in some department stores. Specialty stores would be excellent outlets for the new lines by Estée Lauder and Britt. Customers likely expect to find Estée Lauder lines of scarves, leather, and accessories in women's apparel, gift, or leather stores. Britt's line of green cosmetics would fit nicely in a cosmetics specialty store such as Sephora.

Sephora, France's leading perfume and cosmetic chain—a division of the luxury goods conglomerate LVMH (Louis Vuitton–Moët Hennessy)—is an example of an innovative specialty store concept. In Canada, prestigious cosmetics are typically sold in department stores. Each brand has a separate counter and a commissioned salesperson is stationed behind the counter to help customers. Sephora is a cosmetic and perfume specialty store offering a deep assortment in a self-service, 550–840-square-metre format. Its stores provide more than 15 000 SKUs and more than 200 brands, including its own, private-label brand. Merchandise is grouped by product category, with the brands displayed alphabetically so customers can locate them easily. Customers are free to shop and experiment on their own. Product testing is encouraged. The knowledgeable salespeople, always available to assist customers, are paid a salary by Sephora, unlike department store cosmetic salespeople, who are compensated in part by incentives provided by the vendors. The low-key, open-sell environment results in customers spending more time shopping.

Category Specialists A **category specialist** offers a narrow variety but a deep assortment of merchandise. Some are like large specialty stores, such as Paderno (home and kitchen tools) or Chapters Indigo (books); others resemble discount stores in appearance and have similar low prices but offer a more concentrated assortment of goods, such as Future Shop (consumer electronics) or RONA (home improvement). Most category specialists use a self-service approach, but some, such as Home Depot,

---

general merchandise retailer
May be a *discount store, specialty store, category specialist, department store, drugstore, off-price retailer,* or *extreme value retailer*; may sell through multiple channels, such as the Internet and catalogues.

discount store
Offers a broad variety of merchandise, limited service, and low prices.

specialty store
Concentrates on a limited number of complementary merchandise categories in a relatively small store.

category specialist
Offers a narrow variety but a deep assortment of merchandise.

Sephora is an innovative specialty store that sells cosmetics.

provide extensive customer service. Because category specialists offer such an extensive assortment in a particular category, they can so overwhelm the category that other retailers have difficulty competing; in these cases, the specialists are frequently called **category killers**.

category killer
Offers an extensive assortment in a particular category, so overwhelming the category that other retailers have difficulty competing.

Department Stores   Department stores refer to those retailers that carry many different types of merchandise (broad variety) and lots of items within each type (deep assortment), offer some customer services, and are organized into separate departments to display their merchandise. Department stores often resemble a collection of specialty shops, including women's, men's, and children's clothing and accessories; home furnishings and furniture; and kitchenwares and small appliances.

With the demise of Eaton's, the largest remaining department store chains in Canada are Sears and The Bay. Other store chains are very diverse. Some, such as Sears, carry less expensive products and compete more closely with discount stores, whereas others, such as Holt Renfrew, sell expensive, exclusive merchandise and compete with high-end specialty store chains.

drugstore
A specialty store that concentrates on health and personal grooming merchandise, though pharmaceuticals may represent more than 60 percent of its sales.

Department stores have lost market share to specialty stores, discount stores, and category specialists in recent years. They seem to have gotten stuck in the middle, between those retailers that provide a better value at lower prices and those that offer more complete and fashionable assortments and better customer service, according to consumer perceptions. But they are fighting back with a vengeance. The Bay has begun placing a greater emphasis on high-fashion, private-label merchandise than it did in the past.

Drugstores **Drugstores** are specialty stores that concentrate on health and personal grooming merchandise, though pharmaceuticals often represent more than 60 percent of their sales. The largest drugstore chains in Canada—Shoppers Drug Mart (Pharmaprix in Quebec), Jean Coutu, PharmaSave and London Drugs[8]—face a major challenge because of the low margins they earn on prescription drugs; health insurance companies and government programs pay most of the cost of many prescriptions, and the health insurance companies negotiate substantially lower prices with drugstores. These drugstores therefore are attempting to make up for their lost profits on prescriptions by concentrating their efforts on nonpharmaceutical products. General merchandise has long been a staple in drugstores, but food, and particularly fresh food such as milk and fruit, are relatively new additions to their assortment.[9]

Off-Price Retailers **Off-price retailers**, such as Winners, Designer Depot, and HomeSense, offer an inconsistent assortment of merchandise at relatively low prices. They typically buy from manufacturers or other retailers with excess inventory or at the end of a season for one-fourth to one-fifth the original wholesale price. Because of the way these retailers buy, customers can never be confident that the same type of merchandise will be in stock each time they visit the store. Different bargains also will be available on each visit. To improve their offerings' consistency, some off-price retailers complement their opportunistically bought merchandise with merchandise purchased at regular wholesale prices. In addition to their low prices, the key to off-price retailers' success is the treasure hunt environment they create.

Extreme value retailers are a subset of off-price retailers and one of the fastest growing retailing segments. **Extreme value retailers**, such as Dollarama, are general merchandise discount stores found in lower-income urban or rural areas. They are much smaller than traditional discount stores, usually less than 840 square metres.

Stores such as Home Depot are known as category specialists because they offer a narrow variety but a deep assortment of merchandise.

off-price retailer
A type of retailer that offers an inconsistent assortment of merchandise at relatively low prices.

L03

extreme value retailer
A general merchandise discount store found in lower-income urban or rural areas.

Creating a Retail Strategy

In a time when more and more Canadian consumers are value conscious, retailers need strategies that deliver. Today's consumers shop at any retailer or through any retailing channel they feel provides the best value for their money. And the lines between the different types of retailers are increasingly becoming blurred as retailers expand the range of their merchandise and services. For example, Walmart, and to a lesser extent Shoppers Drug Mart and Canadian Tire, are moving into the grocery business. Thus, it is extremely important for retailers to develop effective retailing strategies and market positioning in order to differentiate themselves in the increasingly competitive landscape and give customers a compelling reason to shop at their stores.

In developing an effective retailing strategy, many of the principles we discussed in Chapter 7 on segmentation, targeting, and positioning can be very helpful. Retailers must first obtain a deep understanding of the consumers in their markets—their attitudes, behaviours, and preferences. Then they must use this knowledge of their consumers to develop market segments and select those segments they want to serve. Retailers that try to be all things to all people often end up not being able to serve

House&Home
STYLE FOR LIVING™

GLUCKSTEINHOME

25%ff

All pillows and
mattress pads
Reg. $12.99 to $99.99
Sale $9.74 to $74.99
Also: 40% off All duvets
by GLUCKSTEINHOME
and HOUSE & HOME.
Reg. $99.99 to $619.99
Sale $59.99 to $371.99
Shown: GLUCKSTEINHOME.
Selection will vary by store.

50%ff

New! All
window panels
& drapery
hardware
After sale $9.99 to $169.99
Sale $4.99 to $84.99

*You can get House &
Home private-label
bedding only at The Bay.*

any particular segment appropriately and soon find themselves in serious trouble. Once the target market is selected, retailers must develop product merchandising, pricing, promotion, and place strategies to reach and serve these consumers. These elements must be closely coordinated so that they portray a consistent and clear positioning so consumers know what type of customers the retailer is targeting and how they want to serve them. For example, a retailer such as Harry Rosen, which wants to be perceived as a high-end clothing retailer, carries high-quality clothing, offers personalized services, and charges premium prices for its merchandise. Harry Rosen's store image and atmospherics (place) also portray an image of affluence and professionalism—an image that is consistent with its customers' perceptions of themselves.

Recognizing the importance of creating effective retailing strategies, Loblaw has created many different store formats for different target customers. For example, Loblaw's Real Canadian Superstores are for customers who want high-quality products, a wide range of product assortments, and high levels of service, and are willing to pay a premium; but, Loblaw's No Frills stores are for customers who want to pay much lower prices and don't mind narrower product assortments and less service.

We now examine in more detail how retailers use the four Ps in their retail strategy to create value for consumers.

Product

A typical grocery store carries 30 000 to 40 000 different items; a regional department store might carry as many as 200 000. Providing the right mix of merchandise and services that satisfies the needs of the target market is one of retailers' most fundamental activities. Offering assortments gives customers choice and helps them attract new and existing customers. For example, The Bay added designer shoe lines to its mix when its analysis showed that footwear sales trends were rising, while clothing and accessory sales were falling.[10] And HMV Canada shook up music retailing with the addition of headphones, books, gadgets, and clothing designed to attract teens and twenty-somethings looking to make a fashion statement into its stores.[11]

To reduce transportation costs and handling, manufacturers typically ship cases of merchandise to retailers, such as cartons of mayonnaise or boxes of blue shirts. Because customers generally don't want or need to buy more than one of the same item, retailers break the cases and sell customers the smaller quantities they desire. Manufacturers don't like to store inventory because their factories and warehouses are typically not available to customers. Consumers don't want to store more than they need because it takes up too much space. Neither group likes to store inventory that isn't being used because doing so ties up money that could be used for something else. Retailers thus provide value to both manufacturers and customers by performing the storage function, though many retailers are beginning to push their suppliers to hold the inventory until they need it. (Recall our discussion of just-in-time inventory systems in Chapter 12.)

It is difficult for retailers to distinguish themselves from their competitors through the merchandise they carry because competitors can purchase and sell many of the same popular brands. So many retailers have developed private-label brands (also called store brands), which are products developed and marketed by a retailer and available only from that retailer. For example, if you want House & Home bedding, you have to go to The Bay.

Price

Price helps define the value of both the merchandise and the service, and the general price range of a particular store helps define its image. Although both Banana Republic and Old Navy are owned by The Gap, their images could not be more different. Banana Republic prices its merchandise to attract young professionals, whereas Old Navy aims to satisfy trendy, price-sensitive consumers. Thus, when a manufacturer such as Estée Lauder considers which of these stores is most appropriate for its new line of scarves, leather, and accessories, it must keep customers' perceived images of these retailers' price–quality relationship in mind.

As we showed in Chapter 11, there is much more to pricing than simply adding a markup onto a product's cost. Manufacturers must consider at what price they will sell the product to retailers so that both the manufacturer and the retailer can make a reasonable profit. At the same time, both the manufacturer and the retailer are concerned about what the customer is willing to pay. Canadian Tire has addressed this in part by launching a mobile app for iPhone, BlackBerry, and Android smartphones. The app allows in-store shoppers to scan product bar codes to get price, availability, and product information, as well as ratings and reviews by other customers. Shoppers can also access the Canadian Tire weekly flyer to check out current sales and special pricing.[12] This information can shape customer expectations of price by enabling them to quickly and easily get the most current prices.

Price must always be aligned with the other elements of the retail mix: product, promotion, place, personnel, and presentation. For instance, you would not expect to pay $20 for a chocolate bar sold in your local grocery store, but a limited-edition bar, made of fine Belgian dark chocolate, packaged in a gold-plated keepsake box, sold at Holt Renfrew, might be a real steal at $20. Entrepreneurial Marketing 13.1 describes a man with incredible vision and a concept based on very inexpensive merchandise.

Promotion

Retailers and manufacturers know that good promotion, both within their retail environments and in the media, can mean the difference between flat sales and a growing consumer base. Advertising in traditional media such as newspapers, magazines, and television continues to be important to get customers into the stores. But as seen in Social Media Marketing 13.1, new media vehicles that communicate with consumers electronically are becoming increasingly important. Once in the store, however, retailers use displays and signs, placed at the point of purchase or in strategic areas such as the end of aisles, known as end caps, to inform customers and stimulate purchases of the featured products.

A coordinated effort between the manufacturer and retailer helps guarantee that the customer receives a cohesive message. The extent to which manufacturers work with their retailers to coordinate promotional activities can ensure that both the manufacturer and the retailer can maintain their consistent images. For example, Estée Lauder might work with its most important retailers to develop advertising and point-of-sale signs. It may even help defray the costs of advertising by paying all or a portion of the advertising's production and media costs, an agreement called **cooperative (co-op) advertising**.

Store credit cards and gift cards are more subtle forms of promotion that also facilitate shopping. Retailers also might offer pricing promotions—such as coupons, rebates, in-store or online discounts, or perhaps buy-one-get-one-free offers—to attract

cooperative (co-op) advertising
An agreement between a manufacturer and retailer in which the manufacturer agrees to defray some advertising costs.

Entrepreneurial Marketing 13.1   Giant Tiger Stakes Its Territory

On May 13, 1961, Gordon Reid opened his first Giant Tiger store in Ottawa. The business concept was simple: keep the cost of operation low and sell a large volume of merchandise at everyday low prices. The large general merchandise store aimed to offer everything a customer could need, all under one roof. This all-Canadian company has now grown to 190 stores, employing more than 6500 people, who all work in support of that same original idea.[13]

The main thrusts of Giant Tiger's roaring success are maintaining low rent, using efficient transportation, and keeping the cost of store operations low. Tiger Trucking is the private fleet that transports merchandise for the chain to the majority of stores, which are in Ontario and Quebec. In store, employees work directly with customers on the store floor. Many stores don't even advertise a phone number, because having an employee answer the phone would increase costs and take him or her away from helping customers![14] The company's refund policy is clear: if you present a receipt, you get your money back, no matter how many days have passed.[15]

Each store offers a large assortment of casual clothing and footwear, everyday needs in groceries, cleaning supplies, housewares, stationery, toys, and health and beauty products. The identical quality and fashion items offered by major chain stores are sold at Giant Tiger at lower prices. Discontinued items and one-offs are available frequently for special deals on a store-by-store basis. Beyond the Giant Tiger brand, the GT Boutique (www.gtboutique.com) has been developed to showcase new fashions and trends. A deep-rooted commitment to the community shows that Giant Tiger truly cares about its customers. Along with contributing funds to local charities and supporting fundraising events, many storefronts feature murals that not only beautify, but also bring attention to political issues.[16]

People love to shop at Giant Tiger stores because their merchandise is inexpensive, the stores are conveniently located and easy to shop in, and treasures are found every day among the basics.

The success shows no signs of slowing. A franchise agreement with Northwest Company in 2002 to open 72 new stores made a big impact, with the first 20 stores in cities such as Regina, Winnipeg, Edmonton, and Calgary bringing a flood of success for Giant Tiger.[17] Also, 2005 brought expansion stores in and around the Greater Toronto Area. The 2006 federal government announcement to lower the goods and services tax to 6 percent was even made from an Ottawa-area Giant Tiger store! Press coverage of events like this and returning loyal customers have helped keep Giant Tiger's bottom line strong. Despite tough competitors such as Walmart and Zellers, Giant Tiger is a homegrown retailer that Canadians continue to loyally support.

consumers and stimulate sales. These promotions play a very important role in driving traffic to retail locations, increasing the average purchase size, and creating opportunities for repeat purchases. But retail promotions also are valuable to customers; they inform customers about what is new and available and how much it costs.

In addition to more traditional forms of promotion, many retailers are devoting more resources to their overall retail environment as a means to promote and showcase what the store has to offer. Their displays of merchandise, both in the store and in windows, have become an important form of promotion. For example, Shoppers Drug Mart has redesigned its cosmetics counters as Beauty Boutiques. Since many shopping activities can be rather mundane, those retailers who can distinguish themselves with unusual and exciting store atmospherics add value to the shopping experience. G.A.P. Adventures™, founded by Calgarian Bruce Poon Tip, has opened concept stores in Vancouver, Toronto, Calgary, Melbourne, and New York City where visitors can watch G.A.P. Adventures™ documentaries featuring travellers on expeditions around the world.[18] And Mark's (formerly Mark's Work Wearhouse) installed a custom walk-in freezer in stores to allow customers to test out the warmth of

Social Media Marketing 13.1

Dell Harnesses the Power of Social Media to Drive Sales

Dell is well-known as the company that carved out a niche in the computer industry by selling direct to consumer, first by telephone and then by sales through its website. You'd think that selling online by using social media tools would be a natural progression. But it wasn't so straightforward.

Dell's chief blogger, Lionel Menchaca, wasn't convinced that Twitter had business potential at first. However, trying new social media tools was part of his job so he opened a Twitter account. He tweeted each time he posted on the company blog, Direct2Dell. He soon discovered that when he posted a link on Twitter, people immediately clicked through.[19] He used this learning to justify a commitment to selling through Twitter.

Dell started selling through @DellOutlet in June 2007. Major deals and discounts are tweeted out to Twitter followers multiple times in a week. Stephanie Nelson, who manages the account, says almost every post includes a coupon or a link to a sale, and about half of the posts are Twitter-exclusive deals.[20] Incentives like these helped Dell build its number of followers to more than 1.4 million near the end of 2009.[21]

It took 18 months to generate the first million dollars in sales, but only six months more to double that figure. To date, Dell has earned just over $3 million on Twitter. This pales next to the company's overall revenue ($12.3 billion in the first quarter of 2009 alone).[22] Nevertheless, the model represents high growth potential for the company, with social media opening up a new avenue for developing sales and relationships with its customers.

For Dell, social media is a lead generator and a forum for observing correlations between people making comments about its products and then buying them. The company discovered that people who read customer ratings and reviews were 138 percent more likely to make a purchase.[23]

---

clothing before buying. It's all part of the company's new merchandising strategy. In addition to walk-in freezers, Mark's also lets customers try out anti-slip work boots on ramps in the store that are covered with roof shingles, tiles, rocks or stainless steel to mimic conditions found on construction sites. These features enhance customers' visual and sensory experiences, provide them with educational information, and increase the store's sales potential by enabling customers to "try before they buy."

Sears Canada has also found new ways to better connect with shoppers, especially younger ones. It now offers Skype technology in 10 of its trendy fashion stores. Based on its research, Sears found that many young women shop with friends, with one of them serving as the style expert.[24] Skype allows shoppers to have instant access to a friend's virtual opinion by connecting them to a style expert who isn't physically at the store.

A variety of factors influence whether customers will actually buy once they are in the store, some of which are quite subtle. Consumers' perceptions of value and their subsequent patronage are heavily influenced by their perceptions of the store's "look and feel." Consider the difference between having coffee at Tim Hortons versus Second Cup. In which outlet would you rather spend time socializing with your friends? Music, colour, scent, and crowding can also significantly impact the overall shopping experience.[25] Therefore, the extent to which stores offer a more pleasant shopping experience fosters a good mood, resulting in greater spending.

Personal selling and customer service representatives are also part of the overall promotional package. Retailers must provide services that make it easier to buy and use products. As a part of the Dairy Farmers of Canada's Cooking with Cheese campaign, brand ambassadors were sent to stores armed with handheld scanners. In the stores, the ambassadors could scan items in shoppers' carts on the spot and then print out

Shoppers Drug Mart redesigned its cosmetic counters as Beauty Boutiques to better display and promote merchandise.

A walk-in freezer at Mark's in Edmonton lets customers test out how warm clothing really is before they buy it.

share of wallet
The percentage of the customer's purchases made from a particular retailer.

cheese-friendly recipes and dinner suggestions based on the ingredients.[26] Retail associates, whether in the store, on the phone, or over the Internet, provide customers with information about product characteristics and availability. They can also facilitate the sale of products or services that consumers perceive as complicated, risky, or expensive, such as an air conditioning unit or a diamond ring. Manufacturers can play an important role in getting retail sales and service associates prepared to sell their products. Estée Lauder, for example, could conduct seminars about how to use and sell a new line of cosmetics. In some retail firms, these salesperson and customer service functions are being augmented, or even replaced, by technology used through in-store kiosks, the Internet, or self-checkout lanes.

The knowledge retailers can gain from their store personnel and customer relationship management (CRM) databases is key for developing loyal customers and operating loyalty programs. Traditionally, retailers treated all their customers the same way; but, today, the most successful retailers concentrate on providing more value to their best customers. Using direct salesperson contact, targeted promotions, and services, they attempt to increase their **share of wallet**—the percentage of the customer's purchases made from that particular retailer—with their best customers. For instance, Internet retailers can use consumer information to provide a level of personal service that previously was available only through expensive salespeople in the best specialty stores.

Place

Retailers already have realized that convenience is a key ingredient to success, and an important aspect of this success is convenient locations.[27] As the old cliché claims, the three most important things in retailing are "location, location, location." Many customers choose stores on the basis of where they are located, which makes great locations a competitive advantage that few rivals can duplicate. For instance, once Starbucks saturates a market by opening in the best locations, it will be difficult for a new competitor to break into that same market—where would it put its stores?

In pursuit of better and better locations, retailers are experimenting with different options to reach their target markets. Canada's largest drugstore retailer, Shoppers Drug Mart, now has some stores that are open 24 hours a day so customers can pick up prescriptions and other items at any time.

To offer more convenience, some Shoppers Drug Mart stores are open 24 hours a day so customers can pick up prescriptions or other items at any time.

The Changing Retail Landscape

Now and in the future, success for retailers will mean learning how to compete in a value-driven world. Remember, value doesn't just mean low price. It means getting maximized benefit for the money. Retailers that provide great value, such as Costco, were once known largely as a destination for monthly stock-up trips. But today, they have penetrated the weekly shopping routine. Consumers of all ages, nearly all income groups, and practically all segments have undertaken the "shift to value." Consumers have fundamentally changed their reference points for both price and quality, such that they have been trained to expect significantly lower prices from

Sustainable Marketing 13.1   IKEA's Never Ending List

For most companies, sustainability means taking small steps in the hopes of making a positive long-term impact. However, initiatives by IKEA are taking a giant leap. As the world's largest furniture retailer, any sustainability efforts by IKEA will make a noticeable difference. With more than 10 million customers in Canada, changes in IKEA's 11 Canadian stores make a huge difference.

Since its beginning in 1943 as a household goods catalogue by young entrepreneur Ingvar Kamprad, IKEA has built on a simple concept: "offer quality furniture at the lowest possible price to contribute to helping more people live a better life at home." Since then, IKEA has evolved from a household goods catalogue to a global furniture giant, while still working to help people live a better life.

IKEA has designated preferred parking spaces to reward customers who drive hybrid or fuel-efficient vehicles.

The company embraces sustainability in many ways, from partnerships with other organizations, to its physical stores and its relationships with customers. With the introduction of its Never Ending List in 2010, IKEA publicly demonstrates its commitment to sustainability by outlining its accomplishments and setting goals to expand its sustainability initiatives.[28] The company has international initiatives with UNICEF, Save the Children, and the WWF. It also has a long-standing partnership with Tree Canada. At its retail locations, IKEA has in-store recycling bins and has created green parking spaces to reward customers who drive hybrid or fuel-efficient vehicles. Additionally, it is the first Canadian retailer to begin phasing out incandescent

light bulbs. IKEA not only integrates changes inside its stores, but also takes its initiative outside; it installed solar panels to 150 stores and distribution centres for electricity production.

Along with its in-store efforts, IKEA is making an effort to help customers consume in a more environmentally friendly manner. IKEA has launched a free shuttle bus service in Toronto so that customers can use a more sustainable method of transport and leave their cars at home. In addition, IKEA offers free delivery for customers who use the bus.[29] Its Bag the Bag program encouraged customers to be more environmentally conscious by charging 5 cents for plastic bags. The program raised $280,000, which was donated to Tree Canada.[30] As of 2009, IKEA no longer provides plastic bags. Instead, customers are encouraged to purchase the recyclable blue bag for 59 cents, to cut down on plastic bag waste.

Its sustainability efforts have not gone unnoticed. For two consecutive years, IKEA has been the only retailer to be honoured by Mediacorp Canada as one of Canada's Greenest Employers.[31] It takes its commitment to sustainability very seriously; it releases annual Global Sustainability Reports that highlight IKEA's global development and tracks its progress toward achieving its sustainability goals. IKEA is incorporating environmental, economic, and social responsibility across the organization, taking a huge leap forward.

---

many retailers. As an example, Suzy Shier is known for offering current fashion trends at very affordable prices. In addition, as many people's lifestyles have become more casual, consumers have begun to redefine quality from "good" to just "good enough" for particular items and occasions, such as their casual weekend wardrobe. As their definition of quality changes, so does their definition of value.

Value retailers continue to improve their "shopability," providing more convenient store layouts and shopping experiences that make the task faster and easier. As Sustainable Marketing 13.1 notes, some retailers are committing to publicly stated sustainability measures to help both their stores and their customers embrace greener practices. Value retailers are rapidly expanding, bringing more types of retailers and store locations under fire. The majority of regional and national retailers have not yet felt the full force of the value retailers. But the most vulnerable, the smaller, undifferentiated regional chains, have consistently lost out to value retailers when they arrive in the local market.

Costco attracts people of all ages and income brackets as consumers shift to value retailers.

Various theories have been developed to explain the structure and evolution of the retail industry.[32] The Wheel of Retailing (shown in Exhibit 13.3) offers one view of how new forms of retail outlets compete in the market. Generally, retailers enter with low prices, low margins, and low status. Over time, they add more and more

| **EXHIBIT 13.3** | The Wheel of Retailing |

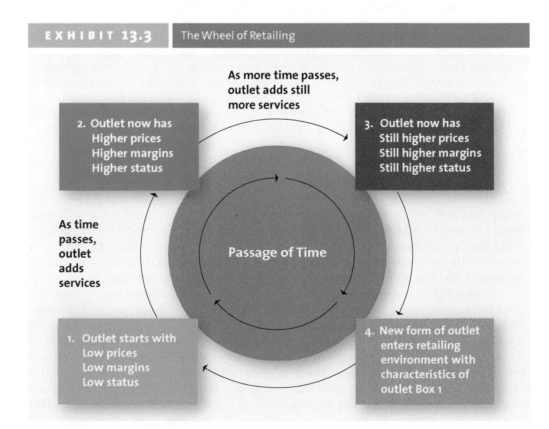

As more time passes, outlet adds still more services

2. Outlet now has
   Higher prices
   Higher margins
   Higher status

3. Outlet now has
   Still higher prices
   Still higher margins
   Still higher status

As time passes, outlet adds services

Passage of Time

1. Outlet starts with
   Low prices
   Low margins
   Low status

4. New form of outlet enters retailing environment with characteristics of outlet Box 1

service and other improvements and thus, are able to raise prices, earn higher margins, and achieve higher status with consumers. For example, the first menu at McDonald's offered only hamburgers, french fries, and milkshakes for takeout. Today, McDonald's has a wide and varied menu, upscale coffee, indoor seating, WiFi access, and play areas for children. The Manhattan location even has a doorman and a grand piano. In Europe, the company is experimenting with a more restaurant-like, sit-down experience. In Wolfratshausen, Germany, McDonald's has a fireplace, leather sofas, wooden floors, vases with flowers, and a McCafé, serving pastry, tiramisu, and cappuccino.[33]

In some Canadian McDonald's outlets, tasteless plastic is being replaced by appealing colours and natural materials, fireplaces, flat-screen TVs, leather chairs, and modern lighting fixtures. Stores are being redesigned, featuring up to four different zones geared to the needs of different target markets; for example, a high-traffic zone for people on the go, a comfortable seating area where customers can linger, and an area specifically for families and large groups.[34] The retrofit is linked to McDonald's strategy to gain a large part of the specialty beverage market, which is dominated by retailers such as Starbucks and Second Cup. By introducing upscale coffee and comfortable seating, McDonald's progresses along the Wheel of Retailing, earning higher margins and gaining higher status. These innovations in products and formats have enabled McDonald's to continue to serve its existing loyal customers and reach out to new target segments while charging competitive prices—key factors for successful retailing. Thus, it is hardly surprising that McDonald's continues to dominate its industry and stave off competition from new entrants.

In the Wheel of Retailing concept, as stores add services and improvements expand the mix of merchandise carried and upgrade their facilities, costs are generally added to the day-to-day operations, which results in higher prices. This change opens up opportunities for new lean, mean entrants at the beginning of the wheel. For example, as a discount store, Walmart entered the Canadian market and undercut established department stores such as Zellers, Kmart, and Woolco. Later, extreme value retailers such as Dollarama entered the market, undercutting existing discount stores such as Walmart.

LO4

Exploring Multichannel Options

So far in this chapter, we have explored the most traditional method for a manufacturer to get merchandise to the ultimate consumer, namely, through retailers. There are, however, other options. For example, Canadian fast-food chain Pizza Pizza gives

McDonald's redesigned restaurant in Scarborough, Ontario, (right) has moved it further along the Wheel of Retailing, compared to early restaurants (left).

customers the choice of ordering in store, by phone, on the company's website, and now through a free app for the iPhone, iPod Touch, and iPad. The app lets customers order and pay for their pizza and then track the guaranteed delivery time.[35] For instance, a manufacturer can sell directly to consumers by using its own stores, kiosks, catalogues, or the Internet. In this section, we explore the relative advantages of each of these options from both a manufacturer's and a retailer's perspective. We also consider the synergies inherent to providing products through multiple channels.

Channels for Selling to Consumers

Each channel—stores, kiosks, catalogues, and the Internet—offers its own unique benefits for selling to consumers (see Exhibit 13.4).

bricks-and-mortar retailer
A traditional, physical store.

Store Channel Traditional stores, or **bricks-and-mortar retailers** as they often are called, offer several benefits to customers that they cannot get when they shop through catalogues or on the Internet.

Browsing. Shoppers often have only a general sense of what they want (e.g., a sweater, something for dinner, a gift) but don't know the specific item they want. They go to a store to see what is available before they decide what to buy. Although some consumers surf the Internet and look through catalogues for ideas, many still prefer browsing in stores.

Touching and feeling products. Perhaps the greatest benefit offered by stores is the opportunity for customers to use all five of their senses—touching, smelling, tasting, seeing, and hearing—when examining products.

Personal service. Sales associates have the capability to provide meaningful, personalized information. Sales people can be particularly helpful when purchasing a complicated product, such as consumer electronics, or something the customer doesn't know much about, such as a diamond ring.

Cash and credit payment. Stores are nearly the only channel that accepts cash payments. Some customers prefer to pay with cash because it is easy, resolves the transaction immediately, and does not result in potential interest payments. Some customers prefer to use their credit or debit card in person rather than send payment information electronically.

Entertainment and social interaction. In-store shopping can be a stimulating experience for some people, providing a break in their daily routine and enabling them to interact with friends.

Instant gratification. Stores have the advantage of allowing customers to get the merchandise immediately after they buy it.

Risk reduction. When customers purchase merchandise in physical stores, it reduces their perceived risk of buying and increases their confidence that any problems with the merchandise will be corrected.

EXHIBIT 13.4	Benefits Provided by Different Channels		
Stores	**Kiosks**	**Catalogues**	**Internet**
• Browsing • Touching and feeling merchandise • Personal service • Cash and credit payment • Entertainment and social interaction • Instant gratification • Risk reduction	• Broader selection • Access to items online that are out of stock in stores • Access to wish lists and gift registries • Access to loyalty program information	• Convenience • Information • Safety	• Broader selection • More information • Personalization

Kiosk Channel   Retailers using a kiosk channel may simply provide store associates with access to the company website so that they can more easily help customers find product information or place orders. Other retailers, such as Chapters, offer self-service kiosks that allow customers to check product selection and availability at its stores. Self-serve movie rental kiosks in grocery stores allow consumers to select, pay for, and take movies home. Of course, today many consumers arrive in store armed with a mobile kiosk in the form of a smartphone capable of accessing product information and even comparing prices at other retailers via the Internet.

Broader selection.   Customers with the ability to shop in a store and look up products at a kiosk generally get access to an expanded assortment of products than are in stock in the store. For example, Staples carries roughly five times as many items online as in stores.

Access to items online that are out of stock in store.   Retailers using in-store kiosks can often save a sale if an item is out of stock or if their location does not carry a broad product assortment.

Access to wish lists and gift registries.   Customers buying gifts can check gift registries for wedding or baby shower gifts as well as wish lists for themselves or the gift recipient.

Access to loyalty program information.   Being able to check the status of a loyalty program and determine whether points are available to be used is a benefit to consumers. It also allows retailers to overcome resource constraints by freeing up staff to provide sales assistance to other customers.

Catalogue Channel   The catalogue channel provides some benefits to customers that are not available from the store or Internet channels. Like all nonstore formats, catalogues offer the convenience of looking at merchandise and placing an order 24-7. However, catalogues have some advantages over other nonstore formats.

Convenience.   The information in a catalogue is easily accessible for a long period of time. Consumers can refer to the information in a catalogue anytime by simply picking it up from the coffee table. The development of magalogs—catalogues with magazine-type editorial content—enhances consumers' desire to keep catalogues readily available. Williams-Sonoma produces a magalog featuring its gourmet cooking tools and foods for sale, along with kitchen tips and recipes.

Information.   Catalogues have information about the products and how they can be used. For example, the IKEA catalogue shows consumers how its products can be put together in a kitchen, office, or child's room.

Safety.   Security in malls and shopping areas is becoming an important concern for many shoppers, particularly the elderly. Nonstore retail formats offer the advantage of enabling customers to view merchandise and place orders from a safe environment—their homes.

Internet Channel   Shopping over the Internet provides the convenience offered by catalogues and other nonstore formats. However, the Internet, compared with store and catalogue channels, also has the potential to offer a greater selection of products and more personalized information about products and services in a relatively short amount of time. It also offers sellers the unique opportunity to collect information about how consumers shop—information that they can use to improve the shopping experience across all channels.

Broader selection.   One benefit of the Internet channel is the vast number of alternatives available to consumers. By shopping on the Internet, consumers can easily "visit" and select merchandise from a broader array of retailers. People living in London, Ontario, can shop electronically at Harrod's in London, England, in less time than it takes them to visit their local supermarket. Websites typically offer deeper assortments of merchandise (more colours, brands, and sizes) than are available in stores. This offering enables them to satisfy consumer demand for less popular styles, colours, or sizes and still keep their overall inventory costs low.[36]

More information to evaluate merchandise. Using an Internet channel, firms can provide as much information as each customer wants and more information than he or she could get through store or catalogue channels. Customers can drill down through web pages until they have enough information to make a purchase decision. Unlike in catalogues, the information on an electronic channel database can be frequently updated and will always be available—24-7, 365 days per year. Furthermore, the cost of adding information to an Internet channel is likely to be far less than the cost of continually training sales associates.

The depth of information available on a website even can provide solutions to customer problems. Home Depot walks its online customers through the steps of installation and repair projects, thereby giving do-it-yourselfers confidence prior to tackling home improvement tasks. The directions include the level of difficulty and a list of the tools and materials needed to complete the project successfully.

Personalization. The most significant potential benefit of the Internet channel is its ability to personalize the information for each customer economically, whether in terms of personalized customer service or personalized offerings.

Personalized Customer Service Traditional Internet channel approaches for responding to customer questions—such as frequently asked questions (FAQ) pages and offering an 800 number or email address to ask questions—often do not provide the timely information customers are seeking. To improve customer service from an electronic channel, many firms offer live, online chats. The online chat feature provides customers with the opportunity to click a button at any time and have an instant messaging email or voice conversation with a customer service representative. This technology also enables firms to send a proactive chat invitation automatically to customers on the site. The timing of these invitations can be based on the time the visitor has spent on the site, the specific page the customer is viewing, or a product on which the customer has clicked. At Bluefly.com, for example, if a visitor searches for more than three items in five minutes, thereby demonstrating more than a passing interest, Bluefly will display a pop-up window with a friendly face offering help.[37]

Personalized Offering The interactive nature of the Internet also provides an opportunity for retailers to personalize their offerings for each of their customers. For example, at many websites, you can create a personal homepage, such as MyYahoo, that is tailored to your individual needs. Using a cookie, a computer program that provides identifying information, Amazon.ca enhances the shopping experience by serving up personalized homepages with information about books and other products of interest based on visitors' past purchases. Amazon.ca will also send interested customers customized email messages that notify them that their favourite author or recording artist has published a new book or released a new CD. Another personalized offering that online retailers are able to present to customers is recommendations of complementary merchandise. Just as a well-trained salesperson would make recommendations to customers prior to checkout, an interactive web page can make suggestions to the shopper about items that he or she might like to see, such as what other customers who bought the same item also purchased.

Challenges in Selling Merchandise via the Internet

When you buy products from bricks-and-mortar stores, some critical information might include "touch-and-feel" attributes, such as how a shirt fits, the ice cream flavour tastes, or the perfume smells. This information cannot be experienced via the Internet. As a result, e-tailers strive for "look-and-see" attributes, such as colour, style, and things like grams of carbohydrates. Fit can be predicted if the apparel has consistent sizing and the consumer has learned over time which size to buy from a particular brand. Because of the problems of providing touch-and-feel information, apparel retailers experience return rates of more than 20 percent on purchases made through an electronic channel but only 10 percent for purchases made in stores. Whereas some products, such as apparel, can be difficult for customers to purchase over the Internet because of their need to touch, feel, and try on these products, Amazon's offerings do well in the worldwide Internet marketplace.

Role of Brands   Brands provide a consistent experience for customers that helps overcome the difficulty of not being able to touch and feel merchandise prior to purchase online. Because consumers trust familiar brands, products with important touch-and-feel attributes, such as clothing, perfume, flowers, and food, with well-known name brands sell successfully through nonstore channels, including the Internet, catalogues, and TV home shopping.

Consider branded merchandise such as Tommy Hilfiger perfume. Even if you can't smell a sample of the perfume before buying it online, you know that it will smell like your last bottle because the manufacturer of Tommy Hilfiger makes sure each bottle smells the same.

Using Technology   Firms with electronic channels are using technology to convert touch-and-feel information into look-and-see information that can be communicated through the Internet. Websites are going beyond offering the basic image to giving customers the opportunity to view merchandise from different angles and perspectives by using 3-D imaging and/or zoom technology.

To overcome the limitations associated with trying on clothing, apparel retailers have started to use virtual models on their websites. These virtual models enable consumers to see how selected merchandise looks on an image with similar proportions to their own and then rotate the model so the "fit" can be evaluated from all angles. The virtual models are either selected from a set of "prebuilt" models or, as H&M (www.hm.com) does, constructed on the basis of the shopper's response to questions about his or her height, weight, facial, leg, and other body dimensions. At Timberland.com, customers can design custom boots in a variety of colours, monograms, sole colours, and stitching.

H&M uses virtual models to overcome the limitations associated with trying on clothing.

Power of the Internet 13.1

How Much Is an Amazon.com Customer Worth?[38]

You may be surprised how much an Amazon.com customer is really worth. Apart from having a well-run Internet business, Amazon has always focused its strategy around its customers. The Internet retailer began as a book e-tailer and now sells almost everything under the sun, including an array of web services. It also allows other merchants to sell goods on its Internet site. So, Amazon sells everything. What else?

Jeff Bezos, the company's founder and CEO, has a well-known "obsession" with customers. The customer experience is an important competitive advantage at Amazon, and the online retailer uses its technology capabilities to enhance that experience for each and every customer. In addition to its proprietary recommendation system, Amazon figures out what its customers want and how to get it to them quickly. In one instance, a customer ordered a $500 PlayStation 3, intending it to be a Christmas present. When the package did not arrive, the customer visited Amazon's site, which provided a link for him to track the package. The tracking software indicated the game system already had been delivered and signed for, but it was nowhere to be found. The logical conclusion was that it had been stolen. The customer contacted Amazon through the site, and with few questions asked, Amazon sent the customer another PS3, without charging additional shipping charges.

In this case, Amazon lost $500 in revenue, plus shipping, on a mistake that was not even its fault. But because it provided the technical means for the customer to find out what happened and then solved the issue, it not only saved this family's Christmas but also probably turned the relieved parent into a loyal Amazon customer for life. In the end, this customer also likely will communicate his extraordinary experience to many other potential Amazon customers.

Furthermore, to combat the challenge that Internet shopping does not immediately give customers the items they buy as store shopping would, Amazon decided to launch a program that allows customers to pay an annual fee of $79 for unlimited two-day free shipping. In one year, it has foregone more than $600 million in shipping revenue. Although some Wall Street analysts may frown on "unnecessary costs" like these, Amazon maintains 72 million active customers, defined as those that spent at least $184 per year on the site. The average spending per customer the previous year was $150.

For Amazon, maintaining a customer-centric company means exploiting the technology it has developed and knowing that money it spends on customer service does not benefit the bottom line in the short term. The customer service failure recovery undertaken for the missing PS3 cost the company a considerable amount of money, but in the long term, the company likely has gained a lifetime customer.

Services Some service providers have been very successful over the Internet, because the look-and-see attributes of their offering can be presented very effectively online. For example, REI Adventures (www.rei.com/adventures) is a subsidiary of REI, the multichannel outdoor sporting goods retailer. You can shop for trips by location, activity, or specialty, such as family, private departures, women, and youth. The site provides biographies of the tour guides in each region and vivid descriptions that make you want to pack your bags and go.

Although Amazon.com began as a bookseller, you can now buy just about anything on its site. But the availability of merchandise alone didn't make Amazon the largest Internet-only retailer. Its commitment to customer service garners loyal and profitable customers, as Power of the Internet 13.1 explains.

Perceived Risks in Electronic Shopping

Although most consumers have had the opportunity to try out electronic shopping, they also have some concerns about buying products through an electronic channel. The two critical perceived risks are (1) the security of credit card transactions on the Internet and (2) potential privacy violations. Although many consumers remain concerned about credit card security, extensive security problems have been rare. Almost all Internet sellers use sophisticated technologies to encrypt communications.[39] In 2006, however, the security encryption systems for TJX Companies, owners of Winners and HomeSense, were hacked, exposing 45.7 million credit and debit cards to theft. As a result, customers are leery, and banks are suing the retailer for neglecting to encrypt this secure information properly.[40]

Ethical Dilemma 13.1 — Protecting Consumer Privacy

The definition of personal privacy depends on which country you're in and with which person you're speaking. Some people define personal information as all information that is not publicly available. Others tend to include both public information (e.g., driver's license, mortgage data) and private details (hobbies, income). Internet retailers need to take the necessary precautions to protect consumer privacy by incorporating privacy safety software such as firewalls and data encryption every time any data is transferred to prevent it from being intercepted.[41]

Canadians rely on government legislation to protect their privacy. The situation in the United States is different: existing legislation for consumer privacy is restricted to the protection of information in government functions and practices in credit reporting, video rentals, banking, and health care. Canada, the European Union, Australia, and New Zealand have more stringent consumer privacy laws. Some of their provisions on consumer privacy include the following:

- Businesses can collect consumer information only if they have clearly defined the purpose for collecting the information, such as completing the transaction.

- The purpose must be disclosed to the consumer from whom the information is being collected.

- The information can be used only for that specific purpose.

- The business can keep the information only for the stated purpose. If the business wants to use the information for another purpose, it must initiate a new collection process.

In Canada, consumers own their personal information so retailers must get consumers to agree explicitly to share this personal information through an opt-in agreement. In contrast, personal information in the United States is generally viewed as being in the public domain and retailers can use it in any way they desire. American consumers must explicitly tell retailers not to use their personal information—they must opt out,[42] something for Canadian consumers to consider when purchasing from U.S. retailers.

There is growing consensus that personal information must be fairly collected, that the collection must be purposeful, and that the data should be relevant, maintained as accurate, essential to the business, subject to the rights of the owning individual, kept reasonably secure, and transferred only with the permission of the consumer. To address these concerns, many Internet sellers that collect customer information now have lengthy privacy policies that state what information is collected, how it will be used, give consumers a choice as to whether they give information, and allow them to view and correct any personal information held by an online retail site. Internet sellers need to assure their customers that information about them is held securely and not passed on to other companies without the customer's permission.

Consumers also are concerned about the ability of Internet sellers to collect information about their purchase history, personal information, and search behaviour on the Internet. Consumers may be worried about how this information will be used in the future. Will it be sold to other firms, or will the consumer receive unwanted promotional materials online or in the mail? To answer these questions, consider Ethical Dilemma 13.1.

Evolution Toward Multichannel Marketing

L05

Traditional store-based and catalogue retailers and some manufacturers are placing more emphasis on their electronic channels and evolving into **multichannel retailers**—that is, retailers that sell merchandise in more than one retail channel (e.g., store, catalogue, and Internet)—for four reasons. First, the electronic channel gives them an opportunity to overcome the limitations of their primary existing format, as we described in the previous sections. Second, by using an electronic channel, they can expand their market reach. Third, providing a multichannel offering builds share of wallet, or the percentage of total purchases made by a customer from a particular seller. Fourth, an electronic channel enables firms to gain valuable insights into their customers' shopping behaviour.

multichannel retailers Retailers that sell merchandise in more than one retail channel (e.g., store, catalogue, and Internet).

Overcoming the Limitations of an Existing Format

One of the greatest constraints facing store-based retailers is the size of their stores. The amount of merchandise that can be displayed and offered for sale in stores is limited. By blending stores with Internet-enabled kiosks, retailers can dramatically expand the assortment offered to their customers. For example, Walmart and Home Depot have a limited number of major appliance floor models in their stores, but customers can use an Internet-enabled kiosk to look at an expanded selection of appliances, get more detailed information, and place orders.

Another limitation that store-based retailers face is inconsistent execution. The availability and knowledge of sales associates can vary considerably across stores or even within a store at different times during the day. This inconsistency is most problematic for retailers selling new, complex merchandise. For example, consumer electronic retailers such as Best Buy find it difficult to communicate the features and benefits of the newest products to all of their sales associates. To address this problem, Best Buy installed kiosks designed to be used by sales associates and customers to obtain product information.

A catalogue retailer can also use its electronic channel to overcome the limitations of its catalogue. Once a catalogue is printed, it cannot be updated with price changes and new merchandise. Therefore, retailers such as Lands' End use Internet sites to provide customers with real-time information about stock availability and price reductions on clearance merchandise.

Expanding Market Presence

With the Internet's low entry costs and constantly improving search engines and shopping bots, smaller niche sources for hard-to-find products, collectibles, and hobbies can expand their trade area—the geographical area that contains the potential customers of a particular retailer or shopping centre—from a few city blocks to the world. The Internet has facilitated market expansions by traditional retailers as well. Not only can a customer in Zurich shop online at Sears.ca or Lee Valley Tools Ltd.

Consumers that shop at multichannel retailers—retailers that sell merchandise in more than one retail channel (such as a Sears Canada store (left), catalogue (middle), and Internet (right)—typically buy more than those who shop in only one retail channel.

(leevalley.com), but a Staples customer can buy a computer online and pick it up at the store. In addition to increasing sales by expanding the current customer base and attracting new customers, multichannel retailers can achieve economies of scale by coordinating their buying and logistics activities across channels and consolidating their marketing information and activities. Generally, consumers who shop at multichannel retailers typically buy more than those who shop in only one retail channel.

Adding an electronic channel is particularly attractive to firms with strong brand names but limited locations and distribution. For example, retailers such as Harrod's, IKEA, and Harry Rosen are widely known for offering unique, high-quality merchandise, but they require customers to travel to England or major cities to buy many of the items they carry. Interestingly, most of these store-based retailers currently are multichannel retailers through their successful catalogue and Internet offerings.

Increasing Share of Wallet[43]

Although offering an electronic channel may draw away some sales from other channels, using it with other channels can result in consumers making more total purchases from the seller. Traditional single-channel retailers can use one channel to promote the services offered by other channels. For example, the URL of a store's website can be advertised on in-store signs, shopping bags, credit card billing statements, POS receipts, and the print or broadcast advertising used to promote the stores. The retailer's electronic channel can be used to stimulate store visits by announcing special store events and promotions. Store-based retailers can leverage their stores to lower the cost of fulfilling orders and processing returned merchandise if they use the stores as "warehouses" for gathering merchandise for delivery to customers. Customers also can be offered the opportunity to pick up and return merchandise at the retailer's stores rather than pay shipping charges. Many retailers will waive shipping charges when orders are placed online or through the catalogue if the customer physically comes to the store. Research has shown that multichannel consumers spend substantially more than those who shop at a single channel—between 25 to 100 percent more![44]

Gaining Insights into Customers' Shopping Behaviours

It is difficult to observe customers' behaviour in stores or when they shop catalogues, because most people prefer not to have sales clerks constantly monitoring them in stores or visiting their homes, pestering them with questions about each action they've taken. Therefore, online retailing provides key insights into the choices consumers make since the data can be collected unobtrusively. However, people often shop differently in the different channels; for example, they might browse extensively online but dash into and out of stores to get what they need. If a retailer gathers data about a customer's actions in all of its channels, it should be able to put together a clearer, more detailed picture of how and why customers patronize—or don't patronize—its channels and offerings.

Will Manufacturers Bypass Retailers and Sell Directly to Consumers?

Disintermediation occurs when a manufacturer sells directly to consumers, bypassing retailers. Retailers are concerned about disintermediation because manufacturers can get direct access to their consumers by establishing a retail site on the Internet. Naturalizer brand shoes and accessories are sold through its website (www.naturalizer. com) and at the same time directly to retailers such as Zappos.com. However, Exhibit 13.5 illustrates why most manufacturers are reluctant to engage in retailing.

Manufacturers lack many of the critical skills necessary to sell merchandise electronically, and retailers are typically more efficient in dealing with customers

EXHIBIT 13.5	Capabilities Needed for Multichannel Retailing			
Capabilities	**Store-Based Retailers**	**Kiosks**	**Catalogue Retailers**	**Merchandise Manufacturers**
Develop assortments and manage inventory	High	High	High	Low
Manage people in remote locations	High	Low	Low	Low
Efficiently distribute merchandise to stores	High	Low	Low	High
Present merchandise effectively in a printed format and distribute catalogues	Medium	Medium	High	Low
Present merchandise effectively on a website	Medium	High	High	Low
Process orders from individual customers electronically	Medium	High	High	Low
Efficiently distribute merchandise to homes and accept returns	Medium	High	High	Low
Integrate information systems to provide a seamless customer experience across channels	Low	Medium	Medium	Low

directly than are manufacturers. They have considerably more experience than manufacturers in distributing merchandise directly to customers, providing complementary assortments, and collecting and using information about customers. Retailers also have an advantage because they can provide a broader array of products and services, such as various brands or special offerings, to solve customer problems. For example, if consumers want to buy the components for a home entertainment centre from a variety of manufacturers, they must go to several different Internet sites and still cannot be sure that the components will work together or arrive at the same time.

Manufacturers that sell directly to consumers risk losing the support of the retailers they bypass. Therefore, many manufacturers, such as Energizer (www.energizer.com), the world's largest producer of batteries and flashlights, use their websites only as a marketing tool to show customers which products are available and then direct them to nearby stores where they can purchase the products.

Learning Objectives Review

LO1   Explain the issues manufacturers consider when choosing retail partners

Because manufacturers want their offerings available where, when, and in the form that customers prefer, they must consider whether customers expect to find their products at specific retailers. For example, customers probably do not expect, or want, to find a value-priced product at a luxury retailer. The manufacturer also must consider the basic channel structure in which it functions, along with the characteristics of the members of that channel. Finally, manufacturers need to determine the distribution intensity they prefer.

LO2 Identify what types of retailers are available to distribute products

Retailers generally fall into one of two categories: food retailers and general merchandise retailers. Each of the categories consists of various formats, including supermarkets, supercentres, warehouse clubs, convenience stores, department stores, discount stores, specialty retailers, drugstores, category specialists, extreme value retailers, and off-price stores.

LO3 Describe how retailers use the four Ps to create value for customers

To develop a coordinated strategy—which represents a key goal for an effective channel partnership between retailers and manufacturers—these functions need to consider the four Ps. Retailers provide customers with a choice of merchandise in the quantities they want to buy and services that facilitate the sale and use of those products. They offer convenient locations to shop and an atmosphere and presentation that enhance the shopping experience. Promotions, both in the store and outside, provide customers with information. Finally, price provides signals to the customer about the image of the store, its merchandise, and its services.

LO4 Describe the multichannel options available to retailers

The various types of retail channels—stores, kiosks, catalogues, and the Internet—each offer their own benefits and limitations, including those related to availability, convenience, and safety, among others. If a retailer adopts a multichannel strategy, it can exploit the benefits and mitigate the limitations of each channel and expand its overall market presence.

LO5 Explain why traditional retailers are evolving into multichannel retailers

The Internet has expanded the market for many retailers, from small, specialty niche retailers to large global retailers. Customers feel particularly comfortable buying commodities and branded merchandise over the Internet because they can easily judge quality and compare prices. Other products that require consumers to touch or feel them are more difficult to sell online. A multichannel strategy offers companies the chance to gain a greater share of customers' wallets and more insight into their buying behaviours, allowing retailers to better determine what their customers want and provide them with convenient shopping options.

Key Terms

- big-box food retailer, 426
- bricks-and-mortar retailer, 438
- category killer, 428
- category specialist, 427
- conventional supermarket, 426
- cooperative (co-op) advertising, 431
- discount store, 427
- drugstore, 428
- extreme value retailer, 429
- general merchandise retailer, 427
- multichannel retailers, 443
- multichannel strategy, 424
- off-price retailer, 429
- retailing, 422
- share of wallet, 434
- specialty store, 427

Concept Review

1. Describe the factors that manufacturers must consider when choosing retail partners.

2. How would a manufacturer's strategy for choosing a retailer change depending on its overall market power and the consistency of the new product with existing offerings?

3. Discuss the types of retailers that operate in Canada and identify some of the issues facing each type.

4. Generally merchandise retailers are classified into several different groups such as discount stores, specialty stores, category killers, and so on. However, it seems that increasingly many of these retailers are looking quite similar. Why is this so and what factors may explain this trend?

5. How do marketers use the four Ps to create value in retailing?

6. How has the retail landscape changed in Canada based on the Wheel of Retailing concept?

7. In this chapter, we discuss the fact that researchers have found that store image and atmospherics exert a huge

impact on customers shopping behaviour. What are the key elements of a store's atmospherics and image and why do you think that they affect consumers so strongly?

8. Explain how the Internet has helped reshape retail marketing strategies. What are some of the unique advantages of physical store retailing, website selling, and kiosks?

9. Discuss the advantages of being a multichannel retailer from the perspectives of both retailers and consumers.

10. Explain why it is important for retailers to develop effective retailing strategy and positioning. How do retailers develop such a strategy? Hint: Look at the various store formats of Loblaw or any national grocery chain.

Marketing Applications

1. How have retail institutions evolved over time according to the Wheel of Retailing concept? Provide an example of a specific retailer that operates within each of the categories identified in the model.

2. Why don't traditional department stores have the same strong appeal to Canadian consumers that they once enjoyed during their height in the last half of the twentieth century? Discuss which types of retailers are now competing with department stores.

3. What do retailers do to increase the value of products and services for consumers? Discuss the extent to which bricks-and-mortar retailers are threatened by Internet-only retailers with regard to these factors.

4. Some argue that retailers can be eliminated from the distribution channel because they only add costs to the final product without creating any value-added services in the process. Do you agree with this perspective? Is it likely that consumers will make most purchases directly from manufacturers in the near future? Provide justification for your answers.

5. Many years ago, the corporations that sold gasoline made the strategic move to include a substantial offering of food items. Today, it is rare to find a gas station that does not sell food items. Into which category of food retailer did these service stations fall? Do you think this was a prudent strategic direction for these corporations? Explain your logic.

6. Identify three categories of products especially suited for sale on the Internet. Identify three categories that are not currently suitable for sale on the Internet. Justify your choices.

7. How does Staples.com or Officedepot.com provide value to their customers beyond the physical products that they sell? Identify some of the ways that the companies have overcome the inhibitors to successful Internet retailing.

8. What options do you have for purchasing food in your town? Under what circumstances would you shop at each option? What would a family with two young children consider while making this choice?

9. You can purchase apparel at a discount store, specialty store, category specialist, off-price retailer, department store, or Internet-only store. From which of these types of stores do you shop? Explain why you prefer one type over another.

10. Suppose you are the confectionary buyer for a regional chain of grocery stores. The store policy is to charge a "substantial" listing fee for the placement of new items. Listing fees were originally designed to cover the costs of placing new products on the shelves, such as adjustments to computer systems and realignment of warehouse and store space. Over the years, these fees have become larger, and they are now a significant source of revenue for the chain. A local minority-owned manufacturer of a popular brand of specialty candy would like to sell to your chain, but claims that the listing fee is too high and does not reflect the real cost of adding their candy. Discuss the ethical implications of such a policy. What should the chain do?

Net Savvy

1. Companies such as Lee Valley Tools have expanded their offerings beyond their original channels to sell through multiple channels. Visit the company's website (www.leevalley.com) and determine in which channels it operates (Internet, stores, and/or catalogue). Discuss the advantages of using a multichannel strategy over a single channel strategy.

2. Using either your own experience or that of a friend, select a familiar Internet website that engages in some form of retailing. Evaluate that website in terms of elements that help or hinder it and summarize the extent to which you think the site is successful in sustaining a retailing Internet presence.

Chapter Case Study

STAPLES, INC.[45]

Staples operates in the highly competitive $240-billion office products market, which historically has been served by traditional office products retailers. The office supply category specialists, including Staples, Office Depot, and Office Max, dramatically changed the landscape of the office supply industry. First, they greatly expanded the use of retail stores and Internet channels as a means of distributing office supply products, capitalizing in part on the significant increase in the number of home offices. Prior to the mid-1980s, office supply customers primarily placed their orders through commissioned salespeople or catalogues.

Warehouse clubs, supermarkets, and full-line discount retailers have begun taking market share away from the big three office supply retailers because of their ability to sell the bulk items at lower prices. Retailers such as Walmart and Costco offer low prices on office supplies, which forces the major office supply retailers to offer more than just products, such as extra services and greater customer service. The big three office supply stores have also expanded their business-to-business (B2B) efforts to sell to other companies, such as Wells Fargo or IBM. Staples Advantage, for example, offers a range of products and services to its more than 66 000 B2B customers.[46]

Company Background

Originally opened in 1986 by executive-turned-entrepreneur Tom Stemberg, Staples has reached sales exceeding $23 billion.[47] Staples has been credited with pioneering the high-volume office products superstore concept. By evolving its original mission of slashing the costs and eliminating the hassles of running an office, to making it easy to buy office products, Staples has become the world's largest office products company.

To distinguish itself in this competitive industry, Staples strives to provide a unique shopping experience to customers in all its market segments. Central to maintaining customer satisfaction is developing strong customer relationship skills and broad knowledge about office products in all associates hired by the company. Therefore, Staples includes formal training as an integral part of the development of its associates. Another truly important aspect of customer service is the availability of merchandise. In the office supply industry, customers have very specific needs, such as finding an ink cartridge for a particular printer, and if the store is out of stock of a needed item, the customer may never come back.

Staples uses various channels of distribution to address the needs of its different segments. Smaller businesses are generally served by a combination of retail stores, catalogues, and the Internet. Retail operations focus on serving the needs of consumers and small businesses, especially through an in-store kiosk that enables customers to order a product that may not be available in the store and receive the product via overnight delivery. In-store kiosks allow them to choose to have the product delivered to their home, business, or local store. If a customer does not want to shop in the store, he or she can visit Staples.com to order required products and select from a much larger assortment. The typical Staples retail store has approximately 8000 SKUs, but Staples.com offers more than 45 000 SKUs. This multichannel approach allows Staples to increase its productivity by stocking only more popular items in stores while still providing customers with access to a great variety of products.

Staples believes that the Internet channel has helped to increase its sales while reducing its overhead costs. It has developed three stand-alone websites: Staples.com, a public website; Quill.com, an e-commerce site for medium-sized businesses; and StaplesLink.com, a secure, customized, e-commerce procurement website for large customers with contracts with Staples. In addition, the company has placed Staples.com kiosks in its stores so that customers can make purchases of any product, even if they are not stocked in the store. Customers can pay for these purchases at the register or through Staples.com and have the product delivered to their home or business. This multichannel approach allows Staples to increase its productivity by stocking only fast moving items in stores but not sacrificing product availability.

Multichannel Integration

Staples' overall goal has been to become the leading office products and service provider by combining its existing experience, extensive distribution infrastructure, and customer service expertise with web-based information technology. As a result, the integration of different channels of distribution into one seamless customer experience has been of particular interest to the company. Staples, like many other multichannel retailers, has found that many customers use multiple channels to make their Staples purchases and that sales increase when customers use more than one channel (customers that shop two channels spend twice as much as a single-channel shopper; a tri-channel shopper spends about three times as much as a single-channel shopper). Therefore, the greater the number of channels a particular customer shops, the greater the overall expenditure he or she is likely to make.

Staples faces several challenges in integrating its channels of distribution, most of which are related to its Internet channel. First, it must consider the extent to which the Internet may cannibalize its retail store sales. The most attractive aspect of the Internet is its potential to attract new customers and sell more to existing customers. But if overall sales are flat—that is, if online retailing only converts retail store sales to Internet sales—Staples suffers increased overhead costs and poorer overall productivity. Second, Staples must be concerned about the stock position of its retail stores compared with that of alternative channels. Since a retail store cannot carry as much merchandise as the Internet channel, the challenge is keeping an appropriate balance between minimizing stockouts and avoiding the proliferation of too many SKUs in the retail stores. Finally, Staples has to contend with price competition both within its own multichannel organization and from outside competitors.

Staples' Added Value Services[48]

Such competition means that Staples must continue to differentiate itself from other office supply retailers by adding extra value to office supplies, which themselves represent commoditized products. For example, its Copy and Print Centres within its big-box stores enable customers to order print jobs and receive the help of an in-store print specialist. To increase this business line further, Staples also has opened stand-alone Staples Copy and Print Centres, which are approximately 185 square metres, compared with its typical 2800-square-metre

Staples adds value for its customers with services such as its Copy and Print Centres.

big-box stores. The small size of these stores allows them to be located in metropolitan areas or places where there would not be sufficient space for a large, big-box store. Customers can order their copies through the Staples website, and then pick them up in the store or have them delivered. The Copy and Print stores also sell basic office supply products that customers may need to pick up at the last minute when they come to collect their print orders.

Questions

1. Assess the extent to which Staples has developed a successful multichannel strategy. What factors have contributed to its success?

2. What are the advantages and disadvantages of using kiosks as a part of its approach?

3. How should Staples assess which SKUs to keep in its stores?

4. How do the Staples Copy and Print Centres differentiate Staples from the competition?

 Practise and learn online with Connect. Connect allows you to practise important concepts at your own pace and on your own schedule, with 24/7 online access to an eBook, practice quizzes, interactivities, videos, study tools, additional resources, and more.

CHAPTER 14

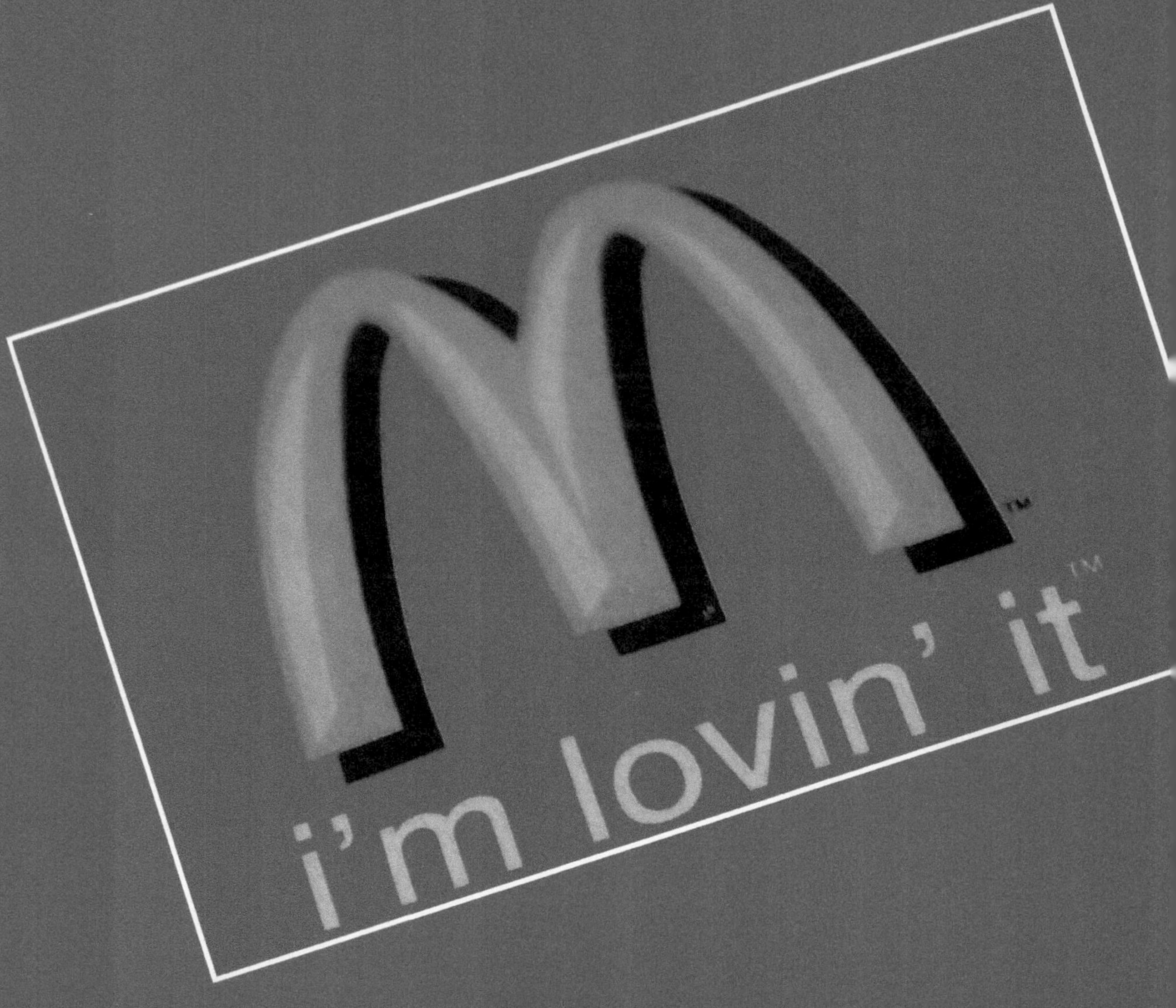

SECTION SEVEN

Value Communication

Integrated Marketing Communications

L aunched in 2003, the McDonald's "I'm Lovin' It" tagline has become the platform for the company's worldwide integrated marketing communications. As the company's most successful and longest-running campaign, "I'm Lovin' It" has outperformed the iconic "You Deserve a Break Today," and "Food, Folks and Fun," in both longevity and sales increases.[1] After only two years, the campaign was credited with sending some 50 million customers to McDonald's daily, a gain of more than two million per day.[2]

When the tagline first launched, ads featured U.S. pop star Justin Timberlake, whose single was used as the theme. The goal was to make "I'm Lovin' It" a full campaign, not just a tagline. As such, the campaign makes use of traditional media such as TV, radio, and print ads, and also incorporates billboards, signage, and sponsorship, ranging from Little League sports to the Olympic Games.

According to the company's chief marketing officer, Mary Dillon, the campaign lifted the relevance of McDonald's and revitalized its image, framing it as a modern and contemporary lifestyle brand.[3] It's not surprising that the company is sticking with the campaign and has asked its myriad of advertising agencies to kick it up a notch to make "I'm Lovin' It" even better. New marketing communication initiatives will see the tagline take prominence over the Golden Arches by having the tagline appear independently and having the Arches introduced later in TV ads. The tagline is being integrated into the action to help celebrate what the company calls "uniquely McDonald's moments."

Given the cost of launching global campaigns, being able to build on one platform helps McDonald's deliver a consistent global message and achieve cost savings. While most countries elected to work with the English version of the tagline, others chose to translate or localize it to adapt

Learning Objectives

After studying this chapter, you should be able to

LO1 Outline the process that firms use to communicate with consumers

LO2 Explain the six tools of integrated marketing communications campaigns

LO3 List the steps in planning an integrated marketing communications campaign

LO4 Describe what appeals advertisers use to get customers' attention

LO5 Identify how firms determine which media to use

LO6 Summarize how firms budget for and measure integrated marketing communications success

it to local culture. For example, in Spanish the tagline is *me encanta*, which translates loosely to "I really like it."[4] The unique musical sound bite featured in ads needs no translation and helps to tie the campaign together around the world.

Although Timberlake has long since been replaced in ads, McDonald's plans to use the "I'm Lovin' It" campaign, with its distinctive "Ba-da-ba-ba-ba" sound bite, to build brand equity and drive sales in the future. .::

---

integrated marketing communications (IMC) Represents the promotion dimension of the four Ps; encompasses a variety of communication disciplines—general advertising, personal selling, sales promotion, public relations, direct marketing, and electronic media—in combination to provide clarity, consistency, and maximum communicative impact.

Throughout the last six chapters, we focused our attention on how firms create value by developing products and services and delivering them to consumers when and where they want to buy them. However, consumers are not likely to come flocking to new products and services unless they are aware of them. Therefore, marketers must consider how to communicate the value of a new product and/or service—or more specifically, the value proposition—to the target market. The chapter vignette about McDonald's illustrates how a firm can develop a communication strategy to increase the relevance and value of its product. Let's begin by examining what integrated marketing communications is, how it has developed, and how it contributes to value creation.

Integrated marketing communications (IMC) represents promotion, the fourth P of the four Ps. It encompasses a variety of communication disciplines—advertising, personal selling, sales promotion, public relations, direct marketing, and electronic media—in combination to provide clarity, consistency, and maximum communicative impact.[5] Rather than consisting of separate marketing communication elements with no unified control, IMC programs regard each of the firm's marketing communications elements as part of a whole, each of which offers a different means to connect with the target audience. This integration of elements provides the firm with the best means to reach the target audience with the desired message, and it enhances the value story by offering a clear and consistent message.

There are three components in any IMC strategy: the consumer or target market, the channels or vehicles through which the message is communicated, and the evaluation of the results of the communication. As shown in our chapter roadmap, in the first section, we focus on *consumers*, examining the communication process: how consumers receive communications, whether via media or other methods, as well as how the delivery of that communication affects a message's form and content. The second section examines the six distinct *tools* of IMC—advertising, personal selling, sales promotion, direct marketing, public relations, and electronic media—and how each is used in an overall IMC strategy. We then identify the steps involved in planning successful campaigns, from identifying a target audience to creating an actual ad and assessing its performance. Although we apply these steps specifically to advertising, the same process can be used when planning sales promotions, direct marketing, public relations, and electronic media. The last section considers how the level of complexity in IMC strategies leads marketers to design new ways to measure the *results* of IMC campaigns.

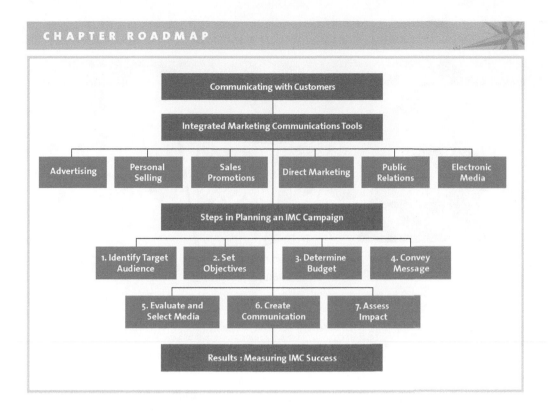

Communicating with Consumers

As the number of communication media has increased, the task of understanding how best to reach target consumers has become far more complex. In this section, we examine a model that describes how communications go from the firm to the consumer, and the factors that affect the way the consumer perceives the message. Then we look at how marketing communications influence consumers—from making them aware that a product or service exists to moving them to buy.

The Communication Process

Exhibit 14.1 illustrates the communication process. Let's first define each component and then discuss how they interact.

The Sender   The message originates from the **sender**, who must be clearly identified to the intended audience. For instance, an organization such as Home Depot working with one of its vendors, Stanley Tools Company, can send a message that it is having a special "Father's Day sale."

In the quest for innovative ways to reach consumers, some marketers have been accused of **deceptive advertising**, which is a representation, omission, act, or practice in an advertisement that is likely to mislead consumers acting reasonably under the circumstances. For example, to promote its film *Godsend*, Lion's Gate Films created a website (www.godsendinstitute.org) to look like a legitimate fertility clinic, disguising the true sender of the message, and deliberately misleading or confusing visitors to the site.

The Transmitter   The sender works with the creative department, whether in-house or from a marketing (or advertising) agency, to develop marketing communications. Stanley likely develops advertising materials with its ad agency and provides the materials to Home Depot. Such an agent or intermediary is the **transmitter**.

sender
The firm from which an IMC message originates; the sender must be clearly identified to the intended audience.

deceptive advertising
A representation, omission, act, or practice in an advertisement that is likely to mislead consumers acting reasonably under the circumstances.

transmitter
An agent or intermediary with which the sender works to develop the marketing communications; for example, a firm's creative department or an advertising agency.

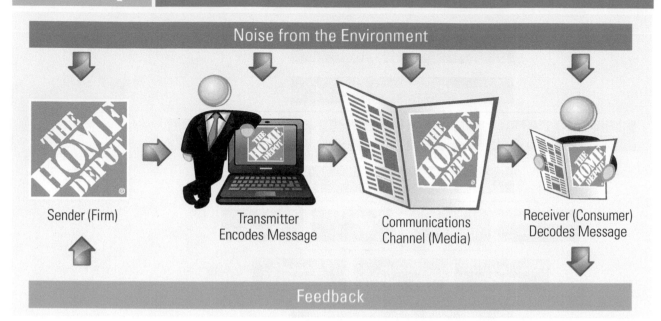

| EXHIBIT 14.1 | The Communication Process |

Noise from the Environment

Sender (Firm)   Transmitter Encodes Message   Communications Channel (Media)   Receiver (Consumer) Decodes Message

Feedback

encoding

The process of converting the sender's ideas into a message, which could be verbal, visual, or both.

communication channel

The medium—print, broadcast, the Internet—that carries the message.

receiver

The person who reads, hears, or sees and processes the information contained in the message or advertisement.

decoding

The process by which the receiver interprets the sender's message.

noise

Any interference that stems from competing messages, a lack of clarity in the message, or a flaw in the medium; a problem for all communication channels.

feedback loop

Allows the receiver to communicate with the sender and thereby informs the sender whether the message was received and decoded properly.

Encoding **Encoding** means converting the sender's ideas into a message, which could be verbal, visual, or both. Home Depot may take out full-page ads in every major newspaper proclaiming, "Amazing Father's Day Deals at 25 Percent Off!" A TV commercial showing men examining and testing tools at Home Depot is another way to encode the message that "there are great deals to be had." As the old saying goes, a picture is worth a thousand words. But the most important facet of encoding is not what is sent but rather what is received. Home Depot shoppers must believe that the sale is substantial enough to warrant a trip to a store.

The Communication Channel The **communication channel** is the medium—print, broadcast, the Internet—that carries the message. Home Depot could transmit through TV, radio, and various print ads, and it realizes that the media chosen must be appropriate to connect itself (the sender) with its desired recipient. So Home Depot might advertise on channels such as HGTV and in magazines such as *Canadian Homes & Cottages*.

The Receiver The **receiver** is the person who reads, hears, or sees and processes the information contained in the message or advertisement. The sender, of course, hopes that the person receiving it will be the one for whom it was originally intended. For example, Home Depot wants its message received and decoded properly by people who are likely to shop in its stores. **Decoding** refers to the process by which the receiver interprets the sender's message.

Noise **Noise** is any interference that stems from competing messages, a lack of clarity in the message, or a flaw in the medium, and it poses a problem for all communication channels. Home Depot may choose to advertise in newspapers that its target market doesn't read, which means the rate at which the message is received by those to whom it has relevance has been slowed considerably. As we have already defined, encoding is what the sender intends to say, and decoding is what the receiver hears. If there is a difference between them, it is probably due to noise.

Feedback Loop The **feedback loop** allows the receiver to communicate with the sender and thereby informs the sender whether the message was received and decoded properly. Feedback can take many forms: a customer's purchase of the item, a complaint or compliment, the redemption of a coupon or rebate, and so forth. If Home Depot observes an increase in store traffic and sales, its managers know that their intended audience received the message and understood that there were great Father's Day bargains to be found in the store.

How Consumers Perceive Communication

The actual communication process is not as simple as the model in Exhibit 14.1 implies. Each receiver may interpret the sender's message differently, and senders often adjust their message according to the medium used and the receivers' level of knowledge about the product or service. And in spite of marketers' best efforts to create clear messages, consumers may not always respond as expected.

Receivers Decode Messages Differently Each receiver decodes a message in his or her own way, which is not necessarily the way the sender intended. Different people shown the same message will often take radically different meanings from it. For example, what does the image on the right convey to you?

If you are a user of this brand, it may convey satisfaction. If you recently went on a diet and gave up your favourite Mexican food, it may convey dismay or a sense of loss. If you have chosen to be a nonuser, it may convey some disgust. If you are a recently terminated employee, it may convey anger. The sender has little, if any, control over what meaning any individual receiver will take from the message.[6]

Senders Adjust Messages According to the Medium and Receivers' Traits Different media communicate in very different ways. So marketers make adjustments to their messages and media depending on whether they want to communicate with suppliers, shareholders, customers, or the general public.[7] Kellogg's would not, for instance, send the same message to its shareholders in a targeted email as it would to its consumers on Saturday morning TV.

Receivers decode messages differently. What does the Taco Bell sign mean to you?

Senders must adjust messages according to the receivers' traits. LG, for instance, uses the ad on the left to target consumers for its Super Blue high-definition players. The ad on the right targets a B2B audience.

Now that we've examined various aspects of the communication process, let's look at the specific tools used in IMC programs.

L02 Integrated Marketing Communications Tools

For any communications campaign to succeed, the firm must deliver the right message to the right audience through the right media. Reaching the right audience is becoming more difficult, however, as the media environment grows more complicated and fragmented. No single communication channel is better than another. The goal of IMC is to use them in a way so that the sum exceeds the total of the parts.

Advances in technology have led to a variety of new media options, such as satellite radio, wireless technology, pop-up and banner ads on websites, brand-sponsored websites, PDA messaging, and text messaging, all of which vie for consumers' attention. Not so long ago, advertisers could reach the masses with media buys on three TV networks. Today, they have to buy on 74 stations to reach the same number of people. Print media have also grown and become more specialized. In Canada, there are currently 124 daily newspapers, 1100 plus community newspapers, well over 1000 consumer magazines, and 900 trade journals.[8]

This proliferation of media has led many firms to shift their promotional dollars from advertising to direct marketing, website development, product placements, and other forms of promotion in search of the best way to deliver messages to their target audiences. Media fragmentation has also occurred on television. Networks are dedicated to certain types of sports (Outdoor Life Network, Golf Channel), to children (YTV), to ethnic minorities (APTN—Aboriginal Peoples Television Network), and to religions (CTS). Each of these channels allows IMC planners to target their desired audience narrowly.

We now examine the individual tools of IMC and the way each contributes to a successful IMC campaign (see Exhibit 14.2). Most of these tools work along a continuum from passive to interactive and can be used either offline or online. Some tools—advertising, personal selling, and sales promotion—appear in detail in the next chapter, and so we discuss them only briefly here.

EXHIBIT 14.2 Integrated Marketing Communications Tools

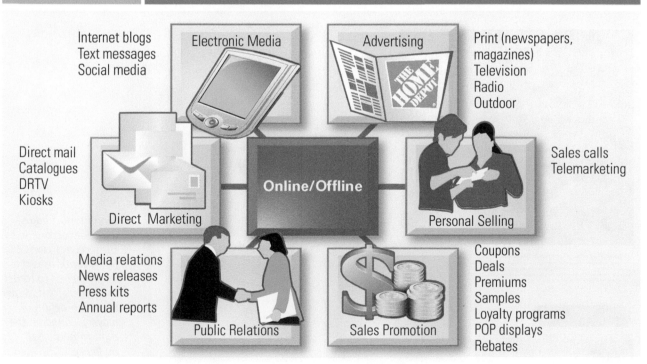

Internet blogs / Text messages / Social media — Electronic Media

Advertising — Print (newspapers, magazines) / Television / Radio / Outdoor

Direct mail / Catalogues / DRTV / Kiosks — Direct Marketing

Online/Offline

Sales calls / Telemarketing — Personal Selling

Media relations / News releases / Press kits / Annual reports — Public Relations

Sales Promotion — Coupons / Deals / Premiums / Samples / Loyalty programs / POP displays / Rebates

Advertising

Perhaps the most visible of the IMC components, **advertising** is a paid form of communication from an identifiable source, delivered through a communication channel, and designed to persuade the receiver to take some action, now or in the future.[9] Traditionally, advertising has been passive and offline; however, these days advertising is increasingly placed online and is interactive. For instance, print ads in newspapers and magazines are offline, with customers simply viewing them (passive). In contrast, banner ads, web-based contests, or online coupons are all offered online and require customers to provide some information or take some action (interactive). Basically, advertising can be either offline or online and either passive or interactive.

In Chapter 15, we discuss the purpose of advertising and its various types, but for now, we note that advertising is extremely effective for creating awareness of a product or service and generating interest. However, advertising can also be used to remind consumers of existing brands. As mentioned in the chapter vignette, the McDonald's "I'm Lovin' It" ads helped revitalize interest in the company's products, driving both traffic and sales.

Mass advertising can entice consumers into a conversation with marketers. However, advertising must break through the clutter of other messages to reach its intended audience. And as marketers attempt to find ways to reach their target audiences, advertising has become increasingly pervasive. Not so long ago, the majority of many firms' promotional budgets was spent on advertising. In the past decade, however, advertising's share of total promotional dollars has fallen as the budgets for other forms of sales promotion, especially direct marketing and public relations, have increased, resulting in a more balanced approach to the use of marketing communications elements.

advertising
A paid form of communication from an identifiable source, delivered through a communication channel, and designed to persuade the receiver to take some action, now or in the future.

Personal Selling

Personal selling is the two-way flow of communication between a buyer and a seller that is designed to influence the buyer's purchase decision. Personal selling can take place in various settings: face to face, video teleconferencing, on the telephone, or over the Internet. Although consumers don't often interact with professional sales people, personal selling represents an important component of many IMC programs, especially in business-to-business (B2B) settings.

The cost of communicating directly with a potential customer is quite high compared with other forms of promotion, but it is simply the best and most efficient way to sell certain products and services. Customers can buy many products and services without the help of a salesperson, but salespeople simplify the buying process by providing information and services that save customers time and effort. In many cases, sales representatives add significant value, which makes the added expense of employing them worthwhile. Chapter 15 devotes more attention to personal selling.

personal selling
The two-way flow of communication between a buyer and a seller that is designed to influence the buyer's purchase decision.

Sales Promotions

Sales promotions are special incentives or excitement-building programs that encourage the purchase of a product or service, such as coupons, rebates, contests, free samples, and point-of-purchase displays. While some sales promotions are offline (e.g., printed coupons or contest entries), others are online (e.g., e-coupons downloaded to a smartphone.) Marketers typically design these incentives for use in conjunction with other advertising or personal selling programs. Many sales promotions, such as free samples or point-of-purchase displays, are designed to build short-term sales; though others, such as contests and sweepstakes, have become integral components of firms' CRM programs as means to build customer loyalty. We discuss such sales promotions in more detail in Chapter 15.

sales promotions
Special incentives or excitement-building programs that encourage the purchase of a product or service, such as coupons, rebates, contests, free samples, and point-of-purchase displays.

Direct Marketing

The component of IMC that has received the greatest increase in aggregate spending recently is **direct marketing**, or marketing that communicates directly with target customers to generate a response or transaction.[10] Direct marketing contains a variety of traditional and new forms of marketing communication initiatives, including offline forms such as direct mail, direct response TV commercials (infomercials), catalogues, and kiosks, as well as online technologies such as email, podcasts, and cellphones. Internet-based technologies have had a profound effect on direct marketing initiatives. Email, for instance, can be directed to specific consumers to inform them about new merchandise, special promotions, confirm receipt of an order and indicate when an order has been shipped. All these initiatives address the customer in very different ways. In some cases, direct marketing initiatives are crucial to the initial success of an IMC plan, while others are used only after consumers identify themselves as wanting to continue the conversation. Unlike mass media, which communicate to a wide audience, direct marketing allows for personalization of the message, a key advantage.

Direct marketing has four defining characteristics: it is targeted, motivates an action, is measurable, and can provide information for the development of a marketing database.[11] It is an information-driven process that enables marketers to narrowly target the appropriate audiences. For example, a company selling a health supplement can use direct marketing to reach only people who subscribe to health-related magazines in an effort to motivate them to take action, such as calling a 1-800 number, visiting a website, or placing a mail order. The company can easily measure the response for each magazine by using uniquely assigned coded coupons, 1-800 numbers, or Internet microsites. The use of response-generating direct marketing forms, such as direct mail, direct response television, or telemarketing can provide meaningful results and allow the evaluation of a marketing campaign in a timely manner.[12]

Direct marketing offers benefits to both buyers and sellers. Companies that use direct marketing campaigns appreciate the ability to sell to a much wider target audience than could be reached with traditional marketing channels. In comparison to personal selling or mass media advertising, the cost of reaching consumers is much lower with direct marketing. As mentioned earlier, one of the defining characteristics of direct marketing is its measurability—campaigns can be closely monitored to track results. Measurability means marketers know who responds to their campaigns,

Direct marketers now use PDAs and cellphones to reach potential customers

Whereas previously companies bought ads on websites related to the product being promoted, for example, a healthy drink on the GNC website, more targeted advertising now pursues a particular customer rather than all visitors to a specific website. For instance, a behavioural advertising firm such as Tacoda can track how a person moves through a web browser, so that it knows when the user frequents certain sites and thus determines the particular interests of that consumer. On the basis of the consumer's interests, firms can then strategically place advertising on specific sites—but only on that person's browser. Other people who visit the same website at the same time will receive different ads, more in line with their own interests.

In a nod to privacy concerns, this method of targeting advertising does not provide personal profiles of consumers, but rather information about their search activity on the browser. Even when multiple users share the same computer, advertising firms can distinguish patterns and identify which user is at the computer at certain times. So,

for instance, if you share your computer with your roommate, advertisers know which of you is using the computer based on your browsing habits. Consumers who don't want their preferences passed on can opt out by changing their browser settings.

As beneficial as this tracking technology may seem for advertisers, it also might enable clever hackers to target computer browsers more easily. In the wrong hands, information about consumers' browsing and purchasing habits might allow others to breach users' privacy and security. Since the technology in some countries requires consumers to opt out, rather than asking them to opt in, it may leave some consumers unaware of everything they are agreeing to when visiting these sites.

Do you believe that your personal privacy is being unjustly invaded by firms that provide you with targeted advertising based on your browsing habits? Or do you think advertising firms engaged in these activities are providing you with information that may make your buying decisions more pleasant and efficient?

allowing them to build rich databases that can be used to cross-sell, tailor offers, and create specific promotions geared to individual customers in future campaigns.

The increased use of customer databases has enabled marketers to identify and track consumers over time and across purchase situations, which has contributed to the rapid growth of direct marketing. Marketers have been able to build these databases thanks to consumers' increased use of credit and debit cards, store-specific credit and loyalty cards, and online shopping, all of which require the buyer to give the seller personal information that becomes part of its database. Because firms understand customers' purchases better when they possess such information, they can more easily focus their direct marketing efforts appropriately. Ethical Dilemma 14.1 details both the benefits and the concerns associated with how firms use such information to market to customers one at a time.

As shown in Exhibit 14.3, direct marketing can take a number of forms, including direct mail/email, catalogues, direct response TV, kiosks, and personal selling. We focus on the first four forms here. Personal selling is addressed in Chapter 15.

Direct Mail/Email   We consider **direct mail** and **email** primarily as targeted forms of communication distributed to a prospective consumer's mailbox or inbox. Mailing lists are a critical component of direct mail. Choose the wrong list and your promotion will be perceived as "junk mail" since the information and offer will not be targeted to the appropriate audience. Canada Post research shows that Canadian households receive an average of 27 pieces of direct mail per week. In spite of such high volumes, addressed mail continues to be welcomed by Canadians—83 percent spend time with addressed direct mail every day and 63 percent are likely to read it as soon as it is received.[13] Most of us receive far more email marketing messages, not all of which are welcome.

For direct mail to be effective, a good contact list is a must and a good offer is also needed to compel consumers to take immediate action. Good offers must be relevant to both consumers and to the product, and are important whether a company

direct mail/email
A targeted form of communication distributed to a prospective customer's mailbox or inbox.

EXHIBIT 14.3 | Forms of Direct Retailing

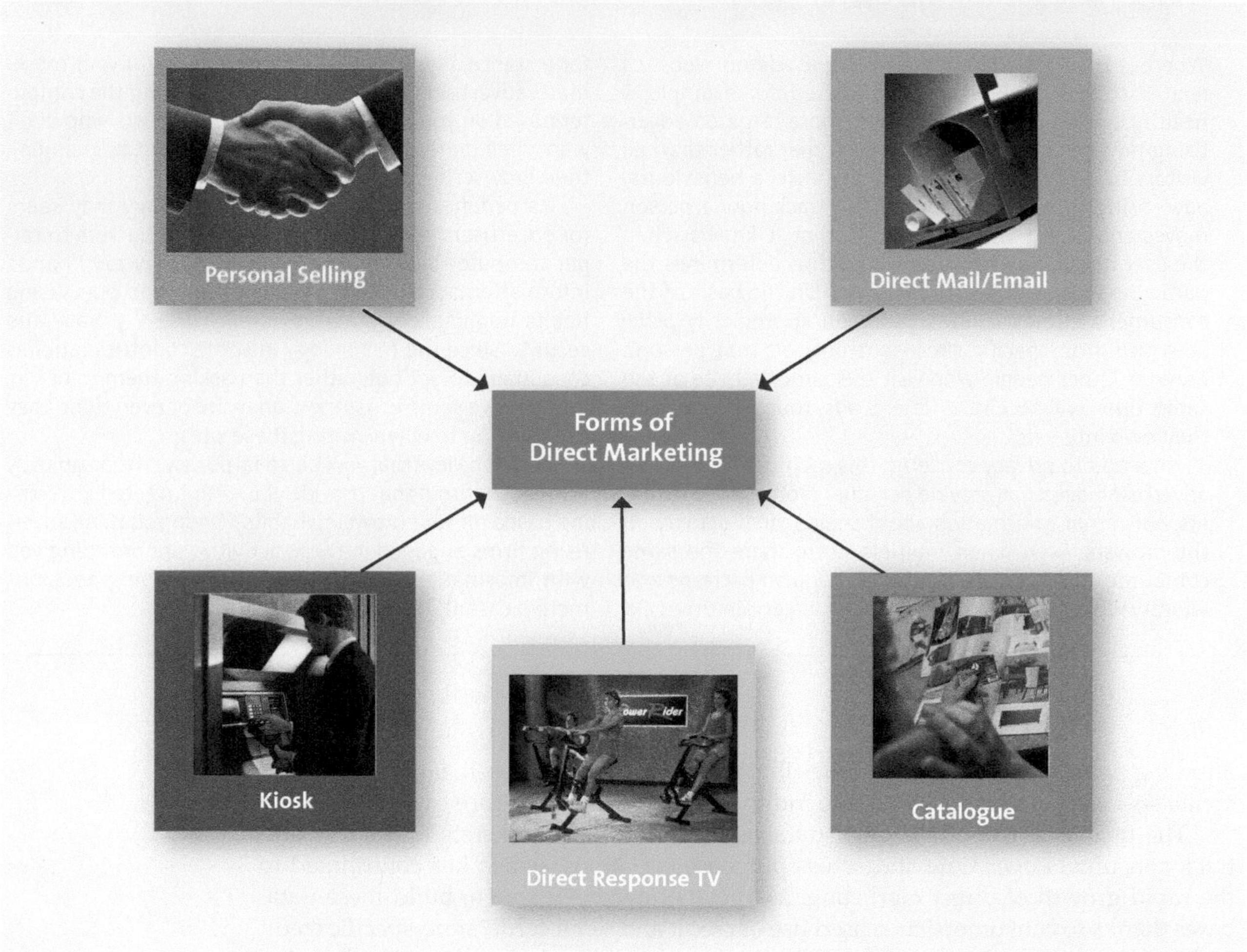

is promoting products to consumers or businesses. But offers don't always involve selling a product. Registered charities rely on direct mail in their fundraising efforts. For example, the Heart and Stroke Foundation of Canada, which receives no operational funding from government sources, uses direct mail extensively to promote its cause. The Foundation's efforts have resulted in the recruitment of more than 140 000 volunteers and 13 million donors[14] and have raised more than $125 million in donations.[15]

Catalogues   Many companies use catalogues to strategically build their business. They represent a medium that Canadians accept, with 80 percent welcoming retail catalogues into their homes. More than half of Canadians have ordered items from catalogues in the past year.[16] Typically, catalogues have been mailed, which can become an issue as a company grows. Although Mountain Equipment Co-op has 2.6 million customers, it mails catalogues to only about 200 000 of them because of the cost and environmental impact. However, it makes catalogues available for download from its website. Today, most companies with physical catalogues, such as IKEA and Business Depot, also offer online catalogues. Despite the ease of online shopping, the vast majority of Canadians still prefer hard-copy catalogues. The Sears *Wish Book* holds fond memories for many adults who remember leafing through its pages as children in anticipation of gifts they might receive.

Catalogues are particularly important for companies with no bricks-and-mortar locations. Toronto-based educational toy company Grand River Toys has never had a

Catalogues are an important communication vehicle that help Sears build its business, allowing consumers to purchase a wide variety of merchandise.

physical store. It started out as a mail order business selling only from its catalogue. As the company grew, it took its catalogue online and added e-commerce capabilities, extending its reach and its sales.

Direct Response TV   **Direct response TV (DRTV)** refers to TV commercials or infomercials with a strong call to action, usually via 1-800 number, return mail address, or website. Although many people may question the effectiveness of this form of direct marketing, DRTV and the Shopping Channel are the two most welcome forms of direct marketing among Canadians.[17] DRTV now accounts for 25 percent of all TV commercials, with the top purchases being exercise products, diet/health/weight merchandise, videos, and beauty products/cosmetics.[18]

Most DRTV ads have short 60- and 120-second formats or are much longer 30-minute infomercials. For many people, the term *infomercial* conjures up images of a late-night TV pitchman telling them how his product slices and dices better than anything on the market. Most infomercials appear to be selling products that seem too good to be true: fitness routines that promise to melt the pounds away, a miracle knife so sharp you'll never have to buy another, or rejuvenating face creams that magically erase wrinkles. Almost everyone has heard of the George Foreman Grill but not nearly as many people recognize Foreman as a heavyweight boxing champion.

direct response TV (DRTV) TV commercials or infomercials with a strong call to action.

The George Foreman Grill is promoted and sold using DRTV infomercials.

DRTV is used for its power to drive results not only through infomercials, but also in shorter format ads. When Canadian Blood Services launched its "Save a Life" campaign, it exceeded targets by more than 50 percent,[19] which was to bring in 2000 new blood donors. More than 3000 new and lapsed donors made appointments to give blood. The new donor drive DRTV campaign took home the Gold award in the DRTV category at the Canadian Marketing Association Awards.[20]

Kiosks   As discussed in Chapter 10, electronic kiosks can be used to facilitate the way services companies deliver their services to customers, for example, allowing passengers at airports to quickly print prebooked tickets. However, kiosks can also be used to sell both services and products to end consumers. For example, after you print your ticket at an airport kiosk, you can get a 10-minute manicure at another kiosk while you wait for your flight. Some kiosks are temporary, such as the kiosks that are set up in malls primarily to sell gift items in the weeks leading up to Christmas. Others kiosks are permanent. For example, Dell's mall kiosks allow shoppers to talk to a Dell representative face to face and find the computer that's just right for them. Consumers can customize their PC, order it, and have it shipped directly to their homes. In Ontario, Virgin Mobile unveiled a network of mall kiosks, which it may use to sell other Virgin products and services in the future.[21] Real estate companies such as Century 21 use kiosks in malls where thousands of potential buyers can connect with property listings. Kiosks from Hallmark allow customers to create their own personalized cards. Disposable cameras and batteries are available at kiosks throughout the Rogers Centre in Toronto.[22] Business marketers use kiosks as well, particularly at trade shows to collect sales leads and to provide information on their products.

Public Relations

Public relations (PR) is the organizational function that manages the firm's communications to achieve a variety of objectives, including building and maintaining a positive image, handling or heading off unfavourable stories or events, and

public relations (PR)
The organizational function that manages the firm's communications to achieve a variety of objectives, including building and maintaining a positive image, handling or heading off unfavourable stories or events, and maintaining positive relationships with the media.

Dell's mall kiosks allow shoppers to find a computer that's just right for them.

Power of the Internet 14.1

Diet Coke and Mentos Viral Blast

Advertising agencies cringe when approached by clients who ask them to create a viral video. When it comes to marketing communications, there simply are no guarantees that consumers will pass along material, no matter how good or how funny. That makes Stephen Voltz, a lawyer, and Fritz Grobe, a professional juggler, unlikely candidates to identify the ingredients of a successful viral video. Yet their company, EepyBird, has spent the last five years developing and refining a proven, repeatable formula and created videos that have won two Emmy Nominations and four Webby Awards.

You may remember one of their first efforts, Experiment #137 (www.eepybird.com/featured-video/the-extreme-diet-coke-mentos-experiments/), which showed the zany duo dropping Mentos mints into giant bottles of Diet Coke, creating geyser-like effects. The video was posted online in June 2006. Two days later, the pair got a call from the *Late Show with David Letterman*. Within only a few years, the video had been viewed more than 120 million times. *Advertising Age* called it "the most important commercial content of 2006." Coca-Cola compared it to "a Superbowl ad at the fraction of the cost."[23] Who would have guessed that a simple video would increase Mentos sales by 20 percent or double the traffic to the Coke website?[24]

The videos changed the lives of Voltz and Grobe and turned EepyBird into a full-time endeavour. They've since made it their mission to explore creativity and how ordinary objects can do extraordinary things.[25] The pair has also experimented with sticky notes, paper airplanes, and shampoo. Besides *Letterman*, they've appeared on *Ellen*, *The Today Show*, and *MythBusters* and performed in Paris, London, Istanbul, Las Vegas, and in New York on Wall Street, and set three Guinness World Records.

Their latest video experiment, a "rocket car" fuelled by Coke Zero and Mentos, was viewed more than a million times in the first two days after being launched in 2010 (www.eepybird.com/featured-video/the-coke-zero-mentos-rocket-car-2d/) The car uses a piston mechanism with 108 six-foot rods inside six-foot tubes, all attached to a bottle of Coke Zero. Mentos provide the pressure to push the rods out of the tubes and propel the car.

Like their earlier videos, the rocket car video has continued to propel their careers, not to mention the Coke and Mentos brands. Voltz and Grobe have become an Internet sensation and now speak and perform all over the world, entertaining consumer audiences and sharing lessons from the front lines of viral videos with corporate audiences.

Experiment #137 created a viral storm for EepyBird, Diet Coke, and Mentos.

maintaining positive relationships with the media. Like advertising, this tactic is relatively passive in that customers do not have to take any action to receive it. However, PR efforts span both offline and online media. PR activities support the other promotional efforts by the firm by generating "free" media attention. For example, McDonald's "I'm Lovin' It" campaign was frequently in the news and discussed in numerous newspaper and magazine articles. While it can be very difficult to convince the media to write about a company or its products and services, this media attention can be crucial to a company's success.

In essence, PR is the free placement of a company's message in the media. Power of the Internet 14.1 examines the viral power of electronic media to quickly spread a message and generate a wealth of valuable publicity for companies and their brands.

Yoplait's "Save Lids to Save Lives" campaign and Champions program both illustrate how a well-orchestrated IMC effort using a combination of promotional and PR campaigns can enhance a firm's image while supporting a worthwhile cause.[26] The "Save Lids to Save Lives" campaign was designed not only to sell yogourt, but also to create a positive association between the brand and a social cause, in this case,

cause-related marketing
Commercial activity in which businesses and charities form a partnership to market an image, product, or service for their mutual benefit; a type of promotional campaign.

breast cancer awareness. This form of promotional campaign is called **cause-related marketing**, which refers to commercial activity in which businesses and charities form a partnership to market an image, product, or service for their mutual benefit.[27] In the "Save Lids to Save Lives" campaign, Yoplait donates a set monetary amount for each special pink yogourt lid that consumers send in to Susan G. Komen for the Cure, a breast cancer foundation.[28]

Integrally linked to the "Save Lids to Save Lives" campaign is Yoplait's Champions program, another PR campaign. The goal of the nationwide Champions program is to identify and recognize "ordinary people doing extraordinary things" in the fight against breast cancer. The 25 individual champions' stories appear in local media, and the program itself often makes the national media. Thus, both initiatives are extremely successful in expanding consumers' knowledge about Yoplait's social commitments, as well as Yoplait's brand awareness.[29]

Designers vie to have celebrities, especially those nominated for awards, wear their fashions on the red carpet. These sightings can create both positive and negative publicity. When Reese Witherspoon wore a Nina Ricci yellow cocktail dress to the Golden Globes, the dress got so much press that the designer's cachet increased significantly. Chanel, Valentino, Zac Posen, and Christian Dior are all red carpet veterans that commonly provide dresses or tuxedos to celebrities, whose images will be broadcast around the world.[30] The placement of designer apparel at media events benefits both the designer and the celebrity. And neither happens by accident. PR people on both sides help orchestrate the events to get the maximum benefit for both parties.

Good PR has always been an important success factor. Yet in recent years, the importance of PR has grown, as the cost of other forms of marketing communications has increased. At the same time, the influence of PR has become more powerful, as consumers have become increasingly skeptical of marketing claims made in other media.[31] In many instances, consumers view media coverage generated through PR as more credible and objective than any other aspects of an IMC program, because the firm does not "buy" the space in print media or time on radio or television.

event sponsorship
A popular PR tool; occurs when corporations support various activities (financially or otherwise), usually in the cultural or sports and entertainment sectors.

For example, TOMS Shoes, a company founded by Blake Mycoskie, illustrates how a well-orchestrated IMC effort, using a combination of promotional and PR campaigns, can enhance a firm's image while supporting a worthwhile cause.[32] Mycoskie took traditional Argentinean shoes, known as *alpargatas*, and began selling and marketing them to consumers outside the generally impoverished nation in which they originated. The company's website proclaims that Mycoskie's inspiration was simple. Noting the comfort of the shoes and the extreme poverty of Argentina, he promises that "With every pair you purchase, TOMS will give a pair of new shoes to a child in need." This message is found on his website and other press vehicles, including a mention as the "Good Guy of the Month" in *O, The Oprah Winfrey Magazine*. TOMS Shoes embraces cause-related marketing. The company is not just about making and selling shoes, but also partners

TOMS Shoes embraces cause-related marketing. For every pair of shoes consumers buy, the company gives a pair of new shoes to a child in need.

with groups such as Insight Argentina, an organization offering volunteer activities in Argentina to help that area address its most pressing social issues.[33]

Another very popular PR tool is event sponsorship. **Event sponsorship** occurs when corporations support various activities (financially or otherwise), usually in the cultural or sports and entertainment sectors. For example, Subaru sponsors the Subaru Ironman Canada Triathlon, regarded as one of the best Ironman events in the world. The race helps Subaru promote its vehicles, which, like athletes, must possess both the versatility to excel in a variety of environments and the durability to outlast the competition.

Firms often distribute a PR toolkit to communicate with various audiences. Some toolkit elements are designed to inform specific groups directly, whereas others are created to generate media attention and disseminate information. We depict the various elements of a PR toolkit in Exhibit 14.4.

Electronic Media

The Internet has had a dramatic impact on how marketers communicate with their customers. **Electronic media** tools range from simple website content to far more interactive features such as corporate blogs, online games, text messaging, social media, and mobile apps. Unlike the other IMC tools discussed previously, these forms of electronic media were designed only for the online world. Marketers are using them more and more often for the following reasons, among others: they can be targeted to specific customer segments, their impact can be easily and quickly measured in real time, modifications can be quickly made to increase their effectiveness, and customers can be engaged to forward the message to their social networks. Entrepreneurial Marketing 14.1 examines a digital marketing agency that understands the power of electronic media to create extraordinary experiences for consumers.

The annual Subaru Ironman Triathlon in Penticton, British Columbia, lets Subaru link the performance and durability of its vehicles to the grueling race.

electronic media
Tools ranging from simple website content to far more interactive features such as corporate blogs, online games, text messaging, social media, and mobile apps.

Websites Firms are increasing their emphasis on communicating with customers through their websites. They use them to build their brand image and educate customers about their products or services and where they can be purchased. Retailers and some manufacturers sell merchandise directly to consumers over the Internet. For example, in addition to selling merchandise, Office Depot's American website has a Business Resource Center that provides advice and product knowledge, as well as a source of networks to other businesses. It includes forms that businesses would use to comply with Occupational Safety and Health Act (OSHA) requirements, to check job applicant records, to estimate cash flow, and to develop a sexual harassment policy; workshops for running a business; and local and national business news. By providing this information on its website, Office Depot reinforces its image as the essential source of products, services, and information for small businesses.

EXHIBIT 14.4	Elements of a PR Toolkit
PR Element	**Function**
Publications: brochures, special-purpose single-issue publications such as books	Inform various constituencies about the activities of the organization and highlight specific areas of expertise
Video and audio: programs, public service announcements	Highlight the organization or support cause-related marketing efforts
Annual reports	Give required financial performance data and inform investors and others about the unique activities of the organization
Media relations: press kits, news releases, speeches, event sponsorships	Generate news coverage of the organization's activities or products/services
Electronic media: websites, email campaigns	Websites can contain all the previously mentioned toolbox elements, while email directs PR efforts to specific target groups

From Driving Range to Digital Agency

When you think about the background needed to head up a digital marketing agency, a career as an LPGA golf pro probably isn't the first thing that comes to mind. Yet those are the skills Critical Mass CEO, Dianne Wilkins, brought to the job. Golf paid her way through university and, after doing her MBA, she taught professional golf management. And it was a golf pro friend who introduced her to company founder Ted Hellard, who hired her in 1998 to go to Sweden and work on a Saab campaign. She served as CEO of the Critical Mass spinoff she established in Stockholm, growing it to 65 employees in only six months.

After two years, Wilkins moved to the firm's Calgary head office where she was later promoted to Canadian CEO. Today, Critical Mass has offices in Calgary, Toronto, Chicago, New York, Nashville, London, and Costa Rica. The company has grown to more than 600 employees, who work with global clients such as AT&T, Budweiser, Infiniti, Las Vegas Convention and Visitors Authority, Moen, and Nissan to bring together creative thinking, smart ideas, and emerging technologies. Wilkins says one of her favourite campaigns is a microsite created for NIKEiD, which allows consumers to interactively design their own shoes, upload the patterns, add the sole of their choice, include their name on the shoe, and have the shoes custom manufactured and delivered to their door.

Although the company focus revolves around all things digital, Wilkins sees "a world where customers no longer consider experiences as online or offline, but focus on the quality of interactions they have with brands."[34] Today, online behaviour has fragmented with dozens of touchpoints. Critical Mass knows each one is important to the total customer experience. Its research division, Curious, helps the company gather consumer insights and mine information from online communities.

Getting and keeping the right people with the right attitude is critical to the company's success. A focus on professional development and office "hives," equipped with Nintendo Wiis, helps employees relax and stay in touch with new technology.[35] Wilkins notes that, in a digital agency, it's important to be focused and stick to a course rather than trying to be all things to all people. That doesn't mean that Wilkins is averse to change, in fact, once the decision to implement change has been made, she says it's critical to drive that change relentlessly.[36]

Wilkins says it's been a fun ride. While her golf handicap may have suffered, Critical Mass has benefited from her leadership. *Marketing Magazine* has named it the number one interactive agency in Canada and one of the top interactive agencies in the world.[37]

Blogs Blogging has risen from obscure, random company postings to a valuable Web addition in virtually no time. A **blog (weblog of Web log)** contains periodic posts on a common web page. A well-received blog can communicate trends, promote special events, create positive word of mouth, connect customers by forming a community, increase sales, improve customer satisfaction because the company can respond directly to customers' comments, and develop a long-term relationship with the company. By its very nature, a blog is supposed to be transparent and contain authors' honest observations, which can help customers determine their trust and loyalty levels. When handled appropriately, blogs can serve as trusted platforms for damage control. A poorly received blog may lead to backlash, decreased customer trust, and tangible but negative economic returns.[38]

> **blog (weblog or Web log)**
> A web page that contains periodic posts; corporate blogs are a new form of marketing communications.

Some universities have started to use student blogs as a recruitment tool to attract undergrads. At the University of Manitoba in Winnipeg, 16 students and alumni have been sharing their experiences at the university through their blogs at www.itsmyfuture.ca. The site attracted more than 60 000 page views by over 6500 visitors in its first four weeks online.[39]

Insincere postings or flogs (fake blogs) that are actually disguised advertising campaigns are problematic. By their very nature, blogs are transparent and contain authors' honest observations, which can help customers determine their trust and loyalty levels. Anything less than total honesty will break that bond and damage the relationship.

When natural and organic grocery store chain Whole Foods Market attempted to purchase its competitor Wild Oats, it was publicly disclosed that its CEO, John Mackey, had been actively blogging on the Yahoo Finance website for eight years. Using the alias Rahodeb (an anagram of his wife Deborah's name), he wrote poorly of Wild Oats, saying that it would probably go into bankruptcy. At the same time, he praised Whole Foods (and himself, noting in one posting that Rahodeb thought Mackey's new haircut was "cute"). Details of this false identification were used to build the case against the Whole Foods takeover of Wild Oats, arguing that Mackey's opinions and statements were strong evidence of his intent to make Whole Foods a monopoly.[40]

Online Games   One particularly successful way to reach younger consumers is through short online games that allow consumers to interact with the site and possibly other players. To celebrate its role as Official Treat Provider to the London 2012 Olympic and Paralympic Games, Cadbury created the website Spots v Stripes, featuring a variety of online sports-related games designed to get the nation playing. Launched in 2010, Spots v Stripes features fun, simple games that anyone can play, for example, Hoop & Glory, Thumb Wrestling, and Paper Plane Dogfight. New games are introduced every three months. Users register on the website (www.spotsvstripes.com), pick a side, and play for a chance to win prizes. Points earned are updated live on Cadbury's Score'o'tron. To appeal to even younger customers, Neopets.com offers games sponsored by a variety of outside companies. Users who agree to receive offers from sponsors are offered help in taking care of their virtual pet. For example, they can earn points by taking consumer surveys or by feeding their Neopet McDonald's products.[41]

Text Messaging   Using the Internet in novel ways has also led to the growth of text messaging (or short message service [SMS]), which is an increasingly important way for marketers to communicate with younger consumers. Tech-savvy customers use their cellphones to obtain sports scores, weather, music videos, and text messages in real time. It thus is a natural evolution for firms to tap into this trend. Recent experiments using text messaging have yielded some impressive results. An average SMS campaign generates a 15-percent response rate, compared with less than half that amount for direct mail. Research also shows that 94 percent of all advertising text messages are read, 23 percent of SMS advertisements are forwarded or shown to other users, and 8 percent of those consumers reply to the text message.[42]

Retailers can send coupons directly to shoppers' cellphones.[43] Redemption rates have been as high as 40 percent, compared with less than 2 percent for many print and online campaigns. Shoppers text a code found on store signs to get the coupon, and then display it on their phone at checkout. While this technology is still very new, Canadian retailers are beginning to adopt it because of interest from consumers. Customers can buy products instantly by using text messages, a process that eliminates the need to go to a store or even visit a website. If consumers see an ad for a coat in a magazine, they can order it by sending the text code that appears next to the item through their cellphone or PDA. Not limited to merchandise, some concert halls are using this technology to sell tickets. After the devastating earthquake in Haiti, some charities solicited and received donations through text messages.

Social Media   Social media refers to a broad spectrum of online communities and social networking sites, such as YouTube, Facebook, and Twitter. Marketers can use social media to engage their customers in a proactive dialogue, as seen in many of the Social Media Marketing boxes throughout this book. When it comes to social media, there is considerably more transparency and honesty than in most other forms of marketing communication. And, because members share so much personal information, marketers can tailor messages and applications to very specific and desirable target markets. For example, TD Canada Trust launched a Facebook application called Split It, an online calculator that allows roommates to divide household expenses. New Brunswick's Mount Allison University is using Facebook groups and student-made videos on YouTube (commissioned and paid for by the university) to recruit future students.[44]

Mobile Apps   With the advent of smartphones, apps (applications) have become very popular. Apps are used for a variety of purposes, from games and advertising to business applications, or even to order a pizza and then track its delivery. Apple's App Store boasts the world's largest collection of mobile apps, with more than 350 000 applications, including a wide range of categories such as music, cooking, travelling, the great outdoors, learning tools for students, and business. CIBC was the first Canadian bank to introduce an iPhone banking app that allows customers to access their bank accounts. RIM launched BlackBerry App World, which has specially designed business and personal smartphone applications. There's even an eBay app to let BlackBerry users search, bid, buy, and check their accounts from virtually anywhere. The Android Marketplace has experienced huge growth, making it one of the fastest-growing mobile application stores on the market today.

Over time, technology will continue to improve, and other new means of communicating with consumers will be added to the IMC channel mix. Let's now look at the steps in planning an IMC campaign that achieves the organization's strategic objectives.

L03   Steps in Planning an IMC Campaign

Designing a successful IMC campaign requires a great deal of planning. Exhibit 14.5 shows some of the key steps in the planning process, each of which helps ensure that the intended message reaches the right audience and has the desired effect. As mentioned earlier, these steps can be used for all IMC tools. To simplify things, let's examine each of these steps as they pertain to an advertising campaign.

1. Identify Target Audience

Who is the target audience for this ad, men or women?

The success of an advertising campaign depends on how well the advertiser can identify its target audience. Firms conduct research to identify their target audience, and then use the information they gain to set the tone for the advertising program and help them select the media they will use to deliver the message to that audience.

During this research, firms must keep in mind that their target audience may or may not be the same as current users of the product. Think about jewellery. Research shows that in a typical year, some 43 percent of the North American adult population—more than 95 million people—purchase jewellery. Although women have a significantly higher purchase incidence (48 percent) and purchase more often than men (36 percent), men spend significantly more money on their jewellery purchases than do women. Perhaps it is no surprise that the majority of men's jewellery purchases are gifts.[45]

Some advertising messages also may be directed at portions of audiences who are not part of the marketer's target market but who participate in the purchase process. Chrysler, for instance, runs ads for its minivans during Saturday morning children's viewing hours. These ads are designed to build brand awareness on the part of the children, who, Chrysler hopes, will influence their parents' purchase of a minivan.[46] Honda reached 18 to 34 year olds directly with an integrated campaign, discussed in Social Media Marketing 14.1, that reflected its target audience's interest in music.

Social Media Marketing 14.1 — Civic Nation Mix-Off "Mixes" IMC

To re-energize the Civic brand with the 18- to 34–year-old demographic, Honda launched the Civic Nation mix-off. The new integrated marketing communications campaign incorporates a combination of offline and online techniques. TV, radio, online, and out-of-home advertising are used to drive online traffic to the CivicNation.ca microsite.

Members of the Civic Tuner Nation culture are very much into music. Visitors to the site are invited to use a sound track mixer to create a 30-second "Anthem for the Nation" by using samples by local hip-hop celeb Saukrates in a variety of music genres, including electronica, hip hop, and electro-pop. According to Ravi Dindayal, director of interactive at Grip, the agency that put the campaign together, Civic owners are "high creators of content."[47] The mixer allows users to mix different instruments and publish their new tracks onto a website where others can vote on them.

Honda's social media marketing efforts didn't stop at allowing people to vote on the Civic Nation microsite. To help contestants earn more votes, Honda ensured that users could post their tracks to blogs, Facebook, Myspace, and Twitter. Not only did the tactic increase the reach of the campaign, it also improved the viral aspect of the contest.

The contest offered a grand prize linked to one of the most popular DJs in Canada, DJ Starting from Scratch.

The winning anthem aired for two weeks as the intro to Scratch's show on the Traffic Flow MixShow on Flow 93.5, a radio station with a highly urban and multicultural demographic.[48] Because he had a diverse audience, Scratch was seen as a good fit for building on the Civic Nation multicultural brand image.

Honda's Civic Nation mix-off contest allowed fans to create and vote on music tracks.

2. Set Objectives

As with any strategic undertaking, firms need to understand the outcome they hope to achieve before they begin. These objectives can be short-term, such as generating inquiries, increasing awareness, and prompting trial. Or they can be long-term in nature, such as increasing sales, market share, and customer loyalty. Driving traffic and sales was the primary and long-term goal of the McDonald's "I'm Lovin' It" campaign; but, in the short term, McDonald's needed to establish heightened brand awareness. Thus, the campaign was designed to get consumers' attention through TV, print, and billboard advertisements. Both short- and long-term goals should be explicitly defined and measured. We discuss how firms measure IMC success later in this chapter.

Campaign objectives are derived from the overall objectives of the marketing program and clarify the specific goals that the ads are designed to accomplish. Generally, these objectives appear in the **advertising plan**, a section of the firm's

advertising plan
A section of the firm's overall marketing plan that explicitly outlines the objectives of the advertising campaign, how the campaign might accomplish those objectives, and how the firm can determine whether the campaign was successful.

EXHIBIT 14.5 | Steps in Planning an IMC Campaign

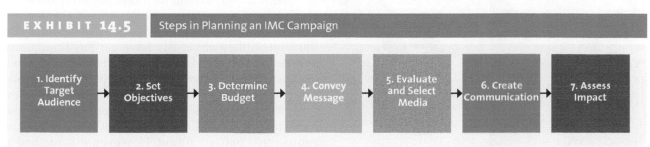

1. Identify Target Audience → 2. Set Objectives → 3. Determine Budget → 4. Convey Message → 5. Evaluate and Select Media → 6. Create Communication → 7. Assess Impact

overall marketing plan that explicitly outlines the objectives of the advertising campaign, how the campaign might accomplish those objectives, and how the firm can determine whether the campaign was successful.[49] An advertising plan is crucial because it will later serve as the metric against which advertising success or failure is measured.

All marketing communications aim to achieve certain objectives: to inform, persuade, and remind customers. These objectives are examined in more depth in Chapter 15. Communication objectives also need to consider focus—for example, does the company hope to stimulate demand for a new product or service or to increase awareness for the company in general?

When setting advertising objectives, the overarching strategy used is one of push versus pull. However, marketers also have to consider other factors, such as the nature of the market (consumer versus business), the nature of the product (simple versus technologically complex), and the stage in the product life cycle (PLC). Generally, when advertising to consumers, the objective is a **pull strategy** in which the goal is to get consumers to pull the product into the supply chain by demanding retailers carry it. **Push strategies** also exist and are designed to increase demand by focusing on wholesalers, distributors, or salespeople, who push the product to consumers via distribution channels. These campaigns attempt to motivate the seller to highlight the product, rather than the products of competitors, and thereby push the product onto consumers.

Once the advertising campaign's objectives are defined, the firm sets the advertising budget.

3. Determine Budget

Firms use a variety of methods to plan their marketing communications budgets (see Exhibit 14.6). Because all the methods of setting a promotional budget have both advantages and disadvantages, no one method should be used in isolation.[50] Budgeting is not a simple process. It may take several rounds of negotiations among the company's managers, who are each competing for resources for their own areas of responsibility.

The **objective-and-task method** determines the budget required to undertake specific tasks to accomplish communication objectives. To use this method, marketers first establish a set of communication objectives, and then determine which media best reach the target market and how much it will cost to run the number and types of communications necessary to achieve the objectives. This process—set objectives, choose media, and determine costs—must be repeated for each product or service. The sum of all the individual communication plan budgets becomes the firm's total marketing communications budget.

In addition to the objective-and-task method, three rule-of-thumb methods: **competitive parity method**, **percentage-of-sales method**, and **affordable method** of budgeting can be used to set budgets.

These rule-of-thumb methods use prior sales and communication activities to determine the present communication budget. Although they are easy to implement, they obviously have various limitations, as noted in Exhibit 14.6. While small companies often use the affordable budgeting method, it generally results in underspending and thus may not accomplish the company's sales objectives. Large companies such as Coca-Cola and PepsiCo may use the competitive parity method. However, this method is

pull strategy
Designed to get consumers to pull the product into the supply chain by demanding retailers carry it.

push strategy
Designed to increase demand by focusing on wholesalers, distributors, or salespeople, who push the product to consumers via distribution channels.

objective-and-task method
An IMC budgeting method that determines the cost required to undertake specific tasks to accomplish communication objectives; process entails setting objectives, choosing media, and determining costs.

This ad informs consumers about Winners' accessories selection.

EXHIBIT 14.6	Budgeting Methods

Method	Definition	Limitations
Objective and Task	The communication budget is set based on the cost of specific tasks required to achieve stated communication objectives.	• It can be difficult to identify the specific tasks that will achieve the objectives and, as a result, it is the most difficult method to use.
Competitive Parity	A method of determining a communications budget in which the firm's share of the communication expenses is in line with its market share.	• Prevents firms from exploiting the unique opportunities or problems they confront in a market. • If all competitors use this method to set communication budgets, their market shares will stay approximately the same over time.
Percentage-of-Sales	A method of determining a communications budget that is based on a fixed percentage of forecasted sales. For example, a company with $2.5 million in projected sales that allocates 3.5% to advertising would have a budget of $87,500.	• Assumes the percentage used in the past, or by competitors, is still appropriate for the firm. • Does not take into account new plans (e.g., to introduce a new line of products in the current year).
Affordable Budgeting	A method of determining a communications budget based on what is left over after other operating costs have been covered. That is, marketers forecast their sales and expenses, excluding communication, during the budgeting period. The difference between the forecast sales, minus expenses plus desired profit is applied to the communication budget (i.e., the budget is the money available after operating costs and profits).	• Assumes communication expenses do not stimulate sales and profit.

competitive parity method
A method of determining a communications budget in which the firm's share of the communication expenses is in line with its market share.

percentage-of-sales method
A method of determining a communications budget that is based on a fixed percentage of forecasted sales.

affordable method
A method of determining a communications budget based on what is left over after other operating costs have been covered.

setting a budget based on market share, which may result in PepsiCo being outspent. The percentage-of-sales method is popular as well, and standard percentages are sometimes used in some product categories, as shown in Exhibit 14.7. Since everyone needs to eat, the grocery industry needs to spend only a small percentage—around 1 percent—of its revenues on advertising, whereas the toy and game industry must spend about 11 percent.

When selecting the various budgeting methods for marketing communications, firms must first consider the role that advertising plays in their attempt to meet their overall promotional objectives. Second, advertising expenditures vary over the course of the PLC, with considerably higher levels of spending during the introduction stage. Third, the nature of the market and the product influence the size of advertising budgets. For example, advertising for the Scion was less than 14 percent of the total promotional budget because Toyota used so many kinds of nontraditional media to get the attention of its young target customers. For other products or services, the advertising portion of the total promotional budget may be as high as 95 percent. It all depends on the objectives of the overall IMC campaign.

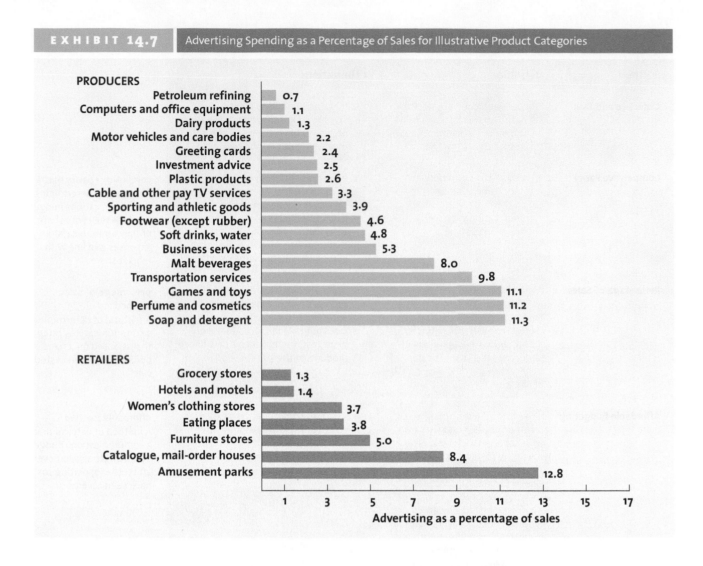

EXHIBIT 14.7 | Advertising Spending as a Percentage of Sales for Illustrative Product Categories

PRODUCERS

Petroleum refining	0.7
Computers and office equipment	1.1
Dairy products	1.3
Motor vehicles and care bodies	2.2
Greeting cards	2.4
Investment advice	2.5
Plastic products	2.6
Cable and other pay TV services	3.3
Sporting and athletic goods	3.9
Footwear (except rubber)	4.6
Soft drinks, water	4.8
Business services	5.3
Malt beverages	8.0
Transportation services	9.8
Games and toys	11.1
Perfume and cosmetics	11.2
Soap and detergent	11.3

RETAILERS

Grocery stores	1.3
Hotels and motels	1.4
Women's clothing stores	3.7
Eating places	3.8
Furniture stores	5.0
Catalogue, mail-order houses	8.4
Amusement parks	12.8

Advertising as a percentage of sales

The nature of the market also determines the amount of money spent on advertising. For instance, less money is spent on advertising in B2B marketing contexts than in B2C markets. Personal selling, as we discuss in Chapter 15, likely is more important in B2B markets.

4. Convey Message

In this step, marketers determine what they want to convey about the product or service. First, the firm determines the key message it wants to communicate to the target audience. Second, the firm decides what appeal would most effectively convey the message. We present these decisions sequentially but, in reality, they must be considered simultaneously.

The Message The message provides the target audience with reasons to respond in the desired way. A logical starting point for deciding on the advertising message is to tout the key benefits of the product or service. The message should communicate the product's problem-solving ability clearly and in a compelling fashion. In this context, advertisers must remember that products and services solve problems, whether real or perceived. That is, people are not looking for 1/4-inch drill bits; they are looking for 1/4-inch holes.[51] Because there are many ways to make a 1/4-inch hole, a firm such as Black and Decker must convey to consumers that its drill bit is the best way to get that hole.

Another common strategy differentiates a product by establishing its unique benefits. This distinction forms the basis for the **unique selling proposition (USP)**, which is often the common theme or slogan in an advertising campaign. Briefly, a good USP communicates the unique attributes of the product and thereby becomes a snapshot of the entire campaign. Some of the most famous USPs include the following: Ford, "Built Tough"; Red Bull, "Gives You Wings"; Nike, "Just Do It."

The selling proposition communicated by the advertising must be not only *unique* to the brand, but also *meaningful* to the consumer; it furthermore must be *sustainable* over time, even with repetition.

The Appeal According to early theories of rhetoric (the study of principles and rules of composition), an argument may use three main types of appeals: logos (logical), ethos (ethical), and pathos (emotional). Likewise, advertisers use different appeals to portray their product or service. Although advertising tends to combine the types of appeals into two broad categories: rational and emotional. Moral appeals are sometimes considered as a third category. Marketers, especially those who work in non-profit organizations, often use this type of message. Since moral appeals can be rational or emotional, they are not addressed as a separate category.

Is Black and Decker doing a good job of selling a solution?

L04

Rational appeals. **Rational appeals** help consumers make purchase decisions by offering factual information and strong arguments built around relevant issues that encourage consumers to evaluate the brand favourably on the basis of the key benefits it provides.[52] Rational appeals focus on consumers' sense of reasoning, logic, and learning. Kimberly-Clark, for example, relies heavily on rational appeals to sell Kleenex Anti-Viral tissues. Note the copy used on the company's website:

> Only KLEENEX® Anti-Viral Tissue has a moisture-activated middle layer that is scientifically proven to kill cold and flu viruses. When moisture from a runny nose, cough or sneeze comes in contact with KLEENEX® Anti-Viral Tissue's special middle layer, cold and flu viruses are trapped and killed.[53]

This appeal is perfectly suited to this type of product. The source of its competitive advantage is a tangible feature of the product. By stressing the superior benefits of this product over regular facial tissue, the advertising copy directly delivers a rational persuasive message.[54]

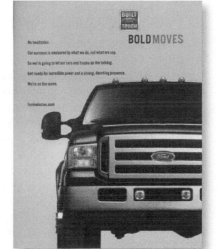

unique selling proposition (USP)
A strategy of differentiating a product by communicating its unique attributes; often becomes the common theme or slogan in the entire advertising campaign.

The unique selling proposition establishes a product or firm's unique benefits in an advertising campaign. Ford's USP is "Built Tough."

Firms use emotional appeals to satisfy consumers' emotional desires rather than their utilitarian needs, such as this one which uses sex appeal.

Emotional appeals. An **emotional appeal** aims to satisfy consumers' emotional desires rather than their utilitarian needs. The key to a successful emotional appeal is the use of emotion to create a bond between the consumer and the brand. The emotions most often invoked in advertising include fear appeal and humour appeal, but also safety, happiness, love (or sex), comfort, and nostalgia. Companies must pay attention to cultural influences because humour is not perceived the same way across different cultural groups and sexual appeals are taboo in some cultures.

Let's look again at Kimberly-Clark's Kleenex line. The company uses a completely different and emotional appeal for its regular facial tissue. Facial tissues can be closely tied to emotional moments that create the need to wipe away tears of joy or sorrow, and Kleenex attempts to reinforce this emotional trigger by sponsoring the TNT Tearjerker Movie. Unlike the Anti-Viral campaign, this campaign relies on the implied need for Kleenex during dramatic films. Tangible product features do not even appear in the emotional appeal because they are no longer the persuasive mechanism used to deliver the selling message, as they are in rational appeals.

Although the term *emotion* often conveys the image of tears, many other effective emotional appeals are used in advertising, ranging from sex appeal (e.g., Tag Body Spray), need for affiliation, need for guidance (e.g., Betty Crocker), and attention (e.g., cosmetics). People need a sense of self-esteem, so advertisements for Bowflex and Jenny Craig tend to feature celebrities or regular people talking about how much better they feel about themselves after they've joined the program and lost weight. Weight loss ads also tend to play a bit on consumers' fears, showing "before and after" pictures as if the heavier version were a horror to behold. Political candidates also use fear appeals for issues as mundane as garbage removal and as serious as sexual predators. Clearly, fear appeals often work best when the threat appears to be directed toward children or some other innocent victim.

LO5

5. Evaluate and Select Media

rational appeal
Helps consumers make purchase decisions by offering factual information and strong arguments built around relevant issues that encourage consumers to evaluate the brand favourably on the basis of the key benefits it provides.

emotional appeal
Aims to satisfy consumers' emotional desires rather than their utilitarian needs.

The content of an advertisement is tied closely to the characteristics of the media that firms select to carry the message, and vice versa. **Media planning** refers to the process of evaluating and selecting the **media mix**—the combination of the media used and the frequency of advertising in each medium—that will deliver a clear, consistent, compelling message to the intended audience.[55] For example, Zellers may determine that a heavy dose of television, radio, print, and billboards is appropriate for the back-to-school selling season between August and September each year.

Because the **media buy**, the actual purchase of airtime or print pages, is generally the largest expense in the advertising budget, marketers must make their decisions carefully. TV advertising is by far the most expensive. Total ad spending in Canada is $12.6 billion per year. With the exception of online advertising, which has grown dramatically, advertising expenditures per medium have remained relatively constant over time: TV, 23 percent; direct mail, 11 percent; newspapers, 14 percent; radio, 10 percent; yellow pages, 9 percent; magazines, 5 percent; and online, 11 percent.

Other media, such as out-of-home advertising (e.g., billboards, bus wraps, posters) account for the remainder.[56] To characterize these various types of media, we again use a dichotomy: mass and niche media.

Mass and Niche Media   **Mass media** channels include national newspapers, magazines, radio, and television, and are ideal for reaching large numbers of anonymous audience members. **Niche media** channels are more focused and are generally used to reach narrower segments, often with unique demographic characteristics or interests. Cable TV, direct mail, and specialty magazines such as *Skateboarder* or *CosmoGirl* all provide examples of niche media. In some cases, niche media offer advertisers the opportunity to change and even personalize their messages, which is generally not an option with mass media. For example, magazine advertisers can print response cards with the name of the subscriber already on the card or change advertisements to reflect local differences, such as climate or preferences.

Choosing the Right Medium   For each class of media, each alternative has specific characteristics that make it suitable for meeting specific objectives (see Exhibit 14.8). For example, consumers use different media for different purposes, to which advertisers should match their messages. Television is used primarily for escapism

media planning
The process of evaluating and selecting the *media mix* that will deliver a clear, consistent, compelling message to the intended audience.

media mix
The combination of the media used and the frequency of advertising in each medium.

media buy
The actual purchase of airtime or print pages.

mass media
Channels, such as national newspapers, magazines, radio, and television, that are ideal for reaching large numbers of anonymous audience members.

niche media
Channels that are focused and generally used to reach narrow segments, often with unique demographic characteristics or interests.

EXHIBIT 14.8	Types of Media Available for Advertising	
Medium	**Advantages**	**Disadvantages**
Television	• Has wide reach • Incorporates sound and video	• Has high cost • Has cluttered airways • May increase awareness of competitor's products
Radio	• Is relatively inexpensive • Can be selectively targeted • Has wide reach	• Is not limited by constraints of video • Is not likely to attract consumers' focused attention as TV does • Has short exposure periods
Magazines	• Are very targeted • Reach wider audience if subscribers pass them along to others	• Are relatively inflexible • Have long lead times
Newspapers	• Are flexible • Are timely • Can localize	• Can be expensive in some markets • Can involve potential loss of control over placement • Have short lifespans
Internet	• Can be linked to detailed content • Is highly flexible and interactive • Allows for specific targeting	• Cannot easily compare costs to other media • Is becoming cluttered • Can be blocked by software prohibiting delivery
Out-of-Home	• Is relatively inexpensive • Offers opportunities for repeat exposure • Is easy to change	• Is not easily targeted • Has placement problems in some markets • Has very short exposure time
Direct Mail	• Is highly targeted • Allows for personalization	• Is relatively expensive • Is often considered "junk mail"

MINI Cooper has developed an innovative method of advertising to its current customers with this interactive billboard. Owners receive an RFID chip–embedded key fob (upper right corner). Every time a customer passes the billboard, he or she receives a customized message.

and entertainment, so most TV advertising relies on a mix of visual and auditory techniques. Out-of-home advertising can also be effectively used to deliver a message. MINI Cooper developed an innovative method of advertising to its current customers in select cities through an interactive billboard. Owners received an RFID chip–embedded key fob. Every time they passed by the billboard, they received a customized message that displayed their name on the billboard.

Communication media also vary in their ability to reach the desired audience. For instance, radio is a good medium for products such as grocery purchases or fast food because many consumers decide what to purchase either on the way to the store or while in the store. Because many people listen to the radio in their cars, it becomes a highly effective means to reach consumers at a crucial point in their decision process. Each medium also varies in its reach and frequency. Advertisers can determine how effective their media mix has been in reaching their target audience by calculating the total gross rating points (GRP) (reach $\times$ frequency) of the advertising schedule, which we discuss later in this chapter.

Determining the Advertising Schedule   Another important decision for the media planner is the **advertising schedule**, which specifies the timing and duration of advertising. There are three types of schedules:[57]

- A **continuous** schedule runs steadily throughout the year and therefore is suited to products and services that are consumed continually at relatively steady rates and that require a steady level of persuasive or reminder advertising. For example, P&G advertises its Tide brand of laundry detergent continuously.

- **Flighting** refers to an advertising schedule implemented in spurts, with periods of heavy advertising followed by periods of no advertising. This pattern generally functions for products whose demand fluctuates, such as tennis racquets, which manufacturers may advertise heavily in the months leading up to and during the summer.

- **Pulsing** combines the continuous and flighting schedules by maintaining a base level of advertising but increasing advertising intensity during certain periods. For example, furniture retailer Ikea advertises throughout the year but boosts its advertising expenditures to promote school supplies in August.

advertising schedule
Specifies the timing and duration of advertising.

continuous advertising schedule
Runs steadily throughout the year and therefore is suited to products and services that are consumed continually at relatively steady rates and that require a steady level of persuasive or reminder advertising.

flighting advertising schedule
Implemented in spurts, with periods of heavy advertising followed by periods of no advertising.

pulsing advertising schedule
Combines the continuous and flighting schedules by maintaining a base level of advertising but increasing advertising intensity during certain periods.

6. Create Communication

After the advertiser has decided on the message, type of ad, and appeal, its attention must shift to the actual creation of the advertisement. During this step, the message and appeal are translated creatively into words, pictures, colours, and/or music. Often, the execution style for the ad will dictate the type of medium used to deliver the message. For example, in one ad campaign, crash tests demonstrating the safety of Toyota cars rely on the visual impact of the crash, softened by children who egg on the tester to "Do it again, Bob." This style of execution works only on television. Therefore, it is common for advertisers to make decisions about their message and appeal, the appropriate medium, and the best execution concurrently.

IKEA uses a pulsing strategy when it sets its advertising schedule. It advertises throughout the year but has more advertising directed at the back-to-school market in August.

Automobile manufacturers and their dealers advertise by using many media vehicles, taking care that the media fits the message. To demonstrate an image, they may use television and magazines. To promote price, they can use newspapers and radio. To appeal to specific target markets, they can use some of the electronic media vehicles described earlier. When using multiple media to deliver the same message, however, advertisers must maintain consistency across the execution styles—that is, integrated marketing—so the different executions deliver a consistent and compelling message to the target audience.

Although creativity plays a major role in the execution stage, advertisers must be careful not to let their creativity overshadow the message. Whatever the execution style, the advertisement must be able to attract the audience's attention, provide a reason for the audience to spend its time viewing the advertisement, and accomplish what it set out to do. In the end, the execution style must match the medium and objectives. An additional complication in Canada is the necessity to design advertising messages in two official languages. And, as mentioned earlier, Canada's multicultural population means that companies must carefully consider cultural influences so as not to alienate groups with inappropriate messages.

Print advertising can be especially difficult because it is a static medium: no sound, no motion, and only one dimension. Instead, print relies on several key components that appear in most ads: the *headline*, or large type designed to draw attention and be read first; the *body copy*, which represents the main text portion of the ad; the *background* for the ad, usually a single colour; the *foreground*, which refers to everything that appears on top of the background, and the *branding*, which identifies the sponsor of the ad. The advertiser must convey its message by using compelling visuals and limited text.

One particularly effective ad in the Stupid.ca print and online campaign won two Gold awards at the Cassies, the Canadian Advertising Success Stories. The campaign was based on insights that kids think parents are lame, teachers are pathetic, and the government is worse. The campaign needed a single, blunt message that kids would relate to. This message, developed in part by an advisory panel of kids, boiled down to a single defining thought: smoking is just about the stupidest thing you can do. It was delivered in a tone that was honest and funny, not preachy. The results were positive, with 91 percent of kids saying that the ads would help prevent their peers from smoking. Better yet, a Statistics Canada study showed that smoking rates declined by 2 percent among 12 to 17 year olds, and there was a 9-percent increase in the number of kids who never started to smoke at all.[58]

For radio and television, some important execution elements include identifying the appropriate talent (actors or singers) to deliver the message and choosing the correct music and visuals. In 1974, when Jell-O brand was introducing its pudding line, it looked for a spokesperson viewed as credible, trustworthy, and likeable; it found Bill Cosby.[59] For more than 30 years, Cosby has been the voice and image of the Jell-O brand because he possesses all the features Jell-O was looking for, along with an immediately recognizable voice and image. Cosby has been featured in more than 70 television, 50 radio, and innumerable print advertisements for the pudding. This continuing relationship has made Cosby the longest-running active spokesperson for any brand.

As the spokesperson for the Jell-O brand, Bill Cosby's voice and image have kept the brand's image credible, trustworthy, and likeable for more than 30 years.

L06

pretesting
Assessments performed before an ad campaign is implemented to ensure that the various elements are working in an integrated fashion and doing what they are intended to do.

tracking
Includes monitoring key indicators, such as daily or weekly sales volume, while the advertisement is running to shed light on any problems with the message or the medium.

posttesting
The evaluation of an IMC campaign's impact after it has been implemented.

7. Assess Impact by Using Marketing Metrics

The effectiveness of an advertising campaign must be assessed before, during, and after the campaign has run. **Pretesting** refers to assessments performed before an ad campaign is implemented to ensure that the various elements are working in an integrated fashion and doing what they are intended to do.[60] **Tracking** includes monitoring key indicators, such as daily or weekly sales volume, while the advertisement is running to shed light on any problems with the message or the medium. **Posttesting** is the evaluation of the campaign's impact after it has been implemented. At this last stage, advertisers assess the sales and/or communication impact of the advertisement or campaign.

Measuring sales impact can be especially challenging because of the many influences other than advertising on consumers' choices, purchase behaviour, and attitudes. These influences include the level of competitors' advertising, economic conditions in the target market, socio-cultural changes, and even the weather, all of which can influence consumer purchasing behaviour. Advertisers must try to identify these influences and isolate those of the particular advertising campaign.

For frequently purchased consumer goods in the maturity stage of the PLC, such as cola, sales volume offers a good indicator of advertising effectiveness. Because their sales are relatively stable, and if we assume that the other elements of the marketing mix and the environment have not changed, we can attribute changes in sales volume to changes in advertising.

For other types of goods in other stages of the PLC, sales data offer but one of the many indicators that marketers need to examine to determine advertising effectiveness. For instance, in high-growth markets, sales growth alone can be misleading because the market as a whole is growing. In such a situation, marketers measure sales relative to those of competitors to determine their relative market share. Firms find creative ways to identify advertising effectiveness; for example, digital cable allows them to present a specific advertisement to certain neighbourhoods and then track sales by local or regional retailers.

Some product categories experience so many influences that it is almost impossible to identify advertising's contribution to any individual consumer's choice to purchase a particular product, especially for addictive products such as cigarettes and alcohol or those with potentially negative health consequences, such as fast food or high-sugar breakfast cereals. The European Union is even facing demands for a ban on fast-food ads and other forms of food advertising to children. Although many people firmly believe that advertising for these products contributes significantly to obesity in children, academic research has not been able to show a causal relationship. Other factors, such as parental and peer influence, tend to reflect a higher causality relationship than does advertising.[61]

| Sustainable Marketing 14.1 | **Ideas That Build Sustainability** |

Advertising agency Quarry Integrated Communications (www.quarry.com) helps its clients build their brands through innovative research, advertising, branding, PR, sales, online, and digital media. Although the company's roots go back to an agricultural base, it has successfully expanded to a wide variety of industries and has worked with companies such as Bell, RIM, Sprint, Budget, Wyndham Hotels and Resorts, and FedEx.

Quarry's long-time tagline has been "Ideas That Build." When the company moved its head office from Waterloo, Ontario, to nearby St. Jacobs, sustainable ideas built its new work environment. "If you're going to be a business in a community, it's your responsibility to help that community sustain itself," says chairman and CEO Alan Quarry. That idea is not just his personal philosophy, it's written into the company's core values.

The company joined Sustainable Waterloo, a not-for-profit group that guides organizations in Waterloo Region toward a more environmentally sustainable future, as a way to focus its efforts and achieve meaningful and measurable results related to its sustainability strategy.[62] However, the company's commitment to sustainability began many years earlier. While recruiting new talent, the company found that prospective employees were becoming more environmentally enlightened about the type of organization they wanted to join. Quarry realized it needed to make changes and started with small efforts. It gave compact fluorescent light bulbs to employees and eliminated bottled water and polystyrene cups in the office. A "cardigan contest" helped employees generate

enthusiasm and warmth when the heat was turned down in the office. To mark the company's thirty-fifth anniversary, employees planted 100 trees in a nearby conservation area. Transit passes were given to employees to encourage them to leave their cars at home.

Sustainable thinking naturally flowed through to the design of the company's new headquarters, where the guiding principle was R4: Rethink, Reduce, Reuse, and Recycle. Wherever possible, materials from the existing site were re-used. Movable walls were used throughout the building. All new finishes have recycled content or are sustainable in their longevity and maintenance, including carpets, porcelain tile, acrylic panels, and solid surface countertops. Additional windows were added to the north side of the building to increase access to daylight. A secure bike room was built and showers were installed for employees who wanted to cycle to work. Air-cleaning snake plants were placed throughout the office, and environmentally friendly soaps are used in the kitchens and washrooms. Even new seating was sourced from a company that manufactures with 100-percent Forest Stewardship Council–certified wood products, in support of responsible forest management.

Alan Quarry says these initiatives make employees feel good about the company and were the right thing to do. Although he hasn't calculated the payback, he views the company's sustainability efforts as generating positive ROI or, as he likes to say, return on involvement.

Quarry's new office was designed to be both sustainable and functional.

One internal campaign to increase an advertising agency's environmental scorecard wasn't measured by conventional methods. Instead, as presented in Sustainable Marketing 14.1, success was measured by how good it made employees feel about the company.

Results: Measuring IMC Success

Earlier, we examined how marketers set strategic goals before implementing any IMC campaign. Once a firm has decided how to set its budget for marketing communications and its campaigns have been developed and implemented, it reaches the point that it must measure the success of the campaigns. Each step in the IMC process can be measured to determine how effective it has been in motivating consumers to move to the next step in the buying process. However, the lagged effect, a delayed response to a marketing communication campaign, influences and complicates marketers' evaluations of a promotion's effectiveness, as well as the best way to allocate marketing communications budgets. Because of the cumulative effect of marketing communications, it may take several exposures before consumers are moved to buy, so firms cannot expect too much too soon. They must invest in the marketing communications campaign with the idea that it may not reach its full potential for some time. In the same way, if firms cut marketing communications expenditures, it may take time before they experience a decrease in sales.

When measuring IMC success, the firm should examine when and how often consumers have been exposed to various marketing communications. Specifically, they use measures of *frequency* and *reach* to gauge consumers' *exposure* to marketing communications. For most products and situations, a single exposure to a communication is not enough to generate the desired response. Therefore, marketers measure the **frequency** of exposure—how often the target audience is exposed to a communication within a specified period of time. The other measure used to determine consumers' exposure to marketing communications is **reach**, which describes the percentage of the target population exposed to a specific marketing communication, such as an advertisement, at least once.[63] Marketing communications managers usually state their media objectives in terms of **gross rating points (GRP)**, which represents reach multiplied by frequency (GRP = reach × frequency). This measure can be used for various media advertising—print, radio, or television.

GRP can be measured for print, radio, or television but, when comparing the calculations, they must refer to the same medium. Suppose that Unilever, the maker of Sunsilk, places five advertisements in *Flare* magazine, which reaches 50 percent of the "fashion forward" target segment. The total GRP generated by these five magazine ads is 50 reach × 5 advertisements = 250 GRP. Now suppose that Sunsilk includes 15 TV ads as part of the same campaign, run during the program *Lost*, which has a rating of 9.2. The total GRP generated by these 15 advertisements is 138 (9.2 reach × 15 ads = 138 GRP). However, ads typically appear during more than one TV program, so the total GRP equals the sum of the GRP generated by each program.

Although GRP is an adequate measure for TV and radio ads, assessing the effectiveness of any web-based communications efforts in an IMC campaign generally requires web tracking software to indicate how much time viewers spend on particular web pages and the number of pages they view. **Click-through tracking** measures how many times users click on banner advertising on websites. All these performance metrics can be easily measured and assessed by using tools such as Google Analytics. Facebook also helps companies see who has been visiting their fan pages, what these people are doing on the fan pages, and who is clicking on their ads. With access to this information, marketers can better customize the content on their pages. Online couponing is a promotional web technique in which consumers print a coupon directly from a site and then redeem the coupon in a store. Another promotional web technique is online referring, in which consumers fill out an interest or order form and are referred to an offline dealer or firm that offers the product or service of interest. All these methods can be easily measured and assessed.

As IMC programs become more sophisticated, measurement is not the only concern. Marketers need to worry about a host of legal and ethical issues, which we will examine in the next chapter.

frequency
Measure of how often the target audience is exposed to a communication within a specified period of time.

reach
Measure of consumers' exposure to marketing communications; the percentage of the target population exposed to a specific marketing communication, such as an advertisement, at least once.

gross rating points (GRP)
Measure used for various media advertising—print, radio, or television; GRP = reach × frequency.

click-through tracking
Measures how many times users click on banner advertising on websites.

Real Marketer Profile: AMI SHAH

I attended Wilfrid Laurier University for my undergraduate degree, a Bachelor of Business Administration. It was a great program, as I received both thorough theoretical and practical exposure to the business world through the academic and co-op programs. Through the program, I decided to focus my career in marketing.

I landed my first job at Procter & Gamble while still at university. After meeting with individuals at the company, I felt like I fit in with the company; we had similar values. I joined the P&G family and looking back, I am really happy I took the job, as I loved my experience there.

My career in marketing began as an assistant business manager. I undertook the challenge to turn around two marginally performing hair colour brands: Natural Instincts and L'Image. Collaborating with my multifunctional team, I evaluated the marketing mix and then developed and implemented unique strategies to increase market share for each brand. This effort resulted in the Natural Instincts brand growing by 15 percent during my first year versus nearly flat sales growth in the previous three years, and the L'Image business delivering sales 12 percent higher than forecasted.

When promoted to business manager at P&G, I was given the opportunity to lead the launch of Perfect 10, a new brand that would revolutionize hair colour technology for the first time in over 50 years. This project was a significant accomplishment for me because it was extremely high profile and was the most demanding project I've led to date. Specifically, I faced a number of challenges: condensed timelines, budget constraints, supply chain issues, and a downsized launch team. However, after six months of dedicated work, I was able to overcome these obstacles and successfully executed the launch plans.

While still at P&G, I took a leave of absence for six months to volunteer and work abroad in Vietnam and India. During that time, I ended up finding innovative social enterprises and traded my expertise in marketing for the opportunity to learn about their experiences as social entrepreneurs in developing markets.

After a number of years of work experience, I decided to return to school to obtain my MBA at INSEAD, an international program that has campuses in France and Singapore. This was a great experience, as it put all my work experience into perspective and helped guide me toward my interest in leveraging my experience in a more entrepreneurial and socially conscious organization.

After my master's degree, I also got the chance to work with my own family businesses, one in the retail industry and the other in the wholesale business. This was a neat experience because when you're working with your own money, you quickly learn to be very pragmatic. At the same time, I learned I also had the flexibility to test and learn new tools really quickly. For example, our retail store (www.shalimardesigns.com) quickly increased sales by 10 percent when we established a stronger presence on Google and through social media tools.

Since then, I've taken the role as a brand manager at a new and dynamic consumer packaged goods company, Planet People. I joined the small company, co-founded by a fellow alum of INSEAD, to launch two eco-friendly lines of cleaning products: iQ and Gloves Off. Both feature nontoxic and safe cleaning formulas; however, what makes iQ unique is that it's delivered in unique concentrated cartridges. This packaging allows the consumer to re-use their bottle by just refilling it with tap water and using a concentrate cartridge to make another bottle. By doing this, consumers can reduce plastic waste by 80 percent. I'm really excited to work on iQ, as it's a product that I really believe in. It's also already getting some great recognition, including being selected for a Green Award for Best Green Packaging.

Work at Planet People has been a great experience so far, but it is very different from my experience at P&G. The challenge here is to deliver best-in-class marketing with limited funds, resources, and research. It means relying more on my gut instinct, being very hands-on and creative, and being more flexible, as I never know what the next day will bring me.

There's so much about marketing I love! Beyond it being such a dynamic, interactive, and fun field to work in, I love that as a marketer you really need to understand *who* your consumer is. My best marketing plans are rooted in deep consumer understanding and ensuring my plans consider the key insights and consumer trial barriers. The fun part of acquiring this understanding is actually meeting and talking to consumers. From conducting formal focus groups or shop-alongs for P&G to doing ad hoc in-store demos for Planet People, by interacting with consumers, asking them questions and getting to know them, I feel I've been able to make decisions for my brands that will best meet the consumer's needs and drive results for my business.

Learning Objectives Review

LO1 Outline the process that firms use to communicate with consumers

On the surface, marketing communications look simple: People become aware of a product or service, then grow interested, then desire it, and finally take an action such as purchasing it. But it isn't quite that simple. First, there is the cumulative effect of marketing communications, or messages a company has sent to consumers. Even ads from the past help influence consumers' actions in the future. Second, messages are encoded, and everyone interprets commercial messages differently, thus making it difficult for a marketer to be assured that a particular, clear signal is getting through. Third, to be effective, marketers must adjust their messages to fit the media, or communications channel, and the receiver's knowledge level. Lastly, consumers receive and decode the messages.

LO2 Explain the six tools of integrated marketing communications campaigns

The six tools of IMC campaigns are advertising, personal selling, sales promotions, direct marketing, public relations, and electronic media. In the past, most of a firm's promotional budget was spent on advertising. Although advertising still demands a sizable portion, other media channels have taken up a substantial chunk of the total budget. While the cost of personal selling to reach potential customers directly is quite high, it remains the best and most efficient way to sell certain products and services. Sales promotions are incentives or programs that promote immediate purchase. Many drive sales in the short run, while others exist as part of a company's customer loyalty programs. Direct marketing expenditures are growing because the number of direct marketing media options has increased in recent years; direct mail, infomercials, alternative media such as catalogues, and other new communication technologies such as PDAs and cellphones are all expanding. Public relations also has become increasingly important as other media forms become more expensive and as consumers grow more skeptical of commercial messages. Finally, electronic media have spawned some innovative new ways to promote products and services.

LO3 List the steps in planning an integrated marketing communications campaign

Firms (1) identify their target market; (2) set objectives; (3) determine the budget; (4) convey the message; (5) evaluate

and select the media; (6) create the communication; and (7) assess the impact of the ad.

LO4 Describe what appeals advertisers use to get customers' attention

Advertising appeals are either rational or emotional. Rational appeals influence purchase decisions with factual information and strong arguments built on relevant key benefits that encourage consumers to evaluate the brand favourably. Emotional appeals indicate how the product satisfies emotional desires rather than utilitarian needs.

LO5 Identify how firms determine which media to use

Firms can use mass media channels such as newspapers or television to reach large numbers of anonymous audience members. Niche media, such as cable TV, direct mail, and specialty magazines, are generally used to reach narrower segments with unique demographic characteristics or interests. When choosing the media, firms must match their objectives to the media. Also, certain media are better at reaching a particular target audience than others.

LO6 Summarize how firms budget for and measure integrated marketing communications success

Planning an IMC budget should encompass a combination of factors. The process could start by setting the overall IMC budget as a percentage of sales. Then, the firm might examine what other firms are spending on similar product categories. When it gets down to planning the budget for individual product categories or items, the firm should set its objectives for the campaign and allocate enough money to meet those objectives.

Marketers rely on a mix of traditional and nontraditional measures to determine IMC success. Because potential customers generally need to be exposed to IMC messages several times before they will buy, firms estimate the degree to which customers are exposed to a message by multiplying frequency (the number of times an audience is exposed to a message) by reach (the percentage of the target population exposed to a specific marketing communication). Measuring Internet IMC effectiveness requires different measures, such as click-through tracking, which measures how many times users click on banner advertising on websites.

Key Terms

- advertising, 459
- advertising plan, 471
- advertising schedule, 478
- affordable method, 473
- blog (weblog or Web log), 468
- cause-related marketing, 466

- click-through tracking, 482
- communication channel, 456
- competitive parity method, 473
- continuous advertising schedule, 478
- deceptive advertising, 455

- decoding, 456
- direct mail, 461
- direct marketing, 460
- direct response TV (DRTV), 463
- electronic media, 467
- email, 461

- emotional appeal, 476
- encoding, 456
- event sponsorship, 466
- feedback loop, 456
- flighting advertising schedule, 478
- frequency, 482
- gross rating points (GRP), 482
- integrated marketing communications (IMC), 454
- mass media, 477
- media buy, 477

- media mix, 477
- media planning, 477
- niche media, 477
- noise, 456
- objective-and-task method, 472
- percentage-of-sales method, 473
- personal selling, 459
- posttesting, 480
- pretesting, 480
- public relations (PR), 464
- pull strategy, 472
- pulsing advertising schedule, 478

- push strategy, 472
- rational appeal, 476
- reach, 482
- receiver, 456
- sales promotions, 459
- sender, 455
- tracking, 480
- transmitter, 455
- unique selling proposition (USP), 475

Concept Review

1. Briefly describe the marketing communication process and identify the possible sources of noise at each stage of the process.

2. What is meant by integrated marketing communications?

3. Describe the IMC tools marketers use in campaigns.

4. Explain the differences between advertising and sales promotion.

5. Describe some of the elements in a PR toolkit. Why would a company include PR in its IMC mix?

6. Identify some of the key electronic media that marketers use to communicate with their customers. How are these media changing the nature of the communication between the firm and its customers?

7. What are the steps involved in developing an IMC campaign? Briefly explain each step.

8. Describe why a company would use a pull strategy versus a push strategy in its marketing communications.

9. Briefly describe the two main appeals of advertising.

10. Explain the three different ways marketers measure the success of their marketing communications. What types of information does each method provide?

Marketing Applications

1. The designer jean company Juicy Couture has embarked on a new IMC strategy. It has chosen to advertise on the NBC *Nightly News* and in *Time* magazine. The message is designed to announce new styles for the season and uses a 17-year-old woman as the model. Evaluate this strategy.

2. It's holiday time, and you've decided to purchase a jewellery item for a friend at Birks. Evaluate how the company's advertising, personal selling, public relations, and electronic media might influence your purchase decision. How might the relative importance of each of these IMC tools be different if your parents were making the purchase?

3. Choose one of the ads featured in this book and explain whether it uses a rational or emotional appeal.

4. Bernard's, a local furniture company, targets its marketing at college and university students with apartments and households of young people purchasing their first furniture items. If you worked for Bernard's, what type of media would you use for your advertising campaign? Justify your answer.

5. Should Bernard's use continuous, pulsing, or flighting for its advertising schedule? Why?

6. Suppose you saw your instructor for this course being interviewed on TV about the impact of gift certificates on upcoming holiday's sales. Is this interview part of your university's IMC program? If so, do you believe it benefits the university? How?

7. A retail store places an ad for yoga pants in the local newspaper. The sales of the featured pants increase significantly for the next two weeks; sales in the rest of the sportswear department go up as well. What do you think are the short- and long-term objectives of the ad? Justify your answer.

8. As an intern for Michelin tires, you have been asked to develop an IMC budget. The objective of the IMC strategy is to raise Michelin's market share by 5 percent in Canada in the next 18 months. Your manager explains, "It's real simple; just increase the budget 5 percent over last year's." Evaluate your manager's strategy.

9. McDonald's spends millions of dollars on advertising. Discuss how it can assess the impact of its advertising by using marketing metrics.

10. You heard a friend talking about GNC's healthy drinks and decided to visit its website. Assume that GNC used the services of behavioural advertising firm Tacoda to track how consumers move through its website and to create more targeted advertising. Would you view these efforts as an invasion of privacy? Do you believe this action constitutes an ethical IMC strategy? How will it affect your attitude toward GNC and the likelihood that you will purchase its products?

Toolkit

RETURN ON MARKETING EXPENDITURES

Suppose Jay Oliver (marketing manager of Transit sneaker store) is considering two search engine marketing options to reach out to new customers to market Transit. In particular, he is using Google AdWords, a search engine marketing tool that allows firms to show up in searches based on the keywords potential customers use. Transit is targeting young adults ages 17 to 28. The sneaker market accounts for about $500,000,000 sales annually, and the target market is about 35 percent of that. Transit's gross margins are 20 percent. Oliver estimates that Transit will capture a 2-percent market share of the target market with a $500,000 advertising and keyword budget (option 1) and a 3-percent market share with a $1,000,000 advertising and keyword budget (option 2). Which marketing plan produces the higher ROI for the year? Use the toolkit provided on Connect to assess the ROI of the two options.

Net Savvy

1. View the website of Taxi (www.taxi.ca), a well-known IMC consulting firm. The site contains a lot of information about what IMC is and how it can be used effectively by a wide variety of companies. Of particular interest is the case studies section. Locate the case studies link, read a case, and discuss the following: What were the goals of the IMC campaign? Which IMC components were used in that particular campaign? How do those components contribute to the success of the IMC campaign in achieving its stated goals?

2. The Canadian Marketing Association (CMA) is the primary source of information about direct marketing activities for both academics and practitioners. The website for the CMA (www.the-cma.org) contains information about direct marketing practices and self-regulation. How many different target markets does the CMA address on its home page? Click on the Consumer Information tab. What services does the CMA provide for consumers? Why do you think it offers those services? Now return to the home page and click on the Marketing Resources tab and check out some of the articles, case studies, or white papers and reports.

Chapter Case Study

DOVE WIDENS THE DEFINITION OF REAL WOMEN . . . AND MEN

In a world where media depictions of beauty are based on physical attractiveness and airbrushed images, the Dove Campaign for Real Beauty has been a breath of fresh air. The campaign, which uses "real" women, not models, was launched by Unilever in Canada in early 2004. Based on research that came out of a global study of 3200 women, Unilever learned that 76 percent wished advertising used more realistic portrayals of beauty. Only 2 percent of women surveyed felt comfortable calling themselves "beautiful."

According to Sharon MacLeod, the marketing manager of the Dove brand, Unilever's approach to IMC is to build a campaign around one true consumer insight. The insight that sprang from the research study was that the current definition of beauty was too narrow and that women wanted it to change. So Dove set out on a mission to widen the definition of beauty. The Campaign for Real Beauty is based on a belief that beauty comes in different shapes, sizes, and ages, and that *real* beauty can be genuinely stunning.

Work on the campaign began with Unilever sending letters to 58 well-known female photographers around the world that asked, "What do you think defines a beautiful woman?" MacLeod says the company was overwhelmed with the response and submissions of photos of women and children of all ages, sizes, and ethnic backgrounds. A photo exhibition was launched, with 67 of the photos (including some by Annie Leibovitz) provided at no charge. Donations by attendees went to the Dove Self-Esteem Fund, created to help women and girls celebrate their individual beauty.

As the campaign evolved, the message was delivered via a variety of marketing communication tools: print and TV ads, billboards, free-standing inserts, websites, sampling, direct mail, in-store promotion, and public relations.

A good IMC strategy must ensure that each tool supports and extends the same integrated and consistent message that is delivered by all the other elements in the campaign. Some people erroneously think that IMC means that you always have to do the same thing. But MacLeod says you do the same thing in a different way so you deliver an integrated message. It's important to have a consistent look, feel, and tone. "We're very conscious about Dove's tone of voice," she says. "Dove's brand personality is honest, straight forward, simple. She talks to you like a friend. There's never any puffery."

Examine any of the Dove communications and it's easy to see consistency; they have predominantly white backgrounds, simple designs, and real women. The overriding message is "Be Beautiful, Be Yourself."

The results of the campaign were impressive, with 100 percent of people who attended the photo exhibit making a link back to the Dove brand. In its first two months, the website campaignforrealbeauty.ca had 50 000 hits. Unilever had to add staff to its call centre because interest generated in the campaign was the highest in the company's history. But more importantly, according to MacLeod, the campaign got people talking. It engaged them in debate, helping to reframe how people think about beauty.

MacLeod says the global study pointed out how a lack of self-esteem affects young girls and holds them back from being successful in life. As a result, Dove funded a website (www.realme. ca) developed by the National Eating Disorder Information Centre, designed for young women to explore issues related to self-worth and body image. The company launched and continues to run Real Beauty Workshops for girls aged 8 to 12 in major cities across Canada to help adult female role models foster self-esteem in girls. The company also sponsored the Girls 20 Summit, held during the G20 Summit 2010 in Toronto, which brought girls together from around the world. Identified as leaders in their countries, the girls took part in a mentoring camp to give them the skills to mentor a younger generation of girls.

The *Little Girls* TV ad, developed in Canada and aired during the 2006 Super Bowl, helped to start a dialogue between women and the game's predominantly male audience. To further the dialogue, Dove aired a 75-second film called *Evolution*, which showed the transformation of an attractive but plain woman into a glamorous supermodel, using makeup and post-camera editing. It was viewed by millions of people within days of being posted on YouTube and was featured by Ellen DeGeneres and other TV hosts. It won numerous accolades, including two Grand Prix Awards at the Cannes Lions International Advertising Festival in 2007, and generated more than $150 million in PR and media coverage in the first six months after it was released.[64]

In 2010, the brand that initiated a global conversation about real beauty sparked a very different conversation about real men. The company used the Super Bowl again, this time to launch the Dove Men + Care product line. Research from a newly commissioned global study provided insights for campaign advertising. MacLeod says the research reported that 80 percent of Canadian men believe that they are falsely portrayed in advertising. They feel they are stereotypically depicted as rich, power-hungry, sports stars, resulting in 71 percent of them finding it difficult to relate to images of men their age in advertising.

In reality, men become comfortable in their own skin through life experiences. They enjoy strong relationships, are committed to their families, lead interesting lives, and define success on their own terms. In fact, 92 percent of fathers globally said they were more comfortable because they've had children and 89 percent of men in a committed relationship said finding a partner was key to becoming comfortable with who they are.[65] Toronto gender expert Michael Kaufman, who worked on the campaign, says men don't often talk about their feelings. However, his work with men found that "deep down, they feel they can not live up to the expectations and demands of manhood as they are portrayed in media and popular culture today."

The Dove Campaign for Real Beauty achieved consistency by using predominantly white backgrounds, simple designs, and "real" women, not models.

And so the Dove Men + Care campaign set about to boldly raise wider questions about what a "real man" is. The Super Bowl ad, *A Journey to Comfort*, featured a man's journey through life and being comfortable in his own skin. Like the Campaign for Real Beauty ads, "real" men were used for the Men + Care ad, not models. "Each time we've gone out and spoken to men, they tell us the campaign is very refreshing," say MacLeod. "They are very open to it and welcome the celebration of men who are not portrayed in a stereotypical fashion."

For a new product launch, MacLeod says it's important to have a good campaign but equally important to have a superior product. The Men + Care line builds on the Dove brand promise of mildness and moisturization. With the company's expertise in skin care, Dove has delivered a product to combat the number one issue for men: dry, itchy skin. Products are specially formulated with Micro Moisture, a patented ingredient that addresses skin irritation.

To date, the Men + Care product launch has been very successful, exceeding MacLeod's expectations. You can expect campaigns—for men and for women—to run as long-term initiatives that will continue to evolve as Unilever listens to consumers, hears what they have to say, and then acts on it.

Dove's Men + Care product line combats skin irritation, while the campaign raises questions about what a "real man" is.

Questions

1. The Dove Campaign for Real Beauty set an objective to widen the definition of beauty rather than an objective to sell products. How did using an IMC campaign help to achieve this objective?

2. In what ways did Dove create value for its target market?

3. The Campaign for Real Beauty has received a lot of publicity. What IMC tools will be the most important for this campaign in the future?

4. Would the same IMC tools be appropriate for use with the Men + Care product line or will Dove have to take a different approach?

 Practise and learn online with Connect. Connect allows you to practise important concepts at your own pace and on your own schedule, with 24/7 online access to an eBook, practice quizzes, interactivities, videos, study tools, additional resources, and more.

CHAPTER 15

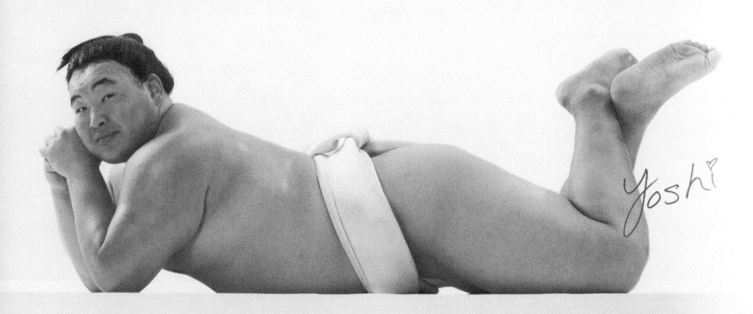

Yoshi

Three-time world champion Byamba poses for the Sexy Subaru campaign. Source: (both images) DDB Canada.

Advertising, Sales Promotions, and Personal Selling

When Don Durst joined Subaru Canada as senior vice-president of sales and marketing, consumers were unfamiliar with its products, ads were imported from the United States, and overall market share was uninspiring. After organizing focus groups across the country, Durst discovered that although the company had been in Canada for 30 years, most people thought Subaru was a Korean brand. "When we told them [that Subaru is Japanese], their attitude toward the vehicle skyrocketed,"[1] he says. Still, consumers thought the Forester looked dated. Although the vehicle was a sensible choice for the target market—families with young children—buying an SUV represented conformity and a loss of personal identity.

To combat this sentiment, Subaru introduced a newly designed Forester in 2008, positioning it as the antithesis of sensible.[2] In contrast to the competition, the Forester was portrayed as playful, fun, and downright sexy with a campaign theme of "Japanese SUVs Just Got a Little Sexier." Sumo wrestlers, an icon of Japanese culture, were used to highlight Subaru's heritage. The sumos were shown in stereotypical situations, for example, in the archetypal sexy carwash scene or in classic pin-up poses.

The company's aggressive campaign goals were to increase annual sales by 47 percent and dealership traffic by 12 percent. A new TV ad, the *Car Wash*, created by DDB Canada, was seeded to YouTube a month before the official launch of the campaign. The ad opens with a new Subaru Forester driving into a car wash, as "Fire in the Disco" by Electric Six plays. Starting in slow motion, sumo wrestlers wash the car. Of course, they end up having a water fight. The ad set a new recall record at a 74-percent level. Magazine and newspaper advertising featured the sumos in a variety of sexy poses, including one ad that simulated a centrefold pullout. Other advertising vehicles included a microsite (sexySubaru.ca), online banner ads, and virtual billboards in Xbox 360 games.

Since one advertising objective was to drive traffic to the dealership, consumers were greeted on arrival by a life-sized sumo cut-out that introduced them to the new Forester. The campaign theme was continued at the Toronto AutoShow, where attendees were invited to have their picture taken as part of the Subaru Sexy Forester Photo Shoot. The shoot made Subaru's booth one of the most visited and talked about by consumers and the media. The campaign was covered by news media, including Citytv and CP24, and generated social media buzz on Facebook and Flikr.[3]

The advertising campaign exceeded all expectations, generating a 15-percent increase in showroom traffic and sales that rose a whopping 132 percent from the previous year.[4] It also grew Subaru's share of the SUV segment by four points to 11 percent. The campaign was a winner in all respects, picking up numerous awards at the Canadian Marketing Awards, including being voted the best campaign of 2009. Sales grew seven times faster than the rest of the SUV category, proving that consumers embrace the Forester as a sexy choice. .::

In the previous chapter, we discussed the tools of integrated marketing communications (IMC) and the steps involved in planning a campaign. While we briefly touched on all of these tools in Chapter 14, we now focus our attention on three elements in particular: advertising, sales promotions, and personal selling, as shown in our chapter roadmap. We begin by introducing the AIDA model, which is the process, or mental stages, marketers try to move consumers through as they are making purchase decisions. As a consumer, you are exposed only to the end product—for example, a finished advertisement—yet many decisions must take place before you actually get to see an ad. We discuss some of these decisions, starting with determining the advertising objectives and the focus of advertisements. We consider some of the regulatory and ethical issues in advertising and those arising from the use of new forms of marketing communications. Then we move on to examine sales promotions and how they add value both as consumer promotions and in the trade channel. The chapter concludes with an examination of how companies use personal selling to influence the buyer's purchase and a look at how companies manage their sale forces.

Advertising

As we saw in Chapter 14, marketing communication is not a straightforward process. After being exposed to an advertisement, consumers go through several steps before actually buying or taking some other action. There is not always a direct link between a particular marketing communication and a consumer's purchase.

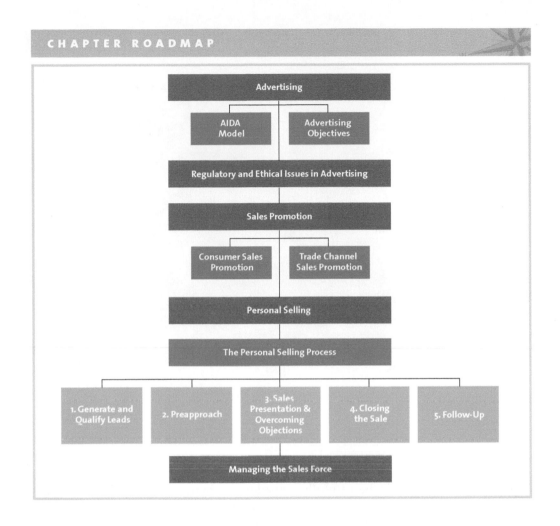

CHAPTER ROADMAP

The AIDA Model

To create effective advertising, marketers must understand how marketing communications work. Generally, marketing communications move consumers step-wise through a series of mental stages, for which there are several models. The most common is the **AIDA model** (Exhibit 15.1),[5] which suggests that **a**wareness leads to **i**nterest, which leads to **d**esire, which leads to **a**ction. At each stage, the consumer makes judgments about whether to take the next step in the process. Customers actually have three types of responses, so the AIDA model is also known as the "think, feel, do" model. In making a purchase decision, consumers go through each of the AIDA steps to some degree, but the steps may not always follow the AIDA order. For instance, during an impulse purchase, consumers may "feel" and "do" before they "think."

Awareness   Even the best marketing communication can be wasted if the sender doesn't gain the attention of the consumer first. Brand awareness refers to a potential customer's ability to recognize or recall that the brand name is a particular type of retailer or product/service. Thus, brand awareness is the strength of the link between the brand name and the type of merchandise or service in the minds of customers.

There are a number of awareness metrics, from aided recall to top-of-mind awareness. **Aided recall** occurs when consumers recognize the brand when its name is presented to them. **Top-of-mind awareness**, the highest level of awareness, occurs when a brand has a prominent place in people's memories that triggers a response without them having to put any thought into it. For example, RIM has top-of-mind awareness if a consumer responds "BlackBerry" when asked about

AIDA model
A common model of the series of mental stages through which consumers move as a result of marketing communications: **a**wareness leads to **i**nterest, which leads to **d**esire, which leads to **a**ction.

aided recall
Occurs when consumers recognize the brand when its name is presented to them.

top-of-mind awareness
A prominent place in people's memories that triggers a response without them having to put any thought into it.

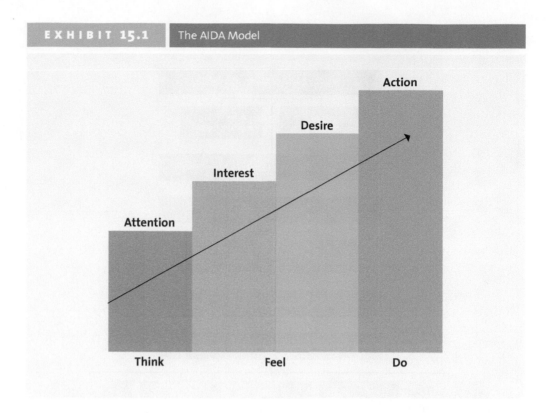

EXHIBIT 15.1   The AIDA Model

Canadian-made smartphones. High top-of-mind awareness means that a particular brand will probably be carefully considered when customers decide to shop for that product or service. Manufacturers, retailers, and service providers build top-of-mind awareness by having memorable names; repeatedly exposing their name to customers through advertising, locations, and sponsorships; and using memorable symbols.

When Toyota introduced the Yaris, a smaller, well-designed car that Toyota wanted to appeal to younger customers, the carmaker swarmed consumers with notifications. In addition to traditional print and TV advertising, the Yaris appears on its own Myspace page, the Yaris website, and direct messages sent to cellphones. Then, playing on the popularity of the Fox network's show *Prison Break*, Yaris sponsored a special advertisement in *TV Guide* in which pictures of the Yaris models appear to be tattooed on a man's chest—just as a crucial plot point hinges on a tattoo in *Prison Break*.[6] With this multichannel approach, Toyota ensured that not just those looking for a new car, but also anyone interested in television would get to know its new product line. Even if someone passed over or ignored one of the communication channels, another channel would likely catch the potential customer's attention.

Interest   Once the consumer is aware that the company or product exists, communication must work to increase his or her interest level. It isn't enough to let people know that the product exists; consumers must be persuaded that it is a product worth investigating. Marketers do so by ensuring that the ad's message includes attributes that are of interest to the target audience. To appeal to younger consumers hoping to find a car with good fuel efficiency, Toyota's ads for the Yaris show it plucking a single coin from a piggy bank or smashing a "spider" with gas pumps for legs.[7] Through these communications, Toyota hopes to pique consumers' interest so much that they do something about it.

Desire   After the firm has piqued the interest of its target market, the goal of subsequent messages should move the consumer from "I like it" to "I want it." For instance, in addition to emphasizing the car's fuel efficiency and affordability, Toyota tries to make the Yaris appear tough to differentiate it from "softer" fuel-efficient cars and thus make the car seem unique.[8]

Action   The ultimate goal of any marketing communication is to drive the receiver to action. If the message has caught consumers' attention and made them interested enough to consider the product as a means to satisfy a specific desire of theirs, they likely will act on that interest by making a purchase.

This step-by-step model applies particularly well to expensive, high-involvement products, such as a new car. As discussed in Chapter 5, the consumer decision process is more complex for specialty products and shopping products. However, for other types of products, the advertising process appears more circular, such that marketers and consumers engage in ongoing dialogue in which marketers provide messages either to induce or respond to consumers' initial comments or feedback.[9]

The Lagged Effect   Sometimes consumers don't act immediately after receiving a marketing communication because of the **lagged effect**—a delayed response to a marketing communication campaign. It generally takes several exposures to an ad before a consumer fully processes its message.[10] In turn, measuring the effect of a current campaign becomes more difficult because of the possible lagged response to a previous one.[11] Suppose you purchased a Yaris right after reading through the advertisement contained in *TV Guide*. The advertising insert may have pushed you to buy, but other communications from Toyota, such as TV ads and articles in automotive magazines that you saw weeks earlier, probably also influenced your purchase.

lagged effect
A delayed response to a marketing communication campaign.

Advertising Objectives

LO1

As noted in Chapter 14, advertising is a paid form of communication from an identifiable source, delivered through a communication channel, and designed to persuade the receiver to take some action, now or in the future.[12] This definition provides some important distinctions between advertising and other forms of promotion, which we discussed in the previous chapter. First, unlike public relations, advertising is not free; someone has paid, with money, trade, or other means, to get the message shown. Second, advertising must be carried by some medium: television, radio, print, the Internet, T-shirts, sidewalks, and so on. Third, legally, the source of the message must be known or knowable. Fourth, advertising represents a persuasive form of communication, designed to get the consumer to take some action. That desired action can range from "Don't drink and drive" to "Buy a new Mercedes."

Some activities that are called advertising really are not, such as word-of-mouth advertising. Even political advertising technically is not advertising because it is not for commercial purposes and thus is not regulated in the same manner as true advertising.

Advertising encompasses an enormous industry and clearly is the most visible form of marketing communications—so much so that many people think of *marketing* and *advertising* as synonymous. Global advertising expenditures are projected to exceed $600 billion, with half that amount being spent in the United States alone. It is not just a perception that advertising is everywhere; it *is* everywhere.[13]

Yet how many of the advertisements that you were exposed to yesterday do you remember today? Probably not more than three or four. As you learned in Chapter 5, perception is a highly selective process. Consumers simply screen out messages that are not relevant to them. When you notice an advertisement, you may not react to it; or, even if you react to it, you may not remember it later. Say you remember seeing it—you still may not remember the brand or sponsor of the advertisement, or, worse yet (from the advertiser's point of view), you may remember it as an advertisement for another product.[14]

To get you to remember their ad and the brand, advertisers must first get your attention. As we discussed in Chapter 14, the increasing number of communication channels and changes in consumers' media usage have made the job of advertisers far more difficult.[15] As the chapter vignette demonstrated, advertisers attempt to use creativity and a mix of promotional elements that offer better opportunities to reach their target markets. As a consumer, you are exposed only to the end product: the finished advertisement. But many actions must take place before you actually get to see an ad, as the Toolkit at the end of this chapter will show you.

As mentioned in the previous chapter, all advertising campaigns aim to achieve certain objectives: to inform, persuade, and remind customers. Another way of looking at advertising objectives is to examine an ad's focus. Is the ad designed to stimulate demand for a particular product or service, or is its focus, more broadly, the institution in general? Marketers use ads to stimulate demand for a product category or an entire industry, or for a specific brand, firm, or item. Let's look at the broad overall objectives of informing, persuading, and reminding.

informative advertising Communication used to create and build brand awareness, with the ultimate goal of moving the consumer through the buying cycle to a purchase.

Informative Advertising   **Informative advertising** communicates to create and build brand awareness, with the ultimate goal of moving the consumer through the buying cycle to a purchase. Such advertising helps determine some important early stages of a product's life cycle (PLC; see Chapter 8), particularly when consumers have little information about the specific product or type of product. Retailers often use informative advertising to tell their customers about an upcoming sales event or the arrival of new merchandise. Subaru used informative advertising to change brand perception of the Forester, as discussed in chapter vignette.

Domestic travel in Canada accounts for $59 billion in spending. Yet Canadians spent close to $30 billion travelling abroad in 2008 because of marketing efforts by major international tourist destinations. The Canadian Tourism Commission (CTC) wanted to show Canadians another side of our country to entice them to spend even more of their vacation dollars at home. In 2009, the CTC launched the "Locals Know" campaign, featuring lesser known spots across the country with headlines that read, "Where is this?" Many of the print ads featured exotic locations, for example, Liard Hot Springs in British Columbia, swimmers in the tropical blue water of Georgian Bay, and sand dunes in Saskatchewan. TV ads featured user-generated content, including surfing in the Lachine Rapids in Quebec and dog sledding in the Northwest Territories. Viewers were encouraged to visit LocalsKnow.ca. The informative advertising campaign resulted in an estimated 2.7 million Canadians travelling at home and generating about $700 million in tourism revenues. Considering the $8 million cost of the campaign, with 150 percent ROI, the marketing effort has been CTC's strongest ever.[16]

persuasive advertising Communication used to motivate consumers to take action.

Persuasive Advertising   When a product has gained a certain level of brand awareness, firms use **persuasive advertising** to motivate consumers to take action. Persuasive advertising generally occurs in the growth and early maturity stages of the PLC, when competition is most intense, and attempts to accelerate the market's acceptance of the product. In later stages of the PLC, persuasive advertising may be used to reposition an established brand by persuading consumers to change their existing perceptions of the advertised product. Firms often use persuasive advertising to convince consumers to take action: switch brands,[17] try a new product, or even continue to buy the advertised product.

Through focus group research, the Canadian Forces (CF) learned that one of its key target markets, young men, were looking for action, rather than a soft "there's no life like it" type of pitch about career opportunities. As a result, the Department of National Defence (DND) launched an action-oriented campaign, putting gritty combat life front and centre. The TV ads and website showed soldiers patrolling war-torn streets in Afghanistan and used the tagline "Fight Fear, Fight Distress, Fight Chaos . . . Fight with the Canadian Forces." The ads proved to be very persuasive, as the number of applicants rose 40 percent to 40 000, and 12 862 full-time and reserve members were

The "Locals Know" campaign by the Canadian Tourism Commission featured exotic images, such as the tropical blue water of Georgian Bay.

recruited between April 2006 and March 2007.[18] DND followed these ads with a second series of TV ads designed to showcase the work of the CF at home in the Arctic and offshore. Ads showed soldiers on rescue missions and patrolling offshore, such as a civilian aircraft crash in the north (*Hard Landing*) and a Navy (*Drug Bust*) operation.[19] The rescue perspective of *Hard Landing* was new to most focus group respondents, who did not previously picture the CF helping in crisis situations and emergencies. The *Drug Bust* ad, through its portrayal of the CF as a protector on the home front, was credited for diversifying respondents' view of the career options associated with the CF.[20] A survey conducted by Ipsos Reid showed that Canadians who saw soldiers responding to natural disasters (such as the 2010 earthquake in Haiti) perceived those serving in the CF as helpful humanitarians who carried shovels instead of weapons.[21]

reminder advertising Communication used to remind consumers of a product or to prompt repurchases, especially for products that have gained market acceptance and are in the maturity stage of their life cycle.

Reminder Advertising Finally, **reminder advertising** is communication used to remind consumers of a product or to prompt repurchases, especially for products that have gained market acceptance and are in the maturity stage of their life cycle. For instance, have you ever gone to a restaurant with a group of friends and ordered a Coke when you really wanted iced tea? In this case, the product has achieved top-of-mind awareness. Just the sight of a reminder ad, like a Coca-Cola logo on an umbrella may be enough to stimulate the desired response. Entrepreneurial Marketing 15.1 discusses a unique form of reminder advertising on hangers, exposing consumers to product ads each time they hang up their clothes.

This umbrella reminds consumers to order a Coke.

Kruger, formerly Scott Paper, faced a challenge. Its licensing agreement with Kimberly-Clark for use of the Cottonelle name was set to expire in June 2007. So it introduced a new brand of toilet paper called Cashmere. Knowing that Kimberly-Clark was expected to reintroduce Cottonelle at some point in the future, Kruger

| Entrepreneurial Marketing 15.1 | **Responsible Advertising Hangs on the Smart Hanger** |

Leigh Meadows has an unusual piece of advice for entrepreneurs: listen to your children. Her six-year-old son, Jacob, got upset when she threw old metal hangers in the garbage. When she explained that they couldn't be recycled, he asked why someone didn't make hangers out of paper.[22] His question was her inspiration for a new product, the smart hanger (www.thesmarthanger.com). The hanger is made from 100-percent Forest Stewardship Council–approved recycled paper, including 90-percent post-consumer content: in other words, the paper has had a previous life as another product. Meadows says that's a pretty big deal, as some "green" coffee cups are made up of only 10 percent post-consumer content.

Only 10 percent of the population reuses wire hangers. Metal, plastic, and other paperboard hangers don't meet recycling standards, resulting in about 350 million hangers going to landfill each year. Before designing her hanger, Meadows approached the City of Toronto to learn about what materials are recyclable to ensure that her product would be environmentally friendly not only from the cradle to the grave, but also from "cradle to cradle."

To understand the shape and strength requirements of the hangers, Meadows spent time working in a dry cleaning plant. In late 2009, after two years of research and planning, her Toronto-based company, Media Hook, launched the smart hanger. Having a Brampton-based manufacturer produce the hanger was a big plus for Meadows, whose mission is to manufacture Canadian-made, practical, and sustainable alternatives to environmentally damaging products.[23]

Meadows began her career as an entrepreneur in her native London, England, where she bought an insurance brokerage when she was only 21 years old. She now describes herself as a serial entrepreneur who starts the new venture process by making a list of what she wants to achieve. Then she looks for businesses that are ailing or are very small but have the potential to be a lot bigger. In the case of the smart hanger, her list focused on the environment and leaving a legacy, something her son would be proud of.

Even though Meadows felt the smart hanger had the potential to be a success, to make it financially viable,

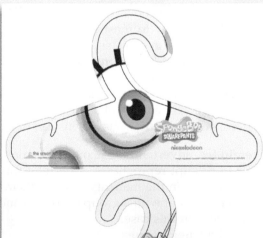

she needed it to do double duty. The obvious answer was to advertise on the hangers, a great way to directly reach consumers in their homes and ensure they will be exposed to the message. Consumers see the message multiple times: when they bring their dry cleaning home, and every time they get dressed and hang the clothing up again. A media engagement study showed that hanger advertising places well above brand recall for TV ads, free-standing inserts, and online ads.[24]

Since her slogan is "Responsible Advertising Hangs on It," Meadows targeted companies and retailers that wanted to make an environmental difference.[25] The space is an ideal vehicle for socially responsible messages. Media Hook signed a contract with the Ontario Fabricare Association, formerly The Dry Cleaners and Launderers Institute of Ontario, to distribute smart hangers.[26]

The company's big break came when Meadows was named runner up in a special "Greenvention" episode of the hit TV show *Dragon's Den* in June 2010. The win opened previously closed doors and led to a contract with Global Edge Brands, which is now the exclusive North American distributor of the hangers. The company is a national leader in the licensed apparel industry and gives Media Hook access to retailers. Although people associate dry cleaners with hangers, Meadows says the retail market contributes more hangers to landfills since many clothes get shipped to stores pre-hung.

Other deals include a contract with Adidas to provide hangers to locker rooms of fitness clubs. In addition, after listening to her son, who suggested that SpongeBob SquarePants should be on hangers, Meadows now has a licensing deal with Nickelodeon. Under Armour will use the smart hanger for the launch of a new environmentally friendly clothing line, and deals are in the works with Sears and other retailers. Media Hook is also looking to develop sales promotion initiatives, such as coupons to drive traffic to advertiser's websites.

Not only is the smart hanger a functional product, it's also an effective advertising platform and an environmental solution that makes Meadows's son proud of her.

Leigh Meadows's six-year-old son Jacob was the inspiration for The Smart Hanger.

needed not only to build brand awareness, but also to remind consumers about Cashmere in a way that stood out. Given its female target market, the company focused on fashion, an idea relevant to their lives. TV and print ads showed a model wearing a dress that appeared to be made of cashmere but was, in fact, made of toilet paper. The tagline for the ads—"Cashmere. Now in Bathroom Tissue"—helped to remind the target consumer to take care of herself. Top-of-mind awareness showed significant improvement and market share grew to a historical high of 27.3 percent in May 2007, up from 23.3 percent one year earlier.[27] Current advertising continues to leverage the fashion connection and a new, more competitive tagline of "Nothing Feels like Cashmere." In spite of Cottonelle's return to the Canadian market in 2008, Kruger was able to protect its market share, which grew to more than 30 percent according to Nielsen MarketTrack.

Focus of Advertisements   To help determine the focus for advertisements, many companies consider the stages in the AIDA model discussed earlier. Some companies will focus their efforts on attracting awareness, for example, in the case of a new product introduction. If consumers are already aware of a product or service, the company will need to build interest and then desire. Lastly, they need to ensure that consumers will be motivated to take action as a result of the company's advertising efforts.

The ad campaign's objectives determine the specific ad's focus. **Product-focused advertisements** are used to inform, persuade, or remind consumers about a specific product or service. The focus of **institutional advertisements** is to inform, persuade, and remind consumers about issues related to places, politics, an industry, or a particular corporation. Some advertisements are designed to generate demand for the product category (e.g., the ironic "Stop Cooking with Cheese!" campaign) or an entire industry (e.g., Dairy Farmers of Canada), while others are designed to generate demand for a specific brand (e.g., Cracker Barrel cheese), firm (e.g., Kraft), or item.

Perhaps the best-known campaign to build demand for a product category is the long-running institutional campaign "Got Milk?" which encourages milk consumption by appealing to consumers' needs to affiliate with the milk-moustached celebrities shown in the ads.[28] While early campaigns focused on building awareness and knowledge, subsequent campaigns have tried to move consumers further along the buyer readiness continuum. A more recent incarnation of the "Got Milk?" campaign, titled "Bones," highlights the beneficial properties of milk for building strong bones. This new focus represents a switch to a more informative appeal, combined with a

product-focused advertisements
Used to inform, persuade, or remind consumers about a specific product or service.

institutional advertisements
Used to inform, persuade, and remind consumers about issues related to places, politics, an industry, or a particular corporation.

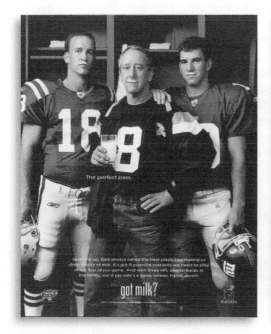 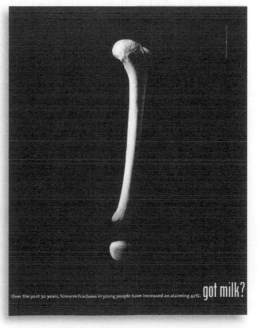

One of the best-known campaigns for generating demand is the "Got Milk?" campaign (left). "Bones" (right), the latest incarnation of the campaign, has a more informative appeal, combined with a mild emotional fear appeal.

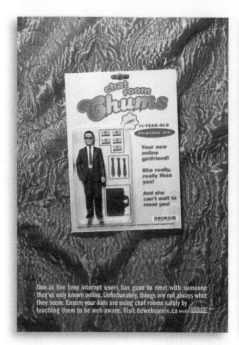

Public service advertising, for causes such as Internet safety, focus on public welfare and generally are sponsored by nonprofit institutions, civic groups, religious organizations, trade associations, or political groups.

public service announcement (PSA)
Advertising that focuses on public welfare and generally is sponsored by nonprofit institutions, civic groups, religious organizations, trade associations, or political groups; a form of *social marketing*.

social marketing
The application of marketing principles to a social issue to bring about attitudinal and behavioural change among the general public or a specific population segment.

mild emotional fear appeal in its assertion that failing to drink milk can lead to medical problems, perhaps a necessary focus to convince consumers to buy milk.

A special class of demand advertising is the **public service announcement (PSA)**, which focuses on public welfare and generally is sponsored by nonprofit institutions, civic groups, religious organizations, trade associations, or political groups.[29] PSAs represent a form of **social marketing**, which is the application of marketing principles to a social issue to bring about attitudinal and behavioural change among the general public or a specific population segment.[30] Because PSAs are a special class of advertising, under the Canadian Radio-television and Telecommunications Commission rules, broadcasters must devote a specific amount of free airtime to them. Some of the most successful PSA campaigns include wildfire prevention (Smokey the Bear), smoking cessation (Stupid.ca), Internet safety (BeWebAware.ca), and breast cancer screening (Breast Cancer Society of Canada).

Because they often are designed by top advertising agencies for nonprofit clients, PSAs usually are quite creative and stylistically appealing. For example, what is your reaction to the Internet safety campaign BeWebAware.ca from the Media Awareness Network? The Ottawa-based nonprofit organization is designed to educate parents about the risks and benefits of letting their kids surf in cyberspace. Supported by Microsoft Canada and Bell Canada, ads highlight eye-opening statistics—such as the fact that 25 percent of kids have been asked to meet someone they've only met online—and encourage people to check out BeWebAware.ca, a website created to help parents get involved in monitoring their children's online activity. One print ad shows a middle-aged man at a computer, typing away in a kids' chat room. The accompanying copy reads, "To 12 year old Lisa, he was simply 11 year old Jenny."

Regardless of whether the advertising campaign's objective is to inform, persuade, or remind, or to focus on a particular product or the institution in general, each campaign's objectives must be specific and measurable. For a brand awareness campaign, for example, the objective might be to increase brand awareness among the target market by 50 percent within six months. Another campaign's goal may be to persuade 10 percent of a competitor's customers to switch to the advertised brand.

L02 ## Regulatory and Ethical Issues in Advertising

IMC brings together many diverse forms of communication under one umbrella. But, in Canada, each form of communication media traditionally has been regulated separately. For example, rather than ban cigarette advertising completely, the federal 1997 Tobacco Act imposed numerous restrictions, including a phased-in ban on tobacco sponsorship of events.[31] However, in 2007, the Supreme Court of Canada struck down the tobacco industry's appeal to remove the advertising ban and also opened the door to new advertising. Companies are allowed to advertise in places where only people over the age of 18 are permitted and in magazines where adults account for more than 85 percent of their readership.[32] We begin this section by detailing the various agencies that regulate the different forms and media for advertising. Then we discuss some controversies surrounding new forms of potential deception.

In Canada, the regulation of advertising involves a complex mix of formal laws and informal restrictions designed to protect consumers from deceptive practices. Many federal and provincial laws, as well as a wide range of self-regulatory agencies and agreements, affect advertising (see Exhibit 15.2). The primary federal agencies that regulate advertising activities are the Competition Bureau, the Canadian Radio-television and Telecommunications Commission (CRTC), the Food and Drug Act, and Advertising Standards Canada. In addition to these agencies, marketers must adhere to other pieces of legislation such as the Consumer Packaging and Labelling Act and the Tobacco Act.

The Competition Bureau enforces the Competition Act, the most comprehensive legislation affecting the marketing activities of companies in Canada. The Competition Act maintains and encourages competition while protecting consumers from misleading and deceptive advertising practices. The CRTC controls the advertising industry and governs broadcast media and licensing. The CRTC must approve all TV and radio advertisements before they can be broadcast. The Food and Drug Act prohibits the advertising or selling of unsafe or misbranded foods, cosmetics, and drugs. It also requires companies to adhere to regulations regarding health claims. Although used for many years in the United States, diet-related health claims for food products, related to risk reduction of heart disease, cancer, osteoporosis, and high blood pressure, have only recently been allowed in Canada. The Consumer Packaging and Labelling Act requires manufacturers, packers, and distributors to disclose full information about their products. All pre-packaged products must be labelled in both French and English and bear the quantity in metric and imperial for weight, volume, or measures.

Many product categories fall under self-regulatory restrictions or guidelines. For example, Advertising Standards Canada (ASC) is a self-regulating body that monitors voluntary industry codes. Advertising to children is regulated primarily

EXHIBIT 15.2	Agencies that Regulate Advertising	
Agency/Legislation	**General Purpose**	**Specific Jurisdiction**
Competition Bureau Canada The Competition Act (1986)	Enforces federal laws that ensure businesses in Canada operate in a fair and equitable manner.	Enforces laws relating to misleading advertising and deceptive marketing practices.
Canadian Radio-television and Telecommunications Commission (CRTC; 1968)	Regulates and supervises all aspects of the Canadian broadcasting system, and regulates telecommunications common carriers and service providers that fall under federal jurisdiction.	Enforces restrictions on broadcasting material. Also administers codes that have an impact on specific categories of advertising, for example, the Code for Broadcast Advertising of Alcoholic Beverages.
Health Canada Food and Drug Act (1954)	Regulates food, drugs, cosmetics, and medical devices.	Establishes standards and requirements for the safety and sanitation of products. Regulates the labelling of food products pertaining to nutrition labelling, nutrient content, and health claims.
Advertising Standards Canada (ASC; 1957)	Monitors voluntary advertising industry codes.	Administers the Canadian Code of Advertising Standards, the Gender Portrayal Guidelines, and the Broadcast Code for Advertising to Children.

Is this billboard ad an example of puffery or deception?

puffery
The legal exaggeration of praise, stopping just short of deception, lavished on a product.

through self-regulatory mechanisms designed by ASC and its Broadcast Code for Advertising to Children. The exception is the province of Quebec, where all advertising to children under the age of 13 is prohibited under the Quebec Consumer Protection Act. Messages with no promotional or selling intent are protected by the Charter of Rights and Freedoms.

Recently, to make matters even more complicated for advertisers whose products sell in the United States, state Attorneys General's offices have begun to assert their authority to regulate advertising in their states. The European Union also has increased its regulation of advertising for EU member nations. Many of these state and European regulations are more restrictive than existing federal or self-regulatory requirements.

Another difference between advertising regulations in Canada and the European Union pertains to **puffery**, the legal exaggeration of praise, stopping just short of deception, lavished on a product.[33] In Canada, consumers are viewed as rational and capable of evaluating advertising claims. Does a certain sneaker brand really make you run faster and jump higher? Does Papa John's pizza really have "better ingredients" that make "better pizza"? In the European Union, however, puffery is considered deception. For instance, Kraft had no problem advertising its orange-flavoured drink Tang surrounded by oranges in North America. But in Germany, the ad was declared deceptive because there are no oranges in Tang. Advertisers must understand these differences to keep from violating EU advertising laws.

Some companies are criticized simply because of their large advertising budgets. Consumers often complain that prices would be lower if companies didn't spend so much money promoting their products. Ethical Dilemma 15.1 discusses numerous companies that have come under fire for expenditures to advertise Product (RED) collections.

Advertising and direct marketing must adhere to different guidelines than PR. For instance, in the case of *Kasky v. Nike*, Nike claimed that a letter to the editor written by its CEO was part of a PR campaign and thus not an advertising message.[34] Unfortunately for Nike, the California courts felt otherwise and found that Nike's letter was an advertisement, which meant that the claims made in the letter had to be substantiated.

Stealth Marketing

stealth marketing
A strategy used to attract consumers that employs promotional tactics which deliver a sales message in unconventional ways, often without the target audience knowing that the message even has a selling intent.

Stealth marketing is a strategy used to attract consumers that employs promotional tactics which deliver a sales message in unconventional ways, often without the target audience knowing that the message even has a selling intent.[35] Stealth marketing can take many forms and use many different communication channels, and as marketers find more innovative ways to communicate with their target markets, they have crossed into uncharted waters. Consumers thus are starting to lose confidence that they can distinguish a commercial message from a noncommercial one.

With new media, it can become extremely difficult for consumers to determine whether they are viewing a promotional message or factual information. Consider the marketing communications Vancouver-based Lions Gate Entertainment used for the horror movie *Godsend*, which included a website (www.godsendinstitute.org), as well as traditional movie promotions. However, the website never clearly indicated that it was designed to promote a movie. The film *Godsend* is about cloning, and

| Ethical Dilemma 15.1 | Seeing (RED) |

Shortly after its launch, Product (RED) stirred controversy in spite of the fact that it was working to fight three of the world's most devastating diseases. The Global Fund to Fight AIDS, Tuberculosis, and Malaria was established in 2002, with the support of world leaders and UN Secretary General Kofi Annan.[36] Four years later, at the 2006 World Economic Forum, Bono and Bobby Shriver announced Product (RED), an economic initiative designed to deliver private sector money to the Global Fund.

Converse, Motorola, Apple, GAP, and other companies created special edition RED products in support of this cause. For example, Apple produced a 4GB iPod nano RED Special Edition, while American Express introduced a RED credit card. A portion of the proceeds from RED-branded products goes to the Global Fund, for example, 10 percent of a $25 iTunes gift card, 5 to 15 percent of a Converse product's profits or 50 percent of the profits from Gap's sales of RED collections. The Product (RED)–themed ads featured glamourous celebrities, such as Penelope Cruz and Christy Turlington, clad in red Gap clothing and suggested consumers could change the world simply by buying a Gap T-shirt.

It didn't take long for the news to break that more than US$100 million had been spent by companies on advertising their RED collections, while only US$18 million had been donated to the Global Fund. Critics claimed the $100 million used for advertising should have simply been donated directly to the cause. Product (RED) promoters argued the initiative was a long-term one, designed to build over time and that one year after launch was too soon to measure its success. They claimed $25 million was raised (not $18 million) and that the donation was five times the amount given to the Global Fund by the private sector in the previous four years.[37] And they pointed out that money spent to promote RED products would otherwise have been spent promoting products that made no contribution to the Global Fund at all.[38]

As of May 2011, Product (RED) claims it has raised more than $170 million to help eliminate AIDS in Africa, with 100 percent of these funds going directly to

programs.[39] The long-term impact of the Product (RED) launch and the value of the publicity generated by thousands of magazine, newspaper, and online articles, and hours of TV news coverage, including a profile on *The Oprah Winfrey Show*, remain to be seen. Before the controversy struck, most people didn't even know the Global Fund existed. Still, the issue has many observers seeing (RED) and questioning whether companies are simply using the cause to their advantage. Is it ethical to profit from a nonprofit cause?

Glamourous celebrities such as Penelope Cruz appeared in Gap ads promoting its Product (RED) clothing.

when people conducted a Google search for "cloning," the web page for the Godsend Institute—not a real institute but rather the setting for the film—would appear in the results list.

The site looks very much like a website for a legitimate fertility clinic and includes online tours of the facilities and testimonials from parents who had been patients at the centre. Family snapshots supposedly portray the children Godsend has cloned from dying siblings. The effect is dramatic—and completely fake. Nowhere on the site is there a disclaimer stating the site's true purpose. Tom Ortenberg, president of film releasing for Lions Gate, stated that the *Godsend* site is "a million dollar idea" built for only about $10,000, in that the site resulted in millions of hits and generated a lot of publicity.[40]

Marketers have also begun to employ actual consumers to be, in essence, salespeople for their brands. The average person has 56 word-of-mouth conversations every week. Organizations such as TheInfluencers.ca are dedicated to helping start, seed, and spread these conversations among Canada's opinion leaders.[41] For example, Dare Foods ran a program to launch its Simple Pleasures Baked Cookie Bars. Participants received 12 boxes of cookie bars to sample and share with friends and were expected to provide feedback to Dare. The goal for companies is to have such programs become a launching point for **viral marketing**, a marketing phenomenon that encourages people to pass along a marketing message to other potential consumers.[42] There are no current regulations on viral campaigns; the laws that cover deceptive practices have never had to address this new form of marketing.

viral marketing
A marketing phenomenon that encourages people to pass along a marketing message to other potential consumers.

The use of online games also has been quite effective at getting children's attention and drawing them to firms' websites—as well as at drawing criticism from children's media watchdog groups. These groups believe that the websites do not inform children that the games contain branded messages. One of the most controversial is www.neopets.com, which offers games sponsored by various corporations. Children who sign up receive offers from these sponsors and site users get assistance in taking care of their Neopets, virtual animals they adopt when they register with the site.[43] They can earn points by taking consumer surveys or feeding their Neopet McDonald's products. Young girls, who make up most of the site's visitors, spend an average of 3.5 hours a month on the site.

As sites like Neopet become more popular with children, children's media watchers begin to ask: Can children distinguish between entertainment and commercial content?[44] For now, again, there are no formal regulations for children's websites, other than those designed to protect children's privacy online. However, regulators are examining the practices used on these sites to determine whether any current regulations are being violated and whether such practices need to be regulated. In the meantime, marketers will continue their quest to find more innovative ways to reach their target audiences by using both traditional and nontraditional methods.

L03 Sales Promotion

Advertising rarely provides the only means to communicate with target customers. As we discussed in Chapter 14, a natural link appears between advertising and sales promotion. Sales promotions are special incentives or excitement-building programs that encourage consumers to purchase a particular product or service, typically used in conjunction with other advertising or personal selling programs. In the context of IMC campaigns, advertising generally creates awareness, interest, and desire, while the value in sales promotions is in closing the deal. Many sales promotions, such as free samples or point-of-purchase (POP) displays, attempt to build short-term sales, whereas others, such as loyalty programs, contests, and sweepstakes, have become integral components of firms' long-term customer relationship management (CRM) programs, which they use to build customer loyalty. In this section, we examine the various tools firms use for their sales promotions and how those tools complement the advertiser's efforts to achieve its strategic objectives.

The tools of any sales promotion can be focused on either channel members, such as wholesalers or retailers, or end-user consumers. Just as we delineated for advertising, when sales promotions are targeted at channel members, the marketer is employing a push strategy; when it targets consumers themselves, it is using a pull strategy. Some sales promotion tools can be used with either a push or pull strategy. We now consider each of the tools and how they are used.

Consumer Sales Promotions

Exhibit 15.3 displays the many different types of tools used in consumer sales promotions, along with their advantages and disadvantages. We will discuss how marketers choose which tool to use based on their specific marketing objectives. Then, we examine some ways in which IMC programs make use of sales promotions.

Coupons   A coupon offers a discount on the price of specific items when they're purchased. Coupons are issued by manufacturers and retailers in newspapers, magazines, and free-standing inserts, on products, on shelves, at the cash register, over the Internet, and by mail. They are commonly used in supermarkets, but other retailers, such as department stores and restaurants, also use coupons to pull customers away from the competition. Some retailers even accept coupons from competitors. More than 300 billion coupons are distributed every year in North America, yet only about 2 percent of them are ever redeemed.[45] However, these redemption rates vary dramatically depending on how consumers obtain the coupon. A segment of the market, the diehard "coupon clippers," devote a great deal of time and effort to searching for, clipping, and redeeming coupons. Many coupon clippers have streamlined this process by using the Internet, which offers entire forums dedicated to coupon sharing and management (e.g., www.couponforum.com). Nonetheless, many consumers dislike the cumbersome coupon process, which is why redemption rates on coupons are so low. In response, coupon distribution has been declining in recent years.[46]

EXHIBIT 15.3	Types of Consumer Sales Promotions		
Promotion	**Objective**	**Advantages**	**Disadvantages**
Coupons	Stimulate demand.	● Encourages retailer support. ● Allows for direct tracing of sales.	● Has low redemption rates. ● Has high cost.
Deals	Encourage trial.	● Reduces consumer risk. ● Retaliates against competitive action.	● May reduce perception of value.
Premiums	Build goodwill.	● Increases perception of value.	● Results in consumers that buy for premium not the product. ● Has to be carefully managed.
Contests	Increase consumer involvement.	● Generates excitement.	● Requires creativity. ● Must be monitored.
Sweepstakes	Encourage higher consumption.	● Minimizes brand switching among existing consumers.	● Sales often decline after.
Samples	Encourage trial.	● Offers direct involvement.	● Has high cost to the firm.
Loyalty Programs	Encourage repurchase.	● Creates loyalty.	● Has high cost to the firm
POP Displays	Increase brand trial.	● Provides high visibility. ● Provides in-store support.	● Is difficult to get a good location in the store. ● Can be costly to the firm.
Rebates	Stimulate demand.	● Increases value perception.	● Is easily copied by competitors. ● May just advance future sales.
Product Placement	Demonstrate product uses.	● Displays products nontraditionally. ● Introduces new products.	● May not provide firm with control over display. ● Can result in product being overshadowed.

MediaCart delivers point-of-sale promotions from a shopping cart.

Coupons carried in newspapers, magazines, in-store displays, and direct mail have very low redemption rates of only 1 to 2 percent, whereas those downloaded from the Internet experience a 56-percent redemption rate. The reason for this dramatic difference is that consumers seek out online coupons for specific items or stores, whereas many people who have no interest in purchasing the product receive traditional coupons.

Some companies are starting to send coupons to consumers on their mobile phones. Although almost a third of consumers would like to receive mobile coupons, only about 1 percent of advertisers currently offer them.[47] These coupons come packed with information about the customers who use them. While the coupons look standard, their bar codes can be loaded with a startling amount of data, including identification of the customer, Internet address, Facebook page information, and even the search terms used to find the coupon. MediaCart is a new product that delivers point-of-sale advertising from a shopping cart. Although it doesn't provide paper coupons in a traditional way, it does inform customers about special deals as they pass them in the aisle. Each video screen is embedded with an RFID chip that interacts with chips installed on store shelves. In addition to providing advertising and special offers, it can record shopping habits, shopper dwelling times, and how shoppers travel through the store—all critical information that the retailer can use to provide a better shopping experience for customers and thus increase sales.

Online coupon sites and daily deal sites, such as Groupon, WagJag, and Living Social, have changed the way some businesses offer promotions. The Cellar Bar and Grill in Bedford, Nova Scotia, sold 200 half-price vouchers worth $20 for only $10 through Kijiji's Daily Deals site.[48] While the coupon offer drew in new customers, the challenge for the bar's owner, Cathy Levangie, will be to entice the bargain seekers to return and pay full price. Facebook Deals also offers online coupons to Canadians through retail partners such as Chapters Indigo, H&M, Wind Mobile, and Town Shoes.[49] Consumers simply post their location to their Facebook page while they are out and about to access special deals from retailers in the area.

deal
A type of short-term price reduction that can take several forms, such as a "featured price," a price lower than the regular price; a "buy one, get one free" offer; or a certain percentage "more free" offer contained in larger packaging.

Deals   A **deal** refers generally to a type of short-term price reduction that can take several forms, such as a "featured price," a price lower than the regular price; a "buy one, get one free" offer; or a certain percentage "more free" offer contained in larger packaging. Another form of a deal involves a special financing arrangement, such as reduced percentage interest rates or extended repayment terms. Deals encourage trial because they lower the risk for consumers by reducing the cost of the good, but they can also alter perceptions of value.

premium
An item offered for free or at a bargain price to reward some type of behaviour, such as buying, sampling, or testing.

Premiums   A **premium** offers an item for free or at a bargain price to reward some type of behaviour, such as buying, sampling, or testing. These rewards build goodwill among consumers, who often perceive high value in them. Premiums can be distributed in a variety of ways. They can be included in the product packaging, such as the toys inside cereal boxes; placed visibly on the package, such as a coupon for free milk on a box of Cheerios; handed out in the store; or delivered in the mail, such as the free perfume offers Victoria's Secret mails to customers.

Furthermore, premiums can be very effective if they are consistent with the brand's message and image and highly desirable to the target market. Finding a premium that meets these criteria at a reasonable cost can be a serious challenge. At fast-food restaurants such as McDonald's and Burger King, for instance, the average order cost is around $5, while the average premium distributed costs less than 50 cents.

Contests A **contest** refers to a brand-sponsored competition that requires some form of skill or effort. In Canada, you cannot give a prize away by chance alone. There must also be a skill component, which is why skill-testing questions are used, making the game one of mixed chance and skill. The effort required by these contests often keeps participation lower than that for other forms of promotion. The ESPN website has a page with numerous sports-related contests. Some of them include "Get Me to the World Cup sponsored by Sony" and "Player of the Month presented by Kia."[50] For the Get Me to the World Cup contest, contestants are required to create and upload a short video demonstrating why they should be sent to the World Cup. The site also provides a number of sample videos, including one by Kobe Bryant.

To be effective, contests must be advertised and enjoy high levels of retailer or dealer support. SportChek ran an online contest to drive up its membership database and increase store traffic. Shoppers received unique contest-entry PIN codes on their receipts. They got a discount coupon when they registered at GetIntoGear.ca. In the first week, 3000 people registered for the contest and sent information about it to friends 1000 times.[51]

Contests are often used to drive sales, as seen in Social Media Marketing 15.1. They can also be used to draw attention to a company's initiatives and even to promote environmental causes. Sustainable Marketing 15.1 discusses how Nabob's "Green Bean Initiative" promotional contest helped to showcase its commitment to making positive change in the world of coffee growers worldwide.

Sweepstakes A form of sales promotion that offers prizes based on a chance drawing of entrants' names, **sweepstakes** do not require the entrant to complete a task other than buy a ticket or fill out a form. Often the key benefit of sweepstakes is that they encourage current consumers to consume more if the sweepstakes form appears inside the packaging or with the product. Unlike contests, sweepstakes winners are determined by a random draw. Reader's Digest Canada runs an annual national sweepstakes for which it invites both subscribers and others to enter.

Samples **Sampling** offers potential customers the opportunity to try a product or service before they make a buying decision. Distributing samples is one of the most costly sales promotion tools but also one of the most effective. Quick-service restaurants and grocery

This sales promotion deal for Payless ShoeSource is a short-term price promotion that encourages consumers to buy a second pair of shoes at one-half off.

contest
A brand-sponsored competition that requires some form of skill or effort.

sweepstakes
A form of sales promotion that offers prizes based on a chance drawing of entrants' names.

sampling
Offers potential customers the opportunity to try a product or service before they make a buying decision.

The Look Fab Studio temporarily offered free beauty tips, makeovers, and workshops from industry experts such as celebrity makeup artist Paul Venoit. Pop-up retail stores are set in temporary locations to generate excitement about a brand or product.

Social Media Marketing 15.1   New Dimensions in Sales Promotions

Sales promotions exist to help create awareness, interest, and desire, while also working to directly drive increased sales volume for the brand or product. Often this is a very fun and creative element of consumer marketing, and the better a contest, coupon, or loyalty program can grab the attention of a consumer, the better the promotion. It makes perfect sense that social media are being easily integrated into many different promotions to expand their effectiveness.

Some promotions choose to layer an added social media element onto a traditional promotion model. The "Alexander Keith's Birthday" promotion aimed to promote the consumption of Alexander Keith's Pale Ale to celebrate his birthday on October 5. Typically, this promotion was supported by mass TV media, posters, banners, and even light-up countdown signs in bars and pubs; online microsites counting down the days; and on-pack banners advertising the celebrations. In fall 2009, social media was added to the mix: Canadians were invited to create a virtual birthday card on Facebook and get their friends to sign it. The card with the most signatures had the chance to win $5000 or a trip to Halifax, Keith's birthplace.[52] The Facebook contest resulted in more than 50 000 Facebook fans and 1500 birthday cards,[53] resulting in countless consumer interactions with the beer, a commodity product.

Many companies and brands take this approach when they begin using social media. It's much easier for marketers to gain company support when they simply add a few extra elements onto an already successful promotional model. Once the value of the social media add-ons can be assessed, they can be further explored. Black Diamond Cheestrings offer another example of a traditional promotion that was extended with social media. The brand ran the "Cheesy's Lucky Lunchbox" campaign, with consumers receiving a unique PIN code inside each package of Cheestrings. By entering this PIN code online, consumers had the chance to instantly win free prizes, such as lunch boxes, pencil cases, and notebooks, and to win eight grand-prize trips to the Bahamas.[54] Traditionally, the prizes would have been claimed and fulfilled by mailing them

out. However, in this case, social media was integrated into the campaign by having @Cheesy on Twitter announce each prize winner. This allowed winners to confirm their prizes before receiving them and gave them a chance to see their names in lights and—Black Diamond hopes—to develop a stronger appreciation of the Cheestrings brand.

Other promotions are centred exclusively on social media tools. One of the most popular and successful examples was the Doritos Guru contest. The campaign launched a new, unnamed flavour of chips into full distribution, with chip bags that featured little more than a question mark and contest details. The challenge: name the new chip flavour and post a 30-second commercial on YouTube to promote it.[55] The winner would receive $25,000, permanently name the new chip, and would also have their spot considered for TV media. Notably, the winner also received a percentage of future sales revenue for the new flavour. Social media was woven throughout the entire promotion. The videos were posted on YouTube and Doritos.ca, and shared through Facebook and Twitter to spread the word and gain votes. The general public was invited to view the videos and vote for their favourite. The promotion was immensely popular, attracting 2100 different video entries, 30 000 Facebook fans, and more than 1.5 million unique visitors on YouTube. It has become a clear success story in the realm of social media promotions.[56]

A number of Canadian brands have echoed this type of program with their own "make a video contest." Canada Post asked its 62 000 employees to make a video promoting postal services such as XpressPost and Smart Moves for the chance to win a trip to the 2010 Vancouver Olympic Games.[57] Other promotions, such as Virgin's "Second Best Job in the World Contest,"[58] Aylmer's TryTheSauce.ca, and Herbon's GetYourHerbon.ca, ask consumers to create their own viral video, post it, and spread the word to friends via social media to earn votes and win a prize.

No matter what the objective of a sales promotion is, social media can be brought into the media mix. The challenge is to make sure it fits well and adds value to the promotion.

stores frequently use sampling. For instance, Starbucks provides samples of new products to customers. Costco uses so many samples that customers can eat an entire meal. Sometimes trial-size samples come in the mail or are distributed in stores. P&G set up a pop-up retail outlet, Look Fab Studio, in the upscale Yonge and Bloor area of Toronto for a single month. The temporary beauty boutique allowed visitors to benefit from free samples, beauty tips, makeovers, and workshops from industry experts, such as celebrity makeup artist Paul Venoit.[59] One of the key purposes of the Look Fab Studio was to help establish P&G as an authority on beauty and to position its beauty brands.

loyalty program
Specifically designed to retain customers by offering premiums or other incentives to customers who make multiple purchases over time.

Loyalty Programs   As part of a sales promotion program, **loyalty programs** are specifically designed to retain customers by offering premiums or other incentives to customers that make multiple purchases over time. Such sales promotions are growing

| Sustainable Marketing **15.1** | **Nabob: Blending Quality with Sustainability[60]** |

When it comes to our planet, even the smallest changes can make a positive difference to sustainability in the long run. This is the Nabob Coffee Company's new stance. But Nabob is not just making small changes; it is also making huge companywide changes at all levels to align its brand with its new sustainability philosophy. Nabob has come a long way since it was established in 1896 by two determined grocers who started blending premium imported beans. In 1994, Kraft acquired Nabob, which is now the largest premium roast and ground coffee brand in Canada.

Nabob has had a long journey of success and is now embarking on a new endeavour of supporting environmental, social, and economic sustainability. The company is committed to recognizing the role it plays in safeguarding coffee-growing environments and improving the lives of coffee growers worldwide; it knows it must balance the needs of producers and consumers with the long-term health of the environment. Its slogan "Better Beans. Better Coffee. Better Planet" demonstrates the recent focus on sustainability and making a positive impact on the world by changing coffee production for the better. One of the company's small changes is the creation of a new canister made from recyclable materials. In addition, Nabob now sources Rainforest Alliance Certified coffee beans. The Rainforest Alliance is an organization that invests in the conservation of biodiversity and the quality of life of local people in their environment. It has developed a socio-economic certification program for agriculture, which is based on more than 200 criteria. These criteria are focused on creating respect for people and the environment, along with considering rural traditions and local culture.

To encourage consumers to become involved in sustainability efforts, the company launched the "Nabob Green Bean Initiative" promotional contest. The contest, which ran in the spring of 2010, generated excitement and awareness

about Nabob's increased commitment to sustainability. The cross-Canada contest required entrants to write a 1200-word essay creatively describing the actions their community could take and explaining how the Nabob Green Bean Initiative would have a positive impact on their community. Initiatives included such things as investing in solar panels or adding more recycling bin containers to a community facility. The winning community received $10,000 to bring their Nabob Green Bean Initiative to fruition.

This contest took Nabob's commitment to supporting sustainability one step further by encouraging consumer involvement. And it put Nabob on the path of integrating sustainability in all aspects of its organization, including its marketing communications strategy.

Nabob is committed to safeguarding coffee-growing environments and the lives of coffee growers.

increasingly popular and are often tied to long-term CRM systems. In Canada, some of the most popular loyalty programs include Canadian Tire "Money," Aeroplan, Air Miles, and the Shoppers Drug Mart Optimum program.

Point-of-Purchase Displays   **Point-of-purchase (POP) displays** are merchandise displays located at the point of purchase, such as at the checkout counter in a grocery store. Marketers spend almost as much on POP materials as they do on consumer magazine advertising, but the key to a successful POP is to make the display "pop out" in a crowded store. In addition, manufacturers must encourage retailers to feature and use the POP displays to maximize their investments. The use of shelf displays along with other promotional tactics led to the successful launch of XOXO, a new brand of wine. Shying away from traditional wine drinkers, the brand was targeted to women looking to complement a "Girl's Night In." Eye-catching on-shelf displays coupled with simple but recognizable packaging were an instant hit, selling 36 000 bottles in just four weeks. In-store sampling produced a conversion rate of 35 to 50 percent, much higher than the 15 to 20 percent expected from such trials.[61]

point-of-purchase (POP) display
A merchandise display located at the point of purchase, such as at the checkout counter in a grocery store.

POP displays are merchandise displays located at the point of purchase, such as at the check-out counter in a grocery store.

Rebates   Rebates refer to a particular type of price reduction. Many products, such as cellphones, now offer significant mail-in rebates that may lower the price of the phone to $0 or even less. Firms offer such generous rebates because the likelihood that consumers will actually apply for the rebate is low, even though consumers indicate that rebate offers are a factor in their purchase decisions. The firms thus garner considerable value from rebates because they attract consumers with a minimal risk that the firm will have to pay off all the rebates offered. Consumers may consider the rebate during their purchase decision process but then never redeem it—an added bonus for the seller.

Recently, heavy rebate users, such as Best Buy, have begun scaling back their programs.[62] Like any promotional tool, too much of a good thing can be a problem. Best Buy found that consumers were becoming increasingly annoyed by having to mail in the rebate forms and wait to receive their money. Many were requesting that the rebate be given at the time of purchase and wondering why this immediate promotion was not possible. In addition, a growing number of lawsuits claim rebate cheques were never sent to consumers and that rebate offers contain overly detailed clauses that cause consumers to have to submit and resubmit their claims.[63]

product placement
Inclusion of a product in nontraditional situations, such as in a scene in a movie or TV program.

Product Placement   When marketers use **product placement**, they include their product in nontraditional situations, such as in a scene in a movie or TV program. The first visible movie product placement was Hershey's Reese's Pieces in the film *ET*. The product actually became part of the storyline, offered the candy high levels of visibility, and resulted in a large increase in sales.[64]

Although Hershey's did not pay to place Reese's Pieces in *ET*, other firms have been more than willing to shell out for product placements. Companies spend approximately $4.38 billion on product placements in television and movies annually (e.g., Sony laptops in the James Bond feature *Casino Royale*). For their deals with *American Idol*, Ford and Coca-Cola paid approximately $30 million each to gain product placements and advertising space.[65] *So You Think You Can Dance Canada* judges sit behind prominently displayed Aquafina bottles. Especially because consumers who

How much do you think Aquafina had to pay So You Think You Can Dance Canada *to get this product placement?*

use digital video recorders report that they skip televised commercials 72.3 percent of the time, product placement is becoming increasingly important. Moreover, research shows that consumers recall product placements relatively well.[66]

Trade Channel Sales Promotions

Although sales promotions are often associated with coupons, contests, and other consumer tactics, far more money is spent on trade channel sales promotions than on consumer sales promotions. Trade channel promotions help convince retailers and wholesalers to stock a new brand, give it eye-level shelf space, and promote it in their flyers and other advertisements. As mentioned earlier, many types of consumer sales promotions can also be used for channel members. Additional trade channel promotions include discounts and allowances, co-operative advertising, and sales force training, each of which is briefly described in this next section.

Discounts and Allowances Discounts and allowances are effective incentives used to maintain or increase inventory levels in the distribution channel. Manufacturers sometimes offer a case allowance, for example, a discount or dollar amount taken off each case ordered during a specific time period. Alternatively, retailers may receive a set quantity of products free, for example, one case at no charge with an order of 10 cases. A merchandise allowance may be offered in return for extra in-store support or for featuring the product in some way by the retailer. For instance, if a store agreed to run an ad with a coupon promoting a specific product, the merchandise allowance may provide a discounted case price for orders received during the promotional period.

Co-operative Advertising One of the important functions retailers perform is promoting products to consumers. Co-operative (co-op) advertising helps to compensate trade channel members for money they spend promoting products and encourages them to feature products more often. Generally, manufacturers will pay 50 percent of the cost of advertising up to an agreed limit. This limit is usually determined based on the amount of business a retailer does with a manufacturer. To ensure high-quality advertisements are placed at the local level, some companies will provide a selection of final ads to choose from, ready to place in a variety of media or adapt as necessary.

Sales Force Training Because retailers have contact with end consumers and are ultimately responsible for selling the products they carry, manufacturers may offer to train the retailer's sales staff. This training gives a company's sales force more in-depth product knowledge, which enhances their confidence in the product and increases the likelihood of future sales. When VitalScience Corp. launched its derma-glow skin care line, it trained cosmeticians at Shoppers Drug Mart, since they were the staff members who would most likely field questions about the new product. Other training activities might include providing manuals or brochures, sales meetings, or field visits. Manufacturers sometimes run contests to help motivate trade channel members to sell their products.

Using Sales Promotion Tools

Marketers must be careful in their use of promotions, especially those that focus on lowering prices. Depending on the item, consumers may stock up when items are offered at a lower price, which simply shifts sales from the future to now and thereby leads to short-run benefits at the expense of long-term sales stability. For instance, using sales promotions such as coupons to stimulate sales of household cleaning supplies may cause consumers to stockpile the products and decrease demand for those products in the future. But a similar promotion used with a perishable product such as Danone yogourt should increase its demand at the expense of competitors like Yoplait.

pop-up stores
Temporary storefronts that exist for only a limited time and generally focus on a new product or a limited group of products offered by a retailer, manufacturer, or service provider; give consumers a chance to interact with the brand and build brand awareness.

cross-promoting
Efforts of two or more firms joining together to reach a specific target market.

The tools connected to sales promotions are as varied as the imaginations of the marketers who devise them, and new forms are constantly popping up. For example, **pop-up stores**—such as P&G's Look Fab Studio in Toronto discussed earlier or the Diet Coke Lounges that popped up in Canadian malls—exist only for a limited time and generally focus on a new product or a limited group of products offered by a retailer, manufacturer, or service provider. These temporary storefronts give consumers a chance to interact with the brand and build brand awareness, but they are not designed primarily to sell the product. Instead, consumers who have visited the pop-up, the company hopes, will follow up with a visit to either another retailer that carries the products or the company's website.[67]

Retailers tend not to mind manufacturers' pop-up stores because most are designed to drive traffic to the retailers through give-aways of coupons and samples. Because pop-ups are short-lived, they don't pose any long-term competition to retailers.

Many firms are also realizing the value of **cross-promoting**, when two or more firms join together to reach a specific target market. To achieve a successful cross-promotion, the two products must appeal to the same target market and together create value for consumers. Burger King, for instance, ran a three-firm cross-promotion: Motts Strawberry-Flavored Applesauce, designed to attract health-conscious parents; Star Wars memorabilia, designed to attract collectors and fans of the movie; and BK King of the Courts 3-on-3 College Basketball Tournament, designed to attract university students and fans of U.S. college basketball. Each of these cross-promotions targets a different market and attempts to create value in a slightly different way for Burger King consumers. However, the ultimate, overall goal for Burger King is to generate increased sales and greater brand loyalty.

The goal of any sales promotion is to create value for both the consumers and the firm. By understanding the needs of its customers, as well as how best to entice them to purchase or consume a particular product or service, a firm can develop promotional messages and events that are of interest to and achieve the desired response from those customers. Traditionally, the role of sales promotion has been to generate short-term results, whereas the goal of advertising was to generate long-term results. As this chapter demonstrates, though, both sales promotion and advertising can generate both long- and short-term effects. The effective combination of both types of activities leads to impressive results for the firm and the consumers.

Evaluating Sales Promotions by Using Marketing Metrics

Many sales promotion opportunities undertaken by retailers are initiated by manufacturers. For example, Sharp might offer the following special promotion to Costco: during a one-week period, Costco can order 37-inch Sharp Aquos LCD HDTVs at $300 below the standard wholesale price. However, if Costco elects to buy these HDTVs at the discounted price, then it must feature them prominently on its web page for $1099.00 ($325 below the suggested retail price). In addition, Costco must agree to purchase enough of this particular model to have front-of-store displays in each of its stores.

Before Costco decides whether to accept such a trade promotion and promote the Sharp HDTV to its customers, it needs to assess the promotion's impact on its own profitability. Such a promotion may be effective for Sharp but not for Costco.

To evaluate a trade promotion, retailers consider

- the realized margin from the promotion
- the cost of the additional inventory carried because of buying more than the normal amount of the product
- the potential increase in sales from the promoted merchandise
- the long-term impact on sales of the promotion

- the potential loss suffered when customers switch to the promoted merchandise from more profitable TVs
- the additional sales made to customers attracted to the store by the promotion

When the HDTV's price is reduced to $1099.00, Costco will sell more Sharp HDTVs than it normally does. But Costco's margin on the HDTVs will be less because the required retail discount of $325 isn't offset by the normal wholesale discount of $300. In addition, Costco might suffer losses because the promotion encourages customers to buy these special HDTVs, which have a lower margin than Costco makes on its other HDTVs. In contrast, the promotion may attract customers who don't normally shop at Costco but who will visit to buy the Sharp HDTV at the discounted price. These customers might buy additional merchandise, providing a sales gain to the store that it wouldn't have realized if it hadn't promoted this item.

Many salespeople now rely on virtual offices, which enable them to communicate via the Internet with colleagues and customers.

Personal Selling

Almost everyone is engaged in some form of selling. On a personal level, you sell your ideas or opinions to your friends, family, employers, and professors. Even if you have no interest in personal selling as a career, a strong grounding in the topic will help you in numerous career choices. Consider, for instance, Tony D'Souza, a very successful labour attorney. He worked his way through university selling alpaca sweaters to fraternities across the country. Although he loved his part-time job, D'Souza decided to become an attorney. When asked whether he misses selling, he said, "I use my selling skills every day. I have to sell new clients on the idea that I'm the best attorney for the job. I have to sell my partners on my legal point of view. I even use selling skills when I'm talking to a judge or jury." In this chapter though, we take a straightforward business perspective on selling.

LO4

The Scope and Nature of Personal Selling

Personal selling is the two-way flow of communication between a buyer (or buyers) and a seller that is designed to influence the buyer's purchase decision. Personal selling can take place in various situations: face to face, via video teleconferencing, on the telephone, or over the Internet. More than one million people are employed in sales positions in Canada,[68] including those involved in B2B transactions—such as manufacturers' representatives selling to retailers or other businesses—and those completing B2C transactions—such as retail salespeople, real estate agents, and insurance agents. Salespeople are referred to in many ways: as sales representatives or reps; account executives; or agents. And, as Tony D'Souza found, most professions rely on personal selling to some degree.

Salespeople don't always get the best coverage in popular media. In Arthur Miller's play *Death of a Salesman*, the main character, Willy Loman, leads a pathetic existence and suffers from the loneliness inherent in being a travelling salesman.[69] Unfortunately, this powerful Pulitzer Prize–winning piece of literature weighs heavily

Professional selling can be a very lucrative career and is very visible to management.

on our collective conscious and often overshadows the millions of hard-working professional salespeople who have fulfilling and rewarding careers and who add value to their firm and provide value for their customers.

Professional selling can be a satisfying career for several reasons. First, many people love the lifestyle. Salespeople are typically out on their own. Although they occasionally work with their managers and other colleagues, salespeople are usually responsible for planning their own day. This flexibility translates into an easier balance between work and family than many office-bound jobs can offer. Many salespeople now rely on virtual offices, which enable them to communicate via the Internet with colleagues and customers. Because salespeople are evaluated primarily on the results they produce, as long as they meet and exceed their goals, they experience little day-to-day supervision.

Second, the variety of the job often attracts people to sales. Every day is different, bringing different clients and customers, often in a variety of places. Their issues and problems and the solutions to those problems all differ and require creativity.

Third, professional selling and sales management can be a very lucrative career. Sales is among the highest-paying careers for college and university graduates, and compensation often includes perks, such as the use of a company car and bonuses for high performance. A top performer can have a total compensation package of more than $150,000; even lower-level salespeople can make well over $50,000. Although the monetary compensation can be significant, the satisfaction of being involved in interesting, challenging, and creative work is rewarding in and of itself.

Fourth, because salespeople are the front-line emissaries for their firm, they are very visible to management. Because it is fairly straightforward for management to identify top performers, those high-performing salespeople who aspire to management positions are in a good position to get promoted.

Personal Selling and Marketing Strategy

Although personal selling is an essential part of many firms' IMC strategy, it offers its own unique contribution to the four Ps. Because of the one-to-one nature of sales, a salesperson is in a unique position to customize a message for a specific buyer—a preplanned sales presentation or demonstration can be altered at any time as the need arises. In a personal selling situation, the salesperson can probe the buyer for his or her potential reservations about a product or service, educate the buyer when appropriate, and ask for the order at the appropriate time. Unlike other types of promotion, the sales presentation can be directed toward those customers with the highest potential. This highly directed approach to promotion is important because experts estimate that the average cost of a single B2B sales call is about $392.[70]

As we discussed in Chapter 12, building strong distribution channel relationships is a critical success factor. Who in the organization is better equipped to manage this relationship than the salesperson, the firm's front-line representative? The most successful salespeople are those who build strong relationships with their customers. They don't view themselves as being successful if they make a particular sale or one transaction at a time. Instead, they take a long-term perspective. Thus, building on the strategic relationship concept introduced in Chapter 12, **relationship selling** is a sales philosophy and process that emphasizes a commitment to maintaining the relationship over the long term and investing in opportunities that are mutually beneficial to all parties. Relationship salespeople work with their customers to find mutually beneficial solutions to their wants and needs. An IBM sales team, for instance, may be working with your university to provide you with the computer support and security you need.

Research has shown that a positive customer–salesperson relationship contributes to trust, increased customer loyalty, and the intent to continue the relationship with the salesperson.[71] To help build strong relationships, many firms undertake

relationship selling
A sales philosophy and process that emphasizes a commitment to maintaining the relationship over the long term and investing in opportunities that are mutually beneficial to all parties.

active CRM programs that identify and focus on building loyalty with the firm's most valued customers. Because the sales force interacts directly with customers, its members are in the best position to help a firm accomplish its CRM objectives.

CRM programs have several components. There is a customer database or data warehouse. Whether the salesperson is working for a retail store or managing a selling team for an aerospace contractor, he or she can record transaction information, customer contact information, customer preferences, and market segment information about the customer. Once the data has been analyzed and CRM programs developed, salespeople can help implement the programs. For instance, bankers use a "high-touch approach" in which they frequently call on their best customers or contact them by phone. A salesperson can contact customers when there are new products or changes to existing product lines. He or she can probe customers about what they liked or disliked about their recent transactions with the firm. Or the purpose of the call can be purely social. If done properly, customers will feel special and important when a salesperson calls just to see how things are going.

A good CRM system provides salespeople with the information they need to suggest specific items and services to individual customers.

The Value Added by Personal Selling

Why have salespeople in the supply chain? They are expensive, and as we discuss later in this chapter, they can be a challenge to manage. Some firms, such as retailers, have made the decision not to use a sales force and become, for the most part, almost completely self-service. But those that use personal selling as part of their IMC program do so because it adds value to their product or service mix—that is, personal selling is worth more than it costs. Personal selling adds value by educating and providing advice, and by saving customers time and simplifying things for them.[72]

Salespeople Educate and Provide Advice Imagine how difficult it would be to buy a new suit, a diamond engagement ring, or a plasma TV without the help of a salesperson. Similarly, UPS wouldn't dream of investing in a new fleet of airplanes without the benefit of Boeing's selling team. Sure, it could be done, but customers see the value in and are willing to pay indirectly for the education and advice salespeople provide. Retail salespeople can provide valuable information about how a garment fits, new fashions, or directions for operating products. Boeing's sales team can provide UPS with the technical aspects of the aircraft, as well as the economic justification for the purchase.

Internet travel services such as Expedia are great for booking relatively simple trips. But when multiple people and multiple destinations are involved, a good travel agent can earn his or her weight in gold.

Five years ago, many observers thought that travel agents and other service providers would be replaced by more efficient Internet services, and the Internet has certainly changed the way many consumers make travel decisions. Thousands use sites such as Expedia.ca and

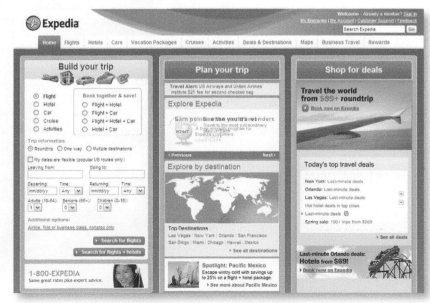

Travelocity.ca or visit airlines, rail, hotels, and car rental firms online to make reservations directly. But when planning to visit an exotic locale or booking a complicated trip or cruise, or for those who don't feel comfortable buying online, travel agents add significant value. They can help with itineraries, give helpful tips, and even save the customer money.

Salespeople Save Time and Simplify Buying Time is money! Customers perceive value in time and labour savings. In many grocery and drugstore chains, salespeople employed by the vendor supplying merchandise straighten stock, set up displays, assess inventory levels, and write orders. In some cases, such as with baked goods or soft drinks, salespeople and truck drivers even bring in the merchandise and stock the shelves. These are all tasks that retail employees would otherwise have to do.

Sometimes, however, turning over too many tasks to suppliers' salespeople can cause problems. If they take over the inventory management function, for instance, they may buy a suboptimal quantity of competitors' products. They might also place competitor products in disadvantageous shelf positions. Salespeople can help facilitate a buying situation, but they shouldn't take it over.

L05   The Personal Selling Process

Although selling may appear a rather straightforward process, successful salespeople follow several steps. Depending on the sales situation and the buyer's readiness to purchase, the salesperson may not use every step, and the time required for each step will vary depending on the situation. For instance, if a customer goes into The Bay already prepared to purchase some chino pants, the selling process will be fairly quick. But if IBM is attempting to sell personal computers for the first time to a university, the process may take several months. With this in mind, let's examine each step of the selling process (see Exhibit 15.4).

Step 1: Generate and Qualify Leads The first step in the selling process is to generate a list of potential customers (**leads**) and assess their potential (**qualify**). Salespeople

leads
A list of potential customers.

qualify
The process of assessing the potential of sales leads.

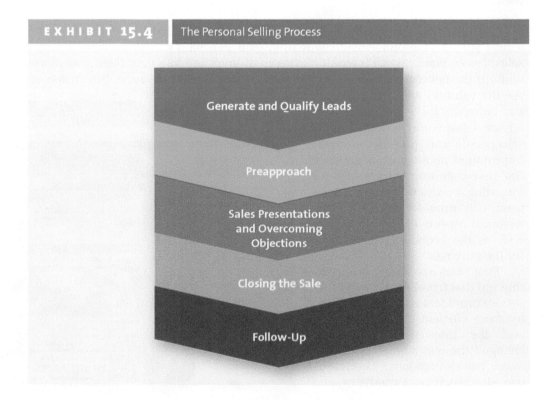

EXHIBIT 15.4   The Personal Selling Process

Generate and Qualify Leads

Preapproach

Sales Presentations and Overcoming Objections

Closing the Sale

Follow-Up

who already have an established relationship with a customer will skip this step, and it is not used extensively in retail settings. In B2B situations, however, it is important to work continually to find new and potentially profitable customers.

Salespeople generate leads in a variety of ways.[73] They can discover potential leads by talking to their current customers and networking at events such as industry conferences or chamber of commerce meetings. The Internet has been a boon for generating leads. For instance, salespeople can gather information collected on the firm's website or Google a few keywords and instantly generate enough potential leads to keep them busy for weeks. Another excellent forum for finding leads are **trade shows**, which are major events attended by buyers who choose to be exposed to products and services offered by potential suppliers in an industry. For instance, the Canadian Meeting and Incentive Travel Group hosts the Incentive-Works Show at the Metro Toronto Convention Centre every August. More than 475 exhibit booths, representing more than 700 companies, from a variety of domestic and international destinations; hotels; resorts; meeting/incentive travel services; and business gifts, premium, and reward merchandise exhibit at the show.[74]

Cold calls are a method of prospecting in which salespeople telephone or go to see potential customers without appointments. **Telemarketing** is similar to a cold call, but it always occurs over the telephone. Sometimes professional telemarketing firms, rather than the firm's salespeople, make such calls. However, cold calls and telemarketing have become less popular than they were in the past. First, the success rate is fairly low because the potential customer's need has not been established ahead of time. As a result, these methods can be very expensive. Second, both federal and provincial governments have begun to regulate the activities of telemarketers. Federal rules prohibit telemarketing to consumers whose names appear on the national Do-Not-Call list, which is maintained by the Canadian Marketing Association. Even for those consumers whose names are not on the list, the rules prohibit calling before 8:00 a.m. or after 9:00 p.m. (in the consumer's time zone) or after the consumer has told the telemarketer not to call. Federal rules also prohibit unsolicited fax messages and unsolicited telephone calls, as well as email messages to cellphones.

After salespeople generate leads, they must qualify those leads by determining whether it is worthwhile to pursue them and attempt to turn the leads into customers. In a retail setting, qualifying potential can be a very dangerous and potentially illegal practice. Retail salespeople should never "judge a book by its cover" and assume that a person in the store doesn't fit the store's image or cannot afford to purchase there. Imagine going to an upscale jewellery store to purchase an engagement ring, only to be snubbed because you are dressed in your everyday, casual school clothes. But in B2B settings, where the costs of preparing and making a presentation can be substantial, the seller must assess a lead's potential. Salespeople should consider, for instance, whether the potential customer's needs pertain to a product or a service. They should also assess whether the lead has the financial resources to pay for the product or service.

Step 2: Preapproach

The **preapproach** occurs prior to meeting the customer for the first time and extends the qualification of leads procedure described in Step 1. Although the salesperson has learned about the customer

A great place to generate leads is at a trade show.

trade shows
Major events attended by buyers who choose to be exposed to products and services offered by potential suppliers in an industry.

cold calls
A method of prospecting in which salespeople telephone or go to see potential customers without appointments.

telemarketing
A method of prospecting in which salespeople telephone potential customers.

Retail salespeople should never "judge a book by its cover" and assume that a person in the store doesn't fit the store's image or cannot afford to purchase there.

preapproach
In the personal selling process, occurs prior to meeting the customer for the first time and extends the qualification of leads procedure; in this step, the salesperson conducts additional research and develops plans for meeting with the customer.

during the qualification stage, in this step, he or she must conduct additional research and develop plans for meeting with the customer. Suppose, for example, a management consulting firm wants to sell a bank a new system for finding chequing account errors. The consulting firm's salesperson should first find out everything possible about the bank: How many cheques does it process? What system is the bank using now? What are the benefits of the consultant's proposed system compared with the competition? The answers to these questions provide the basis for establishing value for the customer.

Having done the additional research, the salesperson establishes goals for meeting with the customer; it is important that he or she know ahead of time exactly what should be accomplished. For instance, the consulting firm's salesperson can't expect to get a commitment from the bank that it will buy on the first visit. But a demonstration of the system and a short presentation about how the system would benefit the customer would be appropriate.

Step 3: Sales Presentation and Overcoming Objections

The presentation.   Once all the background information has been obtained and the objectives for the meeting are set, the salesperson is ready for a person-to-person meeting. Let's continue with our bank example. During the first part of the meeting, the salesperson needs to get to know the customer, get his or her attention, and create interest in the presentation to follow. The beginning of the presentation may be the most important part of the entire selling process, because this is when the salesperson establishes exactly where the customer is in his or her buying process (see Exhibit 15.5). (For a refresher on the B2B buying process, see Chapter 6.) Suppose, for instance, the bank is in the first stage of the buying process, need recognition. It would not be prudent for the salesperson to discuss the pros and cons of different potential suppliers because

EXHIBIT 15.5 | Aligning the Personal Selling Process with the B2B Buying Process

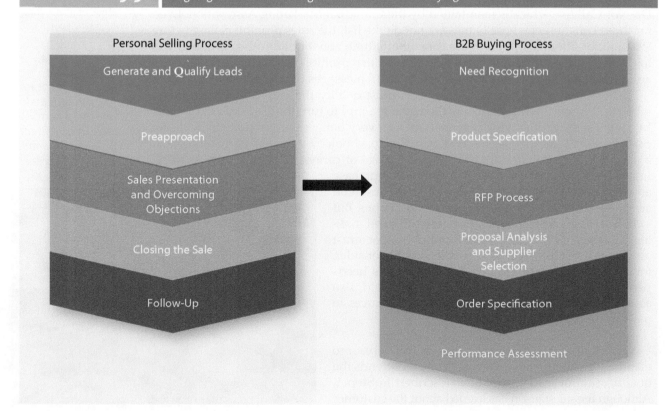

doing so would assume that the customer already had reached Stage 4, proposal analysis and supplier selection. By asking a series of questions, however, the salesperson can assess the bank's need for the product or service and adapt or customize the presentation to match the customer's need and stage in the decision process.[75]

Asking questions is only half the battle; carefully listening to the answers is equally important. Some salespeople, particularly inexperienced ones, believe that to be in control, they must do all the talking. Yet it is impossible to really understand where the customer stands without listening carefully. What if the COO says, "It seems kind of expensive"? If the salesperson isn't listening carefully, he or she won't pick up on the subtle nuances of what the customer is really thinking. In this case, it probably means that the COO doesn't see the value in the offering.

When the salesperson has a good feel for where the customer stands, he or she can apply that knowledge to help the customer solve its problem or satisfy its need. The salesperson might begin by explaining the features or characteristics of the system that will reduce chequing account errors. It may not be obvious, based solely on these features, however, that the system adds value beyond the bank's current practices. Using the answers to some of the questions the customer posed earlier in the meeting, he or she can clarify the product's advantages over current or past practices, as well as the overall benefits of adopting the new system. The salesperson might explain, for instance, that the bank can expect a 20-percent decrease in chequing account errors and that, based on the size of the bank and the number of cheques it processes per year, this improvement would represent $2 million in annual savings. Because the system costs $150,000 per year and will take only three weeks to integrate into the current system, it will add significant and almost immediate value.

Handling objections.   An integral part of the sales presentation is handling objections that the buyer might have about the product or service. Although objections can arise during each stage of the selling process, they are very likely to occur during the sales presentation. Customers may raise objections pertaining to a variety of issues, but they usually relate in some way to value, such as that the price is too high for the level of quality or service.

Good salespeople know the types of objections buyers are likely to raise. They may know, for instance, that their service is slower than competitors' or that their selection is limited. Although not all objections can be forestalled, effective salespeople can anticipate and handle some of them. For example, when the bank COO said the cheque service seemed expensive, the salesperson was ready with information about how quickly the investment would be recouped.

Similar to other aspects of the selling process, the best way to handle objections is to relax and listen, and then to ask questions to clarify any reservations. For example, the salesperson could respond to the COO's objection by asking, "How much do you think the bank is losing through chequing account errors?" Her answer might open up a conversation about the positive trends in a cost/benefit analysis. Such questions are usually more effective than trying to prove the customer's objection is not valid because the latter approach implies the salesperson isn't really listening and could lead to an argument. In an attempt to handle objections and start the process of closing the sale, a salesperson may offer creative deals or incentives that may be unethical.

Step 4: Closing the Sale   **Closing the sale** means obtaining a commitment from the customer to make a purchase. Without a successful close, the salesperson goes away empty-handed, so many salespeople find this part of the sales process very stressful. Although losing a sale is never pleasant, salespeople who are involved in a relationship with their customers must view any particular sales presentation as part of the progression toward ultimately making the sale. An unsuccessful close on one day may just be a means of laying the groundwork for a successful close the next meeting.

Although we have presented the selling process in a series of steps, closing the sale rarely follows the other steps so neatly. However, good salespeople listen

closing the sale
Obtaining a commitment from the customer to make a purchase.

Power of the Internet 15.1   **Phishing for Sales**

Internet crime is big business, estimated at $3.6 billion per year. And there are many ways to steal. One of the most popular methods of committing fraud on the Internet is phishing, or sending emails falsely claiming to be a legitimate business soliciting information to scam users into surrendering private information that will be used for identity theft.[76] The emails direct users to visit a bogus website that looks like the real company's, where they are asked to update personal information, such as passwords and credit card, social security, and bank account numbers, that the legitimate organization already has. The website is set up to steal the user's information. The phishing emails come from a variety of both "real" and invented phoney sources, including banks, auction sites set up to look like eBay or PayPal, and charities. It is estimated that more than 3.6 million adults lose money every year as a result of phishing.[77]

Another scam entails the use of gift cards. A criminal uses cash earned by illegal activity to buy phone or gift cards. The criminal then sells the cards at a discounted value on auction sites. Thieves also rip off gift card numbers while cards are on a store display. Then when the proper owner of the card tries to use it, the funds are already spent. To counter this activity, major retailers do not display gift cards, or activate them only at the time of purchase.

A notorious but easy method of scamming both buyers and sellers has been on auction sites. Sellers post stolen or nonexistent merchandise on the sites but never ship it to the winner. This is relatively rare, since experienced buyers know that they should check out the seller and, in the case of eBay, buy only from those with numerous positive feedbacks. Fraudulent buyers can play havoc with Internet auctions. One popular tactic is to get the seller to use a fictitious escrow company. (Escrow companies are independent third parties that hold/disburse money from the buyer and seller.) Once the sale is consummated, the buyer supposedly sends payment to the fictitious escrow company. But the money is never sent. The escrow company notifies the seller that the money has "safely" arrived. Then the seller sends the merchandise to the buyer but never gets paid.

---

carefully to what potential customers say and pay attention to their body language. Reading these signals carefully can help salespeople achieve an early close. Suppose that our hypothetical bank, rather than being in the first step of the buying process, was in the final step of negotiation and selection. An astute salesperson will pick up on these signals and ask for the sale.

Step 5: Follow-Up   With relationship selling, the sale is never really over, even after it has been made. The attitudes customers develop after the sale become the basis for how they will purchase in the future. The follow-up therefore offers a prime opportunity for a salesperson to solidify the customer relationship through great service quality.

When customers' expectations are not met, they often complain—about deliveries, the billing amount or process, the product's performance, or after-sale services such as installation or training. Effectively handling complaints is critical to the future of the relationship. As we noted in Chapter 10, the best way to handle complaints is to listen to the customer, provide a fair solution to the problem, and resolve the problem quickly.

The best way to nip a postsale problem in the bud is to check with the customer right after he or she takes possession of the product or immediately after the service has been completed. This speed demonstrates responsiveness and empathy; it also shows the customer that the salesperson and the firm care about customer satisfaction. Finally, a postsale follow-up call, email, or letter takes the salesperson back to the first step in the sales process for initiating a new order and sustaining the relationship.

Unfortunately, the Internet has become fertile ground for scam artists and thieves who pose as prospective buyers or sellers on auction sites, as explained in Power of the Internet 15.1.

Managing the Sales Force

Like any business activity involving people, the sales force requires management. **Sales management** involves the planning, direction, and control of personal selling

sales management
Involves the planning, direction, and control of personal selling activities, including recruiting, selecting, training, motivating, compensating, and evaluating, as they apply to the sales force.

activities, including recruiting, selecting, training, motivating, compensating, and evaluating, as they apply to the sales force.[78] Managing a sales force is a rewarding yet complicated undertaking. In this section, we examine how sales forces can be structured, some of the most important issues in recruiting and selecting salespeople, sales training issues, ways to motivate and compensate salespeople, and finally, how to evaluate salespeople.

Sales Force Structure

Imagine the daunting task of putting together a sales force from scratch. Will you hire your own salespeople, or should they be manufacturer's representatives? What will be each salesperson's primary duties? Will the salespeople work together in teams? We examine these issues here.

Company Sales Force or Manufacturer's Representative A company sales force is composed of people who are employees of the selling company. **Independent agents**, also known as **manufacturer's representatives**, are salespeople who sell a manufacturer's products on an extended contract basis but are not employees of the manufacturer. They are compensated by commissions and do not take ownership or physical possession of the merchandise.

independent agents (or manufacturer's representative) Salespeople who sell a manufacturer's products on an extended contract basis but are not employees of the manufacturer; also known as *manufacturer's representatives* or *reps*.

Manufacturer's representatives are useful for smaller firms or firms expanding into new markets because such companies can achieve instant and extensive sales coverage without having to pay full-time personnel. Good sales representatives have many established contacts and can sell multiple products from noncompeting manufacturers during the same sales call. Also, the use of manufacturers' representatives facilitates flexibility; it is much easier to replace a rep than an employee and much easier to expand or contract coverage in a market with a sales rep than with a company sales force.

Company sales forces are more typically used for established product lines. Because the salespeople are company employees, the manufacturer has more control over what they do. If, for example, the manufacturer's strategy is to provide extensive customer service, the sales manager can specify exactly what actions a company sales force must take. In contrast, because manufacturer's representatives are paid on a commission basis, it is difficult to persuade them to take any action that doesn't directly lead to sales.

Although the life of a professional salesperson is highly varied, salespeople generally play three important roles: order getting, order taking, and sales support.

Recruiting and Selecting Salespeople

When the firm has determined how the sales force will be structured, it must find and hire salespeople. Although superficially this task may sound easy, it must be performed carefully because firms don't want to hire the wrong person because salespeople are very expensive to train.

The most important activity in the recruiting process is to determine exactly what the salesperson will be doing and what personal traits and abilities a person should have to do the job well. For instance, a Coca-Cola sales rep who goes to Safeway to pitch a new product will typically need significant sales experience, coupled with great communication and analytical skills. Coke's order takers, who process routine orders, need to be reliable and able to get along with many different types of people in the stores, from managers to customers.

When recruiting salespeople, is it better to look for candidates with innate sales ability, or can a good training program make anyone a successful salesperson? By a margin of 7 to 1 in a survey of sales and marketing executives, respondents believed that training and supervision are more critical determinants of selling success than the salesperson's inherent personal characteristics.[79] Yet some of those same respondents noted that certain personal traits are important for successful sales careers.

Good salespeople, particularly in difficult selling situations such as door-to-door sales, don't easily take no for an answer. They keep coming back until they get a yes.

Those traits, as identified by managers and sales experts[80] are personality, optimism, resilience, self-motivation, and empathy.

Sales Training

All salespeople benefit from training about selling and negotiation techniques, product and service knowledge, technologies used in the selling process, time and territory management, and company policies and procedures.

Firms use varied methods to train their salespeople, depending on the topic of the training, what type of salesperson is being trained, and the cost versus the value of the training. For instance, an on-the-job training program is excellent for communicating selling and negotiation skills because managers can observe the sales trainees in real selling situations and provide instant feedback. They can also engage in role-playing exercises in which the salesperson acts out a simulated buying situation and the manager critiques the salesperson's performance.

A much less expensive training method is the Internet. Online training programs have revolutionized the way training happens in many firms. Firms can provide new product and service knowledge, spread the word about changes in company policies and procedures, and share selling tips in a user-friendly environment that salespeople can access anytime and anywhere. Distance learning sales training programs through teleconferencing enable a group of salespeople to participate with their instructor or manager in a virtual classroom. While online sales training may never replace the one-on-one interaction of on-the-job training for advanced selling skills, it is quite effective and efficient for many other aspects of the sales training task.

Motivating and Compensating Salespeople

An important goal for any effective sales manager is to get to know his or her salespeople and determine what motivates them to be effective. Some salespeople prize their freedom and like to be left alone, whereas others want attention and are more productive when they receive accolades for a job well done. Still others are motivated primarily by monetary compensation. Great sales managers determine how best to motivate each of their salespeople according to what is most important to each individual. Although sales managers can emphasize different motivating factors, the methods used to compensate salespeople are fairly standardized and can be divided into two categories: financial and nonfinancial.

Financial Rewards   Salespeople's compensation usually has several components. Most salespeople receive at least part of their compensation as a salary, a fixed sum of money paid at regular intervals. Another common financial incentive is a commission, money paid as a percentage of the sales volume or profitability. A bonus is a payment made at management's discretion when the salesperson attains certain goals; bonuses usually are given only periodically, such as at the end of the year. A sales contest is a short-term incentive designed to elicit a specific response from the sales force. Prizes might be cash or other types of financial incentives.

Nonfinancial Rewards   As we have noted, good salespeople are self-motivated. They want to do a good job and make the sale because it makes them feel good. But this good feeling also can be accentuated by recognition from peers and management. Nonfinancial rewards should have high symbolic value, as plaques, pens, or rings do. Free trips or days off are also effective rewards. More important than what the reward is, however, is the way it is operationalized. For instance, an award should be given at a sales meeting and publicized in the company newsletter. It should also be done in good taste, because if the award is perceived as tacky, no one will take it seriously.[81]

Evaluating Salespeople

Salespeople's evaluation process must be tied to their reward structure. If salespeople do well, they should receive their just rewards. Considering this guiding principle, how should sales managers evaluate their salespeople? The answer is never easy because measures must be tied to performance, and there are many ways to measure performance in a complex job such as selling. For example, evaluating performance on the basis of monthly sales alone fails to consider how profitable the sales were, whether any progress was made to build new business that will be realized sometime in the future, or the level of customer service the salesperson provided. Because the sales job is multifaceted, with many contributing success factors, sales managers should use multiple measures.[82]

Sales, profits, and the number of orders represent examples of objective evaluation measures. However, such measures do not provide an adequate perspective for a thorough evaluation because there is no means of comparison with other salespeople. For this reason, firms use ratios such as profit per customer, orders per call, sales per hour, or expenses compared to sales as their objective measures. Subjective evaluation measures seek to assess salespeople's behaviour—what they do and how well they do it—and reflect one person's opinion about another's performance. Thus, subjective evaluations can be biased and should be used cautiously and only in conjunction with multiple objective measures.

Personal selling is an integral component of some firms' IMC strategy. Although it doesn't make sense for all firms, it is widely used in B2B markets, as well as in B2C markets in which the price of the merchandise is relatively high and customers need some one-to-one assistance before they can buy. Because of the relatively high expense of maintaining a personal selling force, it is important that salespeople be adequately trained, motivated, and compensated.

Learning Objectives Review

L01 Describe advertising and the objectives of advertising

Advertising is a paid form of communication from an identifiable source, delivered through a communication channel, that is designed to persuade consumers to take action. All advertising campaigns are designed to either inform, persuade, or remind customers. Ads can also be used to stimulate demand for a particular category or industry, or for a specific brand, firm, or item.

L02 Summarize the regulatory and ethical issues of concern to advertisers

Advertising is regulated by a plethora of federal and provincial agencies. The most important agencies are the Competition Bureau, which protects consumers against general deceptive advertising; the Canadian Radio-television and Telecommunications Commission, which has jurisdiction over radio, television, wire, satellite, and cable, and covers issues regarding the use of tobacco products; and Health Canada, whose Food and Drug Act regulates food, drugs, cosmetics, and medical devices. Advertising Standards Canada maintains a strict broadcast code regarding advertising to children.

If a message is designed to promote or sell a product or service, it is generally considered to have an economic motivation, but if the message has no promotional or selling intent, it is fully protected by the Charter of Rights and Freedoms. The line becomes blurred, however, when normally noncommercial venues are used to sell something. Another practice that is causing a stir emerges when the sender of a commercial message is not clearly identified. Activities such as bogus websites or certain stealth marketing programs, in which the identity of the sponsor of an activity or event is intentionally kept from prospective customers, can be considered deceptive promotional practices.

L03 Explain how sales promotions supplement a firm's IMC strategy

Sales promotions are special incentives or excitement-building programs that encourage purchase and include coupons, rebates, contests, free samples, and POP displays. They either push sales through the channel, as is the case with contests directed toward retail salespeople, or pull sales through the channel, as coupons and rebates do. Sales promotions usually occur in conjunction with other elements of a firm's IMC strategy, such as price promotions or loyalty programs. Trade channel sales promotions include discounts and allowances, co-op advertising, and sales force training.

L04 Describe personal selling and how it adds value for customers

Personal selling is the two-way flow of communication between a buyer and a seller and can take place in a variety of situations. Although the cost of an average B2B sales call is expensive (about $390), many firms believe they couldn't do business without their sales force. Customers can buy many products and services without the help of a salesperson, but in many other cases, it is worth the extra cost built into the price of a product to be educated about the product or get

valuable advice. Salespeople can also simplify the buying process and therefore save the customer time and hassle.

L05 Identify the steps in the personal selling process

Although we discuss selling in terms of steps, it truly represents a process, and the time spent in each step varies according to the situation. In the first step, the salesperson generates a list of viable customers. During the second step, the preapproach, the salesperson gathers information about the customer and prepares for the presentation. The third step, the sales presentation, consists of a personal meeting between the salesperson and the customer. Through discussion and by asking questions, the salesperson learns where the customer is in its buying process and tailors the discussion around what the firm's product or service can do to meet that customer's needs. During the fourth step, closing the sale, the salesperson asks for the order. Finally, during the follow-up, the salesperson and support staff solidifies a long-term relationship by making sure the customer is satisfied with the purchase and by addressing any complaints. The follow-up therefore sets the stage for the next purchase.

Key Terms

- AIDA model, 493
- aided recall, 493
- closing the sale, 519
- cold calls, 517
- contest, 507
- cross-promoting, 512
- deal, 506
- independent agents, 521
- informative advertising, 496
- institutional advertisements, 499
- lagged effect, 495
- leads, 516
- loyalty program, 508

- manufacturer's representative, 521
- persuasive advertising, 496
- point-of-purchase (POP) display, 509
- pop-up stores, 512
- preapproach, 518
- premium, 506
- product placement, 510
- product-focused advertisements, 499
- public service announcement (PSA), 500

- puffery, 502
- qualify, 516
- relationship selling, 514
- reminder advertising, 497
- sales management, 520
- sampling, 507
- social marketing, 500
- stealth marketing, 502
- sweepstakes, 507
- telemarketing, 517
- top-of-mind awareness, 493
- trade shows, 517
- viral marketing, 504

Concept Review

1. What is advertising?

2. What is the AIDA model? How does the AIDA model facilitate the planning and execution of marketing communications?

3. What are the three primary objectives of advertising?

4. List and explain some of the potential regulatory and ethical issues firms should consider when developing their marketing communications strategy.

5. What is sales promotion? What are the main objectives of sales promotion?

6. List six different kinds of consumer sales promotion tactics and discuss the advantages and disadvantages of each.

7. Describe the different kinds of sales promotion targeted to distribution channel members. Why are these trade channel promotions necessary? Are they ethical?

8. What is personal selling? Describe the steps in the personal selling process. Which stage do you consider to be the most important and why?

9. What is sales management? Why is sales management considered a complicated task?

10. What are the main considerations involved in recruiting, training, and compensating salespeople?

Marketing Applications

1. Choose one of the ads featured in this book and identify its page number. What are the objectives of this ad? Does the ad have more than one objective? Explain your answer.

2. Using the steps in the AIDA model, explain why a potential consumer who views advertising by designer jean company Parasuco may not be ready to go out and purchase a new pair of jeans.

3. Suppose Lexus is introducing a new line of light trucks and has already created the advertising campaign. How would you assess the effectiveness of the campaign?

4. Suppose now Lexus is planning a sales promotion campaign to augment its advertising campaign for the new line of light trucks. Which sales promotion tools do you believe would be the most effective? Why?

5. How would the Lexus sales promotion differ if it was geared to a business organization with a fleet of company owned trucks?

6. Choose an ad that you believe unreasonably overstates what the product or service can do. (If you can't think of a real ad, make one up.) Explain whether the ad is actually deceptive or just puffery. How would your answer change if you lived in France?

7. You are invited to your six-year-old niece's birthday party and bring her the new superhero doll being advertised on TV. She's thrilled when she unwraps the gift but is in tears a short time later because her new doll is broken. She explains that, on TV, the doll flies and does karate kicks, but when she tried to play with the doll this way, it broke. You decide to call the manufacturer, and a representative tells you he is sorry your niece is so upset but

that the ad clearly states the doll does not fly. The next time you see the televised ad, you notice very small print at the bottom of the screen that states the doll does not fly. You decide to write a letter to Advertising Standards Canada about this practice. What information should you include in your letter?

8. "Salespeople just make products cost more." Agree or disagree with this statement and discuss why you've taken that position.

9. Choose an industry or a specific company that you would like to work for as a salesperson. How would you generate and qualify leads?

10. You have taken a summer job in the windows and doors department of a large home improvement store. During sales training, you learn about the products, how to best address customers' needs, why the lifetime value of the customer concept is so important to a store like this, and how to sell the customer the best product to fit their needs regardless of price point. One day your manager informs you that you are to recommend Smith Windows to every window customer. Smith Windows are more expensive than other brands and don't really provide superior benefit except in limited circumstances. The manager is insistent that you recommend Smith Windows. Not knowing what else to do, you recommend Smith Windows to customers who would have been better served by lower cost windows. The manager rewards you with a sales award. Later, the manager tells you that he received an all-expenses-paid cruise for his family from Smith Windows. What, if anything, should you do with this information?

Toolkit

MAKE AN ADVERTISEMENT

Suppose you have been hired to develop a new ad for a product or service to help target the college and university student market. These ads will appear in student newspapers around the world. Use the toolkit provided on Connect to develop the ad.

Net Savvy

1. Go to the website for Concerned Children's Advertisers (www.cca-kids.ca), an agency that produces and delivers social messaging campaigns on issues of challenge in children's lives. Click on the About CCA tab and examine the history and activities of the organization. How does the role it plays in responsible advertising complement the formal regulation of other agencies? Now look under the News tab. Choose one of the PSAs

and discuss how these ads are used to deliver CCA's message.

2. Go to www.couponsaver.com and identify five of the products featured. How effective are coupons for selling these products? Why? What are the benefits to the seller of using CouponSaver.com over other IMC options? How do you think CouponSaver.com makes money?

Chapter Case Study

JIGSAW: A MENACE TO YOUR PHONE[83]

The televised trailers for Lions Gate Entertainment's *Saw* films seem scary enough, with their images of toes being cut off and screaming actors, along with flashes of the films' frightening trap-maker, Jigsaw. Yet to maintain the buzz surrounding the film series between the third and fourth installations, the movie studio went much further.

Lions Gate wanted to push the DVD release of *Saw III* and therefore engaged in an elaborate plan, fitting for the detailed games and traps that frequent the movies themselves, that would send images of the blood-soaked torture flick to millions of fans' cellphones. The market for slasher movies tends to include younger men, most of whom likely viewed the film during its theatrical release. But to induce them to think about the movie again for the DVD release, Lions Gate and its advertising agency, Initiative, created ads that could double as entertainment. As the executive vice-president of Initiative noted, "Advertising and content are really not that different, especially in the entertainment space."[84]

Working with MobiTV, a company that offers subscribers live television on their cellphones, the company created a 24-7 *Saw III* channel that provided never-before-seen outtakes, behind-the-scenes footage, and cast interviews. To tout the channel, MobiTV also ran interactive ads on its own service. If users were watching, say, the Discovery Channel on their phones, they might see an ad for the *Saw* channel. Thus, the campaign increased awareness of not only the DVD release, but also the advertising for the DVD release in a virtual cycle of attention building.

Not satisfied to rely just on consumers who subscribe to MobiTV, the campaign also reached out to another form of entertainment widely accessed by the target market: comedians. It may seem that comedy and movies focusing on dismemberments and violence have little in common, but by prompting comedians, such as Richard Villa, to mention the movie in their stand-up routines and sketches, an entirely different group of viewers were, in turn, prompted to remember their affection for the films.

Comedy not an odd enough partner for horror? What about a musical? Lions Gate also teamed up with Warcon Records to produce a *Saw III*–themed live music show in support of both the film and its soundtrack. "A Musical Evening Inspired by the Soundtrack of *Saw III*" took over New York's Webster Hall, featuring appearances by bands from the film's soundtrack, with headlining acts such as Helmet, The Smashup, and Hydrovibe. Shawnee Smith, the actress who plays Amanda in the *Saw* movies, served as the emcee. For the performance, the hall installed a special museum, displaying film props, torture devices, and the creepy Billie puppet. And of course, attendees could join the Circle of Blood fan club.[85]

Fans of this calibre certainly are not willing to let the producers of the film have all the fun. Inspired by these creative efforts, various fans push the product themselves, in a form of advertising specially enabled by modern technology. Myspace even hosts a *Saw* music video, posted by a member who calls himself "Saw III."[86]

The result of these varied and innovative marketing communications? The *Saw* franchise continues to rake in movie dollars. In particular, for its DVD release, *Saw III* became the top-selling and top-rented release of the week, and the halo effect of its success pushed the DVDs of the first two films into the top 20, according to Nielsen. And now the creators of *Saw* have released the sixth movie in the series—a sure sign that advertising efforts have paid off.

Questions

1. How effective do you think Lions Gate's advertising through nontraditional media channels has been for its films?

2. The *Saw* movies tend to appeal mostly to younger, male viewers. Therefore, is Lions Gate's strategy a long- or short-term strategy? Why?

3. Identify and link the various advertising and promotion tactics used by Lions Gate to the AIDA model described in this chapter. How effective do you think these tactics are to its success?

Lions Gate uses multiple media channels to advertise its Saw *films.*

 Practise and learn online with Connect. Connect allows you to practise important concepts at your own pace and on your own schedule, with 24/7 online access to an eBook, practice quizzes, interactivities, videos, study tools, additional resources, and more.

SECTION EIGHT
Marketing in the Global Environment

CHAPTER 16 Global Marketing

Global
Marketing

"The world is a global village" is something we have all heard at one time or another. But what does it actually mean for marketers? Simply put, it means that the economies of the world are interconnected and interdependent and thus competition is global, the marketplace is global, and that to be successful, firms must look beyond their borders for opportunities to grow and expand. Indeed, Canada's small economy is another reason why companies must look to the global market for growth and expansion. Let's look at one of Canada's success stories in the highly competitive high-tech sector: Research In Motion (RIM), the maker of the BlackBerry and the PlayBook.[1]

The BlackBerry, launched in 2002, is the brainchild of Mike Lazaridis, who developed the concept for it based on a paper he wrote in three hours on a computer in his basement. Within a year of its launch, the BlackBerry became a household name in Canada and the United States. Today, it's a household name around the world and, according to Interbrand, "Blackberry created the [smartphone] category." Since 2002, RIM has sold more than 100 million devices worldwide and has close to 50 million subscribers, averaging an annual growth rate of 80 percent. The BlackBerry is available through 550 telecom carriers and distribution partners in over 175 countries. More than 250 000 organizations around the world use the BlackBerry Enterprise Server. RIM also partners with technology providers such as IBM and Microsoft to integrate tools and platforms into the device. More recently, RIM started to partner with companies such as eBay and Yahoo to develop applications to bring the services of these companies to the BlackBerry.

According to Steve Yankovich, vice-president of platform business solutions and mobile at eBay, the eBay application

Learning Objectives

After studying this chapter, you should be able to

LO1 Identify the factors that aid the growth of globalization

LO2 Explain the components of a country market assessment

LO3 Describe the various market entry strategies

LO4 List the similarities of and differences between a domestic marketing strategy and a global marketing strategy

LO5 Explain how ethical issues affect global marketing practices

for BlackBerry smartphones allows users to search, bid, buy, and check their eBay activity virtually anywhere. The app leverages the BlackBerry Push Service to allow users to be wirelessly notified of the status of eBay listings in real time. With alerts, eBay buyers can be notified when they have won an item or have been outbid, or when an auction for a listing they are interested in is ending soon. eBay sellers can be notified when their sale ends and can be provided with the buyer's information and the sale price. All notifications are directed to the user's BlackBerry email inbox and, because the BlackBerry operating system supports multitasking, it is simple to use: users can simply click on the email notification to automatically launch or switch to the eBay application.

Clearly, the BlackBerry benefits many different stakeholders, including consumers, telecom carriers, marketers, technology providers, and, of course, RIM. Indeed, RIM's growth and financial performance so far has been phenomenal and despite intense competition it has managed to secure its position as the market leader. This type of performance by a Canadian company on a global scale is uncommon. The company's success begs the question, how did they do that? Expanding globally within a decade to more than 175 countries and partnering with over 550 carriers and distributors around the world is quite the feat. What are some of the challenges RIM must have had to overcome along the way, and what are some of the challenges it faces on a daily basis as it tries to manage and expand its global presence? .::

The increasing globalization of markets affects all companies—large, small, medium, and entrepreneurial—in Canada, and around the world. Many Canadian companies find themselves becoming part of the global supply chain. Competition is no longer local, provincial, or even national; it is global. Canadian companies have to compete with other global companies not only for raw materials, labour, knowledge, and other inputs, but also for markets for their products. Most people don't think about how globalization impacts their daily lives, but just take a minute and read the labels on the clothing you are wearing right now. Chances are that most of the items, even if they carry Canadian or U.S. brand names, were manufactured in another part of the world, such as China, India, Thailand, Mexico, Brazil, and dozens of other developing countries.

In Canada, the market has evolved from a system of local and provincial marketplaces, to national markets, to geographically regional markets (e.g., Canada and the United States together), to international markets, and finally to global markets. According to the Government of Canada and the Business Development Bank of Canada, **globalization** refers to the increased flow of goods, services, people, technology, capital, information, and ideas around the world. Its impacts are economic, political, social, cultural, and environmental.[2] Global markets are the result of several fundamental changes, such as reductions or eliminations of trade barriers by country governments, the decreasing concerns of distance and time with regard to moving

globalization
Refers to the increased flow of goods, services, people, technology, capital, information, and ideas around the world; has economic, political, social, cultural, and environmental impacts.

products and ideas across countries, the standardization of laws across borders, and globally integrated production processes.[3] For instance, consider the lululemon pants that you own. It is possible that lululemon athletica buys its raw materials from a supplier in one country and its sewing machines and washers from a supplier in another country, while its workers come from a third country, and its marketers are placed in several countries around the world where its pants are sold (i.e., customers are spread across the globe). Thus, globalization creates great interdependency among firms and divisions of firms spread around the world.

Globalization has not only created economies of scale because of the global scale in which research, production, and marketing are performed, but also made it possible for many market niches that are not profitable at the provincial or national level to become profitable at the global level. For instance, Gennum of Burlington, Ontario, which makes specialized parts for the hearing instrument industry, found that the Canadian market is too small for its products; however, on a global scale, it can profitably serve this market niche. To exploit global market niches, it has design, R&D, and sales offices in Japan, Taiwan, Korea, and the United Kingdom. Indeed, many Canadian companies are part of the global supply chain, supplying inputs and raw materials rather than marketing finished products.

These fundamental changes have paved the way for marketing to flourish in other countries. The elimination of trade barriers and other governmental actions, for instance, allows goods and ideas to move quickly and efficiently around the world, which in turn facilitates the quick delivery of goods to better meet the needs of global consumers. When examining countries as potential markets for global products, companies must realize that these different countries exist at very different stages of globalization. The World Bank ranks countries according to their degrees of globalization on the basis of a composite measure that examines whether the factors necessary to participate in the global marketplace are present. Countries that score

CHAPTER ROADMAP

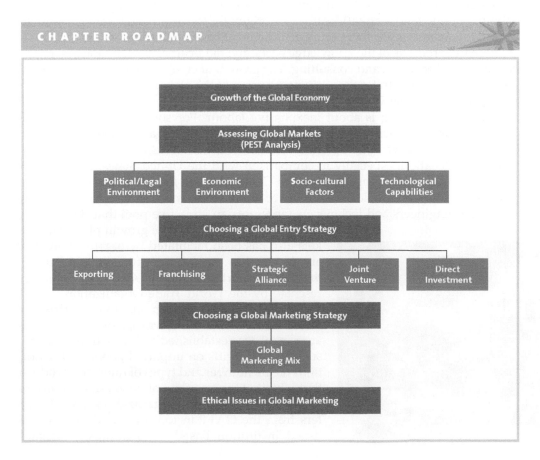

high on the scale represent the best markets for globalized products and services; those lowest on the scale represent the most troublesome markets.

Most Canadians tend to take access to global products and services for granted. When we walk into Starbucks, we expect to find our favourite Jamaican Blue Mountain coffee ground and ready for us. But think about the process through which coffee came from a mountainside in Jamaica to your town. Or, think about how all the products sold at dollar stores such as A Buck or Two, Dollarama, Dollar Giant, and Everything for a Dollar Store (EFADS) can be produced, transported halfway around the world, and sold for a dollar or less. We will be examining these topics in this chapter.

We begin by looking at the growth of the global economy and the forces that led to it. We'll see how firms assess the potential of a given market, make decisions to go global, and choose markets in which to sell globally. Then we explore how to build the marketing mix for global products and consider some of the ethical issues of globalization. The chapter roadmap illustrates the sequence of this chapter content.

LO1

globalization of production (or offshoring) Refers to manufacturers' procurement of goods and services from around the globe to take advantage of national differences in the cost and quality of various factors of production (e.g., labour, energy, land, capital).

General Agreement on Tariffs and Trade (GATT) Agreement established to lower trade barriers, such as high tariffs on imported goods and restrictions on the number and types of imported products that inhibited the free flow of goods across borders.

The World Bank Group provides loans, policy advice, technical assistance, and knowledge sharing services. James Wolfensohn, the former World Bank president, is shown here.

Growth of the Global Economy: Globalization of Marketing and Production

Changes in technology, especially communications technology, have been the driving force for growth in global markets for decades. The telegraph, radio, television, computer, and, now, Internet increasingly connect distant parts of the world. Today, communication is instantaneous. Sounds and images from across the globe are delivered to TV sets, radios, computers, and smartphones in real time, which enables consumers in all parts of the world to observe how others live, work, and play.

The **globalization of production**, also known as **offshoring**, refers to manufacturers' procurement of goods and services from around the globe to take advantage of national differences in the cost and quality of various factors of production (e.g., labour, energy, land, capital).[4] Although originally focused on relocating manufacturing to lower cost producer countries, the practice of offshoring has now grown to include the products of the knowledge economy: medical services, financial services, technological services, and consulting. The growth of cities such as Bangalore, India, for instance, demonstrates the rapid progression of the globalization of production of both products and services.[5]

Not all offshoring is about inexpensive labour. For some companies, such as IBM, offshoring reflects its constant, global hunt for talent, as it makes an effort to reduce costs. Krakow, Poland, which receives heavy investments from IBM, may be a low-cost location, especially in comparison with the United States, but it cannot compare to the cost-savings available in China or India. However, Krakow also has invested heavily in technical education for its students, and the highly trained group of 150 000 engineers and technicians represents an attractive pool that IBM can tap

to support its business.[6] The growth of global markets also has been facilitated by organizations that are designed to oversee their functioning. Perhaps the most important of these organizations is represented by the World Trade Organization (WTO), which replaced **General Agreement on Tariffs and Trade** (**GATT**; www.gatt.org) in 1994. The GATT agreement was established to lower trade barriers, such as high tariffs on imported goods and restrictions on the number and types of imported products that inhibited the free flow of goods across borders.

The **World Trade Organization (WTO)** differs from the GATT in that the WTO is an established institution based in Geneva, Switzerland, instead of simply an agreement. In July 2008, there were 153 members in the WTO that accounted for 97 percent of global trade.[7] Furthermore, the WTO is the only international organization that deals with the global rules of trade among nations. Its main function is to ensure that trade flows as smoothly, predictably, and freely as possible. The WTO also administers trade agreements, acts as a forum for trade negotiations, settles trade disputes, reviews national trade policies, and assists developing countries in their trade policy issues through technical assistance and training. For instance, in 2010, Japan filed a WTO dispute against Canada with regard to Ontario's renewable energy program, which was launched in 2009.[8] The Ontario government created a new incentives program to get renewable energy producers to develop and market innovative clean technologies that would contribute to the elimination of coal-powered generators and the creation of new "clean" jobs. The incentives program for producers of energy from clean, renewable sources, such as the sun and wind, offered guaranteed, above-market prices. Japan complained that the price guarantees offered by the Ontario program are really a subsidy to these businesses, which violates Canada's obligations under international trade law. This dispute could take years to settle by the WTO, especially if Canada challenges it.

The **International Monetary Fund** (**IMF**; www.imf.org) was established as part of the original GATT. The primary purpose of the IMF is to promote international monetary cooperation and facilitate the expansion and growth of international trade. The **World Bank Group** is a development bank that provides loans, policy advice, technical assistance, and knowledge-sharing services to low- and middle-income countries in an attempt to reduce poverty.[9] Along with the IMF, it is dedicated to fighting poverty and improving the living standards of people in the developing world. Thus, the key difference between the IMF and the World Bank is that the IMF focuses primarily on maintaining the international monetary system, whereas the World Bank concentrates on poverty reduction through low-interest loans and other programs. For instance, the World Bank is the largest external funding source of education and HIV/AIDS programs.

Both these organizations affect the practice of global marketing in different ways; but, together, they enable marketers to participate in the global marketplace by making it easier to buy and sell, by financing deserving firms, by opening markets to trade, and by raising the global standard of living, which allows more people to buy goods and services. The financing assistance provided by both the World Bank and the IMF make it possible for firms in the developed world to market their products to developing countries.

However, a diverse group of nongovernmental organizations, religious groups, and advocates for workers and the poor have condemned these organizations. The primary criticism of the World Bank is that it is merely a puppet of Western industrialized nations that use World Bank loans to assist their globalization efforts. Others argue that the World Bank loans too much money to developing countries, which makes it almost impossible for these often debt-ridden nations to repay their loans.[10]

Globalization obviously has its critics, and those critics very well may have a point. But globalization also has been progressing at a steady and increasing pace. With that development in mind, let's look at how firms determine in which countries to expand their operations.

Assessing Global Markets

Because different countries, at their various stages of globalization, offer marketers a variety of opportunities, firms must assess the viability of a variety of international markets. This assessment is done through an environmental analysis similar to what is described in Chapter 3. As illustrated in Exhibit 16.1, four sets of factors are often used to assess a country's market: **political/legal, economic, socio-cultural,** and **technology and infrastructure** factors. The acronym *PEST* is used as shorthand to refer to these

World Trade Organization (WTO)
Replaced the GATT in 1994; differs from the GATT in that the WTO is an established institution based in Geneva, Switzerland, instead of simply an agreement; represents the only international organization that deals with the global rules of trade among nations.

International Monetary Fund (IMF)
Established as part of the original *General Agreement on Tariffs and Trade (GATT)*; primary purpose is to promote international monetary cooperation and facilitate the expansion and growth of international trade.

World Bank Group
A development bank that provides loans, policy advice, technical assistance, and knowledge-sharing services to low- and middle-income countries in an attempt to reduce poverty.

LO2

| EXHIBIT 16.1 | Components of a Country Market Assessment |

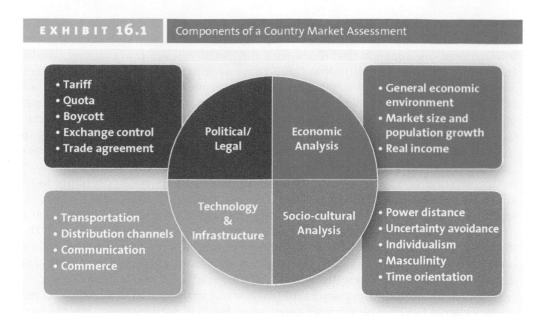

Political/Legal
- Tariff
- Quota
- Boycott
- Exchange control
- Trade agreement

Economic Analysis
- General economic environment
- Market size and population growth
- Real income

Technology & Infrastructure
- Transportation
- Distribution channels
- Communication
- Commerce

Socio-cultural Analysis
- Power distance
- Uncertainty avoidance
- Individualism
- Masculinity
- Time orientation

---

trade sanctions
Penalties or restrictions imposed by one country over another country for importing and exporting of goods, services, and investments.

factors. Analysis of these four factors offers marketers a more complete picture of a country's potential as a market for products and services. Although we describe each factor separately, it is important to note that marketers consider them together in order to obtain a complete picture of a country's marketing potential. In fact, marketers often have to make trade-offs between these factors when entering or doing business in a foreign market. For instance, Canadian oil and mining companies may enter markets where the economic opportunity is great but the political risks are higher.

Analyzing the Political and Legal Environment

Governmental actions, as well as the actions of nongovernmental political groups, can significantly influence firms' ability to sell goods and services, because they often result in laws or other regulations that either promote the growth of the global market or close off the country and inhibit growth. Policies aimed at restricting trade and global marketing are called protectionist policies, and those that encourage global trade and marketing are referred to as trade liberalization policies. In this section, we discuss various forms of protectionist and liberalization policies. These issues include trade sanctions such as tariffs, quotas, boycotts, exchange controls, and trade agreements (see Exhibit 16.2).

| EXHIBIT 16.2 | Government Actions |

Government Actions
- Tariff
- Quota
- Boycott
- Exchange Control
- Trade Agreement
- Trade Sanctions

Trade Sanctions **Trade sanctions** are penalties or restrictions imposed by one country over another country for importing and exporting of goods, services, and investments. In February 2011, Canada imposed sweeping trade sanctions on Libya because of escalating human rights abuses by the Libyan government on its citizens. Some of the measures announced include a ban on all goods exported from Canada to Libya and a ban on all goods imported from Libya into Canada.[11] An embargo is a form of trade sanction that prohibits trading with a certain country or trading in specific goods (e.g., oil embargo) by other signatory countries.

Tariffs   A **tariff** (also called a **duty**) is a tax levied on a good imported into a country. In most cases, tariffs are intended to make imported goods more expensive and thus less competitive with domestic products,[12] which in turn protects domestic industries from foreign competition. In other cases, tariffs might be imposed to penalize another country for trade practices that the home country views as unfair. One of the best known cases in Canada occurred in 2002, when the United States imposed a whopping 19.31-percent duty on Canadian softwood lumber exported to the United States because the U.S. softwood industry claimed that Canada was subsidizing Canadian softwood lumber and Canadian lumber producers were **dumping**—the practice of selling a good in a foreign market at a price that is lower than its domestic price or below its cost—low-cost softwood lumber on the U.S. market. The duty increased the prices of Canadian lumber sold in the United States by 27 percent, making it difficult for Canadian companies to compete with U.S. lumber producers.[13] In 2010, the Government of Canada basically made Canada a tariff-free zone for industrial manufacturers by eliminating all tariffs on machinery, equipment, and goods imported into Canada for further manufacturing. When fully implemented, this change will provide $300 million in annual duty savings for Canadian business to support investment and growth and create jobs.[14]

tariff (or duty)
A tax levied on a good imported into a country.

dumping
The practice of selling a good in a foreign market at a price that is lower than its domestic price or below its cost.

Quotas   A **quota** designates the maximum quantity of a product that may be brought into a country during a specified time period. Many Canadian quotas on foreign-made textiles were eliminated in 2005, which reduced the cost of imported apparel products sold in Canada. Some firms have chosen to redistribute the bulk of these savings to consumers—in Walmart's case, 75 percent of them—whereas others, such as bebe, are planning to distribute only 25 percent and keep the rest as profit.[15]

quota
Designates the maximum quantity of a product that may be brought into a country during a specified time period.

Tariffs and quotas can impose a potentially devastating blow on a firm's ability to sell products in another country. Tariffs artificially raise prices and therefore lower demand, and quotas reduce the availability of imported merchandise. Conversely, tariffs and quotas benefit domestically made products because they reduce foreign competition. In the case of softwood lumber, tariffs and quotas benefit U.S. lumber producers and reduce competition from Canadian lumber producers. Unfortunately, U.S. consumers end up paying higher prices for U.S. softwood lumber rather than benefiting from cheaper Canadian lumber and Canadian lumber producers lost huge market share.

Boycott   A **boycott** pertains to a group's refusal to deal commercially with some organization to protest against its policies. Boycotts might be called by governments or nongovernmental organizations, such as trade unions, human rights, or environmental groups. For example, the United States continues to impose economic sanctions against Cuba and Iran, and in 2010 Canada imposed its own sanctions on Iran.

boycott
A group's refusal to deal commercially with some organization to protest against its policies.

Many quotas on foreign-made textiles have been eliminated. Some firms have chosen to redistribute the bulk of these savings to consumers—in Walmart's case (left), 75 percent of the savings; whereas other firms, such as bebe (right), are planning to redistribute only 25 percent of the savings and keep the rest as profit.

exchange control
Refers to the regulation of a country's currency *exchange rate*.

exchange rate
The measure of how much one currency is worth in relation to another.

countertrade
Trade between two countries where goods are traded for other goods and not for hard currency.

trade agreement
Intergovernmental agreement designed to manage and promote trade activities for specific regions.

trading bloc
Consists of those countries that have signed a particular trade agreement.

The increase in value of the Canadian dollar against the U.S. dollar has made Canadian exports to the United States more expensive, and imports from the United States less expensive.

Exchange Control   **Exchange control** refers to the regulation of a country's currency **exchange rate**, the measure of how much one currency is worth in relation to another.[16] A designated agency in each country, often the central bank, sets the rules for currency exchange. In Canada, the Bank of Canada sets the rules for the currency exchange rates. In recent years, the value of the Canadian dollar against the U.S. dollar has increased significantly, from around CAD$0.60 for US$1.00 in 2001, to CAD$1.10 in November 2007. Since then, the exchange rate has fluctuated between CAD$0.76 and CAD$1.10. The rise of the Canadian dollar has had a twofold effect on the ability of Canadian firms to conduct global business. For Canadian firms that depend on U.S. imports of finished products, raw materials, or services, the cost of doing business has gone down dramatically. However, U.S. buyers find the costs of Canadian goods and services much more expensive than they were before. This tends to have a negative impact on Canadian manufacturing exports to the United States, as Americans will find that their dollar can buy them far less in Canada while Canadians will find that they can buy more in the United States with their Canadian dollars.

A method of avoiding an unfavourable exchange rate is to engage in counter-trade. **Countertrade** is trade between two countries where goods are traded for other goods and not for hard currency. For instance, the Philippine government has entered into a countertrade agreement with Vietnam. The Philippine International Trading Corp. is importing rice and paying for half of it with fertilizer, coconuts, and coconut by-products.[17] A study of Canadian executives' attitudes to countertrade found that although the majority sees the benefit of countertrade, they are lukewarm to being involved in the practice.[18]

All the restrictions on trade and global marketing discussed so far are deemed protectionist since they, in one way or another, protect a country's domestic industry from foreign competition. A country may also implement protectionist policies for social, economic, or political reasons. The Canadian government, for example, provides subsidies to farmers and technology companies in order for these industries or specific firms to grow and compete globally. Bombardier, a Canadian global firm, benefits substantially from government subsidies.

Not all government policies are protectionist. Often, governments will implement policies and agreements to foster global trade and marketing. We now turn our attention to these agreements.

Trade Agreements   Marketers must consider the trade agreements to which a particular country is a signatory or the trading bloc to which it belongs. A **trade agreement** is an intergovernmental agreement designed to manage and promote trade activities for a specific region, and a **trading bloc** consists of those countries that have signed the particular trade agreement.[19]

Some major trade agreements cover two-thirds of the world's international trade: the European Union (EU), the North American Free Trade Agreement (NAFTA), the Central America Free Trade Agreement (CAFTA), Mercosur, and the Association of Southeast Asian Nations (ASEAN).[20] These trade agreements are summarized in Exhibit 16.3. The European Union represents the highest level of integration across individual nations, whereas the other agreements vary in their integration levels.

European Union. The European Union is an economic and monetary union that currently contains 27 countries, as illustrated in Exhibit 16.4. Croatia, Iceland, Macedonia, and Turkey head a list of official candidate countries, but they have not yet been granted full

EXHIBIT 16.3	Trade Agreements
Name	**Countries**
European Union	Austria, Belgium, Bulgaria, Cyprus, Czech Republic, Denmark, Estonia, Finland, France, Germany, Greece, Hungary, Ireland, Italy, Latvia, Lithuania, Luxembourg, Malta, the Netherlands, Poland, Portugal, Romania, Slovakia, Slovenia, Spain, Sweden, United Kingdom of Great Britain
NAFTA	Canada, Mexico, the United States
CAFTA	Costa Rica, the Dominican Republic, El Salvador, Guatemala, Honduras, Nicaragua, the United States
Mercosur	Full members: Argentina, Brazil, Paraguay, Uruguay, Venezuela
ASEAN	Brunei Darussalam, Cambodia, Indonesia, Laos, Malaysia, Myanmar, Philippines, Singapore, Thailand, Vietnam

membership. More countries are officially recognized as potential candidates.[21] The European Union represents a significant restructuring of the global marketplace. By dramatically lowering trade barriers between member nations within the union, the complexion of the global marketplace has changed.

Having one currency, the euro, across Europe has simplified the way many multinational firms market their products. For instance, prior to the conversion to the euro on January 1, 1999, firms were unable to predict exchange rates and this made

EXHIBIT 16.4	Map of the European Union[22]

The European Union has resulted in lowering trade barriers and strengthening global relationships among member nations.

it difficult to set consistent prices across countries in Europe. The introduction of the euro has eliminated price fluctuations because of currency exchange rates. Now products can be preticketed for distribution across Europe. Patent requirements were also simplified since one patent application could cover multiple countries. Similarly the rules governing such things as data privacy and transmission, advertising, and direct selling have been streamlined and simplified, allowing seamless trade.

North American Free Trade Agreement (NAFTA). NAFTA is limited to trade-related issues, such as tariffs and quotas, among Canada, Mexico, and the United States. For example, the softwood lumber and the split-run magazine disputes between Canada and the United States, two NAFTA partners, were resolved through the WTO.

Central American Free Trade Agreement (CAFTA). CAFTA is a trade agreement between Costa Rica, the Dominican Republic, El Salvador, Guatemala, Honduras, Nicaragua, and the United States.[23]

Mercosur. Translated from Spanish, *Mercosur* means the Southern Common Market. This group covers most of South America. In 1995, Mercosur member nations created the Free Trade Area of the Americas (FTAA), primarily in response to NAFTA.

Association of Southeast Asian Nations (ASEAN). Originally formed to promote security in Southeast Asia during the Vietnam War, ASEAN changed its mission to building economic stability and lowering trade restrictions among the six member nations in the 1980s.

These trading blocs affect how Canadian firms can conduct business in the member countries. Some critics contend that such blocs confer an unfair advantage on their member nations because they offer favourable terms for trade, whereas others believe they stimulate economies by lowering trade barriers and allowing higher levels of foreign investment.

Political Risk Analysis Before a company decides to engage in global marketing, it must conduct a political risk analysis—assessing the level of political, socio-economic, and security risks of doing business with a country. Such analysis usually involves weighing the likelihood of certain events, such as change in government, violence, and the imposition of restrictive trade policies, taking place over a specific period of time. This type of analysis requires sophisticated expertise, which most companies do not possess. Thus, they rely on government agencies (e.g., Export Development Canada, Foreign Affairs and International Trade Canada) and private companies that specialize in political risk analysis to provide information and guidance. Political risk analysis helps to reduce the risk of a company losing its investment or goods and the possibility of harm to its employees.

Analyzing the Economic Environment

The greater the wealth of people in a country, generally, the better the opportunity a firm will have in that particular country. A firm conducting an economic analysis of a country's market must look at three major economic factors: general economic environment, market size and population growth, and real income (see Exhibit 16.5).

Evaluating the General Economic Environment Generally, healthy economies provide better opportunities for global marketing expansions. A firm can measure the relative health of a particular country's economy in several ways. Each way offers a slightly different view, and some may be more useful for some products and services than for others.

To determine the market potential for its particular product or service, a firm should use as many measures as it can obtain. One measure is the relative level of imports and exports. Canada, for example, enjoys a trade surplus, while the United States suffers a trade deficit. A **trade deficit** means that the country imports more goods than it exports. Firms would prefer to manufacture in a country, such as Canada, that has a **trade surplus**, or a higher level of exports than imports, because it signals a greater opportunity to export products to more markets.

trade deficit
Results when a country imports more goods than it exports.

trade surplus
Results when a country exports more goods than it imports.

EXHIBIT 16.5 | Economic Analysis

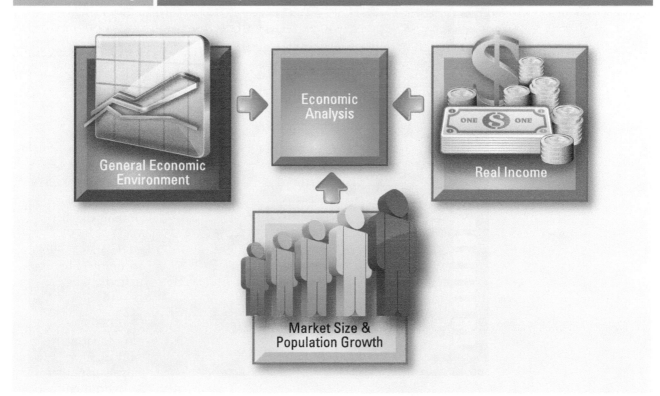

gross domestic product (GDP)
The market value of the goods and services produced by a country in a year; the most widely used standardized measure of output.

purchasing power parity (PPP)
A theory that states that if the exchange rates of two countries are in equilibrium, a product purchased in one will cost the same in the other, expressed in the same currency.

The most common way to gauge the size and market potential of an economy, and therefore the potential the country has for global marketing, is to use standardized measures of output. One of the most widely used measures is **gross domestic product (GDP)**, which is defined as the market value of the goods and services produced by a country in a year. So what does the size of a country's GDP have to do with global marketing? GDP growth means that production and consumption in the country is expanding, therefore, there are greater marketing opportunities for most goods and services. When GDP growth is slowing, it means that the economy is contracting, or that production and consumption are falling, and marketing opportunities for certain goods and services will decline.

Another frequently used measure of an overall economy is the **purchasing power parity (PPP)**, a theory that states that if the exchange rates of two countries are in equilibrium, a product purchased in one will cost the same in the other, expressed in the same currency.[24] A novel measure that employs PPP to assess the relative economic buying power among nations is *The Economist's* Big Mac Index, which suggests that exchange rates should adjust to equalize the cost of a basket of goods and services, wherever it is bought around the world. Using McDonald's Big Mac as the market basket, Exhibit 16.6 shows that the cheapest burger is in China, where it costs $1.45, compared with an average Canadian price of $3.68. This difference implies that the

EXHIBIT 16.6	Big Mac Index: Local Currency Under (−)/Over (+) Valuation Against the Dollar

Chinese yuan is undervalued by 61 percent: that is, the Chinese yuan is priced too low relative to the Canadian dollar. In this case, the undervalued yuan makes China's exports to Canada cheaper than they would otherwise be, thereby providing an unfair trade advantage to China. It also makes Canadian exports to China more expensive.

These various measures help marketers understand the relative wealth of a particular country; however, as scholars have argued, they may not give a full picture of the economic health of a country because they are based solely on material output.[25] As a corollary measure to those described previously, the United Nations has developed the **human development index (HDI)**, a composite measure of three indicators of the quality of life in different countries: life expectancy at birth, educational attainment, and whether the average incomes, according to PPP estimates, are sufficient to meet the basic needs of life in that country. For marketers, these measures determine the lifestyle elements that ultimately drive consumption (recall that Chapter 5 discussed the influence of consumer lifestyle on consumption). The HDI is scaled from 0 to 1: those countries that score lower than 0.5 are classified as nations with low human development, those that score 0.5 to 0.8 have medium development, and those that score above 0.8 are classified as having high human development. Exhibit 16.7 shows a map of the world with the various HDI scores. Higher HDI means greater consumption levels, especially of discretionary goods and services.

These macroeconomic measures provide a snapshot of a particular country at any one point in time. Because they are standardized measures, it is possible to compare countries across time and to identify those that are experiencing economic growth and increased globalization.

Although an understanding of the macroeconomic environment is crucial for managers facing a market entry decision, of equal importance is the understanding of economic measures of individual income and household size.

Evaluating Market Size and Population Growth Rate Global population has been growing dramatically since the turn of the twentieth century (see Exhibit 16.8). It is estimated that by 2011, the world population will reach 7 billion people. From a marketing perspective, however, growth has not been equally dispersed. Less-developed nations, by and large, are experiencing rapid population growth, while many developed countries are experiencing either zero or negative natural population growth. Population growth in many developed countries, such as Canada, is attributed to high levels of immigration. The countries with the highest purchasing power today may become less attractive in the future for many products and services because of stagnated growth.

human development index (HDI)
A composite measure of three indicators of the quality of life in different countries: life expectancy at birth, educational attainment, and whether the average incomes are sufficient to meet the basic needs of life in that country.

EXHIBIT 16.7 Global Human Development Index Scores

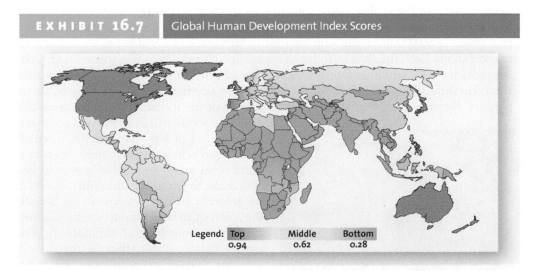

Legend: Top 0.94   Middle 0.62   Bottom 0.28

Source: www.nationmaster.com/red/graph/eco_hum_dev_ind-economy-human-development-index&int=1&b_map=1#.

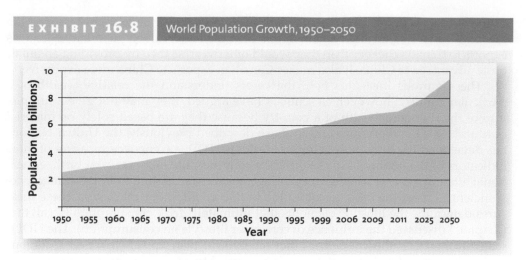

| EXHIBIT 16.8 | World Population Growth, 1950–2050 |

Source: www.prb.org/Content/NavigationMenu/PRB/Educators/Human_Population/Population_Growth/Population_Growth.htm.

Another aspect related to population and growth pertains to the distribution of the population within a particular region; namely, is the population located primarily in rural or urban areas? This distinction determines where and how products and services can be delivered. Long supply chains, in which goods pass through many hands, are necessary to reach rural populations and therefore add costs to products. India's 1.1 billion people live overwhelmingly in rural areas, though the population is moving toward urban areas to meet the demands of the growing industrial and service centres located in major cities such as Bangalore and New Delhi. This population shift, perhaps not surprisingly, is accompanied by rapid growth in the middle class.[26] Another major trend in India involves the age of the population; more than half of India's citizens are younger than 25 years.[27] In Canada, in contrast, the median age is 39.7 years.[28]

Evaluating Real Income   Real income—income adjusted for inflation—affects consumers' buying power, and thus will influence the marketing mixes companies develop for their overseas markets. For instance, two-thirds of the Chinese population earn less than $25 per month, so when P&G wanted to sell its Head & Shoulders shampoo in China, it had to modify both the package and price to make it affordable to Chinese consumers. P&G had to forgo its usual bottle and package Head & Shoulders in single-use packets, which made the shampoo affordable and practical for the Chinese market.[29] Coke and Pepsi also made adjustments to their products and prices to be able to compete in India. For example, in the town of Jagadri in Northwest India, which is composed of 60 000 residents who are mostly farmers, Coke and Pepsi are battling for market share. Each firm has introduced repackaged products to win this market. Coke is producing a 200-millilitre bottle that sells for 12 cents at small shops, bus stops, and roadside stands in order to offer a more affordable alternative to Pepsi. Why battle for Jagadri? Because each firm knows that 70 percent of the Indian population, some 700 million people, still lives in rural areas and has incomes of less than $42 per month.[30] If they can win in Jagadri, they can win in other rural areas, and the only way to win is to make the product affordable. Power of the Internet 16.1 shows how Pepsi is using the Internet to reach out to young Chinese consumers. Speaking of affordability, who would believe that Africa is the fastest-growing market for cellphones, given the negative stereotypes of poverty in Africa?

Coke and Pepsi are battling for market share in India.

Power of the Internet 16.1

PepsiCo Engages the Chinese over the Web

Pepsi has red aspirations: it wants to be China's cola of choice, but it currently has achieved only a 30-percent market share and continues to trail the most popular "red" cola, Coke, which enjoys 50 percent of the market. But things, as they often do, are changing. Pepsi has begun using the Internet to engage Chinese consumers and, in doing so, has earned a great response.

In the past few years, use of the Internet among Chinese consumers has increased dramatically. Although there are only 384 million Chinese consumers online, which places the Internet penetration rate at approximately 28 percent of the country, these users tend to be affluent urban consumers—exactly those consumers that most foreign brands want to target.[31]

"Pepsi is always looking to raise the bar in terms of consumer engagement," says Chris Tung, vice-president of Pepsi brand marketing in the Greater China Region.[32] To this end, Pepsi is using various approaches to reach Chinese consumers over the Internet. First, it posts online videos in an attempt to find popular and inexpensive brand promoters within the Chinese market. The Back Dorm Boys gained international online prominence with their lip-synched YouTube videos and appealed to a particularly enormous following in China.

Pepsi teamed up with this comic group to create additional videos for its Chinese website (www.pepsi.cn) and then featured their talents on a Pepsi Max TV spot. By using the Internet to find spokespeople, Pepsi not only saved itself money, but also extended its appeal to a young, cola-drinking audience.[33]

Second, Pepsi offers online competitions to Chinese consumers. In one of its most successful competitions, Pepsi solicited photos that people had taken of themselves rooting for Team China during the Olympics. The competition, by far the largest online event that Pepsi has ever created, prompted 2.46 million photo submissions and tallied more than 140 million votes. The prize? To have one's photo placed on Pepsi cans all over China.[34]

Third, for its fourth annual Creative Challenge in China, Pepsi partnered with Tencent, China's Internet giant, to offer Chinese web users the ability to tweet, blog, and IM their birthday wishes to China. The campaign received nearly 34 million entries, more than 17 million of which resulted from Pepsi's use of Taotao.com, the Twitter-like site, for submissions. This number was an increase of nearly 6 million entries from the previous year.[35]

To combat Coke's dominant market share in China, Pepsi uses the Internet to promote its products with celebrities such as soccer star David Beckham.

Today, one in 10 Africans is a cellphone user. The main reason for this explosive growth is a combination of government policy—many African governments privatized their telephone monopolies—and fierce competition among cellphone operators, which led to dramatic price decreases for airtime and a handset.[36]

Analyzing Socio-cultural Factors

While companies wishing to enter global markets can buy commercially available reports about the political, economic, and technological situation in a country fairly easily, they find it more difficult to acquire cultural information. Understanding another country's culture is crucial to the success of any global marketing initiative. Culture, or the set of values, guiding beliefs, understandings, and ways of doing things shared by members of a society, exists on two levels: visible artifacts (e.g., behaviour, dress, symbols, physical settings, ceremonies) and underlying values (thought processes, beliefs, and assumptions). Visible artifacts are easy to recognize, but businesses often find it more difficult to understand the underlying values of a culture and appropriately adapt their marketing strategies to them.[37] Even global companies with many years of experience operating in a country occasionally end up offending their customers, which causes the companies huge embarrassment, lost sales, and financial losses. Several examples of these cultural gaffes are presented in this section for illustrative purposes.

One important cultural classification scheme that firms can use is Geert Hofstede's cultural dimensions concept, which sheds more light on these underlying values. Hofstede believes cultures differ on five dimensions:[38]

1. **Power distance**: Willingness to accept social inequality as natural.
2. **Uncertainty avoidance**: The extent to which the society relies on orderliness, consistency, structure, and formalized procedures to address situations that arise in daily life.
3. **Individualism**: Perceived obligation to and dependence on groups.
4. **Masculinity**: The extent to which dominant values are male-oriented. A lower masculinity ranking indicates that men and women are treated equally in all aspects of society; a higher masculinity ranking suggests that men dominate in positions of power.[39]
5. **Time orientation**: Short- versus long-term orientation. A country that tends to have a long-term orientation values long-term commitments and is willing to accept a longer time horizon for, say, the success of a new product introduction.

Business relationships in China often are formalized by just a handshake, and trust and honour are often more important than legal arrangements.

To illustrate two of the five dimensions, consider the data and graph in Exhibit 16.9. Power distance is on the vertical axis and individualism is on the horizontal axis. Several Latin American countries cluster high on power distance but low on individualism; Canada, the United States, Australia, and the United Kingdom, in contrast, cluster high on individualism but low on power distance. Using this information, firms should expect that if they design a marketing campaign that stresses equality and individualism, it will be well accepted in the English-speaking countries, all other factors being equal. The same campaign, however, might not be as well received in Latin American countries.

Another means of classifying cultures distinguishes them according to the importance of verbal communication.[40] In Canada, the United States, and most European countries, business relationships are governed by what is said and written down, often through formal contracts. In countries such as China and South Korea, however, most relationships rely on nonverbal cues, so that the situation or context means much more than mere words. For instance, business relationships in China often are formalized by just a handshake, and trust and honour are often more important than legal arrangements.

EXHIBIT 16.9 | Country Clusters

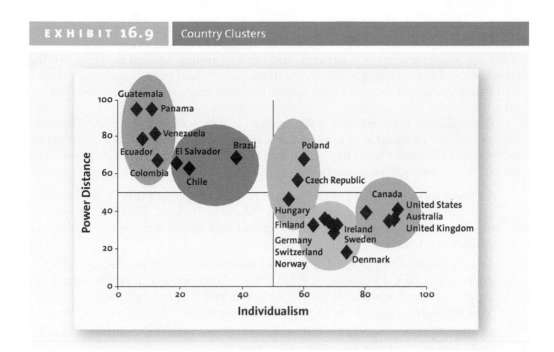

Source: Based on data available at www.geert-hofstede.com. Data from: Geert Hofstede, *Culture's Consequences*, 2nd edition (Thousand Oaks: Sage, 2001). Copyright © Geert Hofstede, reproduced with permission.

Overall, culture affects every aspect of consumer behaviour: why people buy, who is in charge of buying decisions, and how, when, and where people shop. Essentially, understanding consumer behaviour is about understanding consumers' culture, particularly in global marketing. For example, in India, McDonald's sells it Maharajah Mac made from lamb instead of beef because the cow is sacred in Hindu culture. In Israel, McDonald's Kosher restaurants use the blue and white colours of Israel's flag instead of the yellow and red of its Golden Arches.[41] Similarly, Coca-Cola developed a new drink, Vitango, to be sold in Africa, and P&G developed its Nutristar for Venezuelan consumers.[42] Both companies claim that

In Israel, McDonald's Kosher restaurants use the blue and white colours of Israel's flag.

their soft drinks have special health benefits for their customers in these markets. In North America, people often use their BlackBerrys almost everywhere—in subways, lobbies, restaurants, ballparks, and hockey arenas, as well as while driving. However, in Japan, typing away on the BlackBerry when in company—say during a sit-down dinner or a child's little league baseball game—could be viewed as bad manners.[43]

The challenge for marketers is that culture is very subtle, and a failure to recognize the subtleties could lead to very embarrassing and costly mistakes. The following examples illustrate what happens when marketers have a poor understanding of the culture of their global markets.[44]

- A Canadian importer of Turkish shirts destined for Quebec used a dictionary to help him translate into French the label "Made in Turkey." His final translation was "Fabrique en Dinde." True, *dinde* means turkey, but it refers to the bird not the country, which in French is *Turquie.*

- An Otis Engineering Corp. display at a Moscow exhibition produced as many snickers among the Russians as it did praise. Company executives were not happy to learn that a translator had rendered in Russian a sign identifying "completion equipment" as "equipment for orgasms."

- Japan's Olfa Corp. sold knives in the United States with the warning "Caution: Blade extremely sharp. Keep out of children."

- In one country, the popular Frank Perdue Co. slogan, "It takes a tough man to make a tender chicken," read in the local language something akin to "It takes a sexually excited man to make a chicken affectionate."

- One company in Taiwan, trying to sell diet food to expatriates living there, urged consumers to buy its product to add "roughage" to their systems. The instructions claimed that a person should consume enough roughage until "your tool floats." Someone dropped the *s* from *stool.*

- A Hong Kong dentist once advertised, "Teeth extracted by the latest Methodists."

- A hotel in notoriously polluted Mexico City proclaimed, "The manager has personally passed all the water served here."

- General Motors's promotion in Belgium for its car that had a "body by Fisher" turned out to be, in the Flemish translation, "corpse by Fisher."

- Colgate introduced a toothpaste in France called Cue, which was the name of a local porn magazine.

- Since McDonald's operates more than 28 000 restaurants in over 25 countries, you would expect the company to be aware of the cultures of its various markets, right? It didn't seem so in India. McDonald's knew that the cow is a sacred religious symbol in India but used beef flavouring for its fries. When consumers learned about this, there were huge protests and a major lawsuit. McDonald's apologized, changed its practices, and made a large charitable donation to appease Indian consumers.

Analyzing Technology and Infrastructure Capabilities

infrastructure
The basic facilities, services, and installations needed for a community or society to function, such as transportation and communications systems, water and power lines, and public institutions such as schools, post offices, and prisons.

The next component of any market assessment is a technology and infrastructure analysis. **Infrastructure** is defined as the basic facilities, services, and installations needed for a community or society to function, such as transportation and communications systems, water and power lines, and public institutions such as schools, post offices, and prisons. Marketers are especially concerned with four key elements of a country's infrastructure: transportation, distribution channels, communications, and commerce.

These four components are essential to the development of an efficient marketing system. First, there must be a system to transport goods throughout the various markets

Sustainable Marketing 16.1 — Bombardier: Moving Forward Responsibly[45]

Canada's Bombardier is a global transportation company that operates in more than 60 countries on five continents. It is a world-leading manufacturer of innovative transportation solutions, from commercial aircraft and business jets to rail transportation equipment, systems, and services. Its revenues for the fiscal year 2010 were US$19.4 billion. Bombardier's 62 900 employees around the globe do everything from R&D to the design, manufacture, sales, and support stages for a broad range of world-class products in aerospace and rail transportation. Some high-profile projects include a fully automated people mover in the Beijing airport and high altitude railcars for a railway to Lhasa, Tibet.

Bombardier has made sustainability an integral part of its global business strategy, implementing a wide range of initiatives across the entire global organization. According to Pierre Beaudoin, president and CEO of Bombardier, "Our ongoing investments attest to our belief that excellence in corporate social responsibility makes business sense in all economic cycles. That is why we made corporate social responsibility a key element of our new business strategy." The company also actively promotes the UN Global Compact's principles of social responsibility and has embedded these principles in its Code of Ethics and Business Conduct. To demonstrate its commitment and to measure and communicate its progress, Bombardier has undertaken to produce an annual report card,

Moving Forward Responsibly, detailing its many initiatives and accomplishments.

On the product innovation side, for example, Bombardier has developed the all-new *CSeries* commercial aircraft. When the *CSeries* takes flight in 2013, it will burn up to 20 percent less fuel and generate up to 20 percent less carbon dioxide emissions than other aircraft in its class. Similarly, the *ZEFIRO* portfolio features the world's most economical and eco-friendly high-speed trains. It includes *ECO4* technologies, which can yield overall energy savings of up to 50 percent.

Between 2004 and 2009, Bombardier successfully achieved its goal of reducing its water consumption by 35 percent, energy consumption by 17 percent, and greenhouse gas emissions by 10 percent. The progress made by Bombardier in the area of sustainability has earned it a spot on two prestigious Dow Jones Sustainability Indexes and, for the second time, on the Carbon Disclosure Project (CDP), the world standard for carbon disclosure methodology and process. The CDP named Bombardier one of the 10 Canadian Climate Disclosure Leaders.

In keeping with its theme of Moving Forward Responsibly, Bombardier has indentified four areas in which it will make additional investments over the next few years: community investment, stakeholder engagement, employee volunteering, and corporate social responsibility reporting and communication.

---

and to consumers in geographically disperse marketplaces. Second, distribution channels must exist to deliver products in a timely manner and at a reasonable cost. Third, the communications system must be sufficiently developed to allow consumers access to information about the products and services available in the marketplace. Fourth, the commercial infrastructure consists of the legal, banking, and regulatory systems that allow markets to function. Marketers, especially those that are interested in offshoring research, production, and marketing will be particularly interested in the technical sophistication of the workforce of the country. Generally, a more sophisticated work force means that a higher proportion of product design, development, and marketing activities can be decentralized to the foreign country.

For a country to be a viable option for a new market entry, firms must assess its transportation, distribution channels, communications, and commerce.

Sustainable Marketing 16.1 highlights how Canada's Bombardier, a world leader in the transportation industry, is implementing sustainable business practices across its global operations with great success.

After marketing managers have completed the four parts of the market assessment, they are better able to make informed decisions about whether a particular country possesses the necessary characteristics to be considered a potential market for the firm's products and services. In the next section, we detail the market entry decision process, beginning with a discussion of the various ways firms might enter a new global market.

L03 Choosing a Global Entry Strategy

When a firm has concluded its assessment analysis of the most viable markets for its products and services, it must then conduct an internal assessment of its capabilities. As we discussed in Chapter 2, this analysis includes an assessment of the firm's access to capital, the current markets it serves, its manufacturing capacity, its proprietary assets, and the commitment of its management to the proposed strategy. These factors ultimately contribute to the success or failure of a market expansion strategy, whether at home or in a foreign market. After these internal market assessments, it is time for the firm to choose its entry strategy.

A firm can choose from many approaches when it decides to enter a new market. These approaches vary according to the level of risk the firm is willing to take. Many firms actually follow a progression in which they begin with less risky strategies to enter their first foreign markets and move to increasingly risky strategies as they gain confidence in their abilities, as illustrated in Exhibit 16.10. Generally, profit potential increases with higher levels of risks. We examine these different approaches that marketers take when entering global markets, beginning with the least risky.

Exporting

exporting
Producing goods in one country and selling them in another.

Exporting means producing goods in one country (exporting country) and selling them in another (host country). This entry strategy requires the least financial risk but also allows for only a limited return to the exporting firm. Global expansion often begins when a firm receives an order for its product or service from another country, in which case it faces little risk because it can demand payment before it ships the merchandise. By the same token, it is difficult to achieve economies of scale when everything has to be shipped internationally. The Italian bicycle component manufacturer Campagnolo sells relatively small but expensive bicycle parts all over the world. Because its transportation costs are relatively small compared with the cost of the parts, the best way for it to service any market is to export from Italy. Exporting generally provides less employment for citizens of the host country than either joint venture or direct investment.

Exporting may take two forms: indirect or direct. Indirect exporting occurs when the exporting firm sells its goods in the host country through an intermediary; for

EXHIBIT 16.10 | Entry Strategies

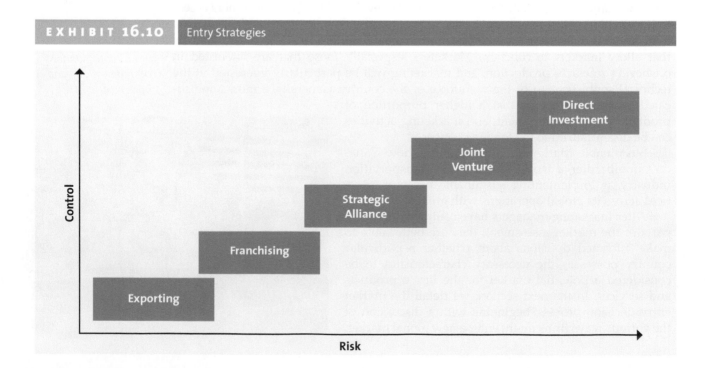

example, RIM sells its BlackBerry in Japan through NTT DOCOMO, Japan's largest cellphone operator.[46] This approach carries the least risk and probably returns the least profit for the exporting company. This approach is likely to be used when the company has limited contacts in the foreign country but wants to market to that country. Direct exporting is when the exporting company sells its products in the host country directly without the intermediaries. This approach carries more risk and offers greater returns to the exporting firm than indirect exporting. For example, Christie Digital, a firm based in Kitchener, Ontario, is a manufacturer of a variety of display technologies and solutions for cinema, large audience environments, control rooms, business presentations, training facilities, 3-D and virtual reality, simulation, education, media, and government. Christie has installed more than 75 000 projection solutions in the United States, the United Kingdom, Japan, China, and many other countries around the world.[47] Similarly, Cognos, an Ottawa-based company of business intelligence tools and applications, sells its solutions to businesses around the world by using its own sales force.

In Canada, the latest data currently available show that there were 45 260 exporters in 2007. However, the top five Canadian exporters account for 25 percent of Canada's export and the top 50 Canadian exporters account for 50 percent of Canada's exports. The remaining 45 210 exporters are responsible for the remaining 50 percent. Almost three-quarters (72.6 percent) of Canadian exporters had exports of less than $1 million. More than two-thirds (67.3 percent) of Canada's exports come from two sectors: manufacturing and wholesale trade.[48] Exhibit 16.11 lists some of Canada's largest global corporations. Examples of the importance of global trade to these companies' success and growth can be observed from their dependence on foreign revenues and profitability. For instance, in 2010, RIM derived more than 90 percent of its revenues from outside of Canada; for Magna International, this number was 33 percent; for Bank of Nova Scotia, 35 percent; for Bombardier, 39 percent; and for Potash Corporation of Saskatchewan, 17 percent.[49]

Franchising

Franchising is a contractual agreement between a firm, the franchisor, and another firm or individual, the franchisee. A franchising contract allows the franchisee to operate a business—a retail product or service firm or a B2B provider—using a name and format developed and supported by the franchisor. Many of the best-known retailers in Canada are also successful global franchisers, including McDonald's, Pizza Hut, Starbucks, Domino's Pizza, KFC, and Holiday Inn, all of which have found that global franchising entails lower risks and requires less investment than does opening units owned wholly

| **EXHIBIT 16.11** | A Sample of Canada's Global Corporations |

Company	Industry	Sales ($B)	Profits ($B)	Company	Industry	Sales ($B)	Profits ($B)
Encana	Oil & Gas Operations	30.6	5.94	Agrium	Chemicals	10.03	1.32
PowerCorp	Diversified Financials	30.05	0.7	RIM	Technology Hardware & Equip.	9.48	1.79
RBC	Banking	30.01	3.52	Potash Corp.	Chemicals	9.45	3.5
Manulife Financial	Insurance	26.73	0.4	ACE Aviation	Transportation	8.98	-0.1
George Weston	Food Markets	25.99	0.67	Talisman Energy	Oil & Gas Operations	7.94	2.85
Suncor Energy	Oil & Gas Operations	24.37	1.73	Barrick Gold	Materials	7.91	0.82
Magna International	Consumer Durables	23.7	0.07	TransCanada	Utilities	6.98	1.22
Petro-Canada	Oil & Gas Operations	22.51	2.54	Nexen	Oil & Gas Operations	6.67	1.39
Onex	Diversified Financials	21.77	-0.23	AbitibiBowater	Materials	6.65	-1.05
BNS	Banking	21.62	2.54	SNC-Lavalin	Construction	5.76	0.25
TD Canada Trust	Banking	20.8	2.88	Teck Cominco	Materials	5.59	0.53
Husky Energy	Oil & Gas Operations	20.01	3.04	Saputo	Food, Drink, & Tobacco	4.54	0.23
BBD	Aerospace & Defense	19.56	0.94	Addax Petroleum	Oil & Gas Operations	3.76	0.78
Couche-Tard	Food Markets	17.17	0.21	Gold Corp	Materials	2.42	1.48
BMO	Banking	15.37	1.57	Cameco	Materials	2.32	0.36
Enbridge	Oil & Gas Operations	13.07	1.08	Tim Hortons	Hotels, Restaurants, & Leisure	1.66	0.23
Empire	Food Markets	11.98	0.21	Kinross Gold	Materials	1.62	-0.81
Can N Res	Oil & Gas Operations	11.47	4.04	Yamana Gold	Materials	1.05	0.43
CIBC	Banking	11.15	-0.37	Angico–Eagle Mines	Materials	0.33	0.07

These franchise logos are recognized around the world.

by the firm. However, when it engages in franchising, the firm has limited control over the market operations in the foreign country, its potential profit is reduced because it must be split with the franchisee, and, once the franchise is established, there is always the threat that the franchisee will break away and operate as a competitor under a different name. In Canada, more than 78 000 franchise operations employ more than 1.5 million people and generate in excess of $100 billion in annual sales.[50]

Entrepreneurial Marketing 16.1 describes how White Spot, one of Canada's oldest restaurant chains, successfully used franchising to expand its operations into Asia.

Strategic Alliance

strategic alliance
A collaborative relationship between independent firms, though the partnering firms do not create an equity partnership; that is, they do not invest in one another.

Strategic alliances refer to collaborative relationships between independent firms, though the partnering firms do not create an equity partnership; that is, they do not invest in one another. For example, Star Alliance constitutes one of the most complex strategic alliances in the world, with 27 airline members representing different countries: Adria Airways (Slovenia), Aegean Airlines (Greece), Air Canada, Air China, Air New Zealand, All Nippon Airways (Japan), Asiana Airlines (South Korea), Austrian Airlines, Blue1 (Finland), BMI (United Kingdom), Brussels Airlines (Belgium), Continental Airlines (USA), Croatia Airlines, EgyptAir, LOT (Poland), Lufthansa (Germany), Scandinavian Airlines (Denmark, Norway, and Sweden), Singapore Airlines, South African Airways, Spanair (Spain), Swiss International Air Lines, TAM Airlines (Brazil), TAP Portugal, Thai Airways International, Turkish Airlines, United Airlines (United States), and US Airways.[51]

What began as a series of bilateral agreements among five airlines grew over time into Star Alliance, which now acts as a separate legal entity in which each member is a stakeholder but no member is an equity owner in the others. Star Alliance

The Star Alliance is a strategic alliance with 27 airline members, including Air Canada.

Entrepreneurial Marketing 16.1

A Place That Really Hits the Spot[52]

More than 80 years ago, a lone entrepreneur, Nat Bailey, started White Spot, in the midst of the Depression of the 1920s. Recognizing an opportunity to serve hungry sightseers and tourists at Vancouver's Lookout Point, Nat Bailey converted his 1918 Ford Model T into a moving lunch counter. The travelling lunch counter was so successful that within a short time he needed hired help to meet customer demand. In 1928, the first White Spot drive-in was opened on Granville Street at 67th Avenue in Vancouver. White Spot became so popular that most Vancouverites, and soon visitors to the city, recognized Nat and his trademark bow tie. The restaurant became the place where celebrities dined and people celebrated special occasions, such as anniversaries and birthdays or even a first date.

By the 1960s, White Spot had 10 locations and introduced a new logo. During Expo '86, White Spot was the host restaurant at the BC Pavilion. It opened two concepts, one of which hosted visiting dignitaries, such as Prince Charles and Princess Diana, while the other served guests from around the world. In the early 2000s, White Spot expanded into Alberta and underwent another redesign, which was intended to give it a new identity and reach out to a younger demographic. The redesign provided a fresh new look on the outside. Granville Island started brewing beer exclusively for White Spot: Nat Bailey Pale Ale and Lager. To go with the new brew, White Spot introduced lounges, providing guests with a more social setting and a variety of alcohol offerings that appeal to a younger target market. While the award-winning Triple "O" burger, shakes, and fresh-cut fries are still wildly popular, many customers love the freshly prepared salads, pastas, steaks, and chicken dishes. And all restaurants now offer a wide selection of beverages, including a variety of wines, martinis, margaritas, Caesars, and the ever-popular Nat Bailey Pale Ale and Lager.

In 2008, White Spot achieved another milestone in culinary innovation and quality when it became the first restaurant to offer all components of a full indentured Red Seal apprenticeship certification program in-house for cooks. The Red Seal certification is a nationally recognized symbol of quality and is the standardized certification for Canadian tradespeople, such as those in the culinary arts. White Spot's entrepreneurial endeavours did not end there but rather continued in a bold way: it moved into Asia rather than into other provinces of Canada.

In November 2003, White Spot opened its first Asian location in the Admiralty District of Hong Kong in Pacific Place. Why Asia? A few years earlier, White Spot's executives observed an odd spike in sales of its mushroom burgers and quickly figured out that Asian expat university students were responsible for the sales pattern.

Something in the combination of mushrooms, sweet buns, and tangy relish appealed to Asian palates. That was the "aha moment" for White Spot's executives. They realized that if Asian consumers like the taste here, they would love it there. And the rest is history.

Thus began White Spot's leap into Asia. The restaurant is located in a high-end food court named Great, considered a "triple A" location in Hong Kong. According to Warren Erhart, White Spot's CEO, when entering a new market, it is important to find the best possible site available; success is about "location, location, location."[53] Today, White Spot has several restaurants in Hong Kong and Bangkok and is continually evaluating other opportunities in Asia.

According to Erhart, new markets must be analyzed on a country-by-country basis since countries have different rules that need to be considered. For example, some countries (e.g., Thailand and South Korea), have protectionist policies regarding the import of beef products. In addition, costs have to be controlled in new markets just as they do in the domestic market, which was another reason why White Spot led in Asia with its Triple O's brand, which has fewer products and a more simplified system.[54]

White Spot's expansion into Asia has been through franchising. To some extent this has led to measured growth, since the company must find suitable franchisees before it can open other locations. Because of the risks associated with franchising, White Spot has taken steps to protect the reputation of its brand. It provides franchisees with experienced supervisors for support and Asia-based compliance. White Spot also completes operations reviews and has a mystery shopper program. Regular plant inspections at food suppliers are standard operating procedures. Franchisees are responsible for spending a percentage of their sales on brand and local marketing, and White Spot provides assistance with "off the shelf" and specific location marketing programs to ensure consistency for brand look and feel.

Further, White Spot has modified its marketing mix strategy to suit the Asian market and as a way of maintaining its high standards. For example, it has added a number of menu items that complement the system and the tastes of the local market. In British Columbia, the company's salmon burger is extremely popular; but, in Hong Kong, white fish is more popular than salmon, so White Spot created a fish burger made with cod from New Zealand. In contrast, White Spot currently ships its relish, pickles, and beef gravy from Vancouver to Asia, because these ingredients were difficult to replicate in Hong Kong.

coordinates the members on projects of mutual interest, such as helping members in their individual brand-building efforts by creating value through their membership in the Alliance. This plan offers passengers benefits from individual airlines when they purchase from alliance partners. For instance, an Air Canada frequent flier member could earn Aeroplan miles by flying Spanair. This coalition also allows seamless booking and other transactions across the Alliance membership.

Joint Venture

joint venture
Formed when a firm entering a new market pools its resources with those of a local firm to form a new company in which ownership, control, and profits are shared.

A **joint venture** is formed when a firm entering a new market pools its resources with those of a local firm to form a new company in which ownership, control, and profits are shared. In addition to sharing the financial burden, the local partner offers the foreign entrant greater understanding of the market and access to resources such as vendors and real estate. Tesco, the U.K. supermarket, finance, telecom, and insurance superstar, entered China through a joint venture in which it has purchased a 50-percent share in Ting Hsin—which owns and operates the 25-store hypermarket chain Hymall—for $250 million.[55] China usually requires joint ownership from entering firms, as do many other countries, though these restrictions are loosened as a result of WTO negotiations. Problems with this entry approach can arise when the partners disagree or if the government places restrictions on the firm's ability to move its profits out of the foreign country and back to its home country. Problems can arise with joint ventures if the objectives, responsibilities, and benefits of the venture are not clearly defined from the outset. Conflicts could also arise if larger partners benefit more than smaller partners, which could threaten the venture. Differences in organizational cultures, management styles, and leadership, as well as disagreements about marketing and investment policies, could seriously affect the performance of the venture.

Two variants of joint ventures are contract manufacturing and management contracting. Contract manufacturing is when a foreign firm contracts with a local firm in the host market to manufacture the product. For example, NutraLab Canada is a contract manufacturer that has provided original equipment manufacture (OEM) and private label service for vitamin, natural health, and dietary supplement products

Tesco, the U.K. supermarket chain, has a joint venture in China in which it has purchased a 50-percent share in Ting Hsin—which owns and operates the 25-store hypermarket chain Hymall.

for more than 10 years.[56] NutraLab Canada produces many of the pharmaceutical softgels, capsules, liquid, and tablets that we consume.

Management contracting is when the domestic firm provides management consulting and advice to a foreign firm. For example, many Canadian technology companies will supply their technology to firms and governments in developing countries with a specific agreement that only the Canadian supplier can maintain the technology or provide know-how regarding technology use and repair. Management contracting is a low-risk method of entering a country's market without setting up operations in the country. It also generates returns immediately upon execution of the agreement. Management contracting tends to be long-term since it extends over the life of the technology.

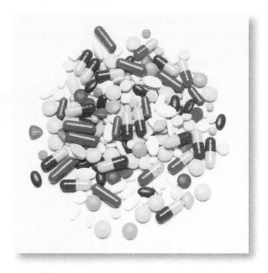

Direct Investment

Direct investment requires a firm to maintain 100-percent ownership of its plants, operation facilities, and offices in a foreign country, often through the formation of wholly owned subsidiaries. This entry strategy requires the highest level of investment and exposes the firm to significant risks, including the loss of its operating and/or initial investments. For example, a dramatic economic downturn caused by a natural disaster or war, political instability, or changes in the country's laws can increase a foreign entrant's risk considerably. Many firms believe that in certain markets, these potential risks are outweighed by the high potential returns; with this strategy, none of the potential profits must be shared with other firms. In addition to the high potential returns, direct investment offers the firm complete control over its operations in the foreign country.

Hundreds of Canadian mining, manufacturing, and technology companies have direct investments in several countries around the world. For example, Barrick Gold is the world's largest gold producer, with a portfolio of 25 operating mines, advanced exploration and development projects in South America, North America, Africa, and Australia. Similarly, Bombardier has direct investments in Japan, the United States, Denmark, and Ireland.[57]

As we noted, each of these entry strategies entails different levels of risk and rewards for the foreign entrant. But even after a firm has determined how much risk it is willing to take, and therefore how it will enter a new global market, it still must establish its marketing strategy, as we discuss in the next section.

A sample of the kinds of products NutraLab contract manufactures on behalf of drug companies.

direct investment
When a firm maintains 100-percent ownership of its plants, operation facilities, and offices in a foreign country, often through the formation of wholly owned subsidiaries.

Choosing a Global Marketing Strategy   L04

Just like any other marketing strategy, a global marketing strategy includes two components: determining the target market(s) to pursue and developing a marketing mix that will sustain a competitive advantage over time. In this section, we examine marketing strategy as it relates specifically to global markets.

Target Market: Segmentation, Targeting, and Positioning

Global segmentation, targeting, and positioning (STP) is more complicated than domestic STP for several reasons. First, firms considering a global expansion have much more difficulty understanding the cultural nuances of other countries. Second, subcultures within each country also must be considered. Third, consumers often view products and their role as consumers differently in different countries.[58]

A product or service often must be positioned differently in different markets. For example, Tang, the fruit-flavoured drink produced by Kraft, is positioned as a low-priced drink in the United States; but, such a positioning strategy would not work in Brazil,

Tropicana uses a global positioning strategy that stresses around the world that Tropicana is fresh-squeezed Florida orange juice.

where fresh orange juice already is a low-priced drink. Consequently, Kraft promotes a pineapple-flavoured Tang and positions it as a drink for special occasions. In a similar fashion, McDonald's generally competes on convenience and low price; but, in countries such as China and India, where consumers already have lower-priced and more convenient alternatives, McDonald's positions itself as an "American" restaurant.[59]

The most efficient route is to develop and maintain a global positioning strategy; one position means only one message to get out. For instance, Tropicana is the bestselling orange juice brand in the United States and owns 6 percent of the global juice market. Tropicana's parent company, PepsiCo, therefore takes a global positioning strategy that stresses around the world that Tropicana is fresh-squeezed Florida orange juice.[60]

When it identifies its positioning within the market, the firm then must decide how to implement its marketing strategies by using the marketing mix. Just as firms adjust their products and services to meet the needs of national target market(s), they must alter their marketing mix to serve the needs of global markets.

The Global Marketing Mix

The PEST factors described earlier in this chapter, as well as consumers' psychological, social, and situational factors, influence how marketers configure the marketing mix and implement their marketing strategy. In this section, we explore the four Ps (product, place, promotion, price) from a global perspective.

Global Product or Service Strategies

There are three potential global product strategies:

- Sell the same product or service in both the home country market and the host country.
- Sell a product or service similar to that sold in the home country but include minor adaptations.
- Sell totally new products or services.

The strategy a firm chooses depends on the needs of the target market. The level of economic development and differences in product and technical standards help determine the need for product adaptation. Cultural differences such as food preferences, language, and religion also play a role in product strategy planning. For example, Nestlé recently created 20 unique flavours of KIT KAT for Japanese consumers; in Japan, KIT KAT is one of the top confectionary brands. By creating flavours that reflect the local produce and tastes of different regions of Japan, Nestlé aims to promote its unique KIT KAT as regional souvenirs. KIT KAT varieties now range from yubari melon from Hokkaido Island, to green beans and cherries from Tohoku in northeastern Japan, to yuzu fruit and red potatoes from Kyushu/Okinawa region at the southern-most tip of the country. The Kanto region, including Tokyo, contributed the sweet potato, blueberry, and soy sauce flavours. Wasabi-flavoured white chocolate KIT KAT is also quite popular with Japanese consumers.[61]

The level of economic development also affects the global product strategy because it relates directly to consumer buying behaviour. For instance, sales of Apple's iPhone soared in North America from the day it was released; however, it has failed miserably in India. It is estimated that only about 20 000 iPhones have been sold in India in the first six months following the phone's launch, even though

Indian cellphone providers have added 20 million subscribers during that same six-month period. There are several reasons for the iPhone's disastrous sales performance, but the reason of affordability really stands out. The iPhone, priced at $700, is far beyond the reach of even many middle-class Indian consumers. This price tag is in stark contrast to the $199 price tag available in Canada and the United States with a two- or three-year contract. According to observers in India, the price of three iPhones is equivalent to the cost of a Nano, the $2,000 car that Tata Motors launched in India in 2009.[62]

In contrast, recognizing that the millions of low-income consumers in India cannot afford to buy its larger-size Cadbury chocolates, Cadbury introduced its Cadbury Dairy Milk Shots, which are pea-sized chocolate balls with a sugar shell to protect them from the heat. They were launched this year and cost only two rupees, or about four cents, for a 5-gram packet. Cadbury also sells other candies, such as Eclair caramels, for two cents to make them more accessible to consumers. The chocolate market is worth close to $500 million a year, and Cadbury controls about 70 percent of the market, so it is no wonder that the company goes to great lengths to serve its Indian customers.[63]

Some firms also standardize their products globally but use different promotional campaigns to sell them. The original Pringles potato chip product remains the same globally, as do the images and themes of the promotional campaign, with limited language adaptations for local markets. However, the company does change Pringles' flavours in different countries, including paprika-flavoured chips, which are sold in Italy and Germany.[64] McCain Foods, which markets frozen potato specialties in 100 countries, localizes its product by,

for instance, calling french fries *chips* in the United Kingdom and developing local advertising for markets by region.[65]

Because an iPhone costs $700, Indian consumers can buy the Nano car for the price of three iPhones.

Manufacturers are not the only ones that must adapt their offering. On the retail side, for example, Whole Foods is making shopping an experience in the United Kingdom to compete with the local organic supermarket chains.

Despite persistent differences across borders, marketers have found a growing convergence in tastes and preferences in many product categories. Starbucks is a good example of a company that has both influenced and exploited this global convergence in tastes. Even in China and Great Britain, traditional strongholds for tea marketers, coffee is quickly gaining as the beverage of choice. Increasingly, because of the Internet and other information technologies, there seems to be not only a convergence of taste among youths, but also the emergence of global homogenous segments. That is, groups of consumers from around the world now share similar buying characteristics. One study identified the "global teen segment," which they describe as teenagers from around the world—from Japan to Vancouver, London, Beijing, and San Francisco—who generally buy the same brand name clothing, electronics, and accessories; listen to the same music; and eat the same food. Such trends make it easier for marketers to target these consumers with standardized products.[66]

Global Pricing Strategies Determining the selling price in the global marketplace is an extremely difficult task.[67] Many countries still have rules governing the competitive marketplace, including those that affect pricing. For example, in parts of Europe, including Belgium, Italy, Spain, Greece, and France, promotional sales are allowed only twice a year, in January and in June or July. In most European countries, retailers can't sell below cost, and they can't advertise reduced prices in advance of sales or discount items until they have been on shelves for more than a month. For firms such as Walmart and other discounters, these restrictions threaten their core competitive positioning as the lowest-cost provider in the market. Other issues, such as tariffs, quotas, anti-dumping laws, and currency exchange policies, can also affect pricing decisions.[68]

Competitive factors influence global pricing in the same way they do home country pricing, but because a firm's products or services may not have the same positioning in the global marketplace as they do in their home country, market prices must be adjusted to reflect the local pricing structure. Spain's fashion retailer Zara, for instance, is relatively inexpensive in the European Union but is priced about 65 percent higher in North America, putting it right in the middle of its moderately priced competition.[69] Since it is important for Zara to get its fashions to the consumers in a timely manner, it incurs additional transportation expenses, which it passes on to its North American customers. In the case of Apple's iPhone in India, it seems that the $700 price tag has very little to do with the cost of production and more to do with trading rules, competition, and local Indian resellers, who seem to have different goals than Apple for the iPhone. Finally, as we discussed earlier in this chapter, currency fluctuations impact global pricing strategies.

Global Distribution Strategies Global distribution networks form complex value chains that involve intermediaries, exporters, importers, and different transportation systems. These additional intermediaries typically add cost and ultimately increase the final selling price of a product. As a result of these cost factors, constant pressure exists to shorten distribution channels wherever possible.

The number of firms with which the seller needs to deal to get its merchandise to the consumer determines the complexity of a channel. In most developing countries, manufacturers must go through many different types of distribution channels to get their products to end users, who often lack adequate transportation to shop at central shopping areas or large malls. Therefore, these consumers shop near their homes at small, family-owned retail outlets. To reach these small retail outlets, most of which are located far from major rail stations or roads, marketers have devised a variety of creative solutions. In the Amazon jungle in Brazil, for instance, Avon products are sometimes delivered by canoe. Alternatively, Unilever's strategy in India is a prime example of how a global company can adopt its distribution network to fit local conditions. Unilever trained 25 000 Indian women to serve as distributors, who in turn extended Unilever's reach to 80 000 villages across India. The program generates $250 million each year in villages that otherwise would be too costly to serve.[70]

Global Communication Strategies   The major challenge in developing a global communication strategy is identifying the elements that need to be adapted to be effective in the global marketplace. For instance, even though Japan has one of the world's most sophisticated digital-media markets, Nestlé took a low-tech route to promote its unique 20 flavours of KIT KAT, which are sold as souvenirs in railway stations, airports, and expressway service shop areas. Nestlé was struck by the discovery that KIT KAT sounds similar to the Japanese phrase *Kitto Katsu*, which means "surely win." The company realized the chocolate bar could be paired with the tradition of sending students good-luck wishes before they take tough higher-education entrance exams. So it partnered with Japan's postal service to create Kit Mail, a postcard-like product sold only at the post office that could be mailed to students as an edible good-luck charm. Nestlé decorates post offices with a cherry blossom theme that coincides with Japan's annual exam period. It also stocks a sales point in each post office, a move that became possible when Japan's postal service was privatized in 2007. Nestlé noted that, if post offices were still government-owned, the company probably could not have done this: "The post office is a great distribution channel for KIT KAT, because there is no competition, unlike in convenience stores or supermarkets," said Mr. Kageyama, CEO of JWT Japan, Nestlé Japan's advertising agency.[71]

Distribution can be challenging in some countries if the transportation infrastructure is inadequate. In the Amazon jungle in Brazil, for instance, Avon products are sometimes delivered by canoe.

Media availability also varies widely; some countries offer only state-controlled media. Advertising regulations differ too. In an attempt at standardization, the European Union recently recommended common guidelines for its member countries regarding advertising to children, and it is currently reviewing a possible ban on "junk food" advertising.[72]

Differences in language, customs, and culture also complicate marketers' ability to communicate with customers in various countries. Language can be particularly vexing for advertisers. For example, in the United Kingdom and Australia, a thong is a sandal; whereas in Canada, it can also be an undergarment. To avoid the potential embarrassment that language confusion can cause, firms spend millions of dollars to develop brand names that have no pre-existing meaning in any known language, such as Accenture (a management consulting firm) or Avaya (a subsidiary of Lucent Technologies, formerly Bell Labs).

Within many countries, there are multiple variants on a language. For example, in China, where there are three main languages, firms such as Mercedes-Benz adapted its name for each language: it is pronounced *peng zee* in Cantonese for Hong Kong; *peng chi* in Mandarin for Taiwan; and *ben chi* in Mandarin for mainland China. Other firms, such as Nokia, only use one name in China, pronounced *nuo jee ya* in Mandarin.[73] As China continues to develop, having more than one name to represent a product or service will become increasingly inefficient. Unlike these companies, RIM markets its BlackBerry by using the same name around the globe.

Even with all these differences, many products and services serve the same needs and wants globally with little or no adaptation in their form or message. Firms whose products have global appeal, such as Coca-Cola, can develop global advertising campaigns, an advantage that results in significant savings. According to Coca-Cola's advertising firm, McCann-Erickson, over a 20-year period, it saved Coca-Cola $90 million by reusing advertisements it had already created and by changing only a few elements for different local markets.[74] Although Microsoft is an example of a company that sells products with global appeal, it sees the benefit of connecting with local markets. Social Media Marketing 16.1 describes how Microsoft is using social media to communicate with its global customer base.

Nestlé's Kit Mail could be mailed to students as an edible good-luck charm.

Other products require a more localized approach because of cultural and religious differences. In a classic advertisement for Longines watches, a woman's bare arm and hand appear, with a watch on her wrist. The advertisement was considered too risqué for predominantly Muslim countries, where women's bare arms are never displayed in public. The company changed the advertisement to show a gloved arm and hand wearing the same watch.

Regulatory actions in the host country can also affect communication strategies. For example, the WTO has become involved in several cases that involve firms' rights to use certain names and affiliations for their products and promotions. Several products in the European Union have established worldwide brand recognition on the basis of where they are made. For instance, the European Union currently allows only ham made in Parma, Italy, to be called Parma ham and sparkling wine made in the Champagne region of France to be called Champagne. However, the European Union has also refused to grant requests from non-EU countries for similar protection, notably Florida orange juice.[75] The WTO is expected to ask the European Union to either remove all such protections or grant them to non-EU countries as well. In one case, similar arguments have even led to a global beer brawl, in which the American beer giant Budweiser must contend with claims by the tiny, 700-year-old Czech brewery Budvar that the U.S. company stole its name. The two companies coexisted in an uneasy truce before the fall of the Berlin Wall, because Budweiser could not access Budvar's Eastern European market, and Budvar could not easily get its products out of that area. But since then, the competition between the two has heated up, leading some countries to provide exclusive registrations to one of the two and other countries to place them both on shelves. Most indications suggest the WTO will deny both companies' claims to the exclusive use of the Budweiser/Budvar names, meaning that someday soon; consumers may have to clarify what they mean when they say, "I'll have a Bud."[76]

L05 Ethical Issues in Global Marketing

Although ethical issues abound domestically, an extra layer of complexity arises for global marketing. Firms that market globally must recognize that they are, in essence, visitors in another country and, as such, must be aware of the ethical concerns of their potential customers, both at home and abroad. In this section, we examine three areas of particular concern: environmental concerns, labour issues, and impact on host country culture.

Environmental Concerns

environmental concerns Include, but are not limited to, the excessive use of natural resources and energy, refuse from manufacturing processes, excess trash created by consumer goods packages, and hard-to-dispose-of products such as tires, cellphones, and computer monitors.

People throughout the world are worried about the amount of waste being generated, especially in developed countries. Current **environmental concerns** include, but are not limited to, the excessive use of natural resources and energy, refuse from manufacturing processes, excess trash created by consumer goods packages, and hard-to-dispose-of products such as tires, cellphones, and computer monitors.

Social Media Marketing 16.1

Microsoft: Strengthening Its Local Presence via Social Media

A multimillion-dollar global company with customers in more than 90 countries cannot possibly build a unique, personal relationship with each and every one of its consumers. Instead, Microsoft's challenge is to find a way to share news, updates, information, and resources with consumers in a way that they will find meaningful and relevant. Social media is a big part of Microsoft's solution.

To maintain a high-impact global presence, Microsoft has developed a four-step process of listening and responding to consumers.[77] Its first step is simply to *monitor* organically occurring activities. A team of experts search the Internet, using Twitter, Digg, Delicious, and Boardreader and other tools to track, measure, and analyze any relevant online conversations. These experts want to determine whether the conversations indicate satisfied or dissatisfied customers.

The team sifts through all the news and conversations worldwide to *detect* real issues, such as dissatisfied customers, or glaring issues, such as a recurring problem with a piece of software. They determine whether some sort of interaction is needed by monitoring the frequency of repeat complaints online and also by watching out for warning signs of issues that the company would not otherwise be aware of without the use of social media.

After actionable issues have been identified, Microsoft begins working on solutions. Finding a solution usually starts by having a representative join a conversation, for example, by tweeting back to a dissatisfied customer to gain more information. In most cases, the issue can be resolved right away; but, if not, the team works to *manage* the customer's expectation while it investigates further.

The final element of this process is the management of Microsoft's *influencer-enablement program*. This fancy term describes using the same tools in the first three steps of its review process to identify the most valuable influencers: those people with the most web traffic or strong leadership positions online. Instead of attempting to affect each and every customer, Microsoft concentrates its efforts on these influencers, sharing new product information with them and giving them direct access to the Microsoft team.

Implementing these steps has resulted in a number of positive factors for Microsoft. It has been able to build strong relationships with more than 2000 third-party communities and to develop a large group of Microsoft advocates.[78] As well, it has successfully created a local presence, despite being a large international player. Lastly, it has been able to gain clear insights into the ways that consumers use its products every day. Without social media at the heart of this entire program, Microsoft would not have been able to achieve the same results, nor would it have the ability to respond quickly.

Many developed countries produce almost two tonnes of household and industrial waste per person per year![79] Although developing countries do not produce nearly the same level of waste, much of the waste in these areas is not properly disposed of.

Global Labour Issues

Global labour issues, especially concerns about working conditions and wages paid to factory workers in developing countries, have become increasingly prominent.[80] Many large U.S. firms, such as Nike, PepsiCo, and Walmart, have been questioned by various groups, including nongovernmental organizations and human rights activists, about the degree to which workers the companies employ are paid less than a living wage or forced to work long hours in poor working conditions.[81]

In this context, high prices offer no guarantee of a supply chain free of sweatshops. Recently, Apple has been repeatedly questioned about the working conditions in the manufacturing plants that produce iPods and iPhones. Even though iPod boxes proudly state that the music player was designed in California,

global labour issues
Includes concerns about working conditions and wages paid to factory workers in developing countries.

Many developed countries produce almost two tonnes of household and industrial waste per person per year that requires proper disposal.

Apple's iPhones, iPods, iPads, and other products are hugely popular among Canadians and Americans, to such an extent that there are usually back orders and long lineups at retailers whenever they are released. However, how many of us read the label to find out where these products are manufactured? Although designed in the United States, the products are manufactured in China and elsewhere. Where they are produced is not necessarily a problem. What is problematic for Apple, are the repeated claims in the media of the deplorable working conditions in Chinese factories. News agencies reported 10 recent suicides at Apple's Foxconn factory. Apple's CEO, Steve Jobs, was quoted as saying, "Although every suicide is tragic, Foxconn's suicide rate is well below the China average and we are all over this."[83] Issues such as fair wages and labour conditions must be especially important to Apple, because the core demographic for the iPod and its other innovative products consists of creative people who are willing to tailor their purchasing to a political viewpoint.[84] Apple simply cannot afford to have its affluent customers wondering whether Apple is profiting from human suffering.

In response to pressure from consumers, Apple has begun investing in social responsibility and has joined an industry group, the Electronic Industry Citizenship Coalition (EICC), which supports the EICC Code of Conduct. This Code of Conduct, signed by a group of companies, including the founding firms Hewlett-Packard, Dell, and IBM, exacts a promise to ensure safe labour conditions, workers' rights, and environmental responsibility in the global electronics supply chain.[85] Apple acknowledges that social responsibility is an ongoing process and now conducts audits and monitors suppliers to ensure safer working conditions.[86] Do you think Apple's claims that suicide rates in its factory are below that of the China average and that embracing the EICC Code of Conduct is an appropriate and ethical response to the suicide situation at Foxconn?

the entire manufacturing process has been subcontracted to Taiwanese and Chinese manufacturers.[82] Because Apple does not own the plants in which its goods are produced, it must negotiate with factory owners to improve or ensure adequate working conditions and wages, while at the same time attempting to get the cheapest prices. Because Apple negotiates very hard on price, suppliers sometimes try to make money by paying labourers less, making them work long hours, or providing them with unsafe working conditions. As discussed in Ethical Dilemma 16.1, labour conditions for Chinese workers in "iPod city" recently became so deplorable that many Chinese workers resorted to committing suicide and several high-profile strikes protested their working conditions.

Impact on Host Country Culture

cultural imperialism
The belief that one's own culture is superior to that of other nations; can take the form of an active, formal policy or a more subtle general attitude.

The final ethical issue involves **cultural imperialism,** or the belief that one's own culture is superior to that of other nations. Cultural imperialism can take the form of an active, formal policy or a more subtle general attitude.[87] Critics of U.S. firms entering foreign markets claim that U.S. products and services overwhelm the local culture, often replacing its foods, music, movies, and traditions with those of the West.

In Iran, for example, the ruling clerics have forbidden the celebration of Valentine's Day.[88] Despite strict Iranian laws regarding the interactions of men and women, especially unmarried men and women, Valentine's Day has become a popular holiday among the youth market. These Iranians were exposed to Valentine's Day through the Internet and satellite television, two information sources the government cannot control. Holiday-themed products arrive through underground distribution channels and are displayed in local shops. Risking legal action, florists, gift shops, and restaurants make special accommodations for the holiday. Many parents sponsor Valentine parties with both men and women in attendance. Apparently, there is no stopping love. Half the Iranian population is younger than 25 years of age, and this youth market has embraced the holiday and continues to celebrate it in traditional Western ways.

For other Iranians though, this type of celebration represents a threat to Iran's culture. Many U.S. firms find themselves squarely in the middle of this cultural conflict.[89] Various countries around the world encompass competing desires: the desire to modernize and participate in the global marketplace versus the desire to hold on to traditional cultural values and ways of life. There is no simple way to resolve these dilemmas. Firms that enter new markets simply must tread lightly to ensure that their business practices, products, and services do not create any unnecessary friction or offence in the host country.

When Western firms enter foreign markets, they must be cognizant of the host country's culture.

Real Marketer Profile: NIGEL VANDERLINDEN

I am RIM's senior director of Global Business Development. My primary objective is to expand RIM's global channel reach. This is achieved by leading a team of business development and carrier implementation professionals to establish and enable new partnerships with network operators. I am also tasked with evangelizing Enhanced Edge (E-EDGE) technology and devices to network operators. This work involves close cooperation with network equipment and services vendors.

I completed an Honours Bachelor of Business Administration degree at Wilfrid Laurier University (WLU). My course focus at WLU was primarily marketing. I also completed a diploma program in International Business at Queen's University International Study Centre in Hailsham, East Sussex, in the United Kingdom.

While I was at Laurier, I completed two co-op terms at RIM, both in the area of business development. RIM hired me immediately after graduation.

My first role at RIM as a full-time employee was that of inside sales account manager for the OEM Radio Module

Team. I was responsible for managing the early phases of the sales funnel/process—that is, lead generation/new opportunities, initial communication, and qualification/fact finding.

One of the most exciting and interesting projects I've worked on was when I was tasked with establishing RIM's footprint in the Middle East and Africa. The role required me to move to RIM's EMEA headquarters in the United Kingdom, although I spent three to four months a year in Dubai. I developed an extensive network of mobile operators and strategic channel partners across the region.

Since then, I've returned to RIM's global headquarters in Waterloo, Ontario, after spending three years in the United Kingdom. I now have a global mandate and a team of business development and carrier implementation professionals. I am also the proud father of a busy 15 month old!

I love working in marketing. Deal making is my drug!

Learning Objectives Review

L01 **Identify the factors that aid the growth of globalization**

Technology, particularly in communications, has facilitated the growth of global markets. Firms can communicate with their suppliers and customers instantaneously, easily take advantage of production efficiencies in other countries, and bring together parts and finished goods from all over the globe. International organizations such as the World Trade Organization, the International Monetary Fund, and the

World Bank Group also have reduced or eliminated tariffs and quotas, worked to help people in less-developed countries, and facilitated trade in many areas.

L02 **Explain the components of a country market assessment**

First, firms must determine whether the proposed country has a political and legal environment that favours business. Second, firms must assess the general economic environment. For instance, countries with a trade surplus, strong domestic and national products, population growth, and income growth tend to be favourable prospects. Third, firms should be cognizant of the socio-cultural differences between their home and host countries and adapt to those differences to ensure successful business relationships. Fourth, firms should assess a country's technology and infrastructure capabilities. To be successful in a particular country, the firm must have access to adequate transportation, distribution channels, and communications.

L03 **Describe the various market entry strategies**

Firms have several options for entering a new country, each with a different level of risk and control. Direct investment is the most risky but also has the potential to be the most lucrative. Firms that engage in a joint venture with other firms already operating in the host country share the risk and obtain knowledge about the market and how to do business there. A strategic alliance is similar to a joint venture, but the relationship is not as formal. A less risky method of entering a new market is franchising, in which, similar to domestic franchise agreements, the franchisor allows the franchisee to operate a business using its name and strategy in return for a fee. The least risky method of entering another country is exporting.

L04 **List the similarities of and differences between a domestic marketing strategy and a global marketing strategy**

The essence of a global marketing strategy is no different than that of a domestic strategy. The firm starts by identifying its target markets, chooses specific markets to pursue, and crafts a strategy to meet the needs of those markets. However, additional issues make global expansion more difficult. For instance, the company needs to ask the following questions: Should the product or service be altered to fit the new market better? Does the firm need to change the way it prices its products in different countries? What is the best way to get the product or service to the new customers? How should the firm communicate its product or service offering in other countries?

L05 **Explain how ethical issues affect global marketing practices**

In particular, firms must be cognizant of the impact their businesses have on the environment. When producing merchandise or employing service personnel in another country, companies must be certain that the working conditions and wages are fair and adequate, even if the workers are employed by a third party. Finally, marketers must be sensitive to the impact their business has on the culture of the host country.

Key Terms

- boycott, 535
- countertrade, 536
- cultural imperialism, 560
- direct investment, 553
- dumping, 535
- duty, 535
- environmental concerns, 558
- exchange control, 536
- exchange rate, 536
- exporting, 548
- General Agreement on Tariffs and Trade (GATT), 532

- global labour issues, 559
- globalization, 530
- globalization of production, 532
- gross domestic product (GDP), 540
- human development index (HDI), 541
- infrastructure, 546
- International Monetary Fund (IMF), 533
- joint venture, 552
- offshoring, 532
- purchasing power parity (PPP), 540

- quota, 535
- strategic alliance, 550
- tariff, 535
- trade agreement, 536
- trade deficit, 539
- trade sanctions, 534
- trade surplus, 539
- trading bloc, 536
- World Bank Group, 533
- World Trade Organization (WTO), 533

Concept Review

1. What is globalization? What are the factors that facilitate globalization? Explain how globalization has influenced marketing in Canada.

2. List and describe the four components of market assessments firms must conduct to evaluate the viability of different global markets.

3. Which of the four components of market assessment do you think are often most difficult to assess? Why?

4. List the five types of strategies companies can use to enter global markets. Compare these strategies in terms of level of risk, expected return, and control.

5. Discuss the advantages and disadvantages of using a global product strategy (i.e., offering the same product both at home and in overseas markets).

6. What are the primary considerations marketers should use in deciding whether to customize its four Ps to specific markets?

7. What is political risk? Why is it important to assess political risks? How is political risk assessed? List two or three organizations in Canada that provide marketers with political risk assessments.

8. Protectionist policies restrict trade and global marketing while trade agreements facilitate global marketing. Explain the reasons why a country may want to impose protectionist policies in some industries and liberalize other industries.

9. Explain how measures such as GDP, PPP (i.e., the Big Mac Index), and HDI help marketers decide whether to enter a global market. What are the weaknesses of these measures?

10. Explain how useful Hofstede's five dimensions of culture are to our understanding of different cultures around the world. Where and how can marketers learn about the culture of a country to which they are interested in marketing?

Marketing Applications

1. The World Trade Organization, World Bank, and International Monetary Fund all work in different ways to facilitate globalization. What role(s) does each organization play in the global marketplace?

2. Cervélo is a high-end Canadian bicycle manufacturer. Assume the company is considering entering the United Kingdom and Chinese markets. When doing its market assessment, what economic factors should Cervélo consider when making its decision? Which market do you expect will be more lucrative for Cervélo? Why?

3. Now consider the political, economic, and legal systems of China versus the United Kingdom. Explain why you think one country might be more hospitable to Cervélo than the other.

4. Volkswagen sells cars in many countries throughout the world, including Mexico and Latin America. How would you expect its market position to differ in those countries compared with that in Canada?

5. Global brands that gain status on a local level have the best of both worlds: local loyalty with all the advantages of global connections. How do huge global companies such as McCain Foods, Philips, and McDonald's achieve multi-local status?

6. What is cultural imperialism? Why would a recording company such as Def Jam Recordings need to be aware of and sensitive to this issue?

7. Provide an example of a potentially ethically troubling practice by a foreign firm doing business in Canada.

8. Many Canadian and U.S.-based firms are relocating their production facilities and services overseas (outsourcing or offshoring). Why do you believe they are doing so? Do the benefits outweigh the potential losses of Canadian and U.S. jobs? Why or why not?

9. Assume you work for a Canadian-based financial services firm that positions itself as having experts that personally manage the clients' accounts. The clients are unaware that most of the tax preparation work, the bookkeeping, and other record keeping are done by a company in India. The local office simply reviews the file and signs the cover letters. Yet as your manager pointed out, there is still only one person that *manages* each account. After recent news stories about the practice of offshoring sensitive transactions such as tax preparation, clients have been commenting about how grateful they are to have a local firm. What, if anything, should you tell your clients about the firm's practice of offshoring?

10. Canadian companies such as Tim Hortons and lululemon have expanded their global presence through company-owned stores. In what instances might these companies consider using joint ventures as their global market entry strategy into new markets?

Net Savvy

1. For many small businesses, the idea of entering a foreign market is frightening. The Government of Canada, as well as most provincial and territorial governments, now offers assistance designed specifically for small business owners. Two such government departments are Foreign Affairs and International Trade Canada (DFAIT) and Industry Canada. Visit Industry Canada's Canada Business website at www.canadabusiness.ca and examine the types of services it provides for Canadian businesses wishing to do business in a foreign country. Evaluate the usefulness of the information provided.

2. McCain Foods is a global brand; but, it alters its products and promotions to accommodate local tastes in each country. Go to www.mccain.ca and visit the Canadian site. Then click through to the South American site, the U.S. site, and the site for France. How are these three websites different from the Canadian site? What products are different? What promotional elements are different?

Chapter Case Study

LULULEMON: REVOLUTIONIZING THE GLOBAL ATHLETICS AND SPORTS APPAREL INDUSTRY[90]

In 1998, Chip Wilson, the creative mind behind the lululemon athletica brand, started his yoga-inspired athletic apparel manufacturing and retailing business in Kitsilano, a trendy Vancouver neighbourhood. His original goal was to have one store in Kitsilano, and never grow beyond that. But within a few years, lululemon was transformed into a global brand and a great Canadian success story in the athletic and sportswear industry.

lululemon has experienced exponential growth since its creation in 1998. By 2010, it had expanded around the world to 128 stores, 122 of which are company-owned and 14 are franchises. There are 44 stores in Canada, 78 in the United States, and 11 corporate-owned stores and 4 show-rooms in Australia.[91] It also has 14 showrooms and plans to open another 22 to 27 stores in Canada and the United States in fiscal 2011. In addition, three corporate-owned stores are branded ivivva athletica, which specialize in dance-inspired apparel for female youths.

lululemon's revenue also grew exponentially, from $40.7 million in 2004 to $711.7 million in 2010,[92] representing a compound annual growth rate of 61 percent. The company's earnings are reported in U.S. dollars, therefore, a stronger Canadian dollar works in the firm's favour for its U.S. sales. Its revenues increased by 11 percent, or $13.5 million, because of the appreciation of the Canadian dollar. However, as more and more of its earnings are from Canada, the strong Canadian dollar will have a negative impact on its earnings. The company's workforce increased by more than 175 percent between 2007 and 2011, from around 1650 employees in January 2007 to 4572 employees in January 2011.[93]

lululemon retail stores are primarily at street locations, in lifestyle centres, and in malls next to premium retailers such as Banana Republic, Lacoste, Cartier, Gucci, and Whole Foods Market. In addition to company-owned stores and franchises, lululemon also sells directly to consumers through its e-commerce website, which was launched in 2009, and through wholesalers: premium yoga studios, health clubs, and fitness centres. Sales through its e-commerce website accounted for 9 percent of revenues in 2010. The e-commerce site is designed to enhance its brand image and make its products accessible in more markets beyond physical stores. lululemon's premium wholesalers offer an alternative distribution channel for some core customers and enhance its brand image. Strategically, the wholesale channel was never meant to be a big contributor to overall sales (actual contribution is about 2 percent annually) but, like the company's e-commerce site, this channel was designed to build brand awareness, especially in new markets, including those outside of North America.

The market for athletic apparel is highly competitive. Competitors include established companies who are expanding their production and marketing of performance products, as well as frequent new entrants to the market. lululemon competes directly with wholesalers and retailers of athletic apparel such as Nike, Adidas, Reebok, Under Armour, and even Walmart. It also competes with retailers that focus specifically on women's athletic apparel, including lucy activewear, The Gap's Athleta collection, and bebe's Sport collection.

The athletic apparel industry mainly competes on the basis of brand image and recognition, product quality, innovation, style, distribution, and price. From its very beginning, lululemon's approach to sports clothing was different from the industry standard. When global brands in the 1990s focused primarily on men and made only minor changes to the men's lines to create women's clothing, lululemon developed sport clothing specifically for women. Similarly, when sports clothing was designed primarily for comfort and functionality, lululemon offered customers not only comfortable and functional clothing, but also fashionable clothing made of breathable fabric. lululemon offered products that capitalized on the growing trends of female participation in sports, specifically yoga, and the demand for clothing made from sustainable materials. lululemon successfully competed on the basis of its premium brand image, its focus on women, and its technical product innovation. Its vertical retail distribution strategy also differentiates it from competitors and enables the company to more effectively control its brand image.

So far, lululemon has successfully stolen market share from established global companies that have dominated the market for years. It has become a major force within the industry even though its line of sportswear goods and accessories are not cheap relative to the competition. If you want a pair of lululemon pants, prepare to fork over about $100 and another $50 for a top.

By any metric, lululemon's success on the international stage within such a short period of time is phenomenal, especially since many excellent Canadian companies have failed in the United States and other global markets.

lululemon's marketing activities are designed to create brand awareness primarily through word of mouth from customers and community ambassadors: yoga instructors, personal trainers, or up-and-coming athletes from the local community endorse its products. These ambassadors wear lululemon merchandise and their photographs are usually displayed in stores so customers can see them. The company also uses these professionals to gain insights and feedback on designs and other aspects of its products. Rarely, if ever, does lululemon follow the lead of competing brands, such as Nike or Adidas, and use expensive celebrity endorsements. lululemon does however use hard-hitting, even controversial, promotional events, such as when it opened its Kingston, Ontario, store, where it offered free clothing to the first 30 customers who entered the store naked or topless.[94] It also relies on local and national media for free publicity of its events, merchandise, and company story.

Customers are individuals that work, play, and share lululemon's vision of creating healthier, happier, and more fun lives!

In addition to its unique marketing campaigns, lululemon takes great care in choosing where to establish its stores and who to partner with, either through franchises or joint ventures. Its understanding of the culture of new markets and the manner in which it enters those markets and connects with customers are also important elements of its strategy. lululemon "eyes global markets but seeks local advice"[95]; that is, it works closely with its customers—yogis and athletes in local communities—for continuous research and product feedback. These customers help lululemon set the standard in technical fabrics and functional designs. It has cultivated strong relationships with the local communities where it operates. For example, it encourages interactions with local communities at its regular meetings with local designers. It has developed a strong local organization by partnering with local companies. For example, most of its Australian stores are franchises, although the company recently increased its equity interest in its Australian joint venture partner, New Harbour Yoga Pty, from 13 percent to 80.3 percent. The increased ownership is widely viewed as providing the foundation for lululemon's expansion in the Australian market and to test its ability to support strategic international expansion over the longer term.

In terms of its sourcing strategy, lululemon does not own or operate manufacturing facilities, nor does it contract directly with third-party vendors for fabrics and finished goods. The fabric used in its products is sourced by its manufacturers from a limited number of pre-approved suppliers. The company works with a group of approximately 35 manufacturers, 10 of which produced approximately 85 percent of its products in 2009. No single manufacturer produced more than 25 percent of the products. Approximately 75 percent of its products are produced in China, 8 percent in Southeast Asia, 5 percent in Canada, and the remaining 12 percent in the United States, Israel, Peru, and Taiwan. North American manufacturers provide the company with the speed–to-market necessary to respond quickly to changing trends and increased demand. Distribution of finished products in North America is done centrally from distribution facilities in Vancouver, British Columbia, and Sumner, Washington. Merchandise is typically shipped to stores through third-party delivery services multiple times per week, providing a steady flow of new inventory.

Despite its excellent growth record and strong brand image, things have not always gone smoothly for lululemon. For example, in 2007, *The New York Times* reported that the alleged beneficial health claims by lululemon regarding the therapeutic benefits of its VitaSea line were untrue based on independent tests. The firm's customers were angry, and some even threatened filing lawsuits against the company for making false claims. lululemon responded with independent laboratory–testing that substantiated its claims; however, later, the Competition Bureau of Canada required the firm to remove all related claims from its products. Then, in 2008, lululemon closed its operations in Japan because of weakness in that market. In 2009, it faced two high-profile class-action lawsuits from employees in the United States. Three former hourly company employees alleged that lululemon violated various California Labor Code sections by requiring employees to wear lululemon clothing during working hours without reimbursing them for the cost of the clothing and by paying certain bonus payments in the form of lululemon gift cards redeemable only for lululemon merchandise. In another case, a former hourly company employee filed a class action lawsuit and alleged that lululemon violated various California Labor Code sections by failing to pay employees for certain rest and meal breaks and "off the clock" work. lululemon settled both cases.

Looking ahead, lululemon's CEO Christine Day notes that the major challenges facing the company's management team are decisions about how many stores and showrooms to open, the balance between online and retail selling, and the best strategy for growth abroad. With a long-tem goal of expanding the firm's global footprint, senior executives must decide whether to grow by opening company-owned stores or franchises, or by acquiring or partnering with foreign firms through joint ventures. Senior executives know that partnering with companies with significant experience and proven success in the target country is to their advantage. However, they also realize that they may have to give up some control if they pursue the partnership route. For example, franchisees are independent business operators and are not lululemon employees, and the management team cannot exercise control over the day-to-day operations of their retail stores. The most they can do is provide training and support to franchisees, and set and monitor operational standards. In terms of revenue growth, lululemon's senior executives believe that the first priority remains growing existing stores, the second priority is e-commerce, and the third priority is new store openings, especially outside of North America.

Questions

1. What factors do you think are responsible for the phenomenal success of lululemon? Are the reasons for its success sustainable over the next decade?

2. Given the nature of lululemon's sourcing, manufacturing, and marketing strategies, discuss how the PEST factors could influence the company's success and performance in the future.

3. Discuss how socio-cultural considerations influence the success of lululemon.

4. Why do you think that the fallout from *The New York Times* story regarding lululemon's misleading claims was short-lived?

5. lululemon recognizes revenues in Canada in Canadian dollars but reports its worldwide revenues in U.S. dollars. Assuming that in 2013 its Canadian revenues were $500 million, what impact would a 10-percent depreciation of the Canadian dollar relative to the U.S. dollar have on the earnings it reports in U.S. dollars?

6. As stated at the end of the case, management is faced with two major decisions regarding the future of lululemon. One decision pertains to the mode of entry into new global markets (i.e., establish company-owned stores, franchises, or joint ventures). The second decision concerns where to focus its efforts for revenue growth (i.e., first at existing stores, then at e-commerce, and then at new stores). Discuss the advantages and disadvantages of the various options. What course of action would you recommend?

 Practise and learn online with Connect. Connect allows you to practise important concepts at your own pace and on your own schedule, with 24/7 online access to an eBook, practice quizzes, interactivities, videos, study tools, additional resources, and more.

glossary

*Glossary entries marked with an asterisk appear in Chapter 17, the online chapter of this book.

administered vertical marketing system A supply chain system in which there is no common ownership and no contractual relationships, but the dominant channel member controls the channel relationship.

advanced shipping notice An electronic document that the supplier sends the retailer in advance of a shipment to tell the retailer exactly what to expect in the shipment.

advertising A paid form of communication from an identifiable source, delivered through a communication channel, and designed to persuade the receiver to take some action, now or in the future.

advertising allowance Tactic of offering a price reduction to channel members if they agree to feature the manufacturer's product in their advertising and promotional efforts.

advertising plan A section of the firm's overall marketing plan that explicitly outlines the objectives of the advertising campaign, how the campaign might accomplish those objectives, and how the firm can determine whether the campaign was successful.

advertising schedule Specifies the timing and duration of advertising.

affective component A component of *attitude* that reflects what a person feels about the issue at hand—his or her like or dislike of something.

affordable method A method of determining a communications budget based on what is left over after other operating costs have been covered.

AIDA model A common model of the series of mental stages through which consumers move as a result of marketing communications: **a**wareness leads to **i**nterests, which lead to **d**esire, which leads to **a**ction.

aided recall Occurs when consumers recognize the brand when its name is presented to them.

alpha testing An attempt by the firm to determine whether a product will perform according to its design and whether it satisfies the need for which it was intended; occurs in the firm's R&D department.

associated services The nonphysical attributes of the product, including product warranties, financing, product support, and after-sale service; also called *augmented product*.

attitude A person's enduring evaluation of his or her feelings about and behavioural tendencies toward an object or idea; consists of three components: *cognitive, affective,* and *behavioural.*

augmented product See *associated services.*

autocratic buying centre A buying centre in which one person makes the decision alone, though there may be multiple participants.

B2B (business-to-business) The process of selling merchandise or services from one business to another.

B2C (business-to-consumer) The process in which businesses sell to consumers.

baby boomers Generational cohort of people born after World War II; are between the ages of 48 and 66.

bait and switch A deceptive practice of luring customers into the store with a very low advertised price on an item (the bait), only to aggressively pressure them into purchasing a higher-priced item (the switch) by disparaging the low-priced item, comparing it unfavourably with the higher-priced item, or professing an inadequate supply of the lower-priced item.

behavioural component A component of *attitude* that comprises the actions a person takes with regard to the issue at hand.

behavioural segmentation Groups consumers based on the benefits they derive from products or services, their usage rate, their user status, and their loyalty.

benefit segmentation Groups consumers based on the benefits they derive from products or services.

beta testing Having potential consumers examine a product prototype in a real-use setting to determine its functionality, performance, potential problems, and other issues specific to its use.

big-box food retailer Comes in three types: supercentre, hypermarket, and warehouse club; larger than a *conventional supermarket*; carries both food and nonfood items.

blog (weblog or Web log) A web page that contains periodic posts; corporate blogs are a new form of marketing communications.

boycott A group's refusal to deal commercially with some organization to protest against its policies.

brand The name, term, design, symbol, or any other features that identify one seller's good or service as distinct from those of other sellers.

brand association The mental links that consumers make between a brand and its key product attributes; can involve a logo, slogan, or famous personality.

brand awareness Measures how many consumers in a market are familiar with the brand and what it stands for; created through repeated exposures of the various brand elements (brand name, logo, symbol, character, packaging, or slogan) in the firm's communications to consumers.

brand dilution Occurs when a brand extension adversely affects consumer perceptions about the attributes the core brand is believed to hold.

brand equity The set of assets and liabilities linked to a brand that add to or subtract from the value provided by the product or service.

brand extension The use of the same brand name for new products being introduced to the same or new markets.

brand licensing A contractual arrangement between firms, whereby one firm allows another to use its brand name, logo, symbols, or characters in exchange for a negotiated fee.

brand loyalty Occurs when a consumer buys the same brand's product or service repeatedly over time rather than buying from multiple suppliers within the same category.

brand personality Refers to a set of human characteristics associated with a brand, which has symbolic or self-expressive meanings for consumers.

brand repositioning (rebranding) A strategy in which marketers change a brand's focus to target new markets or realign the brand's core emphasis with changing market preferences.

break-even point The point at which the number of units sold generates just enough revenue to equal the total costs; at this point, profits are zero.

breakthroughs See *pioneers.*

bricks-and-mortar retailer A traditional, physical store.

business ethics* Refers to a branch of ethical study that examines ethical rules and principles within a commercial context, the various moral or ethical problems that might arise in a business setting, and any special duties or obligations that apply to persons engaged in commerce.

business-to-business (B2B) marketing The process of buying and selling goods or services to be used in the production of other goods and services, for consumption by the buying organization, or for resale by wholesalers and retailers.

buyer The buying centre participant who handles the paperwork of the actual purchase.

buying centre The group of people typically responsible for the buying decisions in large organizations.

C2C (consumer-to-consumer) The process in which consumers sell to other consumers.

cash discount Tactic of offering a reduction in the invoice cost if the buyer pays the invoice prior to the end of the discount period.

category killer Offers an extensive assortment in a particular category, so overwhelming the category that other retailers have difficulty competing.

category specialist Offers a narrow variety but a deep assortment of merchandise.

cause-related marketing Commercial activity in which businesses and charities form a partnership to market an image, product, or service for their mutual benefit; a type of promotional campaign.

channel conflict Results when supply chain members are not in agreement about their goals, roles, or rewards.

click-through tracking Measure how many times users click on banner advertising on websites.

closing the sale Obtaining a commitment from the customer to make a purchase.

cobranding The practice of marketing two or more brands together, on the same package or promotion.

cognitive component A component of *attitude* that reflects what a person believes to be true.

cold calls A method of prospecting in which salespeople telephone or go to see potential customers without appointments.

communication channel The medium—print, broadcast, the Internet—that carries the message.

communication gap A type of *service gap*; refers to the difference between the actual service provided to customers and the service that the firm's promotion program promises.

compensatory decision rule Is at work when the consumer is evaluating alternatives and trades off one characteristic against another, such that good characteristics compensate for bad ones.

competitive intelligence (CI) Used by firms to collect and synthesize information about their position with respect to their rivals; enables companies to anticipate changes in the marketplace rather than merely react to them.

competitive parity A firm's strategy of setting prices that are similar to those of major competitors.

competitive parity method A method of determining a communications budget in which the firm's share of the communication expenses is in line with its market share.

competitor orientation A company objective based on the premise that the firm should measure itself primarily against its competition.

competitor-based pricing method An approach that attempts to reflect how the firm wants consumers to interpret its products relative to the competitors' offerings.

complementary products Products whose demand curves are positively related, such that they rise or fall together; a percentage increase in demand for one results in a percentage increase in demand for the other.

concentrated (or niche) segmentation strategy A marketing strategy of selecting a single, primary target market and focusing all energies on providing a product to fit that market's needs.

concept testing The process in which a concept statement that describes a product or a service is presented to potential buyers or users to obtain their reactions.

concepts Brief written descriptions of a product or service; its technology, working principles, and forms; and what customer needs it would satisfy.

conclusive research Provides the information needed to confirm preliminary insights, which managers can use to pursue appropriate courses of action.

consensus buying centre A buying centre in which all members of the team must reach a collective agreement that they can support a particular purchase.

consultative buying centre A buying centre in which one person makes the decision, but he or she solicits input from others before doing so.

consumer decision rules The set of criteria consumers use consciously or subconsciously to quickly and efficiently select from among several alternatives.

consumer products Products and services used by people for their personal use.

consumerism* A social movement aimed at protecting consumers from business practices that infringe upon their rights.

contest A brand-sponsored competition that requires some form of skill or effort.

continuous advertising schedule Runs steadily throughout the year and therefore is suited to products and services that are consumed continually at relatively steady rates and that require a steady level of persuasive or reminder advertising.

contractual vertical marketing system A system in which independent firms at different levels of the supply chain join together through contracts to obtain economies of scale and coordination and to reduce conflict.

contribution per unit Equals the price less the variable cost per unit; variable used to determine the break-even point in units.

control phase The part of the strategic marketing planning process when managers evaluate the performance of the marketing strategy and take any necessary corrective actions.

convenience goods/services Products or services for which the consumer is not willing to spend any effort to evaluate prior to purchase.

conventional supermarket Offers groceries, meat, and produce with limited sales of nonfood items, such as health and beauty aids and general merchandise, in a self-service format.

cooperative (co-op) advertising An agreement between a manufacturer and retailer in which the manufacturer agrees to defray some advertising costs.

core customer value The basic problem-solving benefits that consumers are seeking.

corporate and product line brands The use of a combination of family brand name and individual brand name to distinguish a firm's products.

corporate brand (family brand) The use of a firm's own corporate name to brand all of its product lines and products.

corporate social responsibility (CSR)* Refers to the voluntary actions taken by a company to address the ethical, social, and environmental impacts of its business operations and the concerns of its stakeholders.

corporate vertical marketing system A system in which the parent company has complete control and can dictate the priorities and objectives of the supply chain; it may own facilities such as manufacturing plants, warehouse facilities, retail outlets, and design studios.

cost of ownership method A value-based method for setting prices that determines the total cost of owning the product over its useful life.

cost-based pricing method Determines the final price to charge by starting with the cost, without recognizing the role that consumers or competitors' prices play in the marketplace.

countertrade Trade between two countries where goods are traded for other goods and not for hard currency.

country culture Entails easy-to-spot visible nuances that are particular to a country, such as dress, symbols, ceremonies, language, colours, and food preferences, and more subtle aspects, which are trickier to identify.

coupon Provides a stated discount to consumers on the final selling price of a specific item; the retailer handles the discount.

cross-price elasticity The percentage change in demand for Product A that occurs in response to a percentage change in price of Product B; see *complementary products*.

cross-promoting Efforts of two or more firms joining together to reach a specific target market.

cross-shopping The pattern of buying both premium and low-priced merchandise or patronizing both expensive, status-oriented retailers and price-oriented retailers.

cultural imperialism The belief that one's own culture is superior to that of other nations; can take the form of an active, formal policy or a more subtle general attitude.

culture The shared meanings, beliefs, morals, values, and customs of a group of people.

cumulative quantity discount Pricing tactic that offers a discount based on the amount purchased over a specified period and usually involves several transactions.

customer excellence Involves a focus on retaining loyal customers and excellent customer service.

customer lifetime value (CLV) The expected financial contribution from a particular customer to the firm's profits over the course of their entire relationship.

customer orientation Pricing orientation that explicitly invokes the concept of customer value and setting prices to match consumer expectations.

customer relationship management (CRM) A business philosophy and set of strategies, programs, and systems that focus on identifying and building loyalty among the firm's most valued customers.

customer service Specifically refers to human or mechanical activities firms undertake to help satisfy their customers' needs and wants.

data Raw numbers or other factual information of limited value.

deal A type of short-term price reduction that can take several forms, such as a "featured price," a price lower than the regular price; a "buy one, get one free" offer; or a certain percentage "more free" offer contained in larger packaging.

deceptive advertising A representation, omission, act, or practice in an advertisement that is likely to mislead consumers acting reasonably under the circumstances.

decider The buying centre participant who ultimately determines any part of or the entire buying decision—whether to buy, what to buy, how to buy, or where to buy.

decision heuristics Mental shortcuts that help consumers narrow down choices; examples include price, brand, and product presentation.

decline stage Stage of the product life cycle when sales decline and the product eventually exits the market.

decoding The process by which the receiver interprets the sender's message.

delivery gap A type of *service gap*; the difference between the firm's service standards and the actual service it provides to customers.

demand curve Shows how many units of a product or service consumers will demand during a specific period at different prices.

democratic buying centre A buying centre in which the majority rules in making decisions.

demographic segmentation The grouping of consumers according to easily measured, objective characteristics such as age, gender, income, and education.

demographics Characteristics of human populations and segments, especially those used to identify consumer markets, such as age, gender, income, race, ethnicity, and education.

derived demand The linkage between consumers' demand for a company's output and its purchase of necessary inputs to manufacture or assemble that particular output.

determinant attributes Product or service features that are important to the buyer and on which competing brands or stores are perceived to differ.

differentiated segmentation strategy A strategy through which a firm targets several market segments with a different offering for each.

diffusion of innovation The process by which the use of an innovation, whether a product or a service, spreads throughout a market group over time and over various categories of adopters.

direct investment When a firm maintains 100-percent ownership of its plants, operation facilities, and offices in a foreign country, often through the formation of wholly owned subsidiaries.

direct mail A targeted, printed form of communication distributed to a prospective customer's mailbox.

direct marketing Marketing that communicates directly with target customers to generate a response or transaction.

direct response TV (DRTV) TV commercials or infomercials with a strong call to action.

discount store Offers a broad variety of merchandise, limited service, and low prices.

dispatcher The person who coordinates deliveries to distribution centres.

distribution centre A facility for the receipt, storage, and redistribution of goods to company stores or customers; may be operated by retailers, manufacturers, or distribution specialists.

distribution channel The institutions that transfer the ownership of and move goods from the point of production to the point of consumption.

distribution intensity The number of channel members to use at each level of the supply chain.

distributive fairness Pertains to a customer's perception of the benefits he or she received compared with the costs (inconvenience or loss) that resulted from a service failure.

diversification strategy A growth strategy whereby a firm introduces a new product or service to a market segment that it does not currently serve.

downsizing Exiting markets, reducing product portfolios, or closing certain businesses or store or plant locations.

drugstore A specialty store that concentrates on health and personal grooming merchandise, though pharmaceuticals may represent more than 60 percent of its sales.

dumping The practice of selling a good in a foreign market at a price that is lower than its domestic price or below its cost.

duty See *tariff*.

early adopters The second group of consumers in the diffusion of innovation model, after *innovators*, to use a product or service innovation; generally don't like to take as much risk as innovators.

early majority A group of consumers in the diffusion of innovation model that represents approximately 34 percent of the population; members don't like to take much risk and therefore tend to wait until bugs are worked out.

economic situation Economic changes that affect the way consumers buy merchandise and spend money; see *inflation, foreign currency fluctuations, interest rates,* and *recession*.

elastic Refers to a market for a product or service that is price sensitive; that is, relatively small changes in price will generate fairly large changes in the quantity demanded.

electronic data interchange (EDI) The computer-to-computer exchange of business documents from a retailer to a vendor and back.

electronic media Tools ranging from simple website content to far more interactive features such as corporate blogs, online games, text messaging, social media, and mobile apps.

email A targeted, electronic form of communication distributed to a prospective customer's inbox.

emotional appeal Aims to satisfy consumers' emotional desires rather than their utilitarian needs.

empowerment In the context of service delivery, means allowing employees to make decisions about how service is provided to customers.

encoding The process of converting the sender's ideas into a message, which could be verbal, visual, or both.

English auction Goods and services are simply sold to the highest bidder.

environmental concerns Include, but are not limited to, the excessive use of natural resources and energy, refuse from manufacturing processes, excess trash created by consumer goods packages, and hard-to-dispose-of products such as tires, cellphones, and computer monitors.

esteem needs Allow people to satisfy their inner desires.

ethical climate* The set of values within a marketing firm, or in the marketing division of any firm, that guides decision making and behaviour.

ethnography An observational method that studies people in their daily lives and activities in their homes, work, and communities.

evaluative criteria Consist of a set of salient, or important, attributes about a particular product that are used to compare different alternative products.

event sponsorship A popular PR tool; occurs when corporations support various activities (financially or otherwise), usually in the cultural or sports and entertainment sectors.

everyday low pricing (EDLP) A strategy companies use to emphasize the continuity of their retail prices at a level somewhere between the regular, nonsale price and the deep-discount sale prices their competitors may offer.

exchange The trade of things of value between the buyer and the seller so that each is better off as a result.

exchange control Refers to the regulation of a country's currency *exchange rate*.

exchange rate The measure of how much one currency is worth in relation to another.

exclusive distribution Strategy of granting exclusive rights to sell to one or very few retail customers so no other customers can sell a particular brand.

exclusive geographic territories Territories granted to one or very few retail customers by a manufacturer using an exclusive distribution strategy; no other customers can sell a particular brand in these territories.

experience curve effect Refers to the drop in unit cost as the accumulated volume sold increases; as sales continue to grow, the costs continue to drop, allowing even further reductions in the price.

experimental research A type of quantitative research that systematically manipulates one or more variables to determine which variable has a causal effect on another variable.

exploratory research Attempts to begin to understand the phenomenon of interest; also provides initial information when the problem lacks any clear definition.

exporting Producing goods in one country and selling them in another.

extended problem solving A purchase decision process during which the consumer devotes considerable time and effort to analyzing alternatives; often occurs when the consumer perceives that the purchase decision entails a great deal of risk.

external locus of control Refers to when consumers believe that fate or other external factors control all outcomes.

external reference price A higher price to which the consumer can compare the selling price to evaluate the purchase.

external search for information Occurs when the buyer seeks information outside his or her personal knowledge base to help make the buying decision.

extranet A collaborative network that uses Internet technology to link businesses with their suppliers, customers, or other businesses.

extreme value retailer A general merchandise discount store found in lower-income urban or rural areas.

financial risk Risk associated with a monetary outlay; includes the initial cost of the purchase, as well as the costs of using the item or service.

first movers Product pioneers that are the first to create a market or product category, making them readily recognizable to consumers and thus establishing a commanding and early market share lead.

fixed costs Those costs that remain essentially at the same level, regardless of any changes in the volume of production.

flighting advertising schedule Implemented in spurts, with periods of heavy advertising followed by periods of no advertising.

focus group A research technique in which a small group of persons (usually 8 to 12) comes together for an intensive discussion about a particular topic, with the conversation guided by a trained moderator using an unstructured method of inquiry.

foreign currency fluctuations Changes in the value of a country's currency relative to the currency of another country; can influence consumer spending.

franchisee See *franchising*.

franchising A contractual agreement between a *franchisor* and a *franchisee* that allows the franchisee to operate a retail outlet, using a name and format developed and supported by the franchisor.

franchisor See *franchising*.

frequency Measure of how often the target audience is exposed to a communication within a specified period of time.

functional needs Pertain to the performance of a product or service.

gatekeeper The buying centre participant who controls information or access to decision makers and influencers.

General Agreement on Tariffs and Trade (GATT) Agreement established to lower trade barriers, such as high tariffs on imported goods and restrictions on the number and types of imported products that inhibited the free flow of goods across borders.

general merchandise retailer May be a *discount store, specialty store, category specialist*, department store, *drugstore, off-price retailer*, or *extreme value retailer*; may sell through multiple channels, such as the Internet and catalogues.

generation X Generational cohort of people between the ages of 36 and 47.

generation Y Generational cohort of people between the ages of 13 and 32; the biggest cohort since the original postwar baby boom.

generational cohort A group of people of the same generation—typically have similar purchase behaviours because they have shared experiences and are in the same stage of life.

generic A product sold without a brand name, typically in commodities markets.

geodemographic segmentation The grouping of consumers on the basis of a combination of geographic, demographic, and lifestyle characteristics.

geographic pricing The setting of different prices depending on a geographical division of the delivery areas.

geographic segmentation The grouping of consumers on the basis of where they live.

global labour issues Includes concerns about working conditions and wages paid to factory workers in developing countries.

globalization Refers to the increased flow of goods, services, people, technology, capital, information, and ideas around the world; has economic, political, social, cultural, and environmental impacts.

globalization of production Refers to manufacturers' procurement of goods and services from around the globe to take advantage of national differences in the cost and quality of various factors of production (e.g., labour, energy, land, capital); also known as *offshoring*.

goods Items that can be physically touched.

green marketing Involves a strategic effort by firms to supply customers with environmentally friendly merchandise.

grey market Employs irregular but not necessarily illegal methods; generally, it legally circumvents authorized channels of distribution to sell goods at prices lower than those intended by the manufacturer.

gross domestic product (GDP) The market value of the goods and services produced by a country in a year; the most widely used standardized measure of output.

gross rating points (GRP) Measure used for various media advertising—print, radio, or television; *GRP = reach × frequency*.

growth stage Stage of the product life cycle when the product gains acceptance, demand and sales increase, and competitors emerge in the product category.

habitual decision making A purchase decision process in which consumers engage with little conscious effort.

high/low pricing A *pricing strategy* that relies on the promotion of sales, during which prices are temporarily reduced to encourage purchases.

horizontal price fixing Occurs when competitors that produce and sell competing products collude, or work together, to control prices, effectively taking price out of the decision process for consumers.

human development index (HDI) A composite measure of three indicators of the quality of life in different countries: life expectancy at birth, educational attainment, and whether the average incomes are sufficient to meet the basic needs of life in that country.

hypothesis A statement or proposition predicting a particular relationship among multiple variables that can be tested through research.

ideal point The position at which a particular market segment's ideal product would lie on a *perceptual map*.

ideas Include thoughts, opinions, philosophies, and intellectual concepts.

implementation phase Where marketing managers identify and evaluate different opportunities by engaging in a process known as segmentation, targeting, and positioning. They then develop and implement the marketing mix by using the four Ps.

improvement value Represents an estimate of how much more (or less) consumers are willing to pay for a product relative to other comparable products.

impulse buying A buying decision made by customers on the spot when they see the merchandise.

income effect Refers to the change in the quantity of a product demanded by consumers because of a change in their income.

inconsistent A characteristic of a service: its quality may vary because it is provided by humans.

independent agents Salespeople who sell a manufacturer's products on an extended contract basis but are not employees of the manufacturer; also known as *manufacturer's representatives* or *reps*.

in-depth interview A research technique in which trained researchers ask questions, listen to and record the answers, and then pose additional questions to clarify or expand on a particular issue.

individual brands The use of individual brand names for each of a firm's products.

inelastic Refers to a market for a product or service that is price insensitive; that is, relatively small changes in price will not generate large changes in the quantity demanded.

inflation Refers to the persistent increase in the prices of goods and services.

influencer The buying centre participant whose views influence other members of the buying centre in making the final decision.

information Data that has been organized, analyzed, interpreted, and converted into a useful form for decision makers.

informative advertising Communication used to create and build brand awareness, with the ultimate goal of moving the consumer through the buying cycle to a purchase.

infrastructure The basic facilities, services, and installations needed for a community or society to function, such as transportation and communications systems, water and power lines, and public institutions like schools, post offices, and prisons.

initiator The buying centre participant who first suggests buying the particular product or service.

innovation The process by which ideas are transformed into new products and services that will help firms grow.

innovators Those buyers who want to be the first to have the new product or service.

inseparable A characteristic of a service: it is produced and consumed at the same time—that is, service and consumption are inseparable.

institutional advertisements Used to inform, persuade, and remind consumers about issues related to places, politics, an industry, or a particular corporation.

intangible A characteristic of a service; it cannot be touched, tasted, or seen like a pure product can.

integrated marketing communications (IMC) Represents the promotion dimension of the four Ps; encompasses a variety of communication disciplines—general advertising, personal selling, sales promotion, public relations, direct marketing, and electronic media—in combination to provide clarity, consistency, and maximum communicative impact.

intensive distribution A strategy designed to get products into as many outlets as possible.

interest rates Represent the cost of borrowing money.

internal locus of control Refers to when consumers believe they have some control over the outcomes of their actions, in which case they generally engage in more search activities.

internal reference price Price information stored in the consumer's memory that the person uses to assess a current price offering—perhaps the last price he or she paid or what he or she expects to pay.

internal search for information Occurs when the buyer examines his or her own memory and knowledge about the product or service, gathered through past experiences.

International Monetary Fund (IMF) Established with the original *General Agreement on Tariffs and Trade (GATT)*; primary purpose is to promote international monetary cooperation and facilitate the expansion and growth of international trade.

introduction stage Stage of the product life cycle when innovators start buying the product.

Inventory A characteristic of a service: it is perishable and cannot be stored for future use.

involvement The consumer's degree of interest or concern in the product or service.

joint venture Formed when a firm entering a new market pools its resources with those of a local firm to form a new company in which ownership, control, and profits are shared.

just-in-time (JIT) inventory systems Inventory management systems designed to deliver less merchandise on a more frequent basis than traditional inventory systems; the firm gets the merchandise "just in time" for it to be used in the manufacture of another product; also known as *quick response (QR)* systems in retailing.

knowledge gap A type of *service gap*; reflects the difference between customers' expectations and the firm's perception of those expectations.

laggards Consumers who like to avoid change and rely on traditional products until they are no longer available.

lagged effect A delayed response to a marketing communication campaign.

late majority The last group of buyers to enter a new product market.

lead time The amount of time between the recognition that an order needs to be placed and the arrival of the needed merchandise at the seller's store, ready for sale.

lead users Innovative product users who modify existing products according to their own ideas to suit their specific needs.

leader pricing Consumer pricing tactic that attempts to build store traffic by aggressively pricing and advertising a regularly purchased item, often priced at or just above the store's cost.

leads A list of potential customers.

learning Refers to a change in a person's thought process or behaviour that arises from experience and takes place throughout the consumer decision process.

lifestyles Refers to the way a person lives his or her life to achieve goals; a component of *psychographics*.

limited problem solving Occurs during a purchase decision that calls for, at most, a moderate amount of effort and time.

listing allowances Fees paid to retailers simply to get new products into stores or to gain more or better shelf space for their products.

locational excellence Involves a focus on a good physical location and Internet presence

logistics management The integration of two or more activities for the purpose of planning, implementing, and controlling the efficient flow of raw materials, in-process inventory, and finished goods from the point of origin to the point of consumption.

loss leader pricing Loss leader pricing takes the tactic of *leader pricing* one step further by lowering the price below the store's cost.

love (social) needs Relate to our interactions with others.

loyalty program Specifically designed to retain customers by offering premiums or other incentives to customers who make multiple purchases over time.

loyalty segmentation Strategy of investing in retention and loyalty initiatives to retain the firm's most profitable customers.

macroenvironmental factors Aspects of the external environment—culture, demographics, social trends, technological advances, economic situation, and political/legal environment (CDSTEP)—that affect companies.

manufacturer brands (national brands) Brands owned and managed by the manufacturer.

manufacturer's representative See *independent agents*.

markdowns Reductions retailers take on the initial selling price of the product or service.

market Refers to the groups of people who need or want a company's products or services and have the ability and willingness to buy them.

market development strategy A growth strategy that employs the existing marketing offering to reach new market segments, whether domestic or international or segments not currently served by the firm.

market growth rate The annual rate of growth of the specific market in which the product competes.

market penetration pricing A pricing strategy of setting the initial price low for the introduction of the new product or service, with the objective of building sales, market share, and profits quickly.

market penetration strategy A growth strategy that employs the existing marketing mix and focuses the firm's efforts on existing customers.

market positioning Involves the process of defining the marketing mix variables so that target customers have a clear, distinct, desirable understanding of what the product does or represents in comparison with competing products.

market segment A group of consumers who respond similarly to a firm's marketing efforts.

market segmentation The process of dividing the market into distinct groups of customers where each individual group has similar needs, wants, or characteristics—who therefore might appreciate products or services geared especially for them in similar ways.

marketing A set of business practices designed to plan for and present an organization's products or services in ways that build effective customer relationships.

marketing ethics* Refers to those ethical problems that are specific to the domain of marketing.

marketing mix (four Ps) Product, price, place, and promotion—the controllable set of activities that a firm uses to respond to the wants of its target markets.

marketing plan A written document composed of an analysis of the current marketing situation, opportunities and threats for the firm, marketing objectives and strategy specified in terms of the four Ps, action programs, and projected or pro forma income (and other financial) statements.

marketing planning process A set of steps a marketer goes through to develop a marketing plan.

marketing research A set of techniques and principles for systematically collecting, recording, analyzing, and interpreting data that can aid decision makers involved in marketing goods, services, or ideas.

marketing strategy Identifies a firm's target market(s), a related marketing mix—the four Ps, and the bases upon which the firm plans to build a sustainable competitive advantage.

mass customization The practice of interacting on a one-to-one basis with many people to create custom-made products or services; providing one-to-one marketing to the masses.

mass media Channels, such as national newspapers, magazines, radio, and television, that are ideal for reaching large numbers of anonymous audience members.

maturity stage Stage of the product life cycle when industry sales reach their peak, so firms try to rejuvenate their products by adding new features or repositioning them.

maximizing profits strategy A mathematical model that captures all the factors required to explain and predict sales and profits, which should be able to identify the price at which its profits are maximized.

media buy The actual purchase of airtime or print pages.

media mix The combination of the media used and the frequency of advertising in each medium.

media planning The process of evaluating and selecting the *media mix* that will deliver a clear, consistent, compelling message to the intended audience.

micromarketing An extreme form of segmentation that tailors a product or service to suit an individual customer's wants or needs; also called *one-to-one marketing*.

mission statement A broad description of a firm's objectives and the scope of activities it plans to undertake; attempts to answer two main questions: What type of business is it? and What does it need to do to accomplish its goals and objectives?

modified rebuy Refers to when the buyer has purchased a similar product in the past but has decided to change some specifications, such as the desired price, quality level, customer service level, and options.

monopolistic competition Occurs when many firms sell closely related but not homogeneous products; these products may be viewed as substitutes but are not perfect substitutes.

monopoly Occurs when only one firm provides the product or service in an particular industry.

motive A need or want that is strong enough to cause the person to seek satisfaction.

multichannel retailers Retailers that sell merchandise in more than one retail channel (e.g., store, catalogue, and Internet).

multichannel strategy Selling in more than one channel (e.g., store, catalogue, kiosk, and Internet).

need A person feeling physiologically deprived of basic necessities, such as food, clothing, shelter, and safety.

need recognition The beginning of the consumer decision process; occurs when consumers recognize they have an unsatisfied need and want to go from their actual, needy state to a different, desired state.

negative word of mouth Occurs when consumers spread negative information about a product, service, or store to others.

new buy In a B2B setting, a purchase of a good or service for the first time; the buying decision is likely to be quite involved because the buyer or the buying organization does not have any experience with the item.

niche media Channels that are focused and generally used to reach narrow segments, often with unique demographic characteristics or interests.

noise Any interference that stems from competing messages, a lack of clarity in the message, or a flaw in the medium; a problem for all communication channels.

noncompensatory decision rule Is at work when consumers choose a product or service on the basis of a subset of its characteristics, regardless of the values of its other attributes.

noncumulative quantity discount Pricing tactic that offers a discount based on only the amount purchased in a single order.

North American Industry Classification System (NAICS) codes A classification scheme that categorizes all firms into a hierarchical set of six-digit codes.

objective-and-task method An IMC budgeting method that determines the cost required to undertake specific tasks to accomplish communication objectives; process entails setting objectives, choosing media, and determining costs.

observation An exploratory research method that entails examining purchase and consumption behaviours through personal or video camera scrutiny.

odd prices Prices that end in odd numbers, usually 9, such as $3.99.

off-price retailer A type of retailer that offers an inconsistent assortment of merchandise at relatively low prices.

offshoring See *globalization of production*.

oligopolistic competition Occurs when only a few firms dominate a market.

one-to-one marketing See *micromarketing*.

operational excellence Involves focus on efficient operations and excellent supply chain management.

organizational culture Reflects the set of values, traditions, and customs that guides a firm's employees' behaviour.

panel research A type of quantitative research that involves collecting information from a group of consumers (the panel) over time; data collected may be from a survey or a record of purchases.

perceived value The relationship between a product or service's benefits and its cost.

percentage-of-sales method A method of determining a communications budget that is based on a fixed percentage of forecasted sales.

perception The process by which people select, organize, and interpret information to form a meaningful picture of the world.

perceptual map Displays, in two or more dimensions, the position of products or brands in the consumer's mind.

performance risk Involves the perceived danger inherent in a poorly performing product or service.

personal selling The two-way flow of communication between a buyer and a seller that is designed to influence the buyer's purchase decision.

persuasive advertising Communication used to motivate consumers to take action.

physiological needs Relate to the basic biological necessities of life: food, drink, rest, and shelter.

physiological (safety) risk Risk associated with the fear of an actual harm should the product not perform properly.

pioneers New product introductions that establish a completely new market or radically change both the rules of competition and consumer preferences in a market; also called *breakthroughs*.

planning phase Where marketing executives and other top managers define the mission and objectives of the business, and evaluate the situation by assessing how various players, both inside and outside the organization, affect the firm's potential for success.

point-of-purchase (POP) display A merchandise display located at the point of purchase, such as at the checkout counter in a grocery store.

political/legal environment Comprises political parties, government organizations, and legislation and laws that promote or inhibit trade and marketing activities.

pop-up stores Temporary storefronts that exist for only a limited time and generally focus on a new product or a limited group of products offered by a retailer, manufacturer, or service provider; give consumers a chance to interact with the brand and build brand awareness.

positioning The mental picture that people have about a company and its products or services relative to competitors.

positioning statement Expresses how a company wants to be perceived by consumers.

postpurchase dissonance An internal conflict that arises from an inconsistency between two beliefs, or between beliefs and behaviour; buyer's remorse.

posttesting The evaluation of an IMC campaign's impact after it has been implemented.

preapproach In the personal selling process, occurs prior to meeting the customer for the first time and extends the qualification of leads procedure; in this step, the salesperson conducts additional research and develops plans for meeting with the customer.

predatory pricing A firm's practice of setting a very low price for one or more of its products with the intent of driving its competition out of business; illegal under the Competition Act.

premarket test Conducted before a product or service is brought to market to determine how many customers will try and then continue to use it.

premium An item offered for free or at a bargain price to reward some type of behaviour, such as buying, sampling, or testing.

premium pricing A competitor-based pricing method by which the firm deliberately prices a product above the prices set for competing products to capture those consumers who always shop for the best or for whom price does not matter.

prestige products or services Those that consumers purchase for status rather than functionality.

pretesting Assessments performed before an ad campaign is implemented to ensure that the various elements are working in an integrated fashion and doing what they are intended to do.

price The overall sacrifice a consumer is willing to make—money, time, energy—to acquire a specific product or service.

price bundling Consumer pricing tactic of selling more than one product for a single, lower price than what the items would cost sold separately; can be used to sell slow-moving items, to encourage customers to stock up so they won't purchase competing brands, to encourage trial of a new product, or to provide an incentive to purchase a less desirable product or service to obtain a more desirable one in the same bundle.

price discrimination The practice of selling the same product to different resellers (wholesalers, distributors, or retailers) or to the ultimate consumer at different prices; some, but not all, forms of price discrimination are illegal.

price elasticity of demand Measures how changes in a price affect the quantity of the product demanded; specifically, the ratio of the percentage change in quantity demanded to the percentage change in price.

price fixing The practice of colluding with other firms to control prices.

price lining Consumer market pricing tactic of establishing a price floor and a price ceiling for an entire line of similar products and then setting a few other price points in between to represent distinct differences in quality.

price skimming A strategy of selling a new product or service at a high price that *innovators* and *early adopters* are willing to pay to obtain it; after the high-price market segment becomes saturated and sales begin to slow down, the firm generally lowers the price to capture (or skim) the next most price-sensitive segment.

price war Occurs when two or more firms compete primarily by lowering their prices.

pricing tactics Short-term methods, in contrast to long-term pricing strategies, used to focus on company objectives, customers, costs, competition, or channel members; can be responses to competitive threats (e.g., lowering price temporarily to meet a competitor's price reduction) or broadly accepted methods of calculating a final price for the customer that is short term in nature.

primary data Data collected to address the specific research needs/questions currently under investigation. Some primary data collection methods include focus groups, in-depth interviews, and surveys.

private exchange Occurs when a specific firm, either buyer or seller, invites others to join to participate in online information exchanges and transactions; can help streamline procurement or distribution processes.

private-label brands (store brands) Brands developed and marketed by a retailer and available only from that retailer.

procedural fairness Refers to the customer's perception of the fairness of the process used to resolve complaints about service.

product Anything that is of value to a consumer and can be offered through a marketing exchange.

product category An assortment of items that the customer sees as reasonable substitutes for one another.

product design See *product development*.

product development Entails a process of balancing various engineering, manufacturing, marketing, and economic considerations to develop a product; also called *product design*.

product development strategy A growth strategy that offers a new product or service to a firm's current target market.

product excellence Involves a focus on achieving high-quality products and effective branding and positioning.

product life cycle Defines the stages that new products move through as they enter, get established in, and ultimately leave the marketplace and thereby offers marketers a starting point for their strategy planning.

product line A group of products that consumers may use together or perceive as similar in some way.

product line breadth The number of product lines, or variety, offered by the firm.

product line depth The number of categories within a product line.

product lines Groups of associated items, such as those that consumers use together or think of as part of a group of similar products.

product mix The complete set of all products offered by a firm.

product placement Inclusion of a product in nontraditional situations, such as in a scene in a movie or TV program.

product-focused advertisements Used to inform, persuade, or remind consumers about a specific product or service.

profit orientation A company objective that can be implemented by focusing on *target profit pricing*, *maximizing profits*, or *target return pricing*.

projective technique A type of qualitative research in which subjects are provided a scenario and asked to express their thoughts and feelings about it.

prototype The first physical form or service description of a new product, still in rough or tentative form, that has the same properties as a new product but is produced through different manufacturing processes, sometimes even crafted individually.

psychographics This segmentation base delves into how consumers describe themselves; allows people to describe themselves by using those characteristics that help them choose how they occupy their time (behaviour) and what underlying psychological reasons determine those choices.

psychological needs Pertain to the personal gratification consumers associate with a product or service.

psychological risk Associated with the way people will feel if the product or service does not convey the right image.

PSYTE clusters The grouping of all neighbourhoods in Canada into 60 different lifestyles clusters.

public relations (PR) The organizational function that manages the firm's communications to achieve a variety of objectives, including building and maintaining a positive image, handling or heading off unfavourable stories or events, and maintaining positive relationships with the media.

public service advertising (PSA) Advertising that focuses on public welfare and generally is sponsored by nonprofit institutions, civic groups, religious organizations, trade associations, or political groups; a form of *social marketing*.

puffery The legal exaggeration of praise, stopping just short of deception, lavished on a product.

pull strategy Designed to get consumers to pull the product into the supply chain by demanding retailers carry it.

pulsing advertising schedule Combines the continuous and flighting schedules by maintaining a base level of advertising but increasing advertising intensity during certain periods.

purchasing power parity (PPP) A theory that states that if the exchange rates of two countries are in equilibrium, a product purchased in one will cost the same in the other, expressed in the same currency.

pure competition Occurs when different companies sell commodity products that consumers perceive as substitutable; price usually is set according to the laws of supply and demand.

push strategy Designed to increase demand by focusing on wholesalers, distributors, or salespeople, who push the product to consumers via distribution channels.

qualify The process of assessing the potential of sales leads.

quantity discount Pricing tactic of offering a reduced price according to the amount purchased; the more the buyer purchases, the higher the discount and, of course, the greater the value.

quick response (QR) An inventory management system used in retailing; merchandise is received just in time for sale when the customer wants it; see *just-in-time (JIT) inventory systems*.

quota Designates the maximum quantity of a product that may be brought into a country during a specified time period.

radio frequency identification (RFID) tags Tiny computer chips that automatically transmit to a special scanner all the information about a container's contents or individual products.

rational appeals Help consumers make purchase decisions by offering factual information and strong arguments built around relevant issues that encourage consumers to evaluate the brand favourably on the basis of the key benefits it provides.

reach Measure of consumers' exposure to marketing communications; the percentage of the target population exposed to a specific marketing communication, such as an advertisement, at least once.

rebate A consumer discount in which a portion of the purchase price is returned to the buyer in cash; the manufacturer, not the retailer, issues the refund.

receiver The person who reads, hears, or sees and processes the information contained in the message or advertisement.

recession A period of economic downturn when the economic growth of the country is negative for at least a couple of consecutive quarters.

reference group One or more persons an individual uses as a basis for comparison regarding beliefs, feelings, and behaviours.

reference price The price against which buyers compare the actual selling price of the product and that facilitates their evaluation process.

relational orientation A method of building a relationship with customers based on the philosophy that buyers and sellers should develop a long-term relationship.

relationship selling A sales philosophy and process that emphasizes a commitment to maintaining the relationship over the long term and investing in opportunities that are mutually beneficial to all parties.

relative market share A measure of the product's strength in a particular market, defined as the sales of the focal product divided by the sales achieved by the largest firm in the industry.

reliability The extent to which the same result is achieved when a study is repeated under identical situations.

reminder advertising Communication used to remind consumers of a product or to prompt repurchases, especially for products that have gained market acceptance and are in the maturity stage of their life cycle.

reps See *independent agents*.

request for proposals (RFP) A process through which buying organizations invite alternative suppliers to bid on supplying their required components.

resellers Marketing intermediaries that resell manufactured products without significantly altering their form.

retailers Sell products directly to consumers.

retailing The set of business activities that add value to products and services sold to consumers for their personal or family use; includes products bought at stores, through catalogues, and over the Internet, as well as services such as fast-food restaurants, airlines, and hotels.

reverse auction The buyer provides specifications to a group of sellers, who then bid down the price until the buyer accepts a specific bid.

reverse engineering Involves taking apart a competitor's product, analyzing it, and creating an improved product that does not infringe on the competitor's patents, if any exist.

ritual consumption Refers to a pattern of behaviours tied to life events that affect what and how people consume.

safety needs Pertain to protection and physical well-being.

sales management Involves the planning, direction, and control of personal selling activities, including recruiting, selecting, training, motivating, compensating, and evaluating, as they apply to the sales force.

sales orientation A company objective based on the belief that increasing sales will help the firm more than will increasing profits.

sales promotions Special incentives or excitement-building programs that encourage the purchase of a product or service, such as coupons, rebates, contests, free samples, and point-of-purchase displays.

sample A segment or subset of the population that adequately represents the entire population of interest.

sampling The process of picking a sample; offers potential customers the opportunity to try a product or service before they make a buying decision.

scanner research A type of quantitative research that uses data obtained from scanner readings of UPC codes at checkout counters.

seasonal discount Pricing tactic of offering an additional reduction as an incentive to retailers to order merchandise in advance of the normal buying season.

secondary data Pieces of information that have been collected prior to the start of the focal project.

selective distribution Lies between the intensive and exclusive distribution strategies; uses a few selected customers in a territory.

self-actualization Occurs when you feel completely satisfied with your life and how you live.

self-concept The image a person has of himself or herself; a component of *psychographics*.

self-values Goals for life, not just the goals one wants to accomplish in a day; a component of *psychographics* that refers to overriding desires that drive how a person lives his or her life.

sender The firm from which an IMC message originates; the sender must be clearly identified to the intended audience.

seniors North America's fastest-growing generational cohort; people aged 65 and older.

service gap Results when a service fails to meet the expectations that customers have about how it should be delivered.

service quality Customers' perceptions of how well a service meets or exceeds their expectations.

services Intangible customer benefits that are produced by people or machines and cannot be separated from the producer.

share of wallet The percentage of the customer's purchases made from a particular retailer.

shopping goods/services Products or services, such as apparel, fragrances, and appliances, for which consumers will spend time comparing alternatives.

situation analysis Is the second step in a marketing plan; uses a SWOT analysis that assesses both the internal environment with regard to its **s**trengths and **w**eaknesses and the external environment in terms of its **o**pportunities and **t**hreats.

situational factors Factors affecting the consumer decision process; those that are specific to the purchase and shopping situation and temporal state that may override, or at least influence, psychological and social issues.

size discount The most common implementation of a quantity discount at the consumer level; the larger the quantity bought, the less the cost per unit (e.g., per gram).

social marketing The application of marketing principles to a social issue to bring about attitudinal and behavioural change among the general public or a specific population segment.

social media The use of Internet tools to easily and quickly create and share content to foster dialogue, social relationships, and personal identities.

social needs Relate to one's interactions with others.

specialty goods/services Products or services toward which the customer shows a strong preference and for which he or she will expend considerable effort to search for the best suppliers.

specialty store Concentrates on a limited number of complementary merchandise categories in a relatively small store.

standards gap A type of *service gap*; pertains to the difference between the firm's perceptions of customers' expectations and the service standards it sets.

stealth marketing A strategy used to attract consumers that employs promotional tactics which deliver a sales message in unconventional ways, often without the target audience knowing that the message even has a selling intent.

stock keeping units (SKUs) Individual items within each product category; the smallest unit available for inventory control.

store brands See *private-label brands*.

STP The processes of segmentation, targeting, and positioning that firms use to identify and evaluate opportunities for increasing sales and profits.

straight rebuy Refers to when the buyer or buying organization simply buys additional units of products that had previously been purchased.

strategic alliance A collaborative relationship between independent firms, though the partnering firms do not create an equity partnership; that is, they do not invest in one another.

strategic business unit (SBU) A division of the company that can be managed somewhat independently from other divisions a division of the company that can be managed somewhat independently from other divisions since it markets a specific set of products to a clearly defined group of customers.

strategic relationship (partnering relationship) A supply chain relationship that the members are committed to maintaining long term, investing in opportunities that are mutually beneficial; requires mutual trust, open communication, common goals, and credible commitments.

structured questions Closed-ended questions for which a discrete set of response alternatives, or specific answers, is provided for respondents to evaluate.

substitute products Products for which changes in demand are negatively related—that is, a percentage increase in the quantity demanded for Product A results in a percentage decrease in the quantity demanded for Product B.

substitution effect Refers to consumers' ability to substitute other products for the focal brand, thus increasing the price elasticity of demand for the focal brand.

supply chain The group of firms and set of techniques and approaches firms use to make and deliver a given set of goods and services.

supply chain conflict (channel conflict) Results when supply chain members are not in agreement about their goals, roles, or rewards.

supply chain management Refers to a set of approaches and techniques firms employ to efficiently and effectively integrate their suppliers, manufacturers, warehouses, stores, and transportation intermediaries into a seamless value chain in which merchandise is produced and distributed in the right quantities, to the right locations, and at the right time.

survey A systematic means of collecting information from people that generally uses a *questionnaire*.

sustainable competitive advantage Something the firm can persistently do better than its competitors that is not easily copied and thus can be maintained over a long period of time.

sweepstakes A form of sales promotion that offers prizes based on a chance drawing of entrants' names.

syndicated data Data available for a fee from commercial research firms such as SymphonyIRI Group, National Purchase Diary Panel, Nielsen, and Leger Marketing.

target market The customer segment or group to whom the firm is interested in selling its products and services.

target marketing/targeting The process of evaluating the attractiveness of various segments and then deciding which to pursue as a market.

target profit pricing A pricing strategy implemented by firms when they have a particular profit goal as their overriding concern; uses price to stimulate a certain level of sales at a certain profit per unit.

target return pricing A pricing strategy implemented by firms less concerned with the absolute level of profits and more interested in the rate at which their profits are generated relative to their investments; designed to produce a specific return on investment, usually expressed as a percentage of sales.

tariff A tax levied on a good imported into a country; also called a *duty*.

technological advances Technological changes that have contributed to the improvement of the value of both products and services in the past few decades.

telemarketing A method of prospecting in which salespeople telephone potential customers.

test marketing Introduces a new product or service to a limited geographical area (usually a few cities) prior to a national launch.

top-of-mind awareness A prominent place in people's memories that triggers a response without them having to put any thought into it.

total cost The sum of the *variable* and *fixed costs*.

tracking Includes monitoring key indicators, such as daily or weekly sales volume, while the advertisement is running to shed light on any problems with the message or the medium.

trade agreement Intergovernmental agreement designed to manage and promote trade activities for specific regions.

trade deficit Results when a country imports more goods than it exports.

trade sanctions Penalties or restrictions imposed by one country over another country for importing and exporting of goods, services, and investments.

trade shows Major events attended by buyers who choose to be exposed to products and services offered by potential suppliers in an industry.

trade surplus Results when a country exports more goods than it imports.

trading bloc Consists of those countries that have signed a particular trade agreement.

transactional orientation Regards the buyer–seller relationship as a series of individual transactions, so anything that happened before or after the transaction is of little importance.

transmitter An agent or intermediary with which the sender works to develop the marketing communications; for example, a firm's creative department or an advertising agency.

tweens Generational cohort of people who are not quite teenagers but are not young children either (ages 9 to 12); they're in beTWEEN.

undifferentiated segmentation strategy (mass marketing) A marketing strategy a firm can use if the product or service is perceived to provide the same benefits to everyone, with no need to develop separate strategies for different groups.

uniform delivered pricing The shipper charges one rate, no matter where the buyer is located.

unique selling proposition (USP) A strategy of differentiating a product by communicating its unique attributes; often becomes the common theme or slogan in the entire advertising campaign.

universal product code (UPC) The black and white bar code found on most merchandise.

unsought product/services Products or services consumers either do not normally think of buying or do not know about.

unstructured questions Open-ended questions that allow respondents to answer in their own words.

user The person who consumes or uses the product or service purchased by the buying centre.

validity The extent to which a study measures what it is supposed to measure.

value Reflects the relationship of benefits to costs, or what the consumer *gets* for what he or she *gives*.

VALS™ A psychographical tool offered by Strategic Business Insights that classifies consumers into eight segments: innovators, thinkers, believers, achievers, strivers, experiencers, makers, or survivors.

value-based marketing Focuses on providing customers with benefits that far exceed the cost (money, time, effort) of acquiring and using a product or service while providing a reasonable return to the firm.

value-based pricing method An approach that focuses on the overall value of the product offering as perceived by consumers, who determine value by comparing the benefits they expect the product to deliver with the sacrifice they will need to make to acquire the product.

variable costs Those costs, primarily labour and materials, which vary with production volume.

vertical marketing system A supply chain in which the members act as a unified system; there are three types: *administrated*, *contractual*, and *corporate*.

vertical price fixing Occurs when parties at different levels of the same marketing channel (e.g., manufacturers and retailers) collude to control the prices passed on to consumers.

viral marketing A marketing phenomenon that encourages people to pass along a marketing message to other potential consumers.

voice-of-customer (VOC) program An ongoing marketing research system that collects customer insights and intelligence to influence and drive business decisions.

want The particular way in which a person chooses to satisfy a need, which is shaped by a person's knowledge, culture, and personality.

wholesalers Those firms engaged in buying, taking title to, often storing, and physically handling goods in large quantities, and then reselling the goods (usually in smaller quantities) to retailers or industrial or business users.

World Bank Group A development bank that provides loans, policy advice, technical assistance, and knowledge-sharing services to low- and middle-income countries in an attempt to reduce poverty in the developing world.

World Trade Organization (WTO) Replaced the GATT in 1994; differs from the GATT in that the WTO is an established institution based in Geneva, Switzerland, instead of simply an agreement; represents the only international organization that deals with the global rules of trade among nations.

zone of tolerance The area between customers' expectations regarding their desired service and the minimum level of acceptable service—that is, the difference between what the customer really wants and what he or she will accept before going elsewhere.

endnotes

Chapter 1

1. Information for this chapter vignette was gathered from Research In Motion's annual reports, 2001–2011, which are available on the company's website, www.rim.net (accessed April 22, 2011).

2. Geoff Duncan, "Android Gains Smartphone Market Share Through January," www.digitaltrends.com/mobile/android-gains-smartphone-market-share-through-january/ (accessed May 20, 2010).

3. Marguerite Reardon, "RIM's strategy to stay on top in smartphones," http://news.cnet.com/8301-30686_3-20004753-266.html (accessed May 15, 2010).

4. Christine Persaud, "Smartphones to Reach 300M by 2013," www.marketnews.ca/content/index/page?pid=5573 (accessed May 20, 2010); LuAnn LaSalle, "Canadians increasingly migrating to smartphones," www.theglobeandmail.com/news/technology/canadians-increasingly-migrating-to-smartphones/article1245184/ (accessed May 15, 2010).

5. comScore, "Mobile Device Popularity Surges," www.marketingcharts.com/interactive/mobile-device-popularity-surges-12020/comscore-smartphone-penetration-marketshare-feb-2010jpg/ (accessed May 20, 2010).

6. The Canadian Marketing Association, www.the-cma.org (accessed December 17, 2007). More discussion on marketing is provided by Stephen L. Vargo and Robert F. Lusch, "Evolving to a New Dominant Logic for Marketing," *Journal of Marketing* 68 (January 2004), pp. 1–17; and George S. Day, John Deighton, Das Narayandas, Evert Gummesson, Shelby D. Hunt, C.K. Prahalad, Roland T. Rust, and Steven M. Shugan, "Invited Commentaries on 'Evolving to a New Dominant Logic for Marketing,'" *Journal of Marketing* 68 (January 2004), pp. 18–27. Also see W. Stephen Brown et al., "Marketing Renaissance: Opportunities and Imperatives for Improving Marketing Thought, Practice, and Infrastructure," *Journal of Marketing*, 69, no. 4 (2005), pp. 1–25.

7. The idea of the four Ps was conceptualized by E. Jerome McCarthy, *Basic Marketing: A Managerial Approach* (Homewood, IL: Richard D. Irwin, 1960). Also see Walter van Watershoot and Christophe Van den Bulte, "The 4P Classification of the Marketing Mix Revisited," *Journal of Marketing* 56 (October 1992), pp. 83–93.

8. www.bottledwaterweb.com (accessed April 22, 2011).

9. Bottled Water Free Campus, www.sustainable.uottawa.ca/index.php?module=CMS&id=52 (accessed August 5, 2010).

10. Based on David Simchi-Levi, Philip Kaminsky, and Edith Simchi-Levi, *Designing and Managing the Supply Chain: Concepts, Strategies and Case Studies*, 2nd ed. (New York: McGraw-Hill/Irwin, 2003); and Michael Levy and Barton A. Weitz, *Retailing Management*, 6th ed. (New York: McGraw-Hill/Irwin, 2007).

11. Interview with president of The Country Grocer, Ottawa, Ontario; Lisa Morrison, *EMBA Consulting Report*, University of Ottawa, 2006.

12. "Toyota Plans European Shutdown," www.cbc.ca/news/business/story/2011/04/13/business-toyoa-europe.html (accessed April 22, 2011); "Toyota Faces Vehicles Shortage, U.S. Dealers Told," www.cbc.ca/news/business/story/2011/04/11/business-toyota-vehicles.html (accessed April 22, 2011).

13. "How companies manage sustainability: McKinsey Global Survey Results," www.mckinseyquarterly.com/How_companies_manage_sustainability_McKinsey_Global_Survey_results__2558 (accessed April 22, 2011).

14. "What is Social Media? A not so critical review of concepts and definitions," http://blog.metaroll.com/2008/11/14/what-is-social-media-a-not-so-critical-review-of-concepts-and-definitions/ (accessed April 22, 2011); Joseph Thornley, "Social Media isn't just about Facebook," www.itworldcanada.com/blogs/ahead/2009/04/08/social-networking-isnt-just-about-facebook/48460/ (accessed April 22, 2011); Joseph Thornley, "What is Social Media?" http://propr.ca/2008/what-is-social-media/ (accessed April 22, 2011).

15. comScore, "Social Media Usage," 2009, www.comscore.com.

16. Websites such as www.whymilk.com and www.milkdelivers.org/campaign/index.cfm provide examples of this popular campaign.

17. George S. Day, "Aligning the Organization with the Market," *Marketing Science Institute* 5, no. 3 (2005), pp. 3–20.

18. Dhruv Grewal, Kent B. Monroe, and R. Krishnan, "The Effects of Price Comparison Advertising on Buyers' Perceptions of Acquisition Value and Transaction Value," *Journal of Marketing* 62 (April 1998), pp. 46–60; Kent B. Monroe, *Pricing: Making Profitable Decisions*, 3rd ed. (New York: McGraw-Hill, 2004).

19. www.carmencreek.com/index.shtml (accessed August 4, 2010); www.ic.gc.ca/app/ccc/srch/nvgt.do?lang=eng&prtl=1&sbPrtl=&estblmntNo=234567058950&profile=cmpltPrfl&profileId=501&app=sold (accessed August 4, 2010); www.newswire.ca/en/releases/archive/February2008/27/c6491.html (accessed August 4, 2010); www.bilawchuk.com/portfolio/SBW_magazine Final Final Final Proof 0912.pdf (accessed August 4, 2010).

20. Shelley Emling, "Low-Cost Flying No Longer Just a U.S. Sensation," *Atlanta Journal* December 26, 2003: F1.

21. In 2005, the *Journal of Marketing* ran a special section entirely devoted to relationship marketing. The section included these articles: William Boulding et al., "A Customer Relationship Management Roadmap: What Is Known, Potential Pitfalls, and Where to Go," *Journal of Marketing* 69, no. 4 (2005), pp. 155–166; Jacquelyn S. Thomas and Ursula Y. Sullivan, "Managing Marketing Communications with Multichannel Customers," *Journal of Marketing* 69, no. 4 (2005), pp. 239–251; Lynette Ryals, "Making Customer Relationship Management Work: The Measurement and Profitable Management of Customer Relationships," *Journal of Marketing* 69, no. 4 (2005), pp. 252–261; and Martha Rogers, "Customer Strategy: Observations from the Trenches," *Journal of Marketing* 69 no. 4 (2005), pp. 262–263.

22. Rajendra K. Srivastava, Tasadduq A. Shervani, and Liam Fahey, "Marketing, Business Processes, and Shareholder Value: An Embedded View of Marketing Activities and the Discipline of Marketing," *Journal of Marketing* 63 (special issue, 1999), pp. 168–179; R. Venkatesan and V. Kumar, "A Customer Lifetime Value Framework for Customer Selections and Resource Allocation Strategy," *Journal of Marketing* 68, no. 4 (October 2004), pp. 106–125; V. Kumar, G. Ramani, and T. Bohling, "Customer Lifetime Value Approaches and Best Practice Applications," *Journal of Interactive Marketing* 18, no. 3 (Summer 2004), pp. 60–72; and J. Thomas, W. Reinartz, and V. Kumar, "Getting the Most Out of All Your Customers," *Harvard Business Review* (July–August 2004), pp. 116–123.

23. Hennes & Mauritz AB, www.hm.com (accessed May 22, 2011).

24. Zara, www.zara.com (accessed May 22, 2011).

25. This box was prepared using Ward Hanson and Kirthi Kalyanan, *Internet Marketing & E-Commerce* (Thomson/South-Western, 2007); http://blog.buzzoodle.com/index.php/2008/09/03/evolution-of-internet-marketing/ (accessed April 20, 2011); http://ezinearticles.com/?A-Brief-History-of-Internet-Marketing&id=434488 (accessed April 20, 2011); http://en.wikipedia.org/wiki/Internet_marketing (accessed April 20, 2011).

26. Royal Ford, "Automobila: Toyota Makes Emotional Appeal with Zippy New Line," *Boston Globe* March 13, 2003: E1; Zachary Rodgers, "Toyota Bows Web/Mobile Gaming Campaign for Scion," *Clickz*, July 8, 2004: www.clickz.com; "Forehead Advertising Goes Mainstream with Toyota," *Adrants* (April 8, 2004): www.adrants.com; and Jason Stein, "Scion National Launch Gets Offbeat Support," *Automotive News* 78, no. 6104 (2004), p. 18.

27. Example based on Loblaw Company Limited Supply Chain Management, www-acad.sheridanc.on.ca/syst35412/patenime/intro.htm (accessed March 29, 2007).

28. "HP Canada Social Investment," www.hp.com/canada/corporate/philanthropy/home.html (accessed April 23, 2011).

29. "Understanding the Power Behind Today's Leading Brands—2011 Harris Poll EquiTrend," www.harrisinteractive.com; Calvert, "Corporate Responsibility and Investor Confidence Survey," November 18, 2003: www.harrisinteractive.com. Also see The Trustees of Boston College, "The State of Corporate Citizenship in the United States: 2003," July 2003; Luisa Kroll and Allison Fass, "The World's Billionaires," www.forbes.com (accessed March 29, 2007).

30. http://dictionary.reference.com/search?q=Entrepreneurship (accessed May 16, 2005).

31. www.forbes.com/2007/03/07/billionaires-worlds-richest_07billionaires_cz_lk_af_0308billie_land.html (accessed December 17, 2007).

32. Harpo Productions, www2.oprah.com/about/press/about_press_bio.jhtml (accessed April 23, 2011).

33. This case was written by Priya Persaud in conjunction with the textbook authors (Ajax Persaud and Shirley Lichti) for use in a class discussion; it was not written as an illustration of effective or ineffective marketing practices.

34. Omar El Akkad, "RIM makes a play for its future," The Globe and Mail, www.theglobeandmail.com/globe-investor/rim-makes-a-play-for-its-future/article1987760/ (accessed May 23, 2011); Omar El Akkad and Iain Marlow, "RIM puts its PlayBook in motion," The Globe and Mail, www.theglobeandmail.com/news/technology/tech-news/rim-puts-its-playbook-in-motion/article1990919/ (accessed May 23, 2011).

35. Ben Rooney, "RIM PlayBook Gets Lukewarm Reception," The Wall Street Journal, http://blogs.wsj.com/tech-europe/2011/04/15/rim-playbook-gets-lukewarm-reception/?KEYWORDS=Playbook (accessed May 23, 2011).

36. Rooney, "RIM PlayBook."

37. Akkad, "RIM makes a play for its future."; Akkad and Marlow, "RIM puts its PlayBook in motion."

38. Rooney, "RIM PlayBook."

39. Tony Bradley, "Pros and Cons of BlackBerry PlayBook for Business PC World," www.pcworld.com/businesscenter/article/225222/ (accessed May 23, 2011).

40. Akkad, "RIM makes a play for its future."; Akkad and Marlow, "RIM puts its PlayBook in motion."

41. "RIM Announces Retail Channels for BlackBerry PlayBook" (press release), http://press.rim.com/release.jsp?id=4914 (accessed May 23, 2011).

42. "RIM Announces" (press release).

43. www.rim.com (accessed May 23, 2011).

44. www.apple.com and www.rim.com (accessed April 25, 2011).

45. D. Grewal and M. Levy, Marketing, 3rd ed. (New York: McGraw-Hill, 2011).

46. "RIM Announces" (press release); www.apple.com (accessed April 25, 2011).

47. Akkad, "RIM makes a play for its future"; Akkad and Marlow, "RIM puts its PlayBook in motion."

48. Akkad, "RIM makes a play for its future"; Akkad and Marlow, "RIM puts its PlayBook in motion."

49. Akkad, "RIM makes a play for its future."

50. Bradley, "Pros and Cons."

Chapter 2

1. Disney, www.wdisneyw.co.uk/palmickey.html (accessed October 14, 2004); Disney, "Mickey Mouse," http://disney.go.com/vault/archives/characterstandard/mickey/mickey.html; Disney, "Fact Book and Annual Report," http://disney.go.com/corporate/investors (accessed 2003); Debra D'Agostino, "Walt Disney World Resorts and CRM Strategy," eWeek.com December 1, 2003.

2. New York Times quote from Stephanie Startz, "Disney to Rebrand Mickey Mouse," www.brandchannel.com/home/post/2009/11/05/Disney-To-Rebrand-Mickey-Mouse.aspx (accessed August 5, 2010); Carmine Gallo, "How Disney Works to Win Repeat Customers," www.businessweek.com/print/smallbiz/content/nov2009/sb20091130_866423.htm (accessed August 5, 2010).

3. Startz, "Disney to Rebrand."

4. www.marketingpower.com/live/mg-dictionary.php?SearchFor=marketing+plan&Searched=1 (accessed August 31, 2006).

5. Donald Lehman and Russell Winer, Analysis for Marketing Planning, 5th ed. (Burr Ridge, IL: McGraw-Hill/Irwin, 2001); David Aaker, Strategic Market Management, 6th ed. (New York: John Wiley, 2001).

6. Andrew Campbell, "Mission Statements," Long Range Planning 30 (1997), pp. 931–933.

7. Alfred Rappaport, Creating Shareholder Value: The New Standard for Business Performance (New York: Wiley, 1988); Robert C. Higgins and Roger A. Kerin, "Managing the Growth-Financial Policy Nexus in Marketing," Journal of Marketing 59, no. 3 (1983), pp. 19–47; and Roger Kerin, Vijay Mahajan, and P. Rajan Varadarajan, Contemporary Perspectives on Strategic Market Planning (Boston: Allyn & Bacon, 1991), Chapter 6.

8. Tom Hortons, "About Us," www.timhortons.com/ca/en/about/faq.html (accessed April 23, 2011).

9. Datamonitor, "The Walt Disney Company," www.datamonitor.com/companies/company/?pid=8C7AE530-4ECC-4EF5-AC18-370E646FD097 (accessed December 17, 2007).

10. Datamonitor.

11. Datamonitor.

12. Datamonitor.

13. Lisa D'Innocenzo, "Frito Lay Canada: Potato Chips . . . for Dinner?" Strategy Magazine (January 2007), p. 11.

14. Andrew Martin, "Decaf Being Joined by De-Heartburn" The New York Times March 14, 2007; www.folgers.com/pressroom/press_release_05122006.shtml (accessed December 17, 2007).

15. www.leevalley.com (accessed April 30, 2007); "Conversations on working and well-being: Working by the Golden Rule: Lee Valley Tools," www.vifamily.ca/library/social/lee_valley.html (accessed April 30, 2007); "Lee Valley Tools Case Study," www.nerac.com/research-victories/lee-valley-tools-case-study/ (accessed April 30, 2007); A visit to Lee Valley Tools: A Company built on Innovation and Customer Service, www.woodcentral.com/shots/shot643.shtml (accessed April 30, 2007).

16. Interview with owner of The Country Grocer.

17. Bios from W network, www.wnetwork.com/Shows/TheCupcakeGirls/CharacterBios.aspx (accessed August 5, 2010); http://cupcakestakethecake.blogspot.com/2009/06/cupcake-reality-show-cupcake-girls.html (accessed August 5, 2010).

18. Ajax Persaud and Judith Madill, Assessing the Marketing Capability of the Websites of Canadian Non-Profit Organizations, World Social Marketing Conference, Dublin, Ireland, January 2011.

19. www.adstandards.com (accessed December 17, 2007).

20. Based on an article by Carly Weeks, "Charities' cash conundrum," The Globe and Mail, www.theglobeandmail.com/life/charities-cash-conundrum/article1504383/ (accessed August 5, 2010).

21. Human Resources and Skills Development Canada. "Social Participation—Charitable Donations" http://www4.hrsdc.gc.ca/.3ndic.1t.4r@-cng.jsp?iid=69 (accessed May 22, 2011).

22. "Fairmont Hotels and Resort Case Study." www.accenture.com/Global/Services/By_Industry/Travel/Client_Successes/FairmontCrm.htm (accessed April 20, 2007).

23. Globe and Mail Report on Business Special Case Studies with Concordia University, "Can sustainability be luxury's new gold standard?" May 2010: http://news.concordia.ca/pdf/GlobeMail_Feb26.pdf (accessed July 9, 2011).

24. www.loblaw.ca/en/abt_corprof.html (accessed April 30, 2007). ® President's Choice, PC Financial, PC are registered trademarks of Loblaws Inc., used with permission.

25. This discussion is adapted from Roger A. Kerin et al., Marketing, 7th ed. (Burr Ridge, IL: McGraw-Hill/Irwin, 2003), p. 39.

26. Farris et al., *Marketing Metrics: 50+ Metrics Every Executive Should Master* (Upper Saddle River, NJ: Prentice Hall, 2006), p. 17.

27. Relative market share = brand's market share ÷ largest competitor's market share. If, on the one hand, there are only two products in a market, A and B, and product B has 90 percent market share, then A's relative market share is 10 ÷ 90 = 11.1 percent. If, on the other hand, B has only 50 percent market share, then A's relative market share is 10 ÷ 50 = 20 percent. Farris et al., *Marketing Metrics*, p. 19.

28. Kerin, Mahajan, and Varadarajan, *Contemporary Perspectives on Strategic Market Planning*; See also Susan Mudambi, "A Topology of Strategic Choice in Marketing," *International Journal of Market & Distribution Management* (1994), pp. 22–25.

29. www.fairmont.com (accessed April 30, 2007).

30. Sharon Adams, "Hotels Sweeten the Pot for Travellers," *National Post* April 16, 2007: IS2.

31. www.fairmont.com (accessed April 30, 2007).

32. Hollie Shaw, "Forever 21 Targets Canadian Teens," *National Post*, April 15, 2007: FP1.

33. "The Cisco Mobile Office Solution Power's Fairmont's Hotel E-Business Strategy for Mobile Professionals," www.cisco.com (accessed April 30, 2007); Jens Traenhart, "Fairmont's Award-Winning Website Increases Online Bookings and Brand Awareness," www.blastradius.com (accessed April 30, 2007).

34. www.fairmont.com (accessed April 30, 2007).

35. Christina Valhouli, "Fairmont Hotel and Resorts," www.forbes.com/travel/2004/02/05/cx_cv_0205feat.html (accessed April 30, 2007).

36. Cynthia Montgomery, "Creating Corporate Advantage," *Harvard Business Review* 76 (May–June 1998), pp. 71–80; Shelby Hunt and Robert Morgan, "The Comparative Advantage Theory of Competition," *Journal of Marketing* 59, no. 2 (1995), pp. 1–15; Kathleen Conner and C.K. Prahalad, "A Resource-Based Theory of the Firm: Knowledge versus Opportunism," *Organizational Science* 7 (September–October 1996), pp. 477–501; David Collins and Cynthia Montgomery, "Competing on Resources: Strategy for the 1990s," *Harvard Business Review* 73 (July–August 1995), pp. 118–128; William Werther and Jeffrey Kerr, "The Shifting Sands of Competitive Advantage," *Business Horizons* 38 (May–June 1995), pp. 11–17; "10 Quick Wins to Turn Your Supply Chain into a Competitive Advantage," http://marketindustry.about.com/library/bl/bl_ksa0112.htm?terms=competitive+advantage (January 2002); Market Forward Inc., "Multi-Channel Integration: The New Market Battleground," www.pwcris.com (March 2001).

37. Michael Treacy and Fred Wiersema, *The Disciplines of Market Leaders* (Reading, MA: Addison Wesley, 1995).

38. Bios from W Network, www.wnetwork.com/Shows/TheCupcakeGirls/CharacterBios.aspx (accessed August 5, 2010); http://cupcakestakethecake.blogspot.com/2009/06/cupcake-reality-show-cupcake-girls.html (accessed August 5, 2010).

39. Gerrard Macintosh and Lawrence Lockshin, "Market Relationships and Store Loyalty: A Multi-Level Perspective," *International Journal of Research in Marketing* 14 (1997), pp. 487–497.

40. Venkatesan and Kumar, pp. 106–125; Kumar, Ramani, and Bohling, pp. 60–72; J. Thomas, W. Reinartz, and V. Kumar (2004), "Getting the Most Out of All Your Customers," *Harvard Business Review* (July–August 2004), pp. 116–23.

41. Jo Marney, "Bringing Consumers Back for More," *Marketing Magazine* 33 (September 10, 2001); Niren Sirohi, Edward McLaughlin, and Dick Wittink, "A Model of Consumer Perceptions and Store Loyalty Intentions for a Supermarket Marketer," *Journal of Marketing* 74, no. 3 (1998), pp. 223–247.

42. Rosemarky McCracken, "Rewards Have Their Own Virtues, *National Post* April 26, 2007: IS1.

43. Mary Jo Bitner, "Self Service Technologies: What Do Customers Expect?" *Marketing Management* (Spring 2001), pp. 10–34; Mary Jo Bitner, Stephen W. Brown, and Matthew L. Meuter, "Technology Infusion in Service Encounters," *Journal of Academy of Marketing Science* 28, no. 1 (2000), pp. 138–49; Matthew L. Meuter et al., "Self-Service Technologies: Understanding Customer Satisfaction with Technology-Based Service Encounters," *Journal of Marketing* 64, no. 3 (2000), pp. 50–64;

A. Parasuraman and Dhruv Grewal, "The Impact of Technology on the Quality-Value-Loyalty Chain: A Research Agenda," *Journal of the Academy of Marketing Science* 28, no. 1 (2000), pp. 168–174.

44. "TELUS Consumer Solution: Smart Desktop," www.cipa.com/award_winners/winners_06/Telus.html (accessed April 30, 2007).

45. S. A. Shaw and J. Gibbs, "Procurement Strategies of Small Marketers Faced with Uncertainty: An Analysis of Channel Choice and Behavior," *International Review of Market, Distribution and Consumer Research* 9, no. 1 (1999), pp. 61–75.

46. www.gallaugher.com/Netflix Case.pdf (accessed April 27, 2010); www.netflix.com/MediaCenter?id=5206 (accessed April 28, 2010); www.hd-report.com/2010/03/04/netflix-vs-blockbuster-why-is-netflix-winning/ (accessed April 28, 2010).

47. "Netflix, Paramount sign Canadian rights deal," www.theglobeandmail.com/globe-investor/netflix-paramount-sign-canadian-film-rights-deal/article1959932/ (accessed April 23, 2011).

48. David Carey, "Canadian CIOs test social networking waters," www.itworldcanada.com/news/canadian-cios-test-social-networking-waters/139201 (accessed April 23, 2011).

49. David Lei and John Slocum Jr., "Strategic and Organizational Requirements for Competitive Advantage," *Academy of Management Executive* (February 2005), pp. 31–46.

50. Maria Halkias, "Penney Remakes Culture to Remake Image," *The Dallas Morning News* February 12, 2007.

51. "The Top 100 Brands," *BusinessWeek*, www.businessweek.com/pdfs/2003/0331_globalbrands.pdf (accessed August 29, 2006); "Best Canadian Brands 2006," *Report on Business & Interbrand*, www.ourfishbowl.com/images/surveys/Interbrand_BCB2006.pdf (accessed July 9, 2011).

52. WestJet Airlines, www.westjet.com (accessed April 23, 2011); www.newswire.ca/en/releases/archive/April2007/23/c8051.html (accessed April 30, 2007).

53. This case was written by Stacy Biggar in conjunction with the textbook authors (Shirley Lichti and Ajax Persaud) for class discussion; it was not written as an illustration of effective or ineffective marketing practices. Stacy Biggar is a research associate with Professor Shirley Lichti.

54. www.globesports.com/servlet/story/RTGAM.20070428.wspt-TorFC-loses-28/GSStory/GlobeSportsSoccer/home (accessed May 25, 2011).

55. "Kansas City Ruins Toronto FC's First Home Game," www.usatoday.com/sports/soccer/mls/2007-04-28-kansascity-toronto_N.htm (accessed May 25, 2011).

56. www.citynews.ca/news/news_10409.aspx (accessed May 25, 2011).

57. Telephone interview between Ajax Persaud and Stacy Biggar, and Paul Beirne (Toronto FC's director of business operations), May 14, 2007.

58. www.citynews.ca/news/news_10409.aspx (accessed May 25, 2011).

59. Telephone interview with Paul Beirne.

60. Jonathan Paul, "Overall Winner—Frenzied fans fuel Toronto FC," www.strategymag.com (accessed April 23, 2011).

61. Paul, "Overall Winner."

62. http://toronto.fc.ca (accessed May 25, 2011).

63. www.righttoplay.com/International/Pages/Home.aspx (accessed May 25, 2011).

64. "TFC a Success Story in the Making," www.thestar.com/Sports/article/208302 (accessed May 25, 2011); Paul, "Overall Winner."

65. "Toronto FC erupts to score 1st win," www.cbc.ca/sports/soccer/story/2007/05/12/mls-chi-tor.html (accessed May 25, 2011).

66. "Toronto FC erupts."

67. Paul, "Overall Winner."

68. Paul, "Overall Winner."

Appendix 2A

1. This appendix was written by Tom Chevalier, Britt Hackmann, and Elisabeth Nevins Caswell in conjunction with the textbook authors (Dhruv Grewal and Michael Levy) for class discussion; it was not written as an illustration of effective or ineffective marketing practices.

2. "How to Write a Marketing Plan," www.knowthis.com/tutorials/principles-of-marketing/how-to-write-a-marketing-plan.htm (accessed May 16, 2008); also see "Marketing Plan Online," www.quickmba.com/marketing/plan/ (accessed May 16, 2008); "Marketing Plan," www.businessplans.org/Market.html (accessed May 18, 2008).

3. Roger Kerin, Steven Hartley, and William Rudelius, *Marketing* (New York: McGraw-Hill/Irwin, 2008), p. 53.

4. Kerin, Hartley, and Rudelius, p. 54; "How to Write a Marketing Plan."

5. This list of sources largely comes from the *Babson College Library Guide* May 12, 2008, http://www3.babson.edu/Library/research/marketingplan.cfm (accessed May 15, 2008). Special thanks to Nancy Dlott.

6. This marketing plan presents an abbreviated version of the actual plan for PeopleAhead. Some information has been changed to maintain confidentiality.

7. Publishers' and Advertising Directors' Conference, September, 21, 2005.

8. Mintel International Group, "Online Recruitment–US," January 1, 2005, www.marketresearch.com (accessed September 1, 2005).

9. Corzen Inc., www.wantedtech.com (accessed May 17, 2004).

10. Mintel International Group, "Online Recruitment–US."

Chapter 3

1. Q1 2010 Canadian Tire Corporation Earnings Conference Call, http://corp.canadiantire.ca/EN/Investors/EventsPresentations/Pages/QuarterlyWebcast.aspx (accessed August 5, 2010).

2. Canadian Tire Outlines Strategy for Growth Focused on Core Business, http://www.newswire.ca/en/releases/archive/April2010/07/c8276.html (accessed August 6, 2010).

3. "Canadian Tire maintains growth strategy," Canwest News Service October 3, 2007: www.canada.com/vancouversun/news/business/story.html?id=38979fb4-178f-4f3b-b009-435b918dc558&k=18791 (accessed August 5, 2010).

4. "Canadian Tire Corporation, Limited," www.referenceforbusiness.com/history/Ca-Ch/Canadian-Tire-Corporation-Limited.html (accessed August 6, 2010).

5. "Canadian Tire Corporation, Limited."

6. "2010 Strategic Objectives, Strengthen the core, Create a great CTR with a strong automotive division," http://corp.canadiantire.ca/EN/Investors/CorporateInformation/Pages/BusinessStrategy.aspx (accessed August 5, 2010).

7. Q1 2010 Canadian Tire Corporation Earnings Conference Call.

8. Q1 2010 Canadian Tire Corporation Earnings Conference Call.

9. Q1 2010 Canadian Tire Corporation Earnings Conference Call.

10. Peter F. Drucker, *The Essential Drucker* (New York: Harper Collins, 2001).

11. www.crestcanada.com and www.colgate.com (accessed April 23, 2011).

12. Matt Fish, "Silicon Belly: The Value of Competitive Intelligence," November 10, 2003: http://lexis-nexis.com (accessed September 6, 2006).

13. Steve Mossop, "Companies Not Spending Enough on Business Intelligence Activities," www.ipsos-na.com/news/pressrelease.cfm?id=2874 (accessed May 10, 2007).

14. Steven Gray, "Gillette in a Lather over Schick's Challenge for $1.7 Billion Razor Market," *Seattle Times* January 14, 2004.

15. Jack Neff, "Gillette, Schick Fight with Free Razors," *Advertising Age* 74, no. 48, p. 8.

16. Andrew Caffey, "Gillette Wins Legal Fight with Schick," *Knight Ridder Tribune Business News* April 30, 2005.

17. Caffey, "Gillette Wins."

18. Jean Abelson, "For Fusion, Gillette Plans a Super Bowl Blitz," *Knight Ridder Tribune Business News* January 27, 2006: 1.

19. "Air Canada, WestJet Settle Spying Lawsuit," www.cbc.ca/canada/calgary/story/2006/05/29/ca-westjet-settlement-20060529.html (accessed May 15, 2007).

20. www.nau.com (accessed April 29, 2010); Polly Labarre, "Leap of Faith," *Fast Company* June 2007.

21. Michael Solomon, *Consumer Behavior: Buying, Having and Being* (Upper Saddle River, NJ: Prentice Hall, 2006).

22. Rob Gerlsbeck, "Research: A Distinct Shopping Society," www.marketingmag.ca/magazine/current/quebec_rpt/article.jsp?content=20070625_69884_69884 (accessed June 25, 2007).

23. John Feto, "Name Games," *American Demographics*, February 15, 2003.

24. "Orthodox," *American Demographics*, May 2004, p. 35.

25. Dhru Grewal and Michael Levy, *Marketing*, 2nd U.S. ed. (Boston: McGraw-Hill/Irwin, 2010), pp. 50–51.

26. "2005 YTV Tween Report, Solutions Research Group, A Corus Entertainment Inc. Company," www.corusmedia.com/ytv/research/index.asp (accessed May 15, 2007); J.K. Wall, "Tweens Get Retailers into Parents' Wallets," *Knight Ridder Tribune Business News* September 12, 2003: 1. Research attributed to WonderGroup in Cincinnati.

27. The term *speeders* was coined by Cynthia Cohen, president of Strategic Mindshare.

28. www.statscan.ca (accessed May 15, 2007).

29. Pamela Paul, "Getting Inside Gen Y," *American Demographics* 23, no. 9.

30. Noah Rubin Brier, "Move Over Prime-Time!" *American Demographics* (July/August 2004), pp. 14–20; John Hoeffel, "The Next Baby Boom," *American Demographics* (October 1995), pp. 22–31.

31. www.statscan.ca (accessed May 15, 2007); James Tenser, "Ageless Aging of Boom-X," *Advertising Age* 77, no. 1 (January 2, 2006), pp. 18–19; Tabitha Armstrong, "GenX Family Values," *The Lane Report* January 1, 2005: 41.

32. "Lesley Young, Portrait of the New Family," www.marketingmag.ca/magazine/current/feature/article.jsp?content=20040315_61585_61585 (accessed May 11, 2007).

33. Michael Weiss, "Chasing Youth," *American Demographics* (October 2002), pp. 35–41.

34. www.statscan.ca (accessed May 15, 2007).

35. Social Welfare Research Institute, "Good Tidings for a New Year: The $41 Trillion Transfer of Wealth Is Still Valid," www.bc.edu/research/swri/meta-elements/ssi/wcvol3.html.

36. www.statscan.ca (accessed May 15, 2007).

37. Kristin Davis, "Oldies but Goodies; Marketers, Take Note: Baby Boomers Have Lots of Money to Spend," *U.S. News & World Report* (Washington edition), March 14, 2005: 45.

38. www.statscan.ca (accessed April 23, 2011).

39. www.statscan.ca (accessed April 23, 2011).

40. www.statscan.ca (accessed April 23, 2011).

41. www.hammacher.com (accessed May 3, 2010).

42. http://europe.nokia.com/ovi-services-and-apps/nokia-money (accessed May 4, 2010).

43. Steve Kerstetter, *The Affordability Gap: Spending Differences between Canada's Rich and Poor, Canadian Centre for Policy Alternatives* (September 2009) www.policyalternatives.ca/sites/default/files/uploads/publications/National_Office_Pubs/2009/Spending_Patterns,_Low_Incomes.pdf (accessed July 9, 2011).

44. www.statscan.ca (accessed April 23, 2011); U.S. Bureau of the Census, www.census.gov/population/www/socdemo/educ-attn.html.

45. www.statscan.ca (accessed April 23, 2011).

46. Bethany Clough, "Home-Improvement Store Empower Female Customers with Do-It-Herself Tools," *Knight Ridder Tribune Business Service* March 20, 2005: 1; Fara Warner, "Yes, Women Spend (And Saw and Sand)," *The New York Times* February 29, 2004: C1.

47. www.statscan.ca (accessed April 23, 2011).

48. www.statscan.ca (accessed April 23, 2011); *OECD Employment Outlook 2010.* Chart LMF1.5.A: Gender gap in median earnings of full-time employees, www.oecd.org/dataoecd/1/35/43199347.xls (accessed May 25, 2011).

49. www.theglobeandmail.com/servlet/story/RTGAM.20071205.wcensusmain1005/BNStory/census2006/home (accessed December 18, 2007).

50. www.statscan.ca (accessed May 15, 2007).

51. "Tapping into the Hot Chinese and South Asian Marketplace," *Ipsos Ideas*, www.ipsos-ideas.com/article.cfm?id=3391 (accessed May 15, 2007).

52. Rebecca Harris, "Skin Deep, Canada's Big Banks Have Taken Great Strides to Reach Newcomers to the Country. But, They Need to Look Beneath the Surface to Truly Connect to Multicultural Consumers," *Marketing Magazine* January 29, 2007.

53. Harris, "Skin Deep."

54. "How Sobey's is taking on Loblaws," www.theglobeandmail.com/report-on-business/rob-magazine/top-1000/how-sobeys-is-taking-on-loblaws/article1603663/ (accessed April 23, 2011); Andy Holloway, "Getting Fresh," *Canadian Grocer* (June/July 2010), p. 23; "Sobeys Inc. Launches FreshCo. Discount Stores" (press release), www.sobeyscorporate.com/App_Themes/SobeysCorporate/media/en/Sobeys-Inc-Launches-FreshCo-Discount-Stores.pdf (accessed April 23, 2011).

55. "How Sobey's,"; Holloway, "Getting Fresh," p. 23; "Sobeys Inc. Launches FreshCo."

56. "How Sobey's,"; Holloway, "Getting Fresh," p. 23; "Sobeys Inc. Launches FreshCo."

57. This section draws heavily from Jacquelyn A. Ottman, *Green Marketing: Opportunity for Innovation* (Chicago, IL: NTC Publishing, 1997), also available online at www.greenmarketing.com.

58. Jeremy Lloyd, "Polar Bear Tweets Make Environmental Stand," www.marketingmag.ca/english/news/marketer/article.jsp?content=20091007_143731_9936 (accessed August 6, 2010); http://polartweets.com (accessed August 6, 2010).

59. http://polartweets.com (accessed November 28, 2009).

60. Centre for Science in the Public Interest, "Guidelines for Marketing Food to Kids Proposed" (press release), January 5, 2005.

61. Kristin Laird (2010), "BullFrog Invites Consumers to Pay More," www.marketingmag.ca/english/news/marketer/article.jsp?content=20100422_145930_3524 (accessed August 6, 2010).

62. "Massive Epsilon E-mail Breach Hits Citi, Chase, and many more," www.pcworld.com/article/224147/massive_epsilon_email_breach_hits_citi_chase_many_more.html (accessed April 23, 2011).

63. www.statscan.ca (accessed April 23, 2011).

64. Martin Peers, "Buddy, Can You Spare Some Time?" *The Wall Street Journal* January 26, 2004: B1, B3.

65. Peers, "Buddy, Can You Spare."

66. www.thenorthface.com/webapp/wcs/stores/servlet/TNFAttachmentDisplay?langId=-1&storeId=207&attachment =/corporate/about_us/company_news/articles/

67. www.cbc.com (accessed April 24, 2011).

68. www.yourdictionary.com (accessed September 5, 2006).

69. www.bankofcanada.ca/en/ (accessed May 15, 2007).

70. Heather Scoffield, "Outlook Dims as Rates Fall to Record Low," http://v1.theglobeandmail.com/servlet/story/LAC.20090121.RECONOMY21/TPStory/Business (accessed August 6, 2010).

71. "BP Won't Pay Dividends This Year," http://money.cnn.com/2010/06/16/news/bp.dividend.fortune/index.htm (accessed August 6, 2010); Steve Hargreaves, "Oil spill damage spreads through Gulf economies," http://money.cnn.com/2010/05/30/news/economy/gulf_economy/index.htm (accessed August 6, 2010).

72. This case was written by the textbook authors (Ajax Persaud and Shirley Lichti) for use in a class discussion; it was not written as an illustration of effective or ineffective marketing practices. It is based on publicly available information.

73. This case was developed by using the following sources: Frederic Lardinois, "EReader and E-book Market Ready for Growth," www.readwriteweb.com/archives/report_ereader_and_ebook_market_ready_for_growth.php (accessed April 24, 2011); www.kobobooks.com/about_us (accessed April 24, 2011); "The 30 Benefits of E-books," http://epublishersweekly.blogspot.com/2008/02/30-benefits-of-ebooks.html (accessed April 24, 2011); Anton Shilov, "E-books Industry Set to Raise," www.xbitlabs.com/news/multimedia/display/20091107152810_Electronic_Book_Industry_Set_to_Explode_in_2010_Analysts.html (accessed April 24, 2011); "The Great Canadian Debate: Future of eBooks in Canadian Retail," http://knol.google.com/k/the-great-canadian-ebook-debate# (accessed April 24, 2011); "Looking into the Future: Price, Color, Video—and the End of the Chain Bookstore," www.readwriteweb.com/archives/report_ereader_and_ebook_market_ready_for_growth.php (accessed August 6, 2010); Paul Miller, "Kobo's $149 eReader gets reviewed" www.engadget.com/2010/04/11/kobos-149-ereader-gets-reviewed/ (accessed July 9, 2011); Mark Medley, "Testing the Kobo e-reader," http://network.nationalpost.com/NP/blogs/afterword/archive/2010/04/17/testing-the-kobo-ereader.aspx#ixzz0rrO1c7T (accessed April 24, 2011); "Test drive of Canadian company's new e-book hardware," cbc.ca (accessed April 24, 2011); Forrester Research Inc. through

74. Associated Press, "Amazon says e-book sales pass paper," www.marketingmag.ca/news/media-news/amazon-says-e-book-sales-pass-paper-27662 (accessed May 19, 2011).

Chapter 4

1. Adapted from Natalia Williams, "For the Love of Jam," *Strategy Magazine*, www.strategymag.com/articles/magazine/20050701/mediaed.html?word=e.d.&word=smith (accessed April 24, 2011); www.edsmith.com/web/edsmith.nsf/eng/WhatsNew (accessed April 24, 2011).

2. A. Parasuraman, Dhruv Grewal, and R. Krishnan, *Marketing Research* (Boston: Houghton Mifflin, 2004), p. 9.

3. Holly Bailey, "Where the Voters Are," *Newsweek* 143, no. 13 (March 29, 2004), p. 67.

4. www.whirlpool.com/home.jsp (accessed November 12, 2004); Parasuraman, Grewal, and Krishnan, *Marketing Research*; Greg Steinmetz and Carl Quintanilla, "Whirlpool Expected Easy Going in Europe, and It Got a Big Shock," *The Wall Street Journal* April 10, 1998: A1, A6.

5. "AquaSteam," www.whirlpool.co.uk/app.cnt/whr/en_GB/pageid/pgdswprmhome001/rqpg/detail/id/293 (accessed February 5, 2008).

6. Erhard K. Valentin, "Commentary: Marketing Research Pitfalls in Product Development," *Journal of Product & Brand Management* 3, no. 4–6 (1994), pp. 66–69.

7. www.legermarketing.com/eng/qui.asp (accessed April 24, 2011).

8. Augustine Fou, "Metrics, Metric, Everywhere," www.clickz.com/3634816 (accessed August 6, 2010).

9. Jim Barnes, "Dangers of Dumbing Down Customer Research," www.customerthink.com/article/dangers_of_dumbing_down_customer_research? (accessed August 6, 2010).

10. Barnes, "Dangers of Dumbing Down."

11. Barnes, "Dangers of Dumbing Down."

12. Barnes, "Dangers of Dumbing Down."

13. Edward G. Carmines and Richard A. Zeller, *Reliability and Validity Assessment (Quantitative Applications in the Social Sciences)* (London, UK: Sage University Press, 1979).

14. Carmines and Zeller, *Reliability and Validity Assessment*.

15. Virginia Galt, "Embedding Sustainability in Company Culture," www.theglobeandmail.com/report-on-business/your-business/business-categories/sustainability/embedding-sustainability-in-company-culture/article1548519/ (accessed August 6, 2010).

16. Emily Nelson, "P&G Wants the Truth: Did You Really Brush Your Teeth?" *The Globe and Mail* June 1, 2001: M2.

17. Nelson, "P&G Wants the Truth."

18. Lisa D'Innocenzo, "Cosying Up to Shoppers to Really Get the Consumer's POV—And a Gain in a Competitive Edge–Talk-Face-To-Face," *Strategy* (November 2006), p. 32.

19. "Our Brands," www.jny.com/brand.jsp?event=brands (accessed February 2, 2008).

20. Ross Tucker, "L.E.I. Gets New Look for Back-to-School," *Women's Wear Daily* July 5, 2007 (accessed electronically February 2, 2008).

21. Allison Fass, "Collective Opinion," Forbes.com November 11, 2005, www.forbes.com/forbes/2005/1128/076.html (accessed July 9, 2011).

22. Elisabeth A. Sullivan, "Be Sociable," *Marketing News* January 15, 2008; Sarah Perez, "Despite Recession, More Than 50% of Marketers Increase Spending on Social Media," www.readwriteweb.com/enterprise/2009/03/despite-recession-more-than-50-of-marketers-increase-spending-on-social-media.php (accessed December 3, 2009).

23. "Client Story: Kraft," www.communispace.com/assets/pdf/C_Cli_casestudy_kraft_final.pdf (accessed April 6, 2010).

24. Sarah Needleman, "For Companies, a Tweet in Time Can Avert PR Mess," *The Wall Street Journal* August 3, 2009.

25. Adapted from A. Parasuraman, D. Grewal, and R. Krishnan, *Marketing Research* (Boston: Houghton Mifflin, 2004), p. 64.

26. Stanley E. Griffis, Thomas J. Goldsby, and Martha Cooper, "Web-Based and Mail Surveys: A Comparison of Response, Data and Cost," *Journal of Business Logistics* 24, no. 2 (2003), pp. 237–259; Chris Gautreau, "Getting the Answers," *The Greater Baton Rouge Business Report* 22, no. 29 (September 28, 2004), p. 17; Alf Nucifora, "Weaving Web Surveys That Work," *njbiz* 15, no. 46 (November 11, 2002), p. 28.

27. https://pulse.asda.com (accessed April 15, 2010); Joel Warady, "Asda Takes the 'Pulse of the Nation,'" *Retail Wire* (July 16, 2009).

28. Based on Perez, "Despite Recession."

29. This example was based on information taken from Coinstar's website (www.coinstar.com) and a case study about Coinstar, available on the SPSS Inc. website, www.spss.com (accessed September 18, 2006).

30. For a more thorough discussion of effective written reports, see Parasuraman, Grewal, and Krishnan, *Marketing Research*, Chapter 16.

31. "Canadian Privacy Legislation," www.media-awareness.ca/english/issues/privacy/canadian_legislation_privacy.cfm (accessed June 1, 2007).

32. This case was written by Priya Persaud in conjunction with the textbook authors (Ajax Persaud and Shirley Lichti) for use in a class discussion, it was not written as an illustration of effective or ineffective marketing practices. Priya Persaud is a student research assistant on this book. This case was prepared on April 20, 2011.

33. www.shoelessjoes.com (accessed August 6, 2010).

34. www.shoelessjoes.com (accessed August 6, 2010).

35. "Shoeless Joe's gains access to real-time customer data," *Direct Marketing* (September 2009). www.dmn.ca (accessed August 6, 2010).

36. "Shoeless Joe's gains access."

Chapter 5

1. "Worldwide Sales of TMC Hybrids Top 3 Million Units," http://media.toyota.ca/pr/tci/en/worldwide-sales-of-tmc-hybrids-193419.aspx (accessed June 2, 2011).

2. David Wigder, "Hybrids Shift into Mass Market, Marketing & Strategy Innovation" www.futurelab.net/blogs/marketing-strategy-innovation/2007/04/hybrids_shift_into_the_mass_ma.html (accessed April 24, 2011).

3. Dhruv Grewal et al., "The Internet and the Price-Value-Loyalty Chain," *Journal of Business Research* 56 (May 2003), p. 391.

4. See Henry Assael, *Consumer Behaviour and Marketing Action* (Boston: Kent Publishing, 1987); John A. Howard and Jadish Sheth, *The Theory of Consumer Behaviour in Marketing Strategy* (Upper Saddle River, NJ: Prentice Hall, 1989); Philip Kotler, Gary Armstrong, and Peggy Cunningham, *Principles of Marketing*, 6th Can. ed. (Toronto: Pearson, 2005), pp. 279–280.

5. Pamela Sebastian, "'Aspirational Wants' Form the Basis of a Modern Retailing Strategy," *The Wall Street Journal* October 15, 1998: A1; Barry Babin, William Darden, and Mitch Griffin, "Work and/or Fun: Measuring Hedonic and Utilitarian Shopping Value," *Journal of Consumer Research* 20 (March 1994), pp. 644–656.

6. "Christian Louboutin Styles for the Uptown Girl," http://www.newshoefashion.com (accessed April 24, 2011); Cindy Clark, "Christian Louboutin's Red-Soled Shoes Are Red-Hot," *USA Today*, www.usatoday.com/life/lifestyle/fashion/2007-12-25-louboutin-shoes_N.htm (accessed April 24, 2011).

7. www.bloomberg.com/news/2011-04-07/louboutin-sues-yves-saint-laurent-over-red-sole-shoes-trademark-violation.html (accessed April 24, 2011).

8. Brian T. Ratchford, Debabrata Talukdar, and Myung-Soo Lee, "The Impact of the Internet on Consumers' Use of Information Sources for Automobiles: A Re-Inquiry," *Journal of Consumer Research* 34, no. 1 (2007), pp. 111–119; Glenn J. Browne, Mitzi G. Pitts, and James C. Wetherbe, "Cognitive Shopping Rules for Terminating Information Search in Online Tasks," *MIS Quarterly* 31, no.1 (2007), pp. 89–104.

9. "Canadian Product Reviews," http://forum.smartcanucks.ca/canadian-product-reviews/ (accessed December 3, 2009).

10. Lyndsie Bourgon, "Enter Social Media: The Twitterari effect," www.canadianbusiness.com/after_hours/lifestyle_activities/article.jsp?content=20091123_10010_10010 (accessed November 28, 2009).

11. Bourgon, "Enter Social Media."

12. Bourgon, "Enter Social Media."

13. "Recall Hits Toyota Sales; GM, Ford see double digit-gains," www.usatoday.com/money/autos/2010-02-02-auto-sales-january_N.htm (accessed April 24, 2011).

14. The term *determinance* was first coined by James Myers and Mark Alpert nearly three decades ago. www.sawtoothsoftware.com/productforms/ssolutions/ss12.shtml (accessed September 4, 2006).

15. www.sawtoothsoftware.com/productforms/ssolutions/ss12.shtml (accessed September 4, 2006).

16. Jim Oliver, "Finding Decision Rules with Genetic Algorithms," www.umsanet.edu.bo/docentes/gchoque/MAT420L07.htm (accessed June 2004).

17. Paul S. Richardson, Alan S. Dick, and Arun K. Jain, "Extrinsic and Intrinsic Cue Effects on Perceptions of Store Brand Quality," *Journal of Marketing* 58 (October 1994), pp. 28–36; Rajneesh Suri and Kent B. Monroe, "The Effects of Time Constraints on Consumers' Judgments of Prices and Products," *Journal of Consumer Research* 30 (June 2003), pp. 92–104.

18. Merrie Brucks, Valerie A. Zeithaml, and Gillian Naylor, "Price and Brand Name as Indicators of Quality Dimensions for Consumer Durables," *Journal of the Academy of Marketing Science* 28, no. 3 (2000), pp. 359–74; Niraj Dawar and Philip Parker, "Marketing Universals: Consumers' Use of Brand Name, Price, Physical Appearance, and Retailer Reputation as Signals of Product Quality," *Journal of Marketing* 58 (April 1994), pp. 81–95; William B. Dodds, Kent B. Monroe, and Dhruv Grewal, "Effects of Price, Brand, and Store Information on Buyers' Product Evaluations," *Journal of Marketing Research* 28 (August 1991), pp. 307–319.

19. Mary Jo Bitner, "Servicescapes: The Impact of Physical Surroundings on Customers and Employees," *Journal of Marketing* 56 (April 1992), pp. 57–71; Dhruv Grewal and Julie Baker, "Do Retail Store Environmental Factors Affect Consumers' Price Acceptability? An Empirical Examination," *International Journal of Research in Marketing* 11 (1994), pp. 107–115; Eric R. Spangenberg, Ayn E. Crowley, and Pamela W. Henderson, "Improving the Store Environment: Do Olfactory Cues Affect Evaluations and Behaviors?" *Journal of Marketing* 60 (April 1996), pp. 67–80; Kirk L. Wakefield and Jeffrey G. Blodgett, "Customer Response to Intangible and Tangible Service Factors," *Psychology and Marketing* 16 (January 1999), pp. 51–68.

20. www.expedia.com/daily/service/about.asp?rfrr=-1087 (accessed September 4, 2006); www.expedia.ca (accessed May 17, 2007).

21. Ruby Roy Dholakia and Miao Zhao, "Retail Web Site Interactivity: How Does It Influence Customer Satisfaction and Behavioral Intentions?" *International Journal of Retail & Distribution Management* 37 (2009), pp. 821–838.

22. Claire Cain Miller, "Closing the Deal at the Virtual Checkout Counter," *The New York Times* October 12, 2009 (accessed electronically December 13, 2009).

23. Youngme Moon and John A. Quelch, "Starbucks: Delivering Customer Service," *Harvard Business Review* (July 31, 2003).

24. A.H. Maslow, *Motivation and Personality* (New York: Harper & Row, 1970).

25. Michael Levy and Barton A. Weitz, *Retailing Management*, 6th ed. (Burr Ridge IL: Irwin/McGraw-Hill, 2007), Chapter 4.

26. "2005 YTV Tween Report, Solutions Research Group, A Corus Entertainment Inc. Company," www.corusmedia.com/ytv/research/index.asp (accessed May 15, 2007).

27. Sandra Yin, "Kids; Hot Spots," *American Demographics* (December 1, 2003); Peter Francese, "Trend Ticker: Trouble in Store," *American Demographics* (December 1, 2003).

28. L. Hamzaoui and M. Zahaf, *Exploring the decision making process of Canadian organic food consumers* (working paper WP 2006-31), Telfer School of Management, University of Ottawa, 2006.

29. A. Kristallis and G. Chryssohoidis, "Consumers' willingness to pay for organic food: Factors that affect it and variation per organic product type." *British Food Journal* 107, no. 5 (2005), pp. 320–343.

30. Leila Hamzaoui Essoussi and Mehdi Zahaf, "Clustering organic food consumers using purchasing patterns." *European Journal of Management* 9, no. 1 (Spring 2009), p. 202.

31. L. Zepeda and J. Li, "Characteristics of organic food shoppers." *Journal of Agricultural and Applied Economics* 39, no. 1 (2007), pp. 17–28.

32. "Survey Reveals Teen Spending Habits, Retail Brand Perceptions," http://money.cnn.com/news/newsfeeds/articles/newstex/VNU-0016-16243010.htm (accessed May 20, 2007).

33. Rebecca Harris, "Skin Deep, Canada's Big Banks Have Taken Great Strides to Reach Newcomers to the Country. But, They Need to Look Beneath the Surface to Truly Connect to Multicultural Consumers," *Marketing Magazine* January 29, 2007.

34. "Collaborative Consumption," Wikipedia.com (accessed April 24, 2011); Rachel Botsman and Roo Rogers, *What's Mine Is Yours: The Rise of Collaborative Consumption* (New York: Harper Collins, 2011).

35. "Collaborative Consumption"; Botsman and Rogers, *What's Mine Is Yours*.

36. "Montreal's Bixi Rental Bikes are Rolling," www.cbc.ca/consumer/story/2009/05/12/montreal-bixi.html (accessed August 6, 2010).

37. The concept of atmospherics was introduced by Philip Kotler, "Atmosphere as a Marketing Tool," *Journal of Retailing* 49 (Winter 1973), pp. 48–64.

38. Anna S. Mattila and Jochen Wirtz, "Congruency of Scent and Music as a Driver of In-Store Evaluations and Behavior," *Journal of Retailing* 77, no. 2 (Summer 2001), pp. 273–289; Teresa A. Summers and Paulette R. Hebert, "Shedding Some Light on Store Atmospherics; Influence of Illumination on Consumer Behavior," *Journal of Business Research* 54, no. 2 (November 2001), pp. 145–150; for a review of this research, see Joseph A. Bellizzi and Robert E. Hite, "Environmental Color, Consumer Feelings, and Purchase Likelihood," *Psychology and Marketing* 9, no. 5 (September–October 1992), pp. 347–363; J. Duncan Herrington and Louis Capella, "Effects of Music in Service Environments: A Field Study," *Journal of Services Marketing* 10, no. 2 (1996), pp. 26–41; Richard F. Yalch and Eric R. Spangenberg, "The Effects of Music in a Retail Setting on Real and Perceived Shopping Times," *Journal of Business Research* 49, no. 2 (August 2000), pp. 139–148; Michael Hui, Laurette Dube, and Jean-Charles Chebat, "The Impact of Music on Consumer's Reactions to Waiting for Services," *Journal of Retailing* 73, no. 1 (1997), pp. 87–104; and Julie Baker, Dhruv Grewal, and Michael Levy, "An Experimental Approach to Making Retail Store Environmental Decisions," *Journal of Retailing* 68 (Winter 1992), pp. 445–460; Maxine Wilkie, "Scent of a Market," *American Demographics* (August 1995), pp. 40–49; Spangenberg, Crowley, Henderson, "Improving the Store Environment"; Paula Fitzgerald Bone and Pam Scholder Ellen, "Scents in the Marketplace: Explaining a Fraction of Olfaction," *Journal of Retailing* 75, no. 2 (Summer 1999), pp. 243–263.

39. Abercrombie and Fitch, http://en.wikipedia.org/wiki/Abercrombie_&_Fitch (accessed May 20, 2007).

40. Julie Baker et al., "Wait Expectations, Store Atmosphere and Store Patronage Intentions," *Journal of Retailing* 79, no. 4 (2003), pp. 259–268.

41. Jagdish Sheth, Banwari Mittal, and Bruce I. Newman, *Customer Behavior: Consumer Behavior and Beyond* (Fort Worth, TX: The Dryden Press, 1999); J. Paul Peter and Jerry C. Olson, *Consumer Behavior and Marketing Strategy* (McGraw-Hill/Irwin, 2007); Michael R. Solomon, *Consumer Behavior: Buying, Having, and Being* (Toronto: Prentice Hall, 2009).

42. Karen M. Stilley, J. Jeffrey Inman, and Kirk L. Wakefield, "Planning to Make Unplanned Purchases? The Role of In-Store Slack in Budget Deviation," *Journal of Consumer Research*, DOI: 10.1086/651567; R. Puri, "Measuring and Modifying Consumer Impulsiveness: A Cost-Benefit Accessibility Framework," *Journal of Consumer Psychology* 5 (1996), pp. 87–113.

43. This case was written by Kate Woodworth in conjunction with Dhruv Grewal and Michael Levy for use in a class discussion; it was not written as an illustration of effective or ineffective marketing practices.

44. Statistics Canada, *Canadian Health Measures Survey 2007–2009*, www.statcan.gc.ca (accessed April 25, 2011).

45. www.statcan.gc.ca (accessed April 25, 2011).

46. Vauhini Vara, "New Gadets Aim to Help Users Watch Their Weight," *The Wall Street Journal Online* May 12, 2005.

47. http://jennycraig.com/programs/ (accessed April 19, 2010).

48. Geoff Williams, "Weight Watchers Sues Jenny Craig for Misleading Ads: Let the Mudslinging Begin," *walletpop.com*, January 20, 2010.

49. Jennifer LaRue Huget, "Weight Watchers and Jenny Craig Offer Programs for Men Who Want to Shed Pounds," *The Washington Post*, March 25, 2010.

Chapter 6

1. This chapter vignette is based on www.rbcroyalbank.com (accessed April 24, 2011).

2. Arun Sharma, R. Krishnan, and Dhruv Grewal, "Value Creation in Markets: A Critical Area of Focus for Business-to-Business Markets," *Industrial Marketing Management* 30, no. 4 (2001), pp. 391–402; Ajay K. Kohli and Bernard J. Jaworski, "Market Orientation: The Construct, Research Propositions, and Managerial Implications," *Journal of Marketing* 54, no. 2 (1990), pp. 1–13; John C. Narver and Stanly F. Slater, "The Effect of Market Orientation on Business Profitability," *Journal of Marketing* 54, no. 4 (1990), pp. 20–33.

3. www.magna.com (accessed April 24, 2011).

4. "Our Mission and Vision," www.burtsbees.com (accessed April 24, 2011).

5. "Burt's Bees Focuses on Production Efficiency," *Cosmetics Design*, November 2, 2006.

6. www.retailcouncil.org/training/publications/canadianretailer/crmediakit11.pdf (accessed June 3, 2011).

7. www.statcan.ca (accessed April 24, 2011).

8. Based on Naomi Carniol, "Printer Impresses Clients with Eco-changes," www.theglobeandmail.com/report-on-business/your-business/business-categories/sustainability/printer-impresses-clients-with-eco-changes/article1525300/ (accessed April 24, 2011).

9. www.charityvillage.com (accessed April 24, 2011).

10. www.pwgsc.gc.ca (accessed April 24, 2011).

11. https://buyandsell.gc.ca and www.merx.com (accessed June 3, 2011).

12. www.merx.com (accessed April 24, 2011).

13. "Bombardier Announces up to $4.7 Billion in orders at the Paris Air Show," *Reuters* June 24, 2011, www.reuters.com/article/2011/06/25/idUS20538+25-Jun-2011+HUG20110625 (accessed July 17, 2011).

14. "Bombardier Bank," www.canadianbusiness.com/article.jsp?content=20040329_59236_59236 (accessed April 24, 2011).

15. www.shepherd.ca (accessed May 21, 2007); www.shepherd.ca; "RoyNat Capital Entrepreneurial Profile," *Financial Post* May 7, 2007: FP12.

16. www.census.gov/epcd/naics02/SICN02E.HTM#S48; www.census.gov/epcd/www/naics.html; www.census.gov/epcd/naics02/N2SIC51.HTM.

17. This illustration, which exemplifies how Toyota works with its suppliers, is based on Jeffrey K. Liker and Thomas Y. Choi, "Building Deep Supplier Relationships," *Harvard Business Review* (December 2004), pp. 104–114.

18. Toyotasupplier.com (accessed September 6, 2006).

19. Toyotasupplier.com (accessed September 6, 2006).

20. Tilting Pixels on the Web is based on a personal interview between Matt Inglot (CEO of Tilted Pixels) and Shirley Lichti, June 25, 2010.

21. www.marketingpower.com/live/mg-dictionary-view435.php. These definitions are provided by www.marketing-power.com (the American Marketing Association's website). We have bolded our key terms.

22. Amber Bowerman, *The Economics of Donation*, www.avenuecalgary.com/articles/page/item/the-economics-of-donations (accessed April 25, 2011); Value Village, www.valuevillage.com/downloads/SaversValueVillagePressKits.pdf (accessed April 25, 2011).

23. Kimberly Maul, "More B-to-B companies Find That Social Media Is an Essential Business Platform," PRweekus.com, June 2009; Ellis Booker, "B-to-B Marketers Apply Analytics to Social Media," *BtoB* April 12, 2010; Elisabeth A. Sullivan, "A Long Slog," *Marketing News* February 28, 2009.

24. www.tweetdeck.com (accessed July 20, 2010).

25. Daniel B. Honigman, "Make a Statement," *Marketing News* May 1, 2008.

26. Sarah Mahoney, "Staples Launches Small-Biz Incentive Plan," *Marketing Daily* January 5, 2010.

27. Susan Kuchinskas, "Data-Based Dell," *Adweek Magazine's Technology Marketing* 23, no. 6 (September 2003), p. 20.

28. Barton A. Weitz, Stephen B. Castleberry, and John F. Tanner, *Selling Building Partnerships*, 5th ed. (Burr Ridge, IL: McGraw-Hill/Irwin, 2003), p. 93.

29. Kate Maddox, "Marketers Face Challenges from Economy to Ecology," www.btobonline.com/apps/pbcs.dll/article?AID=/20071210/FREE/71210002/1109/FREE#seenit (accessed June 3, 2011).

30. "Microsoft's Looking Glass Will Let Marketers Peer into a Real-Time Social Stream," www.techcrunch.com/2009/09/23/microsofts-looking-glass-will-let-marketers-peer-into-the-social-stream/ (accessed April 25, 2011); Demonstration video available at "Microsoft Looking Glass Helps Businesses Catch the Social Media Wave at Advertising Week 2009," http://community.microsoftadvertising.com/blogs/analytics/archive/2009/09/23/microsoft-lookingglass-helps-businesses-catch-the-social-media-wave-at-advertising-week-2009.aspx (accessed December 2, 2009); Video Demonstration of Microsoft's Looking Glass, www.youtube.com/watch?v=kSGO6SfaFRQ; "Canadians CIOs test social networking waters," www.itworldcanada.com/news/canadian-cios-test-social-networking-waters/139201 (accessed December 3, 2009).

31. Amanda C. Kooser, "Virtual Trade Shows Take Care of Some Very Real Business," *Entrepreneur* August 2007.

32. K.C. Laudon and C.G. Traver, *E-Commerce: Business, Technology, Society*, 2nd ed. (Boston: Pearson, 2004).

33. www.Guru.com (accessed January 3, 2008).

34. www.Guru.com (accessed January 3, 2008).

35. David Whitford, "Hired Guns on the Cheap," *Fortune Small Business* January 3, 2008; Sandy Jap, "An Exploratory Study of the Introduction of Online Reverse Auctions," *Journal of Marketing* 67, no. 3 (July 2003), accessed electronically; R. Tassabehji et al., "Reverse E-auctions and Supplier-Buyer Relationships: an Exploratory Study," *International Journal of Operations and Production Management* 26, no. 2 (2006), pp. 1–19; Sandy Jap, "Going Going, Gone," *Harvard Business Review* 78, no. 6, accessed electronically; "Reverse Auctions Gain Momentum as Cost Tool-Chipmakers Grudgingly Join in Online Bids," *Spencer Chin* (March 3, 2003), p. 1.

36. This case was written by Ajax Persaud and Shirley Lichti based on an interview with Sean Humphrey (marketing director of *The Globe and Mail*), July 14, 2010. This case is for use in a class discussion; it was not written as an illustration of effective or ineffective marketing practices.

37. Andy Macaulay, founder and former CEO of zig, a company based in Waterloo, Ontario. Presentation at Wilfrid Laurier University.

Chapter 7

1. "Heritage," www.thecocacolacompany.com/heritage/chronicle_birth_refreshing_idea.html (accessed June 5, 2010).

2. Coca-Cola Company, "Coca-Cola Announces Plans to Launch Coca-Cola Zero" (press release), March 21, 2005 (accessed June 5, 2010).

3. Betsy McKay, "Zero Is Coke's New Hero," *The Wall Street Journal* April 17, 2007 (accessed electronically January 14, 2008).

4. "The Chronicle of Coca-Cola," www.thecocacolacompany.com/heritage/chronicle_global_business.html (accessed June 5, 2010).

5. Kate Fitzgerald, "Coke Zero," *Advertising Age*, November 12, 2007 (accessed electronically January 14, 2008).

6. "Brands," www.thecocacolacompany.com/brands/index.html (accessed June 5, 2010).

7. Kate MacArthur, "Coke bets on Zero to Save a Cola Category." *Advertising Age*, January 1, 2007 (accessed electronically January 14, 2008).

8. Melanie Shortman, "Gender Wars," *American Demographics* (April 2002), p. 22.

9. Sheth, Mittal, and Newman, *Customer Behavior*.

10. Tamara Mangleburg et al., "The Moderating Effect of Prior Experience in Consumers' Use of User-Image Based versus Utilitarian Cues in Brand Attitude," *Journal of Business & Psychology* 13 (Fall 1998), pp. 101–113; M. Joseph Sirgy et al., "Direct versus Indirect Measures of Self-Image Congruence," *Journal of the Academy of Marketing Science* 25, no. 3 (1997), pp. 229–241.

11. Sheth, Mittal, and Newman, *Customer Behavior*.

12. VALS1, the original lifestyle survey, assessed general values and lifestyles. The VALS survey focuses more on values and lifestyles related to consumer behaviour and thus has more commercial applications. Another lifestyle segmentation system is Yankelovich's Monitor Mindbase (yankelovich.com).

13. www.strategicbusinessinsights.com/vals/applications/apps-pos.shtml (accessed June 6, 2010).

14. Michael D. Lam, "Psychographic Demonstration: Segmentation Studies Prepare to Prove Their Worth," *Pharmaceutical Executive*, January 2004.

15. Kathleen Krhialla, "CRM Case Study: The Analytics That Power CRM at Royal Bank [of Canada]," www.teradata.com/library/pdf/towergroup_020701.pdf (accessed June 6, 2010).

16. "About Us," www.corporateknights.ca/about-us/61-about-us/56-about-us.html (accessed June 8, 2010).

17. Erin Millar and Ben Colli, "The new liberal education: Sustainability," http://oncampus.macleans.ca/education/2009/12/18/the-new-liberal-education-sustainability/ (accessed June 8, 2010).

18. "Sustainability Pledge," www.sustain.ubc.ca/campus-sustainability/getting-involved/student-involvement/ubc-sustainability-pledge (accessed June 7, 2010).

19. "flyPhone," www.fireflymobile.com/flyphone/?osCsid=164huuvku66c55l78deg4g75 (accessed June 6, 2010).

20. A.M. Tomczyk, "Firefly Mobile: Calling all Tweens," *BusinessWeek Online* November 8, 2008.

21. Stowe Shoemaker and Robert Lewis, "Customer Loyalty: The Future of Hospitality Marketing," *Hospitality Management* 18 (1999), p. 349.

22. V. Kumar and Denish Shah, "Building and Sustaining Profitable Customer Loyalty for the 21st Century," *Journal of Retailing* 80, no. 4 (2004), pp. 317–330.

23. Rebecca Harris, "Canadians Love Loyalty," *Marketing Daily* May 31, 2007.

24. Aricanada.com (accessed June 1, 2007).

25. Michael J. Weiss, *The Clustered World* (Boston: Little, Brown, 2000).

26. PSYTE Advantage, www.tetrad.com/pricing/can/psyteadvantage.html (accessed June 1, 2007).

27. www.tetrad.com/demographics/canada/environics/prizmce.html (accessed June 1, 2007).

28. Pete Jacques, "Aspirational Segmentation," *LIMRA's MarketFacts Quarterly* 22 (Spring 2003), p. 2[0].

29. G.R. Iyer et al., "Linking Web-Based Segmentation to Pricing Tactics," *Journal of Product & Brand Management* 11, no. 5 (2002), pp. 288–302; B. Jaworski and K. Jocz, "Rediscovering the Consumer," *Marketing Management* (September/October 2002), pp. 22–27; L. Rosencrance, "Customers Balk at Variable DVD Pricing," *Computer World* September 11, 2000: 4; M. Stephanek, "None of Your Business: Customer Data Were Once Gold to E-Commerce. Now, Companies are Paying a Price for Privacy Jitters," *BusinessWeek* June 26, 2000: 78; D. Wessel, "How Technology Tailors Price Tags," *The Wall Street Journal* June 23, 2001: A1.

30. www.aa.com/content/AAdvantage/programDetails/eliteStatus/main.jhtml (accessed March 3, 2005).

31. www.microsoft.com/info/cookies.htm (accessed September 30, 2005).

32. www.lasenza.com (accessed December 18, 2007).

33. Dhruv Grewal, "Marketing Is All about Creating Value: 8 Key Rules," in *Inside the Mind of Textbook Marketing* (Boston: Aspatore Inc., 2003), 79–96.

34. James L. Heskett, W. Earl Sasser Jr., and Leonard A. Schlesinger, *The Service Profit Chain: How Leading Companies Link Profit and Growth to Loyalty, Satisfaction, and Value* (New York: Simon & Schuster Adult Publishing Group, 1997); Christopher D. Ittner and David F. Larcker, "Are Nonfinancial Measures Leading Indicators of Financial Performance? An Analysis of Customer Satisfaction," *Journal of Accounting Research* 35 (Supplement 1998), pp. 1–35; Thomas O. Jones and E. Earl Sasser Jr., "Why Satisfied Customers Defect," *Harvard Business Review* (November/December 1995), pp. 88–99; A. Parasuraman and Dhruv Grewal, "The Impact of Technology on the Quality-Value-Loyalty Chain: A Research Agenda," *Journal of the Academy of Marketing Science* 28, no. 1 (2000), pp. 168–174; Frederick F. Reichheld, "Loyalty-Based Management," *Harvard Business Review* 2 (March/April 1993), pp. 64–73; Frederick F. Reichheld, "Loyalty and the Renaissance of Marketing," *Marketing Management* 2, no. 4 (1994), pp. 10–21; Frederick F. Reichheld and Phil Schefter, "E-Loyalty," *Harvard Business Review* (July/August 2000), pp. 105–113; Anthony J. Rucci, Richard T. Quinn, and Steven P. Kirn, "The Employee-Customer-Profit Chain at Sears," *Harvard Business Review* (January/February 1998), pp. 83–97; Roland T. Rust, Valarie Zeithaml, and Katherine N. Lemon, *Driving Customer Equity* (New York: The Free Press, 2000); Russell S. Winer, "A Framework for Customer Relationship Management," *California Management Review* 43, no. 4 (2001), pp. 89–105; Valarie Zeithaml, Roland T. Rust, and Katherine N. Lemon, "The Customer Pyramid: Creating and Serving Profitable Customers," *California Management Review* 43, no. 4 (2001), pp. 118–142.

35. Datamonitor: Hallmark Cards, Inc., "Greeting Cards Facts and Figures," *Souvenirs, Gifts & Novelties* (May 2005).

36. lasenza.com (accessed December 18, 2007).

37. Marie Driscoll, "Abercrombie & Fitch: Power Shopper," *Standard & Poor's Equity Research*, October 30, 2007 (accessed electronically January 16, 2008).

38. Nicholas Kohler, "Abercrombie & Fitch: Come Shop in Our Dungeon," *Maclean's* (November 13, 2006) (accessed electronically June 6, 2010).

39. B. Joseph Pine, *Mass Customization: The New Frontier in Business Competition* (Cambridge, MA: Harvard Business School Publishing, 1999); James H. Gilmore and B. Joseph Pine, eds., *Markets of One: Creating Customer-Unique Value through Mass Customization* (Cambridge, MA: Harvard Business School Publishing, 2000).

40. "The Founder," www.chezcora.com/a/01-belle-histoire/1-3-fondatrice2.htm (accessed June 7, 2010).

41. Sabritir Ghosh, "Made to Order," *Report on [Small] Business* (September 2009), www.theglobeandmail.com/report-on-business/your-business/start/franchising/made-to-order/article1265158/ (accessed June 7, 2010).

42. "The Founder," www.chezcora.com/a/01-belle-histoire/1-3-fondatrice2.htm (accessed June 7, 2010).

43. Vanessa O'Connell, "Fashion Journal: Bubble Gum at Bergdorf's," *The Wall Street Journal* February 15, 2007 (accessed electronically January 15, 2008).

44. Vanessa O'Connell, "Fashion Bullies Attack—in Middle School." *The Wall Street Journal* October 25, 2007 (accessed electronically January 15, 2008).

45. Jean Halliday, "Maloney Wants Volvo Viewed as Both Safe and Luxurious," *Advertising Age* 75, no. 12 (2004), p. 22.

46. www.jacob.ca, www.lasenza.com, and www.abercrombie.ca (accessed June 1, 2007).

47. "Avis: We Try Harder," www.buildingbrands.com/didyouknow/16_avis_we_try_harder.php (accessed December 18, 2007).

48. "McDonald's legal cases," http://en.wikipedia.org/wiki/McDonald's_legal_cases (accessed December 18, 2007).

49. Crane et al., *Marketing*, 6th Can. ed. (Whitby, ON: McGraw-Hill Ryerson, 2006), p. 243.

50. "McDonald's Global Sales Advance 4.8%: Burger Giant Now Top Seller of Chicken," *Bloomberg News* (accessed June 1, 2007).

51. Gogi Anand et al., "Can Junk Food Be Healthy? A Consumer Behaviour Response to Repositioning Junk Food as a Healthy Alternative" (unpublished paper for WLU Consumer Behaviour Project), Wilfrid Laurier University, Waterloo, Ontario, 2007.

52. Stephen Brown, Robert V. Kozinets, and John F. Sherry Jr., "Teaching Old Brands New Tricks: Retro Branding and the Revival of Brand Meaning," *Journal of Marketing* 67, no. 2 (July 2003), p. 19.

53. Chuck Salter, "Whirlpool Finds Its Cool," *Fast Company* 95 (June 2005), p. 73.

54. Christine Bittar, "Cosmetic Changes beyond Skin Deep," *Brandweek*, May 17, 2000, pp. 20, 22.

55. Lisa Granatstein, "Back to Cool," *Mediaweek*, June 21, 2004, pp. 25–26.

56. Brian Wansink, "Making Old Brands New," *American Demographics* (December 1997), pp. 53–58.

57. Wansink, "Making Old Brands New."

58. This case was written by Shirley Lichti, the textbook co-author, for the basis of class discussion; it was not written as an illustration of effective or ineffective marketing practices.

59. Matt Semansky, "M&M Goes Downtown with Uptown," www.marketingmag.ca/daily/20071017/topstory.html (accessed October 16, 2007).

Appendix 7A

1. V. Kumar, A. Petersen, and R.P. Leone, "How Valuable Is the Word of Mouth?" *Harvard Business Review* (October 2007), pp. 139–146; V. Kumar and Morris George, "Measuring and Maximizing Customer Equity: A Critical Analysis," *Journal of the Academy of Marketing Science* 35, no. 2 (June 2007), pp. 157–171; V. Kumar, Denish Shah, and Rajkumar Venkatesan, "Managing Retailer Profitability: One Customer at a Time!" *Journal of Retailing* 82, no. 4 (October 2006), pp. 277–294; V. Kumar, "Profitable Relationships," *Marketing Research: A Magazine of Management and Applications* 18, no. 3 (Fall 2006), pp. 41–46; V. Kumar, "Customer Lifetime Value: A Databased Approach," *Journal of Relationship Marketing* 5, no. 2/3 (2006), pp. 7–35; Sunil Gupta et al., "Modeling Customer Lifetime Value," *Journal of Service Research* 9 (November 2006), pp. 139–155; V. Kumar, R. Venkatesan, and Werner Reinartz, "Knowing What to Sell, When and to Whom," *Harvard Business Review* (March 2006), pp. 131–137; Werner Reinartz, J. Thomas, and V. Kumar, "Balancing Acquisition and Retention Resources to Maximize Profitability," *Journal of Marketing* 69 (January 2005), pp. 63–79; R. Venkatesan and V. Kumar, "A Customer Lifetime Value Framework for Customer Selection and Resource Allocation Strategy," *Journal of Marketing* 68 (October 2004), pp. 106–125; V. Kumar and J. Andrew Petersen, "Maximizing ROI or Profitability: Is One Better Than the Other," *Marketing Research: A Magazine of Management and Applications* 16, no. 3 (Fall 2004), pp. 28–34; V. Kumar, G. Ramani, and T. Bohling, "Customer Lifetime Value Approaches and Best Practice Applications," *Journal of Interactive Marketing* 18, no. 3 (Summer 2004), pp. 60–72; J. Thomas, Werner Reinartz, and V. Kumar, "Getting the Most out of All Your Customers," *Harvard Business Review* (July–August 2004), pp. 116–123; Werner Reinartz and V. Kumar, "The Impact of Customer Relationship Characteristics on Profitable Lifetime Duration," *Journal of Marketing* 67 (January 2003), pp. 77–99; Werner Reinartz and V. Kumar, "The Mismanagement of Customer Loyalty," *Harvard Business Review* (July 2002), pp. 86–97; W. Reinartz and V. Kumar, "On the Profitability of Long Lifetime Customers: An Empirical Investigation and Implications for Marketing," *Journal of Marketing* 64 (October 2000), pp. 17–32.

2. We have made some minor adjustments to the formula suggested by Gupta et al., "Modeling Customer Lifetime Value."

3. Sunil Gupta and Donald R. Lehmann, *Managing Customers as Investments* (Philadelphia, PA: Wharton School Publishing, 2005); Gupta et al., "Modeling Customer Lifetime Value."

Chapter 8

1. About Inventables, www.inventables.com/about (accessed June 9, 2010).

2. www.dove.com.

3. "Thinking outside the cardboard box," www.metronews.ca/vancouver/live/article/264794 (accessed June 10, 2010).

4. "Doing the Right Thing," www.frogbox.com/therightthing.php (accessed June 10, 2010).

5. A number of articles on variety seeking are available. For example, see Andrea Morales et al., "Perceptions of Assortment Variety: The Effects of Congruency between Consumer's Internal and Retailer's External Organization," *Journal of Retailing* 81 no. 2 (2005), pp. 159–169.

6. Koen Pauwels et al., "New Products, Sales Promotions, and Firm Value: The Case of the Automobile Industry," *Journal of Marketing* 68, no. 4 (October 2004), p. 142.

7. Kalpesh Kaushik Desai and Kevin Lane Keller, "The Effects of Ingredient Branding Strategies on Host Brand Extendibility," *Journal of Marketing* 66, no. 1 (January 2002), pp. 73–93.

8. Rajesh K. Chandy, Jaideep C. Prabhu, and Kersi D. Antia, "What Will the Future Bring? Dominance, Technology Expectations, and Radical Innovation," *Journal of Marketing* 67, no. 3 (July 2003), pp. 1–18; Harald J. van Heerde, Carl F. Mela, and Puneet Manchanda, "The Dynamic Effect of Innovation on Market Structure," *Journal of Marketing Research* 41, no. 2 (May 2004), pp. 166–183.

9. Clayton M. Christensen and Michael E. Raynor, *The Innovator's Solution* (Boston: Harvard Business School Press, 2003).

10. Philip Kotler, *Marketing Management*, 11th ed. (Upper Saddle River, NJ: Prentice-Hall, 2003), pp. 330–331. Kotler's work was based on the following research: William T. Robinson and Claes Fornell, "Sources of Market Pioneer Advantages in Consumer Goods Industries," *Journal of Marketing Research* 22, no. 3 (August 1985), pp. 305–317; Glen L. Urban et al., "Market Share Rewards to Pioneering Brands: An Empirical Analysis and Strategic Implications," *Management Science* 32 (June 1986), pp. 645–659; and G.S. Carpenter and Kent Nakamoto, "Consumer Preference Formation and Pioneering Advantage," *Journal of Marketing Research* 26, no. 3 (August 1989), pp. 285–298.

11. Raji Srinivasan, Gary L. Lilien, and Arvind Rangaswamy, "First in, First out? The Effects of Network Externalities on Pioneer Survival," *Journal of Marketing* 68, no. 1 (January 2004), p. 41.

12. Cyndee Miller, "Little Relief Seen for New Product Failure Rate," *Marketing News* June 21, 1993: 1, 10; "Flops," *BusinessWeek* (August 16, 1993), p. 76ff; Lori Dahm, "Secrets of Success: The Strategies Driving New Product Development at Kraft," *Stagnito's New Products Magazine* 2 (January 2002), p. 18ff.

13. www.marketingpower.com (accessed September 18, 2006).

14. www.appleinsider.com/articles/04/11/29/ipod_adoption_rate_faster_than_sony_walkman.html (accessed December 23, 2007).

15. Eliot Van Buskirk, "Apple iPad Reaches '1 Million Sold' Twice as Fast as iPhone," www.wired.com/epicenter/2010/05/apple-ipad-reaches-one-million-sold-twice-as-fast-as-iphone/ (accessed June 9, 2010).

16. www.quickmba.com (accessed September 16, 2006).

17. Michael Arndt, "The Challenges for McDonald's Top Chef," www.businessweek.com/innovate/content/sep2009/id20090914_256776.htm?link_position=link41 (accessed June 9, 2010).

18. Subin Im and John P. Workman Jr., "Market Orientation, Creativity, and New Product Performance in High-Technology Firms," *Journal of Marketing* 68, no. 2 (April 2004), p. 114.

19. Standard & Poor's Industry Surveys, Healthcare: Pharmaceuticals, June 24, 2004.

20. Geoffrey York and Simon Avery, "China's got RedBerry," www.theglobeandmail.com/servlet/story/RTGAM.20060411.wredberry11/BNStory/Business/home (accessed June 11, 2007).

21. Glen L. Urban and John R. Hauser, "'Listening In' to Find and Explore New Combinations of Customer Needs," *Journal of Marketing* 68, no. 2 (April 2004), p. 72; Steve Hoeffler, "Measuring Preferences for Really New Products," *Journal of Marketing Research* 40, no. 4 (November 2003), pp. 406–420.

22. Glen L. Urban and John R. Hauser, *Design and Marketing of New Products*, 2nd ed. (Upper Saddle River, NJ: Prentice Hall, 1993), pp. 120–121.

23. Interview with Jevin Eagle (executive vice-president of merchandising and marketing at Staples), June 18, 2009.

24. http://mystarbucksidea.force.com/apex/ideaList?lsi=2 (accessed June 9, 2010).

25. Lisa D'Innocenzo, "Frito Lay Canada: Potato chips … for dinner?" www.strategymag.com/articles/magazine/20070101/biz.html (accessed June 12, 2007).

26. D'Innocenzo, "Frito Lay Canada."

27. www.betterproductdesign.net/tools/user/leaduser.htm (accessed November 12, 2004); Eric von Hippel, "Successful Industrial Products from Consumers' Ideas," *Journal of Marketing* 42, no. 1 (January 1978), pp. 39–49; Eric von Hippel, "Lead Users: A Source of Novel Product Concepts," *Management Science* 32 (1986), pp. 791–805; Eric von Hippel, *The Sources of Innovation* (New York: Oxford University Press, 1988); Glen L. Urban and Eric von Hippel, "Lead User Analysis for the Development of Industrial Products," *Management Science* 34 (May 1988), pp. 569–582.

28. Karl T. Ulrich and Steven D. Eppinger, *Product Design and Development*, 2nd ed. (Boston: Irwin-McGraw-Hill, 2000).

29. www.marketingpower.com (accessed September 18, 2006).

30. Ulrich and Eppinger, *Product Design and Development*, p. 166.

31. Ely Dahan and V. Srinivasan, "The Predictive Power of Internet-Based Product Concept Testing Using Visual Depiction and Animation," *Journal of Product Innovation Management* 17 (2000), pp. 99–109.

32. www.marketingpower.com (accessed September 18, 2006).

33. Ulrich and Eppinger, *Product Design and Development*.

34. Ellen Byron, "A Virtual View of the Store Aisle," *The Wall Street Journal* October 3, 2007.

35. Tonya Vinas, "P&G Seeks Alternatives to Animal Tests," *Industry Week* 253, no. 7 (July 2004), p. 60; "EU to Ban Animal Tested Cosmetics," www.cnn.com (accessed March 31, 2006); www.leapingbunny.org; Gary Anthes, "P&G Uses Data Mining to Cut Animal Testing," www.computerworld.com (accessed December 6, 1999).

36. Noriko Suzuki, "The Truth about the Body Shop," www.tsujiru.net/compass/compass_1996/reg/suzuki_noriko.htm (accessed June 12, 2007).

37. www2.acnielsen.com/products/crs_bases2.shtml (accessed September 20, 2006).

38. Kotler, *Marketing Management*.

39. Emily Wexler, "McDonald's Plans to Win," www.strategyonline.ca/articles/magazine/20090901/bizmcdonalds.html (accessed June 9, 2010).

40. Patricia Sellers, "P&G: Teaching an Old Dog New Tricks," *Fortune* (May 31, 2004), pp. 166–180.

41. Norma Ramage, "Testing, testing 1-2-3," www.marketingmag.ca/magazine/current/in_context/article.jsp?content=20050718_69775_69775 (accessed June 12, 2007).

42. www.infores.com/public/us/analytics/productportfolio/bscannewprodtest.htm (accessed April 2, 2006).

43. J. Daniel Sherman and William E. Souder, "Managing New Technology Development," http://books.google.com/books?id=6p3hdSUXOlsC&pg=PA104&lpg=PA104&dq=kellogg+% 22toast+ems%22&source=web&ots=xP30aQrfMe&sig=YA xE8134Djzngytp3DcC_H8g_FA (accessed June 12, 2007).

44. D'Innocenzo, "Frito Lay Canada."

45. Product Development Management Association, *The PDMA Handbook of New Product Development*, 2nd ed., Kenneth K. Kahn, ed. (New York: John Wiley & Sons, 2004).

46. Ashwin W. Joshi and Sanjay Sharma, "Customer Knowledge Development: Antecedents and Impact on New Product Success," *Journal of Marketing* 68, no. 4 (October 2004), p. 47.

47. BestNewProducts.ca maintains a list of best new products launched each year. The products listed were winners in the 4th Annual Best New Products Awards, a competition judged by 10 000 Canadian consumers coast to coast.

48. "BlackBerry Pearl 8130 smartphone," www.businessonthego1.com/english/wp_blackberry_bb8130.asp (accessed January 12, 2008).

49. Yuhong Wu, Sridhar Balasubramanian, and Vijay Mahajan, "When Is a Preannounced New Product Likely to Be Delayed?" *Journal of Marketing* 68, no. 2 (April 2004), p. 101.

50. www.pdma.org (accessed September 15, 2006).

51. Theodore Levitt, *Marketing Imagination* (New York: The Free Press, 1986).

52. Donald R. Lehmann and Russell S. Winer, *Analysis for Marketing Planning*, 6th ed. (Boston: McGraw-Hill/Irwin, 2004).

53. Urban and Hauser, *Design and Marketing*.

54. www.organicearthday.org/DelMonteFoods.htm (accessed June 10, 2010); www.delmonte.com/Products/ (accessed June 10, 2010).

55. Miriam Jordan and Jonathan Karp, "Machines for the Masses; Whirlpool Aims Cheap Washer at Brazil, India and China; Making Due with Slower Spin," *The Wall Street Journal* December 9, 2003: A19.

56. Om Malik, "The New Land of Opportunity," *Business 2.0*, July 2004, pp. 72–79.

57. Claire Briney, "Wiping Up the Market," *Global Cosmetic Industry* 172, no. 4 (April 2004), pp. 40–43.

58. Kara Swisher, "Home Economics: The Hypoallergenic Car; Wave of Cleaning Products Caters to Finicky Drivers; Premoistened Auto Wipes," *The Wall Street Journal* (eastern edition; May 6, 2004): D1.

59. www.toiletwand.com (accessed September 20, 2006).

60. "Popularity of virtual rock 'n' roll fuels second national gaming tour," www.newswire.ca/en/releases/archive/February2009/24/c3087.html (accessed November 15, 2009).

61. Jonathan Paul, "Pepsi amps it up on campuses," www.strategyonline.ca/articles/magazine/20091101/maoysilver.html?page=2 (accessed November 15, 2009).

62. www40.statcan.ca/l01/cst01/arts28.htm (accessed June 12, 2007).

63. "Vinyl lovers spur new boom for old medium," www.cbc.ca/consumer/story/2007/01/03/vinyl-boom.html (accessed June 12, 2007).

64. "Vinyl lovers spur new boom."

65. Kevin J. Clancy and Peter C. Krieg, "Product Life Cycle: A Dangerous Idea," *Brandweek*, March 1, 2004, p. 26; Nariman K. Dhalla and Sonia Yuseph, "Forget the Product Life-Cycle Concept," *Harvard Business Review* (January–February 1976), p. 102ff.

66. Peter Golder and Gerard Tellis, "Cascades, Diffusion, and Turning Points in the Product Life Cycle," *MSI* Report No. 03-120, 2003.

67. Jay Bolling, "DTC: A Strategy for Every Stage," *Pharmaceutical Executive*, November 2003, pp. 110–117.

68. This case is based on a case written by Colin Fox in conjunction with the textbook authors (Ajax Persaud and Shirley Lichti) for use in a class discussion; it was not written as an illustration of effective or ineffective marketing practices.

69. www.apple.com/investor/ (accessed November 27, 2007).

70. Tom Hormby, "Birth of the PowerBook: How Apple Took Over the Portable Market in 1991," *Low End Mac*, November 23, 2005, http://lowendmac.com/orchard/05/1123.html (accessed October 6, 2008).

71. Wingfield, Nick, "A New Wireless Player Hopes to Challenge iPod," *The Wall Street Journal* April 9, 2007.

72. Frank Rose, "Battle for the Soul of the MP3 Phone," *Wired*, November 24, 2005.

73. Lev Grossman, "Invention of the Year: iPhone," *Time*, October 31, 2007, www.time.com/time/business/article/0,8599,1678581,00.html (accessed November 24, 2005).

74. John Barber, "Why old media loves Apple's newest thing," *The Globe and Mail* January 28, 2010: B1.

75. Barber, "Why old media."

76. Associated Press, "Apple Sells 300,000 iPads on First Day," www.marketingmag.ca/english/news/marketer/article.jsp?content=20100405_151859_9012 (accessed June 12, 2010).

77. Eliot Van Buskirk, "Apple iPad Reaches '1 Million Sold' Twice as Fast as iPhone," www.wired.com/epicenter/2010/05/apple-ipad-reaches-one-million-sold-twice-as-fast-as-iphone/ (accessed June 9, 2010).

78. "Apple Sells Two Million iPads in Less Than 60 Days," www.apple.com/pr/library/2010/05/31ipad.html (accessed June 12, 2010).

79. Barrie McKenna, "The new tech king: Consumers help Apple steal Microsoft's crown," *The Globe and Mail* May 27, 2010: A1.

Chapter 9

1. www.unileverusa.com/ourbrands/personalcare/dove.asp (accessed June 6, 2007).

2. Karen Mazurkesich, "Dove Story," www.strategymag.com/articles/magazine/20070101/dove.html?word=dove&wor d=story (accessed June 6, 2007).

3. American Marketing Association, *Dictionary of Marketing Terms* (Chicago, IL: American Marketing Association, 2004), available at www.marketingpower.com/live/mg-dictionary-view329.php?.

4. "All Colgate Toothpastes," www.colgate.com (accessed September 16, 2006).

5. William P. Putsis Jr. and Barry L. Bayus, "An Empirical Analysis of Firms' Product Line Decisions," *Journal of Marketing Research* 38, no. 1 (February 2001), pp. 110–118.

6. Bruce G.S. Hardie and Leonard M. Lodish, "Perspectives: The Logic of Product-Line Extensions," *Harvard Business Review* (November–December 1994), p. 54.

7. John A. Quelch and David Kenny, "Extend Profits, Not Product Lines," *Harvard Business Review* (September–October 1994), pp. 153–160.

8. Rekha Balu, "Heinz to Trim Its Work Force as Much as 9%," *The Wall Street Journal* February 18, 1999: ProQuest Document ID 39039688.

9. Naoko Fujimura and Mike Firn, "Starbucks Says Via Sales May Pass $1 Billion Globally," www.businessweek.com/news/2010-04-13/starbucks-says-via-sales-may-pass-1-billion-globally-correct-.html (accessed May 30, 2010).

10. "Starbucks Introduces Starbucks®Natural Fusions Naturally Flavored Coffee in Grocery Stores Nationwide," http://news.starbucks.com/article_display.cfm?article_id=388 (accessed May 30, 2010).

11. "J&J to Buy Skin-Care Business," *The Wall Street Journal* December 18, 1998: 1.

12. http://scjohnson.com/products/ (accessed September 20, 2006).

13. Louis Lee, "Jean Therapy, $23 a Pop," *BusinessWeek*, June 28, 2004, pp. 91, 93.

14. Ernest Beck, "Unilever to Cut 25,000 Jobs, Close Factories—Consumer-Goods Company to Focus on Core Brands in Restructuring Asian," *The Wall Street Journal* February 23, 2000: 2.

15. www.rbc.com/aboutus/index.html (accessed June 6, 2007).

16. www.rbcroyalbank.com/RBC:RmcqJo71A8UAAWzg3w8/products/deposits/view-all-bank-accounts.html (accessed June 6, 2007).

17. Kevin Lane Keller, *Strategic Brand Management: Building, Measuring, and Managing Brand Equity*, 2nd ed. (Upper Saddle River, NJ: Prentice Hall, 2003).

18. This discussion on the advantages of strong brands is adapted from Keller, *Strategic Brand Management*, pp. 104–112; Elizabeth S. Moore, William L. Wilkie, and Richard J. Lutz, "Passing the Torch: Intergenerational Influences as a Source of Brand Equity," *Journal of Marketing* 66, no. 2 (April 2002), p. 17.

19. Angela Y. Lee and Aparna A. Labroo, "The Effect of Conceptual and Perceptual Fluency on Brand Evaluation," *Journal of Marketing Research* 41, no. 2 (May 2004), pp. 151–165.

20. www.interbrand.com/best_brands_2004.asp (accessed September 14, 2006). The net present value of the earnings over the next 12 months is used to calculate the value.

21. David A. Aaker, *Managing Brand Equity* (New York: Free Press, 1991).

22. "Best Global Brands 2009," http://issuu.com/interbrand/docs/bgb2009_magazine_final (accessed May 30, 2010).

23. Polo Ralph Lauren Corporate Report 2004, http://media.corporate-ir.net/media_files/NYS/RL/reports/04ar/PRL2004AR.pdf (accessed September 16, 2006).

24. David A. Aaker, "Measuring Brand Equity Across Products and Markets," *California Management Review* 38 (Spring 1996), pp. 102–120.

25. http://en.wikipedia.org/wiki/List_of_generic_and_genericized_trademarks (accessed December 22, 2007).

26. Keller, *Strategic Brand Management*.

27. Jennifer L. Aaker, "Dimensions of Brand Personality," *Journal of Marketing Research* 34, no. 3 (August 1997), pp. 347–356.

28. Kevin Lane Keller, "Conceptualizing, Measuring, and Managing Customer-Based Brand Equity," *Journal of Marketing* 57, no. 1 (January 1993), pp. 1–22.

29. Dave Larson, "Building a Brand's Personality from the Customer Up," *Direct Marketing*, October 2002, pp. 17–21.

30. www.marketingpower.com/live/mg-dictionary.php?SearchFor=brand+loyalty&Searched=1 (accessed September 17, 2006).

31. Russ Martin, "Nutella Launches Better Breakfast Challenge," www.marketingmag.ca/english/news/pr/article.jsp?content=20090512_173532_9460 (accessed May 30, 2010).

32. Martin, "Nutella Launches."

33. James H. McAlexander, John W. Schouten, and Harold F. Koenig, "Building Brand Community," *Journal of Marketing* 66, no. 1 (January 2002), pp. 38–54.

34. Christine Bittar, "Big Brands: Stronger than Dirt," *BrandWeek*, June 23, 2003, pp. S52–S53.

35. "President's Choice Continues Brisk Pace," *Frozen Food Age*, March 1998, pp. 17–18.

36. Laura Liebeck, "Private Label Goes Premium," *Discount Store News* (November 4, 1996): F38; "New Private-Label Alternatives Bring Changes to Supercenters, Clubs," *DSN Retailing Today*, February 5, 2001, p. 66.

37. www.marketinghalloflegends.ca/visionaries_david_nichol.php (accessed June 7, 2007).

38. Michael Levy and Barton A. Weitz, *Retailing Management*, 6th ed. (New York: McGraw-Hill/Irwin, 2007).

39. www.pg.com.

40. Harvey Schacter, "What's in a name? Plenty," *The Globe and Mail* May 5, 2004: C4.

41. Eve Lazarus, "New beer goes with flies and a croak," www.marketingmag.ca/magazine/marketingdaily/article.jsp?content=20060914_102950_5424 (accessed June 7, 2007).

42. For recent research on brand extensions, see Subramanian Balachander and Sanjoy Ghose, "Reciprocal Spillover Effects: A Strategic Benefit of Brand Extensions," *Journal of Marketing* 67, no. 1 (January 2003), pp. 4–13; Kalpesh Kaushik Desai and Kevin Lane Keller, "The Effects of Ingredient Branding Strategies on Host Brand Extendibility," *Journal of Marketing* 66, no. 1 (January 2002), pp. 73–93; Tom Meyvis and Chris Janiszewski, "When Are Broader Brands Stronger Brands? An Accessibility Perspective on the Success of Brand Extensions," *Journal of Consumer Research* 31, no. 2 (September 2004), pp. 346–357.

43. David Aaker, "Brand Extensions: The Good, the Bad, and the Ugly," *Sloan Management Review* 31 (Summer 1990), pp. 47–56.

44. www.braun.com (accessed June 10, 2011).

45. www.dell.com (accessed June 10, 2011).

46. www.fritolay.com/consumer.html (accessed June 10, 2011).

47. Vanitha Swaminathan, Richard J. Fox, and Srinivas K. Reddy, "The Impact of Brand Extension Introduction on Choice," *Journal of Marketing* 65, no. 3 (October 2001), pp. 1–15.

48. Jennifer Aaker, Susan Fournier, and S. Adam Brasel, "When Good Brands Do Bad," *Journal of Consumer Research* 31, no. 1 (June 2004), pp. 1–16.

49. Hoover's Company Information, *Hoover's Online*, 2004; Melissa Master, "Overreaching," *Across the Board* (March/April 2001), pp. 20–26; David Taylor, *Brand Stretch: Why 1 in 2 Extensions Fail and How to Beat the Odds* (New York: John Wiley & Sons, 2004); Melanie Wells, "Red Baron," *Forbes*, July 3, 2000, p. 150.

50. www.hoovers.com/virgin-group/—ID__41676—/free-cofactsheet.xhtml (accessed August 30, 2005).

51. Barbara Loken and Deborah Roedder John, "Diluting Brand Beliefs: When Do Brand Extensions Have a Negative Impact?" *Journal of Marketing* 57, no. 3 (July 1993), pp. 71–84.

52. Aaker, "Brand Extensions," pp. 47–56.

53. David A. Aaker and Kevin Lane Keller, "Consumer Evaluations of Brand Extensions," *Journal of Marketing* 54, no. 1 (January 1990), pp. 27–41.

54. Susan M. Broniarczyk and Joseph W. Alba, "The Importance of the Brand in Brand Extension," *Journal of Marketing Research* 31, no. 2 (May 1994), pp. 214–228.

55. www.ritzcarlton.com/corporate/about_us/history.asp (accessed September 16, 2006).

56. Kate Fitzgerald, "A New Addition to Cobranding's Menu," *Credit Card Management*, 16 (November 2003), pp. 40–44.

57. This section is based on Akshay R. Rao and Robert W. Ruekert, "Brand Alliances as Signals of Product Quality," *Sloan Management Review* 36 (Fall 1994), pp. 87–97.

58. Kristen Laird, "Joe Fresh begins relationship with Barbie," www.marketingmag.ca/english/news/marketer/article.jsp?content=20101103_164846_9592 (accessed April 27, 2011).

59. "FedEx Expands Alliance with Kinko's," *Journal of Commerce* (August 11, 2000), p. WP.

60. "FedEx and Kinko's to Deliver Increased Threat," *DSN Retailing Today*, May 17, 2004, p. 17.

61. T. Kippenberger, "Co-Branding as a Competitive Weapon," *Strategic Direction* 18 (October), pp. 31–33.

62. "Sprinkles on your doughnut . . . or your ice cream?," *The Globe and Mail* June 12, 2009: B7.

63. Tom Blacket and Bob Boad, eds., *Branding: The Science of Alliance* (London: Macmillan Press, 1999).

64. David A. Aaker, *Brand Portfolio Strategy* (New York: The Free Press, 2004).

65. Keller, *Strategic Brand Management*.

66. Doug Desjardins, "LIMA Foresees Huge 2nd Half for Entertainment Properties," *DSN Retailing Today*, June 21, 2004, pp. 6, 37.

67. "NASCAR Launches New Stock Car Racing Series in Canada and National Title Sponsorship Agreement with Canadian Tire," www.newswire.ca/en/releases/archive/September2006/12/c5003.html (accessed June 7, 2007).

68. Keller, *Strategic Brand Management*.

69. www.lacoste.com (accessed June 10, 2011).

70. Dwight Oestricher, "Marvel: Powerhouse Potential? Other Heroes Spawned by Spider-Man Creator Could Pay Off," *The Wall Street Journal* May 8, 2002: B9ff.

71. Anna Wilde Mathews, "Lord of the Things—Separate Companies Hold Rights to the Products from 'Rings' Books, Films," *The Wall Street Journal* December 17, 2001: B1ff.

72. William Makely, "Being the Beauty, Being the Brand," *Global Cosmetic Industry* (January 2004), pp. 28–30.

73. "Corby's Annual Report 2009," p. 6, www.corby.ca/annualreports/237934acc243818cb2.pdf (accessed November 11, 2009).

74. Kristen Laird, "Corby Has Social Media Fun with Polar Ice," www.marketingmag.ca/english/news/marketer/article.jsp?content=20090820_172203_940.

75. www.cdnaids.ca/polarice/english.html (accessed November 11, 2009).

76. "Packages: Tracing an Evolution," *Packaging Digest* (December 2003), pp. 37–42.

77. www.packagingdigest.com/articles/200605/6.php (accessed June 8, 2007).

78. Annette Bourdeau, "A green future: Three eco-friendly trends you should be keeping an eye on," www.strategymag.com/articles/magazine/20070501/what.html?word=biodegradable&word=palm&word=fibre-based&word=packaging (accessed June 7, 2007).

79. Annette Bourdeau, "P&G rallies allies (and foes)," www.strategymag.com/articles/magazine/20071001/upfronttide.html (accessed December 22, 2007).

80. Sustainable Agriculture, www.thecoca-colacompany.com/citizenship/sustainable_agriculture.html (accessed May 30, 2010).

81. David Ebener. "Green message in a bottle," *The Globe and Mail* November 17, 2009: B3.

82. "Sourcing," www.thecoca-colacompany.com/citizenship/plantbottle_sourcing.html (accessed May 30, 2010).

83. "The Coca-Cola Company PlantBottle™ Packaging Receives Prestigious Global Award," www.thecoca-colacompany.com/presscenter/nr_20100525_plantbottle_award.html (accessed May 30, 2010).

84. "Frequently Asked Questions," www.thecoca-colacompany.com/citizenship/plantbottle_faq.html (accessed May 30, 2010).

85. "Danone Expands Goodies Low-Fat Line of Desserts," *Marketing*, February 12, 2004, p. 4; www.landwriter.co.uk/landwriter/premium/TemplateParser.asp?ald=3778&page=FreeTemplate (accessed August 30, 2005).

86. www.smartspot.com/about/criteria/ (accessed June 8, 2007).

87. Laura Penny, "When Health Meets Hedonism," *The Globe and Mail* June 2, 2007: F7.

88. This case was written by Jeanne L. Munger and Julie Rusch in conjunction with the U.S. textbook authors (Dhruv Grewal and Michael Levy) for use in a class discussion; it was not written as an illustration of effective or ineffective marketing practices. Jeanne Munger is an associate professor at the University of Southern Maine.

89. www.bandaid.com/brand_story.shtml; www.bandaid.com/new_products.shtml; Christine Bittar, "J&J Stuck on Expanding BAND-AID® Franchise," *Brandweek*, March 3, 2003, p. 4; Richard Gutwillig, "Billion-Dollar Bandages," *Supermarket Business*, August 15, 2000, p. 58; "United States Top 10 First Aid Tape/Bandages/Gauze Brands Ranked by Dollar Sales and Unit Volume for 2003," *Chain Drug Review*, June 21, 2004, p. 238; Andrea M. Grossman, "Personal and Beauty Care: News Bites," *Drug Store News*, January 11, 1999, p. 61; "O-T-C Health Care: United States Over-the-Counter Heath Care Product Sales in Dollars and Percent Change for 2003," *Chain Drug Review*, May 24, 2004, p. 32.

90. Christine Bittar, "J&J Stuck on Expanding Band-Aid Franchise," *Brandweek* 44, no. 9 (March 3, 2003), p. 4.

Chapter 10

1. "Got-Junk Owner named Entrepreneur of the Year," www.canada.com/vancouversun/news/business/story.html?id=a6494cd4-321b-4fdf-ba33-ff55b3e11429 (accessed June 13, 2010).

2. Matt Semansky, "1-800-Got-Junk? Makes a Beer Run," www.marketingmag.ca/daily/20070320/national2.html (accessed June 13, 2007).

3. "Got-Junk Owner named Entrepreneur of the Year," www.canada.com/vancouversun/news/business/story.html?id=a6494cd4-321b-4fdf-ba33-ff55b3e11429 (accessed June 13, 2010).

4. Eve Lazarus, "Trash Talk," www.marketingmag.ca/magazine/current/in_context/article.jsp?content=20070226_68767_68767 (accessed June 13, 2007).

5. "Junk Collection Environmental Audit," www.1800gotjunk.com/ca_en/Files/System Wide Audit Summary.pdf (accessed June 13, 2010).

6. Leonard L. Berry and A. Parasuraman, *Marketing Services: Competing through Quality* (New York: The Free Press, 1991), p. 5.

7. Valarie A. Zeithaml, A. Parasuraman, and Leonard L. Berry, *Delivering Quality Service: Balancing Customer Perceptions and Expectations* (New York: The Free Press, 1990).

8. "myFinanceTracker from RBC a first for Canada," www.clickweekly.com/articles/June 1_2010/RBC.htm (accessed June 13, 2010).

9. Konrad Yakabuski, "The Greatest Canadian Company on Earth," *Report on Business Magazine* (September 2007), p. 57.

10. "Cineplex Entertainment Launches Online Social Networking Community, mycineplex," www.reuters.com/article/pressRelease/idUS92039+03-Sep-2008+MW20080903 (accessed online November 17, 2009).

11. Canadian Press, "Blockbusters boost Cineplex bottom line," www.marketingmag.ca/english/news/marketer/article.jsp?content=20090212_165501_2552 (accessed November 17, 2009).

12. M. Levy, Jerry Gotlieb, and Gopal Iyer, *Developing a Deeper Understanding of Post-Purchase Perceived Risk and Repeat Purchase Behavioral Intentions in a Service Setting* (unpublished working paper), Babson College, 2006; Mary Jo Bitner, Stephen W. Brown, and Matthew L. Mueter, "Technology Infusion in Service Encounters," *Journal of the Academy of Marketing Science* 28, no. 1 (2000), pp. 138–149; Jerry Gotlieb, Dhruv Grewal, Michael Levy, and Joan Lindsey-Mullikin, "An Examination of Moderators of the Effects of Customers' Evaluation of Employee Courtesy on Attitude toward the Service Firm," *Journal of Applied Social Psychology* 34 (April 2004), pp. 825–847.

13. Choice Hotels, "Special Guest Policies," 2004, www7.choice-hotels.com/ires/en-US/html/GuestPolicies?sid=hPTj.2R60 elpGw.7 (accessed September 10, 2006).

14. "Privacy Concerns Fail to Slow Social Activity," www.emarketer.com/Article.aspx?R=1007773 (accessed July 1, 2010).

15. "It's Quit Facebook Day. Who will dare delete their profile?" www.theglobeandmail.com/news/technology/personal-tech/its-quit-facebook-day-who-will-dare-delete-their-profile/article1586482/ (accessed May 31, 2010).

16. "Youth Don't Trust Social Networking Sites," www.marketingmag.ca/english/news/media/article.jsp?content=20100528_163244_13916 (accessed June 10, 2010).

17. David Brown, "Marketers Out of 'Experimentation' Phase with Facebook, Zuckerberg Tells Festival," *Marketing@Cannes* June 24, 2010: www.marketingmag.ca/english/news/cannes/article.jsp?content=20100624_101039_7692 (accessed June 28, 2010).

18. Brown, "Marketers Out of 'Experimentation.'"

19. Brown, "Marketers Out of 'Experimentation.'"

20. www.clubmed.com (accessed June 13, 2011).

21. Rebecca Harris, "Confident Customers," www.marketingmag.ca/magazine/current/in_context/article.jsp?content=20060410_76174_76174 (accessed June 17, 2007).

22. Greg Michetti, "Webify Your Workout," www.backbone-mag.com/Magazine/Hot_Tech_12310602.asp (accessed June 17, 2007).

23. Andrew Willis, "Sports fan munchies fatten Cineplex's bottom line," www.theglobeandmail.com/servlet/story/LAC.20070104.RCINEPLEX04/TPStory/Entertainment (accessed June 17, 2007).

24. Steve Ladurantaye, "Introducing the biggest outdoor water park in Canada," www.theglobeandmail.com/report-on-business/your-business/start/location/introducing-the-biggest-outdoor-water-park-in-canada/article1598930/ (accessed June 13, 2010).

25. "Waterpark Industry General & Fun Facts," www.waterparks.org/otherArticles/Waterpark Industry General & Fun Facts.pdf (accessed June 13, 2010).

26. Ladurantaye, "Introducing the biggest outdoor water park in Canada," www.theglobeandmail.com/report-on-business/your-business/start/location/introducing-the-biggest-outdoor-water-park-in-canada/article1598930/ (accessed June 13, 2010).

27. Ladurantaye, "Introducing."

28. "Canada's Largest Theme Waterpark Gearing up for Big Splash Grand Opening," www.calypsopark.com/_files/press_release_042010.pdf (accessed June 13, 2010).

29. The discussion of the Gap Model and its implications draws heavily from Michael Levy and Barton A. Weitz, *Retailing Management*, 6th ed. (Burr Ridge, IL: Irwin/McGraw-Hill, 2007) and also is based on Deon Nel and Leyland Pitt, "Service Quality in a Retail Environment: Closing the Gaps," *Journal of General Management* 18 (Spring 1993), pp. 37–57; Zeithaml, Parasuraman, and Berry, *Delivering Quality Customer Service*; Valerie Zeithaml, Leonard Berry, and A. Parasuraman, "Communication and Control Processes in the Delivery of Service Quality," *Journal of Marketing* 52, no. 2 (April 1988), pp. 35–48.

30. Kenneth Clow, David Kurtz, John Ozment, and Beng Soo Ong, "The Antecedents of Consumer Expectations of Services: An Empirical Study across Four Industries," *The Journal of Services Marketing* 11 (May–June 1997), pp. 230–248; Ann Marie Thompson and Peter Kaminski, "Psychographic and Lifestyle Antecedents of Service Quality Expectations," *Journal of Services Marketing* 7 (1993), pp. 53–61.

31. Zeithaml, Parasuraman, and Berry, *Delivering Quality Customer Service*.

32. Rebecca Harris, "Marketing 2.0," www.marketingmag.ca/magazine/current/feature/article.jsp?content=20070430_69539_69539 (accessed June 17, 2007).

33. Harris, "Marketing 2.0."

34. Harris, "Marketing 2.0."

35. Leonard Berry and A. Parasuraman, "Listening to the Customer—The Concept of a Service-Quality Information System," *Sloan Management Review* 38, no. 3 (1997), pp. 65–77; A. Parasuraman and Dhruv Grewal, "Serving Customers and Consumers Effectively in the 21st Century" (working paper), University of Miami, Coral Gables, Florida, 1998.

36. Teena Lyons, "Complain to Me—If You Can," *Knight Ridder Tribune News* December 4, 2005: 1.

37. www.enermodal.com/Canadian/company_profile.html (accessed June 14, 2010).

38. www.enermodal.com/Canadian/news/EEL-Newsroom-Fifth.pdf (accessed June 14, 2010).

39. "Sustainable Waterloo," *The Record* (special advertising feature), March 20, 2010: D4.

40. www.enermodal.com/Canadian/company_building.html (accessed June 14, 2010).

41. www.enermodal.com/Canadian/company_green_policies.html (accessed June 14, 2010).

42. Joanna LaFleur, "Business Motivations for Sustainability," www. enermodal.com/Canadian/news/EEL-Newsroom-Sustainability.pdf (accessed June 14, 2010).

43. Diane Jermyn, "The Top 50 Greenest Employers," www. theglobeandmail.com/report-on-business/the-top-50-greenest-employers/article1543083/ (accessed June 14, 2010).

44. www.nwa.com/plan/index.html (accessed September 20, 2006).

45. "2009 Financial Report," www.westjet.com/pdf/investorMedia/ financialReports/WestJet2009AR_financialReport.pdf (accessed June 15, 2010).

46. Joe Castaldo, "Just be nice: providing good customer service," www. canadianbusiness.com/managing/strategy/article.jsp?conte nt=20061009_81513_81513 (accessed June 17, 2007).

47. www.westjet.com/guest/en/experience/onTimePerformance.shtml (accessed June 15, 2010).

48. Jim Poisant, *Creating and Sustaining a Superior Customer Service Organization: A Book about Taking Care of the People Who Take Care of the Customers* (Westport, CT: Quorum Books, 2002); "People-Focused HR Policies Seen as Vital to Customer Service Improvement," *Store* (January 2001), p. 60; Michael Brady and J. Joseph Cronin, "Customer Orientation: Effects on Customer Service Perceptions and Outcome Behaviors," *Journal of Service Research* (February 2001), pp. 241–251; Michael Hartline, James Maxham III, and Daryl McKee, "Corridors of Influence in the Dissemination of Customer Oriented Strategy to Customer Contact Service Employees," *Journal of Marketing* 64, no. 2 (April 2000), pp. 25–41.

49. Conrad Lashley, *Empowerment: HR Strategies for Service Excellence* (Boston: Butterworth/Heinemann, 2001).

50. "Future Success Powered by Employees," *DSN Retailing Today* 44 (January 2006), pp. 22–24.

51. www.marketwire.com/press-release/The-Keg-Royalties-Income-Fund-Announces-June-2010-Cash-Distribution-TSX-KEG.UN-1274712.htm (accessed June 15, 2010).

52. Alicia Grandey and Analea Brauburger, "The Emotion Regulation behind the Customer Service Smile," in *Emotions in the Workplace: Understanding the Structure and Role of Emotions in Organizational Behavior*, eds. R. Lord, R. Klimoski, and R. Kanfer (San Francisco: Jossey-Bass, 2002); Mara Adelman and Aaron Ahuvia, "Social Support in the Service Sector: The Antecedents, Processes, and Consequences of Social Support in an Introductory Service," *Journal of Business Research* 32 (March 1995), pp. 273–282.

53. Colin Armistead and Julia Kiely, "Creating Strategies for Managing Evolving Customer Service," *Managing Service Quality* 13, no. 2 (2003), pp. 64–171; www.robertspector.com/NordWay_extract.html (accessed September 20, 2006).

54. Barton Goldenburg, "Customer Self-Service: Are You Ready?" *CRM Magazine* (May 2004), www.destinationcrm.com/articles/default. asp?ArticleID=4011 (accessed September 20, 2006).

55. Rhett H. Walker et al., "Technology-Enabled Service Delivery: An Investigation of Reasons Affecting Customer Adoption and Rejection," *International Journal of Service Industry Management* 13, no. 1 (2002), pp. 91–107; Mary Jo Bitner, Steven W. Brown, and Matthew L. Meuter, "Technology Infusion in Service Encounters," *Journal of the Academy of Marketing Science* 28, no. 1 (2000), pp. 138–149; Stephen W. Brown, "Service Recovery through IT," *Marketing Management* 6 (Fall 1997),
pp. 25–27; P.A. Dabholkar, "Technology-Based Service Delivery: A Classification Scheme for Developing Marketing Strategies," in *Advances in Services Marketing and Management*, Vol. 3, eds. T.A. Swartz, Deborah E. Bowen, and Stephen W. Brown (Greenwich, CT: JAI Press, 1994), pp. 241–271.

56. "Everyone's Internet = Poor Service & False Advertising," *Complaints.com* June 11, 2000: www.complaints.com (accessed September 20, 2006).

57. Subimal Chatterjee, Susan A. Slotnick, and Matthew J. Sobel, "Delivery Guarantees and the Interdependence of Marketing and Operations," *Production and Operations Management* 11, no. 3 (Fall 2002), pp. 393–411; Piyush Kumar, Manohar Kalawani, and Makbool Dada, "The Impact of Waiting Time Guarantees on Customers' Waiting Experiences," *Marketing Science* 16, no. 4 (1999), pp. 676–785.

58. K. Douglas Hoffman, Scott W. Kelley, and H.M. Rotalsky, "Tracking Service Failures and Employee Recovery Efforts," *Journal of Services Marketing* 9, no. 2 (1995), pp. 49–61; Scott W. Kelley and Mark A. Davis, "Antecedents to Customer Expectations for Service Recovery," *Journal of the Academy of Marketing Science* 22 (Winter 1994), pp. 52–61; Terrence J. Levesque and Gordon H.G. McDougall, "Service Problems and Recovery Strategies: An Experiment," *Canadian Journal of Administrative Sciences* 17, no. 1 (2000), pp. 20–37; James G. Maxham III and Richard G. Netemeyer, "A Longitudinal Study of Complaining Customers' Evaluations of Multiple Service Failures and Recovery Efforts," *Journal of Marketing* 66, no. 3 (October 2002), pp. 57–71; Amy K. Smith, Ruth N. Bolton, and Janet Wagner, "A Model of Customer Satisfaction with Service Encounters Involving Failure and Recovery," *Journal of Marketing Research* 36, no. 3 (August 1999), pp. 356–372; Scott R. Swanson and Scott W. Kelley, "Attributions and Outcomes of the Service Recovery Process," *Journal of Marketing Theory and Practice* 9 (Fall 2001), pp. 50–65; Stephen S. Tax and Stephen W. Brown, "Recovering and Learning from Service Failure," *Sloan Management Review* 40, no. 1 (1998), pp. 75–88; Stephen S. Tax, Stephen W. Brown, and Murali Chandrashekaran, "Consumer Evaluations of Service Complaint Experiences: Implications for Relationship Marketing," *Journal of Marketing* 62, no. 2 (April 1998), pp. 60–76; Scott Widmier and Donald W. Jackson Jr., "Examining the Effects of Service Failure, Customer Compensation, and Fault on Customer Satisfaction with Salespeople," *Journal of Marketing Theory and Practice* 10 (Winter 2002), pp. 63–74; Valarie A. Zeithaml and Mary Jo Bitner, *Services Marketing: Integrating Customer Focus across the Firm* (New York: McGraw-Hill, 2003).

59. James Maxham III, "Service Recovery's Influence on Consumer Satisfaction, Positive Word-of-Mouth, and Purchase Intentions," *Journal of Business Research* (October 2001), pp. 11–24; Michael McCollough, Leonard Berry, and Manjit Yadav, "An Empirical Investigation of Customer Satisfaction after Service Failure and Recovery," *Journal of Service Research* (November 2000), pp. 121–137.

60. "Correcting Store Blunders Seen as Key Customer Service Opportunity," *Stores* (January 2001), pp. 60–64; Stephen W. Brown, "Practicing Best-in-Class Service Recovery: Forward-Thinking Firms Leverage Service Recovery to Increase Loyalty and Profits," *Marketing Management* (Summer 2000), pp. 8–10; Tax, Brown, and Chandrashekaran, "Customer Evaluations"; Amy Smith and Ruth Bolton, "An Experimental Investigation of Customer Reactions to Service Failures and Recovery Encounters: Paradox or Peril?" *Journal of Service Research* 1 (August 1998), pp. 23–36; Cynthia Webster and D.S. Sundaram, "Service Consumption Criticality in Failure Recovery," *Journal of Business Research* 41 (February 1998), pp. 153–159.

61. Ko de Ruyter and Martin Wetsel, "The Impact of Perceived Listening Behavior in Voice-to-Voice Service Encounters," *Journal of Service Research* (February 2000), pp. 276–284.

62. Hooman Estelami, "Competitive and Procedural Determinants of Delight and Disappointment in Consumer Complaint Outcomes," *Journal of Service Research* (February 2000), pp. 285–300.

63. Michael Tsiros, Anne Roggeveen, and Dhruv Grewal, *Compensation as a Service Recovery Strategy: When Does It Work?* (unpublished working paper), Babson College, 2006. Amy K. Smith, Ruth N. Bolton, and Janet Wagner, "A Model of Customer Satisfaction with Service Encounters Involving Failure and Recovery," *Journal of Marketing Research* 36 (August 1999), pp. 356–372. Scott R. Swanson and Scott W. Kelley, "Attributions and Outcomes of the Service Recovery Process," *Journal of Marketing: Theory and Practice* 9 (Fall 2001), pp. 50–65.

64. This case was written by Colin Fox and Britt Hackmann in conjunction with the textbook authors for use in a class discussion; it was not written as an illustration of effective or ineffective marketing practices; Suzanne Marta, "As Ritz Opening Nears, Every Detail Counts," *Knight Ridder Tribune Business News* August 6, 2007; Jack Gordon, "Redefining Elegance," *Training* 44, no. 2 (2007), pp. 14–20; Jennifer Saranow, "Turning to Luxury Hotels for Service Ideas; Companies Lacking in Customer Savvy Try the Special Touch," *The Wall Street Journal* July 19, 2006.

65. "Luxury Hotels—Business Is Up and Hotels Are Upgrading," *BusinessWeek* January 20, 2008 (accessed electronically February 26, 2008).

66. "Fact Sheet," http://corporate.ritzcarlton.com/en/Press/FactSheet.htm (accessed June 13, 2010).

67. "Our History," http://corporate.ritzcarlton.com/en/About/OurHistory.htm (accessed June 13, 2010).

68. "Working at the Ritz Carlton," http://corporate.ritzcarlton.com/en/Careers/WorkingAt.htm (accessed June 13, 2010).

Chapter 11

1. "Company Profile," http://cineplexgalaxy.disclosureplus.com/SiteResources/ViewContent.asp?DocID=3&v1ID=&RevID=238&lang=1 (accessed June 23, 2010).

2. David Friend, "Cineplex plans to wow audiences with bigger screens, enhance sound," www.canadianbusiness.com/markets/headline_news/article.jsp?content=b3403333&utm_source=markets&utm_medium=rss (accessed June 23, 2010).

3. "Q1 2010 Final Report," http://cineplexgalaxy.disclosureplus.com/SiteResources/data/MediaArchive/pdfs/reports_filings/q1 2010 report final.pdf (accessed June 23, 2010).

4. Kent B. Monroe, *Pricing: Making Profitable Decisions*, 3rd ed. (New York: McGraw-Hill, 2003); Dhruv Grewal, Kent B. Monroe, and R. Krishnan, "The Effects of Price Comparison Advertising on Buyers' Perceptions of Acquisition Value and Transaction Value," *Journal of Marketing* 62 (April 1998), pp. 46–60.

5. "American Shoppers Economize, Show Greater Interest in Nutrition and Awareness of Food Safety Issues, According to Trends in the United States: Consumer Attitudes and the Supermarket 2003," www.fmi.org/media/mediatext.cfm?id=534 (accessed December 10, 2005). A key finding was that low price was the third most important feature in selecting a supermarket; it was viewed as important by 83 percent of respondents; see also "The New Value Equation," *Supermarket News* 50 (June 10, 2002), p. 12.

6. Anthony Miyazaki, Dhruv Grewal, and Ronnie Goodstein, "The Effects of Multiple Extrinsic Cues on Quality Perceptions: A Matter of Consistency," *Journal of Consumer Research* 32 (June 2005), pp. 146–153; William B. Dodds, Kent B. Monroe, and Dhruv Grewal, "The Effects of Price, Brand, and Store Information on Buyers' Product Evaluations," *Journal of Marketing Research* 28 (August 1991), pp. 307–319.

7. Robert J. Dolan, "Note on Marketing Strategy," *Harvard Business School* (November 2000), pp. 1–17; Dhruv Grewal and Larry D. Compeau, "Pricing and Public Policy: An Overview and a Research Agenda," *Journal of Public Policy & Marketing* 18 (Spring 1999), pp. 3–11.

8. www.paradigm.com/en/paradigm/company/ (accessed June 1, 2010).

9. Monroe, *Pricing: Making Profitable Decisions*.

10. www.corporate.canada.travel/en/ca/research_statistics/trends_outlook/tib/tib.html (accessed June 23, 2010).

11. www.marketingpower.com/mg-dictionary-view669.php? (accessed September 19, 2006).

12. Ruth N. Bolton and Venkatesh Shankar, "An Empirically Derived Taxonomy of Retailer Pricing and Promotion Strategies," *Journal of Retailing* 79, no. 4 (2003), pp. 213–224; Rajiv Lal and Ram Rao, "Supermarket Competition: The Case of Every Day Low Pricing," *Marketing Science* 16, no. 1 (1997), pp. 60–80.

13. A.R. Rao, M.E. Bergen, and S. Davis, "How to Fight a Price War," *Harvard Business Review* 78 (March–April 2000), pp. 107–116.

14. Rao, Bergen, and S. Davis, "How to Fight a Price War."

15. Tara Perkins and Tavia Grant, "White-label Cash Kings," www.globeinvestor.com/servlet/WireFeedRedirect?cf=GlobeInvestor/config&vg=BigAdVariableGenerator&date=20070423&archive=rtgam&slug=wrabm_Bsection23 (accessed June 18, 2007).

16. Perkins and Grant, "White-label Cash Kings."

17. Tavia Grant and Tara Perkins, "Red flags on white-label ABMS," www.theglobeandmail.com/servlet/story/RTGAM.20070424.wxrabm24/BNStory/Business (accessed June 18, 2007).

18. Perkins and Grant, "White-label Cash Kings."

19. www.ndp.ca/endatmfees (accessed June 18, 2007).

20. *Merriam-Webster's Dictionary of Law*, 1996.

21. "Fujitsu Institutes New Warranty Policy For Plasmavision® Monitors," May 15, 2002, www.plasmavision.com/buying_online.htm (accessed January 25, 2005).

22. Joseph P. Bailey, "Electronic Commerce: Prices and Consumer Issues for Three Products: Books, Compact Discs, and Software," *Organization for Economic Cooperation and Development, OECD, GD* 98 (1998), p. 4; J. Yannis Bakos, "Reducing Buyer Search Costs: Implications for Electronic Marketplaces," *Management Science* 43, no. 12 (1997), pp. 1676–1692; Erik Brynjolfsson and Michael D. Smith, "Frictionless Commerce? A Comparison of Internet and Conventional Retailers," *Management Science* 46, no. 4 (2000), pp. 563–585; Rajiv Lal and Miklos Sarvary, "When and How Is the Internet Likely to Decrease Price Competition?" *Marketing Science* 18, no. 4 (1999), pp. 485–503; Xing Pan, Brian T. Ratchford, and Venkatesh Shankar, "Can Price Dispersion in Online Markets be Explained by Differences in E-Tailer Service Quality?" *Journal of the Academy of Marketing Science* 30, no. 4 (2002), pp. 433–445; Michael D. Smith, "The Impact of Shopbots on Electronic Markets," *Journal of the Academy of Marketing Sciences* 30, no. 4 (2002), pp. 446–454; Michael D. Smith and Erik Brynjolfsson, "Consumer Decision-Making at an Internet Shopbot: Brand Still Matters," *The Journal of Industrial Economics* 49 (December 2001), pp. 541–558; Fang-Fang Tang and Xiaolin Xing, "Will the Growth of Multi-Channel Retailing Diminish the Pricing Efficiency of the Web?" *Journal of Retailing* 77, no. 3 (2001), pp. 319–333; Florian Zettlemeyer, "Expanding to the Internet: Pricing and Communications Strategies When Firms Compete on Multiple Channels," *Journal of Marketing Research* 37 (August 2000), pp. 292–308; Dhruv Grewal et al., "The Internet and the Price-Value-Loyalty Chain," *Journal of Business Research* 56 (May 2003), pp. 391–398; Gopalkrishnan R. Iyer et al., "Linking Web-Based Segmentation to Pricing Tactics," *Journal of Product & Brand Management* 11, no. 4/5 (2002), pp. 288–302.

23. Tim Kildaze, "Ninety-nine bucks for $400 worth of organic meat. Seriously?," *The Globe and Mail* April 16, 2011: M1.

24. Independent Equity Research Corp., "Coastal Contacts Inc. Update Report" (eResearch coastal contacts.pdf), http://eresearch.ca/profile.asp?companyID=437 (accessed June 24, 2010).

25. Mary Biti, "Clearly a Winning Strategy," http://investors.coastalcontacts.com/mediacoverage.asp?ticker=T.COA&report=show&id=6151&lang=EN&title=null (accessed June 24, 2010).

26. Eve Lazarus, "Trevor Linden Plays with Clearly Contacts," www.marketingmag.ca/english/news/marketer/article.jsp?content=20100528_164119_13472 (accessed June 24, 2010).

27. Biti, "Clearly a Winning Strategy."

28. "The Timeline," http://investors.coastalcontacts.com/custommessage.asp?ticker=t.coa&message=fifth&title=null (accessed June 24, 2010).

29. Amy Verner, "Carried Away with Eco-bags," http://www.theglobeandmail.com/life/work/article103771.ece (accessed June 23, 2007).

30. Thomas T. Nagle and Reed K. Holden, *The Strategy and Tactics of Pricing*, 3rd ed. (Upper Saddle River, NJ: Pearson, 2002).

31. http://twitter.com/iwearyourshirt (accessed November 17, 2009).

32. "Man makes living by selling the shirt on his back," www.reuters.com/article/lifestyleMolt/idUSTRE5A50K620091106 (accessed November 17, 2009).

33. Lisa E. Bolton, Luk Warlop, and Joseph W. Alba, "Consumer Perceptions of Price (Un)Fairness," *Journal of Consumer Research* 29 (March 2003), pp. 474–491; Margaret C. Campbell, "Perceptions of Price Unfairness: Antecedents and Consequences," *Journal of Marketing Research* 36 (May 1999), pp. 187–199; Peter R. Darke and Darren W. Dahl, "Fairness and Discounts: The Subjective Value of a Bargain," *Journal of Consumer Psychology* 13, no. 3 (2003), pp. 328–338; Sarah Maxwell, "What Makes a Price Increase Seem 'Fair'?" *Pricing Strategy & Practice* 3, no. 4 (1995), pp. 21–27.

34. A. Biswas, E.J. Wilson, and J.W. Licata, "Reference Pricing Studies in Marketing: A Synthesis of Research Results," *Journal of Business Research* 27, no. 3 (1993), pp. 239–256; A. Biswas, "The Moderating Role of Brand Familiarity in Reference Price Perceptions," *Journal of Business Research* 25 (1992), pp. 251–262; A. Biswas and E. Blair, "Contextual Effects of Reference Prices in Retail Advertisements," *Journal of Marketing* 55 (1991), pp. 1–12; Larry D. Compeau and Dhruv Grewal, "Comparative Price Advertising: An Integrative Review," *Journal of Public Policy & Marketing* 17 (Fall 1998), pp. 257–273; Rajesh Chandrashekaran and Dhruv Grewal, "Assimilation of Advertised Reference Prices: The Moderating Role of Involvement," *Journal of Retailing* 79, no. 1 (2003), pp. 53–62; David M. Hardesty and William O. Bearden, "Consumer Evaluations of Different Promotion Types and Price Presentations: The Moderating Role of Promotional Benefit Level," *Journal of Retailing* 79, no. 1 (2003), pp. 17–25.

35. Dhruv Grewal, Kent B. Monroe, and R. Krishnan, "The Effects of Price Comparison Advertising on Buyers' Perceptions of Acquisition Value and Transaction Value," *Journal of Marketing* 62 (April 1998), pp. 46–60.

36. Noreen M. Klein and Janet E. Oglethorpe, "Reference Points in Consumer Decision Making," in *Advances in Consumer Research*, Vol. 14, eds. Melanie Wallendorf and Paul Anderson (Provo, UT: Association for Consumer Research, 1987), pp. 183–187.

37. J.E. Urbany, W.O. Bearden, and D.C. Weilbaker, "The Effect of Plausible and Exaggerated Reference Prices on Consumer Perceptions and Price Search," *Journal of Consumer Research* 15 (1988), pp. 95–110.

38. Michael Levy and Barton A. Weitz, *Retailing Management*, 6th ed. (Burr Ridge, IL: Irwin/McGraw-Hill, 2007).

39. Sonia Verma, "Can Canadian perfume help Afghanistan break its poppy habit?" *The Globe and Mail* March 19, 2010; A1.

40. Trisse Laxley, "A Fragrance with a Political Scent," *The Globe and Mail* March 19, 2010: A18.

41. Verma, "Can Canadian perfume help?"

42. Andrea Nemetz, "Opportunity blossoms," www.the7virtues.com/AnyNewsM/1177760.html (accessed June 24, 2010).

43. Nemetz, "Opportunity blossoms."

44. Robert Schindler, "The 99 Price Ending as a Signal of a Low-Price Appeal," *Journal of Retailing* 82, no. 1 (2006).

45. Merrie Brucks, Valerie A. Zeithaml, and Gillian Naylor, "Price and Brand Name as Indicators of Quality Dimensions for Consumer Durables," *Journal of the Academy of Marketing Science* 28, no. 3 (2000), pp. 359–374; William B. Dodds, Kent B. Monroe, and Dhruv Grewal, "Effects of Price, Brand, and Store Information on Buyers' Product Evaluations," *Journal of Marketing Research* 28 (August 1991), pp. 307–319.

46. Brucks, Zeithaml, and Naylor, "Price and Brand Name as Indicators"; Niraj Dawar and Philip Parker, "Marketing Universals: Consumers' Use of Brand Name, Price, Physical Appearance, and Retailer Reputation as Signals of Product Quality," *Journal of Marketing* 58 (April 1994), pp. 81–95; Dodds, Monroe, and Grewal, "Effects of Price, Brand, and Store Information"; Paul S. Richardson, Alan S. Dick, and Arun K. Jain, "Extrinsic and Intrinsic Cue Effects on Perceptions of Store Brand Quality," *Journal of Marketing* 58 (October 1994), pp. 28–36; Anthony Miyazaki, Dhruv Grewal, and Ronnie Goodstein, "The Effect of Multiple Extrinsic Cues on Quality Perceptions: A Matter of Consistency," *Journal of Consumer Research* 32 (June 2005), pp. 146–153.

47. "Our Commitment," http://waterontap.ca/our_commitment.php (accessed June 28, 2010).

48. "Frequently Asked Questions," http://waterontap.ca/faqs.php#Q3 (accessed June 28, 2010).

49. This section draws from Levy and Weitz, *Retailing Management*.

50. Sha Yang and Priya Raghubir, "Can Bottles Speak Volumes? The Effect of Package Shape on How Much to Buy," *Journal of Retailing* 81, no. 4 (2005), pp. 269–281.

51. "Competition Bureau Investigation Leads to $1-Million Settlement with Suzy Shier Inc.," www.competitionbureau.gc.ca/internet/index.cfm?itemID=305&lg=e (accessed June 24, 2007).

52. Compeau and Grewal, "Comparative Price Advertising"; Larry D. Compeau, Dhruv Grewal, and Diana S. Grewal, "Adjudicating Claims of Deceptive Advertised Reference Prices: The Use of Empirical Evidence," *Journal of Public Policy & Marketing* 14 (Fall 1994), pp. 52–62; Dhruv Grewal and Larry D. Compeau, "Comparative Price Advertising: Informative or Deceptive?" *Journal of Public Policy & Marketing* 11 (Spring 1992), pp. 52–62; Larry Compeau, Joan Lindsey-Mullikin, Dhruv Grewal, and Ross Petty, "An Analysis of Consumers' Interpretations of the Semantic Phrases Found in Comparative Price Advertisements," *Journal of Consumer Affairs* 38 (Summer 2004), pp. 178–187.

53. Joanna Grossman, "The End of Ladies Night in New Jersey," *Find Law's Legal Commentary*, 2004, http://writ.news.findlaw.com/grossman/20040615.html (accessed November 29, 2005); Joyce Howard Price, "'Ladies' Night Ruled Discriminatory," *The Washington Times* 2004, www.washingtontimes.com/national/20040602-111843-2685r.htm (accessed November 29, 2005).

54. Joe Schneider, "Victory is Sweet in BC price-fixing case," *The Globe and Mail* April 13, 2010: B13.

55. This case was written by Elisabeth Nevins Caswell in conjunction with the textbook authors (Dhruv Grewal and Michael Levy) for use in a class discussion; it was not written as an illustration of effective or ineffective marketing practices; David Kravets, "Like Amazon's DRM-Free Music Downloads? Thanks Apple," *Wired.com*, September 25, 2007 (accessed January 20, 2008); Kevin Kelleher, "Let the MP3 Price Wars Begin," TheStreet.com September 28, 2007: www.thestreet.com/newsanalysis/technet/10381387.html (accessed January 20, 2008).

Chapter 12

1. www.zara.ca (accessed June 28, 2010); Pankaj Ghemawat and Jose Luis Nueno, "Zara: Fast Fashion," *Harvard Business School Case Number 9-703-497* (April 1, 2003), www.inditex.com/english/home.htm (accessed July 20, 2006); Guillermo D'Andrea and David Arnold, "Zara," *Harvard Business School Case Number 9-503-050* (March 12, 2003); www.gapinc.com/financmedia/financmedia.htm (accessed March 13, 2005); www.hm.com/us/start/start/index.jsp# (accessed June 4, 2005); www.benetton.com/press/ (accessed September 3, 2006); Stephen Tierney, "New Look's Supply Chain Obsession," *Frontline Solutions* 12, no. 6 (October 2003), pp. 24–25.; David Bovet and Joseph Martha, "E-Business and Logistics Unlocking the Rusty Supply Chain," *Logistics Quarterly* 6, no. 4 (Winter 2000), pp. 1–3; Jane M. Folpe, "Zara Has a Made-to-Order Plan for Success," *Fortune* 142, no. 5 (September 2000), pp. 80–82; Carlta Vitzthum, "Just-in-Time Fashion: Spanish Retailer Zara Makes Low-Cost Lines in Weeks by Running Its Own Show," *The Wall Street Journal* (Eastern Edition), May 18, 2001: B1.

2. Carol Toller, "The push for pull," *Report on Business Magazine* October 2009: 13.

3. Rebecca Harris, "Buy a coffee, remember a veteran," www.marketingmag.ca/magazine/current/the_briefing/article.jsp?content=20041101_64784_64784 (accessed January 2, 2008).

4. "Royal Canadian Mint Raises $3,000 for the Canadian Breast Cancer Foundation," www.mint.ca/store/news/royal-canadian-mint-auction-raises-3000-for-the-canadian-breast-cancer-foundation-5800042?cat=News+Releases&nId=700002&nodeGroup=About+the+Mint (accessed June 2, 2010).

5. Shirley Lichti, "When it comes to packaging, it pays to be different," www.marketingmagic.ca/articles/Packaging.htm (accessed January 2, 2008).

6. "The Pop Shoppe Story," http://thepopshoppe.com/#/The Pop Shoppe Story/ (accessed June 28, 2010).

7. Renee Alexander, "The Pop Shoppe Pops Back," www.businessweek.com/innovate/content/dec2005/id20051216_985463.htm (accessed June 28, 2010).

8. Blair Matthews, "The Pop Shoppe Returns to the Market," http://duxelle.info/soft-drink-industry-analysis/the-pop-shoppe-returns-to-the-market (accessed June 28, 2010).

9. Joanna Pachner, "Retro Cool: Entrepreneur revives the Pop Shoppe," www.theglobeandmail.com/report-on-business/your-business/start/financing/retro-cool-entrepreneur-revives-the-pop-shoppe/article1589947/ (accessed June 13, 2010).

10. www.marketingpower.com/live/mg-dictionary.

11. Based on David Simchi-Levi, Philip Kaminsky, and Edith Simchi-Levi, *Designing and Managing the Supply Chain: Concepts, Strategies and Case Studies*, 2nd ed. (New York: McGraw-Hill/Irwin, 2003); Michael Levy and Barton A. Weitz, *Retailing Management*, 5th ed. (New York: McGraw-Hill/Irwin, 2004).

12. www.marketingpower.com/live/mg-dictionary. Definition from the Council of Logistics Management.

13. Bloomberg, "Nestle to sail Amazon rivers to reach consumers," *The Globe and Mail* June 18, 2010: B8.

14. Michael Posner, "He brought Hush Puppies to Canada and took his dogs on the road for the soft sell," *The Globe and Mail* November 26, 2009: S7.

15. Shirley Won, "Arctic Glacier Seeks to Ice Competition," *The Globe and Mail* May 29, 2007.

16. Emily York, "Social Media Allows Giants to Exploit Niche Markets," http://adage.com/article?article_id=137870 (accessed November 24, 2009).

17. York, "Social Media Allows Giants."

18. York, "Social Media Allows Giants."

19. Omar El Akkad, "Google bookstore plan could be boon to Canada," *The Globe and Mail* May 5, 2010: B1.

20. Frederic Lardinois, "Is Google Getting Ready to Enter the eBook Market?" www.readwriteweb.com/archives/is_google_getting_ready_to_enter_the_ebook_market.php (accessed June 27, 2010).

21. J.R. Raphael, "Google Editions: Bringing E-Books to Your Browser," www.pcworld.com/article/195594/google_editions_bringing_ebooks_to_your_browser.html (accessed June 27, 2010).

22. "Google sparks e-books fight with Kindle," www.reuters.com/article/idUSTRE59E28H20091015 (accessed June 27, 2010).

23. Jon Pareles, "The Once and Future Prince," www.nytimes.com/2007/07/22/arts/music/22pare.html?pagewanted=all (accessed January 3, 2008).

24. Thomas W. Gruen, Daniel S. Corsten, and Sundar Bharadwaj, "Retail out of Stocks: A Worldwide Examination of Extent, Causes, and Consumer Responses" (unpublished working paper), May 7, 2002; Nirmalya Kumar, "The Power of Trust in Manufacturer-Retailer Relationships," *Harvard Business Review* (November–December 1996), pp. 92–106; Mark E. Parry and Yoshinobu Sato, "Procter & Gamble: The Wal-Mart Partnership," University of Virginia case #M-0452 (1996).

25. www.marketingpower.com/live/mg-dictionary.

26. Canadian Franchise Directory, www.franchisedirectory.ca (accessed June 28, 2007).

27. "Franchise Guide Fast Facts," www.canadianfranchisedirectory.ca/franchiseguide.aspx (accessed June 27, 2010).

28. Ghemawat and Nueno, "ZARA: Fast Fashion."

29. www.marketingpower.com/live/mg-dictionary.

30. Sharyn Leaver, Joshua Walker, and Tamara Mendelsohn, "Hasbro Drives Supply Chain Efficiency with BPM," *Forester Research*, July 22, 2003.

31. Erin Anderson and Anne Coughlan, "Structure, Governance, and Relationship Management," in *Handbook of Marketing*, eds. B. Weitz and R. Wensley (London, UK: Sage, 2002).

32. Erin Anderson and Barton Weitz, "The Use of Pledges to Build and Sustain Commitment in Distribution Channels," Journal of Marketing Research 29 (February 1992), pp. 18–34.

33. This section draws from Levy and Weitz, *Retailing Management*, Chapter 10.

34. "Frito Lay Canada," www.pepsico.ca/en/Purpose/ES_ENG_FLC.html (accessed June 29, 2010).

35. "High-Efficiency Fleet at Frito Lay Canada" (pdf provided by Frito Lay Canada June 28, 2010).

36. "Frito Lay Canada is Canada's First Food Manufacturer to Introduce Zero-Emission Electric Vehicles into Delivery Fleet," http://smr.newswire.ca/en/frito-lay-canada/frito-lay-canada-is-canadas-first-food-manufacturer (accessed June 29, 2010).

37. "Frito Lay Canada," www.pepsico.ca/en/Purpose/ES_ENG_FLC.html (accessed June 29, 2010).

38. Larry Kellam, "P&G Rethinks Supply Chain," *Optimize* (October 2003), p. 35.

39. This case was written by Jeanne L. Munger in conjunction with the U.S. textbook authors (Dhruv Grewal and Michael Levy) for use in a class discussion; it was not written as an illustration of effective or ineffective marketing practices. Jeanne Munger is an associate professor at the University of Southern Maine.

40. Mellissa S. Monroe, "Wal-Mart Is Rewriting Rules, Dominating World's Supply Chain," *Knight Ridder Tribune Business News* November 10, 2003: 1.

41. Richard J. Schonberger, "The Right Stuff, Revisited," *MSI* 21, no. 9 (September 2003), p. 26.

42. Sharon Gaudin, "Some Suppliers Gain from Failed Wal-Mart RFID Edict," *Computer World* April 28, 2008.

43. Stephanie Rosenbloom, "Wal-Mart Unveils Plan to Make Supply Chain Greener," *The New York Times* February 26, 2010.

44. William B. Cassidy, "Wal-Mart Tightens the Chain," *The Journal of Commerce* (January 18, 2010).

Chapter 13

1. Stephen Fenech, "Apple's Theme Park," *Herald Sun* May 28, 2008; www.apple.com (accessed May 28, 2008); Jerry Useem, "Apple: America's Best Retailer," *Fortune* March 8, 2007.

2. David Chartier, "Apple Retail Stores Stomping Competition Foot by Foot," *InfiniteLoop* January 8, 2008.

3. Deloitte and Stores Media, "Top 250 Global Retailers 2008," www.stores.org/global-powers-retailing-top-250 (accessed July 4, 2011).

4. "Retail Sales in Canada," www.stockresearchportal.com/Canada/RetailSales.aspx (accessed July 1, 2010).

5. www.retailcouncil.org/news/media/profile/print/default.asp (accessed January 4, 2008).

6. This chapter draws heavily from Michael Levy and Barton A. Weitz, *Retailing Management*, 7th ed. (Burr Ridge, IL: McGraw-Hill/Irwin, 2009), Chapters 2 and 3.

7. "Nutrition Center," www.petesfrootique.com/LorieMcNeil.asp (accessed June 23, 2007).

8. "Shoppers Drug Mart Opens its 1,000th Drug Store in Canada," www.shoppersdrugmart.ca/english/corporate_information/investor_relations/press_releases/articles/april_26_2007.html (accessed June 25, 2007).

9. "An Industry That's Regaining Its Fighting Trim," *Chain Drug Review* June 7, 2004: 20.

10. Marina Strauss, "The Bay steps up its game with a focus on shoes," *The Globe and Mail* June 5, 2010: B3.

11. Marina Strauss, "HMV Moves Beyond Music," *The Globe and Mail* June 14, 2010: B1.

12. "Canadian Tire introduces new barcode app," *Click! Weekly* November 30, 2010.

13. "About Giant Tiger—History," www.gianttiger.com/en/about_gt/history/index.php (accessed June 20, 2007).

14. "Facts and Questions," www.gianttiger.com/en/faq.php (accessed June 20, 2007).

15. "Facts and Questions."

16. "Community/Murals," www.gianttiger.com/en/community/murals/ (accessed June 20, 2007).

17. "The North West Company: Alberta," www.northwest.ca/BackOffice/DesktopDefault.aspx?tabindex=0&tabid=10080 (accessed June 20, 2007).

18. Wes Lafortune, "Concept Retailing Trend Costly But Growing," www.businessedge.ca/article.cfm/newsID/11401.cfm (accessed June 24, 2007).

19. Shel Israel, "In Business, Early Birds Twitter Most Effectively," www.businessweek.com/managing/content/oct2009/ca2009106_370257.htm (accessed November 21, 2009).

20. www.businessinsider.com/henry-blodget-twitter-sells-3-million-of-computers-for-dell-2009-6 (accessed November 21, 2009).

21. http://twitter.com/dellOutlet (accessed November 21, 2009).

22. Nicholas Kolakowski, "Twitter helps Dell sell on Outlet site," www.eweek.com/c/a/Web-Services-Web-20-and-SOA/Twitter-Helps-Dell-Sell-on-Outlet-Site-654941/ (accessed November 21, 2009).

23. Anyd Sernovitz, "Andy's Answers: How Dell finds ROI from social media," http://smartblogs.com/socialmedia/2011/04/06/andys-answers-how-dell-generating-roi-from-social-media/ (accessed May 1, 2011).

24. Marina Straus, "Does this blouse make Sears look plugged-in?," *The Globe and Mail* April 22, 2011: B4.

25. Julie Baker et al., "The Influence of Multiple Store Environment Cues on Perceived Merchandise Value and Patronage Intentions," *Journal of Marketing* 66 (April 2001), pp. 120–141; Eric R. Spangenberg, Ayn E. Crowley, and Pamela W. Henderson, "Improving the Store Environment: Do Olfactory Cues Affect Evaluations and Behaviors?" *Journal of Marketing* 60 (April 1996), pp. 67–80; Michael K. Hui and John E.G. Bateson, "Perceived Control and the Effects of Crowding and Consumer Choice on the Service Experience," *Journal of Consumer Research* 18 (September 1991), pp. 174–184.

26. "Shelf Help: A Guide to Shopper Marketing," *Strategy Magazine* (July 2010), p. S56.

27. Leonard Berry, Kathleen Seiders, and Dhruv Grewal, "Understanding Service Convenience," *Journal of Marketing* 66 (July 2002), pp. 1–17.

28. "IKEA Canada Launches New Sustainability Program—The Never Ending List," www.newswire.ca/en/releases/archive/February2010/02/c6012.html (accessed July 28, 2010).

29. "Greener Ways to Get Here," http://theneverendinglist.ikea.ca/en/Greener-Ways-to-Get-Here.html (accessed July 28, 2010).

30. "Blue Bag Program," http://theneverendinglist.ikea.ca/en/Blue-Bag-Program.html (accessed July 28, 2010).

31. "Top Green Employers," http://theneverendinglist.ikea.ca/en/Top-Green-Employers.html (accessed July 28, 2010).

32. For descriptions of the Wheel of Retailing theory, see Stanley Hollander, "The Wheel of Retailing: What Makes Skilled Managers Succumb to the 'Prosper, Mature, and Decay' Pattern?" *Marketing Management* (Summer 1996), pp. 63–65; Stephen Brown, "Postmodernism, the Wheel of Retailing, and Will to Power," *The International Review of Retail, Distribution, and Consumer Research* (July 1995), pp. 387–412; Arieh Goldman, "Institutional Change in Retailing: An Updated Wheel of Retailing," in *Foundations of Marketing Channels*, eds. A. Woodside et al. (Austin, TX: Lone Star, 1978), pp. 193–201. For a description of the Accordion Theory, see Stanley C. Hollander, "Notes on the Retail Accordion," *Journal of Retailing* 42 (Summer 1966), pp. 20–40, 54. For a description of the Dialectic Process theory, see Thomas J. Maronick and Bruce J. Walker, "The Dialectic Evolution of Retailing," in *Proceedings: Southern Marketing Association*, ed. Barnett Greenberg (Atlanta: Georgia State University, 1974), p. 147. For descriptions of Natural Selection theory, see A.C.R. Dreesmann, "Patterns of Evolution in Retailing," *Journal of Retailing* (Spring 1968), pp. 81–96; Murray Forester, "Darwinian Theory of Retailing," *Chain Store Age* (August 1995), p. 8. A summary of these theories can be found in Michael Levy and Barton A. Weitz, *Retailing Management*, 6th ed. (Burr Ridge, IL: Irwin/McGraw-Hill, 2007).

33. Reuters, "Would You Like Fries with your Tiramisu?" www.theglobeandmail.com/servlet/story/LAC.20070628.RTICK28SEC/TPStory/Business (accessed June 28, 2007).

34. Paul Brent, "McLatte Anyone?" *Marketing Magazine* December 10, 2007: 10.

35. Amit Shilton, "Convenience is Key for Pizza Pizza's new app," *The Globe and Mail* April 5, 2011: B9.

36. "Can't Find That Dress on the Rack? Retailers Are Pushing More Shoppers to the Net," *Knowledge@Wharton*, November 1, 2006.

37. Kenneth Hein, "Study: Web Research Nets In-Store Sales," *Brandweek*, May 7, 2007 (accessed electronically December 24, 2007).

38. Brad Stone, "Amazon Accelerates Its Move to Digital," *The New York Times* April 7, 2008; Joe Nocera, "Put Buyers First? What a Concept," *The New York Times* January 5, 2008.

39. Sandra Forsythe et al., "Development of a Scale to Measure the Perceived Benefits and Risks of Online Shopping," *Journal of Interactive Marketing* 20, no. 2 (2006), pp. 55–75.

40. Jon Brodkin, "TJX Breach: Rethinking Corp. Security," *Network World* 24, no. 13 (2007) (accessed electronically December 14, 2007).

41. Forsythe et al., "Development of a Scale."

42. Brodkin, "TJX Breach."

43. For more information on approaches for increasing share of wallet, see Tom Osten, *Customer Share Marketing* (Upper Saddle River, NJ: Prentice Hall, 2002).

44. Barry Berman and Shawn Thelen, "A guide to developing and managing a well-integrated multi-channel retail strategy," *International Journal of Retail & Distribution Management* 32, no. 3 (2004), p. 4.

45. This case was written by Jeanne L. Munger (University of Southern Maine) in conjunction with the U.S. textbook authors (Dhruv Grewal and Michael Levy) for use in a class discussion; it was not written as an illustration of effective or ineffective marketing practices. The authors thank Max Ward, vice-president of technology at Staples, who provided valuable input for the development of this case. They also acknowledge that parts of the case are based on information provided by W. Caleb McCann (in collaboration with J.P. Jeannet, Dhruv Grewal, and Martha Lanning), "Staples," in *Fulfillment in E-Business*, ed. Petra Schuber, Ralf Wolfle, and Walter Dettling (Germany: Hanser, 2001), pp. 239–252 (in German).

46. www.staplescontract.com/stapleslinktour/index.asp (accessed April 6, 2010).

47. *"2008 Staples Annual Report"* (accessed electronically March 23, 2010).

48. Interview with Demos Parneros (Staples' vice-president of stores) and Jevin Eagle (executive vice-president of merchandising and marketing), June 21, 2009.

Chapter 14

1. Emily Bryson York, "McDonald's Unveils 'I'm Lovin' It' 2.0," http://adage.com/article?article_id=143453 (accessed July 28, 2010).

2. Kate MacArthur, "McD's to Shops: Make 'Lovin' It' More Than Tag," http://adage.com/article?article_id=107083 (accessed July 28, 2010).

3. MacArthur, "McD's to Shops."

4. Randall Frost, "Lost in Translation," www.brandchannel.com/features_effect.asp?pf_id=340 (accessed July 28, 2010).

5. T. Duncan and C. Caywood, "The Concept, Process, and Evolution of Integrated Marketing Communication," in *Integrated Communication: Synergy of Persuasive Voices*, eds. E. Thorson and J. Moore (Mahwah, NJ: Lawrence Erlbaum Associates, 1996); http://jimc.medill.northwestern.edu/2000/pettegrew.htm.

6. Deborah J. MacInnis and Bernard J. Jaworski, "Information Processing from Advertisements: Toward an Integrative Framework," *Journal of Marketing* 53, no. 4 (October 1989), pp. 1–23.

7. Deborah J. MacInnis, Christine Moorman, and Bernard J. Jaworski, "Enhancing and Measuring Consumers' Motivation, Opportunity," *Journal of Marketing* 55, no. 4 (October 1991), pp. 32–554. Joan Meyers-Levy, "Elaborating on Elaboration: The Distinction between Relational and Item-Specific Elaboration," *Journal of Consumer Research* 18 (December 1991), pp. 358–367.

8. Canadian Media Directors' Council, "Media Digest," 2010, www.cmdc.ca/pdf/MediaDigest_1010.pdf (accessed July 16, 2011).

9. American Marketing Association, *Dictionary of Marketing Terms* (Chicago, IL: American Marketing Association, 2008).

10. http://online.wsj.com/article/SB1000142405274870348100457464690 4234860412.html; George E. Belch and Michael A. Belch, *Advertising and Promotion: An Integrated Marketing Communications Perspective* (New York: McGraw-Hill, 2007).

11. Ruth Stevens, "Crash Course in Direct Marketing," www.marketingprofs. com/premium/seminar_detail.asp?adref=semsrch&semid=104 (accessed June 25, 2007).

12. Canadian Media Directors' Council, "Media Digest."

13. *Marketing Research Group Fact Sheet: Canadian Consumer Attitudes to Direct Mail (Part II)*, www.canadapost.ca/business/prodserv/mdm/market-e.asp (accessed June 26, 2007).

14. Heart & Stroke Foundation of Canada, "About Us," ww2.heartandstroke. ca/Page.asp?PageID=88&CategoryID=10& Src=about (accessed June 26, 2007).

15. Heart & Stroke Foundation of Canada, "Annual Report 2006," ww2. heartandstroke.ca/Images/HSFC_AR_2006_ eng.pdf (accessed June 26, 2007).

16. "Marketing and Selling Solutions: Catalogues," www.canadapost. ca/tools/pdf/getpdf.asp?pdf=/offerings/catalogue_mail/pdf/cat-e. pdf&lang=e (accessed June 26, 2007).

17. "Marketing Research Group Fact Sheet: Canadian Consumer Attitudes to Direct Mail (Part II)," www.canadapost.ca/business/prodserv/mdm/market-e.asp (accessed June 26, 2007).

18. "Direct Response Television," www.direct-response-television.com (accessed June 26, 2007).

19. "Canadian Blood Services & Northern Lights to Present at Interactive Marketing Conference," www.nldrtv.com/news/CBS_CaseStudy_ PressRelease.htm (accessed June 26, 2007).

20. "Northern Lights and Canadian Blood Services Capture Gold at CMA Awards," www.nldrtv.com/news/CMA_PressRelease.htm (accessed June 26, 2007).

21. Paul-Mark Rendon, "Virgin Builds on Buzz," www.marketingmag.ca/magazine/current/feature/article. jsp?content=20051212_73030_73030 (accessed June 26, 2007).

22. "About Rogers Centre," www.rogerscentre.com/inaround/visitors/policies/index.html (accessed June 26, 2007).

23. "Video Sponsorships," www.eepybird.com/video-sponsorships/ (accessed July 28, 2010).

24. "The Original Coke & Mentos Sensation," www.eepybird.com/original-coke-mentos-sensation/ (accessed July 28, 2010).

25. "Inside the EepyLab," www.eepybird.com/about/ (accessed July 28, 2010).

26. wwwyoplait.com/breastcancer_lids.aspx (accessed September 22, 2006).

27. Jackie Huba, "A Just Cause Creating Emotional Connections with Customers," 2003, www.inc.com/articles/2003/05/25537.html.

28. www.yoplait.com/breastcancer_lids.aspx (accessed October 25, 2004).

29. www.coneinc.com/Pages/buzz3.html (accessed October 22, 2004).

30. Katherine Rosman, "And the Loser Is … Fashion," *The Wall Street Journal* January 9, 2008.

31. Carl Obermiller and Eric R. Spangenberg, "On the Origin and Distinctness of Skepticism toward Advertising," *Marketing Letters* 11, no. 4 (2000), p. 311.

32. www.tomsshoes.com/ourcause.aspx (accessed July 31, 2010).

33. www.insightargentina.org (accessed July 31, 2010).

34. "Critical Mass," www.dmnews.com/critical-mass/article/136612/ (accessed July 31, 2010).

35. Annette Bourdeau, "Critical Mass: The Unagency," www.strategyonline. ca/articles/magazine/20070601/bizcritical.html (accessed July 31, 2010).

36. www.criticalmass.com/about/news/profile-dianne-wilkins-ceo-critical-mass.htm (accessed July 31, 2010).

37. Christina Reynolds, "Q & A with Ted Hellard Founder and Chairman of Critical Mass Inc," excerpted from the *Calgary Herald*, www.criticalmass. com/about/news/259.htm (accessed July 31, 2010).

38. "iUpload Takes Datamations First Blogging Win," February 28, 2006, www. itmanagement.eartweb.com (accessed April 19, 2006); Nicole Ziegler

Dizon, "Corporations Enter into World of Blogs," *San Francisco Gate* June 6, 2006, www.sfgate.com (accessed September 26, 2006); Mark Berger, "Annie's Homegrown: 'Bernie's Blog' Case Study," www.backbonemedia. com (accessed September 26, 2006); "Corporate Blogging Survey," www. backbonemedia.com (accessed September 26, 2006).

39. Carey Toane, "U of M Using Student Blogs as Recruitment Tool," www. mediaincanada.com/articles/mic/20071129/recruitment.html (accessed January 5, 2008).

40. Bret A.S. Martin, Bodo Lang, and Stephanie Wong, "Conclusion, Explicitness in Advertising: The Moderating Role of Need for Cognition and Argument Quality on Persuasion," *Journal of Advertising* 32, no. 4 (2004), pp. 57–65.

41. www.consideryourselfwarned.com (accessed September 20, 2006); www.childrennow.org/newsroom/news-04/cam-ra-05-03-04.cfm (accessed October 11, 2004).

42. Michael Singer, "Microsoft, SINA Send SMS Message to China," 2004, http://internetnews.com/ent-news/article.php/1585181 (accessed September 25, 2006).

43. Jayne O'Donnell, "Teens Targeted with Cellphone Marketing," *USA Today* March 20, 2007.

44. Elizabeth Church, "Newsfeed Update: Universities Sign onto Facebook," *The Globe and Mail* December 26, 2007: A14.

45. http://retailindustry.about.com/library/bl/q2/bl_um041701.htm (accessed September 26, 2006).

46. www.inastrol.com/Articles/990601.htm (accessed September 26, 2006).

47. Garine Tcholakian, "Honda tunes into Civic Nation via anthem mix-off," hwww.mediaincanada.com/articles/mic/20091015/hondatuner.html (accessed November 17, 2009).

48. Tcholakian, "Honda tunes into Civic Nation."

49. http://advertising.utexas.edu/research/terms/index.asp#O (accessed September 26, 2006).

50. This section draws from Michael Levy and Barton A. Weitz, *Retailing Management*, 6th ed. (Burr Ridge, IL: McGraw-Hill/Irwin, 2007).

51. Theodore Leavitt, *The Marketing Imagination* (New York: The Free Press, 1986).

52. George E. Belch and Michael A. Belch, *Advertising and Promotion: An Integrated Marketing Communications Perspective*, 7th ed. (New York: McGraw-Hill/Irwin, 2007).

53. www.kleenex.com/us/av/index.asp (accessed September 26, 2006).

54. Martin, Lang, and Wong, "Conclusion, Explicitness in Advertising."

55. http://wps.prenhall.com/ca_ph_ebert_busess_3/0,6518,224378-,00. html.

56. The Television Bureau of Canada, www.tvb.ca/pages/nav2_htm (accessed August 1, 2010).

57. William F. Arens, *Contemporary Advertising*, 8th ed. (New York: McGraw-Hill, 2003).

58. "Cassies Canadian Advertising Success Stories 2006," http://cassies.ca/winners/2006Winners/winners_04.html (accessed July 4, 2007).

59. www.kraftfoods.com/jello/main.aspx?s=&m=jlo_news_jun04.

60. Dean M. Krugman et al., *Advertising: Its Role in Modern Marketing* (New York: The Dryden Press, 1994), pp. 221–226.

61. Stanford L. Grossbart and Lawrence A. Crosby, "Understanding Bases of Parental Concern and Reaction to Children's Food Advertising," *Journal of Marketing* 48, no. 3 (1984), pp. 79–93; Brian M. Young, "Does Food Advertising Influence Children's Food Choices? A Critical Review of Some of the Recent Literature," *International Journal of Advertising* 22, no. 4 (2003), p. 441.

62. "Celebrating Carbon Commitments," *Sustainable Waterloo's 2009 Report*, http://www.sustainablewaterloo.org/index.php?p=2009report (accessed July 28, 2010).

63. www.riger.com/know_base/media/understanding.html (accessed November 15, 2004).

64. Matt Semansky and David Brown, "It's an Evolution at the Marketing Awards," www.marketingmag.ca/daily/20070330/topstory.html (accessed June 29, 2007).

65. Dove Men+Care Media Kit, pdf provided by Unilever via Harbinger, a marketing consulting and communications company (accessed July 30, 2010).

Chapter 15

1. Mary Dickie, "Don Durst, the Change Provoker," www.strategyonline.ca/articles/magazine/20081201/moydurst.html (accessed August 4, 2010).

2. "Cassies 2009 Cases, Brand/Case: Subaru Forester," http://cassies.ca/caselibrary/winners/2009pdfs/26_C09_Forester_Web.pdf (accessed August 4, 2010).

3. "Cassies 2009 Cases, Brand/Case: Subaru Forester."

4. "Sexy Sumos sizzle at 2009 CMA Awards," www.newswire.ca/en/releases/archive/November2009/30/c6106.html (accessed August 4, 2010).

5. E.K. Strong, *The Psychology of Selling* (New York: McGraw-Hill, 1925).

6. Karl Greenber, "Toyota Promotes Yaris in 'TV Guide,' Fox Deal," *Marketing Daily* October 3, 2007: http://publications.mediapost.com/index.cfm?fuseaction=Articles.showArticle&art_aid=68554 (accessed February 14, 2008).

7. Seth Stevenson, "Toyota's Violent Yaris Car Ads," July 6, 2007, www.npr.org/templates/story/story.php?storyId=5538263 (accessed February 14, 2008).

8. Stevenson, "Toyota's Violent Yaris Car Ads."

9. William F. Arens, Michael F. Weigold, and Christian Arens, *Contemporary Advertising*, 11th ed. (New York: McGraw-Hill, 2008), p. 255.

10. John Philip Jones, "What Makes Advertising Work?" *The Economic Times* July 24, 2002.

11. www.legamedia.net/lx/result/match/0591dfc9787c111b1b24dde6d61e43c5/index.php.

12. Jef I. Richards and Catherine M. Curran, "Oracles on 'Advertising': Searching for a Definition," *Journal of Advertising* 31, no. 2 (Summer 2002), pp. 63–77.

13. www.brandweek.com/bw/news/financial/article_display.jsp?vnu_content_id=1001615315 (accessed September 26, 2006); "Global Ad Spending Expected To Grow 6%," *Brandweek*, December 6, 2005.

14. Raymond R. Burke and Thomas K. Srull, "Competitive Interference and Consumer Memory for Advertising," *Journal of Consumer Research* 15 (June 1988), pp. 55–68; Kevin Lane Keller, "Memory Factors in Advertising: The Effect of Advertising Retrieval Cues on Brand Evaluation," *Journal of Consumer Research* 14 (December 1987), pp. 316–333; Kevin Lane Keller, "Memory and Evaluation Effects in Competitive Advertising Environments," *Journal of Consumer Research* 17 (March 1991), pp. 463–477; Robert J. Kent and Chris T. Allen, "Competitive Interference Effects in Consumer Memory for Advertising: The Role of Brand Familiarity," *Journal of Marketing* 58, no. 3 (July 1994), pp. 97–106.

15. Anthony Bianco, "The Vanishing Mass Market," *BusinessWeek*, July 12, 2004, pp. 61–68.

16. "Cassies January 24, 2011 Official Winners Guide," http://cassies.ca/winners/2011Winners/winners.html (accessed May 4, 2011).

17. Matthew Shum, "Does Advertising Overcome Brand Loyalty? Evidence from the Breakfast Cereal Market," *Journal of Economics and Management Strategy* 13, no. 2 (2004), pp. 77–85.

18. Rob Gerlsbeck, "The Military Draws Recruits by Putting Combat Life Front and Centre," *Marketing Magazine*, November 26, 2007, p. 22.

19. Department of National Defence, "Decima DND Advertising Pre-Test Revised reportv2.pdf," p. 21.

20. Department of National Defence, "Final Report DND Advertising Pre-Test Winter 2008.doc," p. 22.

21. Department of National Defence, "Decima DND Advertising."

22. Kelly Gadzala, "Entrepreneur credits her son, 6, for eco-savvy idea," www.mytowncrier.ca/entrepreneur-credits-her-son-6-for-eco-savvy-idea.html (accessed August 3, 2010).

23. "Media Hook," www.thesmarthanger.com/media_hook.html (accessed August 2, 2010).

24. Mike Friskney, "E-Hanger In Home Media wears green well," *Direct Marketing* (June 2010), p. 6.

25. Diane Jermyn, "No more (environmentally insensitive) wire hangers," www.theglobeandmail.com/report-on-business/your-business/business-categories/sustainability/no-more-environmentally-insensitive-wire-hangers/article1654921/ (accessed August 2, 2010).

26. "Toronto firm launches recyclable clothes hanger," www.cbc.ca/consumer/story/2009/09/16/smart-hanger.html (accessed August 2, 2010).

27. "Cashmere," *Strategy Magazine*, November 2007, p. 48.

28. www.gotmilk.com/fun/decade/year_1993.html (accessed September 26, 2006).

29. http://advertising.utexas.edu/research/terms/index.asp#P (accessed November 15, 2004).

30. www.grantstream.com/glossary.htm (accessed September 26, 2006).

31. "The Battle to Ban Advertising," www.idrc.ca/en/ev-28820-201-1-DO_TOPIC.html (accessed July 2, 2007).

32. Grant Robertson, "Tobacco Ban Stays, But Expect Ad Blitz Anyway," www.theglobeandmail.com/servlet/ArticleNews/freeheadlines/LAC/20070629/TOBACCO29/national/National (accessed July 2, 2007).

33. http://advertising.utexas.edu/research/terms/index.asp#O (accessed September 26, 2006).

34. Richard Kielbowicz and Linda Lawson, "Unmasking Hidden Commercials in Broadcasting: Origins of the Sponsorship Identification Regulations 1927–1963," 2004, www.law.indiana.edu/fclj/pubs/v56/no2/Kielbowicz Finals round IV.pdf (accessed September 4, 2005).

35. www.onpoint-marketing.com/stealth-marketing.htm (accessed September 20, 2006).

36. "The Global Fund," www.joinred.com/globalfund/ (accessed July 4, 2007).

37. "Letter to the Editor," www.joinred.com/archive/adage/ (accessed July 4, 2007).

38. "Point/Counter Point," www.joinred.com/archive/adage/pcp.asp (accessed July 4, 2007).

39. "The Latest (RED) Results," www.joinred.com/red/ (accessed May 4, 2011).

40. www.cnn.com/2004/TECH/internet/04/26/godsend.controversy.reut/ (accessed September 5, 2005).

41. The Influencers, "What We Do," www.theinfluencers.ca/whatwedo.php (accessed July 2, 2007).

42. www.marketingterms.com/dictionary/viral_marketing/ (accessed September 26, 2006).

43. K. Onah Ha, "It's a Neopet World: Popular Site for Kids Stirs Controversy," *San Jose Mercury News* September 14, 2004.

44. Christopher Reynolds, "Game Over," *American Demographics* 26, no. 1 (2004), pp. 35–39.

45. This section draws from Tom Duncan, *Principles of Advertising and IMC*, 2nd ed. (Burr Ridge, IL: Irwin/McGraw-Hill, 2005).

46. "Merger and Acquisition Activity Impacts Coupon Promotion Volume, Study Finds," *The Food Institute Report*, March 5, 2001, p. 4.

47. "Mobile Coupons Find More Favor with Consumers than Advertisers," *Internet Retailer*, May 11, 2008.

48. Wency Leung, "Online coupon sites turn up the heat on restaurants," *The Globe and Mail* May 4, 2011: p. L1.

49. Simon Houpt, "There could be a deal right where you are standing," *The Globe and Mail* February 1, 2011: p. B9.

50. http://sports.espn.go.com/espn/contests/index (accessed April 16, 2010).

51. Annette Bourdeau, "Sport Chek, Contiki and Subaru Rally for Data," www.strategymag.com/articles/magazine/20070601/sportchek.html (accessed July 5, 2007).

52. Paul Crowe, "Alexander Keith's Birthday," http://adjoke.blogspot.com/2009/09/alexander-keiths-birthday.html (accessed October 22 2009).

53. Crowe, "Alexander Keith's Birthday."

54. "Cheesy's Luky Lunchbox," www.cheestrings.ca/luckylunchbox/ (accessed November 23, 2009).

55. Meliata Kuburas, "Students 'scream cheese' at Doritos Guru coronation," www.mediaincanada.com/articles/mic/20090504/doritosguru.html (accessed November 28, 2009).

56. Ben Lucier, "Doritos GURU contest update: Cast your vote as semi-finalists fight for millions!," www.benlucier.ca/work/marketing/doritos-guru-contest-update-cast-your-vote-as-semi-finalists-fight-for-millions/ (accessed November 28, 2009).

57. Amy Bostock, "Canada Post goes viral with video contest aimed at increasing product line awareness," www.clickweekly.com/articles/October 27_2009/lead.htm (accessed October 21, 2009).

58. Colin Hunter, "Laurier grad lands the world's second best job—Virgin intern," www.youtube.com/watch?v=2-cLys9ZK40 (accessed June 12, 2009).

59. "Pop-up branding," www.strategymag.com/articles/magazine/20070601/escapism.html (accessed July 3, 2007).

60. "Nabob Over the Years," www.nabob.ca/en/history.html (accessed July 27, 2010).

61. Paul-Mark Rendon, "Agency of the Year," *Capital C Blog*, http://capitalc.typepad.com/my_weblog/agency_of_the_year/index.html (accessed June 25, 2007).

62. www.msnbc.msn.com/id/7357071/ (accessed September 26, 2006).

63. www.engadget.com/entry/1234000103038638/ (accessed September 26, 2006).

64. www.itvx.com/SpecialReport.asp (accessed September 26, 2006).

65. Bill Shepard, "Jumping on the Brand Wagon: The Allure of Product Placement," *Wisconsin Business Alumni Update* 25, no. 1 (June 2007).

66. www.itvx.com/SpecialReport.asp (accessed September 26, 2006).

67. Betsy Spethmann, "For a Limited Time Only," *Promo: Ideas, Connections and Brand*, 2004, http://promomagazine.com/mag/marketing_limited_time/.

68. Statistics Canada, *Canada Year Book*, (Ottawa, 2005).

69. This section draws from Mark W. Johnston and Greg W. Marshall, *Relationship Selling and Sales Management* (Burr Ridge, IL: Irwin/McGraw-Hill, 2004).

70. www.workz.com/content/view_content.html?section_id=557&content_id=7086 (accessed April 15, 2008).

71. Michael Beverland, "Contextual Influences and the Adoption and Practice of Relationship Selling in a Business-to-Business Setting: An Exploratory Study," *Journal of Personal Selling and Sales Management* (Summer 2001), p. 207.

72. Bill Stinnett, *Think Like Your Customer*, 1st ed. (Burr Ridge, IL: McGraw-Hill, 2004).

73. Johnston and Marshall, *Relationship Selling and Sales Management*.

74. IncentiveWorks, "Canada's Meetings & Promotions Show," www.meetingscanada.com/cmits_pi/exhibitinfo_cmits.jsp (accessed June 24, 2007).

75. Barton A. Weitz, Harish Sujan, and Mita Sujan, "Knowledge, Motivation, and Adaptive Behavior: A Framework for Improving Selling Effectiveness," *Journal of Marketing* (October 1986), pp. 174–191.

76. www.webopedia.com/TERM/P/phishing.html (accessed January 11, 2008).

77. Catherine Holahan, "'Tis the Season for Scams," *BusinessWeek Online* December 26, 2007: 1.

78. www.marketingpower.com/live/mg-dictionary.

79. Rene Y. Darmon, "Where Do the Best Sales Force Profit Producers Come From?" *Journal of Personal Selling and Sales Management* 13, no. 3 (1993), pp. 17–29.

80. Julie Chang, "Born to Sell?" *Sales and Marketing Management* (July 2003), p. 36.

81. Johnston and Marshall, *Relationship Selling and Sales Management*, p. 368; Bill Kelley, "Recognition Reaps Rewards," *Sales and Marketing Management* (June 1986), p. 104 [reprinted from Thomas R. Wotruba, John S. Macfie, and Jerome A. Collem, "Effective Sales Force Recognition Programs," in *Industrial Marketing Management* 20, pp. 9–15].

82. For a discussion of common measures used to evaluate salespeople, see Johnston and Marshall, *Churchill/Ford/Walker's Sales Force Management* (McGraw-Hill/Irwin, 2005), p. 482.

83. This case was written by Elisabeth Nevins Caswell in conjunction with the textbook authors (Dhruv Grewal and Michael Levy) for use in a class discussion; it was not written as an illustration of effective or ineffective marketing practices.

84. "Best Laid Plans," *Adweek* (special report) June 18, 2007: www.mediaweek.com/mediaweek/images/pdf/MediaPlan6_18.pdf (accessed March 3, 2008).

85. "Lionsgate and Warcon Records Promote 'Saw III' with Live Musical Event," October 13, 2007, www.indiescene.net/archives/lionsgate_films/lionsgate_and_warcon_records_p.htm (accessed March 3, 2008).

86. http://vids.myspace.com/index.cfm?fuseaction=vids.channel&ChannelID=77571500 (accessed March 3, 2008).

Chapter 16

1. This chapter vignette is based on the following: "RIM's 2010 Annual Report," available at rim.com (accessed April 24, 2011); "eBay and RIM Offer eBay Application for BlackBerry Smartphones in Six More Countries," www.marketwire.com/press-release/eBay-and-RIM-Offer-eBay-Application-for-BlackBerry-Smartphones-in-Six-More-Countries-NASDAQ-RIMM-1283829.htm (accessed April 24, 2011); Fran Foo, "BlackBerry Ban Hits Travellers to the Middle East," www.theaustralian.com.au/business/blackberry-ban-hits-travellers-to-the-middle-east/story-e6frg8zx-1225901829388 (accessed August 6, 2010).

2. Business Development Bank of Canada, www.bdc.ca (accessed April 24, 2011).

3. Pierre-Richard Agenor, *Does Globalization Hurt the Poor?* (Washington, DC: World Bank, 2002); "Globalization: Threat or Opportunity," International Monetary Fund, www.imf.org/external/np/exr/ib/2000/041200.htm#II (accessed on September 18, 2006).

4. Charles W.L. Hill, *Global Business Today*, 3rd ed. (New York: Irwin McGraw-Hill, 2004).

5. David Rosenbaum, "Next Stop, New Delhi: The Strategic Debate Over Off-Shoring is Over," *CIO* 19, no. 8, (February 1, 2006) p. 1.

6. Jack Ewing, "Why Krakow Still Works for IBM," *BusinessWeek,* September 25, 2007 (accessed electronically January 7, 2008).

7. "Members and Observers," www.wto.org/english/thewto_e/whatis_e/tif_e/org6_e.htm (accessed July 5, 2011).

8. "Japan starts WTO dispute with Canada on clean power," www.reuters.com/article/2010/09/13/us-trade-japan-canada-idUSTRE68C2RN20100913 (accessed April 25, 2011).

9. "About Us," http://web.worldbank.org/WBSITE/EXTERNAL/EXTABOUTUS/0,,pagePK:50004410~piPK:36602~theSitePK:29708,00.html (accessed July 5, 2011).

10. For a full description of criticisms of the IMF, see www.imf.org/external/np/exr/ccrit/eng/cri.htm. For a list of criticisms of the World Bank, see www.artsci.wustl.edu/~nairobi/wbissues.html (accessed August 28, 2005).

11. "Canada Imposes Wide Range of Sanctions against Libya," www.theglobeandmail.com/news/politics/canada-imposes-wide-range-of-sanctions-against-libya/article1922800/ (accessed April 25, 2011).

12. David L. Scott, *Wall Street Words: An A to Z Guide to Investment Terms for Today's Investor* (Boston: Houghton Mifflin, 2003).

13. www.international.gc.ca/eicb/softwood/menu-en.asp (accessed May 26, 2007).

14. "Budget 2010: Leading the Way on Jobs and Growth," www.budget.gc.ca/2010/home-accueil-eng.html (accessed August 6, 2010).

15. www.bloomberg.com/apps/news?pid=10000103&sid=ajtpC2UYVKwk&refer=us.

16. http://en.wikipedia.org/wiki/Exchange_rate.

17. "Philippines Implement Countertrade Program for Vietnamese Rice," *Asia Pulse Pte Limited,* April 27, 2005.

18. Nicolino Strizzi and G.S. Kindra, "A Survey of Canadian Countertrade Practices with Asia-Pacific Countries," *Revue Canadienne des Sciences de l'Administration*, 1997.

19. http://ucatlas.ucsc.edu/trade/subtheme_trade_blocs.php (accessed March 5, 2005).

20. www.unescap.org/tid/mtg/postcancun_rterta.pps#1.

21. http://ec.europa.eu/enlargement/countries/index_en.htm (accessed January 8, 2008).

22. http://en.wikipedia.org/wiki/European_Union (accessed May 19, 2010); www.nationsonline.org/oneworld/europe_map.htm (accessed May 19, 2010).

23. www.fas.usda.gov/itp/CAFTA/cafta.asp (accessed July 5, 2011).

24. http://en.wikipedia.org/wiki/Purchasing_power_parity (accessed September 19, 2005); O'Sullivan-Sheffrin, *Macroeconomics: Principles and Tools activeBook*, 3rd ed. (Upper Saddle River, NJ: Prentice Hall, 2002).

25. http://hdr.undp.org/reports/global/2001/en/. Nobel Prize–winning economist Amartya Sen has proposed that developing countries should also be measured according to the capabilities and opportunities that people within that particular country possess.

26. T.N. Ninan, "Six Mega-Trends That Define India's Future," *Rediff.com*, January 6, 2007 (accessed January 7, 2007).

27. "India," *The CIA World Factbook*, December 13, 2007 (accessed electronically January 8, 2008).

28. "Canadians in Context—Aging Population," http://www4.hrsdc. gc.ca/.3ndic.1t.4r@-eng.jsp?iid=33 (accessed April 25, 2011).

29. "Who's Getting It Right? American Brands in the Middle Kingdom," *Time* 164, no. 17 (October 25, 2004), p. A14; "Cracking China," www. chiefexecutive.net 199 (June 2004); Normandy Madden and Jack Neff, "P&G Adapts Attitude towards Local Markets," *Advertising Age* (Midwest region edition) 75, no. 8 (February 23, 2004), p. 28; www. pg.com.eg/history4.cfm.

30. "Rural India, Have a Coke," www.businessweek.com/magazine/ content/02_21/b3784134.htm.

31. "China: Online Marketing Comes of Age," *BusinessWeek*, June 12, 2007 (accessed electronically January 10, 2008).

32. "Pepsi China aim to receive over 30 million entries for the latest Pepsi Creative Challenge," www.contagiousmagazine.com/2009/09/ pepsi_4.php (accessed April 25, 2011); China Internet Statistics, www. internetworldstats.com/asia.htm (accessed July 27, 2010); David Bum, "One In Ten Chinese Internet Users 'Drink' Pepsi," www.adpulp.com/ archives/2009/10/one_in_ten_chin.php (accessed August 6, 2010).

33. Normandy Madden, "Chinese Net Stars Tapped by Brands," *Ad Age China* September 20, 2006 (accessed electronically January 10, 2008).

34. Loretta Chao and Betsy Mckay, "Pepsi Steps into Coke Realm: Red, China," *The Wall Street Journal* September 12, 2007: B4 (accessed electronically January 9, 2008).

35. "Pepsi China aim to receive over 30 million entries for the latest Pepsi Creative Challenge," www.contagiousmagazine.com/2009/09/pepsi_4. php (accessed April 25, 2011).

36. "Cellphones Catapult Rural Africa to 21st Century," www.nytimes. com/2005/08/25/international/africa/25africa.html (accessed December 18, 2007).

37. Training Management Corporation (TMC), *Doing Business Internationally: The Cross Cultural Challenges, Seminar and Coursebook* (Princeton, NJ: Trade Management Corporation, 1992).

38. Geert Hofstede, "Management Scientists Are Human," *Management Science* 40 (January 1994), pp. 4–13; Geert Hofstede and Michael H. Bond, "The Confucius Connection from Cultural Roots to Economic Growth," *Organizational Dynamics* 16 (Spring 1988), pp. 4–21; Masaaki Kotabe and Kristiaan Helsen, *Global Marketing Management* (Hoboken, NJ: John Wiley & Sons, 2004).

39. www.geert-hofstede.com (accessed September 10, 2006).

40. Donghoon Kim, Yigang Pan, and Heung Soo Park, "High versus Low Context Culture: A Comparison of Chinese, Korean and American Cultures," *Psychology and Marketing* 15, no. 6 (1998), pp. 507–521.

41. www.brandchannel.com/features_effect.asp?pf_id=261.

42. Betsy Mckay, Procter & Gamble, "Coca-Cola Formulate Vitamin Drinks for Developing Countries," *The Wall Street Journal*, cited at www. chelationtherapyonline.com/articles/p9.htm (accessed May 26, 2007).

43. Amy Chozick, "Japan Finally Opens," *The Globe and Mail* September 26, 2006.

44. Laurel Delaney, "Global Marketing Gaffes," March 19, 2002, www. marketingpofs.com (accessed December 18, 2007).

45. www.bombardier.com (accessed August 6, 2010).

46. Amy Chozick, "Japan Finally Opens."

47. www.christiedigital.com (accessed December 18, 2007).

48. Statistics Canada (accessed electronically April 25, 2011).

49. Compiled from the annual reports for 2010 of the respective companies.

50. Canadian Franchise Association, www.cfa.com (accessed April 25, 2011).

51. Angela Andal-Ancion and George Yip, "Smarter Ways to Do Business with the Competition," *European Business Forum* (Spring 2005), pp. 32–37.

52. www.whitespot.com (accessed April 25, 2011); Patrick Brethour, "Burgers go from Burnaby to Bangkok" (interview with Warren Erhart, president of White Spot Restaurants), www.theglobeandmail.com/report-on-business/your-business/start/franchising/burgers-go-from-burnaby-to-bangkok/article1336289/ (accessed April 25, 2011).

53. Brethour, "Burgers go from Burnaby."

54. Brethour, "Burgers go from Burnaby."

55. "Joint Venture with Ting Hsin Brings Tesco to China," *MMR* 11, no. 11 (July 26, 2004), p. 13.

56. www.nutralab.ca (accessed April 25, 2011).

57. Bruce D. Keillor, Michael D'Amico, and Veronica Horton, "Global Consumer Tendencies," *Psychology and Marketing* 18, no. 1 (2001), pp. 1–20.

58. www.consumerpsychologist.com/food_marketing.htm.

59. http://ro.unctad.org/infocomm/anglais/orange/market.htm; www. tropicana.com/index.asp?ID=27.

60. Glenn Collins, "Going Global Involves More Than Many US Companies Think," *The New York Times* January 2, 1997: C10.

61. Normandy Madden, "Soy-Sauce-Flavored Kit Kats? In Japan, They're No. 1," http://adage.com/globalnews/article?article_id=142461 (accessed August 6, 2010)

62. Mehul Srivastava, "Apple's iPhone, an Indian Flop, Prepares for China," www.businessweek.com/print/globalbiz/content/apr2009/ gb2009041_266236.htm (accessed August 6, 2010).

63. Sonya Misquitta, "Cadbury Redefines Cheap Luxury—Marketing to India's Poor, Candy Maker Sells Small Bites for Pennies," http://online.wsj.com/ article/SB124440401582092071.html (accessed August 6, 2010).

64. www.pringles.it.

65. "Local Success on a Global Scale," www.brandchannel.com/features_ effect.asp?pf_id=261 (accessed December 18, 2007).

66. H.M. Hayes, P.V. Jenster, and N.-E. Aaby, *Business Marketing: A Global Perspective* (Boston: Irwin/McGraw-Hill, 1996).

67. Mary Anne Raymond, John F. Tanner Jr., and Jonghoon Kim, "Cost Complexity of Pricing Decisions for Exporters in Developing and Emerging Markets," *Journal of International Marketing* 9, no. 3 (2001), pp. 19–40.

68. Terry Clark, Masaaki Kotabe, and Dan Rajaratnam, "Exchange Rate Pass-Through and International Pricing Strategy: A Conceptual Framework and Research Propositions," *Journal of International Business Studies* 30, no. 2 (1999), pp. 249–268.

69. "Fashion Conquistador," *BusinessWeek*, September 4, 2006 (accessed electronically January 31, 2008).

70. Satish Shankar et al., "How to Win in Emerging Markets," *Bain Briefs* November 29, 2007 (accessed electronically January 9, 2008).

71. Madden, "Soy-Sauce-Flavored Kit Kats?"

72. www.aeforum.org/latest.nsf.

73. www.brandchannel.com/features_effect.asp?pf_id=274 (accessed on July 5, 2011).

74. Charles W.L. Hill, *Global Business Today*, 3rd ed. (New York: Irwin McGraw-Hill, 2004).

75. Paul Meller, "The W.T.O. Said to Weigh In on Product Names," *The New York Times* November 18, 2004: 1; Mark Jarvis, "Which Bud's for You?" *BrandChannel* January 5, 2004: www.brandchannel.com/start1.asp?fa_ id=191 (accessed September 5, 2005); Paul Byrne, "Austrian Court Rules in Favor of Anheuser Busch," *PR Newswire* December 31, 2004.

76. Meller, "The W.T.O. Said."

77. Kimberly Smith, "Case Study: Tips from Microsoft on Cultivating Customer Satisfaction & Loyalty on a Global Scale," www.marketingprofs.com/casestudy/143 (accessed November 28, 2009).

78. Smith, "Case Study: Tips from Microsoft."

79. "Disposable Planet," *BBC News*, http://news.bbc.co.uk/hi/english/static/in_depth/world/2002/disposable_planet/waste/statsbank.stm (accessed September 5, 2005).

80. Alladi Venkatesh, "Postmodernism Perspective for Macromarketing: An Inquiry into the Global Information and Sign Economy," *Journal of Macromarketing* 19, no. 12 (1999), pp. 15–169.

81. Michael R. Czinkota and Ilkka A. Ronkainen, "An International Marketing Manifesto," *Journal of International Marketing* 11, no. 1 (2003), pp. 13–27.

82. Bruce Einhorn, "Apple's Chinese Supply Lines," *BusinessWeek,* January 8, 2008 (accessed electronically January 9, 2008); "Responsible Supplier Management," www.apple.com/supplierresponsibility/ (accessed January 9, 2008).

83. "Steve Jobs and 'The Maker,'" www.marketwatch.com/story/steve-jobs-china-problem-2010-07-04 (accessed August 6, 2010).

84. "Steve Jobs and 'The Maker.'"

85. Arik Hesseldahl, "Apple Answers 'Sweatshop' Claims," *BusinessWeek,* August 21, 2006 (accessed electronically January 9, 2008).

86. "Electronic Industry Code of Conduct," www.eicc.info/code.html (accessed January 9, 2008).

87. http://users.aber.ac.uk/pjm04/linguisticimperialism.html#culturalimperialism.

88. Farnaz Fassihi, "As Authorities Frown, Valentine's Day Finds Place in Iran's Heart; Young and in Love Embrace Forbidden Holiday; A Rush on Red Roses," *The Wall Street Journal* February 12, 2004: p. A1.

89. Fassihi, "As Authorities Frown."

90. This case was written by Ajax Persaud and Shirley Lichti for use in a class discussion; it was not written as an illustration of effective or ineffective marketing practices.

91. This case is based on information from lululemon's SEC 10K Filings and complemented with information from the following sources: www.lululemon.com (accessed April 25, 2011); http://en.wikipedia.org/wiki/lululemon (accessed May 23, 2007); www.mindspring.com/~wilma-munsey/uhcw/BBCNews (accessed May 23, 2007); http://sev.prnewswire.com/retail/20061003/LAM02203102006-1.html (accessed May 23, 2007); www.hoovers.com/lululemon/--ID__156721--/free-cofactsheet.xhtml (accessed May 23, 2007); Laura Bogomolny, "Toned and Ready," *Canadian Business* (April 24–May 7, 2006), pp. 59–63; Martha Strauss, "As It Stretches, Lululemon Tries Not to Bend, *The Globe and Mail* October 2, 2006.

92. lululemon's SEC 10K Filings with the SEC (accessed May 5, 2011).

93. lululemon's SEC 10K Filings.

94. Competition Bureau, "Lululemon Vitasea Clothing." www.competitionbureau.gc.ca/eic/site/cb-bc.nsf/eng/02517.html (accessed July 16, 2010).

95. Georgie Binks, "Taking it all off, even if you don't want to," *CBC News ViewPoint,* www.cbc.ca/news/viewpoint/vp_binks/20051212.html (accessed August 12, 2010)

Chapter 1

Photos/ads: p. 2, BlackBerry®, RIM®, Research In Motion®, SureType®, SurePress™ and related trademarks, names and logos are the property of Research In Motion Limited and are registered and/or used in the U.S. and countries around the world; p. 7, © Rex Features [2005] all rights reserved/The Canadian Press; p. 8, Courtesy of Clearly Canadian; p. 9, AP Photo/Mark Allan/The Canadian Press; p. 10, Courtesy of The Country Grocer; p. 11, Courtesy of Parasuco Jeans Ltd.; p. 15 (top), Nico Tondini/Getty Images; p. 15 (bottom), Courtesy National Fluid Milk Processor Promotion Board; Agency: Lowe Worldwide, Inc.; p. 17, © Scottish Viewpoint/GetStock.com; p. 19 (top), The Canadian Press/Steve White; p. 19 (bottom), Courtesy EasyJet; p. 20, Courtesy of Honda North America, AFP/Getty Images; p. 22, McGraw-Hill Companies, Inc./Gary He, photographer; p. 23, Courtesy Scion, Toyota Motor Sales, U.S.A., Inc.; p. 26 (top), The Canadian Press/Chris Young; p. 26 (bottom), Thomas Cooper/Getty Images; p. 29, BlackBerry®, RIM®, Research In Motion®, SureType®, SurePress™ and related trademarks, names and logos are the property of Research In Motion Limited and are registered and/or used in the U.S. and countries around the world.

Exhibits: Exhibit 1.8, Jason Reed/Getty Images; © Digital Visions/PunchStock; © Edward Rozzo/Corbis; Andrew Ward/Life File/Getty Images; © Roy McMahon/Corbis; © Brand X Pictures/PunchStock; BananaStock/JupiterImages; Digital Vision/Getty Images; Exhibit 1.10, apple.com and rim.com (accessed April 25, 2011); Exhibit 1.11, RIM's Website, http://press.rim.com/release.jsp?id=4914 and Apple.com.

Chapter 2

Photos/ads: p. 34, Janette Pellegrini/Stringer/Getty Images; p. 41, © Tracy Leonard; p. 43, Courtesy of Frito-Lay Inc.; p. 44, © The Procter & Gamble Company. Used by permission; p. 45, The Canadian Press/Mark Abraham; p. 47, Courtesy of Lee Valley Tools Ltd.; p. 49, Getty Images; p. 50, McGraw-Hill Companies, Inc.; p. 55, © Mhryciw/Dreamstime.com/getstock.com; p. 57, Roger Tully/Stone/Getty Images; p. 60, Photo courtesy of Kelli Wood; p. 65, The Canadian Press/Toronto Sun/Dave Thomas.

Boxes: Social Media Marketing 2.1, David Carey, "Canadian CIOs tests social networking waters," www.itworldcanada.com/news/canadian-cios-test-social-networking-waters/139201.

Chapter 3

Photos/ads: p. 84, Used by permission of Canadian Tire Corporation; p. 90 (both), © M. Hruby; p. 91, Courtesy Nau, Inc.; p. 93, Courtesy MINI USA; p. 94, Jack Hollingsworth/Getty Images; p. 95 (top), © JuanSilva 2010/Getty Images; p. 95 (bottom), © Chuck Savage/CORBIS; p. 96, Photo by Brian Bahr/Getty Images; p. 98, Courtesy of Hammacher Schlemmer, www.hammacher.com; p. 99 (top), The Canadian Press/Don Denton; p. 99 (bottom), Jochen Sand/Digital Vision/Getty Images; p. 100, © Tracy Leonard; p. 101, Courtesy of Ford Motor Company; p. 104 (top), © ANP [2008] all rights reserved/The Canadian Press; p. 104 (bottom), AP Photo/Ric Feld; p. 106, Courtesy Domino's Pizza, LLC; p. 108, Caz Shiba/Digital Vision/Getty Images.

Chapter 4

Photos/ads: p. 116, © Tracy Leonard; p. 119, © Bill Aron/PhotoEdit; p. 120, Courtesy Whirlpool Corporation; p. 121, Purestock/Getty Images; p. 122, altrendo images/Getty Images; p. 129 (top), © Marnie Burkhart/Corbis; p. 129 (bottom), The McGraw-Hill Companies, Inc./John Flournoy, Photographer; p. 130, © Andrew Rubtsov/alamy/getstock.com; p. 131, © 2006 The LEGO Group; p. 134, The McGraw-Hill Companies, Inc./John Flournoy, Photographer; p. 141, Courtesy Coinstar, Inc.; p. 146, The Canadian Press/Steve White.

Boxes: Social Media Marketing 4.1, Perez, Sarah, *Despite Recession*, More Than 50% of Marketers Increase Spending on Social Media, http://www.readwriteweb.com/enterprise/2009/03/despite-recession-more-than-50-of-marketers-increase-spending-on-social-media.php (accessed December 3, 2009.).

Chapter 5

Photos/ads: p. 148, Justin Sullivan/Getty Images; p. 152, Photo by Timothy A. Clary/AFPGetty Images; p. 155, © M. Hruby; p. 156, Andrew Wakeford/Getty Images; p. 157 (top), © M. Hruby; p. 157 (bottom), Bloomberg via Getty Images; p. 159, Courtesy of Expedia, Inc.; p. 161, Getty Images; p. 164 (left), Courtesy Taco Bell; p. 164 (right), McGruff ® and Scruff ® are a part of the National Crime Prevention Council's ongoing crime prevention education campaign; p. 165 (top), The McGraw-Hill Companies, Inc./Andrew Resek, photographer; p. 165 (bottom), Copyright © Ron Kimball/Ron Kimball Stock. All rights reserved; p. 167, Thinkstock/JupiterImages; p. 170, The Canadian Press/Mario Beauregard; p. 171, AP Photo/Rick Bowmer/The Canadian Press; p. 172, © Richard Cummins/Corbis; p. 178, © M. Hruby.

Chapter 6

Photos/ads: p. 180, Used by permission of Toyota Canada; p. 184, Courtesy of Burt's Bees, Inc.; p. 185, Reprinted with permission from MERX; p. 189 (left), Royalty-Free/Corbis; p. 189 (right), © Comstock Images/Alamy; p. 190, Used by permission of Toyota Canada; p. 191 (top), GRANTLAND®. Copyright Grantland Enterprises; www.grantland.net; p. 191 (bottom), © Toyota Motor Engineering & Manufacturing North America; p. 193, © Worth Canoy/Icon SMI/Corbis; p. 195, GRANTLAND®. Copyright Grantland Enterprises; www.grantland.net; p. 198, Courtesy stickK.com; p. 202, Courtesy of Ryan Burgio and The Stryve Group.

Chapter 7

Photos/ads: p. 210, © M. Hruby; p. 216 (both), Courtesy The Gillette Company; p. 218, © Benetton Group SPA; Photo by; Oliviero Toscani; p. 219 (top), © Catherine Wessel/Corbis; p. 219 (bottom, both), Ryan McVay/Getty Images; p. 222, Used by permission of Wilfrid Laurier University; p. 224 (left), Stockbyte/Punchstock Images; p. 224 (middle), Getty Images; p. 224 (right), Ryan McVay/Getty Images; p. 225, Ed Taylor/Taxi/Getty Images; p. 227, La Senza Girl Spring 2008 website homepage; p. 228 (left), © Jerry Arcieri/Corbis; p. 228 (right), The McGraw-Hill Companies, Inc./Andrew Resek, photographer; p. 229 (left), Courtesy of Canadian Tire Corporation; p. 229 (right), Courtesy Carhartt, Inc.; p. 230 (top), Courtesy Hallmark Cards, Inc.; p. 230 (bottom), Courtesy of Kettleman Bagel Co.; p. 233, Photo by Michael Loccisano/FilmMagic for Paul Wilmot Comunications/Getty Images; p. 234, Used with permission of Cora; p. 235, Photo by Oli Scarff/Getty Images; p. 237, Courtesy of Volvo of North America; p. 238, Green Giant for Business Wire via Getty Images; p. 240 (left), Photo by Doug Benc/Getty Images; p. 240 (right), Photo by Ezra Shaw/Getty Images; p. 241, Photo provided by MABE Canada Inc; p. 242, ® Registered Trademark/tm Trademark of Whirlpool, U.S.A., Whirlpool Canada LP licensee in Canada. Trademarks and photograph used with permission of Whirlpool Corporation; p. 246, Courtesy of M&M Meat Shops; p. 247, The Canadian Press/Paul Chiasson.

Exhibits: Exhibit 7.8 (left to right), © Digital Vision, © Bananastock/Punch Stock, Royalty-free/Corbis, © Digital Vision.

Appendix 7A: p. 250, © Don Mason/CORBIS.

Chapter 8

Photos/ads: p. 252 (top left), © Michael Newman/Photo Edit; p. 252 (top right), Courtesy Tivo, Inc.; p. 252 (bottom left), Courtesy Polaroid Corporation; p. 252 (bottom right), © The Procter & Gamble Company. Used by Permission; p. 257 (both), Used with permission from FrogBox; p. 258 (top), © M. Hruby; p. 258 (bottom), Courtesy Dyson, Inc.; p. 259, Photo by Caroline Bittencourt/LatinContent/Getty Images; p. 260 (all), Courtesy of NewProductWorks, www.newproductworks.com; p. 262, Photo by Paul Thomas/PhotodiscGreen/Getty Images; p. 263, BlackBerry®, RIM®, Research In Motion®, SureType®, SurePress™ and related trademarks, names and logos are the property of Research In Motion Limited and are registered and/or used in the U.S. and countries around the world; p. 264, © 2011 Elizabeth Anne Shoes; p. 265, AP PHOTO/Jim Mone, file; p. 267 (top), © Tracy Leonard; p. 267 (bottom), Photo Courtesy of Staples,

Inc.; p. 268, Photo by Dave Hogan/Getty Images; p. 269, AP Photo/Nick Wass; p. 271, Courtesy of Petro Canada; p. 272, Used with permission from Canadian Living; p. 274 (top), Photo by Ryan McVay/Photodisc Blue/Getty Images; p. 274 (bottom), Comstock Images/Alamy; p. 277 (top), Used with permission of PepsiCo Beverages Canada; p. 277 (bottom), © M. Hruby; p. 278, Courtesy KFC Corporation; p. 279, Gourmantra Foods Inc. Owners: Rachna Prasad, Moa Prasad, & Retha Prarsad; p. 283, The McGraw-Hill Companies, Inc./Lars A. Niki, photographer, p. 285, Used with permission from Globe and Mail.

Chapter 9

Photos/ads: p. 286 (both), Used by permission of Unilever Canada Inc.; p. 289 (right), Michael Blann/Digital Vision/Getty Images; p. 292, Used with permission of Starbucks Corporation; p. 295, © K. Rousonelos; p. 296 (top), The Canadian Press/Richard Lam; p. 296 (bottom), Photo by Linda Davidson/The Washington Post/Getty Images; p. 298, © M. Hruby; p. 299, p. AP PHOTO/Mary Altaffer/The Canadian Press; p. 300, Used with permission from Ferrero Canada Ltd.; p. 301, DOVE is a trademark owned or used under license by Unilever Canada, Toronto, Ontario M4W 3R2; p. 302, McGraw-Hill Companies; p. 303, Courtesy General Electric company; p. 304, © Tracy Leonard; p. 305 (top), © M. Hruby; p. 305 (bottom), © GK Custom Research, LLC; p. 306, Photo by Stephane L'hostis/Getty Images; p. 308 (both), Lacoste S.A.; p. 309, THE COCO-COLA COMPANY; p. 311, © M. Hruby; p. 312 (bottom), © Parmalat Canada Inc. Used with permission; p. 313, © Pure Fun Confections Inc.; p. 314, Photo courtesy of Stacey Biggar; p. 317, © M. Hruby.

Chapter 10

Photos/ads: p. 320, The Canadian Press; p. 324, Dynamic Graphics/Jupiter Images; p. 325, Photo by David McNew/Getty Images; p. 327, Courtesy Enterprise Rent-A-Car; p. 328 (top), Courtesy of Nerds On Site; p. 328 (bottom), Courtesy NCR Corporation; p. 329, © Buddy Mays/CORBIS; p. 330, Calypso Theme Waterpark Limoges Canada © Copyright 2011 p. 331, © Dan Holmberg/CORBIS; p. 334, © Dynamic Graphics Group/Creatuas/Alamy; p. 336, Courtesy of Enermodal; p. 337, Niko Guido/Getty Images; p. 339, The Canadian Press; p. 342, © Royalty-free/CORBIS; p. 343, © Michael Newman/PhotoEdit, Inc.; p. 344, Photo courtesy of Byron Pascoe; p. 347, Royalty-Free/CORBIS.

Exhibits: Exhibit 10.1 (left to right), © Jose Fuste Rage/CORBIS, The McGraw-Hill Companies, Inc./Andrew Resek, photographer, John A. Rizzo/Getty Images, © Charles Bowman/Alamy, Photodisc, Brand X Pictures/Getty Images.

Chapter 11

Photos/ads: p. 350, 2007 Twentieth Century Fox - All Rights Reserved/get-stock.com; p. 354, Enrique Marcarian/Reuters/Corbis; p. 355, Lucas Oleniuk/GetStock.com; p. 356, Courtesy Ryanair Holdings plc; p. 357 (both), Courtesy Paradigm Electronics, Inc.; p. 358 (left), The Canadian Press/Tom Hanson; p. 358 (right), The Canadian Press/Alessandra Tarantino/AP Photo; p. 359, The Canadian Press/Andrew Vaughan; p. 360, © David Young-Wolff/PhotoEdit, Inc.; p. 363 (left), The Canadian Press/Adrian Wyld; p. 363 (right), Inti St Clair/Photodisc Red/Getty Images; p. 366, Vladislav Kochelaevskiy/Alamy/getstock.com; p. 367, Used with permission from Coastal Contacts Inc.; p. 368, Photo by Mario Tama/Getty Images; p. 369 (top), Courtesy Ferrari; p. 369 (bottom), BlackBerry®, RIM®, Research In Motion®, SureType®, SurePress™ and related trademarks, names and logos are the property of Research In Motion Limited and are registered and/or used in the U.S. and countries around the world; p. 370, Courtesy of iwearyourshirt.com; p. 372, Photo by Michael Nagie/Getty Images; p. 373, Courtesy Sears, Roebuck and Co; p. 374, Used with permission from The 7 Virtues; p. 375, © Jeff Greenberg/PhotoEdit; p. 376, Image supplied courtesy of The Regional Municipality of Waterloo; p. 380, © M. Hruby; p. 381, © Jeff Greenberg/PhotoEdit, Inc.; p. 382, © Tom Prettyman/PhotoEdit.

Exhibits: Exhibit 11.6 (top to bottom), © Brand X Pictures/PunchStock, Ingram Publishing/SuperStock, Steve Cole/Getty Images, © Corbis - All Rights Reserved.

Chapter 12

Photos/ads: p. 388 (both), Courtesy of Zara International, Inc.; p. 392, Used with permission of The Royal Canadian Mint and the Canadian Breast Cancer Foundation; p. 393, © Tracy Leonard; p. 395, Courtesy The Stanley Works; p. 399, Photo by Stephen Chemin/Getty Images; p. 402 (top), © Jeff Greenberg/PhotoEdit; p. 402 (bottom), © Susan Van Etten/PhotoEdit; p. 403, © Tessuto E Colore srl; p. 405, © Thinkstock/Alamy/Getty Images; p. 407, © Gianni Giansanti/Sygma/Corbis; p. 410, p. 411, Courtesy of Harry Rosen Inc.; p. 412, David Buffington/Getty Images; p. 413, Photodisc Red/Getty Images; p. 414, Used by permission of Frito Lay Canada; p. 415, Photo courtesy of Mark Montpetit.

Exhibits: Exhibit 12.5 (left box), AP Photo/Mike Wintroath, The Canadian Press/Boris Spremo, The Canadian Press/Steve White, The Canadian Press/Boris Spremo, (middle box) The Canadian Press/Don Denton, AP Photo/Carolyn Chappo; (right box) Photo by Stephanie Paschal/Rex Features, © INF [2004] all rights reserved/The Canadian Press.

Chapter 13

Photos/ads: p. 420, © Tracy Leonard; p. 424 (top), The Canadian Press/Mel Evans/AP Images; p. 424 (bottom), Courtesy of Moores Clothing for Men; p. 428, Courtesy Sephora USA, Inc.; p. 429, AP Photo/Ric Feld; p. 432, Courtesy of Giant Tiger Stores Limited; p. 433, © Copyright 2008 of Shoppers Drug Mart Inc. Shoppers Drug Mart is a registered trademark of 911979 Alberta Ltd., used under licence; p. 434 (top), Used with permission of Canadian Tire Corporation; p. 434 (bottom), © Copyright 2008 of Shoppers Drug Mart Inc. Shoppers Drug Mart is a registered trademark of 911979 Alberta Ltd., used under licence; p. 435, IKEA Canada; p. 436, The Canadian Press/Ted S. Warren/AP Photo; p. 437 (left), © James Leynse/Corbis; p. 437 (right), The Canadian Press/Rene Macura/AP Photo; p. 441, Courtesy of H&M, Hennes & Mauritz LP; p. 444 (left), The Canadian Press; (middle and right), Used with permission of Sears Canada Inc.; p. 450, AP Photo/DamianDovarganes.

Chapter 14

Photos/ads: p. 452, © India Images/getstock.com; p. 457 (top), © M. Hruby; p. 457 (bottom, both), Courtesy LG Electronics; p. 460, Chris Ratcliffe/Bloomberg via Getty Images; p. 462, Courtesy Sears, Roebuck and Co; p. 463 (bottom), Martin Oeser/AFP/Getty Images; p. 464, AP Photo/Harry Cabluck; p. 465, Photo courtesy of EepyBird.com; p. 466, Donato Sardella/WireImage/Getty Images; p. 467, The Canadian Press/Mark Brett; p. 470, Courtesy The Diamond Trading Company; Agency: J. Walter Thompson U.S.A., Inc.; p. 471, Ian Shipley HR/GetStock.com; p. 475 (top), Courtesy of The Black & Decker Corporation; p. 475 (bottom), Courtesy Ford Motor Company; p. 476, Courtesy of BBH Tokyo; p. 478, Courtesy MINI USA; p. 479 (top), Courtesy IKEA; p. 479 (bottom), © Mitchell Gerber/CORBIS; p. 483, Photo provided by Ami Shah; p. 488 (top), DOVE is a trademark owned or used under license by Unilever Canada, Toronto, Ontario M4W 3R2; p. 488 (bottom), Used by permission of Unilever Canada Inc.

Exhibits: Exhibit 14.3 (left to right), Geostock/Getty Images, Stockbyte/Punch Stock Images, Keith Brofsky, Photo by Time Life Pictures/Long Photography Inc./Time Life Pictures/Getty Images, Christopher Kerrigan.

Chapter 15

Photos/ads: p. 497 (top), © John Hayes; p. 497 (bottom), Vasil Boglev/Alamy/getstock.com; p. 498, Used with permission of Leigh Meadows; p. 500 (top left), Courtesy National Fluid Milk Processor Promotion Board: Agency Lowe Worldwide, Inc.; p. 500 (top right), California Milk Processor Board; Agency: Goodby, Silverstein & Partners; p. 500 (bottom, both), Courtesy of Microsoft Corporation; p. 502, © Bill Aron/PhotoEdit, Inc.; p. 503, Photo by David Paul Morris/Getty Images; p. 506, Courtesy David Brice; p. 507 (top), Courtesy Payless Shoe Source, Inc.; p. 507 (bottom), Photo by John M. Heller/Getty Images; p. 509, National Geographic/Getty Images; p. 510 (top), © Michael Newman/PhotoEdit; p. 510 (bottom), Photo courtesy of CTV; p. 513 (top), © Royalty-Free/Corbis; p. 513 (bottom), © Royalty-Free/Corbis; p. 515 (top), Daniel Acker/Bloomberg news/Landov; p. 515 (bottom), © 2006 Expedia, Inc. All rights reserved; p. 517 (top), © Royalty-Free/Corbis; p. 517 (bottom), Photo by Evan Agostini/Getty Images; p. 522, © Royalty-Free/Corbis; p. 527, Courtesy Initiative Public Relations.

Box: Entrepreneurial Marketing 15.1, Used with permission of Leigh Meadows.

Chapter 16

Photos/ads: p. 528, H. John Maier Jr./Contributor; p. 532, AP Photo/Jose Luis Magana/The Canadian Press; p. 535 (left), Photo by Tim Boyle/Getty Images; p. 535 (right), © Gail Mooney/CORBIS; p. 536, © 2007 Canadian Press Images; p. 538, © Digital Vision/Getty Images; p. 542, AFP/Getty Images; p. 543, Courtesy Pepsi-Cola Company; p. 544, Polka Dot Images/Jupiterimages; p. 545, © Ronen Zvulun/Reuters/Corbis; p. 547, AP Photo/Greg Baker; p. 550 (top, both), Courtesy YUMI Brands, Inc.; p. 550 (bottom), The Canadian Press/Larry MacDougal; p. 552, Bloomberg via Getty Images; p. 553, Image Source/Getty Images; p. 554, The McGraw-Hill Companies, Inc./Andrew Resek, photographer; p. 555 (top), Courtesy of Apple; p. 555 (bottom), REUTERS/Arko Datta/Corbis; p. 557 (top), H. John Maier Jr./Contributor; p. 557 (bottom), Used with permission from Nestlé Japan; p. 559, © Digital Vision; p. 561 (top), AFP/Getty Images; p. 561 (bottom), AFP/Getty Images; p. 565, The Canadian Press/Richard Lam.

company index